Encyclopedia of the Harlem Literary Renaissance

LOIS BROWN

 Facts On File, Inc.

Encyclopedia of the Harlem Literary Renaissance

Facts On File, Inc.
132 West 31st Street
New York NY 10001

Library of Congress Cataloging-in-Publication Data

Brown, Lois, 1966–
Encyclopedia of the Harlem literary renaissance / Lois Brown.
p. cm.
Includes bibliographical references and index.
ISBN 0-8160-4967-X (hardcover : alk. paper)
1. American literature—African American authors—Encyclopedias.
2. African Americans—Intellectual life—20th century—Encyclopedias.
3. Authors, American—20th century—Biography—Encyclopedias. 4. Harlem
(New York, N.Y.)—Intellectual life—Encyclopedias. 5. African American
intellectuals—Biography—Encyclopedias. 6. African American authors—
Biography—Encyclopedias. 7. American literature—20th century—
Encyclopedias. 8. African Americans in literature—Encyclopedias. 9. Harlem
Renaissance—Encyclopedias. I. Title
PS153.N5B675 2005
810.9'896'07307471—dc22
2004022097

CONTENTS

ACKNOWLEDGMENTS

Completion of a project such as this depends on the support, counsel, and expertise of colleagues, librarians, research assistants, and friends. I offer sincere thanks to my Mount Holyoke College students Abigail Horne, Stacy Pringle, Florence Rice, Jennifer Roberts, Rachel Schaefer, and Emily Uecker for their enthusiastic research assistance that has enriched this volume. Thanks to Leigh Golden, Taran Schindler, and the staff at the Beinecke Rare Book and Manuscript Library, the librarians in the Rare Books Department at the Boston Public Library, and the librarians of Mount Holyoke College and of the Five College Consortium for providing access to instrumental resources and to archival materials. For permission to reproduce photographs by Carl Van Vechten housed in the James Weldon Johnson Memorial Collection of Negro Arts and Letters, I thank Bruce Kellner and the Van Vechten Trust. Many thanks also to Donal O'Shea, Dean of the Faculty at Mount Holyoke, for funds that aided the research for the volume and for his much appreciated and enthusiastic endorsements of the life of the mind.

Edgar and Jean Brown, Anna Brown-Bryant, Michael Bryant, Carolyn Collette, Greta Heintzelman, Amy Martin, Lynda Morgan, Lauret Savoy, Alycia Smith-Howard, Sally Sutherland, and Kathy Washburn have offered friendship, good counsel, and timely and spirited words of encouragement throughout this period of writing, research, and compilation. For these bolstering and generous gifts, I thank them sincerely. Finally, for his wisdom, his invaluable perspectives on the academic life, and his inspiring love of history, I thank Peter Monson.

INTRODUCTION

The Harlem Renaissance was an era of spirited intellectual debate, innovative creative ventures, unprecedented collaboration, and vibrant cultural engagement. Writers, editors, artists, critics, patrons, and readers alike immersed themselves in enterprising literary and artistic ventures in the years after World War I through to 1940. The pioneering works of drama and fiction, sobering political critiques, and ambitious periodicals produced during this time confirmed the diversity, complexity, and seemingly infinite richness of African-American experiences. This volume, which focuses primarily on the diverse literary history and figures associated with the period, strives to illuminate the connections between writers and regions. The entries assembled here also suggest the political, racial, and cultural contexts that shaped the works and agendas of the period's earnest, determined, and eloquent personalities.

Many Harlem Renaissance figures were multifaceted professionals who combined careers in areas such as education, politics, and medicine with their literary pursuits. As a result, the Harlem Renaissance was a literary movement that was infused with explicit political and social awareness. Writers strategized about how best to combat racial violence, economic and political disenfranchisement, and federal malaise in the face of rising threats to African-American civil rights. They collaborated on private literary projects and public activist agendas that targeted the pernicious racism that fueled stereotypes and racial tension throughout the nation. As Zora Neale Hurston, recalling a heated conversation with Alain Locke, Langston Hughes, and Louise Thompson about representa-

tions of authentic African-American culture, noted spiritedly in a 1934 letter to Eslanda Goode Robeson, "I have steadily maintained that the real us was infinit[e]ly superior to the synthetic minstrel version, and once they have had a glimpse, the imitation is rapidly losing ground" (Hurston 300). In addition, as members of the Harlem Renaissance explored the worlds beyond American borders, they not only satisfied their own keen intellectual curiosity but also developed powerful perspectives on pan-African experiences and insights about the best ways to marshal the energies of like-minded compatriots.

As historian Bruce Kellner and others have observed, the use of the phrase "Harlem Renaissance" suggests incorrectly that the movement was based solely in Harlem and in Manhattan. New York City did serve as the most visible base for the intense social and literary networks that so defined the period. It was there, after all, that the definitive periodical publications the *Crisis, Opportunity,* and *Messenger* were based. Writers such as Countee Cullen, Jessie Fauset, Langston Hughes, Helene Johnson, and Dorothy West flocked to the city to capitalize on the growing interest in and market for African-American productions. Yet, other writers such as Zora Neale Hurston, Arna Bontemps, and Anne Spencer were based in cities and countries well beyond the borders of Harlem. Wallace Thurman, one of the period's most energetic and successful writers and editors, recognized the need to depart from that frenetic place in order to produce. Although he "miss[ed] the chats" he had had with "certain kindred spirits" and the "occasional mad nights experienced in Harlem," Thurman confided on one occasion in his friend and collaborator William Jourdan Rapp that if he remained in New York City, "no work would be done" (Thurman 149). While some, like Thurman, departed from the city in order to preserve their creative genius, others like Georgia Douglas Johnson and Eugene Gordon established well-known and nurturing literary communities in other urban centers. Johnson's Washington, D.C., salon, Gordon's productive Boston literary club known as the Saturday Evening Quill Club, and the Black Opals of Philadelphia represented some of the best-known East Coast centers of literary activity. It was with poet Georgia Douglas Johnson that Alice Dunbar-Nelson, Alain Locke, and others delighted regularly in "much poetry and discussion and salad and wine and tea" (Hull 185). Lesser known but equally valuable Harlem Renaissance communities flourished as far away as Texas, the Midwest, and throughout the West. Writers such as Claude McKay, Langston Hughes, and Nella Larsen were among the many whose work was enriched from time spent in dynamic and transitory expatriate communities abroad in countries such as France, Morocco, Russia, and Portugal.

Many of the individuals associated with the Harlem Renaissance became part of a larger movement to showcase black culture and to overcome the oppressive racial politics of the day. Yet, as much of the correspondence and primary works reveal, writers of color dealt with the racial imperatives and realities of their time in different ways. Some, like Jean Toomer, openly defied the automatic racial categorization of their work and selves. Others, like Arna Bontemps and Jessie Fauset, were committed to providing children of African descent with vivid, regal, and grounding literature that inspired and educated them to transcend the narrow and stultifying effects of Jim Crow segregation and misleading, or simply nonexistent, accounts of African-American culture and African history. The unrelenting federal scrutiny of individuals such as W. E. B. DuBois, Langston Hughes, A. Philip Randolph, and Paul Robeson raised the stakes of the Renaissance. While this was the period of many celebrated landmark events such as the staging of the first African-American play on Broadway, it also was the period in which many had occasion to rally to protest lynching, to support innocent victims such as the Scottsboro Boys, and to examine their support for or distance from the women and men among them who regarded language and performance as powerful tools with which to achieve literary and political emancipation.

This volume benefits enormously from the recent renaissance in African-American literature and scholarship that has made available a stunning array of primary works by well-known and long-lost figures of the Harlem Renaissance period. Access to primary works energizes any critical field of study, and a number of recent anthologies, collections of letters, and volumes of collected works have further rejuvenated the fields of African-American and American studies. Scholars continue to build on the pioneering work of literary reconstruction begun by scholars such as James Hatch, Nathan Huggins, Bruce Kellner, David Levering Lewis, Kathy Perkins, Ann Allen Shockley, Ted Shine, and Mary Helen Washington, all of whom have demonstrated the undeniable allure of this literary period, its debt to the viable African-American tradition that began in the 18th century, and its formative influence on contemporary African-American writing. Recently edited volumes such as Emily Bernard's *Remember Me to Harlem: The Letters of Langston Hughes and Carl Van Vechten* (2001), Carla Kaplan's *Zora Neale Hurston: A Life in Letters* (2002), William Maxwell's *Complete Poems: Claude McKay* (2004), Amritjit Singh and Daniel Scott's *The Collected Writings of Wallace Thurman: A Harlem Renaissance Reader* (2003), Thomas Wirth's *Gay Rebel of the Harlem Renaissance: Selections from the Work of Richard Bruce Nugent* (2002), and the multivolume series initiated by Henry Louis Gates, Jr., and Jennifer Burton dedicated to the writings of African-American women writers from 1910 through 1940, shed new light on the fellowship, tensions, and inspiring literary production that were at the core of the movement.

The recent intense scholarly production and research in the field has resulted in the republication of a diverse number of materials that have long been obscured or otherwise unavailable. This reference guide acknowledges and incorporates many of these new works and groundbreaking scholarly finds in its presentation of the Harlem Renaissance. It is informed by the invaluable work of scholars who have provided deliberate reconsiderations of major journals and their contributors. These newly assembled volumes of primary writings offer absorbing perspectives on the meaningful and substantial forums that W. E. B. DuBois, Jessie Fauset, Charles Johnson, Chandler Owen, A. Philip Randolph, and others generated for creative production and political self-expression. Publications such as Sondra Wilson's anthologies of writings published in *The Crisis, The Messenger,* and *Opportunity,* respectively, Lionel Bascom's *A Renaissance in Harlem: Lost Essays of the WPA, by Ralph Ellison, Dorothy West, and Other Voices of a Generation* (2001), Craig Gable's *Ebony Rising: Short Fiction of the Greater Harlem Renaissance Era* (2004), Marcy Knox's *The Sleeper Wakes: Harlem Renaissance Stories by Women* (1993), and Lorraine Elena Roses and Ruth Elizabeth Randolph's, *Harlem's Glory: Black Women Writing, 1900–1950* (1996) continue to provide scholars with new primary materials with which to reconsider the scope, mission, and intensity of the Harlem Renaissance. In addition, biographies such as Valerie Boyd's *Wrapped in Rainbows: The Life of Zora Neale Hurston* (2003), Christine Rauchfuss Gray's comprehensive study, *Willis Richardson: Forgotten Pioneer of African-American Drama* (1999), David Levering Lewis's double Pulitzer Prize-winning volumes on W. E. B. DuBois, and Thadious Davis's biography of Nella Larsen not only reveal the prolific, seemingly irrepressible energy and vision of the movement but also perform vital acts of literary recovery that re-introduce figures whose names might be familiar but whose circumstances, backgrounds, and lives continue to warrant scrupulous reconstruction and nuanced examination.

This book includes references to many women writers, those who have come to be regarded as definitive examples of the feminist literary enterprise of the day as well as many who have existed on the fringes of Harlem Renaissance studies. The information presented here owes much to the scholarship and intellectual rigor of individuals such as Elizabeth Brown-Guillory, Marcy Knox, Kathy Perkins, Lorraine Elena Roses, Ruth Elizabeth Randolph, Alice Walker, and Sondra Wilson. These and other scholars have been determined to honor the influence, efforts, and successes of writers whose productivity ranged

from the publication of several poems to the founding of journals.

The landmark act of Harlem Renaissance-related feminist recovery is, for many, Alice Walker's much-heralded and documented commitment to mark the life and writings of Zora Neale Hurston. Walker's tireless efforts, which culminated in a challenging and decisive act of placing a tombstone on the long-neglected Florida grave of the writer, have encouraged many to emulate her passionate and unapologetic pursuit of figures without whom our understanding of the period continues to be incomplete. Roses and Randolph note that they were compelled to correct enduring "male literary myopia" that accommodated notions that the Harlem Renaissance was "primarily a male event" and to catalog the long-obscured women, some of whom "were so undocumented that it was a challenge to verify that they had ever existed." (Roses 4, 5) In addition to the biographical profiles of women writers and discussions of their works, the volume also includes some brief entries that signal the still elusive nature of some works and figures. These are incorporated here in an effort to mark a place, however tenuous, for both the authors and the writings.

Scholars continue to debate which years mark the beginning and end of the Harlem Renaissance. Many critics agree that the period spanned the 1920s and ended with the onset of the Great Depression. Historian Nathan Huggins has suggested that the Renaissance began as early as 1914, while scholars David Levering Lewis and Bruce Kellner use central political events such as the 1917 silent march through Harlem and the 1935 Harlem Riot to frame the period. Victor Kramer and Robert Russ suggest that the Harlem Renaissance should not be regarded as a movement that spanned only the decades of the 1920s and 1930s. They argue that its influences and its principal writers have informed American and African-American literary and cultural studies well into the late 20th century.

This volume acknowledges the ongoing debate about the life span of the movement. While it uses 1920 to 1940 as its primary chronological guide, it includes references to relevant works and events that occurred before and after those dates. The majority of entries focus on the artists, works, and issues of the day. However, in an effort to contextualize the period and its evolution, impact, and legacies, the book also includes citations that shed light on the editors, publishers, mentors, patrons, and critics who were active members of the Harlem Renaissance literary and arts communities. Also included is information about the literary organizations, informal and recognized networks, and competitions that figured prominently in the lives of many artists. In addition to its entries on authors, works, publications, events, locations, and organizations, this volume includes a selected bibliography of Harlem Renaissance-era works by leading figures of the movement. It also includes a bibliography of major secondary publications, many of which are cited throughout the text. The chronology offers a general overview of the literary publications and key historical events of the time.

"Oh, if you knew my dreams! my vaulting ambition! How I constantly live in fancy in seven league boots, taking mighty strides across the world, but conscious all the time of being a mouse on a treadmill," declared Zora Neale Hurston in 1926 to Annie Nathan Meyer, her advocate and a Barnard College trustee (Hurston 77). Hurston's dueling perspectives, which reveal the tension between dazzling transcendence and sobering reality, articulate both the seductive possibilities and the unavoidable realities with which she and her contemporaries grappled. This volume has been inspired by these competing tensions that compelled participants in the Harlem Renaissance to craft eloquent testimonies of the nation's collective past and their own present, sustained them in the face of unexpected tragedies, and allowed them to nurture "vaulting ambition" that catapulted them onto the broad stage of American literary history.

Bibliography

Hurston, Zora Neale, to Eslanda Robeson. 18 April 1934. In *Zora Neale Hurston: A Life in Letters*, edited by Carla Kaplan, 300. New York: Doubleday, 2002.

Hurston, Zora Neale, to Annie Nathan Meyer. 15 January 1926. In *Zora Neale Hurston: A Life in Letters*, edited by Carla Kaplan, 77. New York: Doubleday, 2002.

Hull, Gloria, ed. *Give Us Each Day: The Diary of Alice Dunbar-Nelson*. New York: W. W. Norton, 1984. 185.

Roses, Lorraine Elena, and Ruth Elizabeth Randolph, eds. *Harlem's Glory: Black Women Writing, 1900–1950*. Cambridge, Mass.: Harvard University Press, 1996. 4, 5.

Thurman, Wallace, to William Jourdan Rapp. Undated. In *The Collected Writings of Wallace Thurman: A Harlem Renaissance Reader*, edited by Amritjit Singh and Daniel M. Scott III, 149. New Brunswick, N.J.: Rutgers University Press, 2003.

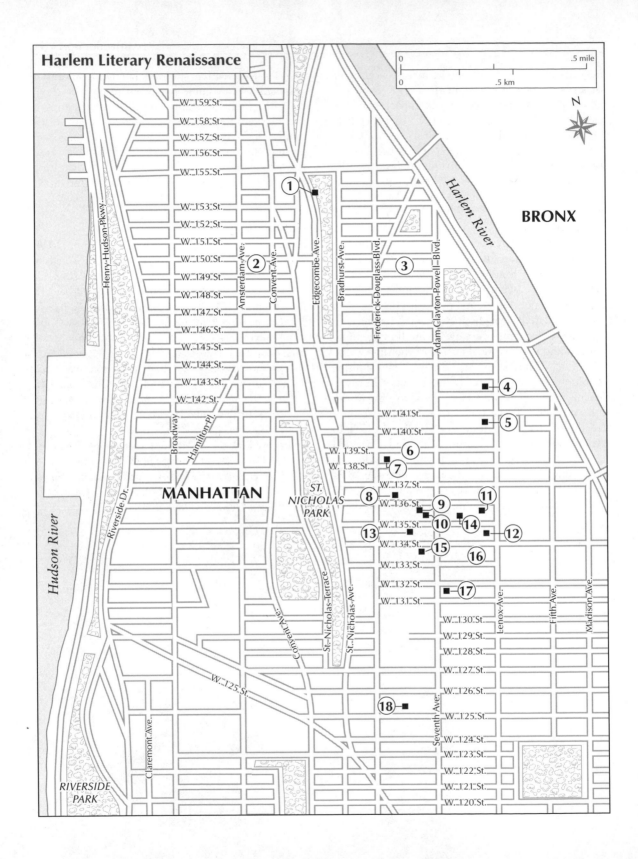

Harlem Literary Renaissance

W. 159 St.
W. 158 St.
W. 157 St.
W. 156 St.
W. 155 St.

W. 153 St.
W. 152 St.
W. 151 St.
W. 150 St.
W. 149 St.
W. 148 St.
W. 147 St.
W. 146 St.
W. 145 St.
W. 144 St.
W. 143 St.
W. 142 St.

W. 141 St.
W. 140 St.
W. 139 St.
W. 138 St.
W. 137 St.
W. 136 St.
W. 135 St.
W. 134 St.
W. 133 St.
W. 132 St.
W. 131 St.
W. 130 St.
W. 129 St.
W. 128 St.
W. 127 St.
W. 126 St.
W. 125 St.
W. 124 St.
W. 123 St.
W. 122 St.
W. 121 St.
W. 120 St.

Henry-Hudson Pkwy.
Amsterdam Ave.
Convent Ave.
Edgecombe Ave.
Bradhurst Ave.
Frederick Douglass Blvd.
Adam Clayton Powell Blvd.
Harlem River
Broadway
Hamilton Pl.
Riverside Dr.
Claremont Ave.
Convent Ave.
St. Nicholas Terrace
St. Nicholas Ave.
Seventh Ave.
Lenox Ave.
Fifth Ave.
Madison Ave.

BRONX

MANHATTAN

ST. NICHOLAS PARK

Hudson River

RIVERSIDE PARK

0 .5 mile
0 .5 km

1. **409 Edgecombe Avenue:** Upscale apartment building in the Sugar Hill district that was home to luminaries such as Aaron Douglas, W. E. B. DuBois, Walter White, and Thurgood Marshall.

2. **Sugar Hill:** 145th–155th Streets between Amsterdam and Edgecombe Avenues. Location of notable buildings.

3. **Dunbar Apartments:** Seventh to Eighth Avenues at West 149th to 150th Streets. Residents included W. E. B. DuBois, A. Philip Randolph, Matthew Henson, and other leading figures of the period.

4. **Cotton Club:** 644 Lenox Avenue. Famous nightclub where legendary entertainers such as Cab Calloway, Bill "Bojangles" Robinson, and Ethel Waters performed.

5. **Savoy Ballroom:** 596 Lenox Avenue. One of the best-known clubs in Harlem and the place where the dance known as the Lindy Hop was created; it spanned a city block.

6. **Striver's Row:** 138th and 139th Streets between Seventh and Eighth Avenues. Lined with homes designed by Stanford White; named in honor of its residents who represented the upwardly mobile African-American professional class of doctors, lawyers, and artists.

7. **Abyssinian Baptist Church:** 132–142 West 138th Street. Founded in 1808 and relocated to Harlem in 1922 during the tenure of its pastor Rev. Adam Clayton Powell, Sr.

8. **Niggerati Manor:** 267 West 136th Street. The boarding house where the journal *Fire!!* originated, dubbed "Niggerati Manor" by Zora Neale Hurston.

9. **National Urban League:** 202–206 West 136th Street. From 1917, the Manhattan offices of the National Urban League and its official publication, *Opportunity.*

10. **United Negro Improvement Association:** 2305 Seventh Avenue (near 136th Street). Headquarters of UNIA and its official publication, *The Negro World,* from 1916 to 1918.

11. **Dark Tower:** 108–110 West 136th Street. Sophisticated salon and nightclub established by heiress A'Lelia Walker in 1929 in the townhouse that was once the home of her mother, millionaire and entrepreneur Madam C. J. Walker, and headquarters of the Walker School of Hair.

12. **135th Street Branch, New York Public Library:** Lenox Avenue and 135th Street. Location of the Schomburg Library.

13. **National Association for the Advancement of Colored People:** 224 West 135th Street. Headquarters of the NAACP and *The Crisis.*

14. **YMCA:** 181 West 135th Street. Important African-American community center that served also as a hotel, lecture hall, and theater.

15. **St. Philip's Episcopal Church:** 210–216 West 134th Street. Founded in 1818; relocated to Harlem in 1911.

16. **Jungle Alley:** 133rd Street, between Lenox and Seventh Avenues. Location of the Nest Club, Connie's Inn, and Barron's Exclusive Club.

17. **Lafayette Theatre:** 132nd Street and Seventh Avenue. First New York City venue to desegregate its seating and the home of the Lafayette Players, the first professional stock theater company in Harlem.

18. **Apollo Theater:** 253 West 125th Street. One of America's most famous theaters.

Abbott, Robert Sengstacke (1870–1940)

Editor and founder of the CHICAGO DEFENDER, the influential newspaper that encouraged African Americans in the South to migrate north for better living conditions and economic possibilities. Abbott, whose parents were former slaves, studied printing at Hampton Institute. He used the earnings from his printing business to fund his law school education at the Kent College of Law in CHICAGO and graduated in 1900. Five years later he began publishing the *Chicago Defender*, a weekly publication that Pullman porters disseminated regularly throughout the South despite the outrage of white southerners who were determined to prevent a mass exodus of underpaid, disenfranchised African-American workers.

Historians estimate that during its heyday in the 1920s the newspaper reached some 250,000 readers nationwide, many of them working-class African Americans. Abbott published a number of contemporary writers, including LANGSTON HUGHES and Gwendolyn Brooks. In 1929 Abbott founded ABBOTT'S MONTHLY, a magazine that published works by a number of Harlem Renaissance writers. The periodical lasted for four years but succumbed eventually to the economic upheaval of the Great Depression.

Robert S. Abbott, founder of the *Chicago Defender* *(Yale Collection of American Literature, Beinecke Rare Book and Manuscript Library)*

Bibliography

DeSantis, Alan D. "A Forgotten Leader: Robert S. Abbott and the *Chicago Defender* from 1910–1920." *Journalism History* 23, no. 2 (1997): 63–71.

Jordan, William G. *Black Newspapers and America's War for Democracy.* Chapel Hill: The University of North Carolina Press, 2001.

Ottley, Roi. *The Lonely Warrior: The Life and Times of Robert S. Abbott.* Chicago: H. Regnery Co., 1955.

Abbott's Monthly

A CHICAGO-based magazine founded by ROBERT SENGSTACKE ABBOTT, founder and editor of the CHICAGO DEFENDER, in September 1929, just one month before the devastating stock-market crash. Despite the timing of its debut, Abbott sold 50,000 copies of the first issues and quickly became the best-selling African-American magazine to date.

The monthly magazine, which, according to the *Detroit Independent,* "outstripped the imagination of all," published a variety of Harlem Renaissance-era writers and artists, including LANGSTON HUGHES and Robert Hayden. Widespread African-American unemployment and poverty during the depression contributed to the magazine's demise in 1933.

Bibliography

Johnson, Abby Arthur, and Ronald Maberry Johnson. *Propaganda & Aesthetics: The Literary Politics of African American Magazines in the Twentieth Century.* Amherst: University of Massachusetts, 1979.

Ottley, Roi. *The Lonely Warrior: The Life and Times of Robert S. Abbott.* Chicago: H. Regnery Co., 1955.

Abyssinian Baptist Church

Founded in 1808 by the Reverend Thomas Paul, the pioneering minister of BOSTON's African Baptist Church, the Abyssinian Baptist Church was the first African-American Baptist church in New York State. In 1920 the congregation purchased land on 138th Street, between LENOX AVENUE and Seventh Avenue. Intense tithing by its members resulted in the construction of an impressive structure with Gothic and Tudor features, a pulpit of Italian marble, and gorgeous stained glass windows.

The pastor of the Abyssinian Baptist Church during the 1920s was ADAM CLAYTON POWELL, SR. He was succeeded by his son Adam Clayton Powell, Jr., who went on to become a popular city councilman in 1941 and a congressman whose New York constituency elected him to serve in the U.S. House of Representatives for 14 terms.

Bibliography

Abyssinian Baptist Church website. Available online URL: http://www.abyssinian.org.

Gore, Bob. *We've Come This Far: The Abyssinian Baptist Church—A Photographic Journal.* New York: Tabori & Chang, 2001.

Advancing South, The: Stories of Progress and Reaction   Edward Mims (1926)

A social science volume by Edward Mims on economic, educational, and social conditions in the South. In this volume, Mims proposed that the African-American press was the "greatest single power in the Negro race" (268). ALAIN LOCKE reviewed the book in the December 1926 issue of OPPORTUNITY.

Bibliography

Locke, Alain. *Opportunity* (December 1926).

Mims, Edward. *The Advancing South: Stones of Progress and Reaction.* New York: Doubleday, Page, 1926.

Africa

The continent of Africa figures prominently in the literary, political, artistic, and social imagination of Harlem Renaissance writers and artists. ALAIN LOCKE urged writers to consider ways in which African history and traditions might shape their work. CARTER G. WOODSON crafted an impressive argument about the greatness of Africa in *The African Background Outlined, or Handbook for the Study of the Negro,* his respected 1936 history and bibliographic review of materials relating to Africa. MARCUS GARVEY advocated that African Americans establish themselves there. Poets such as COUNTEE CULLEN conjured up haunting images of black people's empowering past in a mythic Africa. W. E. B. DuBois treated issues relating to European colonialism in Africa and to PAN-AFRICANISM. Other writers, such as LANGSTON HUGHES and JAMES WELDON JOHNSON, did not focus on African and primitive subjects, however; they preferred to concentrate on black American issues and encourage sustained attention to, and analysis of, black issues and African-American contexts.

Bibliography

Jones, Norma Ramsay. "Africa, as Imaged by Cullen & Co." *Negro American Literature Forum* 8, no. 4 (winter 1974): 263–267.

African Black Brotherhood

A political organization that was affiliated with the COMMUNIST PARTY. This socialist group was part of a larger African-American political movement that saw several groups like the Garvey-related UNIVERSAL NEGRO IMPROVEMENT ASSOCIATION (UNIA) and the NATIONAL ASSOCIATION FOR THE ADVANCEMENT OF COLORED PEOPLE (NAACP) founded to promote race unity and advancement. CLAUDE MCKAY, the acclaimed West Indian writer, recognized the value of the group, and WILFRED A. DOMINGO organized its publicity and propaganda dissemination.

Bibliography

Howe, Irving, and Lewis Coser. *The American Communist Party: A Critical History.* New York: Da Capo Press, 1974.

Naison, Mark. *Communists in Harlem during the Depression.* New York: Grove Press, 1985.

African Orthodox Church

Founded by MARCUS GARVEY in 1921. The church, which combined rituals from Garvey's Catholic faith and the Episcopalian tradition, promoted worship of a black God and other religious figures such as the Madonna and Christ who were rendered as African. The Reverend George Alexander McGuire, a well-known BOSTON minister who served as chaplain for Garvey's UNIVERSAL NEGRO IMPROVEMENT ASSOCIATION, was appointed to lead the church, which ultimately closed in 1935.

Bibliography

Cronon, E. David. *Black Moses: The Story of Marcus Garvey and the Universal Negro Improvement Association.* Madison: University of Wisconsin Press, 1987.

Clarke, John Henrik, ed. *Marcus Garvey and the Vision of Africa.* New York: Vintage Books, 1974.

Aftermath Mary Burrill (1928)

A play by MARY (MAMIE) BURRILL that was performed in May 1928 by the HARLEM-based KRIGWA PLAYERS during the National Little Theatre Tournament. It was published in 1919 in the *LIBERATOR*, the journal founded by MAX EAST-MAN. The script, which features black dialect, tells the tragic story of John, a heroic World War II veteran who returns to his South Carolina family only to find that his father has been lynched by a white mob. Mam Sue, his mother, and Millie, his sister, struggle with the decision to ruin his short leave by telling him about his father's awful fate. The play ends as John, bitter about his military service in defense of white America, prepares to confront the racist men who killed his father. Burrill's play is part of a substantial group of Harlem Renaissance works that grapple with the horrors of LYNCHING and its wrenching effects on African-American families.

Bibliography

Gates, Henry Louis, and Jennifer Burton, eds. *Zora Neale Hurston, Eulalie Spence, Marita Bonner, And Others: The Prize Plays and Other One-Acts Published in Periodicals.* New York: G. K. Hall, 1996.

Schroeder, Patricia. "Remembering the Disremembered: Feminist Realists of the Harlem Renaissance." In *Realism and the American Dramatic Tradition,* edited by William Demastes, 91–106. Tuscaloosa: University of Alabama Press, 1996.

Airs from the Wood-Winds Bessie Calhoun Bird (1935)

A collection of poems by BESSIE CALHOUN BIRD of Philadelphia that contained a forward by ARTHUR HUFF FAUSET, a fellow writer of the city. Alpress, a Philadelphia-based company, published 300 copies of Bird's only book. Bird published this volume, which contained poems on traditional themes such as love and nature, at a time when members of the PIRANEAN CLUB and Beaux Art Club, the two literary and arts groups of which she was a member, were meeting regularly at her home to discuss writing and art.

Bibliography

Jubilee, Vincent. *Philadelphia's Afro-American Literary Circle and the Harlem Renaissance.* Ann Arbor, Mich.: University Microfilms, 1982.

Aldridge, Ira Frederick (1807–1867)

A British-American actor celebrated for his impressive dramatic accomplishments throughout

Europe. Aldridge, the grandson of a Senegalese prince became a British citizen and dazzled countless audiences. His sophisticated performances of classical dramas were powerful challenges to the continued cultural and social disenfranchisement of people of color.

Ira was born in New York City to Daniel and Lurona Aldridge, free people of color. His father was a straw vendor and preacher, and both his parents endeavored to provide their children a good education. As a student at the African Free School in the city, Aldridge frequently won prizes for oratory, and it was there that he began to realize his dramatic potential. In 1852, he married Margaret Gill, an Englishwoman. In 1865, one year after her death, he remarried. His second wife was Amanda Pauline von Brandt, a Swede. He had four children: Ira Daniel, Luranah, Ira Frederick, and Amanda. Aldridge died in Lodz, Poland on 10 August 1867.

Aldridge's love for the stage blossomed when he began working in local city theaters. He also immersed himself in the African Theatre, a company that free people of color established in New York City in 1820. He took advantage of an opportunity to leave America, because there were so few possibilities there for his full advancement and development in the theater. He was 17 when he arrived in London, as the valet of James and Henry Wallack, actors whom he had met in America. Eventually, he enrolled at the University of Glasgow, Scotland, where he excelled in his studies and achieved recognition for excellence in Latin. Henry Wallack provided a key reference for Aldridge that helped him to acquire an engagement at the Royal Coburg Theatre in London. It was there, in October 1825, that Aldridge made his debut as Oronooko in the play *The Revolt of Surinam, or A Slave's Revenge.*

Aldridge became famous as a Shakespearean actor and was especially well known for his performances as Othello. He gradually began to play white roles and, in so doing, significantly broadened his repertoire and his impact on the European dramatic tradition. During the course of his career, he performed throughout Europe in such roles as Macbeth, King Lear, Richard III, and Shylock. Scholar Errol Hill notes that he introduced Shakespeare to people who never before had seen

his plays staged. Aldridge, who appeared in at least 30 European nations, also was the first Shakespearean actor to perform in Serbia and Croatia. He earned impressive honors and awards. These included the White Cross of Switzerland in 1854, admission to the National Dramatic Conservatory of Hungary in 1858, the Imperial Jubilee de Tolstoy Medal in 1858, and knighthood in the House of the Royal Saxon Ernestinischen in 1858.

Aldridge often experienced racism during his career, but he refused to allow it to curtail his professional development. He was denied access to prominent theaters and forced to accept engagements in lesser-known playhouses. Yet, as Hill notes, Aldridge's career constituted "substantial proof to the proponents emancipation that, given the opportunity, the black man could rise from the degradation of slavery to the highest levels of artistic expression" (Hill, 18–19). He was well apprised of racial matters and did not hesitate to use his position to challenge slavery as well. He gave financial support to antislavery organizations and, on one occasion, he purchased and freed a family of five fugitive slaves who had been captured and were being auctioned.

Aldridge's impressive accomplishments motivated aspiring African-American actors and companies during the Harlem Renaissance. The ALDRIDGE PLAYERS, a group established in the mid-1920s, honored the great tragedian by choosing his name for their company. HOWARD UNIVERSITY established the Ira Aldridge Theatre Building on its campus. In 1923, JAMES WELDON JOHNSON rallied African Americans to raise $1,000 for the Ira Aldridge Memorial Chair, a position affiliated with the Shakespeare Memorial Theatre in Stratford-upon-Avon.

Bibliography

Hill, Errol. *Shakespeare in Sable: A History of Black Shakespearean Actors.* Amherst: University of Massachusetts Press, 1984.

Lindfors, Bernth, " 'Nothing Extenuate, nor Set Down aught in Malice': New Biographical Information on Ira Aldridge." *African American Review* 28, no. 3 (fall 1994): 457–472.

Marshall, Herbert and Mildred Stock. *Ira Aldridge: The Negro Tragedian.* Carbondale: Southern Illinois University Press, 1968.

Peyton, Fountain. *A Glance at the Life of Ira Frederick Aldridge.* Washington, D.C.: R. K. Pendleton, 1917.

Aldridge Players

A small African-American theater group in NEW YORK CITY whose name paid tribute to Ira Aldridge, the great 19th-century tragedian who was "the most famous of Negro actors" and "had few equals in the part of Othello, the Moor" (Negro Year Book, 1925–1926: 354). The Aldridge Players presented three superior productions during the summer of 1926. THEOPHILUS LEWIS, the highly respected MESSENGER theater critic, praised the company for their versions of three FRANK WILSON plays, *SUGAR CAIN, Color Worship,* and *Flies.*

Bibliography

Lewis, Theophilus. "Theatre." *The Messenger* (August 1926).

Marshall, Herbert. *Ira Aldridge, the Negro Tragedian.* Carbondale: Southern Illinois University Press, 1968.

Alexander, Lewis (1900–1945)

An actor, poet, and editor born in WASHINGTON, D.C., on 4 July 1900. Alexander, a student at both HOWARD UNIVERSITY and the UNIVERSITY OF PENNSYLVANIA, immersed himself in African American theater in New York. He collaborated with several groups, including the ALDRIDGE PLAYERS, HOWARD UNIVERSITY PLAYERS, and ETHIOPIAN ART PLAYERS. His poems, inspired by Japanese haiku and traditional poetical forms, were not especially race-conscious. They appeared in *FIRE!!, OPPORTUNITY,* the *SATURDAY EVENING QUILL,* and in *CAROLING DUSK,* the 1927 collection of poems by African-American writers edited by COUNTEE CULLEN. In 1927 Alexander was the editor of the *Carolina Magazine* issue that was devoted to works by African-American writers.

Bibliography

Hughes, Langston, and Arna Bontemps, eds. *The Poetry of the Negro, 1756–1970.* 1949, reprint, Garden City, N.Y.: Doubleday, 1970.

Alexander, Raymond Pace (1898–1975)

Born in Philadelphia, Pennsylvania, Alexander earned a bachelor of science degree from the UNIVERSITY OF PENNSYLVANIA in 1920 and an LL.B. degree from HARVARD Law School in 1923. During his legal career, which included a presidency of the National Negro Bar Association and a lengthy tenure on the Philadelphia Court of Common Pleas, he published essays on African Americans and the law. In February 1923 he published in *OPPORTUNITY* a forthright indictment of Harvard's racist residential policy that barred African-American students from the campus dormitories. His September 1931 essay on "The Negro Lawyer" was a spirited call to African-American lawyers, whom he regarded as essential defenders of black social, civil, and legal rights.

Bibliography

Alexander, Raymond Pace. "Voices from Harvard's Own Negroes." *Opportunity* (February 1923).
———. "The Negro Lawyer." *Opportunity* (September 1931).

Alexander Pushkin Poetry Prize

A literary award named in honor of Alexander Pushkin (1799–1837), the celebrated Russian poet, and one of the many poetry prizes offered by *OPPORTUNITY* magazine, the official publication of the Urban League. Winning entries included "Golgotha Is a Mountain" by ARNA BONTEMPS in 1926.

Alfred A. Knopf, Inc.

The highly respected publishing house established in 1915, founded by ALFRED ABRAHAM KNOPF, a COLUMBIA UNIVERSITY graduate, native of NEW YORK CITY, and cofounder of the journal *AMERICAN MERCURY.*

Knopf gained a reputation for excellence and contributed much to literary history and scholarship through its attention to emerging and established authors in and beyond America. The publishers gained much respect for their promotion of European writers such as Albert Camus, Franz Kafka, André Gide, and Thomas Mann. The press also prided itself on its list of important American authors who included Willa Cather, Ezra Pound, and Wallace Stevens. Books by Knopf soon came to be recognized by the distinctive Borzoi symbol. Inspired by the Russian wolfhound and suggested by Knopf's wife and instrumental coworker, Blanche Wolf Knopf, the image signaled the press's commitment to literary excellence.

Knopf published the works of many leading writers of the Harlem Renaissance. It produced THE WEARY BLUES (1926), the first volume of poems by LANGSTON HUGHES, and went on to publish several additional Hughes works such as the writer's first novel, NOT WITHOUT LAUGHTER (1930). Other Harlem Renaissance works that the press published included WALTER WHITE's FIRE IN THE FLINT (1924), RUDOLPH FISHER's THE WALLS OF JERICHO (1928), and NELLA LARSEN's QUICK-SAND (1928) and PASSING (1929).

Poet CLAUDE MCKAY had mixed encounters with the press. He was confident that Knopf would publish SPRING IN NEW HAMPSHIRE (1922), his first American book, but they did not. The press later rejected Color Scheme, his first book manuscript but one filled with graphic images and obscenity. McKay never published the work; he destroyed it and began work on HOME TO HARLEM, the novel published by HARPER & BROTHERS that invigorated his career in the United States.

Bibliography

Alfred A. Knopf Quarter Century. New York: Plimpton Press, 1940.

Knopf, Alfred A. Portrait of a Publisher 1915–1965. Vol. 1: Reminiscences and Reflections. New York: The Ty-pophiles, 1965.

Lewis, Randolph. "Langston Hughes and Alfred A. Knopf, Inc., 1925–1935." Library Chronicle of the University of Texas 22, no. 4 (1992): 52–63.

Moore, Heather, and Lewis Randolph, eds. "The Education of a Publisher: Selections from the Memoirs of Alfred A. Knopf." Library Chronicle of the University of Texas 22, no. 4 (1992): 8–49.

Tebbel, John William. Between Covers: The Rise and Transformation of Book Publishing in America. New York: Oxford University Press, 1987.

Alhambra Theatre

A popular entertainment venue located at 126th Street and Seventh Avenue. It became especially well known because it was there in 1926 that the celebrated Blackbirds production, starring Florence Mills and Bill Robinson, played.

The theater also was home to dramatic stock companies and troupes such as the All Star Colored Civic Repertory Company, which was in residence during May and June of 1927. The Alhambra Players, whose members included accomplished veterans of the stage and of film, were based at the theater from 1928 through 1931. Its members included Evelyn Preer, Charles Moore, and J. Lawrence Criner, and the troupe offered "half-hour 'playlet[s],'" which complemented the main entertainment of silent films or vaudeville shows.

According to theater historian Bernard Peterson, the Alhambra "booked some black acts, but had a regular policy of racial discrimination" (Peterson, 10). That policy eventually lapsed in the early 1920s, and the theater managers actively began to solicit African American patrons.

Bibliography

Peterson, Bernard L. ed. The African American Theatre Directory, 1816–1960: A Comprehensive Guide to Early Black Theatre Organizations, Companies, Theatres, and Performing Groups. Westport, Conn.: Greenwood Press, 1997.

Allen, Cleveland (1887–1953)

A journalist who wrote for the New York Age, the pro–BOOKER T. WASHINGTON paper edited by T. THOMAS FORTUNE, and was the New York agent for the CHICAGO DEFENDER and the Indianapolis Freeman. Allen, who studied music at NEW YORK UNIVERSITY and the Angelus Academy of Music, also lectured and published articles on African-American folk music in scholarly music journals.

Bibliography

Pride, Armistead Scott, and Clint C. Wilson. A History Of The Black Press. Washington, D.C.: Howard University Press, 1997.

Simmons, Charles. The African American Press: A History of News Coverage During National Crises, with Special Reference to Four Black Newspapers, 1827–1965. Jefferson, N.C.: McFarland & Co., 1998.

Vogel, Todd, ed. *The Black Press: New Literary and Historical Essays*, New Brunswick, N.J.: Rutgers University Press, 2001.

All God's Chillun Got Wings Eugene O'Neill
(1924)
A controversial play by white playwright EUGENE O'NEILL about an interracial marriage between an African-American intellectual man and a white woman. The script, which O'Neill wrote with the actor PAUL ROBESON in mind for its leading role, drew considerable fire and protest from whites, including then-mayor of New York City Jimmie Walker, because of its challenge to conservative social mores. Robeson performed in the Greenwich Village Theatre shows that began in August 1924. *The NEW YORK TIMES* praised him for the "admirable force" that he brought to the leading role. O'Neill's play, like *IN ABRAHAM'S BOSOM* (1926) by PAUL GREEN, was part of the growing canon of white-authored plays about African-American-related themes.

Bibliography
Frank, Glenda. "Tempest in Black and White: The 1924 Premier of Eugene O'Neill's *All God's Chillun Got Wings*." *Resources for American Literary Study* 26, no. 1 (2000): 75–89.

Kramer, Victor, and Robert Russ, eds. *The Harlem Renaissance Re-Examined*. Troy, N.Y.: Whitson Pub., 1997.

O'Neill, Eugene. *All God's Chillun Got Wings; and Welded*. New York: Boni & Liveright, 1924.

The New York Times, 19 August 1924, p. 9.

Along This Way James Weldon Johnson
(1933)
The first work of African-American autobiography to be reviewed in *The New York Times*, *Along This Way* is the 1933 autobiography of JAMES WELDON JOHNSON, the executive secretary of the NATIONAL ASSOCIATION FOR THE ADVANCEMENT OF COLORED PEOPLE (NAACP) and the highly respected editor of several anthologies of African-American writing. Johnson, who penned the anonymous 1912 edition of the *AUTOBIOGRAPHY OF AN EX-COLOURED MAN*, affixed his name to his only fictional work when it was republished in 1927. Some critics suggest that he published *Along This Way*, in part, to dispel the rumors that the fictional *Autobiography*, which chronicled the life of an unnamed protagonist who decides to pass for white, was based on his own life.

The memoir, which Johnson dedicated to his wife, Grace Nail Johnson, "in love and comradeship," was divided into four sections. It offers detailed genealogical information and informative accounts of Johnson's life, developing awareness of racism, literary endeavors, experiences in the world of commercial songwriting, personal relationships, and political work within and beyond the NAACP, the organization to which he devoted much of his life.

Bibliography
Johnson, James Weldon. *Along This Way: The Autobiography of James Weldon Johnson*. 1933, reprint, New York: Da Capo Press, 2000.

Levy, Eugene. *James Weldon Johnson, Black Leader, Black Voice*. Chicago: University of Chicago Press, 1973.

Alpha Kappa Alpha, Inc.
The first Greek-letter sorority founded by African-American women in the United States. Founded in January 1908 at HOWARD UNIVERSITY by undergraduate students led by Ethel Hedgeman Lyle, the organization grew into an influential network that implemented vital social programs, lobbied for black political rights, and supported racial uplift throughout and beyond the years of the Harlem Renaissance. Members were part of key Renaissance-era institutions such as the NATIONAL ASSOCIATION FOR THE ADVANCEMENT OF COLORED PEOPLE (NAACP) and the YOUNG WOMEN'S CHRISTIAN ASSOCIATION (YWCA).

Bibliography
Parker, Marjorie. *Alpha Kappa Alpha in the Eye of the Beholder*. Washington, D.C.: Alpha Kappa Alpha Sorority, 1979.

———. *Alpha Kappa Alpha through the Years, 1908–1988*. Chicago: Mobium Press, 1990.

Ross, Lawrence. *The Divine Nine: The History of African American Fraternities and Sororities*. New York: Kensington Books, 2000.

American Mercury

A monthly literary magazine founded by H. L. MENCKEN, journalist, and George Jean Nathan, theater critic, in 1924. The periodical, which offered spirited and satiric articles on contemporary American life and society, also published key writers of the Harlem Renaissance. Its November 1924 publication of COUNTEE CULLEN's "The Shroud of Colour" resulted in good critical attention for the emerging young poet.

Bibliography

Bontemps, Arna. *The Harlem Renaissance Remembered: Essays Edited with a Memoir*. New York: Dodd, Mead, 1972.

Singleton, Marvin Kenneth. *H. L. Mencken and the American Mercury Adventure*. Durham, N.C.: Duke University Press, 1962.

American Negro Academy (1897–1928)

Founded on March 5, 1897, the American Negro Academy (ANA) was the first major African-American learned society. Established in WASHINGTON, D.C., by Alexander Crummell, its officers and members represented the intellectual and professional elite of the day. Individuals associated with the organization included Crummell, its first president; Paul Laurence Dunbar, one of the five founding members; W. E. B. DUBOIS, ALAIN LOCKE, and CARTER G. WOODSON. In addition to its platforms on race, the ANA produced biographical and social history monographs including *The Social Evolution of the Black South* (1911) by W. E. B. DuBois.

Bibliography

Cromwell, John W. "American Negro Academy," *African Times and Orient Review* 2 (November–December 1913): 243–244.

Moss, Alfred A. Jr. *The American Negro Academy: Voice of the Talented Tenth*. Baton Rouge: Louisiana State University Press, 1981.

Amsterdam News

A leading New York City–based newspaper and the first African-American newspaper to have unionized workers. James Henry Anderson, a native of South Carolina, founded the paper in 1909. By the late 1920s, it was highly respected for its coverage of New York City issues and its uncompromising analysis of racism. The name of the paper was inspired by the name of Anderson's neighborhood and the community in which he began publication.

Anderson was an extremely enterprising journalist. According to Clint Wilson, he "parlayed a $10 investment, six sheets of paper and two pencils into his venture and launched one of the most influential publications in the annals of the Black press" (Wilson, 1). With the help of Edward A. Warren, his business partner, Anderson was able to expand the paper and its offices. On the eve of the Harlem Renaissance, the *Amsterdam News* offices had moved from 135th Street to Seventh Avenue.

In 1921, Warren's widow, Sadie, and his daughter Odessa agreed to maintain Warren's financial and professional commitments to the paper. The newspaper staff included WILLIAM KELLEY, THELMA BERLACK, and R. LIONEL DOUGHERTY. Journalist and writer EUGENE GORDON suggested that the *Amsterdam News* was the best African-American newspaper in the country. The newspaper continues to be published out of its Harlem offices.

Bibliography

Gordon, Eugene. "The Negro Press." *Annals* [of the American Academy of Political and Social Sience] 140 (November 1928).

Ottley, Roi, and William Weatherby, eds. *The Negro in New York: An Informal Social History*. New York: Praeger, 1969.

Pride, Armistead Scott, and Clint C. Wilson. *A History of the Black Press*. Washington, D.C.: Howard University Press, 1997.

Wilson, Clint C. II. "History of Amsterdam News." Available online. URL: http://www.amsterdamnews.org/News/aboutus. Accessed December 2004.

Anderson, Garland (ca. 1886–1939)

A Kansas-born playwright who was working as a bellhop in San Francisco when he completed *Appearances* (1925), a sobering play about an African-American man falsely accused of raping a white woman. With this work, Anderson became the first African-American playwright to see his full-length work produced on BROADWAY. Following his historic dramatic accomplishment, Anderson published UNCOMMON SENSE (1937) and traveled to England. He invented a popular malted milk beverage during his sojourn in London.

Anderson, Marian (1902–1993)

A Philadelphia native who became one of the best-known concert singers of her day. She displayed poise and professionalism throughout her career, especially when confronted with racism. The most dramatic test of Anderson's composure occurred in 1939, when the Daughters of the American Revolution refused to grant Anderson access to Constitution Hall in Washington, D.C. Intervention from Eleanor Roosevelt, Harold Ickes, and others led to Anderson's historic concert at the Lincoln Memorial. During her 30-year career, Anderson received numerous awards, including a JULIUS ROSENWALD FELLOWSHIP and the NAACP's prestigious SPINGARN MEDAL.

Bibliography

Anderson, Marian. My Lord, What a Morning: An Autobiography. 1956, reprint, Urbana: University of Illinois Press, 2002.

Keiler, Allan. Marian Anderson: A Singer's Journey. New York: Scribner, 2000.

Southern, Eileen. The Music of Black Americans: A History. New York: W. W. Norton, 1997.

Anderson, Sherwood (1876–1941)

The white Ohio-born author who became a well-known member of the Chicago Renaissance and who began publishing regularly in avant-garde magazines such as THE SEVEN ARTS, accepted invitations from JESSIE FAUSET and JEAN TOOMER to participate in the dynamic arts movement that was the Harlem Renaissance. While he did not accept ALAIN LOCKE's invitation to submit a piece to THE NEW NEGRO, the seminal collection of writings by and about African-American culture, identity, and art, Anderson did agree to provide Jessie Fauset with a piece that could be included in the CRISIS symposium on the representation of African Americans in art.

Jean Toomer tried to enlist Anderson's support for a magazine that would celebrate African-American artists, scholarship, and culture. Toomer's overtures resulted in a productive but sometimes trying relationship between the two. Anderson's contact with Toomer led to his involvement in the publication of CANE. While Toomer acknowledged his high regard for Anderson's work and noted that works such as Winesberg, Ohio and Triumph of the Egg had influenced his own literary visions and regionalist sensibilities, he did chafe against Anderson's tendency to emphasize his black identity.

Bibliography

Anderson, David. Critical Essays on Sherwood Anderson. Boston: G. K. Hall, 1981.

Anderson, Mark. "Sherwood Anderson and Jean Toomer," Negro American Literature Forum 9 (summer 1975).

Howe, Irving. Sherwood Anderson. Stanford: Stanford University Press, 1966.

Scruggs, Charles. "The Reluctant Witness: What Jean Toomer Remembered from Winesburg, Ohio." Studies in American Fiction 28, no. 1 (spring 2000): 77–100.

Townsend, Kim. Sherwood Anderson. Boston: Houghton Mifflin, 1987.

Andrew, Joseph Maree

The occasional pseudonym of MARITA BONNER. She published several works under this name, including "One Boy's Crisis," a short story that appeared in the November 1927 CRISIS, and "And I Passed By," a piece that CHARLES S. JOHNSON selected for inclusion in Ebony and Topaz: A Collectanea (1927).

Bibliography

Flynn, Joyce, and Joyce Occomy Striklin. Frye Street & Environs: The Collected Works of Marita Bonner. Boston: Beacon Press, 1987.

Andrews, Regina M. Anderson (Ursula Trelling) (1901–1993)

A woman whose work at the NEW YORK PUBLIC LIBRARY (NYPL) and friendships with figures like ETHEL RAY NANCE, secretary to NAACP leader JAMES WELDON JOHNSON, placed her at the heart of the Harlem Renaissance.

The daughter of William Grant, a lawyer, and Margaret Simons Anderson, Andrews attended both WILBERFORCE UNIVERSITY and the UNIVERSITY OF CHICAGO. She earned her master's in library science from the Library School of COLUMBIA UNIVERSITY. In 1936 Andrews became the first African-American supervising librarian at the NYPL 135th Street Branch.

Andrews was known for hosting gatherings for artists and writers in the SUGAR HILL apartment that she shared with Louella Tucker and Ethel Nance, secretary to OPPORTUNITY editor CHARLES S. JOHNSON. Andrews also was one of the visionary leaders in the African-American theater movement that flourished during the Harlem Renaissance. She collaborated with CRISIS editor W. E. B. DuBois and the writer and artist Gwendolyn Bennett to found the Crigwa Players. This group, which later became the HARLEM EXPERIMENTAL THEATRE, was based in the basement of the NYPL branch in which Andrews worked. The troupe staged two of her plays during the early 1930s.

Andrews was also an accomplished playwright and scholar. She wrote several plays, a children's book, library-related articles, and was the coeditor of a historical chronology of African Americans in New York City. Like NELLA LARSEN and MARITA BONNER, Andrews used a pseudonym when she pursued her creative goals. She wrote plays under the name of URSULA TRELLING. Her 1931 work, CLIMBING JACOB'S LADDER, was inspired by the tireless antilynching activist IDA B. WELLS BARNETT. W. E. B. DuBois encouraged Andrews to polish the piece and when presented with the revised version, he declared that the play was "thrilling." She based her 1933 play *Underground* on the antebellum Underground Railroad, the extensive abolitionist network that helped enslaved African Americans escape to freedom. The Drama Committee of the New York Public Library also produced the play. These and other works such as *The Man Who Passed* and *Matilda* displayed Andrews's

A May 1925 photograph of (left to right) Langston Hughes, Charles Johnson, E. Franklin Frazier, Rudolph Fisher, and Hubert Delany taken at the Sugar Hill apartment of Regina Andrews and her apartment mates Louella Tucker and Ethel Nance *(Yale Collection of American Literature, Beinecke Rare Book and Manuscript Library)*

continued interest in African-American social and political dilemmas and self-determination. She continued to publish well after the Harlem Renaissance. In 1971 she coedited with Ethel Ray Nance the *Chronology of African Americans in New York, 1621–1966.*

Throughout her career and in the years beyond the Harlem Renaissance, Andrews maintained close ties to leading race organizations and broadened her influence by participating in groups like the New York State Commission for Human Rights.

Bibliography

Hatch, James V., and Omanii Abdullah. *Black Playwrights, 1823–1977: An Annotated Bibliography of Plays.* New York: Bowker, 1977.

Huggins, Nathan. *Harlem Renaissance.* New York: Oxford University Press, 1973.

Regina Andrews Papers, Schomburg Center for Research in Black Culture, New York Public Library.

Antar of Araby Maude Cuney Hare (1930)

A play written by MAUDE CUNEY HARE just six years before her untimely death due to cancer. In this work, Hare reflected her long-standing interest in anthropology and the ways in which African traditions and perspectives permeated Western culture. She produced a provocative pan-Africanist meditation in this romantic drama based on Antar, a foundational figure in the Arab literary tradition. In her play, the blackness and low social station of the dark-skinned slave-poet Antar have thwarted his ambitions. His frustrations are further highlighted when he gains a chieftain's daughter for his wife. Hare's depictions of caste prejudice and the slave man's innate noble qualities resonated with ongoing Harlem Renaissance–era debates about and representations of caste, prejudice, and black self-determination as illustrated in other notable works such as *DARK PRINCESS* by W. E. B. DuBois, *AUTOBIOGRAPHY OF AN EX-COLOURED MAN* by JAMES WELDON JOHNSON, and *QUICKSAND* by NELLA LARSEN.

Bibliography

Kramer, Victor, and Robert Russ, eds. *The Harlem Renaissance Re-Examined.* Troy, N.Y.: Whitson, 1997.

Anthology of American Negro Literature

A series of anthologies published by the Modern Library. V. F. CALVERTON, a white Marxist intellectual who supported African-American artistic and literary efforts, edited the first volume, which appeared in 1929.

Bibliography

Kramer, Victor, and Robert Russ, eds. *The Harlem Renaissance Re-Examined.* Troy, N.Y.: Whitson, 1997.

Anthology of Magazine Verse

A popular anthology that WILLIAM STANLEY BRAITHWAITE, a Boston poet and journalist, inaugurated in 1913. To be chosen for inclusion in the highly selective journal, which stands as a reliable index of the 20th-century American poetical tradition, was an indication of artistic potential and conferred a measure of success on all who were published.

Braithwaite believed that it was more productive to focus on talent than on race. He included a wide variety of Harlem Renaissance writers in the annual anthologies but made no effort to privilege black writers of the period.

Anthology of Verse by American Negroes, An White and Jackson, eds. (1924)

An anthology edited by NEWMAN IVEY WHITE and WALTER CLINTON JACKSON, two white Southerners who wanted to promote good race relations. The volume, which spanned the black poetical tradition, included works by Phillis Wheatley and more contemporary 20th-century poets like WILLIAM STANLEY BRAITHWAITE. Also included were works by COUNTEE CULLEN, GEORGIA DOUGLAS JOHNSON, GEORGE MARGETSON, and JAMES WELDON JOHNSON. The three-year lag between the completion of the manuscript in 1921 and its publication in 1924, however, prevented the editors from providing a truly current and comprehensive set of works by many Harlem Renaissance writers. The book is an especially good resource because of its informative biographical profiles of each poet.

"Antropoi" John F. Matheus (1928)

A short story by JOHN F. MATHEUS set in the West Virginia countryside that addresses the tension between Americans of African descent and European immigrants who are better able to assimilate into the dominant white culture.

"Antropoi" chronicles the division and then restored connection between Bushrod Winter, a man born free in Ohio in the last year of the Civil War, and Demetrius Pappaniasus, a Greek immigrant whose brown-skinned Syrian wife and children symbolize the problematic notion of whiteness in America. White privilege, racial segregation, and the Ku Klux Klan severely test the solidarity and the conceptions of citizenship of both men. Matheus's story, which appeared in the August 1928 issue of OPPORTUNITY, underscored the pathos associated with assimilation, ethnicity, and racial alienation.

Apollo Theater

Formerly known as Seamon's Music Hall, the Apollo Theater is located on 125th Street between Seventh and Eighth Avenues in HARLEM.

It offered audiences upscale entertainment featuring such talented performers as Benny Carter's orchestra but also presented comedy acts that tended to veer away from the more decorous musical presentations. Theater historian Bernard Peterson notes that the theater "regularly emphasized a vaudeville policy, with films only 'sandwiched' in between live performances" (Peterson, 17). One of the popular shows booked at the Apollo during the Harlem Renaissance was the 1933 production of *Blackbirds*, starring Bill Robinson, Lionel Monagas, and Edith Wilson.

The Apollo is one of the best-known theaters in America and continues to be synonymous with African-American talent.

Bibliography

Anderson, Jervis. *This Was Harlem: A Cultural Portrait, 1900–1950.* New York: Farrar Straus Giroux, 1982.

Peterson, Bernard L. ed. *The African American Theatre Directory, 1816–1960: A Comprehensive Guide to Early Black Theatre Organizations, Companies, The-atres, and Performing Groups.* Westport, Conn.: Greenwood Press, 1997.

Appearances Garland Anderson (1925)

A play originally entitled *Don't Judge by Appearances* that enjoyed 23 BROADWAY performances in fall 1925 and secured for GARLAND ANDERSON, who had completed it in less than one month, the honor of being the first African-American playwright to have a full-length play on Broadway. Anderson, who was working as a bellhop in San Francisco when he wrote the script, crafted a daring story about Carl Sanderson, an African-American bellhop falsely accused by a woman of rape. The similarities between Anderson and his protagonist, represented by their occupations and the modest variation in surnames, infuse the drama with additional realism and tension. The drama is further complicated by the fact that the accuser ultimately is revealed to be a woman of color in league with an attorney who is determined to persecute Sanderson.

The primary setting for the three-act play is the Hotel Mount Shasta, a San Francisco hotel. The prologue introduces two judges and Carl, the bellhop who believes that "if he, with color, lack of education, lack of money and all against him, can work his dream out in real life, it will prove that other people with greater advantages can naturally do greater things." Judge Thornton instructs Carl to share his dream of achievement with the skeptical Judge Robinson, and the bellhop's account marks the transition into Act One and into the play itself. *Appearances* focuses mainly on Carl's plight as a man unfairly accused of a crime. It also incorporates secondary plots that focus on the white characters who are grappling with suspicious business partners, courtships, and marital problems.

Carl Sanderson, a bookish young man, represents African-American intellectual and social potential. An earnest and conscientious worker, he is engaged to Elsa Buford, the hotel's acting housekeeper, who also is a law student. Anderson reveals, however, that the couple's high professional goals and their generally impressive demeanor are not enough to protect them from racial prejudice and mob violence. One evening, Carl becomes the unfortunate target of a robbery. Elsie Benton, a white Utah woman who is posing as a widow but has deserted her husband and young son, accosts him on the street. She demands money from Sanderson, and, when he refuses her, she pretends that she has been violated and begins to scream for help. A mob quickly forms, and the true circumstances of the situation quickly are obscured. One week later, Sanderson is on trial. After a series of witnesses—including Rufus, the comedic and loquacious newly hired hotel porter—offer details about the events, Sanderson is exonerated.

Following his ordeal, Sanderson immerses himself in writing. His explanation to the hotel guests who have supported him, who are also writers, may reveal Anderson's own creative process. Sanderson notes that he "dreamed a play" and that it evolved from "just a jumble of thoughts that gradually straightened itself out, then characters came into being and . . . as they talked I put it down on paper." "All my thoughts and all they said," he muses, "were filled with a big message." Theater historians James Hatch and Ted Shine note that Anderson's bold message about African-American honor and conviction had to accommodate "a dénouement for Broadway's satisfaction" (Hatch and Shine, 101) and that the comedic, stereotypical figure of Rufus, provided that necessary foil. Hatch and Shine recognize the value of Anderson's work and insist that he "wrote for a white audience, attempting to give them something better than what they usually saw of the black man" (Hatch and Shine, 101).

Anderson's access to the New York theater world was financed in part by Al Jolson. Jolson made arrangements for Anderson's first visit to New York City, and while there, the aspiring playwright was able to have a reading of his play that generated financial backing and piqued interest in his work. The play was presented at the Waldorf before an audience of some 600 guests and Anderson "sat near by in his bellhop uniform" (Hatch and Shine, 100).

Anderson's play emerged at a time when Broadway productions avoided interracial casts and when directors often used blackface to circumvent the use of actors of color. As a result, before its successful launch, the play did provoke some white actors to abandon the project. Scholar Allen Woll notes that two "leading ladies [Myrtle Tannehill and Nedda Harrigan] left the show because they discovered 'there were going to be three Negroes in the cast'" (Woll, 10). Scholars note that despite its groundbreaking achievement, *Appearances* did not appeal to African-American audiences. Critic Benjamin Brawley seemed unfazed by the play's historic staging on Broadway and noted that "[w]hen one turns to original Negro effort in the drama he finds that most of the work that has been produced has not yet gone beyond the range of experiment and that there is great room for advance in technique" (Brawley, 280). According to Brawley, *Appearances* was "not really a racial drama" because it was "dominated by the idea that all things are possible to him that believeth and who will make the best use of his powers." It was this simplistic optimism, suggested Brawley, that diminished the play's impact and explained why it "had hardly the strength to hold the public interest for any length of time" (Brawley, 281).

Following its Broadway run at the Frolic Theater, the play moved on to Chicago and to various West Coast venues, including Seattle and San Francisco. In 1930, *Appearances* was staged briefly in London.

Bibliography

Abdul, Raoul. "The Negro Playwright on Broadway." In Lindsay Patterson, *Anthology of the American Negro in the Theatre: A Critical Approach.* New York: Publishers Company, 1970.

Brawley, Benjamin. *The Negro Genius: A New Appraisal of the Achievement of the American Negro in Literature and the Fine Arts.* New York: Biblio and Tannen, 1966.

Hatch, James V., and Ted Shine. *Black Theater U.S.A.: Forty-five Plays by Black Americans.* New York: The Free Press, 1974.

Woll, Allen. *Dictionary of the Black Theatre: Broadway, Off-Broadway, and Selected Harlem Theatre.* Westport, Conn.: Greenwood Press, 1983.

April Grasses Marion Vera Cuthbert (1936)

Published by the New York City–based Woman's Press, this volume of poems by MARION VERA CUTHBERT surprised critics. Cuthbert, a COLUMBIA UNIVERSITY Ph.D. who was well known for her strident activism in civil rights and women's rights circles, produced a volume that was essentially raceless. Cuthbert's focus recalls the consistent effort of

other Harlem Renaissance writers such as COUN-
TEE CULLEN and WILLIAM STANLEY BRAITHWAITE
who stressed the importance of recognizing the productions rather than the race of African-American
writers.

Arlen, Harold (1905–1986)

A white songwriter who was employed by the
COTTON CLUB and cowrote such notable hits as
"Stormy Weather" for Ethel Waters in 1933. He
also cowrote the lyrics and music used in *St. Louis
Woman,* the musical comedy on which COUNTEE
CULLEN and ARNA BONTEMPS collaborated.

Bibliography

Haskins, James. *The Cotton Club.* New York: Random
House, 1977.

Associated Negro Press

Founded in 1919 by CLAUDE ALBERT BARNETT, an
Illinois native, TUSKEGEE INSTITUTE graduate, and
expert on African art. Barnett's organization, based
on the Associated Press news service, provided articles and information relating to African Americans to 500-plus black newspapers and magazines
during the 1920s. During the post-World War II
era, the Associated Negro Press provided information to African publications as well. The service
closed soon after Barnett's death in 1967.

Bibliography

Vincent, Theodore. *Voices of a Black Nation: Political
Journalism in the Harlem Renaissance.* Trenton, N.J.:
Africa World Press, 1973.

Association for the Study of Negro Life and History

Organized by CARTER G. WOODSON and four colleagues in CHICAGO in 1915. The association was
dedicated to promoting the study of African and
African-American history and culture, supporting research, publishing works relating to these fields, and
fostering harmonious relations between whites and
people of color. One of its most impressive and important contributions was the formation of the JOUR-
NAL OF NEGRO HISTORY, a journal that appeared

first in 1916 and is still published today. In 1937 the
organization, bolstered by private donations and
funds from supporters of black ventures like Julius
Rosenwald, the sponsor of the ROSENWALD FEL-
LOWSHIP, began publishing the *Negro History Bulletin.*

Bibliography

Conyers, James, ed. *Carter G. Woodson: A Historical
Reader.* New York: Garland, 2000.
Goggin, Jacqueline. *Carter G. Woodson: A Life in Black
History.* Baton Rouge: Louisiana State University
Press, 1993.
Woodson, Carter G. *Ten Years of Collecting and Publishing
the Records of the Negro.* Washington, D.C.: Associa-
tion for the Study of Negro Life and History, 1925.

Atlanta

The capital city of Georgia that is home to several
African-American colleges and universities, including Spelman College, MOREHOUSE COLLEGE,
and Clark-Atlanta University, founded in 1988
when the historic ATLANTA UNIVERSITY merged
with Clark College.

Prominent Harlem Renaissance figures had for-
mative years in and enjoyed strong ties with the city.
W. E. B. DuBois, WILLIAM STANLEY BRAITHWAITE,
JAMES WELDON JOHNSON, and GEORGIA DOUGLAS
JOHNSON all had ties to Atlanta University. The
African-American journal, *Voice of the Negro,* edited
by JESSE MAX BARBER, was founded there in 1904.
This was also the city in which BOOKER T. WASH-
INGTON delivered his 1895 "Atlanta Exposition Ad-
dress," the speech in which he reaffirmed his
blueprint for racial accommodationism.

W. E. B. DuBois and his first wife, Nina, suffered a tragic loss due to the city's segregated practices and unequal facilities for African Americans.
The couple was unable to secure medical treatment for their sick son, Burghardt, because of the
paucity of African-American physicians and the
entrenched segregation of white Atlanta hospitals.
As a result, their first child and only son succumbed to diphtheria.

Bibliography

Kuhn, Clifford, Harlon Joye, and E. Bernard West. *Living
Atlanta: An Oral History of the City, 1914–1948.*
Athens: University of Georgia Press, 1990.

Lewis, David Levering. *W. E. B. DuBois: Biography of a Race, 1868–1919*. New York: Henry Holt and Company, 1993.

Atlanta University

The alma mater and intellectual home of pioneering American writers, activists, and intellectuals, Atlanta University was established in 1865 by Northern Congregationalist missionaries.

JAMES WELDON JOHNSON, an NAACP leader, is one of its best-known graduates. Joseph Bibb, founder of the *Chicago Whip*, enrolled there, and GEORGIA DOUGLAS JOHNSON, the Washington, D.C., poet, furthered her studies there as well. In 1897 W. E. B. DuBois, a sociology Ph.D. from HARVARD UNIVERSITY, began his 13-year tenure there. In 1935 WILLIAM STANLEY BRAITHWAITE joined the faculty as a professor of creative writing, a position that he held for 10 years. The institution is known now as Clark Atlanta University following its 1988 merger with Clark College, one of the city's historically black institutions.

Bibliography

Bacote, Clarence. *The Story of Atlanta University. A Century of Service, 1865–1965*. Atlanta: Atlanta University Press, 1969.

Lewis, David Levering. *W. E. B. DuBois: Biography of a Race, 1868–1919*. New York: Henry Holt and Company, 1993.

Atlantic Monthly, The

A highly respected "magazine of literature, art, and politics" that was founded in Boston in November 1857. James Russell Lowell, a Harvard University graduate, poet, and literary critic, was the first editor and served from 1857 through 1861. The writer William Dean Howells, whose poetry, fiction, and literary reviews appeared in the journal, eventually became one of its best-known editors. From 1871 and throughout his tenure as editor, Howells encouraged a diverse group of writers, including Stephen Crane, Paul Laurence Dunbar, Sarah Orne Jewett, CHARLES CHESNUTT, and Edith Wharton. During the 19th century, prominent writers such as Nathaniel Hawthorne, Harriet Beecher Stowe, and Mark Twain published memorable pieces in the journal. In 1869, Stowe's controversial essay on Lord Byron appeared and prompted some 15,000 readers to cancel their subscriptions. Two years later, in 1871, the journal paid Bret Harte the impressive sum of $10,000 for 12 stories. Twain's writing on his adventures aboard American steamboats, on which he based his 1883 book entitled *Life on the Mississippi*, appeared in the *Atlantic* in 1875.

Charles Chesnutt was the first African-American writer to be published in the monthly periodical. During the 1920s the *Atlantic* began publishing articles of a more political nature, including essays by African-American figures such as BOOKER T. WASHINGTON. It also published the works of Harlem Renaissance writers such as RUDOLPH FISHER, who made his literary debut with "The City of Refuge," the short story that appeared in 1925.

Attaway, William (1911–1986)

A novelist, playwright, and composer who began to publish in the last years of the Harlem Renaissance. Two years after he published his first novel, *Let Me Breathe Thunder* (1939), he completed BLOOD ON THE FORGE (1941). Between 1950 and 1985, Attaway published works that included two books on music and two scripts, one of which focused on the Atlanta serial killings of African-American boys.

Critics have drawn parallels between Attaway's works of sobering realism and those written by ARNA BONTEMPS and RICHARD WRIGHT. His first novel focused on white transients and offered a compelling account of depression-era life. It was Attaway's second work of fiction, however, that revealed his capacity for generating riveting accounts of African-American life and experiences. His tale about three southern brothers who join the black migration to the North is a tragic story about the crisis of black masculinity, the social tensions surrounding integration, and the sometimes overwhelming and inhumane demands of the American urban workplace.

At the Coffee House George S. Schuyler (1925)

A sparse one-act play by GEORGE S. SCHUYLER that appeared in the June 1925 issue of *The MESSENGER*.

The three characters, identified only by the generic titles "The Woman," "The Man," and "The Waitress," speculate about whether or not there are African Americans who resemble the bevy of Negro characters in contemporary writing. The shabbily dressed couple reappears in the second scene as "faultlessly dressed" individuals. Schuyler suggests that their improved self-presentation and apparent material privilege is a sign of how well they have profited from the market for black stereotypes.

Bibliography

Peplow, Michael. *George S. Schuyler*. Boston: Twayne Publishers, 1980.

"Attic Romance" Florence Marion Harmon
(1929)

A short story by FLORENCE MARION HARMON that appeared in the second annual edition of the African-American and Boston-based literary magazine, the SATURDAY EVENING QUILL.

The plot centers on a lonely artist who tries to deal with his feelings of attraction toward his neighbor. Janet Murray, an artist, moves into the top floor of Carleton Chambers. Her downstairs neighbor is completely annoyed by her presence. Not only does she wear vivid colors that distract him, but the smell of her cooking prevents him from "forget[ting] the existence of the green-smock girl." He eventually makes her acquaintance by going up to borrow some lace that he hopes to use in one of his art projects. He begins to give in to his interest in her. However, it is only when he happens to pass her door and see her posing dramatically before a "tall, dark young man sprawled in her most comfortable chair," that he realizes his feelings. When he finds out later that the man is Murray's brother and not a suitor, the artist asks her out to dinner immediately. He also requests that she wear the "ravishing evening gown of green velvet" and the "huge green feather fan" that she donned and paraded before her brother. Murray demurs, and the story closes as she insists that they concentrate on their newfound interest and celebrate the present moment.

Harmon's story and its focus on romance, the professional woman, and the power of domesticity contributed to ongoing debates about the evolving role of women during the Harlem Renaissance. Her representation of a woman whose pursuit of art does not detract from her desirability or her interest in social relationships does much to underscore the realities with which women and men of the day were contending.

Aubrey, John

An unidentified African-American student and writer at Williams College used this pseudonym. Scholars have yet to identify Aubrey, who attended the same school as STERLING BROWN and ALLISON DAVIS. Aubrey's "VIRGINIA IDYLL," a tragic short story about an impoverished African-American family in the South, appeared in the April 1931 issue of OPPORTUNITY.

Aunt Sara's Wooden God Mercedes Gilbert
(1938)

The first and only novel published by MERCEDES GILBERT, an extremely talented and multifaceted woman who enjoyed successes as an actress, playwright, composer, and songwriter. In his introduction to the novel, LANGSTON HUGHES hailed the realism of Gilbert's work and described it as "an authentic everyday story of thousands of little families below the Mason-Dixon line, bound to the soil by poverty and blackness, but living their enclosed lives always in the hope that someday some one of them may escape the family group and go on to higher things." Hughes recommended the novel and assured readers who enjoyed ZORA NEALE HURSTON's JONAH'S GOURD VINE that they would find this novel appealing. Despite Hughes's enthusiasm, the book garnered few reviews and disappeared into relative obscurity until it was republished in the 1980s.

Set in the rural town of Byron, Georgia, this local-color novel traces the unfortunate and ultimately dissolute life of a cherished child named William. The only son of the now-widowed Aunt Sara and the figure to whom the title's term "wooden god" applies, William is a mulatto and the illegitimate son of Aunt Sara and one of her white employers. His half brother, Jim, the son of Sara and her husband John Carter, is a farmer. Gilbert's narrative about William, the favored but ultimately unworthy son, is set forth in a sequence of events that recall the tragic realism of Paul Laurence Dunbar's *Sport of the Gods* (1902) and descriptive accounts of a young man's descent into the world of gambling, liquor, and danger. Jim remains devoted to his mother, in spite of her preferential treatment of his brother and the victimization that he suffers at the hands of William. Gilbert's tragic portrait and searing social realism are softened by the traces of African-American resilience, determination, and love.

Bibliography

Gilbert, Mercedes. *Selected Gems of Poetry, Comedy, and Drama and Aunt Sara's Wooden God.* Introduction by Susanne Dietzel. New York: G. K. Hall, 1997.

Roses, Lorraine Elena, and Ruth Elizabeth Randolph, *Harlem Renaissance and Beyond: Literary Biographies of 100 Black Women Writers, 1900–1945.* Boston: G. K. Hall, 1990.

Autobiography of an Ex-Coloured Man
James Weldon Johnson (1912, 1927)

A gripping novel by JAMES WELDON JOHNSON published anonymously in 1912. Through the characters, the majority of whom are nameless, the author portrayed the limitations placed on African-American potential and self-expression and the consequences of living in a highly stratified and racially segregated world. The novel received little critical attention when it was published first by a small BOSTON press. Fifteen years later, in 1927, ALFRED A. KNOPF, the prestigious New York–based publishing house, reprinted the work under Johnson's name, and it garnered immediate praise and attention. Many believed that the work was Johnson's thinly veiled autobiography. The book did contain richly detailed scenes drawn from Johnson's own experiences, including a character's plans to attend ATLANTA UNIVERSITY, the author's alma mater, and the main character's work in a Florida tobacco factory. Despite these striking similarities, however, Johnson asserted that the novel was not an account of his own life story.

Six of the most important characters are the unidentified protagonist, a light-skinned African-American boy who is ultimately orphaned, his mother, two schoolmates, and the hero's white wife and the mother of his two children who dies prema-turely. The story, which moves back and forth between the South and North, underscores the chaos and indecisiveness that the main character endures as he tries to make a steady life for himself. The novel begins as he and his mother leave the Georgia town, in which his white father lives, for the North. In Connecticut the protagonist discovers that despite his light skin, he is indeed black. His ensuing crisis of self is exacerbated by the death of his mother. He returns to the South to begin music studies at Atlanta University, but the theft of his tuition money forces him to make new plans. After a stint in a cigar factory, he returns to the North and settles in New York, where he begins working for a mysterious millionaire. He is embroiled in a murderous love triangle and once again flees to the South. There, he witnesses a lynching by a white mob and is determined to protect himself from such vulnerability in the white world. He returns to New York once again, begins a lucrative business life as a white man, falls in love with a white woman who ultimately accepts his racial heritage, marries her, and begins a family. The novel ends as the protagonist, fully aware of his true identity and the pressing need to maintain his personal fiction, contends with the guilt and worry that continue to plague him.

As critic Nathan Huggins notes, the protagonist "succeeds like a Horatio Alger hero" and weathers the several tests of his honor and manhood. His decision to pass comes after he witnesses a series of racial injustices, the most dramatic of which is the lynching of a man by a white mob. The protagonist confesses his true racial identity to the woman he loves but refuses to acknowledge the overtures from childhood friends like Shiny, the promising African-American student whom he meets years later and who immediately realizes that his old friend has chosen a new life and identity for himself. The guilt and worry that plague the novel's main character embody the twoness of the American Negro of which W. E. B. DuBois wrote just 12 years earlier in his illuminating work *SOULS OF BLACK FOLK* (1903). Johnson's novel about PASSING is part of the significant body of passing literature produced during the Harlem Renaissance.

Bibliography

Fleming, Robert. *James Weldon Johnson.* Boston: Twayne Publishers, 1987.

Goellnicht, Donald. "Passing as Autobiography: James Weldon Johnson's *The Autobiography of an Ex-Coloured Man.*" *African American Review* 30, no. 1 (1996): 17–33.

Huggins, Nathan. *Harlem Renaissance.* New York: Oxford University Press, 1971.

Levy, Eugene. *James Weldon Johnson: Black Leader, Black Voice.* Chicago: University of Chicago Press, 1973.

Pisiak, Roxanna. "Irony and Subversion in James Weldon Johnson's *The Autobiography of an Ex-Coloured Man.*" *Studies in American Fiction* 21 (spring 1993): 83–96.

Price, Kenneth, and Lawrence Oliver. *Critical Essays on James Weldon Johnson.* New York: G. K. Hall, 1997.

Autumn Love Cycle, An Georgia Douglas Johnson (1928)

The third volume of poetry published by GEORGIA DOUGLAS JOHNSON, a prolific poet and playwright who was at the center of the WASHINGTON, D.C., Harlem Renaissance literary movement. ALAIN LOCKE wrote the introduction to the collection that Johnson dedicated to ZONA GALE, the white writer who had encouraged her to write plays and who also had supported Jessie Fauset's writing efforts.

Regarded as the most autobiographical, mature, and polished of Johnson's published works, *An Autumn Love Cycle* is believed to have been prompted by a love affair. It contains "I Want to Die While You Love Me," one of her most anthologized poems and the one that OWEN DODSON read at Johnson's funeral. The book, published by the lesser known New York City press of Harold Vinal, Limited, included a portion of a unadorned and whimsical title sketch by MARY EFFIE LEE NEWSOME and Johnson's sincere overture to Gale in which she thanked her for the "appreciation, encouragement and helpful criticism" that had "so heartened me." She also thanked Locke and the white writer CLEMENT WOOD for their "helpful criticism and suggestions" as she prepared the volume for publication.

The foreword to the volume, like that which W. E. B. DuBois contributed to Johnson's second collection BRONZE (1922), was both complementary and somewhat suspect. Locke, who was well known as a misogynist and who invested much more energy in advancing the careers of men than he did women, praised Johnson for choosing "with singular felicity, indeed with the felicity of instinct, her special domain in art." The domain and the writerly task to which he referred was "the documenting of the feminine heart." Such work was as "welcome as it is rare," he suggested, because "the emotions of woman, time-old though they be and hackneyed over as in a sense they really are, are still but half expressed." In closing, he refrained from suggesting that the volume of poems had significant intellectual heft. "Whatever the philosophical yield," he wrote, "we are grateful for the prospect of such lyricism."

The collection is divided into five sections, each of which contributes to the cycle suggested by the book's title. "Cycle," the first section and the largest group of poems, is followed by "Contemplation," "Intermezzi," "Penseroso," and finally, "Cadence." As Johnson scholar Gloria Hull notes, the collection is organized around "the organic process of the romance" (Hull, 175). Johnson abandons the highly structured classical language and conventions that she used in earlier work and employs free verse to generate compelling and authentic meditations on emotional awakening, anticipation, desire realized, and unwavering devotion. The volume is enriched by the evolution of the speaker, a woman who offers unmediated perspectives on her emotions, ego, and undulating levels of self-confidence. In "Cycle," the speaker moves from a state of painful solitude and suspense into the early stages of interaction with a beloved. The first poem, "I Closed My Shutters Fast Last Night," is, despite its melancholy, a romantic account of single life. "I left my lagging heart outside / Within the dark alone," recalls the speaker who then reveals that the natural world tends to that aching heart and does so well. "Upon my sleepless couch I lay / Until the tranquil morn / Came through the silver silences / To bring my heart forlorn / Restoring it with calm caress / Unto its sheltered bower." Words such as "Oh night of love" confirm the arrival of passion and the speaker's transition into "groves of strange content" and her enjoyment of "kisses" and "rapt ecstatic hours." Yet, by "Preview," she is doubting her ability to prevail in the face of competition. "I fear my power impotent / To hold you leal and full content," she writes, "I tremble lest some stranger friar / Arrest you,—cause you to compare / The meagre charms which I possess / With some resplendent loveliness." The section closes as the speaker reaches a distressing but ultimately helpful state of awareness. In "Delusion," she laments that she has been "blind," deceived by "your hand . . . the last word, the dear word, / The soul's entity." The section's final poem, "Sunset," thus returns to the barricaded home that emerged in the section's first works. Now, she acts "as one who closes up the house and goes uncaring where / He may forget the scenes of home 'mid foreign climes and air," and declares without fanfare, "I bar the chamber of my heart and seal the past within."

The 11 poems in "Contemplation" range from self-indulgent notes about the innate neediness of women, the painful aftermath that so often follows the loss of a lover, and the assurance that her feelings, though difficult, signal her ability to love and to feel. "Since I have known the purple gleam / That lifts above me," she wonders, "can I deem / The way unlighted—when I go / Encircled by love's afterglow?" The burgeoning sense of self-possession that marks "Contemplation" flourishes in "Intermezzi." Here, innocence is no longer a hallmark of love; instead, it is the notion of woman's choice that becomes the dominant mode. On the heels of this emancipatory state, however, comes "Penseroso," the second-to-last section and the one in which the reality of loss finally becomes unavoidable. The speaker is still well fortified, however, to withstand the melancholy and the reality that she confronts. In the plainly titled poem "Armor," she states directly, "You cannot hurt me any more / For I am armored now / And I can look into your face / With cool, unfevered brow." The poems of "Cadence" reveal the speaker's desire to prevail and her efforts to maintain her emotional composure about a love affair in which she was wholly absorbed. In the poem "Offering," she notes primly, "I seek no token of you dear" before confessing that "when for you the final sun / Moves toward the darkening West, / I shall be lingering to place / Love's flower on your breast." The volume closes as the earnest speaker remains fully intent on establishing the terms on which the relationship truly will end. "Consider me a memory—a dream / That passed away," she advises. "Consider

me a melody / That served its simple turn / Or but the residue of fire / That settles in the urn," she recommends in "Recessional." Yet, the incurable romantic cannot divorce herself from the past, and in the volume's final meditation, "Afterglow," she indulges her feelings for the last time. "I would give a thousand worlds / To live it all again!" she declares in a statement that suggests both passion and recklessness.

ALICE DUNBAR-NELSON, Johnson's close friend and a talented writer herself, noted the publication of *Autumn Love Cycle* in her diary. The entry for 18 December 1928 is brief but telling: "Have fun reading Georgia's new book of poems—*Autumn Love Cycle*" (Hull, *GUTD* 284). Johnson also received praise from her contemporaries. JEAN TOOMER, to whom she had sent verses for consideration, insisted that Johnson's work "come[s] nearer [to] my heart than anything I've read." Yet, scholar Claudia Tate suggests that Toomer's passionate response was less than sincere and that he was "unbeknownst to Johnson . . . a patronizing reader of her work" who believed that any "lyric gift" that she did have was impeded by "too much poetic jargon, too many inhibitions" (Tate, xxx).

Johnson's verse is powerful for its humanization of women and its evolving considerations of feminist thought. Her efforts to chronicle love also produce subtle commentaries on the development of independent thought and the power of choice. Such work counters the images of silenced or oppressed women who populate the works of writers like Jean Toomer and CLAUDE MCKAY and enrich the overall consideration of gendered experience during the Harlem Renaissance.

Bibliography

Hull, Gloria, ed. *Give Us This Day: The Diary of Alice Dunbar-Nelson*. New York: W. W. Norton & Company, 1984.

Hull, Gloria. *Love, Sex, and Poetry: Three Women Writers of the Harlem Renaissance*. Bloomington: Indiana University Press, 1987.

Tate, Claudia. Introduction in *The Selected Works of Georgia Douglas Johnson*. New York: G. K. Hall & Co., 1997.

B

"Backslider, The" Rudolph Fisher (1927)

An engaging story by RUDOLPH FISHER published in 1927, the year in which he began his NEW YORK CITY medical practice. Like the other three short stories that he published that same year, "The Backslider" was set in HARLEM. The protagonist, Ebenezer Grimes, is a young man who suffers greatly for his perceived sins. Fisher contemplates the nature of hypocrisy and the power of self-confidence in this tale about a young man's coming of age.

The story begins as Ebenezer, who also is known as Eben, timidly makes his way into a storefront church. The building, which is a converted rowhouse, "wore the saintlier garb of a proper convert: an uncompromising halo from a globe-light over the doorway; windows stained with tissue-paper, red and green in squares" (Fisher, 108). The parishioners include Sister Gassoway, a "big, shiny and round" woman, and Brother Hezekiah Mosby, "a sexton, usher and chorister" who usually "flit[s] about like a worrisome little black fly, grinning, whispering, buzzing useless greetings, questions, confidences" (Fisher, 108). Presiding over the meeting is Senior Deacon Crutchfield, a "magnificent man, big, hearty, bass-voiced, with an engaging smile and a painfully powerful handshake" (Fisher, 109).

Eben, a southerner who has been raised in the church, regrets that in New York he has become a "sinful backslider" and failed to "advanc[e] to high office" (Fisher, 109). His worst fears are realized when the congregation votes to expel him because he has been seen frequenting a local bar and emerging in a drunken stupor. Clearly shaken by the proceedings, Eben ends up at the Rodent, the very club

that has caused his downfall. It is a nondescript place, "nothing but a transformed cellar—not too much transformed" (Fisher, 111). Eben has been robbed in the Rodent, but Lil, a charitable young woman who works in the bar, also has befriended him. She advises Eben to join another church, one that is "not so tight—with a broader mind" and with a "long name, like Episcopalian or Utilitarian or something" (Fisher, 112).

The story gains momentum as Eben endeavors to save Lil from being arrested for unpaid debts. He plans to burglarize a barber shop but instead steals a purse from an apartment. Police pursue him when they receive a tip from Spider Webb, the con man who stole Eben's paycheck during his first visit to the Rodent. Eben narrowly escapes arrest and on his way to return the purse, sees a crowd gathered about a police van. He waits with them to see the individuals being arrested for bootlegging and gambling. He is taken aback when he sees Deacon Crutchfield, one of the leaders of the illegal activities, being led out to the wagon.

Eben is beside himself when he realizes that hypocrites have engineered his recent expulsion from the church. He exults in the fact that he has not been refused access to God and plans to "backslide on de Devil" now that he has acquired a second chance. The story ends on a romantic and mildly humorous note as Eben wonders "ef Lil would backslide too" (Fisher, 118).

"The Backslider" reflects Fisher's talent for crafting accessible tales about earnest southerners who have to content with the corrupting influences of the urban North.

Bibliography

Fisher, Rudolph. "The Backslider." In *The Short Fiction of Rudolph Fisher*, edited by Margaret Perry. Columbia: University of Missouri Press, 1987.

McCluskey, John Jr. *The City of Refuge: The Collected Stories of Rudolph Fisher*. Columbia: University of Missouri Press, 1987.

Perry, Margaret, ed. *The Short Fiction of Rudolph Fisher*. New York: Greenwood Press, 1987.

"Back to Africa" Movement

A philosophy and plan associated with MARCUS GARVEY, the Jamaican leader who established the UNIVERSAL NEGRO IMPROVEMENT ASSOCIATION, an organization that advocated his platform that African Americans would be able to establish themselves and to flourish in AFRICA rather than in the white Western world.

Bibliography

Cronon, Edmund. *Black Moses: The Story of Marcus Garvey and the Universal Improvement Association*. Madison: University of Wisconsin Press, 1987.

Hill, Robert, and Barbara Blair. *Marcus Garvey, Life and Lessons: A Centennial Companion to the Marcus Garvey and Universal Negro Improvement Association Papers*. Berkeley: University of California Press, 1987.

Bagnall, Robert W. (1864–1943)

A graduate of the BISHOP PAYNE DIVINITY SCHOOL who became an Episcopal priest before he joined the NAACP staff as director of branches. He combined a career in the ministry with racial activism and writing. Several of his essays, including "The Spirit of the K.K.K.," which appeared in the September 1923 issue, were published in *THE CRISIS*.

Bibliography

Hughes, Langston. *Fight for Freedom: The Story of the NAACP.* New York: Norton, 1962.

Baker, George (Father Divine) (1880–1965)

The well-known founder and beloved leader of the Peace Mission, an organization that encouraged African Americans to believe in a God of color, peace, and prosperity, even in the face of the GREAT DEPRESSION and entrenched American racism. Baker, who moved his mission from Long Island to HARLEM in 1933, offered 15-cent meals, affordable lodgings, and spiritual support to African Americans in need. During the 1930s he protested racial violence and segregation, and he encouraged the organization's members to achieve economic independence and to uphold strict moral codes.

Bibliography

Burnham, Kenneth. *God Comes to America: Father Divine and the Peace Mission Movement*. Boston: Lambeth Press, 1979.

McKay, Claude. *Harlem: Negro Metropolis*. 1940; reprint, New York: Harcourt Brace Jovanovich, 1968.

Watts, Jill. *God, Harlem, U.S.A.: The Father Divine Story*. Berkeley: University of California Press, 1992.

Baker, Josephine (1906–1975)

A dynamic artist in the vibrant New York arts and entertainment scene during the 1920s and 1930s, Baker worked as a singer and dancer with leading composers and musicians, including Noble Sissle and Eubie Blake. Ultimately, though, Baker preferred the reception she received in France, where she appeared in *La Revue* (1925) and at the *Folies-Bergère*, and established her primary residence there rather than in the United States. She was awarded the Legion of Honor and the Medallion of the City of Paris.

Bibliography

Baker, Jean-Claude, and Chris Chase. *Josephine: The Hungry Heart*. New York: Random House, 1993.

Rose, Phyllis. *Jazz Cleopatra: Josephine Baker in Her Time*. New York: Doubleday, 1989.

Wood, Ean. *The Josephine Baker Story*. London: Sanctuary, 2000.

Baker, Ray Stannard (1870–1946)

A journalist and writer who also published under the name of David Grayson, Stannard was one of the whites whose support of and interest in African Americans prompted ZORA NEALE HURSTON to coin the term "NEGROTARIANS." Baker was the first of six sons born to Joseph Stannard and Alice

Potter Baker. He grew up in Lansing, Michigan, and maintained close links to his home state. He graduated in 1889 from Michigan Agricultural College in East Lansing and in 1892 began law school studies at the University of Michigan. When he left the university before completing his degree, he relocated to Chicago, where he hoped to realize his dreams of writing a successful novel. Baker's turn to journalism occurred in Chicago, where he began working as a reporter at the *Chicago News-Record*.

Baker joined the staff of *McClure's*, an influential journal that Ida Tarbell, one of his fellow staffers, characterized as "an exacting little mistress" (Semonche, 123). There, according to biographer John Semonche, he gained a reputation for being "a perceptive, fair, trustworthy and open-minded journalist" and became "convinced that he was making a contribution to the long-neglected education of the American people" (Semonche, 124). Baker focused on labor issues primarily, even when prompted by his editors Samuel S. McClure and John S. Phillips to diversify his writing interests. He also was interested in issues related to "the Negro and lawlessness" (Semonche, 124). During the late 1890s, he documented the Pullman strike and became a staunch advocate of the strikers. A committed muckraker, he contributed essays in 1904, to the ground-breaking *McClure's* series on race.

During the Harlem Renaissance period, Baker published several volumes on Woodrow Wilson, whose politics he wholeheartedly endorsed. These included *What Wilson Did at Paris* (1919), *Woodrow Wilson and World Settlement* (1922), and when he became Wilson's designated biographer, the multivolume sets entitled *The Public Papers of Woodrow Wilson* (1925–27) and the Pulitzer Prize–winning collection, *Woodrow Wilson: Life and Letters* (1927–39).

Baker, who married Jessie Beal in 1896, relocated with his wife and four children from East Lansing to Amherst, Massachusetts, in 1910. Following his death as a result of heart disease, he was buried in the local Wildwood Cemetery in Amherst.

Bibliography

Baker, Ray. *Native American: The Book of My Youth.* New York: Charles Scribner's Sons, 1941.

Bannister, Robert. *Ray Stannard Baker: The Mind and Thought of a Progressive.* New Haven, Conn.: Yale University Press, 1966.

Ray Stannard Baker Papers, Library of Congress; Jones Library in Amherst, Massachusetts; and Princeton University Library.

Semonche, John. *Ray Stannard Baker: A Quest for Democracy in Modern America, 1870–1918.* Chapel Hill: University of North Carolina Press, 1969

Baldwin, William (fl. 1920s)

One of the influential literary figures who lent his support to the Harlem Renaissance celebrations of emerging writers. Baldwin was one of the figures OPPORTUNITY editor CHARLES S. JOHNSON invited to the legendary 1924 dinner at the Civic Club that was organized to mark the publication of JESSIE FAUSET's first novel but instead, much to Fauset's dismay, turned into a celebration of several leading men of the day such as ALAIN LOCKE.

Ballad of the Brown Girl, The: An Old Ballad Retold Countee Cullen (1927)

A stirring ballad by COUNTEE CULLEN that in 1927 was reprinted in an elaborate and decorative monograph with illustrations. Cullen first published the poem while an undergraduate at New York University. In 1924 it earned second place in the Witter Bynner Undergraduate Poetry Contest sponsored by the Poetry Society of America. Poet LANGSTON HUGHES would compete in and win the Witter Bynner Contest in 1926. *The New York Times*, which recognized enthusiastically Cullen's achievement in a full-length column about the 20-year old writer, noted that he was "one of 700 undergraduates, representing sixty-three colleges and universities" to have their work judged by Carl Sandburg, Alice Corbin, and WITTER BYNNER. Cullen, who was interviewed for the piece, noted that he was "interested in poetry for poetry's sake, and not for propaganda purposes." "In spite of myself," he added, "however, I find that I am actuated by a strong sense of race consciousness. This grows upon me, I find, as I grow older: and although I struggle against it, it colors my writing, I fear, in spite of everything I do." Cullen dedicated the 1927 volume, published by HARPER &

BROTHERS, to Witter Bynner. His brother Charles provided the illustrations and evocative decorations in the volume.

The Ballad of the Brown Girl is Cullen's revision of a British ballad entitled "The Tragical Ballad of the Unfortunate Loves of Lord Thomas and Fair Eleanor: Together with the Downfall of the Brown Girl" that is believed to have been created during the 17th-century reign of King Charles II. Numerous versions of the song exist and range from folk renditions performed throughout English areas such as Devon, Yorkshire, and Staffordshire, in Scotland, and throughout Ireland as well. Scottish versions, according to folk and music historians, also revised the title to "Fair Annet." It is the sad and violent story of a flawed love triangle that is doomed by color prejudice.

Written in traditional ballad meter, Cullen's 200-line version focuses upon Lord Thomas, a would-be hero, who is torn between two women. He seeks advice from his mother and, while he kneels at her side, describes the two very different women for whom he has feelings. The first is Fair London, a "lily maid, / And pride of all the south" who is "full shy and sweet as still / Delight when nothing stirs." Lord Thomas admits that his "soul can thrive on love of her / And all my heart is hers." While such a straightforward announcement would seem to clarify matters, his mother requests information about the second woman. "Is she as sweet and fair," she asks, to which the young suitor replies that "[s]he is the dark Brown Girl who knows / No more-defining name." She later is described as having "hair . . . black as sin is black" and "eyes . . . black as night is black / When moon and stars conspire" and a mouth that "was one red cherry clipt / In twain." Lord Thomas comments on the social rejection she has faced and that "bitter tongues have worn their tips / In sneering at her shame." When he confesses, however, that "there are lands to go with her, / And gold and silver stores," his mother, who "loved the clink of gold, / The odor and the shine / Of larders bowed with venison / And crystal globes of wine," insists that he marry the Brown Girl.

The bride-to-be, innocent of the materialistic rather than emotional motives behind Lord Thomas's proposal, prepares for her wedding day. She comes to him "as might / A queen to take her throne." The regality of the Brown Girl is not feigned; according to the narrator, she "comes of kings." Just moments after Lord Thomas and the Brown Girl "have made the holy vow / To share one board and bed," Fair London appears. In a sign of great foreboding, Lord Thomas leaves the side of his bride and escorts his former sweetheart into the feast. Although she says that she has come to toast him and his new bride, she promptly insults the Brown Girl, protests interracial marriage, and raises the ugly specter of racial segregation. "I think she's might brown," she says caustically, "Why didn't you marry a fair bright girl . . . only the rose and the rose should mate, / Oh never the hare and hound." When her groom fails to defend her honor, the Brown Girl takes matters into her own hands. She uses a serpentine dagger that is part of her costume to kill her rival. Lord Thomas then turns on his wife and uses her own hair to strangle her in a savage moment that, given the onlookers, is highly evocative of a LYNCHING. In the moments that follow, he sinks quickly into madness, chides his mother for her greed and self-interest, commands his guests to "[g]o dig one grave to hold us all," and kills himself with the same dagger that ended Fair London's life. His last instruction before dying is that the Fair London be placed by his side and that the Brown Girl be laid at his feet. The poem, a tortured account of racism and racial hierarchy, ends with an eerie bucolic scene: ". . . in the land where the grass is blue, / In a grave dug deep and wide, / The Brown Girl sleeps at her true lord's feet, / Fair London by his side."

Cullen adapted the original version of the poem to reflect American and African-American issues. There are a number of differences between the plots. In the original, the Brown Girl uses a penknife, rather than a dagger that "a dusky queen, / In a dusky dream-lit land" once used to end her life because of her unrequited love. Even more significant differences emerge as well. The British version includes details of Lord Thomas decapitating the Brown Girl, flinging her head aside, and making absolutely no provisions to bury her alongside himself and the white woman whom he loves. The Brown Girl of Cullen's poem has considerably more agency and self-possession. Although she is doubly victimized—scorned in public and abandoned in private. It is her grand, though publicly unacknowledged, ancestry that enables her to rage at injustice but control her passions in the face of desertion. The British ballad ends with a striking image of a red rose growing out of the bosom of Fair Eleanor, who is buried in the choir section of the church, and a briar emanating from the heart of the faithless Lord Thomas, who is also buried in the church. Cullen's version reflects his effort to recoup the ballad and use it to explore the tensions among high romance, segregation, and social hierarchy. The work also reflects his steady interest in contemplating the value and lingering powers of a mythic and romantic African past.

Bibliography

Cullen, Countee. *The Ballad of the Brown Girl, An Old Ballad Retold with Illustrations and Decorations by Charles Cullen.* New York: Harper & Brothers, 1927.

Ferguson, Blanche. *Countee Cullen and the Negro Renaissance.* New York: Dodd, Mead, 1966.

"Negro Wins Prize in Poetry Contest." *New York Times,* 2 December 1923, E1.

Shucard, Alan. *Countee Cullen.* Boston: Twayne, 1984.

Vaughan Williams, R., and A. L. Lloyd, eds. *The Penguin Book of Folk Songs.* London: Penguin, 1959.

Balo: A One-Act Sketch of Negro Life
Jean Toomer (1924)

A one-act folk play that JEAN TOOMER wrote for the HOWARD UNIVERSITY PLAYERS, the drama troupe based at HOWARD UNIVERSITY in WASHINGTON, D.C. It was included in the program for the 1923–24 season at the Howard Theatre. The play is one of two of Toomer's works that was staged during his lifetime. It was included in *Plays of Negro Life,* the anthology that Howard University professors T. MONTGOMERY GREGORY and ALAIN LOCKE published in 1927.

A portrait of religious fervor and transcendence, the play is set in Georgia at a time when the harvests are poor and farming families find themselves depending on their modest savings for sustenance. The cast includes Will and Susan Lee, both of whom live in the shadow of an antebellum "old frame mansion" that "stands, or rather, the ghost of it, in the direct vision of [their] front door"

(Toomer, 219). The play is marked for its simplicity of setting and its minimalist plot. As critic Frederik Rusch notes, *Balo* "has only the slightest plot and little individual character development" (Rusch, 116).

The Lees and their sons, Tom and Balo, are hard-working individuals. The boys return home from a night spent boiling sugarcane and preparing syrup. When they arrive home at dawn, they prepare to rest and read a few verses from the Bible before they sleep. This is the first occasion when Balo slips into a spiritual reverie. Balo, whom Michael Krasny describes as a "frenziedly devout" boy "who experiences a somnambulistic outburst of religious passion' (Krasny, 103) takes pleasure in the verses from a chapter in the Gospel of Matthew and repeats the phrase, 'An' th' floods came, an' th' winds blew," several times. While the boys are sleeping, their parents receive a visit from Mr. Jennings, a white man whose family lives in close proximity to the Lees. In the course of the conversation, Jennings reveals that Balo has been "actin' like he was crazy" and repeating the phrase "White folks ain't no more'n niggers when they gets ter heaven." While Jennings laughs about this, the location and the inherent racial tensions of the South make this an auspicious moment.

The second set of interactions in the play revolve around visits from cousins and their families. The group, which now includes some six children ranging in age from two and a half years to 12 years, eventually begins to sing hymns and discuss spiritual matters. Four more people appear, and the group members begin to play a game of cards, even though they hesitate because it may be a worldly act that could offend Will, their host. He "turns his gaze into the fire, and by his silence gives consent" (Toomer, 224). As they play, conversation drifts back to Bible stories and, without warning, Balo "jumps to his feet" and begins to declare, "Jesus, Jesus, I've found Jesus" (Toomer, 224). His exclamations prompt those playing the card games to cease their activity and they "file out, heads lowered, in sheepishness and guilt" (Toomer, 224).

James Hatch and Ted Shine suggest that *Balo* is "more a sketch than a play" and that "it is also more honest than most folk drama" (Hatch and Shine, 218). The character of Balo, they suggest, achieves "sensitivity and . . . tenderness . . . in the theater or our imagination" and that, as such, presents a mighty challenge to a "flesh-and-blood actor" who aspires to fill the role. It is a play in which, as Michael Krasny argues, "Toomer's central concern is the forces which inhibit, pervert, and destroy innate spirituality" (Krasny, 104).

Balo reflects, as Rusch proposes, what Toomer "found most exciting in the rural South, the archaic folk elements still intact in Georgia, the dialectical, musical, and agricultural traditions" (Rusch, 118). The work anticipates Toomer's representation in *Cane* of African-American intimacy with the natural world.

Bibliography

Hatch, James V., and Ted Shine, eds. *Black Theater U.S.A.: Forty-Five Plays by Black Americans.* New York: The Free Press, 1974.

Krasny, Michael. "Design in Jean Toomer's *Balo*." *Negro American Literature Forum* 7, no. 3 (autumn 1973): 103–104.

Rusch, Frederik L. "Jean Toomer's Early Identification: The Two Black Plays," *MELUS* 13, nos. 1/2 (spring 1986): 115–124.

Toomer, Jean. *Balo: A One-Act Sketch of Negro Life.* In *Black Theater U.S.A.: Forty-Five Plays by Black Americans,* edited by James V. Hatch and Ted Shine, 218–224. New York: The Free Press, 1974.

Banana Bottom Claude McKay (1933)

CLAUDE MCKAY's third and final novel. It is the story of a young woman who must overcome personal upheaval as she negotiates the tensions between her West Indian identity and her experiences in the British colonial world.

Set in Jamaica and in England, the novel focuses on Bitta Plant, a young woman from the Jamaican countryside whose name suggests fragility, a potential for growth, and bitterness. Bitta, a survivor of rape, by a man (Crazy Bow) twice her age, is given opportunities to recover from the trauma by a British missionary couple, the Craigs. Malcolm and Priscilla Craig, longtime friends of the family, intervene before Bitta's father relocates his 12-year-old daughter. They take responsibility for Bitta, bring her up as their own daughter, and provide her with numerous educational and cultural opportunities in Europe. Additional challenges for Bitta emerge when she returns to her homeland and begins to realize the sharp contrasts between "civilized" society and her folk world. Her cultural rehabilitation continues as she encounters Squire Gensir, a man whose name suggests a claim to gentility and whose character McKay based on Walter Jekyll, the English mentor and folklorist who encouraged McKay's literary development. Gensir encourages Bitta to reevaluate her adopted middle-class perspectives, and this begins when she attends a tea in Banana Bottom. The effects of her reconnection with the community are manifold. Ultimately, Bitta ends her engagement to Herald Newton Day, a young man whose education in the missionary schools and aspirations for a career in the ministry make him a seemingly appropriate mate for the Europeanized Bitta. Rather than "herald a new day," Bitta falls in love with and marries Jubban, a man who works for her father and who eventually becomes a successful farmer in his own right. This alliance, which contributes to "the formal exorcism of Bitta's demon of Western culture" (Tillery, 131), represents the triumph of folk culture.

Literary critic Amritjit Singh proposes that the "resolution in *Banana Bottom* is achieved at a great loss of complexity; by choosing a rural Jamaican setting for his novel, McKay bypasses many urban and international issues raised in *HOME TO HARLEM* and *BANJO*" (Singh, 54). Yet, McKay scholar Tyrone Tillery suggests that the novel represents McKay's effort to "advance the theme he had unsuccessfully begun in *Home to Harlem* and carried through *Banjo*: that Western civilization was the Negro's cultural hell and should be rejected in favor of the simple values of the 'folk'" (Tillery, 129). The novel, which is enriched by McKay's development of a female protagonist, speaks eloquently to his interest in evoking and confirming the rich and emancipatory nature of the West Indies and the folk communities of that world.

Bibliography

Cooper, Wayne. *Claude McKay: Rebel Sojourner in the Harlem Renaissance.* New York: Schocken Books, 1987.

Hathaway, Heather. *Caribbean Waves: Relocating Claude McKay and Paule Marshall.* Bloomington: Indiana University Press, 1999.

McKay, Claude. *Banana Bottom*. 1933, reprint, Chatham, N.J.: The Chatham Bookseller, 1970.

Singh, Amritjit. *The Novels of the Harlem Renaissance: Twelve Black Writers, 1923–1933*. University Park: Pennsylvania State University Press, 1976.

Tillery, Tyrone. *Claude McKay: A Black Poet's Struggle for Identity*. Amherst: University of Massachusetts Press, 1992.

Banjo: A Story Without a Plot
Claude McKay (1929)

A novel inspired by CLAUDE MCKAY's own experiences and interactions with the laborers, seamen, and itinerants whom he met while in the French port city of Marseille in 1926. *Banjo* attempts to articulate the meanings of racial differences, and it explores the tension between private artistic vision and the public politics of representation. The novel features Ray and Banjo, two characters whom McKay developed first in HOME TO HARLEM (1928), the controversial novel that he published just one year earlier.

Banjo is a novel in which McKay takes great pains to underscore the differences between white and African-American culture. The subtitle, "A Story Without a Plot," signals the potential itinerancy of the work, not just of the primary characters themselves. McKay uses Lincoln Agrippa Daily, known also as Banjo, to represent blackness as an extremely natural state that is represented well by music and by seemingly immediate, unthinking responses to the world. The story is set in Marseille, a place that will not only host a Pan-African conference but one that is also home to cabarets and prostitutes. The glaring juxtaposition here establishes the first of many binary oppositions that exist in the novel. Banjo, characterized in one review as "the unthinking negro" of the book, pursues a relatively carefree life as an itinerant musician. Ray welcomes his interaction with Banjo, a figure who is even more free-spirited than his old friend Jake in *Home to Harlem*. Banjo, who is also a master of the instrument after whom his nickname is derived, persuades Ray to accompany him on his adventures. Together, the two immerse themselves in the lower-class communities of the city. They survive interactions with Satanists, the gruesome deaths of several compatriots, and trou-bling interactions with West Africans who suffer at the hands of aggressive French police.

By the novel's end, Ray is the character who has sustained the most ambitious conversations about race, art, materialism, European racism, and racial stereotypes. In contrast, it is Banjo who appears to test his friend's theories and who gravitates toward action rather than speculation, toward immersion rather than purposeful objectivity. Ultimately, Ray does not allow his penchant for intellectual inquiry to keep him from the streets. The novel closes as he and Banjo decide to leave the city and continue their travels together elsewhere.

McKay, who was traveling abroad during the period in which he wrote and then revised the novel, had to contend with major and unsolicited editorial revisions of his work. When he received the proofs, he was struck by what he regarded as excessive changes to his writing. "I am a poet and have always striven conscientiously to find words to say exactly what I see and feel," he wrote in a letter to editor Eugene Saxton at the press. He insisted that he "took a long time to write *Banjo* in the face of real difficulties, writing and re-writing to find the right words to rend the atmosphere and the types that moved in it" and suggested that the editors had "wantonly compromise[d] the character of my writing by replacing my personal words with cheap two- and three-syllabled stock words" (Cooper, 253). He won the right to have his original prose restored, although the publishers charged him for this second round of editing.

Reviewers welcomed the reemergence of Ray, a character who they believed "bobs up again in *Banjo* to rescue Mr. McKay's second novel from . . . 'the sink of naturalism'" (*NYT*, 12 May 1929, BR5). Recent scholarship on McKay and this novel, however, suggests that the work is part of McKay's deliberate effort to "antagoniz[e] the American black intellectual establishment" and to generate a work in which the "sterility and the perversion of materialistic white culture . . . are . . . repeatedly summarized, analyzed, and denounced" (Giles, 84). There is continued debate about whether or not the novel is a purposeful representation of African-American life. One early review of the work suggested that "[i]n spite of some too-picturesque writing in which the color is slapped on with several trowels, and in spite of an occasional internal formlessness deriving from apostrophes to jazz rhythms, *Banjo* has definite form." "The book follows two curves," wrote the unidentified *New York Times* reviewer as he went on to note that the novel tracks "the carefree Banjo who occupies the centre of the stage until the midpoint of the story is reached, only to drift away into a minor position, and that of Ray, who more and more usurps the major position in the story" (*NYT*, 12 May 1929, BR5). McKay's reviewers tended to hope that the author would develop more complicated issues for his characters and stage more intense moral dilemmas in the novels. "[H]e doesn't give his people enough problems to test them," lamented one critic in 1928, but McKay scholar James Giles insists that "there are more complexities in the characterization of *Banjo* than may at first appear and more than most critics have recognized" (Giles, 87). The novel is a kaleidoscopic picaresque, one that privileges the perspectives of young men of color. It provides unpretentious accounts of life abroad and combines its vivid tales of raucous life with subtle commentaries on the ways in which colonialism continues to factor in the lives of people of color.

Bibliography

Cooper, Wayne. *Claude McKay: Rebel Sojourner In the Harlem Renaissance*. New York: Schocken Books, 1987.

Giles, James R. *Claude McKay*. Boston: Twayne Publishers, 1976.

Barber, Jesse Max (1878–1949)

The outspoken journalist who single-handedly managed the *Voice of the Negro*, an ATLANTA-based African-American literary and social history journal founded in 1904. During his tenure as editor, Barber published works by CHARLES CHESNUTT, Pauline Hopkins, W. E. B. DUBOIS, GEORGIA DOUGLAS JOHNSON, MARY CHURCH TERRELL, and other progressive race writers and activists.

Barber was one of the early members of the NIAGARA MOVEMENT and the NAACP; he served as the president and executive director of the Philadelphia branch of the organization in the 1920s. His propensity for straightforward analysis and his public critiques of BOOKER T. WASHING-

TON complicated his professional and personal life. Washington labeled him as a troublemaker and actively lobbied against Barber whenever he could. Barber eventually became a dentist in Philadelphia and stated that this was the only profession in which he could establish himself beyond Washington's reach.

Bibliography

Johnson, Abby Arthur, and Ronald Maberry Johnson. *Propaganda & Aesthetics: The Literary Politics of African American Magazines in the Twentieth Century*. Amherst: University of Massachusetts, 1979.

Barnard College

Founded in 1889, this New York City women's college was one of the original members of the Seven Sisters consortium. In 1900 it officially became part of the COLUMBIA UNIVERSITY system. The most well-known Harlem Renaissance writer to enroll at Barnard was ZORA NEALE HURSTON. Annie Nathan Meyer, one of the college's founders, helped to facilitate Hurston's enrollment at the school on scholarship beginning in 1925. Hurston, the lone African-American student at the college, produced sophisticated work that caught the attention of FRANZ BOAS, the eminent anthropology scholar. Hurston soon took graduate courses with Boas and prepared for her pioneering fieldwork and research under his supervision.

Bibliography

A History of Barnard College, Published in Honor of the Seventy-Fifth Anniversary of the College. New York: Barnard College, 1964.

Horowitz, Helen. *Alma Mater: Design and Experience in the Women's Colleges from Their Nineteenth-Century Beginnings to the 1930s*. New York: Knopf, 1984.

Kendall, Elaine. *'Peculiar Institutions': An Informal History of the Seven Sisters Colleges*. New York: Putnam, 1976.

Barnes, Albert Coombs (1872–1951)

A successful physician, art collector and graduate of the UNIVERSITY OF PENNSYLVANIA Medical School who grew up in poverty in Philadelphia. His pharmaceutical invention of Argyrol made him a millionaire. He used his money to begin and to maintain the Barnes Collection, an impressive array of Impressionist and post-Impressionist paintings, including works by Renoir, Matisse, Cezanne, and Picasso. He began publishing articles on art in OPPORTUNITY, the official National Urban League magazine, during the 1920s. He also contributed to SURVEY GRAPHIC and to THE NEW NEGRO, the anthology edited by ALAIN LOCKE.

Bibliography

McCardele, Carl. "The Terrible Tempered Barnes." The Saturday Evening Post 21 (March 1942).

Barnett, Claude Albert (1889–1967)

Barnett, an Illinois native who attended TUSKEGEE INSTITUTE and who, for a time, sold advertisements for the CHICAGO DEFENDER, founded the ASSOCIATED NEGRO PRESS in 1919 in order to streamline the distribution of newsworthy information and articles to African-American newspapers, such as the New York Amsterdam News and the Chicago Defender, throughout the United States. After World War II, Barnes provided information to a number of African newspapers as well.

Bibliography

Hogan, Lawrence. A Black National News Service: The Associated Negro Press and Claude Barnett, 1919–1945. London: Associated University Presses, 1984.

Meier, August, and Elliott Rudwick, eds. The Claude A. Barnett Papers: The Associated Negro Press, 1918–1967. Frederick, Md.: University Publications of America, 1986.

Barthé, Richmond (1901–1989)

A Chicago art institute student from 1924 through 1928 and a member of the National Academy of Arts and Letters, Barthé is recognized as one of the first modern artists to depict African Americans in his sculpture and hailed as the "most talented and prolific African American sculptor of his generation" (Wirth, 25).

Born in Bay St. Louis, Mississippi, he was raised in Louisiana by parents of mixed African, French, and Native American heritage. According to scholar Thomas Wirth, Barthé became a houseboy for a wealthy New Orleans family, and it was during his residency with them that he attracted the attention of one of his two important early mentors. Neighbor Lyle Saxon and Barthé's minister became enthusiastic sponsors of his work and financed his schooling at the Art Institute of Chicago (Wirth, 25).

Barthé moved in Harlem Renaissance circles that included ARNA BONTEMPS, LANGSTON HUGHES, WALLACE THURMAN, CARL VAN VECHTEN, and ALAIN LOCKE. Locke, who was a member of the homosexual community of the period, encouraged his friend BRUCE NUGENT to make Barthé's acquaintance, assuring his friend that he "always liked" the man and "instantly sensed his genius" (Wirth, 25). Barthé and Nugent maintained a close friendship that may have developed into a short-lived relationship at one point. The correspondence that they exchanged during their decades-long relationship included some tender letters. In 1978 Barthé, recalling a memorable and early opportunity to watch Nugent perform in a 1927 production of PORGY, wrote to say, "I love you with the kind of love that will last forever" (Wirth, 25).

Barthé went on to win a HARMON FOUNDATION AWARD and was a two-time recipient of the prestigious JULIUS ROSENWALD FELLOWSHIP. He was commissioned to create what many expected would be an inspiring and awesome bronze monument in honor of JAMES WELDON JOHNSON. The project was derailed, however, when military needs prompted the government to appropriate all metals for the war effort. A number of his works are part of the Schomburg Collection of the NEW YORK PUBLIC LIBRARY and the collections of the Metropolitan Museum of Art.

By the late 1950s, Barthé was residing in Jamaica, where, according to Langston Hughes, he was living "like a feudal lord" and taking advantage of the relatively inexpensive cost of maintaining domestic help.

Bibliography

Wirth, Thomas. Gay Rebel of the Harlem Renaissance: Selections from the Work of Richard Bruce Nugent. Durham: Duke University Press, 2002.

Basshe, Em Jo

A playwright whose gender was debated by the New York City columnists who reviewed the 1927 play *EARTH*. The play featured a performance by Daniel Haynes, a new star in the theater of the day. Haynes was an aspiring southern minister whose turn to the stage once he arrived in New York City brought him major success.

The *MESSENGER* theater critic THEOPHILUS LEWIS dismissed the shows at the 52nd Street Theatre as a poor imitation of black drama. The play chronicled the awful existence of a bereaved mother who had lost six children, consulted a voodoo priest in order to resurrect her favorite child, and after being blamed for a fire near her village, killed the priest and then died. In his impatient remarks, Lewis also claimed that contrary to what *THE NEW YORK TIMES* reviewer proposed, Basshe was in fact a man.

Batouala René Maran (1921)

A controversial novel by RENÉ MARAN that was publicized highly in *NEGRO WORLD*, the magazine disseminated by MARCUS GARVEY's UNIVERSAL NEGRO IMPROVEMENT ASSOCIATION. The novel, quickly translated into English, drew attention primarily because of its graphic descriptions of native life in the French Congo. Despite its lurid details, however, it seemed to appeal to readers interested in strengthening their familiarity with African culture.

Bibliography

Irele, F. Abiola. *Literature and Ideology in Martinique: René Maran, Aimé Césaire, Frantz Fanon.* Buffalo, N.Y.: State University of New York at Buffalo, 1972.
Ojo-Ade, Femi. *René Maran, the Black Frenchman: A Bio-Critical Study.* Washington, D.C.: Three Continents Press, 1984.

Beale Street: Where the Blues Began
George Washington Lee (1934)

The book by GEORGE WASHINGTON LEE that was selected to be a BOOK-OF-THE-MONTH CLUB selection in 1934. *Beale Street* chronicled the life and experiences of musician W. C. HANDY (who provided the introduction to the text), provided a history of the blues musical tradition, and described the evolution of Beale Street in Memphis.

Bearden, Romare Howard (1914–1988)

A painter whose career began in the early 1940s as the Harlem Renaissance came to a close. During the mid- to late 1930s, however, Bearden was very much involved in the New York City world of vibrant arts and literary culture. He pursued his formal study of art at the Art Student League from 1936 through 1937 and in 1943 enrolled in courses at Columbia University.

Bibliography

Schwartzman, Myron. *Romare Bearden, His Life & Art.* New York: H. N. Abrams, 1990.
Washington, M. Bunch. *The Art of Romare Bearden: The Prevalence of Ritual.* New York: Abrams, 1973.

Beasley, Delilah Leontium (1871–1934)

An enterprising journalist who was publishing articles in well-known newspapers such as the *Cleveland Gazette* by the time she was 15 years of age. She maintained a regular column in the *Oakland Tribune* for 20 years, from 1910 through 1930.

Born in Cincinnati, Ohio, Beasley was forced to rely on her own wits after the death of her parents. She eventually settled in California, where she conducted extensive research for *The Negro Trail-Blazers of California* (1919), her important history of African-American achievements in the state. Beasley's professional accomplishments make her one of the inspiring examples of African-American journalism and illuminate the scope and diversity of African-American women journalists of the 1920s and 1930s.

Bibliography

Beasley, Delilah. *The Negro Trail-Blazers of California.* 1919; reprint, New York: G. K. Hall, 1997.

Beavers, Louise (1902–1962)

The actress who made her debut in the 1927 film version of *Uncle Tom's Cabin*, based on the influential 1852 antislavery novel of the same name by Harriet Beecher Stowe. Beavers starred in the

1934 *Imitation of Life* as the domestic servant and business partner of the character played by Claudette Colbert. The film was based on the 1933 novel of the same name written by FANNIE HURST.

Becton, George Wilson (1890–1933)

An evangelist, writer, and associate of the Reverend FREDERICK CULLEN, pastor of the Salem Methodist Episcopal Church and adoptive father of COUNTEE CULLEN, the poet. Before his death at the hands of mobsters, Becton founded *The Menu*, a quarterly magazine to which Countee Cullen contributed the poem "If You Should Go."

Bibliography

Ferguson, Blanche. *Countee Cullen and the Negro Renaissance.* New York: Dodd, Mead, 1966.

"Belated Romance"   Florence Marion Harmon (1928)

A romantic short story by FLORENCE MARION HARMON. Published in the Boston-based SATURDAY EVENING QUILL, the annual periodical that featured the work of SATURDAY EVENING QUILL CLUB members, the story portrayed the earnest efforts of two mature gentlemen who were both determined to win the hand of an aristocratic spinster.

In the story, Josiah Beede and his wife, Mary, are concerned about their neighbor, Miss Sabina Corning. In response to her husband's musings about Sabina's financial and domestic affairs, Mary Beede suggests that Sabina be married off "before she becomes more of a spinster than she is now." Her brother-in-law Seth Beede, who has been a longtime boarder in their home, overhears her comment and is prompted to reconsider his feelings for the neighbor. Seth promptly seeks out Henry Holcomb, a local man whom he thought had won the heart of the still-unmarried Sabina. Henry returns to Sabina's home, and much to her surprise, he proposes. When she rejects Holcomb, Seth Beede makes a beeline for her home. Finally, after many years of waiting and wondering, he asks her if he had in any way "marred" their earlier understanding and whether or not there is a reason that they should not wed. Sabina suggests that nothing stands in their way. When he leaves her

home, Seth is triumphant. He "went out into the night with a look of exultation on his face—like a martyr who offered himself for sacrifice, but found that the cause for which he had offered himself did not exist" (63).

"Belated Romance" is an entertaining story about African-American courtship that maintains a discernible air of gentility.

Benchley, Robert C. (1889–1945)

A highly regarded humorist, writer, editor of VANITY FAIR, and drama critic for the *New Yorker*. He was one of the well-known literary personalities whom CHARLES S. JOHNSON invited to judge the entries in the first literary contest sponsored by OPPORTUNITY and the NATIONAL URBAN LEAGUE. Also on that panel were the noted poet WITTER BYNNER and the novelist FANNIE HURST.

Bennett, Gwendolyn (1902–1981)

A Texas-born teacher, artist, and poet whose father abducted her from her mother's Washington, D.C., home and raised her in Harrisburg, Pennsylvania, and Brooklyn, New York. A graduate of PRATT INSTITUTE and COLUMBIA UNIVERSITY, Bennett taught art at HOWARD UNIVERSITY and at the Tennessee Agricultural and Industrial College before becoming assistant editor of OPPORTUNITY and an editorial board member of FIRE!! From September 1926 through May 1928, she authored "THE EBONY FLUTE" a monthly literary society column in *Opportunity*. JACOB LAWRENCE was one of the students she taught during her tenure as director of the Harlem Art Center. Her literary and artistic career ended in 1941 when she was targeted by the RED SCARE and branded a communist.

Bennett's artwork appeared on the covers of *CRISIS* and *Opportunity*. Her poem "Song" was included in THE NEW NEGRO (1925), the critically acclaimed anthology edited by ALAIN LOCKE that helped to institutionalize the Harlem Renaissance that was unfolding. Bennett was one of only eight women whose writings were included in the collection. Her poems, which have never been collected in a single volume, were published in JAMES WELDON JOHNSON'S THE BOOK OF AMERICAN NEGRO

POETRY (1922) and COUNTEE CULLEN's edited collection CAROLING DUSK (1925), as well as AMERICAN MERCURY, THE CRISIS, THE MESSENGER, Opportunity, and Fire!! In addition to her 21 installments of "The Ebony Flute," her works include the short story "Wedding Day," extant paintings, sketches, and cover art, and the poems "Dear Things," "Epitaph," "Hatred," "Heritage," "Lines Written at the Grave of Alexander Dumas," "Purgation," "Quatrains," "Song" "To a Dark Girl," "Sonnet–2," "Tokens," and "To Usward."

During the Harlem Renaissance, Bennett was hailed for the "delicate poignant lyrics" of her poems. Many of her poetical works convey her fascination with a haunting and empowering African past. Their power is rooted in Bennett's deliberate and sobering contemplations of American slavery and its enduring effect on African Americans. Bennett used rhyming couplets and conventional rhyme schemes to endow works such as "On a Birthday" (1925) with especially playful messages. Her use of free verse in the majority of her poetical works, however, reinforced the unique and meditative qualities of her poems.

Bennett's poems were published widely in journals of the period, and many reflected the Renaissance interest in delineating black experience and celebrating the seductive and intriguing aspects of black identity. Bennett's poem "Heritage," which predates Countee Cullen's similarly titled poem, is reminiscent of LANGSTON HUGHES's often-anthologized poem "The Negro Speaks of Rivers." It underscores the romanticism that prevailed during the Renaissance and that was rooted in notions of an uncorrupted African past. Several of Bennett's poems feature speakers who evolve from lonely spectators to earnest participants in the worlds around them. Bennett's insistent message about the life-changing power of experience reflects her belief in a people's need for their history and the allure of the past.

Bennett's poems frequently portray the plight and triumphs of outsiders. Poems such as "To a Dark Girl," "Lines Written at the Grave of Alexander Dumas," and "Song" are peopled by individuals whose isolation fuels their desire for racial solidarity and uplift. Bennett's representations of loss and exile reveal her efforts to communicate a deliberate sense of mourning about racial oppression and black disenfranchisement. In poems such as "Ha-

tred," however, Bennett creates formidable female characters who are intent on self-control and gaining mastery of the natural world.

In the New Negro anthology, "Song" appeared in the section entitled "Music" alongside poems by Langston Hughes and Claude McKay, and essays on Negro spirituals and jazz by Locke and JOEL AUGUSTUS ROGERS, respectively. Like other Bennett works, this poem celebrated the ways in which African-American music transcended slavery and offered generations a real connection to their past. Bennett merged images of spirited camp meetings with those of provocative dancing girls. The exuberance of the poem, symbolized by its use of ellipses and indentations, is threatened by references to the chains of slavery and metaphorical bondage of blackface minstrelsy. The poem closes, however, with what will become characteristic Bennett exhortations. "Sing a little faster, / Sing a little faster, / Sing!" urges the speaker, whose insistence here stands in stark contrast to the description of an indulgent creative process in the poem's first lines. The call for creative production and the inextricable link between African-American history and black creativity in this poem become defining elements in Bennett's future works. Over the course of her literary career, Gwendolyn Bennett's poems, fiction, and prose writings reflected her passion for black history, her steady belief in female agency, and her unwavering commitment to exhort her race.

Bibliography

Govan, Sandra. "Kindred Spirits and Sympathetic Souls: Langston Hughes and Gwendolyn Bennett in the Harlem Renaissance" in C. James Trotman (ed.), Langston Hughes: The Man, His Art, and His Continuing Influence. New York: Garland Publishers, 1995.
———. "After the Renaissance: Gwendolyn Bennett and the WPA Years," MAWA Review 3, no. 2 (December 1988): 27–31.
Gwendolyn Bennett Papers, Schomburg Center for Research in Black Culture, New York Public Library.

Berlack, Thelma (1906–unknown)

After showing exceptional promise in journalism while still a Florida high school student, Berlack went on to study journalism at NEW YORK UNIVERSITY. While still an undergraduate, she began writing society columns for the *PITTSBURGH COURIER*. Her career included a long-standing editorial position at the highly respected NEW YORK CITY offices of the *AMSTERDAM NEWS*.

Bethune, Mary McLeod (1875–1955)

A woman whose life embodied the fortitude, optimism, determination, and potential of African Americans in post-slavery America. The 15th child of 17 born to Sam and Patsy McLeod, former slaves who gained their freedom during the Civil War, Mary McLeod established a national reputation for academic excellence, entrepreneurial ingenuity, and political savvy. She was the founder of a school that by 1916 was known as the Daytona Normal and Industrial Institute for Negro Girls and that eventually became part of BETHUNE-COOKMAN COLLEGE. Her grandson eventually became a librarian at the college.

Despite her distance from the bustling Harlem scene, Bethune supported and established close ties to a number of leading writers and figures of the period. When LANGSTON HUGHES closed his February 1932 poetry reading at the school with a rendition of "The Negro Mother," Bethune reportedly exclaimed "My son! my son!" as she thanked him. In his second memoir, *I Wonder As I Wander*, Hughes described her as a woman "joyfully clothed in African dignity."

Bethune, who was widowed in 1918, was a leader in national and African-American political circles. She was a vice president in the NATIONAL ASSOCIATION FOR THE ADVANCEMENT OF COLORED PEOPLE, president of the NATIONAL ASSOCIATION OF COLORED WOMEN, and president of the national Council for Negro Women. Presidents Herbert Hoover and Franklin Roosevelt both called on her expertise and appointed her to serve on committees relating to children's health and welfare.

Bibliography

Bethune, Mary McLeod. *Building a Better World: Essays and Selected Documents*. Audrey Thomas McCluskey and Elaine M. Smith, eds. Bloomington: Indiana University Press, 1999.

Holt, Rackham. *Mary McLeod Bethune*. Garden City, N.J.: Doubleday, 1964.

Mary McLeod Bethune Papers, Bethune Foundation, Bethune-Cookman College Archives, and the Amistad Research Center.

Peare, Catherine. *Mary McLeod Bethune*. New York: Vanguard Press, 1951.

Bethune-Cookman College

This pioneering coeducational college resulted from the merger of the Daytona Normal and Industrial Institute for Negro Girls, founded in 1904, with the all-male Cookman Institute, founded in 1872, in Jacksonville, Florida. In 1923 it was officially named Bethune-Cookman College, in honor of MARY MCLEOD BETHUNE, the legendary educator and the only woman to have founded a historically black college in the United States.

In its early years, the college functioned as a high school and offered junior college–level classes. By 1931, it had become a two-year college, and in 1947, it was accredited as a four-year institution of higher learning. Bethune retired from the post of president in 1942. The school continues to thrive and today is part of the impressive consortium of historically black colleges and universities.

Bibb, Joseph Dandridge (1891–unknown)

The Georgia-born attorney who helped to found the *CHICAGO WHIP*, an extremely successful African-American newspaper that achieved a circulation of nearly 70,000 within 10 years of its beginnings. Educated at a number of schools, including ATLANTA UNIVERSITY and HARVARD UNIVERSITY, Bibb graduated in 1918 with a law degree from YALE UNIVERSITY.

"Bidin' Place" May Miller (1937)

A short story by MAY MILLER SULLIVAN, the woman who encouraged ZORA NEALE HURSTON to attend HOWARD UNIVERSITY and who comforted GEORGIA DOUGLAS JOHNSON as she lay dying. "Bidin' Place," which appeared in the April 1937 issue of *Arts Quarterly*, was a first-person account of a sobering encounter between an unnamed white traveler and the tragic families he meets when car trouble leaves him stranded in rural North Carolina.

The narrator, whose account is reminiscent of an anthropological report, finds himself alone on an "eerie road that stretched like a band of tinsel ribbon into the distant mistiness." Shortly after he sets out, the narrator comes to a "mean hovel that not even the sportive moonlight could trick into semblance of a decent abode." Despite his plea for accommodations, the man is turned away when the father of the house informs him that the family is battling an illness that already has claimed the life of one of the children. The father directs him to seek out Ma Grady, a midwife who lives nearby with a person referred to only as "Mose." The traveler offers five dollars to the "wizened gray woman" who has "kinky hair, crackled skin and filmy eyes [that] harmoniously blen[ded] in a washed-out neutral tone," and she promptly accepts it. After drinking a potion that she gives to him to ward off his chill, the man clambers into a bed with Mose, a "hulking straight figure under the ragged covers" who "fortunately lay very still with his face turned toward the wall." The next morning, while the traveler has his car repaired, he finds out from the mechanics that the man with whom he shared a bed was Ma Grady's dead son. He also learns that she needed five dollars in order to provide the best funeral arrangements possible for her son. The story ends on a contemplative note as the narrator, who has survived a night alongside a corpse and unwittingly contributed vital funds to a grieving mother, considers the dramatic events and the ways in which decisions and interactions can be shaped by circumstance and need.

Big Sea, The: An Autobiography
Langston Hughes (1940)

This memoir by LANGSTON HUGHES, rich in anecdotes, fascinating details, and personal commentary, was published in 1940. The first of his formal autobiographical accounts, the volume was based in part on the 1925 materials entitled "L'histoire de ma vie," which he produced to satisfy CARL VAN VECHTEN's repeated suggestion that he pen an account of his life story. He published a second memoir, *I Wonder As I Wander*, in 1956.

Dedicated to Emerson and Toy Harper, the volume is divided into three sections entitled "Twenty-one," "Big Sea," and "Black Renaissance." The epigraph that prefaces the work signals the optimism

and willingness to entertain the unexpected: "Life is a big sea / full of many fish. / I let down my nets / and pull." The sections include a number of chapters or "stories," as Hughes refers to them, some of which had been published previously in AMERICAN MERCURY, *Scribner's*, OPPORTUNITY, ABBOTT'S MONTHLY, *The Brooklyn Daily Eagle*, and *Debate*. The memoir opens with an account of the often-quoted scene in which the 21-year-old Hughes is standing on the deck of the SS *Malone* just off Sandy Hook, New Jersey, and tosses all of the "books I had had at Columbia, and all the books I had lately bought to read." About this moment, which he admits may seem "melodramatic," he recalls that "then it was like throwing a million bricks out of my heart when I threw the books into the water" (31). This unforgettable moment of liberation leads to a series of adventures that begin with his voyage to Africa.

"Twenty-one," the first section, is devoted primarily to accounts of Hughes's family life, his ancestry, childhood experiences of religion, early reading life, time in Mexico with his father, and transition to life at Columbia in New York City. The last lines of "Beyond Sandy Hook," the first story in the volume, refer to Hughes's distress that when he reached Africa aboard the SS *Malone*, the "Africans looked at me and would not believe I was a Negro." Hughes acknowledges this slight but in the next story reveals that the Africans' assessments are in fact correct. "You see, unfortunately, I am not black," he writes in the opening lines of "Negro," the second recollection of *The Big Sea*. He then begins to outline his ancestry and absorbing antebellum family history in the second story. The genealogy and family lore that he shares in "Negro" include details about Sheridan Leary, his maternal grandmother's first husband who died alongside John Brown at the ill-fated 1859 raid on Harper's Ferry.

"Big Sea," the second section, constitutes the high adventure portion of the memoir. It is in this portion of the book that Hughes resumes the story of the SS *Malone* with which he began the autobiography. In "Africa," the first chapter, he recalls his observations about the symbolic and real implications of trade. "We brought machinery and tools, canned goods, and Hollywood films," he writes. "We took away riches out of the earth, loaded by human hands. We paid very little for the labor. We paid but little more for the things we took away.

The white man dominates Africa. He takes produce and lives, very much as he chooses. The yield of the earth for Europe and America. The yield of men for Europe's colonial armies" (95). Hughes's observations about the inequities perpetuated by colonialism lead to additional musings about the racial tensions that he experiences and witnesses aboard the ship. He provides details about his shipmates, such as "Manuel, the Filipino boy from Mindanao, who served the passengers." He was an earnest worker "because he was hoping they would tip him well when the boat got to New York. Manuel wanted to marry a Mexican girl," Hughes reveals, "and put a big payment down on new furniture for their flat" (111). Hughes returns home to Cleveland, Ohio, with a monkey named Jocko that his mother, who refers to it as a "Congo devil," promptly sells to a local pet shop as soon as Hughes makes plans to go again to sea. When his firing by a racist steward inadvertently saves his life because the ship is blown up by an undetected mine in the Black Sea, Hughes celebrates and takes advantage of his new opportunities to live in France. He settles in Paris, makes friends with young people like Mary, a woman with "soft, doe-brown" skin who reads the CRISIS, is familiar with his poems, and shares with him an appreciation for CLAUDE MCKAY, "the Negro poet, in London" and his volume SPRING IN NEW HAMPSHIRE. The section closes with anecdotes about his arrival in the United States, his first encounters with members of the Harlem Renaissance, and his relocation to WASHINGTON, D.C. In "Washington Society," Hughes recalls that he "landed with a few poems," shared them with COUNTEE CULLEN, gained access to a NATIONAL ASSOCIATION FOR THE ADVANCEMENT OF COLORED PEOPLE party at the club owned by Happy Rhone, and promptly found himself immersed in conversations with such influential civil rights and literary figures as WALTER WHITE, JAMES WELDON JOHNSON, and CARL VAN VECHTEN.

In "Black Renaissance," the third and final section of the autobiography, Hughes provides a documentary overview of the Harlem Renaissance. He describes performances such as the musical revue *Shuffle Along,* considers the influence of actors Charles Gilpin, Rose McClendon, PAUL ROBESON, and others, and his own firsthand interactions with writers while living in the room-

ing house that came to be known as "Niggerati Manor" with Wallace Thurman. He also provides scintillating assessments of figures like Thurman, whom he describes as "a strangely brilliant black boy, who had read everything, and whose critical mind could find something wrong with everything he read" and who "had read so many books because he could read eleven lines at a time. He would get from the library a great pile of volumes that would have taken me a year to read," recalls Hughes, "But he would go through them in less than a week, and be able to discuss each one at great length with anybody" (182). Hughes also devoted several passages to accounts of decadent and memorable social events ranging from the annual Hamilton Club Lodge Ball, where "men dress as women and women as men" (208) and which he attended with heiress A'LELIA WALKER, to the funeral of Florence Mills that included "a beautiful procession, with the chorus girls from her show marching all in gray, and an airplane releasing flocks of blackbirds overhead" (209).

In his postscript to *The Big Sea,* Hughes considered once again the epigraph with which he began the volume. "Literature is a big sea full of many fish," he writes. "I let down my nets and pulled. I'm still pulling." Hughes reaffirms his commitment to life as a writer. "I would have to make my own living again," he decides, as the 1920s end and, according to him, so too does the Harlem Renaissance. "I determined to make it writing. I did. Shortly poetry became bread; prose, shelter and raiment. Words turned into songs, plays scenarios, articles, and stories" (250).

Bibliography

Berry, Faith, ed. *Langston Hughes: Before and Beyond Harlem.* Westport, Conn.: Lawrence Hill & Company, 1983.

McLaren, Joseph, ed. *The Collected Works of Langston Hughes.* Vol. 13: *Autobiography—The Big Sea.* Columbia: University of Missouri Press, 2001.

Rampersad, Arnold. *The Life of Langston Hughes: I, Too, Sing America.* Vol. 1: *1902–1941.* New York: Oxford University Press, 1986.

Billy Pierce Studio

A pioneering dance studio. Billy Pierce's story was the basis of ELMER A. CARTER's May 1930 OPPOR-

TUNITY article, "He Smashed the Color Line: A Sketch of Billy Pierce."

Bird, Bessie Calhoun (1906–unknown)

A member of the ambitious African-American literary circle in Philadelphia whose members regularly published in BLACK OPALS, their literary magazine. Bird's colleagues included other Philadelphia writers such as NELLIE BRIGHT and MAE COWDERY. Like GEORGIA DOUGLAS JOHNSON in WASHINGTON, D.C., and REGINA ANDERSON in NEW YORK CITY, Bird hosted gatherings of Philadelphia-area writers and artists in her home. She was an active member of the local PIRANEAN CLUB and the Beaux Arts Club, and her first and only published collection of poems appeared when the Piranean Club was at its peak. Although Bird focused on traditional themes such as nature and feelings, she crafted works that prompted ARTHUR HUFF FAUSET, a fellow Philadelphian who wrote an introduction to AIRS FROM THE WOOD-WINDS, to characterize them as "zephyrs."

"Bird in the Bush, The" Theophilus Lewis (1926)

A short story by THEOPHILUS LEWIS, drama critic for THE MESSENGER, that appeared in that magazine in January 1926. The character Marie Steele is a woman caught between her competing desire for economic security and passionate romance. Bascom, a thoroughly boring man, is courting her when she meets Lester, a charming and self-confident potential suitor. Ultimately, though, Marie convinces herself that "a good husband [isn't] to be sniffed at" and chooses Bascom. Lewis's entertaining but sobering portrait anticipated the plight of Helga Crane, the tragic heroine of NELLA LARSEN's QUICKSAND, and the self-defeating and confining decisions that she makes about marriage.

Birth of a Nation (1915)

The controversial 1915 film by D. W. Griffith that appeared first as *The Clansman* and was screened in NEW YORK CITY for the first time in March of that year. The script, inspired by Thomas Dixon's novel *The Clansman*, celebrated the Ku Klux Klan and the Confederacy. It mocked celebrated northern antislavery leaders, indicted interracial relationships, and perpetuated numerous African-American stereotypes. The film elicited extensive protests from individuals and from organizations such as the NATIONAL ASSOCIATION FOR THE ADVANCEMENT OF COLORED PEOPLE. Emmett Scott, the secretary to Booker T. Washington, was so outraged by the film that he created a film company to produce *Birth of a Race*, a counter-narrative to the Griffiths production. The NAACP waged a lengthy four-year battle against Griffith's film. In addition to organizing marches, the organization petitioned city officials for injunctions against the shows and generally rallied African Americans and their supporters to fight against the racism that prompted interest in and the production of such offensive material.

Bibliography

Fleener-Marzec, Nickieann. *D. W. Griffith's The Birth of a Nation: Controversy, Suppression, and the First Amendment As It Applies to Filmic Expression, 1915–1973.* New York: Arno Press, 1980.

Silva, Fred, comp. *Focus on Birth of A Nation.* Englewood Cliffs, N.J.: Prentice-Hall, 1971.

Birthright Thomas Stribling (1922)

A work by THOMAS STRIBLING, a Tennessee lawyer and reporter, and recognized as the first significant novel by a white American writer in which the protagonist was African American. The plot revolves around the life of Peter Siner, a mixed-race Tennessee native who travels north to Harvard for school. He eventually returns to "Hooker's Bend," where he concludes that his African heritage dooms him to tragic powerlessness. JESSIE FAUSET believed that Stribling's work illuminated the ready market for good literature by and about African Americans. Like Pauline Hopkins, the turn-of-the-20th-century novelist who claimed that African Americans were most capable of generating informed, engaging race stories, Fauset urged her peers that they "who are better qualified to present that truth than any white writer try to do so."

Bishop Payne Divinity School

Named after Bishop Daniel A. Payne, a freeborn minister in the African Methodist Episcopal Church and the person who secured the financial autonomy of WILBERFORCE UNIVERSITY. Located in Virginia, the divinity school was the alma mater of such figures as ROBERT W. BAGNALL, a high-ranking NAACP official who combined a career in the ministry with race work and a writing career that saw several race-related essays published during the Harlem Renaissance.

"Black" Nellie Rathborne Bright (1927)

A prizewinning essay in which NELLIE RATHBORNE BRIGHT described and analyzed her travel experiences in Europe. Bright noted the lack of European anxiety about her color but provided ample proof of pervasive racism. Her encounter with a Nigerian who is traumatized by his experiences in America prompts Bright to realize the multifaceted nature of race and blackness.

Black and White (1932)

A Russian film project on American race relations, sponsored by the MESCHRABPOM FILM CORPORATION. The company invited several Harlem Renaissance writers to Russia to create and perform in the production. The group of 22 who boarded the ship *Europa* included writers, actresses, COMMUNIST PARTY members, social workers, and teachers, among them LANGSTON HUGHES, LOUISE THOMPSON, DOROTHY WEST, TED POSTON, Henry Moon, Allen McKenzie, TAYLOR GORDON, Mollie Lewis, Sylvia Garner, Wayland Rudd, Juanita Lewis, and Thurston Lewis. Shortly after their arrival, the group discovered that the project was not what they had thought, and they disbanded after a few months.

Black and White Tangled Threads
Zara Wright (1920)

A novel by ZARA WRIGHT that recalls *Iola Leroy or the Shadows Uplifted,* the pioneering 1892 novel of racial awareness and uplift by Frances Ellen Watkins Harper. Wright's southern tale about mixed-race heroines and their historically

Langston Hughes and Louise Thompson in 1933 aboard the *Europa* as they sail to Russia to participate in *Black and White,* a film project sponsored by the Meschrabpom Film Corporation *(Yale Collection of American Literature, Beinecke Rare Book and Manuscript Library)*

kind, formerly slave-owning white neighbors, revises the traditional racial uplift plot, however. When Zoleeta discovers that she is not white, she accepts her racial heritage but devotes herself not to improving the lot of African Americans but to enlightening white southerners about their prejudices.

Published eight years after the anonymously authored AUTOBIOGRAPHY OF AN EX-COLOURED MAN and nine years before NELLA LARSEN's PASSING, this work is part of the continuing tradition of literature about the social upheaval and remedies brought to bear on the American history of miscegenation, interracial alliances, and mixed-race identity.

Black Boy **Jim Tully and Frank Dazey** (1926)
A play in which the casting of PAUL ROBESON in
the lead role appeared to be the only redeeming aspect of the production. The play, written by Jim
Tully and Frank Dazey about a young man who enjoys fleeting fame as a champion boxer, opened at
the Comedy Theatre in October 1926.

Black Christ and Other Poems, The
Countee Cullen (1929)
Published shortly after COUNTEE CULLEN's return
to the United States after a GUGGENHEIM FEL-
LOWSHIP year in Paris, this was the celebrated author's third published volume. It contained
politically charged works that addressed contemporary issues such as LYNCHING, controversial cases
such as the Sacco-Vanzetti trial, and the painful
legacies of war represented by such haunting sites
as the grave in Paris at the Arc de Triomphe that is
dedicated to the Unknown Soldier.

The volume included a number of pieces
shaped by traditional English poetic conventions
and "The Black Christ," a lengthy narrative piece
in which Cullen explored the subject of lynching
from a spiritual perspective. "Hopefully dedicated
to White America," the narrative poem chronicles
the powerful effect that the victim of white mob
violence is able to have when he reappears to his
grieving family and urges them to rely on God for
justice. Despite the title's suggestion, Cullen does
not imagine a black savior. Instead, he draws on
the parallels between the crucifixion and resurrection of Christ and his ability to direct an enduring,
patient love toward his attackers.

The set of 47 poems appeared in three sections,
entitled "Varia," "Interlude," and "Color." The third
and final section, which was the shortest with only
four poems, contained the moving and explosive
poem "The Black Christ." The volume, like Cullen's
previous works, was published by HARPER &
BROTHERS and included provocative art deco images by the white artist Charles Cullen. The poet
dedicated the book to "Three Friends": Edward,
Roberta, and Harold. "To the Three for Whom the
Book" was the first poem in the volume, and it extended Cullen's dedicatory tribute. The lengthy and
vivid narrative that evoked an intense mythological
landscape and mighty figures such as Theseus,

Medusa, and the Minotaur celebrated "three rare /
Friends whom I love / (With rhymes to swear / The
depths whereof)" (ll. 92–95). Cullen went even further, justifying his dedication to kindred spirits who
"have not bent / The idolatrous knee, / Nor worship
lent / To modern rites, / Knowing full well / How a
just god smites / The infidel" (ll. 97–103). Immediately following this poem was "Tribute," which
Cullen dedicated to his mother. He honored the
lessons that he had learned from her and cited the
powerful "intervention of your face" as the only
force that "[s]pared him with whom was my most
bitter feud" (ll. 11–12).

The first section included poems informed by
history and by political realities. These included
"At the Etoile (At the Unknown Soldier's Grave in
Paris)," "Two Epitaphs," which included a poem
"For the Unknown Soldier," and "For a Child Still-
born," "Not Sacco and Vanzetti." The poems
about Paris and the Unknown Soldier were inspired by Cullen's time in Paris as a Guggenheim
Fellow. In the poem "At the Etoile," Cullen celebrated the universality that accompanied the soldier's anonymity: "Each bit of moving dust in
France may strike / Its breast in pride, knowing he
stands for him" (ll. 11–12). In "Two Epitaphs," the
second, and much more cryptic tribute to the soldier, Cullen's narrator insisted again on the enor-
mity of the soldier's symbolic life and death. "Not
one stilled heart in that torn breast / But a myriad
millions" (ll. 3–4) he insisted, going on to note
that those many hearts could sleep in "Unknown
but not unhonored rest" (l. 1).

Following the set of observant and politically
astute poems in section one were a number of more
personal meditations conveyed primarily in the first
person. These included "One Day I Told My Love,"
a tender poem about a vulnerable lover whose
sweetheart does not abuse his heart but instead
does "a gentle thing" and advises that " 'The proper
place for a heart . . . / 'Is back in the sheltering
breast' " (ll. 13, 15–16). Other confessional poems,
such as "Lesson" and "The Simple Truth," recognized the powerful assets that others brought to relationships. In the latter, the speaker addresses his
"level-headed lover who / Can match my fever
while the kisses last" (l. 5). The beloved elicits respect because he or she is "never shaken through
and through" and because his or her "roots are firm

after the storm has passed" (ll. 6–7). In "Valedictory" the speaker rallies in the face of desertion and vows to "write no more" of the one who makes "vows . . . / Out of a haughty heart" and will no longer "tremble for my sake / Nor writhe beneath the smart / Of hearing on an alien tongue / Tolled lightly and in play" (ll. 8, 9–13). In his pointed response to the Sacco-Vanzetti trial, Cullen blasted the accusers and those responsible for dragging out the case for some seven years. "These men who do not die, but send to death, / These iron men whom mercy cannot bend / Beyond the lettered law," he wrote, "These are the men I should not care to be" (ll. 1–3, 14).

Reviews, as they had been for his previous works, were good, and the impact of the book continued to be felt years after its publication. Cullen's biographer, Blanche Ferguson, notes that in 1945 Eleanor Roosevelt called the book to the attention of the American public and suggested that its title poem be "required reading for every American student as soon as he became mature enough to understand it" (Ferguson, 115). Cullen clearly took pride in the book; just before his untimely death in 1946, he selected some 24 poems from *The Black Christ* for inclusion in *On These I Stand*, a posthumously published volume of collected poems that he had carefully selected and arranged to have published with his longtime publisher, Harper & Brothers.

Bibliography

Ferguson, Blanche. *Countee Cullen and the Negro Renaissance.* New York: Dodd, Mead, 1966.
Shucard, Alan. *Countee Cullen.* Boston: Twayne, 1984.

Black Damp John Matheus (1929)

Published in the April 1929 issue of *Carolina Magazine*, this play was set in a West Virginia coal mine, where a racially and ethnically mixed group of miners grappled with the demands of the job and their various motivations to work in the shafts.

The miners Big Steve Johnson, Foots Williams, and Goosy Woods are good men, who are determined to earn enough to give their children and their sisters a chance to make something of themselves. Twenty-six-year-old Johnson takes out a letter that he has just received from his 18-year-old

sister and reads it to his friends. As they prepare for another day of grueling work, they fend off the aggressive overtures of the fireboss. Just before they descend into the mines, they learn that a white Prohibition officer was killed the night before. A police officer named Dawson arrives at the mine, determined to arrest the two African-American miners. Big Steve insists that he be allowed to work his shift and to earn at least one more day's wages in order to support his sister. The men intimidate the officer, and their coworkers assure him that the two suspects will indeed return and go peaceably with him.

The play intensifies as an explosion breaks out in the mine and traps Johnson, Woods, and Dawson down below. As they struggle to make it to safety, the three men each reveal something important about themselves. Johnson and Woods recall their home life and deliver moving accounts of their childhood experiences. Dawson, however, reveals the truth about the murder of the Prohibition officer and confesses that he is, in fact, the murderer. Just as he delivers this shocking revelation, two rescuers appear in the mine. In a savage twist, they decide that they can only rescue one of the three men there, and they take Dawson, the guilty man, and leave the two upstanding, innocent men to die.

Black Damp, inspired by Matheus's own exposure to miners during his childhood, was one of 11 plays published in the special African-American drama issue of *Carolina Magazine*. The play appeared alongside works by LEWIS ALEXANDER, EULALIE SPENCE, MAY MILLER SULLIVAN, and WILLIS RICHARDSON. It was performed more than two decades later in Cleveland in the 1950s.

"Black Dress, The" Dorothy West (1934)

A "short short story" about friendship and performance by Bostonian DOROTHY WEST that appeared in the May 1934 issue of *OPPORTUNITY*, the official monthly magazine of the NATIONAL URBAN LEAGUE.

The story begins as the first-person narrator, a childhood friend of Margaret Johnson, contemplates how best to entice her friend Margaret back to her hometown to see the father from whom she has been estranged for years. Margaret, an actress who has to defend her love of the theater and her desire to have a career on the stage, writes to say that she will visit her friend whom she has not seen in some 12 years. Unfortunately, Margaret's father passes away before she arrives. The narrator has, however, inadvertently given the hospital Margaret's home address in response to their request for information about next-of-kin. She hopes that Margaret has left home before the message arrives and vows not to spoil the Christmas holiday by telling her friend this sad news on the first evening that she arrives. The two are reunited with much enthusiasm, and the narrator is convinced that her friend has not been informed about her father's death. That night they share a delightful and festive evening together. "I shall never forget our happy evening," promises the narrator. "She was like a sprite, never still. She fell in love with small Margaret. Once she said fiercely to the shining faces [of the children], 'Be happy. Let nothing stand in the way of your being happy.'" Later that night, the two women prepare for bed having relegated the narrator's husband to a cot downstairs. Margaret opens her suitcase and takes out a black dress that she intends to wear to the funeral. The narrator is dumbfounded by what is revealed to have been Margaret's impressive performance. "My throat went dry," she recalls. "For the first time in my life I was going to sleep with a stranger."

West's brief story conveys well the kind of performance and deception that can shatter illusions of domestic harmony and notions of true friendship. It is in keeping with her other stories that explore the nature of family relationships and the strong-willed women who survive the most trying, and potentially devastating, of circumstances.

Blacker the Berry, The Wallace Thurman (1929)

A compelling meditation on intraracial color consciousness, this novel on the African-American middle class generated critical acclaim for its author WALLACE THURMAN. He explored the psychological, emotional, and financial effects of color prejudice as practiced within the black community.

Over the course of the novel's five sections, entitled "Emma Lou," "Harlem," "Alva," "Rent Party," and "Pyrrhic Victory," respectively, Emma Lou, the darkest-skinned child in an emphatically light-skinned family, suffers exclusion, alienation, and dismissal in and beyond her own family. The novel begins with a character who has a promising sense of herself as she takes part in her high school graduation but is a woman under siege. "More acutely than ever before Emma Lou began to feel that her luscious black complexion was somewhat of a liability," notes the narrator, "and that her marked color variation from the other people in her environment was a decided curse." The child of a light-skinned mother and "old black Jim Morgan," her dark-skinned father, Emma Lou is rendered the "alien member of the family and of the family's social circle" and has to endure a "moaning and grieving over the color of her skin." She is

Cover illustration by Aaron Douglas of Wallace Thurman's 1929 novel, *The Blacker the Berry,* Macauley Company *(Yale Collection of American Literature, Beinecke Rare Book and Manuscript Library)*

the descendant of free mulattos and the grand-daughter of Boise's Blue Vein society, a group that is open only to people who are light-skinned enough to pass and to show the blue veins in their wrists. Following graduation, she travels further west to Los Angeles, where her kindly Uncle Joe hopes that she will be able to avoid "stupid color prejudice such as she had encountered among the blue vein circle in her home town." She enrolls at the University of California, Los Angeles, and has the opportunity, and burden at times, of negotiating new relationships with the few students of color on campus.

Despite her optimism and readiness to thrive, Emma Lou suffers the sting of intraracial exclusion and her uneven experiences in California prompt her to leave school and head to HARLEM. There she experiences more direct racism as she searches for gainful employment and suffers the taunts of men who stand on the sidewalk appraising the girls and women who pass by. The "Harlem" section closes after Emma Lou endures a long lecture from a well-meaning employment agency clerk about the values of higher education and hears a crude man named Fats suggest to his buddies that he would never pursue a girl like her because he "don't haul no coal." Emma Lou surrenders her goal of doing administrative white-collar work and accepts a job as a maid to Arline Strange, a white actress who, at the time that Emma Lou joins her, is playing the part of a mulatto heroine. When she takes a temporary leave from the job because Arline is called away due to a family emergency, Emma Lou begins a series of destructive behaviors. She spends hours fussing with her hair and then resorts to trying a number of remedies designed to lighten the skin. She makes herself sick by eating arsenic wafers that "were guaranteed to increase the pallor of one's skin" and jeopardizes her clear complexion by slathering on the peroxide-based "Black and White" ointment that produces only "blackheads, irritating rashes, and a burning skin." She endures a difficult relationship with a man named Alva, whose penchant for drink and wild parties jeopardizes Emma Lou's reputation and results in her losing her rental accommodations. Thanks to Arline Strange's intervention, Emma Lou obtains a job as a maid to Clere Sloan, a retired actress who is married to Campbell Kitchen,

a writer "who had become interested in Harlem" and "along with Carl Van Vechten was one of the leading spirits in this 'Explore Harlem; Know the Negro'" crusade. It is clear that Emma Lou can find no sanctuary in New York City, despite its large and diverse African-American community, the opportunities to teach, and myriad prospects for entertainment. She finally extricates herself from the unhealthy relationship that she resumes with Alva and his sickly child and prepares to live up to her new motto: "Find—not seek."

Thurman suggests that even while victimized because of her skin tone, Emma Lou has imbibed the same cultural biases and prejudices used against her. Thurman uses Emma's desire for a satisfying romance to explore the alienation and self-doubt that she experiences time and time again. He suggests that Emma is in fact victimized by the society that jeers her in the streets, makes disparaging remarks about her marriageability, and focuses on a flawed racial aesthetic rather than individual merits and potential. The character of Truman Walter, a figure whose Christian name and fictional circumstances bear a striking resemblance to the author's identity, offers sharp critiques of the social and cultural desires that fuel intraracial intolerance. Ultimately, Emma survives several demeaning social encounters and disappointing encounters with men, including a tortured relationship with a mixed-race Filipino named Alva, and contemplates the best way to restore her own agency and self-confidence. The novel closes as she considers the value of returning to her childhood home, a place that both defines and challenges the notion that racial solidarity is either predictable or available.

The novel begins with two epigraphs that underscore the competing interpretations of race in general, and dark skin tone in particular. The first one that Thurman uses is taken from an African-American folk saying that proposes that "[t]he blacker the berry / The sweeter the juice." The second, excerpted from a COUNTEE CULLEN poem, states hauntingly, "My color shrouds me in." Writer Shirley Taylor Haizlip suggests that the novel is "an important story for our times and for the future. One that should be kept alive, told, and retold, in the context of how black self-hate, black rage is created and how black self-love, black empowerment can triumph" (Haizlip, 14).

Bibliography

Haizlip, Shirley Taylor. Introduction. *The Blacker The Berry.* 1929; reprint, New York: Simon and Schuster, 1996.

Singh, Amritjit. *The Novels of the Harlem Renaissance: Twelve Black Writers, 1923–1933.* University Park: Pennsylvania State University Press, 1976.

Wright, Shirley Haynes. *A Study of the Fiction of Wallace Thurman.* Ann Arbor, Mich.: University Microfilms International, 1983.

"Black Fronts" Marita Bonner (1938)

A set of three fictional vignettes by MARITA BONNER that appeared in the July 1938 issue of *OPPORTUNITY.* The chaotic narratives focus on the domestic distress brought on by extravagant lifestyles, the economic upheaval of the Great Depression, and all-around family stress. The first, entitled "Front A," relates the tragic story of Big Brother, a man whose family has sacrificed greatly so that he could become a lawyer. "He was a lawyer," asserts the narrator in the opening lines of the story before making the grim observation that "[h]e had not had a case since 1932. This was 1935." The story follows Big Brother's increasingly desperate decline, dependence on his family, and inability to prevent his wife Rinky Dew from spending beyond their means. The vignette ends, however, with a more sympathetic account of the couple's independent stress and an indication that they are completely distracted by their inability to overcome the pressures of the life in which they find themselves.

"Front B" and "Front C," the second and third installments in "Black Fronts," are made up of vivid dialogues between unidentified speakers. The conversations in "Front B" are between a domestic worker and her employer, and they veer wildly around issues of employment, social status, and ethnic stereotypes. The first involves the two women, both of whom are African American. The domestic worker is frustrated by the fact that her employer does not leave her to complete her tasks. She also is annoyed that she is being watched so carefully and unable to filch a few items for her own family. "Front C" is a series of pained observations that the employer makes about the demands of motherhood and her need to prevent theft in her own home.

The stories reflect Bonner's ongoing interest in domestic upheaval and the negotiations that many women are forced to make in order to maintain an air of normalcy in the face of overwhelming demands or social realities.

Black Horseman, The Willis Richardson (1929)

A play about intrigue, deception, and military might that dramatist WILLIS RICHARDSON adapted for high school students. The play was selected for inclusion in *PLAYS AND PAGEANTS FROM THE LIFE OF THE NEGRO,* an anthology that Richardson had edited.

The play, set in the African region of Numidia, opens as King Massinissa of East Numidia is trying to uncover the real reason why Syphax, a prince of West Numidia, has come to the court. The conversation between the guards Claudius and Eubonius establishes the intrigue and what will become a growing suspicion that the African empire is threatened with invasion or co-optation. The king's three daughters have taken matters into their own hands and have determined, through stealth and eavesdropping, that Syphax has come with plans to wed their father to a white Carthaginian princess and to initiate major changes in the governance of the state. It is the princesses who lodge a successful appeal to the king that prevents him from accepting a suspicious demotion to the rank of prince and the loss of his territory. "Think a moment, Sire," says the princess Casintha, "Of how your people love you, think of how / Your soldiers fought to give you power here / In Africa, the nation's treasure house." Her sister Rosioba lodges a forceful plea for racial solidarity and raises the specter of unappealing racial differences. "Think of the strangers you would tarry with," she declares, "then think of us, your own dark women who / Love you as they love life; but most of all / Think of a pale, cold bride whose kisses are / But shadows of a kiss, whose love would be / An empty dream of love, and give him 'no' / For an answer." The princesses successfully persuade the king to abandon his plans to marry the Carthaginian princess, arrangements that they are sure could "weaken Africa" and "[e]nslave Numidia." King Massinissa preserves his kingdom, rejects the suspicious overtures from imposters who pose as messengers from Scipio Africanus, and prepares to lead his kingdom into an even greater moment of triumph and power.

The Black Horseman, which Richardson described as one of the "neo-romances" included in the anthology, provides students and children with romantic historical images. It was part of the larger Harlem Renaissance-era movement to generate enriching and diverse materials for performance groups and their audiences.

Bibliography

Richardson, Willis. *Plays and Pageants from the Life of the Negro.* Washington, D.C.: The Associated Publishers, Inc., 1930.

Black King, The (1932)

A Southland film, directed by Bud Pollard, that offered a negative and demeaning image of MARCUS GARVEY as an ineffectual, illiterate leader.

Black Magic Thelma Duncan (1931)

A play by THELMA DUNCAN, a HOWARD UNIVERSITY graduate and teacher. The comedy, which included African-American dialect, focused on a married couple, moments of miscommunication, and groundless suspicions, and it merited inclusion in the 1931 edition of *The Yearbook of Short Plays*.

Black Manhattan James Weldon Johnson (1930)

An accessible work of social and cultural history by JAMES WELDON JOHNSON that highlighted the contributions, communities, and long-standing history of African Americans in the city. Published by ALFRED A. KNOPF, the same firm that reprinted Johnson's *AUTOBIOGRAPHY OF AN EX-COLOURED MAN* in 1927, *Black Manhattan* represented Johnson's most extensive historical effort to date.

The book is based in part on Johnson's 1925 *SURVEY GRAPHIC* essay "The Making of Harlem." ALAIN LOCKE republished this same essay later that year in the highly recognized anthology entitled *THE NEW NEGRO*, a highly regarded collection of works by African-American writers. In his preface to the *Black Manhattan*, Johnson assured readers that it was "not my intention to make this book in any strict sense a history. I have attempted only to etch in the background of the Negro in latter-day New York," he stated, "to give a cut-back in projecting a picture of Negro Harlem" (vii). He relied on the research assistance of Richetta Randolph, the memories and anecdotes of William Foster and Irving Jones, and the expansive collection of African-American materials that were part of the impressive Schomburg Collection held at the 135th Street Branch of the NEW YORK PUBLIC LIBRARY.

Black Manhattan's 22 chapters included overviews of New York history from the 17th century to the 20th, accounts of African-American educational opportunities since the establishment of the first free schools for people of color, and the history of residential patterns that transformed areas such as HARLEM and the borough of Brooklyn into thriving, lively places. In his cultural profiles, Johnson provided detailed notes about sports figures, stage and vaudeville actors, and contemporary entertainers such as his own brother J. Rosamond Johnson and Bob Cole, Big JIM EUROPE, W. C. HANDY, and PAUL ROBESON. The final chapters were devoted to contemporary Harlem during the age of the Renaissance. In these narratives, Johnson considered the impact of writers, most of them male, the importance of literary prizes offered by the major journals *OPPORTUNITY* and *THE CRISIS*, and the significant role that Harlem could play and was playing in the "public opinion about the Negro" (xvii).

Johnson began with a bold characterization of Harlem. It was "not merely a colony or a community or a settlement," he declared in his first chapter, "not at all a 'quarter' or a slum or a fringe—but a black city, located in the heart of white Manhattan, and containing more Negroes to the square mile than any other spot on earth." With confidence, he insisted that Harlem "strikes the uninformed observer as a phenomenon, a miracle straight out of the skies." In his commentary about the Harlem Renaissance period, Johnson acknowledged the links between political realities and cultural endeavors. He recounted graphic details about race riots, such as the one that occurred in the summer of 1917 and in which one of his close friends suffered at the hands of the police when he sought protection from the unchecked white mob raging indiscriminately against African Americans. Johnson also documented the rise of the periodical press and the "new vigour" with which they proceeded to represent issues of importance to Americans of color. Of journals such as *THE MESSENGER, NEGRO WORLD,* and *THE EMANCIPATOR,* he noted that that they were "edited and written by men who had a remarkable command of forcible and trenchant English, the precise style for their purpose." Finally, Johnson concluded the volume by asserting that "The Negro in New York still has far, very far yet, to go and many, very many things yet to gain. He still meets with discriminations and disadvantages. But New York guarantees her Negro citizens the fundamental rights of citizenship," and the state "protects them in the exercise of those rights." Johnson invoked the frequently overlooked and underestimated history of African-American perseverance, triumph, and patriotism that he had presented in his volume as he generated an inspired closing statement.

As Johnson scholar Richard Fleming notes, many reviewers suggested that Johnson's volume was a good but not especially innovative compilation of facts and that "the strictly historical matter of the book could have been produced by any competent researcher" (Fleming, 85). According to Fleming, though, the strength of *Black Manhattan* lay in the firsthand experiences and accounts that Johnson incorporated into his discussions of history, culture, literature, and politics.

Bibliography

Fleming, Robert. *James Weldon Johnson.* Boston: Twayne Publishers, 1987.

Johnson, James Weldon. *Black Manhattan.* 1930; reprint, New York: Arno Press, 1968.

Price, Kenneth, and Lawrence Oliver. *Critical Essays on James Weldon Johnson.* New York: G. K. Hall, 1997.

Black Man's Verse **Frank Marshall Davis** (1935)

A powerful collection of poems by FRANK MARSHALL DAVIS and the first of three that Davis published with the Black Cat Press of CHICAGO. The volume reflected Davis's independent spirit; Davis refused to include an introduction or prefatory remarks by any well-known writers. The collection of poems, most of which reflected Davis's experimental work with free verse, tapped into popular culture and also addressed issues of particular urgency such as LYNCHING.

The book was praised widely and successfully identified Davis as an emerging talent of the period. It included poems such as "Lynched (Symphonic Interlude for Twenty-one Selected Instruments," "Cabaret," "Chicago's Congo," "Ebony Under Granite," and "What Do You Want America?" In addition to positive reviews in *THE NATION, BLACK MAN'S VERSE* was heralded by major Harlem Renaissance figures such as ALAIN LOCKE. Davis's work was included in the 1941 *Negro Caravan* anthology edited by STERLING BROWN, ULYSSES LEE, and ARTHUR DAVIS.

Critics long have considered Davis in relation to influential writers such as LANGSTON HUGHES and RICHARD WRIGHT, whom he met and came to know well while living in Chicago. In 1941, Sterling Brown and his co-editors suggested to readers of *Negro Caravan* that Davis was one of the "[r]ecent poets of promise" and that *Black Man's Verse* was a book of "powerful social criticism" (Brown, 282). More recently, scholar James Smethurst has suggested that Davis, Hughes, and Wright "significantly urbanized and proletarianized the Communist-influenced concept of the vernacular" (Smethurst, 29). The volume reflects Davis's social consciousness and desire to merge political reality with literary forms. *Black Man's Verse* earned Davis a prestigious JULIUS ROSENWALD FELLOWSHIP in 1937.

Bibliography

Brown, Sterling. *The Negro Caravan: Writings by American Negroes.* New York: Dryden Press, 1941.

Smethurst, James. *The New Red Negro: The Literary Left and African American Poetry, 1930–1946.* New York: Oxford University Press, 1999.

Black No More: Being an Account of the Strange and Wonderful Workings of Science in the Land George Schuyler (1931)

A scathing satire by GEORGE SCHUYLER about race, white privilege, and many African-American political organizations and leading figures that appeared at the midway point of the Harlem Renaissance. Schuyler spared no one in this aggressive and scandalous story about a doctor who has invented "Black No More," a treatment that transforms skin color, and the hopeful dark-skinned people who flock to use this remedy to succeed in the color-conscious, segregated worlds in which they live. The novel is dedicated to "all Caucasians in the great republic who can trace their ancestry back ten generations and confidently assert that there are no Black leaves, twigs, limbs or branches on their family trees."

The main characters include Dr. Junius Crookman, the "Black No More" inventor; Max Disher, the young black man who uses the treatment to marry a white southern girl and take advantage of white anxieties about race; and Bunny Brown, Disher's friend and the person who marries the last "real" black girl in America. Other characters, such as Shakespeare A. Beard, Santop Licorice, and Sissereta Blandish are caricatures that are clearly based on leading political figures such as W. E. B. DuBois, MARCUS GARVEY, and Madame C. J. Walker, respectively.

The novel opens as Max Disher watches an interracial crowd enter a nightclub to celebrate New Year's Eve. Disher, the ultimate observer, is quickly subjected to the narrator's scrutiny as he laments the fact that he has no date with whom to celebrate the holiday. Described as a "tall, dapper" man with "smooth coffee-brown" skin, Disher also has "negroid features [with] a slightly satanic cast" to them, and there is an "insolent nonchalance about his carriage." Bunny Brown, a fellow World War I veteran who now works as a bank teller, joins him. Both men, who are known among their Harlem peers as "gay blades," share three preferences that the narrator insists are "essential to the happiness of a colored gentleman: yellow money, yellow women and yellow taxis." While Disher vows to date dark-skinned women now that he has suffered so at Minnie's hands, Bunny calls his attention to a "tall, titian-haired girl who had seem-

ingly stepped from heaven or the front cover of a magazine." Unfortunately, he suffers the double insult of being rejected by Minnie, his "high 'yallah' flapper" girlfriend, and by Helen Givens, the stunning white woman from ATLANTA he sees in the cabaret. Frustrated by the desire whom people like Helen have for frequenting African-American venues, but casting aspersions on the people of color with whom they come into contact there, Disher agrees to try the innovative Black No More treatment that Bunny has learned about in the newspaper.

Disher, motivated by images of a new life and social opportunities, makes sure that he is the first man in Harlem to be treated in the newly opened clinic. He arrives well ahead of the 4,000 people who eventually converge on the Dr. Crookman's offices. The process, which involves a "formidable apparatus" that requires he be lashed to a chair that "resembled a cross between a dentist's chair and an electric chair," frightens him, but once he is manhandled into the unit by "two husky attendants," he realizes that there is "no retreat. It was either the beginning or the end." Transformed into a white-skinned person, he is a new man, one for whom whiteness now meant "no more expenditures for skin whiteners; no more discrimination; no more obstacles in his path. He was free! The world was his oyster and he had the open sesame of a pork-colored skin!" Disher changes his name to Fisher and heads south in search of Helen.

While the narrative follows the evolution of Disher, it also attends to the impact that the whitening process has upon Dr. Crookman, the son of an Episcopal clergyman, and his wife, who "though poor, were proud and boasted that they belonged to the Negro aristocracy." Crookman is a scholarly and political man, one who "prided himself above all on being a great lover of his race." His invention is part of his plan to enact modern emancipation, and he is motivated by his philosophy that "if there were no Negroes, there could be no Negro problem. Without a Negro problem, Americans could concentrate their attention on something constructive." Crookman, who is married to a "white girl with remote Negro ancestry, of the type that Negroes were wont to describe as being 'able to pass for white,'" believes that his Black No More process is not solely about racial aesthetics. He is convinced, rather, that it has everything to do with the overhaul of American society. He also is convinced that with his process "it would be possible to do what agitation, education and legislation had failed to do." He does not anticipate the overwhelming impact that the process will have on African-American culture, businesses, organizations, or families, however. Almost overnight, the churches lose their congregations; donations to anti-lynching campaigns cease; and political groups who have benefited financially from donations meant to finance protests of mob law, disenfranchisement, and segregation now find themselves bankrupt and without any justified campaigns.

Disher survives a number of wild escapades including adventures that involve his infiltration of and membership in the Knights of Nordica, a KU KLUX KLAN–like organization. He eventually merges his northern experience with his southern plan when he collaborates with the Reverend Givens, the Imperial Grand Wizard of the white supremacist group. Givens, who is a "short, wizened, almost-bald, bull-voiced, ignorant ex-evangelist," agrees on a scheme that will use the Black No More process to detect and guard against the infiltration of the group and larger Southern society by nonwhite "whites." It is serendipitous, of course, that Givens's daughter, who attends the Knights of Nordica meetings, is the same woman whom Disher saw first in Harlem and has gone south to find.

Disher marries Helen, but he is leery of their ability to have children. She bears their first child, despite his efforts to organize trips and exercise routines for her that he hopes will bring on a miscarriage and prevent the threat of any startling racial revelations. The child is born and, as Disher suspected, his newborn son does not have pure, white skin but is in fact a "chubby, ball of brownness." Max confesses to Helen, the woman he loves so intensely despite her "prejudices and queer notions," that he has some Negro ancestry. Although she reacts favorably, happy that she has "money and a beautiful, brown baby," Disher's domestic situation and that of the nation as a whole begin to unravel wildly. Since it is now impossible to determine who is or is not an authentic white person, social chaos and political upheaval prevail. Once it is revealed that "authentic" whites are in fact duskier than the individuals who have used the Black No More process, individuals begin to seek ways to stain their skins, rather than whiten them, in order to prove their true identities. "It became the fashion for [the upper class] to spend hours at the seashore basking naked in the sunshine and then . . . lord it over their paler, and thus less fortunate, associates," comments the narrator. Ultimately, Disher, also known as Fisher, escapes with his family to Mexico. He leaves behind a country that is in the throes of reversing its racial makeup and on the verge of reinstating the same hierarchies and prejudices that Dr. Crookman aspired to dissolve.

Black No More and Schuyler's other writings about racial anxieties, such as "NEGRO-ART HOKUM," have suggested to some critics that the author was promoting a theory of assimilation. Yet, as scholar Harry McKinley insists persuasively, Schuyler was much more intent on critiquing the "destructiveness and foolishness of America's obsession with skin color," and the novel "underscored Schuyler's conviction that simply 'getting white' as do virtually all the Negroes in the novel, would not solve the race's problems" (McKinley, 187).

Bibliography

McKinley, Harry. *When Black Is Right: The Life and Writings of George S. Schuyler.* 1988; reprint, Ann Arbor, Mich.: University Microfilms International, 1990.

Peplow, Michael. *George S. Schuyler.* Boston: Twayne Publishers, 1980.

Black Opals

A PHILADELPHIA-based literary magazine established in the spring of 1927 and produced by a close-knit group of the city's African-American intellectual and professional elite. Despite its apparent literary and cultural value, there were only three issues produced, and the magazine lasted for just one year. Described by W. E. B. DuBois as a "little brochure," the magazine stressed its desire to publish aspiring young, school-age African Americans. It also fostered the talents of adult writers, many of whom were active participants in the PIRANEAN CLUB and the Beaux Arts Club, two well-organized African-American literary societies in the city. Among them were BESSIE BIRD, MAE COWDERY, NELLIE RATHBORNE BRIGHT, and ARTHUR HUFF FAUSET, who was the step-brother of CRISIS editor JESSIE FAUSET and the editor of the first issue. The magazine also published works by MARITA BONNER, LANGSTON HUGHES, Jessie Fauset, and other Renaissance writers.

Bibliography

Johnson, Abby Arthur, and Ronald Maberry Johnson. *Propaganda & Aesthetics: The Literary Politics of African American Magazines in the Twentieth Century.* Amherst: University of Massachusetts, 1979.

Jubilee, Vincent. *Philadelphia's Afro-American Literary Circle and the Harlem Renaissance.* Ann Arbor, Mich.: University Microfilms, 1980.

Black Sadie T. Bowyer Campbell (1928)

A novel by T. BOWYER CAMPBELL about a woman known as Black Sadie and her life as a dancer. Campbell, a missionary, began writing the book when his ambitious plans for religious outreach began to fail. Houghton Mifflin accepted the manuscript for publication on the basis of two paragraphs.

Bowyer described the novel as "a story of Colored people in three social and economic brackets: in Virginia some two decades after the emancipation, in the north as house servants with higher wages, and lastly entering into professional and creative work."

NELLA LARSEN penned a rather frank and ironic review of the work for OPPORTUNITY. In her article, Larsen noted that the novel was "an awkwardly written and disorderly book," filled with "inaccuracies that would therefore make much of the book very amusing—especially to the Negro reader." As scholar Anna Brickhouse notes, Larsen dismissed Campbell's work, referring to it impatiently as "twaddle concerning the inherent qualities of the Negro" (Brickhouse, 538).

Bibliography

Brickhouse, Anna. "Nella Larsen and the Intertextual Geography of *Quicksand*." *African American Review,* 35, no. 4 (winter, 2001): 533–560.

Campbell, T. Boyer. "Thomas Bowyer Campbell." Catholic Authors.com. URL: http://www.catholicauthors.com/campbell.html. Accessed January 2005.

Larsen, Nella. "Black Sadie." *Opportunity* (January 1929): 24.

Black Thunder Arna Bontemps (1936)

One of the earliest 20th-century novels about an American slave revolt, *Black Thunder* represented ARNA BONTEMPS's attempt to revisit the story of the thwarted 1800 Gabriel Prosser rebellion in Virginia. He chose to re-create the story of the rebellion after encountering the substantial collection of slave narratives in the library of FISK UNIVERSITY.

Bontemps's account revolved around the characters of Gabriel Prosser, his brothers, Solomon and Martin, his love interest, Juba, his ally and a free man, Mingo, his white owner, Thomas Prosser, and the two slaves who betrayed him, Ben and Pharaoh. The revolt, which is thwarted, in part by a storm, is motivated by Prosser's desire to avenge the beating death of an elderly slave man on his plantation. Like Nat Turner, the leader of the 1831 slave revolt in Southampton, Virginia, Prosser outlines his rationale and list of potential victims. He and his supporters agree to spare any whites who are Quakers, Methodists, or Frenchmen. Ultimately, though, their plan is not realized. In the chaos that follows, Gabriel escapes, but he eventually surrenders in order to save one of his loyal supporters.

The novel is divided into five books, entitled "Jacobins," "Hand Me Down My Silver Trumpet," "Mad Dogs," "A Breathing of the Common Wind," and "Pale Evening . . . A Tall Slim Tree." Bontemps used historical documents as he recreated the life of Prosser and the tumultuous events that Prosser engineered. Set in Richmond, Virginia, the novel focuses on Gabriel, a man whom reviewers have described as "a mischievous slave who is subjected to cruel and excessive punishment" or as a man with "a thirst for freedom, for himself and his kind" and "a man of destiny" (Tompkins, BR7). Bontemps's character emerges early in the novel as part of the plantation owned by the white man Thomas Prosser. Gabriel is "almost a giant for size" with "features . . . as straight as a Roman's, but he was not a mulatto. He was just under twenty-four and the expression of hurt pride that he wore was in keeping with his years and station. He was too old for joy, as a slave's life went . . . too young for despair as black men despaired in 1800" (16). Gabriel, who recalls his older brothers's herculean efforts to escape, is motivated to organize a revolt in the wake of a slave owner's brutal murder of an enslaved man. His love interest, Juba, is a "tempestuous brown wench" (29) who listens often to Gabriel's ruminations about freedom. When he finally begins to plan, Gabriel's leadership is marked by his economy of language and precise instructions. In meeting with his coconspirators, there are "[n]o greetings, no useless words passed . . . No preliminary words, no Biblical extenuations preceded the essential plans" (59). Ben, an enslaved coachman who curries favor with his master and relishes the status that he achieves once he has revealed what he knows about the planned revolt, betrays the group. He witnesses the hangings of the perpetrators but is unable to remain completely immune from the awful proceedings. "A mournful dignity bow[s]" his head and "though his shoulders stood back fairly strong . . . his lips parted now and again and his tongue slipped between them, but they were never moistened. They remained as white as if they had been painted" (169).

Black Thunder is perhaps the earliest African-American historical novel to focus on a slave conspiracy and rebellion. The most notable 19th-century work about slave rebellions and resistors that preceded his was *Dred, or Tales of the Dismal Swamp* (1856) by Harriet Beecher Stowe. *Black Thunder* certainly predates *The Confessions of Nat Turner,* the controversial 1967 novel by white writer William Styron that prompted a general outcry among African Americans for what were deemed to be unsavory and problematic depictions of Nat Turner. Bontemps's novel also builds an important bridge between the 19th-century slave narratives and memoirs such as *Incidents in the Life of a Slave Girl* (1861) by Harriet Jacobs that allude to rebellions and African-American resistance and 20th-century considerations of enslavement. Kirkland Jones, Bontemps's biographer, reiterates this point, noting that "Bontemps succeeded in showing, contrary to the propaganda of many non-black writers of the post-Reconstruction and pre-Harlem Renaissance periods, that African Americans as a whole did not accept injustice lying down" (Jones, 81). Bontemps also made a deliberate effort to contextualize the African-American struggle and to relate it quite specifically to the French Revolution and history of resistance. The character Monsieur Creuzot, who owns a print shop in town, provides white

European perspectives on enslavement and the prevailing American rationalizations of the pernicious system. In his conversations, Creuzot contemplates the inconsistencies of American ideology and practice, noting that although he has read works such as Jefferson's *Notes on Virginia* and has kept abreast of arguments advanced by leading public figures associated with the College of William and Mary, "it all seems hopeless in this country" (21). The novel ends with the scene in which Gabriel is murdered. That the proceedings are reported through the eyes of the man who betrayed him underscores the limits of racial solidarity and suggests that slavery will persist as an unrelenting reality.

Bontemps wrote the novel while living in Watts, California, where he and his family had relocated to live with his parents. He did not have the luxury of a study in which to write but was determined to proceed with the novel. He had to write "the book in longhand on the top of a folded-down sewing machine in the extra bedroom" of his parents' home because there was no convenient place where he might set up his typewriter. These circumstances, however trying, were much less oppressive than the hostile Alabama community in which Bontemps had been teaching recently. Knowing that he could not "tell them about Gabriel's adventure," Bontemps made the decision to leave the white Seventh-Day Adventist school community that scrutinized his reading materials, questioned his friendships with writers who visited or wrote to him, and finally demanded that he prove his blind patriotism and civic docility by burning his books publicly. In a 1972 autobiographical essay, Bontemps recalled that during the year in which he wrote the novel, he was "brooding over a subject matter so depressing that [he] could find no relief until it resolved itself as *Black Thunder*" (Bontemps, 260). Reviewer Lucy Tompkins encouraged readers who might be "looking for a sort of prose spiritual on the Negroes themselves" to seek out the novel, which she believed offered a tribute that "one could not find . . . more movingly sung" (Tompkins, BR7). Bontemps created an inspiring character, one whose honor, fidelity to his race, and earnest hope for a viable life as a free man would inform subsequent accounts of these tumultuous antebellum times.

Bibliography

Bontemps, Arna. "The Awakening: A Memoir" [1972]. In *Remembering The Harlem Renaissance*. Cary Wintz, ed. New York: Garland Publishing, Inc., 1996. 235–260.

Davis, Mary Kemp. "From Death unto Life: The Rhetorical Function of Funeral Rites in Arna Bontemps' Black Thunder," *Journal of Ritual Studies* 1, no. 1 (winter 1987): 85–101.

Egerton, Douglas. *Gabriel's Rebellion: The Virginia Slave Conspiracies of 1800 and 1802.* Chapel Hill: University of North Carolina Press, 1993.

Levecq, Christine. "Philosophies of History in Arna Bontemps' Black Thunder (1936)," *Obsidian III: Literature in the African Diaspora* 1, no. 2 (fall-winter 2000): 111–130.

Tompkins, Lucy. "*In Dubious Battle* and Other Recent Works of Fiction," *New York Times* 2 (February 1936): BR7.

Weil, Dorothy. "Folklore Motifs in the Arna Bontemps' Black Thunder," *Southern Folklore Quarterly* 35 (1971): 1–14.

Black Velvet Willard Robertson (1927)

A play by Willard Robertson that ran at the Liberty Theatre in the fall of 1927. At the center of this drama was an obstreperous white Confederate Civil War officer who tried actively to thwart African-American advancement, in and beyond his own life. Over the course of three acts, he sanctions the murder of a pro-black labor leader in the North, endorses the LYNCHING of a young black man, and tries to prevent his grandson from marrying a young woman of color.

"Blades of Steel" Rudolph Fisher (1927)

Published in the ATLANTIC MONTHLY, this short story by pioneering physician RUDOLPH FISHER focused on an intense and potentially deadly rivalry between two men and the lifesaving interventions of an unlikely heroine.

The story opens in a thriving HARLEM barbershop, where Eight-Ball Eddy Boyd readies himself for a haircut. Just as he prepares to sit down in the barber's chair, however, he is pulled back by Dirty Cozzens, a man with whom he has had a long-standing feud. The narrator makes an effort to describe the two men, both of whom bear nicknames that were inspired by their skin color. Dirty Cozzens, the villain of the piece, is "a peculiar genetic jest," a man from whom "[h]eredity had managed to remove his rightful share of pigment." His gray hair and eyes and light skin prompt others to regard him as "Dirty Yaller," and it is not long before he is simply known as "Dirty." His rival, Eight-Ball, has a name inspired by the eight-ball used in the game of pool. "His skin," notes the narrator, "was as dark as it is possible for skin to be, smooth and clean as an infant's." Eight-Ball is also a much more appealing figure than Dirty, for he is "beautifully small, neither heavy nor slight, of proud erect bearing, perfect poise, and a silhouette-like clean-cutness."

There are two major altercations between the two men, and it is an alert hairdresser named Effie, who manages to derail Dirty's threats and to empower Eight-Ball on each occasion. At the Barber's Ball, Effie and Eight-Ball are once again confronted by Dirty and completely dismayed by the covert attacks that he continues to make on them with a razor. When Effie refuses to dance with him, Dirty slices the back of Eight-Ball's jacket. He also slashes two of the tires of the car that belongs to Eight-Ball's boss. In the final confrontation between the two men, it is Effie who slips a safety-razor into the hand of her sweetheart so that he can defend himself against Dirty. The slashes on Dirty's face are the first that he has ever received at the hands of an opponent, and he is thoroughly cowed by the injuries. The story ends as Eight-Ball marvels at the subtle but effective intervention of Effie, an attentive woman whose femininity is in no way undermined by her street smarts and courage.

The story is one of several evocative portraits of Harlem life that established Fisher as one of the period's most talented writers. "Blades of Steel" is especially powerful for its realistic images, innovative plot twists, and absorbing accounts of everyday life.

Bibliography

McCluskey, John Jr. *The City of Refuge: The Collected Stories of Rudolph Fisher.* Columbia: University of Missouri Press, 1987.

"Blind Alley" Alvira Hazzard (1929)

A short story about intraracial jealousy by ALVIRA HAZZARD, published in April 1929 issue of the BOSTON publication SATURDAY EVENING QUILL.

Neighbors and a community that take no pleasure in seeing the transformative power of love or in seeing the uplift of African-American people undo Phil Howard and the young Miss Carlen. Miss Carlen is a motivated young woman who is determined to fulfill her dream of becoming a nurse. She does not want to settle for an approximation of that role but craves to one day be "a nurse in a spotless white dress and cap." The visions that she has of herself are "overwhelming," and she revels in them as she "[r]ock[s] back and forth with her little hands clasped tightly in her lap to keep them from fluttering."

Phil Howard cannot believe his luck when he finds out that Miss Carlen likes him. He regards her as a lady whose high station demands that he prove himself worthy. His growing affection for her prompts him to think grandly and to develop "well-laid plans for her happiness." These daydreams "gave him strength." Unfortunately, Miss Carlen's neighbor, Carrie Morris, cannot bring herself to contribute to the obvious romance. She fails to pass along Miss Carlen's messages to Phil, and thus she prevents them from meeting for a long-awaited outing. In addition, Carrie torments Phil, telling him that she has spoken to Miss Carlen and revealed the truth about him. Devastated that he cannot reach her and that she may have turned against him, Phil stumbles into a local pool hall to regain his composure. There, he is taunted by "Half Pint," a man who is "dwarfed, black as a hole, [and] shrewd as a diplomat." The crowd is totally surprised when Phil responds to Half-Pint's insults and hits him to the floor "with the coolness and disdain of a victorious gladiator." Phil's composure signals that his love affair with Miss Carlen has had a wonderful effect, and it is the only fleeting sign that the two may find each other again.

Blood on the Forge William Attaway (1941)
A novel by WILLIAM ATTAWAY, author of the Harlem Renaissance–era novel Let Me Breathe Thunder (1939). This work, like the 1940s works by RICHARD WRIGHT, represented the intensified turn toward social realism and sociological dramas during the post–Harlem Renaissance period.

"Blue Aloes" Ottie Beatrice Graham (1924)
A CRISIS short story by OTTIE BEATRICE GRAHAM that appeared in the July 1924 issue alongside works by ARNA BONTEMPS, JESSIE FAUSET, and LANGSTON HUGHES.

The story, set in an unidentified Southern town, features Joseph, a 20-year-old man, recently returned from the North, whose recklessness and disrespect endangers Melrose, the love of his life, and alienates her from her maternal kin. "Who can account for an impulse?" asks the narrator as the story opens and Joseph appears and readies himself for a quick dip in the Little River. After immersing himself in the waters that flow by Aloe House, he calls out to Melrose, a beautiful young woman who lives with Granna, her forbidding grandmother who is known for her cultivation of aloes. Granna, not Melrose, appears by the banks of the river and chides Joseph for courting her charge. The conflict escalates dramatically. Joseph yells, taunts the grandmother, calls her "old Ashface," and threatens to "take [Melrose] from the South and superstition!" Perhaps his worst action is to tip over a set of tubs filled with the drippings from a precious set of blue aloes that Granna obtained from the islands. As the interchange between the two grows more heated, the grandmother characterizes Joseph as an "[u]ngrateful yaller devil," rips off a string of aloes that she wears around her neck, and sprays him with the liquid of blue aloes. She also alludes to the threat of another woman and insists that neither one of them come back to her when the interloper intrudes on their romance.

In the moments following Granna's attack on Joseph, Melrose comes to the aid of her hot-headed suitor who, "[f]or a moment . . . thought he was blinded." She takes him to the river, where they "bathed the bruised eyes. Then they started off to the future, empty handed, looking not behind them." The two marry and establish a home for themselves in the house that Joe has inherited from his father. They plan to stay there until Melrose is healed of a nagging cough and then head North. The two often paddle down the Little River, but when Melrose's condition weakens her, Joseph begins to paddle alone during the evenings. On one of his outings, he finds himself seduced by the sounds of piano music and eventually by the sight of a woman in the windows of the mansion that sits on a nearby hill within view of the river. The woman so resembles Melrose that Joseph thinks of her as Melrose's "second self." On one of his encounters, the unnamed woman drops an ornate paddle into his boat. Melrose identifies it as a precious object, one made of aloe wood with lapis lazuli stones in its handle. Melrose eventually suspects that the mysterious woman has entranced her husband. She follows him more than once and finally confronts the woman, who has hair that is "[b]lack—deep, black like crows . . . gently pushed, red lips . . . [and] eyes like dark, melted pansies." The encounter is unsettling because it appears that the women are in fact mother and daughter. When they meet, "[t]hey stood like stone, these women. Stone images reflected in a mirror. Melrose had not seen her close before. She had not seen Melrose ever. Bout now a look of knowing flitted across her face, than a look of awful fear, and she backed to the steps and turned and ran. Leaped like a frightened deer. Midway she wheeled again. Melrose had not moved." The woman flees the mansion and reappears only when the townspeople lay her dead body on a porch swing after she falls into the path of an oncoming horse and carriage after attempting to kill a white man. In the wake of the woman's demise, the town begins to generate rumors about the strained family connections among Melrose, Joseph, and the mysterious woman. The couple attempts to find Granna, in part to make restitution and also perhaps to understand the lingering connection that they feel to the woman from the mansion. Unfortunately, when they return to Aloe House, "Granna was not there. Nothing was there." The story ends here, without any comforting resolution for the confused lovers or any clarification about how Melrose's long-estranged mother returned to the area.

Graham blended mysticism, folk superstition, and elements of seduction in her lengthy tale. "Blue Aloes" is part of the larger oeuvre of American folktales that writers such as CHARLES CHESNUTT elevated during the early 20th century and the mystical tales of tragic romance penned by Graham's peers such as LANGSTON HUGHES. She hints at the disregarded and underestimated powers of matriarchs, especially those of African descent whose knowledge of plants' and medicines' powers hint at their greater powers of folk magic and intervention. In "Blue Aloes," Graham suggests that traditional African kinship ties can be irrevocably undermined and lost when brash youth assert themselves and fail to recognize the ancestral power and influence of the elders.

Blue Blood Georgia Douglas Johnson (1926)

A riveting, fast-paced, and award-winning one-act play that GEORGIA DOUGLAS JOHNSON completed just one year after she became a widow and began her writing life in earnest. The play was published first in 1927 by the New York company Appleton-Century. Eleven years later, the company included it in the 1938 edition of *Fifty More Contemporary One-Act Plays*, edited by Frank Shay. Johnson used the melodramatic tragic romance form to craft a memorable exposé of sexual bondage, incest, and the dangers of color-consciousness within the black community.

The play opens as Mrs. Bush and Mrs. Temple, two single mothers, prepare for the marriage between their daughter and son, respectively. As they begin to bicker about which child is benefiting more from the union of two light-skinned people, the mothers discover that Captain Winfield McCallister of Atlanta, Georgia, has victimized them both. They are devastated to realize that a marriage between their children will amount to incest and that it cannot be allowed. The women concentrate on finding a quick and believable way to prevent the ceremony scheduled for that evening. May is whisked away by Randolph Strong, an aptly named, long-suffering, and dark-skinned physician whom May had spurned because of his color. Johnson provides no heavy-handed critique of intraracial color prejudice, nor does she rage against the tragic history of sexual concubinage suffered by black women of the South. Nonetheless, she delivers a jarring play that succeeds precisely because of its shocking coincidences.

Bibliography

Hull, Gloria. *Love, Sex, and Poetry: Three Women Writers of the Harlem Renaissance.* Bloomington: Indiana University Press, 1987.

Sullivan, Megan. "Folk Plays, Home Girls, and Back Talk: Georgia Douglas Johnson and Women of the Harlem Renaissance," *College Language Association Journal,* 38, no. 4 (June 1995): 404–419.

Blues: An Anthology (1926)

An assortment of music selected by W. C. HANDY for this folio-size publication published by the well-known Harlem Renaissance press of ALBERT and CHARLES BONI. In this often republished history of the blues, Handy included some works that he himself had arranged. The illustrations in the volume were done by Miguel Covarrubias, the talented Mexican caricaturist who designed the cover-sketch for LANGSTON HUGHES's 1925 THE WEARY BLUES and who composed many other memorable Harlem Renaissance images.

Boas, Franz (1858–1942)

The accomplished German-born anthropologist with whom ZORA NEALE HURSTON studied during her college years at BARNARD COLLEGE in the 1920s. This cofounder of the American Anthropological Association and former teacher who trained well-known specialists such as Melville Herskovits and Margaret Mead, recognized Hurston's potential for scholarship and after seeing one of her term papers, hired her and began to train her to conduct anthropological research. It was her studies with Boas that shaped Hurston's pioneering fieldwork in the American South and in the West Indies, research that gave THEIR EYES WERE WATCHING GOD and other impressive works their distinctive flair.

Bibliography

Hyatt, Marshall. *Franz Boas, Social Activist: The Dynamics of Ethnicity.* New York: Greenwood Press, 1990.

Stocking, George. *A Franz Boas Reader: The Shaping of American Anthropology, 1883–1911.* Chicago: University of Chicago Press, 1982.

Williams, Vernon. *Rethinking Race: Franz Boas and his Contemporaries.* Lexington: University Press of Kentucky, 1996.

"Bodies in the Moonlight" Langston Hughes (1927)

A short story by LANGSTON HUGHES in which the circumstances and certain actions of the romantic protagonist seem quite autobiographical. Like Hughes did when he sailed for AFRICA in 1923 aboard the *West Hesseltine,* the main character, an unnamed boy, admits that he has "thrown all . . . school books overboard" at the beginning of his first sea voyage. While on the trip that recalls Hughes's own six-month journey to West Africa, the young sailor vies for the affections of a Nunuma, a provocative West African girl. His competition, however, is Porto Rico, an extremely burly and aggressive sailor. Ultimately, provoked by Nunuma's charms and seductive invitations, the two men fight each other. The young sailor is wounded, and the story ends as he regains consciousness aboard ship. The story appeared in the April 1927 issue of the MESSENGER.

Bibliography

Gates, Henry Louis Jr., and Kwame Anthony Appiah, eds. *Langston Hughes: Critical Perspectives Past and Present.* New York: Amistad, 1993.

Miller, R. Baxter. *The Art and Imagination of Langston Hughes.* Lexington: University Press of Kentucky, 1989.

"Boll Weevil Starts North, The: A Story" Benjamin Young (1926)

A story told from the perspective of a relatively powerless northern spectator as he travels by train through the Black Belt South on his way to Ohio. In this short story by BENJAMIN YOUNG that appeared in the February 1926 issue of OPPORTUNITY, the nameless narrator watches as Elder Scott, an elderly farmer and church man, suffers the loss of his life savings and believes that he has been victimized by a young man from his own community. In this depressing story about an inadvertently misplaced item and derailed life plans, Young also provides rich details about the black migration to the North and proves that harmful racial stereo-types, so quickly applied by both whites and blacks in certain situations, are unreliable and faulty.

Boni, Albert (1892–1981) and Charles (unknown)

The two men who founded the Boni publishing firm that later incorporated HORACE LIVERIGHT and became the publishing house of BONI & LIV-ERIGHT. They participated in events such as the NAACP literary contest celebrations, gatherings that celebrated black writers of the period and facilitated productive relationships among them, publishers, and patrons. It was their firm that in 1925 published ALAIN LOCKE's influential anthology THE NEW NEGRO.

Bibliography

Johnson, Abby Arthur, and Ronald Maberry Johnson. *Propaganda & Aesthetics: The Literary Politics of African American Magazines in the Twentieth Century.* Amherst: University of Massachusetts, 1979.

Boni & Liveright Publishers

The press headed by ALBERT and CHARLES BONI and HORACE LIVERIGHT. Characterized as a "young daring, unconventional" press, it established a solid reputation for itself by publishing THEODORE DREISER, Ezra Pound, William Faulkner, and other major white writers.

Boni and Liveright also achieved prominence as one of the presses that made significant contributions to the Harlem Renaissance. JEAN TOOMER's CANE (1923) was one of the first African-American works that the press published. One year later, Horace Liveright oversaw the publication of THERE IS CONFUSION, the first novel of JESSIE FAUSET. The press took its commitment to authors seriously and in Fauset's case, generated extensive publicity for the novel that launched her career. They created many enthusiastic advertisements and when sales proved to be good, invested quickly in a second edition of the book. Boni and Liveright set a new standard in the publishing industry in their treatment of African-American writers, a point noted by Floyd Calvin in the *Pittsburgh Courier.* Calvin was convinced that the publicity "mark[s] the beginning of a new era in the treatment of colored authors" (Sylvander, 71). Boni and Liveright also published *TROPIC DEATH* (1926) by ERIC WALROND.

Bibliography

Sylvander, Cheryl. *Jessie Redmon Fauset, Black American Writer.* Troy, N.Y.: Whitson, 1981.

Bonner, Marita Odette (1899–1971)

A prolific writer of fiction, short stories, plays, and essays and known best for her writings of stark and tragic works of social realism.

She was one of four children born to Joseph Andrew Bonner, a machinist, and his wife, Mary Anne Noel Bonner. Sadly, Marita, who was born in Brookline, Massachusetts, was the only Bonner child to survive childhood. After graduating from Brookline High School, where she began to cultivate her interests in music and German, Bonner attended RADCLIFFE COLLEGE. There, she majored in English and comparative literature. Although racially discriminatory college residential policies denied her accommodations in the campus dormitories, she cultivated real school spirit and was one of the college's most enthusiastic students. It was she who composed her class song and also founded the college's chapter of DELTA SIGMA THETA. Bonner's talent earned her a coveted place in the highly selective writing seminar of Professor Charles Copeland. As a result of her continued immersion in creative writing, Bonner began to publish while in college. She also began a lengthy and impressive career as a teacher. While still an undergraduate, she began teaching at Cambridge High School. In 1922, following her graduation, she began teaching in Virginia at the Bluefield Colored Institute. She then relocated to WASHINGTON, D.C., where she joined the faculty at Armstrong High School and taught English from 1925 through 1930.

In the capital, Bonner became part of an active literary circle. She joined the well-known literary salon that GEORGIA DOUGLAS JOHNSON hosted at her home. Attendees at the popular weekly gatherings included LANGSTON HUGHES, RUDOLPH FISHER, RICHARD BRUCE NUGENT, and ANGELINA GRIMKÉ. It was in this supportive environment that Bonner completed some of her best work, including the prize-winning essay "ON BEING YOUNG—A WOMAN—AND COLORED" (1925), the plays THE POT MAKER (1927), THE PURPLE FLOWER (1928), and EXIT, AN ILLUSION (1929) and "THE YOUNG BLOOD HUNGERS" (1928), a perceptive essay on race and social violence. Bonner's works appeared in BLACK OPALS, the short-lived but notable African-American Philadelphia literary magazine, and in two of the leading race journals of the period, the NAACP's CRISIS and the Urban League's OPPORTUNITY. In the years before her 1930 marriage, Bonner, who published regularly, also employed the pseudonym of JOSEPH MAREE ANDREW on several occasions.

Bonner received recognition for her work through the annual *Crisis* and *Opportunity* literary prize contests. In the first *Opportunity* contest, held in 1924, Bonner earned an honorable mention for her story "The Hands" (1925). In 1932, judges FANNIE HURST, STERLING BROWN, and Richard Walsh awarded her innovative short story montage, "A Possible Triad on Black Notes" (1933), an honorable mention in that year's literary contest. One year later, Bonner's "Tin Can" won her first place over works by GEORGE SCHUYLER and Henry B. Jones. Bonner fared equally well in the *Crisis* competitions. Judges Edward Bok, JOEL SPINGARN, and BENJAMIN BRAWLEY awarded her first place in the essay division for "On Being Young—a Woman—and Colored." In 1927 she won the prestigious first prize in the literary art and expression division for a multigenre collection of works that included two plays, a short story, and an essay. Other writers honored that year were BRENDA RAY MORYCK, EULALIE SPENCE, RANDOLPH EDMONDS, and JOHN MATHEUS.

In 1930 Bonner married William Almy Occomy, a Rhode Island native and graduate of BROWN UNIVERSITY. She soon moved with her husband to Chicago, where she would live for just over 40 years, and started a family that eventually included three children: Warwick, William, and Marita Joyce. Bonner returned once again to the classroom and began teaching English at the Philips High School in 1950. She stepped down from that post in 1963. It was her daughter and namesake Marita who would later gather together Bonner's unpublished stories and republish them in the late 1980s. Although far removed from the supportive East Coast circles in which she used to

move, Bonner continued to write. She used CHICAGO as the new backdrop for her stories of African-American life and located several tales in the fictional, multiethnic community of Frye Street. Critic Joyce Flynn characterizes this fictional Depression-era community that Bonner created, and in which she fully invested in her writings, as "a daring symbol of the diversity, novelty, and opportunity available in cities like Chicago and Detroit" (Flynn, xi).

As a playwright, Bonner engaged her audiences directly, often using the second person to draw in her readers and make them witnesses to the events about to unfold. The stage directions for *The Pot Maker*, for instance, begin with a gentle imperative: "See first the room. A low ceiling; smoked walls; far more length than breadth." She then suggests that her readers have an intense familiarity with the place and characters of the piece: "You know there is a garden," she writes, "because if you listen carefully you can hear a tapping of bushes against the window and a gentle rustling of leaves." Bonner sustains the hypnotic quality of her prose and stage directions in her other two plays. In *The Purple Flower*, she evaluates her readers' reactions to the "Sundry White Devils" in the Dante-esque world of the play. "You are amazed at their adroitness," she declares. "Their steps are intricate. You almost lose your head following them." In *Exit*, Bonner's assertions about her readers are extremely forceful; by making her audience part of the set design, they become a vital part of the script and heavily invested in the outcome of the play.

Bonner's penchant for realist fiction and her substantial canon of works based in Chicago's ethnic and minority neighborhoods are believed to have reinforced RICHARD WRIGHT'S literary perspectives. Scholars believe that works such as "Tin Can" anticipate themes that Wright began to explore in his literary career that blossomed in the years after the Renaissance. Bonner created deft and absorbing portraits of African-American women and the demanding and often unsatisfying worlds in which they lived. One of the talented black feminist writers of the Harlem Renaissance, Bonner's works complemented the social visions that writers like NELLA LARSEN, JESSIE FAUSET, and Georgia Douglas Johnson developed in their works. Bonner paid particular attention to the politics of race and caste, the effects of poverty upon the African-American family, and the nature of marriage and domestic life.

This prolific and talented writer appears to have stopped writing shortly after the Harlem Renaissance ended. Her last published story appeared in 1942, the same year in which she joined the Christian Science church. Bonner died tragically when her Chicago apartment was razed by fire.

Bibliography

The Marita Bonner Papers are held in the Schlesinger Library, Radcliffe College, Cambridge, Massachusetts.

Allen, Carol. *Black Women Intellectuals: Strategies of Nation, Family, and Neighborhood in the Works of Pauline Hopkins, Jessie Fauset, and Marita Bonner.* New York: Garland Publishers, 1998.

Flynn, Joyce, and Joyce Occomy Striklin. *Frye Street and Environs: The Collected Works of Marita Bonner.* Boston: Beacon Press, 1987.

Roses, Lorraine Elena, and Elizabeth Randolph. "Marita Bonner: In Search of Other Mothers' Gardens," *Black American Literature Forum* 21, nos. 1–2 (spring-summer 1987): 165–183.

Bontemps, Arnaud (Arna) Wendell

(1902–1973)

A prolific and engaged writer, editor, teacher, librarian, and literary critic of the Harlem Renaissance. His enduring and close professional friendship with LANGSTON HUGHES sheds light on the opportunities and challenges of a writerly professional life during the period. Bontemps was highly regarded for his writings of poetry and historical fiction and became especially influential as a writer of children's books. His numerous collections of fiction and poems for children complemented the landmark efforts of others such as JESSIE FAUSET and W. E. B. DUBOIS, who published works that would educate children of color about African history and African-American culture.

Bontemps was the only son born to Paul Bismark Bontemps, a successful bricklayer, and Maria Carolina Pembroke Bontemps, a schoolteacher, in Alexandria, Louisiana. In the face of threatening racism and aggressive KU KLUX KLAN activity, the Bontemps family, which also included daughter Ruby Sarah, migrated to California when he was three years old. Bontemps, who would return to the South much later in life, eventually migrated from his family's home in California to HARLEM. Bontemps lost his mother when he was 12 years old. He forged close ties to his maternal grandmother and members of his large, extended family who also had relocated to California from Louisiana. Paul Bontemps, a former Catholic who converted to the Seventh-Day Adventist faith and worked as a lay minister of the church, was determined to maintain the family in the face of their loss, however. He continued to shape his children's intellectual and spiritual development. Following the death of Maria Bontemps, Arna became extremely close to his Uncle Buddy, a dynamic figure whose love of stories and passion for storytelling inspired his young nephew. The exciting tales that Bontemps heard from his Uncle Buddy eventually informed his own writing and reflected his strong ties, through family, to the South.

Paul Bontemps's deep religious sensibilities shaped his son's early education. When he was 15, Bontemps enrolled at the predominantly white San Fernando Academy, a boarding school affiliated with the Seventh-Day Adventists. He then attended Pacific Union College, where he earned his B.A. in 1923. Bontemps, an avid reader with a passion for learning, endeavored to continue his studies after his graduation. While working night shifts in the Los Angeles postal system, he took a number of courses at the University of California, Los Angeles.

Both Bontemps and the enterprising future writer and editor WALLACE THURMAN were employed at the same Los Angeles post office. The two, who actually did not meet while working there, eventually became friends because they moved in the same Los Angeles social circle. They shared their enthusiasm for writing and often discussed their own work and ambitions. It was during this early postgraduate period that Bontemps began submitting his poems for publication. His first acceptance letter, for a poem entitled "Hope," came from Jessie Fauset, literary editor of *The* CRISIS. The poem appeared in the August 1924 issue alongside works by Langston Hughes, OTTIE GRAHAM and Fauset. Shortly after his debut publica-

Langston Hughes (right) and Arna Bontemps; photographed by Griffith Davis *(Reproduced by permission of the estate of Griffith Davis)*

tion, Bontemps headed east to NEW YORK CITY at Thurman's urging.

Bontemps supported himself in Harlem as a teacher at the HARLEM ACADEMY, a Seventh-Day Adventist school. In 1926 he married Alberta Johnson, an orphaned Georgia native who had been raised by her grandmother and who had begun her schooling in a Seventh-Day Adventist school in nearby Waycross, Georgia. Bontemps met his future wife when she enrolled in the ninth grade as an older student at the Harlem Academy. The couple, who were devoted to each other and were married for 47 years, had four daughters and two sons: Joan, Camille, Constance, Poppy, Paul, and Arna Jr. As the Great Depression began, Bontemps faced the challenges of relocating from the now-closed Harlem Academy. His exemplary record at the school enabled him to secure a new teaching post in the South, and the Bontemps family were able to relocate their growing family and left Harlem for Huntsville, Alabama.

While in New York City during the 1920s, however, Bontemps immersed himself in the available educational and cultural opportunities and began to forge valuable professional contacts and friendships. In 1926 he received his first formal recognition in two of the most notable Harlem Renaissance literary competitions. His poems "A Garden Cycle" and "Nocturne of the Wharves," which competed against winning works by STERLING BROWN and HELENE JOHNSON, won fourth-place and sixth-place honorable mentions, respectively, in the general poetry competition sponsored by *Opportunity*. In another division of that same literary contest, judges WILLIAM STANLEY BRAITHWAITE, Carl Sandburg, RIDGELY TORRENCE, COUNTEE CULLEN, and others awarded Bontemps and his poem "The Return" the first-place prize in the Alexander Pushkin Category of the *Opportunity* Poetry Prize competition. That same year, Bonner, with "A Nocturne at Bethesda," won first prize over Countee Cullen's "Thoughts in a Zoo" and works by EFFIE LEE NEWSOME and BLANCHE TAYLOR DICKINSON. Six years later, in 1932, Bontemps's devastating and most regularly anthologized short story "A SUMMER TRAGEDY" was the sole winner in the *Opportunity* Literary Contest for which FANNIE HURST, STERLING BROWN, and Richard Walsh served as judges. Bontemps's success as a poet led to his developing interest in writing, and he began work on his first novel, *Chariot in the Sky*, despite the offers from publishers who hoped that he might compile a volume of his poetic works.

Bontemps's affiliation with the Seventh-Day Adventist faith and school system shaped his literary life. He was transferred, for instance, to Huntsville, Alabama, just after his first published novel, GOD SENDS SUNDAY, appeared in 1931. At the Oakwood Junior College, a church-affiliated school, he worked as an English teacher and as a librarian. At a time when he could have capitalized on his burgeoning reputation, Bontemps found himself in an environment in which he had to moderate his love of books and friendships beyond the school circle. His regular correspondence with Hughes, for instance, prompted school officials to caution him against outside, secular, and problematic political stances. He was, on one occasion, instructed to burn his collection of literature and history books that included writings by Frederick Douglass, W. E. B. DuBois, JAMES WELDON JOHNSON, and Wallace Thurman in order to prove his willingness to endorse the conservative political status quo that the school upheld. He refused to do so, and the heightening pressure under which he was placed prompted him to resign his post a year later. In the face of stark economic times and limited financial resources, it was Bontemps's own writing that enabled his family to leave the South. He used his royalties from sales of BLACK THUNDER, his second novel, to finance his move to CHICAGO. There, he joined the faculty at Shiloh Academy, another Seventh-Day Adventist school, from 1935 to 1938. In 1938, he began working with the Works Progress Administration and in the course of his six-year employment with the Illinois Writer's Project, met fellow writer RICHARD WRIGHT.

Bontemps's introduction to the Harlem Renaissance circle came from Countee Cullen, the person who would judge Bontemps's work in literary competitions and later collaborate with him on *St. Louis Woman*, a stage adaptation of Thurman's first novel. Cullen, who also asked Bontemps to be one of his 14 groomsmen when he married NINA YOLANDE DuBOIS in 1928 in one of the most celebrated social events of the Harlem Renaissance period, encouraged Bontemps to join the writer-artist gatherings that were held frequently at the 135TH STREET BRANCH of the NEW YORK PUBLIC LIBRARY. He was able to forge good professional relationships and personal friendships with figures such as Jessie Fauset, the woman who launched his publishing career, REGINA ANDERSON, GWENDOLYN BENNETT, RUDOLPH FISHER, Langston Hughes, ALAIN LOCKE, and many other active members of the thriving African-American community. When Bontemps relocated to Chicago in 1935, Richard

Wright and MARGARET WALKER became part of his new literary and social circle.

Bontemps's friendship with Langston Hughes endured almost as long as his marriage. The two men, who met first in 1924, wrote regularly during their 41-year friendship, and their letters reveal much about the stark realities of pursuing a writing career during the Harlem Renaissance, the evolution of their writing sensibilities, the nature of their diverse and successful collaborations, and their perspectives on leading figures of the day, many of whom were close friends. As Charles Nichols notes in his edition of the selected correspondence, the "letters are most affecting" because they reveal the "good-humored and steady struggle" by the writers "to refine their work and gain a hearing in the world of letters" (Nichols, 11). They exchanged work with each other; offered frank but supportive criticism; shared strategies for professional advancement; critiqued contemporary books, plays, and other cultural events; and mused about the directions of African-American literature as reflected during and after the Harlem Renaissance. In the wake of the publication of POPO AND FIFINA (1932), their first collaborative children's book venture, Bontemps asked his friend about his impressions of the prepublication print. "And how did you like it," he asked. "I was pleasantly surprised. I like the style of the drawings—those that I have seen. But I will not be joyful unless you are too" (Nichols, 18). When Hughes was poised to publish his autobiography THE BIG SEA (1940) with KNOPF, Bontemps encouraged his friend to garner all of the publicity that he could. "Please let me know when *Big Sea* will be published," he wrote. "And have the Knopf publicity man call the attention of Gabriel Heater [sic] of 'We The People' to you about that time. This should put you right in the groove for that program and a good send-off. I intend to write him, too, when the date approaches. The fact that you have an autobiography at this age should be arresting immediately. A few details should do the rest. With or without this, of course, I'm ready to bet a Stetson the book becomes a best seller" (Nichols, 47).

Bontemps's fiction, in particular, reflected his deep interest in African-American history. After the publication of *God Sends Sunday*, an energetic, but tragic, novel about a self-confident African-

American jockey that was inspired by his Uncle Buddy's vivid tales of the South, Bontemps published two substantial works in which he revisited key moments of black self-determination and revolt. The first was BLACK THUNDER: GABRIEL's REVOLT, VIRGINIA 1800, published in 1936 by Macmillan Press. In the novel, which reviewers for *The New York Times* praised for its "simplicity, precision and elasticity of prose" (*NYT*, 2 February 1936: BR7), Bontemps recreated the life of Gabriel Prosser, the slave whose daring revolt against cruel and complicit white slave owners and their families was betrayed. The second, DRUMS AT DUSK, focused on Haiti during the 18th century and the slave revolt that culminated in freedom for its enslaved population. Margaret Wallace, who reviewed the work in *The New York Times*, described Bontemps as "an American Negro novelist and an earnest student of Haitian history" and congratulated him on his rich imagery and the "restrained intensity in [his] prose, which makes the most scenes he might easily have been tempted to overwrite" (*NYT*, 7 May 1939). Bontemps finished the bulk of the manuscript before traveling to Haiti during the year in which he held a JULIUS ROSENWALD FELLOWSHIP. Some critics suggested that the novel would have been enriched further if he had been able to immerse himself in the culture and history before completing the novel.

Bontemps, who eventually turned away from writing historical fiction and toward writing literature for children, developed a significant record of publications in the popular periodical press during the Harlem Renaissance. Short stories such as "Barrel Staves" (1934) and "Dang Little Squirt" (1935) appeared published in the journals CHALLENGE and NEW CHALLENGE, which writer DOROTHY WEST established in the late 1930s. Bontemps was committed to providing African-American children with substantial and absorbing literature. Inspired by his desire to provide such rich materials for his own children and to combat the prevailing literary stereotypes of African Americans and their history, he soon established himself as one of the most highly regarded writers of children's literature. His 16 works for children included collaborations with Langston Hughes, fiction, travel narratives, and histories. The titles included *Popo and Fifina: Children of Haiti* (1932), *You Can't*

Pet a Possum (1934), *Bon-Bon Buddy* (1935), *Slappy Hooper, Sad-Faced Boy* (1937), *The Wonderful Sign Painter* (1946), *Famous Negro Athletes* (1964), and *Mr. Kelso's Lion* (1970).

As the Renaissance came to a close, Bontemps, like Wright and other African-American writers in Chicago, joined the Works Progress Administration. Bontemps returned to graduate school in the early 1940s and earned his master's degree from the University of Chicago Graduate Library School in December 1943. He then became head librarian at FISK UNIVERSITY in Nashville, Tennessee. During his tenure at Fisk, where he impressed the faculty, staff, and students with his generosity, charm, and broad intellectual interests, he was elected to serve on the American Library Association's governing council. He was one of the judges on the Fellowship of the Academy of American Poets panel that in 1953 elected to bestow its highest award to writer William Carlos Williams. He continued to be honored for his own publications and impact on American cultural and literary history.

He retired from the university in 1966 after a distinguished career that included his efforts to collect the papers of Countee Cullen, Langston Hughes, and JEAN TOOMER. In 1972 he was appointed honorary consultant to the Library of Congress. Before his death in 1973, Bontemps accepted the invitation to become a visiting professor and the Beinecke Library chief archivist of the James Weldon Johnson Memorial Collection of Negro Arts and Letters at YALE UNIVERSITY.

Bontemps's canon of works included three novels, many short stories, numerous children's books, anthologies of African-American writing, and African-American histories. In addition to the various literary prizes that he won during his lifetime, Bontemps was also awarded two prestigious national awards that recognized his prodigious creative output and literary excellence. He won GUGGENHEIM FELLOWSHIPs in 1949 and in 1954 for creative writing, three ROSENWALD FELLOWSHIPs, and several honorary degrees from schools that included Morgan State University and Berea College.

Bontemps, who was one of the oldest surviving members of the Harlem Renaissance, continued to publish widely after the period. His later works included poetry anthologies such as *Golden Slippers: An Anthology of Negro Poetry for Young People* (1941) and

The Poetry of the Negro, 1746–1949 (1949), which he coedited with Langston Hughes; collections of short fiction and folklore such as *The Old South: "A Summer Tragedy" and Other Stories of the Thirties* (1973) and the coedited *The Book of Negro Folklore* (1958) with Hughes; biographies that included *Frederick Douglas: Slave, Fighter, Freeman* (1958) and *Young Booker: The Story of Booker T. Washington's Early Days* (1972); and a collection of reflections entitled *The Harlem Renaissance Remembered: Essays* (1972).

At the time of his death from a heart attack in June 1973, Bontemps was affiliated with Fisk University as a writer-in-residence. Funeral services were held at the Chapel on the Nashville campus, and a memorial service was held at the Riverside Church in New York City. Bontemps was survived by his wife, six children, 10 grandchildren, and his sister.

The Arna Bontemps African American Museum in Alexandria, Louisiana, was established in 1988. The site, which opened in the restored Bontemps birthplace and childhood home and is known now as the Arna Bontemps Museum and Cultural Center, was the first African-American museum in Louisiana when it opened.

Bibliography

"Arna Bontemps, Writer, 70, Dies," *New York Times*. 6 June 1973, 50.

Arna Bontemps Papers, George Arents Research Library, Syracuse University; Fisk University Special Collections, Fisk University; Beinecke Library, Yale University.

Flamming, Douglas. "A Westerner in Search of 'Negro-Ness': Region and Race in the Writing of Arna Bontemps." In *Over the Edge: Remapping the American West*, edited by Valerie J. Matsumoto. Berkeley: University of California Press, 1999.

Jones, Kirkland C. *Renaissance Man From Louisiana: A Biography of Arna Wendell Bontemps*. Westport, Conn.: Greenwood Press, 1992.

Nichols, Charles H., ed. *Arna Bontemps–Langston Hughes Letters, 1925–1967*. New York: Paragon House, 1990.

Reagan, Daniel. "Achieving Perspective: Arna Bontemps and the Shaping Force of Harlem Culture," *Essays in Arts and Sciences* 25 (October 1996): 69–78.

Tompkins, Lucy. "'In Dubious Battle' and Other Recent Works of Fiction." *New York Times*, 2 February 1936, BR 7.

Wallace, Margaret. "A Tale of the Slave Revolt in Haiti." *New York Times*, 7 May 1939, BR4.

Book of American Negro Poetry, The
James Weldon Johnson (1922)

The first comprehensive anthology of poetry by 20th-century African-American poets. The editor of the volume, JAMES WELDON JOHNSON, used a JULIUS ROSENWALD FELLOWSHIP to fund a year-long leave from the NAACP during which time he prepared the volume for publication. The table of contents included well-known and emerging poets and often included several poems by each of the writers listed. Johnson chose 40 poets for publication in the anthology; of this number, seven were women: GWENDOLYN BENNETT, ALICE DUNBAR-NELSON, JESSIE FAUSET, GEORGIA DOUGLAS JOHNSON, HELENE JOHNSON, ANNE SPENCER, and Lucy Ariel Williams.

In his introduction, Johnson offered several evaluations of African-American literary practice. He praised the use of authentic Negro sources, noting that several of the featured writers "have dug down into the genuine folk stuff" and made the distinction between this material and "the artificial folk stuff of the dialect school." Johnson lamented the fact that in the body of African-American poetry "not stimulated by a sense of race," he could not identify "one single poem possessing the power and artistic finality found in the best of the poems rising out of racial conflict and contact." Like Pauline Hopkins and Jessie Fauset, he believed that African Americans were best equipped to write, and even responsible for generating, the passionate, incisive race literature that would document the evolution, struggles, and triumphs of the race.

Book of American Negro Spirituals (1925)

A songbook edited by J. Rosamond Johnson, the composer of "Lift Every Voice and Sing," and his brother JAMES WELDON JOHNSON, the writer, NAACP executive, and editor. The volume, published by Viking Press, included an introduction by James and arrangements of the spirituals by J. Rosamond. The popularity of the volume prompted the Johnsons to publish *The Second Book of Negro Spirituals* in 1926.

Book-of-the-Month Club

The national book network that was established in 1926. In 1934 it offered to its members BEALE STREET: WHERE THE BLUES BEGAN by GEORGE LEE. This was the first work by an African-American author that the organization included in its catalog. In 1945 RICHARD WRIGHT's just-published novel *Black Boy: A Record of Childhood and Youth* was one of the selections included in the book club's offerings.

Born to Be Taylor Gordon (1935)

The autobiography of TAYLOR GORDON, a young man from White Sulphur Springs, Montana, and a singer during the 1920s. His story included anecdotes about his colorful work experiences as a chauffeur, cook, messenger, and singer. Well-known Harlem Renaissance personalities endorsed the volume, including CARL VAN VECHTEN, who penned the introduction, and Miguel Covarrubias, who provided the illustrations.

Boston

The Harlem Renaissance had satellite communities of writers beyond NEW YORK CITY. The city of Boston and its suburbs of Brookline and Cambridge, for example, were home to writers, editors, and journalists such as DOROTHY WEST, WILLIAM STANLEY BRAITHWAITE, Florence Marion Henderson, and MARITA BONNER. A number of the black intellectual elite had ties to the city and its educational institutions. HARVARD UNIVERSITY students and graduates included W. E. B. DUBOIS, the school's first African-American Ph.D., JOSEPH DANDRIDGE BIBB, cofounder of the CHICAGO WHIP, and RAYMOND PACE ALEXANDER, a law school graduate. Marita Bonner attended RADCLIFFE COLLEGE.

Like WASHINGTON, D.C., PHILADELPHIA, and HARLEM, Boston also hosted its own Renaissance-era literary salons and literary journals. The SATURDAY EVENING QUILL CLUB, founded in 1925 and led by EUGENE GORDON, sustained a literary journal of the same name. The magazine introduced a number of new writers and strengthened the reputations of others, including Dorothy West, HELENE JOHNSON, and FLORENCE HARMON. Although its membership was open, it was an all-black group. Its membership included Florida Ruffin Ridley, the daughter of the prominent women's club leader Josephine St. Pierre Ruffin, EDYTHE MAE GORDON, the wife of the club president, and Helene Johnson.

Boston Transcript, The

A Boston newspaper for which WILLIAM STANLEY BRAITHWAITE served as a literary critic and book review editor.

Boston University

The Boston-born writer DOROTHY WEST and the poet HELENE JOHNSON attended this private, co-educational university in Boston that was also the alma mater of Martin Luther King, Jr. Established in 1839 in Vermont and then relocated to Boston and renamed in 1867, this was one of the first schools to accept African-American students and women.

Bottomland Clarence Williams and Eva Taylor
(1927)
A play by Clarence Williams and Eva Taylor, two popular radio personalities, about a young woman who journeys north to locate her lost sister in a HARLEM cabaret. Its depictions of the entertainment world contribute to other narratives, such as Paul Laurence Dunbar's *Sport of the Gods*, in which these Harlem venues are associated with seduction, moral corruption, and danger.

Bottom of the Cup John Tucker Battle
and William Perlman (1924)
A play by JOHN TUCKER BATTLE and WILLIAM PERLMAN in which the protagonist, Charles Thompson, returns home from school in the North and makes plans to establish a school for African Americans in his southern hometown. He never realizes his dream; he offers himself up as a victim to a lynch mob in order to protect his family. Written by white playwrights, this play was another

Renaissance-era production that profiled the social chaos and devastating impact that LYNCHING had on American society in general and on African-American families in particular.

'Bout Culled Folkses Lucy Mae Turner
(1938)
A volume of poetry by LUCY MAE TURNER, who was a granddaughter of Nat Turner, the leader of the historic 1831 slave rebellion in Southampton, Virginia. In the modest collection of 38 poems, Turner uses African-American dialect, standard English prose, and a variety of poetical forms. The poems include lively depictions of African-American laborers and portraits of meditative women. Her accounts of washerwomen, hotel employees, and other working-class African Americans are sprightly. They humanize and give voice to these essential but often silenced figures. Turner creates self-confident, optimistic women, and through them she delivers insightful commentary on the politics of domesticity, the nature of white privilege, and African-American survival strategies. Turner pays tribute to her grandfather in the final poem, a tightly framed four-line poem in which she celebrates his decision to die rather than live in a world in which human beings were bought and sold.

Bibliography
Reardon, Joanne, and Kristine Thorsen. *Poetry by American Women, 1900–1975: A Bibliography.* Metuchen, N.J.: Scarecrow Press, 1979.

Bowman, Laura (ca. 1881–1957)
One of the cast members of the historic May 1923 Broadway production of THE CHIP WOMAN'S FORTUNE, the work by WILLIS RICHARDSON that was the first play by an African-American writer to appear on BROADWAY. Bowman also participated in plays produced by the Negro Theatre Guild and the ETHIOPIAN ART PLAYERS. She branched out into film, and her career included parts in two Oscar Micheaux films, *Lem Hawkins' Confession* (1935) and *God's Stepchildren* (1938).

Brain Sweat John Charles Brownell (1934)

A play by JOHN BROWNELL about a man who devotes two years of his life to perfect a money-making scheme. The play was staged at the Longacre Theatre in New York City in March 1934. Robert Ober staged the production; Vail Studios provided the setting; and James Montgomery and Henry Stern produced it.

The three-act play with a cast of 10 and a group of jubilee singers was billed as a "comedy of Negro life." It revolves around Henry Washington, a placid philosopher who has sworn off physical activity and labor in order to create a powerful intellectual project. Washington's wife, Rose, has become the primary wage earner and taken in laundry while her husband has immersed himself in thinking. NEW YORK TIMES drama critic Brooks Atkinson suggested to his readers that "no one believes in Henry's mysterious project for making money by the use of his brain" (*NYT*, 5 April 1934, 24). Yet, Henry ultimately succeeds and proves that "brain sweat" is indeed worthwhile.

When it opened in New York, *Brain Sweat* featured the talented and beloved Carrie McClendon in the role of Rose Washington. Atkinson praised her for performing "with all the delicacy of a sensitive artist" and also remarked that she "has a presence and a grace that are wholly admirable." Of her co-star, Billy Higgins, who played the role of Henry Washington, "the intellectual giant of the family," Atkinson declared that he was "just plump and pompous enough to be a comedian." He noted also that "[w]hen the great project ripens in the last act Mr. Higgins's exultant grin, which measures several miles in linear distance, and his triumphant rocking and his delusions of sepia grandeur are blissfully ludicrous" (*NYT*, 5 April 1934, 24).

Promotional information about the upcoming New York City production called attention to the fact that it had "a Negro cast" (*NYT*, 17 February 1934, 20). When it opened, audiences were presented with "shilly-shallying with a humorous notion for two acts" before the comedy "brighten[ed] into an amusing play at the end, and dismisse[d] in a cheerful frame of mind" (*NYT*, 5 April 1934, 24).

Bibliography

Atkinson, Brooks. "On the Advantages of Using the Mind—'Brain Sweat' With a Negro Cast." *New York Times*, 5 April 1934, 24.

"'Brain Sweat' Due Here on Wednesday." *New York Times*, 29 March 1934, 27.

"Theatrical Notes." *New York Times*, 17 February 1934, 20.

Braithwaite, William Stanley Beaumont (1878–1962)

A Bostonian who became a prominent editor, literary critic, and publisher. Born to mixed-race parents, Braithwaite was forced to end his education prematurely when his father died. His love of literature developed during one of his jobs as a typesetter for a publishing firm in the city. He published two volumes of poetry before he was 30 years of age, *Lyrics of Life and Love* (1904) and *The House of Falling Leaves, with Other Poems* (1908). From 1913 through 1929, he selected the items for inclusion in and published the ANTHOLOGY OF MAGAZINE VERSE and the *Yearbook of American Poetry*. Some writers lobbied him heavily because inclusion in the yearly books enhanced their reputations. In 1918 his literary achievements contributed to his selection for an NAACP SPINGARN MEDAL and an honorary degree from ATLANTA UNIVERSITY.

Braithwaite, whom historian David Levering Lewis identifies as "the dean of African American belles-lettres," was quite outspoken about his distaste for aggressive race poetry. He castigated CLAUDE MCKAY, for example, for his celebrated poem "If We Must Die," a piece written in response to the bloody race riots during the summer of 1919. Like JEAN TOOMER, Braithwaite advocated for poetry that reflected the talents, rather than the race, of a writer. When CANE appeared in 1923, Braithwaite hailed Toomer, its author and a man who fretted in the face of racial objectification, as "a bright morning star of a new day of the Race in literature."

Braithwaite's anthologies, notably devoid of works that were polemical or political, reflected his studied effort to situate African-American poets in a larger context of American poetry. His sentiments ran counter to those expressed by JAMES WELDON JOHNSON and others, however; the

NAACP secretary urged African Americans to realize that their race made it especially important that they develop histories—fictional and otherwise—of their race.

Like W. E. B. DuBois, whom he considered to be a friend, Braithwaite taught at Atlanta University. He was a professor of creative literature for 10 years and continued publishing into his 90s.

Bibliography

Clairmonte, Glenn. "He Made American Writers Famous," *Phylon* 30, no. 2 (1969): 184–190.

Fleming, G. James, and Christian E. Burckel, eds. *Who's Who In Colored America: An Illustrated Biographical Directory of Notable Living Persons of African Descent in the United States.* Yonkers-on-Hudson, N.Y.: Christian E. Burckel & Associates, 1950.

Lewis, David Levering. *W. E. B. DuBois: The Fight For Equality and the American Century, 1919–1963.* New York: Henry Holt and Company, 2000.

Brass Ankles DuBose Heyward (1931)

A play by DuBose Heyward about a woman who is tortured by her black heritage. When she gives birth to a dark-skinned child and learns that her ancestry includes black grandparents, she decides that death would be better than the shame accompanying any confession to her husband. She taunts him with a lie about her adultery, and he kills her and their child. The title, inspired by a southern folk expression, refers to individuals who invoke Native American heritage, rather than African descent, to explain their color.

Bibliography

Slavic, William H. *Dubose Heyward.* Boston: Twayne Publishers, 1981.

Brawley, Benjamin (1882–1941)

A social critic, historian, and teacher who found the Harlem Renaissance distasteful. Born in Columbia, South Carolina, Brawley attended Morehouse College, the University of Chicago, and Howard University. During the years of the Renaissance, Brawley published several works of nonfiction including *A Short History of the American Negro* (1913), *The Negro in Literature and Art* (1918), *A Social History of the American Negro* (1921), and *A Short History of the English Drama* (1921). His essays appeared in *The Crisis,* and he was one of the well-known personalities chosen to judge the entries to the *Opportunity* literary contest in 1927.

Bibliography

Brawley, Benjamin. *Early Negro American Writers; Selections with Biographical and Critical Introductions.* 1935, reprint, Freeport, N.Y.: Books for Libraries Press, 1968.

———. *The Negro Genius: A New Appraisal of the Achievement of the American Negro in Literature and the Fine Arts.* 1939, reprint, New York: Biblo and Tannen, 1972.

Johnson, Abby Arthur, and Ronald Maberry Johnson. *Propaganda & Aesthetics: The Literary Politics of African American Magazines in the Twentieth Century.* Amherst: University of Massachusetts, 1979.

"Bride of God" Octavia Wynbush (1938)

An Octavia Wynbush short story about a young woman who recovers from the betrayal of her fiancé by devoting herself to God.

Published in the October 1938 issue of *The Crisis,* "Bride of God" was one of several stories that Wynbush set in Louisiana. Leah Sommers, the protagonist, is reveling in the natural splendor that has blessed the day of her wedding. The rich imagery of the garden just beyond her Aunt Sabriny's red cottage is highly evocative of a prelapsarian Eden. Leah, whose name recalls the biblical woman whose own marriage involved trickery and disappointment, "moved lightly, gayly among the flowers, caressing the leaves with her long, slender brown fingers, stooping to press her nostrils close to the velvety red, white and delicately pink and yellow roses, bending over the white jasmine throned in their dark green leaves." Yet, while she delights in the "cool fragrance of the clambering honeysuckle vines," Leah's friends and family come to learn that her beau Aleck has married another woman and "done gone 'way wid her."

Leah contemplates suicide, but her aunt catches her on the banks of the Gulf and convinces her that no man is worth dying for and that she may have the chance to fulfill some other plan that God has for her life. It is Aunt Sabriny who suggests that Leah could become a bride of God, a woman devoted to good works and one who does not have to join the convent in order to do so. Leah takes her aunt's advice and for the next 20 years becomes an invaluable member of the community. She remains unmarried even though she has ample opportunity to accept the attentions of other suitors. One night, as she is contemplating the life that she has led and wondering whether or not she might have been wrong to stay single, she is reunited with Aleck. In a rushed conversation, he tells her of his years of misfortune and the fact that he is now on the run from the law because he might have killed a local overseer. He begs Leah to give him shelter from the mob that is in hot pursuit. Before she can agree, he has sequestered himself in the house, and she then directs him to hide himself in the attic. She faces down the would-be lynchers who storm down upon the house and is in the process of fending off the police who arrive shortly thereafter. Aleck emerges and surrenders even though it appears that Leah is on the verge of successfully defending herself and her home from invasion and inspection. The story closes as she tells Aleck that he has not ruined her life because "[n]o man kin spoil the life of a Bride o' God."

Wynbush's story of fugitives and love betrayed, like the controversial NELLA LARSEN story entitled "SANCTUARY," explores the bravery of women and their commitment to racial solidarity even when they have suffered greatly.

"Brief Biography of Fletcher J. Mosely"
Theophilus Lewis (1924)

A tragic love story by THEOPHILUS LEWIS in which a spurned woman employs voodoo to win back her lover but ultimately sets in motion the events that bring about his death by LYNCHING. Lewis's well-paced and evocative prose tells the story of two hotel employees and the racial tensions that make it a microcosm of the larger, volatile white southern world.

Fletcher Josephus Mosely loves Miranda Minatree and eventually asks her to marry him. After proposing, however, Mosely attempts to break off the engagement. Miranda seeks help from a voodoo priestess, who warns her that a spell can bring back and turn away the person in question. When Mosely attempts to steal the ring from his ex-fiancée's room, she mistakes him for a burglar and flings magic powder in his eyes. As he stumbles away, Mosely accidentally enters the room of Anna, a vivacious blonde employee. His boss, who hated to see any hint of familiarity between the two, thinks that she is being attacked. Anna lies about the event and thus justifies the mob's pursuit of Mosely. The story ends with the brief note that Mosely has been lynched and a reference to Miranda, who believes that it was the spell, rather than any unfortunate act of hers, that drove Mosely into the white woman's room.

The story appeared in the July 1924 issue of *The* MESSENGER.

Briggs, Cyril Valentine (1888–unknown)

A founder of the AFRICAN BLACK BROTHERHOOD, a Marxist organization begun sometime before 1920 by West Indian intellectuals that actively protested segregation and racial inequality. Briggs was also the editor of the New York–based AMSTERDAM NEWS, the platform from which he delivered numerous editorials on issues of the day. He lodged a successful suit against MARCUS GARVEY, whom he had supported in earlier years, after the Jamaican leader accused Briggs, an extremely light-skinned black man, of having "white" attitudes.

Bright, Nellie Rathborne (ca. 1902–1976)

Born to West Indian parents in Savannah, Georgia, Nellie Bright grew up in PHILADELPHIA. The daughter of an Episcopal minister, Bright came of age as a writer in the supportive black literary community of the city. After graduating from the Philadelphia School of Pedagogy and the UNIVERSITY OF PENNSYLVANIA, she began teaching in the city's public school system. She soon joined the BLACK OPALS group that included BESSIE BIRD, MAE COWDERY, and ARTHUR HUFF FAUSET, a fellow city school teacher. She published in *Black Opals* and in OPPORTUNITY, the journal in which "BLACK," her essay about her developing racial consciousness, won third prize in the magazine's 1927 literary contest.

"Bright and Morning Star" Richard Wright (1938)

A short story by RICHARD WRIGHT that appeared first in a May 1938 issue of *NEW MASSES*, a Marxist magazine based in New York that opened Wright's eyes to the global and "organized search for the truth of the lives of the oppressed and the isolated." He recalled that his first impression of the magazine was so powerful because "the revolutionary words leaped from the printed page and struck [him] with tremendous force." The work eventually became part of *UNCLE TOM'S CHILDREN*, his 1938 collection of stark novellas.

The plot centered on the courageous and ultimately self-destructive acts of an elderly mother whose ties to the Communist Party endanger her and her son. She is betrayed by a man who relays information that she has provided him to a lynch mob that is determined to unearth the Communist sympathizers and network in its midst. Granny Sue, the matriarch, goes to the public torture of her son, an event made possible by her own conversations with the traitor. When her son begins to give in, she shoots him and then dies when the mob turns on her. This last story in the later versions of *Uncle Tom's Children* was a shocking meditation on nationalistic hysteria, black self-determination, and awesome, unexpected examples of maternal intervention.

Bibliography

Delmar, P. Jay. "Tragic Patterns in Richard Wright's Uncle Tom's Children," *Negro American Literature Forum* 10, no. 1 (spring 1976): 3–12.

Gayle, Addison. *Richard Wright: Ordeal of a Native Son.* Garden City, N.Y.: Anchor Press, 1980.

Oleson, Carole. "The Symbolic Richness of Richard Wright's 'Bright and Morning Star,'" *Negro American Literature Forum* 6, no. 4 (winter 1972): 110–112.

Bright Medallion, The Doris D. Price (1932)

A play in dialect by DORIS D. PRICE in which a young man, who invents a story about his bravery in World War I, dies because he has to live up to the false story of his courage. Published in a collection of plays by University of Michigan students, edited by Kenneth Rowe, the play charts the evolution of Samuel Hunt, a Texan, who finds a World War I medal and claims it as his own. In an effort to maintain the respect of his town and the woman he loves, Samuel rescues a baby from a burning building; he succeeds but dies shortly thereafter from smoke inhalation.

Broadway

The major entertainment location in NEW YORK CITY. By 1925 there were 80 theaters along this route, an increase of 400 percent since 1900, when there had been just 20. While Broadway theaters staged white-authored plays about black life and featured works with black actors, it was not until 1923 that the first major play by an African-American writer was staged on Broadway. *THE CHIP WOMAN'S FORTUNE*, a one-act play by WILLIS RICHARDSON, which had previously performed in HARLEM, opened on Broadway in May 1923.

Broken Banjo, The Willis Richardson (1926)

A searing domestic tragedy, this play by WILLIS RICHARDSON appeared in the March and April 1926 issues of *THE CRISIS*. Richardson, the first African American to see his work staged on BROADWAY, offered readers a painful story about a victimized husband whose wife and in-laws undermine his authority and ultimately reveal his dreadful secret to police.

Matt Turner is the besieged husband, a banjo player who seeks refuge in his home from poverty and the stress of daily life. His wife, Emma, bargains with him for a new pair of shoes when he tries to prevent her relatives from lounging and eating in their home. Her materialism, rather than loyalty to her husband, is the first sign of Matt Turner's imminent demise. Matt threatens Emma's brother and cousin when he finds that they have broken the banjo, his most valued possession. They in turn threaten to reveal him as the murderer of a white man. After much pleading by Matt, they promise not to tell and to allow Matt to leave town. Before he can escape, the two men return with the police. Emma is at her most pathetic as she watches her husband being led away.

The play is a forerunner of the domestic realism that emerges most powerfully in plays by

Lorraine Hansberry and in the fiction of RICHARD WRIGHT.

Bronze: A Book of Verse Georgia Douglas Johnson (1922)

The second book of poetry by GEORGIA DOUGLAS JOHNSON. In 1941 she confessed to ARNA BONTEMPS that she had written *Bronze* to silence those critics who believed her incapable of writing about race. Published by B. J. Brimmer Company in BOSTON, it was a volume of poetry that she regarded as "entirely race conscious." That conviction was strengthened by the introduction to the volume, written by W. E. B. DuBois, a scholar whom Johnson respected and also the man with whom she had had a passionate love affair. In his comments, DuBois prepared readers for the mysterious, mystical work that they might encounter in the collection. He recommended the book to "Those who know what it means to be a colored woman in 1922—and know it not so much in fact as in feeling, apprehension, unrest and delicate yet stern thought" and declared that it was these individuals who "must" read her work. "As a revelation of the soul struggle of the women of a race it is invaluable," DuBois concluded.

Johnson divided 65 poems into nine sections with titles such as "Exhortation," "Supplication," "Motherhood," "Prescience," "Exaltation," and "Appreciations." In addition to new works, she included poems that had appeared previously in *OPPORTUNITY* and the *LIBERATOR*. As Claudia Tate notes in her preface to a recent collection of Johnson's works, while there was a racial veneer on many of the poems, Johnson seemed to be writing more directly about love, loss, and sadness. Her "Author's Note" reinforces this notion. Johnson described *Bronze* as "the child of a bitter earth-wound." She then described her experiences as a writer in direct and spiritual language. "I sit on the earth and sing— sing out, and of, my sorrow," she shared. She continued and provided an increasingly encouraging message to her readers: "Yet, fully conscious of the potent agencies that silently work in their healing ministries, I know that God's sun shall one day shine upon a perfected and unhampered people."

The three poems in "Exhortation" were "Sonnet to the Mantled," "Sonnet to Those Who See

but Darkly," and "Brotherhood." As a whole, the poems constitute a vibrant exhortation of those who find themselves oppressed and weighed down. "Like joyful exiles swift returning home," Johnson's speaker imagined mantled figures shedding their cumbersome cloaks and emerging "Erect, and strong, and visioned, in the day / That rings the knell of Curfew o'er the sway / Of prejudice." The dominant images here recall the well-known Tuskegee University statue by sculptor Charles Keck, unveiled in 1922, in which Booker T. Washington stands over a former slave who is crouching before him. Washington holds a mantle in his hand, but depending on one's perspective on accommodationism and Washington's politics in general, it is possible to argue that he is pulling the cloak away in order to speed the slave's emancipation and progress or keeping it in place so that freedom remains a qualified state for some and an opportunity for power for others. Johnson maintained her focus on the uplift of the masses in the next sonnet. It imagined "Those Who See but Darkly" as individuals whose "gaze uplifting from shoals of despair . . . / Surge to the piping of Hope's dulcet lay, / Souled like the lily, whose splendors declare / God's mazéd paradox—purged of all blight, / Out from the quagmire, unsullied and fair."

"Supplication" represents a noticeable shift in agency from that in the preceding group of poems. There, the poems tend to feature first-person narrations, revealing a speaker who is desperate for protection and endurance. "Let me not lose my dream," pleads one speaker, "Hold me, and guard, lest anguish tear my dreams away!" Yet, the posture of "Supplication" eventually gives way in "Calling Dreams." The speaker reasserts herself, realizing that she cannot just ask but must demand of life "The right to make my dreams come true" so that she can "stride into the morning-break!"

The third section, "Shadow," introduces an observant and world-weary speaker, one struck by the oppression that permeates one's waking and dream life. She exists in a world full of "mad mocking strife" and the "venomed prick of probing knife, / The baleful subtle leer of scorn / That rims the world from morn to morn." The poem "Laocoon" is an additional meditation on the aggressive silencing that individuals endure. "This spirit-choking atmosphere / With deadly serpent-coil / Entwines my soaring-upwardness / And chains me to the soil," the tormented speaker reveals. Her frustration, however, is intense not because of the limitations but because of the intensity of her desire to soar. "[W]hy these glowing forms of hope / That scintillate and shine," she asks, "If naught of all that burnished dream / Can evermore be mine?" The resilience that began to emerge in "Supplication" now takes hold as the speaker reveals her outrage. "My every fibre fierce rebels / Against this servile role," she exclaims, "And all my being broods to break / This death-grip on my soul."

The section entitled "The Mother" includes poems that range from portraits of melancholy mothers to inspired mantras about the destiny of future generations. Poems such as "The Mother," the title poem, "Maternity," and "Black Woman" are heart-wrenching for their laments about the pain of the world and the bleak outlook that exists for innocent babes. Yet, in "Shall I Say, 'My Son You're Branded'," a forceful maternal speaker rejects the notion that she become complicit with the world's oppression. Instead, she tells her son plainly and "with love prophetic" to "dauntlessly arise / Spurn the handicap that clogs you, taking what the world denies." The section ends on a more conventional note, with "Benediction," a poem with a set of straightforward wishes for a successful life. Yet, the poem underscores the unbreakable link between a child and its mother. "Go forth, my son, / Winged by my heart's desire," instructs the confident female figure who narrates the poem.

Johnson's often-anthologized poem "Credo" is the lead poem in the section entitled "Prescience." The manifesto is magnificent and stately, an eloquently expressed code by which to live. "I believe in the ultimate justice of Fate; / That the races of men front the sun in their turn; / That each soul holds the title to infinite wealth / In fee to the will as it masters itself," declares the self-possessed speaker in the opening portion of the 10-line poem. The volume closes with a set of moving tributes to past and current leaders, friends, and heroes. Johnson honors historical figures such as John Brown and some of her contemporaries such as DuBois, EMILIE BIGELOW HAPGOOD, MARY CHURCH TERRELL, RIDGELY TORRENCE, WILLIAM STANLEY BRAITHWAITE, and RICHARD WRIGHT.

The last poem is a tribute to ATLANTA UNIVERSITY, the institution with which she was affiliated during her high school years in Georgia.

Johnson assembled *Bronze* while fully aware of the scrutiny that it would attract. She responded to the call for "race poems" in a dignified manner and preserved her own creative integrity. The poems represent a steady and thoughtful set of perspectives on personal ambition, the will to succeed, and the immunity that can be acquired through self-expression.

Bibliography
Tate, Claudia. "Introduction." In *Georgia Douglas Johnson: The Selected Works of Georgia Douglas Johnson.* Henry Louis Gates, Jr., and Jennifer Burton, eds. New York: G. K. Hall & Company, 1997.

Brooks, Johnathan Henderson (1905–1945)

A minister from Mississippi who showed early promise as a poet and fiction writer. In the autobiographical essay that he contributed to CAROLING DUSK, the 1927 anthology edited by COUNTEE CULLEN and in which three of his poems appeared, Brooks recounted his family's disintegration due to divorce, the economic hardships that he and his mother faced as sharecroppers working for an unethical white farmer, and his mother's heroic efforts to educate her son. Her economy and fortitude enabled Brooks to attend LINCOLN UNIVERSITY, from which he graduated from the high school division in 1925 with "salutary honors," and Tougaloo College.

Brooks's earliest works were religious in nature, and this trend continued in his later writings, most of which he published during his year of ministry in Southern churches. "The Resurrection," "The Last Quarter Moon of the Dying Year," and "O Paean," the three Brooks poems in *Caroling Dusk*, were earnest testaments to God's love and celebratory tributes to nature.

Brooks, Van Wyck (1886–1963)

A white writer who published American literary histories and was known for his commentaries on American cultural affairs. With LANGSTON HUGHES, he was one of the signatories for the journal *NEW MASSES*, a radical magazine that regularly critiqued the class politics of Renaissance-era writers like CLAUDE MCKAY and contributed to calls for racial and social justice.

Broun, Heywood (1888–1939)

A cofounder and the first president of the American Newspaper Guild, which was organized in 1933. Broun was a forthright critic of American government policy, and his opinions frequently resulted in the termination of his employment at various American newspapers. In 1921 LANGSTON HUGHES, who had just began his first year at COLUMBIA UNIVERSITY, attended the Rand School of Social Science lectures that Broun delivered there.

Brown, Hallie Quinn (ca. 1845–1949)

A pioneering educator and writer of detailed African-American women's histories, Brown was the daughter of former slaves, who dedicated themselves to helping other fugitives escape via the Underground Railroad. Brown inherited her parent's commitment to social protest and racial uplift. Her active participation in temperance groups, suffrage organizations, and educational programs dedicated to African-American migrant workers contributed to her election to the presidency of the NATIONAL ASSOCIATION OF COLORED WOMEN in 1920. In 1924 she became the first African-American woman to address a national political convention when she gave a speech in which she supported the candidacy of Warren Harding.

Brown published the bulk of her work during the Harlem Renaissance. Her publications included instructional texts on elocution, borne of Brown's stint as a professor of elocution at WILBERFORCE UNIVERSITY, and two books devoted to African-American women's history: *Our Women: Past, Present, and Future* (1925) and *Homespun Heroines and Other Women of Distinction* (1926). Wilberforce University, the institution on whose behalf she traveled abroad to raise money, presented her with two honorary degrees, a master of science in 1890 and a law degree in 1936.

Brown, Sterling Allen (1901–1989)

Regarded by some critics as the folk poet of the Harlem Renaissance, this talented poet, critic, and teacher was born to former slaves in the District of Columbia. He distinguished himself at DUNBAR HIGH SCHOOL, where his teachers included JESSIE FAUSET, the *CRISIS* literary editor and novelist, and ANGELINA WELD GRIMKÉ, the playwright. His stellar academic career continued during his undergraduate years at Williams College, where he was elected to PHI BETA KAPPA and graduated with honors. He pursued graduate studies in English at HARVARD UNIVERSITY and earned a master's degree in 1923.

Brown began his 40-year tenure in the English Department of HOWARD UNIVERSITY in 1929. He published *SOUTHERN ROAD*, his first volume of poetry, three years later. Despite the praise that Brown received from ALAIN LOCKE and other critics and his repeated publication in *OPPORTUNITY* and other journals, his Howard University colleagues showed disdain for his work. They resisted his use of folk images, dialect, Negro spirituals, and black musical forms like jazz and the blues. They made plain their preference for works that adhered to more standard English and conventional anglicized poetical forms. The Howard criticism, coupled with the economic hardships of the GREAT DEPRESSION, made it difficult for Brown to find a publisher for his second collection of poems; he would not publish another book of verses for some 40 years.

In the late 1930s and in the decades that followed, Brown collaborated with other writers and scholars and produced highly regarded collections of African-American literature. These included *THE NEGRO IN AMERICAN FICTION* and *Negro Poetry and Drama*. In 1941 he, ARTHUR DAVIS, and ULYSSES LEE edited *The Negro Caravan*, a highly respected anthology whose value lay in its presentation of many previously unpublished works by African Americans.

Bibliography

Gabbin, Joanne. *Sterling A. Brown: Building the Black Aesthetic Tradition.* Westport, Conn.: Greenwood Press, 1985.

Sanders, Mark. *Afro-Modernist Aesthetics and the Poetry of Sterling Brown.* Athens: University of Georgia Press, 1999.

———. "Sterling A. Brown and the Afro-Modern Moment," *African American Review* 31, no. 3 (autumn 1997): 393–397.

Skinner, Beverly Lanier. "Sterling Brown: An Ethnographic Perspective," *African American Review* 31, no. 3 (autumn 1997): 417–422.

Brownell, John Charles (1877–1961)

A white playwright and actor whose own plays that appeared on Broadway during the Harlem Renaissance included *The Nut Farm* (1929), BRAIN SWEAT (1934), *Dream Child* (1934), *Her Majesty the Widow* (1934), and *A Woman of the Soil* (1935).

Brain Sweat was a comedy about a man determined to refrain from physical labor in order to achieve a great intellectual feat. The play featured splendid performances by veteran actors Rose McClendon and Billy Higgins. NEW YORK TIMES drama critic Brooks Atkinson suggested that the play's "genial hilarity" was welcome and that it "dismisse[d] the audience in a cheerful frame of mind" (*NYT*, 5 April 1934, 24).

Bibliography

Atkinson, Brooks. "On the Advantages of Using the Mind—'Brain Sweat' with a Negro Cast." *New York Times*, 5 April 1934, 24.

Brownies' Book, The

A magazine for African-American children, produced and published by W. E. B. DUBOIS, JESSIE FAUSET, and AUGUSTUS GRANVILLE DILL from January 1920 through December 1921. Dedicated to "children who with eager look / Scanned vainly library shelf, and nook, / For history or Song of Story / That told of Colored People's glory," the magazine sold for $1.50 per copy and included a diverse array of materials and illustrations, many of the former written, but left unsigned, by Fauset.

Compelled by the lack of material that would educate, inspire, and prepare children for life, the editors and publishers devoted themselves wholeheartedly to this enterprising cultural project. LANGSTON HUGHES, then 18 years old, published his very first work in *The Brownies' Book* and became a regular contributor to the magazine shortly thereafter. Other writers responded to the call for works that would shape the children of the race, including GEORGIA DOUGLAS JOHNSON, JAMES WELDON JOHNSON, NELLA LARSEN, and WILLIS RICHARDSON.

Articles included biographies of black heroes and heroines, articles about geography, poems, and plays. Economic woes and a downturn in subscribers for *The Brownies' Book* and competition from other race periodicals like THE CRISIS, contributed to the cessation of this invaluable resource for African-American children, their parents, and their communities.

Bibliography

Lewis, David Levering. *W. E. B. DuBois: The Fight for Equality and the American Century, 1919–1963*. New York: Henry Holt and Company, 2000.

Sylvander, Cheryl. *Jessie Redmon Fauset, Black American Writer*. Troy, N.Y.: Whitson, 1981.

Brown University

The Ivy League school in Providence, Rhode Island, that was the alma mater of JAY SAUNDERS REDDING and where RUDOLPH FISHER earned both his bachelor's and master's degrees and was elected to PHI BETA KAPPA.

Bruce, John Edward (1856–1924)

Born into slavery in Maryland, John Edward Bruce was one of America's first black nationalists. He refused to let his limited access to formal education hamper him; he became an avid reader and a well-published journalist and writer.

By the early 1900s, Bruce was making deliberate moves to preserve African-American history. He collaborated with ARTHUR SCHOMBURG, one of America's most impressive bibliophiles and the man whose collections formed the basis of the Schomburg Library Archives at the 135TH STREET BRANCH of the NEW YORK PUBLIC LIBRARY. In 1911 Bruce and Schomburg founded the Negro Society for Historical Research.

Bruce was intrigued by the racial philosophies of Marcus Garvey and committed himself to Garvey's organization. He joined the UNIVERSAL NEGRO IMPROVEMENT ASSOCIATION (UNIA) and contributed to NEGRO WORLD, the organization's newspaper. When Bruce died in 1924, Garvey honored his loyal affiliate with a massive funeral parade that included more than 5,000 UNIA members and foreign dignitaries.

Bibliography
Gilbert, Peter, ed. *The Selected Writings of John Edward Bruce, Militant Black Journalist.* New York: Arno Press, 1971.

Bullitt, Louise Bryant (1885–1936)
A Harlem Renaissance patron who, after being widowed by the death of Jack Reed, became the wife of William Bullitt, a Philadelphia millionaire. She helped poet CLAUDE MCKAY to recover from a severe case of influenza when they were both in Paris in December 1923. Her decision to become his patron and to provide him with financial support appears to have begun during that time. During their relationship, McKay sent rough drafts of some of his work to Bullitt, who also promised to disseminate his work to publishers. She had an unhappy second marriage; it ended in divorce, and she died from poor health soon thereafter.

Bibliography
Cooper, Wayne. *Claude McKay: Rebel Sojourner in the Harlem Renaissance.* New York: Schocken Books, 1987.

Burleigh, Harry Thacker (1866–1949)
A recipient of the prestigious NAACP SPINGARN MEDAL in 1917, Burleigh was a talented and accomplished singer and composer. In 1929 this charter member of the American Society of Composers, Authors and Publishers and baritone soloist at St. George's Episcopal Church in New York City published *Old Songs Hymnal,* a collection of Negro songs with arrangements that were accessible to laypeople.

Burrill, Mary (Mamie) (ca. 1882–1946)
Little is known about the background of Mary Burrill, a playwright who published works in the years just before the Harlem Renaissance began. She attended Emerson College in BOSTON, Massachusetts, at two different times, first between 1901 through 1904, and then again in the late 1920s, when she earned her bachelor's degree in literary interpretation in 1929.

A correspondent of ANGELINA WELD GRIMKÉ during their teenage years, Burrill published two plays. The first, AFTERMATH (1919), appeared in the *Liberator* and was performed by the KRIGWA PLAYERS, a drama group organized by W. E. B. DUBOIS, in May 1928. The play "They That Sit in Darkness" (1919) appeared in *Birth Control Review.* Burrill's writing addressed pertinent social issues of the day, including women's health and reproductive rights, race violence, and LYNCHING.

Bursting Bonds William Pickens (1923)
An autobiography by WILLIAM PICKENS, the son of former slaves, who grew up to become a journalist, orator, and assistant to JAMES WELDON JOHNSON at the NAACP. In this memoir, Pickens, who was an eloquent critic of BOOKER T. WASHINGTON and his accommodationist policies, updates and expands *Heir of Slaves,* his 1911 autobiography.

Bush-Banks, Olivia Ward (1869–1944)
The child of a Mormon polygamist who gave the care of his daughter over to her aunt when her mother died, Olivia Ward grew up in Providence, Rhode Island. Her marriage dissolved, and in the wake of her husband's departure, she abandoned her plans to pursue a career in nursing in order to attend more closely to her two daughters. She remarried in the post–World War II era and moved into a new and creative phase in her life. She began teaching drama at the Abyssinia Community Center in HARLEM and hosted multiracial literary and artistic gatherings at her NEW YORK CITY studio.

Bush-Banks published most extensively in the early 1900s, before the Renaissance began. In 1923, however, her poem "The Great Adventure" appeared in the October issue of *The MESSENGER.* She developed close friendships with a number of notable Renaissance figures, including COUNTEE CULLEN, W. E. B. DUBOIS, and PAUL ROBESON.

Butler, Anna Mabel Land (1901–1989)

An editor, journalist, and poet whose father, John Weaver Land, worked as a hotel doorman and was a published poet. Butler grew up in Atlantic City, New Jersey. During the Harlem Renaissance, Butler published poems in the PITTSBURGH COURIER. It was not until the 1950s, however, that she began publishing the first of her three collections of poems.

Butler, Bennie (unknown)

A drama critic for the INTER-STATE TATTLER, a NEW YORK CITY–based newspaper. Butler, who also contributed society column articles and worked as managing editor, paid particular attention to African-American productions.

Bynner, Witter (1881–1968)

A poet and anthologist who supported the efforts of Harlem Renaissance writers. He accepted the invitation issued by CHARLES S. JOHNSON to judge the entries in the first literary contest sponsored by OPPORTUNITY and the NATIONAL URBAN LEAGUE. He participated alongside other recognizable literary personalities, including FANNIE HURST and ROBERT BENCHLEY. In 1925 Bynner was one of the judges in the Opportunity Prize competition and attended the dinner held at the Fifth Avenue Hotel to celebrate the winners.

Bibliography
Bontemps, Arna. The Harlem Renaissance Remembered: Essays Edited with a Memoir. New York: Dodd, Mead, 1972.

By Sanction of Law Henry Joshua Jones (1924)

A novel of interracial romance in the South, written by HENRY JOSHUA JONES, and published by the B. J. Brimmer Company of BOSTON, the same company that in 1922 published GEORGIA DOUGLAS JOHNSON's second volume of poetry, BRONZE. Jones, who dedicated the novel to his father and to Mayor James Curley, "the man [he] revere[d] and most deeply respect[ed]" after his father, offered a forthright preface to his novel. He noted that the book was, in some ways, factual and that he had used discretion when revealing or shrouding the identity of certain locations. He confessed that his novel was a work of racial outreach, one meant to bridge the gaps between the races: "[h]aving lived and battled in a world of prejudice, knowing that under the skin I was and am no white different than any other human being, and knowing the fallacy of race prejudice, also the swiftness with which race prejudice vanishes when we know one another, I have tried to show how all can dwell side by side."

Calloway, Cabell (Cab), III (1907–1994)

An extremely popular and beloved figure of the Harlem Renaissance era. Born on Christmas Day in 1907 in Rochester, New York, he began to study law but turned instead to music. He became the bandleader at the COTTON CLUB shortly after he arrived in HARLEM in 1928.

Calverton, V. F. (Victor Francis Calverton) (1900–1940)

A white Marxist intellectual, an accomplished editor of the *Modern Quarterly,* and the first editor of the ANTHOLOGY OF AMERICAN NEGRO LITERATURE. Born George Goetz, he was the first of three children of Charles and Ida Geiger Goetz, German-Americans who settled in Baltimore, Maryland. Calverton, who adopted this new name in the 1920s in order to protect himself from political prejudice, attended Johns Hopkins University and graduated in 1921. He began graduate studies there but left to become a public school teacher in Baltimore. He married twice. Following his divorce from Helen Letzer, his first wife and the mother of his daughter, Calverton married Nina Melville in 1931. He died in 1940 as a result of pernicious anemia. Calverton was buried in Loudon Park Cemetery in Baltimore.

Calverton was an earnest political activist whose beliefs were shaped by his family's tradition of outspoken critique. He embraced socialism but during his twenties turned to communism. He established the journal *Modern Quarterly* in 1923, just two years after graduating from college. He served as editor of the journal until his untimely death in 1940s. As Calverton scholar Phillip Abbott notes, the journal featured writings by influential political and literary figures such as Leon Trotsky, John Dewey, SHERWOOD ANDERSON, and LANGSTON HUGHES. From 1934 through 1936, MAX EASTMAN worked alongside Calverton as co-editor of the journal. Eastman recalled that he was especially "proud" of this work and that "Calverton had generously offered him an outlet when no publication would print his criticism of Stalinism" (Abbott, 3).

The first volume of the *Anthology of American Negro Literature* appeared in 1929. It included works by well-known writers of the Harlem Renaissance period such as LEWIS ALEXANDER, GWENDOLYN BENNETT, COUNTEE CULLEN, GEORGIA DOUGLAS JOHNSON, JAMES WELDON JOHNSON, Langston Hughes, JOHN MATHEUS, and NELLA LARSEN. Critics Victor Kramer and Robert Russ credit Calverton for his "exceptional independence of white stereotypes." They and others suggest that it was Calverton's Marxist philosophies and appreciation of African-American economic realities that fueled his genuine interest in African-American literature during the Renaissance.

Calverton was a prolific man who was a regular contributor to leading American publications and an author and editor of numerous cultural and literary studies, including *The Bankruptcy of Marriage, American Literature at the Crossroads, Sex in Civilization,* and *Woman's Coming of Age.* Abbott notes that "there was not a major journal in

America, from the *Nation* to the *Saturday Review of Literature* in which Calverton's name did not appear as a contributor or reviewer" (Abbott, 1), At the time of his death, he had just completed *Where Angels Fear to Tread,* a book-length study of American communist colonies and was in fact "at work on the preface until a few minutes before his death" (*New York Times,* 21 November, 1940, 29).

Bibliography

"V. F. Calverton, 40, Author and Editor." *New York Times,* 21 November 1940, 29.

Abbott, Phillip. Leftward Ho! V. F. Calverton and American Radicalism. Westport, Conn.: Greenwood Press, 1993.

Calverton, V. F. *Anthology of American Negro Literature.* New York: The Modern Library, 1929.

Genizi, Haim "V. F. Calverton, a Radical Magazinist for Black Intellectuals, 1920–1940," *Journal of Negro History* 57, no. 3 (July 1972): 241–253.

Kramer, Victor A., and Robert Russ, eds. *The Harlem Renaissance Re-Examined.* Troy, N.Y.: Whitson Pub., 1997.

Schuyler, George. *Black No More: Being an Account of the Strange and Wonderful Working of Science in the Land.* 1930, reprint, New York: Random House, 1999.

Calvin, Floyd Joseph   (1902–1939)

An Arkansas native who became the associate editor of The MESSENGER and the PITTSBURGH COURIER's New York City editor.

Campbell, Hazel Vivian   (fl. 1935)

The elusive author of two memorable stories published in OPPORTUNITY. In "Part of the Pack: Another View of Night Life in Harlem," which appeared in August 1935, and "The Parasites," which appeared in September 1936, Campbell generated alternate views of the glittering, bustling world of HARLEM. She addressed African-American economic realities, the sobering implications of welfare, and the fragility of self-determination. In "Part of the Pack," she meditated on married life and economic survival during the Great Depression. She maintained her focus on the bleak reality facing so many African Americans during that period in "The Parasites." That story was even more disturbing than her first. It suggested that welfare could in fact induce a shameless malaise, a condition that invalidated racial uplift ideology at the heart of the Renaissance. Campbell disappeared from print following the publication of her 1936 story.

Campbell, T. Bowyer   (1887–1976)

A white Virginia-born author, Episcopalian minister, and history professor who was motivated to write fiction because of the literary endeavors of his siblings. A graduate of the College of William and Mary, Campbell went on to attend the Alexandria Seminary in Virginia. He traveled to Shanghai immediately following his graduation but was disenchanted by the limitations of his opportunities to serve as a missionary. Campbell was one of several white authors to take up race-related themes during the Harlem Renaissance, but his work did not garner much praise or critical attention.

Campbell had a love of writing that prompted him to write creative pieces as an undergraduate. He completed at least one play that his collegiate drama club performed, and he also completed what he described as a "sentimental novel shot through with a religious thread" but destroyed the manuscript rather than submit it to a publisher for consideration (Campbell, 1). He began writing regularly when he returned to the United States to begin a novitiate in the Catholic Church. Campbell blended his love of writing with his faith and published book reviews and religious articles in the *Episcopal American Church Monthly.* In 1930 he joined the faculty at Notre Dame and taught history there for nearly two decades. He later became a professor at St. Bede College in Illinois.

Black Sadie, which Campbell began writing in 1927, was a book that Houghton Mifflin hastened to place under contract before Campbell had even completed the majority of the writing. Campbell describes the work as "a story of Colored people in three social and economic brackets: in Virginia some two decades after the emancipation, in the north as house servants with higher wages, and lastly entering into professional and creative work." Nella Larsen reviewed the book for *Opportunity* and provided readers with a frank and ironic assessment. She noted that the novel, which focused primarily on an African-American woman and her life as a dancer, was "an awkwardly written and disorderly book." In addition to containing "inaccuracies," she noted that *Black Sadie* was plagued by "twaddle concerning the inherent qualities of the Negro" that would therefore make much of the book "very amusing—especially to the Negro reader" (Larsen, 24).

Following the publication of *Black Sadie*, Campbell began work on his second novel. *Ole Miss*, which was based on the life of his great-grandmother, whose life spanned all but 10 years of the 19th century, was published in 1929. The GREAT DEPRESSION prompted Houghton Mifflin to refrain from publishing his third novel, originally entitled *Sweet Chariot* but which his British publishers changed to *White Nigger*. While Campbell admitted that he preferred his original title, it is clear that the press saw the opportunity to tap into the increasing commercialization of controversial racial material. Unfortunately for Campbell, however, the book did not fare well in the British market. According to Campbell this was because "the English people see no urgency in that question" of mixed-race identity and racial assimilation (1). Once he had forged new ties to England, where he was writing and also working in Oxford at St. Paul's Church, Campbell continued to write and to shepherd his books through the publishing process. His last novel, *Far Trouble*, was a "story of kidnapping and mystery" set in China, but it did not sell well in England or when an American publisher published it. The disappointing sales prompted Campbell to abandon writing for the time being. Following his retirement from Notre Dame, which was hastened by his adverse reaction to academic pressures at the school that were brought on by World War II, Campbell returned again to writing. He tried unsuccessfully to obtain a publisher for *Sweet Chariot*, completed a book on Virginia, and began his autobiography.

Bibliography

Campbell, T. Bowyer. "Thomas Bowyer Campbell." CatholicAuthors.com. Available online. URL: http://catholicauthors.com/campbell.html. Accessed May 2005.

Larsen, Nella. "Black Sadie," *Opportunity* 7 (January 1929): 24.

Cane Jean Toomer (1923)

The collection of writings by JEAN TOOMER that was published by BONI & LIVERIGHT in 1923. The volume, which included an introduction by WALDO FRANK, Toomer's mentor, seemed destined to become a best seller. Shortly after its publication, COUNTEE CULLEN wrote to Toomer, announcing proudly that he had "bought the first copy of *Cane* which was sold." Having "read every word of it," he declared it to be "a real race contribution, a classical portrayal of things as they are." According to scholar Charles Davis, Toomer would come to believe that it was a portrait of what was, a "swan song" of the South and of his ability to represent that world in his writing.

Divided into three sections, *Cane* included works previously published in a variety of magazines. The first two sections included short fiction, poems, and vignettes. The third was a lengthy prose narrative about a tormented northern schoolteacher who confronts his racial nightmares and his fears of LYNCHING in the South. Toomer offered nuanced sketches of black life that ultimately revealed disturbing motifs of sterility, predation, alienation, and disregard. In ways, these themes testified to Toomer's own struggles to define himself and assert a humanity and identity not predetermined by sociocultural notions of race and black manhood. *OPPORTUNITY* editor Charles Johnson's assessment of the volume reinforced Toomer's goal. Although he pronounced first that Toomer had emerged "triumphantly the Negro artist," he went on to declare that the writer was "detached from propaganda, sensitive only to beauty" and that he had bestowed upon "the peasant a passionate charm" (Bontemps, 243).

The first section, represented by a portion of a circle that the subsequent sections will add to and complete, focuses intently on African-American folk and rural life in Georgia. The opening piece in the volume, "Karintha," signals the unconventional gaze that Toomer will cast upon this landscape. It begins with the following epigraph that reappears in the text proper: "Her skin is like dusk on the eastern horizon, / O can't you see it, O can't you see it, / Her skin is like dusk on the eastern horizon / When the sun goes down." The inversion of the natural, the fact that dusk is best seen on the western horizon, suggests the elusive nature of the woman featured in the story and hints at a backward glance that, while informative, is not based on straightforward assessment. Karintha, a young girl who is "perfect as dusk when the sun goes down," is a girl to whom the men of the community are drawn. Each generation finds something deeply appealing about the young girl who "at twelve, was a wild flash that told the other folks just what it was to live." By the time she has matured and become a woman, Karintha "carries beauty" and has been married "many times." She maintains her role as the raison d'etre for the men of her community: the "[y]oung men run stills to make her money . . . they all want to bring her money." Yet Karintha, who never speaks in the piece, remains an unknown entity, one who bears the desires of others and whose body only hints at her perspectives on the world. Other pieces in the first section hint at the violence of the South, even if it is presented as a rich, natural world. The short prose piece "Becky" features a vicious community that outcasts a white woman who bears mixed-race children out of wedlock. She dies much as she lives, on the outskirts of town without any discernible emotional or practical support.

The violence of the South only intensifies in poems like "Portrait in Georgia" and short stories such as "Blood Burning Moon." Toomer focuses increasingly on the perilous nature of relationships and the complicity of the earth that absorbs the blood of those who are victimized. Tom Burwell defends the honor of Louisa, the woman he loves, who is raped by a white man named Bob Stone. When he mortally wounds Stone, it is only a matter of time before a self-righteous crowd of whites lynches him. Toomer does not spare his readers the graphic details of Tom's death by a slow-burning fire. Louisa, despite her recent trauma at the hands of Stone, is oblivious to the awful murder unfolding in town and does not hear the mob's noise, even though it "echoed against the skeleton stone walls and sounded like a hundred yells. Like a hundred mobs yelling." That she is impervious to the events is troubling but consistent with Toomer's portraits of women throughout the volume.

In the second section, Toomer shifts his attention to urban scenes and makes specific references to the cities of Washington, D.C., and Chicago. The inhabitants of these places do not fare much better than their southern comrades. They live in a fast-paced and uncaring world, one that still scrutinizes their actions and renders them impotent and unattractive. The title character in "Rhobert," for instance, is a "banty-bowed, shaky, ricket-legged man" who is overpowered by the weight of his house. "Life is a murky, wiggling, microscopic water that compresses him," observes the narrator, who documents Rhobert's inevitable decline. In "Avey," a prose piece that features a first-person narration, the protagonist is still unable to triumph despite the fact that he has a voice. He is unable to charm Avey, who has feelings for another. Even though she does show tenderness toward Robert, the narrator places the burden of emotional connection upon her: "I wanted her to love me passionately as she did him," he laments. "I gave her one burning kiss. Then she laid me in her lap as if I were a child." The tragic ineptitude only progresses, and the piece closes without any satisfying resolution that signals the narrator's advancement or chance of obtaining happiness. The story "Bona and Paul," which completes the section, is an especially painful chronicle of an interracial relationship that does not survive. Bona, an assertive young white woman, has several interactions with Paul, a young man with a "red-brown" face. The two do not survive the real world even though Paul eventually attempts to assert that he and Bona will find happiness. When he leaves her momentarily to confront a "knowing" look in the eyes of a doorman, he insists that he is ready to claim Bona and marshal the richness of the natural world as he celebrates their romance. Unfortunately, when he returns to the place where he left her, Bona is gone, and Paul, like so many of Toomer's thwarted protagonists, is once again alone.

The final installment in *Cane* is "Kabnis," a lengthy work that he dedicated to Waldo Frank. The piece revolves around a man named Kabnis, who is sequestered in a southern cabin where the walls are permeated by the voice of the outside world. As the piece opens, Kabnis, lying on a bed, begins to listen to the noises that come through the cracks in the wooden panels. The "cracks between the boards are black," intones the narrator, before adding that "[t]hese cracks are the lips the night winds use for whispering. Night winds in Georgia are vagrant poets, whispering." The song that Kabnis then hears has a "weird chill" to it and refers to a deadly "White-man's land" where imperatives govern the lives of people of color: "Niggers, sing. / Burn, bear black children / Till poor rivers bring /Rest, and sweet glory / In Camp Ground." Kabnis is uneasy in the South and hardly at home in his temporary quarters in which rats appear and must be killed. As the piece proceeds, Kabnis's experience of the South only becomes more unappealing. He is plagued by the gruesome stories of lynchings and the murders of unborn children snatched from their dead mothers' bellies. When he is targeted directly as an outsider and receives an ominous message that instructs him to leave, he slips into extreme anxiety. The narrator outlines his reaction in staccato phrases: "Fear squeezes him. Caves him in. As a violent external pressure would. Fear flows inside him. It fills him up. He bloats." "Kabnis" ends without any dramatic resolution, a fact that reflects Toomer's self-confessed confusion about the best way to conclude the volume. While the trek through the nation from South to North and back again to the South has been concluded, there is no comfort in the image of a cyclical journey or the specter of closure. *Cane* is a haunted volume, one in which individuals find little peace and are unable to transcend the persistent and seemingly innate violence of the post-slavery world in which they live.

Like CLAUDE MCKAY, LANGSTON HUGHES, NELLIE RATHBORNE BRIGHT, and other writers of the period, Toomer drew material for his work from his own travels and experiences in the South. In a 1922 letter to the *LIBERATOR*, one of the magazines in which portions of *Cane* had appeared previously, Toomer confessed that "a deep part of [his] nature, a part that [he] had repressed, sprang suddenly to life and responded" to the "rich dusk beauty" and "folk-songs com[ing] from the lips of Negro peasants." Indeed, one of the major strengths of the volume is the blend of literary and narrative styles and genres. As critic Harold Bloom suggests, *Cane* is "one of the most remarkable novels of its time because of its prose-poetic language, its amalgamation of literary genres, and its rich evocation of the lives of both northern and southern black Americans." *Cane* still is hailed for its piercing, haunting, and evocative sketches of life in the Black Belt region of the South and for African Americans in the urban North. Toomer assembled a memorable set of testimonies that constituted a powerful record of dehumanization, racial objectification, and a defiantly evocative American culture.

Bibliography

Bloom, Harold, ed. *Black American Prose Writers of the Harlem Renaissance*. New York: Chelsea House Publishers, 1994.

Bontemps, Arna. "The Awakening: A Memoir." In *Remembering the Harlem Renaissance*, edited by Cary Wintz. 1972, reprint, New York: Garland Publishing, 1996. 235–260.

Bowen, Barbara. "Untroubled Voice: Call-and-Response in *Cane*," *Black American Literature Forum* 16, no. 1 (spring 1982): 12–18.

Caldeira, Maria Isabel. "Jean Toomer's *Cane*: The Anxiety of the Modern Artist," *Callaloo* 25 (autumn 1985): 544–550.

Foley, Barbara. "In the Land of Cotton: Economics and Violence in Jean Toomer's *Cane*." *African American Review* 32, no. 2 (summer 1998): 181–198.

Ikonné, Chidi. *From Du Bois to Van Vechten: The Early New Negro Literature, 1903–1926*. Westport, Conn.: Greenwood Press, 1981.

Caroling Dusk: An Anthology of Verse by Negro Poets Countee Cullen (1927)

COUNTEE CULLEN, the editor of *Caroling Dusk*, took great pains to introduce his collection of works by African-American writers of the period. "I have called this collection an anthology of verse by Negro poets rather than an anthology of Negro verse," he wrote, "since this latter designation would be more confusing than accurate. Negro poetry . . . in the sense that we speak of Russian, French, or Chinese poetry, must emanate from some country other than this in some language other than our own" (xi). Cullen's assertions underscored the effort by some Harlem Renaissance writers to have black writers recognized, celebrated, and confronted as Americans, individuals with long-standing histories of industry, patriotism, and excellence. His remarks also revealed his belief that AFRICA, as a conceptual and mythical state, was not the most reliable resource from which American writers of color could or should draw.

The volume, published by HARPER & BROTHERS, included "decorations" by AARON DOUGLAS and was dedicated to fellow anthology editor and poet WILLIAM STANLEY BRAITHWAITE, "Poet and Friend, Whom Those Who Know Him Delight to Honor." The book included writing published in a variety of well-known works, magazines, and journals, and by particular publishing houses. Included in the lengthy list were Dodd, Mead and Co., ALFRED A. KNOPF, B. J. Brimmer, VANITY FAIR, THE ATLANTIC MONTHLY, The Carolina Magazine, THE CRISIS, and FIRE!! The Acknowledgements list alone confirmed for readers the breadth of writing by African Americans, as well as a sense of the patrons and institutional supporters of these works.

Cullen included autobiographical profiles for each of the writers included. The contributors ranged from well-known and prolific artists such as WILLIAM STANLEY BRAITHWAITE, ANGELINA WELD GRIMKÉ, LANGSTON HUGHES, and CLAUDE MCKAY, to lesser-known writers like George Leonard Allen, WESLEY CURTWRIGHT, and LULA LOWE WEEDEN.

Bibliography

Cullen, Countee. *Caroling Dusk: An Anthology of Verse by Negro Poets.* New York: Harper & Brothers, 1927.

Ferguson, Blanche. *Countee Cullen and the Negro Renaissance.* New York: Dodd, Mead, 1966.

Shucard, Alan. *Countee Cullen.* Boston: Twayne, 1984.

Carter, Elmer Anderson (1890–1973)

A HARVARD UNIVERSITY–educated teacher, writer, veteran, and member of Alpha Phi Alpha, who began his professional life as a math instructor at Prairie View State College in Texas. Carter joined the staff of three different national branches of the NATIONAL URBAN LEAGUE before arriving in NEW YORK CITY, where, in 1928, he became the editor of the organization's publication OPPORTUNITY. He held this important and demanding position until 1942.

Bibliography

Fleming, G. James, and Christian E. Burckel. *Who's Who In Colored America: An Illustrated Biographical Directory of Notable Living Persons of African Descent in the United States.* Yonkers-on-Hudson, N.Y.: Christian E. Burckel & Associates, 1950.

Carter, Eunice Roberta Hunton
(1899–1970)

The daughter of William Alpheus Hunton and ADDIE D. WAITES HUNTON, Eunice Carter was a Smith College graduate and Fordham University Law School graduate whose family moved from ATLANTA to Brooklyn, New York, in the wake of the 1906 race riots. She graduated from Smith, where she earned a bachelor's degree, a master's degree, and cum laude honors, in 1921. She graduated from law school in 1931 and passed the New York State bar examination three years later. After beginning a groundbreaking career in the district attorney's office where she became the first African-American woman to serve as district attorney, Hunton became one of New York City's first African-American women judges. Her alma mater, Smith College, awarded her an honorary degree, doctor of laws, in 1938. Carter was recognized for her "distinguished record as an undergraduate . . . followed by seventeen years of public service" and was hailed for the significant ways in which "her brilliant abilities have been devoted to the welfare of her city and have brought high credit to her college and her race" (NYT, 21 June 1938, 15).

Eunice Hunton married Dr. Lisle Carter, who became an executive director of the National Urban League and later received a federal appointment to a post in the Department of Health, Education, and Welfare. The Carters lived at 409 Edgecombe Avenue, one of Harlem's most well-known apartment buildings and the residence that was home to members of the professional and literary elite such as W. E. B. DuBois, the influential scholar and editor of *Crisis;* future Supreme Court justice THURGOOD MARSHALL; and RUDOLPH FISHER, a pioneering physician, medical researcher, and novelist.

Carter, who later became a member and chair of the board of trustees of the NATIONAL COUNCIL OF NEGRO WOMEN, contributed four works to OPPORTUNITY: "Digression" (December 1923), "Replica" (September 1924), "Who Gives Himself" (December 1924), and "The Corner" (April 1925). She also published several book reviews, including evaluations of

Eugene O'Neill's play ALL GOD'S CHILLUN GOT WINGS and Wallace Thurman's THE BLACKER THE BERRY. Carter's literary pursuits diminished as she immersed herself in her burgeoning legal career, which continued to thrive in the years following the Harlem Renaissance.

Bibliography

"Four Women Get Honors at Smith." *New York Times,* 21 June 1938, 15.

Carver, George Washington (ca. 1861–1943)

A 1922 SPINGARN MEDAL winner, this former slave, who was raised by his owner after his enslaved mother was abducted by slave traders, went on to become a horticultural and agricultural genius. He earned degrees from Iowa State College before joining the faculty at TUSKEGEE INSTITUTE. He was recognized for the stunning number of inventions he developed during his research on the peanut and the sweet potato. He used his research to help southern sharecroppers and farmers to replenish their fields, diversify their crops, and harvest larger yields.

Bibliography

Adair, Gene. *George Washington Carver.* Philadelphia: Chelsea House, 1988.

Bontemps, Arna. *The Story of George Washington Carver.* Evanston, Ill.: Row, Peterson, 1954.

Holt, Rackham. *George Washington Carver; An American Biography.* Garden City, N.Y.: Doubleday, 1963.

Nelson, Marilyn. *Carver: A Life in Poems.* Asheville, N.C.: Front Street, 2001.

Casey, Patrick

One of two pseudonyms that the writer, editor, and playwright WALLACE THURMAN used during his career.

"Caucasian Storms Harlem, The"
Rudolph Fisher (1927)

An autobiographical essay by RUDOLPH FISHER, a brilliant Brown University honor student and roentgenology physician. Fisher, who managed to write and publish while enduring the rigors of medical school at COLUMBIA UNIVERSITY College of Physicians and Surgeons, reminisced about his Harlem experiences and encounters with artists and writers of the day. His essay provided a cultural and social blueprint of Harlem in its heyday.

Caught Eloise Bibb Thompson (1920)

A play written by ELOISE ALBERTA VERONICA BIBB THOMPSON and staged by the Playcrafters at the Gamut Club.

Caution-Davis, Ethel (1880–1981)

A 1912 graduate of Wellesley College, active member of the NAACP, and poet whose works appeared in a number of central Harlem Renaissance publications, including THE CRISIS, THE BROWNIES' BOOK, and in 1926, the highly regarded ANTHOLOGY OF MAGAZINE VERSE, edited by WILLIAM STANLEY BRAITHWAITE. Critics Lorraine Roses and Ruth Randolph note that while she refrained from large-scale considerations of race matters, Caution-Davis did not eliminate such issues from her work.

Bibliography

Roses, Lorraine Elena, and Ruth Elizabeth Randolph. *Harlem Renaissance and Beyond: Literary Biographies of 100 Black Women Writers, 1900–1945.* Boston: G. K. Hall & Co., 1990.

Century, The

A quarterly journal edited by CARL VAN DOREN and published in New York between July 1913 and August 1929. W. E. B. DuBois regarded this magazine as one that African Americans should disregard because of the discernible prejudice it had toward the race.

Century Magazine

The continuation of THE CENTURY, a New York–based periodical edited by CARL VAN DOREN.

Challenge newspaper

A militant newspaper, first published in 1916, that provided HARLEM readers and writers with especially outspoken evaluations of contemporary political, cultural, and social issues.

Challenge journal

A literary journal founded in 1934 and edited by Bostonian DOROTHY WEST that was renamed *NEW CHALLENGE* in 1937 and continued for additional years. GEORGIA DOUGLAS JOHNSON praised West's vision, describing it as "away and beyond superior to any Little Magazine that we have yet launched." Years later, noted scholar Harold Cruse dismissed the publication, calling it "very undistinguished" and charging that its editors had failed to observe the real Renaissance. West was an astute editor, however; it was during her tenure that "Blueprint for Negro Writing," the foundational cultural literary essay by RICHARD WRIGHT appeared in the magazine. During its existence, which involved a renaissance of its own in 1934, West and her editors published writings by CLAUDE McKAY, ARNA BONTEMPS, ZORA NEALE HURSTON, and others.

Bibliography

Johnson, Abby Arthur, and Ronald Maberry Johnson. *Propaganda & Aesthetics: The Literary Politics of African American Magazines in the Twentieth Century.* Amherst: University of Massachusetts, 1979.

Chanler, Robert (1872–1930)

On at least one occasion, he was a judge on a panel that included CARL VAN VECHTEN, Chanler's Greenwich Village neighbor, in a lively and risqué drag costume competition at the Savoy Ballroom.

Charbonneau, Louis (unknown)

Author of *Mambu, et son amour,* a novel that Sterling Brown reviewed in the January 1926 issue of *OPPORTUNITY.* Brown praised the work of this French writer, whose novel received the Prix Coloniale for its realistic, rather than stereotyped, portraits of African scenes and the relations between native men and women.

Bibliography

Brown, Sterling. "Two African Heroines." *Opportunity* (January 1926): 24.

Chesnutt, Charles Waddell (1858–1932)

A teacher, lawyer, and writer who secured a reputation as a gifted novelist in the late 19th and early 20th centuries. During the Harlem Renaissance, Chesnutt published such works as "The Marked Tree," a short story published in the December 1924 and January 1925 issues of *THE CRISIS,* and the essay "Post-Bellum—Pre-Harlem" published in 1931. The title of the latter captured Chesnutt's provocative place between two very distinct eras in American and African-American literary and cultural history. In 1928 the NAACP awarded this author of four novels, more than 50 short pieces of fiction and nonfiction, the SPINGARN MEDAL for his "work as a literary artist depicting the life and struggles of Americans of Negro descent, and for his long and useful career as scholar, worker and freeman of one of America's greatest cities." Chesnutt died in 1932.

Bibliography

Andrews, William L. *The Literary Career of Charles W. Chesnutt.* Baton Rouge: Louisiana State University Press, 1980.

Chesnutt, Helen. *Charles Waddell Chesnutt, Pioneer of the Color Line.* Chapel Hill, University of North Carolina Press, 1952.

Keller, Frances R. *An American Crusade: The Life of Charles Waddell Chesnutt.* Provo, Utah: Brigham Young University Press, 1978.

Chicago

An industrial city to which many southern blacks migrated during the 1920s and 1930s. The city was home to the influential *CHICAGO DEFENDER* and ROBERT ABBOTT, its enterprising editor-in-chief, to JOSEPH BIBB, editor of the *Chicago Whip,* and to IDA B. WELLS BARNETT, who took over the editorship of the *Chicago Conservator* following her marriage to Chicago attorney Ferdinand Barnett. The writers RICHARD WRIGHT, MARGARET WALKER, and ARNA BONTEMPS lived and met each other there before moving on to different cities and countries in the 1930s. REGINA ANDREWS, who enrolled at the UNIVERSITY OF CHICAGO, was one of the Harlem Renaissance figures who attended school in the city in which CARTER G. WOODSON and four colleagues founded the ASSOCIATION FOR THE STUDY OF NEGRO LIFE AND HISTORY in 1915.

Chicago Defender

One of the most highly regarded, valued, and informative African-American newspapers in print before, during, and after the Harlem Renaissance. Credited especially with rallying southern blacks to migrate north, this newspaper founded in 1905 by ROBERT ABBOTT paid close attention to issues that affected, shaped, and informed African-American life.

Bibliography

Johnson, Abby Arthur, and Ronald Maberry Johnson. *Propaganda & Aesthetics: The Literary Politics of African American Magazines in the Twentieth Century.* Amherst: University of Massachusetts, 1979.

Chicago Whip

An African-American newspaper founded in CHICAGO by JOSEPH DANDRIDGE BIBB and other colleagues. Unlike its fellow city paper the *CHICAGO DEFENDER*, whose readership was comprised primarily of blue-collar African Americans, the *Whip* catered to middle-class blacks.

Bibliography

Kramer, Victor, and Robert Russ, eds. *The Harlem Renaissance Re-Examined.* Troy, N.Y.: Whitson, 1997.

Chinaberry Tree, The: A Novel of American Life Jessie Fauset (1931)

The third novel published by JESSIE FAUSET in which she attempted to explore the stigmas of illegitimacy, interracial romance, and the tortured psyche of a mixed-race woman in a small northern town.

Fauset wrote the novel while living in NEW YORK CITY and taking an early-morning French class at COLUMBIA UNIVERSITY. She published the work with the New York City–based firm of Frederick A. Stokes and dedicated it to "Ellen Winsor, My Friend." In a 1932 interview that was published in the *SOUTHERN WORKMAN*, Fauset credited her schedule as the primary force that enabled her to finish the novel. "And never would I have got my novel done in such good season if it hadn't been for taking that French course and being thereby forced to get up early every day," she told

journalist Marion Starkey (Davis, xvii). Her diligence paid off; the novel further intensified her reputation as a writer of merit. "If Jessie Fauset's two earlier novels had not already established her as one of the more interesting and important of the Negro novelists," read the *New York Times* review of the novel, "*The Chinaberry Tree*, would certainly do so." She was praised for "writ[ing] with discretion and artistic fidelity" and for refraining from the impulse to "exploit the obviously dramatic or sensational phases of Negro life . . . She has chosen . . . to portray the sensitive and cultivated Negro, whose handicaps and problems, as far as they are specifically racial, have been forced on him from the outside by the accidental fact of his inclusion in a predominantly white society" (*NYT*, 10 January 1932, BR7).

The novel focuses on the lives, relationships, and trials of the women in the Strange family. The surname immediately marks the women as different and alien, and it hints at the twisted and demanding past that continues to impact their lives. The protagonist Laurentine Strange lives with her mother Sarah Strange, also known as Sal, in the town of Red Brook, New Jersey. Laurentine is the child of the long-term relationship between Sal and the now-deceased Colonel Francis Halloway, her white employer. When Melissa Paul, a young, brash niece and the daughter of Sal's sister Judy, "a pretty, rather rawboned girl, bold and tactless," (Fauset 3) comes north to stay with the two women, the issues of paternity, romance, and domestic fantasy come to the fore. Like her sister, Judy also has transgressed. Her social scandal revolves around the affair that she had with a married man nearly two decades earlier. Over the course of the novel, Laurentine struggles to find acceptance and love. She is plagued and undermined by the idea of her illegitimacy. The loud claims of legitimacy, and thus desirability, that her cousin Melissa makes contribute to Laurentine's melancholy. Yet, Laurentine strives to locate the honor in interracial relationships like that of her parents which existed beyond and in defiance of rigid, fiercely protected codes of white gentility and social decorum.

The novel's title refers to a chinaberry that grows in the Stranges' garden. The tree, like the family surname, also maintains the focus on the power of the past and the ways in which it roots itself in the present day. A member of the mahogany family and a tree that is native to China, it is known for being invasive, because its seeds are easily spread by birds and animals, and it is drought resistant. It produces yellow leaves in the autumn and yellow berries during winter. The tree featured in the novel grows from a sapling to a towering specimen, and it is Francis Holloway who brings it to Red Brook from Alabama. It becomes "the visible measure of Frank's love for Sal" despite his inability to openly declare his deep feelings for her (Davis, xxv). Every day, Aunt Sal sits under the tree "on the circular hexagonal seat which ran around it and remembered. Laurentine too used to sit under the tree and thought that she could not remember any time in her life when it had not cast its shadow on the side lawn" (Fauset, 2). Fauset's novel suggests that time does provide women like Sal and future generations with increased opportunities for redemption and public affirmations of their virtue. Laurentine ultimately marries Dr. Denleigh, a man who focuses on the woman she is, rather than on the allegedly illicit circumstances of her birth.

According to some critics, *The Chinaberry Tree* was the weakest of Fauset's novels. While Fauset herself admitted that she preferred her first two books, she offered a persuasive assessment of the goals she tried to reach. "In the story of Aunt Sal, Laurentine, Melissa and the Chinaberry Tree," she wrote in her Author's Foreword to the novel, "I have depicted something of the homelife of the colored American who is not being pressed too hard by the Furies of Prejudice, Ignorance, and Economic Injustice. And behold he is not so vastly different from any other American, just distinctive" (Fauset, ix). The novel prompted many in the Harlem Renaissance community to praise Fauset for creating what ALAIN LOCKE referred to as "one of the accomplishments of Negro fiction" (Davis, xxxi). In his review, Locke suggested that Fauset "handle[d]" the "tragedy of mixed blood" and that she did so "very competently, with conviction, force and reserve" (Davis, xxxi). ZONA GALE, who authored the introduction to the book, reinforced the growing notion that Fauset was a writer concerned with propriety and respectability. "She foregoes the color, the richness, the possibility of travesty and comedy and the popular appeal of the uneducated Negro with his di-

alect and idiom, his limited outlook," she observed. "She has turned to this other field," noted Gale, one "less spectacular and, to the 'General Public' less convincing because so little standardized" (Fauset, vii). Gale also referenced Fauset's sophisticated background and "her American and European experiences" as she underscored the impressive class motifs that, according to her, represented a new and important constituency among American readers and African-American characters. "From the homes of the thousands of the members of the National Federation of Colored Women to the homes of college professors at Hampton or Tuskegee, Howard or Wilberforce," she insisted, "these Americans are trying for a life of reason and culture" and "such people are to be met, not only in New York and Chicago, but in the smaller towns of the East, the Middle West, and the South" (Fauset, viii).

Thadious Davis, who suggests that Fauset's Sarah is a modern-day version of Nathaniel Hawthorne's Hester Prynne, notes also that the novel illustrates "the bounded lives and subjectivities" of the Strange women whose "carefully structured family drama . . . has the overlay of Greek tragedy" (Davis, xxi). Indeed, there are many powerful links between Fauset's novel and others. As Davis also notes, Fauset's use of the chinaberry tree becomes a useful model for ZORA NEALE HURSTON, who endows a pear tree in her celebrated *THEIR EYES WERE WATCHING GOD* (1937) with great social and sexual significance (Davis, xxv). More recently, the children's fiction writer William Miller continued the connection in his historical fiction entitled *Zora Hurston and the Chinaberry Tree*, a tale based on Zora's response to the death of her mother and the comforting horizons that she is able to see when she climbs a chinaberry tree to escape the oppressive sadness of her family home.

The Chinaberry Tree is one of Fauset's most evocative novels, a work in which she grapples most deliberately with the complicated legacies of slavery, caste, and racial segregation.

Bibliography

"*The End of Desire* and Other Works of Fiction." *New York Times*, 10 January 1932, BR7.

Davis, Thadious. "Introduction" in *Jessie Redmon Fauset—The Chinaberry Tree: A Novel of American Life*. New York: G. K. Hall, 1995.

Fauset, Jessie. *The Chinaberry Tree. A Novel of American Life.* 1931; reprint, New York: G. K. Hall, 1995.

Johnson, Abby Arthur. "Literary Midwife: Jessie Redmon Fauset and the Harlem Renaissance." *Phylon* 39, no. 2 (1978): 143–153.

Sylvander, Cheryl. *Jessie Redmon Fauset, Black American Writer.* Troy, N.Y.: Whitson Publishing Company, 1981.

Chip Woman's Fortune, The
Willis Richardson (1923)

The play by WILLIS RICHARDSON that became the first work by an African-American playwright to be performed on BROADWAY.

There are five characters in this one-act play about a family whose patriarch may lose his job if he fails to make payments on a Victrola he has bought on credit from a friend of his boss. The drama is set in the cramped and sparse quarters of the family home, where the "floor is without covering and the walls are without pictures." The Victrola functions as an important decorative prop, as well as a luxurious item that fuels the domestic dreams of its family members, especially Silas, the husband, and Emma, his teenaged daughter. The family conspires to coax their long-nonpaying boarder into giving them the money that he owes them. The family finds out that Aunt Nancy, the chip woman who collects bits of coal and wood in order to raise funds, has been saving for the day when her incarcerated son will be freed. Undaunted by her admirable and inspiring self-sacrifice, they appeal to her for the money that he owes them. Her son Jim appears, gives the family $15 as a way of thanking them for caring for his mother, and then divides his "inheritance" with the family so that they can pay off the collections men.

The play is in keeping with later Richardson plays like "THE BROKEN BANJO" (1926). Like the works of MARITA BONNER, ERIC WALROND, DOROTHY WEST, and others, it is part of the sizable number of Harlem Renaissance commentaries on black domestic life and the various costs associated with social stability and material culture.

Bibliography

Rauchfuss, Christine Gray. *Willis Richardson: Forgotten Pioneer of African American Drama.* Westport, Conn.: Greenwood Press, 1999.

"Cholo Romance, A" Eric Walrond (1924)

A short story by ERIC WALROND written in dialect. Its romance plot and thwarted would-be hero conjure up scenes found in LANGSTON HUGHES's 1927 short story "BODIES IN THE MOONLIGHT." In this story that appeared in the June 1924 issue of *OPPORTUNITY*, the protagonist over-invests in the life of a young African-Indian girl whom he meets. Sure that she is about to be abducted by a white slaver, he choreographs a potentially successful intervention. By the story's end, however, he comes to realize that the eloquent man whom he has thought of as a villain is indeed the father of Maria, the young woman he wanted to save.

The moral of the story seems to lie in its assertion that culture and environment can overshadow, and even obscure, the blood ties between people. It is a disciplinary tale about the danger of cultural and racial stereotypes.

Bibliography

Parascandola, Louis, ed. *Winds Can Wake Up the Dead: An Eric Walrond Reader.* Detroit: Wayne State University Press, 1998.

Church Fight, The Ruth Gaines-Shelton (1925)

One of the earliest published African-American comedies and a prize-winning play by RUTH GAINES-SHELTON.

Gaines-Shelton early establishes the biblical and religious import of the play by naming members of the cast after the biblical figures Ananias and Judas. That there will be tension between "the brethren" and "the sisters" is confirmed through the cast names as well. The women are identified, for the most part, as stereotypes and for the types of behaviors that they exhibit. One of the central characters, Sapphira, is joined by her fellow church members Meddler, Experience, Take-It-Back, and Two-Face.

The play proceeds quickly as the aggrieved brethren descend upon Sapphira's home and try to concoct a "church fight" that will enable them to terminate the services of Parson Procrastinator. The conversation reveals a startling degree of hypocrisy as some of the women reveal that they are willing to lie about the parson's behavior in order to have him fired. Just as they begin to convince themselves that he may be living above his means, and thus shaming his poor congregation, the parson himself appears at the house. In an instant, the annoyed parishioners begin to praise him, and no one will own up to making any allegations against him. The play ends as the group stands for a prayer that asks God to "smile down in tender mercies upon those who have lied, and those who have not lied . . . and direct Parson Procrastinator's feet toward the railroad track." The lack of resolution prompts the group to disintegrate once more, and the curtain comes down before any cohesive and sincere plan for the church can be developed.

Judges EUGENE O'NEILL, Charles Burroughs, and Lester Walton awarded Gaines-Shelton second prize in the 1925 CRISIS literary contest. First and third prizes went to WILLIS RICHARDSON for THE BROKEN BANJO and to MYRTLE SMITH LIVINGSTON for FOR UNBORN CHILDREN, respectively. The Church Fight was a pointed satire on church politics and a humorous critique of human nature.

Bibliography
Brown-Guillory, Elizabeth. Their Place on the Stage: Black Women Playwrights in America. New York: Praeger, 1990.

"City of Refuge" Rudolph Fisher (1925)

Written by RUDOLPH FISHER during his medical training at Columbia University and published in the February 1925 issue of THE ATLANTIC MONTHLY, the prestigious New England literary magazine in which CHARLES CHESNUTT was the first African-American writer to see his works published. This was the first story that Fisher, who went on to write a diverse number of short stories, essays, and novels, published.

A story about black migration, the lure of the streets, and social violence in and beyond the South, "City of Refuge" told the tale of King Solomon Gillis, a man whose regal name belied his need to escape the threat of LYNCHING in North Carolina. HARLEM is the "city of refuge" to which Gillis flees, but it eventually proves to be anything but a sanctuary. The first sight that he beholds when he arrives in Harlem is that of an African-

American police officer intimidating a white motorist. The role reversals are stunning, but they also suggest how vulnerable Gillis might be in this wholly unfamiliar environment. Ultimately, he becomes a pawn in a drug ring, is threatened with arrest, and attacks the officers who want to take him into custody. In the melee that ensues, Gillis realizes that the officer he is fighting is the same man whom he saw disciplining the white driver. The story closes as he smiles, seemingly aware of the ironic justice and injustice of his situation.

Bibliography
Lenz, Gunter. "Symbolic Space, Communal Rituals, and the Surreality of the Urban Ghetto: Harlem in Black Literature from the 1920s to the 1960s," Callaloo 35 (spring 1988): 309–345.

McCluskey, John Jr. The City of Refuge: The Collected Stories of Rudolph Fisher. Columbia: University of Missouri Press, 1987.

Civic Club

An entertainment venue in HARLEM that, unlike the COTTON CLUB, freely admitted both black and white patrons. It was there in 1924 that OPPORTUNITY editor CHARLES S. JOHNSON hosted what became a legendary pre-Harlem Renaissance party: a celebration to honor JESSIE FAUSET and to mark the publication of THERE IS CONFUSION, her first novel.

Clark, Mazie Earhart (1874–1958)

A poet whose poems reflected her feelings of great personal loss. Clark lost her mother when she was five years old and later in life lost her husband prematurely as well. She published her poems, some of which were elegies for the World War I dead, in a number of periodicals and in at least two collected volumes: LIFE'S SUNSHINE AND SHADOWS (1929), for which she used the pseudonym Fannie B. Steele, and GARDEN OF MEMORIES (1932).

Bibliography
Roses, Lorraine Elena, and Ruth Elizabeth Randolph. Harlem Renaissance and Beyond: Literary Biographies of 100 Black Women Writers, 1900–1945. Boston: G. K. Hall & Co., 1990.

"Clay" John Matheus (1926)

A startling local-color short story by JOHN MATHEUS that appeared in the October 1926 edition of OPPORTUNITY. It is set in a southern country town whose black and white residents congregate in the town center on market day. The plot develops as a volatile conflict erupts between an aggressive white man and Dick Rivers, one of the vendors whom he charges with theft. The vendor attempts to defend himself but is left dead at the end of the struggle. The unjustified death of this black man prompts Jarvis Singlreed, the white undertaker who has watched the entire scene from his upstairs office nearby, to be overcome by his fear of an African-American uprising. Matheus suggests that the undertaker's death is representative of a larger and collective white "dread of black rebellion, black usurpation, black self assertion." These fears go unrealized, however, as the market, its black and white vendors, and customers reappear for another day of sales without comment.

Clifford, Carrie Williams (1862–1934)

A native of Chillicothe, Ohio, and a leader in the women's club movement of Ohio, Clifford eventually moved to WASHINGTON, D.C., where she immersed herself in its Harlem Renaissance–era community of writers and intellectuals. She married William H. Clifford, an attorney and a member of the Ohio state legislature, and with him had two sons. In Washington, D.C., Clifford became known for her Sunday salon gatherings, weekend meetings at her home that included fellow D.C. resident GEORGIA DOUGLAS JOHNSON, her aristocratic women's club colleague MARY CHURCH TERRELL, W. E. B. DUBOIS, and others together.

Clifford, an avid reader, pursued her passion for literature before the Harlem Renaissance. She founded in Ohio a literary reading group called the Minerva Reading Club and, with her fellow members immersed herself in writing and the arts. Clifford published two volumes of poetry. The first was *Race Rhymes* (1911), and the second, THE WIDENING LIGHT (1922), appeared during the Harlem Renaissance. She also contributed short fiction, essays, and poems to the pioneering Boston periodical *The Colored American Magazine*, to Alexander's *Magazine*, and to the leading Harlem Renaissance-era journals THE CRISIS and OPPORTUNITY.

Throughout her life, Clifford was a dedicated reformer. She worked tirelessly for political change and was an energetic advocate of female suffrage and women's rights. She did not shy away from using poetry as a political vehicle through which to indict southern apologists of racism, to encourage continued African-American advancement, or to reveal the lingering and unacceptable examples of race prejudice. Even the titles of Clifford's poems confirmed the deliberate and pointed nature of her writing. Works such as "A Reply to Thomas Dixon," a poem that made reference to the white southern author of the pro-white novel *The Leopard's Spots*, and "We'll Die For Liberty" suggest the deliberate and pointed style of her work.

Bibliography

Clifford, Carrie W. *The Widening Light.* Introduction by Rosemary Clifford Wilson. New York: Crowell, 1971.

Clifford, Carrie Williams, and Carrie Law Morgan Figgs. *Writings of Carrie Williams Clifford and Carrie Law Morgan Figgs with an introduction by P. Jane Splawn.* New York: G. K. Hall & Co., 1997.

Climbing Jacob's Ladder Regina Andrews (1931)

A play about LYNCHING by REGINA ANDREWS who felt compelled to write a play about the horrific acts of violence that she found so "incomprehensible" when she heard about them during her childhood. Andrews was impressed by the antilynching activism of IDA B. WELLS BARNETT and WALTER WHITE, the NAACP assistant secretary with whom Andrews worked.

Andrews shared with W. E. B. DUBOIS an early draft of the work about a lynching that is performed while churchgoers worship nearby. He urged her to make revisions. Once he saw the staged work, DuBois wrote to her and congratulated her on a "thrilling" production that had "gripped the audience" and that he had "enjoyed immensely."

Bibliography

Mitchell, Loften. *Voices of the Black Theatre.* Clifton, N.J.: J. T. White, 1975.

Clouds and Sunshine Sarah Lee Brown Fleming (1920)
A collection of poems by SARAH LEE BROWN FLEMING, the first African-American schoolteacher in Brooklyn. Published in Boston by the Cornhill Press, the volume included dialect poetry, race poetry, and standard English forms.

Bibliography
Roses, Lorraine Elena, and Ruth Elizabeth Randolph. *Harlem Renaissance and Beyond: Literary Biographies of 100 Black Women Writers, 1900–1945.* Boston: G. K. Hall & Co., 1990.

Coal Dust Shirley Graham (1930)
A one-act play by SHIRLEY GRAHAM, who later became the second wife of W. E. B. DuBois. The Karamu Theatre staged this unpublished work in 1938.

Bibliography
Roses, Lorraine Elena, and Ruth Elizabeth Randolph. *Harlem Renaissance and Beyond: Literary Biographies of 100 Black Women Writers, 1900–1945.* Boston: G. K. Hall & Co., 1990.

Cohen, Octavus Roy (1891–1959)
A white writer whose inflammatory stereotypes of African Americans and use of dialect in his fiction enraged writers like STERLING BROWN, who saw that these denigrations of black identity made it necessary for African-American writers to provide corrective and ennobling versions of black life and authentic portraits of African Americans.

Bibliography
Kramer, Victor, and Robert Russ, eds. *The Harlem Renaissance Re-Examined.* Troy, N.Y.: Whitson, 1997.

Coleman, Anita Scott (1890–1960)
A Mexican-born writer who grew up in the American Southwest. The child of a Cuban father and a formerly enslaved mother who gained her freedom when her husband bought her, Coleman went on to publish short stories, essays, and poems in a number of prominent Renaissance-era periodicals such as THE CRISIS and *The* MESSENGER. She published one volume of poetry, SMALL WISDOM (1937), but did so under the pseudonym of Elizabeth Stapleton Stokes. Her writing was especially evocative in style and voice. In works such as "Unfinished Masterpieces," a short story published in the March 1927 issue of *The Crisis*, she used the second person to create arresting narratives that engaged her readers and purported to tell their stories.

Color Countee Cullen (1925)
The first published volume of poetry by COUNTEE CULLEN. The volume, which was published by HARPER & BROTHERS, prompted extremely positive critical reviews and enthusiastic outpourings from members of his Harlem Renaissance circle. Cullen dedicated the work to his adoptive parents, the Reverend FREDERICK CULLEN and his wife Carolyn. The volume included a number of previously published works culled from a diverse array of journals that testified to Cullen's prodigious publication record. The journals in which works had already appeared included THE AMERICAN MERCURY, *The Bookman*, CRISIS, *Folio, Poetry: A Magazine of Verse*, THE MESSENGER, *The Southwestern Christian Advocate*, SURVEY GRAPHIC, THE WORLD TOMORROW, and VANITY FAIR.

Cullen divided the volume into four sections. The first, entitled "Color," included the frequently anthologized sonnet "Yet Do I Marvel" and "Heritage," the lengthy meditation on origins, migration, and memory, as well as "Brown Boy to Brown Girl," "Black Magdalens," "Simon the Cyrenian Speaks," "Saturday's Child" and "Pagan Prayer." The second section, "Epitaphs," included an array of poems dedicated to a range of people. Cullen offered tributes to his grandmother, influential writers such as Paul Laurence Dunbar and Joseph Conrad, and individuals who represented specific perspectives or moods. The latter poems bore rather generic titles such as "For a Fool," "For a Philosopher," "For a Skeptic," and "For a Wanton." The third and fourth sections of the book, which were the two shorter sections in the volume, were entitled "For Love's Sake" and "Varia," respectively. In "For Love's Sake," Cullen included eight poems including "If You Should Go," "To One Who Said Me Nay," and "Spring Reminiscence."

The 13 poems in "Varia" included "Suicide Chant" and "In Memory of Col. Charles Young" as well as religious poems based on Judas Iscariot and the Virgin Mary and a tribute to John Keats, the British Romantic poet.

Cullen's foreword to the volume was a vivid 13-stanza poem in which he addressed his readers, considered his own mortality, made a plea for his own biography, and offered his perspectives on how his collection might best serve readers. He characterized *Color* as "Juice of the first / Grapes of my vine," as a "red rose," and as "[s]eed of my sowing / And work of my days." His most explicit directive to readers corresponded with the natural images that he used to describe his work. "Drink while my blood / Colors the wine," he urged, "Reach while the bud / Is still on the vine." Cullen's foreword also revealed his early concern with his literary reputation and the record of his accomplishments. "A little while, / Too brief at most, / And even my smile / Will be a ghost," he mused before asking "who shall trace / The path I took?" His concern about having the story of his life told and passed on is a noticeable theme in the poem. "Who shall declare / my whereabouts; / Say if in the air / My being shouts / Along light ways, / Or if in the sea, / Or deep earth stays / The germ of me?" he asked pointedly. In the last stanzas of his prefatory poem, Cullen encouraged readers to consider the volume as a timeless and incorruptible means of recovering his youth. He insisted that readers "Turn to this book / Of the singing me" in order to get "a springtime look / At the wintry tree."

Herbert Gorman, who reviewed Cullen's first volume for *The New York Times,* was convinced that the book revealed Cullen's "unmistakable lyric gift that is out of the ordinary." He was equally insistent that "it is not often that men of his blood reveal so deep and so modern a sensitivity to the poetic urge, and consequently his excellence stands out all the more vividly." While Gorman's enthusiastic praise of Cullen was merited, his comments reveal the widespread unfamiliarity with the long-established African-American poetical tradition that included powerful and eloquent 18th- and 19th-century poets such as Jupiter Hammon, George Moses Horton, James Monroe Whitfield, and Daniel Payne. Recognizing Cullen's already well-established record of excellence, Gorman noted that "[t]here is much that is arresting here, love poems that are sensitive and compelling and faint satire that is unmistakably piercing" (*NYT,* 8 November 1925, X15). Poet STERLING BROWN regarded the volume highly because it contained the "most polished lyricism of modern Negro poetry" (Wintz, 118). Cullen also received high praise for *Color* from his peers and the recognized deans of the Harlem Renaissance period such as W. E. B. DuBois and ALAIN LOCKE, both of whom were unanimous in their praise for the work and its powerful example of sophisticated African-American literary endeavor.

The wider African-American response to *Color* revealed an intriguing focus on the book's contribution to the literary racial aesthetic of the day. As critic Michael Lomax notes, a number of well-known writers and civil rights leaders praised the volume for its racial commentaries. Jessie Fauset, who described the poems as "beautifully done," admitted that she was "convinced" of Cullen's ability to express "colored-ness in a world of whiteness" and hoped aloud that "he will not be deflected from continuing to do that of which he has made such a brave, and beautiful beginning" (Lomax, 241). WALTER WHITE of the National Association for the Advancement of Colored People suggested that Cullen's "race and its sufferings give him depth and an understanding of pain and sorrow" (Lomax 240). Cullen's debut volume inspired many and revealed the poet's own double consciousness, his awareness of his burgeoning identity as one of America's best poets and his role as an African-American writer at a time when one's representations of race frequently were used to define the quality, range, and power of a writer's work.

Bibliography

Brown, Sterling. "Contemporary Negro Poetry." In *Remembering the Harlem Renaissance,* edited by Cary Wintz. New York: Garland Publishing, Inc., 1996: 108–129.

Davis, Arthur. "The Alien-and-Exile Theme in Countee Cullen's Racial Poems." *Phylon (1940–1956)* 14, no. 4 (1953): 390–400.

Gorman, Herbert. "A Poet of the Plains." *New York Times,* 8 November 1925, X15.

Huggins, Nathan. *Harlem Renaissance.* New York: Oxford University Press, 1971.

Lomax, Michael. "Countee Cullen: A Key to the Puzzle." In *Harlem Renaissance Re-Examined: A Revised and Expanded Edition*, edited by Victor Kramer and Robert Russ. Troy, N.Y.: Whitson, 1997, 239–247.

Colored Woman in a White World, A
Mary Church Terrell (1940)

"This is the story of a colored woman living in a white world," declared the teacher, activist, feminist, and women's club leader MARY CHURCH TERRELL in the introduction to her compelling autobiography. "It cannot possibly be like a story written by a white woman. A white woman has only one handicap to overcome—that of sex. I have two—both sex and race" (Terrell, Introduction). Published when Terrell, a native of Memphis, Tennessee, was in her late seventies, the book provided rich and detailed accounts of her life and activism, and the prevalence of American racism.

Originally entitled *A Mighty Rocky Road*, the autobiography contains 42 chapters that offer richly informative accounts of her early life, schooling, family life, marriage to Robert Terrell, the first African-American municipal judge in WASHINGTON, D.C., and her career. In addition, chapters such as "Notable Lecture Engagements," "With Frederick Douglass and Paul Dunbar at the World's Fair," and "The Secretary of War Suspends Order Dismissing Colored Soldiers at My Request" provide engaging and illuminating accounts of her social improvement work, community leadership, and political activism.

In her account of how she came to join the NATIONAL ASSOCIATION FOR THE ADVANCEMENT OF COLORED PEOPLE, Terrell remembered that she "traveled a thousand miles to attend its first meeting in New York City." Although she was lecturing in the South when she received the invitation to join the organization's meeting in New York, Terrell recalled, "eagerly did I respond to that call. Such an organization was sorely needed at that time," she insisted, and "it was my duty, as it certainly was my pleasure, to render any assistance in my power" (Terrell, 194).

In addition to the accounts of positive experiences, however, Terrell endeavors to remind her readers that she has been "obliged to refer to incidents which have wounded my feelings, crushed my pride, and saddened my heart." She does insist, however, that in spite of these accounts she does "not want to be accused of 'whining'" (Terrell, Introduction). "I have not tried to arouse the sympathy of my readers by tearing passion to tatters, so as to show how wretched I have been. The many limitations imposed upon me and the humiliations to which I have been subjected speak for themselves" (Terrell, Introduction).

H. G. Wells, the prolific English author whose works included *The War of the Worlds*, knew Terrell well. He agreed to become the "godfather of her literary offspring" and to write the preface to her memoir. Wells accepted, despite the fact that he was well known for his "obstinate refusal[s] to write prefaces for books" and his strong opinion that "generally . . . a Preface does a book more harm than good" (Wells, Preface). Writing from London, he characterized Terrell as one who had "lived her life through a storm of burning injustices" and invited readers to "[t]urn over the pages of this plucky, distressful woman's naive story of the broadening streak of violence, insult and injustice in your country, through which she has been compelled to live her life" (Wells, Preface). Wells did seem to contradict Terrell's own claim that her story was unique because of her race. "[I]f she had been born a sensitive and impressionable white girl in a village on some English estate," he wrote, "destined normally to be an under-housemaid and marry an under-gardener, she would have had almost the same story to tell, if not in flamboyant colors then in aquatint. . . . She would have struggled to independence and self-respect against handicaps less obvious but more insidious" (Wells, Preface). He also recognized that Terrell would challenge this idea and imagined that she would retort, "the fact remains that the colours of the inferiority and superiority struggle in Europe are not so intense as in the American scene, that the contrasts . . . see[m] to be fading" (Wells, Preface).

Scholar Nellie McKay notes that Terrell's biography "has much to teach us about the complexity of black life in this country and it helps us to better comprehend the many roles that black reformers, women and men, played in shaping the politics that led to the black explosions of the

1950s and 1960s in the black revolution of [the twentieth] century" (McKay, xxxiv).

Bibliography

Jones, Beverly. *Quest for Equality: The Life and Writings of Mary Church Terrell, 1863–1954.* Brooklyn, N.Y.: Carlson Pub., 1990.

Mary Church Terrell Papers, Moorland-Spingarn Collection, Howard University, and the Library of Congress.

McKay, Nellie. Introduction to *A Colored Woman in a White World.* 1940, reprint, New York: G. K. Hall & Co., 1996.

Terrell, Mary Church. *A Colored Woman in a White World.* 1940, reprint, New York: G. K. Hall & Co., 1996.

Wells, H. G. Preface to *A Colored Woman in a White World.* 1940, reprint, New York: G. K. Hall & Co., 1996.

Color Struck: A Play in Four Scenes
Zora Neale Hurston (1926)

A provocative play about insecurity, internalized racism, and devotion by ZORA NEALE HURSTON that was published in the first issue of *FIRE!!*, the short-lived but dynamic magazine of which WALLACE THURMAN was the editor. Hurston's play was one of two works included in that issue; the second was "SWEAT," a story of one's woman's painful triumph over her husband and his acts of domestic and emotional abuse.

The play opens as a boisterous group en route to a cakewalk contest in St. Augustine, Florida, boards a segregated train in Jacksonville. The group, which is described as "a happy lot of Negroes . . . dressed in the gaudy, tawdry best of the 1900s" includes Effie, a young mulatto girl who is traveling without her partner, Sam. When quizzed about his absence, she explains quite righteously that "the man dat don't buy me nothin' tuh put in mah basket, ain't goin' wid me tuh no cake walk." The train begins to leave as the group realizes that John and Emmaline, the couple favored to win, have yet to board. The two run for the train and with some effort manage to board. It becomes clear that Emmaline is prepared to sacrifice much for the sake of her uncontrollable jealousy. Convinced that her partner, John, was smiling at Effie, she in-

sists that they take another streetcar even if it jeopardizes their chances of reaching the train station on time.

Over the course of the play, Emmaline's jealousy becomes increasingly oppressive. In response, John defends his interactions with the few women who approach them and insists that he is being courteous, not flirtatious. Once the cakewalk competition begins, Emmaline becomes convinced that winning will only make her partner and beau more attractive to the "yaller wenches" with whom she is fighting an endless and often imaginary fight. In a moment of pique, she allows John to go on stage without her, and it is Effie who takes her place. It is no surprise that the newly matched couple then win the competition.

The final scene of the play, set some 17 years later, opens in Effie's dilapidated home, a "one-room shack in an alley." Emmaline is there nursing her sick daughter when she answers a knock at the door. Much to her surprise, it is her former cakewalk partner John. Recently widowed, he has come in search of the woman he loved sincerely so many years ago. He is unfazed by the fact that Emmaline bore her daughter out of wedlock and that the child is clearly of mixed race. He insists that he wants to marry Emmaline and welcomes the chance to become a father to her daughter. The couple agrees to marry the very next day. Once that arrangement is made, John convinces Emmaline to bring a doctor, gives her money for the fee, and sits with the girl while her mother is away. Emmaline returns, but when she sees John with his hand on the girl's forehead, she explodes. Her irrational and poisonous ideas about his unchecked desire for light-skinned women resurface, and she accuses him of preying on her daughter. John cannot fathom the depths of her paranoia and self-hatred. "She so despises her own," he marvels, "that she can't believe any one else could love it." He leaves, disappointed that after 20 years of waiting, he will never be united with the woman he loves. The play closes as Emmaline sinks into a rocking chair and lapses into sobs.

Hurston's play advanced her further into Harlem Renaissance circles and identified her as one of the rising talents of the movement. She reveled in her good fortune and the recognition that she received as a triple winner in the 1925 *Opportunity* literary awards. In what reigns as one of the most memorable scenes of the period, she arrived at the awards dinner on May 1 wearing "a long, richly colored scarf draped across her shoulders . . . strode into the room—jammed with writers and arts patrons, black and white— . . . flung the colorful scarf around her neck with a dramatic flourish and bellowed a reminder of the title of her winning play: 'Coloooooor Struuckkk!'" Biographer Valerie Boyd suggests that with this "exultant entrance," Hurston "literally stopped the party for a moment, just as she had intended" and that "[i]n this way, Zora Neale Hurston made it known that a bright and powerful presence had arrived" (Boyd, 97–98). The popularity of Hurston's play was not limited to the *Opportunity* awards. It also had great appeal to newly formed theater groups such as the NEGRO ART THEATRE OF HARLEM. In November 1925, Hurston wrote to tell Annie Nathan Meyer, the woman who supported her application to BARNARD COLLEGE, that the group was "fairly launched now and the first program will include my 'Color Struck'" and that she hoped Meyer would "find time to come" (Kaplan, 69). Hurston's favorite portion of the play was the opening scene on the railway car. In an August 1929 letter to LANGSTON HUGHES, she asked, enthusiastically, "Dont you think that was the best part of the play? Do you think it could be made a good skit separated from the rest?" (Kaplan, 147).

David Levering Lewis characterizes the play as a work of "searing, complex irony" (Lewis, 195), but others have disagreed. Biographer Robert Hemenway suggests that the play "is an apprentice work," "not an effective drama," and that the "only memorable scene is a cakewalk" (Hemenway, 47). While Hurston's own preference for the lively opening scene may reinforce Hemenway's perspective, the play does tackle the deadly issue of self-loathing. It also explores, quite strategically, the notion of racial performance both through the cakewalk as a form of accepted public racial entertainment and through the socially constructed roles of single-race and mixed-race individuals.

Bibliography

Boyd, Valerie. *Wrapped in Rainbows: The Life of Zora Neale Hurston.* New York: Scribner, 2003.

Hemenway, Robert. *Zora Neale Hurston: A Literary Biography.* Urbana: University of Illinois Press, 1977.

Kaplan, Carla. *Zora Neale Hurston: A Life in Letters.* New York: Doubleday, 2002.

Lewis, David Levering. *When Harlem Was in Vogue.* New York: Knopf, 1981.

Colson, William N. (unknown)

A writer and MESSENGER editor who contributed book reviews to the magazine that A. PHILIP RANDOLPH and CHANDLER OWEN established in NEW YORK CITY in 1917.

Columbia University

The Ivy League university in NEW YORK CITY that was an all-male undergraduate school until 1983. Its sister school was BARNARD COLLEGE, the institution where ZORA NEALE HURSTON pursued her studies before branching out into anthropology coursework with Franz Boas, an eminent Columbia University anthropology professor, in the 1920s.

LANGSTON HUGHES enrolled at Columbia in 1921 but left after his first year. ROMARE BEARDEN studied at Columbia in 1943 and GWENDOLYN BENNETT studied here for two years before going on to PRATT INSTITUTE. MARION VERA CUTHBERT, a Kent Fellowship recipient, earned her master's degree and Ph.D. at Columbia in 1931 and 1942, respectively.

Comedy, American Style Jessie Fauset (1933)

The last of JESSIE FAUSET's four novels and a work based on her short story "DOUBLE TROUBLE," which was published in the August 1923 issue of THE CRISIS. Published by the New York–based company of Frederick A. Stokes, the publisher who produced three of her other works, the novel maintains Fauset's interest in black gentility, caste prejudice, and women's identity. The novel's focus on the anxieties and aspirations of the black middle class led some critics to underestimate its pointed critique of caste prejudice, conceptions of self, and the damaging social motivations that could affect African-American families.

Fauset's novel is fashioned in the form of a play in several acts. In chapters with titles such as "The Plot," "The Characters," "Curtain," and others named after the children in the novel, Fauset chronicles the evolution of a woman whose heightened color consciousness results in much distress and pain for her family. Olivia Carey, desperate to preserve herself from racial stereotyping, places undue emphasis on her light-skinned, ethnically ambiguous identity. She is a character whom one reviewer described emphatically as "a peculiarly repulsive and cold-blooded villainess . . . who wrecks her own and her children's lives because of her half-crazed obsession on the subject of color" (*NYT,* 19 November 1933, BR19). Olivia chooses Christopher Carey as her husband and does so not because she loves him but because she believes that they will produce children who are extremely light-skinned and, for all her intents and purposes, white. Unfortunately for her, this man who "might easily have been taken for the average American" (Fauset, 25) frustrates his wife's claims on whiteness by maintaining friendships with a number of dark-skinned individuals.

The couple's three children grapple with their mother's color prejudice in different ways. The daughter Teresa accepts her mother's efforts to catapult her into white society and does not resist when she is sent away from Philadelphia to Christies, an elite boarding school. She lives as a white girl among her schoolmates who "of course, unquestionably accepted her as white." She is able to maintain her facade without pain, it seems, because "the absence of any other colored girl took away any sense of strain or disloyalty to her own" (Fauset, 71). Teresa denies her love for Henry Bates, who is a student at the Massachusetts Institute of Technology but a man whose skin color and race consciousness make him unacceptable to Olivia Carey. When Teresa attempts to persuade Henry to pass as a Mexican rather than live his life as he has done proudly and with relish, he abandons the relationship. She then agrees to a loveless marriage to Professor Aristide Pailleron, a Frenchman whom she meets in Toulouse while enrolled in classes and recovering there with her mother from her failed relationship with Henry. As she considers her married life and the upheaval with which she must contend when her demanding mother-in-law comes to live with them, Teresa "dwelt in some wonder on her mother's ambitions." She is taken aback by the limits of her life but acquiesces and

"settled into an existence that was colorless, bleak and futile" (Fauset, 183).

The Members of the Carey family, with the exception of Olivia, cherish Oliver, the child whose bronze-colored skin is the darkest of any family member. Their embrace of him contrasts sharply with his mother's denial that he is her child. Her reaction to the child is fueled by the fact that she regards him as "the totality of that black blood which she so despised" and the fact that "[i]n her own eyes it frightened and degraded her to think that within her veins, her arteries, her blood-vessels, coursed enough black blood to produce a child with skin as shadowed as Oliver's" (Fauset, 205). She is shocked when she sees the

Dust jacket cover of *Comedy, American Style* (1933), the last of four novels by Jessie Fauset *(Yale Collection of American Literature, Beinecke Rare Book and Manuscript Library)*

infant child and even more undone when she realizes that her carefully cherished eugenistic plan has been undone by her own body and the genes that she inherited from Lee Blanchard, her long-deceased brown-skinned father. As a result of his distressing relationship with his mother, Oliver inhabits what Fauset refers to as "a double world" (Fauset, 187) that includes "chilly spaces, those blank moments when his mother's indifference, her almost obvious dislike, cast their shadows about him" (Fauset, 199). His paternal grandparents, like his father, endeavor to teach him the proud and inspiring history of the race. Yet, what Oliver craves most is the love of his family. He is devastated when his sister Teresa writes to let him know that her marriage to a white man prevents her from acknowledging her brown-skinned brother and thus her true identity. Eventually, he commits suicide, unable to stave off the awful years of his mother's unrelenting rejection and the accumulated slights that oppress his spirit and deny him the opportunity to express himself fully.

The couple's son Christopher is blessed by his marriage to Phoebe, a steady, self-confident woman who often is taken for white because she has inherited her father's features. "My color is my father's gift," she tells Llewellyn Nash, her unsuspecting suitor with whom she breaks off a relationship once she reveals her racial background. Christopher proposes marriage to her and admits that he hopes that she will be a wife and a companion who will help him to "restore" his father in the wake of his youngest son's suicide. The couple disregard Olivia's "dissatisfaction with the young folk's plan of moving into a street which recently had received a considerable influx of Negroes" (Fauset, 299) and begin to build a life for themselves. When Chris Carey experiences an unexpected reversal of fortune, she opens her own home to her in-laws. Despite his wife's good intentions, however, she who had "welcomed the idea of assisting the man she loved, found herself overwhelmed by the reality of the idea" and becomes increasingly exhausted both physically and emotionally (Fauset, 304). On the verge of an extramarital affair with a former sweetheart in New York, however, she remembers the tender vows of her earnest husband

and returns to Philadelphia. When she does, she finds that Olivia, the main source of tension in the home, has left for France. Ultimately, Olivia is left destitute and friendless in France, unable to take comfort in any of the relationships that she has manipulated so deliberately over the years.

Fauset's title, which quickly proves ironic, enables readers to appreciate the "frustrated, ill-adjusted and doomed" characters of the novel (*NYT,* 19 November 1933, BR19). *The New York Times* review of the work called attention to the fact that Fauset was featuring Philadelphia and veering away from the typical HARLEM and southern backdrops chosen by many other authors. The review, which called attention to Fauset's own racial background, insisted that it understood Fauset's perspectives on race and identity. "Miss Fauset obviously believes," asserted the anonymous reviewer, "that happiness is open only to those who unreservedly accept their racial heritage, and who do not warp and waste themselves in an endeavor to be white." The review ultimately concluded with the observation that the novel "could, however, have been written with more subtlety and skill," and it bemoaned the fact that Fauset's "style is somewhat unfortunate, frequently sentimental, frequently strained and stiff, and in her effort to prove a point she loads the dice in a way that is too reminiscent of the outright propagandist." Nonetheless, the article's author did concede that "Miss Fauset's thesis is a provocative one," that she "handles it intelligently and honestly," and that she "wisely stresses [her characters's] humanity rather than their race" and in so doing "forces one to face their problems as they themselves see them" (*NYT,* 19 November 1933, BR19). Carolyn Sylvander, Fauset's biographer, proposes that with this novel, the enterprising literary editor and midwife of the Harlem Renaissance concluded a substantive and realistic appraisal of African-American social and domestic realities. *Comedy, American Style* is an impressive consideration of racial identities and the politics of African-American domesticity.

Bibliography
Lupton, Mary Jane. "Clothes and Closure in Three Novels by Black Women," *Black American Literature Forum* 20, no. 4 (winter, 1986): 409–421.

Singh, Amritjit. *The Novels of the Harlem Renaissance: Twelve Black Writers, 1923–1933*. University Park: The Pennsylvania State University Press, 1976.

Sylvander, Cheryl. *Jessie Redmon Fauset, Black American Writer*. Troy, N.Y.: Whitson Pub. Co., 1981.

Come Seven Octavus Roy Cohen (1920)

A comedy by OCTAVUS ROY COHEN, a white writer who capitalized on the interest in African-American themes and generated numerous works that included black stereotypes. His play was in many respects a modern blackface show; all of the African-American characters were played by white actors.

Communist Party

The Communist Party in the United States of America (CPUSA) was a political organization that appealed to a number of Harlem Renaissance writers, activists, and personalities. Based in HARLEM, the organization promoted assimilationist platforms in the North and black separatist agendas in the South. Although it made every effort to marshal the political potential of Harlem's black voting population, the CPUSA was a satellite Russian organization. As a result, CLAUDE MCKAY and others realized that involvement with the organization could mark them as agents of a foreign power and make them vulnerable to federal investigation in an increasingly nationalistic America. Individuals who became involved in or associated with the CPUSA included WILFRED ADOLPHUS DOMINGO, editor of *NEGRO WORLD*; PAUL ROBESON, who was stripped of his passport and denied the right to travel; W. E. B. DUBOIS, who became an official member in 1961; and LANGSTON HUGHES, who eventually distanced himself from the organization in an effort to protect himself and his career.

Bibliography

Klehr, Harvey, John Haynes, and Kyrill Anderson. *The Soviet World of American Communism*. New Haven: Yale University Press, 1998.

Paul Mishler. *Raising Reds: The Young Pioneers, Radical Summer Camps, and Communist Political Culture in the United States*. New York: Columbia University Press, 1999.

Compromise: A Folk Play Willis Richardson (1925)

Published in ALAIN LOCKE's *THE NEW NEGRO* (1925), this play by WILLIS RICHARDSON was performed by the KRIGWA PLAYERS, a dramatic troupe organized by W. E. B. DUBOIS. The play is set in the Maryland home of a widowed woman who struggles to defend her family's honor in the wake of a white man's murder of her son. Jane Lee has a bizarre and lengthy interaction with Ben Carter, the white neighbor who pays off her husband, who drank himself to death after his son's accidental shooting. Mr. Lee's acceptance of the $100 payoff constitutes the first compromise of the play. When she discovers that her daughter is pregnant by Carter's son, Jane attempts to broker another deal with Ben Carter. He reneges on his agreement to educate her children, however, when one of Jane's sons defends his sister's honor and breaks her young lover's arm in the process. Carter, a murderer who has yet to "pay" for the death of Lee's son, now threatens to have her son imprisoned for assault. The play ends as Jane sits at the table, fingering a loaded shotgun, and laments her own deadly compromise, however honorable and beneficial it may have been, with Carter.

Bibliography

Locke, Alain. *The New Negro: Voices of the Harlem Renaissance*. 1925; reprint, New York: Arno Press, 1968.

Peterson, Bernard. "Willis Richardson: Pioneer Playwright." *Black World* 24, no. 6 (1975): 40–48, 86–88.

"Conjure Man" Octavia Wynbush (1938)

A "weird story of hatred, jealousy, murder and revenge from the bayou country in rural Louisiana" by writer OCTAVIA WYNBUSH that appeared in the March 1938 issue of *THE CRISIS*. Published alongside the Gwendolyn Brooks poem entitled "Little Brown Boy" and GEORGE PADMORE's article "Fascism in the West Indies," "Conjure Man" traced a tangled history of love and betrayal that culminated in a tragic and desperate end for a lonely woman.

"Conjure Man," like Wynbush's story "The Conversion of Harvey," is set in the bayous of

Louisiana. Its protagonist is Seremba, a widowed woman known now as Maum Semba. Some 40 years earlier, she was embroiled in a tense love triangle as a young woman when she stole the heart of Bob Moore, the fiancé of Amanda Hartwell. Some time later, Amanda marries a man named Wesson, and the two couples seem to have gone their separate ways. Maum Semba and her husband, Bob, have six children, and their youngest, a daughter named Lucille, eventually becomes engaged to Amanda Wesson's son, Andrew. In a savage turn of events that mirrored the betrayal and emotional mayhem in which her own parents were once involved, however, Amanda's fiancé abandons her on their wedding day. Lucille succumbs to the "scorching humiliation" of her sweetheart's faithlessness and dies. Her mother is awfully affected by her daughter's demise and "shrivelled . . . into a mummified version of her former self."

The story opens as a dismayed Maum Semba learns that Andrew Wesson, his wife, and his mother, Amanda, will be building a grand, new home directly in front of her "dilapidated cabin with its run-to-weeds garden in which she had lost interest since the death of her husband two years ago." Outraged by what she regards as an unbearable "punishment," Maum Semba seeks the help of a witch doctor known as Old Elias. She asks him to help her to "get shet of a enemy." He offers her a set of charms for the exorbitant fee of twenty-five dollars and requires that she obtain three items from Amanda, the enemy whom Maum Semba refuses to name. Maum Semba is quite innovative about obtaining the lock of hair, writing sample, and piece of clothing from the woman whose heart she helped to break. Once she does, she is able to imitate the spell against the Wessons, and she asks that the newly constructed mansion burn to the ground. She is overcome when it does, and upon returning to her cabin falls into a deep sleep. When she awakes, she finds that she has been burglarized and that her closely guarded life savings have been stolen. She seeks out Old Elias for help, but when she discovers on his floor the key to her treasure box, she realizes that he has stolen from her and may also have rigged the fire that destroyed the Wesson home. The story concludes as Maum Semba, a broken woman, is forced to realize just how much her jealousy and long-ago seduction may have cost her.

"Conjure Man" is reminiscent of earlier Harlem Renaissance works such as "THE BRIEF BIOGRAPHY OF FLETCHER J. MOSELY" (1924), a memorable story by THEOPHILUS LEWIS, in which a woman seeks help from a witch doctor in order to deal with a frustrating love affair. Wynbush is especially adept at crafting riveting tales of intrigue and southern folk life, and "Conjure Man" is one of her best local-color stories.

Bibliography

Roses, Lorraine Elena, and Ruth Elizabeth Randolph. *Harlem Renaissance and Beyond: Literary Biographies of 100 Black Women Writers, 1900–1945.* Boston: G. K. Hall & Co., 1990.

Conjure-Man Dies, The: A Mystery Tale of Dark Harlem Rudolph Fisher (1932)

A dynamic novel by RUDOLPH FISHER and one of the earliest published non-serialized mystery novels by an African American. Fisher, who died tragically at the age of 37, completed the book just two years before he passed away. *The Conjure-Man Dies* sparked memorable plays during and long after the Harlem Renaissance ended. The writers COUNTEE CULLEN and ARNA BONTEMPS collaborated to stage one of the first dramatic versions of the novel; it was performed shortly after Fisher's death by the Federal Theatre Project.

The Conjure-Man Dies featured some of the memorable primary characters who appeared in *THE WALLS OF JERICHO* (1928), his first novel. In this next work, Fisher focused on the adventures of Dr. John Archer, a physician, who finds himself on the trail of a murderer in HARLEM. Bubber Brown, a former sanitation worker posing as a private detective who specializes in "affairs of the heart" with special expertise in issues involving "cheaters and backbiters" (48), summons Archer to attend to Mr. Frimbo, a conjure-man who was trained in the arts at HARVARD UNIVERSITY. The conjure-man is an African king, who tells fortunes to clients in his apartment above a local mortuary owned by Stanley Crouch, his landlord. Customers seek out N'Gana Frimbo at the third-floor apartment in the 130th Street apartment that he occupies. The building's features are dark and mysterious and "about the place hovered an oppressive silence, as if those who entered here were warned beforehand not to speak above a whisper" (4).

Customers sit with N'Gana Frimbo, the conjure-man who advertises himself as a "psychist," in a "chamber" that is kept "almost entirely in darkness" by "black velvet drapes" that hang from the ceiling to the floor. The only light in the room comes from a "single strange source . . . a device which hung low over a chair behind a large desk-like table" that shines directly upon patrons but shrouds the conjure-man in shadows (6). The novel becomes a murder mystery when one patron discovers that the conjure-man to whom he is directing his questions is dead. Over the course of the novel, Archer begins working with Perry Dart, a NEW YORK CITY police detective assigned to the homicide. Dart represents a new era in the criminal justice system; he is the highest-ranking African-American officer and one of only 10 men of color who serve on the Harlem force. A "Manhattanite by birth," he has a good knowledge of the city, and "having himself grown up with the black colony, knew Harlem from lowest dive to loftiest temple" (14).

The novel takes on a new twist when Frimbo's body goes missing from the mortuary. As the detectives deal with that news, they encounter yet another mystery. Frimbo comes back to life in the midst of an interrogation that is being staged in what was believed to be the murder scene. Detective Dart, Martha Crouch, and others stare "with utterly unbelieving eyes at the figure that sat in the chair from which the dead body had been removed: a black man wearing a black robe and a black silk head-band; a man with fine, almost delicate features, gleaming, deep-set black eyes, and an expression of supreme intelligence and tranquility" (169). Frimbo insists that this is not the first time that he has "outwitted death" and insinuates himself into the murder investigation. The stalwart Harlem detectives, however, suspect that Frimbo may be guilty of murdering his own servant, N'Ogo. The real villain is ultimately revealed, and it is Stanley Crouch, a cuckolded man who succeeds in striking again, killing N'Gana Frimbo, who has seduced Martha, his wife.

Fisher maintains an absorbing narrative, one that, according to one of his contemporary reviewers, "takes on such varied aspects as time goes on that the reader is kept busy wondering who, if anybody, has been murdered—to say nothing of the how and the why" (Anderson, BR 13). As scholar Adrienne Gosselin notes, Fisher successfully creates a character inspired by the legendary detective Sherlock Holmes and one who even outdoes the classic detective created by Sir Arthur Conan Doyle. In addition, suggests Gosselin, Fisher uses the novel to examine the evolving African-American middle class, one that is "[n]o longer grounded in equal marriage or moral rectitude" but rather "increasingly materialist, having fully appropriated the values of the petit bourgeois" (Gosselin, 614–615).

Reviewer Isaac Anderson celebrated the novel and was encouraged by the fact that Fisher did "not make the mistake, so common with Caucasian authors, of making all his Negroes comic" (Anderson, BR13). Fisher's innovative modernist text appeared six years after *The Haunting Hand* by Walter Roberts, which is recognized as the first non-serialized African-American detective novel. Pauline Hopkins, an accomplished editor at the *Colored American Magazine* and author of *Hagar's Daughter* (1901–1902), published the earliest serialized African-American mystery novel. Fisher's work renewed interest in the mystery novel and demonstrated yet another multifaceted version of life in Harlem.

Recent productions of *Conjure-Man Dies* include January 2001 performances at the New Federal Theatre in Manhattan and by the Kuntu Repertory Theatre of the University of Pittsburgh, which ended its 2001–2002 season with a presentation of Fisher's work. Recently optioned by the well-known actor Morgan Freeman, the novel may also become a major feature film.

Bibliography

Anderson, Isaac. "New Mystery Stories." *New York Times*, 31 July 1932, BR 13.

Fisher, Rudolph. *The Conjure-Man Dies, a Mystery Tale of Dark Harlem.* 1932, reprint, New York: Arno Press, 1971.

Gosselin, Adrienne. "The World Would Do Better to Ask Why Is Frimbo Sherlock Holmes?: Investigating Liminality in Rudolph Fisher's The Conjure-Man Dies." *African American Review* 32, no. 4. (winter 1998): 607–619.

Soitos, Stephen F. *The Blues Detective: A Study of African American Detective Fiction.* Amherst: University of Massachusetts Press, 1996.

Connelly, Marc(us) Cook (1890–1980)

A white playwright whose highly successful Pulitzer Prize–winning play GREEN PASTURES (1930) shed new light on the cultural work and racial intervention that dramatists could achieve.

Born Marcus Cook in McKeesport, Pennsylvania, on December 13, 1890, he was the son of Mabel Fowler Cook and Patrick Joseph Connelly, both of whom were actors. His father passed away in 1902, and Connelly cut short his schooling in order to work and to provide financial support for his mother. In 1930, he married Madeline Hurlock, an actress who had begun her film career in the 1920s and appeared in a variety of productions ranging from silent films to comedies. The couple divorced in 1935. Hurlock's subsequent marriage to the playwright Robert Sherwood prompted Cook to note that his former wife was "the only person I know who married two Pulitzer Prize playwrights" (Whitman, D15).

Connelly collaborated successfully with other playwrights and established an especially highly respected name for himself as collaborator with fellow playwright George Kaufman. The two men produced a number of plays, including *Dulcy* (1921), which opened at the Frazee Theatre, *To the Ladies* (1922), and *Beggar on Horseback* (1924). At the opening of *Green Pastures*, Connelly declined to make a speech to the audience following their enthusiastic response to the play. Once he overcame the "stupor" brought on by the "uncommon huzza" that they bestowed upon him, Connelly announced that "[y]ears ago George Kaufman and I made a pact. If either of us dared address a first-night audience, the other was privileged to open fire immediately with an elephant gun. Mr. Kaufman happens to be sitting on the aisle in Row B. I bid you good night" (Whitman, D15). Connelly later focused on films, musical productions, fiction writing, teaching, and traveling. His diverse pursuits included helping to found *The New Yorker*, joining the faculty of the Yale University School of Drama and serving as the United States commissioner to UNESCO and as president of the National Institute of Arts and Letters.

Connelly's *Green Pastures*, a racialized adaptation of Old Testament biblical tales, is regarded by critics such as Bernard Sobel, writing in 1940, as "one of the great and most beloved plays of our time" (Sobel, 389). At the time, some producers declined to pursue the work. According to Alden Whitman, some "feared that the play . . . might offend blacks and clergymen, as being sacrilegious" (Whitman, A1). Although now regarded as a mildly offensive work because of its use of racial stereotypes, the play was a successful stage production that featured African-American actors, music, and choirs.

Bibliography

Kramer, Victor, and Robert Russ, eds. *The Harlem Renaissance Re-Examined.* Troy, N.Y.: Whitson, 1997.

Mantle, Burns. *Contemporary American Playwrights.* New York: Dodd, Mead, & Company, 1938.

Sobel, Bernard. *The Theatre Handbook and Digest of Plays.* New York: Crown Publishers, 1940.

Whitman, Alden. "Marc Connelly, Playwright, Dies; Won Fame with 'Green Pastures.'" *The New York Times*, 22 December 1980, A1, D15.

Connie's Inn

A delicatessen for which Fats Waller was a delivery boy. It became one of Harlem's most frequently patronized cabarets, and LOUIS ARMSTRONG was one of its best-known headliner artists.

Bibliography

Watson, Steven. *The Harlem Renaissance: Hub of African-American Culture, 1920–1930.* New York: Pantheon Books, 1995.

Contempo

The unofficial University of North Carolina at Chapel Hill student newspaper that was published from 1931 through 1934. It devoted an issue to African-American writing and received submissions from COUNTEE CULLEN, LANGSTON HUGHES, and others. Hughes's contribution of "Christ in Alabama," a poem inspired by the SCOTTSBORO Boys case, made it difficult for the paper's authors to host or raise the promised honorarium for Hughes when he went to the school to give a poetry reading.

Bibliography

Bernard, Emily. *Remember Me to Harlem: The Letters of Langston Hughes and Carl Van Vechten.* New York: Knopf, 2001.

"Conversion of Harvey, The"   Octavia
Wynbush (1936)

A tender short story by OCTAVIA WYNBUSH about one young man's efforts to experience a genuine spiritual conversion and his community's response to what they perceive as his hardness of heart.

Published in the March 1936 issue of THE CRISIS, "The Conversion of Harvey" was an earnest *bildungsroman* that featured Harvey, a boy of 14 who lives in a close-knit community that includes his family, his outspoken grandmother, and members of the Roughnecks, a gang to which Harvey belongs. The story opens as Harvey finds himself in the heart of the Devil's Swamp, a place that is an apt metaphor for the place in which he believes he and his soul may be forever constrained. Harvey is a meditative young person, one for whom "the weight of sin and wretchedness" is an awful burden. He, like the majority of people in the community, has been participating in the revival services of the Jerusalem Church. Unlike the members of his gang, he has yet to surrender himself to the spiritual call or to provide "wonderful testimony" of his conversion that could "set the meeting on fire." His resistance prompts a variety of responses. His grandmother believes he is "harborin' some secret sin," his Uncle Butler tries to comfort him by insisting that he "aint in earnest," and one of his younger siblings taunts him with the explanation that "you must go to sleep when you kneel at the mourner's bench, Harvey. You know you're too lazy to stay awake 'cept only when you're moving or eating." He is grateful that his parents, Reuben and Jean, do not chastise or tease him about his predicament.

The whole family attends the last night of the revival together. While they are engaged in lively conversation en route, Harvey "walked along rapidly, head sunk on his chest, hands deep in his pockets, oblivious of the rest of the family." He is painfully aware of the social stigma that will follow him if he fails to accept Christ as his savior and hopes desperately that his prayers will lead to his social and religious redemption. Unfortunately, despite his repeated prayers, the laying on of hands, and the focused attention of various other believers, Harvey does not experience any kind of reassuring spiritual vision. Much to his grandmother's dismay, he is forced to announce to the congregation that he has not been saved. His declaration prompts a major family argument and an unrelenting tirade against him by his grandmother. His father, a usually quiet man who in 18 years has never raised his voice against his mother-in-law, comes to his son's defense. Reuben's heroic intervention forces Grandma Brown to leave the house rather than "to sacrifice her dignity." He then takes his son aside, praises him for being honest about his state of mind, and reminds Harvey that spiritual redemption is not necessarily a public matter. The story ends as father and son marvel at the beauties of the natural world and the ways in which "Jes' as God don' use the same way to make a summer day pretty, He don' use the same way wid us."

Wynbush's story explores the dynamics of southern folk community and presents a moving account of a young man's efforts to conform to the spiritual expectations of his family and world. "The Conversion of Harvey" is especially powerful for its attentive and persuasive representation of burgeoning masculinity and sensitive patriarchy that succeeds where religion and matriarchy do not.

Cook, Will Marion   (1869–1944)

A gifted and successful musician who received his training at Oberlin Conservatory and went on to produce popular songs and to collaborate with leading writers of the day such as Paul Laurence Dunbar.

Born in WASHINGTON, D.C., he began studies in music and the violin at Oberlin Conservatory, his mother's alma mater, at the age of 13. Two years later, he traveled to Germany and continued his musical studies there at the University of Berlin. One of his instructors there was the internationally acclaimed violinist Joseph Joachim. Cook would later study with Antonin Dvorák at the National Conservatory of Music after he returned to the United States.

Cook became well known for the music and libretto that he composed for *Clorindy, or the Origin of the Cakewalk* with Paul Laurence Dunbar. He collaborated with his son Mercer Cook on *St. Louis Woman,* the musical adaptation that WALLACE THURMAN and COUNTEE CULLEN developed for GOD SENDS SUNDAY (1931), Thurman's first novel. Cook composed the music, and his son wrote the libretto.

Bibliography

Peterson, Bernard L. Jr. *A Century of Musicals in Black and White: An Encyclopedia of Musical Stage Works By, About, or Involving African Americans.* Westport, Conn.: Greenwood Press, 1993.

Cooped Up **Eloise Bibb Thompson** (1924)

A play by ELOISE ALBERTA VERONICA BIBB THOMPSON that won her an honorable mention in the 1924–25 OPPORTUNITY literary contest. It was staged at the Lafayette Theatre and also produced by the ETHIOPIAN ART PLAYERS.

Bibliography

Arata, Esther, and Nicholas Rotoli, eds. *Black American Playwrights, 1800 to the Present: A Bibliography.* Metuchen, N.J.: Scarecrow Press, 1976.

Cooper, Anna Julia (ca. 1858–1964)

A pioneering scholar, teacher, and feminist whose works lay the foundation for 20th-century African-American debates about the cultural, educational, and political potential of the race. Educated at Oberlin College, Cooper went on to teach at WILBERFORCE UNIVERSITY, to serve as principal at the famed DUNBAR HIGH SCHOOL in WASHINGTON, D.C., and to found Ferlinghuysen University, a night school for African Americans. Her most famous publication is the 1892 *A Voice from the South by a Black Woman of the South,* a collection of insightful and visionary feminist essays.

In 1925, Cooper became the fourth African-American woman to earn a Ph.D. when she graduated from the SORBONNE, in Paris. That same year, she published *Charlemagne Voyage à Jerusalem et a Constantinople* with a French press. Cooper was a prolific writer and formidable thinker. During the Harlem Renaissance, she published essays in THE

CRISIS and other journals, and in 1951, she published a biography of the influential Grimké family.

Bibliography

Lemert, Charles, and Esme Bhan, eds. *The Voice of Anna Julia Cooper: Including a Voice from the South and Other Important Essays, Papers, and Letters.* Lanham, Md.: Rowman & Littlefield, 1998.

Roses, Lorraine Elena, and Ruth Elizabeth Randolph, *Harlem Renaissance and Beyond: Literary Biographies of 100 Black Women Writers, 1900–1945.* Boston: G. K. Hall & Co., 1990.

Washington, Mary Helen. "Anna Julia Cooper: The Black Feminist Voice of the 1890s." *Legacy: A Journal of American Women Writers* 4, no. 2 (fall 1987): 3–15.

Copeland, Josephine (unknown)

A Louisiana-born poet who published two poems and then seems to have disappeared from the literary scene. The first, "Negro Folk Song," was published in the May 1940 issue of THE CRISIS. It was a mournful meditation on unrealized dreams. The second, "The Zulu King: New Orleans," appeared in ARNA BONTEMPS's 1941 edited collection of poetry entitled *Golden Slippers.* It was a richly detailed poem inspired by Mardi Gras celebrations in Copeland's home state.

Bibliography

Roses, Lorraine Elena, and Ruth Elizabeth Randolph, *Harlem Renaissance and Beyond: Literary Biographies of 100 Black Women Writers, 1900–1945.* Boston: G. K. Hall & Co., 1990.

Copper Sun **Countee Cullen** (1927)

The second volume of poems that COUNTEE CULLEN published and the collection that followed the significant success of his debut volume entitled COLOR (1925). The volume, published by HARPER & BROTHERS, included illustrations by the well-known white art deco illustrator Charles Cullen. Countee Cullen, who had offered his first book as a tribute to his parents, dedicated this volume to YOLANDE DUBOIS, whom he referred to not by name but as "The Not Impossible Her." Like *Color, Copper Sun* included a number of previously published poems that had appeared in journals such as THE Crisis, FIRE!!, *Harper's Magazine,* THE NA-TION, OPPORTUNITY, *The Bookman, The Carolina Magazine,* and PALMS.

The volume consisted of five sections: "Color," "The Deep in Love," "At Cambridge," "Varia," and "Juvenilia." The first section, "Color," began with the poem "From the Dark Tower," a work that recalled Cullen's regular column in *Opportunity* and that he dedicated to *Opportunity* editor CHARLES S. JOHNSON. The highly evocative poem was both an exhortation and a lament. The first stanza began with the promise that "We shall not always plant while others reap / The golden increment of bursting fruit." The speaker went on to assure his audience that African Americans were not doomed to perpetual service, literary or otherwise, for others. "Not everlasting while others sleep / Shall we beguile their limbs with subtle brute," he promised before insisting that "We were not made eternally to weep." The opening poem signaled Cullen's racial awareness and accommodated some of his critics who believed that it was in his race poetry that Cullen conveyed the most powerful messages. Yet, in the volume, Cullen also veered away from producing narrowly defined racial pieces and offered instead a multifaceted set of meditations on art, life, love, and relationships.

A number of poems provided intense perspectives on African Americans and subjected the narrative subjects like "The Brown Girl" to unrelenting scrutiny. The narrator in the poems often acted as a heroic advocate but also was given to acting the role of outraged defender. In "Threnody for a Brown Girl," Cullen's speaker claimed comfort in knowing that the young woman had become part of a new world, one that recognized and responded to her gifts. "Weep not, you who love her," the speaker instructed, "Life who was not loth to trade her / Unto death, has done / Better than he planned, has made her / Wise as Solomon. / Now she knows the Why and Wherefore, / Troublous Whence and Whither, / Why men strive and sweat, and care for / Bays that droop and wither" (ll. 1, 25–32). Now the young woman had gained understanding of racism, social hierarchies, and social injustice; she knows, asserted the speaker, "why fevered blisters / Made her dark hands run / While her favored, fairer sisters / Neither wrought nor spun" (ll. 41–44). Other poems,

like "Colors" and "The Litany of the Dark People" celebrated the power of transcendence and faith that could enable African Americans to overcome the mean-spirited world in which they lived.

Cullen's collection of love poems included personal tributes to Fiona Braithwaite, daughter of the literary critic WILLIAM STANLEY BRAITH-WAITE, and to Yolande DuBois, his future wife. In addition to these, Cullen included poems about the loss of love such as "To One Who Was Cruel" or the satirical "In Memoriam," which critiqued the notion of loss. The poem suggested that such pain was unavoidable but noted bitingly that the speaker realized now that the one who was gone was "the path I had to take / To find that all / That lay behind its loops and bends / Was a bare blank wall" (ll. 1–4). Others, like "A Song of Sour Grapes" were more direct and offered unflinching rejection: "I wish your body were in the grave, / Deep down as a grave may be," insisted the outraged lover, whose tirade concluded with the wish that "your mother had never borne, / Your father's seed to fruit / That meadow rats had gnawed his corn / Before it gathered root" (ll. 1–2, 9–12).

The section entitled "At Cambridge," which Cullen dedicated "With grateful appreciation to Robert Hillyer," his former instructor at HARVARD UNIVERSITY and later a winner of a PULITZER PRIZE, included eight poems that ranged from classical lyric to sonnets on the demands of education and dramatic meditations on confinement. Cullen had worked closely with Hillyer on the eight poems that he included in the volume and the works shed light on the continuing evolution of his craft and talents.

Herbert Gorman, who had published an enthusiastic review of Cullen's debut volume in 1925, was delighted to recommend *Copper Sun* to audiences. In his NEW YORK TIMES review entitled "Countee Cullen Is a Poet First and a Negro Afterward," Gorman suggested that *Copper Sun* "reveals a profounder depth than *Color*" and that the book was enriched by "a primitive naiveté." "There are times," he observed, "when [Cullen] is the more obvious negro poet sentimentalizing about himself and his people, but the admirable aspect of his work is the direct evidence in *Copper Sun* that he transcends this limitation time and again and becomes sheer poet" (*NYT,* 21 August 1927, BR5).

Reviewers in *The Nation* echoed Gorman's lead, noting that "Best of all [Cullen] can forget that he is of the colored race and be just 'poet' most of the time" (Ferguson, 92). Alain Locke, however, phrased it more deliberately in the January 1926 response that he published in *Opportunity*. "Ladies and gentlemen," he proclaimed, "A genius! Posterity will laugh at us if we do not proclaim [Cullen] now" (Lomax, 240). It is clear, though, that Cullen never forgot his racial identity nor divorced himself from the racially insistent nature of the Harlem Renaissance in which he came of age.

Bibliography

Countee Cullen Papers, Amistad Research Center, Dillard University.

Ferguson, Blanche. *Countee Cullen and the Negro Renaissance.* New York: Dodd, Mead, 1966.

Lomax, Michael. "Countee Cullen: A Key to the Puzzle." In *Harlem Renaissance Re-Examined: A Revised and Expanded Edition*, edited by Victor Kramer and Robert Russ. Troy, N.Y.: Whitson, 1997. 239–247.

Shucard, Alan. *Countee Cullen.* Boston: Twayne, 1984.

"Cordelia the Crude" Wallace Thurman
(1926)

A memorable short story by WALLACE THURMAN that appeared in the November 1926 debut issue of *FIRE!!* The story, told from the perspective of an unwitting first-person narrator, traces the devolution and inadvertent moral corruption of a 16-year-old girl who ultimately becomes a prostitute in NEW YORK CITY.

Cordelia is the rebellious daughter of parents who "decided to be lured to New York by an older son who had remained there after the demobilization of the war time troops." She is an especially assertive 16-year-old, "matronly mature" and "an undisciplined, half-literate product of rustic South Carolina." Once in New York, she refuses to attend school or to seek employment and thoroughly undermines her parents's efforts to ease her transition into urban life. Her resistance ultimately means that her mother, who has five other children at home, has to seek day work.

Cordelia develops a reputation as a "fus' class chippie" after she begins spending time at the Roosevelt Motion Picture Theatre that is located on 145th Street and Seventh Avenue, near her home. She has become adept at entertaining and rebuffing the advances of male theater patrons. Those whom she likes are able to sit with her during the show, cuddle, and make plans for "an after-theater rendezvous." When the unnamed narrator meets her, he is encouraged by her response. "[S]he noticed my pursuit," he recalls, "and thinking that I was eager to play the game, let me know immediately that she was wise, and not the least bit averse to spooning with me during the evening's performance." While he delights in the company and "played up to her with all the fervor, or so [he] thought, of an old timer," he fails to take physical advantage of her. After the show, the innocent narrator walks her home. They kiss on the stair landings as they make their way to her apartment, and when they reach the front door, the narrator gives her two dollars. She stares at him "foolishly," as if unsure of the transaction. Six months later, when he encounters her at a party, he is somewhat taken aback by the sight of Cordelia "savagely careening in a drunken abortion of the Charlestown and surrounded by a perspiring circle of handclapping enthusiasts." When he pursues her afterward, he hears her describe him to a group of girls as "The guy who gimme ma' firs' two bucks."

The story provides a vivid image of social life among young people in Harlem even as it explores the more sobering issues of prostitution and wanton behavior. The narrator appears to send a young girl, whom he has described as "physically, if not mentally . . . a potential prostitute," toward an unfortunate life. Thus, Thurman suggests that all can be complicit in social degradation and that innocence can exist on both sides of the moral line.

"Cordelia the Crude" is part of the rich collection of Harlem Renaissance writings about African-American migration and life in the urban North. The startling conclusion also counters the stereotypical image of inevitable sexual depravity.

Bibliography

Perkins, Huel. "Renaissance 'Renegade': Wallace Thurman," *Black World* 25, no. 4 (1976): 29–35.

Singh, Amritjit, and Daniel Scott, eds. *The Collected Writings of Wallace Thurman: A Harlem Renaissance Reader.* New Brunswick, N.J.: Rutgers University Press, 2003.

Wright, Shirley Haynes. *A Study of the Fiction of Wallace Thurman.* Ann Arbor, Mich.: University Microfilms International, 1983.

"Corner, The" Eunice Hunton Carter (1925)

"The Corner" was one of several prose narratives that EUNICE HUNTON CARTER, a successful lawyer and noted feminist, published in OPPORTUNITY during the Harlem Renaissance. In it, she considers the ways in which the true riches and splendor of HARLEM escape those like her friend who lives ensconced in a "doll's house of white enamel and soft blues." She also observes the ways in which "alien pleasure seekers" who drive in for entertainment fail to appreciate the "life" of the black city. "They had missed a chance of seeing life when they didn't stop and watch the boy on the corner who for clapping companions in front of the drug store was doing a dance that was a bit of Buck and Wing, a bit of 'Charleston' and many other things," she notes. She finally abandons her post in her friend's home, lured down to the street by the "heated argument" about philosophy in which a group of college students are completely engaged. The piece ends with a final lament about the cultural invasion of Harlem. The speaker sees another lot of "pleasure seekers" whom she is convinced "heard nothing but their own maudlin laughter, they saw nothing but their own vacuous faces. They passed on to the cabarets," she writes, "illegitimate offspring of their own resorts, looking for life, Harlem life, and blindly, feverishly rushing by it."

Cotter, Joseph Seamon, Jr. (1895–1919)

A poet and playwright whose great promise as a writer was cut short when, at the age of 24, he committed suicide rather than die of tuberculosis. The son of JOSEPH COTTER, SR., an established poet and friend of Paul Laurence Dunbar, he wrote most of his poems while he battled the sickness he had contracted while studying at FISK UNIVERSITY. Before his death, he published a collection of poems entitled *The Band of Gideon* (1918) and a one-act play *On the Fields of France* in THE CRISIS.

Bibliography

Payne, James, ed. *Complete Poems: Joseph Seamon Cotter, Jr.* Athens: University of Georgia Press, 1990.

Cotter, Joseph Seamon, Sr. (1861–1946)

An industrious teacher and poet who overcame great odds to become a respected school administrator and published poet. A mixed-race child whose father was a wealthy, white Louisville citizen, Cotter inherited his love of literature from his mother. His friendship with Paul Laurence Dunbar encouraged him to write and to incorporate dialect into his works. The father of JOSEPH SEAMON COTTER, JR., outlived his son, an aspiring poet, who died tragically in 1919. During the Harlem Renaissance, the 77-year old Cotter Sr., an author of plays, poems, and autobiographical musings, published a volume of his collected poems. One year later, he published another volume entitled *Sequel to the 'Pied Piper of Hamelin' and Other Poems* (1939).

Bibliography

Shockley, Ann Allen. "Joseph S. Cotter, Sr.: Biographical Sketch of a Black Louisville Bard." *College Language Association Journal* 18 (1975): 327–340.

Cotton Club

One of the best-known clubs of the Harlem Renaissance, the Cotton Club was an exclusive establishment that catered almost exclusively to whites. As historian Steven Watson notes, the club provided whites with a highly regulated opportunity to experience African-American culture. It was only out of respect for DUKE ELLINGTON, one of its most highly respected and long-standing performers, that the club relaxed its segregationist policy. Located on Lenox Avenue, the Cotton Club presented stunning shows featuring African-American performers such as Ethel Waters, CAB CALLOWAY, and other well-known artists of the day.

Bibliography

Watson, Steven. *The Harlem Renaissance: Hub of African-American Culture, 1920–1930.* New York: Pantheon Books, 1995.

"Coulev' Endormi" John Matheus (1929)

A tale of an exotic dancer whose performances prompt comparisons to a *coulev endormi,* or sleeping serpent. Written by JOHN MATHEUS and published in the December 1929 issue of OPPORTUNITY, the story is set in HAITI and relates the story of a mysterious woman whose sensuous performances in a bar prove to be inspired by her tragic love life. Matheus creates a number of nameless archetypes in this story about desire, voyeurism, and sexual objectification.

Cowdery, Mae Virginia (ca. 1909–1953)

A PHILADELPHIA native whose works caught the attention of leading Harlem Renaissance figures including LANGSTON HUGHES, CHARLES S. JOHNSON, and ALAIN LOCKE. In 1927, at the age of 18, she won the Krigwa Poem Prize and had already seen three poems published in BLACK OPALS, the Philadelphia-based African-American literary magazine. She went to New York to study at the PRATT INSTITUTE and while there immersed herself in the lively arts and literature circles of the Renaissance. She published works in the major black periodicals of the era, THE CRISIS and OPPORTUNITY, and was also featured in respected anthologies including CHARLES S. JOHNSON's EBONY AND TOPAZ (1927) and BENJAMIN BRAWLEY's edition of The Negro Genius (1939). In 1936 Alpress, the same Philadelphia publisher who printed the works of BESSIE CALHOUN BIRD, another Philadelphia poet and member of the Black Opals literary circle, published her volume, WE LIFT OUR VOICES AND OTHER POEMS. Cowdery committed suicide in 1953.

Bibliography

Roses, Lorraine Elena, and Ruth Elizabeth Randolph. *Harlem Renaissance and Beyond: Literary Biographies of 100 Black Women Writers, 1900–1945.* Boston: G. K. Hall & Co., 1990.

Crane, (Harold) Hart (1899–1932)

A highly respected poet and writer who, like a number of other well-known white writers of the time, began to incorporate African-American characters and themes into his work as the Harlem Renaissance began to thrive. Crane is best known for his ambitious work "The Bridge," a poem completed in 1930 that represents his efforts to combine modernism, American romanticism, and symbolist and post-impressionist styles.

Born in Garretsville, Ohio, in 1899, Crane was the only child of Clarence Arthur and Grace Hart Crane. In 1909, the marital problems of his parents resulted in his relocation to Cleveland to live with his grandmother. Crane suffered greatly as a result of his parents' intense emotional conflict, and as a young man, he struggled with depression and alcoholism. In 1932, morose and alone, while sailing from Veracruz to New York, he jumped overboard and drowned.

In 1915, he published his first poem, and shortly thereafter he journeyed to NEW YORK CITY with a family friend in the hope that he could immerse himself in the literary world and improve his writing. He did so without financial support from his father, who did not approve of his vocation. Crane struggled to provide for himself and even returned home to work in one of his father's Akron, Ohio, shops. Tensions prompted him to abandon that job, however, and he decided to pursue journalism instead.

One of Crane's most evocative poems is "Black Tambourine," a work in which he establishes parallels between the life of the narrator and that of an African-American man who is relegated to obscurity in a cellar. Crane's focus on the plight of African Americans was influenced by his proximity to the chefs and waiters who worked in the Cleveland tearoom and shop that his father ran. As Crane biographer Philip Horton notes, the "only diversion left to [Crane] during the dark, monotonous days in the basement was the society of the Negro waiters and chefs in the kitchen." "He enjoyed their high animal spirits and rich humor," suggests Horton, "and was in the habit of taking coffee and toast with them each morning during their breakfast hour, though he himself prepared his own breakfast at home before leaving for work" (Horton, 89–90). Crane saw parallels between himself and African Americans who so often had to contend with alienation and exclusion. In a letter to friend Gorham Munson, he explained that "Black Tambourine" was "a description and bundle of insinuations, suggestions bearing on the negro's place somewhere between man and beast." "The value of the poem," he confessed, "is only, to me, in what a painter would call its 'tactile' quality,—an entirely aesthetic feature. A propagandist for either side of the negro question could find anything he wanted to in it. My only declaration in it is that I find the negro (in the popular mind) sentimentally or brutally 'placed' in this midkingdom" (Hammer and Weber, 64).

Crane was part of the literary group that included SHERWOOD ANDERSON, WALDO FRANK, VAN WYCK BROOKS, and James Oppenheim, cofounders of the journal *SEVEN ARTS*. Frank, with whom Crane had a close friendship, published a posthumous collection of Crane's poems in 1933. In 1937 Phillip Horton published a biography that was enriched by contributions from Crane's estranged mother and from his correspondence.

Bibliography

Hammer, Langdon, and Brom Weber, eds. *O My Land, My Friends: The Selected Letters of Hart Crane.* New York: Four Walls Eight Windows, 1997.

Brown, Susan Jenkins. *Robber Rocks: Letters and Memories of Hart Crane, 1923–1932.* Middletown, Conn.: Wesleyan University Press, 1969.

Fisher, Clive. *Hart Crane: A Life.* New Haven, Conn.: Yale University Press, 2002.

Horton, Philip. *Hart Crane: The Life of an American Poet.* New York: Viking Press, 1957.

Unterecker, John. *Voyager: A Life of Hart Crane.* New York, Farrar, Straus and Giroux, 1969.

Crigwa Players

A theater group that W. E. B. DUBOIS founded in the 1920s with the help of the librarian and playwright REGINA ANDREWS and the writer and artist GWENDOLYN BENNETT.

The word *Crigwa* was an acronym for "*Crisis* Guild of Writers and Artists," a phrase that asserted DuBois's connection to *THE CRISIS.* The name of the group also underscored the importance of the arts and the support that the official journal of the NATIONAL ASSOCIATION FOR THE ADVANCEMENT OF COLORED PEOPLE offered to aspiring writers.

The troupe, which met in the basement of the 135th Street Library, received support from the branch librarian ERNESTINE ROSE. The group, which soon changed its name to KRIGWA PLAYERS, later became the HARLEM EXPERIMENTAL THEATRE.

See also KRIGWA PLAYERS.

Bibliography

Mitchell, Loften. *Voices of the Black Theatre.* Clifton, N.J.: J. T. White, 1975.

Crisis, The

The first of the three influential New York City–based African-American periodicals that flourished during the Harlem Renaissance. Founded in 1910 and edited for 24 years by W. E. B. DUBOIS, the magazine was an invaluable forum in which writers, artists, politicians, and intellectuals of all races could publish their work, debate the issues of the day, and mark the significant achievements of the day. Hailed by David Levering Lewis, DuBois's biographer, as "one of the most remarkable journals of opinion and propaganda in America," *The Crisis* had more than 100,000 readers during its peak years.

Like the journal *OPPORTUNITY* that was the official magazine of the NATIONAL URBAN LEAGUE,

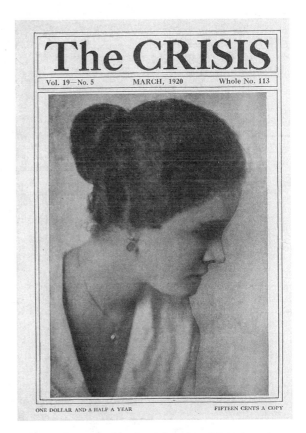

Portrait of Georgia Douglas Johnson published on the cover of the September 1927 issue of *The Crisis,* New York National Association for the Advancement of Colored People *(Yale Collection of American Literature, Beinecke Rare Book and Manuscript Library)*

The Crisis was the publication produced by and for the NATIONAL ASSOCIATION FOR THE ADVANCEMENT OF COLORED PEOPLE (NAACP). During the Harlem Renaissance, its staff was made up of talented and multifaceted writers and thinkers, including JESSIE FAUSET, the visionary and perceptive literary editor, AUGUSTUS GRANVILLE DILL, coeditor of *The BROWNIES' BOOK* with Fauset. The journal established an extremely popular and rewarding annual literary competition whose winners included LANGSTON HUGHES and COUNTEE CULLEN. In 1924 the magazine began awarding the Amy Einstein Spingarn Prizes in Literature and Art, a prestigious award endowed by Spingarn that further recognized the talent and potential of African-American writers.

Bibliography

Lewis, David Levering. *W. E. B. Du Bois: The Fight For Equality and the American Century, 1919–1963.* New York: Henry Holt and Company, 2000.

Wilson, Sondra Kathryn, ed. *The Crisis Reader: Stories, Poetry, and Essays from the N.A.A.C.P.'s Crisis Magazine.* New York: The Modern Library, 1999.

Crisis Guild of Writers and Artists

The drama troupe established by W. E. B. DuBois with help from REGINA ANDREWS. The acronym *Crigwa* in the name "CRIGWA PLAYERS" was derived from this group. It was later changed to *Krigwa*.

Crisis prizes in literature and art

Awards that *THE CRISIS*, the official publication of the NATIONAL ASSOCIATION FOR THE ADVANCEMENT OF COLORED PEOPLE, awarded in 1925 for the first time. These prizes, which solicited submissions from aspiring and established artists and writers, acknowledged, encouraged, and celebrated the works of African Americans. JOEL and AMY SPINGARN provided the first funds for the competition when they sent $300 to *Crisis* editor W. E. B. DuBois for the prizes.

DuBois was the first to develop the idea of literary prizes. Yet, his competitor, *OPPORTUNITY* editor CHARLES S. JOHNSON, who in September 1924 announced that his journal would be holding a

prize competition, preempted him. According to David Levering Lewis, DuBois's biographer, Johnson's usurpation of the idea "was an early example of [his] gloved ruthlessness. For the pragmatic sociologist who believed that 'literature has always been a great liaison between races,'" notes Lewis, "appropriation of a rival's idea was hardly even a misdemeanor if it promoted racial progress through the arts" (Lewis, 97–98).

DuBois and his indispensable associate JESSIE FAUSET endeavored also to recognize formally the work of artists as well. In 1925 the prizes were awarded in the categories of short stories, poetry, plays, and essays. By 1927 the prizes were given only in two categories: poetry and literary art and expression. In 1928 *The Crisis* was soliciting submissions for the Charles Waddell Chesnutt Honoraria, which provided winners with a substantial $50 prize each month. As scholar Cary Wintz notes in his study of the period, *The Crisis* intensified further its support for writers when it "persuaded a number of black banks and insurance companies to fund 'economic' prizes for literary and artistic creations that portrayed black economic development" (Wintz, 144).

The prestige that accompanied the award was generated in large part by the esteemed judges that served on the prize committees. *The Crisis* assembled interracial panels that included literary stars, race leaders, and political activists. DuBois also included newly established Harlem Renaissance writers and artists. In 1925, judges included WILLIAM STANLEY BRAITHWAITE, LESLIE PINCKNEY HILL, SINCLAIR LEWIS, MARY WHITE OVINGTON, and JOEL SPINGARN. In 1926, judges included CHARLES CHESNUTT, Otelia Cromwell, JAMES WELDON JOHNSON, and LANGSTON HUGHES.

Winners of *The Crisis* prizes received considerable attention, and many were able to capitalize on the celebrity and attention to their works. Winners, many of whom also won prizes in the *Opportunity* contests also, included MARITA BONNER, ARNA BONTEMPS, ANITA SCOTT COLEMAN, COUNTEE CULLEN, GEORGIA DOUGLAS JOHNSON, JOHN MATHEUS, EFFIE LEE NEWSOME, and EDWARD SILVERA. In addition to first, second, and third prizes, the judges dispensed "honorable mention" awards. In so doing, they broadened the scope of the competition and were able to endorse and to acknowledge the efforts of many writers. Access to the works of lesser-known writers of the Harlem Renaissance is made possible, in part, because their work was recognized and subsequently published in *The Crisis*.

Bibliography

Lewis, David Levering. *When Harlem Was in Vogue*. New York: Knopf, 1981.

Wintz, Cary. *Black Culture and the Harlem Renaissance*. Houston: Rice University Press, 1988.

"Criteria of Negro Art" Symposium (1926)

The series of published articles solicited by W. E. B. DuBois and facilitated by JESSIE FAUSET during DuBois's editorship at *The Crisis*.

The series appeared over a period of seven months and seven issues in 1926. It was inspired by "Criteria for Negro Art," the impassioned lecture that DuBois delivered at the 1926 annual conference of the NATIONAL ASSOCIATION FOR THE ADVANCEMENT OF COLORED PEOPLE. DuBois called for a responsible racially conscious and uplifting tradition of art and literature and protested the notion that African Americans could afford to produce art simply for the sake of doing so. The *Crisis* series was an effort to stimulate further discussion of the need for substantial, politically effective, and refined art rather than reckless, self-indulgent, racially irresponsible art that could impede, rather than enhance, the efforts of DuBois and others to secure respect and rights for the race.

DuBois and Jessie Fauset, the literary editor at *Crisis*, distributed questionnaires to 20 white and African-American writers and scholars. The respondents represented a wide range of influential publishers, writers, and scholars. The group included COUNTEE CULLEN, JOHN FARRAR, DUBOSE HEYWARD, ALFRED KNOPF, SINCLAIR LEWIS, H. L. MENCKEN, JOEL SPINGARN, CARL VAN VECHTEN, and WALTER WHITE.

Bibliography

Lewis, David Levering. *W. E. B. Du Bois: The Fight for Equality and the American Century, 1919–1963*. New York: Henry Holt and Company, 2000.

"Cross Crossings Cautiously" Anita Scott Coleman (1930)

Published in the June 1930 issue of *OPPORTUNITY*, this short story by ANITA SCOTT COLEMAN was a tragic tale of African-American vulnerability and white paranoia. Sam Timons is an unwitting victim when he sympathizes with an outspoken little girl whose neglectful parents refuse to take her to the circus. Having told their child that she can go if she can find a companion, young Claudia persuades Sam to take her. The two set off, and Sam ignores the sinking feeling he has as he passes railroad warning signs that advise pedestrians and other travelers to "Cross Crossings Cautiously." The advice, as it is soon revealed, pertains to more than the danger of passing trains. Timons is spotted holding hands with the child, and the incident is reported to the child's mother, who immediately feigns fear and anxiety. Coleman includes no details of Sam's LYNCHING and chooses to focus instead on the innocence of the little girl who wonders about the whereabouts of her "circus man" and is wholly unaware of the murderous act of racism that has been committed in her name.

Crowninshield, Francis (Frank) Welch (1872–1947)

As editor of *VANITY FAIR* during the 1920s and 1930s, Frank Crowninshield oversaw the earliest publication of African-American writers, art, and images in a mainstream American magazine. His decision to publish writers such as COUNTEE CULLEN contributed immensely to the national reputation of Harlem Renaissance figures.

Born in Paris on June 24, 1872, he was one of three children born to Helen Fairbanks and Frederic Crowninshield, a painter and art instructor whose appointments included the museum school at Boston's Museum of Fine Arts. In the late 1890s, when he was in his early thirties, Frank Crowninshield, became the publisher of the *Bookman*, a literary review. By 1900, he had become an assistant editor of the magazine. Before joining *Vanity Fair*, he worked also at *Munsey's Magazine* as an assistant editor and then at CENTURY MAGAZINE as the art editor. He never married, believing that "[m]arried men . . . make very poor husbands" but also, according to his secretary Jeanne Ballot, because he "felt as if he had to make every girl in the world feel as if she were the only girl in the world" (Amory, 138).

Crowninshield was the first editor of *Vanity Fair.* His tenure began in 1914, shortly after the publishing house of Condé Nast founded the magazine as *Dress and Vanity Fair* in 1913. He continued in the post until 1936 and, according to Cleveland Amory, oversaw the magazine's evolution into "the central rendezvous of a Café Society without the Café" (Amory, 137). He had strong connections in the literary world, most notably his relationship with poet Edna St. Vincent Millay, for whom he became a longtime and influential patron. In addition to providing key emotional support, Crowninshield also published Millay's work, under her pseudonym, in *Vanity Fair.* A collector of contemporary art, Crowninshield in 1929 became a founder of the Museum of Modern Art in New York City.

Crowninshield came to be regarded as "the last of Society's acknowledged 'arbiters' " (Amory, 20) and as "the last of the species known as 'gentleman'" (Amory, 20). Just two years before he died, he lamented the current social trends that were leading to the end of "real Society." "Nowadays the only qualification for membership," he noted, "is to own, or rent, a dress suit—and soon we won't even do that" (Amory, 20). He died in 1947. Following the funeral in the St. James Episcopal Church in New York City, he was buried in the historic Mount Auburn Cemetery in Cambridge, Massachusetts.

Bibliography

Amory, Cleveland. *Who Killed Society?* New York: Harper & Brothers, 1960.

Cheney, Anne. *Millay in Greenwich Village.* University: The University of Alabama Press, 1975.

C'ruiter John Matheus (1926)

A 1926 play by JOHN MATHEUS in which the younger generation in a family of sharecroppers in rural Georgia heeds the call of northern recruiters and prepares to join the great black migration. Matheus's play was part of a substantial migration literature produced in post–Civil War America.

Matheus develops only four characters in this play. By keeping the cast to a minimum, he is able to hone in on the emotional and domestic implications of the migration, the hardships, and the cherished aspects of black southern life. Sonny, the 23-year-old grandson of Granny, knows that he has a chance to better himself and provide for his young wife if he goes to work in a Detroit munitions factory. He eventually succeeds in coaxing his grandmother to join them, but at the last minute, when she realizes that the family dog has to be left behind, she refuses to go. The scene closes with the haunting image of the elderly woman sitting alone in her cabin.

Cullen, Countee Porter (1903–1946)

A literary prodigy whose early intellectual prowess and stunning publication record represented the best of the Harlem Renaissance. A poet, playwright, author of children's books, and novelist, Cullen acquired impressive honors during his relatively short but entirely productive literary career. By the time of his untimely death at the age of 42 in 1946, he had energized the American literary scene, documented key social and cultural trends of the times, and contributed undeniably to the richness and diversity of the era.

Cullen was the adopted son of the Reverend FREDERICK CULLEN, a civil rights activist, the president of the Harlem branch of the National Association for the Advancement of Colored People, and an influential minister of the Salem Methodist Episcopal Church in New York, and his wife, Carolyn Belle Mitchell Cullen. He joined the Cullen family after the death of Amanda Porter, the woman whom some scholars identify as his grandmother, and with whom he was living in the Bronx, in 1917. Cullen maintained that he was a native of New York City while others, including friends, suggested that he was born in Louisville, Kentucky, or in Baltimore, Maryland. As scholar Gerald Early notes, Cullen's undergraduate transcript lists New York City as his birthplace. Other scholars suggest that the writer embraced the city once he began to achieve literary acclaim there. Cullen was relatively circumspect about personal details and never provided any specific accounts of his early childhood. Cullen's birth mother was Elizabeth Thomas Lucas, who died in Louisville in 1940; the identity of his father was unknown. The poet went by the name Countee Porter until he was adopted by the Cullens. His biographer Blanche Ferguson notes that the Cullens, who had no children of their own, regarded Countee, who was a solicitous and intelligent child, as a "gift from God" (Ferguson, 11). The family remained close; in 1926, for instance, following his graduation from Harvard, Frederick Cullen, who received the splendid gift from his church of a trip to the Middle East, took the extended trip, which included stops in Italy and France, with his son. On board, the two had the opportunity to talk more with fellow passengers ALAIN LOCKE, Dorothy Peterson, and ARTHUR HUFF FAUSET, who were traveling to Europe.

Cullen excelled as a student at DEWITT CLINTON HIGH SCHOOL in NEW YORK CITY, which he attended from 1918 through 1921. He was the editor of the school newspaper, an honor society member, a senior class officer, and an associate editor of the *Magpie,* the literary magazine with which James Baldwin, one of Cullen's future students, would one day be affiliated. Cullen demonstrated his literary talents while in high school, and his victory in a Women's Clubs–sponsored citywide literary competition signaled his potential. Cullen, a voracious reader who had already pored over the Reverend Cullen's substantial private collection of theological works, was a regular patron at Harlem's 135th Street Branch of the New York Public Library. There, he had the opportunity to talk regularly with librarian ERNESTINE ROSE about books and authors.

In 1921, he enrolled at NEW YORK UNIVERSITY, and he graduated PHI BETA KAPPA in 1925. Cullen's college years were extremely rewarding because it was there that he began to write the majority of poems that later would be organized into his first three published collections. Cullen, who had gained recognition for his prize-winning entries in the prestigious Witter Bynner Undergraduate Poetry Contests, published poems regularly in the college magazine, as well as national periodicals such as *American Mercury, Bookman, Century, CRISIS, The Nation, OPPORTUNITY,* and *PALMS,* and had seen the publication of *COLOR,* his first volume of poems while still an undergraduate, clearly was already enjoying a successful writing career.

Portrait of Countee Cullen that the poet inscribed to Carl Van Vechten in February 1925 *(Yale Collection of American Literature, Beinecke Rare Book and Manuscript Library)*

Immediately following his graduation from New York University, Cullen began master's programs in English and in French at HARVARD UNIVERSITY. His graduation from Harvard in 1925 meant that he joined the ranks of a number of Ivy League educated writers that included W. E. B. DUBOIS, ZORA NEALE HURSTON, and RUDOLPH FISHER. He went on to win major literary prizes, including the HARMON FOUNDATION Gold Medal, and prizes in *Opportunity* literary competitions. In 1926, Cullen joined the editorial staff of *Opportunity* as assistant editor. He wrote book reviews and was a regular contributor himself of poems and the author of "The Dark Tower," the monthly column that commented on various social, literary, and cultural events of the day. The regular installments began in December 1926 and lasted through September 1928. Cullen also included moving obituary notes and tributes to prominent and beloved figures such as Florence Mills and Clarissa Scott Delany. He worked with the editor CHARLES S. JOHNSON and with the staff of *Opportunity* until 1928, the year in which he won a GUGGENHEIM FELLOWSHIP and married.

During his years in Harlem, Cullen was at the center of lively literary and cultural circles. The heiress A'LELIA WALKER, daughter of the highly successful entrepreneur Madam C. J. Walker, was a major social figure, and her friendship with Cullen meant that he often had invitations to her memorable and frequent soirées. Walker's home on 136th Street, which fondly became known as "The Dark Tower," was the site of many gatherings that included writers, artists, musicians, critics, potential patrons, and publishers.

In April 1928, Cullen married YOLANDE DuBOIS, the only surviving child of W. E. B. DuBOIS, to much acclaim. The lavish wedding ceremony occurred in his father's church, with his father presiding. The wedding announcements underscored the collective sense of Cullen's professional potential and that, with his bride's lineage, the marriage represented a marriage of two American families with imposing literary and intellectual traditions. "The marriage of Countee Cullen, negro poet and recent winner of a Guggenheim Foundation fellowship, to Miss Nina Yolande Du Bois, daughter of Dr. W. E. B. Du Bois, editor of *The Crisis,* will take place April 9" (*NYT,* 26 March 1928, 15) read the announcement in the *New York Times.* At the time of the wedding, DuBois was an art and English teacher at Baltimore's Douglas High School. According to David Levering Lewis, the historian and Pulitzer Prize–winning biographer of W. E. B. DuBois, DuBois made every effort to collaborate with his future son-in-law in order to preserve the propriety of the occasion. According to Lewis, the two men met for lunch at the Civic Club in order to finalize the details about the guest list, reception format, and hour of the service. Both men attempted to persuade Yolande to reduce the number of bridesmaids from 15 to six, but she prevailed, had 16 attendants, and also succeeded in inviting some 1,500 guests, rather than the more modest number of 500, to the ceremony. The wedding, which took place on Easter Monday, represented a virtual who's who of African-American society and the Harlem Renaissance circles. DuBois's bridesmaids included members of The Moles, the social club to which DuBois herself belonged (Ferguson, 99). Among the young women from the social and professional elite were Mae Miller, the daughter of HOWARD UNIVERSITY dean Kelly Miller, Harriet

Pickens, the daughter of a high-ranking National Association for the Advancement of Colored People officer, and Constance Murphy, a member of the family that ran the influential *Baltimore Afro-American* newspaper. The writer ARNA BONTEMPS, whom Cullen introduced to the thriving New York literary and cultural scene; William Alphaeus Hunton, Jr., the brother of writer EUNICE HUNTON CARTER; and LANGSTON HUGHES and HAROLD JACKMAN were among the 14 groomsmen. The reception, which originally was scheduled to be held at the Madame Walker Studio, was relocated to the rectory at Salem Methodist Church.

Despite the pomp and circumstance of the ceremony and the massive press coverage that included two pages of photographs in *The Crisis* and detailed accounts in the *INTER-STATE TATTLER* and *AMSTERDAM NEWS,* the marriage began to dissolve shortly after the service. The honeymoon in PHILADELPHIA did not go well, and within two months, Cullen's ocean voyage to Europe without his wife and with Harold Jackman, a handsome, close bisexual friend, prompted a revival of rumors about his homosexuality. Cullen, who was en route to Paris as a Guggenheim Fellow, attempted to explain that Yolande had responsibilities that made it necessary to delay her departure and that his father would be accompanying the men on the voyage. Nonetheless, the marriage failed, and the couple, who attempted reconciliations, finally divorced in 1930. The dissolution did not affect Cullen's future submissions to *The Crisis,* the journal edited by his former father-in-law and in which his poetry had appeared often. DuBois assured him that the magazine would continue to welcome and to publish his work. It was nearly a decade before Cullen remarried. His second wife, Ida Mae Roberson, was a sister of Orlando Roberson, a well-known singer who was affiliated with the Claude Hopkins Orchestra and later with the Ink Spots. Writer Arna Bontemps, with whom Cullen enjoyed a good professional and social relationship, noted that not only was "Countee's wife Ida . . . quite lovely: petite, dainty, very friendly, very devoted to Cullen" but that "as a result Countee is writing as of old" (Nichols, 95). The couple, who married in September 1940, enjoyed six years together before Cullen died from high blood pressure and uremic poisoning in January 1946. It was Ida Cullen who met with

Arna Bontemps at Fisk University and decided to donate her late husband's papers to the school. Bontemps, who was chief archivist at the time, noted that "Countee's literary effects" would become part of the "collection of Negroana: letters, manuscripts, the books of his library, everything that was still with him at his death." Although, according to Bontemps, Cullen had "given much away previously . . . much remained" and would be housed, "beside the forthcoming [Charles] Chesnutt collection" (Nichols, 282).

Cullen's first volume of poetry appeared in 1925. *Color,* published by HARPER & BROTHERS, was heralded as the work of a new star, a young man whose work embodied the aspirations of the TALENTED TENTH and represented the unlimited potential of African Americans. Included in this volume was "Yet Do I Marvel," one of his most well-known pieces, about the irony of being born black and a poet. He used his Guggenheim and Harmon Foundation awards to fund a year in France. Two years later, in 1927, he published two works: *COPPER SUN,* a volume whose painful love poetry is believed to have been inspired by the breakdown of his marriage, and *THE BALLAD OF THE BROWN GIRL,* an ornate and highly decorative monograph version of a previously published poem. He also edited *CAROLING DUSK: AN ANTHOLOGY OF VERSE BY NEGRO POETS,* a volume in which he asserted his belief in the importance of creative versatility for black writers and decried any notion that they have a responsibility to write race literature. Cullen's protestations, however, in no way minimized the force of his most race-conscious poems, works in which he challenged race prejudice, racism, and inequality.

In 1929, he produced *THE BLACK CHRIST AND OTHER POEMS,* a volume that included a long narrative poem about the powerful resurrection of a LYNCHING victim and the solace he offered to his mourning, traumatized family. Cullen scholars note that the poet's productivity diminished steadily after the publication of *The Black Christ* but that he did continue to pursue creative projects. Cullen published *ONE WAY TO HEAVEN* (1932), his first and only novel with Harper, the press with which he worked exclusively throughout his career. In the *New York Times,* reviewer Elizabeth Brown noted that many white readers had "not yet reached the stage where we can appreciate any story about colored people at its face value without always straining to find it some sort of presentation of Negro life" and that it was thus "an impertinence to say that Mr. Cullen paints a convincing picture of life in Harlem; but one can at least say that the picture is sometimes amusing, sometimes very moving, and at all times interesting" (*NYT,* 28 February 1932, BR7). Ultimately, the novel was not a major critical success and was hampered by its two competing and seemingly unrelated plot lines. The first revolved around a tragic love affair between an earnest domestic named Mattie Johnson and an unreliable con man named Sam Lucas. The novel, set in Harlem, also allowed Cullen to portray the lively social and intellectual circles of the community and of the time. The character Constancia Brandon, for instance, was seen as a thinly veiled version of A'Lelia Walker. Cullen attempted to transform the novel into a play, but the stage version of the work did not become a significant public endeavor.

W. E. B. DuBois, believed that Cullen was a writer whose "career was not finished" and "did not culminate." Writing in the *Chicago Defender* in January 1946, DuBois noted movingly that Cullen's career "was halted in mid-flight and becomes at once inspiration and warning to the American Negro group" (Lomax, 246). Cullen scholar Alan Lomax suggests that Cullen in fact "refus[ed] to accept race as a basic and valuable segment of his total identity" and that this "was an evasion which prevented him from further straightforward and clear development" (Lomax, 246). Cullen's career, like that of JEAN TOOMER, was undoubtedly informed by the writer's interest in incorporating race into his works but reflected the writer's determination to prevent it from becoming the overarching theme in all of his work.

In 1934, Cullen began an 11-year career as a teacher of English and French at Frederick Douglass Junior High School in New York City. There, one of his students was James Baldwin, the future acclaimed novelist and essayist. It was Cullen who encouraged Baldwin's love of literature and served as the adviser to the high school literary club to which Baldwin belonged. Cullen continued to publish during his tenure at the school. In 1935, he produced *THE MEDEA AND SOME POEMS.* In the early 1940s, Cullen published two short story collections entitled THE LOST ZOO (1940) and *My Lives and How I Lost Them* (1942). His love of theater continued throughout his later career, and his final effort, published posthumously in August 1946, was a one-act play coauthored with Owen Dodson entitled *The Third Fourth of July* and published in the journal *Theatre Arts*.

One of Cullen's most successful creative ventures came during the waning years of the Renaissance when he collaborated with Arna Bontemps. In 1939, the two completed *St. Louis Woman*, a dramatic and musical production of Bontemps's 1931 novel *God Sends Sunday*. The two men also worked closely on the project with Langston Hughes, who on one occasion referred to the work as "beautiful" and admitted that as it progressed he "like[d] it better and better" (Nichols, 37). The adaptation was staged in New York City at the Martin Beck Theatre. It opened in March 1946 and enjoyed more than 100 performances before it closed in early July 1946. The show, directed by Rouben Mamoulian, with set and costume designs by Lemuel Ayers, featured a cast that included the actress Pearl Bailey.

Some 3,000 people attended funeral services for Cullen after he died at age 42 on 9 January 1946. The service for the "leading Negro poet," as he was described in the *New York Times* coverage of the event, was held at Salem Methodist Church, the longtime church of his father, the Reverend Frederick Cullen, located at Seventh Avenue and West 129th Street. Cullen, who was living in Tuckahoe, New York, at the time of his death, was buried in the Woodlawn Cemetery, the resting place of other prominent New York figures, such as FIORELLO LA GUARDIA. His death was a shock to many, including Langston Hughes, who wrote to his longtime friend Arna Bontemps to ask "What happened to Countee?" and noted that "Everyone in L.A. was shocked at the news" (Nichols, 203). A number of leading figures of the Harlem Renaissance attended the service, including Arna Bontemps, WILLIAM STANLEY BRAITHWAITE, the prizefighter and *Native Son* star actor Canada Lee, ALAIN LOCKE, RIDGELY TORRENCE, CARL VAN VECHTEN, and RICHARD WRIGHT. The presiding minister, Charles Trigg, and the principal at Frederick Douglass Junior High School, George Zuck-

erman, delivered eulogies. Rev. Trigg "extolled Mr. Cullen for his devoutness, his calmness and inward serenity, his untiring work in his poetry and teaching, his loyalty to his friends and his respect for all humanity." Zuckerman, who recalled Cullen's 11-year teaching career at the school on West 140th Street, also "noted especially his extracurricular work in creative poetry with the pupils."

Bibliography

Countee Cullen Papers, Amistad Research Center, Tulane University.

Bronz, Stephen. *Roots of Racial Consciousness. The 1920s: Three Harlem Renaissance Authors*. New York: Libra, 1964.

Early, Gerald. *My Soul's High Song: The Collected Writings of Countee Cullen, Voice of the Harlem Renaissance*. New York: Doubleday, 1991.

Ferguson, Blanche. *Countee Cullen and the Negro Renaissance*. New York: Dodd, Mead, 1966.

Lewis, David Levering. *When Harlem Was in Vogue*. New York: Knopf, 1981.

Lomax, Michael. "Countee Cullen: A Key to the Puzzle." In *The Harlem Renaissance Re-Examined*, edited by Victor Kramer and Robert Russ. Troy, N.Y.: Whitson, 1997. 239–248.

Nichols, Charles H., ed. *Arna Bontemps-Langston Hughes Letters, 1925–1967*. New York: Paragon House, 1990.

Powers, Peter. "'The Singing Man Who Must Be Reckoned With': Private Desire and Public Responsibility in the Poetry of Countee Cullen." *African American Review* 34, no. 4 (winter 2000): 661–678.

Shucard, Alan. *Countee Cullen*. Boston: Twayne, 1984.

Cullen, Frederick Asbury (1868–1946)

The Reverend Frederick Cullen was pastor at the Salem Methodist Episcopal Church in New York City and the adoptive father of COUNTEE CULLEN, the acclaimed and prolific Harlem Renaissance poet. In 1928, the Reverend Cullen presided over the wedding ceremony of his son and YOLANDE DUBOIS.

Bibliography

Lewis, David Levering. *When Harlem Was in Vogue*. New York: Knopf, 1981.

Cunard, Nancy (1897–1965)

The British editor of *Negro: An Anthology* (1934), a collection of impressive scope that included a variety of articles relating to black life. She solicited contributions from well-known Harlem Renaissance writers, many of whom she included in the volume. JEAN TOOMER, who had by this time decided that he would not identify himself as a Negro, declined her invitation. Cunard was a spirited rebel, one whose communist affiliations were a direct rejection of her family's shipping fortune, and whose interracial relationship was, among other things, a means to challenge social prejudice.

Bibliography

Ford, Hugh. *Nancy Cunard: Brave Poet, Indomitable Rebel 1896–1965.* Philadelphia: Chilton, 1968.

Cuney, (William) Waring (1906–unknown)

A musician who trained at the prestigious New England Conservatory of Music in BOSTON, Cuney published regularly during the Harlem Renaissance. Born in WASHINGTON, D.C., he went on to attend HOWARD UNIVERSITY in the city. He later enrolled at LINCOLN UNIVERSITY in Pennsylvania. He won first prize in the 1926 literary contest sponsored by OPPORTUNITY. While a music student in Boston, he enjoyed the distinction of seeing seven of his poems included in COUNTEE CULLEN's 1927 volume, *CAROLING DUSK: AN ANTHOLOGY OF VERSE BY NEGRO POETS* while he was a music student in Boston. WILLIAM STANLEY BRAITHEWAITE included Cuney's work in one of his highly selective volumes of the *ANTHOLOGY OF MAGAZINE VERSE*. In 1931 JAMES WELDON JOHNSON included eight of Cuney's poems in *THE BOOK OF AMERICAN NEGRO POETRY*. He also published in *The Forum* and in *PALMS*.

Cuney, whom scholars regard as a talented but minor poet of the Harlem Renaissance, enjoyed a delightful and lively friendship with LANGSTON HUGHES, whom he met while living in Washington, D.C. Arnold Rampersad, Hughes's biographer, reports that Cuney, Hughes, and BRUCE NUGENT became inseparable and were prone to staging dramatic farces that ranged from pretending to speak foreign languages to walking in public without shoes. It was Cuney, a Lincoln University graduate himself, who suggested to Langston Hughes that he attend Lincoln University. Hughes, who found himself depressed by the weather and stodgy Washington, D.C. environment, took his friend's advice and enrolled at Lincoln in 1926.

Cuney was one of the writers who published in the promising but short-lived black journal, *FIRE!!*. His poem "Death Bed" appeared alongside works by Hughes, ZORA NEALE HURSTON, Countee Cullen, and GWENDOLYN BENNETT, and drawings by AARON DOUGLAS. His works were diverse in theme and style and ranged from spiritual reflections to understated romantic commentaries on love and rejection. His poem "Dust," like Hughes's "The Negro Speaks of Rivers," offers a powerful contemplation of the ancient African past from which American Negroes had been so abruptly severed. Cuney also recognized the rigors of daily life endured by so many African Americans; works like "True Love" offered respectful and ennobling tributes to those like the unwavering female subject in the poem who transcended the grim realities and managed to love "in a tenement / Where the only music / She hears / Is the cry of street car brakes / And the toot of automobile horns / And the drip of a kitchen spigot / All day." Cuney's work contributed to the substantial canon of black domestic literature that produced a powerful comment on black life in the early 20th century.

Bibliography

Cullen, Countee. *Caroling Dusk: An Anthology of Verse by Negro Poets.* New York: Harper & Brothers Publishers, 1927.

Rampersad, Arnold. *The Life of Langston Hughes: I, Too, Sing America.* Vol. 1: *1902–1941.* New York: Oxford University Press, 1986.

Curtwright, Wesley (1910–unknown)

This Brunswick, Georgia, native migrated north to HARLEM after his father died. In the city, he enrolled in HARLEM ACADEMY, the Seventh-Day Adventist school in which ARNA BONTEMPS began teaching in 1924. By 1927, the 17-year-old student poet had published in *OPPORTUNITY* and the *MESSENGER* and had been selected for inclusion in COUNTEE CULLEN's 1927 anthology, *CAROLING DUSK: AN ANTHOLOGY OF VERSE BY NEGRO*

POETS. What little is known about his circumstances is based on the biographical profile included in *Caroling Dusk*.

Bibliography

Cullen, Countee. *Caroling Dusk: An Anthology of Verse by Negro Poets*. New York: Harper & Brothers Publishers, 1927.

Cuthbert, Marion Vera (1896–1989)

Born in St. Paul, Minnesota, Cuthbert pursued college and graduate studies in the East. She graduated from BOSTON UNIVERSITY in 1920 and used a Kent Fellowship to fund her master's program at COLUMBIA UNIVERSITY. In 1942 she earned her Ph.D. at Columbia. She devoted herself primarily to a career in education and social outreach; she was the dean of Talladega College from 1927 through 1930 and an active participant and board member with the YOUNG WOMEN'S CHRISTIAN ASSOCIATION (YWCA).

Cuthbert published at least three works during the Harlem Renaissance. In 1933, she penned JULIETTE DERRICOTE, a memorial tribute to the FISK UNIVERSITY dean and YWCA administrative member whose death was due in large part to ATLANTA hospitals whose racist exclusionary policies allowed them to refuse treatment to her, a car accident victim. In 1936, Cuthbert published APRIL GRASSES, a volume of poetry that prompted critics to comment on the absence of race-related works. A second work, *Democracy and the Negro*, also appeared that year. She was a forthright social critic who recognized, alongside her Harlem Renaissance peers, that while the evolution of American society was a "slow and painful" process, "the whole structure of democracy may fail unless its basic tenets are adhered to and serfdom abolished in a country designed for free men" (Cuthbert, 1).

Bibliography

Cuthbert, Marion Vera. "The Negro Today." *Church and Society* (January 1932): 1–2.
Roses, Lorraine Elena, and Ruth Elizabeth Randolph. *Harlem Renaissance and Beyond: Literary Biographies of 100 Black Women Writers, 1900–1945*. Boston: G. K. Hall & Co., 1990.

"Cynthia Goes to the Prom" Eric Walrond (1923)

A short story about a high school girl whose prom serves as the backdrop for her coming of age in an unpredictable and prejudiced world. Narrated by an omniscient and rather animated narrator, the story follows Cynthia, a popular girl whose race has not impeded her social relations at her predominantly white high school. When she decides to attend her prom, she is subjected to increasingly aggressive acts of racism. The insults culminate in a scene in which her white schoolmates watch and refuse to help her when a coat clerk humiliates her. This work by ERIC WALROND appeared in the November 1923 issue of OPPORTUNITY.

D

Dandridge, Raymond Garfield
(1882–1930)

A poet from Cincinnati who overcame severe physical handicaps and paralysis to make a name for himself as a poet and critic. The literary editor for the *Cincinnati Journal*, he published three volumes of poetry, two of which appeared in the most vibrant years of the Harlem Renaissance. THE POET AND OTHER POEMS was published in 1920; ZALKA PEETRUZA AND OTHER POEMS appeared in 1928.

In 1922 five Dandridge poems were selected for inclusion in JAMES WELDON JOHNSON's THE BOOK OF AMERICAN NEGRO POETRY, the most comprehensive survey of works by African-American poets. According to the biographical profile that preceded the five Dandridge poems included in Johnson's anthology, Dandridge wrote most of his poems while confined to his bed. A number of his poems, including " 'Ittle Touzle Head," "Sprin' Fevah," and "De Drum Majah" were dialect poems, works inspired by his appreciation for the dialect compositions of Paul Laurence Dunbar.

Bibliography

Johnson, James Weldon. *The Book of American Negro Poetry*. New York: Harcourt, Brace and Company, 1922.

Dark Princess W. E. B. DuBois (1928)

W. E. B. DUBOIS described his second novel, *Dark Princess*, as "a romance with a message" and "a story of the great movement of the darker races for self-expression and self-determination." Published by HARCOURT, BRACE & COMPANY in April 1928, the novel was priced at $2 per copy and provided him with an advance of $500.

The book, which eventually sold 4,500 of the 5,000 copies printed initially, did not sell briskly. As historian Herbert Aptheker notes, biannual statements confirm that the average number of books purchased during each six-month period between 1930 and 1933 was 40 copies (Aptheker, 20). The book was reviewed widely and signaled DuBois's importance as much as the general initial interest in reading a novel by the esteemed and scholarly editor of THE CRISIS. Writing for the Denver-based *Rocky Mountain News*, George Burns described the novel as "a searching exposition of that age-old cry of man for an answer to life, not alone of the dominating white man, but of the man who not only must solve the forces of life, but also must contend with the restrictions imposed on him by fellow human beings" (Aptheker, 22). The NEW YORK TIMES suggested that although the plot was "flamboyant and unconvincing" there was "real meat in the *Dark Princess* and such proof of the author's power that it seems a pity he is not using his talent to show the natural ability of the colored man or his nobility of character, as in *Porgy*, rather than to dwell, oversensitively, on social injustices which are inevitable in any period of racial transition and development—of white or black" (Aptheker, 25). The *New Republic* reviewer challenged the suggestion articulated in the *New York Times*, however, suggesting that "[i]t is worth noting that this author is one of the few who can write about minority and 'queer' races as if they were men rather than types. He is conscious of the individual as the individual is of himself" (Aptheker, 24).

DuBois began the novel with a lengthy and florid dedication. "To Her High Loveliness TITANIA XXVII By Her Own Grace Queen of Faerie," he wrote, "Commander of the Bath; Grand Medallion of Merit; Litterarum Humanarum Docor; Fidei Extensor; etc., etc. Of Whose Faith and Fond Affection This Romance Was Surely Born." He divided the story into four parts entitled "The Exile," "The Pullman Porter," "The Chicago Politician," and "The Maharajah of Bwodpur," respectively. The novel begins in a mode of high anxiety and disruption because the honor student Matthew Towns has been denied the opportunity to continue his medical studies at the University of Manhattan since white patients will not be willing to have a man of color tend to them in obstetrics. Outraged by the hypocrisy of the institution and fed up with the limitations placed on African Americans regardless of their demonstrated ability or potential, he abandons America and sets sail for Europe. A man of "tall, lean form and dark brown face," he soon finds himself in Germany, where he instinctively defends the honor of a beautiful woman of color when a crude white American threatens her. He finds himself sharing his autobiography with the woman whom he comes to know as Princess Kautilya of Bwodpur, India, and is intrigued by her provocative questions about African-American survival and their strategies for advancement in an age of ruthless segregation. Eventually, he is initiated into the princess's plans to stage a systematic reevaluation of the Negro in America and of "the relative ability of all classes and peoples." Part One closes as she tells him of her pending trip to America, "to see for myself," she explains, "if slaves can become men in a generation. If they can—well, it makes the world new for you and me."

In "The Pullman Porter" section, DuBois intensifies the mystery of *Dark Princess* as Towns becomes an undercover agent for Princess Kautilya. He meets the enigmatic Mr. Perigua who intends to counter lynchings by staging targeted bombings of the lynch mobs. In an effort to realize his scheme, Perigua arranges for Towns to become a Pullman porter, work the popular New York–Atlanta route, and recruit allies among the men. Despite his insistence that he had no interest in America, Towns works spiritedly as an observer for the princess. He endures awful work conditions, racism, and insults so that he can provide her with reliable assessments of the condi-

tion of the Negro. He characterizes his first report as a "hasty but careful survey of the attitude of my people in this country, with regard to the possibility of their aid to a movement looking toward righting the present racial inequalities in the world, especially along the color line." In it, he concludes that "American Negroes are a tremendous social force, an economic entity of high importance" despite the fact that "[t]heir power is at present partly but not wholly dissipated and dispersed into the forces of the overwhelming nation about them." In a dizzying turn of events, however, Towns becomes committed to leading a strike that never materializes and to allowing a bombing of a train that he then prevents when he realizes that the princess is aboard. The section closes as he is found guilty of providing aid to the would-be murderers and is sentenced to 10 years of hard labor at Joliet Prison in Illinois. The princess sees him just before he is interned, and he instructs her to visit his aged mother in Virginia. "Make her life's end happy for her," he cautions the princess as he bids her to be discreet about his whereabouts.

Over the course of the last two sections of the novel, Towns is awarded a pardon, thanks to the enterprising efforts of Sarah Andrews and the ambitious politician Sammy Scott for whom she works. Towns marries Sarah shortly after his release and allows himself to be groomed for public office. He increasingly accommodates her political agenda and, through her persistence, advances systematically through the political system. Yet, he abandons the career and his wife when he is reunited unexpectedly with the princess, who is masquerading as a leader of a trade union, and decides that "[t]he world was one woman and one cause." Their shared tales of sacrifice fuel their passionate love affair further. Both have assumed different identities and worked alongside people who constitute the masses whom the princess hopes to band together. Eventually, pressed by demands from her native land, she returns to Virginia, where she seeks counsel from Towns's mother. It is this unsung elder who provides the rich and idealistic young woman with a renewed sense of global purpose and personal commitment to Matthew, the man with whom she hopes to "build a world . . . where the Hungry shall be fed, and only the Lazy shall be empty." The novel closes as the pair is reunited once again in Virginia after Matthew appears at the divorce proceedings in Chicago and finds Sarah now paired off with her former boss.

Matthew finds his beloved in Virginia with their son, whom she has named Madhu, and the two are wed in a moving ceremony. Immediately thereafter, the child is feted in what is reminiscent of the efforts to find the Christ child born to Mary. The novel ends as Madhu is hailed as "Messenger and Messiah to all the Darker Worlds!"

The final note in the text is delivered by an envoy who declares with apparent relish that "[t]he tale is done and night is come" and bids the sprites help him to return his magic cape to the Queen of Faeries who "lent [it] to me for a season." DuBois's invocation of Shakespeare's *Midsummer Night's Dream* brings the involved tale of intrigue, solidarity, intimidation, and social evolution to a formal close.

The formal African-American response to *Dark Princess* came in DuBois's own journal, *The Crisis*, and from established leaders of the Harlem Renaissance movement such as ALAIN LOCKE. ALLISON DAVIS, who provided the *Crisis* review, offered readers an earnest appraisal of the work. He contextualized the novel in relation to the larger African-American experience of "great suffering" and collective survival of "common tragedy." Davis made a point of setting *Dark Princess* apart from some of the most controversial novels recently published: The book "will not appeal to the same public which enjoyed *NIGGER HEAVEN* and *HOME TO HARLEM*," he insisted. "All those who have a high faith in the destiny and nature of the Negro, therefore, ought to read it." Alain Locke, whose assessment was published in the *New York Herald Tribune*, noted the limitations of form but focused instead on the political implications of the work. He regarded *Dark Princess* as a "skyscraper problem novel of the Negro intellectual and the world radical" and suggested that not only should readers regard the book as a "document" but that it also "should be widely read" (Aptheker, 28).

Bibliography

Aptheker, Herbert. Introduction to *Dark Princess: A Romance.* 1928, reprint, Millwood, N.Y.: Kraus-Thomson Organization Limited, 1974, 5–29.

Lewis, David Levering. *W. E. B. DuBois: The Fight for Equality and the American Century, 1919–1963.* New York: Henry Holt and Company, 2000.

Dark Tower

A fashionable literary salon named in honor of the *OPPORTUNITY* magazine column of the same name,

YOU are cordially invited to be one of a small group meeting at the residence of Miss A'Lelia Walker, 110 West 136th Street, on Thursday afternoon, February 21, at four o'clock, to hear in advance a talk on the plans and program of an important Negro Theatre which will soon be opened in New York.

Mr. Raymond O'Neil, Director of the Ethiopian Art Theatre, will address the group.

Mr. James Weldon Johnson will preside.

From four to five P.M.

A'LELIA WALKER
ARTHUR B. SPINGARN
GRACE NAIL JOHNSON

An invitation to participate in one of the many gatherings that socialite heiress A'Lelia Walker hosted at her home *(Yale Collection of American Literature, Beinecke Rare Book and Manuscript Library)* which was written by COUNTEE CULLEN. Located in HARLEM on West 136th Street, the salon's hostess was A'LELIA WALKER, daughter of Madam C. J. Walker, the self-made and first black woman millionaire. Walker hoped that writers and artists would benefit from the open sessions and art exhibitions at her home. The location was eventually redesigned into a popular restaurant and nightclub that was open to both African-American and white patrons.

Davis, Allison (1902–1983)

A graduate of Williams College, HOWARD UNIVERSITY, and the UNIVERSITY OF CHICAGO, this WASHINGTON, D.C., native and psychologist was also a published poet and professor. His poems appeared in *THE CRISIS,* and at the end of the Renaissance he coauthored *Children of Bondage: The Personality Development of Negro Youth in the Urban South* (1940), a lengthy social psychology study of African-American children's development, with John Dollard.

Davis authored the *Crisis* review of W. E. B. DuBois's 1928 novel *Dark Princess,* a text that he declared a "sane and balanced work, purged of any rash and strident 'aggressiveness' " (Aptheker, 27).

Bibliography

Aptheker, Herbert. Introduction to *Dark Princess: A Romance.* 1928; reprint, Millwood, N.Y.: Kraus-Thomson Organization Limited, 1974, 5–29.

Davis, Arthur P. (1904–1996)

Davis was a regularly published *Norfolk Gazette* columnist and a literary critic with unwavering theories about race and talent. In 1941, just after the close of the Harlem Renaissance, Davis collaborated with STERLING BROWN and ULYSSES LEE to publish *The Negro Caravan: Writings by American Negroes.* The three coeditors used this collection, which numbered more than 1,000 pages, to assert their belief that race was neither a determining nor defining characteristic of a writer or a literary tradition.

Davis, Frank Marshall (1905–1987)

A journalist, editor, and poet whose first book, *BLACK MAN'S VERSE* was published in 1935 and deemed a critical success. Davis regarded poetry as "a subjective way of looking at the world" and believed that "[a]ll poetry worthy of the name is propaganda" (Tidwell, "Interview," 107).

Davis was born in Arkansas City, Kansas. His parents divorced while he was still an infant. He attended Friends University in Wichita before transferring to Kansas State Agricultural College, where he studied journalism. He published three books of poetry during the Harlem Renaissance period: *Black Man's Verse* (1935), *I AM THE AMERICAN NEGRO* (1937), and *THROUGH SEPIA EYES* (1938). A fourth book, *47th Street,* appeared in 1948, the same year in which Davis relocated to Hawaii.

Davis began writing poetry in college at the urging of Ada Rice, his English professor. His work soon earned him membership in the American College Quill Club. His success, he recalled in an interview with his biographer, transformed him into "a curiosity" and he became "known as 'the poet who looks like a prizefighter'" (Tidwell, "Interview," 105).

ARNA BONTEMPS suggested that the "main quality" of Davis's poetry was "ruggedness." "Perhaps this is not surprising," Bontemps continued, "in a poet who worked with street construction gangs in his youth and who has since lived the rough-and-tumble life of a newspaper man" (Bontemps, 357). Major American poets such as Carl Sandburg, Edgar Lee Masters, FENTON JOHNSON, LANGSTON HUGHES, and STERLING BROWN inspired Davis. In addition to liking Sandburg's "hard, muscular poetry," Davis also was impressed by Edgar Lee Masters. Masters's "economy of words and ability to knife through to the heart" made an impression on Davis, who also admitted that he "had not patience with [Masters's] rhyme" (Tidwell, Interview, 105).

Davis's biographer John Edgar Tidwell notes that Davis "emerged in the 1930s as one of the foremost Black practitioners of social realism in poetry" (Tidwell, "Interview," 105). His development as a poet benefited enormously from his contacts with other Harlem Renaissance–era writers while he was living in Chicago. When he moved there in 1934, RICHARD WRIGHT urged Davis to join the League of American Writers. In addition, he discussed writing with MARGARET WALKER, Gwendolyn Brooks, Fenton Johnson, and Wright while participating with them in a short-lived writing group. Davis's links to Wright continued. He recalled that in addition to selling Wright his first camera, he "also read the galley proofs of *Native Son* (part of which was left out by the publisher as too pornographic for that era).

Davis's long-time residency in Chicago minimized his links to the larger literary Harlem Renaissance world. That distance did not bother Davis, who had no desire to be part of what he regarded as the "Effete East" (Tidwell, "Interview," 106). While he never was immersed in the African-American literary communities on the East Coast, Davis did enjoy some contact with successful writers of the Harlem Renaissance. He considered Langston Hughes a friend and enjoyed his meetings with STERLING BROWN, ZORA NEALE HURSTON, CLAUDE MCKAY, and JAMES WELDON JOHNSON. Although he never met W. E. B. DUBOIS, did have a memorable conversation with ALAIN LOCKE about the African-American literary movement with which Locke was so involved. He recalled that Locke, "a dapper, fastidious little man" had told him that the Harlem Renaissance "would have blown up in everybody's faces had it not been for free gin in the big posh apartments on Park Avenue and the personal efforts of Carl Van Vechten" (Tidwell, "Inteview," 106).

Davis generated his principal source of income from articles he wrote for an array of African-American publications. He was executive editor at the ASSOCIATED NEGRO PRESS between 1935 and 1947 and contributed to the *Negro Digest,* the *CHICAGO WHIP,* and other African American Chicago-based papers. Before moving to Hawaii in the 1940s, he published two additional volumes of poetry: *I AM THE AMERICAN NEGRO* (1937) and *THROUGH SEPIA EYES* (1938).

Davis passed away in 1987. Since his death, his book, *Livin' the Blues: Memoirs of a Black Journalist and Poet* (1992) and *Black Moods: Collected Poems* (2002) have been published.

Bibliography

Bontemps, Arna. "Negro Poets, Then and Now." *Phylon* 11, no. 4 (1950): 355–360.

Tidwell, John Edgar. "An Interview with Frank Marshall Davis." *Black American Literature Forum* 19, no. 3 (autumn 1985): 105–108.

———, ed. *Livin' the Blues: Memoirs of a Black Journalist and Poet—Frank Marshall Davis.* Madison: University of Wisconsin Press, 1992.

Davis, Robert Hobart (1869–1942)

An editor affiliated with *Munsey Magazine,* a NEW YORK CITY–based weekly magazine that the formidable publisher Frank Munsey founded in 1889. Davis, who joined the staff of in 1904, began working as the fiction editor. Davis also contributed to other Munsey periodicals, including *Argosy, Cavalier,* and *All-Story.* He was credited with publishing the works of many promising and emerging writers and continues to be regarded as the figure who transformed the short story into one of a highly successful commercial form. One of his best-known protégés was O. Henry; Davis also was an important supporter of Max Brand, Dorothy Canfield, and Fannie Hurst.

In 1924 Davis accepted CHARLES S. JOHNSON's invitation to judge entries in the first *OPPORTUNITY* literary contest. In the personal comment published in the September 1924 informational article about the competition, Davis stressed his interest in "the work of Negro writers" and noted that he would "like to do whatever [he could] to encourage them in their development." Davis was a dynamic and well-connected figure for aspiring Harlem Renaissance writers to know. He was, according to scholar Abe Ravitz, a "thorough pragmatist who regarded all stories as merchandise and magazine buyers as consumers of a given product, Davis counseled his stable of writers to give the public what it wants, most especially to strike at the heart" (Ravitz, 13).

Bibliography

Ravitz, Abe. *Imitations of Life: Fannie Hurst's Gaslight Sonatas.* Carbondale: Southern Illinois University Press, 1997.

Wilson, Sondra Kathryn, ed. *The Opportunity Reader: Stories, Poetry, and Essays From the Urban League's Opportunity Magazine.* New York: The Modern Library, 1999.

Davis, Sadie Warren (unknown–1946)

The owner of the highly respected NEW YORK CITY–based *AMSTERDAM NEWS.* The African-American newspaper was founded in 1909. Noted for the extensive coverage it provided on race-related matters, the newspaper's staff during the 1920s and 1930s included WILLIAM KELLEY, THELMA BERLACK, and R. LIONEL DOUGHERTY, and their collaborative efforts contributed to the paper's reputation for excellence and forthright defenses of the race.

Bibliography

Pride, Armistead Scott, and Clint C. Wilson. *A History of the Black Press.* Washington, D.C.: Howard University Press, 1997.

"Days" Brenda Ray Moryck (1928)

A short story by BRENDA RAY MORYCK that appeared in the June 1928 issue of THE CRISIS. Moryck tackled the controversial issue of residential segregation and racial stereotypes in this story about an African-American couple who move into a predominantly Greek, Irish, and Italian community. The white immigrant families and descendants are convinced that the dark-skinned attorney and his light-skinned, albeit clearly privileged, wife are going to ruin their neighborhood. By year's end, however, the couple, through unselfconscious example, has succeeded in inspiring their white neighbors to take pride in their property and themselves.

Deacon's Awakening, The Willis Richardson (1920)

A dynamic one-act play by WILLIS RICHARDSON, one of the leading American dramatists of the Harlem Renaissance. Published in the November 1920 issue of THE CRISIS, the play focuses on women's political empowerment and is regarded as a pioneering feminist drama of the period.

The play, which is set in WASHINGTON, D.C., focuses on the tensions that arise when a women's group called the Voting Society challenges the conservative patriarchal perspectives of their church's board of deacons. The deacon Dave Jones, whose wife Martha and daughter Ruth are passionately committed to women's suffrage, draws the unfortunate task of spying on the upcoming meeting of the society. His wife learns of the pending treachery and successfully thwarts his under-

cover mission by arranging for him to visit a sick neighbor. One of his fellow deacons, however, does gather information on the women participants and reports to the group and to Deacon Jones. In one of the most memorable scenes of the play, the deacon confronts his wife and is dismayed by the eloquent resistance that she displays. Martha is one of the primary advocates of women's suffrage and, with her daughter, has been actively educating local women about their political rights and responsibilities. The deacon insists that she "can't make [him] believe in a woman voting" and she tells him, quite confidently, that he will "believe in it of [his] own accord when [he] wake[s] up." As the play proceeds, the deacon is hard-pressed to ignore the democratic principles that his wife is advancing or the emancipatory domestic politics in which she fervently believes. She rejects the narrow-minded notion that women should content themselves with only housework and child-rearing and refuses to accommodate the deacon's board or her husband on this point.

Christine Rauchfuss Gray suggests that despite the illuminating presentation of women's rights and empowerment, *The Deacon's Awakening* reflects Richardson's inability to represent fully independent women. She does propose, however, that the play establishes important precedents for later Richardson plays, those in which women who "[a]lthough they may be under the control of men . . . exert what power they can in their circumstances" (72). The play was the first work that Richardson published in *The Crisis*, and it signaled his willingness to explore controversial and meaningful domestic issues. It also hinted at the significant impression and formative influence that his talented teachers, the playwrights MARY BURRILL and ANGELINA GRIMKÉ, had upon him while he was attending the renowned M Street School in Washington, D.C.

Bibliography

Gray, Christine Rauchfuss. *Willis Richardson, Forgotten Pioneer of African-American Drama.* Westport, Conn.: Greenwood Press, 1999.

Dear Lovely Death Langston Hughes (1931)

A collection of poems by LANGSTON HUGHES. Its title was chosen by AMY SPINGARN at a time when Hughes was despondent about his potential loss of sponsorship by CHARLOTTE OSGOOD MASON, the patron whom ALAIN LOCKE, ZORA NEALE HURSTON, and others referred to as "Godmother." Amy Spingarn's press, Troutbeck, published 100 numbered copies of the Hughes volume on handmade paper that also included Spingarn's sketch of the author on its frontispiece.

Bibliography

Bernard, Emily. *Remember Me to Harlem: The Letters of Langston Hughes and Carl Van Vechten*. New York: Knopf, 2001.

Rampersad, Arnold. *The Life of Langston Hughes: I, Too, Sing America*. Vol. 1, *1902–1941*. New York: Oxford University Press, 1986.

Death Dance, The Thelma Duncan (ca. 1921)

The first play by THELMA DUNCAN, written while she was a student at HOWARD UNIVERSITY in WASHINGTON, D.C. The University Players, a drama group at Howard, produced this one-act musical. It told the story of Kamo, a heroic young African man who survives the treachery of a jealous medicine man. Kamo's ability to survive doses of a potion called "ordeal" enables him to win the love of the dancer named Asumana.

Bibliography

Roses, Lorraine Elena, and Ruth Elizabeth Randolph. *Harlem Renaissance and Beyond: Literary Biographies of 100 Black Women Writers, 1900–1945*. Boston: G. K. Hall & Co., 1990.

"Death Game, The" Edwin Drummond Sheen (1927)

The second-place winner in the 1926 THE CRISIS literary contest, this short story by EDWIN DRUMMOND SHEEN was a grim account of an unreliable woman, her earnest suitor, and the troublemaker who ends her life. Against the backdrop of a dilapidated CHICAGO neighborhood, Nell engages in reckless relationships. This thrice-married woman who killed her last husband could improve her life by being true to Joe Nixon, a man who loves her. Nixon discovers Nell's treachery, and he confronts Shug Lewis, her lover. The two

men begin a card game that will decide which man will kill the other and win Nell's affections. Shug ends up killing Nell, the inconstant and damaged woman, instead.

Delaney, Sara (Sadie) Marie (1889–1958)

Educated at City College in New York, Delaney earned her library certificate from the NEW YORK PUBLIC LIBRARY school and went on to become a highly effective bibliotherapist at the Veteran's Administration Hospital in Tuskegee, Alabama. During her time in NEW YORK CITY, Delaney lived in the STRIVER'S ROW neighborhood and participated in the multifaceted activities of the Renaissance. Delaney believed that books were essential to recovery. Her resourcefulness, determination, and vision completely transformed the meager holdings of the hospital library from 200 to some 4,000 books.

Delany, Clarissa M. Scott (1901–1927)

A poet, essayist, and teacher whose works appeared in THE CRISIS, OPPORTUNITY, and the COUNTEE CULLEN anthology, CAROLING DUSK (1927). Her poems, which included works like "Joy," "Solace," and "Interim" were rather simplistic narratives about nature and suppressed feelings.

The Wellesley-educated writer and scholar was the daughter of Eleanora Baker Scott and Emmett Scott, the devoted longtime secretary of BOOKER T. WASHINGTON. She graduated PHI BETA KAPPA from the prestigious women's college in 1923. After an enjoyable postgraduate year spent traveling through Europe, she joined the faculty at the WASHINGTON, D.C., DUNBAR HIGH SCHOOL, the highly selective school that was the alma mater of many accomplished Harlem Renaissance writers including JEAN TOOMER, MAY MILLER SULLIVAN, and RICHARD BRUCE NUGENT. Delany would later confess that "though . . . children were interesting, teaching was not [her] *metier*," despite her immersion in the school's intellectually stimulating environment.

Delany's untimely death prevented her from becoming a full-fledged and prolific member of the Harlem Renaissance. The four works that she did publish, however, earned her recognition from leading figures of the Harlem Renaissance period.

Despite her demonstrated ability to conduct research, Delany chose a "career" as a wife, a pursuit that she characterized as "interesting and absorbing." She wed Hubert Delany, an attorney, in 1926 and the couple relocated to New York City. There, Delany pursued a career in social work and was affiliated with both the NATIONAL URBAN LEAGUE and the Woman's City Club of New York. Delany, who also was a member of DELTA SIGMA THETA, died prematurely at the age of 26.

Bibliography

Cullen, Countee. *Caroling Dusk: An Anthology of Verse by Negro Poets.* New York: Harper & Brothers Publishers, 1927.

Delta Sigma Theta Sorority, Inc.

Founded in 1913 by HOWARD UNIVERSITY students, this African-American sorority became an important advocate of social change and black economic and intellectual advancement. Its membership expanded considerably during the Harlem Renaissance years. Prominent members included JESSIE REDMAN FAUSET.

Bibliography

Giddings, Paula. *In Search of Sisterhood: Delta Sigma Theta and the Challenge of the Black Sorority Movement.* New York: Morrow, 1988.

"Deserter from Armageddon, A"
Theophilus Lewis (1924)

A story of spiritual distress and anxiety by THEOPHILUS LEWIS that is linked directly to the willful and flirtatious behavior of Rosalie, the young wife of Roscoe Joyful. Roscoe is an industrious man who is pushed to the brink by his wife's perpetual disappearances to go dancing. One night he follows her to a barn dance and becomes convinced that the man she has met there is actually Satan. Shortly after he leaves in disgust, Rosalie makes her way home and reports that the barn caved in and that a fire broke out. Her experience, which essentially presents her falling into the fires of Hell, leaves her haunted by the image of her dance partner. Roscoe leaves to secure medical help and returns to find his wife dead. The burn mark on her breast reinforces his belief that Satan has snatched her and that his tortured prayers to God were inadequate and unheard.

The story appeared in two installments in the 1924 March and April issues of the MESSENGER, the magazine for which Lewis was the long-standing theater critic.

Dewitt Clinton High School

The NEW YORK CITY high school that counted influential writers of the Harlem Renaissance and the next generation of African-American literary talent among its graduates. COUNTEE CULLEN attended the school from 1918 through 1921. During his years there, he was the editor of the school newspaper and actively involved on the board of the *Magpie*, the school's literary magazine. Cullen went on to teach at Frederick Douglass Junior High School, where he taught the future novelist and essayist James Baldwin. Baldwin completed his precollege education at Dewitt Clinton. JESSIE FAUSET, writer and visionary literary editor of *THE CRISIS*, taught French at Dewitt Clinton from 1927 through 1944.

Bibliography

Sylvander, Cheryl. *Jessie Redmon Fauset, Black American Writer.* Troy, N.Y.: Whitson Publishing Company, 1981.

Dickinson, Blanche Taylor (1896–unknown)

A well-published poet from Kentucky whose works appeared in most of the leading African-American newspapers and periodicals of the era, including the *CHICAGO DEFENDER*, the *PITTSBURGH COURIER*, *THE CRISIS*, and *OPPORTUNITY*. She published regularly and was awarded literary prizes by both *The Crisis* and *Opportunity*. In 1926 her poem "That Hill," which placed alongside the first-place work "A Nocturne at Bethesda" by ARNA BONTEMPS and "Thoughts In A Zoo" by COUNTEE CULLEN, was one of two works that judges Babette Deutsch, JAMES WELDON JOHNSON, and LANGSTON HUGHES awarded an honorable mention. In 1927 her work was included in *EBONY AND TOPAZ: A COLLECTANEA*, the impressive and selective anthology that *Opportunity* editor CHARLES S. JOHNSON produced in part to represent the evolution and direction of the African-American literary tradition. Countee Cullen included six of her poems in CAROLING DUSK: AN ANTHOLOGY OF VERSE, including the autobiographical poem "Revelation" about a young girl who, like Dickinson, took great pleasure from walking with crowds in public.

In her open and casual autobiographical commentary that preceded the poems in *Caroling Dusk*, Dickinson revealed that her favorite poets were Countee Cullen, GEORGIA DOUGLAS JOHNSON, and Edna St. Vincent Millay. Her "favorite pastime" was "walking along a crowded street," and her "favorite exertion" involved efforts to "perfect [her] technique" as a writer of short stories.

Dickinson's poems reflect her familiarity with the Bible, her interest in women's survival strategies, and her belief in self-assertion.

Bibliography

Roses, Lorraine Elena, and Ruth Elizabeth Randolph. *Harlem Renaissance and Beyond: Literary Biographies of 100 Black Women Writers, 1900–1945.* Boston: G. K. Hall & Co., 1990.

Dill, Augustus Granville (1881–1956)

A 1908 graduate of HARVARD UNIVERSITY and member of the NATIONAL ASSOCIATION FOR THE ADVANCEMENT OF COLORED PEOPLE (NAACP), whose work as a sociology student was instrumental to W. E. B. DuBois. A native of Ohio, Dill became a vital contributor to the Atlanta Studies publication series that DuBois produced during his tenure at ATLANTA UNIVERSITY. Dill, whose scholarship earned him a rarely bestowed master's degree from the university, followed DuBois to NEW YORK CITY, where he established the official NAACP magazine, THE CRISIS.

Dill was one of the first editorial staff members of *The Crisis.* He worked closely with W. E. B. DuBois, editor and founder of the periodical, and with JESSIE FAUSET, literary editor and the colleague with whom he coedited THE BROWNIES' BOOK, a children's magazine. DuBois and Dill founded a press together, but DuBois made the decision to terminate Dill's employment at the magazine in the wake of Dill's arrest on sexual molestation charges.

Bibliography

Lewis, David Levering. *W. E. B. DuBois: Biography of A Race, 1868–1919.* New York: Henry Holt and Company, 1993.
———. *W. E. B. DuBois: The Fight for Equality and the American Century, 1919–1963.* New York: Henry Holt and Company, 2000.

Dismond, Geraldyn (Gerry Major)
(1894–unknown)

A teacher, Red Cross worker during World War I, and popular Harlem Renaissance–era columnist. Dismond, who earned her Ph.D. from the UNIVERSITY OF CHICAGO in 1915, provided up-to-date social commentary for the leading African-American newspapers of the era, including the AMSTERDAM NEWS, the *Chicago Bee*, and the *Baltimore Afro-American*. She was a pioneering radio personality who became the first African-American female to provide announcements for a commercial radio station. She used the pseudonym Gerry Major while serving as editor of the INTER-STATE TATTLER and was known widely because of her longtime role as society editor for *Jet Magazine*.

Divine, Father   *See* BAKER, GEORGE.

Dodge, Mabel (1879–1962)

A wealthy white woman who was determined to become the patron and love interest of JEAN TOOMER. Dodge was married to her fourth husband, Tony Luhan, when she discovered Jean Toomer. She embraced Toomer's Gurdjieffian beliefs, pursued him, and encouraged his attentions by bestowing large sums of money upon him.

Bibliography

Lewis, David Levering. *When Harlem Was in Vogue.* New York: Knopf, 1981.

Dodson, Owen (Vincent) (1914–1983)

A poet, playwright, and novelist who pursued careers as a writer and teacher. He graduated from the YALE UNIVERSITY School of Drama with a master's of fine arts. He began teaching theater at the college level and enjoyed stints at ATLANTA UNIVERSITY and Hampton Institute, two historically black colleges and universities. While teaching, Dodson continued to prepare his work for the stage. His master's thesis inspired "Divine Comedy," his first play and a work staged at Yale. Another Renaissance-era piece was entitled "Garden of Time," a verse drama in which he revisited the story of Medea.

Over the course of his career and in the years beyond the Harlem Renaissance, Dodson wrote a diverse number of works and was still publishing just before his death in 1983.

Bibliography

Lewis, David Levering. *When Harlem Was in Vogue*. New York: Knopf, 1981.

Domingo, Wilfred Adolphus (1889–1968)

The West Indian–born black nationalist and editor of *Negro World*, the newspaper of the UNIVERSAL NEGRO IMPROVEMENT ASSOCIATION that was established in the United States by MARCUS GARVEY of Jamaica. Domingo eventually cut ties with Garvey, whom he saw as an unpredictable threat to African-American domestic interests, and became a highly regarded contributor of essays and nonfictional prose pieces to the *Messenger*. The anti-West Indian sentiments of that magazine, founded by A. PHILIP RANDOLPH and CHANDLER OWEN in 1917, ultimately prompted Domingo to establish his own publication, the *EMANCIPATOR*. He became one of the period's black Communists and began contributing his time and writing skills to the AFRICAN BLACK BROTHERHOOD, a socialist organization affiliated with the COMMUNIST PARTY.

Bibliography

Lewis, David Levering. *When Harlem Was in Vogue*. New York: Knopf, 1981.

"Door Stop"   May Miller (1930)

A short story by MAY MILLER SULLIVAN that appeared in the May 1930 issue of *Carolina Magazine*, the student literary magazine of the University of North Carolina at Chapel Hill.

"Double Trouble"   Jessie Fauset (1923)

A short story by JESSIE FAUSET, literary editor of *THE CRISIS* whose setting and plot rehearsed some of the same racial tensions that Fauset would address several years later in *PLUM BUN*, her 1929 novel.

The story, which appeared in the August and September 1923 issues of the magazine and included illustrations by artist Laura Wheeler, was set in Edendale, New Jersey, a community with a strictly observed social and racial hierarchy. The protagonists, Angelique Murray and Malory Fordham, are high school students and in love with each other. They are part of the African-American community that lives in close connection with the upper-class white community made up of "a wealthy and leisure class of whites, men of affairs, [and] commuters having big business interests in Philadelphia, Trenton, Newark, and even New York." The young couple, however, is unable to express freely their affection for one another because of the watchful nature of the community and the Murray family's general prohibition against boys. When the two are seen together at a local picnic, they begin to realize the widespread resistance to their involvement. Malory does not understand his family's prejudice against Angelique but is determined "like many another fond lover to acquaint others with his treasure to show off not only this unparalleled gem, but himself too." The two are unable to spend time together that afternoon, and the obstructions that arise prompt Malory to insist that Angelique accompany him home the next day in order to meet his family. This planned introduction does not take place either, and she is forced to leave the front porch and wander home alone. When Malory then fails to keep their regular appointment and seems to run from her, she pursues him desperately. She wonders whether it is the stigma of her cousin Laurentine's illegitimacy and the relationship between her Aunt Sal and her white employer Ralph Courtney that has forced the Fordhams to reject her. When she finally confronts Malory, however, she is shocked to learn that she is in fact his half sister. Angelique is devastated by the news that her mother stole away with Malory's father and that her reputation is forever linked to the unseemly affair that her mother allowed between herself and the patriarch of a respectable family of

color. The story ends somewhat obliquely as Angelique now grasps at the chance to be saved by another young man named Asshur, who has promised
to return to Edendale and to save her.

Fauset's tale of class stratification, complicated
intraracial romances, and stigma further broadened the scope of Harlem Renaissance literature
that explored African-American family lives and
community dynamics. Fauset used the specter of
incest to intensify the traditional plot of the tragic
mulatto and to consider the devastating effects of
seduction and secrecy within middle-class communities of color.

Dougherty, Romeo Lionel (1906–1944)

An energetic reporter whose life was cut short.
Dougherty, who published under the name "Lionel
Dougherty," was a journalist who worked on the
staff of three East Coast papers. He began his ca-
reer as a *Brooklyn Eagle* reporter, became the AMS-
TERDAM NEWS sports and drama editor, and finally
served for a time as the editor and manager of the
Washington Sun.

Douglas, Aaron (1888–1979)

A talented painter whose works established his
reputation as one of the most well-known artists of
the Harlem Renaissance. He won major arts fellowships sponsored by a number of foundations
supportive of African-American arts efforts, including the Barnes Foundation Fellowship. His career began in the 1920s, and it was the commission
to illustrate THE NEW NEGRO, edited by ALAIN
LOCKE, that began his lengthy and influential participation in the Harlem Renaissance. Like ZORA
NEALE HURSTON, LANGSTON HUGHES, and
Locke, Douglas enjoyed the financial support of
CHARLOTTE OSGOOD MASON, a wealthy white
patron of the period.

Douglas's art graced the pages of a variety of
first-rate publications. His works, which appeared in THE CRISIS, VANITY FAIR, and the
AMERICAN MERCURY, also secured his contracts
to provide illustrations for books by prominent
Harlem Renaissance–era writers. Douglas worked
with JAMES WELDON JOHNSON, Alain Locke,
CARL VAN VECHTEN, and many others. The

Works Progress Administration (WPA) commissioned his murals for the NEW YORK PUBLIC LI-
BRARY branch in HARLEM. In these murals, which
he entitled *Aspects of Negro Life,* Douglas provided
powerful images of black life. He designed posters
for the KRIGWA PLAYERS, the drama troupe that
W. E. B. DuBois established in Harlem. Douglas,
who earned his bachelor's degree in fine arts from
the University of Kansas, later became a professor
of art at FISK UNIVERSITY.

Bibliography
Henderson, Harry Brinton. *A History of African-Ameri-
can Artists: From 1792 to the Present.* New York:
Pantheon Books, 1993.
Kirschke, Amy. *Aaron Douglas: Art, Race, and the Harlem
Renaissance.* Jackson: University Press of Missis-
sippi, 1995.

"Drab Rambles" Marita Bonner (1927)

"Drab Rambles" was made up of two carefully rendered stories about the plight of African-American
workers. MARITA BONNER's stories, which appeared
in the December 1927 issue of OPPORTUNITY, were
powerful commentaries on the unwarranted humiliations visited upon African Americans and critiques
of the limited understanding that whites had of the
extent of their own privilege and insensitivity.

The first section, prefaced by Bonner's mystical invocation, "I am you and I am myself," focused
on a hard-working man named Peter Jackson,
whose life of toil has ruined his heart. He suffers
the rudeness of the hospital staff for a time but ultimately chastises his doctor for his thoughtless statements about his health and options for recovery.

The second narration follows the character
Madie Frye, a diligent laundry worker who is forced
to hide her first child, born of the unwanted sexual
advances from a former white male employer, while
she works. The tragedy here is that Madie is ac-
costed again and left to wonder how she will juggle
raising two children and the pressing demands of a
labor-intensive job. Bonner's narrator is an ardent,
albeit helpless, champion of these two powerful
archetypes. The piece closes with a haunting warning that seems directed toward whites in particular:
"the blood will flow back to you—and you will
care," announces the narrator. Bonner's critique

was part of the tradition of piercing works of domestic realism produced by a number of Harlem Renaissance writers.

Bibliography

Roses, Lorraine Elena, and Ruth Elizabeth Randolph. *Harlem Renaissance and Beyond: Literary Biographies of 100 Black Women Writers, 1900–1945.* Boston: G. K. Hall & Co., 1990.

Draper, Muriel (1891–1956)

An American whose British literary salon counted Pablo Casals and Henry James among its attendees. When she returned to the United States in the 1920s, Draper started a literary salon that catered to Harlem Renaissance writers and artists. She became a patron and editor; it was she who edited BORN TO BE, the lively autobiography by TAYLOR GORDON. She published her own autobiography, *Music at Midnight,* in 1929.

Bibliography

Muriel Draper Papers, Beinecke Library, Yale University.

Dream Keeper and Other Poems, The
Langston Hughes (1932)

Published by KNOPF in 1932, this volume of poems by LANGSTON HUGHES was prompted by a request from Effie Lee Power, a librarian and nationally recognized figure in the field of children's literature, for works that would appeal to children. Hughes wrote new pieces for this collection but also drew from THE WEARY BLUES and FINE CLOTHES TO THE JEW, two of his earlier works. Helen Sewell provided the illustrations to this book that Hughes dedicated to Gwyn Clark, his beloved stepbrother.

Bibliography

Rampersad, Arnold. *The Life of Langston Hughes: I, Too, Sing America.* Vol. 1, *1902–1941.* New York: Oxford University Press, 1986.

Dreiser, Theodore (1871–1945)

A white writer of naturalism whose best literary success occurred during the Harlem Renaissance. The Indiana-born author of *Sister Carrie* (1900)

and *Jennie Gerhardt* (1911) published his novel *An American Tragedy,* a work inspired by a well-known murder case of the period, in 1925.

Dreiser traveled with LANGSTON HUGHES when the League of American Writers commissioned both men to represent the organization at the Congress for Peace Action and Against Bombing of Open Cities. Dreiser proved to be an unreliable partner; Hughes was the one who kept their appointments. In 1933, Dreiser was one of several well-known writers who agreed to donate work to the auction and benefit for the SCOTTSBORO Boys that Hughes was involved in organizing.

Bibliography

Bernard, Emily. *Remember Me to Harlem: The Letters of Langston Hughes and Carl Van Vechten.* New York: Knopf, 2001.
Rampersad, Arnold. *The Life of Langston Hughes: I, Too, Sing America.* Vol. 1, *1902–1941.* New York: Oxford University Press, 1986.

"Drenched in Light" Zora Neale Hurston (1924)

A short story by ZORA NEALE HURSTON that appeared in the December 1924 issue of OPPORTUNITY, one of several stories that she published while attending HOWARD UNIVERSITY, but the first to appear in a national magazine.

The story revolves around Isis Watts, an irrepressible 11-year-old girl whose well-meaning antics are often misunderstood. A protagonist who recalls the child protagonist Frado in Harriet Wilson's *Our Nig* (1859), Isis ends up entertaining a white couple with her grand dreams and imaginings about her future life. She escapes punishment and detention when her temporary new guardians persuade the grandmother to let them take Isis with them to dance downtown.

The figure of the strong female matriarch, the young girl whose coming of age is a painful process of containment, and the female desire for unmediated self-expression establish early similarities to later Hurston works, especially THEIR EYES WERE WATCHING GOD and her autobiography DUST TRACKS ON A ROAD. It was this story that Hurston used to establish her first contacts in HARLEM when she arrived in NEW YORK CITY in 1925.

Bibliography

Campbell, Josie. *Student Companion to Zora Neale Hurston.* Westport, Conn.: Greenwood Press, 2001.

Hemenway, Robert. *Zora Neale Hurston: A Literary Biography.* Urbana: University of Illinois Press, 1977.

Drums at Dusk Arna Bontemps (1939)

A historical novel and the third work of fiction for adults by ARNA BONTEMPS. The work, which Bontemps proposed to complete while a Rosenwald Fellow in 1938, continued to explore themes related to the enslavement of peoples of African descent. Like BLACK THUNDER, the novel about Gabriel Prosser and his foiled slave rebellion of 1800, this book also focused on a slave revolt and the complicated politics of black self-emancipation. Bontemps recreated the stories surrounding the slave revolt that Toussaint Louverture led in HAITI and against French colonial slave owners and military forces.

The publication of *Drums at Dusk* coincided with the 150th anniversary of the fall of the Bastille. Like *Black Thunder*, Bontemps's novel about Gabriel Prosser and his efforts to organize a slave revolt, *Drums at Dusk* also made connections between the French revolution and African-American resistance during the antebellum period.

The novel, criticized for its thinly constructed plot, revolved around the romance between Celeste Juvet, a young woman of French descent, and Diron Desautels, an ardent antislavery aristocrat with ties to Les Amis de Noirs, a French abolitionist group dedicated to ameliorating the plight of the enslaved Africans on the island. Known as an "exuberant society of violent anti-slavery partisans" (5), the group adhered to the ideal that "All men are born and continue free and equal as to their rights" (5). Desautels makes overtures to the enslaved people when he can, insisting that "[t]here are thousands in Paris who abhor slavery" and encouraging them to seek him out if "ever you blacks feel strong enough to help yourselves" because they will "have the active sympathy of many *blancs,* including myself" (53). Reviewers noted that the bulk of the novel focused on white characters. By maintaining his focus on the white European slave-owning class, Bontemps relegated Louverture and the larger plans for resistance to the background. In so doing, Louverture maintains a mythical presence; when he emerges, he appears as a highly ordered and rational man. More than midway through the novel, as the revolt rages and households are thrown into disarray, Louverture, a coachman, appears. Bontemps describes him as a man who is "not a great one for the sort of havoc this night was producing; his mind was offended by messiness, confusion and turmoil" (150). The hero of the Haitian Revolution is not a bloodthirsty general. In the novel, he exists as an almost unwilling hero, one who "hadn't the power to draw a brawling sword" but one who is "thrilled by the prospect" of saving an oppressed people and also "ready and anxious to meet a military foe if by doing so he could strike a blow for the freedom of the blacks" (150). Bontemps provides a most nuanced and subtle fictional portrait of Toussaint Louverture, the impressive and accomplished leader of the rebellion that culminated in freedom for the enslaved people of the island.

Bontemps completed *Drums at Dusk* before he traveled to Haiti on a JULIUS ROSENWALD FELLOWSHIP. While there, he found it necessary to make only minor changes to his representations of the island and its history. Once the book was completed, Bontemps was involved in an innovative radio preview of the novel. Bontemps spoke with Ethel Reid Winser, director of the CHICAGO-based radio program "Know Your Authors" during an interview that then was aired with additional details about the book (Jones 94). Critics suggest that the novel only would have been strengthened had he in fact allocated substantial time for research in Haiti and then incorporated more of his observations of island life and Haitian historical facts into the work. Yet, as biographer Kirkland Jones notes, financial constraints did not make it possible for Bontemps to proceed in this manner. Reviewer Charles Poore commented on the "moderation" that he detected in the novel about "a melodramatic time" and urged Bontemps to consider writing a sequel (Poore, 18). Bontemps's restraint in the novel was noticeable, prompting another reviewer to observe that "[a]s for Toussaint, who is worth a novel to himself, we take leave of him at the tantalizing moment when it occurs to him that his great chance has come, that once the frenzy of revenge has spent itself this rabble of freed slaves will be a tool ready to his hand" (*NYT*, 7 May 1939, BR4). Bontemps's style and historical reserve may have piqued the interest of readers enough that they themselves probed into Haitian history.

Bibliography

"A Tale of the Slave Revolt in Haiti." *New York Times*, 7 May 1939, BR4.

James, C. L. R. *The Black Jacobins; Toussaint L'Ouverture and the San Domingo Revolution.* New York: Vintage Books, 1963.

Jones, Kirkland C. *Renaissance Man from Louisiana: A Biography of Arna Wendell Bontemps.* Westport, Conn.: Greenwood Press, 1992.

Poore, Charles. "Books of the Times." *New York Times*, 13 May 1939, 18.

DuBois, William Edward Burghardt (W. E. B. DuBois) (1868–1963)

The eminent scholar and teacher, prolific writer, accomplished editor, and tireless activist whose deliberate leadership and advocacy and visionary efforts to create purposeful dialogue about political, social, and intellectual matters shaped the Harlem Renaissance in explicit and enduring ways. The sociopolitical works and philosophies of DuBois, who has long been regarded as the most influential African-American intellectual of the 20th century, continue to enrich contemporary analyses of race, class, and political thought.

Born in Great Barrington, Massachusetts, DuBois was the son of Mary Sylvania Burghardt and Alfred DuBois, a Haitian whose ancestry included white French Huguenots. He grew up in the protective and professionally ambitious New England world of his maternal kin. The valedictorian of his 13-member senior class at Great Barrington High School, he delivered the graduation speech on New England abolitionist Wendell Phillips. In the wake of his mother's death shortly after his graduation from high school, DuBois received financial support and counsel from his high school teachers about the next stages of his academic development. While he aspired to attend HARVARD UNIVERSITY, DuBois matriculated at FISK UNIVERSITY in Nashville, Tennessee. He graduated with

honors in 1888 and then realized his long-held dream to attend school in Cambridge, MASSACHUSETTS. He began a second bachelor's degree program at Harvard University and earned a B.A. and an M.A. degree before pursuing a two-year course in sociology and economics in Germany at the University of Berlin. Financial constraints prevented him from earning a degree from the university, and he returned to Massachusetts. In 1895, he became the first African American to earn a Ph.D. from Harvard. His thesis, "The Suppression of the Slave Trade," earned him university honors and was published as part of the highly selective Harvard Historical Series. Throughout his life, he maintained close and sometimes fractious relationships with leading scholars and educational institutions throughout the North and South. In addition to teaching at WILBERFORCE UNIVERSITY, he was a member of the faculty at ATLANTA UNIVERSITY and the UNIVERSITY OF PENNSYLVANIA.

DuBois married Nina Gomer, a Wilberforce student of African-American and German heritage whom he had met at the school. The couple had two children. Their son, Burghardt, died tragically during infancy. Their only daughter, NINA YOLANDE DUBOIS, a FISK UNIVERSITY graduate and teacher, married poet COUNTEE CULLEN in a service that was touted as the African-American social event of the year. Their union was short-lived, however, and she later remarried. Yolande passed away in 1960, and DuBois was forced to confront the overwhelming loss of both children. Following the death of his first wife in 1950, DuBois married SHIRLEY GRAHAM, an accomplished playwright who shared his nationalist vision and worked alongside him to support pan-Africanist dialogue, social reform, and political freedom for all people. At the invitation of Kwame Nkrumah, a graduate of LINCOLN UNIVERSITY and the first president of an independent Ghana, the couple settled in Accra, Ghana. DuBois became a Ghanaian citizen at 95, in 1963 just before his death there. Nkrumah presided over the formal state funeral given in honor of DuBois. DuBois's descendants include a grandson, DuBois Williams, and an adopted son, David DuBois.

DuBois linked his political activism to African-American institutional efforts. In 1897, he collaborated with Alexander Crummell, Paul Laurence

Dunbar, ALAIN LOCKE, and CARTER G. WOODSON to form the AMERICAN NEGRO ACADEMY, the nation's first significant African-American learned society. The organization promoted intellectual debate and was committed to publishing works by notable and emerging scholars of color. DuBois's study, *The Social Evolution of the Black South,* appeared in 1911. Later in his life, and during the last 10 years of the Harlem Renaissance, DuBois intensified his participation in pan-Africanist circles. He organized international pan-Africanist conferences in FRANCE, England, and the United States that provided important platforms from which leading scholars and political activists could question colonial practices and ideology and explore avenues that would result in effective pan-African unity and solidarity. DuBois continued his political agitation in the years following the Harlem Renaissance and worked with such organizations as the Council on African Affairs.

DuBois's long-standing relationship to the NATIONAL ASSOCIATION FOR THE ADVANCEMENT OF COLORED PEOPLE (NAACP) began in the early 1900s when he became part of the Niagara Movement, a gathering of some 60 intellectuals, political figures, and reformers, such as Harvard graduate and newspaper editor WILLIAM MONROE TROTTER, Mary Talbert, Atlanta University president JOHN HOPE, and journalist JESSE MAX BARBER. When the NAACP was founded in 1910 and based in New York, DuBois joined the organization as the director of the organization's publications and as the first editor of its flagship monthly, THE CRISIS.

DuBois founded and edited *The Crisis,* the first of the major Harlem Renaissance journals to appear, in 1910. THE MESSENGER, founded by Chandler Owen and A. Philip Randolph, began publication seven years later, and OPPORTUNITY, the journal of the National Urban League, was founded 13 years later in 1923. It was not his first journal venture. In 1905 he established *Moon,* a weekly journal that lasted through 1906, and the *Horizon,* a monthly periodical published from 1907 through 1910. During his 24-year tenure as *Crisis* editor, DuBois was dedicated to using the journal as a forum in which to promote intense and rigorous debates about national and global issues relating to such pressing contemporary realities such as World War I, poverty, black migration, racial disen-

W. E. B. DuBois, author, scholar, public intellectual, civil rights leader, and *The Crisis* editor *(Yale Collection of American Literature, Beinecke Rare Book and Manuscript Library)*

franchisement, and LYNCHING. His editorials were noted for their uncompromising stand on racial aesthetics, the priorities of the NEW NEGRO, trends in African-American literature, and the responsibilities of African-American writers. Historian Nathan Huggins asserts that "[i]n regard to violence and injustice against the Negro, no one was a more ruthless muckraker than Du Bois" (Huggins, 28). He did not shy away from exposing the hypocrisy of federal officials and policy and was determined to provide readers with the most informative statistical and narrative assessments related to issues such as mob violence and discrimination against African Americans in the military. He was especially outspoken against Woodrow Wilson, the president who approved segregation in all federal offices and authorized the 1918 execution of soldiers alleged to have participated in race riots in Houston. His combative critiques led to potential charges of sedition, and in order to minimize the threat to the NAACP, and by extension to himself and *The Crisis*, DuBois tempered his outrage in his published editorials.

DuBois was attentive to intraracial political matters as well. He had little patience for MARCUS GARVEY, the Jamaican-born leader of the increasingly popular back-to-Africa movement and the Universal Negro Improvement Association. Nathan Huggins notes that DuBois was especially frustrated by and opposed to Garvey's efforts because PAN-AFRICANISM as a movement and an ideology had been "a lifelong commitment" and because "the problems were much too complex and torturous to be given into the hands of one whose ego tended to make its own realities." DuBois began formal efforts to advance pan-Africanism in 1919 when he began to organize against colonial governments in Africa and to work toward the independence of all African nations. He was instrumental in organizing international conferences, the first of which was held in Paris in 1919 during the Versailles Peace Conference. In his explication of the differences between the two men, Huggins notes that DuBois worked to "achieve a careful balance of Negro integration in the American society" while Garvey "simply announced a kind of black separatism even to the point of collusion with the Ku Klux Klan" (Huggins, 47).

When JESSIE FAUSET joined the staff of *The Crisis*, she invigorated the journal, developed its focus on literary matters, and provided a welcoming and respected forum in which writers of the period could showcase their work. DuBois worked closely with Fauset, a prolific writer, attentive editor, and mentor extraordinaire who became known as a literary midwife of the Harlem Renaissance. The two were cocreators of *THE BROWNIES' BOOK*, one of the most deliberate efforts during the period to create an appealing, empowering, literature for children of color that sparked their imaginations, provided intriguing details about African history and culture, and was free of damaging racial stereotypes. The literary focus of the journal also allowed DuBois to cultivate relationships with contemporary writers and artists, many of whom had incisive political agendas and perspectives as well. Writer ARNA BONTEMPS, who in 1941 saw DuBois deliver a lecture in CHICAGO on "This War and the Darker Races," testified to the elder scholar's lasting ap-

peal. In a letter to Langston Hughes, Bontemps noted that DuBois "spoke . . . to an overflow crowd—at 50¢ a head" and that the lecture was "[v]ery deep, scholarly and enlightening" (Nichols, 80). Bontemps, also intrigued by DuBois's plans to publish an *Encyclopedia of the Negro*, invited him to Chicago to meet with potential contributors and was able to say proudly that "progress was made" (Nichols, 77). The two men shared a number of similar ideas, a reality that on at least one occasion prompted Bontemps to lament the quick pen of the respected activist. In 1939, when Bontemps was planning to compose an essay on the African-American press, DuBois published a forthright analysis in the *Chicago Defender*. The piece, which Bontemps confessed "takes some of the steam out of my plan to a Negro press article," insisted that "the black press is a symptom, not a disease; a result of the Negro's lack of participation in American life, not a cause of anything. The thing to treat is the condition which makes the daily press insufficient for the needs of Negroes," wrote Bontemps in his overview of DuBois's essay.

Writer CLAUDE MCKAY admired DuBois but, as scholar Wayne Cooper notes, "found DuBois too aloof and formal for any genuine friendship to develop between them" (Cooper, 141). McKay, who developed a passionate interest in Russian politics and the Russian Revolution, also was somewhat put off by DuBois's "sneering" at the historic moment in Russian history that he believed was "the greatest event in the history of humanity" (Cooper, 141). In turn, DuBois struggled to acknowledge *HOME TO HARLEM* (1927), a novel that "nauseated" him and contained such grimy portraits of Harlem life that he felt "distinctly like taking a bath" (Lewis, 214). In response to *CANE* by JEAN TOOMER, DuBois noted that the volume could have benefited immensely had Toomer had a deeper familiarity with the South and with Georgia, but he went on to celebrate Toomer as one who might soon be regarded "as a writer who first dared to emancipate the colored world from the conventions of sex" and whose portraits of women and relationships were "painted with a frankness that is going to make his black readers shrink and criticize; and yet they are done with a certain splendid, careless truth" (Turner, 50). Writer ZORA NEALE HURSTON was conflicted about DuBois, an influential man whom she addressed as the "Dean of American Negro Artists" (Kaplan, 518), whose influence she recognized, and whose editorial evaluations she sought out. Her contact with him included correspondence in which she asked whether certain of her plays might be of interest to Krigwa, the theater group with which he was affiliated, and in which she agreed to contribute to his *Encyclopedia Africana* "if you will tell me what you wan[t]" (Kaplan, 374).

DuBois was active in cultural circles and was an outspoken advocate of a race-based theater. He used his position at *The Crisis* to encourage playwrights to create works that reflected the complexity of African-American life and that explored universal and wide-ranging social and creative issues. DuBois's recommendations became the foundation for the little theater movement, a tradition that encouraged communities to generate small companies that were rooted in and involved the neighborhoods in which they were based. DuBois collaborated in 1927 with Regina Andrews, a librarian at the 135th Street branch of the NEW YORK PUBLIC LIBRARY, to create the KRIGWA PLAYERS.

DuBois also sponsored annual *Crisis* literary contests that, like those held by CHARLES S. JOHNSON's NATIONAL URBAN LEAGUE publication *Opportunity*, recognized emerging writers, and helped to model acceptable race literature. DuBois enlisted the aid of leading American writers—white and black—as well as NAACP leaders and notable public figures who supported the organization's efforts to foster African-American talent. Judges included BENJAMIN BRAWLEY, CHARLES CHESNUTT, Otelia Cromwell, LESLIE PINCKNEY HILL, JAMES WELDON JOHNSON, EUGENE O'NEILL, MARY WHITE OVINGTON, JOEL SPINGARN, and H. G. Wells. Prizes were offered for fiction, poetry, plays, and essays. Winners included MARITA BONNER, ARNA BONTEMPS, ANITA SCOTT COLEMAN, COUNTEE CULLEN, RUDOLPH FISHER, RUTH GAINES-SHELTON, LANGSTON HUGHES, and WILLIS RICHARDSON.

DuBois also pursued several intense and intimate relationships with women who were central to the Harlem Renaissance movement. Biographer David Levering Lewis notes that when DuBois's wife left for Paris in the spring of 1929 to comfort her daughter in the wake of her disastrous marriage to Countee Cullen, DuBois began to enjoy a "social life that was emotionally so much more rewarding" (Lewis, 266). His "serial affairs" included a previous "star-crossed love affair" with Jessie Fauset; relationships with ETHEL RAY NANCE, the longtime secretary at *Opportunity* who worked alongside Charles S. Johnson; GEORGIA DOUGLAS JOHNSON, the WASHINGTON, D.C., poet and beloved, accommodating mentor of many writers and scholars in the capital; Mildred Bryant Jones, a Fisk University graduate and chair of the music department at the Wendell Phillips High School, the leading African-American public school in Chicago; and Virginia Alexander, a graduate of the Woman's Medical College of Pennsylvania whom Lewis suggests "might [have] become the second Mrs. DuBois and for whom he felt a special passion and admiration" (Lewis, 272). Colleagues continued to respect his privacy, and DuBois's liaisons did not jeopardize his high public standing.

DuBois published significant works of sociology, political critique, and fiction in the years before the Harlem Renaissance. Included among the 21 independently authored volumes and 15 edited collections that he produced during his lifetime were the influential study *The Philadelphia Negro* (1899), the illuminating collection of essays *Souls of Black Folk* (1903), a biography of John Brown, and the novel *The Quest of the Silver Fleece* (1911). His most influential work, SOULS OF BLACK FOLK (1903), cemented his reputation as an intellectual and as the main challenger to the accommodationist philosophies of Booker T. Washington.

DuBois's powerful evaluations of African-American psychological, social, economic, intellectual, and political realities proved integral to the founding of the NAACP, which grew out of the 1905 Niagara meetings in Buffalo, New York. In *Souls of Black Folk*, DuBois emphasized an investment in the intellectual and political advancement of people of color. The lasting impression of DuBois's eloquent compilation of essays on racial awakening, the rejuvenating purity and power of the African-American folk, and the need to cultivate and maintain a talented tenth capable of spearheading the race's advancement, led to his appointment as editor of *The Crisis* once the NAACP was established. During his tenure, circulation increased one hundred fold during a 10-year period, growing from 1,000 copies in the first printing to some 100,000 by 1919. He resigned in 1934, following a series of policy disagreements with the NAACP that included a difference of opinion about how best to protect African-American economic, educational, and political progress.

During the Harlem Renaissance, he published the first of his three autobiographies. *Dark Water: Voices from Within the Veil* appeared in 1921. His novel *DARK PRINCESS* appeared in 1928 and represented DuBois's effort to model the literary and racial aesthetic that he believed most appropriate and politically useful for the period. In the late 1930s, DuBois's editorials appeared regularly in the African-American newspapers including the New York-based *AMSTERDAM NEWS* and the *PITTSBURGH COURIER*. Additional works that contributed to the rich and multifaceted scholarship on African-American and pan-African culture, politics, and tradition included *Africa: Its Place in Modern History* (1930), *Black Reconstruction: An Essay Toward a History of the Part Which Black Folk Played in the Attempt to Reconstruct Democracy in America, 1860–1880* (1935), and *Black Folk, Then and Now: An Essay in the History and Sociology of the Negro Race* (1939).

Following his departure from *The Crisis*, DuBois became chair of the Atlanta University Sociology Department in 1934. There, he founded and edited *Phylon Magazine* for the next 10 years, until 1944. His significant publication record in the years after the Harlem Renaissance included continued publication in the African-American press and newspapers such as the *Chicago Tribune*. He published respected works on Africa including *The World and Africa: An Inquiry into the Part Which Africa Has Played in World History* (1947). He also returned to fiction and published works such as the trilogy *The Ordeal of Mansart* (1957), *Mansart Builds a School* (1959), and *Worlds of Color* (1961).

DuBois received high national and international honors and recognition for his unwavering commitment to social and political reforms and equality. He was the recipient of the Spingarn Medal, the NAACP's highest honor, in 1932. His many honors included honorary degrees from numerous schools such as the University of Berlin, HOWARD UNIVERSITY, Morgan State College, and Fisk University. Elected to the National Institute of Arts and Letters in 1943, he also was honored by the Liberian government, which made him Knight

Commander of the Liberian Humane Order of African Redemption. DuBois was awarded the Lenin Peace Prize in Moscow in 1959.

DuBois was a resilient public figure, a man who refused to compromise his standards of intellectual excellence and political morality. His fortitude, multifaceted leadership in the arts, education, and politics underscored the complexity of African-American experiences. His professional example inspired and required many writers to articulate their agendas as aspiring public intellectuals and women and men of their race.

The W. E. B. DuBois papers are held in several libraries and archives. The majority of his papers are held in the Special Collections Department, University of Massachusetts, Amherst. Additional archives holding DuBois's papers include Fisk University Library and Atlanta University.

Bibliography

Aptheker, Herbert. *The Legacy of W. E. B. DuBois*. White Plains, N.Y.: Krause International Publications, 1989.

Cooper, Wayne. *Claude McKay: Rebel Sojourner in the Harlem Renaissance*. New York: Schocken Books, 1987.

Coviello, Peter. "Intimacy and Affliction: DuBois, Race, and Psychoanalysis," *Modern Language Quarterly* 64, no. 1 (2003): 1–32.

DuBois, Shirley Graham. *His Day Is Marching On: A Memoir of W. E. B. DuBois*. New York: Lippincott, 1971.

DuBois, W. E. Burghardt. *Souls of Black Folk*. 1903; reprint, New York: Bantam Books, 1989.

Huggins, Nathan. *Harlem Renaissance*. New York: Oxford University Press, 1971.

Kaplan, Carla. *Zora Neale Hurston: A Life in Letters*. New York: Doubleday, 2002.

Lewis, David Levering. *W. E. B. DuBois: Biography of a Race, 1868–1919*. New York: Henry Holt and Company, 1993.

———. *W. E. B. DuBois: The Fight for Equality and the American Century, 1919–1963*. New York: Henry Holt and Company, 2000.

———, and Deborah Willis. *A Small Nation of People: W. E. B. DuBois and African American Portraits of Progress*. New York: Amistad, 2003.

Marable, Manning. *W. E. B. DuBois, Black Radical Democrat*. Boston: Twayne, 1986.

Nichols, Charles H., ed. *Arna Bontemps–Langston Hughes Letters, 1925–1967.* New York: Paragon House, 1990.

Rampersad, Arnold. *The Art and Imagination of W. E. B. DuBois.* New York: Schocken Books, 1990.

Turner, Darwin T. "W. E. B. DuBois and the Theory of a Black Aesthetic." In *Harlem Renaissance Re-Examined: A Revised and Expanded Edition,* edited by Victor Kramer and Robert Russ. Troy, N.Y.: Whitson Pub., 1997. 45–64.

Wintz, Cary. *African American Political Thought: Washington, Du Bois, Garvey, and Randolph.* Armonk, N.Y.: M. E. Sharpe, 1996.

DuBois, (Nina) Yolande (1900–1960)

The only surviving child of W. E. B. DuBois and Nina Gomer DuBois, his first wife. Described by David Levering Lewis, a DuBois biographer, as "outstandingly ordinary—a kind, plain woman of modest intellectual endowment," Yolande graduated from FISK UNIVERSITY in 1924 and pursued a career in teaching. She is perhaps best known for her short-lived marriage to COUNTEE CULLEN. The ceremony in the Salem Methodist Episcopal Church with Cullen's adoptive father presiding, was, without a doubt, the most impressive African-American social event of the year. The marriage lasted less than a year; Yolande married a second time and bore a son, DuBois Williams. She died of a heart attack in 1960, and W. E. B. DuBois was devastated by the loss of his daughter. Shortly after he buried his daughter in Great Barrington, Massachusetts, alongside her mother and infant brother, he left for GHANA, where he died in 1963.

Bibliography

Lewis, David Levering. *W. E. B. DuBois: Biography of A Race, 1868–1919.* New York: Henry Holt and Company, 1993.

———. *W. E. B. DuBois: The Fight For Equality and the American Century, 1919–1963.* New York: Henry Holt and Company, 2000.

———. *When Harlem Was in Vogue.* New York: Knopf, 1981.

Dunbar Apartments

One of Harlem's most prestigious addresses, the Dunbar Apartments were built by Roscoe Conkling Bruce, the son of the black Reconstruction-era senator from Mississippi. There were more than 500 apartments in the development located between 149th and 150th Streets and from Seventh to Eighth Avenues. Some of the most significant figures of the Renaissance who lived there at some time included COUNTEE CULLEN, W. E. B. DuBois, and PAUL ROBESON.

Dunbar Garden Players

A small theater group whose name honored Paul Laurence Dunbar. During its short performance life that began in 1929, it produced at least two plays. EULALIE SPENCE directed the company's production of *Before Breakfast* by EUGENE O'NEILL and *Joint Owners of Spain* by Alice Brown.

Dunbar High School

One of the most famous schools in WASHINGTON, D.C. Known for its impressive teachers, rigorous courses, and stellar students, the school counted a number of leading Harlem Renaissance writers and activists among its students and faculty. This was the alma mater of JEAN TOOMER, RICHARD BRUCE NUGENT, STERLING BROWN, MAY MILLER, and CLARISSA SCOTT. Teachers included JESSIE FAUSET, ANNA JULIA COOPER, ANGELINA WELD GRIMKÉ, CLARISSA SCOTT DELANY, MARY BURRILL, and EVA DYKES, one of the first African-American women to earn a Ph.D. in America.

Bibliography

Watson, Steven. *The Harlem Renaissance: Hub of African-American Culture, 1920–1930.* New York: Pantheon Books, 1995.

Dunbar-Nelson, Alice Ruth Moore (1875–1935)

A spirited, highly motivated, and self-confident writer born in New Orleans. Like many other Harlem Renaissance figures, she attended several schools including Cornell University and the UNIVERSITY OF PENNSYLVANIA, two Ivy League schools. She pursued the teaching course of study at Straight

College (which has since become Dillard University). Dunbar-Nelson's literary career began in the 1890s when she published collections of short stories and poetry to much critical acclaim. Her correspondence with Paul Laurence Dunbar, begun when she wrote him to praise his poems, eventually led to marriage in 1898. The union lasted for four years before they separated; Paul Dunbar died of complications from tuberculosis in 1906.

Dunbar-Nelson relocated to Wilmington, Delaware. She began her 18-year teaching appointment at Howard High School, where she eventually became English Department chair. In 1918, she published "Hope Deferred" in THE CRISIS and also penned a play entitled *Mine Eyes Have Seen*. Like ANNA JULIA COOPER, who founded a night school for working African Americans, Dunbar-Nelson diversified her educational outreach and established the Delaware Industrial School For Colored Girls in 1924.

Although she produced the bulk of her writing before the Harlem Renaissance, Dunbar-Nelson provided models of regionalist and domestic fiction that surely influenced other writers of the period. She remained committed to African-American excellence, education, and intellectual development.

Bibliography

Hull, Gloria, ed. *Give Us This Day: The Diary of Alice Dunbar-Nelson*. New York: W. W. Norton & Company, 1984.

———. *Love, Sex, and Poetry: Three Women Writers of the Harlem Renaissance*. Bloomington: Indiana University Press, 1987.

Roses, Lorraine Elena, and Ruth Elizabeth Randolph. *Harlem Renaissance and Beyond: Literary Biographies of 100 Black Women Writers, 1900–1945*. Boston: G. K. Hall & Co., 1990.

Dunbar News

The newspaper published by the residents of the Dunbar Apartments on Seventh and Eighth Streets in HARLEM. The biweekly publication grew from announcements about issues and events pertinent to residents to literary columns that included, on at least one occasion, a poem submitted by LANGSTON HUGHES.

Dunbar Speaker and Entertainer

One of two anthologies that ALICE MOORE DUNBAR-NELSON, the author and former wife of Paul Laurence Dunbar, produced. Published in 1920, the volume, like *Masterpieces of Negro Eloquence* (1914), provided materials that could be used to support oratorical training.

Bibliography

Dunbar, Mrs. Paul Laurence, W. S. Scarborough, and Reverdy C. Ransom. *Paul Laurence Dunbar, Poet Laureate of the Negro Race*. Philadelphia: Reverdy C. Ransom, 1914.

Duncan, Thelma (1902–unknown)

Educated at HOWARD UNIVERSITY, the WASHINGTON, D.C., school that counted LEWIS ALEXANDER, ZORA NEALE HURSTON, MAY MILLER, and GWENDOLYN BENNETT among its students and faculty, Duncan graduated with honors in music. She, like Hurston, enjoyed a fruitful start to her writing career at the school; her first play, THE DEATH DANCE, was performed first by the Howard drama group, University Players.

Duncan, a St. Louis, Missouri, native, gave every impression that she would become an established playwright of the Harlem Renaissance. She wrote *Sacrifice* in 1930 and *Black Magic*, a comedy, in 1931. Unfortunately, Duncan disappeared from the literary scene after completing that work.

Bibliography

Roses, Lorraine Elena, and Ruth Elizabeth Randolph. *Harlem Renaissance and Beyond: Literary Biographies of 100 Black Women Writers, 1900–1945*. Boston: G. K. Hall & Co., 1990.

Dust Tracks on a Road Zora Neale Hurston (1942)

The engagingly vivid but controversial autobiography that the accomplished writer ZORA NEALE HURSTON published shortly after the end of the Harlem Renaissance.

Hurston began work on her memoir because her publisher urged her to do so. She was quite open with friends and colleagues about the reservations that she had about the project. In a February 1943 letter to Hamilton Holt, the president of Rollins College, she declared, "Truly I am glad that you liked *Dust Tracks*. I did not want to write it at all, because it is too hard to reveal one's inner self, and still there is no use in writing that kind of book unless you do" (Kaplan, 478).

As Maya Angelou notes in her foreword to a recent edition of the work, not only did Hurston "choose to write her own version of life in *Dust Tracks on a Road*" but what Hurston reports "is enough to convince the reader that [she] had dramatic adventures and was a quintessential survivor" (Angelou, viii). Angelou's generous evaluation hints at one of the key features of the autobiography: Hurston's liberal use of mythic images and narratives. Indeed as Lynn Domina points out, "in her folklore, that is, she tells her own story, while in her autobiography, she includes much 'lore'" (Domina, 197).

Hurston's champion, the writer Alice Walker, is one of several critics who believe that *Dust Tracks* fails to match the intensity and authenticity of Hurston's other works. Her evaluation echoes scholar Robert Hemenway's suggestion that the work reflects Hurston's deep conflict about genre and her own writing goals. Yet, as Hurston biographer Valerie Boyd cautions, "readers cannot dismiss *Dust Tracks* unless they also are willing to dismiss LANGSTON HUGHES's THE BIG SEA and RICHARD WRIGHT's *Black Boy*—two other autobiographies published in the 1940s in which black writers engaged in mythmaking about their lives" (Boyd, 355).

Some 5,000 copies of *Dust Tracks* sold during its first publication run, and, despite its controversial presentation, it was awarded the Anisfield-World Award in Racial Relations and an award of $1,000 from the *Saturday Review*. The prize committee deemed it "the best book of the year concerned with racial problems in the field of creative literature" (Kaplan, 438) and featured the book on its February 1943 cover.

Bibliography

Angelou, Maya. Foreword to *Dust Tracks on a Road*, by Zora Neale Hurston. New York: HarperPerennial, 1991.

Boyd, Valerie. *Wrapped in Rainbows: The Life of Zora Neale Hurston*. New York: Scribner, 2003.

Domina, Lynn. "'Protection in My Mouf': Self, Voice, and Community in Zora Neale Hurston's *Dust Tracks on a Road* and *Mules and Men*." *African American Review* 31, no. 2 (1997): 197–209.

Kaplan, Carla. *Zora Neale Hurston: A Life in Letters*. New York: Doubleday, 2002.

Hemenway, Robert. *Zora Neale Hurston: A Literary Biography*. Urbana: University of Illinois Press, 1977.

Dykes, Eva Beatrice (1893–1986)

A RADCLIFFE COLLEGE–educated scholar who in 1921 became one of the first black women to receive a Ph.D. in America. Dykes graduated from DUNBAR HIGH SCHOOL and from HOWARD UNIVERSITY in WASHINGTON, D.C., the city of her birth. Following graduate studies at Radcliffe, where she earned an A.B., A.M., and Ph.D., she returned to teach at both of her alma maters in the nation's capital. Her publications, the bulk of which appeared in the 1940s, included *The Negro in English Romantic Thought* and scholarly articles that appeared in leading humanities journals.

Bibliography

Roses, Lorraine Elena, and Ruth Elizabeth Randolph. *Harlem Renaissance and Beyond: Literary Biographies of 100 Black Women Writers, 1900–1945*. Boston: G. K. Hall & Co., 1990.

E

Earth Em Jo Basshe (1927)

A play by EM JO BASSHE that *MESSENGER* theater critic THEOPHILUS LEWIS blasted as a "Broadway forgery of Negro drama." It starred Daniel Haynes, a former aspiring minister whose turn to drama when he reached NEW YORK CITY brought him immediate acclaim.

Bibliography

Patterson, Lindsay. *Anthology of the American Negro in the Theatre: A Critical Approach.* New York: Publishers Company, 1967.

Eastman, Crystal (1881–1928)

A pioneering feminist, lawyer, socialist, and activist who was a cofounder of the National Civil Liberties Bureau, the organization that became the American Civil Liberties Union in 1920. CLAUDE MCKAY worked with Eastman, who was the cofounder and coeditor of the *LIBERATOR,* the periodical whose chief editor was MAX EASTMAN, Crystal Eastman's younger brother. The Eastmans published many of McKay's early poems, including "If We Must Die," his powerful 1919 exhortation of African Americans. McKay later joined the staff of the magazine that was the new incarnation of the *MASSES,* a periodical banned by the government because of its open criticism of national policies.

Bibliography

Cooper, Wayne. *Claude McKay: Rebel Sojourner in the Harlem Renaissance.* New York: Schocken Books, 1987.

Eastman, Max Forrester (1883–1969)

An intrepid socialist activist, dynamic chief editor of the *LIBERATOR,* and longtime friend of poet CLAUDE MCKAY. He believed in the potential value of socialism and was an outspoken critic of United States policies during the World War I. His activism led to two trials for espionage; neither case resulted in a guilty verdict.

Eastman, together with his accomplished and enterprising sister CRYSTAL EASTMAN, offered wholehearted support and literary exposure to McKay. Eastman published some of McKay's earliest poems in the pages of the *Liberator,* a magazine that later became known as the most impressive avant-garde literary magazine of the period. In addition, Eastman provided the preface to his collection of poems entitled *HARLEM SHADOWS* and often read McKay's work-in-progress.

Eastman published a number of works on socialism, Russian politics, and Russian history through the 1930s. He died in Barbados in 1969.

Bibliography

Cooper, Wayne. *Claude McKay: Rebel Sojourner in the Harlem Renaissance.* New York: Schocken Books, 1987.

Eastman, Max. *Love and Revolution: My Journey Through an Epoch.* New York: Random House, 1965.

Eatonville

The childhood home of ZORA NEALE HURSTON and the first town in the United States to be incorporated and recognized as a self-governing black community. Located in Florida, this all-black town was where John Hurston was elected mayor. It was there that Zora Hurston's mother died in 1904 and where the future novelist, the sixth of seven children, struggled to find domestic and familial stability in the wake of her mother's death and her father's subsequent remarriage. Eatonville emerges in a number of Hurston's works, perhaps most memorably in her 1937 novel THEIR EYES WERE WATCHING GOD.

Bibliography

Boyd, Valerie. *Wrapped in Rainbows: The Life of Zora Neale Hurston.* New York: Scribner, 2003.

Campbell, Josie. *Student Companion to Zora Neale Hurston.* Westport, Conn.: Greenwood Press, 2001.

Hemenway, Robert. *Zora Neale Hurston: A Literary Biography.* Urbana: University of Illinois Press, 1977.

"Eatonville Anthology, The"   Zora Neale Hurston (1926)

A series of local-color sketches that ZORA NEALE HURSTON, a native of EATONVILLE, Florida, published in the September and October 1926 issues of THE MESSENGER. In the 14 vignettes, Hurston introduces a number of households, most of them marked by some kind of marital tension. In these sketches, or what biographer Valerie Boyd refers to as "the literary equivalent of Hurston's animated storytelling sessions at Harlem parties" (Boyd, 140), Hurston provides intriguing and disturbing glimpses of everyday life, marital troubles, and community politics. The majority of protagonists in the pieces are women who range from long-suffering wives of adulterous husbands to local vamps to independent single mothers.

The first story in "The Eatonville Anthology" is "The Pleading Woman," a lively set of observations about a melodramatic and hypocritical woman named Mrs. Tony Roberts, who "just loves to ask for things." Despite the fact that her husband "gives her all he can rake and scrape, which is considerably more than most wives get for their housekeeping," Mrs. Roberts "goes from door to door begging for things" (59). The community essentially provides her with meals for her children, in spite of her less-than-grateful responses to their charity that soon suggest a kind of obsessive-compulsive disorder

rather than a deliberate domestic strategy. Other stories, such as "Turpentine Love," the concise three-paragraph account of Jim Merchant and the wife he loves, and the untitled third story about Becky Moore, an unmarried mother of "eleven children of assorted colors and sizes," provide oblique commentaries on how individuals and communities deal with potentially unsettling situations or characteristics. Jim Merchant waits patiently and without fanfare until his sweetheart is "cured" of her penchant for fits before he marries her. Becky Moore emerges as the victim of men who simply will not propose. "She has never stopped any of the fathers of her children from proposing," notes the narrator, whose indictment then turns to the other women of the town who refuse to interact with her or let their children play with hers.

Other stories reveal a more troubling aspect of domestic life. "Tippy," for instance, is about a dog that will not die, despite the fact that he has "been sentenced to death dozens of times, and the sentences executed upon him." The stoic narrator calls attention to the dog's resilience, noting, "[i]n spite of all the attempts upon his life, Tippy is still willing to be friendly with anyone who will let him." The theme of long-suffering survivors also extends to the wronged wife in "The Head of the Nail" who defies everyone's expectations and beats the brazen vamp named Daisy Taylor, who is seducing her husband, so badly that Taylor leaves town immediately. Additional works that explore problematic community passivity include the untitled ninth and tenth works about devoted female churchgoers who suffer domestic abuse and live without ever seeing their church intervene on their behalf.

The collection is a forerunner of works such as "SWEAT" (1926) and Hurston's 1937 novel THEIR EYES WERE WATCHING GOD, which is set in Eatonville and includes some of the characters introduced in the magazine sketches. The collection, as biographer Valerie Boyd notes, includes tales that Hurston came to know of while living in Eatonville and others that were well-known and part of the larger African-American culture. In form, the vignettes model the presentation that RICHARD WRIGHT chooses for his 1940 autobiographical sketches entitled "Ethics of Living Jim Crow."

Bibliography

Boyd, Valerie. *Wrapped in Rainbows: The Life of Zora Neale Hurston.* New York: Scribner, 2003.

Hemenway, Robert. *Zora Neale Hurston: A Literary Biography.* Urbana: University of Illinois Press, 1977.

Hurston, Zora Neale. *The Complete Stories.* New York: HarperCollins, 1995.

Ebony and Topaz: A Collectanea
Charles S. Johnson, ed. (1927)

A volume of creative and nonfiction works selected by CHARLES S. JOHNSON, the respected editor of OPPORTUNITY. Johnson described *Ebony and Topaz* as a "fairly faithful reflection of current interests and observations in Negro life." He addressed potential concerns of African-American readers, whom he thought "will doubtless quarrel with certain of the Negro characters who move in these pages." Insisting that "in life some Negroes are distasteful to other Negroes," Johnson argued that readers should "[a]ccep[t] the materials of Negro life for their own worth" and celebrate the fact that "Negro writers, removed by two generations from slavery, are now much less self-conscious, less interested in proving that they are just like white people, and, in their excursions into the fields of letters and art, seem to care less about what white people think, or are likely to think about the race." L. HOLLINGSWORTH WOOD, NATIONAL URBAN LEAGUE president, *Opportunity* editorial board member, and member of the FISK UNIVERSITY Board of Trustees, reinforced Johnson's forceful message about African-American creative autonomy. In his foreword to the collection, Wood emphasized that the collection had the potential to perform some powerful cultural work. It was a "challenging collection," he suggested, because it "focuses, as it were, the appraising eyes of white folks on the Negro's life and of Negroes on their own life and development in what seems . . . a new and stimulating way."

Johnson selected works by a number of rising stars and lesser-known figures in the Harlem literary and artistic circles. He also provided historical perspective by including works by influential writers from earlier periods, including Phillis Wheatley's "To a Gentleman, on His Voyage to Great Britain for the Recovery of His Health"

and facsimile reproductions of manuscript pages written by Paul Laurence Dunbar. Contemporary writers included ARTHUR HUFF FAUSET, JESSIE FAUSET, GEORGIA DOUGLAS JOHNSON, HELENE JOHNSON, MARITA BONNER writing as JOSEPH MAREE ANDREW, ALAIN LOCKE, BRENDA MORYCK, and ANNE SPENCER. Striking art work by AARON DOUGLAS, Charles Cullen, and Richard Bruce appeared alongside facsimile reproductions of famous paintings from the impressive art collection of Albert C. Barnes and pamphlets such as Wheatley's poem "An Elegy." Johnson also included works on African-American themes and history by white writers, including "The Runaway Slave at Pilgrim Point" by Elizabeth Barrett Browning, "Gullah" by Julia Peterkin, and *On the Road One Day, Lord,* a one-act play by Paul Green.

There were a considerable number of poems published in the volume and a fairly balanced representation of works by women and men of the period. The set included "Divine Afflatus" by Jessie Fauset, "Requiem" by Georgia Douglas Johnson, "Idolatry" and "The Return" by ARNA BONTEMPS, "And One Shall Live in Two" and "A Student I Know" by Jonathan Brooks, "A Sonnet to a Negro in Harlem" by Helene Johnson, "Effigy" by LEWIS ALEXANDER, and other works by Anne Spencer, FRANK HORNE, Lois Augusta Cuglar, and George Chester Morse. The modest array of short fiction included "Jumby" by Arthur Huff Fauset, "General Drums" by JOHN MATHEUS, "Tokens" by GWENDOLYN BENNETT, and "Verisimilitude" by John P. Davis. The two plays in the collection were *On the Road One Day, Lord* by PAUL GREEN and *The First One—A Play in One Act* by ZORA NEALE HURSTON. Nonfiction works included the essay "The Negro in the Jazz Band" by Jose Salaverria and translated from the Spanish by Dorothy Peterson, "The Natural History of Race Prejudice" by Ellsworth Faris, "John Henry—A Negro Legend" by Guy Johnson, and "Racial Self-Expression" by E. FRANKLIN FRAZIER.

This strength of this collection lay in its breadth, the intensity of the works included, and the timeliness of its publication. Johnson noted that the contents represented four discernible themes and areas of concern. The first was devoted to African-American folk life, and the works depicted lives "full of strong colors, of passions, deep and fierce, of struggle, disillusion—the whole gamut of life free from the wrappings of intricate sophistication." The second grouping was specifically historical and included biographical profiles that examined "long gone figures who flashed like bright comets across a black sky" and "some of the rare and curiously interesting fragments of careers and art which constitute that absorbing field of the past now being revealed through the zeal and industry of Negro scholars." The third category of works were devoted to "racial problems and attitudes," and the final section included essays that "touch boldly and with a striking candor some of the ancient racial foibles: and "lack[ed] conspicuously the familiar tears of self-pity and apology." *Ebony and Topaz* reasserted the legitimacy of the Harlem Renaissance by placing it in the larger context of an African-American literary and arts tradition.

Bibliography

Johnson, Charles. *Ebony and Topaz: A Collectanea.* 1927; reprint, North Stratford, N.H.: 2000.

"Ebony Flute, The"

The monthly column that GWENDOLYN BENNETT, a talented artist, poet, and teacher, published in OPPORTUNITY from September 1926 through May 1928. CHARLES S. JOHNSON, the magazine's editor, commissioned Bennett to provide up-to-date and informal commentary on the literary events, personalities, and news of the day. The title of her column was taken from a line in the poem "Harlem" by William Rose Benet, in which the speaker declares his desire "to sing Harlem on an ebony flute."

Bennett used the column to publicize poetry competitions, to honor literary prizewinners, to review books and plays, and to provide information about black literary clubs in and beyond NEW YORK CITY.

Bibliography

Johnson, Abby Arthur, and Ronald Maberry Johnson. *Propaganda & Aesthetics: The Literary Politics of African American Magazines in the Twentieth Century.* Amherst: University of Massachusetts, 1979.

Echoes from the Hills Bessie Woodson Yancey (1939)

The first and only collection of poems by Bessie Woodson Yancey, a Virginia teacher. The volume reflected Yancey's love of nature, included works written in dialect, and offered positive, encouraging meditations on the beauty and strength of African Americans. Yancey may have published more in the years after the Renaissance; indeed, at least one poem appeared later in the PITTSBURGH COURIER.

Bibliography

Roses, Lorraine Elena, and Ruth Elizabeth Randolph. *Harlem Renaissance and Beyond: Literary Biographies of 100 Black Women Writers, 1900–1945.* Boston: G. K. Hall & Co., 1990.

"Echo from Tolouse, An" Idabelle Yeiser (1926)

An engaging travel essay by IDABELLE YEISER, a COLUMBIA UNIVERSITY Ph.D., published in the July 1926 issue of THE CRISIS.

The two-page narrative focuses primarily on her impressions of the city and does not include any specific details about how she fared as a woman of color. Frustrated by the fact that she was socializing with Americans and English-speakers in Paris, she readily pursued the opportunity to study at the University of Toulouse. Yeiser readily offered her perspectives to *Crisis* readers and provided historical, political, and cultural details about the city. She outlined its impressive educational history, praised its multicultural population, and celebrated the rich social life that could be enjoyed. "Never once have I regretted coming to Toulouse," she declared. "On the contrary I shall regret leaving it. It is like a magic bag. One can draw at random, but the result is always a prize."

Yeiser was a graduate of the UNIVERSITY OF PENNSYLVANIA, a writer, and a teacher who traveled throughout Europe and North Africa in 1925 and 1926. She published additional articles about her encounters with Africans, including the prizewinning "Letters" in OPPORTUNITY.

Bibliography

Jubilee, Vincent. *Philadelphia's Afro-American Literary Circle and the Harlem Renaissance.* Ann Arbor, Mich.: University Microfilms, 1982.

Edmonds, Sheppard Randolph (1900–1983)

Born in Lawrenceville, Virginia, this college professor and playwright graduated from Oberlin College and earned a master's degree from COLUMBIA UNIVERSITY. He pursued additional studies at YALE UNIVERSITY and used a JULIUS ROSENWALD FELLOWSHIP to fund his studies abroad in 1938 at the University of Dublin and at the London School of Speech and Drama.

A prolific playwright and essayist, Edmonds published plays, articles, reviews, and literary criticism during his tenure as a professor of drama at historically black schools in the South: Dillard University, Florida A & M University, ATLANTA UNIVERSITY, and Hampton Institute. In 1930 he published SHADES AND SHADOWS; four years later, SIX PLAYS FOR THE NEGRO THEATRE; and in 1942 *The Land of Cotton and Other Plays*, his third drama collection.

In 1948 the NATIONAL URBAN LEAGUE recognized Edmonds, a member of the League, the NAACP, and the Omega Psi Phi fraternity, for his art.

Bibliography

Fleming, G. James, and Christian E. Burckel. *Who's Who in Colored America: An Illustrated Biographical Directory of Notable Living Persons of African Descent in the United States.* Yonkers-on-Hudson, N.Y.: Christian E. Burckel & Associates, 1950.

Edward, H. F. V. (1898–1973)

Little biographical information is known about H. F. V. Edward. Details about his life emerge through his connections with *The Crisis*, the journal of the NATIONAL ASSOCIATION FOR THE ADVANCEMENT OF COLORED PEOPLE. Edward joined the staff of *The Crisis* as bookkeeper and manager of advertising following a depressing stint in the New York State Employment Service during the Depression. His job, which placed him in the HARLEM branch office, was to find job vacancies. Inspired by W. E. B. DUBOIS and the writers who had connections with *The CRISIS*, Edward decided to pursue a writing career himself and "give vent to my experience in the seeming hopelessness of the Hoover era."

Job Hunters, a dire one-act that was his only published play, appeared in the December 1931 issue of *The Crisis*. The cast included unnamed characters who represented the faceless unemployed of the era and the activists who worked on their behalf. The play recalled Edward's own depressing interactions with unemployed men and women during the Depression.

Set in a Harlem public employment office, the play begins with a nameless "Official" preparing for a day with job seekers. The man is jaded, not at all ready to endure one more day of "people's troubles and moanings." His attitude underscores the evils and the seemingly predictable inhumanity of bureaucracy. While he refuses to open the office a few minutes before its official opening time of eight o'clock, the man muses that his office "is where men sit and hear each other groan." Edward relocates the hopelessness of the job seekers to the employment officers themselves as he introduces an earnest sociology student. Warren Thomas announces himself as an Ivy League sociology student with socialist beliefs. "I believe public employment offices are essential," he declares before the Official directs him to a chair from which he might watch the day's proceedings. Thomas appears to believe more in the idea of the system than in the actual practice of helping others to find work.

Over the course of the play, the Official interviews a host of jobless men. Unfortunately, the encounters tend to undermine the men's ability to get jobs. One of the men, Clarence White, is a high school graduate who makes the mistake of confiding in the Official. When asked why he lost a former position that he had held for three years, White reveals that his boss was demanding overtime hours but failing to pay him. To compensate himself, White "took it out in goods" and had to leave when he was caught "stealing." Rather than recognize White's disadvantaged position as an overtaxed worker, the Official prepares to use the information against his client. "Now when I am asked about references I shall be informed about the situation," he responds blandly but menacingly before dismissing Mr. White.

The play provides additional examples of bureaucratic insensitivity and disregard. Edward focuses entirely on men who are mistreated and disrespected by a system that should, in principle, support their efforts to become successful providers. The play concludes with pointed references to a riot in CHICAGO prompted by unemployment and pressing social needs. Ultimately, Edward offers a pained exposé of social services and the plight of the working poor and unemployed.

Bibliography

Hatch, James. *Black Theatre, U.S.A.; Forty-five Plays by Black Americans, 1847–1974.* New York: Free Press, 1974.

Edwards, Eli

One of several pseudonyms used by poet and novelist CLAUDE MCKAY. The name "Eli Edwards" was based on the first letters in the names of his wife Eulalie Imelda Lewars. Biographer Wayne Cooper also suggests that McKay developed the pseudonym as a tribute to his mother, Hannah Ann Elizabeth Edwards.

McKay used this pseudonym during a period of economic hardship. In 1917, three years after his marriage to Lewars ended, he published poems, including "Invocation" and "The Harlem Dancer," under this name.

Bibliography

Cooper, Wayne. *Claude McKay: Rebel Sojourner in the Harlem Renaissance.* New York: Schocken Books, 1987.

Giles, James R. *Claude McKay.* Boston: Twayne Publishers, 1976.

McKay, Claude. *A Long Way from Home.* New York: Arno Press, 1969.

Edwards, Eulalie Imelda (unknown)

Born Eulalie Lewars in Jamaica, she was the childhood sweetheart and wife of Jamaican-born poet and novelist CLAUDE MCKAY. The couple, who married on July 30, 1914, in Jersey City, New Jersey, settled in NEW YORK CITY. The marriage was short-lived. After six months, a pregnant Edwards returned to Jamaica, where she bore their daughter, Rhue Hope McKay.

Bibliography

Cooper, Wayne. *Claude McKay: Rebel Sojourner in the Harlem Renaissance.* New York: Schocken Books, 1987.

Elijah's Raven Shirley Lola Graham DuBois (1930)

An unpublished three-act comedy by SHIRLEY LOLA GRAHAM DuBois, written in 1930 during her tenure as a music teacher at Morgan College, now Morgan State University. The KARAMU PLAYERS performed the play during DuBois's two-year residency at the Yale Drama School in New Haven on a JULIUS ROSENWALD FELLOWSHIP and in 1942.

Bibliography

"Shirley Lola Graham DuBois." *Dictionary of American Biography, Supplement 10: 1976–1980.* New York: Scribners, 1995.

Roses, Lorraine Elena, and Ruth Elizabeth Randolph. *Harlem Renaissance and Beyond: Literary Biographies of 100 Black Women Writers, 1900–1945.* Boston: G. K. Hall & Co., 1990.

Ellington, Edward Kennedy (Duke Ellington) (1899–1974)

An extremely popular Harlem Renaissance–era composer, bandleader, and entertainer. Ellington, who began performing professionally when he was 17 years of age, established himself in NEW YORK CITY in the early 1920s. His bands, which ranged in size from sextets to 14-piece ensembles, produced some of the most well-known pieces of the age including "Black and Tan Fantasy" (1927) and "Mood Indigo" (1930). He enjoyed a lengthy engagement at the COTTON CLUB, the famous establishment that became synonymous with Harlem Renaissance gaiety and entertainment, from 1927 through 1932 and again from 1937 through 1938. The 1935 film *Symphony in Black* was based on Ellington's "A Rhapsody of Negro Life."

Bibliography

The Ellington Papers are located at the Smithsonian Institution in the Ellington Collection and at Yale University Library in the Ellington Papers.

Lawrence, A. H. *Duke Ellington and His World: A Biography*. New York: Routledge, 2001.

Nicholson, Stuart. *Reminiscing in Tempo: A Portrait of Duke Ellington*. Boston: Northeastern University Press, 1999.

Rattenbury, Ken. *Duke Ellington: Jazz Composer*. New Haven, Conn.: Yale University Press, 1990.

Ellison, Ralph Waldo (1914–1994)

A southern-born writer whose lengthy sojourn in NEW YORK CITY during the 1930s launched his writing career and influenced his literary works and political ideas in the post-Harlem Renaissance period.

Ellison was born in Oklahoma City, Oklahoma, to Lewis Alfred and Ida Millsap Ellison in 1914. His father, a Spanish-American War veteran and member of the Twenty-Fifth U.S. Colored Infantry, deliberately named his son after the 19th-century poet and philosopher Ralph Waldo Emerson. According to biographer Lawrence Jackson, Lewis Ellison often would declare that he was grooming his son to become a poet. Ralph Ellison was the grandson of four former slaves, including Alfred Ellison, a former South Carolina slave who became a local community leader in South Carolina during the Reconstruction. Ellison was three years old when his father died. His mother provided vital emotional support and intellectual encouragement for her children. She shepherded them through potentially debilitating racist encounters and provided her children with impressive examples of gracious fortitude and race pride.

Ellison became a voracious reader during his childhood. He graduated from the segregated Douglass High School with honors in 1932. After plans to attend Langston University and participate in the well-known school band failed to materialize, Ellison pursued admission to TUSKEGEE INSTITUTE located in Alabama. Ellison matriculated 17 years after the passing of BOOKER T. WASHINGTON, the school's founder. When Ellison arrived, Robert Russa Moton, a Hampton Institute graduate and future HARMON medal and SPINGARN MEDAL winner, was the school's president. At Tuskegee, Ellison studied music with William Dawson in the school's impressive and richly equipped Music School.

During his years at Tuskegee, Ellison had the opportunity to learn about and see performances of creative works by Harlem Renaissance artists. On one occasion, he attended a program that included a presentation of LANGSTON HUGHES's stirring poem "The Negro Speaks of Rivers" and works from SOUTHERN ROAD, the first published volume of poetry by STERLING BROWN and a work that was infused with rich African-American folk traditions, spirituals, and other musical forms.

In 1936, at the end of his junior year, Ellison journeyed to New York on the advice of trusted Tuskegee teachers. He hoped to earn money enough to cover the tuition costs of his senior year. The trip North was an eventful turning point for Ellison. He arrived on Independence Day and quickly was introduced to the vibrant and opinionated world of Harlem Renaissance literary and political circles. Hazel Harrison, one of his most important college professors, the sculptress AUGUSTA SAVAGE, the poet LANGSTON HUGHES, and the teacher and activist LOUISE THOMPSON facilitated Ellison's immersion into Harlem Renaissance circles.

Almost immediately after arriving in New York City, he introduced himself to ALAIN LOCKE and to Langston Hughes in the lobby of the Harlem YMCA on 135th Street. Hughes, impressed by Ellison's literary knowledge, recommended a number of contacts and locations for the young man to seek out. He facilitated Ellison's studies with RICHMOND BARTHÉ, the critically acclaimed sculptor whose commissions included installations and murals for the New York Treasury. Hughes also introduced the aspiring writer to RICHARD WRIGHT. It was encouragement from Wright, a veteran editor and forceful writer, that led to Ellison's first published works appearing in NEW CHALLENGE. He began with book reviews and soon moved on to short fiction. "Hymie's Bull," his first published work, was a tale of dreadful interracial confrontations on the railroads. It was a bittersweet professional debut since Ellison lost his mother Ida under tragic circumstances. Wright continued to support Ellison and was responsible for Ellison's employment by the New Deal's Federal Writers Project. Ellison's assignments for the organization required him to do research at the Schomburg

Library, an intellectual and creative hub of the Harlem Renaissance community.

Ellison's writing career began just as the Harlem Renaissance began to wane. This novelist, essayist, journalist, and magazine editor published in a number of established journals of the era, including NEW MASSES, Negro Quarterly, and NEW CHALLENGE. By the end of the Harlem Renaissance, he was experiencing a newfound literary and critical autonomy. No longer reliant on Wright, Ellison began to develop his own literary voice. In 1944 he won a JULIUS ROSENWALD FELLOWSHIP and began work on Invisible Man, the work that would win the 1953 National Book Award and that prompted the CHICAGO DEFENDER to recognize Ellison as the writer "symbolizing the best in American Democracy." Ellison's life was marked by outstanding honors that included membership in the American Academy of Arts and Letters and in 1953 the Medal of Honor, the nation's highest civilian honor. He was a recognized professor and enjoyed appointments at Bard College, Rutgers University, and NEW YORK UNIVERSITY before he passed away in Harlem at 80 years of age.

Ellison's major works include his first novel, Invisible Man (1953), the essay collections entitled Shadow and Act (1964) and Going to the Territory (1986), and two posthumously published works, Flying Home and Other Stories (1996) and Juneteenth (1996).

Bibliography

Benston, Kimberly W., ed. Speaking for You: The Vision of Ralph Ellison. Washington, D.C.: Howard University Press, 1987.

Jackson, Lawrence. Ralph Ellison: Emergence of Genius. New York: John Wiley & Sons, Inc., 2002.

Nadel, Alan. Invisible Criticism: Ralph Ellison and the American Canon. Iowa City: University of Iowa Press, 1988.

Sundquist, Eric, ed. Cultural Contexts for Ralph Ellison's Invisible Man. Boston: Bedford Books of St. Martin's Press, 1995.

"El Tisico"   Anita Scott Coleman (1920)

A short story by ANITA SCOTT COLEMAN published in the March 1920 issue of The CRISIS, one of three short stories that Coleman published in

the NAACP journal edited by W. E. B. DuBois. The poem "Attar" by poet GEORGIA DOUGLAS JOHNSON appeared immediately after Coleman's tale. "El Tisico's" account of the railroad and the treatment that an African-American family experienced was in sharp contrast to "Hymie's Bull," RALPH ELLISON's first published short story and harrowing tale of the violence that African-American boys endured at the hands of aggressive white riders and railroad workers.

Coleman's story is told in the first person by an observant railroad man whose colleagues are debating the definitions of patriotism. While an Irish engineer named O'Brady insists that patriotism is "a thing men put before their wives," another man declares that it pales in comparison to "love-making and women." Eventually, Sam Dicks, a "grizzled old trainman, who had more yarns in his cranium, than a yellow cur has fleas on a zig-zag trail between his left ear and his hind right leg," speaks up. He relates a compelling story about an African-American family with a sick infant who boarded a train in Mexico. The mother, sure that her child was dying, was desperate that he last until the train crossed the border. Once word spread to the engineer, "the greatest dare devil and the squarest that ever guided a throttle," the train raced through the Mexican countryside "faster than a whirligig in a Texas cyclone." The train pulled into Nogales, but the coach with the worried family "landed fair and square upon American soil." Sam Dicks's attentive audience is struck by the heroics of one of their own and the mother's steadfast wish that her son die at home. They pepper him with questions about the outcome. He is only to pleased to tell them that the youngest musician in the talented trio that they have been listening to is the child in question. It appears that the young man has never fully recovered and, according to Dicks, is "what the Mexicans call, 'el Tisico.'" The word, which means "tubercular," signals the perennial vulnerability of the young man.

Coleman, who was herself born in Mexico to Cuban and African-American parents, delivers several messages with this economical and evocative story. First, she underscores the ways in which African Americans are central to debates about patriotism. White immigrants and white men, unable to agree about the concept, finally concur when they learn from an African-American woman, a delicate individual described as a "little fluttery thin thing, all heart and eyes." Although the American child survived his childhood sickness, his perpetual ailments suggest his inability to become entirely well on American soil. In "El Tisico," Coleman considers vital questions of entitlement, patriotism, and national unity.

Bibliography

Coleman, Anita Scott. "El Tisico." *The Crisis* (March 1920): 252–253.

Roses, Lorraine Elena, and Ruth Elizabeth Randolph. *Harlem Renaissance and Beyond: Literary Biographies of 100 Black Women Writers, 1900–1945*. Boston: G. K. Hall & Co., 1990.

Emancipator

The short-lived weekly magazine founded in NEW YORK CITY by WILFRED A. DOMINGO, a Jamaican radical with Socialist ties. Domingo started his career in publishing in 1919 as editor of the *NEGRO WORLD*, the newspaper produced by MARCUS GARVEY. Domingo and Richard B. Moore, his coeditor and the colleague who helped to promote the journal, obtained financial support for the magazine from several labor unions. The magazine lasted for less than two months, but during that time it lodged detailed critiques of Garvey and the UNIVERSAL NEGRO IMPROVEMENT ASSOCIATION. Garvey, who fired Domingo because of his contrary politics, regarded the *Emancipator* as a direct impediment to the Black Star Steamship Line, which would facilitate his program to return African Americans to Africa and to organize profitable global economic relationships between peoples of African descent.

Bibliography

Moore, Richard B. "The Critics and Opponents of Marcus Garvey." In *Marcus Garvey and the Vision of Africa*. John Henrik Clarke, ed. New York: Vintage, 1974.

Turner, W. Burghardt, and Joyce Moore Turner, eds. *Richard B. Moore, Caribbean Militant in Harlem: Collected Writings, 1920–1972*. Bloomington: Indiana University Press, 1988.

Emilie Hapgood Players

The theater group that in April 1917 became the first to present African-American life to BROADWAY audiences and the first to use African-American actors to perform plays about African-American issues on Broadway. EMILIE BIGELOW HAPGOOD, a prominent NEW YORK CITY philanthropist, intellectual, and influential participant in the New York theater world, founded the Players troupe. The performances of Inez Clough and Opal Cooper prompted George Jean Nathan, a highly regarded drama critic, to propose that they were among the top 10 actors of the season.

On 5 April 1917, the day before America entered World War I, the Players performed *GRANNY MAUMEE, SIMON THE CYRENIAN*, and *THE RIDER OF DREAMS* at the Garden Theatre located in Madison Square Garden. The playwright was the white writer RIDGELY TORRENCE. Emilie Bigelow Hapgood was the producer. The director was Robert Edmond Jones, a man whom Hapgood praised in a published letter to *THE NEW YORK TIMES* for having in "play after play, galvanized [the] stage into a peculiar and electric and organic life, creating an atmosphere which lifts both actor and audience into a spirit which some do not comprehend or even observe, except in a half realized feeling like, 'there is also present a dream quality which hangs like the thin veil of softening mist between the audience and the stage.'"

The writer and activist JAMES WELDON JOHNSON asserted in *BLACK MANHATTAN*, that the Players' performances represented the "most important single event in the entire history of the Negro in the American Theatre." According to Johnson, critics were extremely impressed by the productions. It appears, however, that the coincidence of the war and the production's opening and audience resistance to seeing serious black drama contributed to the plays' short-lived run.

Bibliography

Curtis, Susan. *The First Black Actors on the Great White Way*. Columbia: University of Missouri Press, 1998.

Johnson, James Weldon. *Black Manhattan*. 1930, reprint, New York: Arno Press and *The New York Times*, 1968.

"Emmy" Jessie Fauset (1912–1913)

A gripping romance by JESSIE FAUSET and the first of her fictional works to appear in *THE CRISIS*. "Emmy," which appeared in two parts in the December 1912 and January 1913 issues of *Crisis*, is set in Plainville, a central Pennsylvania town, and in the city of PHILADELPHIA. It chronicles the ways in which two young people, Emmy Carrel and Archie Ferrers, her childhood sweetheart, grapple with troubling lessons about race, racism, and white privilege and their eventual honorable triumph in the face of social and racial prejudice. Fauset's emphasis on the protagonists' physical beauty underscores her critique of shallow ideas about racial exceptionalism. The story reflects Fauset's lifelong interest in the politics of romance, the ways in which African-American domesticity is beset by racial realities, and her efforts to explore how facts and fictions about black identity constrain, influence, and emancipate whites and people of color.

The story, which constitutes a male and female *bildungsroman*, first locates African-American female experience of inter- and intraracial prejudice within the school and home. Emmy is the daughter of an industrious and talented unmarried mulatto woman and the granddaughter of a woman enslaved in New Orleans and the white man who helped her to escape to HAITI and FRANCE. In Plainville, Pennsylvania, Emily is one of two children of color; in a series of potentially humiliating encounters, her teacher and white schoolmates insist on her blackness and reveal their unwavering belief in her inferiority. Emmy grapples with the coded messages and confrontations and, with Archie, her impoverished light-skinned beau, wonders about the role of color and the hurtful dimensions of exclusion.

Archie Ferrers learns his lessons about race in a series of workplace encounters and in the urban world of Philadelphia. He loses jobs because he defends dark-skinned employees and receives several cautions from white employers urging him to let well enough alone. A well-meaning white patron arranges a job for Ferrers at his family's prestigious engineering firm but urges Ferrers not to reveal his racial identity. Eventually Ferrers is spotted in town with Emmy, his fiancée, and he is tortured by the prejudice that her presence elicits in social situations. The tension intensifies when Ferrers's supervisor, who finds favor with his employee and wants to groom him for partnership in the firm, incorrectly assumes that Emmy is Ferrers's mistress rather than his fiancée. Ferrers attempts to postpone his marriage in order to secure a major promotion, but Emmy rejects his logic and his love. The two are reunited after Ferrers is fired when he reveals his love for Emmy and his true identity. Just as they mourn the heartache brought on by what Emmy refers to as "color," a telegram arrives with news of Ferrers' reinstatement and a pending apology from his employer.

Its tidy conclusion aside, "Emmy" is an absorbing tale about socialization in early 20th-century America and an earnest portrait of private struggles against prejudice in the public sphere.

Bibliography

McLendon, Jacquelyn Y. *The Politics of Color in the Fiction of Jessie Fauset and Nella Larsen.* Charlottesville: University Press of Virginia, 1995.

Sylvander, Carolyn Wedin. *Jessie Redmon Fauset, Black American Writer.* Troy, N.Y.: Whitson Pub. Co., 1981.

Wall, Cheryl A. *Women of the Harlem Renaissance.* Bloomington: Indiana University Press, 1995.

Emperor Jones, The Eugene O'Neill (1921) *play*

A play by EUGENE O'NEILL, originally entitled *The Silver Bullet*, that in the 1920s became a signature piece for actor, singer, and activist PAUL ROBESON. The play was inspired by Haitian history and chronicled the adventures of Brutus Jones, an escaped convict and former Pullman porter. With help from a Cockney trader named Henry Smithers, Jones uses trickery and plays on the superstitions of West Indian island natives in order to become ruler. Eventually this despot, who has raided the island of its riches, attempts to leave. However, he is overwhelmed by the supernatural world and by haunting scenes of his African family's enslavement and is finally killed by the natives whom he has oppressed.

The play was performed first in GREENWICH VILLAGE at the Provincetown Playhouse and also was staged at the LAFAYETTE THEATRE in

HARLEM. Paul Robeson, who in the 1920s joined the PROVINCETOWN PLAYERS, a theater group that was closely affiliated with O'Neill, appeared in the title role in the London production of the play. Robeson, whom critics praised for his dynamic and powerful performance, traveled with the show back to New York for its 1924 repeat run at the Provincetown Playhouse. In 1933, Robeson starred in the film version of *The Emperor Jones*.

Bibliography

Black, Stephen A. *Eugene O'Neill: Beyond Mourning and Tragedy*. New Haven, Conn.: Yale University Press, 1999.

Duberman, Martin. *Paul Robeson*. New York: Knopf, 1989.

Dubost, Thierry. *Struggle, Defeat or Rebirth: Eugene O'Neill's Vision of Humanity*. Jefferson, N.C.: McFarland & Company, Inc., 1997.

Robeson, Paul, Jr. *The Undiscovered Paul Robeson: An Artist's Journey*. New York: J. Wiley, 2001.

Emperor Jones, The (1932) *opera*

Based on EUGENE O'NEILL's 1921 play *THE EMPEROR JONES*, the opera by Russian-born musician and composer Louis Gruenberg with a libretto by the American playwright Kathleen de Jaffa. The opera was performed for the first time in NEW YORK CITY at the Metropolitan Opera House in January 1933. During the 1933 and 1934 seasons, the work that received much acclaim was performed 11 times. Unlike the play and film that starred PAUL ROBESON, the New York productions featured Lawrence Tibbett, a white baritone, in the title role.

The opera made its European premier in Amsterdam, Holland, in 1934. This production featured Jules Bledsoe, an acclaimed Texas-born African-American baritone, pianist, and composer whose performance credits included a prominent role in the 1930 New York run of *Showboat*. He was immensely popular in the title role of Emperor Jones.

Bibliography

Baker, Theodore, and Nicolas Slonimsky. *Baker's Biographical Dictionary of Musicians*. New York: Schirmer Books, 1978.

Cuney-Hare, Maud. *Negro Musicians and Their Music*. 1936, reprint, New York: G. K. Hall & Co., 1996.

Gruenberg, Louis. *The Emperor Jones: Opera in Two Acts, a Prologue, an Interlude and Six Scenes*. New York: F. Rullman, 1932.

Lynette Geary. "Bledsoe, Julius Lorenzo Cobb." *The Handbook of Texas Online*. Available online. URL: http://www.tsha.utexas.edu/handbook/online/articles/view/BB/fbl22.html. Accessed May 20, 2005.

Emperor Jones, The (1933) *film*

The 1933 film adaptation of EUGENE O'NEILL's *THE EMPEROR JONES* was directed by Dudley Murphy and produced by John Krimsky and Gifford Cochran. The film starred PAUL ROBESON in the title role, and its supporting cast included Rex Ingram, Fredi Washington, and Frank Wilson. The deletion of potentially controversial scenes, such as the one in which Robeson's character struck a white man, were balanced by the incorporation of several songs performed by Robeson.

Bibliography

Bogle, Donald. *Toms, Coons, Mulattoes, Mammies and Bucks: An Interpretive History of Blacks in American Films*. New York: Continuum, 1989.

Duberman, Martin. *Paul Robeson*. New York: Knopf, 1989.

Leab, Daniel. *From Sambo to Superspade: The Black Experience in Motion Pictures*. Boston: Houghton Mifflin, 1975.

Robeson, Paul Jr. *The Undiscovered Paul Robeson: An Artist's Journey*. New York: J. Wiley, 2001.

Environment Mercedes Gilbert (1931)

One of three plays written by MERCEDES GILBERT, a Florida-born novelist, composer, and actress. Gilbert, who became famous for her BROADWAY stage performances, also starred in silent films, including *Body and Soul* opposite PAUL ROBESON. *Environment* was published first in 1931 in Gilbert's collection of her own works, *SELECTED GEMS OF POETRY, COMEDY, AND DRAMA*.

The three-act drama, written in rather self-conscious prose, documents the trials of a southern family whose migration to the urban North ruins their family bond and jeopardizes their collective future. The patriarch, James Williams, is demoralized by the racism that prevents him from finding work. Driven to drink, he ultimately becomes a fugitive from the law when he is falsely accused of murder. He flees, but as a result, his wife Mary Lou and son, Henry, are targeted and harassed by the police. His daughter, Edna May, becomes a drug addict, and the family seems destined for annihilation. A corrupt, upper-class lawyer named Charles Jackson is one of several men who sexually harass Mary Lou and try to compromise her honor and moral standards.

Gilbert's critique of the North as a direct threat to African-American domestic stability is borne out by the Williams's return to North Carolina. The son, Henry, who has survived his stint with an urban gang, is engaged to be married. The daughter, Edna May, reappears, having recovered from drug addiction, and with news of James William's exoneration and imminent return to the family. In the last scene, Gilbert reveals that Henry's future father-in-law is the villain who endangered the family. The ensuing attack on the unsavory opportunist allows the Williams family to regain their honor and demonstrate their capacity to overcome the social evil of the larger society and within the race.

Bibliography

Hatch, James V., and Ted Shine. *Black Theater U.S.A.: Forty-Five Plays by Black Americans.* New York: The Free Press, 1974.

Roses, Lorraine Elena, and Ruth Elizabeth Randolph. *Harlem's Glory: Black Women Writing, 1900–1950.* Cambridge: Harvard University Press, 1996.

Espionage Act

Passed by Congress in June 1917 once America entered World War I and amended in 1918, the Espionage Act punished individuals found guilty of compromising American military positions and national defense, or inciting resistance to the American government. Punishments included fines of up to $10,000 and up to 20 years imprisonment.

Harlem Renaissance editor MAX EASTMAN, editor of *NEW MASSES,* was one of the first figures arrested under the act. The journal, identified as a socialist publication, was targeted for its anti-American articles and cartoons. Despite vigorous

efforts by Eastman and others, the publication could not prove that it was supporting the war effort and eventually was forced to cease publication.

Other prominent figures targeted by the Espionage Act included Eugene Debs, a labor organizer and Socialist presidential candidate, and Emma Goldman, a Russian-born anarchist and antiwar activist who was ultimately stripped of her American citizenship and deported to Russia.

Bibliography

Cantor, Milton. *Max Eastman.* New York: Twayne Publishers, 1970.

Kohn, Stephen. *American Political Prisoners: Prosecutions under the Espionage and Sedition Acts.* Westport, Conn.: Praeger Publishers, 1994.

O'Neill, William. *The Last Romantic: A Life of Max Eastman.* New York: Oxford University Press, 1996.

Essentials Jean Toomer (1931)

A work of aphorisms that JEAN TOOMER, the author of *CANE,* published privately in 1931. In the first republished edition of the work, the editor Rudolph Byrd notes that the work reflects but is not overly defined by Toomer's belief in the philosophies of Armenian-born mystic GEORGES GURDJIEFF.

Essentials, divided into 64 untitled sections, is evocative of many literary and cultural traditions. It includes spiritual and emotional directives, as well as suggestions about how best to deal with conflict, stress, and moral dilemmas. The work contributes to an established American literary tradition informed by the wise and pithy sayings of influential and enterprising Americans. The aphorisms of Benjamin Franklin and Abraham Lincoln, for instance, are well known and used frequently to characterize events, motivations, and a variety of human behaviors. Toomer's venture into this genre reflects his deep investment in Gurdjieff's philosophies about conscious, even hyperconscious, existence.

The first section in the volume begins with five declarative statements about human potential. The entry that read, "These are my first values: Understanding, Conscience, and Ability," suggested a mantra that Toomer himself might have been applying. The very last entry in *Essentials* is not an entirely uplifting principle. Toomer writes, "It is our task to suffer a conscious apprenticeship in the stupidities and abnormalities of mankind." The statement offers a final emphasis on awareness but is tempered by the references to frustrating limitations of others.

Essentials signaled Toomer's transition away from the ordered world of institutional publishing. In 1931 he collaborated with fellow Gurdjieff adherents to found a press that would "encourage, secure, publish, and distribute quality literature dealing with all phases of spiritual experience . . . essential experience, experience concerned with and leading to the full balanced growth and development of human beings." Essentials was the first book produced by the Lakeside Press based in CHICAGO. Unfortunately, it also was the only work to appear under the imprint.

Toomer, whose resistance of racial categorization was well documented, refused to have Essentials incorporated into the collection of African-American holdings at the Schomburg Library in New York. This solitary work from the Lakeside Press continued to reflect its author's increased isolation from the mainstream African-American literary community.

Bibliography

Benson, Brian, and Mabel Dillard. *Jean Toomer*. Boston: Twayne Publishers, 1980.

Toomer, Jean. *Essentials*. 1931; reprint, Rudolph Byrd, ed. Athens: University of Georgia Press, 1991.

"Eternal Quest, The" Anita Scott Coleman (1931)

A short story by ANITA SCOTT COLEMAN about the power of faith and the awesome inspiration that ordinary folk can deliver to those who are attentive and willing to learn from their examples.

Published in the August 1931 issue of OPPORTUNITY, the story begins with the tragic tale of Dr. Evan Given, a London surgeon who suffers the awful loss of his wife and then, 17 years later, the death of their only child. In response to the "burdensome grief" that overcomes him and because he is a man who believes in life after death, he ends his medical practice and devotes himself to the "study of science—the science of faith." He devotes himself to solving questions such as "What is this thing faith . . . Why does it suffice for some . . . Why is it

insufficient for others . . . [and] Why believing as I do that God is the giver, and therefore has a Divine right to take when and as He wills, am I rebellious because He has bereft me of mine?" One day, while he is traveling in America, he is invited to consult on a medical case that has defied physicians. He arrives at the hospital to find a patient identified only as "No. 60 in ward 400." The man is a giant, "easily six foot ten" and the "span of his shoulders came near to over-taxing the width of the white iron cot" on which he lies. He is restrained because of his delirium "but yet the strong thongs were proving inadequate, the motions of the man lifted the cot until it tossed about like a frail craft on a windy sea." Given announces that nothing medical can be done for the man who continues to repeat the word *mommer*. He tells the nursing staff to locate and to bring in the patient's mother so that he can die in peace. The woman, whom the narrator describes as "a small woman, a tightly shriveled hard little person, not unlike a black walnut" consults with Given for a moment and then proceeds to tend to her son. She talks to him, instructs him to cease making trouble for the staff, and then instructs the nurses to release her child from the restraints so that he can "die free." Within moments, the man slips into "his final sleep, peacefully as a babe." Given watches, awe-struck by the woman's ability to "meet death" and to give thanks to God that her son has been released from his pain. The story ends as the doctor marvels at the woman's belief in God's ability to sustain her and at the poise that she displays in the face of imminent financial hardship now that her son is no longer able to provide for her.

The story's title suggests, in part, that for some the effort to understand or to locate faith is in fact an eternal quest. The uncomplicated, unwavering faith of the devoted mother in "The Eternal Quest" provides readers with an exemplary tale of African-American family bonds and empowering spiritual strength that may not be easily reproduced or captured by others.

Ethiopian Art Players

A theater group founded in CHICAGO in 1923 by Raymond O'Neil and Mrs. SHERWOOD ANDERSON during a period that saw a number of experimental theater troupes and companies established in cities such as NEW YORK CITY, Chicago, and WASHINGTON, D.C. The Ethiopian Art Players included PAUL ROBESON, and it is the organization that scholars credit with establishing Robeson as a formidable actor. Other prominent Harlem Renaissance-era figures associated with the group included writer LEWIS ALEXANDER.

The company achieved much during an early 1920s run in New York City. It performed at the LAFAYETTE THEATRE in HARLEM under the name "The Negro Folk Company." In Manhattan the group appeared at the Frazee Theatre, a venue named after theater producer Harry Frazee, also the owner of the Boston Red Sox who authorized the 1920 trade of player Babe Ruth to the New York Yankees.

The company is perhaps best known for its New York run that included a staging of WILLIS RICHARDSON's THE CHIP WOMAN'S FORTUNE, the first play by an African American to be performed on Broadway. In 1923, the same year in which the NATIONAL URBAN LEAGUE began to publish OPPORTUNITY, the group performed two plays at the Frazee Theatre. The first of eight scheduled performances of Oscar Wilde's "Salome" opened on 7 May 1923 with a 13-member cast that included Lewis Alexander, George Jackson, Evelyn Preer, Marion Taylor, and WALTER WHITE. One week later, on 15 May, six members of the troupe appeared in The Chip Woman's Fortune. There were 31 performances, and the cast on opening night included Laura Bowman, Solomon Bruce, Sydney Kirkpatrick, Evelyn Preer, Arthur Ray, and Marion Taylor. The May 1923 New York City engagement also included performances of The Comedy of Errors by William Shakespeare.

Some years later, Lindsay Patterson, writing for The New York Times in an article chronicling the history of African-American theater, noted that the Ethiopian Art Players were, despite their historic efforts, greeted "with almost the same derision" directed toward the 19th-century New York City–based African Grove Company just over 100 years earlier.

Bibliography
Johnson, James Weldon. Black Manhattan. 1930, reprint, New York: Arno Press and The New York Times, 1968.

Patterson, Lindsay. "To Make the Negro a Living Human Being." The New York Times, 18 February 1968, 92.

Ethiopian Art Theatre
A theater troupe founded in 1922 by white producer Raymond O'Neil and a number of African-American actors. The troupe also performed as the Colored Folk Theatre and as the Negro Folk Theatre. It demonstrated the breadth of black dramatic talent through its productions of diverse works that included medieval romances, Shakespearean plays, Oscar Wilde plays, and contemporary drama. One of the most accomplished members of the troupe included the film and stage actress Evelyn Preer, who played the lead roles in WILLIS RICHARDSON's THE CHIP WOMAN'S FORTUNE and in the production of Oscar Wilde's Salome. Others included Lewis Alexander, Laura Bowman, Marion Taylor, and Coy Applewhite. The troupe disbanded in 1923.

In May 1923, the company arrived in NEW YORK CITY to perform new works by the white playwright Willis Richardson. Segregated seating and the allocation of balcony seats only for black theatergoers at the Frazee Theatre on BROADWAY threatened to disrupt the performances. The insistent resistance of black drama critics and patrons forced the theater to rescind its biased seating policy.

Critics recognized the talent of the company. The New York Post drama critic W. E. Clark declared that the performances were "among the best that has been seen in New York City this season." However, the first serious stage presentations of black life were undermined by disrespectful audiences, some of whom talked loudly during the play and others who had to be ejected from the premises. In addition, according to the historian David Krasner, the company frequently performed plays other than those billed for the evening. The unexpected changes were due in part to the manager O'Neil, who wanted to profit from the "novelty" of black actors performing classic and mainstream plays.

Bibliography
Krasner, David. A Beautiful Pageant: African American Theatre, Drama, and Performance in the Harlem

Renaissance, 1910–1927. New York: Palgrave Macmillan, 2002.

Europe, James Reese (Big Jim Europe)
(1881–1919)

A dynamic figure on the eve of the Harlem Renaissance, James Europe was a talented conductor and composer who organized the 369th Infantry Band and led the triumphant World War I veteran musicians in the historic black military march up FIFTH AVENUE and into HARLEM.

Europe's talent and successful entrepreneurial efforts resulted in a rousing postwar tour with the Hellfighters, as the band also was known. The group, which popularized ragtime, toured America and performed for enthusiastic military and civilian audiences.

Bibliography

Anderson, Jervis. *This Was Harlem: A Cultural Portrait, 1900–1950.* New York: Farrar, Straus and Giroux, 1982.

Badger, Reid. *A Life in Ragtime: A Biography of James Reese Europe.* New York: Oxford University Press, 1995.

Cooper, Michael L. *Hell Fighters: African American Soldiers in World War I.* New York: Dutton, 1997.

Schneider, Mark. *"We Return Fighting": The Civil Rights Movement in the Jazz Age.* Boston: Northeastern University Press, 2002.

"Everlasting Stain, The" Kelly Miller (1920)

An article by KELLY MILLER that appeared in the 27 November 1920 issue of the *Cleveland Advocate.* Miller, who was the first African-American graduate student in mathematics and the first black student admitted to Johns Hopkins University, offered a forthright critique of the racial hysteria that, he proposed, secured the election of Warren Harding to the presidency. Miller also called attention to the prevailing public anxiety about blackness. "Why should it be considered more heinous than any crime to possess a trace of Negro blood?" he asked pointedly, before proceeding to challenge racially prejudiced valorizations of white figures like Shakespeare and demonizations of black figures such as Alexandre

Dumas, Frederick Douglass, and Paul Laurence Dunbar.

Bibliography

Miller, Kelly. "The Everlasting Stain." *Cleveland Advocate,* 27 November 1920, 8.

Exceeding Riches and Other Verse
J. Pauline Smith (1922)

The only known published work by Detroit, Michigan, poet J. PAULINE SMITH. Published in 1922 by the African Methodist Episcopal Book Concern in Philadelphia, the volume included poems that had already appeared in a number of Detroit publications such as the *Detroit Free Press* and the *Detroit Leader,* and in the nationally known Philadelphia African Methodist Episcopal publication, *The Christian Recorder.*

The majority of Smith's poems focused on religious and spiritual matters. She decried the influence of materialism and worldly concerns and exhorted her readers to focus on the transformative power of religious faith. Other poems reflected her patriotism and literary appreciation of classical poets such as Robert Browning.

Bibliography

French, W. P., M. J. Singh, and G. E. Fabre. *Afro-American Poetry and Drama, 1760–1975: A Guide to Information Sources.* Detroit: Gale Research Co., 1979.

Porter, Dorothy. *North American Negro Poets: A Bibliographical Checklist of Their Writings, 1760–1944.* Hattiesburg, Miss.: Book Farm, 1945.

Reardon, Joan, and Kristine A. Thorsen. *Poetry by American Women, 1900–1975: A Bibliography.* Metuchen, N.J.: Scarecrow Press, 1979.

Rush, Theressa Carol Myers, and Esther Arata. *Black American Writers Past and Present: A Biographical and Bibliographical Dictionary.* Metuchen, N.J.: Scarecrow Press, 1975.

Exit, an Illusion Marita Bonner (1929)

A one-act play by MARITA BONNER that appeared in the October 1929 issue of *THE CRISIS.*

The play's foreword, marked for its deliberate use of the second-person pronoun "you," is a detailed set of descriptions that emphatically situate the reader and audience in the scene. The play is set in a studio apartment that reflects the social upheaval and moral confusion in the lives of the two characters.

After a precise orientation of the untidy space, Bonner reveals the occupants and comments disparagingly on the ambiguous relationship between them. The female protagonist is Dot, a woman who is "thin . . . almost as pale as the sheets" and suffering from uneasy sleep. On the floor next to her is Buddy, a man whose "high poised features," according to the narrator, mark him as a "keen black man."

Over the course of the play, Dot prepares for an evening out with a man named Exit Mann. The puns on his name are not lost on Buddy, who suspects that the light-skinned Dot is passing and dating a white man. In a murderous rage, Buddy threatens to kill the woman, whom he cannot admit to loving, and her suitor. In the final scene, Dot's beau appears but shadows about him conceal his identity. Buddy, frustrated by racial inequity and his conflicted emotions, shoots in the direction of the couple. The beau finally turns and reveals a dead Dot in his arms. At this moment, Exit Mann is revealed. The figure in a dark coat and hat now appears to have the "hollow eyes and fleshless cheeks" of Death. Bonner's final scene repeats the first; the couple is sleeping fitfully in the same positions in which they appeared first. Dot dies in her bed as Buddy, shocked by her passing, professes his love for her.

"Exit, an Illusion" is a stark and pointed meditation on racial anxiety and the effects of social and racial inequality. Bonner's terse portrayal of strained social relations between men and women underscores the life-threatening impact of poverty and hints at the nightmarish domestic upheaval that accompanies racial passing.

Bibliography

Allen, Carol. *Black Women Intellectuals: Strategies of Nation, Family, and Neighborhood in the Works of Pauline Hopkins, Jessie Fauset, and Marita Bonner.* New York: Garland, 1998.

Bonner, Marita. "Exit, an Illusion." *Crisis* (October 1929): 335–336, 352.

Flynn, Joyce, and Joyce Occomy Striklin. *Frye Street and Environs: The Collected Works of Marita Bonner.* Boston: Beacon Press, 1987.

"Marita Odette Bonner." Lorraine Elena Roses and Ruth Elizabeth Randolph. *Harlem Renaissance and Beyond: Literary Biographies of 100 Black Women Writers, 1900–1945.* Boston: G. K. Hall & Co., 1990.

Roses, Lorraine Elena, and Elizabeth Randolph. "Marita Bonner: In Search of Other Mothers' Gardens." *Black American Literature Forum* 21, nos. 1–2 (Spring–Summer 1987): 165–183.

Eyes of the Old, The Doris D. Price (1932)

One of four known plays by DORIS D. PRICE, published in 1932 with Price's THE BRIGHT MEDALLION in a collection entitled *University of Michigan Plays.* The volume, edited by George Wahr, included selections of University of Michigan student work produced in classes with English professor Kenneth Thorpe Rowe. Little is known about Price, but records confirm that sisters in the Detroit chapter of DELTA SIGMA THETA produced *The Eyes of the Old* and *The Bright Medallion.*

The Eyes of the Old focuses on three generations of women in the South: Grandma Matthews, her daughter Lillian, and her granddaughter Carrie Jackson. Grandma Matthews, whose blindness does not prevent her from seeing the error of her granddaughter's ways, attempts to prevent Carrie from abandoning school and eloping. The strong and visionary matriarch in Price's drama argues for education and against the evils of single motherhood. The play's title is taken from Grandma Matthews's prescient observation that "young folks born wid der eyes of der ole" are the only individuals who are able to overcome the follies of youth and to succeed.

Bibliography

French, W. P., M. J. Singh, and G. E. Fabre. *Afro-American Poetry and Drama, 1760–1975: A Guide to Information Sources.* Detroit: Gale Research Co., 1979.

Roses, Lorraine Elena, and Ruth Elizabeth Randolph. *Harlem's Glory: Black Women Writing, 1900–1950.* Cambridge: Harvard University Press, 1996.

F

"Fairy Story, A" Caroline Bond Stewart Day (1919)

A short story for children by Caroline Bond Stewart Day, a sociologist, teacher, and writer. The work appeared in the October 1919 issue of THE CRISIS.

Day crafted a fast-paced and suspenseful North African fairy tale for her readers. Set in "the wild and hilly country of Morocco," the tale has characteristic features of classic fairy tales such as a motherless child, evil stepsister, scheming stepmother, arranged marriage, and prince who could only be released from a magic spell by a kiss. Day revitalized the genre, however, by providing new racial and cultural standards for beauty, desirability, and romance. Her protagonist Ean is a "beautiful little princess" with "copper-colored skin and black hair that was exceedingly curly," "bright black eyes" and "teeth [that] gleamed like pearls between her full, red lips." In contrast to tales that yoke evil characters to dark or black colors, "A Fairy Story" transfers qualities that hint of European standards of beauty to her villainous character. Maga, her jealous stepsister, has "very pale olive skin," "a thin nose," and "long, straight, black hair."

Ean is a kind and considerate princess whose father arranges for her to marry an ugly, old man who happens to be the most powerful leader in North Africa. If she refuses, the chief will wage war on Ean's tribe. As she surrenders to her fate, her jealous step-relatives prepare to veil Maga and allow her to wed the chief, a rich man whose extremely unattractive features nobody has actually ever seen. On the way to her ritual bath, Ean kisses the pet ostrich that she rescued and has protected from heartless children who wanted to stone it. Within moments, a "handsome young Arab prince on a white horse" rescues her. As Day remarks to her readers, "Of course, you know that this was the enchanted Prince who had been disguised as an ostrich."

Day's short story complemented the mission that JESSIE FAUSET developed during her editorial years at The Crisis. Fauset and W. E. B. DuBois, Crisis editor-in-chief, actively developed and encouraged writers to produce uplifting and inspiring race works for children of color. Day's revision of the traditional European fairy tale was a prime example of the innovative and absorbing narratives that The Crisis included in its issues.

Day, a RADCLIFFE COLLEGE graduate and pioneering social anthropologist, published this piece during a year in which she worked in NEW YORK CITY in organizations providing support to African-American military families. Later, in 1919, she relocated to Texas, where she began teaching college-level English, first in Waco and then in Houston.

Bibliography

Caroline Bond Day Papers, Peabody Museum, Harvard University.

Day, Caroline Bond. "A Fairy Story," Crisis (October 1919): 290–291.

Farrar, John Chipman (1896–1974)

A YALE UNIVERSITY–educated poet, literary critic, editor of The Bookman, and original partner in the publishing house Farrar, Straus and Giroux. With the poet Robert Frost, Farrar was instrumental in the founding of the Breadloaf Writer's Conference at Middlebury College and served as its first director.

Born in Burlington, Vermont, to Edward and Sally Wright Farrar, he enrolled at Yale University following a stint in the armed services, where he served as an aviation inspector in the air corps during World War I. He graduated in 1919, the same year in which he won the Yale Younger Poets Prize for his volume entitled *Forgotten Shrines*. He married Margaret Petheridge, the crossword editor for *THE NEW YORK TIMES*, in 1926. The couple had four children.

Farrar had a long career as a writer and in publishing. In addition to his early years as a reporter for *The New York World*, he served as editor of *The Bookman*, a literary journal established by George Doran. He made his move to publishing in the late 1920s and until just a few years before his death, serving as chairman of the board of Farrar, Straus and Giroux. His own Harlem Renaissance–era works included the memoir entitled *Songs for Children* (1921), books of poetry such as *The Middle Twenties* (1924), and *Songs for Johnny-Jump-Up* (1930), as well as edited collections of *The Bookman Anthology of Verse* (1922) and *The Bookman Anthology of Essays* (1923).

CHARLES S. JOHNSON, the editor of *OPPORTUNITY*, invited Farrar to serve as one of the judges in the first *Opportunity* literary prize contest held in 1924. Farrar, who in 1922 helped found the first American chapter of Poets, Essayists and Novelists (PEN), was delighted to participate. He was committed to identifying promising writers and welcomed the opportunity to learn firsthand about the emerging group of African-American authors.

Father Divine's Peace Mission

An extremely successful interracial mission established in HARLEM in 1933. The mission provided food and shelter and disseminated the ministry and racial uplift philosophies of Father Divine (GEORGE BAKER), an enigmatic and influential minister and cultist.

Bibliography

Reid, Ira. "Negro Movements and Messiahs, 1900–1949." *Phylon* 10, no. 4 (1949): 362–369.

Watts, Jill. *God, Harlem U.S.A.: The Father Divine Story.* Berkeley: University of California Press, 1992.

Weisbrot, Robert. *Father Divine and the Struggle for Racial Equality.* Urbana: University of Illinois Press, 1983.

Fauset, Arthur Huff (1899–1963)

A historian, writer, teacher, and school principal who became a leading figure in PHILADELPHIA during the Harlem Renaissance. Born in Flemington, New Jersey, to Redmond and Bella Fauset, he was the younger half brother of accomplished writer and scholar JESSIE REDMON FAUSET. He earned his B.A., M.A., and Ph.D. from the UNIVERSITY OF PENNSYLVANIA and went on to serve in the U.S. Army during World War II. He began teaching in the Philadelphia public schools during his college years, and his career spanned nearly 30 years, from 1918 through 1946. A fellow in the American Anthropological Association, he was published regularly in the leading New York-based periodicals *OPPORTUNITY* and *THE CRISIS*, and in *BLACK OPALS*, the Pennsylvania black literary arts journal. In 1926 *Opportunity* awarded him one of its literary prizes, and he became one of the select writers to publish in *FIRE!!*, the ambitious but short-lived periodical founded by LANGSTON HUGHES, ZORA NEALE HURSTON, BRUCE NUGENT, and AARON DOUGLAS. He enjoyed a longtime friendship with ALAIN LOCKE and, like Hurston and Hughes, received monies from CHARLOTTE OSGOOD MASON to support his writing and research of black culture.

In addition to his extensive periodical publications, Fauset published four works of nonfiction. His first book, *For Freedom: A Biographical Sketch of the American Negro*, appeared in 1927 and was followed three years later by *Folklore from Nova Scotia*, a collection of essays and observations. In 1938 he published *Sojourner Truth: God's Faithful Pilgrim*, one of the earliest modern biographies and the first black-authored study of the inspired former slave and evangelist. In 1942 Fauset published *Black Gods of the Metropolis: Negro Religious Cults of the Urban North*. It was a revision of "A study of five Negro religious cults in the Philadelphia of today," his University of Pennsylvania doctoral thesis. In 1969 he collaborated with NELLIE RATHBORNE BRIGHT, a fellow University of Pennsylvania alumna and member of the *Black Opals* literary circle. *America: Red, White, Black, Yellow* was published posthumously by Publishing & Supply Company, the first press to distribute his work.

Fauset's writing reflected his deep interest in religiosity and its redemptive power for black Americans. His biography of Sojourner Truth focused on her religious development. Carter G. Woodson reviewed the book for the *American Historical Review* in 1939. In addition, Fauset's anthropological research in African-American culture and religion informed his writing projects. His essay "American Negro Folk Literature" was included in Locke's influential *New Negro*. In *Black Gods* he proposed that African-American churches of all denominations were vital and empowering places for people of color.

Bibliography

Woodson, Carter. "Arthur Huff Fauset: Sojourner Truth, God's Faithful Pilgrim." *American Historical Review* 44, no. 2 (1939): 403.

Fauset, Jessie Redmon (1882–1961)

Hailed as the "midwife" of the Harlem Renaissance, Jessie Redmon Fauset was an accomplished writer, editor, scholar, teacher, and mentor. Her visionary efforts, mentoring, and outreach to emerging writers intensified the intellectual and creative output of the period. A prolific writer in her own right, Fauset's career reflected her keen evaluations of social tensions, racial ideals, and the creative challenges and opportunities for American writers of color during the era. She believed that "[t]o be a Negro in America posited a dramatic situation" but that "there are breathing-spells, in-between spaces where colored men and women work and love and go about their ways with no thought of the 'problem'" (*NYT,* 10 January 1932, BR7).

The most prolific and published author of the era, Fauset was born in New Jersey to Redmon and Annie Seamon Fauset. When her mother died and her father remarried, Jessie became part of a large family. Her stepmother, Bella Huff, had three children of her own and, with Redmon Fauset, went on to have three additional children. One of Jessie

Fauset's closest relations was her half brother ARTHUR HUFF FAUSET, who, like his sister, pursued a literary career and was dedicated to encouraging the collective literary endeavors of his Philadelphia community.

A gifted student, Jessie Fauset graduated from the Philadelphia High School for Girls in 1900. She gained admission to Bryn Mawr College, but once the school determined her race, it made every effort to prevent her from enrolling. As a result, the school helped to negotiate her acceptance to Cornell University. Fauset attended the Ivy League school in Ithaca, New York, and graduated Phi Beta Kappa in 1905. She became the first African-American woman to graduate from Cornell University and the first elected to PHI BETA KAPPA. She remained especially proud of her scholarly accomplishments, and her Phi Beta Kappa key, which she wore on a necklace, is evident in many of the photographs that were taken of her in later life. Her undergraduate studies focused on languages, and Fauset later continued her scholarship at the UNIVERSITY OF PENNSYLVANIA and at the SORBONNE.

Following her graduation from Cornell, Fauset returned to Pennsylvania with an interest in teaching. Unfortunately, ingrained racial prejudice prevented her from acquiring a position in the segregated public school system. After gaining employment at a school in Baltimore, Maryland, for one year, she relocated to WASHINGTON, D.C., and joined the faculty of the renowned M Street High School. Like her half brother, Arthur, she taught in the public schools but was forced to pursue teaching positions in Washington, D.C., when denied employment in Philadelphia because of her race. Fauset taught French for 14 years at the legendary M Street High School, also known as the DUNBAR HIGH SCHOOL, where Sorbonne Ph.D. and pioneering feminist scholar Anna Julia Cooper was headmistress. At the institution, Fauset was part of a formidable intellectual and literary elite that, in addition to Cooper, included fellow teachers and scholars EVA BEATRICE DYKES and MARY CHURCH TERRELL.

In 1918 Fauset began graduate studies at the University of Pennsylvania, and she completed a master's degree in 1919. Her early correspondence with W. E. B. DuBois, whose scholarship and activism she admired greatly, prompted her relocation

Jessie Fauset, Langston Hughes, and Zora Neale Hurston at Tuskegee Institute, Tuskegee, Alabama, 1927 *(Yale Collection of American Literature, Beinecke Rare Book and Manuscript Library)*

to New York City, where she accepted a position as literary editor at THE CRISIS. Fauset's leadership role in the Harlem Renaissance was facilitated by her prominent position in the NATIONAL ASSOCI- ATION FOR THE ADVANCEMENT OF COLORED PEOPLE and *The Crisis*, its official publication. She began working with W. E. B. DuBois, *Crisis* editor and a longtime correspondent and inspiration, in 1919.

At *The Crisis*, Fauset became responsible for the day-to-day management of the magazine, played a central role in the preparation of THE BROWNIES' BOOK, a children's periodical, and cul- tivated new literary talent. Fauset is credited with having discovered successful writers such as LANGSTON HUGHES and CLAUDE MCKAY. It was Fauset who sent ARNA BONTEMPS his first literary acceptance letter, and her encouragement prompted the aspiring writer to leave California and head East to participate fully in the Renais- sance. Fauset's commitment to literary matters meant that *The Crisis* began to showcase more lit- erary material and to pursue meaningful debates about literary trends and issues. The journal's turn toward annual literary competitions was directly linked to Fauset's own influence, and it allowed the NAACP to further enrich its offerings to mem- bers and the public at large. She took advantage of her position and used it to generate thoughtful cri- tiques of her contemporaries. While her close col- league DuBois published a less-than-glowing introduction to BRONZE (1922), GEORGIA DOU- GLAS JOHNSON's first volume of poems, Fauset took the time to address the work in the regular *Crisis* column "Notes on New Books." Fauset sug- gested that "Mrs. Johnson seems to me to hear a message, a message that gains through being softly but intensely insinuated between the lines of her poems" and in deference to Johnson, quoted the Washington, D.C.–based writer when she invoked "the saving grace of the motherheart" and hoped that it would "save humanity" (Hull, 164). In re- sponse to COLOR (1925), COUNTEE CULLEN's first published collection of poems, Fauset asserted that she was "convinced" of the poet's ability to articu- late the complexities of African Americans' experi- ences. "He has the feelings and the gift to express colored-ness in a world of whiteness," she wrote in *The Crisis*, "I hope he will not be deflected from

continuing to do that of which he has made such a brave and beautiful beginning" (Lomax, 241).

Fauset's deft handling of a professional and lit- erary career also served as a role model for writers such as Countee Cullen, Langston Hughes, NELLA LARSEN, and CLAUDE MCKAY, whose work she published during her time at *The Crisis*. According to Larsen biographer Thadious Davis, "Fauset's background, credentials, achievement, and style impressed Nella Larsen Imes, who saw in Fauset a reflection of the accomplished woman that she herself wanted, and intended, to be" (Davis, 143). Her correspondence with writers is a documented part of the Harlem Renaissance record and reflects the great esteem in which many, like Langston Hughes, held her. In 1963, as he was preparing to take a collection of his papers to the library at YALE UNIVERSITY, Hughes noted to his lifelong friend Arna Bontemps that he had come across "a real treasure trove of Jessie Fauset letters, from the one accepting my first poem to 10 to 12 years thereafter" (Nichols, 460). Many years earlier, when Claude McKay was hospitalized after suffer- ing a stroke, Hughes informed Bontemps and urged him to "Tell Fauset" (Nichols, 133). Fauset's close ties to the 135th Street Branch of the NEW YORK PUBLIC LIBRARY and its energetic staff in- cluding REGINA ANDERSON ANDREWS, also in- creased her ability to effectively build professional contacts and sustain the creative enterprises of so many.

During her tenure at *The Crisis*, Fauset collab- orated with DuBois on one of the most significant ventures to produce substantive and appealing lit- erature for and about children of color. As Fauset declared in the dedicatory notice that appeared in the first volume, *The Brownies' Book* was created to fill the insistent void in works by and about peoples of African descent. According to Fauset, the publi- cation was expressly for "children, who with eager look / Scanned vainly library shelf and nook, / For History or Song or Story / That told of Colored People's glory" (Davis, 132). The volumes included numerous short stories, puzzles, biographies, and poetry, and it was Fauset herself who authored a majority of the pieces published in the 24 issues of *The Brownies' Book*. The journal for children also included works by other writers such as Nella Larsen, from whom Fauset solicited submissions, and who contributed autobiographical sketches of her Danish childhood and games that helped to diversify further the messages about the range of African-American origins and backgrounds.

Fauset left *The Crisis* in 1926, after which she began graduate studies, enjoyed international travel, and returned to teaching. Fauset taught French at the DEWITT CLINTON HIGH SCHOOL in New York City, the same institution that Countee Cullen attended.

Fauset was an accomplished writer and published in a variety of genres. Her works include travel essays, short stories, novels, poems, essays, and reviews. She translated the poetical works of French West Indian poets and crafted absorbing essays on her experiences in Paris as a student and later as a delegate to the Pan-African Congresses of the early 1920s. Fauset's poems were published in respected collections of African-American poetry and in literary journals. JAMES WELDON JOHNSON selected five of Fauset's poems for inclusion in his 1921 edited collection, THE BOOK OF AMERICAN NEGRO POETRY: "La Vie C'est la Vie," "Christmas Eve in France," "Dead Fires," "Oriflamme," and "Oblivion."

Fauset's fiction included works that were compelling black female *bildungsromans*, stories about coming of age and often painful negotiations of race and class that people of color experienced. Her short fiction, much of which appeared in *The Crisis*, included "EMMY," "DOUBLE TROUBLE," and "THE SLEEPER WAKES." These stories reflected Fauset's interest in romance and the ways in which women grappled with their desires, unrequited love, and the highly regulated social forums in which they developed relationships.

Fauset published four novels between 1924 and 1933, and her work was part of a growing canon of African-American literary realism. The first, THERE IS CONFUSION, was published in 1924 by BONI & LIVERIGHT, the same house that published JEAN TOOMER's CANE one year earlier. The book sold well and was reprinted in 1929, the same year in which Fauset published PLUM BUN: A NOVEL WITHOUT A MORAL. The book's publication is at the heart of one of the most legendary events of the Harlem Renaissance period. In an effort to mark Fauset's achievement, OPPORTUNITY editor CHARLES S. JOHNSON hosted a festive gathering at the CIVIC CLUB. The event drew a number of leading figures of the period including writers, editors, activists, and publishers, such as Georgia Douglas Johnson, W. E. B. DuBois, HORACE LIVERIGHT, CARL VAN DOREN, ALICE DUNBAR-NELSON, and WALTER WHITE. It quickly became a larger celebration of African-American creativity and intellectual prowess. According to historian Arnold Rampersad, however, Fauset was outraged by the slights that she received on that night. Although the evening was touted as a celebration of Fauset's debut novel, Johnson swiftly reoriented the focus of the evening. Apparently, "to Fauset's barely suppressed but justified fury, given her vastly superior record, Johnson . . . hailed as the 'virtual dean of the movement' his own key adviser in cultural matters: the distinguished Howard University professor, Alain Leroy Locke" (Rampersad, 96). ALAIN LOCKE benefited even more on that evening because this also was the occasion that facilitated his conversation with SURVEY GRAPHIC founder PAUL KELLOGG. The meeting between the two men ultimately led to the March 1925 Harlem issue of the magazine and Locke's pioneering anthology THE NEW NEGRO in 1925.

The title of *Plum Bun*, Fauset's second book and a narrative about the conflicts that racial passing raises for families of color, was inspired by a well-known nursery rhyme that referred to leaving home for the market in order to buy a plum bun. Indeed, the work reflected the kinds of transitions between home and the outside world as well as the pressures of the social marketplace in which individuals were confronted by their own appetites and desires.

During the summer of 1931, Fauset completed her third novel, THE CHINABERRY TREE: A NOVEL OF AMERICAN LIFE, and *Selected Writings*, which appeared later that year. As Fauset biographer Cheryl Sylvander notes, the novel was inspired by a story with which Fauset had become familiar during her childhood and which she first considered in her previously published short story entitled "DOUBLE TROUBLE." After some resistance from her publisher, Frederick A. Stokes Company, Fauset succeeded in acquiring an introduction from writer ZONA GALE and an affirmation of her own focus on middle-class African Americans who defied prevailing stereotypes. Fauset's fourth and final work, COMEDY, AMERICAN STYLE, was published in 1933. Critics have hailed the work for its forthright critique of the social pressures that African Americans face and the aspirations that they foster for themselves and their families. The novel's format, evocative of a stage play, was reminiscent of the format with which the writer had experimented in *The Chinaberry Tree*.

In each of her four novels, Fauset focused on issues of self-definition, racial discrimination, black family dynamics, and passing. *There Is Confusion* chronicles the lives of two families and their efforts to overcome racial discrimination and the demands of mixed-race identities. *Plum Bun*, regarded by many scholars as Fauset's best and most polished work, focused on a family in which some members were able to pass while others were not. The novel is especially powerful in its account of the bittersweet loss of home and the personal destruction of the daughter and mother who abandon the family in search of social privilege and freedoms. Fauset's last two novels, both of which were published by Frederick A. Stokes Company, had to overcome initial resistance at the press. According to Fauset, her editors doubted that the eloquent, self-sufficient, and capable African Americans whom Fauset depicted in her novels actually existed. *The Chinaberry Tree* and *Comedy, American Style* employed new literary forms. The former invoked classical Greek tragedy, and the latter was modeled on a dramatic script and included sections identified as "Acts" and formal descriptions of "The Plot" and "The Characters."

Fauset was a member of DELTA SIGMA THETA, and in this capacity attended the 1921 Second Pan-African Congress in Europe. In April 1929 Fauset married Herbert Harris, an insurance agent with the Victory Life Insurance Company and a World War I veteran. The couple was hosted at numerous teas held in their honor. The couple wed in Fauset's New York apartment, and some 200 guests attended the reception at the nearby Utopia Neighborhood House. The marriage, which received much publicity in the local newspapers including the AMSTERDAM NEWS, which published an article on its front page, apparently prompted Alain Locke to make what ZORA NEALE HURSTON referred to as "one of the best wise cracks of the year" and a comment so inappropriate that "if

Jessie ever hears of it he will have to live abroad for a long time" (Kaplan, 136). When Harris died in 1958, Fauset moved to the Philadelphia home of her half brother. She lived there until her death on April 30, 1961.

Fauset's modest NEW YORK TIMES obituary emphasized her educational credentials and the range of works that she published during her lifetime. In addition, it noted that "Miss Fauset's characters were usually Negroes of 'background and ambition'" and that "racial discrimination was one of her themes" (*NYT*, 3 May 1961). A memorable 1928 *New York Times* editorial on "New Negro Leadership" hailed Fauset as a writer who provided "stimulation for all in [her] subtle poetry and ambitious prose" (*NYT*, 15 April 1928). Fauset continues to be celebrated today for her dynamic professional example, her commitment to education, her enterprising efforts to increase awareness of African-American accomplishments, and her unwavering investment in the development of the African-American literary tradition.

Bibliography

Davis, Thadious M. *Nella Larsen, Novelist of the Harlem Renaissance: A Woman's Life Unveiled.* Baton Rouge: Louisiana State University Press, 1994.

"The End of Desire and Other Works of Fiction." *New York Times*, 10 January 1932, BR7.

Hull, Gloria. *Love, Sex, and Poetry: Three Women Writers of the Harlem Renaissance.* Bloomington: Indiana University Press, 1987.

Johnson, James Weldon. *The Book of American Negro Poetry.* New York: Harcourt, Brace and Company, 1922.

Jones, Sharon. *Rereading the Harlem Renaissance: Race, Class, and Gender in the Fiction of Jessie Fauset, Zora Neale Hurston, and Dorothy West.* Westport, Conn.: Greenwood Press, 2002.

Kaplan, Carla. *Zora Neale Hurston: A Life in Letters.* New York: Doubleday, 2002.

Lomax, Michael. "Countee Cullen: A Key to the Puzzle." In *The Harlem Renaissance Re-Examined*, edited by Victor Kramer and Robert Russ. Troy, N.Y.: Whitson Pub., 1997, 239–248.

Nichols, Charles H., ed. *Arna Bontemps—Langston Hughes Letters, 1925–1967.* New York: Paragon House, 1990.

Rampersad, Arnold. *The Life of Langston Hughes: I, Too, Sing America.* Vol. 1, *1902–1941.* New York: Oxford University Press, 1986.

Sylvander, Cheryl. *Jessie Redmon Fauset, Black American Writer.* Troy, N.Y.: Whitson Pub. Co., 1981.

Wall, Cheryl. *Women of the Harlem Renaissance.* Bloomington: Indiana University Press, 1995.

Fernandis, Sarah Collins (1863–1951)

A teacher and social welfare activist who was born in Maryland to Caleb and Mary Jane Collins. She attended the Hampton Normal and Agricultural Institute and composed the alma mater song that still is used today. She graduated from Hampton in 1882. In 1906 she enrolled in the New York School of Philanthropy, the institution that is now the COLUMBIA UNIVERSITY School of Social Work.

Fernandis pursued a career in teaching and was employed in public schools throughout the South. At one point, her teaching assignment in Florida was organized by the Woman's Home Missionary Society of Boston, a regional chapter of the national organization dedicated to the support of American women and children. In the early 1900s she was a tireless advocate for the poor of WASHINGTON, D.C. Her efforts on behalf of the community in the Bloodfield area resulted in a settlement program that included day care facilities, domestic training classes, and a public library. In Baltimore she founded the Co-Operative Civic League, an African-American branch of the white Women's Civic League, and supported efforts to improve urban life for families and children in the area. In the years leading up to and following World War I, Fernandis intensified her activism and civil rights work. She published numerous articles in the *SOUTHERN WORKMAN,* the Hampton University journal dedicated to racial and ethnic matters that also published writers such as CHARLES CHESNUTT. These writings documented her campaigns for fair housing, racial uplift, and community development.

Fernandis, who married John Fernandis in 1902, was a well-published community leader when she published her first and only volume of poetry in 1925. *Poems* and *Vision* included a number of pieces published previously in the *Southern Workman.* In 1924 her work was chosen for inclusion in AN ANTHOLOGY OF VERSE BY AMERICAN NEGROES, the

collection edited by NEWMAN IVEY WHITE and WALTER CLINTON JACKSON. Fernandis, who wrote extensively about her work in black settlements, was an impassioned poet. In poems such as "The Children's Open Door," she raised public awareness about poverty. Other works recalled her experiences of black solidarity and triumph. Patriotism was another key theme for Fernandis. She composed several works in honor of black soldiers, including "The Troops at Carrizal," a poem about the Tenth Cavalry troops who fought against Mexican soldiers at Carrizal, Mexico. "Our Colored Soldiery" and "Our Allegiance" were rousing poems that applauded African-American patriotism in the face of continued racism and disenfranchisement.

Bibliography
"Alma Mater." Hampton University. Available online. URL: http://www.hamptonu.edu/about/alma_mater.htm. Accessed May 20, 2005.

Roses, Lorraine Elena, and Ruth Elizabeth Randolph. *Harlem's Glory: Black Women Writing, 1900–1950.* Cambridge, Mass.: Harvard University Press, 1996.

Rush, Theressa, Carol Myers, and Esther Arata. *Black American Writers Past and Present: A Biographical And Bibliographical Dictionary.* Metuchen, N.J.: Scarecrow Press, 1975.

Yenser, Thomas, ed., *Who's Who in Colored America.* Brooklyn: Yenser, 1932.

Ferris, William Henry (1874–1941)

A writer and ordained minister whose activities during the Harlem Renaissance were linked closely to MARCUS GARVEY and the UNITED NEGRO IMPROVEMENT ASSOCIATION (UNIA).

Born in New Haven, Connecticut, to David and Sarah Ann Ferris, he went on to graduate from YALE UNIVERSITY in 1895. He earned master's degrees at Yale and at HARVARD UNIVERSITY and studied for two years at the Harvard Divinity School. In the early 1910s Ferris pastored churches in North Carolina and Massachusetts.

Ferris's turn toward politics included writing stints at the *Boston Guardian,* the fiercely anti-accommodationist paper edited by WILLIAM MONROE TROTTER. He also worked with W. E. B. DuBois on matters relating to the Niagara Movement, and with JOHN EDWARD BRUCE and the

AMERICAN NEGRO ACADEMY and the Negro Society for Historical Research. When Ferris joined the UNIA he did so with a controversial publication record and respected scholarly credentials. In 1913 he authored *The African Abroad, or, His Evolution in Western Civilization, Tracing His Development Under Caucasian Milieu*. The two-volume work was the result of Ferris's extensive travels and studies of African history.

In 1919 Ferris became the literary editor of *NEGRO WORLD*, the official publication of the UNIA. Under his leadership, the weekly newspaper flourished. CARTER G. WOODSON, historian and founder of the ASSOCIATION FOR THE STUDY OF NEGRO LIFE AND HISTORY, said that Ferris was largely responsible for making the colorful weekly the most "widely circulated Negro newspaper which has been published in the Western hemisphere." Ferris became fully immersed in the Garvey movement and figured prominently in financial ventures such as the Negro Factories Corporation initiatives in the 1920s that led to the purchase of laundry factories, grocery stores, and restaurants.

Ferris published several essays in the 1920s. In 1922 he published "The Negro Renaissance" and "Negro Composers and Negro Music—Is There Race in Music?" In 1923 "The Philosophy and Opinions of Marcus Garvey" appeared.

Bibliography

Burkett, Randall. *Black Redemption: Churchmen Speak for the Garvey Movement*. Philadelphia: Temple University Press, 1978.

Martin, Tony. *African Fundamentalism: A Literary and Cultural Anthology of Garvey's Harlem Renaissance*. Dover, Mass.: Majority Press, 1991.

Rashidi, Runoko. "William Henry Ferris: The African Abroad." The Global African Community. Available online. URL: http://www.cwo.com/~lucumi/ferris.html. Accessed May 20, 2005.

Fifteenth Regiment of New York National Guard

A group of soldiers whose regiment became the 369th United States Infantry and the first African-American regiment to see action in France during World War I. Their story was included in *Scott's Official History of the American Negro in the World War* (1919), written by Emmett Scott, special adjutant to the secretary of war and longtime private secretary of BOOKER T. WASHINGTON. The regiment's adaptability and military expertise won them high praise from skeptical officers and members of the Department of War.

The regiment, known as the "Fighting Fifteenth" and the "Hell Fighters," embodied the bravery and patriotism that underscored African-American efforts to secure civil rights in postwar America. In February 1919 the regiment returned from France to New York. The striking parade of the 1,300 soldiers and their 18 officers in strict formation up FIFTH AVENUE and into HARLEM marked what historian David Levering Lewis has defined as the beginning of the New Negro Renaissance, the precursor of the Harlem Renaissance.

Bibliography

Ellis, Mark. *Race, War, and Surveillance: African Americans and the United States Government during World War I*. Bloomington: Indiana University Press, 2001.

Little, Arthur. *From Harlem to the Rhine: The Story of New York's Colored Volunteers*. New York: Haskell House, 1974.

Scott, Emmett. *Scott's Official History of the American Negro in the World War*. 1919, reprint, New York: Arno Press, 1969.

Schneider, Mark Robert. *"We Return Fighting": The Civil Rights Movement in the Jazz Age*. Boston: Northeastern University Press, 2002.

Fifth Avenue

A major New York City thoroughfare. It is immortalized in Harlem Renaissance history by the February 1919 march of the FIFTEENTH REGIMENT OF NEW YORK NATIONAL GUARD, or 369th U.S. Infantry, upon its victorious return from combat in France during World War I. The 1,300-member regiment and its 18 officers were led by Bill "Bojangles" Robinson as drum major, and by JAMES REESE EUROPE, the leader of the 369th military band.

Bibliography

Anderson, Jervis. *This Was Harlem: A Cultural Portrait, 1900–1950*. New York: Farrar, Straus and Giroux, 1982.

Watson, Steven. *The Harlem Renaissance: Hub of African-American Culture, 1920–1930*. New York: Pantheon Books, 1995.

Figgs, Carrie Law Morgan (1878–1968)

A published poet and playwright who was born in Valdosta, Georgia, to the Reverend James and Lucinda Morgan. She attended Edward Waters College in Jacksonville, the first Florida college founded for African Americans and the oldest independent school of higher learning in the state. Following graduation, she married William Figgs, a porter and a Mason, in Jacksonville and worked as a schoolteacher in the city for just over 20 years. After the Figgs family moved to CHICAGO in 1920, Figgs became an increasingly prominent member of the African Methodist Episcopal church, a leading community activist, and a respected entrepreneur and owner of the Commonwealth Real Estate Employment Company, based in the family home. In Chicago, Figgs rose through the ranks of the Heroines of Jericho, an organization that was open only to the wives of Masons.

In 1920 Figgs published POETIC PEARLS, her first work and first book of poems with the Edward Waters College Press, the publishing house of her alma mater. The 25 poems included works dedicated to her parents, and religious meditations, as well as commentaries on social relations and family dynamics. In her introduction to the volume, Figgs noted that during her years of travel and service as a teacher and Masonic officer, she had "observe[d] much" and was "[t]herefore . . . sending this little book out into the world." The work received favorable reviews from various figures including the president of WILBERFORCE UNIVERSITY, who characterized the book as "a very fine contribution." Figgs proved herself an advocate of unsung heroes in poems such as "Why Slight the Working Girl" and "After the Honeymoon," in which she championed earnest but mistreated working persons. Figgs also included "The Bull Frog's Song," a poem written when she was 14 years old. Like other poems in the collection, it had four-line stanzas and an irregular rhyme scheme. The "Tribute to the Business Men of Jacksonville" and "The Negro Has Played His Part" revealed Figgs's earnest contributions to

racial uplift and efforts to exhort African Americans who, she claimed, had "boldly played [their] part" in American history.

One year later, in 1921, Figgs self-published NUGGETS OF GOLD, a collection of poems priced at fifty cents. Included in the preface were excerpts from letters she had received from readers of *Poetic Pearls*. It was these positive responses and the "enormous sales" and "popular favor" of her first book that she said "inspired me to send to you *Nuggets of Gold*." Figgs noted that the encouraging assessments of her first work had prompted her to generate another volume. This collection of 20 poems maintained her focus on African-American progress, positive work ethics, and the importance of faith and morality. It began with a celebration of her own family in the title poem, "My Nuggets of Gold," in which she declared, "I own three golden nuggets. / Two boys and a girl; / Who fondly call me mother; / I'm the happiest woman in the world."

Two years later, in 1923, Figgs produced the self-published collection SELECT PLAYS: SANTA CLAUS LAND, JEPTHAH'S DAUGHTER, THE PRINCE OF PEACE, BACHELOR'S CONVENTION. The title page made a pointed note that "Production of these Plays is FREE to Amateurs, but the sole *Professional Rights* are reserved by the *Author*. *Moving Picture Rights reserved*." Two of the four works were based on biblical stories, one was a children's play, and another was a contemporary "comedy drama."

Santa Claus Land was a short, two-act play for children that emphasized the value of curiosity and useful virtues such as patience. In *Bachelor's Convention*, Figgs crafted a pointed satire of patriarchal society and suggested that women needed to have more freedom from domestic responsibilities. *Select Plays* also included two biblical plays that examined inspiring stories from the Old and New Testaments about self-sacrifice, sanctification and holiness, and female virtue.

Figgs's contributions to the Harlem Renaissance reflected the ongoing interest in racial uplift that peaked in the late 1890s with the formation of the NATIONAL ASSOCIATION OF COLORED WOMEN. Her philanthropic work and religious outreach manifested themselves in her writings and further secured her reputation as a respected elder in her Chicago community.

Bibliography

Clifford, Carrie Williams, and Carrie Law Morgan Figgs. *Writings of Carrie Williams Clifford and Carrie Law Morgan Figgs with an introduction by P. Jane Splawn.* New York: G. K. Hall & Co., 1997.

Roses, Lorraine Elena, and Ruth Elizabeth Randolph. *Harlem's Glory: Black Women Writing, 1900–1950.* Cambridge, Mass.: Harvard University Press, 1996.

Finding a Way Out Robert Russa Moton
(1920)

Published in 1920, the autobiography of Robert Russa Moton (1867–1940), a successful graduate of Hampton Institute, and winner of both the HARMON FOUNDATION AWARD, in 1930, and the SPINGARN MEDAL, in 1932. Moton returned to Hampton in 1890 and served as a commandant for 25 years before moving to TUSKEGEE INSTITUTE, where he succeeded BOOKER T. WASHINGTON as president and principal. He published two additional works, *What the Negro Thinks* (1929) and, as commission chair, a *Report of the United States Commission on Education in Haiti, October 1, 1930.*

Moton hoped that his autobiography, which began with stories of his African great grandparents and their abduction into slavery, would "encourag[e] any member of my race to greater faith in himself, as well as in other selves, both white and black; and shall help him to make his life count for the very most in meeting and solving the great human problem which we in this country call the 'race problem.'" He also hoped that accounts of his exhaustive work as a civil rights advocate and race representative, commissioned by the federal government to investigate race-related matters ranging from experiences of black troops abroad in World War I to prospects of education in Haiti, would encourage black and white youth to work for "securing justice and a fair opportunity for the humblest American citizen, whatever his race or colour" (vii).

Bibliography

James, Felix. "Robert Russa Moton and the Whispering Gallery after World War I," *Journal of Negro History* 62, no. 3 (1977): 235–242.

Matthews, Carl S. "The Decline of the Tuskegee Machine, 1915–1925: The Abdication of Political Power." *South Atlantic Quarterly* 75, no. 4 (1976): 460–469.

Moton, Robert Russa. *Finding a Way Out: An Autobiography.* New York: Negro Universities Press, c. 1920 (1969 printing).

———. *Report of the United States Commission on Education in Haiti, October 1, 1930.* Washington, D.C.: U.S. Govt. Printing Office, 1931.

———. *What the Negro Thinks.* New York: Doubleday, Doran and Company, Inc., 1929.

Pamphile, Leon D. "America's Policy-Making in Haitian Education, 1915–1934." *Journal of Negro Education* 54, no. 1 (1985): 99–108.

Fine Clothes to the Jew Langston Hughes
(1927)

In 1927, poet LANGSTON HUGHES, a student at LINCOLN UNIVERSITY, completed his second collection of poems. It appeared one year after the publication of THE WEARY BLUES, his first volume of poems. Hughes dedicated *Fine Clothes* to CARL VAN VECHTEN, the mentor whose support and advocacy helped to ensure the publication in 1926 of *The Weary Blues*, his first book, by ALFRED A. KNOPF. *Fine Clothes to the Jew* was published in the early stages of Hughes's three-year patronage relationship with philanthropist CHARLOTTE OSGOOD MASON.

The controversial title of the volume was taken from "Hard Luck," a poem included in the volume. "Hard Luck" was one of 17 poems in the volume that Hughes wrote "after the manner of the Negro folk-songs known as *Blues.*" In the prefatory note that he included, Hughes reminded his readers that the "mood of the *Blues* is almost always despondency, but when they are sung people laugh." In "Hard Luck," Hughes's realistic speaker considered the limited options available to an individual when "hard luck overtakes you." There is "[n]othin' for you to do," he insists, "When hard luck overtakes you / Nothin' for you to do. / Gather up yo' fine clothes / An' sell 'em to de Jew." The poem, which focuses first on the Jewish-owned pawn and trade shops in NEW YORK CITY, then chronicles the potentially self-destructive efforts of the hard-luck individual who is "so low down" that if he "was a mule" with a "wagon to haul," he would be unable to do so because he "[a]in't even got a stall." With the "dollar an' a half" from the pawn shop, advises the world-wise speaker, "Go to de bootleg's / Git some gin to make you laugh." Historians suggest that had his publishers insisted, Hughes would have changed the name of the collection. Others note that the publishing house did resist Hughes's choice of title but that they desisted after Carl Van Vechten, whose novel NIGGER HEAVEN focuses on the grim realities of working- and lower-class African Americans, lobbied them to leave the original phrase intact. Hughes himself addressed the history of the book and its title in his 1940 autobiography THE BIG SEA. There, he recalled that he "called it *Fine Clothes to the Jew*, because the first poem, 'Hard Luck,' a blues, was about a man who was often so broke he had no recourse but to pawn his clothes— to take them, as the Negroes say, to 'the Jew's' or 'Uncle's.' Since the whole book was largely about people like that, workers, roustabouts, and singers . . . people up today and down tomorrow, working this week and fired the next, beaten and baffled, but determined not to be wholly beaten, buying furniture on the installment plan, filling the house with roomers to help pay the rent, hoping to get a new suit for Easter—and pawning that suit before the Fourth of July—that was why I called my book *Fine Clothes to the Jew*." (Hughes, 202). Hughes was quick to realize, however, that "it was a bad title" because not only was "it confusing" but "many Jewish people did not like it." "I don't know why the Knopfs let me use it," he wrote, "since they were very helpful in their advice about sorting out the bad poems from the good, but they said nothing about the title. I might just as well have called the book *Brass Spitoons,* which is one of the poems [in the collection] I like best" (Hughes, 202).

The collection included poems inspired by Hughes's own experiences. In "Homesick Blues," a poem printed first in the June 1926 issue of *Measure* and then reprinted in *Fine Clothes,* the poet recalled his childhood habit of wandering down to the Lawrence, Kansas, railroad station and imagining the adventures that he might have. This particular poem was informed both by Hughes's longing to travel and his appreciation of the Negro migrations of the age: "I went down to de station. / Ma heart was in ma mouth. / Went down to de station. / Heart was in ma mouth. / Lookin' for a box

car / To roll me to de South." Hughes also addressed unspeakable issues relating to sexuality, promiscuity, and domestic violence. Poems such as "Red Silk Stockings," one that encouraged a young woman to don her stockings and "let de white boys / Looks at yo legs" revealed the dire nature of black poverty. The female subject of the poem was, according to the narrator, forced toward this kind of work. "Ain't nothin to do for you nohow, / round this town,—You's too pretty" declared the narrator, lodging a direct critique of black economic oppression and the toll it took on African-American women in particular.

JULIA PETERKIN, one of the contemporary reviewers, praised Hughes for focusing on the "joys and woes of dish-washers and bell-hops, crap-shooters and cabaret girls, broken women and wandering men, and without losing their strong racial flavor . . . mold[ing] them into swift patterns of musical verse." Others, such as historian and *Pittsburgh Courier* contributor JOEL AUGUSTUS ROGERS, dismissed the book and its sickening "trash." The strength of Hughes's portraits of the underclass contributed to his growing reputation as one of the most promising poets of the age. However, his use of dialect and the blues in the volume elicited strong criticism in the African-American press. The CHICAGO WHIP declared that the volume confirmed Hughes's identity as "The poet lowrate of Harlem" rather than its poet laureate (Hughes, 203). The AMSTERDAM NEWS went even further, using a headline to declare "Langston Hughes—The Sewer Dweller" (Hughes, 203). Arnold Rampersad, Hughes's biographer, suggests, however, that the volume was an innovative project and that the volume's focus on the black masses represented a pioneering gesture in American poetics. Yet, the emphatic and overwhelming negative immediate response to the work reveals the intense desire of many to advance images of African-American propriety, gentility, and stability. This reality was confirmed by Eustace Gay's 5 February 1927 review of the work in the *Philadelphia Tribune.* It is "bad enough to have white authors holding up our imperfections to public gaze," he wrote. "Our aim ought to be to present to the general public, already mis-informed both by well-meaning and malicious writers, our higher aims and aspirations, and our better selves" (Hughes,

205). Hughes was unfazed, confident in his tribute to the real people whom he encountered and whose lives he examined with genuine interest and a keen gaze. *Fine Clothes to the Jew* still stands as a volume that is valuable for its sustained realism and the insights that it provides about 1920s conceptions of African-American identity and domesticity, and the intraracial anxieties about notions of the black primitive and the struggling underclass.

Bibliography
Chinitz, David. "Rejuvenation through Joy: Langston Hughes, Primitivism, and Jazz." *American Literary History* 9, no. 1 (spring 1997): 60–78.

Hughes, Langston. *The Big Sea: An Autobiography*, edited by Joseph McLaren. 1940, reprint, Columbia: University of Missouri Press, 2002.

Rampersad, Arnold. "Langston Hughes's *Fine Clothes to the Jew*." *Callaloo* (winter 1986): 144–158.

Firbank, Arthur Annesley Ronald
(1886–1926)

A wealthy and eccentric London-born novelist whose novel *Sorrow in Sunlight* (1924) was distributed in America with the title PRANCING NIGGER. The work focused on a fictionalized Caribbean empire and the social ambitions of its inhabitants. Critics have hailed the book for its critique of racism and its sympathetic portrait of the characters who endure a variety of social stresses, such as illicit affairs and tragic heartbreak, and quests for spiritual comfort in the face of personal loss.

CARL VAN VECHTEN introduced Firbanks's works to American audiences during the 1920s and of these, *Prancing Nigger* was the most popular among white readers because of its racial themes. GWENDOLYN BROOKS reviewed the work in the June 1926 issue of OPPORTUNITY.

Bibliography
Benkovitz, Miriam J. *A Bibliography of Ronald Firbank*. Oxford: Clarendon Press, 1982.

Brophy, Brigi. *Prancing Novelist: A Defense of Fiction in the Form of a Critical Biography in Praise of Ronald Firbank*. New York: Barnes & Noble, 1973.

Canning, Richard. "Notes Toward a Biography of Ronald Firbank," *James White Review* 17, no. 4 (fall 2000): 5–13.

Clark, William Lane. "Degenerate Personality: Deviant Sexuality and Race in Ronald Firbank's Novels." In *Camp Grounds: Style and Homosexuality*, edited by David Bergman. Amherst: University of Massachusetts Press, 1993. 134–155.

Potoker, Edward M. *Ronald Firbank*. New York: Columbia University Press, 1969.

Fire!!

The journal *Fire!!* represented the collective efforts of leading writers and artists of the Harlem Renaissance era. The cofounders and contributors to the magazine, which debuted in November 1926, were responding to the call for African-American initiatives in the arts that LANGSTON HUGHES had articulated in his 1925 essay "The Negro Artist and the Racial Mountain." Hughes, AARON DOUGLAS, ZORA NEALE HURSTON, and BRUCE NUGENT met in Harlem at the rooming house on West 136th Street known as NIGGERATI MANOR to prepare the publication.

The founders, who located their editorial offices at 314 West 138th Street, planned to produce quarterly issues, "Devoted to the Younger Negro Artists," priced at $1. In New York the writer Bruce Nugent was one of the supporters who helped to disseminate the magazine throughout the city. Hughes recalled that the unemployed Nugent would walk through GREENWICH VILLAGE collecting monies from the few bookstores that displayed and sold the magazine but that he would inevitably spend the profits before he returned to the *Fire!!* offices. The magazine, which required $1,000 to produce and printed only one issue, was conceived in part to establish a distinctive new voice in African-American letters.

The premier issue included works by writers already recognized and celebrated by Harlem Renaissance audiences. WALLACE THURMAN, who provided the financial resources for the magazine and spent some four years paying off the start-up costs despite initial $50 pledges from the founders, published "CORDELIA THE CRUDE," a story deemed offensive by many readers because of its focus on a teenage prostitute. GWENDOLYN BENNETT contributed "WEDDING DAY," one of the two short stories she published during her career. Zora Neale Hurston published the play COLOR STRUCK: A

PLAY IN FOUR SCENES and "SWEAT," a powerful story about a besieged but ultimately triumphant southern laundress. The section entitled "Flame from the Dark Tower" featured poems by LEWIS ALEXANDER, ARNA BONTEMPS, COUNTEE CULLEN, WARING CUNEY, Langston Hughes, HELENE JOHNSON, and EDWARD SILVERA. Richard Bruce contributed several items to the issue, including part one of *Smoke, Lillies and Jade,* a work that critics have hailed as the first published African-American work with homosexual themes. ARTHUR HUFF FAUSET contributed an essay entitled "Intelligentsia," and Aaron Douglas, whose striking artwork graced the cover of the magazine, published three additional drawings and some "Incidental Art Decorations" in the issue.

The majority of first-edition copies of the short-lived journal were destroyed when a fire spread through the building in which they were being stored. Facsimile copies of the journal were created in 1982 by the Fire!! Press.

Bibliography

Cobb, Michael. "Insolent Racing, Rough Narrative: The Harlem Renaissance's Impolite Queers." *Callaloo: A Journal of African-American and African Arts and Letters* 23, no. 1 (winter 2000): 328–351.

Henry, Matthew. "Playing with Fire!!: Manifesto of the Harlem Niggerati." *Griot: Official Journal of the Southern Conference on Afro-American Studies, Inc.* 10, no. 2 (fall 1992): 40–52.

Hughes, Langston. *The Big Sea: An Autobiography.* New York: Knopf, 1940.

"Fire and Cloud"   Richard Wright (1938)

A prize-winning short story by RICHARD WRIGHT. It was awarded the first prize of $500 in a 1937 contest sponsored by *Story* and then awarded the O. Henry Memorial Award in 1938. The work was published first in 1938 in *Story* and then republished in UNCLE TOM'S CHILDREN: FOUR NOVELLAS, the acclaimed 1938 collection of Wright fiction.

HARPER & BROTHERS, the original publishers, reissued the volume two years later, in 1940, and included an additional novella *Bright and Morning Star,* and Wright's memorable autobiographical essay "The Ethics of Living Jim Crow."

"Fire and Cloud" documents the political awakening of Dan Taylor, a minister whose sense of self and his ability to advocate for his community have been compromised by white racism and intimidation. In the face of a life-threatening drought, Taylor must decide whether he will join his congregation and the black community in a protest march. The white local government asks him to dissuade the community and when he fails to do so, subjects him to a brutal whipping. It is in the midst of this violence that Taylor experiences a powerful epiphany. He takes his place at the head of the protest march and, with his community, succeeds in obtaining food for the desperate citizens.

The story was one of Wright's most powerful illustrations of the rigors and dangers of black southern folk life. It has been hailed for its realism, critique of capitalism, and celebration of the emancipatory benefits of collective, or communist, action.

Bibliography

Gayle, Addison. *Richard Wright: Ordeal of A Native Son.* Garden City, N.Y.: Anchor Press/Doubleday, 1980.

Tuhkanen, Miko Juhani. "A (b)igger's place": Lynching and Specularity in Richard Wright's "Fire and Cloud" and "Native Son." *African American Review* 33 (spring 1999): 125–133.

"Fire and the Cloud, The"   Zora Neale Hurston (1934)

A short story by ZORA NEALE HURSTON that appeared in CHALLENGE in September 1934. The journal, founded by DOROTHY WEST in 1934, published Hurston's Harlem Renaissance contemporaries and also is known for being the periodical in which RICHARD WRIGHT's seminal essay, "A Blueprint for Negro Writing," first appeared.

Hurston's story should not be confused with Wright's story "FIRE AND CLOUD" published in the 1940 collection UNCLE TOM'S CHILDREN. Hurston's story would later evolve into her 1939 novel MOSES, MAN OF THE MOUNTAIN. The short story features Moses in an illuminating and reflective conversation about his leadership with a lizard. Hurston uses folklore and vivid personification to revisit the emancipation of the Hebrew slaves from their Egyptian bondage. Hurston biographer Valerie Boyd notes that the short story reveals the evolution of Hurston's interest in using Moses as a vehicle through which to celebrate and explore African-American history and culture.

Bibliography

Boyd, Valerie. *Wrapped in Rainbows: The Life of Zora Neale Hurston.* New York: Scribner, 2003.

Caron, Timothy. "'Tell Ole Pharaoh to Let My People Go': Communal Deliverance in Zora Neale Hurston's *Moses Man of the Mountain,*" *Southern Quarterly* 36, no. 3 (spring 1998): 47–60.

Morris, Robert. "Zora Neale Hurston's Ambitious Enigma: Moses, Man of the Mountain," *CLA Journal* 40, no. 3 (March 1997): 305–335.

"Fire by Night" Rudolph Fisher (1927)

This short story by RUDOLPH FISHER appeared in the December 1927 issue of *McClure's* magazine. It is marked for its personification of a vicious NEW YORK CITY, one in which the description of LENOX AVENUE is particularly vivid. Fisher imagines the street, at the heart of HARLEM, as totally besieged and ambushed: "Ugly, cheap little shops attack it, cluster like scavenging vermin about it. Trucks crush blindly, brutally over it, subway eats wormily into it. Waste clutters over it, odors fume up from it, sewer-mouths gape like wounds in its back. Swift changes of complexion come—pallor—grayness—lividity. Then, less than a mile beyond its start, the Avenue turns quite black."

Fire in the Flint Walter White (1924)

The first of two novels by WALTER WHITE, a major figure in the Harlem Renaissance and prominent officer of the NATIONAL ASSOCIATION FOR THE ADVANCEMENT OF COLORED PEOPLE (NAACP). The book grew out of White's intensive antilynching work and activism for the NAACP and complemented his extensive journalistic writings on the brute violence and inhumanity of lynching.

The novel was published in 1924, just two years after the Dyer Anti-Lynching Bill was passed in the House of Representatives but blocked by a filibuster in the Senate. The NAACP, which from its inception committed itself to the creation of antilynching legislation, supported the bill and worked tirelessly for its passage. White's novel may

be considered, in part, a reflection of his earnest commitment to the organization's efforts.

White was on staff at the NAACP as national assistant secretary in 1919 when the organization published *Thirty Years of Lynching in America, 1889–1918.* Documented lynchings in the 20th century were on the decline when White published, but as historians have noted, there were significant numbers of killings that went unreported. In 1919, following the end of World War I, racial unrest increased; there were 83 lynchings. By 1933, the number of documented attacks stood at 28.

The novel chronicled the life of Kenneth Harper, a doctor who, after completing his medical training at HARVARD UNIVERSITY, decides to return home to Georgia. Harper, who grew up in the segregated South, confronts the rigid, racist structures of the South. He allies himself with a group of sharecroppers and supports their attempts to create an empowering cooperative. The local white response, represented by the KU KLUX KLAN, pits Harper against the life-threatening racial caste of the early 20th century.

Bibliography

Janken, Kenneth Robert. *White: The Biography of Walter White, Mr. NAACP.* New York: The New Press, 2003.

White, Walter. *Rope and Faggot: A Biography of Judge Lynch.* Knopf, 1929; reprint, Kenneth Janken (ed.), Notre Dame, Ind.: University of Notre Dame, 2001.

Zangrando, Robert L. *The NAACP Crusade Against Lynching, 1909–1950.* Philadelphia: Temple University Press, 1980.

First International Convention of the Negro Peoples of the World

Organized by MARCUS GARVEY and the UNIVERSAL NEGRO IMPROVEMENT ASSOCIATION (UNIA), the convention was held in HARLEM throughout August 1920. The unprecedented gathering of Africans and African Americans included a staggering parade through Harlem. It was during this event that the red, green, and black flag symbolizing African unity was adopted. Hailed by the *NEGRO WORLD*, the official UNIA newspaper, as a "unique and glorious achievement," the convention succeeded in rallying people to Garvey's ambitious plans for black solidarity and a back-to-Africa initiative. The convention formalized the UNIA, elected officers, and established salaries for organization members.

Bibliography

Cronon, Edmund. *Black Moses: The Story of Marcus Garvey and the Universal Negro Improvement Association.* Madison: University of Wisconsin Press, 1955.

Hill, Robert, ed. *The Marcus Garvey and Universal Negro Improvement Association Papers.* Berkeley: University of California Press, 1983.

First World War

The conflict that began in 1914 and ended in 1918 was won with heroism, sacrifice, and patriotic contributions from some 350,000 African-Americans soldiers. One hundred and seventy-one soldiers in units that fought alongside the French and against German troops received the prestigious French Legion of Honor medal. African Americans faced pervasive racism within the segregated American military. By the war's midpoint, much public and community protest had resulted in black access to officer's training. More than 600 African-American captains and first and second lieutenants were commissioned to serve during the war. Veterans in the Harlem Renaissance community included CHARLES S. JOHNSON, the founder of OPPORTUNITY and an officer in the NATIONAL URBAN LEAGUE.

In February 1919, the all-black 369th Infantry, a regiment that began as the FIFTEENTH REGIMENT OF NEW YORK NATIONAL GUARD, returned to New York City. The first regiment of African-American soldiers to see action in France during the war and the most decorated of all American military units was a magnificent and impressive sight to behold. The march took the 1,300-strong regiment and its 18 officers north along FIFTH AVENUE and into Harlem. The return of black veterans, many of whom had experienced less racism in Europe, contributed to heightened resistance to American segregation and JIM CROW laws. Tensions throughout the nation escalated and in the summer of 1919, culminated in the "RED SUMMER," three months of uprisings and riots in urban cities.

A number of Harlem Renaissance writers focused on the war, black veterans, and issues of patriotism and citizenship. The 1918 one-act play *Mine Eyes Have Seen* by ALICE DUNBAR-NELSON was published in THE CRISIS and performed at Howard High School in WASHINGTON, D.C., that same year. Set in 1918, the short play illuminated the debates about the use and validity of black participation in the war. MARY BURRILL's 1919 drama AFTERMATH, published in the LIBERATOR, focused on a young veteran who returns to his South Carolina home only to find that his father has been lynched. Burrill's play highlighted the uneasy and often invalidating white national response to black soldiers and African-American contributions to the war effort.

Poet CLAUDE MCKAY penned the rousing poem "If We Must Die" in 1919 as soldiers returned en masse to American and to Harlem. His poem, reprinted in the 1922 poetry collection HARLEM SHADOWS, was used as an anthem for black courage. The sonnet articulated the militancy, self-assertion, and pride with which many African Americans, buoyed by the inspiring record of black troops, were determined to overcome oppression in America. In 1928 McKay published HOME TO HARLEM, a best-selling novel that focused on the adventures and assimilation of a young veteran into a vibrant, unpredictable Harlem world.

Bibliography

Barbeau, Arthur. *The Unknown Soldiers: Black American Troops in World War I.* Philadelphia: Temple University Press, 1974.

Little, Arthur. *From Harlem to the Rhine: The Story of New York's Colored Volunteers.* New York: Haskell House, 1974.

Scott, Emmett. *Scott's Official History of the American Negro in the World War.* 1919; reprint, New York: Arno Press, 1969.

Shack, William. *Harlem in Montmartre: A Paris Jazz Story between the Great Wars.* Berkeley: University of California Press, 2001.

Fisher, Rudolph John Chauncey
(1897–1934)

A prolific writer, talented musician, and accomplished physician, Fisher enjoyed one of the most multifaceted professional careers of any writer in the Harlem Renaissance. He wrote engaging fiction and was the first African-American man to publish a detective novel. His literary triumphs, which included making his debut in THE AT-LANTIC MONTHLY, energized the New York City circles in which he moved and inspired his peers.

Fisher was the last of six children born in WASHINGTON, D.C., to John and Glendora Fisher. The family, who suffered the devastating early deaths of three of the children, moved to Providence, Rhode Island. Fisher excelled in his studies at Classical High School, from which he graduated with honors in 1915. He stayed in Providence to attend BROWN UNIVERSITY and distinguished himself while there. He was awarded prestigious university prizes for public speaking and for studies in German. In 1919, when he graduated with a degree in English, he also delivered the oration on Class Day and was the student speaker at Com-

Rudolph Fisher, physician and author *(Yale Collection of American Literature, Beinecke Rare Book and Manuscript Library)*

mencement that year. At Commencement, Fisher had the opportunity to meet PAUL ROBESON, an emerging vocalist and then-Rutgers University student. The two men, who became close friends in the years to come, hatched a plan to raise funds for their next academic ventures. According to Robeson biographers Sheila Boyle and Andrew Buni, the two " 'toured the eastern seaboard' in 1919 to earn money for college tuition" (Boyle and Buni, 82). Despite their entrepreneurial spirit, however, they failed to turn a profit from the musical venture that featured Fisher on the piano and Robeson as vocalist and needed to get emergency funds from Fisher's father in order to finance their passage home. One year later, in 1920, he completed requirements for a master's degree in biology from Brown. He then relocated to Washington, D.C., where he enrolled at HOWARD UNIVERSITY, earned his medical degree, and graduated summa cum laude in 1924.

Fisher completed a one-year internship at the Freedmen's Hospital in 1925 and advanced medical training at the Columbia University College of Physicians and Surgeons in NEW YORK CITY in 1927. His areas of specialization included roentgenology, bacteriology, and pathology. The PHI BETA KAPPA graduate from Brown University and Howard University Medical School graduate eventually settled in HARLEM. During the course of his medical career, Fisher enjoyed appointments at leading hospitals and busy health agencies in New York City. These included the Bronx Hospital, Mt. Sinai, the International Hospital, and Montefiore Hospital and Vincent Sanitarium as well as the New York City Health Department, where he worked as an X-ray technician for four years, from 1930 through 1934. He was highly respected as a physician and enjoyed an active professional life that included the presidency of the New York branch of the Howard Medical Club and memberships in medical societies such as the Queens Clinical Society and the North Harlem Medical Association. Fisher also served in the military as a first lieutenant with the Medical Corps of the National Guard's New York 369th Infantry.

Fisher married Jane Ryder in September 1924, and the couple had one son, Hugh. The family lived on Edgecombe Avenue in one of Harlem's most well-known apartment buildings. At 409

Edgecombe, they were part of a residential community that included many members of the African-American professional and intellectual elite. As the writer and educator Katherine Butler Jones recalls, Fisher, who lived on the 13th floor of the building, "was a brilliant man, a real genius" (Boyd, 35). Fisher's untimely death in 1934 at age 37 was officially attributed to intestinal ailments. Many scholars have considered that his death was hastened by his exposure to harmful X-rays through his work as a roentgenologist in his own New York City practice, city hospitals, and his pioneering research in radiology. David Levering Lewis characterized Fisher's demise as "maddeningly avoidable" and blamed it on his "exposure to his own x-ray equipment" (Lewis, 304). Fisher scholar John McCluskey, whose research on the pioneering physician-writer has involved conversations with his widow Jane, however, refutes this notion and suggests that Fisher did not succumb because of overexposure to X-rays.

Fisher's passions for literature and for science prompted him to realize his potential in both fields. In an August 1927 interview published in *McClure's*, Fisher declared frankly that his early degrees fanned his interests in the arts and in the sciences. Ultimately, he "studied medicine to heal" what he referred to as his "fractured ambition." He went on to note that his medical degree "saved my life by permitting me to write both fiction and articles for literary journals and research reports for the scientific journals" (Tignor, 87).

One of the most widely published writers of the era, Fisher published 15 short stories, two novels, and additional book reviews, research papers, and essays in leading journals such as *The Atlantic Monthly*, THE CRISIS, *McClure's*, OPPORTUNITY, *Story*, and SURVEY GRAPHIC. In addition, he penned a stage adaptation of his second novel, THE CONJURE-MAN DIES, that opened at the Lafayette Theatre in New York City in the spring of 1936.

He soon saw his work published in leading periodicals of the day, including key journals of the Harlem Renaissance period such as *The Crisis, Opportunity*, and *Survey Graphic* and in mainstream journals such as *The Atlantic Monthly* and *McClure's*. He worked closely with Paul Robeson and composed many of the musical arrangements for the Negro spirituals that Robeson performed.

Fisher made his publishing debut with "THE CITY OF REFUGE," a notable short story published in the prestigious *Atlantic Monthly*. It was later included in the *Best Short Stories of 1925*, edited by Edward O'Brien, and in THE NEW NEGRO, the impressive collection of promising and accomplished Harlem Renaissance–era writers edited by ALAIN LOCKE. A second story, "THE SOUTH LINGERS ON" also was included in *The New Negro*; it appeared with the new title "Vestiges: Harlem Sketches." In 1927 his short story "HIGH YALLER" won first prize in the contest sponsored by philanthropist AMY SPINGARN. At the awards ceremony held at the Renaissance Casino, located at 138th Street and Seventh Avenue, Fisher was feted together with WILLIS RICHARDSON, Ruth Shelton, COUNTEE CULLEN, and LANGSTON HUGHES, whose work also received recognition and prizes in the annual contest. This also was the year in which he published his only essay. "THE CAUCASIAN STORMS HARLEM," a satiric autobiographical essay prompted by the exclusion of African Americans from Harlem clubs, recalled Fisher's own encounters with leading writers and artists of the day. The engaging reflection appeared in the August 1927 issue of AMERICAN MERCURY.

KNOPF published THE WALLS OF JERICHO, Fisher's first novel, in 1928. Reviewers praised Fisher for his "undoubted literary knack" and for the "force and felicity of his expositions and descriptions" of African-American characters and communities (*NYT*, 5 August 1928, 54). His second novel, *The Conjure-Man Dies: A Mystery Tale*, was published in 1932 and promptly translated into French in 1936. A second French edition appeared in 2001. In 1936 Fisher completed a dramatic adaptation of the novel as part of the Federal Theater Project. The three-act play, which opened in March 1936 and closed in on July 4 of that year, brought thousands to the LAFAYETTE THEATRE in Harlem. Scholar Eleanor Tignor notes that some 83,000 people saw the show that was based on the first non-serialized detective novel by an African American to feature a black sleuth. The substantial cast included Lional Monagas in the role of Dr. John Archer, Irving Ellis as Jinx Jenkins, Dooley Wilson as Detective Sergeant Perry Dart, and Fritz Weller as the enigmatic N'Gana Frimbo, the conjure man.

Many of Fisher's peers recognized his talents and did not hesitate to praise his work and example. ZORA NEALE HURSTON was extremely enthusiastic about the prospect of seeing her work published alongside Fisher's in the new journal that DOROTHY WEST was attempting to establish. In a March 1934 letter to West, Hurston did not hesitate to reveal her high opinion of Fisher, a writer whom she believed was "greater than the Negroes rate him generally." According to Hurston, some tended to underestimate Fisher because "he is too honest to pander to our inferiority complex and write 'race' propaganda" (Kaplan, 297). One of the most memorable stories about Fisher revolves around a taxi ride that he took with Paul Robeson, Juilliard School graduate and teacher Edwin Coates, and New York City School deputy superintendent Frank Turner. Scholars of both Robeson and Fisher record that in response to the driver's recklessness and near misses on the dark, rainy night, Robeson finally urged him to slow down. "Be careful," he intoned. "If anything happens to any of us, you will set the race back three generations" (Boyle and Buni, 102; McCluskey, xi). Contemporary reviews of his work also tended to praise Fisher for what one writer referred to as his "undoubted literary knack" (NYT, 5 August 1928, 54).

In a January 1933 radio interview that was later published in the PITTSBURGH COURIER, Fisher described himself as a writer whose works would historicize and document the culture and traditions of this vibrant and evolving location. A prizewinning student in elocution and debate during his college years, Fisher continued to demonstrate his facility with language in his writing. As scholars like Leonard Deutsch have noted, personification was the figurative device that Fisher used most, and he used it to bring the city alive. Most of his works contain evocative descriptions of well-known Harlem locations and underscore the vitality and personality of the place.

Like writers JESSIE FAUSET, NELLA LARSEN, WALLACE THURMAN, and others, Fisher explored issues of intraracial tension and racial passing in his works. His prizewinning short story "High Yaller" is part of the significant body of Harlem Renaissance-era work on passing, assimilation, and race pride. Like Hurston, Fisher also was known for crafting memorable portraits of the African-American folk. His focus on the ways in which ordinary people grappled with the transition from rural southern life to the fast-paced and often unfeeling urban world contributed much to ongoing discussions of African-American assimilation and advancement. Fisher also developed intense portraits of class struggle and difference. During 1927, his most prolific year, he published "BLADES OF STEEL," a grim story that introduced readers to the seedy and vicious world of pool halls and bars. In addition to his extensive collection of published works, Fisher also completed but did not publish at least two other dramas and several short stories. The plays *The Vici Kid* and *Golden Slippers* and the short fiction that includes undated works such as "Across the Airshaft," "The Lindy Hop," "One Month's Wages" and "Skeeter" are held in the John Hay Library at Brown University and also by his family. Fisher took great pride in his ability to portray African-American life, and as Fisher scholar John McCluskey notes, Fisher took great pleasure in the prospect of being regarded as "Harlem's interpreter." While Fisher was quite frank about his desire to protect his creative freedom and avoid obligatory race fiction just because of his own racial identity, he recognized the value of probing and evocative stories about people of color. "If I should be fortunate enough to become known as Harlem's interpreter," he declared in 1933, "I should be very happy" (McCluskey, xxxix). His literary example continued to inspire writers in the years beyond the Harlem Renaissance. Fisher's surviving kin note that he aspired to generate a novel that would tell the story of African-American migration, assimilation, and success. While his life was cut short and Fisher was prevented from realizing the trilogy of great African-American novels that he had envisioned, he did succeed in modeling for many the innovative and compelling methods by which one could document the significant migrations and transformations of American people of color.

Bibliography

"The Walls of Jericho and Other Works of Fiction." *New York Times*, 5 August 1928, 54.

Boyd, Herb. "Once a Harlemite, Always a Harlemite." *Amsterdam News* (10 April 2003): 35.

Boyle, Sheila Tully, and Andrew Buni. *Paul Robeson: The Years of Promise and Achievement.* Amherst: University of Massachusetts Press, 2001.

Clarke, John Louis. "Mystery Novel Writer Is Interviewed Over the Radio." *Pittsburgh Courier,* 21 January 1933.

Deutsch, Leonard. "'The Streets of Harlem;' The Short Stories of Rudolph Fisher." *Phylon* 40, no. 2 (1979): 159–171.

Gosselin, Adrienne. "The World Would Do Better to Ask Why Is Frimbo Sherlock Holmes?: Investigating Liminality in Rudolph Fisher's *The Conjure-Man Dies.*" *African American Review* 32, no. 4 (winter 1998): 607–619.

Kaplan, Carla. *Zora Neale Hurston: A Life in Letters.* New York: Doubleday, 2002.

McCluskey, John, ed. *The City of Refuge: The Collected Stories of Rudolph Fisher.* Columbia: University of Missouri Press, 1987.

McGruder, Kevin. "Jane Ryder Fisher." *Black Scholar* 23, no. 2 (1993): 20–25.

Rudolph Fisher Newsletter: Online News and Resources for Rudolph Fisher & the Harlem Renaissance. Available online. URL: http://www.fishernews.org. Accessed June 2005.

Tignor, Eleanor. "Rudolph Fisher." In *Dictionary of Literary Biography:* New York: Gale Group, 1987, 86–96.

Fisk University

The oldest university in Nashville, Tennessee, Fisk was founded in 1866 with an early mission to educate former slaves. In 1952 it became the first historically black institution to have a chapter of PHI BETA KAPPA established on its campus. The Jubilee Singers, founded in 1871 to raise funds for the school and to preserve African-American songs, brought national and international attention to the school.

Fisk played a central role in the lives of Harlem Renaissance writers and scholars. NELLA LARSEN attended the school for one year in 1907; her ex-husband, Elmer Imes, studied physics and graduated from Fisk in 1903. Adelaide Allen Brown, the mother of the writer, educator, and future Fisk professor STERLING BROWN, was one of the school's graduates. Sociologist George Edmund Haynes earned his B.A. there in 1903, and the renowned singer Roland Hayes enrolled and studied voice at Fisk with Jennie Robinson.

Prominent writers and editors shaped the humanities, arts, and social science programs at Fisk in the 1920s and 1930s in particular. W. E. B. DuBois, the cofounder of the NATIONAL ASSOCIATION FOR THE ADVANCEMENT OF COLORED PEOPLE, *CRISIS* editor, and the first African-American Ph.D. at HARVARD UNIVERSITY, graduated from Fisk in 1888. JAMES WELDON JOHNSON, a former secretary of the NAACP, taught creative writing there until his death in a car accident in 1938. AARON DOUGLAS, the pioneering artist of the Harlem Renaissance, founded the Fisk Art Department and was chair until 1966. ALAIN LOCKE, respected scholar and editor of *THE NEW NEGRO* anthology, was a visiting professor. CHARLES S. JOHNSON, founder of *OPPORTUNITY* and officer in the NATIONAL URBAN LEAGUE, joined the Sociology Department at Fisk in 1926. In 1946 he became the first African-American president of the institution. E. FRANKLIN FRAZIER, the accomplished sociologist and author of *The Negro in the United States,* was a member of the Fisk faculty during Johnson's tenure as chair.

In 1934 ZORA NEALE HURSTON began conversations with Fisk President Thomas Jones, who encouraged her to apply for a faculty appointment. Hurston, who had just visited the campus to see her friends Charles Johnson, James Weldon Johnson, and Lorenzo Dow Turner, was enthusiastic about the prospect. The position in the drama department did not materialize, however. Hurston biographer Valerie Boyd suggests that the school became wary of Hurston's reputation for being assertive and outspoken.

In 1943, soon after the close of the Harlem Renaissance, writer ARNA BONTEMPS became the head librarian and under his leadership began an impressive African-American literary collection that included papers by COUNTEE CULLEN, CHARLES S. JOHNSON, JEAN TOOMER, and the musical collection of CARL VAN VECHTEN.

Bibliography

Jones, Thomas. *Progress at Fisk University: A Summary of Recent Years.* Nashville: Fisk University, 1930.

Richardson, Joe. *A History of Fisk University, 1865–1946.* Tuscaloosa: University of Alabama Press, 1980.

Fleming, Sarah Lee Brown (1875–1963)

The first black woman elected "Mother of the Year" in Connecticut, Fleming was also the first

African-American teacher in Brooklyn, New York. In addition to her teaching career, Fleming pursued writing and began to publish on the eve of the Harlem Renaissance. While not a part of the most active literary circles, Fleming contributed to the momentum of the black literary arts movement during the 1920s.

Fleming's first and only novel, *Hope's Highway*, was published in 1918. A novel of racial uplift, it tackles issues of prejudice and racial solidarity. Scholars have celebrated the recently republished work for its innovative treatment of these popular themes.

In 1920 Fleming published CLOUDS AND SUNSHINE, her sole collection of poems. Dedicated to her children, the volume included 27 works divided into three distinct sections. Like Paul Laurence Dunbar, who experimented with traditional English and black dialect forms, Fleming developed poems that reflected her skills in both linguistic styles. In addition to the sections that showcased formal mainstream English and black dialect, the volume included a final section entitled "Race Poems" that celebrated black history and exhorted readers to persist in spite of their struggles.

In 1926 Fleming contributed two biographical profiles of black women to *Our Women: Homespun Heroines and Other Women of Distinction.* Fleming's entries on Eliza Gardner, AME Zion leader and abolitionist, and Josephine St. Pierre Ruffin, leading Boston club woman, were part of the rich collection of profiles compiled by HALLIE QUINN BROWN, an internationally known civil and women's rights activist and educator.

Bibliography

Fleming, Sarah Lee Brown. *Hope's Highway and Clouds of Sunshine.* New York: G. K. Hall & Co., 1995.

McLendon, Jacquelyn. "Sarah Lee Brown Fleming." In *African American Authors, 1745–1945: A Bio-Bibliographical Critical Sourcebook,* edited by Emmanuel Nelson. Westport, Conn.: Greenwood, 2000.

Flight Walter White (1926)

Published in 1926, one year before author WALTER WHITE won a GUGGENHEIM FELLOWSHIP, *Flight* traced a mixed-race woman's uneasy journey to self-realization and racial acceptance. The novel, published by ALFRED A. KNOPF, coincided with other significant literary events in 1926, including the debut of *FIRE!!*, the explosive but short-lived journal, CARL VAN VECHTEN's controversial novel *NIGGER HEAVEN,* and the publication of *THE WEARY BLUES,* LANGSTON HUGHES's first collection of poems.

Written during White's tenure as acting secretary at the NAACP, the novel focuses on the struggles of protagonist Annette Angela Daquin, also known as Mimi. She survives the death of her father, an unexpected pregnancy, and a tumultuous trip northward from ATLANTA to PHILADELPHIA and NEW YORK. In the urban North, she passes for white but eventually abandons her white husband and their community for HARLEM.

This novel, White's second, was a major factor in his selection for a Guggenheim Award in 1927.

Bibliography

Brooks, Neil. "We Are Not Free! Free! Free!: *Flight* and the Unmapping of American Literary Studies." *College Language Association Journal* 41, no. 4 (June 1998): 371–386.

Janken, Kenneth Robert. *White: The Biography of Walter White, Mr. NAACP.* New York: The New Press, 2003.

Waldron, Edward. *Walter White and the Harlem Renaissance.* Port Washington, N.Y.: Kennikat Press, 1978.

White, Walter. *A Man Called White: The Autobiography of Walter White.* New York: Viking Press, 1948.

Flight of the Natives, The Willis Richardson (1927)

A stirring one-act play by WILLIS RICHARDSON, the first African-American writer to see his work produced on BROADWAY. It was published in 1927 in *PLAYS OF NEGRO LIFE: A SOURCEBOOK OF NATIVE AMERICAN DRAMA,* a volume coedited by ALAIN LOCKE and MONTGOMERY GREGORY. Artist AARON DOUGLAS produced a haunting illustration of a man and natural world in silhouette that appeared opposite the title page.

The play is set in the cabin of an enslaved South Carolina family and their friends in 1860, on the eve of the Civil War. The characters include two married couples, Mose and Pet and Tom and

Sallie, as well as a mulatto slave named Luke, a slave informer named Jude, and a white slave owner named John. The play begins as the men and women speculate on the fate of a runaway named Slim. They challenge Jude, who has shared details of the man's escape route with the master, but who insists on keeping company with them. The master appears and attempts to intimidate the slaves. He threatens to sell them away because of their harsh treatment of the tattler. Once he leaves the cabin, however, the light-skinned slave Luke reappears in the clothes of the master. Richardson does not specify how the young man has come into possession of his master's wardrobe or keys held by Jude. He stresses the looming heroic potential of this figure as the play ends. The two couples and Luke begin their journey to freedom, and it is in response to Luke's "commanding gesture" that the group begins its exodus.

Bibliography

Gray, Christine Rauchfuss. *Willis Richardson: Forgotten Pioneer of African-American Drama.* Westport, Conn.: Greenwood Press, 1999.

Patton, Venetria K., and Maureen Honey, eds. *Double-Take: A Revisionist Harlem Renaissance Anthology.* New Brunswick: Rutgers University Press, 2001.

Florida Negro, The Zora Neale Hurston (date unknown)

An unpublished work by the anthropologist and novelist ZORA NEALE HURSTON. The collection of folktales and songs was written during her tenure with the Federal Writers' Project (FWP), which she joined seven months after publishing her acclaimed work THEIR EYES WERE WATCHING GOD (1937). Hurston, like other writers who were able to prove their need of financial support, was hired to collect materials for the national project. She traveled throughout Florida working as a field researcher and writer and earned $63 a month for her efforts. Hurston's penchant for innovative outreach and entrepreneurial efforts to support the artistic ventures of black musicians prompted Henry Alsberg, the national director of the Federal Writers' Project, to suggest that Hurston be appointed editor of the volume and receive a substantial increase in salary. The current director, a white woman named Carita Dogget Corse, who both hired and admired Hurston, compromised somewhat in order to prevent racial upheaval in her offices. She promoted Hurston to the position of "Negro editor" and increased Hurston's travel allowance but did not provide any office space for the writer.

The volume included chapters devoted to the arts, religion, folklore, and music. Among the essays that Hurston completed were "Go Gator and Muddy the Water," a discussion of African-American folk materials, and "Negro Mythical Places," an essay on imaginary restful places. According to biographer Valerie Boyd, one of Hurston's most riveting submissions was "The Ocoee Riot," an account of a 1920 attack by whites on blacks in a town near Hurston's own home of EATONVILLE. Hurston's graphic descriptions of the mob violence ultimately prompted the white editors of the Florida guidebook series to include only minute portions of the essay.

Despite the bulk and breadth of Hurston's essays, the FWP editors used only a small portion of her writings. These informative and descriptive writings were published in full for the first time in 1993 and have enjoyed new critical attention.

Bibliography

Bordelon, Pamela, ed., *Go Gator and Muddy the Water: Writings by Zora Neale Hurston from the Federal Writers' Project with Biographical Essays by Pamela Bordelon.* New York: W. W. Norton, 1999.

Boyd, Valerie. *Wrapped in Rainbows: The Life of Zora Neale Hurston.* New York: Scribner, 2003.

Felker, Christopher. "'Adaptation of the Source': Ethnocentricity and 'The Florida Negro'" in Steve Glassman and Kathryn Lee Seidel eds., *Zora in Florida.* Orlando: University of Central Florida, 1991. 146–158.

Findlay, James, and Margaret Bing. "Touring Florida Through the Federal Writer's Project." Broward County Library. Available online. URL: http://www.co.broward.fl.us/library/bienes/lii10213.htm. Accessed May 20, 2005.

Hemenway, Robert. *Zora Neale Hurston: A Literary Biography.* Urbana: University of Illinois Press, 1977.

"Flower of the South" Gertrude Schalk (1930)

A short story about culture shock and LYNCHING by GERTRUDE SCHALK. Published in the 1930 issue of the annual SATURDAY EVENING QUILL, the story chronicled the growing enchantment and rapid disillusion that an Englishman experienced while visiting the South.

The Honorable Hugh Stanhope Wiltshire is visiting a southern plantation where he is the guest of a senator and his daughter Betty. Wiltshire is quite taken by the charm and hospitality of his hosts. He has fallen in love with Betty and plans to propose. While in the South, however, Wiltshire also is increasingly struck by the fact that the region has "such ugly black pages in [its] history." Wiltshire's dismay is linked to the evidence of racial mixing and the production of illegitimate children of color. He has an eye-opening conversation with one of the older women of color, and she tells him quite frankly about the entrenched practice of rape and intimidation that perpetuates the sexual oppression of African-American women by white men. She also tells him that most white southerners have, unbeknownst to them, a significant African-American heritage. "Dey's moah black blood in dem dan yuh could shake a stick at," she says emphatically.

The story begins to climax when word of an impending lynching reaches the manor. Wiltshire accompanies the senator, who is quite cavalier about the lawlessness that has been unleashed and the likelihood that an innocent man may be denied a rightful trial and murdered by a mob. Wiltshire looks on in horror as the lynching proceeds; his distress is intensified even more, however, when he spies Betty cheering on the bloodthirsty mob. He immediately departs the scene and blocks out the sound of Betty's calls to him. He is deeply affected by the awful events and, in order to survive the moment, steels himself against all that has enchanted him there. He "folded his arms. His ears were closed to the South, and his eyes were sick of its warmth and beauty, and his soul shrunk within him," reports the narrator.

Schalk's short story was part of a consistent effort by Harlem Renaissance writers to document the horrors and effects of LYNCHING. The social critique in "Flower of the South" is intensified further by the use of an outside observer who is systematically shorn of his romantic illusions about the United States and driven to reject, rather than tolerate, the racial injustice.

"Fog" John Matheus (1925)

A short story by JOHN MATHEUS that won first prize in the 1925 short story contest sponsored by OPPORTUNITY, the official publication of the NATIONAL URBAN LEAGUE.

Published during his tenure as a professor of the Romance languages at what is now West Virginia State College, the story focused on a purposeful fog and its transformative effect on society. The primary action involves a group of travelers who are forced to occupy close quarters on a train that slows to a near halt because of the thick fog that comes down upon it. The fog becomes a powerful social antidote. It is so thick and "impenetrable" that it prevents people from "recognizing their neighbor ten feet ahead, whether he be Jew or Gentile, Negro or Pole, Slav, Croatian, Italian, or one hundred per cent American." Aboard the train, however, passengers still are able to focus on their ethnic, racial, social, and religious differences. They make snide remarks about each other, allow their prejudices to govern where they will sit, and generally exhibit less than fraternal behavior.

The crowd of passengers is stunned into kindness and sympathy when the train begins to plunge off a bridge. Many are forced into reveries about their lives and loved ones as they prepare for what seems to be an imminent death in the river below. They are spared however, when it appears that the bridge has not given way entirely. On the banks of the river, even the most xenophobic of passengers becomes humane. The men and women begin to reach out to each other, earnestly helping to calm frightened women and children, and to honor the faith of people with whom they believed they had nothing in common. The story ends as the narrator reports calmly that the "dense, tenacious, stealthy, chilling fog" continued to make its way across the landscape but that "from the hearts and minds of some rough, unlettered men another fog had begun to lift."

"Fog" is a subtle critique of the unnatural sentiments that continued to divide American society throughout the Harlem Renaissance period. Matheus uses this short story to expose the kinds of attitudes that can be transformed and the more accommodating, unified American nation that is within reach.

Fool's Errand Eulalie Spence (1927)

A one-act play by EULALIE SPENCE that the KRIGWA PLAYERS, a drama troupe founded in 1926 by W. E. B. DuBOIS, performed in their first show. Artist AARON DOUGLAS helped to design the sets used for the performances. In 1927 the play won second prize in the National Little Theatre Tournament held at the Frolic Theatre in NEW YORK CITY and first prize in the drama category.

The play, commissioned in part by DuBois, was a comedy that tackled community assumptions and social anxieties. Faced with the possible pregnancy of an unmarried girl, church women insist that the girl and her boyfriend marry. By the play's end, it is revealed that it is the mother of the railroaded bride-to-be who is in fact pregnant. The message about true love, honor, and devotion is illuminated by the innocent young man's decision to marry his sweetheart.

Bibliography

Giles, Freda Scott. "Willis Richardson and Eulalie Spence: Dramatic Voices of the Harlem Renaissance." *American Drama* 5, no. 2 (1996): 1–22.

Perkins, Kathy A. *Black Female Playwrights: An Anthology of Plays before 1950.* Bloomington: Indiana University Press, 1989.

Roses, Lorraine Elena, and Ruth Elizabeth Randolph. *Harlem Renaissance and Beyond: Literary Biographies of 100 Black Women Writers, 1900–1945.* Boston: G. K. Hall & Co., 1990.

Foreign Mail Eulalie Spence (1926)

A prize-winning play by EULALIE SPENCE, writer, teacher, and drama critic for OPPORTUNITY. It was one of numerous dramas penned by the Brooklyn, New York, drama teacher, who taught Joseph Papp, a future influential theater producer. In 1926 the script won second prize in a contest sponsored by the KRIGWA PLAYERS and THE CRISIS. One year later, in 1927, the play won a $200 first prize for best unpublished manuscript in the contest sponsored by the publisher and was soon published by the press. Unfortunately, to date, no extant copies of the work have been located.

Bibliography

Giles, Freda Scott. "Willis Richardson and Eulalie Spence: Dramatic Voices of the Harlem Renaissance." *American Drama* 5, no. 2 (1996): 1–22.

Fortune, Timothy Thomas (1856–1928)

A veteran journalist whose accomplishments included founding NEW YORK AGE, the newspaper for which antilynching activist IDA B. WELLS-BARNETT began writing after threats of mob violence forced her to abandon her own newspaper, *Free Speech*, in Memphis, Tennessee. Fortune, the son of Emanuel and Sarah Jane Fortune, was born into slavery in Marianna, Florida, and witnessed his own father's rise in postbellum Florida politics. The threat of LYNCHING prompted the Fortunes to relocate to Jacksonville, Florida. He later attended HOWARD UNIVERSITY but had to leave school because of financial constraints.

Fortune worked closely with BOOKER T. WASHINGTON and served as ghostwriter for the TUSKEGEE INSTITUTE president. Fortune's own publications included the late-19th-century works *Black and White: Land, Labor, and Politics in the South* (1884) and *The Negro in Politics* (1885). Historians suggest that Fortune's agitation on civil rights and labor practices, coupled with his founding of the Afro-American League, laid the groundwork for important organizations such as the NATIONAL ASSOCIATION FOR THE ADVANCEMENT OF COLORED PEOPLE.

Fortune's role in the Harlem Renaissance peaked in 1923 when he became editor of NEGRO WORLD, the official publication of MARCUS GARVEY's UNIVERSAL NEGRO IMPROVEMENT ASSOCIATION. He maintained this post until his death of nervous collapse and heart disease in 1928.

Bibliography

Allman, Jean, and David Roediger, "The Early Editorial Career of Timothy Thomas Fortune: Class, Nationalism and Consciousness of Africa." *Afro-Americans in New York Life and History* 6, no. 2 (1982): 39–52.

Thornbrough, Emma Lou. *T. Thomas Fortune: Militant Journalist.* Chicago: University of Chicago Press, 1972.

Wolseley, Roland, "T. Thomas Fortune: Dean of Black Journalists." *Crisis* 83, no. 3 (1976): 285–287.

Forum

The magazine that published CARL VAN VECHTEN's "Music After the Great War" and "Adolphe Appia and Gordon Craig." In 1926 ZORA NEALE HURSTON published her folktale "Possum or Pig" there; this decision, according to scholar Valerie Boyd, reflected Hurston's effort to introduce wider audiences to the black folklore tradition. In December 1927 the journal published ALAIN LOCKE's essay "The High Cost of Prejudice," in which he reinforced his beliefs in the TALENTED TENTH and the importance of the New Negro to American and African-American society. "Both as an American and as a Negro," he wrote, "I would much rather see the black masses going gradually forward under the leadership of a recognized and representative and responsible elite than see a group of malcontents later hurl these masses at society in doubtful but desperate strife" (Mason, 315). The controversial story "SANCTUARY" by NELLA LARSEN appeared in the January 1930 issue. The journal supported Larsen when charges arose that she had plagiarized the work.

Bibliography

Boyd, Valerie. *Wrapped in Rainbows: The Life of Zora Neale Hurston.* New York: Scribner, 2003.

Davis, Thadious M. *Nella Larsen, Novelist of the Harlem Renaissance: A Woman's Life Unveiled.* Baton Rouge: Louisiana State University Press, 1994.

Kellner, Bruce. *Carl Van Vechten and the Irreverent Decades.* Norman: University of Oklahoma Press, 1968.

Mason, Ernest D. "Alain Locke." *Dictionary of Literary Biography.* Vol.. 51: *Afro-American Writers from the Harlem Renaissance to 1940,* edited by Trudier Harris. Detroit: Gale Research, Inc., 1987. 313–321.

For Unborn Children Myrtle Livingston (1926)

The only extant play written by MYRTLE LIVINGSTON. A teacher and longtime resident of Colorado, Livingston gained critical attention with her prizewinning drama. In 1925 the work was awarded third prize and $10 in the contest sponsored by philanthropist AMY SPINGARN. It was published in the July 1926 issue of THE CRISIS.

The play, set in an unspecified southern location, features two individuals who must overcome the entrenched family and social resistance to their interracial relationship and pending marriage. Livingston's characters, a white southern woman named Selma and an African-American man named Leroy, are ultimately undone by racism within and beyond their respective families. The play ends on a sobering note that underscores the lack of black social freedom. Even though Leroy has ended his relationship with Selma, a lynch mob enraged by his past actions descends upon his home, determined to kill him.

Livingston's meditation on miscegenation, interracial unions, and LYNCHING complemented the works of other Harlem Renaissance writers. *For Unborn Children* appeared in the same year as WALTER WHITE's *FLIGHT,* a sobering novel on racial passing and miscegenation. Livingston's efforts to illustrate the perpetual threat of lynching placed her in dialogue with playwrights GEORGIA DOUGLAS JOHNSON, ALICE DUNBAR-NELSON, and MARY BURRILL.

Bibliography

Roses, Lorraine Elena, and Ruth Elizabeth Randolph. *Harlem Renaissance and Beyond: Literary Biographies of 100 Black Women Writers, 1900–1945.* Boston: G. K. Hall & Co., 1990.

"Four Lincoln University Poets" (1930)

The Harlem Renaissance figures WARING CUNEY, William Hill, and LANGSTON HUGHES all attended LINCOLN UNIVERSITY. In 1930 the historically black, all-male university sponsored the publication of a pamphlet that featured work by the talented young poets, three of whom had gone on to establish themselves as leading writers of the period. In 1926 Cuney, Hughes, and EDWARD SILVERA contributed to the first issue of the short-lived *Fire!!,* the innovative journal of which Hughes had been a cofounder. It was Cuney, a talented singer and lifelong friend of Hughes, who suggested that the poet attend the Pennsylvania institution. Hughes enrolled in 1926 and graduated three years later. By 1930, Cuney, Hughes, and Silvera had been published in leading venues of the day.

The pamphlet included poems that had been published in prominent poetry collections such as

COUNTEE CULLEN's acclaimed 1927 volume CAR-OLING DUSK and in well-known periodicals such as THE CRISIS and OPPORTUNITY. The publication of Hughes's first novel, NOT WITHOUT LAUGHTER, coincided with the pamphlet's appearance.

In 1954 Hughes collaborated with Cuney and Bruce McWright, another former Lincoln University student, and produced *Lincoln University Poets.*

Bibliography
Berry, Faith. *Langston Hughes: Before and Beyond Harlem.* Westport, Conn.: Lawrence Hill & Company, 1983.

Four Negro Poets Alain Locke, ed. (1927)
A pamphlet edited by ALAIN LOCKE that featured previously published works of COUNTEE CULLEN, LANGSTON HUGHES, CLAUDE MCKAY, and JEAN TOOMER. Simon & Schuster published the collection of diverse works by accomplished poets of the period in 1927. It was part of the "The Pamphlet Poets" series. The affordable paperback pamphlets showcased the works of American poets. Each copy included a biographical profile and brief discussions of the writer's work. Previously featured writers included Emily Dickinson, Edna St. Vincent Millay, and Carl Sandburg.

Published two years after his foundational collection of African-American writing, THE NEW NEGRO, the volume further established Locke's role as a public historian of the Harlem Renaissance. *Four Negro Poets* led to his appointment as editor of additional series on black writers.

France
A vibrant and empowering destination for many Harlem Renaissance writers. It was the country in which many members, including writers like CHARLES S. JOHNSON, celebrated musician JAMES REESE EUROPE, and their fellow soldiers in the legendary 369th Regiment known as the Hellfighters, saw action and became the first black troops to fight in World War I.

Harlem Renaissance–era writers, artists, patrons, and scholars traveled to France. Expatriates included the exotic JOSEPHINE BAKER and pioneering scholar ALAIN LOCKE, and represented the full spectrum of the African-American community. In 1925 the educator and feminist author ANNA JULIA COOPER became the first black woman to earn a Ph.D. when she graduated, at age 67, from the SORBONNE. GUGGENHEIM and HARMON Fellowships enabled poet COUNTEE CULLEN to spend one year in France shortly after the publication of COLOR, his notable first book. CLAUDE MCKAY, suffering from a severe case of influenza while in France, was rescued by his newly acquired patron LOUISE BRYANT BULLITT, who helped him to finish drafts of works in progress. Novelists NELLA LARSEN and Dorothy Peterson also enjoyed short stints in France as did LANGSTON HUGHES, who visited the country as part of the European travels he made before publishing NOT WITHOUT LAUGHTER, his first book of poems. JEAN TOOMER, the author of CANE and follower of G. I. GURDJIEFF, studied at the mystic's Institute for the Harmonious Development of Man.

France also figured in works such as JOSEPH SEAMON COTTER, JR.'s one-act play ON THE FIELDS OF FRANCE, JESSIE FAUSET's last novel, COMEDY, AMERICAN STYLE, and in BANJO, Claude McKay's second novel.

Artist AUGUSTA SAVAGE's study in France was funded by a JULIUS ROSENWALD FELLOWSHIP, and it was there that sculptor Meta Vaux Warrick Fuller was able to work with the renowned Auguste Rodin. The writer GWENDOLYN BENNETT pursued art studies in France before returning to America and the position of assistant editor at OPPORTUNITY. Other Harlem Renaissance artists traveled to France, including William H. Johnson and Lois Maillou Jones.

Shortly after the end of the First World War, NAACP cofounder W. E. B. DUBOIS represented the organization at the 1919 Peace Conference. He then developed plans for Pan-African conferences in France. JESSIE FAUSET, who attended Pan-African Congress meetings in Paris, also featured the nation in her fiction and poems.

Bibliography
Fabre, Michel. *From Harlem to Paris: Black American Writers in France, 1840–1980.* Urbana: University of Illinois Press, 1991.
Woodson, Jon. *To Make a New Race: Gurdjieff, Toomer, and the Harlem Renaissance.* Jackson: University Press of Mississippi, 1999.

Frank, Waldo (1889–1967)

A talented white writer whose involvement with the Harlem Renaissance included stints with contemporary publications and close ties to the writer JEAN TOOMER, with whom he traveled on Toomer's formative journey throughout the South. He was born in New Jersey to Julius and Helen Frank. MARGARET NAUMBERG, the first of his three wives, became the lover and spiritual mentor of Toomer, the author of CANE. Frank was a noted literary critic and editor of the period.

Like ALAIN LOCKE, RUDOLPH FISHER, and JESSIE FAUSET, Frank was a PHI BETA KAPPA scholar. After graduating from YALE UNIVERSITY and a short residency in Paris, Frank arrived in NEW YORK CITY. In 1916 he collaborated with VAN WYCK BROOKS and others to establish the arts journal THE SEVEN ARTS. The antiwar platform of the magazine's editors resulted in federal censure, and The Seven Acts ultimately was forced out of print. A decade later, he was contributing editor on THE NEW REPUBLIC and NEW MASSES. Frank was an outspoken political activist who had ties to the COMMUNIST PARTY. Twice during the 1930s he endorsed and campaigned for Communist Party presidential candidates.

During the 1920s and 1930s, Frank published several novels with BONI & LIVERIGHT, the same firm that published JESSIE FAUSET, JEAN TOOMER, and ERIC WALROND. Works published during the 1920s and 1930s included *The Dark Mother* (1920), *Rahab* (1922), a lynching tragedy entitled HOLIDAY (1923), *Chalk Face* (1924), and *The Bridegroom Cometh* (1938). Frank also wrote two plays, *New Year's Eve* (1929) and *Dot* (1933).

Bibliography

Bittner, William. *The Novels of Waldo Frank.* Philadelphia: University of Pennsylvania Press, 1958.

Carter, Paul. *Waldo Frank.* New York: Twayne Publishers, 1967.

Cooley, John. "White Writers and the Harlem Renaissance." In *The Harlem Renaissance: Revaluations,* edited by Amritjit Singh, Stanley Brodwin, and William Shiver. New York: Garland Press, 1989, 13–22.

Helbling, Mark. "Jean Toomer and Waldo Frank." *Phylon: The Atlanta University Review of Race and Culture* 41 (1980): 167–178.

Trachtenberg, Alan, ed., *Memoirs of Waldo Frank.* Amherst: University of Massachusetts Press, 1973.

Frazier, Edward Franklin (1894–1962)

A pioneering sociologist and educator who began his professional career in the 1930s following his completion of doctoral studies at the UNIVERSITY OF CHICAGO. The first of four children born to James Frazier, a bank messenger, and Mary Clark Frazier, whose work as a domestic supported the family after James's untimely death in 1905, Frazier also was the paternal grandson of a slave who bought his family's freedom. In 1922 he married Mary Winton, a published poet and aspiring lawyer from North Carolina who benefited from professional advice on her writing from the poet COUNTEE CULLEN.

Educated in the segregated Baltimore school system, Frazier went on to attend HOWARD UNIVERSITY on scholarship, and his impressive scholarly efforts earned him the nickname of "Plato." Following graduation from Howard, he began a series of teaching jobs that included posts at TUSKEGEE INSTITUTE. He continued his graduate studies throughout the 1920s and earned a master's degree in sociology from Clark University in Worcester, Massachusetts, in 1920. In 1921 he became the first African-American recipient of the prestigious American Scandinavian Foundation Fellowship and used the award to finance a year of studies at the UNIVERSITY OF COPENHAGEN. In 1923 he began doctoral studies at the University of Chicago, received a prestigious Social Science Research Council Grant to fund his research on the African-American family, and earned his Ph.D. in 1931. In 1940 he joined the elite intellectual circle of Guggenheim Fellows and used his fellowship to develop a comparative study of race relations in Brazil and in the United States. He was the president of the American Sociological Society and, as such, was the first African American to serve as president of a predominantly white professional organization.

Frazier's professional career as a scholar and sociologist included faculty appointments at ATLANTA UNIVERSITY, Carleton College, FISK UNIVERSITY, Howard University, MOREHOUSE COLLEGE, Sarah Lawrence College, New York University, and the University of California at Berkeley. In 1934 he became chair of the Sociology Department at Howard and is credited with revitalizing the curriculum and its programs and with increasing student enrollments.

Frazier wrote prizewinning essays that were published in prominent journals and books of the Harlem Renaissance period. His essays appeared in *The Crisis, The Nation, THE NEW NEGRO* (1925) edited by ALAIN LOCKE, and *Ebony and Topaz* (1927) edited by CHARLES S. JOHNSON, and won prizes in literary contests sponsored by *OPPORTUNITY*. In 1929 his essay "The Mind of the Negro" won first prize in the *Opportunity* contest, which was renamed by its new financial sponsor, CARL VAN VECHTEN, in memory of the accomplished actress Florence Mills.

Frazier's collaborations with Harlem Renaissance figures also involved racial activism and civil rights interventions. In 1935, three years after he completed *The Negro Family in Chicago,* a work based on his doctoral dissertation, he collaborated with Countee Cullen, ASA PHILIP RANDOLPH, and others on a New York City mayoral committee charged with studying the social and economic factors that contributed to the devastating Harlem Riot in 1935. In 1939, at the close of the Renaissance, he published *The Negro Family in the United States,* a volume hailed as one of the most influential scholarly books on black history and culture.

In the years following the Harlem Renaissance, Frazier published highly regarded and influential sociological studies including *Black Bourgeoisie,* the seminal and highly controversial work that was published first in FRANCE in 1955 and in the United States in 1957. His final work, *The Negro Church in America,* was published in 1962 shortly after his death.

Bibliography

Platt, Anthony. *E. Franklin Frazier Reconsidered.* New Brunswick, N.J.: Rutgers University Press, 1991.
Platt, Tony, and Susan Chandler. "Constant Struggle: E. Franklin Frazier and Black Social Work in the 1920s." *Social Work* 33 (July/August 1988): 293–297.
Semmes, Clovis. "E. Franklin Frazier's Theory of the Black Family: Vindication and Sociological Insight." *Journal of Sociology and Social Welfare* 28, no. 2 (June 2001): 3–21.
Teele, James, ed. *E. Franklin Frazier and Black Bourgeoisie.* Columbia: University of Missouri Press, 2002.

Furman, Abraham Loew (unknown)

The lawyer for the New York City–based Macaulay Publishing Company who collaborated with WALLACE THURMAN on *THE INTERNE,* Thurman's third and last novel. Furman met Thurman when the writer was employed as a reader for the company, which opened in 1909 and closed in 1941. Sometimes misidentified as *The Interns,* the novel chronicled the professional coming-of-age of a young white physician named Carl Armstrong. Following the publication of *The Interne,* Thurman was appointed editor-in-chief at the press.

Furman and a brother of the founders later became a prolific writer and editor of literature for children.

Bibliography

Henderson, Mae. "Portrait of Wallace Thurman" in Cary Wintz, ed. *Remembering the Harlem Renaissance.* New York: Garland, 1996. 289–312.
McIver, Dorothy. *Stepchild in Harlem: The Literary Career of Wallace Thurman.* Ann Arbor, Mich.: University Microfilms International, 1983.
Van Notten, Eleanore. *Wallace Thurman's Harlem Renaissance.* Amsterdam: Rodopi, 1994.
West, Dorothy. "Elephant's Dance: A Memoir of Wallace Thurman," *Black World* 20, no. 1 (1970): 77–85.

G

Gaines-Shelton, Ruth Ada (1872–1932)

A playwright and teacher whose career of two decades saw her emerge as a prolific dramatist committed to providing empowering and substantial drama to community groups, churches, and schools.

Born in Glasgow, Missouri, she was the daughter of Rev. George W. and Mary Elizabeth Gaines. Her father, a Civil War soldier, was a former student of Joanna Moore, a devoted missionary teacher. In 1891 Ruth began undergraduate studies at WILBERFORCE UNIVERSITY in Ohio. Following her graduation in 1895, she lived in CHICAGO and helped her father, who was overseeing construction of the Old Bethel A.M.E. Church on Dearborn Street. Later that year, she returned to Missouri and began teaching in the public school system of Montgomery. In 1898, just one year before she withdrew from her teaching post, she married William Obern Shelton. The couple had three children, George Washington, Obern Archibald, and Mary Gloria.

Gaines-Shelton's career as a playwright began in 1899 but flourished in the early and mid-1900s. She identified herself in a 1930 autobiographical profile in *Who's Who in Colored America* as a "[w]riter of plays for Churches [and] Private Theatricals." She was an established local playwright when she won second prize in the 1925 *Crisis* literary contest. Judges EUGENE O'NEILL, Charles Burroughs, and Lester Walton awarded first prize to WILLIS RICHARDSON for *THE BROKEN BANJO*, second prize to Gaines-Shelton for *THE CHURCH FIGHT*, and third prize to MYRTLE SMITH LIV-INGSTON for her play entitled *FOR UNBORN CHILDREN*. Gaines-Shelton's prize-winning play subsequently was published in the May 1926 issue of *THE CRISIS*.

Bibliography

Hatch, James. *Black Theatre, U.S.A.; Forty-five Plays by Black Americans, 1847–1974*. New York: Free Press, 1974.

Moore, Joanne P. *"In Christ's Stead": Autobiographical Sketches*. Chicago: Women's Baptist Home Mission Society, 1902.

Roses, Lorraine Elena, and Ruth Elizabeth Randolph. *Harlem Renaissance and Beyond: Literary Biographies of 100 Black Women Writers, 1900–1945*. Boston: G. K. Hall & Co., 1990.

Gale, Zona (1874–1938)

One of the judges in the first literary contest sponsored by *OPPORTUNITY* and CHARLES S. JOHNSON, its editor, in 1924. Gale, who declared that she was "honored by [the] initiation" and was happy to "accept with pleasure," also judged future contests with figures such as NELLA LARSEN and THEODORE DREISER.

The winner of the 1921 PULITZER PRIZE in drama, Gale was a white writer whose literary career peaked in the years leading up to the Harlem Renaissance. Her writing and professional life, which included an appointment to the Board of Regents of the University of Wisconsin, were rooted in the Midwest.

Born to Charles and Eliza Gale in Portage, Wisconsin, she began writing during childhood. Following graduation from the University of Wisconsin, she worked as a reporter for several newspapers, including the *Milwaukee Journal* and the New York *Evening World*. Gale was engaged for some time to playwright RIDGELY TORRENCE, whose successful works included *Three Plays for a Negro Theater* (1917), but the couple never married. In 1928 she wed banker William Breese.

Gale's connections to the Harlem Renaissance also emerged through her support of some of its most prominent writers. She was an advocate for JESSIE FAUSET when she provided a preface for Fauset's third novel, THE CHINABERRY TREE (1931). The testimony by Gale helped to persuade Fauset's publishers that material about mixed race protagonists was of interest to a broad spectrum of readers. Gale was a longtime and, by some accounts, overbearing mentor for Margery Latimer, the future wife of JEAN TOOMER. It was Gale who introduced the mystic GEORGES IVANOVITCH GURDJIEFF to Toomer's circle.

Bibliography

Derleth, August. *Still Small Voice: The Biography of Zona Gale*. New York: D. Appleton-Century Company, 1940.

Kerman, Cynthia. *The Lives of Jean Toomer: A Hunger for Wholeness*. Baton Rouge: Louisiana State University Press, 1987.

Simonson, Harold. *Zona Gale*. New York: Twayne Publishers, 1962.

Williams, Deborah. *Not in Sisterhood: Edith Wharton, Willa Cather, Zona Gale and the Politics of Female Authorship*. New York: Palgrave, 2001.

Wilson, Sondra Kathryn, ed. *The Opportunity Reader: Stories, Poetry, and Essays from the Urban League's Opportunity Magazine*. New York: The Modern Library, 1999.

"Game" Eugene Gordon (1927)

A jarring short story by EUGENE GORDON, a BOSTON journalist who wrote for the *Boston Post* and was published in leading journals of the Harlem Renaissance such as the AMERICAN MERCURY and OPPORTUNITY. "Game," published in September 1927, was one of two stories awarded first prize in the *Opportunity* literary contest.

The protagonist is Sam Desmond, an overwhelmed man who is harassed by his coworkers at the Greater Boston Meat Market and at home by his wife Marguerite. His wife telephones regularly to demand choice meats for herself and for Mussolini, the cat that she indulges and Sam Desmond despises. Gordon alludes to intraracial caste tensions when he reveals the value that the light-skinned Marguerite has for Desmond. His antagonist Roberts, a dark-skinned deliveryman who delights in calling Desmond "Snow White," once courted Marguerite but suggests that he gave her up in order to avoid unflattering attention.

After suffering relentless emasculating indignities at home and insistent jibes about his marriage at work, Desmond takes revenge on his wife. One day he has to transport the cat, which has become sick by eating one of the fish bones in Desmond's paltry dinner, to the veterinarian. He tells his wife that the cat has died. That evening, as promised, he takes home "game" to his wife, but it is the dressed remains of the cat rather than the venison or rabbit that she has been nagging him to provide.

Bibliography

Wilson, Sondra Kathryn, ed. *The Opportunity Reader: Stories, Poetry, and Essays from the Urban League's Opportunity Magazine*. New York: The Modern Library, 1999.

Garden of Memories Mazie Earhart Clark (1932)

A volume of poems published by MAZIE EARHART CLARK, who also published under the pseudonym Fannie B. Steele. The subtitle of *Garden of Memories* was a loving tribute "Dedicated To My Friends In Memory of My Husband Sgt. George J. Clark" and referred to her husband who, after his death in World War I, was buried in Arlington National Cemetery.

Bibliography

Boelcskevy, Mary Anne Stewart, ed. *Voices in the Poetic Tradition: Clara Ann Thompson, J. Pauline Smith, Mazie Earhart Clark*. New York: G. K. Hall, 1996.

Garland of Poems, A   Clara Ann Thompson
(1926)

A Garland of Poems was the second of two volumes published by CLARA ANN THOMPSON. Produced by the BOSTON-based Christopher Publishing House, the book primarily consisted of religious meditations and patriotic works. Thompson's frank preface included references to her "despotic Muse" and the fact that she felt compelled to write: "I write . . . because I must," she declared.

Like poet SARAH COLLINS FERNANDIS, who honored African-American veterans, Thompson celebrated the triumphant return of black World War I fighters.

Bibliography
Boelcskevy, Mary Anne Stewart, ed. *Voices in the Poetic Tradition: Clara Ann Thompson, J. Pauline Smith, Mazie Earhart Clark.* New York: G. K. Hall, 1996.

Garnett, David (1892–1981)
A white British writer who moved in the high literary circles of the Bloomsbury group. He was the son of Edward and Constance Garnett, both of whom were well known for their literary accomplishments. His father, the son of the Reading Room superintendent at the British Museum, was a publisher whose successes included Joseph Conrad. His mother, a translator, completed an English translation of *War and Peace* by Leo Tolstoy. Following the death of his first wife, Rachel Alice Marshall, Garnett married Angelica Bell, a niece of Virginia Woolf.

During the 1920s, Garnett owned a bookstore in the SoHo area of NEW YORK CITY and developed friendships with a number of Harlem Renaissance–era figures. During that period, he published four novels, including *The Sailor's Return.* Published by KNOPF in 1925, it told the tragic story of a sailor who returns to Dorset, England, with an African princess wife and their mixed-race child, only to see his wife destroyed by racial prejudice. The work, inspired by an 18th-century inn of the same name in East Chaldon, Dorset, gained critical attention and was reviewed in established journals such as the *Dial.* It also piqued the interest of prominent Harlem Renaissance figures such as CARL VAN VECHTEN, who in October 1925 mentioned the newly published work to his close friend, the poet LANGSTON HUGHES.

The novel complemented works by authors such as JESSIE FAUSET, NELLA LARSEN, and WALTER WHITE that focused on the politics and social anxieties relating to interracial relationships and mixed-race identity. *The Sailor's Return* has enjoyed several reincarnations since its publication. In 1978 it became a film directed by Jack Gold and was adapted for the screen by the British playwright James Saunders. In the late 1940s both *The Sailor's Return* and Garnett's *Lady Into Fox* (1922) were adapted by Marie Rambert as narrative ballets that featured the celebrated ballerina Sally Gilmour.

Garnett's friendship with NANCY CUNARD, the wealthy British-born activist and editor whose works included *Negro: An Anthology* (1934), spanned nearly 40 years. Cunard's interracial relationship with Henry Crowder, which resulted in alienation from her family, prompted her to ask Garnett for an autographed copy of *The Sailor's Return,* a work that resonated with her own experiences.

In 1938, Garnett published an edition of the letters of T. E. Lawrence, his close friend and the soldier known as "Lawrence of Arabia." Garnett passed away in 1981 at his home in Montcuq, FRANCE.

Bibliography
"David Garnett, 88, Novelist, Dies; A Member of Bloomsbury Group." *New York Times,* 20 February 1981, A20.

Cunard, Nancy. *These Were the Hours.* Carbondale: Southern Illinois University Press, 1969.

Ford, Hugh. *Nancy Cunard: Brave Poet, Indomitable Rebel 1896–1965.* Philadelphia: Chilton, 1968.

Ousby, Ian. "Garnett, David." In *Cambridge Guide to Literature in English.* Cambridge: Cambridge University Press, 1993.

Garvey, Marcus Mosiah (1887–1940)
An outspoken and influential race leader, entrepreneur, editor, and poet who mobilized thousands in his "BACK TO AFRICA" campaigns during the 1920s. Born to Marcus and Sarah Jane Garvey in St. Ann's Bay, Jamaica, Garvey arrived in the

United States in 1916. He married Amy Ashwood in 1919, but they divorced three years later. In 1922 he married Amy Jacques, and the couple had two sons, Marcus Jacques Garvey and Julius Winston Garvey.

When Garvey established himself in HARLEM in 1916, he attempted to develop further his newly organized UNIVERSAL NEGRO IMPROVEMENT ASSOCIATION (UNIA). The estimated worldwide membership of the organization, dedicated to improving black economic opportunities and intensifying race pride, reached as high as 4 million.

Garvey founded NEGRO WORLD, a weekly newspaper that advanced the cause of PAN-AFRICANISM and highlighted UNIA activities. The organization's message rallied African Americans at a time that saw major social upheaval such as that signaled by the devastating 1917 race riots in St. Louis and the heroic contributions of African Americans in the segregated armed forces of World War I. Garvey called for an independent Africa that was free of colonial governance.

In 1919 he began to build the Black Star Shipping Line, a steamship company designed to facilitate the triumphant return of African Americans to Africa. Members bought $5 shares in the company. He also organized the Negro Factories Corporation and used it to build black-owned businesses in Harlem.

One of the most momentous events associated with Garvey was the FIRST INTERNATIONAL CONVENTION OF THE NEGRO PEOPLES OF THE WORLD. It convened in NEW YORK CITY and included enormous parades that reflected the progress and pride of the race, and Garvey's memorable address to some 25,000 people in Madison Square Garden. It was during this convention that Garvey created the flag of pan-Africanism with its red, green, and black colors. Additional meetings convened throughout the early 1920s and included conventions in Detroit, Michigan. The meetings rallied members, but within a few years the UNIA was under siege because of financial irregularities. In 1922 Garvey was convicted of mail fraud and sentenced to five years in an Atlanta prison. Despite his pending incarceration in 1925, he devised new plans for another steamship enterprise, the Black Cross Navigation and Trading Company. President Calvin Coolidge commuted Garvey's sentence in 1927, but the race leader was deported immediately to Jamaica. He continued to cultivate interest in black enterprise and political autonomy, and in 1929 he hosted another international convention.

In 1921 Garvey founded the AFRICAN ORTHODOX CHURCH and appointed the Reverend George Alexander McGuire as its minister. The church, which existed until 1935, combined elements of the Catholic and Episcopalian faiths and encouraged the worship of a black God, Madonna, and Christ.

During the late 1920s, Garvey published several works of poetry. These included *The Tragedy of White Injustice* (1927), *Selections from the Poetic Meditations of Marcus Garvey* (1927), and *Keep Cool* (1927). He focused often on themes of universal harmony, racial advancement, and individual responsibility. In "Hail, United States of Africa-free!", a poem examining the potential of a united Africa, Garvey celebrated the "Sweet land of our father's noble kin!" and imagined a continent free of European influence: "The treason of the centuries is dead, / All alien whites are forever gone; / The glad home of Sheba is once more free, / As o'er the world the black man raised his head." Other works reinforced his pan-Africanist vision of an empowering and uplifting African sensibility.

In 1934, following his relocation to London, Garvey founded *Black Man*, a monthly publication. Six years later, in January 1940, he was weakened by a serious stroke and died a few months later. He was buried in England.

Bibliography

Cronon, E. David. *Black Moses: The Story of Marcus Garvey and the Universal Negro Improvement Association.* Madison: University of Wisconsin Press, 1987.

Garvey, Amy J., ed. *Philosophy and Opinions of Marcus Garvey.* New York: The Universal Publishing House, 1923–1925.

Hill, Robert, ed. *The Marcus Garvey and Universal Negro Improvement Association Papers.* Berkeley: University of California Press, 1983.

Lewis, Rupert. *Marcus Garvey: Anti-Colonial Champion.* Trenton, N.J.: Africa World Press, 1988.

Stein, Judith. *The World of Marcus Garvey: Race and Class in Modern Society*. Baton Rouge: Louisiana State University Press, 1986.

Stephens, Michelle. "Black Transnationalism and the Politics of National Identity: West Indian Intellectuals in Harlem in the Age of War and Revolution." *American Quarterly* 50, no. 3 (1988): 592–608.

Garvin, Charles H. (1891–1968)

The first African-American physician to be commissioned in the U.S. Army, Garvin was born in Jacksonville, Florida, to Charles and Theresa Garvin on 27 October 1891. In 1920 he married Rosalind West, and the couple had two sons. Following education in the Florida public schools, Garvin earned his B.A. from HOWARD UNIVERSITY in 1911 and his M.D. from the Howard University Medical School in 1915. He was secretary, and later president, of the Alpha Phi Alpha Fraternity from 1912 through 1914.

Following internships at the Freedman's Hospital in WASHINGTON, D.C., he established himself in private practice in Cleveland, Ohio. In 1920 he began an affiliation with the Lakeside Hospital and Dispensary of the Western Reserve University.

In addition to participating in professional medical organizations such as the Cleveland Academy of Medicine and the American Medical Association, Garvin joined the board of the NATIONAL URBAN LEAGUE. He published articles in his area of medical expertise and also contributed related works for lay readers in OPPORTUNITY. These included "White Plague and Black Folk" in August 1913 and "Immunity to Disease Among Dark Skinned Peoples" in August 1926.

Garvin left private practice to join the U.S. Army as the first commissioned black physician. Overseas for nearly one year, he served as captain in the Medical Corps, worked with the 367th Infantry, and was the commanding officer of the 368th Ambulance Corp. His efforts were recorded first by Ralph Tyler, a fellow Ohioan and the first black war correspondent in the world, and then by Emmett Scott in *Scott's Official History of the American Negro in the World War* (1919).

Garvin's civic and political work included participation in the Republican Party. He was part of the Cleveland committee that welcomed those attending the party's national convention in 1923. In 1950 he and John Henrik Clarke, Rosa Guy, and John Oliver Killens founded the Harlem Writers Guild, a literary organization that is still thriving today.

Bibliography

Wilson, Sondra Kathryn, ed. *The Opportunity Reader: Stories, Poetry, and Essays from the Urban League's Opportunity Magazine*. New York: The Modern Library, 1999.

Yenser, Thomas, ed. *Who's Who in Colored America*. New York: Thomas Yenser, 1937.

George, Maude Roberts (ca. 1892–ca. 1945)

An arts advocate, teacher, and music critic for the CHICAGO DEFENDER. Before moving to CHICAGO, she taught at her alma mater, Walden University, formerly known as Central Tennessee College and the school from which Meharry Medical College emerged, in Nashville, Tennessee.

In 1935 George was the seventh president of the National Association of Negro Musicians (NANM), an organization established in 1919. It is the oldest organization dedicated to the study and appreciation of African-American music. In 1919 the contralto Marian Anderson was the first artist to receive an NANM scholarship.

George is credited for her tireless efforts to introduce classical music to students and communities of color. The final NANM convention over which she presided concluded with a rousing concert at the Juilliard School and included performances by the Bronx Symphony Orchestra and the pioneering African-American composer and soloist Florence Price.

Bibliography

Lovett, Bobby. "Walden University." Tennessee State University Libraries and Media Centers. Available online. URL: http://www.tnstate. edu/library/digital/ walden.htm. Accessed May 20, 2005.

"Negro Musicians Elect." *New York Times*, 30 August 1935, 13.

Georgia Nigger John Spivak (1932)

Published in 1932 by investigative journalist JOHN SPIVAK. Spivak joined the ranks of other white writers of the 1920s like OCTAVUS ROY COHEN who considered African-American subject matter in their works. The novel, noted for its graphic details and imagery, focused on the plight of men in a Georgia prison chain gang. Spivak, who covered the KU KLUX KLAN and corporate corruption during his career, used material acquired for his exposé articles on racism and corruption. The novel incorporated stark illustrations of prisoners in their distinctive striped uniforms.

Bibliography

Lichtenstein, Alex. "Chain Gangs, Communism & the 'Negro Question': John Spivak's Georgia Nigger," *Georgia Historical Quarterly* 79 (fall 1995): 633–658.

Gershwin, George (1898–1937)

A prolific composer who collaborated with Harlem Renaissance–era writers and performers such as DuBOSE HEYWARD and Adelaide Hall. Born in Brooklyn, New York, to Morris and Rose Gershwin, he was the younger brother of Ira Gershwin, the musician and lyricist. George was part of a small but growing number of white writers and artists of the day like JOHN SPIVAK, who incorporated African-American scenes and culture into his works. His 1922 one-act opera *George White's Scandals* used HARLEM as a backdrop, and in 1935 he achieved critical acclaim for *PORGY AND BESS*, his opera based on the novel and play by DuBose Heyward. The composer of such well-known works as *Rhapsody in Blue* and *An American in Paris,* he earned a reputation as one of the era's most influential and successful composers and was hailed for his use of documented black musical forms and jazz rhythms. In 1937 Gershwin died at the age of 38 after a failed operation to treat a brain tumor.

ARNA BONTEMPS, the writer and head librarian at FISK UNIVERSITY in the 1940s, established an impressive collection of Gershwin papers and memorabilia. In 1957 the writer and mentor CARL VAN VECHTEN penned the introduction to *The Gershwin Years.*

Bibliography

Gilbert, Steven. *The Music of Gershwin.* New Haven, Conn.: Yale University Press, 1995.

Hollis, Albert. *The Life and Times of Porgy and Bess: The Story of an American Classic.* New York: Knopf, 1990.
Peyser, Joan. *The Memory of All That: The Life of George Gershwin.* New York: Simon & Schuster, 1993.
Schneider, Wayne, ed. *The Gershwin Style: New Looks at the Music of George Gershwin.* New York: Oxford University Press, 1999.

Ghana

Located on the west coast of AFRICA, Ghana, in 1957, became the first African country to achieve its independence from European rule. It had been one of the major African countries targeted by the British, Dutch, and Danish slave trades.

President Kwame Nkrumah became the first president of the Republic of Ghana in 1960. In 1939 he graduated from LINCOLN UNIVERSITY, the alma mater of poet LANGSTON HUGHES and U.S. Supreme Court justice Thurgood Marshall. He continued his education at the UNIVERSITY OF PENNSYLVANIA, from which he earned a master's of science in education and a master's in philosophy. In 1961 Ghana became the adopted homeland of W. E. B. DuBois, the scholar, editor of *THE CRISIS* and cofounder of the NATIONAL ASSOCIATION FOR THE ADVANCEMENT OF COLORED PEOPLE.

Bibliography

A. Adu Boahen. *Ghana: Evolution and Change in the Nineteenth and Twentieth Centuries.* London: Longman, 1975.
Awoonor, Kofi. *Ghana: A Political History from Pre-European to Modern Times.* Accra: Sedco Publishers, 1990.
Birmingham, David. *Kwame Nkrumah: The Father of African Nationalism.* Athens: Ohio University Press, 1998.
Bourret, F. M. *Ghana: The Road to Independence, 1919–1957.* London: Oxford University Press, 1960.
Nkrumah, Kwame. *Africa Must Unite.* London: Heinemann, 1963.

Gift of Black Folk: The Negroes in the Making of America W. E. B. DuBois (1924)

A history of people of African descent, by W. E. B. DuBois, whose accomplishments included pioneering scholarship on African-American history and politics and the editorship of THE CRISIS. Published in BOSTON by the Stratford Company, *Gift of Black Folk* was the second of DuBois's two histories. It appeared nine years after THE NEGRO (1915), his first effort.

Gift of Black Folk dealt with a variety of subjects including the history of black contributions in art, politics, and education. As such, it was part of an established African-American literary effort to chronicle the often underestimated and overlooked contributions of black Americans. DuBois's work recalled foundational 19th-century American texts by early black historians and writers William Cooper Nell, William Wells Brown, and others.

Biographer David Levering Lewis suggests that with the *Gift of Black Folk*, DuBois was challenging a growing post–world war investment in the "ideology of whiteness." The work was part of a concerted effort by black scholars to recuperate the history of blacks in the postbellum and modern age. DuBois's work appeared just two years after *The Negro in Our History* by CARTER G. WOODSON, the founder of the ASSOCIATION FOR THE STUDY OF NEGRO LIFE AND HISTORY and the editor of the JOURNAL OF NEGRO HISTORY. In addition, it preceded additional contemporary publications on the centrality of black history in the newly established *Journal of Negro History* as well as *A Short History of the American Negro* (1927) by BENJAMIN BRAWLEY.

Bibliography

Lewis, David Levering. *W. E. B. Du Bois: The Fight for Equality and the American Century, 1919–1963.* New York: Henry Holt and Company, 2000.

Gilbert, Mercedes (1889–1952)

A talented writer and actress who completed her first impressive works of drama and poems while completing her nursing training. Like NELLA LARSEN, Gilbert combined her professional training with her writing career.

Born in Jacksonville, Florida, Gilbert began writing as a young child. She attended Edward Waters College, a historically black college founded by the African Methodist Episcopal Church in 1866, in Jacksonville, and completed her nurse's training at the historic Brewster Hospital Nurses Training School. In 1901 the former private Florida home became the first Florida hospital for African Americans. In 1922 Gilbert married Arthur Stevenson.

Shortly after she relocated to NEW YORK CITY in 1916, Gilbert began what would become a celebrated and accomplished career in the performing arts. Undaunted by the lack of employment in nursing, she turned to songwriting. This soon led to stage work on and off BROADWAY. Before immersing herself in Broadway productions, Gilbert worked closely with Oscar Micheaux, the novelist and independent film producer whose works marked the beginning of the African-American film tradition. Gilbert starred in *Body and Soul,* a silent melodrama, opposite PAUL ROBESON.

Gilbert made her Broadway debut in January 1927 at the New York City Forrest Theatre in the musical *Lace Petticoat.* Subsequent performances included the musical *Bamboola* (1929) and the plays *Lost* (1927), *How Come, Lawd?* (1937), *The Searching Wind* by Lillian Hellman (1944), and *Tobacco Road* (1950), based on the novel by Erskine Caldwell. Gilbert played Zipporah, the Ethiopian wife of Moses, in MARC CONNELLY's GREEN PASTURES, during the musical's five-and-a-half-year run on Broadway. When in 1935 she joined the cast of MULATTO, the Broadway play by LANGSTON HUGHES that opened at the Vanderbilt Theater in October 1924, the AMSTERDAM NEWS characterized her performance as "epochal."

In 1931, Gilbert produced SELECTED GEMS OF POETRY, COMEDY, AND DRAMA, published by Christopher Publishing House, the same Boston press that produced A GARLAND OF POEMS (1926) by CLARA ANN THOMPSON. She wrote three plays: MA JOHNSON'S HARLEM ROOMING HOUSE, *In Greener Pastures,* and ENVIRONMENT. To date, *Environment,* a melancholy play about a woman dealing with domestic upheaval, is the only extant Gilbert play. In 1938 she published her first and only novel, AUNT SARA'S WOODEN GOD.

As the Harlem Renaissance came to a close, she reasserted herself as a film actress, starring in African-American productions such as *Moon Over Harlem* (1939) with musician Sidney Bechet. In

1949 she wrote and produced, in cooperation with the Jamaica, New York, branch of the NATIONAL ASSOCIATION FOR THE ADVANCEMENT OF COLORED PEOPLE, "Cavalcade of the American Negro." THE NEW YORK TIMES described the show, which included a cast of 30 and a choral ensemble of 40, as "a pageant depicting the history of the Negro in America."

Gilbert's death was noted in *The New York Times*. Her obituary, which listed her many theatrical triumphs, also described her as "a well-known Negro actress" whose credits included "one-woman theatre recitals." A resident of Jamaica, Queens, Gilbert died in March 1952.

Bibliography

"Mercedes Gilbert, Stage, Radio Actress." *New York Times*, 6 March 1952, 31.

"Negro Pageant in Jamaica." *New York Times*, 18 February 1949, 30.

Patton, Charlie. "Old Hospital in Critical Need of Life Support." *Florida Times-Union*, 27 February 2002, B1.

Roses, Lorraine Elena, and Ruth Elizabeth Randolph. *Harlem's Glory: Black Women Writing, 1900–1950*. Cambridge: Harvard University Press, 1996.

"Gilded Six-Bits, The" Zora Neale Hurston (1933)

An engaging and moving story by ZORA NEALE HURSTON about a married couple in EATONVILLE, Florida, who survive betrayal and infidelity. The work appeared in the August 1933 issue of *Story* magazine. This Depression-era work, which helped to sustain the financially strapped writer, quickly led to a book contract with the J. B. Lippincott Company and the 1934 publication of JONAH'S GOURD VINE.

At the beginning of the tale, the protagonists Missy May and her husband Joe Banks relish their intimacy and the loving home that they have created. The question with which Missy May greets her husband Joe, "Who dat chunkin' money in may do'way," sets the stage for the story's stunning upheaval. Though the couple value each other and the monies that they are saving for their future, Missy May finds herself attracted to Otis D. Slemmons, a local ice-cream parlor owner known for the gold accessories with which he adorns his suits. Joe

discovers his wife and Slemmons in the act of adultery; in the chaos that follows, the gold watch charm that Slemmons has used to entice Missy May falls to the floor and is discovered to be nothing more than a gilded six-bit and not the ten-dollar gold coin that she imagined. The couple eventually reunite and, much to their relief and that of Joe's watchful mother, become parents of a son.

The story closes as the couple, once again represented as consumers in the southern public sphere, browse in a white-owned shop. Joe uses the gilded six-bits to buy candy for his wife. As they leave, the proprietor, completely unaware of the marital crises and rehabilitation that have occurred, comments on what he believes to be the perpetual happy-go-lucky personalities of the race.

Bibliography

Bordelon, Pamela. *Go Gator Muddy the Water: Writings By Zora Neale Hurston from the Federal Writers' Project with Biographical Essays*. New York: W. W. Norton & Company, 1999.

Boyd, Valerie. *Wrapped in Rainbows: The Life of Zora Neale Hurston*. New York: Scribner, 2003.

Chinn, Nancy, and Elizabeth Dunn. "The Ring of Singing Metal on Wood: Zora Neale Hurston's Artistry in 'The Gilded Six-Bits.'" *Mississippi Quarterly* 49, no. 4 (fall 1996): 775–790.

Hemenway, Robert. *Zora Neale Hurston: A Literary Biography*. Urbana: University of Illinois, 1977.

Jones, Evora. "The Pastoral and Picaresque in Zora Neale Hurston's 'The Gilded Six-Bits,'" *College Language Association Journal* 35, no. 3 (March 1992): 316–324.

Gingertown Claude McKay (1932)

A collection of short stories. It appeared in the same year as ARNA BONTEMPS's GOD SENDS SUNDAY, JESSIE FAUSET's THE CHINABERRY TREE, and GEORGE SCHUYLER's BLACK NO MORE. McKay began writing the volume when he took up residence in Tangier, Morocco. After weathering some social upheaval brought on by the visit of Anita Thompson, a Harlem socialite, he moved to Xauen, Spain, and completed the collection there. The work included some earlier pieces on Harlem, new writings on rural Jamaica, and two works set in cities reminiscent of Marseilles and Tangier.

Gingertown is sometimes misidentified as a novel and even as a collection of poems. However, it is a set of 12 short stories with settings in HARLEM, Jamaica, and North Africa. Novelist RUDOLPH FISHER, who reviewed it for the New York *Herald Tribune*, remarked that the work focused on the personal and social trials of "displaced people."

Published by HARPER & BROTHERS in the midst of the Depression, the book had disappointing sales. There were a number of positive reviews, but the book also prompted McKay's peers, like the writer Rudolph Fisher, to suggest that McKay was now far removed from the Harlem that he aspired to depict. Critics did applaud the apparent "authenticity and . . . quality of acrid poignancy" of the stories set in Jamaica.

Bibliography

Cooper, Wayne. *Claude McKay: Rebel Sojourner in the Harlem Renaissance*. New York: Schocken Books, 1987.

Gladiola Gardens: Poems of Outdoors and Indoors for Second Grade Readers
Mary Effie Lee Newsome (1940)

The only volume of collected works by the professor, poet, and influential children's literature writer MARY EFFIE LEE NEWSOME. Published at the close of the Harlem Renaissance, the book included poems published previously in THE CRISIS. The celebrated painter Lois Mailou Jones provided the evocative pen-and-ink illustrations of children at play.

The most-often-cited poem of the collection is "Morning Light." With its suspenseful language, Newsome recounts the movements of "dew boys," the children often used by European hunters in Africa to make a path through high grasses. The "little black boy, / A naked black boy" of the poem emerges "Through heavy menace and mystery / Of half-waking tropic dawn."

In 1999 Newsome's poems were republished for the first time since their publication in *The Crisis* and *Gladiola Gardens*.

Bibliography

Bishop, Rudine Sims, comp. *Wonders: The Best Children's Poems of Effie Lee Newsome*. Honesdale, Pa.: Boyds Mill Press, 1999.

Roses, Lorraine Elena, and Ruth Elizabeth Randolph. *Harlem Renaissance and Beyond: Literary Biographies of 100 Black Women Writers, 1900–1945*. Boston: G. K. Hall & Co., 1990.

Goat Alley Ernest Howard Culbertson (1921)

A sobering play about an African-American couple beset by various social injustices. The white playwright Ernest Howard Culbertson joined the group of white writers like Octavus Roy Cohen, John Spivak, and DuBose Heyward who explored black themes in their works.

The play, which one NEW YORK TIMES reviewer reviled, chronicles the unfortunate life of a young girl whose lover is imprisoned. She turns to a life of prostitution, and when he is released, he abandons her and their child. Despite its harrowing reception in the press, the play was recognized for its contributions to African-American drama. ALAIN LOCKE and MONTGOMERY GREGORY selected *Goat Alley* and *Rackey* (1919), an earlier Culbertson play, for inclusion in *Plays of Negro Life* (1927).

Goat Alley opened in June 1921 at the Bijou Theatre in NEW YORK CITY with an all-black cast that included Barrington Carter, Beulah Daniels, Lillian McKee, and William H. Smith. The Toussaint Players revived the work six years later and staged it in April 1927 at the Princess Theatre.

Bibliography

Krasner, David. *A Beautiful Pageant: African American Theatre, Drama, and Performance in the Harlem Renaissance, 1910–1927*. New York: Palgrave Macmillan, 2002.

Locke, Alain, and Montgomery Gregory, eds. *Plays of Negro Life: A Source-Book of Native American Drama*. New York: Harper & Brothers, 1927.

God Sends Sunday Arna Bontemps (1931)

Published by HARCOURT, BRACE in 1931, this was the first novel that ARNA BONTEMPS published. He dedicated the work to "P.B. Bontemps," the initials of both his son Paul Bismarck and of his own father. It reflected the influence of Bontemps's southern heritage and Louisiana home. Bontemps was inspired to write *God Sends Sunday* in part by Joe Ward, his maternal granduncle. After seeking out the man known for his dapper style, Bontemps found himself thoroughly intrigued by Ward's stories of black life and culture.

The novel chronicles the adventures of the jockey Little Augie as he moves across the country through New Orleans, St. Louis, and Mudtown, California. Born on the Red River plantation where he lives with his older sister Leah, the orphan Augie, a "thin, undersized boy, smaller for his years than any other child on the place, [who] had round pop-eyes," has suffered somewhat because of his perceived physical frailty. Despite his inability to toil alongside his peers or elders in the cotton and rice fields, however, he "enjoyed a certain prestige" because he was born with a caul, or "mysterious veil," over his face. Augie also believes firmly in his own destiny and in the supernatural signs that he interprets as signs of his innate luckiness. He eventually stows away on a steamboat that takes him to New Orleans. There, he discovers the world of horse racing and with Bad-foot Dixon, a stable man with a clubfoot, he comes of age in the masculine world of horse training and racing.

Augie's knack for horses provides him great opportunities for financial and romantic successes. His first employer, Horace Church-Woodbine, who greets Augie with the rousing shout "Where's ma black boy?" whenever he is looking for him, gives the young boy his break as a jockey. Augie's success as a jockey is directly related to his relationship with the horses. As the narrator notes, "[w]ith horses he gained a power and authority, which, due to his inferior size and strength, he had never experienced with people . . . after he became a full fledged jockey he became a new person." He starts to walk with a swagger, delights in his newfound financial successes, and begins to contemplate spending his money on the ladies.

Over the course of the novel, Augie proves himself to be an energetic, if not sometimes overly aggressive, ladies' man. In one of his first encounters, with a San Antonio woman named Parthenia, he gets drunk and then punches her twice in the face, leaving her with two black eyes. Unfortunately, Augie's victim affirms his violence and "pretended to admire him for his brutality." In St. Louis, where he reunites with his sister Leah and her several children, he meets Della Green, a "fancy woman" who caters to patrons of a local establishment for "sweet men of the period." Della becomes his new love interest, Augie defends her from the violence of Biglow Brown, another man who fancies Della, and the two eventually go on to win a cakewalk contest with much flair and style.

Despite his apparent freedoms and lavish spending, however, Augie cannot deny his feelings for Florence, a light-skinned dressmaker whom he meets and falls in love with in New Orleans. Augie attempts to provide Della with the same material security and indulgences that his white former employer has bestowed upon his mistress Florence, but it is clear that he continues to be obsessed with the woman he has left behind. The love triangle that emerges here, though, illuminates Augie's political powerlessness. Despite Augie's initial belief that Florence is "a church gal" and "ain't no chippie," he cannot deny that she is the kept mistress of his wealthy white employer. Eventually, in the wake of her abandonment by Mr. Woody, she finally accepts Augie's advances. Their efforts to set up house are thwarted by the white neighbors who tolerated her presence there as a white man's mistress but not as an independent woman of color with an African-American lover. It is not long before Church-Woodbine, known as "Mr. Woody," begins to wreak havoc on Augie and on the couple. Florence's jealous ex-lover, who was forced to give up his relationship with her because of his family's objections, now engineers Augie's failures at the track by rigging the races and horses assigned to the energetic jockey. The story ends tragically. The erstwhile Florence deserts Augie once his losing streak begins, and he becomes an alcoholic. The novel closes as he boards a train that he hopes will take him to Mexico and away from his deteriorating life in the South.

THE NEW YORK TIMES published a lengthy review of the novel and praised Bontemps as a writer who "plows deeply into a rich soil of Negro personality" (*NYT*, 15 March 1931, 60) and "[catches] the light-heartedness and the soft melancholy of the Negro race with such a perfect natural grace that it is only in a second reading that one begins to realize the gem-like qualities of the recorded conversation and the artistic economy in the vividly intense pictures of common life in the Negro quarters" (*NYT*, 15 March 1931, 61). The anonymous reviewer, who characterized Augie as "something of a natural Byronic figure," noted that the protagonist was "too unreflective, however, and with too much simplicity to be tortured for long at a time by the melancholy introspection of supersensitive souls" (*NYT*, 15 March 1931, 61). Despite this gentle criticism, however, the reviewer noted that "A fine unforced imagery flickers in and out of [the novel's] last pages lighting up a touchingly sympathetic portrait of Little Augie in his old age, clinging to the memory of his days of grandeur, but content withal in his indolent life if it were but lighted occasionally by a touch of color or a remnant of beauty" (*NYT*, 15 March 1931, 61). The novel was the first of many Bontemps works to feature what the author himself referred to as the "lonesome-boy theme." Bontemps himself admitted to shying away from first-person narratives but noted that he did invest his writings with rich autobiographical details. The novel's publication in 1931 coincided with the GREAT DEPRESSION and, as a result, did not bring Bontemps great financial reward. Bontemps later revisited *God Sends Sunday* and collaborated with COUNTEE CULLEN on a musical version of the work. The musical comedy *St. Louis Woman*, completed in 1945, was a hit.

Bibliography

Canaday, Nicholas. "Arna Bontemps: The Louisiana Heritage," *Callaloo* (February–October 1981): 163–169.

Jones, Kirkland. *Renaissance Man from Louisiana: A Biography of Arna Wendell Bontemps*. Westport: Greenwood Press, 1992.

"'The Good Earth' and Other Recent Works of Fiction." *New York Times*, 15 March 1931.

God's Trombones: Seven Negro Sermons in Verse James Weldon Johnson (1927)

The 1927 collection of sermons written by JAMES WELDON JOHNSON and illustrated by AARON DOUGLAS and published 12 years after *AUTOBIOGRAPHY OF AN EX-COLOURED MAN* (1912). Johnson, an agnostic, reconstructed key events

and figures in the Bible. Several key experiences of African-American sermons inspired Johnson's volume, including a trip into rural Georgia during his freshman year at ATLANTA UNIVERSITY during which he encountered a minister whose voice recalled a powerful trombone, and another, in 1918 to Kansas City, which influenced Johnson's writing of "The Creation."

A long-standing interest in what Johnson described as "the primitive stuff of the old-time Negro sermon" led him to memorialize the powerful African-American sermon tradition. Johnson realized that the incredible power of the addresses lay not solely in their text but in their delivery. In his preface, Johnson reminded readers that "[t]hese poems would better be intoned than read. But the intoning practiced by the old-time preacher is a thing next to impossible to describe; it must be heard, and it is extremely difficult to imitate even when heard."

The volume includes an essay and eight substantial poems entitled "Listen, Lord—A Prayer," "The Creation," "The Prodigal Son," "Go Down Death—A Funeral Sermon," "Noah Built the Ark," "The Crucifixion," "Let My People Go," and "The Judgement Day." Written in free verse and in standard English, the volume evoked the cadences, spirit, and intensity of African-American churches. The works are based on selections from the Bible and offer evocative retellings of well-known biblical scenes and figures. In his sermon on the Creation, for instance, Johnson introduces readers to an accessible God, one who "sat down— / On the side of a hill where he could think; / By a deep, wide river he sat down; / With his head in his hands, / God thought and thought, / Till he thought: I'll make me a man!"

In addition to evocative images of the Almighty, Johnson included sermons that personified and softened forces such as death that were often regarded as predatory and unfeeling. In "Go Down, Death," Johnson depicted the thoughtful collaboration between God and the angel of death. God, whose "big heart was touched with pit, / With the everlasting pity" at the sight of a suffering mortal, summons "that tall, bright angel standing at this right hand: / Call me Death!" The call goes out, Death appears before God, and in response to the command to "Go Down, Death, and bring her to me," the silent masculinized force "loosed the reins on his pale, white horse, / And he clamped the spurs to his bloodless sides, / And out and down he rode, / Through heaven's pearly gates, / Past suns and moons and stars." When he appears at the bedside of the ailing Sister Caroline, "She saw Old Death. She saw Old Death / Coming like a falling star. / But Death didn't frighten Sister Caroline; He looked to her like a welcome friend." The dying woman is taken "up like a baby, / And she slay in his icy arms / But she didn't feel no chill" until she is placed finally "On the loving breast of Jesus." Johnson imagines a powerful new Trinity, one that now represents human creation, salvation, and death.

Johnson's deliberate prose and animated retellings of well-known stories have contributed to the long-standing popularity of the work. Since its publication, *God's Trombones* has been adapted for the stage and for performance by a variety of groups. In 1994 James Earl Jones and Dorian Harewood appeared in a film version of the work. At Emory University in 1999, the Reverend C. T. Vivian and other prominent ministers performed selections in honor of civil rights leader and Congressman John Lewis.

Bibliography

Fleming, Robert. *James Weldon Johnson.* Boston: Twayne Publishers, 1987.

Johnson, James Weldon. *Along This Way: The Autobiography of James Weldon Johnson.* New York: Penguin Books, 1990.

Levy, Eugene. *James Weldon Johnson: Black Leader, Black Voice.* Chicago: University of Chicago Press, 1973.

Goin' Home Ransom Rideout (1928)

A prize-winning play by RANSOM RIDEOUT that opened on BROADWAY in August 1928 at the Hudson Theatre in NEW YORK CITY. The play, which was produced by Brock Pemberton and required an enormous cast, was an involved and tragic story set in World War I–era FRANCE and billed as an "after-the-war drama." Before its Broadway debut, the play received special recognition from the Pasadena Community Players and was awarded first prize in a contest cosponsored by the Drama League of America and the publishing house of Longmans, Green & Company. The press, which was committed to publishing new material, balked at publishing Rideout's play because it featured a mixed cast and thus deemed it not easily adaptable by all-white drama groups. Although one NEW YORK TIMES review proposed that in the play "coincidence strains credibility," the drama enjoyed 78 performances in the late summer and early fall of 1928.

The frustrated protagonist of "Goin' Home" is Israel du Bois, a New Orleans-born soldier. He woos Lise, his white, French wife and a successful café owner, with exaggerated tales of his military exploits, and American fortune. Lise learns the truth about her husband and the plight of African Americans from Major Edward Powell, a white officer and former family acquaintance of du Bois. After Lise and Powell become romantically involved, Samba Saar, a Senegalese friend of du Bois, is determined to avenge his friend's honor. In a painful ironic twist, du Bois kills his best friend rather than the man who is party to his disenfranchisement in America and who contributes to the erosion of his marriage. The play closes as Powell escorts du Bois, a character whose manhood is constantly under siege, back to America.

The play's conclusion called attention to problematic American racial dynamics and hierarchies. *New York Times* drama critic J. Brooks Atkinson was incensed that "the fearless Senegalese lies stiff, cold, and unmoored in the anteroom" while "with some perfunctory muttering about 'comrades' and some abortive military flourish, [Rideout] calls quits all around and joins the Major and the negro in everlasting liberté, egalité, and fraternité" (*NYT*, 2 September 1928, 83). This "moral equality between a white officer and an emigré New Orleans negro" was recognized as a potentially powerful example for contemporary dramatists. Atkinson also praised Rideout's inclusion of a Senegalese character, a figure with whom the playwright could "contrast the black African of fierce pride and ebony gods with the descendants of American slaves" (*NYT*, 24 August 1928, 5).

The play was promoted in *The New York Times* and reviewed extensively by Atkinson. The following year, Atkinson included *Goin' Home* in his list of plays by white playwrights about Negroes that "frequently develop ideas without sacrificing character" (*NYT*, 3 March 1929, X1). The opening night's cast included a number of accomplished performers including Richard Hale as Israel du Bois, Barbara Bulgakova as Lise, Russell Hicks as Captain Powell, and Clarence Redd as Samba Saar.

Bibliography

Atkinson, J. Brooks. "Black and White." *New York Times*, 2 September 1928, 83.
———. "The Play." *New York Times*, 24 August 1928, 25.

"Golden Penknife, The" S. Miller Johnson
(1925)

An intense and dizzying short story by S. MILLER JOHNSON. It was published in the August 1925 issue of THE MESSENGER, the NAACP magazine whose editors included A. PHILIP RANDOLPH, CHANDLER OWEN, and GEORGE SCHUYLER. Johnson focuses on two young European immigrants whose families enjoy economic success and who are becoming increasingly Americanized because of their good fortune. The Americanization of these Russian immigrant families is defined primarily by material gains, business expansion, and higher social status. Johnson suggests, however, that European assimilation into white America cannot help but involve an increasing and deadly anxiety about African Americans, interracial relationships, and miscegenation.

Anna Paul and Fred Soskii, her fiancé, live with their families in Detroit, Michigan. Fred, the son of Russian parents, is focused on improving his family's grocery store holdings and their reputation in the community. He has traditional views about a wife and family and hopes to "marry a chaste pretty woman and settle down, have one or two kids . . . take out insurance, join the Rotarians, denounce lawbreakers, boost the Y, be patriotic, etc. etc. etc." Johnson's description of Soskii's aspirations suggests that he regards these goals as oppressively pedestrian. In sharp contrast to Soskii's domestic plans, however, are the unconventional ideas and actions of Anna. She was raised as a Catholic and is determined to "conform to her father's and her lover's idea of what a good woman should be." Johnson begins the story with a telling and provocative description of the evolving female protagonist. "Now Anna was a pretty little devil," he writes, "Her lips, pursed as if to invite a kiss, were red enough without rouge; and so were her cheeks. Her eyes, clearly and light and roaming, fairly beamed with loveliness that clamored for wholesome expression." Anna is thoroughly unsettled by puberty and hormones and is plagued by the "enormous struggle between inward natural desires and conventional morality."

The parallel struggles against illicit physical desires, unacceptable sexual activity, and social expectations drive Anna and Fred apart. Her reputation is threatened when she is rumored to be keeping company with any number of men, including figures who are never clearly seen but are imagined to be Negroes or other unacceptable ethnic people such as Turks, Filipinos, or Indians. Fred almost succumbs to the lure of showgirls but becomes the embodiment of virtue as he mourns the loss of his fiancée. Eventually, Fred encounters Anna and her friend, a dark-haired Russian whom she has met and romanced in a bookstore. Egged on by a friend, Fred considers attacking Askof Tervanovitch. He resists the temptation at first but ultimately lies in wait for Anna outside her home. When he confronts her, he demands the answer to one question: "Did you know that fellow's colored you were with tonight?" Blinded by jealousy and romantic incompetence, Fred Soskii invests in an explosive social myth about the racial other in general and about African Americans in particular. Fred murders Anna before she can reveal that her new lover shares their Russian heritage. He uses his foot to turn her lifeless body over in the snow, shrugs his shoulders, and then spits before departing. His heartless gesture is a chilling index of the disgust he feels for Anna's romantic choice and his belief that her dalliance has done irreparable damage to her family.

Johnson offered to *Messenger* readers a vivid exploration of 1920s sexual mores and the burdens of assimilation. The story is a probing examination of social expectations and white anxiety about race and difference. It concludes with haunting suggestions about cultural blindness and its deadly results.

Bibliography

Wilson, Sondra. *The Messenger Reader: Stories, Poetry, and Essays from The Messenger Magazine*. New York: Modern, 2000.

Gooden, Lauretta Holman (unknown)

A native of Sulphur Springs, Texas, Holman early demonstrated her love of writing and poetry while growing up in Texas. The mineral springs of her hometown on the Colorado River attracted a well-known health resort in the 1880s. The small, yet thriving factory town, which had a population of 2,500 in the 1880s, had an African-American population large enough to support two African-American churches. During the Civil War, the county in which Sulphur Springs was located supported secession and eventually gave rise to strong KU KLUX KLAN activity. While the African-American population in the county rose to almost 15 percent of the county's population, Holden's family was part of the migration from Sulphur Springs that led to a steady decrease in the African-American population during the 1920s and 1930s.

Shortly after Holman's birth, her family moved to Texarkana, Texas, the town in which the renowned musician and composer Scott Joplin was raised. Following her marriage to John Gooden, she moved to Dallas and worked alongside her husband in their grocery shop.

In 1936, John Brewer Mason, an accomplished folk historian, writer, teacher, and fellow Texan, published five of Holman's poems in *Heralding Dawn: An Anthology of Verse*, a pioneering anthology of works by Texas poets of color. Mason, who began teaching and then collecting African-American folk materials in the mid-1920s, was an aspiring poet as well and later would become the first African-American member of the Texas Folklore Society. His extensive work to preserve black traditions, dialects, and history merited comparisons to ZORA NEALE HURSTON. Mason's editorial notes on Holman's poems called attention to her "well placed phraseology."

Bibliography

Brewer, John Mason. *Heralding Dawn*. Dallas: June Thomason Printing, 1936.
Grider, Sylvia Ann and Lou Halsell Rodenberger. *Texas Women Writers: A Tradition of Their Own*. College Station: Texas A & M University Press, 1997.
Roses, Lorraine Elena, and Ruth Elizabeth Randolph. *Harlem Renaissance and Beyond: Literary Biographies of 100 Black Women Writers, 1900–1945*. Boston: G. K. Hall & Co., 1990.

Gordon, Edythe Mae Chapman
(ca. 1890–unknown)

A writer, poet, intellectual, and officer of the SATURDAY EVENING QUILL CLUB, a dynamic literary arts group in 1920s BOSTON. Born in WASHINGTON, D.C., she attended the M Street or DUNBAR HIGH SCHOOL whose accomplished faculty during her enrollment from 1912 through 1916 included the feminist philosopher ANNA JULIA COOPER, the writer and Harlem Renaissance mentor JESSIE FAUSET, and the influential historian CARTER G. WOODSON. In 1916 she married EUGENE GORDON, whom she may have met in Washington, D.C., during his enrollment at the Howard University Academy and College.

By 1926 the Gordons were living in Boston. Eugene began a successful career as a local newspaper reporter, and the couple enrolled in special courses at BOSTON UNIVERSITY. Edythe completed nondegree course work at HARVARD UNIVERSITY, undergraduate studies, and a master's program at Boston University. Following her 1934 graduation with a B.Sc. in Religious Education and Social Services, she enrolled in the School of Social Services and earned a master's degree in the summer of 1935. Biographer Lorraine Elena Roses notes that little is known of Gordon's experiences at Boston University; there is, however, one photograph of Gordon and other religious education seniors in the 1934 school yearbook. Gordon's master's thesis was entitled "The Status of the Negro Woman in the United States from 1619–1865." In the preface, Gordon asserts her hope that the work will "stimulate further study in this neglected field of Negro history." She also reveals her efforts to create "a vivid picture of the struggles, cruelties, inhumanities and injustices to which the Negro woman was a victim under the system of chattel slavery which lasted for nearly three hundred years" and to "suggest the present day situation of the Negro woman, and intimate a remedy." Gordon's preface confirmed the depths of her intellectual commitment to creating a revisionist and more inclusive American history. The work also reflects her interest in providing rich historical context for the continued social work and racial uplift efforts of her day.

Gordon was a published poet and writer of short fiction during the 1920s and 1930s. She made her literary debut in the SATURDAY EVENING QUILL, a short-lived but impressive literary magazine founded by a group of writers including HELENE JOHNSON and DOROTHY WEST. During the three-year existence of the magazine, Gordon published a number of poems and short stories. Biographical and editorial notes that accompanied the works in the Quill reveal that Gordon's work was receiving high praise from other quarters. Her first published story in the Quill was "SUBVERSION," a work selected by the O. Henry Memorial Award Prize Committee as one of the most impressive works of short fiction in 1928.

Gordon's short fiction is marked for its economical and pointed accounts of tragic romance, loss, and heartbreak. Her protagonists range from deluded wives to devoted husbands. The home lives of these individuals are often haunted by the unknown as in "IF WISHES WERE HORSES," a short story about Alfred Pomeroy, a hardworking department store clerk who is thoroughly unsettled by his encounter with a fortune-teller. He is perplexed by the prediction, unable to understand how he might be "the maker of his wife's dreams." Without embellishment, Gordon relates Alfred's sudden death. The story closes with the report of his wife's departure on a luxury cruise to Europe; the trip is financed by Alfred's $50,000 life insurance policy. Other stories, including "Hostess," and "Subversion," suggest the searing pain of betrayal and the life-threatening results of infidelity. Gordon's short fiction contributes to the powerful feminist writing about taxing domesticity, the limitations of romance, and the complicated nature of self-destruction.

Gordon's poems focus on traditional themes of love, loss, and natural beauty. She uses the first-person voice often, and the speakers frequently contemplate the possibilities of romance and passion in the natural world. Poems such as "Let Your Rays," "Elysium," "I See You," and "April Night" reveal the heady influence that a vibrant and fertile earth can have on lovers and imaginative individuals. In "Sonnet for June," a four-line poem that offers only a portion of the traditional rhyme scheme of an Italian sonnet, the speaker is transported into an unself-conscious and sensual rhapsody: "I breathe deep draughts from the fragrant earth . . . / Which quickens me with ecstasy and mirth; And all the day, I kneel at your altar." In "April Night," the speaker cries out to June, an ambiguous reference to a woman or to the month. "O glorious-tinted June, have pity!" declares the speaker, who admits to being "ravished" by the "primrose beauty" of the April night. The poem concludes with a submissive and worshipful posture that is characteristic of Gordon's poems: "You are eternal as a mountain pine, / All day, I kneel below your petalled shrine." These and other poems reflect Gordon's romantic sensibilities and fascination with the natural world.

Edythe Gordon filed for divorce from her husband Eugene in 1942 and then essentially disappeared from the public record. However, biographer Lorraine Elena Roses has uncovered poems published in 1938 and evidence that Gordon may have relocated to North Carolina and worked as a social worker. The date and location of Gordon's death have not yet been determined.

Bibliography

Gordon, Edythe Mae. *Selected Works of Edythe Mae Gordon.* Introduction by Lorraine Elena Roses. New York: G. K. Hall & Co., 1996.
Saturday Evening Quill. Boston, Mass.: 1928–1930.

Gordon, Eugene (1890–unknown)

The editor of the SATURDAY EVENING QUILL, a popular but short-lived BOSTON magazine, Gordon was a journalist by trade. A Florida native, he worked at a number of Boston newspapers following his years of schooling at HOWARD UNIVERSITY and BOSTON UNIVERSITY. In 1919 he began writing editorials for the *Boston Post;* by the mid-1920s, he was on staff at the *Boston Globe.*

Gordon was a member of the SATURDAY EVENING QUILL CLUB, a Boston literary club that encouraged and published aspiring authors. The group also included members of the African-American social and literary elite among its members, such as FLORIDA RUFFIN RIDLEY, the daughter of the suffrage leader Josephine St. Pierre Ruffin. The periodical published a majority of Harlem Renaissance women writers, including Florence Harmon Gill, HELENE JOHNSON, and DOROTHY WEST.

Gordon, himself a writer, published articles in *Opportunity,* the journal of the Urban League, and in AMERICAN MERCURY, the monthly magazine founded by H. L. MENCKEN and George Jean Nathan.

Bibliography

Jubilee, Vincent. *Philadelphia's Afro-American Literary Circle and the Harlem Renaissance.* Ann Arbor, Mich.: University Microfilms, 1982.

Gordon, (Emmanuel) Taylor (1893–1971)

The author of BORN TO BE (1929), an absorbing autobiography that chronicled his colorful life experiences in vaudeville, circus life, and his childhood home in the Montana mining town of White Sulphur Springs. Gordon was a writer and singer who, during the 1920s, worked closely in vaudeville and formal concerts with J. Rosamond Johnson, the brother of JAMES WELDON JOHNSON. The son of a former slave and a cook in a Montana mining camp, his was the only African-American family living in the mining boomtown of White Sulphur Springs.

Gordon, who left Montana when he was 17 years old, worked in a number of colorful professions. In addition to working as a waiter and porter, he also did a stint as chauffeur to John Ringling, the circus magnate. His vocal talents catapulted him to fame. He was a member of "The Inimitable Five," a singing group established by J. Rosamond Johnson. Gordon followed in the tradition of the Fisk Jubilee Singers when in the 1920s, he traveled throughout England and FRANCE performing spirituals. His audiences were primarily aristocratic and upper class.

CARL VAN VECHTEN penned the foreword to Gordon's autobiography. He and Gordon met first in the early 1920s when Gordon, like many other aspiring writers and artists of the day, auditioned for the influential cultural broker in his NEW YORK CITY apartment. Gordon's performance led to his 1925 spirituals concert at the Theater Guild, the program for which included a complimentary note from Van Vechten. According to Leon Coleman, it was Van Vechten, impressed by Gordon's tales and adventures, who encouraged Gordon to write his life story. In his praising foreword, Van Vechten,

who described the writer as a "lanky six-feet" figure with a "falsetto voice, molasses laugh . . . and an eye that can see," characterized the book as a "'human document' of the first order."

Professional struggles during the 1930s alienated Gordon from his New York arts circles. His major frustrations included an untidy end to his relationship with J. Rosamond Johnson and the conviction that *Doanda,* his unpublished novel, was being passed off by John Steinbeck as *The Grapes of Wrath.* Gordon suffered a breakdown in 1947 and was admitted to several mental hospitals before returning to White Sulphur Springs under the care of his sister. He died there in 1971.

Bibliography

Coleman, Leon. "Carl Van Vechten Presents the New Negro." In *Harlem Renaissance Re-examined,* edited by Victor Kramer and Robert Russ. Troy, N.Y.: Whitson Publishing Company, 1997.

Gordon, Taylor. *Born to Be.* New York: Covici-Friede Publishers, 1929. Reprint with a new introduction by Robert Hemenway, 1975. Reprint with new introduction by Thadious Davis, 1995.

Lewis, David Levering. *When Harlem Was in Vogue.* New York: Knopf, 1981.

Graham, Ottie Beatrice (1900–unknown)

A Virginia-born playwright and fiction writer who became part of the Harlem Renaissance literary circle in PHILADELPHIA. The daughter of Reverend W. G. Graham, she attended both HOWARD UNIVERSITY and COLUMBIA UNIVERSITY. Her talent for writing earned her several prizes while an undergraduate. She published in both *The Crisis* and *Opportunity* but appears to have pursued more financially stable careers than writing.

Like NELLA LARSEN, JESSIE FAUSET, and others, Graham focused on the legacies of slavery and the complicated politics of mixed-race identity.

Bibliography

Graham, Ottie. "Holiday." *The Crisis,* May 1923, 12–17.
———. "Blue Aloes." *The Crisis* July 1924, 156–162.
———. "Slackened Caprice." *Opportunity,* November 1924, 332–335.
———. "To a Wild Rose." *Opportunity,* June 1923, 59–63.

Roses, Lorraine Elena, and Ruth Elizabeth Randolph. *Harlem Renaissance and Beyond: Literary Biographies of 100 Black Women Writers, 1900–1945.* Boston: G. K. Hall & Co., 1990.

Graham DuBois, Shirley Lola (1906–1977)

A talented musician, biographer, and prolific playwright who composed and produced the first major opera to feature an African-American cast. Graham was born in Indianapolis, Indiana, to Etta Bell Graham and David Graham, an African Methodist Episcopal minister and active NATIONAL ASSOCIATION FOR THE ADVANCEMENT OF COLORED PEOPLE (NAACP) leader. She was educated in Paris and returned to the United States to begin a teaching career and to continue her schooling. In 1923 she married Shadrack McCanns (also spelled McCants), a newspaper editor in Seattle, and the couple had two children before McCann's death three years later.

Graham renewed her acquaintance with W. E. B. DuBois in 1936, almost 15 years after the ATLANTA UNIVERSITY scholar and *CRISIS* editor had lodged overnight with her family in Colorado. During the decades leading up to their marriage in 1951, Graham benefited from DuBois's support for her career. He published her writing in *The Crisis* and wrote strong letters of support that contributed to her winning prestigious fellowships such as the JULIUS ROSENWALD FELLOWSHIP. It was Graham who, following DuBois's forced retirement from ATLANTA UNIVERSITY, arranged for him to relocate to 409 Edgecombe Avenue in HARLEM's prestigious SUGAR HILL district. In 1951, after an impressive and longstanding career as a writer, teacher, and playwright, she married the recently widowed W. E. B. DuBois on St. Valentine's Day in 1951. The couple lived in Brooklyn, New York, until they immigrated to GHANA in 1961.

Graham completed a master's thesis entitled "Survivals of Africanism in Modern Music." Before pursuing undergraduate and master's level degrees in music at Oberlin College, however, Graham studied for one year at the Howard School of Music in WASHINGTON, D.C. In 1929 she joined the faculty at Morgan State College, where she taught music until 1932. As a sophomore at Oberlin, she distinguished herself by completing *TOM-TOM*, a one-act play that was developed further and fashioned into the 1932 opera *Tom-Tom: An Epic of Music and the Negro.* The work was the first major opera written and produced by a woman. It was produced in several formats, including an NBC radio broadcast of an abridged form of the play. The piece was performed in its entirety at the Cleveland Stadium in late June and early July 1932.

Graham was part of the Works Project Administration cultural effort. In 1936 she moved to CHICAGO, joined the Federal Writers' Project, and managed the Prince Theatre, where she worked with African-American casts. Among the works that she adapted for them to perform were *The Mikado* and *Little Black Sambo.* She became a Julius Rosenwald fellow and became affiliated with the Yale University School of Drama in 1938. The prestigious grant enabled Graham to be in residence until 1940. During this two-year period, she completed several plays that revealed the breadth of her talents. In quick succession, she produced the musical *Deep Rivers* (1939), the tragic drama *It's Morning* (1940), a popular radio script, *Track Thirteen* (1940), and the three-act tragedies *ELISHA'S RAVEN* (1941) and *Dust to Earth* (1941).

Graham's career intensified as the Harlem Renaissance came to a close. She was a GUGGENHEIM FELLOWSHIP winner from 1945 to 1947. She began writing biographies of famous African Americans shortly thereafter. In 1946 her biography *Paul Robeson: Citizen of the World* earned the Julian Messner Award, and the forthcoming work, *There Once Was a Slave: The Heroic Story of Frederick Douglass,* based on the antebellum abolitionist and orator, would also win the Messner Award. Other works included biographies of Phillis Wheatley, Pocahontas, Jean Baptiste Pointe de Sable, and Benjamin Banneker. Graham published steadily throughout the 1940s and in 1950 was honored by the National Institute of Arts and Letters for her works.

Her political activities also increased; in 1943 she was appointed to the position of field secretary for the NAACP. Her political work facilitated her renewed acquaintance with W. E. B. DuBois, whom she had met first while a teenager in Colorado Springs and again in the 1930s during her tenure at Tennessee Agricultural and Industrial

State College. She joined the COMMUNIST PARTY USA following the death of her son Robert. She was prompted to make the political commitment in large part because of the devastating racial prejudice that she and her sick son had received in New York City. Robert was denied treatment by three city hospitals because of his race; by the time Shirley Graham had forced a fourth hospital to admit her son, it was too late.

Graham DuBois traveled with her husband to Beijing for a highly controversial visit and then with him to Ghana, where he applied for citizenship status. Following his death in 1963, Graham DuBois lived in Accra until 1967 and then relocated to Cairo, Egypt. The U.S. government barred her return to America, citing her links to the Communist Party. Graham DuBois, suffering from cancer, traveled to Beijing, China, for treatment. She died there in 1977.

Bibliography

Horne, Gerald. *The Lives of Shirley Graham DuBois*. New York: New York University Press, 2000.

Lewis, David Levering. *W. E. B. DuBois: The Fight for Equality and the American Century, 1919–1963*. New York: Henry Holt and Company, 2000.

New York Times obituary, 5 April 1977.

Peterson, Bernard. "Shirley Graham DuBois: Composer and Playwright," *Crisis* (May 1977).

Granny Maumee Ridgely Torrence (1914)

One of the three one-act dramas included in the influential work entitled *Plays for a Negro Theatre* by playwright, poet, editor, and teacher RIDGELY TORRENCE. The collection included *Granny Maumee*, SIMON THE CYRENIAN, and THE RIDER OF DREAMS. Many critics hailed Torrence, a white Ohio playwright, for presenting the first set of sober dramas on African-American life. His works have been regarded as instrumental in facilitating the access of African-American actors to broader mainstream American audiences.

In March 1914 *Granny Maumee*, billed as a "Negro Tragedy," was performed at the Lyceum Theatre on BROADWAY. The play was performed as part of a double bill with *A Woman Killed with Kindness*, by Mark Heywood. This run was presented by the Stage Society of New York and in-

cluded one public performance to benefit the Actor's Fund.

Three years later, in 1917, the Macmillan Company published *Plays for a Negro Theatre*. *Granny Maumee* and its companion pieces from *Plays for a Negro Theatre* were staged at the Garden Theatre and at the Garrick Theatre in NEW YORK CITY throughout April 1917. The producer for these shows was EMILIE BIGELOW HAPGOOD, a respected theater producer and designer. She also was the founder of the EMILIE HAPGOOD PLAYERS, the African-American theater group that provided the first African-American cast for *Granny Maumee*. The opening cast in the April 1914 production of *Granny Maumee* included Lola Clifton, Dorothy Donnelly, and June Mathis. In 1917 the three leading actresses from the Hapgood Players in the opening night cast were Blanche Deas, Marie Jackson-Stuart, and Fannie Tarkington.

The play was included in *PLAYS OF NEGRO LIFE: A SOURCE-BOOK OF NATIVE AMERICAN DRAMA* (1927) edited by Alain Locke and Montgomery Gregory. The edition note states that *Granny Maumee* was performed first by the Stage Society in New York City. It also indicates that the first performance with an African-American cast occurred on April 5, 1917, and featured members of the Hapgood Players.

The play, set in a southern Louisiana cabin in the late 19th century, features three women. Granny Maumee, described plainly as "an old Negro woman," and her two great-granddaughters, Pearl and Sapphie, are haunted by the traumatic lynching death of Sam, who was Granny Maumee's son and the girls' grandfather. Granny Maumee rushed into the fire to save her son but was unable to prevent his death. Pulled from the fire, she sustained terrible burns and was blinded when the fire that had been set to kill an innocent man scorched her eyes. The desperate mother did pull away two pieces of burning wood, and she has saved these as awful and powerful reminders of the violence that was wrought upon her family.

The drama, which uses a vivid southern dialect throughout, turns on the imminent arrival of Sapphie, a character whose name suggests the powerful Sapphira as well as the precious stone. Sapphie is due to appear with her newborn son and husband. When she does arrive, however, she does so without Lightfoot, the father of her child. Her sister, shocked at the identity of the child, describes the infant in her sister's arms as a "light-head merlatter." Sapphie has been seduced by her white male employer, a man descended from the murderer of Granny Maumee's only son.

Sapphie and Pearl are thankful that Granny is blind and will not be able to see the mixed-race child and the first male child born into the family since Sam's death. The sisters soon realize, however, that Granny Maumee is intent on restoring her sight. As she says to Pearl, "Befo' my las' houah deze eyes shill look an' see ergin." The girls are also faced with Granny's pride in the high morality and virtue of the family. She reminds them how, even in the face of enslavement and potentially threatening domestic service arrangements, generations of women in the family have kept themselves "clean er de w'ite streak." She regards this as a mighty defense since "W'ite blood were 'stroying tuh my fambly f'um de beginnin's."

Torrence links Granny's intense color consciousness to her unwavering disdain and hatred for whites. She dons a bright red dress because, as she announces, "Red's de fus coloh er baby notice." Delighted at the prospect of a dark-skinned great-great-grandson, she makes the ominous declaration that "red allers goes wif black. Red neveh go wif w'ite." Her meditation on primary colors and race quickly lead to upsetting recollections of Sam. "I use allers tuh wrop my Sam in red," she notes as, according to the script, her voice grows more and more shrill, "an red's de las' way I seen 'im."

Much to the girls' dismay, Granny does restore her sight. She uses the charred wood from the lynching fire and earnest prayers to beseech heaven for this precious gift. Once she realizes that her request has been granted, though, she is shocked to behold the light-skinned child in her arms. Within moments, she learns of Sapphie's seduction and the father's identity. In a powerful scene that borders on stereotypical folk presentation and evocative human angst, Granny Maumee hypnotizes the girls as she prepares a spell that will ensnare young Lightfoot, who is coming to pay his respects to Granny Maumee and to assure her of his continued financial support of Sapphie. She

plans to use the chains that bound Sam and the wood from his lynching fire to reenact the murder as she kills Lightfoot. As he knocks at the cabin door, Granny Maumee, intent on revenge for her son's death and her great-granddaughter's violation, is halted by an ethereal contact with Sam. She is steadied by his ghostly counsel, which urges her to forgive her enemies so that she can be reunited with her own loved ones. After tense moments of deliberation, Granny Maumee agrees to forgive. The girls wake from their spell-induced stupor just in time to see the figure of Granny Maumee on the floor. The sisters flee in terror, and the play closes with the figure of Granny Maumee alone on the floor of the cabin.

Granny Maumee was part of a significant canon of antilynching plays written during the Harlem Renaissance. Its setting in Louisiana called attention to the awful history of mob and racial violence in that state. Between 1882 and the 1930s, there were almost 300 lynchings of African Americans by whites. The state was ranked third among Southern states; the states of Mississippi and Georgia were first and second, respectively.

Torrence was among the critically acclaimed white writers, like PAUL GREEN and John William Rogers, who addressed racial violence in their works. Despite the political relevance of his work, however, critics such as Benjamin Brawley have proposed that Torrence and other white writers of the Harlem Renaissance era unable to appreciate or explore fully the African-American experience. Yet, the intensified political aesthetic in antilynching plays did succeed in drawing attention to the brutal social violence.

Torrence's subject matter also corresponded to the antilynching dramas that were calling attention to the traumatic American history of mob violence and racial hatred as shown in works such as *RACHEL* by ANGELINA GRIMKÉ, *Mine Eyes Have Seen* (1917) by ALICE DUNBAR NELSON, and *Aftermath* (1919) by MARY BURRILL. In an April 15, 1917, interview published in *THE NEW YORK TIMES*, Torrence described the source of inspiration for his pioneering plays on African-American life and experiences: "I got my knowledge of the negro when I lived in Southern Ohio. I spent my boyhood in Xenia, Ohio. Xenia is a focal point for negro immigration, and it really is more Southern than any part of the South" (*NYT,* 15 April 1917, SM8).

Granny Maumee is one of several Harlem Renaissance–era plays that place women in the foreground of antilynching dramas. Like Granny Maumee, they appear as scarred female survivors of lynchings or as disempowered witnesses. This work, with its noticeable generation gap, comments explicitly on the ruptured genealogy of families who suffered the barbarity of lynching in America.

Bibliography

Gunning, Sandra. *Race, Rape, and Lynching: The Red Record of American Literature, 1890–1912.* New York: Oxford University Press, 1996.

Locke, Alain, and Montgomery Gregory, eds. *Plays of Negro Life: A Source Book of Native American Drama.* 1927; reprint, Westport, Conn.: Negro Universities Press, 1970.

Wells-Barnett, Ida B. *On Lynchings: Southern Horrors, a Red Record, Mob Rule in New Orleans.* Amherst, N.Y.: Humanity Books, 2002.

Graven Images May Miller (1929)

A stirring one-act play for children by MAY MILLER SULLIVAN, the playwright, editor, teacher, and daughter of HOWARD UNIVERSITY dean Kelly Miller. Written in 1929, "Graven Images" was published shortly thereafter in *PLAYS AND PAGEANTS FROM THE LIFE OF THE NEGRO*, edited by fellow playwright WILLIS RICHARDSON. In his introduction to the volume, Richardson described Miller's work as a neo-romance. He added that the play's roles for children and adults meant that the work could be "portrayed by teachers and their pupils." The pedagogical import of Miller's work contributed to her promise as a playwright who would, in Richardson's words, further help to "make the Negro drama worthy of attention."

The play explored the Old Testament history of Moses, his Ethiopian wife Zipporah, and the racism of Moses's siblings Aaron and Miriam. Miller anticipated the historical novel of her friend and fellow Howard University student ZORA NEALE HURSTON. In 1939 Hurston revisited the story of the Jewish leader that included a substantial and lively account of his marital relationship

and the tensions prompted by Zipporah's African heritage in *Moses, Man of the Mountain.* Miller's focus on the interracial dimensions of Moses's family brings together disparate Old Testament references to his wife and sons. In addition, Miller highlights the better-known conflict recorded in the Book of Numbers (Chapter 12: 1–15). In this scene, Moses confronts his jealous siblings, and God transforms Miriam, the one who rejects Zipporah most strongly, into a leper with intensely white skin.

Miller uses interactions between children to highlight the limitations and prejudices of adults. The play begins as Ithamar, a son of Aaron, and other Israelite children discover a golden bull. The group of boys disregards the prohibitions regarding the worship of idols and creates play rituals of worship. They are midway through their speeches and offerings of clothing and hair to the idol when a group of girls comes upon them. As they dictate the girls' inferior position and reinforce prohibitive gender roles, Eliezer, the youngest son of Moses and Zipporah, discovers the group. He is amused by the performance. His laughter and pronouncement that "in Hazderoth little boys and girls dance and worship idols while their parents worship Jehovah" does not endear him to the group. After initial teasing and rejection because of his golden color and the fact that he is "a foreign boy," the mixed-race child of the revered leader of the Israelites becomes the object of worship. Miller makes a fascinating intervention as Eliezer capitalizes on the value of the golden bull and claims the status of precious object for himself:

> Eliezer: I shall make a far better idol than this. (*he springs lightly to the platform in front of the idol*) Look, this idol is gold. (*he strips his tunic off to the waist*) Am I not gold? (*the boys press forward murmuring their assent*) Come feel your idol. It is cold but I am warm. Warm gold. (*the boys press closer*) And see! see! You worship this thing that does not so much as nod his thanks. Its still, but I move, I move.

The Bible contains no direct transcript of the interactions between Miriam and Zipporah. In *Graven*

Images, Miller compensates for this missing dialogue by creating a distressing interaction between Miriam and Zipporah's youngest son. Ithamar turns on his cousin and provokes the violent dialogue between the aunt and Eliezer, her recently arrived nephew. Without hesitation, she challenges both his status as an object worthy of idolization and his status as a person worthy of social position. "This child is no image of God. Jehovah," she declares, "He is black like his mother." She pulls him off the platform and chastises him forcefully: "Black one, you had best hide your shame from the followers of your father and not place your complexion where all may see," she tells the child. Her tirade continues in her conversations with Aaron. She encourages her brother to prepare for his ascension and argues that Moses's marriage invalidates him as a worthy leader. In one of the baldest racist statements in the play, Miller's Miriam declares that "He should lead Israel who is truly an Israelite, one uncontaminated by Ethiopian blood." The racial hysteria that Miller introduces here taps into black Jewish identity as well as American anxieties about miscegenation and racial purity.

In the final scenes, Moses exiles the leprous Miriam from the camp for seven days. Eliezer emerges as a resilient and willful heir to his father's influence. The play closes as the child reinstates his position as a worthy idol. He "sits hugging his knees in delight in anticipation of the coming sport" promised by the imminent arrival of his now-chastened and awed playmates who believe that he, like his father, has the ability to articulate God's will.

"Graven Images" reflected Miller's lifelong efforts to illuminate the enduring presence of African and African-American figures throughout history. The play also reflected Miller's penchant for direct discussion of problematic issues and her use of drama to catalyze audiences and debates about privilege, power, and history.

Bibliography

Boyd, Valerie. *Wrapped in Rainbows: The Life of Zora Neale Hurston.* New York: Scribner, 2003.

Richardson, Willis. *Plays and Pageants from the Life of the Negro.* Washington, D.C.: The Associated Publishers, Inc., 1930.

Great Day   John Wells   (1929)

A musical play based on the novel of the same name by John Wells that debuted at the Cosmopolitan Theatre on BROADWAY in October 1929. *Great Day* featured some actors in blackface and variations of the script. The drama was set in New Orleans, Louisiana, and the characters were embroiled in Louisiana romance, gambling escapades, and the chaos caused when a sugar plantation was flooded by the Mississippi River.

William Cary Duncan wrote the libretto, Vincent Youmans composed the music, and William Rose created the lyrics. Actors Flournoy Miller and Aubrey Lyles appeared in blackface during the play's October 1929 Broadway run.

Great Day, The   Zora Neale Hurston   (1932)

A dynamic and multifaceted cultural performance scripted by ZORA NEALE HURSTON and performed in a one-time show at the John Golden Theatre on West 58th Street in NEW YORK CITY. The work, originally entitled "In the Beginning: A Concert of Negro Secular Music," included dancers and Negro spirituals and lullabies. The performance included two major plots. The first revolved around the lives of workers building a railroad in Florida and featured a number of popular work songs such as "John Henry." As Hurston biographer Valerie Boyd notes, Hurston's presentation of these stirring lyrics illuminated the ways in which these songs constituted impressive declarations of African-American political and cultural strength. The second major plot featured in the performance was set in a rousing juke joint. Performers thrilled the audience at the John Golden Theatre with renditions of well-known blues songs. The final portions of the performance included the Fire Dance, based on Hurston's research in the Bahamas, and a finale that involved a celebratory counterpoint in which singers traded verses of secular and religious songs.

The production, advertised as a single performance only, was enthusiastically reviewed. The New York *Herald Tribune* praised the work, citing its "verve" and "lack of self-consciousness." It included performances by well-known actors such as Leigh Whipper, who performed in IN ABRAHAM'S BOSOM, the 1927 PULITZER PRIZE–winning play by Hurston's friend PAUL GREEN.

Hurston used funds from her patron CHAR-LOTTE OSGOOD MASON to fund the one-night extravaganza of *The Great Day*. Both women hoped that the show would be adapted by a Broadway producer and make sizable profits. It was not picked up, however, and Hurston had to solicit additional funds from the woman known as God-mother in order to meet expenses and performer salaries. The financial disappointment prompted Mason to curtail Hurston's independent dramatic ventures. Yet, Hurston promptly refashioned the work for another opening at the New School in New York City. Despite its convincing vignettes and critical praise, the new and improved show did not bring in profits either. In the wake of two successful but time-consuming and costly theatrical productions as the nation was wracked by the Depression, Hurston turned her attention to the more financially stable profession of teaching.

The Great Day script was recently recovered in a search of Library of Congress copyright records that revealed several long-lost Hurston plays. Hurston had delivered carbon typescripts of this and other dramatic materials in order to secure copyright protection for her work.

Bibliography

Boyd, Valerie. *Wrapped in Rainbows: The Life of Zora Neale Hurston.* New York: Scribner, 2003.

Great Depression

A devastating economic period that began with the October 1929 stock market crash that totaled some $16 billion in losses and lasted through the 1930s. Unemployment, homelessness, and financial disaster left many Americans struggling to survive. Cities like Minneapolis grappled with food riots, and others, like Los Angeles, saw an increase in tensions between American and foreign laborers. Veterans lobbied and marched on WASHINGTON, D.C., in order to secure monies promised through the Bonus Bill, a legislative act designed to relieve the suffering of veterans and their families. Banks collapsed at an alarming rate, and millions of depositors lost their savings and access to funds.

By 1933, historians estimate, approximately one-third of the nation's workforce was unemployed. President Franklin D. Roosevelt, who was elected over the incumbent Herbert Hoover in 1932, instituted a number of new programs such as the Civilian Conservation Corps and National Youth Administration. These and other initiatives, such as the Tennessee Valley Authority that spearheaded hydroelectric projects and the construction of dams, were designed to provide employment and alleviate national anxiety about the economy. The New Deal prompted the creation of the federal Works Progress Administration in 1935. It later became the Works Projects Administration and was in existence until 1943. Many Harlem Renaissance–era writers found employment in this national agency that was established in order to ease unemployment and to provide opportunities for writers and artists. RALPH ELLISON, ZORA NEALE HURSTON, RICHARD WRIGHT, and others were part of the federal effort to record oral histories. Artists such as Charles White and William Henry Johnson were part of the federal art initiatives; White became famous for his historical murals that depicted African-American life and history.

Historians often cite America's involvement in World War II as a major economic catalyst that succeeded in ending the Great Depression. The attacks on Pearl Harbor resulted in massive defense manufacturing that introduced women and minorities into the workforce at unprecedented levels.

The Great Depression affected the Harlem Renaissance in numerous ways. Unemployment rates were higher for African Americans throughout the country, and Harlem residents endured joblessness at a level that was five times higher than that in other areas of NEW YORK CITY. Those who did work were not protected from the hardships of the era; historians note that the salaries of many African-American workers in the city plummeted almost 50 percent. By 1932, 50 percent of families in HARLEM were receiving relief from the city

The financial panic affected Harlem's wealthiest personas as well. VILLA LEWARO, the legendary Hudson River estate of A'LELIA WALKER, the daughter of the self-made millionairess Madam C. J. Walker, was placed on the market just weeks before A'Lelia died of a brain hemorrhage. Harlem Renaissance figures also mobilized to sustain the community during the decade of hardship. The Young Negroes Cooperate League, founded by the journalist and novelist GEORGE SCHUYLER in

1930 and led by Ella Baker, its first national director, promoted the value of African-American buying clubs. Rev. ADAM CLAYTON POWELL, SR., organized the Harlem Citizen's Committee for More and Better Jobs in an effort to secure jobs for African Americans within Harlem.

The arts and cultural scene in Harlem continued to thrive in the face of dire poverty and national upheaval. In 1929, on the eve of the Great Depression, a number of artists, such as WALLACE THURMAN and CLAUDE MCKAY, enjoyed major professional accomplishments. In that year, Thurman published his first novel, THE BLACKER THE BERRY, and saw his play HARLEM reach BROADWAY. A number of writers launched and sustained their promising careers during the 1930s. The early 1930s saw the publication of JAMES WELDON JOHNSON's BLACK MANHATTAN (1930), George Schuyler's pointed satire BLACK NO MORE (1931), JESSIE FAUSET's THE CHINABERRY TREE (1931), RUDOLPH FISHER's pioneering mystery novel THE CONJURE-MAN DIES (1932), Claude McKay's Banana Bottom (1933), and ZORA NEALE HURSTON's first novel, JONAH'S GOURD VINE (1934).

Throughout the 1930s, Harlem Renaissance writers and artists alike forged ahead with significant projects. Aaron Douglas was commissioned to create murals for FISK UNIVERSITY, the Harlem YMCA, and the NEW YORK PUBLIC LIBRARY. In 1931 LANGSTON HUGHES produced SCOTTSBORO LIMITED: FOUR POEMS AND A PLAY IN VERSE, a set of works based on the controversial trial of young men falsely accused of and then imprisoned for rape. Louis Armstrong appeared in the 1932 film A Rhapsody in Black and Blue, and one year later PAUL ROBESON starred in the film version of THE EMPEROR JONES (1933).

From the mid-1930s through the end of the Great Depression, Harlem residents supported political activism and community organizing that would sustain the community. Networks such as the Black Cabinet, a group of community and political leaders determined to ensure equitable New Deal policies, represented the resilience, political acuity, and determination to survive the Great Depression era.

Organizations committed to the production and preservation of African-American literature and arts also maintained their sponsorship during the Great Depression. The Harmon Foundation, the organization that awarded the Harmon Medals, sponsored the successful exhibition of paintings and sculptures by African-American artists at the National Gallery.

The end of the 1930s coincided with the close of the Harlem Renaissance. While the looming reality of a second World War contributed greatly to the end of the vital arts and cultural movement, the cumulative arts production during that decade suggests that the artists and national movement prevailed in the face of the Great Depression.

Bibliography

Dodson, Howard, Christopher Moore, and Roberta Yancy. The Black New Yorkers: The Schomburg Illustrated Chronology. New York: John Wiley & Sons, Inc., 2000.

McElvaine, Robert S. The Great Depression: America, 1929–1941. New York: Times Books, 1984.

Thomas, Gordon, and Max Morgan-Witts. The Day the Bubble Burst: A Social History of the Wall Street Crash of 1929. Garden City, N.Y.: Doubleday, 1979.

Watkins, T. H. (Tom H.) The Hungry Years: A Narrative History of the Great Depression in America. New York: Henry Holt & Company, 1999.

Green, Paul (1894–1981)

One of the most visible white writers and playwrights of the Harlem Renaissance era and author of plays hailed for their representations of African-American life and identity. He was born near Lillington, North Carolina, in 1894 and taught school in his rural community before enrolling at the University at Chapel Hill. Green left college in 1917 to join World War I. During his enlistment, which he began at the rank of private, he rose through the ranks. He left having achieved the rank of sergeant-major. After the war, he returned to school, graduated with a degree in philosophy, and pursued further study in the field at Cornell University. He joined the faculty at his undergraduate alma mater, where he eventually became a professor of dramatic art. He received prestigious awards for his scholarship and creative writing, including the GUGGENHEIM FELLOWSHIP. In 1979 he became the dramatist laureate of North Carolina.

Green's playwriting debut was stupendous. His first staged work, IN ABRAHAM'S BOSOM (1927), won the PULITZER PRIZE in drama. Additional plays were Broadway successes and included a theatrical version of RICHARD WRIGHT's NATIVE SON. He also wrote film scripts, and his credits include the script for *Black Like Me*, based on the autobiographical story of John Griffiths.

Like JULIA PETERKIN, Green believed that his works on African-American life were shaped by his early exposure to people of color. He recalled, in a somewhat romanticized manner, that his "first memories [were] of negro ballads ringing out by moonlight and the rich laughter of the resting blacks, down by the river bottom." His works reflected his deep ties to North Carolina and his interest in racial politics. His biographer Barrett Clark suggests that the play *White Dresses* (1920) was the first to reveal "unmistakable signs of genius." The plot centered on a young white man whose father prevents him from marrying a young woman of color. To prevent any interracial union, the white patriarch arranges for the girl to marry an African-American man against her will. The girl's grandmother counsels her to accept her fate, in large part because it appears that her white true love is in fact her half brother.

Green's work returned to the themes of families in disarray, miscegenation, and thwarted love relationships. The play *In Abraham's Bosom* (1927) revisited these themes as it traced one man's efforts to provide education for his African-American community. By the play's end, the aspiring teacher has inadvertently killed his white half brother. Green's flair for tragic story lines and evocative scenes brought new intensity to the Harlem Renaissance drama community and the larger theater world.

Bibliography

Clark, Barrett. *Paul Green*. New York: Robert M. McBride & Company, 1928.

Krasner, David. *A Beautiful Pageant: African American Theatre, Drama, and Performance in the Harlem Renaissance, 1910–1927*. New York: Palgrave Macmillan, 2002.

Roper, John. *Paul Green, Playwright of the Real South*. Athens: University of Georgia Press, 2003.

Green Pastures, The: A Fable Marc Connelly (1930)

A PULITZER PRIZE–winning play by the white dramatist MARC CONNELLY that delivered an African-American perspective on the Old Testament. The script was based on *Ol' Man Adam an' His Chillun*, a collection of short stories by the white Tennessean Roark Bradford. Bradford, like RIDGELEY TORRENCE, used childhood encounters with African Americans to influence his stories of African-American life.

The Green Pastures opened at the Mansfield Theatre on BROADWAY in February 1930 and had a record run of 640 shows. It won the Pulitzer Prize for Drama later that year. *The Green Pastures* enjoyed five national tours, and in February 1935 it returned to Broadway for 73 shows at the 44th Street Theatre. In 1936 Connelly and the William Keighley produced the film version starring Rex Ingram and George Reed. The play was revived in March and April 1951. Marc Connelly directed the 44 performances that were staged at the Broadway Theatre, and Robert Edmond Jones, the director who worked with a number of African-American-related dramas, was the production designer.

The play's reception confirms that the play appealed to Harlem Renaissance–era audiences. While the theater-going public turned out in droves, many African Americans regarded the work as patronizing and driven by racial stereotypes. Influential figures such as such as W. E. B. DUBOIS and ZORA NEALE HURSTON, however, disagreed with Bradford and Connelly's representation of African-American life and thought. In his August 1930 *CRISIS* review of the play, DuBois suggested that "the difficulty with the Negro on the American stage, is that the white audience . . . demands caricatures" and urged African Americans to protest "the incompleteness of art expression . . . the embargo which white wealth lays on full Negro expression." Two years later, in a summer 1932 letter to NAACP secretary WALTER WHITE and his wife Gladys, Hurston, discussing one of her own folk stories projects, voiced her frustration with *The Green Pastures* and other white-authored works that purported to offer reliable windows into black life. "I want the reader to see why Negroes tell such glorious tales," she wrote. "He has more images within his skull than any other human in circulation. That is why it makes me furious when some ham like . . . Roark Bradford gets off a nothing else but and calls it a high spot of Negro humor and imagery." According to Hurston biographer Valerie Boyd, the accomplished anthropologist writer characterized the play as a "swell sensation" that failed to provide real insights. "Nothing like work and bossy white folks in our heavenly concept," declared Hurston.

Bibliography
Boyd, Valerie. *Wrapped in Rainbows: The Life of Zora Neale Hurston.* New York: Scribner, 2003.

Kaplan, Carla. *Zora Neale Hurston: A Life in Letters.* New York: Doubleday, 2002.

Green Thursday Julia Mood Peterkin (1924)
A collection of short stories written by the teacher and PULITZER PRIZE–winning writer JULIA MOOD PETERKIN. Knopf published the collection, whose title refers also to the Christian holy day of Pentecost. A white native of South Carolina, Peterkin's collection of sketches and short fiction was inspired by her experiences of plantation life on Lang Syne, her family estate.

The vignettes followed the tragic and difficult lives of a family on a small, South Carolina farm. Together, Kildee, his wife Rose, and children Jim, Rose, Sis, and Missie experience loss, love, and domestic trials. Kildee, whose name refers to the killdeer, an African bird, is perpetually thwarted in his ability to farm and make a profit. Determined to triumph, he ignores the community superstition about doing any type of fieldwork on Green Thursday. In the days that follow his inauspicious plowing, his family suffers greatly. He and his wife watch their infant daughter die of burns, and the family descends into a disheartening routine of mistrust and suppressed emotions.

The initial run of 2,000 copies sold out quickly, and more than 5,000 were eventually sold. Peterkin was hailed for her humanizing images of African Americans. *Green Thursday* sharply contrasted the racial stereotypes produced in much white-authored literature of the day. Peterkin received encouragement from the NATIONAL ASSOCIATION FOR THE ADVANCEMENT OF COLORED PEOPLE (NAACP). WALTER WHITE penned a

glowing review of the work, and the NAACP distributed the article to some 200 newspapers. White also sent an autographed copy of his novel *FIRE IN THE FLINT* with a congratulatory note to Peterkin. The September 1924 *NEW YORK TIMES* review of the volume hailed Peterkin as "a literary artist, without any prejudice except the saving artistic predilection for unity and coherent form." *Green Thursday,* proposed the reviewer, reflected "the distillation of a rich, human observation of the secret life of a people who have not yet been understood by the whites, because the whites have always found it easier to laugh at it than to attempt to comprehend it."

Peterkin's work was evocative of Paul Laurence Dunbar's *Sport of the Gods* as well as the local-color fiction of CHARLES CHESNUTT. She succeeded in departing from the tradition of plantation literature and demonstrating the ways in which literature had yet to fully explore African-American identity, history, and culture.

Bibliography
Landess, Tom. *Julia Peterkin.* Boston: Twayne Publishers, 1976.

Williams, Susan Millar. *A Devil and a Good Woman, Too: The Lives of Julia Peterkin.* Athens: University of Georgia Press: 1997.

Greenwich Village
The site of numerous literary, artistic, cultural, and political encounters and events that contributed to the flowering of the Harlem Renaissance. The area in lower Manhattan is located between 14th Street and Houston Street, and stretches west from Washington Square to the Hudson River. The Village, as it is also called, lies west of BROADWAY. It has a long-standing African-American arts history that informs and enriches its Harlem Renaissance history. It was in this area of the city that the African Grove Theatre was located. Founded by a West Indian ice cream parlor owner, the venue was home to the nation's first professional African-American theater troupe, and the site in which famed Negro tragedian and Shakespearean actor IRA ALDRIDGE performed.

Greenwich Village was a Native American marshland that was cleared by Dutch settlers and

Africans enslaved by the Dutch during the early 17th century. In 1713, the area was named Grin'wich, and by the 1780s, the area known as Washington Square Park functioned as a potter's field, or cemetery for indigents, and as an area in which public hangings were conducted. The University of the City of New York, renamed NEW YORK UNIVERSITY in 1896, was established there in April 1831, and its campus encircles the scenic Washington Square Park that also is known for its distinctive arch. Artists and writers congregated in Greenwich Village, and the area became synonymous with avant-garde art and cutting-edge journals and magazines. During the Prohibition era, Greenwich Village was home to numerous speakeasies. Known during the 1920s and 1930s for its bohemian communities, Greenwich Village also was known as a sexually liberated area in which homosexual, lesbian, and bisexual men and women could socialize. During the 1930s the Village also became an enclave for art galleries.

Greenwich Village, HARLEM, and Broadway were among the most vibrant areas of New York City during the 1920s and 1930s. It was in Greenwich Village that CLAUDE MCKAY immersed himself in friendships with MAX EASTMAN and others. The phenomenally talented sculptor RICHMOND BARTHÉ had his studios on West 14th Street in Greenwich Village. It was there that RALPH ELLISON, new to New York City, began studying with the artist who was hailed then as the most accomplished African-American sculptor in history. Ellison moved into the Village shortly after arriving in New York City to raise funds for his senior year at TUSKEGEE INSTITUTE.

Gregory, Thomas Montgomery
(1887–1971)

A teacher, activist, World War I veteran, writer, and one of the first judges for the first literary contest organized by OPPORTUNITY, the literary journal affiliated with the NATIONAL URBAN LEAGUE.

Gregory was born in WASHINGTON, D.C., on 31 August 1887. His father, James Monroe Gregory, was the first student to enroll in the College Department of HOWARD UNIVERSITY. In 1872 he was the valedictorian and one of the three men who graduated in the school's first class. He joined the university faculty as a Latin and mathematics instructor. He eventually became a full professor of Latin and served as dean of the school. James Gregory earned a master's degree from HARVARD UNIVERSITY in 1885, two years before the birth of his son. James Gregory met Frederick Douglass at the family home in New Bedford, the community in which the newly emancipated Douglass had settled with his wife and family.

T. Montgomery Gregory's mother, Fannie Emma Hagan, was a Howard University alumna and devoted much time to students during her husband's tenure on the faculty at Howard. Fannie Hagan met her husband when she enrolled in one of his classes at Howard; they were married one year later in December 1873. Born on July 4, 1856, in Frederick, Maryland, she was a descendant of Robert Brook Taney, the white Supreme Court Chief Justice who ruled in favor of slavery and against enslaved people in the 1859 Dred Scott decision. Fannie Hagan's mother, Margaret, was purchased from the Taney family by a Madagascar native and member of the island country's ruling elite who encountered her during a sojourn in the South.

In 1897, when Gregory was 10, his father James was appointed director of the Bordentown Industrial and Manual Training School, and the family relocated to Bordentown, New Jersey. Gregory continued his education at the prestigious Williston Seminary in Easthampton, Massachusetts, from 1902 through 1906.

Gregory graduated from Harvard University in 1910, a member of the class that also included writer T. S. Eliot. While in Cambridge, he excelled in debate and became captain of the varsity debating team. He accepted a faculty position in the English Department at Howard, his parents' alma mater. He was forced to resign in 1912 following a controversial social incident but was reinstated one year later. When World War I began, he was instrumental in overcoming segregationalist army policies. His efforts to establish an Officer's Training Corp program for African Americans was successful, and the program opened at Fort Des Moines, Iowa. He was assigned to the Military Intelligence division during the war and served at the rank of first lieutenant.

In 1918 Gregory married Hugh Ella Hancock. The couple had six children, who advanced further the family tradition of academic and professional excellence. Daughter Yvonne became a published writer and poet whose works appeared in notable anthologies such as ARNA BONTEMPS's *The Negro Poet*. Sons Eugene and Thomas Montgomery, Jr. followed the example of their father and grandfather and graduated from Harvard in 1897 and 1944, respectively. Their son Hugh was a member of the accomplished Tuskegee Airmen, and his daughter Yvonne is a published writer and poet whose works appeared in notable anthologies such as Arna Bontemps's *The Negro Poet*. The Gregory family also included daughters Mignon and Sheila. The family history of achievement continues today. Nephew Frederick Gregory, a Vietnam veteran, became the first African-American commander of a space shuttle flight when he led a 1989 mission aboard the shuttle *Discovery*. In 2002, he became the chief operating officer at NASA. A grandson of T. Montgomery and Hugh Ella Gregory, Ernest Wilson III, followed the family tradition of attending Harvard. He graduated in 1970 and most recently was a member of the National Security Council during the Clinton administration and his sister Wendy is a USAID representative in Senegal.

During his tenure at Howard, Gregory's professional life in Washington, D.C., took on increasingly public dimensions as he developed new theater opportunities at and beyond the school. In 1919, the year in which he was appointed head of the English department, he founded the HOWARD UNIVERSITY PLAYERS. During the next few years, he made important inroads in American theater and developed major possibilities for African-American actors and dramatists. He promoted work by Howard University students and administrators. In 1920 May Miller, a Howard student and daughter of Kelly Miller, the university's dean, saw her play *Within the Shadow* produced by the Howard University Players. Student OTTIE GRAHAM completed *The King's Carpenters* and *Holiday,* published in THE STYLUS and in THE CRISIS, respectively. In 1921, when he became the first chair of the Dramatic Art and Public Speaking division at the university, Gregory oversaw a symbolic, though not well-attended, production of THE EMPEROR JONES. The show featured Charles Gilpin, the actor who had garnered much praise for his performances in the New York shows produced by

the play's creator, Eugene O'Neill. Gilpin appeared in the powerful title role, and members of the Howard University Players were cast in supporting roles. The event showcased Gregory's ambitious plans to develop a National Negro Theatre. Such an organization would not only foster new talent but also would provide vital support for productions by and about African Americans. These same ambitions fueled Gregory's involvement with the Drama Committee of the National Association for the Advancement of Colored People (NAACP). The committee staged *Rachel* (1916), the lynching drama by Angelina Weld Grimké, at the Myrtilla Miner Normal School in Washington, D.C., on March 3 and 4, 1916. It was the first nonmusical play since the *Drama of King Shotaway* (1823) to be written and performed by African Americans.

In 1924, Gregory was the director of the Dramatics Department at Howard University, his alma mater. He incorporated popular Harlem Renaissance–era dramas into the performance schedule of the Howard University Players. He did not hesitate to feature good works by white playwrights. In addition to staging *The Emperor Jones*, he and the Howard University Players produced RIDGELY TORRENCE's SIMON, THE CYRENIAN for attendees at the World Disarmament Conference.

In addition to directing theater productions and teaching drama, Gregory wrote abou plays and literature throughout the Harlem Renaissance. He coedited PLAYS OF NEGRO LIFE with ALAIN LOCKE, a fellow Harvard University graduate and English department faculty member at Howard. He had partnered with Locke before, when the two founded the *Stylus* literary club at Howard. *Plays of Negro Life* included illustrations and decorations by AARON DOUGLAS and scripts relating to African-American life written by established and emerging playwrights. The volume featured works by four women and 10 men, including GEORGIA DOUGLAS JOHNSON's PLUMES, EUGENE O'NEILL's *The Emperor Jones* and *The Dreamy Kid,* JEAN TOOMER's BALO, Ridgely Torrence's GRANNY MAUMEE, and EULALIE SPENCE's THE STARTER. Locke and Gregory used the volume to call attention to the innovative ways in which African-American actors, playwrights, and subjects were a vital part of what they called "native American drama." Both editors stressed the importance of small Negro theater companies and called for "inner freedom" for Negro dramatists and plays. The editors challenged the social expectations and generic limitations that confronted African Americans. The most promising solution for African-American development, argued Locke, lay in the "folk play," a "rare" form whose value lay in its "deep spiritual penetration into the heart and spirit of Negro life."

Throughout his career, Gregory articulated provocative philosophies about American theater and the African-American dramatic tradition. In 1915 he considered the vital link between racial uplift and artistic achievement in *The Citizen,* a Boston-based journal on whose editorial board he served with poet and writer WILLIAM STANLEY BRAITHWAITE. In 1927 his essay entitled "A Chronology of the Negro Theatre" concluded *Plays of Negro Life,* his coedited volume with Locke. In his assessment of African-American dramatic history, Gregory celebrated the visibility of African-American drama and the fact that it was "now recognized as an important factor in the development of a native American drama." He offered an absorbing retrospective account of the black presence in American theater and celebrated the accomplishments of white and African American dramatists and writers alike. He praised the Hapgood Players, the group founded by theater patron and philanthropist EMILIE HAPGOOD, the 1913 historical pageant entitled *The Star of Ethiopia* that W. E. B. DUBOIS wrote and produced, and called attention to his March 1916 collaborative triumph with the NAACP Drama Committee when they staged Grimké's *Rachel.* He concluded on a note of hard-won satisfaction, pleased that "The New York stage, at least, has evidently come to the point where the Negro play is no longer the season's novelty or exception, but quite on the other hand one of the characteristic features of the developing drama of native themes and manufacture."

T. Montgomery Gregory resigned from Howard University in 1924 to become supervisor of Negro Schools in Atlantic City, New Jersey. He continued to advocate the power and importance of African-American dramatic contributions until his retirement in 1956. He was struck down by leukemia and passed away in Washington, D.C., on 21 November 1971.

Bibliography

Frontline: "Secret Daughter." PBS. Available online. URL: http://www.pbs.org/wgbh/pages/frontline/shows/secret/. Accessed May 20, 2005.

Gregory, Montgomery. "The Drama of Negro Life." In *The New Negro,* edited by Alain Locke. 1925, reprint, New York: Athenaeum, 1968.

Sollors, Werner, Caldwell Titcomb, and Thomas Underwood. *Blacks at Harvard: A Documentary History of African-American Experience at Harvard and Radcliffe.* New York: New York University Press, 1993.

Grimké, Angelina Emily Weld (1880–1958)

A Bostonian, poet, dramatist, writer, and teacher whose namesake was her paternal great-aunt Angelina Grimké, one of two ardent white abolitionist sisters from South Carolina. Grimké produced stirring dramas and short fiction that underscored the violence and devastation of LYNCHING. Her literary activism, for which she is best known, was informed by her family's documented history of abolitionist protest and public service.

Born in BOSTON in February 1880 to ARCHIBALD GRIMKÉ and Sarah Stanley Grimké, Angelina benefited from her father's active participation in prominent Boston legal, social, and political circles. Her aunts Angelina and Sarah Grimké sought out Archibald and his brother Francis when the sisters discovered that the children were the illegitimate mixed-race offspring of their slaveholding brother Henry. The sisters, whose antislavery work prompted their family to disinherit them, supported the education of the two boys. Archibald, a graduate of LINCOLN UNIVERSITY, graduated from HARVARD UNIVERSITY Law School in 1874. He was a respected attorney, American consul to Santo-Domingo, activist, editor, and writer whose biographies of Boston abolitionists William Lloyd Garrison and Charles Sumner were highly regarded. Before his death in 1930, Grimké won the SPINGARN MEDAL for his lifelong efforts to protect African-American rights. Angelina's uncle Francis pursued a career in the ministry and married Charlotte Forten, the PHILADELPHIA-born teacher who worked closely with post–Civil War freed peoples in the South Carolina Sea Islands. Charlotte Forten Grimké also distinguished herself in Salem, Massachusetts, where she was the city's first African-American teacher of white pupils.

Angelina Grimké came of age in Boston and enjoyed close family relations with the family of Theodore Weld, her great-aunt Angelina's husband. She had opportunities to interact with members of Boston's active African-American community; her father was president of the city branch of the NATIONAL ASSOCIATION FOR THE ADVANCEMENT OF COLORED PEOPLE (NAACP) and later became vice president of the organization. In 1902, after completing her early education at prestigious preparatory schools, including Carleton Academy in Northfield, Minnesota, Cushing Academy in Ashburnham, Massachusetts, and at the Boston Normal School of Gymnastics, which later became the Department of Hygiene at Wellesley College, Grimké relocated to Washington, D.C., and began teaching English in public high schools. In 1902, she began a five-year career at Armstrong Manual Training School before moving in 1907 to the prestigious M Street High School, the institution that became DUNBAR HIGH SCHOOL in 1916 and counted ANNA JULIA COOPER and JESSIE FAUSET among its faculty.

Grimké produced much of her writing during the Harlem Renaissance era. Her reputation as a talented writer was confirmed on the eve of the Renaissance. The drama committee of the NAACP chose her lynching drama *Rachel* (1916) as the piece that best exemplified successful race plays. It was staged at the Myrtilla Miner Normal School in Washington, D.C., and contributed much to the intense debates about the nature and focus of African-American writing. Grimké published *Rachel* in 1920. Seven years later, the work appeared in *PLAYS OF NEGRO LIFE* (1927), coedited by NAACP member T. MONTGOMERY GREGORY and his HOWARD UNIVERSITY colleague ALAIN LOCKE.

Rachel focused on the evolution of a sentimental young woman and the distressing epiphanies she experienced as she confronted the evils of the world around her. Ultimately, Rachel, a loving woman on the verge of marriage and motherhood, makes painful, isolating decisions about her own future. She vows never to marry and declares that she has no interest in having children who would have to survive a world of intense racial hatred. The family, whose deeply ironic surname is "Loving," lives in an unidentified Northern city. The widowed mother Mrs. Loving and her two children, Tom and Rachel,

are grappling with the endemic racism and disenfranchisement that undermined much African-American progress in post–Civil War America. Mrs. Loving discloses the tragic story of her husband's death at the hands of a lynch mob.

Over the course of the play, Rachel is devastated by the story of her father's death and outraged further by the treatment that her young adopted son endures at school. She withdraws from public life. She ends her engagement to a devoted young man and develops an emphatic and problematic solution to racial harassment. The young woman who once told her mother that she "love[d] little black and brown babies best of all" and that she "pray[ed] God every night to give [her] . . . little black and brown babies to protect and guard," ultimately suppresses her own maternal instincts as a means to preserve her sanity and self. The play closes with Rachel's wrenching vows of abstinence and total self-control.

Rachel was produced at least two more times after its Washington, D.C., debut and included shows at St. Bartholomew's Church in Cambridge, Massachusetts, and at the Neighborhood Playhouse in New York City. The Grimké papers also reveal that a number of nonprofit and community organizations solicited Grimké for the permission to stage the play. In a letter to her father, Grimké also made reference to a national production of the play and an effort to secure the actor George Gliss for a part in the play. *Rachel* had a deep effect on those who saw it. According to Grimké biographer Gloria Hull, the sculptor Meta Vaux Warrick was moved to write Grimké after she saw the work in Cambridge. Warrick wanted the playwright to know just "how thoroughly you reached me" and mused about how deeply she was struck by the play's "bitterness," and "underlying current of sweetness and delicacy" (Hull, 119). In his 1927 essay on the history of African-American theater, T. Montgomery Gregory, chair of the Howard University English department, recalled that the program for the Washington, D.C., production of Grimké's play signaled its explicit political, rather than artistic, agenda. It stated proudly that the work was ". . . the first attempt to use the stage for race propaganda in order to enlighten the American people relative to the lamentable condition of ten millions of Colored citizens in this free republic." Despite such a clear statement, the committee was divided about racial propaganda in literary and artistic works. While Gregory was part of the NAACP drama committee that arranged for *Rachel's* debut, the play also spurred him to pursue less political and more aesthetic dramatic ventures. He was the Howard University faculty member who was instrumental in the development of the college's drama department.

Grimké's dramas and short fiction were insistently political. In works like *Mara,* her second and final play, and in short stories like "The Closing Door," protagonists struggled to control their bodies in a society that preyed upon the black body and subjected it to lynching and psychological tortures. Grimké revisited themes of self-sacrifice, infanticide, and abstinence. Scholars continue to discuss the circumstances that led to the publication of "The Closing Door" in an 1919 issue of *Birth Control Review.* The journal, which was founded by Margaret Sanger in 1917, provided information about the birth control movement, reprinted Sanger's speeches, and addressed a number of topics relating to women's health.

Grimké's short story revisited *Rachel's* themes of self-restraint and suppression of maternal desires. While it was not a conventional message about birth control, the editors invited Grimké to provide another story. She submitted "Goldie," a story that returned to the terrors of lynching, inspired by a horrific and documented account of a Georgia lynch mob's murder of a pregnant woman and her unborn child.

Grimké published widely in the periodical press before and throughout the Harlem Renaissance. Her poems were featured in the *Boston Sunday Globe* and *Boston Transcript* as well as other newspapers in Virginia such as the *Norfolk Gazette.* In the 1920s she published several poems in *Opportunity,* including "Little Grey Dreams," "Death," "Dusk," and "The Black Finger." Her poems were included in important anthologies, most notably *The New Negro* (1925) edited by Alain Locke and Caroling Dusk (1927) edited by Countee Cullen.

The themes of Grimké's poetry contrast the sobering themes of self-sacrifice, infanticide, and sexual abstinence in her plays and fiction. The majority of her poems revolve around romance, although they do focus on longing and unrequited love. Works such as "El Beso," "The Eyes of My Regret," and "A Mona Lisa" reflect Grimké's deeply romantic sensibility and her unabashed study of human emotions. Like other poets of the Harlem Renaissance, Grimké invokes the natural world and uses it to generate powerful metaphors of female desire and loss.

Scholars have concluded that Grimké, who never wed or bore children, was a lesbian who was unable to fully explore her sexuality in early 20th-century America. Gloria Hull notes that the subjects of Grimké's love poems are women and that these works provide valuable hints about the poet's personal relationships and more general perspectives on relationships. In her detailed critical study of Grimké, Hull cites an unpublished poem in which the speaker declares, "Rose whose heart unfolds, red petaled / Prick her slow heart's stir / Tell her white, gold, red my love is— / And for her, —for her." Hull and scholar Carolivia Herron concur that Grimké was involved with Mamie Burrill, one of her schoolmates. Despite Grimké's request that Burrill be her wife, however, the intense relationship did not last.

Angelina Weld Grimké passed away on 10 June 1958. She was one of the more enigmatic figures to contribute to the Harlem Renaissance. She enriched the literary and artistic communities of Boston and Washington, D.C. Her works reflected a powerful feminist political aesthetic and positioned her at the center of deliberate Harlem Renaissance debates about literary activism and racial uplift.

Bibliography

Angelina Weld Grimké Papers, Manuscript Division, Moorland-Spingarn Research Center, Howard University Library.

Grimké, Angelina W. "A Biographical Sketch of Archibald Grimké." *Opportunity, a Journal of Negro Life* (3 Feb. 1925): 44–47.

Herron, Carolivia, ed. *Selected Works of Angelina Weld Grimké.* New York: Oxford University Press, 1991.

Hull, Gloria T. *Color, Sex, and Poetry: Three Women Writers of the Harlem Renaissance.* Bloomington: Indiana University Press, 1987.

Grimké, Archibald (1849–1930)

The father of Harlem Renaissance poet and playwright Angelina Emily Weld Grimké was one of

BOSTON's most accomplished lawyers, historians, and activists. He was one of three sons born to the enslaved Nancy Weston and her owner, Henry Grimké of South Carolina. He enrolled at LINCOLN UNIVERSITY and earned bachelor's and master's degrees before attending HARVARD UNIVERSITY Law School, from which he graduated in 1874. During his career, he served as consul to Santo Domingo, editor of the *Boston Hub,* and member of the AMERICAN NEGRO ACADEMY, a prestigious intellectual society that Alexander Crummell founded in 1897.

Grimké produced the majority of his published work in the decades before the Harlem Renaissance. These included biographies of William Lloyd Garrison and Charles Sumner, prominent Bostonians and ardent abolitionists. He was, however, actively involved in organizations that were at the core of the movement. In Boston he was the chapter president of the NATIONAL ASSOCIATION FOR THE ADVANCEMENT OF COLORED PEOPLE (NAACP). He later served as vice president of the national organization. The NAACP honored Grimké in 1919 when it awarded him the SPINGARN MEDAL, a prize given to outstanding figures for their impressive contributions to African-American progress and uplift.

Bibliography

Bruce, Dickson. *Archibald Grimké: Portrait of a Black Independent.* Baton Rouge: Louisiana State University Press, 1993.

Grimké, Angelina W. "A Biographical Sketch of Archibald Grimké." *Opportunity* (February 1925): 44–47.

"Grist in the Mill" Wallace Thurman (1926)

A brusque short story by WALLACE THURMAN. It provides acerbic and impatient profiles of the central characters, none of whom seem to possess agency enough to be called protagonists. Colonel Charles Summers and his wife are white southerners who embody the old South. Thurman characterizes the Colonel as "an anachronistic relic from pre-civil war days, being one of those rare sons of a dyed-in-the-wool southern father who had retained all the traditionary characteristics of his patrician papa." Mrs. Summers fares no better. Her servants refer to her as "Worrisum bitch," and she fails to participate in important decisions regarding her husband's health.

When the Colonel is injured during a raid on a gambling camp, he sustains injuries that require a blood transfusion. His wife fails to recommend a suitable donor, and unbeknownst to him, he receives blood from a transient and perennially unlucky man named Zacharia. The hospital staff save the Colonel's life, but because of his stingy ways, they take a perverse pleasure in replenishing, but tainting, his blood with that of an African-American donor.

The accident that injures the Colonel occurs at the same time that Zacharia is caught in a gambling raid and imprisoned for disorderly conduct. He acts the part of the accidental prisoner. He is more intrigued with the sock of coins that he won in the interrupted gambling session than he is about his lasting incarceration in the local jail. In the absence of a real villain, Zacharia is tried and found guilty for the death of a deputy sheriff. On the eve of his execution, Zacharia's request to see the Colonel is granted. Again, this occurs through happenstance. The interview does not succeed in protecting Zacharia, who appears to petition the Colonel for protection. He makes his claim because it is his blood that saved the colonel's life. The Colonel eventually dies of the shock but not before he checks his body for signs of color or finds himself haunted by birds that seem to be cawing the word *nigaw.*

Thurman's tale of stark realism suggests an impatience with social stigma and imagined trauma. "Grist in the Mill" is a disturbing story of two men who both face death and have the power to help each other avoid it. While Thurman exposes the tragic implications of racism and mob law, he also suggests that a wicked fatalism rules the world. The opening lines of the story confirm the tale's inevitable tragedy. "This is indeed an accidental cosmos," writes Thurman. "And to make matters more intriguing, more terrifying, there seems to be a universal accompaniment of mocking laughter, coming from the ethereal regions as well as from the more mundane spheres." Such lines convey the author's dismay and the story's depiction of senseless tragedy and the life-threatening dimensions of enforced racial segregation.

Bibliography

Notten, Eleonore van. *Wallace Thurman's Harlem Renaissance.* Amsterdam: Rodopi, 1994.

Thurman, Wallace. "Grist in the Mill." Richard Barksdale and Kenneth Kinnamon, eds. *Black Writers of America: A Comprehensive Anthology.* Englewood Cliffs, N.J.: Prentice Hall, 1972.

Guggenheim Fellowship

A prestigious fellowship awarded to promising scholars and artists. It was established in 1925 by the Guggenheim family, whose patriarch John Simon Guggenheim was the son of Swiss immigrants. The family made their wealth through a successful lace import business and in silver mining. Awards are distributed to individuals working in a broad number of fields.

The Guggenheim Foundation is among an impressive set of American philanthropic organizations that made deliberate efforts to support African-American arts and scholarship. During the Harlem Renaissance, a number of writers received critical support and endorsement from Guggenheim, as well as from the HARMON FOUNDATION and the ROSENWALD fund. Until recently, it was possible to win more than once, and Harlem Renaissance figures like PAUL GREEN, ZORA NEALE HURSTON, and ERIC WALROND were among those who did.

Winners are selected on the basis of published work and demonstrated excellence in the humanities, social sciences, and sciences. In 1927 WALTER WHITE became the first African American to win an award; his was based on his probing fiction about LYNCHING. In 1930 NELLA LARSEN was the first African-American woman awarded the fellowship. Between 1927 and 1940, awards in literature were made to STERLING BROWN, COUNTEE CULLEN, Paul Green, LANGSTON HUGHES, Zora Neale Hurston, Nella Larsen, and Eric Walrond. E. FRANKLIN FRAZIER won for his work in sociology, and Miguel Covarrubias won the fellowship for his accomplishments in fine arts.

Recipients use the generous stipend to support creative ventures, travel, and literary endeavors. Countee Cullen used his 1928 fellowship to finance a productive and restorative sojourn in France. During his Guggenheim year, he completed THE BLACK CHRIST AND OTHER POEMS.

Langston Hughes planned to use his $1,500 monthly fellowship stipend to support himself as he completed research for a historical novel based on the Haymarket Riot of 1886.

Zora Neale Hurston won back-to-back fellowships in 1936 and 1937. In her letter of acceptance, Hurston declared that it was her "earnest hope and . . . firm determination to add something to human understanding and to art" as a result of being selected. She used her first award to finance a six-month study of the Maroons in Jamaica. She used this research in *Tell My Horse* (1938). Her second award facilitated an eventful though physically debilitating residence in Haiti. She arrived there in March 1937 to complete work on hoodoo practices. In September 1944 she wrote to Dr. Henry Allen Moe of the Foundation asking for consideration of a third application. "I want a recording machine this time, and a good camera to take along," she wrote in a forthright plea. Scholar Carla Kaplan, editor of the first published collection of Hurston's letters, reveals that Hurston's references often threatened to undermine the writer-anthropologist's applications. Both FANNIE HURST and Ruth Benedict suggested that Hurston did not have the discipline to conduct independent fieldwork. The author's publications and use of the fellowships, however, proved them wrong. Hurston's correspondence with the foundation, and in particular with Secretary Moe, reveal the foundation's steady belief in the artists' creative freedom. These documents also illuminate the ways in which the fellowship enriched the intellectual life and pursuits of its recipients.

Bibliography

Davis, John. *The Guggenheims (1848–1988): An American Epic.* New York: Morrow, 1978.

Kaplan, Carla. *Zora Neale Hurston: A Life in Letters.* New York: Doubleday, 2002.

Tanselle, G. Thomas, Peter F. Kardon, and Eunice R. Schwager, eds. *The John Simon Guggenheim Memorial Foundation 1925–2000: A Seventy-fifth Anniversary Record.* New York: John Simon Guggenheim Memorial Foundation, 2001.

Gumby Book Studio Quarterly

A short-lived journal produced by Alexander Gumby, an avid collector of Harlem Renaissance materials. The first and only issue appeared in 1930–31. The publication shared its name with Gumby's legendary Harlem Book Studio on FIFTH AVENUE. The site was an impressive repository of clippings, documents, and materials produced by and relating to Harlem Renaissance figures. Like other engaging figures such as A'LELIA WALKER and GEORGIA DOUGLAS JOHNSON, Gumby's home and studios became lively meeting places for artists, writers, and people interested in the movement.

The Depression had devastating effects on the man nicknamed "The Count" because of his self-indulgence and delight in entertaining. His papers and galley proofs of the magazine are part of the Alexander Gumby scrapbook collection held in the Rare Books and Manuscript Library at COLUMBIA UNIVERSITY.

Gurdjieff, Georges Ivanovitch (1872–1949)

A mystic and teacher whose doctrine emphasized the individual's search for wholeness, the suppression of negative thoughts and feelings, and the exploration of human consciousness on many levels. Born in Armenia to Greek parents, he traveled extensively throughout Europe, Asia, and the United States. His lengthy and intense studies with Buddhist and Sufi teachers enabled him to realize his powers as a spiritual leader and teacher. Following his marriage to Russian Countess Ostrowsky, he established himself in Paris. Gurdjieff founded the Institute for the Harmonious Development of Man in Fontainebleu, FRANCE. The organization attracted a number of prominent figures including the writers HART CRANE, JEAN TOOMER, and Katherine Mansfield.

Toomer is the best-known Harlem Renaissance–era follower of Gurdjieff's teachings. Toomer was introduced first to P. D. Ouspensky, a student of Gurdjieff's, whose ideas were popular among American literary and scholarly circles. Intrigued by the per-

spectives on a heightened receptivity and communion with the universe, Toomer spent the summer of 1924 in France at the Institute for the Harmonious Development of Man. Despite the unpredictable and sometimes alarming protocols of the place, Toomer became further convinced of the relevance and power of the mystic's teachings. He pledged to disseminate Gurdjieff's philosophies in the United States.

When he returned, Toomer organized lectures, supervised dances that incorporated movements choreographed by the mystic, and contributed substantial sums of money to the cause. In New York, Toomer's peers initially responded with interest to his sessions on Gurdjieff's teachings. WALLACE THURMAN, AARON DOUGLAS, and NELLA LARSEN were among those who attended some of the first meetings that Toomer organized. Widespread interest, however, was difficult to achieve, and as scholar Eleonore van Notten notes, Toomer's emphasis on racial transcendence may have alienated potential converts who also were proud race men and women. Toomer eventually became disenchanted with the organization. Finally frustrated with the financial demands that increased as the 1930s progressed, he broke ties with his spiritual teacher and the organization.

Gurdjieff's teachings continue to influence contemporary society. Organizations such as the West Virginia–based Claymont Society for Continuous Education preserve the mystic's legacy and philosophies.

Bibliography

Gurdjieff, George I. *All and Everything.* 3 vols. London: Routledge & Kegan, 1974.

Kerman, Cynthia Earl, and Richard Eldridge. *The Lives of Jean Toomer: A Hunger for Wholeness.* Baton Rouge: Louisiana State University Press, 1987.

Webb, James. *The Harmonious Circle.* New York: G. P. Putnam's Sons, 1980.

H

Haiti

A Caribbean country that shares with the Domican Republic the island of Hispaniola. After Columbus's arrival there in 1492, French, British, and Spanish forces sought to colonize the island that was known as Saint-Domingue and Santo Domingo. In 1791 Haitians, led initially by Toussaint Louverture, overthrew and eventually ousted the French, whose military forces were directed by Napoleon Bonaparte. In 1804, the nation of Haiti was established. Led by General Jean-Jacques Dessalines, it became the first black country to recover its independence from colonial forces. Its historic example of successful slave uprisings and black political autonomy inspired enslaved communities and threatened pro-slavery governments and supporters in the United States. As a result, it was not until 1862, one year after the American Civil War began, that Frederick Douglass, the formerly enslaved American orator and statesman, became the first consular minister sent to Haiti by the United States. American military forces, on orders from President Woodrow Wilson, occupied the island from 1915 until 1934.

Haiti figured prominently in the research and literary imagination of Harlem Renaissance artists and scholars. The best-known figure of the era associated with the island was ZORA NEALE HURSTON, the author of *Tell My Horse*. Hurston used her 1936 the GUGGENHEIM FELLOWSHIP to fund six months of research on Haitian culture, folklore, and voodoo. She lived in Port-au-Prince, the capital, and also journeyed to La Gonâve, one of the islands offshore. It was in Haiti that Hurston wrote and completed her influential novel *THEIR EYES WERE WATCHING GOD* (1937) in seven weeks of intense writing.

The island of Haiti also figures prominently in the significant play *THE EMPEROR JONES* by EUGENE O'NEILL, which went on to showcase the talents of PAUL ROBESON and Jules Bledsoe. ARNA BONTEMPS used Haiti as the backdrop for his novel *Drums at Dusk*. Short stories such as JESSIE FAUSET's "EMMY" and JOHN MATHEUS's "COULEV' ENDORMI" also introduced readers to the mystical and historical Caribbean place.

Scholars such as Robert Russa Moton, the second president of TUSKEGEE INSTITUTE, also published work relating to the island's development. Moton's October 1930 report on Haitian education policy and practice reflected the work of the Commission on Education in Haiti that Moton chaired.

Bibliography

Heinl, Robert Debs, and Nancy Gordon Heinl. *Written in Blood: The Story of the Haitian People, 1492–1971.* Boston: Houghton Mifflin, 1978.

Renda, Mary A. *Taking Haiti: Military Occupation and the Culture of U.S. Imperialism, 1915–1940.* Chapel Hill: University of North Carolina Press, 2001.

Half-Century, The

A CHICAGO-based magazine that appeared first in 1916 and that was aimed at middle-class African-American readers. Anthony Overtown, the entrepreneurial founder of the *Chicago Bee* and the founder of Chicago's first African-American federally chartered bank, started the publication in 1916. Its editor was Katherine Williams Irvin.

The magazine's subtitle, "A Colored Monthly for the Businessman and the Homemaker," signaled its goal to provide articles on business, domestic practices, and material culture that this upwardly mobile constituency might find especially appealing. In addition, *The Half-Century* included works of nonfiction, news, and fiction. *The Half-Century*, which ceased publication in 1925 and merged with Overton's *Chicago Bee*, was one of several well-known African-American periodicals and newspapers based in Chicago, including AB-BOTT'S MONTHLY and the CHICAGO DEFENDER.

Bibliography

Johnson, Abby Arthur, and Ronald Maberry Johnson. *Propaganda & Aesthetics: The Literary Politics of African American Magazines in the Twentieth Century.* Amherst: University of Massachusetts, 1979.

Handy, William Christopher (W. C. Handy) (1873–1958)

A pioneering musician whose compositions and efforts to establish music companies created an important legacy in American blues music. Born in Florence, Alabama, to formerly enslaved parents, Handy showed his talents in music while still a child. He excelled in school and considered pursuing a career in teaching, but the low salary and pressing demands created by sharecropping and farming on his students persuaded Handy to stay focused on music. He taught briefly at Alabama A&M University before immersing himself completely in the music communities of CHICAGO and throughout the South.

Handy enjoyed major success in the decades leading up to the Harlem Renaissance period. His most well-known songs include "Memphis Blues" (1912), "St. Louis Blues" (1914), and "A Good Man Is Hard to Find" (1918), which sold some half a million copies. In 1926 Handy published *Blues: An Anthology.* During the 1930s, he published *Negro Authors and Composers of the United States* (1936) and two years later *The Book of Negro Spirituals* (1938). Handy's autobiography *Father of the Blues*, edited by ARNA BONTEMPS and based on Handy's notes about his life, appeared in 1941.

Handy threatened to sue Bontemps because he was not pleased with the volume. Despite the conflict, Bontemps, who saw no problems with the memoir, included Handy's lyrics in *Golden Slippers* (1942), his anthology of poetry for children.

Bibliography

Handy, W. C. *Father of the Blues: An Autobiography*, edited by Arna Bontemps. 1941, reprint, New York: Da Capo Press, 1985.

"Hannah Byde" Dorothy West (1926)

One of the first two stories that prompted DOROTHY WEST to relocate to NEW YORK CITY and immerse herself in the Harlem Renaissance communities. "Hannah Byde" appeared in the July 1926 issue of THE MESSENGER; its companion piece, the prize-winning short story "THE TYPEWRITER," appeared in the July 1926 issue of OPPORTUNITY.

"Hannah Byde" complements the stark domestic realism in works by EUGENE GORDON, ZORA NEALE HURSTON, NELLA LARSEN, and others. Its central character, Hannah Byde, can hardly be called a protagonist. She is plagued by her powerlessness and the limits that her class position and unsatisfying marriage place on her. Hannah strikes out at her husband George, a man who tries to provide her with luxuries. She rejects him and his efforts, even though he tells her, "Ain't no man livin' c'n do better'n his best."

The story opens on New Year's Eve, a night on which Hannah begins to unravel. She imagines her husband dead, entertains visions of her own funeral, and contemplates how she might kill herself. A newlywed neighbor drops by to listen to records and asks George to come down to her flat to persuade her hardworking physician husband to join them in some New Year's revelry. Left alone, Hannah prepares to cut her throat but faints before she can. When she is revived, the doctor sitting by her bedside encourages her to live and to protect her unborn child. He and his new bride leave George and Hannah to themselves. Hannah reveals her pregnancy, is taken aback by George's delight, and then shuns him. The story closes as she locks herself in the bedroom, "flung herself across the bed and laughed and laughed and laughed."

West explores the domestic frustrations that can undermine a marriage and hints at the earnest potential of hardworking men and husbands. "Hannah Byde" underscores the insidious damage of racism and social alienation.

Bibliography

Jones, Sharon L. *Rereading the Harlem Renaissance: Race, Class, and Gender in the Fiction of Jessie Fauset, Zora Neale Hurston, and Dorothy West.* Westport, Conn.: Greenwood Press, 2002.

West, Dorothy. *The Richer, the Poorer: Stories, Sketches, and Reminiscences.* New York: Doubleday, 1995.

Wilson, Sondra. *The Messenger Reader: Stories, Poetry, and Essays from The Messenger Magazine.* New York: Modern, 2000.

Hapgood, Emilie Bigelow (unknown–1930)

An influential philanthropist and enterprising advocate of African-American theater. The daughter of Anson Bigelow, a successful banker in CHICAGO, married Norman Hapgood, a journalist who went on to become a respected drama critic and historian of the theater. Emilie Hapgood gained access to New York's diverse theater culture through her husband. She frequently accompanied him when he attended plays that he was assigned to review. Norman Hapgood's rise, from drama critic at the *New York Commercial-Advertiser* to editor of *Harper's Weekly,* further increased the couple's social standing and visibility.

Hapgood joined the New York Stage Society and served as president for the years 1914 and 1915. It was during her tenure that RIDGELY TORRENCE's play GRANNY MAUMEE, one of the first BROADWAY plays to explore African-American life, was produced. According to the historian Susan Curtis, Hapgood invested thousands of dollars in the production of *Three Negro Plays* by Torrence. When the plays were staged on Broadway in April 1917, the theater troupe, which included Inez Clough and Opal Cooper, was referred to as the EMILIE HAPGOOD PLAYERS.

Despite her divorce from Norman Hapgood in 1915, Emilie Hapgood maintained her financial commitments to the theater. Her interest in race matters extended beyond the theater. She became an outspoken supporter of African-American vet-erans. In 1917 she founded the Circle of War Relief for Negro Soldiers, an organization designed to compensate for the lack of monies, services, and support directed toward soldiers of color.

Emilie Hapgood died in Rome as a result of complications from influenza and from apoplexy. *The New York Times* report of her death noted her successes as a director and producer. It did not mention, however, her extensive work with Torrence and, by extension, her support of emerging African-American actors and writers. As Curtis notes, the playwright MARY BURRILL suggested in a promotional flyer advertising Torrence's plays that "Mrs. Hapgood's object is to show that there is something beautiful, something truly artistic in this neglected life of the Negro. In that she has succeeded gloriously" (Curtis, 77). Hapgood was an unwavering source of support for playwrights and actors. She was committed to providing a forum in which plays by and about African Americans could be developed and appreciated.

Bibliography

Curtis, Susan. *The First Black Actors on the Great White Way.* Columbia: University of Missouri Press, 1998.

"Emilie Hapgood Dies of a Stroke." *New York Times,* 17 February 1930, 17.

Hapgood Players   *See* EMILIE HAPGOOD PLAYERS.

Happy Rhone's Club

One of the popular nightspots in HARLEM. Located at Lenox Avenue and 143rd Street, the cabaret was one of the first venues to develop a floor show and to hire waitresses. According to historian Bruce Kellner, the club's black and white decor signaled owner Arthur "Happy" Rhone's support of integration.

The NATIONAL ASSOCIATION FOR THE ADVANCEMENT OF COLORED PEOPLE (NAACP) used the club for parties and events. In 1924 LANGSTON HUGHES, who had just returned from an eventful European sojourn that included travel with ALAIN LOCKE, attended an NAACP benefit at the club. Shows included pianists such as Cliff Jackson, jazz performers such as Bennie Morton, vocalists such as Lucille Hegamin and Hannah Scott, and floor shows such as Happy Rhone's All Star Show.

Bibliography

Watson, Steven. *The Harlem Renaissance: Hub of African-American Culture, 1920–1930.* New York: Pantheon Books, 1995.

Harcourt & Brace (Harcourt, Brace & Company)

Founded in 1919 by Alfred Harcourt and Donald Brace, former employees of Henry Holt & Company, Harcourt & Brace published a number of best-sellers. The first novel the company published was SINCLAIR LEWIS's *Main Street,* a work whose sales eclipsed expected projections.

In 1922, at the urging of the firm's cofounder and literary adviser JOEL SPINGARN, the company published *HARLEM SHADOWS,* a collection of poems by CLAUDE MCKAY. In 1934 McKay approached the press to see whether they would reissue an expanded edition of *Harlem Shadows.* Cofounder Donald Brace corresponded directly with the poet. The edition never materialized, in large part because McKay, who had no reliable literary agent working for him, did not want to deal with the direct contract negotiations.

The press was one of the impressive New York City–based publishing houses that solicited and published works of Harlem Renaissance writers. Its representatives were actively involved in the celebrations of authors' accomplishments that the NATIONAL ASSOCIATION FOR THE ADVANCEMENT OF COLORED PEOPLE and NATIONAL URBAN LEAGUE, and their respective journals THE CRISIS and OPPORTUNITY, sponsored.

Hare, Maude Cuney (1874–1936)

A Texas-born musician, writer, teacher, and anthropologist who excelled as a pianist and music professional. She was born in Galveston to Norris Wright Cuney, a successful businessman and Texas politician, and his wife, Adelina Bowie Cuney. She married William Parker Hare in 1904. After her February 1936 death from cancer, she was buried next to her parents in the Lake View Cemetery in Galveston.

After graduating from high school, Cuney studied piano at the New England Conservatory in BOSTON. Following her training, she taught music at a number of institutions, including the Texas Deaf, Dumb and Blind Institute for Colored Youths and the State Normal and Industrial College in Prairie View, Texas. She returned to Boston in the early 1900s and began a career as a performer and lecturer.

Hare published frequently in music journals and general periodicals such as the *Musical Quarterly* and the *Christian Science Monitor.* She contributed regularly to THE CRISIS, the official publication of the NATIONAL ASSOCIATION FOR THE ADVANCEMENT OF COLORED PEOPLE, and served as music editor for the journal. The Crisis Publishing Company published her 1913 biography of her father, *Norris Wright Cuney: A Tribune of the Black People.*

In the late 1920s, Hare established the Allied Arts Center in Boston. There she displayed and sold African-American artwork and supported theater productions by African-American playwrights. Before her death in 1936 she also established the Musical Art Studio in Boston and sponsored additional black theater enterprises.

In 1918, Hare published *The Message of Trees: An Anthology of Leaves and Branches,* a volume of poems that included the work of only one poet of color, Paul Laurence Dunbar. In 1930 Hare published *ANTAR OF ARABY,* a four-act play that chronicled the plight of a dark-skinned, enslaved poet who loved the daughter of an Arab chief. The play was performed in Boston some four years before its publication, and Hare supervised its production. In 1936 Hare published *Negro Musicians and Their Music,* an invaluable history of American music history that reflected her expertise in music, folklore, and history.

Her papers, located at Atlanta University, include unpublished musical arrangements and manuscripts of songs and spirituals.

Bibliography

Hales, Douglas. *A Southern Family in White and Black: The Cuneys of Texas.* College Station: Texas A&M University Press, 2003.

Maude Cuney Hare Papers, Atlanta University Center Archives.

Roses, Lorraine Elena, and Ruth Elizabeth Randolph. *Harlem Renaissance and Beyond: Literary Biographies of 100 Black Women Writers, 1900–1945.* Boston: G. K. Hall & Co., 1990.

Harlem

Harlem is located in upper Manhattan, north of Central Park, and spans less than two square miles. Its main thoroughfares include Seventh Avenue, 125th Street, 135th Street, and LENOX AVENUE. Dutch immigrants and enslaved Africans settled in the rural area in 1658, establishing the village of Nieuw Haarlem.

Historian Steven Watson notes that African-American settlement in Harlem began in 1905 on West 133rd Street. African-American migrations coincided with a staggering collapse in real estate values during the first decades of the 20th century. African Americans now had access to housing in the area, and the area's population increased dramatically. Between 1920 and 1930, the population of Harlem reached approximately 200,000 and represented nearly two-thirds of the city's population of color.

During the Harlem Renaissance, Harlem became known for its landmark cultural and historic buildings. It remains home to the ABYSSINIAN BAPTIST CHURCH, founded in the early 1800s by the Reverend Thomas Paul and a group of black Baptists who were suffering exclusion in predominantly white congregations.

Other vital sites include the Schomburg Library branch of the NEW YORK PUBLIC LIBRARY. It was there that writers like LANGSTON HUGHES met other writers, shared their works at public readings, and made lifelong and influential friendships. The studio of accomplished photographer James Van der Zee was located at 109 West 135th Street. The brothers and photographic partners Morgan and Marvin Smith of Kentucky established a successful studio on 125th Street next to the APOLLO THEATER, the premier venue for jazz performances.

Harlem was a thriving entertainment center during the Harlem Renaissance period. The area was home to the COTTON CLUB and the Savoy Ballroom, as well as the Apollo.

Harlem's well-known residential areas included a boardinghouse at 267 West 136th Street.

It was there that WALLACE THURMAN lived and founded *HARLEM: A FORUM OF NEGRO LIFE.*

Political activism flourished in Harlem. The NATIONAL ASSOCIATION FOR THE ADVANCEMENT OF COLORED PEOPLE established its first branch in Harlem. It was there that MARCUS MOSIAH GARVEY founded the UNIVERSAL NEGRO IMPROVEMENT ASSOCIATION in 1917. In the early 1940s, Harlem was ravaged by race riots, sparked by reports of police brutality. Later, the civil rights leader Malcolm X was assassinated in Harlem's Audubon Ballroom.

Bibliography
Clarke, John Henrik, ed. *Harlem, a Community in Transition.* New York: Citadel Press, 1970.

Lewis, David Levering, *When Harlem Was in Vogue.* New York: Knopf, 1981.

Watson, Steven. *The Harlem Renaissance: Hub of African-American Culture, 1920–1930.* New York: Pantheon Books, 1995.

Harlem Academy

The New York City high school affiliated with the Seventh-Day Adventist denomination. The building was located on 127th Street at Seventh Avenue.

The novelist ARNA BONTEMPS taught English at Harlem Academy from 1924 until 1931. It was his appointment at the church's largest high school that financed Bontemps's move from California to Harlem. Bontemps met and married his wife Alberta Johnson, an Academy student of nontraditional age, in 1926.

The school closed in 1931.

Bibliography
Jones, Kirkland C. *Renaissance Man From Louisiana: A Biography of Arna Wendell Bontemps.* Westport, Conn.: Greenwood Press, 1992.

Harlem: A Forum of Negro Life

WALLACE THURMAN founded the literary periodical *Harlem* in 1928. The journal's offices were located at 2376 Seventh Avenue, which also was the site of a magazine-sponsored bookstore named the Harlem Bookshop. There are conflicting reports about the magazine's sales. It failed to secure vital advertising commitments.

Only one issue of *Harlem* was produced. It appears, however, that the promising journal ceased publication for a number of complicated reasons, including financial difficulties. Unlike established journals such as THE CRISIS, OPPORTUNITY, and THE MESSENGER, *Harlem* was not affiliated with a recognized race organization. This independence and political autonomy reflected a generational difference between artists of Thurman's peer community and the political leaders of the older generation. It also eliminated access to sources of support, distribution, and promotion.

The fate of *Harlem* was almost identical to that of the promising publication FIRE!!, a journal for which Thurman also was editor in chief. *Fire!!* appeared in 1926 and involved his friends and colleagues ZORA NEALE HURSTON, LANGSTON HUGHES, and others. The editors at *Fire!!* were determined to place the work of new and young writers. They refused to publish work that represented the ideology of organizations like the NAACP. In excluding ALAIN LOCKE, W. E. B. DuBois, and others, they threatened to alienate themselves from a significant portion of the Harlem Renaissance community. Yet, such a move toward journalistic exclusivity also underscored the editorial commitment to producing an unfettered creative outlet, one whose message was not overly determined by institutional politics.

The primary organizers of *Harlem* were Scholley Pace Alexander, AARON DOUGLAS, RICHARD BRUCE NUGENT, and WALLACE THURMAN. The men sought financial backing from highly regarded friends such as Dorothy Peterson. Thurman and others also solicited contributions from individuals like Alain Locke who had been pointedly avoided during the promotion and development of FIRE!! As editor in chief, Thurman revised the exclusive publication policy that he had upheld at *Fire!!* As biographer Eleonore van Notten notes, Thurman described his vision of the new journal to friends. In an October 1928 letter to CLAUDE MCKAY, Thurman wrote that he envisioned the magazine as "independent, fearless, and general, trying to appeal to all."

The first and only issue included a variety of materials, many of them authored by Thurman. Additional works included "Two Dollars," a con-troversial story about prostitution by George Little, Thurman's book reviews of NELLA LARSEN's QUICKSAND and Captain Canot's *Adventures of an African Slaver,* and an installment of a signature Thurman piece entitled "Harlem Directory: Where to Go and What to Do When in Harlem."

Bibliography

van Notten, Eleonore. *Wallace Thurman's Harlem Renaissance.* Amsterdam: Rodopi, 1994.

Harlem: A Melodrama of Negro Life in Harlem Wallace Thurman and William Jourdan Rapp (1929)

Billed by THE NEW YORK TIMES as "a negro play with a negro cast, or close to it" (*NYT,* 17 February 1929, 113), *Harlem* was a play written by WALLACE THURMAN and WILLIAM JOURDAN RAPP. The play was the first of several collaborations between Thurman, whose works include *The Blacker the Berry* (1929), and Rapp, a white NEW YORK CITY native, journalist, and playwright. The pair developed plans for a set of three plays produced under the title of *Color Parade. Harlem* was to be followed by JEREMIAH THE MAGNIFICENT and *Harlem Cinderella.*

Thurman and Rapp published an absorbing exposé of the play's evolution about two months after the play opened at the Apollo Theatre, a venue located at Broadway and 42nd Street. Their *New York Times* article, entitled "Detouring 'Harlem' to Times Square," chronicled the playwright' experiences with "play broker[s]" and potential producers. After the promising initial bids on the play from Crosby Gaige and Al Lewis, the play began the first of many transformations. According to Thurman and Rapp, rehearsals for the play that was retitled *Black Belt* were suspended abruptly. When the writers "innocently inquired, 'Why?'" producer Al Lewis declared that there was no "'wow' in [the] third act, and naturally we can't go on until we find one." After months spent contemplating new scenarios that included funerals modeled on the then-successful production of PORGY AND BESS, Rapp and Thurman decided to keep the play intact and to pursue other potential producers.

Their independent efforts led them to a "young actor, play reader, stage manager, vaudeville sketch writer, and occasional director by the name of Chester Erskin." Through Erskin, Thurman and Rapp were introduced to a theater publicist named C. A. Leonard, who then introduced them to "young Edward Blatt, who wanted to become a producer and bought the option sight unseen." "Harlem" was Edward Blatt's first BROADWAY play. He directed the play's debut in February 1929 and its revival a few months later in October 1929. Blatt's lengthy career in the theater spanned the Harlem Renaissance and most recently included the November–December 1970 production of Lorraine Hansberry's *Les Blancs,* for which he was company manager.

Notices about *Harlem* called attention to the play's predominantly African-American cast. The February debut included accomplished veteran actors like Inez Clough, a member of the stock company at the Harlem-based LAFAYETTE THEATRE and a performer whom critics lauded for her groundbreaking performances on Broadway. One of the 10 women included on drama critic George Jean Nathan's best actresses list for 1916–1917, Clough's stage credits included appearances in RIDGELEY TORRENCE's *SIMON THE CYRENIAN* in April 1917.

Following its February 1929 opening, the play traveled to CHICAGO, Detroit, and BOSTON. According to the *New York Times,* the October revival at the Eltinge Theatre on Broadway included members of the New York and Chicago casts.

Bibliography

Curtis, Susan. *The First Black Actors on the Great White Way.* Columbia: University of Missouri Press, 1998.

Harlem Branch of the New York Public Library

Located on West 135th Street in Harlem, this library branch was a rich resource for the Harlem Renaissance community and played an important role during the period.

The chief librarian of the branch in the 1920s was ERNESTINE ROSE. Her tenure began in 1920, the same year in which the NEW YORK PUBLIC LIBRARY hired Catherine Latimer, the first African-American woman employed by the institution. REGINA ANDREWS, Rose's assistant, joined the

staff in 1922 and was appointed circulation librarian. The two women dedicated their resources and site to community uplift and cohesion. They provided invaluable introductions to artists newly arrived in the city. They also made the branch available for readings, drama performances, and cultural gatherings.

The special March 1925 Harlem issue of SURVEY GRAPHIC included a profile of the library in its lengthy overview of Harlem institutions. The editorial noted that the 135th Street Branch "seeks to be what the Carnegie Corporation would call an intelligence center." Holdings at the library included a burgeoning collection of African-American works for students, set aside on its own floor. The article emphasized that the branch, which had an interracial staff of librarians, "has already formed a permanent organization of men and women to lend it support and to preserve and stabilize its policies." Finally, *Survey Graphic* made a call to patrons and potential donors who might have "rare, out-of-print or costly books" that to date had been "lost to the public in garrets or second-hand shops" that would "find their way to a collection so well-founded and so safeguarded for public use." *Survey Graphic* readers were encouraged to contact Ernestine Rose, the branch librarian.

The library's Division of Negro Literature, History, and Prints, which is part of the foundation of the library's current holdings, was established officially in May 1925 under the supervision of Rose. She had campaigned for a formal collection in order to protect and to showcase the impressive and valuable donations to the library from bibliophile ARTHUR SCHOMBURG, Louise Latimer, journalist John E. Bruce, and others. Rose organized community meetings to promote the idea, and Schomburg, JAMES WELDON JOHNSON, Hubert Harrison, and John Nail became officers of the branch. The division celebrated by staging the branch's first exhibit of rare books and materials relating to black culture and history.

The formidable collection of Arthur Schomburg became part of the library collection in 1926. The New York Public Library notes that the NATIONAL URBAN LEAGUE brought the collection to the attention of the Carnegie Corporation. The organization purchased it for $10,000. The collection included some 5,000 books, 3,000 manuscripts,

2,000 etchings, and thousands of other items. The impressive Schomburg collection included Phillis Wheatley manuscripts, the scrapbook of famed Shakespearean actor and tragedian IRA ALDRIDGE, and volumes of Jupiter Hammon's poetry. His collection complemented the library's current rare and special collections that included works by Wheatley, Frederick Douglass, Toussaint Louverture, Paul Laurence Dunbar, and others. Schomburg was appointed curator of the collection in 1932. Forty years later, in 1972, the Harlem Branch of the New York Public Library was renamed the Schomburg Center for Research in Black Culture.

Countless numbers of Harlem Renaissance–era writers, artists, and audiences benefited from their access to and affiliation with the library. Novelist NELLA LARSEN made her transition out of nursing by volunteering at the library. In January 1922 she began working as an assistant at the branch. In the following years, she would be promoted to children's librarian. JESSIE FAUSET, who was working with *THE CRISIS*, and ETHEL RAY NANCE, assistant to Urban League president and *Opportunity* editor CHARLES S. JOHNSON also were among the number of dynamic volunteers at the branch. RALPH ELLISON used the library to facilitate his Federal Writers' Project research on African Americans in New York. The library also was the base for the CRIGWA PLAYERS, a troupe that Regina Andrews and W. E. B. DuBois founded in 1924. The group, which evolved into the Krigwa Players and then became known as the HARLEM EXPERIMENTAL THEATRE, was based in the library. It staged performances, including productions of two Andrews plays, in the 135th Street library basement. The HARLEM SUITCASE THEATRE, a troupe that LANGSTON HUGHES founded in 1937, also used the branch basement for performances.

The 135th Street Branch of the New York Public Library, now known as the Schomburg Library, is still thriving. It continues the impressive legacy established by its thoughtful and visionary leadership during the 1920s and 1930s.

Bibliography

Dodson, Howard, Christopher Moore, and Roberta Yancy. *The Black New Yorkers: The Schomburg Illustrated Chronology.* New York: John Wiley and Sons, 2000.

Sinnette, Elinor Des Verney. *Arthur Alfonso Schomburg, Black Bibliophile & Collector: A Biography.* New York: New York Public Library, 1989.

Harlem Experimental Theatre

The theater company that evolved out of the Krigwa Players, a drama troupe founded by W. E. B. DuBois and REGINA ANDERSON, also known as the Negro Experimental Theatre. The Harlem branch of the NEW YORK PUBLIC LIBRARY was the base for the troupe, which critics hailed. The company set new standards in African-American theater and inspired small troupes around the nation.

The group performed two of Anderson's plays. In 1931 the group performed the sobering antilynching play *CLIMBING JACOB'S LADDER*, and in 1932 the play *Underground*, which revisited the antebellum era, slavery, and the Underground Railroad.

See also CRIGWA PLAYERS; KRIGWA PLAYERS.

Harlemites

A term used to describe residents of HARLEM.

Harlem Liberator

The newspaper that began as the *Negro Champion*. In 1928, GEORGE PADMORE, a Trinidadian pan-Africanist who decided to immerse himself in politics rather than pursue premedical studies, became editor of the *NEGRO CHAMPION*. He had a direct impact on Ghanaian politics as the adviser to Kwame Nkrumah, the figure under whose leadership GHANA became the first African nation to regain its independence.

The *Harlem Liberator* was published weekly from 1933 through 1934. It then became known as the *Negro Liberator* and continued to appear through 1935.

Bibliography

Hooker, James R. *Black Revolutionary; George Padmore's Path from Communism to Pan-Africanism.* New York: Praeger, 1967.

Harlem: Mecca of the New Negro

A special issue of *SURVEY GRAPHIC*, a highly regarded journal of social work, which focused on

Harlem. Editor PAUL KELLOGG invited ALAIN LOCKE to organize and serve as guest editor for the issue's that appeared in March 1925. "The Gist of It," an explanatory article by Kellogg, prefaced the special issue's contents and provided brief remarks about some of the contributors. Kellogg thanked Locke for his "painstaking collaboration in its preparation, for the full length study of *The New Negro* and for many smaller pieces in the mosaic of this number." In addition, Kellogg celebrated Locke for being "a brilliant exemplar of that poise and insight which are happy omens for the Negro's future."

The journal issue was divided into three sections. The first, entitled "The Greatest Negro Community in the World," began with "Harlem" and "Enter the New Negro," two articles by Locke. The four other submissions in the section included works by CHARLES S. JOHNSON, JAMES WELDON JOHNSON, RUDOLPH FISHER, and W. A. Domingo.

Section Two, "The Negro Expresses Himself," was a mix of creative writing and documentary pieces. The section began with artwork by WINOLD REISS. Locke's preface to the work noted that "Concretely in his portrait sketches, abstractly in his symbolic designs, [Weiss] has aimed to portray the soul and spirit of a people." "Youth Speaks" showcased poems by COUNTEE CULLEN, ANNE SPENCER, JEAN TOOMER, LANGSTON HUGHES, and ANGELINA GRIMKÉ. ALBERT BARNES, and Winold Reiss contributed essays on "Negro Art and America" and "Harlem Types," respectively.

Section Three, "Black and White—Studies in Race Contacts," anchored the issue. Prominent thinkers and activists such as MELVILLE HERSKOVITS, KELLY MILLER, and WALTER WHITE offered strong sociological and anthropological analyses of race and culture. Winold Reiss submitted four evocative drawings entitled "Four Portraits of Negro Women." In addition to images of "A Woman from the Virgin Islands," "The Librarian," and "Two Public School Teachers," he included a portrait of GERTRUDE ELISE JOHNSON MCDOUGALD, a New York City educator and social worker.

Reviews were positive and reflected the broad appeal of the material. The journal, eager to publicize its success, included a number of review comments from writers, scholars, and activists in its May 1925 issue. "It is full of valuable stuff," declared H. L. MENCKEN, editor of *AMERICAN MERCURY*. Philanthropist JOEL SPINGARN characterized the issue as "superb" and praised the "picture of the almost unparalleled achievement of a race." WALDO FRANK, a novelist and close friend of Jean Toomer, described the journal as "a most fertile, meaty, fascinating magazine." MARCUS GARVEY did not gush about the work but strove instead to place it in the larger context of informative works about African-American life. "The effort you have made to present partially the life of the race as it strikes you in Harlem is commendable," he wrote.

Alain Locke used the well-received *Survey Graphic* issue as the foundation for his *New Negro Anthology*, a volume that appeared at the end of 1925.

Bibliography
Harlem: Mecca of the New Negro. Survey Graphic. Available online. URL: http://etext.lib.virginia.edu/harlem/. Accessed May 20, 2005.

Harlem: Negro Metropolis Claude McKay (1940)

A history of HARLEM by poet and novelist CLAUDE MCKAY. Produced after the poet's tenure with the Works Progress Administration ended, the volume represented McKay's deliberate decision to complete a work of nonfiction and a comprehensive account of Harlem, its history, and its communities. The book was published by E. P. Dutton and Company, and McKay used his advance from the press to revise materials on Harlem that he had collected during his work with the Federal Writers' Project. The BOOK-OF-THE-MONTH CLUB chose *Harlem* as an alternate selection, but reviews of the work were neither plentiful nor overwhelmingly positive.

Chapters included "The Negro Quarter Grows Up," "Harlem Politician," "The Occultists," and "The Business of Amusements." These contributed to McKay's argument that the area needed substantial revitalization and that its residents would benefit from a significant economic redevelopment plan. The last chapters of the book focused on issues relating to communism and its impact on

Harlem. As biographer Wayne Cooper notes, the book reflected McKay's own anticommunist sensibilities and revealed his own efforts to grapple with party politics and African-American issues. The volume also included profiles and discussions of the prominent cult leader and social activist Father Divine, as well as the political movements and strategies of Marcus Garvey and Sufi Abdul Hamid.

Harlem was enriched by McKay's use of contemporary photographs. The volume included montages like "Types of Harlem Women" that profiled the work of the talented Harlem-based photographers Marvin and Morgan Smith.

Bibliography

Cooper, Wayne. *Claude McKay: Rebel Sojourner In the Harlem Renaissance.* New York: Schocken Books, 1987.

———. *The Passion of Claude McKay: Selected Poetry and Prose, 1912–1948.* New York: Schocken Books, 1973.

Giles, James R. *Claude McKay.* Boston: Twayne Publishers, 1976.

Harlem Renaissance

The term designates the extraordinary flowering in African-American literature, arts, and culture. The Harlem Renaissance, which spanned the 1920s and 1930s, also was known as the New Negro Renaissance.

HARLEM, in NEW YORK CITY, was the principal location of activity associated with the Renaissance. However, other urban centers such as BOSTON, CHICAGO, PHILADELPHIA, and WASHINGTON, D.C., also had active intellectual and creative communities. In addition, the Renaissance had a distinct set of international contexts. These were fueled by the significant presence of West Indian and African immigrants and connections. In addition, political conferences and opportunities for research and writing retreats abroad enabled Harlem Renaissance–era artists to cultivate important links.

The broad American and international networks of artists, writers, patrons, and supporters were impressive. There often were dynamic collaborations, memorable performances, and impressive intellectual forums. The aesthetic sensibility was fueled by the increasingly heightened political awareness of the day. Organizations such as the NATIONAL ASSOCIATION FOR THE ADVANCEMENT OF COLORED PEOPLE (NAACP) and the NATIONAL URBAN LEAGUE were committed to addressing critical national issues such as LYNCHING, segregation, world war, and economics. In addition, the NAACP and Urban League supported unequivocally the continued development of the arts and African-American culture. Individuals benefited from the literary contests, opportunities to publish in the widely circulated journals, such as THE CRISIS, OPPORTUNITY, and THE MESSENGER. Scholars and influential supporters, such as W. E. B. DuBois, ALAIN LOCKE, JESSIE FAUSET, JULIUS ROSENWALD, and CARL VAN VECHTEN, did much to raise awareness and support for aspiring and accomplished artists such as ZORA NEALE HURSTON, AARON DOUGLAS, LANGSTON HUGHES, ARNA BONTEMPS, and CLAUDE MCKAY.

The onset of the GREAT DEPRESSION greatly affected the movement, which remains one of America's most celebrated periods of literary and artistic production.

Bibliography

Huggins, Nathan. *Harlem Renaissance.* New York: Oxford University Press, 1971.

Lewis, David Levering. *When Harlem Was in Vogue.* New York: Knopf, 1981.

Roses, Lorraine Elena, and Ruth Elizabeth Randolph. *Harlem Renaissance and Beyond: Literary Biographies of 100 Black Women Writers, 1900–1945.* Boston: G. K. Hall & Co., 1990.

Harlem Shadows Claude McKay (1922)

A powerful collection of poems by Jamaican-born CLAUDE MCKAY and the first of his works to be published in the United States. The book, published by HARCOUT & BRACE, included an introduction by MAX EASTMAN, a number of works on Jamaica, and a set of powerful protest poems. The best-known of the latter was "If We Must Die," a previously published poem inspired by the race riots of 1919. A number of poems were taken from SPRING IN NEW HAMPSHIRE (1920), the volume of poems that McKay completed and published while in England. *Harlem Shadows* included no dialect poetry, a fact that challenged many to rethink the prevailing stereotypes and expectations that were frequently placed upon writers of color.

McKay grew up in Jamaica, a colonized Caribbean nation that did not gain its independence from Britain until 1962. In the "Author's Word," a prefatory note to the volume, McKay commented on how he had been steeped in British literary traditions. He also mused about the degree to which that European influence and literary traditions were "adequate" but perhaps not entirely suited to meet all of his creative aspirations. Reviews of the book did note the absence of dialect poetry. As biographer Wayne Cooper notes in his discussion of the critical response to *Harlem Shadows*, THE NEW YORK TIMES review praised McKay for his successful and emphatic departure from the dialect poetry tradition of Paul Laurence Dunbar, the poet to whom McKay was by then regularly being compared. According to Cooper, African-American responses to McKay's work were thoroughly enthusiastic. The review by Hodge Kirnon in the NEGRO WORLD, the official newspaper of the MARCUS GARVEY's UNITED NEGRO IMPROVEMENT ASSOCIATION, celebrated McKay's articulations of widespread sentiments and similar experiences by people of color in America. "I daresay many other aliens like myself," confessed Hodge, "have felt and thought in like manner without ever giving [it] expression" (Cooper, 165). WALTER WHITE, secretary of the NATIONAL ASSOCIATION FOR THE ADVANCEMENT OF COLORED PEOPLE, declared that McKay "is not a great Negro poet—he is a great poet" (Cooper, 165).

Harlem Shadows included a significant number of poems on traditional themes such as nature, memory, family, and love. Poems such as "Alfonso, Dressing to Wait at Table" and "Wild May" revealed McKay's talent for crafting evocative portraits of people and their environments. Other poems, including "The Tropics in New York" and "Flame-Heart," tackled issues of acculturation and separation from home and spoke to the American immigrant experience. In "To One Coming North," McKay addressed a prospective immigrant. He offered insightful commentary on how a newly relocated individual's feelings about a new home and environment would evolve. "At first you'll joy to see the playful snow, /Like white moths trembling on the tropic air," he wrote. "Like me you'll long for home," the speaker confessed, "where birds' glad song / Means flowering lanes and leas and spaces dry. . . . /But oh! more than the changeless southern isles, / When Spring has shed upon the earth her charm, / You'll love the Northland wreathed in golden smiles / By the miraculous sun turned glad and warm." Other works, such as "The City's Love," "America," and "The White City," challenged the tendency to mythologize America and ignore the painful disregard that some groups suffered in their new homeland. The eight-line poem entitled "The City's Love" recalled the unpredictable nature of America. "For one brief golden moment rare like wine/ The gracious city swept across the line," confesses the narrator. The speaker goes on to note that the city was "Oblivious of the color of my skin, / Forgetting that I was an alien guest/ . . . bent to me, my hostile heart to win." The poem is powerful for its personification of the city and its swiftly delivered chronicle of the uneasy relationship that can exist between a city and its inhabitants, specifically its inhabitants of color.

The poem that inspired the volume's title, "Harlem Shadows," was a moving tribute and startling address to "a lass / In Negro Harlem" and to girls of color "who pass / To bend and barter at desire's call." The poet lamented as he recalled the sound of "timid little feet of clay, / The sacred brown feet of my fallen race! . . . /In Harlem wandering from street to street." Others, like "On Broadway," gave readers a firsthand look at life in a bustling urban center such as New York. This work, reprinted in ALAIN LOCKE's definitive BOOK OF AMERICAN NEGRO POETRY (1922), contributed to the invaluable literary history of Harlem and the era.

The volume was an impressive set of meditations on American life and African-American experiences. It had a profound effect on the writer ARNA BONTEMPS, who first came across McKay's work while he was in college. As Bontemps noted, the volume represented a significant turning point in American letters because "It was the first time in nearly two decades . . . that any publisher had ventured to offer a book of poems by a living black poet" (*NYT*, 6 June 1973, 50). McKay's deft characterizations of loss and acquisition complemented well his writings on rage and resistance. The volume was an accomplished American literary debut and identified McKay as a promising new leader in the Harlem Renaissance movement.

Bibliography

Cooper, Wayne. *Claude McKay: Rebel Sojourner in the Harlem Renaissance*. New York: Schocken Books, 1987.

Giles, James R. *Claude McKay*. Boston: Twayne Publishers, 1976.

McKay, Claude. *Harlem Shadows*. New York: Harcourt, Brace and Company, 1922.

Harlem Suitcase Theatre

The New York City–based theater that LANGSTON HUGHES established in 1937. An amateur, rather than professional, company, it catered primarily to African-American audiences. Hughes, at the suggestion of sociology scholar and activist LOUISE THOMPSON, located the theater in the hall of the International Workers Order (IWO) above an eatery on West 125th Street called Frank's Restaurant. The theater's set design was simple. It included an arena-type stage, and there were no extensive props. The organization eventually moved to the 135th Street Branch of the NEW YORK PUBLIC LIBRARY. This site was home to the NEGRO EXPERIMENTAL THEATRE, a troupe originally cofounded by REGINA ANDREWS and W. E. B. DUBOIS as the CRIGWA PLAYERS. The Suitcase Theatre thrived for two years and closed shortly after its relocation to the New York Public Library branch in Harlem.

The Harlem Suitcase Theatre enjoyed critical support from a number of prominent writers, political figures, and patrons. The membership lists of various committees demonstrated the serious commitment to realizing Hughes's efforts. Among those contributing time and advice were writer GWENDOLYN BENNETT, artist ROMARE BEARDEN, novelist WARING CUNEY, actor Robert Earl Jones, wife of NAACP chairman Grace Nail Johnson, Louise Thompson, and the Harlem Communist Party spokesman Max Yergan.

According to Hughes scholar Joseph McLaren, the Harlem Suitcase Theatre was committed to performing interracial plays and to presenting works at functions sponsored by labor organizations such as the IWO. Hughes discussed his plans in the press; his comments in the Communist paper, *Daily Worker*, confirmed his desire to showcase African Americans in situations other than the stereotypical and confining domestic or comedic roles into which they were frequently cast.

The first season of the Harlem Suitcase Theatre staged the theater's most successful production. *Don't You Want to Be Free? From Slavery Through the Blues to Now—and Then Some*. The play, by founder Langston Hughes, enjoyed more than 100 performances and included poetry, music, and songs. Hughes drew from previously published works such as THE WEARY BLUES and THE DREAM KEEPER. Hailed as a good example of proletarian theater, it showcased the talents of convincing actors, including Robert Earl Jones, the father of the actor James Earl Jones. It has been revived to much acclaim. Contemporary performances have included shows at St. Louis University in 1998 and at Oberlin College in 2001.

The second season again included works by Hughes. Satiric skits such as *The Em-Fuerher Jones, Colonel Tom's Cabin, Limitations of Life*, and *Scarlet Sister Barry* all had titles that played on well-known or recent works in literature, theater, and film. Thomas Richardson joined the staff during the summer of 1939 and oversaw the first revival of Hughes's *Don't You Want to Be Free?*

The Harlem Suitcase Theatre enabled Hughes and the actors associated with the lively performances to generate timely critiques of contemporary issues and creative works. The organization's history and shared political visions also underscored the inextricable link between politics, race, and art that prevailed during the Harlem Renaissance era.

Bibliography

McClaren, Joseph. *Langston Hughes: Folk Dramatist in the Protest Tradition, 1921–1943*. Westport, Conn.: Greenwood Press, 1997.

Harmon, Florence Marion (1880–1936)

A native of Lynn, Massachusetts, and a member and officer of the SATURDAY EVENING QUILL CLUB, an enterprising BOSTON-based literary group that published the SATURDAY EVENING QUILL, its own annual journal.

Harmon studied at the Gordon College of Theology and Missions in Boston but pursued her writing career at the same time. According to the brief biographical note about her that appeared in the first issue of the *Saturday Evening Quill*, Harmon published at least one short story in her college yearbook and also submitted creative work to the *Boston Post*.

In June 1928 Harmon, who served as secretary for the literary club, published "BELATED ROMANCE" in the first issue of the group's journal. Her short story "ATTIC ROMANCE" appeared in the April 1929 issue.

Harmon Foundation Awards

A prestigious prize awarded by the Harmon Foundation, an organization established by real estate tycoon Elmer Harmon to recognize and encourage African-American achievements.

Awards were announced first in December 1925, and the first prizes were distributed one year later. Recipients were awarded gold and bronze medals and cash prizes of $400 and $100. Winners were considered in the categories of arts, education, industry, literature, education, music, religion, and science. One additional prize of $500 was set aside for accomplished white individuals who made positive contributions to race relations.

The foundation solicited evaluations from prominent reviewers, writers, and artists. When NELLA LARSEN applied for an award in 1928, the judges of the literary entries included editor and poet WILLIAM STANLEY BRAITHWAITE and publisher JOHN CHIPMAN FARRAR.

Winners included COUNTEE CULLEN, whose volume of poems entitled COLOR earned him the first gold medal in literature. Palmer Hayden, a veteran and talented art student who worked as a janitor in order to raise money for his supplies, was given the first prize awarded in art. THE NEW YORK TIMES noted Hayden's accomplishment. A January 1927 article headline read, "Negro Worker Wins Harmon Art Prizes: Gold Medal and $400 Awarded to Man Who Washes Windows to Have Time to Paint."

Other winning artists included 1928 gold medalist Archibald Motley, sculptor Sargent Johnson in 1929, artist and Howard University professor James Lesesne Wells in 1931 for his painting "Flight Into Egypt," and painter John Wesley Hardrick.

The literature winners in 1928 were gold medalist CLAUDE MCKAY for his novel HOME TO HARLEM and bronze medalist Nella Larsen for her novel QUICKSAND. Novelist and activist WALTER WHITE won a bronze medal in literature in 1929. Despite the honor, he was miffed by the panel's decision to forgo a gold medal award that year. It had been an intense debate between the judges, who wanted to award Nella Larsen a second prize; they were unable to do so because competition rules prohibited individuals from being repeat winners in the same category. In 1930 poet LANGSTON HUGHES won gold medal for NOT WITHOUT LAUGHTER, his first novel.

CHARLES S. JOHNSON, editor of *Opportunity* and NATIONAL URBAN LEAGUE president, was awarded the gold medal in 1930 for his contributions to the field of science. ATLANTA UNIVERSITY president JOHN HOPE won the award in 1929 for his distinguished achievements in education.

The Harmon Foundation also committed funds to support African-American artists, raise public awareness of their work, and preserve their creations. The foundation organized the first American exhibition dedicated to African-American art in January 1928. It was held in NEW YORK CITY and began a celebrated tradition of touring exhibits.

Harper & Brothers

A NEW YORK CITY publishing house. Established in 1817 and then named Harper & Brothers in 1833, the press was a distinguished organization. It was the only American publisher of novelist Mark Twain and was the press that founded the influential *Harper's Weekly* and *Harper's Bazaar*.

The company published a number of popular and successful works by well-known authors. Writers who were associated with the organization included Charles Dickens, William Thackeray, and the Brontë sisters. Harper & Brothers published Herman Melville's *Moby-Dick* (1851) and Dickens's *Bleak House* (1853).

Harper & Brothers contributed much to the Harlem Renaissance period through its publication of works by major writers such as COUNTEE CULLEN and CLAUDE MCKAY.

The press established a productive relationship with Countee Cullen, the poet and novelist, which spanned more than a decade. They first published COLOR, a volume of poems, in 1925. In 1927, COPPER SUN, the first volume with "decorations" by Charles Cullen, appeared. Harper & Brothers published Countee Cullen's THE BALLAD OF THE BROWN GIRL that included illustrations and artwork by Charles Cullen in 1927. Also in that year, the press published CAROLING DUSK: AN ANTHOLOGY OF VERSE BY NEGRO POETS, for which Cullen was the editor and artist AARON DOUGLAS provided stunning illustrations. In 1929 the sobering collection THE BLACK CHRIST AND OTHER POEMS appeared. ONE WAY TO HEAVEN (1932) and THE MEDEA AND SOME POEMS (1935) followed a few years later.

Claude McKay's affiliation with Harper & Brothers began in 1928 with the publication of HOME TO HARLEM, a novel regarded by many as the first major work of the Harlem Renaissance. One year later, the press published BANJO: A STORY WITHOUT A PLOT (1929). During the next few years, the press published GINGERTOWN (1932) and BANANA BOTTOM (1933).

Harper & Brothers continued its commitment to publishing African-American literature in the years following the end of the Harlem Renaissance. The press published RICHARD WRIGHT's *Black Boy: A Record of Childhood and Youth* in 1945.

Bibliography
Exman, Eugene. *The Brothers Harper: A Unique Publishing Partnership and Its Impact upon the Cultural Life of America from 1817 to 1853.* New York: Harper & Row, 1965.

Harris, Frank (1855–1931)
The editor of *Pearson's Magazine* who showcased the work of CLAUDE MCKAY in the September 1918 issue of the magazine. Pearson, an Irish immigrant from County Galway, was a multitalented writer. He published plays, short stories, and biographies of Oscar Wilde and George Bernard Shaw. Before he joined the staff at *Pearson's*, Harris

served as editor for prominent publications such as *Vanity Fair* and the *Saturday Review.*

Harris became editor of *Pearson's* in 1916, toward the end of his tumultuous career in literary circles and in publishing. Claude McKay was very familiar with Harris's works, and when the two men met in GREENWICH VILLAGE for the first time, McKay shared many details and scrapbooks of his life and adventures. Pearson published five poems by McKay and provided the author with the invaluable opportunity to pen an informative autobiographical statement. According to McKay biographer Wayne Cooper, the publicity in *Pearson's* buoyed McKay's spirits immensely.

Bibliography
Cooper, Wayne. *Claude McKay: Rebel Sojourner in the Harlem Renaissance.* New York: Schocken Books, 1987.
Pullar, Philippa. *Frank Harris, a Biography.* New York: Simon & Schuster, 1976.
Root, E. Merrill. *Frank Harris.* New York: The Odyssey Press, 1947.

Harris, George Westley (1884–unknown)
An accomplished journalist who became the editor of the AMSTERDAM NEWS, one of the most widely respected newspapers in NEW YORK CITY.

Harris attended two Massachusetts schools. He enrolled at Tufts before going on to HARVARD UNIVERSITY; he graduated in 1907. He was an associate editor at the NEW YORK AGE, the paper founded by T. THOMAS FORTUNE, which began as the *New York Freeman* and became the *Age* in 1887. Harris later worked as an editor at the *New York News.*

In 1923 Harris was one of several editors and prominent race leaders who called for legal investigation of MARCUS GARVEY and his organization, the UNIVERSAL NEGRO IMPROVEMENT ASSOCIATION. In January 1923 the group that included Harris, *Messenger* coeditor Chandler Owen, NAACP Director of Branches ROBERT BAGNALL, NAACP Field Secretary WILLIAM PICKENS, and PACE PHONOGRAPH COMPANY founder Harry Pace submitted a lengthy letter to the attorney general. Garvey blasted Harris and others as "wicked Negroes" and characterized their efforts to censure his organization's activities as behavior that betrayed the race.

Bibliography

Pride, Armistead S., and Clint C. Wilson II. *A History of the Black Press.* Washington, D.C.: Howard University Press, 1997.

Harrison, Hubert Henry (1883–1927)

A native of St. Croix, Virgin Islands, who became a formidable scholar and energetic force in New York publishing and journalism circles. In 1917, Harrison became editor of *Voice: A Newspaper for the New Negro,* a paper that generated spirited debate about radical black politics of the day.

Harrison, who was known to sleep less than four hours a day in order to read as much as he could, immersed himself in various fields of study including politics, economics, and sociology. Like J. A. Rogers and A. PHILIP RANDOLPH, Harrison was one of several well-known public intellectuals who declared themselves to be atheists and agnostics. He was known for his stirring street address to New Yorkers during which he advanced his beliefs about socialism, suggested how African Americans might best advance their political interests, and promoted the *Liberty League,* the political organization that he modeled on socialism but in which issues relating to race would figure most prominently.

Harrison, Juanita (ca. 1891–unknown)

The author of MY GREAT WIDE BEAUTIFUL WORLD (1936), an engaging narrative based on the writer's global travels. Harrison, who was born in Mississippi, was a woman of "slight form [and] fresh olive complexion" who wore her "long hair braided about her head" (*Atlantic Monthly,* October 1935, 434). She worked as a domestic and began writing seriously when one of her employers encouraged her to do so. In her late 30s, Harrison embarked on an impressive voyage that spanned the years 1927 through 1935. She financed her travels by working but emphasized her autonomy and freedom from the personal domestic constraints associated with marriage and family. Her impressive itinerary included sojourns in Burma, Hawaii, Israel, India, and Thailand.

Harrison published portions of *My Great Wide, Beautiful World* in the October and November 1935 issues of THE ATLANTIC MONTHLY. The introductory editorial comments informed readers that Harrison was "an American colored woman who at the age of 36 undertook to work her way around the world." They characterized her working life as a domestic as "sordid, unsparing years" filled with an "endless round of cooking, washing, and ironing in an overburdened household" and noted that it was this grueling experience that "steeled in her the determination to escape, and to see the world." Harrison, like IDABELLE YEISER, JESSIE FAUSET, and MARY CHURCH TERRELL, was an enthusiastic and enterprising traveler. Her colorful and insightful accounts confirm what the *Atlantic* asserted—that "[f]or her there existed no barriers of class or race. She has a faculty for making friends; she believed that everyone would like her and she was not disappointed." Noting that Harrison had finally settled in Hawaii, the editorial introduction closed with the enthusiastic assessment that "Whatever else the journal may be, it is certainly genuine."

While Harrison's entries may have convinced *The Atlantic Monthly* editors of her open-mindedness toward others, the narrative does reveal Harrison's own steady awareness of class and racial tensions. As she prepared to leave NEW YORK CITY and to begin her voyage, for example, she noted that "Our cabins looked good. I always want a upper berth I dont want anybody make it down on me." She challenged others about their elitism and stereotypes. On one occasion, she engaged in pointed conversation with a "Young Student Doctor from a town call 'a Way cross Georgia' Ga" who tended to "keep very much to himself." "I ask him why," Harrison writes, "and he say he do not care to mix with emigrant. I said these are respectful business people going home to visit. He had never been away from his little Georgia Town and read about emigrants at Ellis Island. He has not passport the poor kid is about 19." She was unfazed by her illiteracy and promptly secured the help of fellow passengers when she needed it. "My table mate read the mune [menu] for me," she noted in her June 28, 1927, entry, before going on to record that

"Herr Paul Huttrig are giving me german lessons. I like him because he speak such broken English he is all for America." Harrison's forthright assessments of her fellow passengers foreshadow the detailed and shrewd notes that she will make throughout the diary.

The Macmillan Company published My Great Wide, Beautiful World shortly after the Atlantic Monthly installments appeared. The autobiographical travel narrative, which Harrison completed in conjunction with Mrs. Mildred Morris, is reminiscent of pre-Harlem Renaissance narratives including Mary Seacole's Wonderful Adventures of Mrs. Seacole in Many Lands (1857) and Nancy Prince's Narrative of the Life and Travels of Mrs. Nancy Prince (1850). Harrison was a contemporary of pioneering traveler and anthropologist ZORA NEALE HURSTON, as well as other Harlem Renaissance era individuals such as LANGSTON HUGHES, CLAUDE McKAY, COUNTEE CULLEN, and DOROTHY WEST, whose travels throughout the Caribbean and Europe made a great impact on their perspectives and literary sensibilities.

Bibliography

Harrison, Juanita. "My Great Wide Beautiful World," Atlantic Monthly (October 1935): 434–512; (November 1935): 601–612.

———. My Great, Wide Beautiful World. With preface by Mildred Morris. New York: Macmillan, 1936. Reprinted with introduction by Adele Logan Alexander. New York: G. K. Hall, 1996.

Harvard University

One of the premier educational institutions in the world. Founded in 1636, the university in Cambridge, Massachusetts, admitted men only until the late 1870s. The Harvard annex began admitting female students in 1879. RADCLIFFE COLLEGE, the Harvard school for women, received its charter in 1894. During its first 229 years, Harvard College did not admit African Americans. The Medical School, however, admitted three talented young men of color in 1850. Unfortunately, white students were stridently opposed to the presence of Martin Delany, Daniel Laing, and Isaac Snowden. Student protests prompted the Medical School to expel the three men of color.

The first African-American student to enter Harvard College was Richard T. Greener in 1865. By the time that W. E. B. DuBois entered Harvard College with the class of 1890, the school still was not providing residential quarters for its students of color. DuBois, for instance, lived with a Cambridge family during his tenure at the school.

The history of African Americans at Harvard is most often linked to the graduation of W. E. B. DuBois, who in 1896 became the first African American to earn a Ph.D. DuBois transferred to Harvard from FISK UNIVERSITY and completed two years of study before earning his bachelor of arts in 1890 and a master of arts in 1891. After groundbreaking studies in philosophy and study in Germany, DuBois returned to Harvard and completed the requirements for the Ph.D. He enjoyed an influential career as a scholar and university professor. He was the editor of THE CRISIS and a founding member of the NATIONAL ASSOCIATION FOR THE ADVANCEMENT OF COLORED PEOPLE.

Contemporaries of DuBois included the formidable intellectual and activist WILLIAM MONROE TROTTER. The first student of color elected to PHI BETA KAPPA at Harvard, Trotter went on to graduate magna cum laude in 1895 and earned a master's degree one year later. He is best known for his outspoken challenges to accommodationism and Booker T. Washington. Trotter's newspaper, The Guardian, was a vital political publication and encouraged many Bostonians to take up civil rights activism in the years leading up to the Harlem Renaissance. ALAIN LOCKE graduated in the class of 1908 after a stellar career at Harvard. In 1912 the Phi Beta Kappa scholar became the first African American to win a RHODES SCHOLARSHIP. Six years later, Locke, a graduate student in philosophy, joined an elite Harvard group when he became the third African-American man to earn a Ph.D. there.

Women became part of the Cambridge intellectual society at Harvard through their admittance to Radcliffe College. Caroline Stewart, who later became Caroline Bond Day, attended Radcliffe from 1916 until her graduation with a bachelor's degree in 1919. Day pursued a career in higher education following her graduation. In Texas she was dean of women at Paul Quinn College, and English Department chair at Prairie View

State College. She published fiction and essays in Harlem Renaissance periodicals such as OPPORTUNITY. She continued her scholarly research in anthropology, earning a master's degree from Radcliffe in 1930. The university published her highly respected anthropological studies of racially mixed families in 1932.

MARITA BONNER, a Bostonian and graduate of Brookline High School, was admitted to the Radcliffe class of 1922. While at the college, Bonner, who studied English and Comparative Literature, also excelled in music. Shortly after her graduation, Bonner began her career as a successful author and playwright.

A number of Harlem Renaissance writers were considered members of the intellectual elite by virtue of their Harvard studies and degrees. Other influential figures of the era with impressive scholarly Harvard achievements included CARTER G. WOODSON, who earned his Ph.D. in 1912. WILLIAM FERRIS earned his master's degree from Harvard and began divinity studies there as well. The journalist GEORGE WESTLEY HARRIS earned his bachelor's degree in 1907, and the educator LESLIE PINCKNEY HILL earned both bachelor's and master's degrees from the university. The poet COUNTEE CULLEN attended Harvard immediately after completing his undergraduate studies at NEW YORK UNIVERSITY. Cullen, a Phi Beta Kappa graduate, earned his master's degree in 1926. His residence at Harvard coincided with the publication of COLOR, his first and well-received volume of poems. Poet STERLING BROWN, a Phi Beta Kappa graduate from Williams College, entered Harvard in the fall of 1922. He studied literature and earned his master's degree one year later. The eminent historian John Hope Franklin was a Harvard Ph.D. student in history during the last years of the Harlem Renaissance. Franklin earned his M.A. in 1936 and his Ph.D. in 1941.

Despite the university's implicit and explicit policies on segregation and de facto racism, African Americans and people of color did participate in campus life and influence students, faculty, and the administration. Among those who spoke at Harvard during the Renaissance was MARCUS GARVEY. In 1922 he addressed a meeting of the Nile Club, an organization founded by students of color. The civil rights leader Malcolm X made three important speeches at Harvard before his assassination in 1965. He spoke in 1961 and twice in 1964.

The history of African Americans at Harvard during the Harlem Renaissance era is one of academic excellence, leadership, and high professional accomplishment.

Bibliography

Sollors, Werner, Caldwell Titcomb, and Thomas Underwood, eds. *Blacks at Harvard: A Documentary History of African-American Experience at Harvard and Radcliffe.* New York: New York University Press, 1993.

Hawkins, Walter Everette (1883–unknown)

A poet and one of the self-professed atheists and agnostics in HARLEM who made an impact on the post–World War I environment for African Americans in and beyond New York. Born in Warrenton, North Carolina, he was the son of Ossian and Christiana Hawkins. Despite family hardships that did not facilitate a smooth public school education, Hawkins went on to attend Kittrell College. He graduated in 1901. In 1909 he married Lucile Butler of Wilmington, Delaware. His last known residence was in WASHINGTON, D.C.

Hawkins published frequently in THE MESSENGER, the journal for which he served as official poet. He also contributed work to THE CRISIS and to OPPORTUNITY. Hawkins began publishing some years before the Harlem Renaissance began. His first work, *Chords and Discords*, appeared in 1909. The BOSTON printer R. G. Badger reprinted a revised version of the work in 1920 as the Renaissance began. His later works include *The Child of Night, The Black Soldiers, Where Air of Freedom Is, Guardian, Love's Unchangeableness,* and *Too Much Religion.*

In 1924, editors NEWMAN IVEY WHITE and WALTER CLINTON JACKSON selected three of Hawkins's poems for inclusion in AN ANTHOLOGY OF VERSE BY AMERICAN NEGROES (1924). "Wrong's Reward," "A Spade Is a Spade," and "The Death of Justice" appeared in the volume. Hawkins's work now was part of a historicized literary continuum. The table of contents included works by Phillis Wheatley, George Moses

Horton, Frances Harper, and Paul Laurence Dunbar. Hawkins's contemporaries included T. THOMAS FORTUNE, WILLIAM STANLEY BRAITHWAITE, JAMES WELDON JOHNSON, JESSIE FAUSET, CLAUDE MCKAY, and GEORGIA DOUGLAS JOHNSON.

The first of Hawkins's anthologized works was "Wrong's Reward." It is a three-stanza poem that resonates with classical images and language. In their brief comment on the works, White and Jackson described the poem as one that "shows [Hawkins's] belief in ultimate justice." The high moral message about injustice and the trials of the righteous began with the lofty pronouncement that "It is writ in truth eternal, / And the stars of heaven tell, / That he who dares to do the wrong, / Has pitched his tent toward hell." The message about the wages of sin becomes increasingly apocalyptic in the succeeding stanzas. Hawkins made an effort to acknowledge that "Decked with thorns the right may suffer" and that "Wrong may triumph with his crown." Ultimately, however, the poem asserts that "the dread recoil is coming / To the man who does the wrong."

The second and third poems included in the White and Jackson anthology were written in a more contemporary fashion and language. In these, the speaker reveals himself to be a common man, but one at ease with more educated or socially privileged people. "As I talk with learned people, / I have heard a strange remark," notes the thoughtful narrator. He then goes on to muse about the advice that one should not be "too modest / whatsoever thing is said, / Give to every thing its color, / Always call a spade a spade."

Poems published in *The Messenger* reflected Hawkins's penchant for strident political critique. Works such as "Too Much Religion" and "Here and Hereafter" suggest that empty rhetoric could have deadly consequences for people in need. The poem's speaker complains that "There is too much time for doctrine / Too much talk of church and creeds;/ Far too little time for duty, / And to heal some heart that bleeds." The unself-conscious speaker concludes with the call for "less talk of heaven" and more efforts to "do right a little bit." Despite his status as one of Harlem's most outspoken atheists and agnostics, Hawkins generated poems that invoked God and contemplated religious matters. In "The Voice in the Wilderness,"

Hawkins crafted a pained lament in which the speaker presents a moving portrait of African-American endurance and also recounts the vicious attacks on African Americans. "He to bear the lash and load / Hunger's grip and spoiler's goad;/ Toil and grime his lot by day, / Fill the mart where other's prey" notes the speaker. "This my country? cruel Dame," the speaker goes on to declare. The following sequence of lines underscores the problematic myth that all individuals in America enjoy equality. The embattled speaker contemplates America as "This the land my heart must pride / Where my fathers bled and died! / Land that boasts of slavery, Cruel hate and tyranny?"

Chords and Discords is still considered Hawkins's major work. It includes 47 poems and reflects both the writer's ability to use diverse poetical styles and his interest in subjects ranging from moral issues to historical experiences.

Bibliography

White, Newman Ivey, and Walter Clinton Jackson, eds. *An Anthology of Verse by American Negroes.* Durham, N.C. Moore Publishing Company, 1968.

Hayes, Donald Jeffrey (1904–unknown)

A native of North Carolina, Hayes was a poet who enjoyed critical attention during the 1920s. COUNTEE CULLEN, the editor of CAROLING DUSK: AN ANTHOLOGY OF VERSE BY NEGRO POETS (1927) included Hayes's work in the volume. There were two special issues of *Carolina Magazine* devoted to works by African-American writers. In May 1927, LEWIS ALEXANDER, the honorary editor of the issue, selected Hayes's "Threnody to Alice" for inclusion in the periodical. It appeared alongside writings by ARTHUR HUFF FAUSET, GEORGIA DOUGLAS JOHNSON, ARNA BONTEMPS, and EFFIE LEE NEWSOME. One year later, in the May 1928 issue, Hayes's work appeared again when his poem "Lament" was published. LANGSTON HUGHES and Arna Bontemps published his works in *The Poetry of the Negro, 1746–1949* (1949), and his poems also appeared in Bontemps's collection, *American Negro Poetry* (1969). During the mid- to late 1920s, Hayes also was reported to be preparing "a new literary monthly of the Negro race, called Vision." GWENDOLYN BENNETT, who noted Hayes's efforts in her monthly OPPORTUNITY column, "The Ebony Flute," shared the prospective editor's hope for the journal. Hayes envisioned the journal as one that would "contrast other Negro magazines" and "have no chip on its shoulder, but will attempt to win friends by giving the Negro writer opportunity for development and by presenting work of distinction."

In the late 1960s and early 1970s, the composer and pianist Zenobia Powell Perry incorporated five of Hayes's poems into a work entitled "Threnody song cycle for soprano and piano." In addition, she composed a violin and piano piece based on Hayes's poem "Benediction."

Hayes eventually worked with mentally disabled persons as part of his job with the New Jersey Employment Service.

Bibliography

Bennett, Gwendolyn. "The Ebony Flute." *Opportunity* (September 1926): 292–293.

Hayford, Gladys May Casely (1904–1950)

A Ghanaian poet who made her literary debut in THE ATLANTIC MONTHLY before seeing her works appear in leading Harlem Renaissance–era journals such as THE MESSENGER and OPPORTUNITY. Her father was Joseph Casely Hayford, a Fanti (a black African ethnic group), editor, lawyer, and prominent pan-Africanist. Her mother was Adelaide Smith Casely Hayford, a Sierra Leone native, writer, influential educator, and president of the Sierra Leone branch of MARCUS GARVEY's UNIVERSAL NEGRO IMPROVEMENT ASSOCIATION. Gladys Hayford's education included years at a Welsh college in Colywyn Bay. She and her mother had traveled to the United Kingdom in order to obtain medical care. During Gladys's treatment for a birth defect, she learned English and pursued studies in the British college system. She later taught in the Girls' Vocational School in Sierra Leone that her mother, a graduate of the Hersey Ladies College in the United Kingdom and the Stuttgart Conservatory in Germany, had founded in 1923. Gladys Hayford died in 1950 at the age of 46 from cholera.

Gladys Hayford was convinced that she was destined to write and to do so in ways that bene-

fited her homeland and the peoples of Africa. The author's statement that appeared in COUNTEE CULLEN's CAROLING DUSK with her poems noted that by age 12, she "had the firm conviction that [she] was meant to write for Africa." She believed that in order to combat the evils of colonialism and oppression, it was vital to "imbue our own people with the idea of their own beauty, superiority, and individuality, with a love and admiration for our own country, which has been systematically suppressed." Hayford's poems revealed her skill for fashioning revisionist work that transposed traditional Western themes or images into celebratory African contexts. One of the best examples of this occurs in "Nativity," a poem that appeared first in *Opportunity* in January 1927 and was republished later that year in *Caroling Dusk*. The poem is filled with images that recall the biblical nativity scene with Jesus, Mary, and Joseph. Yet, here, the "Infant born" is one "Wrapped in blue lappah that His mother dyed" and he is "Layed on his father's home-tanned deer-skin hide." Instead of angels that herald the birth, "black bards burst their bonds and sang" and "All the black babies who from earth had fled, / Peeped through the clouds—then gathered round His head, / Telling of things a baby needs to do, / When first he opens his eyes on wonders new." The poem ends with a touching scene that reinforces the matrilineal traditions of Africa. Hayford imagines that in this nativity, "All the black women brought their love so wise, / And kissed the motherhood into [the infant's] mother's eyes."

The poems that Hayford published in American journals provided rich glimpses of African landscapes and peoples. "Rainy Season Love Song," which was highly suggestive of the love poems in the biblical Song of Solomon, featured a young woman named Frangepani, after a tropical tree with gorgeous flowers that often grow in Y-shaped clusters. Hayford's romantic heroine is at one with a powerful natural world. She emerges "[o]ut of the tense awed darkness . . . / Whilst the blades of Heaven flash around her, and the roll of thunder drums." This African woman with a "dusky throat" is one with whom "lightning's in love." Her lover can only wonder if "there's thunder hidden in the innermost parts of [her] soul." Other works, like "The Palm Wine Seller," were evocative of the vivid cultural imagery found in works by CLAUDE MCKAY and Countee Cullen. Hayford was a writer who paid attention to details and had a recognizable talent for creating vivid scenes of daily life and culture.

Hayford's poems provided her with the opportunity to enter at least two prestigious American schools. On one occasion, she sent samples of her work to COLUMBIA UNIVERSITY. The institution promptly offered her a place. Although she began her travels to NEW YORK CITY for school, money troubles caused her to detour. She became a member of a Berlin-based jazz troupe instead. Some years later, her mother Adelaide solicited a friend at RADCLIFFE, the prestigious women's college in Cambridge, Massachusetts, and asked her to evaluate some of her daughter's poems. The friend promptly sent the works on to the editor of *The Atlantic Monthly*, who published them immediately. That publishing triumph prompted the college to offer Gladys admission. In her reminiscences of her daughter, Adelaide Hayford noted that "through my dear daughter's own action, another splendid opportunity was lost."

From 1926 through 1928, Hayford published in the well-known monthly magazines *The Messenger* and *Opportunity*. In the spring and summer of 1926, "Creation," "A Poem," and "Mammy" appeared in *The Messenger*. Hayford's poems appeared twice in *Opportunity*, the official journal of the NATIONAL URBAN LEAGUE. In January 1927 she published "Nativity" under the pseudonym Aquah LaLuah. Later that year, in October, her poem "Rainy Season Love Song," attributed to Gladys Casely Hayford, appeared alongside fiction by EUGENE GORDON and "Ebony Flute," the regular GWENDOLYN BENNETT commentary. In February 1930 her poem "The Palm Wine Seller" appeared in *The Journal of Negro Life*.

Hayford, who also published her works under the pseudonym Aquah LaLuah, saw her poems anthologized in Robert Kerlin's *Negro Poets and Their Poems* (1923), COUNTEE CULLEN's *Caroling Dusk: Poetry by American Negro Poets* (1927), and ARNA BONTEMPS's *Golden Slippers* (1941).

Bibliography

Casely-Hayford, Adelaide, and Gladys Casely-Hayford. *Mother and Daughter: Memoirs and Poems*, edited by Lucilda Hunter. Freetown: Sierra Leone University Press, 1983.

Cromwell, Adelaide. *An African Victorian Feminist: The Life and Times of Adelaide Smith Casely Hayford, 1868–1960*. London: F. Cass, 1986.

Cullen, Countee. *Caroling Dusk: An Anthology of Verse by Negro Poets*. New York: Harper and Brothers, 1927.

Roses, Lorraine Elena, and Ruth Elizabeth Randolph. *Harlem Renaissance and Beyond: Literary Biographies of 100 Black Women Writers, 1900–1945*. Boston: G. K. Hall & Co., 1990.

———. *Harlem's Glory: Black Women Writing, 1900–1950*. Cambridge, Mass.: Harvard University Press, 1996.

Hazzard, Alvira (1899–1953)

A writer, teacher, and member of the SATURDAY EVENING QUILL CLUB, the active New England literary group that shared and published work in its publication, the SATURDAY EVENING QUILL. Hazzard, who never married, was the daughter of John and Rosella Hazzard, of North Brookfield, Massachusetts. Hazzard relocated to BOSTON, where she became a public school teacher and established relationships in the city's thriving black literary community. She later became a Boston City Hospital clerk. She died of leukemia in January 1953.

Hazzard published primarily in the local journal, the *Saturday Evening Quill*, and the majority of her works appeared in 1928 and 1929. She was a multitalented writer who wrote plays, fiction, and some poetry. Her biographical note in the *Quill* noted that she "has seen a number of her plays acted by amateurs" and that she published several short stories in the *Boston Post*, the newspaper where Quill Club president EUGENE GORDON worked as editor. Hazzard's first published work, MOTHER LIKED IT, was published in the April 1928 issue of the *Quill*. Her second play, LITTLE HEADS, was published in the *Quill* exactly one year later. Both works probed the persistence of racial stereotype and the kind of social value and devaluation that the practice causes.

Bibliography

Roses, Lorraine Elena, and Ruth Elizabeth Randolph. *Harlem Renaissance and Beyond: Literary Biographies of 100 Black Women Writers, 1900–1945*. Boston: G. K. Hall & Co., 1990.

————. *Harlem's Glory: Black Women Writing, 1900–1950.* Cambridge: Harvard University Press, 1996.

Heart of a Woman and Other Poems, The
Georgia Douglas Johnson (1918)

The first volume of published poems by WASHINGTON, D.C., poet GEORGIA DOUGLAS JOHNSON. A graduate of ATLANTA UNIVERSITY, in the class of 1896, she married Henry Lincoln Johnson, a Georgia attorney who was appointed recorder of deeds for the District of Columbia in 1912 by President Taft. Despite her husband's belief that wives should concentrate on domestic matters, Georgia Douglas Johnson continued to write, publish, and take a leadership role in Washington's literary and cultural circles.

The Cornhill Company of Boston published *The Heart of a Woman,* a collection of 30 poems that Johnson dedicated to her husband. WILLIAM STANLEY BRAITHWAITE provided the foreword to the volume. The Boston writer and editor praised the deep emotional quality of the works, suggesting that this aspect ensured that the poems were "deeply human." Braithwaite went on to suggest that in the 20th century, the "emancipation of woman is yet to be wholly accomplished" and that the "heart of a woman" was still a realm of mystery for many. "We are yet scarcely aware," he intoned, "of what lies deeply hidden, of mystery and passion, of domestic love and joy and sorrow, of romantic visions and practical ambitions." Braithwaite praised Johnson for the "sense of infinite sympathy" that she produced in her poems and concluded that the poet's own heart was "keyed in the plaintive, knows the sorrowful agents of life and experience which knock and enter at the door of dreams." He concluded his breathless praise for the volume with the declaration that "It is a kind of privilege to know so much about the secrets of woman's nature, a privilege all the more to be cherished when given as in these poems, with such exquisite utterance, with such a lyric sensibility."

The first poem in the collection is "The Heart of a Woman." This popular two-stanza poem of eight lines, which was included in JAMES WELDON JOHNSON's *The BOOK OF AMERICAN NEGRO POETRY* (1922) and many other collections, presents a haunting vision of a woman's heart. The poem suggests that a woman's heart "goes forth with the dawn / As a lone bird, soft winging, so restlessly on / Afar o'er life's turrets and vales does it roam / In the wake of those echoes the heart calls home."

Despite these freedoms and migrations, however, the heart of a woman is not free. Johnson imagines that it "enters some alien cage . . . / And tries to forget it has dreamed of the stars / While it breaks, breaks, breaks on the sheltering bars." Her work invoked the painful imagery of Paul Laurence Dunbar's poem "Sympathy," in which a captive bird beats its wings against the unyielding bars of its cage. The poem is a steady meditation on unrealized ambitions and the pain that can emerge from domesticity. Other poems further advanced Johnson's considerations of dreams unrealized. "The Dream of the Dreamer," one of several two-stanza, eight-line poems in the book, declares that the dreamer's dreams are "life-drops that pass / The break in the heart / To the soul's hour-glass." The poems "Quest" and others contribute to the volume's power. They are a chief vehicle through which Johnson placed an unmistakable emphasis on the finite aspects of life and the seemingly unavoidable extinction of dreams.

Poems such as "Elevation" introduced an uplifting mood into the volume. "Elevation," a six-line poem framed by its a/b/c/b/c/a rhyme scheme, opened with a thoughtful statement that "There are highways in the soul." The poem ends with that same line, but an exclamation point intensifies the statement and transforms it into an exultant assertion.

Other poems, such as "Sympathy," "Mate," and "Mirrored," herald the close ties that can exist between people, whether lovers or family members. "My joy leaps with your ecstasy / In sympathy divine," declares the sensitive speaker of "Sympathy." Johnson's telltale fascination with pain emerges here too. The poem ends with visions of one person's "tears falling . . . like bitter rain" into the heart of the empathetic speaker.

Johnson explored the links between the natural world and humanity in poems such as "Peace," "Pent," "Recall," "Impelled," and "Eventide." In "Pent," the speaker is able to defy the easy use of the natural as a metaphor for human experience. "The rain is falling steadily / Upon the thirsty earth," the narrator declares. Yet, "dry-eyed, I remain," confesses the speaker, "and calm / Amid my own heart's dearth."

JESSIE FAUSET's review of *The Heart of a Woman* appeared in the October 1919 issue of the JOURNAL OF NEGRO HISTORY. Fauset echoed Braithwaite's praise for the sincere poems, noting that "In these days of *vers libre* and the deliberate straining for poetic effect . . . We . . . are glad to return to the softer pipings of old time themes— love, friendship, longing, despair." Fauset predicted that Johnson soon would be among "the best writers of the world" because of her single-minded attention to articulating the human condition. Fauset acknowledged that Johnson's collection of poems transcended race and concentrated instead on "imagination that characterizes any literary person choosing this field as a means of directing the thought of the world." She did make an effort, however, to remind readers of Johnson's accomplishments as a race writer. According to Fauset, Johnson had proved herself capable of ably "portraying the trials and tribulations besetting a despised and rejected people."

Johnson would note many years later that *The Heart of a Woman* was "not at all race conscious" and that some had concluded that she had "no feeling for the race." She took the criticism seriously and produced BRONZE (1922), a collection of poems that were entirely focused on matters of race.

Bibliography

Bloom, Harold. *Black American Women Poets and Dramatists*. New York: Chelsea House Publishers, 1996.

Hull, Gloria T. *Color, Sex, and Poetry: Three Women Writers of the Harlem Renaissance*. Bloomington: Indiana University Press, 1987.

Johnson, Georgia Douglas. *The Selected Works of Georgia Douglas Johnson*. Edited by Claudia Tate. New York: G. K. Hall, 1997.

Heart of the World and Other Poems
Henry Joshua Jones (1919)

The first published volume of poems by HENRY JOSHUA JONES, a writer from South Carolina. Jones was a poet and novelist who published his second volume of poems, *Poems of the Four Seas*, in 1921 and BY SANCTION OF LAW, a novel on race and family matters, in 1924. *Heart of the World* in-

cluded a variety of poems and showcased Jones's perspectives of pressing contemporary issues such as LYNCHING and threats to democracy.

The inspiration for the title of Jones's collection came from a 1918 speech by President Woodrow Wilson. In a speech to the U.S. Senate during which he presented the Treaty of Versailles and plans for the formation of the League of Nations, Wilson asked, "Dare we reject it and break the heart of the world?" The Senate answered yes: The effort to pass the Versailles Treaty failed. Jones's volume, published soon after this landmark address by Wilson, includes poems with military themes and endorses the principles of democracy in a world on the brink of a second world war.

NEWMAN IVEY WHITE and WALTER CLINTON JACKSON, editors of AN ANTHOLOGY OF VERSE BY AMERICAN NEGROES (1924), consulted *Heart of the World* as they prepared their anthology. Although they chose not to include any of Jones's poems in the anthology, they did offer a brief critique of the work. Their comments, which were not overwhelmingly positive, noted that the book is a volume of "good commonplace verse" but that its "main defect is lack of ability to rise above the commonplace in diction, emotion, and thought."

Bibliography

White, Newman Ivey, and Walter Clinton Jackson. *An Anthology of Verse by American Negroes*. Durham, N.C.: The Seaman Printery Incorporated, 1924.

Help Wanted Joseph Mitchell (1929)

A play by JOSEPH MITCHELL, an Alabama-born lawyer and playwright who resided in BOSTON during the Harlem Renaissance era.

Some scholars attribute the work to EULALIE SPENCE, a pioneering dramatist who joined the theater world first through her collaborations with W. E. B. DUBOIS and the KRIGWA PLAYERS in the mid- to late 1920s. The play, whose byline identifies Joseph Mitchell as its author, appeared in the April 1929 issue of the Boston-based SATURDAY EVENING QUILL. The comprehensive bibliography of African-American plays by Esther Arata and Nicholas Rotoli attributes the work to Spence. However, critics Lorraine Roses and Ruth Randolph characterize the piece as "pedestrian" and suggest that it is not the product of Spence's "spirited pen" (295).

The play features five characters, all of whom are caught up in a devastating domestic drama that threatens their livelihoods. Leon and Amy are a young married couple who believe that they have good prospects. Leon is an inventor and has developed a shoe-leather stitching device that will dramatically increase the output of shoe manufacturers. Unfortunately, he is an inventor of color and cannot get anyone in management to meet with him or take his invention seriously.

He is determined to advance himself without sacrificing his high moral standards. His wife suggests that he take advantage of his light skin color and pass. His reaction is swift and seemingly uncompromising. "That's yellow!" he cries. "To get away from my race. After all it has undergone for me. And all I owe it. And as much as it needs me. I must rise or fall with my people. My conscience! My pride! Honey! Good God! No!" Despite his passionate initial objections, however, Leon does give in to his wife's suggestion that he pass for white in order to get a job and to circulate his invention. Unfortunately, he is discovered during a tense strike and is badly beaten. His invention is stolen, and Leon is once again forced to consider demoralizing work as a day laborer in order to sustain his family.

The scholars James Hatch and Leo Hamalian call attention to the dated diction of *Help Wanted*. They do note, however, that the work has a "surprisingly contemporary ambience" (74).

Bibliography

Hatch, James V., and Leo Hamalian. *Lost Plays of the Harlem Renaissance 1920–1940*. Detroit: Wayne State University Press, 1996.

Roses, Lorraine Elena, and Ruth Elizabeth Randolph. *Harlem Renaissance and Beyond: Literary Biographies of 100 Black Women Writers, 1900–1945*. Boston: G. K. Hall & Co., 1990.

"He Must Think It Out" Florida Ruffin Ridley (1928)

A short story by FLORIDA RUFFIN RIDLEY about the dilemmas of a man who discovers his mixed-race ancestry. It was published in the June 1928 issue of the SATURDAY EVENING QUILL, a BOSTON-based journal edited by EUGENE GORDON. Ruffin was the daughter of Josephine St. Pierre Ruffin, a prominent Bostonian and officer in the NATIONAL ASSOCIATION OF COLORED WOMEN. Florida Ruffin, in her sixties when her writings were published, was a Boston schoolteacher and active race woman.

The story revolves around Henry Fitts, an attorney who has lived his life believing that he is a white man. Fitts is a father to a dynamic young daughter named Irene, a girl who is "clear-cut [and] adorable" and who has a "clear responsive mind" and "cultivated taste." Her upbringing has cost him dearly. According to the sympathetic narrator, "It had cost him more than money, and money had never come easily to him. It had cost frayed nerves and anxious days." When Fitts learns that his longtime desire for wealth will finally be realized, he is ecstatic. Finally, he will be able to relax and to recoup his willing, but nevertheless substantial, investments in his daughter.

There is, of course, a complication that Fitts must deal with before he can claim the monies gained from the sale of a valuable piece of land in the city. His colleague Ephraim Gray, a man whose name is symbolic of his mixed-race ancestry, has uncovered the genealogical proof that verifies Fitts's claim. Gray also has discovered that he is a co-heir to the land. When he discovers his link to Gray and thus to an African heritage, Fitts is distraught and wonders, "Of all persons why should this curse come upon *him*, upon him who had always been tolerant and sympathetic? Why hadn't some of those ugly fanatics, Negro haters,—why hadn't they been the ones to suffer?"

The terms of the inheritance require that Fitts reveal his African-American and Native American background. He is unable to comprehend how this might affect his daughter, and he is simply overwhelmed by the prospect of raising the subject with his wife. The story ends as Fitts descends into a panic that is fueled by the specter of his family's social rejection and loss of upward mobility. "He must concentrate!" notes the narrator, "He must think it out. He must think it out alone."

Ridley's story was one of several stirring *Saturday Evening Quill* narratives that dealt innovatively with issues of racial misconception, racial passing, and stereotypes.

Bibliography
Roses, Lorraine Elena, and Ruth Elizabeth Randolph. *Harlem Renaissance and Beyond: Literary Biographies of 100 Black Women Writers, 1900–1945.* Boston: G. K. Hall & Co., 1990.

Henderson, George Wylie (1904–1965)

An Alabama-born novelist and writer of short fiction who moved to NEW YORK CITY in the 1920s and made his literary debut in the *New York Daily News,* the newspaper for which he was working as a printer. Henderson was born in Macon County. He attended TUSKEGEE INSTITUTE and studied the printing trade there before journeying northward to New York. There, he applied the skills learned at Tuskegee and began writing in his spare time.

Henderson's primary publishing outlets were the *New York Daily News* and the *Redbook* magazine. He published OLLIE MISS, the first of his two novels, in 1935. *Jule: Alabama Boy in Harlem,* his last novel, continued the story of primary characters introduced in the first novel. It appeared in 1946, some six years after the Harlem Renaissance period had ended.

Both of Henderson's novels focus on life in the South and are set in his home county of Macon. He explores African-American experiences in the rural South and tackles the potentially overwhelming and self-destructive nature of migration north. *Ollie Miss* focuses on a hardworking woman who is employed as a laborer on the farm of Uncle Alex, an industrious African-American farmer who has managed to purchase his own property. Ollie Miss endures the taunts of her fellow laborers, who include the men who desire her. However, she remains faithful to her sweetheart, Jule.

Jule, a chronicle of the eponymous main character who travels to Harlem, is especially evocative of *The Sport of the Gods,* Paul Laurence Dunbar's tragic 1902 novel of African-American migration. The *Chattanooga Times* endorsed the novel as one that "should be widely read . . . both North and South." The provocative pulp fiction design featured a sultry woman in a revealing, pink dress donning stockings. A light-skinned man in striped pajamas lies on bed in the background, his eyes on her and his face half obscured. The images underscored the plot's intrigue and the angst of its protagonist.

Bibliography
Burns, Loretta. "Voices and Visions from a Land Most Strange: Tuskegee's Literary Heritage." *Alabama English* (spring 1990): 25–34.
Christensen, Peter G. "George Wylie Henderson." In *African American Authors, 1745–1945: A Bio-Bibliographical Critical Sourcebook,* edited by Emmanuel Nelson. Westport, Conn.: Greenwood Press, 2000.
Henderson, George Wylie. *Jule: Alabama Boy in Harlem.* 1946, reprint, Birmingham: University of Alabama Press, 1989.
———. *Ollie Miss.* 1935, reprint, Birmingham: University of Alabama Press, 1988.
Nicholls, David G. *Conjuring the Folk: Forms of Modernity in African America.* Ann Arbor: University of Michigan Press, 2000.

Henry, Thomas Millard (1882–unknown)

Born in Stevensville, Virginia, to William and Adalaide Hamilton Henry in December 1882. He attended Hampton Institute in Virginia, the alma mater of BOOKER T. WASHINGTON, and graduated in 1905. In April 1923, he married Margaret Campbell. He relocated North by the 1930s and lived in New Jersey and New York.

Henry lived in New York, on West 18th Street, during the 1930s. The *Who's Who of Colored Americans* for 1933 through 1937 listed his professions as writer and lecturer. During the 1920s, Henry published a series of poems and essays in OPPORTUNITY and THE MESSENGER, leading African-American journals of the Harlem Renaissance. While living in Asbury Park, New Jersey, he was active in religious and political circles. He was a Baptist Sunday school and Bible classes superintendent for a period of time. In addition, he subscribed to the values and philosophies espoused by MARCUS GARVEY. A registered independent, Henry served as vice president of the Asbury Park branch of the UNIVERSAL NEGRO IMPROVEMENT ASSOCIATION.

Henry's poetry reflects a variety of writing styles that include formal exhortations, panegyrics, and romantic meditations on human potential. He focuses often on the plight and potential of working-class people. In "Dreams Are the Workman's Friends," for example, he transcends the drudgery of hard work by focusing on the "rapture" of dreams that "bring . . . rubies from remote confines" and "throw conditions to the winds." His intense personification of dreams suggests that imagination is a vital defense against potential overwhelming realism. Each of the four stanzas ends with the assertion that "Dreams are the workman's friends." The speaker shares his fascination with dreams and their ability to mobilize and stimulate dreamers who might otherwise be stymied by work and depravity. As the speaker notes, dreams "can awake [the workman's] spirits better than old wines; / To 'waken him to beauty is their plan." Other poems, such as "That Poison, Late Sleep," which appeared in the September 1925 *Messenger,* offered engaging narratives about the plight of overworked and bullied employees. The six-line stanzas, made up of three pairs of rhyming lines, introduce a besieged but resilient young man whose late nights and romantic adventures negatively affect his ability to work. "T'was the time I was spending my wages on Loue," he confesses before outlining the end of one relationship and the start of another. "O that poison, sweet sleep, surely fixed me that day. / It, in one way was bully, but Lord! did it pay? / Why the break with my Loue was some blow to my heart. —My! I dote on my Kate when the wound starts to smart."

Henry's considerations of the working man are complemented by his tributes to the successful writers of the day. "Countee Cullen," published in the October 1924 *Messenger,* for instance, paid high tribute to the poet who was on the verge of publishing his first volume of poems. Henry regarded Cullen like a quintessential mythological figure. "On Pegasus you've flown into a sheen— / A glorious passion has possessed your tongue," the narrator declares in the opening lines of the poem. He goes on to imagine Cullen as a modern-day version of the Romantic poet Byron or like the pioneering writer Paul Laurence Dunbar. By the end of the Italian sonnet, Henry declares himself a "patient" of the writer, one who benefits from the "tonic" and "songs like meat, like medicine, like wine."

Henry's investment in a heroic black literary tradition also imbues one of his most passionate *Crisis* essays. In "Old School of Negro 'Critics' Hard on Paul Laurence Dunbar," published in the October 1924 *Messenger,* Henry bemoans the hardships that poets face. "This land is as far from

being a friend to poets as it is to being a friend to grace," he states forthrightly. He critiques *The Crisis* for failing to republish works by Dunbar, who died in 1906, and lays the fault for this oversight at the feet of the "three gentlemen who sit in the judgement seats for *The Crisis* at present . . . Dr. DuBois, Mr. Braithwaite and Mr. James Weldon Johnson." After making a case for Dunbar's renaissance, Henry closes with a series of dramatic pronouncements on Claude McKay, the poet whom cultural critics most often compared to Dunbar. Henry suggested that while "McKay's poems have more blood and thunder in them than any other Negro's verse," it would be some time before the much celebrated "Jamaica poet" would "reach [Dunbar] in some particular."

Thomas Henry's modest set of publications during the Harlem Renaissance explains his relative obscurity. The passion and engagement of the work, however, contribute much to the ever-increasing sense of the period's diversity of talent and critical opinion.

Bibliography

Wilson, Sondra. *The Messenger Reader: Stories, Poetry, and Essays from* The Messenger *Magazine.* New York: Modern, 2000.

Yenser, Thomas. *Who's Who in Colored America: A Biographical Dictionary of Notable Living Persons of African Descent in America.* New York: Thomas Yenser, 1937.

Her Eulalie Spence (1927)

A one-act play by Eulalie Spence, a prolific and prize-winning New York–based playwright. Spence completed the drama during the especially impressive years of her theatrical debut. Her first public works emerged in connection with W. E. B. DuBois, Regina Andrews, and the Krigwa Players, a dramatic troupe based in the 135th Street Branch of the New York Public Library. In the mid to late 1920s, she captured several awards for her works including second prize in the National Little Theatre Tournament and second place in the 1926 drama contest sponsored by the Krigwa Players and *The Crisis.*

Unfortunately, the play is one of several Spence plays for which there is no extant script.

Bibliography

Roses, Lorraine Elena, and Ruth Elizabeth Randolph. *Harlem Renaissance and Beyond: Literary Biographies of 100 Black Women Writers, 1900–1945.* Boston: G. K. Hall & Co., 1990.

Herskovits, Melville Jean (1895–1963)

The scholar credited as being the first Africanist in the United States and the founder of the field of African-American studies. Born in Ohio, he completed a tour with the medical corps during World War I before turning to anthropological studies. He graduated from the UNIVERSITY OF CHICAGO in 1920 with a degree in history. Like ZORA NEALE HURSTON, Herskovits studied anthropology at COLUMBIA UNIVERSITY with the renowned scholar FRANZ BOAS during the 1920s. He completed his Ph.D. in 1923. One year later, he married Frances Shapiro, a student at the New School for Social Research in New York City, where he was pursuing additional studies. In 1925, Herskovits joined the anthropology department at HOWARD UNIVERSITY, where he worked alongside such scholars as Ralph Bunche and E. FRANKLIN FRAZIER. In 1927, he joined the sociology department at Northwestern University. It was there in 1948 that he established the first African-American studies program in the United States. He went on to become the first president of the African Studies Association, an organization that he helped to establish in the 1950s.

Herskovits is best known for his challenges to claims that African culture was primitive. In addition to maintaining the fact that African culture had an extremely influential impact on African-American life and identity, Herskovits advanced the notion that Africanisms had permeated white culture too. His theses generated controversy among those who believed that his ideas suggested that people of African descent were unable to assimilate fully into other cultures. Others embraced his arguments, based on impressive and extensive fieldwork here and throughout African countries such as Benin, GHANA, and Nigeria, as well as Suriname, Brazil, and HAITI.

Herskovits enjoyed a prominent role in and connection to the Harlem Renaissance. OPPORTUNITY editor CHARLES S. JOHNSON featured Her-

skovits's work regularly in the Urban League monthly periodical. His essay "The Dilemma of Social Patterns" began the section entitled "Black and White: Studies in Race Contacts" in the best-selling March 1925 SURVEY GRAPHIC issue that was devoted to African-American issues and edited by ALAIN LOCKE. Herskovits used the article to chronicle his travels through Harlem and his conclusions about African-American acculturation and the powerful universal dimensions of African-American experience. Having surrendered to the "the whirring cycle of life" in Harlem, he quickly began to ask "Where, then, is the 'peculiar' community of which I had heard so much?" before concluding that "the Negro has become acculturated to the prevailing white culture and has developed the patterns of culture typical of American life." Alain Locke's editorial preface to the article assured readers that "what Mr. Herskovits calls 'complete acculturation' . . . speaks well both for the Negro and for American standards of living that this is so."

In 1927, Herskovits was a highly regarded participant in the Fourth Pan-African Congress. The meeting, held in New York City and led by W. E. B. DUBOIS and RAYFORD LOGAN, benefited much from the organizational efforts of the NATIONAL ASSOCIATION OF COLORED WOMEN and the Women's International Circle for Peace and Foreign Relations, led by ADDIE HUNTON and Annie Dingle. One of the last sessions of the four-day meeting featured Herskovits and William Hansberry, the two contemporary American scholars most knowledgeable about African anthropology.

Herskovits was an influential academic figure for scholar-artists such as Zora Neale Hurston and Katherine Dunham. Dunham, a University of Chicago student, had the opportunity to study with Herskovits at Northwestern before her important anthropological field trips to the West Indies. It was he who recommended that Dunham travel to Jamaica to study the Maroons. Her trip coincided with Hurston's GUGGENHEIM FELLOWSHIP–funded field research of that population.

One of Herskovits's most well-documented connections to the Harlem Renaissance resulted from his association with fellow anthropologist Zora Neale Hurston. She conducted her first anthropological research under the supervision of Boas and

Herskovits. In 1934, Hurston seriously considered relocating to Evanston, where she could further intensify her work with the man regarded as the expert in Haitian culture. Like Boas, Herskovits was an important public supporter of Hurston's work. Her second published work, MULES AND MEN, included a highly complementary recommendation from Herskovits. In January 1935, the new ROSEN-WALD FELLOWSHIP winner wrote to her scholarly mentor with a bold idea. "With what you have and what I have and what both of us can get in the next two years," she wrote, "we can furnish the texts that are so needed in America. You of course, being better trained, at the top and me second to you. You said that we could workup something if you could get the money and now I have it" [Kaplan, 335]. In 1936, Herskovits was one of several eminent scholars whom Hurston used as references in her successful Guggenheim Fellowship application. Yet, he also discouraged her from traveling to Jamaica to do research. When she arrived on the Caribbean island in the fall of that year and discovered Dunham, another Herskovits student whom she thought was much less prepared than she to do research, Hurston wondered about the motives of the eminent senior scholar. By 1937, she was writing Herskovits to update him on her research and to comment on the complicated politics of the granting agencies that sponsored her work and prompted her to wonder about Herskovits's investments in her work.

Herskovits published much before, during, and after the Harlem Renaissance period. His scholarship was based on research conducted throughout AFRICA and the Caribbean. Some of his most influential publications during the era include *The American Negro: A Study in Racial Crossing* (1928) and *Dahomey* (1938). His research on Suriname led to two coauthored books with Frances Herskovits, *Rebel Destiny* (1934) and *Suriname Folk Lore* (1936).

Bibliography
Herskovits, Melville. "The Dilemma of Social Pattern." *Survey Graphic* (March 1925): 676–678.
Kaplan, Carla. *Zora Neale Hurston: A Life in Letters*. New York: Doubleday, 2002.
Lewis, David Levering. *W. E. B. DuBois: The Fight for Equality and the American Century, 1919–1963*. New York: Henry Holt and Company, 1993.
Simpson, George Eaton. *Melville J. Herskovits*. New York; Columbia University Press, 1973.

Heyward, Dorothy Hartzell Kuhns
(1890–1961)

An accomplished playwright from Wooster, Ohio, who is perhaps best known as the dramatist who first scripted the novel PORGY (1927), by her husband, DUBOSE HEYWARD. Her writing later served as the libretto in the George and Ira GERSHWIN production of the work PORGY AND BESS, one of the most popular and long-standing American operas. Dorothy Heywood's most acclaimed dramatizations were based on two novels written by her husband DuBose Heyward. Scholars recognize the Heywards as important figures in Harlem Renaissance–era theater and culture. In particular, their decisions to cast African-American actors, rather than whites in blackface, provided talented African-American performers with long-overdue access to the prestigious world of Broadway.

Dorothy Hartzell Kuhn's family moved often during her childhood. She eventually moved to Cambridge, Massachusetts, and immersed herself in theater workshops with George Pierce Baker at HARVARD UNIVERSITY. She married DuBose Heyward, whom she had met at the MacDowell Colony in Peterborough, New Hampshire, in September 1923. They enjoyed 17 years of marriage before his untimely death due to a heart attack in 1940. Dorothy Heyward passed away in New York City in November 1961. The couple's only child, Jennifer, who became a ballerina, was born in 1930 and passed away in 1984.

Dorothy Heyward's impressive career as a playwright spanned more than 30 years, from 1924 through 1957. In March 1924 she debuted *Nancy Ann*, her first play, at the Forty-ninth Street Theatre in New York City after two residencies at MacDowell, the prestigious New Hampshire writers colony. Subsequent plays included *The Lighted House* (1925), *Love in a Cupboard* (1925), *Porgy* (1927), *Jonica* (1930), and *Cinderelative* (1930). In 1927 *Porgy* opened at the Guild Theatre in New York with PAUL ROBESON in the title role. The play enjoyed a staggering 217 performances before the start of its national tour and its triumphant return to New York City.

Eight years later, in October 1935, the Gershwin production of *Porgy and Bess* opened at the Alvin Theatre in New York City. In January 1939 *Mamba's Daughters*, Dorothy Heyward's second collaboration with her husband DuBose, opened at the Empire Theatre. Based on the novel *Mamba's Daughters: A Novel of Charleston*, which DuBose Heyward published in 1929, the play featured Ethel Waters. Waters became the first African-American actress to appear on Broadway in a leading role.

During the Harlem Renaissance, Heyward also published two novels, *Three-a-Day* (1930) and *The Pulitzer Prize Murders* (1932). She continued to write for the stage after the Harlem Renaissance. She completed *South Pacific* in 1940 and *Set My People Free*, a play based on the Denmark Vesey slave revolt in South Carolina, in 1948. In addition to children's fiction, Heyward started but did not complete her autobiography, a memoir with the working title of *I Am Too Young*.

Bibliography

DuBose and Dorothy Heyward Papers, South Carolina Historical Society, Charleston.

Hutchisson, James M. *DuBose Heyward: A Charleston Gentleman and the World of Porgy and Bess*. Jackson: University Press of Mississippi, 2000.

Slavick, William H. *DuBose Heyward*. Boston: Twayne Publishers, 1981.

Heyward, DuBose (1885–1940)

A southern writer, perhaps best known as the author of PORGY (1925), the novel that inspired the musical *Porgy* and the long-lived GERSHWIN production *Porgy and Bess*. DuBose Edwin Heyward was born in Charleston, South Carolina, to Edwin and Janie Screven Heyward. He was a descendant of Judge Thomas Heyward, one of the signers of the Declaration of Independence. Heyward was part of the growing contingent of white Harlem Renaissance–era writers whose works explored African-American life. His early inspiration to write local-color narratives may have been his mother. She, too, wrote short stories about African Americans and incorporated the Gullah dialect into her works.

Heyward endured a harrowing childhood, brought on by the accidental death of his father

and the subsequent precarious financial situation of his family. He left school at age 14 in order to work. He survived a bout of polio and went on to work on the Charleston waterfront. At age 25, he became a founding partner in a Charleston insurance firm and maintained himself in that business for nearly two decades. Heyward's affluence enabled him to regain his high social standing and to explore his love of writing and of the theater.

In the early 1920s, Heyward's literary career began to flourish. He joined forces with John Bennett and Hervey Allen, also of Charleston, and founded the Poetry Society of South Carolina in 1920. Two years later, in 1922, the friends coauthored *Carolina Chansons*, a collection of poems. Heyward had the opportunity to spend time at the MacDowell Colony in Peterborough, New Hampshire. It was there that he developed a friendship with Julia Peterkin and where he met Dorothy Kuhns, an aspiring playwright and his future wife. He and Kuhns married in September 1923; their daughter, Jennifer, was born in 1930.

Heyward's second book and his first independent effort was *Skylines and Horizons*, a collection of poems that was published in 1924. A number of other works followed in quick succession. Having decided to commit wholeheartedly to writing, Heyward turned his efforts to the first of several works based on racial issues and on African-American life in South Carolina. *Porgy* (1925) is hailed as one of the first novels by a white author to feature prominently African Americans. In 1929, he completed *Brass Ankles*, his first play and a script about miscegenation. His novel MAMBA'S DAUGHTERS: A NOVEL OF CHARLESTON also appeared in 1929. This was followed by the novels *Peter Ashley* (1932), *Lost Morning* (1936), and *Star Spangled Virgin* (1939).

It was DOROTHY HEYWARD who developed her husband's interest in the theater. Her successful dramatization of his novel resulted in *Porgy: A Play in Four Acts*. It was staged in New York City and in London. It then enjoyed a dynamic reemergence as a George and Ira Gershwin opera production entitled *Porgy and Bess* (1935). Scholars regard this work as one of the most influential meditations on African-American life.

In 1939, Dorothy, a veteran playwright, and DuBose completed a dramatization of *Mamba's Daughters*. It was staged in 1939 and starred the talented performer Ethel Waters. When it opened at the Empire Theatre in New York City, the play had historic significance. Waters became the first African-American actress cast in a leading role in a BROADWAY play.

Heyward built on his successful collaborations with his wife, Dorothy, and pursued additional opportunities to write for film and for the stage. In 1933, he completed the film script for THE EMPEROR JONES (1933), the well-known play by EUGENE O'NEILL that featured PAUL ROBESON in its London and New York City productions during the 1920s. In 1934 Heyward wrote the script for *The Good Earth* (1934), based on the novel by Pearl S. Buck.

In 1939 Heyward returned to Charleston as the resident dramatist at the Dock Street Theatre. His tenure there was cut short when he died of a massive heart attack in Tryon, North Carolina, on 16 June 1940.

Bibliography

Dorothy and DuBose Heyward Papers, South Carolina Historical Society, Charleston.
Hutchisson, James M. *DuBose Heyward: A Charleston Gentleman and the World of Porgy and Bess.* Jackson: University Press of Mississippi, 2000.
Slavick, William H. *DuBose Heyward.* Boston: Twayne Publishers, 1981.

"High Ball"   Claude McKay (1927)

A pointed short story about interracial relationships, hypocrisy, and self assertion by CLAUDE MCKAY. "High Ball" was the only story featured in the May 1927 and June 1927 issues of OPPORTUNITY. McKay published "High Ball" in 1927, shortly before HOME TO HARLEM, his controversial first novel, appeared in 1928.

The protagonist of this five-part story is Nation Roe, a talented southerner from Baltimore who has experienced a meteoric rise to acclaim on BROADWAY. A blues singer, he is much sought after for his compositions that included "The Dixie blues; the Charleston blues, the Alabama blues, the Tennessee blues. The honeystick blues, the brown boy blues, the fair chile blues, the beautiful blues, the Harlem blues, blues, blues!" Nation's apparent expertise with the blues seems to contrast

sharply with his success and celebrity in New York. As McKay makes all too clear, however, this blues singer is hardly immune from the melancholy, betrayal, and lost love that are frequently featured subjects in blues songs.

Nation Roe's successes as a performer do not protect him from racism within and beyond his home. He is married to Myra, a "bloated coarse-fleshed woman, with freckled hands, beet colored elbows, dull-blue eyes and lumpy hair of the color of varnish." She is Nation's second wife, and the woman whom he chose over a mild-mannered "walnut-brown" woman with "simple charm." He prefers her worldliness and believes that Myra "brought the alien white world closer to him. The commonplace in her turned his head because to him the commonplace had always been strange." Myra is a steady drinker, addicted to highballs, and prone to hysterics when her whiskey and ginger ale are not readily available.

The plot revolves around Myra's conviction that she is being discriminated against because she is a white woman in an interracial relationship. Nation, determined to uncover the truth about this, turns to George Lieberman, a longtime friend. It is highly ironic that Lieberman, an actor who has made a successful career as a blackface performer, is the one who reveals the quiet antipathy that Nation's friends have for Myra. As the story unfolds, Nation weathers a series of uncomfortable social situations that remind him of his inability to move about freely in American society. Ultimately, he realizes that Myra has been deliberately excluded from the Stunts Annual Dinner, a celebrated social affair that Lieberman helps to organize. Instead of offering a toast, Roe blasts the white audience for their patronizing overtures to him and hurries home to his wife. On the threshold, he finds her having her own party with friends. Before he enters the apartment, he overhears Myra's obnoxious friend Dinah proposing a toast to him. It is a racist toast, however, one that refers to Nation as a "prune, our nation . . . al prune." Angered by his wife's betrayal, he evicts her from the premises. The story closes with the awful image of Nation "knelt down against the liquor stained piano . . . bellow[ing] like a wounded bull." The story offers no uplifting message about assimilation or interracial alliances.

Instead, it suggests the awful isolation that can persist for artists of color in the midst of seeming success.

Bibliography

Cooper, Wayne. *Claude McKay: Rebel Sojourner in the Harlem Renaissance.* New York: Schocken Books, 1987.

Wilson, Sondra Kathryn, ed. *The* Opportunity *Reader.* New York: The Modern Library, 1999.

"High Yaller" Rudolph Fisher (1925)

A prizewinning short story by the talented physician and New York–based writer RUDOLPH FISHER. It appeared in two parts in the October and November 1925 issues of THE CRISIS. In 1926, "High Yaller" earned first place in *The Crisis* literary competition.

The protagonists are Evelyn Brown and Jay MacLeod, an African-American couple whose different skin tones prompt passersby to think of them as an interracial couple. The story begins with a dance staged immediately after a basketball game. Evelyn finds the mad throng unbearable, and it becomes even more so to her when she overhears unflattering comments about her friends. She is accused of choosing to spend her time only with light-skinned women. She flatly denies this charge at first but comes to realize that it is indeed true. Her solution is to integrate herself into the community of darker-skinned people. She urges Jay to escort her to the illegal cabarets and night spots frequented by African Americans. These efforts are thoroughly unsuccessful. The couple consistently are ostracized or ogled because of their seeming mixed race.

One of the more novel twists in the story comes as both Evelyn and Jay face their own personal devils. These figures, which appear to each at night, bait them and encourage each one to abandon the other. Jay's devil is a "young man who looked exactly like Jay, feature for feature, with one important exception: his skin was white." He torments Jay with the idea that there are absolute limits within and beyond the race that dictate his choice of partners. "Beside her you become absolute black," insists the white devil who characterizes Evelyn as a girl who's "too fair for comfort." The devil that visits Evelyn is "a sophisticated young woman who sat familiarly on the edge of the counterpane and hugged her knees as she talked, and who might have been Evelyn over again, save for a certain bearing of self-assurance which the latter entirely lacked." This forthright devil torments Evelyn with the notion that her short courtship with Jay is doomed. She proposes that it is a desperate need for "self-protection" that motivates "the lily-whites," light-skinned African Americans and mixed-race people, to keep company with each other. "Whether you do it consciously or not, you're really trying to prevent painful embarrassment," observes the she-devil. The unsolicited visitor then insists that Evelyn extricate herself from the unrewarding social scene. "Get out. Pass," she insists before Evelyn hastens away to tend to her asthmatic mother.

Ultimately, Evelyn becomes brown in name only. She has survived several uncomfortable and threatening encounters with people who believe that she is white and that she should not be socializing with a man of color. After the death of her mother, she has no more ties to the African-American community and seems to pass away as well. Jay, seated in the segregated balcony of a movie theater, spots her in the white section below. He watches as she, seated next to a man who is "unmistakably white," responds to his effort to hold her hand. Jay is transfixed momentarily as "one white hand close[d] firmly over the other." As he hurries out of the theater, "Yaller Gal's Gone Out of Style," the song that has dogged them both recently, begins to play.

CHARLES CHESNUTT, Sinclair Lewis, and H. G. Wells were the judges in the 1926 *Crisis* literary competition. The three accomplished writers voted unanimously to award Fisher first place. Chesnutt, however, noted that he was not entirely convinced of the story's theme. Since then, however, scholars like John McCluskey have recognized Fisher's deft handling of explosive issues of intraracial tension, caste prejudice, and PASSING.

Bibliography

McCluskey, John, Jr. *The City of Refuge: The Collected Stories of Rudolph Fisher.* Columbia: University of Missouri Press, 1987.

Hill, Leslie Pinckney (1880–1960)

A HARVARD UNIVERSITY–educated teacher and poet from Lynchburg, Virginia. The son of Samuel and Sarah Elizabeth Hill, he attended high school in East Orange, New Jersey, and graduated in 1898. He began his studies at Harvard in 1899 and graduated PHI BETA KAPPA in 1903. He stayed on to earn his master's degree in education in 1904. Years later, in 1929, he received the D. Litt. from LINCOLN UNIVERSITY, the alma mater of U.S. Supreme Court Justice Thurgood Marshall, WARING CUNEY, LANGSTON HUGHES, and EDWARD SILVERA. A member of the Greek fraternity Kappa Alpha Psi, Hill also was elected to membership in Pi Gamma Mu, the social science honor society founded in 1924. He enjoyed memberships in professional societies such as the American Academy of Political and Social Science and the Association of Teachers of Colored Children. He also was an active member of political organizations such as the Committee on Total Disarmament and the American Inter-Racial Peace Committee. He married Jane Ethel Clark from Newark, New Jersey, in June 1907 and the couple had six daughters.

Hill had a steady and accomplished career as an educator. His first appointment was as a lecturer at TUSKEGEE INSTITUTE from 1904 through 1907. He then began a six-year term as principal at the Manassas Industrial School in Virginia. In 1913 he became the president of the Cheyney Training School in Pennsylvania, the oldest historically black institution of higher education in America. During his tenure the school, which was a highly respected teacher's training school when he arrived, became Cheyney University. Hill was its first president.

Hill's career as a writer evolved during his tenure at Cheyney. He published WINGS OF OPPRESSION in 1921. TOUSSAINT L'OUVERTURE, published by The Christopher House in BOSTON, appeared in 1928. Hill was anthologized in major Harlem Renaissance collections of poetry. JAMES WELDON JOHNSON included several of Hill's poems in THE BOOK OF AMERICAN NEGRO POETRY published by HARCOURT & BRACE in 1922. In 1924 nine of his poems were published in NEWMAN IVEY WHITE and WALTER JACKSON's AN ANTHOLOGY OF VERSE BY AMERICAN NEGROES. This high number of works was exceeded only by

the entries for Paul Laurence Dunbar and WILLIAM STANLEY BRAITHWAITE. White and Jackson offered high praise for Hill's poems. In the brief biographical profile and editorial comment included in their anthology, they declared that the majority of poems in Wings of Oppression "show a quality of thought and an adequacy of expression that rank them with the best contemporary poetry written by Negroes."

Hill's poems reflect his forthright perspectives on life, education, community, and spiritual consciousness. His only volume of collected poems, Wings of Oppression, included autobiographical meditations, poems inspired by current events, and works that blended high classical imagery with contemporary scenes of African-American life. Works such as "Tuskegee" represented well the strong faith of the Methodist Episcopal teacher who composed them. "Wherefore this busy labor without rest?" asked the speaker in the opening lines of the Italian sonnet. "But what shall be the end, and what the test?" he mused lines later. The sonnet takes as its primary subject the industrial and training school founded in Alabama by BOOKER T. WASHINGTON. As the poem closes, the narrator delivers a memorable comment on the school's mission and a veiled threat to those who might oppose its important work for African Americans: "If all our toilsome building is in vain, / Availing not to set our manhood free, / If envious hate roots out the seed we sow, / The South will wear eternally a stain." Another poem, "The Teacher," reprinted in the Johnson anthology, was a tidy narrative modeled on a prayer. "Lord, who am I to teach the way / To little children day by day, / So prone myself to go astray?" asks the narrator. The next stanzas record the teacher's efforts to enlighten students about knowledge, power, and love. Yet, because of his humanity, and thus imperfection, the teacher ultimately concludes that "if their guide I still must be / Oh let the little children see / The teacher leaning hard on Thee." Hill also tackled pressing social issues and explosive racial incidents such as LYNCHING. One of Hill's most sobering works was "So Quietly," a moving, jagged poem based on a 1919 lynching in Smithville, Georgia. The epigraph to the poem is a lengthy excerpt from THE NEW YORK TIMES that records the official note that the victim "came to his death at the hands of unidentified men." Hill uses images of blackness to underscore the depravity and unenlightened state of the lynch mob. Their "black design" is achieved in "broad, bright day" and the speaker is outraged by the supposed lack of witnesses to the abduction. His disgust with the pronouncement that essentially exonerates the murderers is reiterated in the poem's last lines. The speaker insists that the corruption that justifies, accommodates, and encourages lynching is "sown, But quietly—now in the open face / Of day, now in the dark—and when it comes, / Stern truth will never write, 'By hands unknown.'" Pinckney's poem was part of a considerable canon of antilynching writing produced during the Harlem Renaissance. This was the era in which the NATIONAL ASSOCIATION FOR THE ADVANCEMENT OF COLORED PEOPLE, under the leadership of JAMES WELDON JOHNSON, become the first organization to maintain detailed records on lynching and advance further the courageous political intervention of activists such as Ida B. Wells Barnett.

Bibliography

Hill, Leslie Pinckney. *Wings of Oppression.* Boston: Stratford, 1921.

Yenser, Thomas. *Who's Who in Colored America: A Biographical Dictionary of Notable Living Persons of African Descent in America, 1933–1937.* Brooklyn, N.Y.: Thomas Yenser, 1937.

Hobby Horse, The

A bookshop that focused primarily on works by and about African-American writers. Established by Douglas Howe on West 136th Street in NEW YORK CITY, the Hobby Horse was a popular gathering place for writers. ZORA NEALE HURSTON was one of the many who frequented the shop that promoted new works by African-American writers and artists.

Holiday Waldo Frank (1923)

A novel by WALDO FRANK that grappled with the violence and savagery of LYNCHING in America. Its plot spans one full day in a southern town called Nazareth. The town's name is an eerie foreshadowing of the crucifixion, or lynching, of John Cloud, a local overseer. The oppressive summer heat prompts the white Virginia Hade to honor Cloud's request that workers be given the day off. Plans for a religious revival coincide with the day's sweltering heat, and the town is gripped in a deadly religious fervor. A suggestive encounter between Cloud and Hade produces misleading evidence of their interaction by the bay. Virginia allows her own self-inflicted wound to be misinterpreted, and her family leads whites of Nazareth as they instigate the horrifying lynching of John Cloud.

Frank scholars such as William Bittner note the heavy-handed religious symbolism of the novel. The initials of the victim John Cloud, for instance, also suggest the name of Jesus Christ. The character Virginia Hade functions in ways similar to that of Judas. Another noteworthy element of the novel emerges in its powerful inverse color symbolism. In *Holiday*, the color black denotes all things good and virtuous while the color white is linked to evil and untruths.

Frank consulted JEAN TOOMER, a writer and friend whom he mentored, on questions relating to African-American culture. The novel's sparse natural imagery is evocative of Toomer's own prose in CANE. Coupled with the racial epithets that Frank uses frequently to refer to African Americans are lines that suggest the haunting and deceptive beauty of southern landscape. The description of Nazareth is a striking example of Frank's stark and alienating prose: "Nazareth. The Gulf of Mexico drains soil from her, blood red, to seas gray with moving. Moving seas of the world move athwart Nazareth standing . . . niggers move, niggers sing . . . a clot of crimson clay. But the trees sway up. And a dark man's eyes peer through the corridor of pine . . ." The novel escalates into melodramatic meditations on violence and racial stereotype. At one point, Virginia Hade berates the night, a time that she insistently equates with African Americans: "Yes, you are black," she declares, "Night, you're a raping nigger! / And the autumn day / with its golden sun / and its copper glow of leaf / and its red earth / I suppose you think you're white." The intense language conveys the impending violence and the community's loss of control.

The publication of *Holiday* also coincided with the publication by BONI & LIVERIGHT of

Toomer's much-celebrated work *Cane*. Toomer's work, which included evocative portraits of southern life, also confronted the specter and reality of lynching.

Bibliography

Bittner, William Robert. *The Novels of Waldo Frank.* Philadelphia: University of Pennsylvania Press, 1958.

Frank, Waldo. Introduction to *Holiday*, by Kathleen Pfeffer. Urbana: University of Illinois Press, 2003.

Holloway, Lucy Ariel Williams

(1905–1973)

An accomplished musician, teacher, and poet who published poems in OPPORTUNITY during the Harlem Renaissance. Her first and only volume of poems, *Shape Them into Dreams: Poems,* was published in 1955.

Holloway was born in Mobile, Alabama, the daughter of H. Roger Williams, a physician and pharmacist, and his wife Fannie. She went on to attend Talladega College before graduating from FISK UNIVERSITY with a degree in music in 1926. She enrolled at OBERLIN CONSERVATORY OF MUSIC and earned another bachelor's degree in music. In 1936, after she had completed her formal studies and had begun teaching music, Holloway married Joaquin Holloway, a U.S. Postal Service worker, with whom she had son, Joaquin Jr. Holloway's career in education and music prompted her to move frequently throughout the South. She taught in Alabama, Florida, and North Carolina. During her lifetime, Holloway was deeply involved in civic, religious, and philanthropic organizations. She was one of five charter members of the Delta Sigma Theta Alumnae Chapter in Durham, North Carolina.

She published in *Opportunity* over the course of several years. Her works appeared sporadically from 1926 through 1935. She made a significant and promising debut in *Opportunity* when she won the 1926 literary contest for her poem "Northboun'." That work was included promptly in CAROLING DUSK: AN ANTHOLOGY OF VERSE BY NEGRO POETS, the 1927 anthology edited by COUNTEE CULLEN. In 1941, ARNA BONTEMPS also included the poem in *Golden Slippers: An Anthology of Negro Poetry for Young Readers.*

Bibliography

Cullen, Countee. *Caroling Dusk: An Anthology of Verse by Negro Poets.* New York: Harper & Row, 1968.

Holloway, Lucy. *Shape Them into Dreams.* New York: Exposition Press, 1955.

Holstein, Casper (1876–1944)

A successful immigrant from St. Croix, Virgin Islands, West Indies, whose generosity financed literary competitions organized by OPPORTUNITY and the NATIONAL URBAN LEAGUE.

Born in Christiansted, St. Croix, Holstein moved to the United States while a teenager. He had a colorful career that included stints in the U.S. Navy and work as a hotel bellhop. He eventually made his fortune in the profitable, albeit dangerous, world of gambling. In 1928, a rival gambling organization headed by Dutch Schultz kidnapped Holstein and demanded a ransom of $50,000 for his safe return. Holstein was eventually forced out of the business.

In the early 1920s, Holstein pledged financial support to *Opportunity*. He wanted to encourage African-American literary talent and to foster opportunities for interracial harmony. The organization believed that Holstein had offered funds for one set of prizes. In 1925, at the awards dinner for the first winners, JAMES WELDON JOHNSON announced another generous Holstein donation and read aloud an enthusiastic letter from the earnest patron. In a letter that was republished in the March 1925 issue of *Opportunity*, Holstein declared himself to be a lifelong "firm and enthusiastic believer in the creative genius of the Black Race" and that "artistic expression among Negroes has been a source of breathless interest to me."

Holstein died in April 1944. More than 2,000 mourners attended his funeral service, held at the Memorial Baptist Church in HARLEM.

Bibliography

Holstein, Casper. "The Virgin Islands." *Opportunity* (October 1925).

Holstein Poetry Prize

A prize named after CASPER HOLSTEIN, an enthusiastic patron of talent. The journal OPPORTUNITY, in conjunction with distinguished independent judges, awarded the prize to recognize literary excellence by Harlem Renaissance writers.

Holstein, a native of St. Croix, entrepreneur, and gambling kingpin, financed the prize. In March 1925, Holstein declared his support for the competition that he believed would help to "bridg[e] the gap between the black and white races in the United States today."

The winners of the 1924 competition, the first that Holstein sponsored, included LANGSTON HUGHES, COUNTEE CULLEN, CLARISSA SCOTT DELANY, and JOSEPH S. COTTER, SR.

Holt, Nora (ca. 1890–1975)

A talented composer and writer who, in 1918, became the first African American to earn a master's degree in music.

Born in Kansas City, Kansas, to the Reverend Calvin and Grace Douglas, she attended Kansas State College and graduated in 1915 with a degree in music. In 1918, the year that she married George Holt, she graduated from the Chicago Musical College. She pursued additional graduate studies in music at the University of Southern California and COLUMBIA UNIVERSITY.

During the Harlem Renaissance era, Holt was the music critic for the CHICAGO DEFENDER. She worked in that capacity from 1917 through 1921. In the early 1940s, she became the music critic for the New York City-based AMSTERDAM NEWS. She was an active member of both the NATIONAL ASSOCIATION FOR THE ADVANCEMENT OF COLORED PEOPLE and of the NATIONAL URBAN LEAGUE.

Holt composed a number of distinctive works; well-known performers such as the celebrated tenor Roland Hayes performed her compositions. She was the founder of the National Association of Negro Musicians.

In addition to publishing *History of Negro Musicians*, she was the publisher and editor of *Music and Poetry Magazine* from 1919 through 1921.

Homespun Heroines Hallie Quinn Brown, ed. (1926)

A substantial collection of biographies of African-American women leaders edited by HALLIE QUINN BROWN. Brown, a graduate of WILBERFORCE UNI-

VERSITY, was an educator who served as dean of women at TUSKEGEE INSTITUTE and professor of elocution at Wilberforce. In 1920 she became the president of the NATIONAL ASSOCIATION OF COLORED WOMEN, an influential organization dedicated to racial uplift and empowerment of African-American women and families. Brown referred to *Homespun Heroines* as a "veritable history" and noted that she had assembled it with the hope that readers would "derive fresh strength and courage from its records to stimulate and cause them to cleave more tenaciously to the truth and to battle more heroically for the right." Entitled *Homespun Heroines and Other Women of Distinction*, the volume included 55 informative individual biographical profiles and a composite biography entitled "California Colored Women Trail Blazers." Brown wrote many of the entries, but there were a substantial number of contributors, including DELILAH BEASLEY, Mary Mossell, Ora B. Stokes, and Maritcha Lyons.

Josephine Turpin Washington, the wife of Tuskegee Institute founder BOOKER T. WASHINGTON, provided the foreword to the volume. She declared that the book was valuable for its "reflection of the wonderful spirit which moved the women who strove and achieved, despite obstacles greater than any which have stood in the way of other upward struggles." The biographies, noted Washington, "breathe aspiration, hope, courage, patience, fortitude, faith."

The dedication page of *Homespun Heroines* included poetry by CLARA ANN THOMPSON. Her lines honored women who "Through all the blight of slavery / . . . kept their womanhood, / And now . . . march with heads erect / To fight for all things good." The Thompson epigraph complemented Brown's earnest dedication to "the many mothers who were loyal in tense and trying times" and to members of the American and Canadian branches of the National Association of Colored Women.

Homespun Heroines presented biographies in chronological order and showcased women leaders in the arts, religion, club movement, business, journalism, politics, and education. There were entries on antebellum activists such as Harriet Tubman and Sojourner Truth and profiles of race leaders such as Josephine St. Pierre Ruffin, Lucy

Thurman, and Margaret Murray Washington. Other entries included profiles of the writers Phillis Wheatley, Frances Harper, and Elizabeth Keckley. The volume was an impressive contribution to the growing field of African-American historiography and American women's history.

Bibliography

Hallie Q. Brown, *Homespun Heroines and Other Women of Distinction.* Introduction by Randall K. Burkett. New York: Oxford University Press, 1988.

Home to Harlem Claude McKay (1928)

The first novel by Jamaican-born writer CLAUDE MCKAY. Published in 1928 by HARPER & BROTHERS, it enjoyed brisk sales, prompted controversial reviews, and contributed to McKay's reputation as a writer with a keen eye for deft cultural critique.

In late 1926 McKay had productive meetings with William Aspenwall Bradley, an influential literary agent who had represented Edith Wharton, Gertrude Stein, and Katherine Anne Porter. The two met in Antibes, FRANCE, where McKay was sojourning with Eliena and MAX EASTMAN. It was Bradley who urged McKay to develop further "Home to Harlem," his short story about a World War I soldier named Jake. McKay, inspired by good writing days and pressing financial needs, completed the novel in less than six months. Eugene Saxton, his editor at Harper, made few changes in the novel, and it was ready for distribution by the winter of 1927.

Claude McKay described his newly published novel *Home to Harlem* as "an impudent dog" that had "moved right in among the best sellers" in New York [Cooper, 237]. The novel quickly exceeded expected sales records. LANGSTON HUGHES congratulated McKay for a work that he really liked and also found "so damned real" [Bernard, 61]. Hughes's ebullience was in stark contrast to the distaste that W. E. B. DuBois, scholar and CRISIS editor, directed toward the work. He openly admitted that the novel "nauseate[d]" him and that "after the dirtier parts of its filth I feel distinctly like taking a bath" [Giles, 69]. Indeed, even Hughes recognized the depths of despair and gritty realism of the book. In a letter to CARL VAN VECHTEN, author of *NIGGER HEAVEN*,

a book that many suggested had been an inspiration for McKay, Hughes offered a memorable description of the novel. "[I]f yours was *Nigger Heaven*," he wrote, "this is *Nigger Hell*."

Home to Harlem polarized the older and younger generations of Harlem Renaissance writers and scholars. DuBois and other establishment figures, such as *OPPORTUNITY* editor and sociologist CHARLES S. JOHNSON and director of the NATIONAL ASSOCIATION FOR THE ADVANCEMENT OF COLORED PEOPLE JAMES WELDON JOHNSON, regarded the novel as an unwholesome work that perpetuated racial stereotypes and denigrated women. McKay's contemporaries, such as Langston Hughes and COUNTEE CULLEN, embraced the work wholeheartedly, encouraged by its vibrancy, unrestrained portrait of middle-class life, and evocations of the jazz era.

McKay dedicated the novel to "My friend Louise Bryant." It was Bryant, a white widow who remarried William Bullitt, a wealthy Philadelphian, who went to McKay's aid when he was suffering badly from influenza in Paris in the early 1920s. The novel's 21 chapters, divided into three sections, center on the life and adventures of Jake, a World War I veteran who returns home to HARLEM, a place that immediately gratifies his senses and enables him to indulge himself. Shortly after he arrives, he begins to spend the pay earned on the awful freighter on which he crossed the Atlantic. He targets a young prostitute in a LENOX AVENUE cabaret who also recognizes him as a viable client because of his "hungry wolf's eyes" (11). The early chapters chronicle Jake's seemingly endless adventures, late-night brawls at various nightclubs, early morning drinking, and reminiscences with men like Zeddy, with whom he considers the benefits and shortfalls of liaisons with women. He has the good fortune to benefit from women like the mulatto woman Congo Rose, "a wonderful tissue of throbbing flesh," who takes him in and allows him to lodge, rent free.

Once he leaves Harlem aboard a train on which he has taken a job as a waiter, Jake has the opportunity to glimpse a larger world and to hear absorbing history of Africans that leaves him longing for more. In his first encounter with Ray, a Haitian waiter on the railroad who has studied at HOWARD UNIVERSITY, he learns of Sappho,

Wordsworth's poems, the real rather than stereo-typed Africa, the French Revolution, and of Tous-saint Louverture. In response to the rich tales about the Haitian Revolution and Louverture's leadership, he can only say, "A black man! A black man! Oh, I wish I'd been a soldier under sich a man!" (132). The implicit message in these chapters does not bode well for the reputation of Harlem, a place in which there is much activity but little intellectual stimulation. Once a man like Jake is isolated or contained in a smaller world, however, he becomes a willing student and a potentially reformed young man.

In Pittsburgh, the friendship between Jake and the itinerant intellectual Ray intensifies. Ray represents another version of the New Negro, a man who makes an effort to read broadly and relishes the opportunity to purchase weekly newspapers such as the *Baltimore Afro-American*, the *Negro World*, the *Chicago Defender*, and the *Pittsburgh Courier*. Ray is struggling to overcome the less-than-satisfying world in which he moves. At one point, he surveys the motley group with whom he is sharing a lodging space and wonders, "Why should he have and love a race?" He realizes that he "ought to love" the "men [who] claimed kinship with him" because of his race, but he "loathed every soul in that great barrack-room, except Jake" (153).

Both Jake and Ray are immersed in the unsavory circles of New York society but move confidently among their encounters with prostitutes, gamblers, alcoholics, and other individuals who threaten to corrupt them. McKay crafts vivid portraits of the jobs that the two men obtain and their inevitable hardships as working-class men. They work as railroad porters and experience firsthand the hypocrisy and implicit disenfranchisement of African-American laborers. Their distressing situations include stays in squalid residential conditions and the temptation to experiment with drugs. The protagonists endure stressful confrontations with each other and those with whom they come in contact. McKay uses these encounters to illuminate inter- and intraracial tensions and to consider the devastating social and psychological effects that white-dominated society can have on people of color. He also suggests the recuperative power of African and African-American peoples. The character Ray performs the role of race historian, but

even he is undermined by the pressing realities of urban American life.

Women figure prominently in *Home to Harlem* but are not powerful or wholesome characters. The opening scenes in the novel present Jake's encounter with a Harlem prostitute. She charges him for her services, but when she becomes quickly enamored of him she refunds his money. Despite feeling a "reaching out and marriage of spirits," he quickly leaves and vows not to return to her. He becomes involved with Congo Rose, a cabaret singer who believes that physical abuse is not inconsistent with a love relationship. The numerous female characters in the novel, many of whom are associated with the wild night world of drink and gambling, also include women who are willing to support Jake despite the reality of physical violence and abandonment.

McKay incorporates autobiographical details of his own life into the character Ray. Both men are immigrants from the West Indies, scholarly individuals with intellectual leanings, and hampered by financial lacking and political maneuverings. Ultimately, Ray proves to be an equally perplexing example of 20th-century masculinity. He has the opportunity to marry Agatha, a proper and intelligent girl. He rejects her, however, and flees to Europe rather than saddle himself with marital expectations and responsibilities. The character Ray reappears in *Banjo*, McKay's next novel and the work that was published one year after *Home to Harlem*. The novel ends with the symbolic and desperate exile of the protagonists from Harlem. Ray has fled to Europe, and Jake makes plans to leave for Chicago as the threat of his arrest for military desertion looms.

Home to Harlem was an invaluable contribution to the Harlem Renaissance. It provoked discussion of black culture, strengthened connections between authors, and undoubtedly enriched debates about African-American identity, history, and progress.

Bibliography

Bernard, Emily. *Remember Me to Harlem: The Letters of Langston Hughes and Carl Van Vechten*. New York: Knopf, 2001.

Cooper, Wayne. *Claude McKay: Rebel Sojourner in the Harlem Renaissance*. New York: Schocken Books, 1987.

Giles, James R. *Claude McKay*. Boston: Twayne Publishers, 1976.

McKay, Claude. *Home to Harlem*. Boston: Northeastern University Press, 1987.

"Hongry Fire"   Marita Bonner (1939)

A short story by MARITA BONNER about the remedy that an invalid mother and wife uses to regain peace and stability in her chaotic household.

Published in the December 1939 issue of THE CRISIS, "Hongry Fire" opens with as a distressed mother worried about the quality of housework that her daughter Margaret is doing for her. Unable to relinquish responsibility for the laundry, cooking, and upkeep of the house entirely, Ma is frustrated by her cardiac condition and the doctor's strict orders that she remain on bed rest. Her condition is tested sorely over the course of the story as she hears frightening tales about her children's clandestine relationships, secret marriages, and slow, but seemingly sure, decline into the fast life of alcohol and socializing.

Ma, a woman who clearly is suffering from her physical limitations and her will to preserve the order in her family, is thoroughly challenged when her son Artie marries a woman named Jule and brings her to live in the home. Jule has an unsavory reputation, and Ma becomes convinced that her new and unwelcome daughter-in-law is corrupting her children. Through a hole in the floor, Ma keeps tabs as best she can on the conversations, plots, and mischief that transpire. Eventually she arrives at a plan to stop Jule, the woman whom she regards as a "hongry fire—burning up the house." She laces a glass of brandy with the sleeping medicine that she herself should be taking and insists that the girl drink. The unsuspecting girl imbibes the beverage and within minutes, Ma listens as Jule stumbles into her room and falls onto the bed. "There was no more humming. There was no more yawning," reports the narrator. Having achieved Jule's death, Ma finally takes "her share" of the medicine and begins to rest, sure that the "fire" not only "slept" but "was out."

"The Hongry Fire" is one of several short stories in which Bonner explored families in crisis and upheaval. Her works tended to contain jarring solutions and tragic ends and underscored the kind of domestic tensions that plagued families of color and the domestic ideals that prompted them to employ dramatic solutions to preserve themselves and their loved ones.

Bibliography

Bonner, Marita. *Frye Street and Environs: The Collected Works of Marita Bonner*, edited by Joyce Flynn and Joyce Occomy Stricklin. Boston: Beacon Press, 1987.

Hope, Hugh

A pseudonym that writer CLAUDE MCKAY frequently used for the articles that he published in the British journal WORKER'S DREADNOUGHT during the early 1920s.

Hope, John (1868–1936)

The president of ATLANTA UNIVERSITY, the first African-American graduate school, alma mater of JAMES WELDON JOHNSON, and the school where W. E. B. DUBOIS and WILLIAM STANLEY BRAITHWAITE were on the faculty. Hope, the first African-American president of Atlanta University, was a recognized leader in American education. It was he who championed the value of liberal arts education for African Americans and thus challenged the emphasis on vocational training espoused by BOOKER T. WASHINGTON. Hope received the William Harmon Award in 1929 for "Distinguished Achievement Among Negroes." The founder of the Commission on Interracial Cooperation, Hope was an essayist whose writing appeared in journals such as OPPORTUNITY, the official journal of the NATIONAL URBAN LEAGUE.

John Hope was born in Augusta, Georgia, to James and Mary Hope, an interracial couple. His father was a wealthy Scottish businessman who lived openly with Mary, a free mulatto woman and the daughter of a formerly enslaved woman. Unfortunately, the family was prevented from claiming James Hope's sizable estate when he died. Unlike two of his sisters who passed for white, John Hope lived as a man of color. He received his education in the North. After completing four years at Worcester Academy in Massachusetts, where he graduated with honors, he earned a bachelor's degree from BROWN UNIVERSITY in 1894. He spent the summers of 1897 and 1898 at the UNIVERSITY OF CHICAGO before returning to Providence, Rhode Island, to complete his master's degree at Brown in 1907.

Hope married Lugenia Burns of Chicago in December 1897. An active social work reformer in Chicago, she became a leader in Atlanta's African-American women's club movement and in the city's settlement house movement. She was the first vice president of the Atlanta branch of the NATIONAL ASSOCIATION FOR THE ADVANCEMENT OF COLORED PEOPLE and spearheaded the effort to establish African-American branches of the YOUNG WOMEN'S CHRISTIAN ASSOCIATION in the South.

Hope was an influential college administrator who championed academic excellence and intellectual opportunity for people of color. Rather than accept a teaching post at TUSKEGEE INSTITUTE, the school founded by Washington, Hope joined the faculty at Roger Williams College in Nashville, Tennessee, where he taught Latin, Greek, and science from 1894 to 1898. In 1898 he became a professor of classics at Atlanta Baptist College, the school that eventually became MOREHOUSE COLLEGE. In 1906, he began a lengthy tenure as president of Morehouse. In 1931 he was appointed president of Atlanta University and served until he passed away in February 1936.

Hope was an outspoken scholar-activist with close ties to the African-American intelligentsia. Among his colleagues and friends was W. E. B. DuBois, editor of THE CRISIS and a former Atlanta University professor. Hope published often on matters relating to African-American education, business, and success. In May 1931, for example, he published "Trained Men for Negro Business" in OPPORTUNITY. His essay was powerful in its incorporation of dramatic statistics about African-American economics and its argument about black enterprise in the face of "economic and social handicaps that the Negro faces in venturing into business." Hope linked black entrepreneurial success to education. He noted that while many institutions had graduated ministers and teachers, the new trend in education was to train "lawyers, doctors, dentists, and social workers who have won confidence by their skill and understanding." Yet, Hope proposed that colleges were

facing "a new and perhaps more difficult task—the training of Negro men and women for careers in business." He advocated preparation for leadership and technical training that would equip more people of color to succeed in business.

Hope's position on education, business, and economic advancement was echoed frequently in the fiction of the Harlem Renaissance. Writers such as JESSIE FAUSET, ALICE DUNBAR-NELSON, and others created sobering narratives about inspiring, talented, and highly educated characters in pursuit of rewarding professional careers.

Playwright RIDGELY TORRENCE penned one of the first biographies of Hope. His history, *The Story of John Hope,* was published in 1948.

Bibliography

Davis, Leroy. *A Clashing of the Soul: John Hope and the Dilemma of African American Leadership and Black Higher Education in the Early Twentieth Century.* Athens: University of Georgia Press, 1998.

Hope, John. *Leadership: The Heart of the Race Problem.* Atlanta, Ga.: Atlanta University, 1931.

John and Lugenia Hope Papers, Atlanta University Center Archives.

Torrence, Ridgely. *The Story of John Hope.* New York, Macmillan Co., 1948.

Hope, Rhonda

A pseudonym that writer CLAUDE MCKAY used while on staff at the WORKER'S DREADNOUGHT in England during the early 1920s.

"Hope Deferred"　Alice Dunbar-Nelson (1914)

A short story published by ALICE DUNBAR-NELSON, an accomplished writer, educator, and activist. "Hope Deferred" appeared in the September 1919 issue of THE CRISIS. Dunbar-Nelson was the former estranged wife of the deceased poet Paul Laurence Dunbar, who died in 1906. Despite her established career as a writer before and after her failed marriage, *The Crisis* identified the story's author as "Mrs. Paul Laurence Dunbar."

The story focuses on the highly demoralizing aspects of racism in 20th-century America. Like JESSIE FAUSET's short story "EMMY," which appeared in *The Crisis* in 1912–13, "Hope Deferred" focuses on the ambitions of an engineer, a talented man who is denied employment because of his race. Dunbar-Nelson chronicles the agonizing downward spiral of Louis Edwards, a newlywed man who is forced to become a strikebreaker and waiter in order to survive. The tragedy of the story is intensified because of Edwards's marriage to Margaret, a gentle, kind, and loving woman. The narrator describes him as a young man, "so young that he had not outgrown his ideals. Rather than allow that to happen, he had chosen one to share them with him, and the man who can find a woman willing to face poverty for her husband's ideals has a treasure far above rubies, and more precious than one with a thorough understanding of domestic science."

Edwards begins working at Adams's restaurant, an establishment owned by a man who "should have been rubicund, corpulent, American; instead he was wiry, lank, foreign in appearance." Adams hires Edwards, and the young husband motivates the staff in the face of violent protest from the striking workers who picket the restaurant. On one fateful day, however, Edwards has to serve Hanan, the man who most recently refused to consider his application for an engineering post. Eventually, the white man looks up and recognizes Edwards. He comments that Edwards has found "work for which [he] would be more fitted than engineering." Edwards manages to restrain himself, but at that very moment, a stone shatters the restaurant window. It hits the serving tray that Edwards is holding, and hot food spills onto Hanan. The catalyst for the event goes unnoticed as Hanan insults Edwards, and the two begin to fight. Edwards is arrested and sentenced to prison. The story closes as Margaret visits him and reassures him of her love and intent to wait for him to be free. Her last words to him, and the final scene of the story, deliver a romantic vision of the South, one that repudiates the false promise that the urban North extends to African Americans. Margaret Edwards counsels her husband to maintain his idealism and reminds him that his prison window "faces the South. . . . Look up and out of it all the while you are here," she advises. "[I]t is there, in our southland, that you will find the realization of your dream," she says.

Dunbar-Nelson's story addresses the segregated and divisive working world of the urban North during the early 20th century. It is a memorable comment on the realities of the Great Migration and a compelling meditation on the limits of assimilation, domestic hardships, and the denigration of talented African Americans.

Bibliography

Hull, Gloria, ed. *Color, Sex, & Poetry: Three Women Writers of the Harlem Renaissance.* Bloomington: Indiana University Press, 1987.
———. *The Works of Alice Dunbar-Nelson.* New York: Oxford University Press, 1988.

Horne, Frank S. (1899–1974)

An optometrist by training who published award-winning poetry in leading Harlem Renaissance journals and anthologies. He was part of the vibrant WASHINGTON, D.C., and NEW YORK CITY literary circles and collaborated with accomplished writers such as GEORGIA DOUGLAS JOHNSON.

Horne was born in New York City in August 1899 to Edwin and Cora Calhoun Horne. He attended the College of the City of New York and graduated in 1921. He excelled in sports and was extremely proud of the fact that he was a varsity track athlete. Although he admitted that he "had a hankering to write" from a very early age, it was in college that he began to write seriously. In the autobiographical note that he published in CAROLING DUSK (1927), the poetry anthology that included several of his poems, Horne admitted that it was during college that he had became "guilty . . . of my first sonnet." He credited CHARLES S. JOHNSON, editor of OPPORTUNITY, and GWENDOLYN BENNETT, poet and cultural critic, for encouraging him to publish.

Horne obtained his doctor of ophthalmology degree from Northern Illinois College of Ophthalmology in 1923. Immediately after graduation and until 1926, Horne practiced ophthalmology in New York City and in CHICAGO. He also pursued additional studies at COLUMBIA UNIVERSITY from 1929 to 1930 and earned a master's degree from the University of Southern California in 1932. He began teaching, and his administrative career in education began shortly thereafter. Soon after he joined the faculty at Fort Valley Normal and Industrial School in Fort Valley, Georgia, he was appointed dean and acting president of the school. In 1935, Horne became an administrative officer in the National Youth Administration and its division on Negro Affairs. He was active in housing administration offices in Washington, D.C., and in New York City. With MARY MCLEOD BETHUNE, president of BETHUNE-COOKMAN COLLEGE, and others, Horne was a valuable and often-consulted member of the Black Cabinet. This group, whose formation was proposed by First Lady Eleanor Roosevelt, was made up of accomplished African-American leaders who offered to President Roosevelt their evaluations of pressing current national issues.

Horne married Frankye Priestly Bunn in August 1930. The couple lived in the Crown Heights area of Brooklyn, a neighborhood of many African-American professionals and activists. He married his second wife, Mercedes Rector of Washington, D.C., in 1950. He was a member of Omega Psi Phi, the NATIONAL URBAN LEAGUE, and the NATIONAL ASSOCIATION FOR THE ADVANCEMENT OF COLORED PEOPLE.

Horne emerged as a poet while he was immersed in public life as an administrator and educator. Like RUDOLPH FISHER, a pioneering physician and scientist in X-ray technology, Horne merged his professional and writing lives. In 1925 his poem "Letters Found Near a Suicide" earned second prize in the Amy Spingarn Contest sponsored by THE CRISIS. During the Harlem Renaissance, Horne published in The Crisis, Opportunity, and WILLIAM STANLEY BRAITHWAITE's annual poetry anthologies.

Horne's poetry often invoked painful religious themes relating to the life of Jesus Christ. Works like "On Seeing Two Brown Boys in a Catholic Church" forecast the trials that people of color inevitably faced. The poem, published in the December 1925 issue of Opportunity, begins with an ominous statement. "'Tis fitting that you be here, / Little brown boys / With Christ-like eyes / And curling hair," muses the narrator. He then goes on to make disturbing predictions about the looming trials that the boys will face. He suggests that the innocent boys study the crucifix hanging in the church, since they too "shall know this thing." In this world, African Americans "shall know Hell, will suffer under Pontius Pilate" and "feel the rugged cut of rough hewn cross / Upon . . . surging shoulder."

Horne's poems also explore visceral emotional trauma brought on by difficult relationships and overwhelming melancholy. "To a Persistent Phantom," published first in Opportunity, revealed a speaker tortured by his inability to suppress the memory of a former love. "I buried you deeper last night," he says, but he soon has obsessive awareness of his sweetheart's charms. "I buried you deeper last night / With fuller breasts / And stronger arms / With softer lips / And newer charms / I buried you deeper last night." The speaker endows the object of his attention with greater physical and emotional strength. By poem's end, the battle between the mourner and the mourned is raging intensely. "[T]hat gay spirit / That once was you / Will tear its soul / In climbing through / Deeper . . . aye, deeper / I buried you deeper last night." The lack of resolution in this affair suggests the speaker's haunting powerlessness even as it demonstrates his purposeful engagement with the past.

Horne's most well-known poem, "Letters Found Near a Suicide" is a lengthy and tortured narrative comprising 11 letters that one person writes to important people in his life. The poem begins with a note entitled "To All of You" that suggests the disturbing ease with which the deceased has slipped away. "My little stone / Sinks quickly / Into the bosom of this deep, dark pool / Of oblivion," he writes. Clearly determined to overcome anonymity in death, the writer notes satisfyingly that "those far shores / That knew me not / Will feel the fleeting, furtive kiss / Of my tiny concentric ripples." The speaker then delivers a series of notes to friends, family, lost lovers, and others with whom he has commiserated about the tragedies of love and life. A tone of indictment emerges in the note "To Telie," about a person who "made my voice / A rippling laugh / But my heart / A crying thing." In the longest note to a male friend with the nickname "Chick," the speaker revels in memories of "far flung days of abandon" and transforms his suicide into an act of athletic triumph. He chronicles the closeness of their friendship, a bond that prompted others to call them "The Terrible Two." The speaker celebrates their triumphs on the playing fields and his ability to "slip through / Fighting and squirming / Over the line / To victory. / You remember Chick? . . ." This note closes on a plaintive note as the speaker implores his chum to remember their good days. "When you gaze at me here," he instructs him, "Let that same light / Of faith and admiration / Shine in your eyes / For I have battered the stark stonewall / Before me . . . I have kept faith with you / And now / I have called my signal."

In fall 1926 Horne collaborated with Georgia Douglas Johnson, the noted Washington, D.C., poet, and with MAY MILLER SULLIVAN, playwright and daughter of HOWARD UNIVERSITY dean KELLY MILLER. The three worked with the KRIGWA PLAYERS on the New York City production of BLUE BLOOD, Johnson's riveting, prize-winning play on incest, sexual oppression, and intraracial caste prejudice.

In 1927, COUNTEE CULLEN selected four of Horne's poems for inclusion in *Caroling Dusk: An Anthology of Verse by Negro Poets.* These included "On Seeing Two Brown Boys in a Catholic Church," "To a Persistent Phantom," "Letters Found Near a Suicide," and "Nigger: A Chant for Children." JAMES WELDON JOHNSON also included Horne poems in his edited anthology THE BOOK OF AMERICAN NEGRO POETRY (1931).

Horne continued to write and publish after the Harlem Renaissance ended. Poems appeared in *The Poetry of the Negro, 1746–1949* edited by ARNA BONTEMPS and LANGSTON HUGHES. In 1964 Horne published *Haverstraw*, a collection of poems. His poems also were included in anthologies such as Charlemae Rollins and Tom O'Sullivan's *Chrismas Gif': An Anthology of Christmas Poems, Songs, and Stories* (1963), a collection of poems that featured numerous Harlem Renaissance era writers such as ZORA NEALE HURSTON, Langston Hughes, and EFFIE LEE NEWSOME.

Bibliography

Cullen, Countee. *Caroling Dusk: An Anthology of Verse by Negro Poets.* New York: Harper & Brothers Publishers, 1927.

Primeau, Ronald. "Frank Horne and the Second Echelon Poets of the Harlem Renaissance." In *Remembering the Harlem Renaissance*, edited by Carry D. Wintz, 371–391. New York: Garland, 1996.

House of Sham, The Willis Richardson (1929)

A stirring one-act play by WILLIS RICHARDSON that exposes the fragility of domesticity and social status. *The House of Sham* was written in 1929 and published in Richardson's edited volume PLAYS AND PAGEANTS FROM THE LIFE OF THE NEGRO (1930). The anthology, produced at the urging of CARTER G. WOODSON, included twelve plays by writers such as MAUDE CUNEY HARE, MAY MILLER, JOHN MATHEUS, and EDWARD McCOO. All of the works were deemed suitable for study and performance by high school students, and none was written in dialect. Richardson's play, one of three that he included in the anthology, was part of a substantial dramatic focus in Harlem Renaissance writing on American family life and the demands of middle-class life.

The Cooper family home, the only set location in the play, is a house of sham. Described as a home that belongs to a "well-to-do colored family," it houses John Cooper, who is a realtor on the verge of bankruptcy, his wife Mrs. Cooper, their spoiled daughter Enid, and their practical niece Joyce Adams. The three other characters are Dr. Bill Holland, a physician and Enid's love interest, Hal Ford, an employee in Cooper's real estate office, and Dorsey, a desperate man who believes that Cooper has swindled him.

The two major story lines of the play both involve bankruptcy—financial and moral. The Cooper family has lived beyond its means. Doing so has resulted in Enid's preference for a rich husband rather than a steady and honest companion. Her mother quickly deflects Hal Ford's interest in her daughter and suggests that he is not worthy of Enid's attentions. In a move that recalls the classic dysfunctional families who are often featured in fairy tales, Mrs. Cooper persuades Ford that he is an acceptable match for her niece Joyce. While Joyce is somewhat dismayed by her aunt's politics, she emerges victorious at the end. It appears that despite appearances to the contrary, Bill Holland is not a wealthy physician. As the play closes, Enid's fiancé abandons her because her family is incapable of providing for him also.

The second major plot line of the play revolves around Dorsey, a man intent on recovering $500 from John Cooper. Sure that he has been overcharged in the recent sale of his home, Dorsey stakes out the Cooper house in order to confront his broker. He threatens to kill Cooper and, when he does find the man at home, barricades himself in the study with the family. Hal Ford has argued in vain with his boss about the deal but restrains himself from challenging Cooper's authority. Mrs. Cooper, determined to stop Dorsey's visits to her house and to protect her husband, decides to use subterfuge to obtain a blank check from her husband that she can then make payable to Dorsey. In a tense showdown that threatens to kill Mr. Cooper, Mrs. Cooper appears to save the day when she hands Dorsey the check. In the moments following the man's departure, John Cooper reveals that he has been dodging creditors, that the family home is on the verge of repossession, and that he has been living a sham. The Cooper family women are dismayed by the prospect of working in order to pay off family debts. Joyce Adams and Hal Ford give thanks for the prospect of their union, a relationship founded on genuine honesty and realism.

The House of Sham focuses on family dynamics and complex social negotiations of class status and intraracial relationships. These primary issues reinforced Richardson's reputation as a writer who was concerned with the kinds of social contracts that both emancipate and constrain individuals. His focus on African-American family life and the pressures that can plague the middle class revealed the great diversity of African-American life and experience.

Bibliography

Gray, Christine Rauchfuss. *Willis Richardson, Forgotten Pioneer of African-American Drama.* Westport, Conn.: Greenwood Press, 1999.

Howard Theater

Located in Washington, D.C., at Seventh and T Streets, the Howard Theater was one of the earliest venues dedicated to showcasing African-American performers and productions. It was the first theater built in America to accommodate African-American audiences and productions.

It opened in 1910 and was primarily a venue in which African-American theater, vaudeville, and jazz performances were held. It closed in 1929 on the eve of the GREAT DEPRESSION. Identified as one of America's historic treasures, the long-abandoned building now is in the process of being revitalized.

Howard University

The alma mater of many accomplished scholars, writers, and artists of the Harlem Renaissance period. Members of the First Congregational Society of WASHINGTON, D.C., founded this historically black university in 1866.

Originally organized to prepare African Americans for the ministry, it soon became a liberal arts school. The institution was named in honor of General Oliver Otis Howard, a Civil War general and the commissioner of the Freedmen's Bureau.

The university, located in the heart of Washington, D.C., was and remains a vital intellectual and cultural forum. Its alumni include the first African-American Supreme Court justice, Thurgood Marshall, and Nobel laureate Toni Morrison. It was on the Howard University campus that the influential African-American Greek sororities and fraternities ALPHA KAPPA ALPHA, DELTA SIGMA THETA, Omega Psi Phi, and Phi Beta Sigma were founded.

A number of leading figures of the Harlem Renaissance were educated at Howard. ZORA NEALE HURSTON enrolled in courses at the school and in 1920 earned an associate's degree. While there, she participated in the literary club founded by professors ALAIN LOCKE and THOMAS MONTGOMERY GREGORY and published her first short story in *STYLUS,* the school's literary magazine. THELMA DUNCAN honed her skills as a writer and dramatist at Howard. There she worked with Professor Thomas Montgomery Gregory, founder of the HOWARD UNIVERSITY PLAYERS, the troupe that also performed her work. She graduated cum laude with a degree in music. Poet, playwright, and writer LANGSTON HUGHES, who lived in Washington, D.C., for a time and eventually left the city to attend LINCOLN UNIVERSITY in Pennsylvania, had deep but unfulfilled hopes of attending Howard. WILLIS RICHARDSON, a celebrated playwright, was admitted to Howard, but his family's dire financial situation required that he forgo the scholarship and begin working. Historian BENJAMIN BRAWLEY and writer LEWIS ALEXANDER also attended the school.

Norris Wright Cuney II, the father of poet WILLIAM WARING CUNEY, attended the Howard University Law School before becoming a federal government worker. His son attended Howard University for a short time before going on to study music in Boston and in Rome. The gifted physician and writer RUDOLPH FISHER attended Howard University Medical School and graduated in 1924 with highest honors.

Howard University faculty made significant contributions to the Harlem Renaissance through their scholarship and pioneering efforts in education. Educator and drama scholar THOMAS MONTGOMERY GREGORY had deep ties to the school. His father, James Monroe Gregory, was one of the three men who made up the first graduating class at Howard. Upon his graduation, James Gregory joined the faculty and lived on campus with his family. T. Montgomery Gregory, a HARVARD UNIVERSITY graduate, joined the faculty in 1910. He became the first chair of the Drama Department when it was established in 1921, and he established the Howard University Players, which became one of the nation's leading college theater troupes. Their productions of works by Howard University students and alumni and of accomplished professional playwrights signaled a vibrant new chapter in American theater history. Like Gregory, writer and folklore expert STERLING BROWN had strong ties to the school. Brown was born on the Howard University campus in 1901. His father, Sterling Nelson Brown, a minister, was a professor of religion there. In 1929 he returned to the school and began a 40-year career there as a professor of English. ALAIN LOCKE joined the faculty at Howard University in 1912. After leaving to complete doctoral work in philosophy at Harvard, he returned to Howard in 1918 and taught until his retirement in 1952. James Porter, an acclaimed art professor and scholar regarded as the father of African-American art history, was a Howard University student and faculty member. He began his studies in 1923 and was appointed lecturer in art immediately after his graduation. His teaching career spanned more than 40 years. The Howard art faculty included GWENDOLYN BENNETT, who taught in the mid-1920s, and James Lesesne Wells, who began teaching in 1929.

KELLY MILLER, sociologist, was dean of the school and the father of MAY MILLER SULLIVAN, a talented drama student at Howard. Edward Christopher Williams, a son-in-law of writer CHARLES CHESNUTT, was head librarian and Professor of German and Romance Languages at Howard.

Bibliography

Dyson, Walter. *The Founding of Howard University.* Washington, D.C.: Howard University Press, 1921.

Logan, Rayford Whittingham. *Howard University: The First Hundred Years, 1867–1967.* New York: New York University Press, 1969.

Howard University Players (Howard Players)

The dramatic troupe that THOMAS MONTGOMERY GREGORY founded at HOWARD UNIVERSITY in 1919. Gregory, who became the first director of Howard's drama department when it was established in 1921, saw the opportunity to advance African-American drama at and beyond Howard. The troupe was part of a larger successful campaign to develop a national African-American dramatic tradition. This troupe, which preceded other influential groups such as the KRIGWA PLAYERS and the HARLEM SUITCASE THEATRE, established important precedents in American theater. The Howard University Players were a pioneering force in African-American and American drama.

The troupe was an invaluable resource for playwrights who were committed to developing serious works about African Americans. It is important to note, however, that the actors frequently demonstrated their professional range by performing theater staples and a variety of well-known dramatic works. These included William Shakespeare's *Hamlet,* Henrik Ibsen's *A Doll's House,* and Anton Chekhov's *The Proposal.*

Like the Krigwa Players, established in 1924 by REGINA ANDREWS and W. E. B. DUBOIS, and the Harlem Suitcase Theatre, founded by LANGSTON HUGHES in 1937, the Howard University Players focused primarily on works by and about African Americans. Their status as a college organization also meant that they had a special responsibility to perform student work. The troupe produced a number of plays written by Howard University women students and alumna. These included De Reath Irene Byrd Beausey, THELMA MYRTLE DUNCAN, OTTIE BEATRICE GRAHAM, MAY MILLER SULLIVAN, and Helen Webb. In 1920 the group produced Miller's *Within the Shadow.* Two years later in 1922, they staged *Genefrede,* a play about the tragic death of Toussaint Louverture's fiancée, written while Webb was a student of Gregory's at

Howard. The troupe performed the work again in 1923 at Howard's Rankin Memorial Chapel as part of a fund-raising effort to establish a theater laboratory. *Genefrede* was published in 1935 in *Negro History in Thirteen Plays* edited by WILLIS RICHARDSON and May Miller. The troupe also performed the one-act play *The Yellow Tree* by De Reath Beausey, a work that was published in *The Crisis* in 1922.

Under Gregory's direction, the Howard University Players also developed successful productions of works by professional playwrights such as PAUL GREEN, EUGENE O'NEILL, Willis Richardson, and RIDGELY TORRENCE. One of their best-known productions featured a collaboration with Charles Gilpin in O'Neill's *THE EMPEROR JONES*. In the 1923–24 season, the troupe produced JEAN TOOMER's one-act play *BALO*.

The Howard University Players were recognized nationally as one of the most innovative college dramatic troupes. George Pierce Baker, drama scholar at Harvard University, insisted that the Howard University Players were one of the top two troupes in the nation. In the years following the Harlem Renaissance, the group gained international status. In 1949, they traveled to Norway, Denmark, Sweden, and Germany as goodwill ambassadors, the first college drama troupe to do so.

"How It Feels to Be Colored Me"
Zora Neale Hurston (1928)
A powerful essay on racial identity and society by ZORA NEALE HURSTON. The essay appeared in the May 1928 issue of *THE WORLD TOMORROW*, a Protestant magazine whose staff at the time included WALLACE THURMAN, Hurston's colleague and collaborator.

The essay is hailed as an especially memorable and insightful meditation on autonomy and the evolution of self. Hurston engages popular myths about racial identity as she works toward an assertion about how history both defines and underestimates African Americans. The piece begins with Hurston's sardonic comment about her ancestry and the ways in which contemporary society contends with blackness. "I am colored," she declares, "but I offer nothing in the way of extenuating circumstances except the fact that I am the only Negro in the United States whose grandfather on

the mother's side was *not* an Indian chief." Hurston's striking opening lines lead to other observations about the ways in which others try to define and limit her identity in the context of slavery. She defies the investment in the dehumanized and powerless figure of the slave, a characterization that is meant to render her "tragically colored." She insists that she is investing in a life of mobility and self-determination. "I do not belong to the sobbing school of Negrohood who hold that nature somehow has given them a low-down dirty deal and whose feelings are all hurt about it," she writes.

Hurston's essay is part of a major canon of African-American coming-of-age narratives such as RICHARD WRIGHT's *Black Boy*, James Baldwin's *Notes of A Native Son*, and fictional accounts such as JESSIE FAUSET's short story "EMMY" and NELLA LARSEN's *PASSING*. Hurston links her racial awareness to performance, the opportunities she had to "speak pieces" and "sing and . . . dance the parse-me-la" for the white people who traveled through and lived outside of the all-black town of EATONVILLE, Florida. She also notes that particular settings or environments provoke her sense of race. While she admits, "I do not always feel colored," she goes on to note that she feels "most colored when . . . thrown against a sharp white background." Her immersion in white environments or situations in which whites subject her every move to scrutiny can be problematic. While she may react powerfully to music, a white companion may remain unmoved. It is at these moments when there is such a sharp contrast in receptivity and response that Hurston imagines that a companion has "only heard what I felt . . . He is so pale with his whiteness then and I am so colored." The essay closes with a dynamic image of humanity like a set of colored bags "of miscellany" filled by God, "the Great Stuffer of Bags."

The circumstances surrounding the publication of the essay were especially fraught with tension for Hurston. She had been engaged in a rather unfortunate exchange with CHARLOTTE OSGOOD MASON, her wealthy and domineering patron. Mason had been angered by Hurston's critique of the recent collection of African-American work songs by HOWARD ODUM and GUY JOHNSON. According to Hurston biographer Valerie Boyd, Mason felt targeted by Hurston's comment that "white people could not be trusted to collect the lore of others" (Boyd, 172). Shortly after the two worked their way through that misunderstanding, Hurston published "How It Feels to Be Colored Me." In addition to its focus on the ways in which whites could fail to appreciate different cultures, the essay suggested Hurston's professional autonomy, a status that was in direct conflict with her relationship with Mason. Her patron also was intent on maintaining complete control of Hurston's finances and had to be reassured that Hurston had not profited from the essay. ALAIN LOCKE, another Mason protégé, supported Hurston's claims that she had used the funds to support the effort to publish *Fire!!*, the short-lived journal that she cofounded with Wallace Thurman, LANGSTON HUGHES, and BRUCE NUGENT. In a June 1928 letter to Locke, Hurston reveals that she actually sent the essay to *The World Tomorrow* in an effort to repay the magazine because of "the debt we owed them on *Fire*."

"How It Feels to Be Colored Me" is a landmark essay about the myths and realities of racial identity and is a vital part of Hurston's considerable canon.

Bibliography

Boyd, Valerie. *Wrapped in Rainbows: The Life of Zora Neale Hurston.* New York: Scribner, 2003.

Hemenway, Robert. *Zora Neale Hurston: A Literary Biography.* Urbana: University of Ilinois, 1977.

Kaplan, Carla. *Zora Neale Hurston: A Life in Letters.* New York: Doubleday, 2002.

Hughes, (James Mercer) Langston
(1902–1967)

One of the most active, most published, and most beloved poets of the Harlem Renaissance. In addition to his collections of poems, short stories, and novels, Hughes was a journalist, historian, essayist, translator, playwright, lyricist, founder of a theater group, and editor. He published frequently in the leading literary and race journals of his time. Identified in 1934 as one of America's most intriguing socially conscious individuals, Hughes also won prestigious prizes, such as the GUGGENHEIM FELLOWSHIP and the SPINGARN MEDAL. He was a literary and cultural ambassador whose travels and lectures heightened awareness of the diversity, talent, and depth of the African-American literary tradition.

He was born James Mercer Langston Hughes in Joplin, Missouri. His parents were James Nathaniel Hughes of Charlestown, Indiana, and Caroline [Carrie] Mercer Langston Hughes of Lawrence, Kansas. Hughes's racially mixed ancestry had especially powerful links to American antebellum and Civil War history. His paternal grandfather was a Civil War soldier, his maternal great-grandfather Ralph Quarles was a white Virginia Revolutionary War captain, and his maternal great-uncle was John Mercer Langston, the first elected African American from Virginia to serve in the House of Representatives.

His father, who worked in the office of a mining company in Joplin, moved out of the family home. He supported the family financially throughout his travels, which included a sojourn in Cuba and a longtime residence in Mexico. When Hughes did see his father there in 1908, an earthquake rocked Mexico City. James Hughes, who eventually settled in Toluca, Mexico, became a prosperous landlord, general manager of a power company, and also was a member of the Mexican bar.

Hughes lived primarily with his mother and maternal grandmother in the years following his father's departure. It was his grandmother Mary Langston, a stern woman of Cherokee heritage, who first immersed Hughes in stories of African-American history. Following her death in 1915, family friends whom he referred to as Aunt and Uncle Reed took in Hughes. Hughes's residence with the Reeds exposed him to Christianity and gave him ample opportunity to develop his faith. He resisted, and throughout his life he considered organized religion a lost cause and never joined a church. Just before his 14th birthday, Hughes left the Reeds and went to live with his newly remarried mother, her husband Homer Clark, and Clark's infant son Gwyn, the brother whom Hughes called Kit. In the fall of 1916, Hughes began high school in Cleveland, the city in which Homer Clark had found work as a building caretaker and janitor.

Hughes completed high school in Cleveland. His four years of study had been enriched by his immersion in books and in artistic and dramatic activities at the Neighborhood Association, a local settlement house in Cleveland run by ROWENA and RUSSELL JELLIFFE. Hughes was an avid reader whose tastes ranged from the works of novelist THEODORE DREISER and the poets Carl Sandburg and Vachel Lindsay to philosophers Arthur Schopenhauer and Friedrich Nietzsche.

Following his graduation from Central High School in 1920, he accepted his father's invitation to return to Mexico. Despite his mother's protests, Hughes reunited with his father. During his time in Mexico, he taught English at a local girls' school and business college. He did not follow his father's suggestions that he study engineering in Europe and return to Mexico. Instead, he returned to NEW YORK CITY to begin classes at COLUMBIA UNIVERSITY. Hughes, who boarded at the YMCA on West 135th Street before overcoming Columbia University prejudice that threatened to deny him a dormitory room, began to explore the vibrant world of Harlem. While Harlem was a thriving and inspiring place for Hughes, Columbia University was not. Despite his best efforts, Hughes was put off by the racism of fellow students on the staff of the student newspaper, felt alienated from many of his classmates, and was bored by his classes. He left after his first year. In the years before he resumed his formal education, Hughes worked as a florist delivery boy, joined the crew of the Africa-bound SS *Malone* as a mess boy, was the personal assistant to historian CARTER G. WOODSON, and was employed as an office helper in the offices of Woodson's ASSOCIATION FOR THE STUDY OF NEGRO LIFE AND HISTORY. Hughes began his studies at LINCOLN UNIVERSITY, the first college established in the North for African-American men, in the spring of 1926. Despite the prospect of studying at HARVARD UNIVERSITY, at the urging of WARING CUNEY and suggestions from ALAIN LOCKE, Hughes chose Lincoln and graduated in 1929. AMY SPINGARN, a dedicated sponsor of African-American arts and the namesake of one of the first literary contests in which Hughes would win awards, offered to finance his education.

Hughes never married. Scholars continue to debate whether or not the writer, who moved in openly gay circles, was a homosexual. There is no confirmation of Hughes's sexual orientation. Biographers such as Arnold Rampersad have profiled Hughes as a man without a significant sexual iden-

tity. Other critics cite contemporary evidence that suggests that the intensely private Hughes was gay. For instance, Hughes's close friend ARNA BONTEMPS once remarked that his friend "never betrayed the mincing or posturing offensive to the straight world." Other Harlem Renaissance figures who were identified as homosexual, such as COUNTEE CULLEN and Alain Locke, tried in vain to develop an intimate relationship with Hughes.

Hughes's promise as a writer and his demonstrated penchant for social influence emerged at an early age. At age 13 he was elected class poet; by his senior year of high school, he was editor of the class yearbook. One major triumph that emerged from his otherwise frustrating time as a Columbia student was his opportunity to meet JESSIE FAUSET, literary editor of *THE CRISIS,* and to benefit from the efforts on his behalf made by AUGUSTUS GRANVILLE DILL, the magazine's business manager.

Hughes, who gave a reading at the Community Church in Manhattan as a result of Dill's outreach, made his literary debut in *The Crisis.* In 1921, he responded to Fauset's invitation and submitted the powerful poem "The Negro Speaks of Rivers" to *The Crisis.* Between his departure from Columbia and his return to college at Lincoln University, Hughes wrote and published works that grew out of his growing awareness of racial prejudice and the limitations placed on people of color in America. His works also were inspired by his observations and experiences of Harlem, where he continued to take advantage of the rich and diverse arts and culture offerings. Alain Locke was impressed by Hughes's poems and made an earnest effort to meet the young poet, whose works embodied the excellence and sophistication of African-American writing that Locke was determined to showcase. In 1924, while working as a busboy in a WASHINGTON, D.C., hotel, Hughes slipped three poems onto the dinner table of Vachel Lindsay, a hotel guest, renowned poet, and one of Hughes's favorite poets. Lindsay, impressed by the works, later interrupted his own poetry reading to share Hughes's works with his audience. Lindsay's promotion of Hughes, coupled with his advice to the aspiring writer to "hide, study, read, and think," was a powerful moment in Hughes's artistic development. Pursued by the press, who were determined to find the "busboy poet," as

Hughes was described, he eventually quit his hotel job and moved back to New York.

Hughes published his first volume of poems just before he began college at Lincoln. He also was the celebrated winner of the first literary competition sponsored by OPPORTUNITY magazine. In May 1925 he won first prize for "The Weary Blues," saw his poem "America" tie for third prize with poems by Countee Cullen, and garnered honorable mention for "The Jester" and "Songs to the Dark Virgin." In August he emerged as a double winner in the first prizes awarded in the Amy Spingarn Contest in Literature and Art. His essay "The Fascination of Cities" won the $40 second prize in the essay contest, and his poems "Cross" and "Minstrel Man" earned the $10 third prize. Hughes continued to win prestigious literary prizes throughout the Harlem Renaissance. These included first place in the 1926 Witter Bynner undergraduate poetry contest and the 1927 PALMS Magazine Intercollegiate Poetry award. In 1931 he won the Harmon gold medal for literature for his first novel, NOT WITHOUT LAUGHTER. In 1935 he was awarded a Guggenheim Fellowship and in 1941 received a JULIUS ROSENWALD FELLOWSHIP.

Hughes enjoyed a steady professional relationship with Knopf, the New York City–based publisher. He published THE WEARY BLUES, his first volume of poems, in 1926. This was followed shortly thereafter by FINE CLOTHES TO THE JEW in 1927, SCOTTSBORO LIMITED: FOUR POEMS AND A PLAY in 1932. His post–Harlem Renaissance publications included *Shakespeare in Harlem* (1942), *Fields of Wonder* (1947), *One Way Ticket* (1949), *Montage of a Dream Deferred* (1951), and *Ask Your Mama* (1961).

Hughes was a master of the short story form. He published several collections, including THE WAYS OF WHITE FOLKS (1934) after traveling through Russia, China, and Japan. He started writing while in Moscow and completed the volume, which was inspired by his readings of D. H. Lawrence, in Carmel, California, while part of a writers community.

Hughes had extremely productive collaborations with major figures of the Harlem Renaissance. His most well-documented friendships and working relationships involve Arna Bon-temps, ZORA NEALE HURSTON, and Carl Van Vechten.

Hughes and Bontemps met in 1924 and one year later began a correspondence that would last until Hughes's death in 1967. During that 42-year period, the writers exchanged some 2,300 letters. The two writers exchanged work, critiqued each other's writing, networked, discussed the works and lives of fellow writers and friends, and encouraged each other tirelessly. The Hughes-Bontemps correspondence provides vital insights into their professional development, gives invaluable commentary on the Harlem Renaissance, and showcases a rich friendship between two gifted, thoughtful, and ambitious individuals.

Hughes and Bontemps made important contributions to American literary history through their edited collections of African-American poetry. In 1949 the two edited *The Poetry of the Negro, 1746–1949*, a volume that documented the evolution of African-American poetry and showcased works by well- and lesser-known Harlem Renaissance poets. These included writers such as GWENDOLYN BENNETT, STERLING BROWN, JOSEPH COTTER, SR., CLARISSA SCOTT DELANY, JESSIE FAUSET, GEORGIA DOUGLAS JOHNSON, JAMES WELDON JOHNSON, EFFIE LEE NEWSOME, and JEAN TOOMER.

One of Hughes's most memorable and explosive alliances was with another longtime friend and correspondent, Zora Neale Hurston. Like Hurston and Alain Locke, Hughes was a beneficiary of CHARLOTTE OSGOOD MASON, a demanding and wealthy patron. During his affiliation with Mason, which lasted from 1927 through 1930, Hughes published NOT WITHOUT LAUGHTER. The relationship ended disastrously and caused Hughes much emotional and financial distress. In 1926 Hughes and Hurston, working alongside WALLACE THURMAN, BRUCE NUGENT, and AARON DOUGLAS, established *Fire!!*, the powerful but short-lived literary journal. Hughes and Hurston collaborated on the play MULE BONE. Subsequent machinations on Hurston's part, coupled with the unauthorized distribution of the work, however, prompted a real conflict between the two literary giants.

Hughes also developed a lifelong relationship with Carl Van Vechten, a dance critic and the author of the controversial novel NIGGER HEAVEN.

Carl Van Vechten (right) and Langston Hughes, New York, February 16, 1963. Photograph by Richard Avedon

Hughes and Van Vechten solidified their friendship in the tumultuous days that followed the
publication of the novel. Hughes was one of the
African-American literati who defended the work
against those who deemed it thoroughly racist.
When Van Vechten was sued for copyright infringement based on his unauthorized inclusion of

blues songs in the novel, it was Hughes who composed new lyrics to be included in the book.

Hughes was one of America's most successful
and prolific playwrights. He combined his love of
theater with work in related fields of film and
music. In 1938 he established the HARLEM SUIT-
CASE THEATRE, a group that contributed to the

tradition of innovative drama inaugurated by the HOWARD PLAYERS based at HOWARD UNIVERSITY under the direction of T. MONTGOMERY GREGORY. The troupe produced his play *Don't You Want to Be Free? From Slavery Through the Blues to Now—and Then Some, Limitations of Life* (1938), *The Em-Fuehrer Jones* (1938), and other works. In 1935, Hughes tackled the issues of miscegenation, family chaos, and betrayal in MULATTO, the play that became the longest-running African-American play on BROADWAY until 1959, when Lorraine Hansberry's *A Raisin in the Sun* broke the record. *Mulatto* was banned in Philadelphia because of its subject matter. Additional Harlem Renaissance-era plays include *Soul Gone Home* (1937), *Little Eva's End* (1938), and *The Organizer* (1939). Hughes produced a substantial number of plays in the 1940s, 1950s, and 1960s including *For This We Fight* (1943), *The Glory Round His Head* (1953), *The Ballad of the Brown King* (1960), *Tambourines to Glory* (1963), and *The Prodigal Son* (1965).

Hughes enjoyed writing sessions with Rosamond Johnson, brother of the novelist and NATIONAL ASSOCIATION FOR THE ADVANCEMENT OF COLORED PEOPLE director JAMES WELDON JOHNSON. Hughes also composed lyrics for musician W. C. HANDY and for Caroline Dudley, who was working on a musical revue entitled *O Blues!* that would showcase African-American folk songs. Hughes continued to work in theater after the Harlem Renaissance. He returned to Cleveland and wrote two dramas for the Jelliffes and the Gilpin Players, their dramatic troupe. The Cleveland plays, written in 1936, were *Little Ham*, a comedy, and *Emperor of Haiti*, a historical drama. His later works included the staging of *The Sun Do Move* in CHICAGO in 1941, lyrics for Kurt Weill and Elmer Rice's Broadway production *Street Scene* (1946), *Black Nativity* (1961), a multi-genre performance piece, a Civil Rights–related drama entitled *Jericho—Jim Crow* (1964), and numerous adaptations of his own writings. In 1957 his series of lively short stories about Jesse B. Semple became *Simply Heavenly*, a Broadway musical. Hughes's foray into film included collaborations with Clarence Muse on the 1939 film *Way Down South*, for which Hughes wrote the screenplay.

In 1930 Hughes published his first novel, NOT WITHOUT LAUGHTER, a fictionalized autobiograph-

ical narrative. In 1932 he collaborated with his close friend Arna Bontemps and published *POPO AND FIFINA*, a children's story about Haiti.

Hughes published THE BIG SEA, the first installment of his two-part autobiography, in 1940. Sixteen years later, he completed *I Wonder As I Wander*. In the decades before his death, Hughes continued to write, travel, and generate illuminating analyses of contemporary issues and world events. As a correspondent for the *Baltimore Afro-American* newspaper, he provided coverage of the Spanish Civil War. In 1942 he became a regular contributor to the CHICAGO DEFENDER. During the 1950s, Hughes, like PAUL ROBESON and Albert Einstein, was targeted by the McCarthyists. Hughes was subpoenaed to testify before Congress but refused to implicate any of his colleagues or friends.

A member of Omega Psi Phi, Hughes also enjoyed memberships in professional societies such as the Authors Guild, Dramatic Guild, American Society of Composers, and PEN. He was awarded the prestigious Spingarn Medal in 1960. In 1961 he was elected to membership in the highly selective National Institute of Arts and Letters. Hughes was awarded honorary degrees from Lincoln University, Howard University, and Case Western Reserve University.

Langston Hughes lived in Harlem in a three-story town house purchased from the royalties earned from his Broadway collaboration with Kurt Weill and Elmer Rice. He died of congestive heart failure and complications from prostate cancer at Polyclinic Hospital, where he recently had undergone surgery. He was alone when he died in his sleep on May 22, 1967. Roy Wilkins, director of the NAACP, mourned the passing of the man "who in his own remarkable way was a crusader for freedom for millions of people." Whitney Young, Jr., NATIONAL URBAN LEAGUE director, remembered Hughes as a "courageous fighter for human rights and dignity." *The New York Times* eulogized Hughes as the "O. Henry of Harlem." The newspaper's tribute to Hughes conveyed his vibrant personality through its colorful quotes in which Hughes defined himself as a man who was "unmarried" and liked "'Tristan,' goat's milk, short novels, lyric poems, heat, simple folk, boats and bull fights" and disliked "'Aida,' parsnips, long novels, narrative poems, cold, pretentious folk, buses, and bridges." In keeping with the stipulations that Hughes dictated in his will, funeral services were held in a Harlem funeral home with music provided by a jazz combo, the Randy Weston Trio.

The full life and stunning career of Langston Hughes underscore the richness, power, and depth of the Harlem Renaissance.

Bibliography

Bernard, Emily, ed. *Remember Me to Harlem: The Letters of Langston Hughes and Carl Van Vechten, 1925–1964.* New York: Knopf, 2001.

Berry, Faith, ed. *Good Morning Revolution: The Uncollected Social Protest Writing of Langston Hughes.* Westport, Conn.: Lawrence Hill, 1973.

———. *Langston Hughes: Before and Beyond Harlem.* Westport, Conn.: Lawrence Hill & Company, 1983.

De Santis, Christopher C. *Langston Hughes and the Chicago Defender: Essays on Race, Politics, and Culture, 1942–62.* Urbana: University of Illinois Press, 1995.

Langston Hughes Papers, James Weldon Johnson Memorial Collection, Beinecke Library, Yale University; Moorland-Spingarn Research Library, Howard University; Fisk University Library; Amistad Collection, New Orleans; and Bancroft Library of the University of California at Berkeley.

Nichols, Charles H., ed. *Arna Bontemps–Langston Hughes Letters, 1925–1967.* New York: Paragon House, 1990.

Rampersad, Arnold. *The Life of Langston Hughes: I, Too, Sing America.* Vol. 1, *1902–1941.* New York: Oxford University Press, 1986.

———. *The Life of Langston Hughes: I Dream a World.* Vol. 2, *1941–1967.* New York: Oxford University Press, 1988.

Wood, Gregory. "Gay Re-Readings of the Harlem Renaissance Poets." In *Critical Essays: Gay and Lesbian Writers of Color,* edited by Emmanuel S. Nelson. Binghamton, N.Y.: Haworth Press, 1993.

"Humor of Teaching, The" Anna Julia Cooper (1930)

One of several essays that philosopher and educator ANNA JULIA COOPER published during the Harlem Renaissance. The accomplished scholar published her most influential work, *A Voice from the South,* in 1892. She maintained the intense feminist perspective on education, culture, society, and politics articulated in *A Voice from the South* throughout her public life.

A highly respected educator and former principal of the prestigious M Street, or DUNBAR HIGH SCHOOL in WASHINGTON, D.C. She was prompted to write "The Humor of Teaching," which appeared in the November 1930 issue of THE CRISIS, in response to an ongoing debate on education published in the magazine.

Cooper proposed that teachers and students in segregated schools suffered in part from flawed and distracting self-imposed standards of excellence. The attention to minute details at the expense of immersion in "the very atmosphere of current life and thought" was, according to Cooper, "a handicap unknown and unsuspected in the teaching body itself." She lamented the fact that many of the teachers in segregated schools were "largely bookfed" and spent too much energy attempting to maintain a potentially unreliable intellectual status quo advanced by white scholars whose work also suffered from the pressures of academic performance. Cooper used her essay "The Humor of Teaching" to call for a return to learning for learning's sake.

Bibliography

Gabel, Leona C. *From Slavery to the Sorbonne and Beyond: The Life and Writings of Anna J. Cooper.* Northampton, Mass.: Smith College, 1982.

Johnson, Karen Ann. *Uplifting the Women and the Race: The Educational Philosophies and Social Activism of Anna Julia Cooper and Nannie Helen Burroughs.* New York: Garland Publishers, 2000.

Hunch, The Eulalie Spence (1927)

A one-act play by EULALIE SPENCE that won second prize in the 1927 literary contest sponsored by OPPORTUNITY. *The Hunch* was one of three Spence entries that earned recognition and awards in that competition. The play further cemented Spence's reputation as a talented playwright.

The play is set in a HARLEM apartment owned by Mrs. Reed, a landlady who rents out a well-appointed room to Mavis Cunningham, a young southern woman. The play opens as Mavis packs and prepares for her wedding to Bert Jackson, a dapper con man who is already married. It turns out that Mavis has played the lottery for her friend and admirer Steve who has traveled to Philadelphia. Mrs. Reed informs Mavis that the number won the lottery and that Steve's 50-cent bet now totals $500. Bert Jackson, whom Mavis has known for only four weeks, arrives on the scene. He suggests that he only placed a 10-cent bet and that the winnings are therefore much less than Mavis expects. As she deals with the disappointment and the prospect of telling her friend Steve that she failed to do what he asked, Steve appears at the door with a mystery woman in tow. He has returned with Mrs. Bert Jackson, the wife of Mavis's fiancé. In the confrontation that ensues, Steve recovers his money and defends Mavis's honor. She considers the shame of being left at the altar and succumbing to the treachery of a city man. Her steady friend refuses to abandon her, and the play closes as the two venture out on the town, and the hero's behavior suggests that Mavis will find true love in him eventually.

The Hunch was published in the May 1927 special issue of *Carolina Magazine* edited by LEWIS ALEXANDER. Its publication coincided with the Broadway production of Spence's play THE FOOL'S ERRAND. Other writers featured in the journal devoted to African-American literature included ARNA BONTEMPS, CARRIE CLIFFORD, WARING CUNEY, ANGELINA WELD GRIMKÉ, LANGSTON HUGHES, and HELENE JOHNSON.

Bibliography

Burton, Jennifer, ed. *Zora Neale Hurston, Eulalie Spence, Marita Bonner, and Others: The Prize Plays and Other One-Acts Published in Periodicals.* New York: G. K. Hall, 1996.

Hunter, Jane Edna (Harris) (1882–1971)

The child of sharecroppers, Jane Edna Harris Hunter was a woman committed to social justice and racial uplift.

She was born in South Carolina to Edward Harris and his wife Harriet Millner Harris. Her father passed away when Jane was 10 years old, and she was sent to live with a relative in order to alleviate the financial burdens on the family. She soon began working as a domestic servant, but the abuse she suffered at the hands of her employer resulted in a collective effort by her neighbors to find her another place of employment. Her second position was much more stable, and it was with this second family that Hunter began to advance her education. At age 14, she began classes at the Ferguson Academy in Abbeville, South Carolina. She graduated from that school, known now as Ferguson-Williams College, in 1900. She continued her studies at Hampton Institute in Virginia. Hunter began a career in nursing while in Charleston, South Carolina, a profession that further enabled her to improve the quality of life and health of the working women with whom she came in contact during her years as a settlement house leader. An excellent student, Hunter pursued studies in law at the Baldwin Wallace College Law School and the Marshall Law School in Cleveland. She passed the Ohio bar exam in 1925.

Jane Harris married Edward Hunter, a man 40 years her senior, but the marriage was over less than a year and a half later. She never remarried.

In 1911, Hunter made her first pioneering contributions in the field of social work and in the history of American settlement houses. She established the Working Girls Association in Cleveland, an organization that was renamed the Phillis Wheatley Association shortly thereafter. The organization offered much-needed housing and services to young and working women of color in the urban center of Cleveland. The need was so great that Hunter had to relocate the mission several times in order to accommodate the women residents. In addition to housing, the Phillis Wheatley Association provided some vocational training and education.

A nominee for the 1927 SPINGARN MEDAL awarded by the NATIONAL ASSOCIATION FOR THE ADVANCEMENT OF COLORED PEOPLE, Hunter was nationally recognized for her community and race leadership. She was awarded honorary degrees by several institutions, including FISK UNIVERSITY and TUSKEGEE INSTITUTE. An officer in the NATIONAL ASSOCIATION OF COLORED WOMEN, she embodied the organization's motto "Lifting As We Climb."

Hunter published her autobiography, A NICKEL AND A PRAYER, in 1940, the same year in which the autobiography THE BIG SEA by

LANGSTON HUGHES and the novel NATIVE SON by RICHARD WRIGHT appeared. She died in 1971.

Bibliography

Jones, Adrienne Lash. *Jane Edna Hunter: A Case Study of Black Leadership, 1910–1950.* Brooklyn, N.Y.: Carlson Publishers, 1990.

Sowash, Rick. *Heroes of Ohio: Twenty-Three True Tales of Courage and Character.* Bowling Green, Ohio: Gabriel's Horn Publishing Company, 1998.

Hunton, Addie D. Waites (1875–1943)

A leader in the racial uplift movement of the early 20th century, Addie Waites Hunton also was a historian, activist, and writer whose essays focused on women's rights, suffrage, and African-American history and politics.

She was born in Norfolk, Virginia, to Jesse and Adelina Lawton Waites. Her mother passed away when she was a young child. Her father, who owned a successful oyster and shipping company, allowed his sister-in-law in Boston to take in his daughter. Hunton completed high school at Boston Latin School before relocating to Philadelphia to attend the Spencerian College of Commerce. There, she became the first African-American female graduate. She pursued a teaching career and was appointed principal at the State Normal and Agricultural College in Alabama. She married William Alphaeus Hunton, the son of a formerly enslaved man who married and raised his family in Chatham, Ontario. Hunton was climbing the ranks of the YOUNG MEN'S CHRISTIAN ASSOCIATION and in 1891 became the first African-American secretary of the Colored Men's Department of the organization's International Committee. The couple married in 1893 after a lengthy courtship. They had four children: Eunice Hunton Carter, William Alphaeus, Jr. and two others who died in infancy.

By the time of the Harlem Renaissance, Hunton was a newly widowed mother of two. Committed to honoring her husband's dedication to African-American uplift, she published his biography. Her tribute, *William Alphaeus Hunton,* was published in 1938.

During World War II she pursued service as a volunteer with the YOUNG WOMEN'S CHRISTIAN ASSOCIATION. She was stationed in southern France. While in FRANCE, she attended the Pan-African Congress held in Paris in February 1919. With the small but intrepid number of African-American YWCA workers who became involved with the war effort abroad, Hunton advocated teaching the troops. She organized literacy programs and established libraries for the use of African-American soldiers. In 1920 Hunton collaborated with her fellow YWCA colleague Kathryn Johnson on a memoir of their time abroad. Their account, *Two Colored Women with the American Expeditionary Forces,* was a remarkable and impressive description of their challenges and experiences abroad.

Hunton was an activist who spearheaded numerous campaigns to secure women's rights and equality for people of color. She was an officer in the NATIONAL ASSOCIATION FOR THE ADVANCEMENT OF COLORED PEOPLE, serving as vice president and field secretary of the organization. She was instrumental to the success of the Fourth Pan-African Congress that convened in New York City in 1927. Hunton died in Brooklyn, New York, in June 1943.

Bibliography

Davis, Elizabeth Lindsay. *Lifting as They Climb.* New York, G. K. Hall, 1996.

Giddings, Paula. *When and Where I Enter.* New York: Morrow, 1984. 87, 102, 166–169.

Hunton, Addie Waites. "Negro Womanhood Defended," *Voice of the Negro* (July 1904): 280–282. Photograph, p. 281.

———. *William Alphaeus Hunton: A Pioneer Prophet of Young Men.* New York: Association Press, 1938.

Hurok, Solomon (Sol Hurok) (1888–1974)

A Russian-born producer and theater manager who worked closely with Harlem Renaissance–era performers and artists.

Known affectionately as the "Mahatma of Music," it was Hurok who discovered MARIAN ANDERSON, the powerful contralto singer who soared to fame. He was deeply involved in the promotion of *Cabin in the Sky,* the successful Broadway musical that starred Katherine Dunham, the choreographer, dancer, and anthropologist who studied with MELVILLE HERSKOVITS and whose research overlapped with but never exceeded that of ZORA NEALE HURSTON.

Hurst, Fannie (1889–1968)

A successful and prolific novelist who also is well-known for her relationship with ZORA NEALE HURSTON, whom she employed as a secretary. Born into a German Jewish family, she was the daughter of Samuel and Rose Koppel Hurst. Raised in Hamilton, Ohio, Hurst attended Washington University in St. Louis, Missouri, before moving to New York City. She began to earn her living as a writer in 1910 and quickly became a highly paid author whose works were published in such popular and well-circulated publications as the *Saturday Evening Post* and *Cosmopolitan*. She had an unconventional marriage with Jacques Danielson, a Russian Jewish pianist with whom she did not live. The couple maintained their marriage in secrecy for several years. They had no children.

Hurst was a prolific writer whose publications included some 18 novels, hundreds of short stories, plays, essays, and an autobiography. She published regularly throughout the Harlem Renaissance and was part of the vibrant social circles that included other white patrons and artists such as CARL VAN VECHTEN and AMY and JOEL SPINGARN. In 1933 Hurst published *IMITATION OF LIFE*, a novel about the interracial collaboration between two women and the painful cost of racial passing. It was adapted quickly as a film and was released in 1934. This first version directed by John Stahl starred Louise Beavers, Claudette Colbert, and Fredi Washington.

Hurst also supported the efforts of institutions such as the NATIONAL URBAN LEAGUE to promote and encourage African-American excellence in the arts. In 1918 she was one of the judges presiding in the first literary contest that *Opportunity* and the Urban League sponsored. With CARL VAN DOREN, EUGENE O'NEILL, and ALAIN LOCKE, she celebrated the accomplishments of Zora Neale Hurston, the triumphant winner of multiple awards. Hurst was the judge who handed Hurston the second-place drama prize for her play *COLOR STRUCK*. Impressed by Hurston's potential, Hurst soon sought out the BARNARD COLLEGE student. Thanks to mediation by Annie Nathan Meyer, founder of Barnard College, Hurst soon agreed to

cover Hurston's tuition costs. She also hired Hurston as a secretary and solicited her evaluations of work-in-progress. Hurston biographer Melba Boyd notes that the two women, whose ages differed by five years, enjoyed a lively and supportive relationship that continued even as the terms of their working relationship changed. Hurst wrote on Hurston's behalf when she applied for a GUGGENHEIM FELLOWSHIP in 1934. Her letter, according to Boyd, was a remarkable combination of potentially destructive compliments. Hurst declared that Hurston was an "erratic worker" but then insisted that she also was "a talented and peculiarly capable young woman" (Boyd, 251). Three years later, Hurston wrote a well-received and positive profile of her longtime associate for the *Saturday Review of Literature*.

Fannie Hurst died in February 1968. Her will provided for an endowed professorship in her name at Brandeis University in Massachusetts and at Washington University, her alma mater, in St. Louis, Missouri.

Bibliography
The Fannie Hurst Collection is housed in the Humanities Research Center, University of Texas at Austin.

Boyd, Valerie. *Wrapped in Rainbows: The Life of Zora Neale Hurston*. New York: Scribner, 2003.

Hurst, Fannie. *Anatomy of Me: A Wanderer in Search of Herself*. Garden City, N.Y.: Doubleday, 1958.

Kroeger, Brooke. *Fannie: The Talent for Success of Writer Fannie Hurst*. New York: Times Books, 1999.

Shaughnessy, Mary Rose. *Myths about Love and Woman: The Fiction of Fannie Hurst*. New York: Gordon Press, 1979.

Hurston, Zora Neale (1891–1960)

A prolific, multifaceted, brilliant, and enigmatic figure of the Harlem Renaissance, Zora Neale Hurston authored groundbreaking anthropological studies, best-selling novels, prizewinning plays, and numerous short stories. Hurston was a tenacious scholar, cultural critic, and artist whose accomplishments underscore the significance of the Harlem Renaissance as a period of unprecedented American literary and artistic development. Throughout the Harlem Renaissance, Hurston excelled as a prolific writer, anthropologist, essayist, editor, dramatist, magazine founder, historian, and teacher.

Zora Neale Hurston was born in Notasulga, Alabama, to John and Lucy Potts Hurston. A granddaughter of formerly enslaved Georgians, Hurston had deep ties to the South and its African-American history and culture. The second daughter and fifth child in her family, she was raised in EATONVILLE, Florida, the nation's first all-black incorporated town. The town elected John Hurston as mayor three times. She was educated at the Robert Hungerford Normal and Industrial School, an institution founded by TUSKEGEE INSTITUTE graduates. When her mother died, Zora's father made arrangements for her to relocate to Jacksonville, Florida, and enroll in the Florida Baptist Academy. Despite the emotional turmoil associated with her devastating loss, Hurston excelled in her studies. She had to leave after a year, despite her father's suggestion that the school adopt his youngest child. She returned to Eatonville, her father, and new stepmother. She left home in 1905, after a series of domestic battles that resulted in the departure of two older brothers.

Zora Neale Hurston was not the only Hurston child to excel as a professional. Clifford Hurston, a MOREHOUSE COLLEGE graduate, became a teacher and settled in Selma, Alabama. Her brother Robert attended Meharry Medical College in Nashville, Tennessee, and went on to establish his own practice. Hurston, who had benefited from her schoolteacher mother's love of learning, went on to attend Morgan Academy, the college preparatory division of the institution now known as Morgan State University. Hurston, who had traveled for two years with a Gilbert and Sullivan troupe before arriving in Baltimore and at the Morgan Academy, planned to continue her studies at Morgan College. However, an encounter with MAY MILLER SULLIVAN, the future playwright and the daughter of HOWARD UNIVERSITY Dean KELLY MILLER, prompted her to set her sights on the elite school in WASHINGTON, D.C. She took courses at Howard Academy to prepare her for the academic transition and began classes at Howard in the fall of 1919. She attended classes through the fall of 1923 but did not graduate. In September 1925, she transferred to BARNARD COLLEGE in NEW YORK CITY. She was the only African-American student enrolled in the school but was thoroughly undeterred by that sobering reality. Hurston's studies with FRANZ BOAS, the renowned anthropologist at COLUMBIA UNIVERSITY, began during her years at Barnard. She earned her B.A. in 1928 and began graduate studies in anthropology at Columbia. She went on to become one of Boas's most well-known and accomplished students.

Hurston married Howard Sheen, a fellow Howard University student, in 1927. When they married, Sheen was completing his last year of studies at the University of Chicago Medical School. In a March 1927 letter to friends DOROTHY WEST and HELENE JOHNSON, Hurston referred to herself as "Mrs. Herbert Arnold Sheen,

Zora Neale Hurston, photographed by Carl Van Vechten. Permission granted by the Van Vechten Trust *(Yale Collection of American Literature, Beinecke Rare Book and Manuscript Library)*

if you please" and noted that "We are all quite happy now." One year later, Hurston was bemoaning the state of her marriage. Her letter to Langston Hughes included the dramatic announcement that she was "going to divorce Herbert . . . He tries to hold me back and be generally obstructive so I have broken off relations since early Jan. and that's that." The marriage ended officially in July 1931. Hurston's second marriage, in 1939 to Albert Price III, also ended in divorce. She met Price, who was 25 years her junior, during her tenure with the Works Project Administration. A native of Jacksonville, Florida, he was a student when the wedding occurred. The marriage broke down amid Hurston's claims that Price did not work and that he failed to offer her adequate support. Price generated counterclaims in which he stated he was afraid of her potential black magic powers and her anger. In 1944, Hurston married a third time. She and James Howell Pitts, a South Carolina native, Cleveland businessman, and Meharry Medical College graduate, were wed in southern Florida near Daytona Beach. Hurston scholars Boyd and Carla Kaplan have uncovered absorbing details about Hurston's marriages, especially her last and most elusive relationship with Pitts. The Hurston-Pitts marriage was the shortest of the three; it lasted only eight months and ended officially on 31 October 1944.

It was while a student at Howard University that Hurston published her first short story. "JOHN REDDING GOES TO SEA" appeared in the STYLUS, the highly regarded college literary magazine that ALAIN LOCKE and T. MONTGOMERY GREGORY established. She took the New York City literary scene by storm when, in 1925, she won two prizes in the first OPPORTUNITY literary contest. FANNIE HURST, one of her patrons, was a judge and was on hand to deliver the prize to Hurston in person. Hurston became a secretary and personal assistant to the acclaimed writer Hurst shortly thereafter. It was Hurst who, at the suggestion of Annie Nathan Meyer, Barnard College founder and Hurston supporter, offered to cover Hurston's tuition. As she had at Howard, Hurston thrived as a writer while immersing herself in her academics. In addition to winning notable literary prizes, she published short fiction in a variety of magazines. The short story "Under the Bridge" appeared in the December 1925 issue of The

X-Ray: The Official Publication of Zeta Phi Beta Sorority, her folktale "Possum" appeared in the September 1926 issue of FORUM, and later in the fall of 1926, she published "THE EATONVILLE ANTHOLOGY," a three-month long series of folktales and folk histories in THE MESSENGER. The play The First One appeared in EBONY AND TOPAZ: A COLLECTANEA, the 1927 anthology edited by sociologist and Opportunity editor CHARLES S. JOHNSON.

Hurston was one of the most visible and generous individuals who moved in Harlem Renaissance circles. She was regularly honored in literary competitions sponsored by the Urban League and its official journal Opportunity. She won in two categories of the 1924–25 Opportunity competition. She received the second prize for "SPUNK" and honorable mention for "Black Death" in the short story contest, and her play COLOR STRUCK tied for second prize with Warren McDonald in the drama category. In 1926 judges ZONA GALE, JEAN TOOMER, CARL VAN DOREN, and others awarded a split second-place prize to her short story "MUTTSY" and to Dorothy West's "THE TYPEWRITER." The prize committee, comprising of David Belasco, T. Montgomery Gregory, PAUL ROBESON, and Stark Young, awarded honorable mention to her plays Color Struck and The First One.

She was known for her unstinting kindness, willingness to house and feed her friends in need, and enthusiasm for artistic ventures. She collaborated with many well-known figures of the period. In 1926 she joined forces with LANGSTON HUGHES, WALLACE THURMAN, AARON DOUGLAS, and BRUCE NUGENT in an effort to generate a dynamic, new literary forum. The journal FIRE!! appeared in November of that year. Hurston's role in the conception and production of the magazine placed her in the ranks of enterprising female journalists and editors such as Mary Ann Shad Cary, Pauline Hopkins, and JESSIE FAUSET.

Hurston collaborated with Langston Hughes on collective ventures such as the Fire!! project and on individual creative projects. Their awareness of each other was intensified because the writers shared a patron in CHARLOTTE OSGOOD MASON. In 1929 they were neighbors in Westfield, New Jersey, a situation produced by Mason's desire to monitor closely the activities of her protégés.

On occasion, the two met up during their travels. In 1927 they met in Alabama, posed for a picture with Jessie Fauset at Tuskegee Institute in front of a statue of BOOKER T. WASHINGTON, and then drove back to New York City in "Sassy Susie," Hurston's car. That year, they collaborated on a musical production entitled *Great Day.* They cowrote MULE BONE: A COMEDY OF NEGRO LIFE IN THREE ACTS. The relationship was strained by Hurston's radical revisions of the work, her anxiety about Hughes's efforts to include and to share profits with their secretary, LOUISE THOMPSON, and Hurston's independent presentation to publishers and others, without Hughes's knowledge, of her single-author version. Hughes was alarmed when he received news of the play's distribution and potential production without his authorization. In a January 1931 letter to friend CARL VAN VECHTEN, he admitted that he was "not at all angry about her actions, because she always has been strange in lots of ways." He continued, admitting "I do hate to see a good Folk-play go to waste, because for some reason I do not know, she no longer wants to work with me." In 1991, 60 years after its completion, the work was staged on BROADWAY.

Hurston developed several productive, though demanding, relationships with patrons and mentors. Her supporters included rich and powerful benefactresses such as Annie Nathan Meyer, founder of Barnard College; Fannie Hurst, writer; the writer, critic, and society figure Carl Van Vechten; and Charlotte Osgood Mason, philanthropist and patron of several Harlem Renaissance figures. The publishing house of J. B. LIPPINCOTT produced all but one of her seven books. Based in PHILADELPHIA, the firm relocated to New York City and was, during its relationship with Hurston, one of the nation's leading publishers of trade books.

Her relationships with contemporary writers were intense. An outspoken and unapologetic figure, Hurston was a generous role model for young writers like Helene Johnson and Dorothy West. COUNTEE CULLEN, with whom she corresponded, often encouraged her, and she in turn provided supportive critiques of his work. Of his debut volume entitled COLOR, she insisted that it was "a wonderful volume of poems" and told him "I just sit and wonder as I read poem after poem and wonder

how you can keep it up so long, I can understand one hitting off a few like that," she marveled, "but I cannot see where it all comes from!" (Kaplan, 84). Wallace Thurman, with whom she collaborated on *Fire!!,* noted in an expansive 1932 letter to Langston Hughes about a number of Harlem Renaissance artists that "Zora should learn craftsmanship and surprise the world and outstrip her contemporaries as well" (Davis, 346). Yet, Hurston did not hesitate to voice her frustration with what she deemed tiresome portraits of African-American life. In response to what she called "me and may honey got two mo' days tuh do de buck" poems that Langston Hughes was writing in the mid 1920s, she found it hard to "refrain from speaking" and decided that she was "at least going to speak to Van Vechten," Hughes's close friend and mentor, about the need for Hughes to develop a more expansive creative and socially conscious repertoire. Hurston also made time to craft professional and public responses to the works of her peers. She published reviews, including a frank assessment of Claude McKay's HARLEM: NEGRO METROPOLIS (1940) in which she noted that the BOOK-OF-THE-MONTH CLUB alternate selection confirmed that McKay "knows what is really happening among the folks," that he had "done an amazing thing . . . been absolutely frank . . . [and] had spoken out about those things Negroes utter only when they are breast to breast, but by tradition are forbidden to break a breath about when white ears are present" (Cooper, 344–345).

Hurston's lives as a scholar and novelist were intertwined thoroughly throughout her life. She wrote THEIR EYES WERE WATCHING GOD (1937), her most popular novel, while she was in HAITI conducting anthropological research. One year later, she published *Tell My Horse,* the book based on that research in the Caribbean. Hurston's meteoric rise in Harlem circles coincided with her steady development as an anthropologist who would soon receive prestigious fellowships to fund her research. Hurston published JONAH'S GOURD VINE, her first novel, in 1934. It was followed by *Their Eyes Were Watching God* (1937), MOSES, MAN OF THE MOUNTAIN (1939), and *Seraph on the Suwanee* (1948). Her anthropological studies, funded by two GUGGENHEIM FELLOWSHIPS, focused on cultural practices in Jamaica and Haiti. *Tell My Horse*

(1938) was an exhaustive account of her work and findings. *Mules and Men,* the first collection of Florida and Alabama folklore published by an African-American woman, appeared in 1935. Hurston's research was one of the many projects funded by her patron Charlotte Osgood Mason.

Hurston's life as an essayist began in 1928 when she published "How It Feels to Be Colored Me." The essay appeared in *The World Tomorrow,* a Protestant magazine that had Hurston's collaborator and friend Wallace Thurman on staff. Hurston's submission was prompted by debts that she, Thurman, Langston Hughes, and others had incurred in their optimistic effort to establish the innovative but short-lived literary magazine *Fire!!* The essay is a genuine index of Hurston's zest for life, a rejection of those who would practice racial essentialism, and a declaration of her intent to live beyond the narrow confines of race. Other essays included the December 1942 "Crazy for This Democracy" and the June 1944 "My Most Humiliating Jim Crow Experience," which appeared in *Negro Digest.*

Hurston published *Dust Tracks on a Road,* her autobiography, in 1942. Howard University awarded Hurston its Distinguished Alumni Award in 1943. She returned to Florida in 1950 after an unfortunate and highly publicized scandal in which she was alleged to have molested a young boy. She spent the last decade of her life working in Florida as a teacher at Lincoln Park Academy in Fort Pierce, a librarian, and a freelance writer. Just before her death, she wrote to Harper Brothers to solicit their interest in her historical novel based on King Herod. Ernest Hemingway suggested to her that she buy land on the Cuban Isle of Pines, but she chose to stay on Merritt Island, where she could write in quiet. Hurston suffered a stroke in 1959 and died in a welfare home in Fort Pierce on January 28, 1960. Her grave was unmarked for decades until writer Alice Walker located the site and honored Hurston with a stately gray headstone that read "Zora Neale Hurston—A Genius of the South."

It is tragic that Hurston's impressive achievements faded into obscurity for years after her death. The renaissance in Hurston studies began in the late 1970s and was initiated by Alice Walker, who claimed Hurston as a powerful literary foremother. The recovery of Hurston's legacy and influence continues. Advances in Hurston scholarship continue, fueled by sophisticated critical studies, scholarly research groups dedicated to advancing the critical assessment of Hurston's works and the publications of comprehensive biographies, a groundbreaking collection of her extensive correspondence, and new editions of the author's diverse and captivating writings.

Bibliography

Boyd, Valerie. *Wrapped in Rainbows: The Life of Zora Neale Hurston.* New York: Scribner, 2003.

Cooper, Wayne. *Claude McKay: Rebel Sojourner in the Harlem Renaissance.* New York: Schocken Books, 1987.

Davis, Thadious M. *Nella Larsen, Novelist of the Harlem Renaissance: A Woman's Life Unveiled.* Baton Rouge: Louisiana State University Press, 1994.

Hemenway, Robert E. *Zora Neale Hurston: A Literary Biography.* Urbana: University of Illinois Press, 1977.

Hurston, Zora Neale. *Dust Tracks on a Road.* New York: Lippincott, 1942.

Kaplan, Carla. *Zora Neale Hurston: A Life in Letters.* New York: Doubleday, 2002.

Kroeger, Brooke. *Fannie: The Talent For Success of Writer Fannie Hurst.* New York: Random House, 1999.

Walker, Alice, ed. *I Love Myself When I Am Laughing . . . A Zora Neale Hurston Reader.* New York: The Feminist Press, 1979.

Zora Neale Hurston Papers, James Weldon Johnson Collection, Beinecke Library, Yale University; Alain Locke Collections, Moorland-Spingarn Research Center, Howard University; Special Collections, Fisk University Library; and Special Collections, University of Florida, Gainesville.

I

I Am the American Negro Frank Davis (1937)

The second volume of poetry published by FRANK DAVIS, a Kansas-born poet and journalist. Davis produced his second book in 1937 shortly after he was appointed executive editor of the CHICAGO-based ASSOCIATED NEGRO PRESS.

The title of Davis's second book signaled his claim on the rights and privileges of all Americans. His assertion was rooted in defining moments of his own life. As a young boy of five, for instance, he had been set upon by a group of white boys who wanted to lynch him. In *I Am the American Negro,* he alerted readers to the type of work that the book contained. Declaring that neither "Fairy words" nor a "Pollyanna mind . . . roam[ed] these pages," he described the poems as "coarse victuals / A couch of rough boards." Davis's poems were realistic and unapologetic re-creations of African-American experiences.

The volume also appeared just after he became the first winner of the JULIUS ROSENWALD FELLOWSHIP, an award designed to support the innovative research and work of African-American artists and scholars.

Bibliography

Davis, Frank Marshall. *I Am the American Negro.* Chicago: The Black Cat Press, 1937.

Tidwell, John Edgar. *Black Moods: Collected Poems—Frank Marshall Davis.* Urbana: University of Illinois Press, 2002.

Idle Head Willis Richardson (1929)

A one-act play by WILLIS RICHARDSON, who in 1923 became the first African-American playwright to have his work produced on BROADWAY. *Idle Head,* published in *Carolina Magazine* in April 1929, appeared some six years after Richardson's Broadway triumph with THE CHIP WOMAN'S FORTUNE.

The play is a domestic tragedy that showcases the desperation produced by racism and poverty. The matriarch of the family is Mrs. Broadus, a widowed mother whose husband was a proud, independent man. She lives with her two children, George and Alice. George, despondent about his lack of employment options, refuses to submit to the widespread racism in the workplace. He helps his mother by picking up the laundry that she does for a wealthy white woman but refuses to use the rear servant's entry when he goes. While sorting the laundry, he discovers a diamond brooch and promptly goes off to pawn it. His motive is to provide his family with much-needed funds and the opportunity to preserve their membership in the local church. Alice discovers the pawn slip in George's pockets, even though her brother and mother have chided her for habitually searching through her sibling's clothes. When the police, alerted by the white employer's chauffeur, return to the Broaduses' apartment, Alice is forced to reveal the incriminating evidence that she holds in her hands. George, inadvertently undone by his sister, is hauled off to jail. In a scene reminiscent of heart-wrenching family dramas such as AFTERMATH (1928) by MAMIE BURRILL, who was Richardson's former English teacher, the play closes as a powerless Mrs. Broadus sinks to her knees in grief.

Richardson underscores George's unwavering blackness by representing his speech in dialect while that of his moderate sister, Alice, is in standard, somewhat stilted English. The two children represent the challenges and competing realities of the future. Richardson's play offers a sobering glimpse into African-American family life and the devastating collateral effects of racism.

Bibliography

Gray, Christine Rauchfuss. *Willis Richardson, Forgotten Pioneer of African-American Drama.* Westport, Conn.: Greenwood Press, 1999.

"If Wishes Were Horses" Edythe Mae Gordon (1929)

A short story by EDYTHE MAE GORDON that appeared in the BOSTON-based SATURDAY EVENING QUILL. The sparse but riveting plot revolves around a husband and father named Fred Pomeroy. During an outing with his daughter, he encounters a fortune-teller who predicts that his wife will have her wishes come true and that he will "be the maker of her dreams." Pomeroy cannot imagine how he, an overworked and underpaid sales clerk, will be able to finance such a promising future. His efforts to publish short fiction have yet to result in acceptance or publication. That night he dies in bed, and several weeks after his passing, his wife Rachel receives an insurance check in the amount of $50,000. The story closes as a neighbor learns of the grand trip that the widowed Rachel Pomeroy is taking with her daughter Dorothea.

Gordon's pointed story is a compelling tale of modern domesticity.

Bibliography

Gordon, Edythe Mae. *Selected Works of Edythe Mae Gordon.* Introduction by Lorraine Elena Roses. New York: G. K. Hall & Co., 1996.

Imitation of Life Fannie Hurst (1933)

A novel by the prolific author FANNIE HURST. Originally entitled *Sugar House,* the book was published in 1933 by HARPER & BROTHERS. Hurst conceived the idea for the novel during her fall 1931 travels to Canada with ZORA NEALE HURSTON, the brilliant writer and anthropologist whose BARNARD COLLEGE studies she financed. The book was released in serial installments in *Pictorial Review* and published separately by Harper. Within three months, Hurst had sold the movie rights to Universal. Director John Stahl produced the 1934 version of the film that starred Louise

Beavers, Claudette Colbert, and Fredi Washington. In 1959 Douglas Sirk directed the remake of *Imitation of Life.* This version featured Lana Turner and Juanita Moore in the main roles. The second film transformed the original relationship between the two protagonists into a problematic hierarchical relationship that reinforced current racial expectations and denigrating stereotypes.

The story followed the evolving partnership of two New Jersey widows, Bea Pullman and Delilah Johnson. Pullman is destitute and overwhelmed by the loss of her husband, the demands of her infant daughter, and the responsibility for caring for her paralyzed father. She hires Johnson as a live-in housekeeper, and the two women do their best to make ends meet. Bea creates a plan to market Delilah's exquisite waffles and maple syrup. The business plan succeeds beyond their wildest dreams. The women become millionaires as their cottage industry becomes a national phenomenon. Despite their financial success, however, both women are challenged by the predicaments in which their daughters find themselves.

Hurst explores the politics of domesticity in the interracial friendship between Bea and Delilah, whose daughters grow up together. Delilah's daughter Peola, a light-skinned girl of color, wants to pass for white. Contemporary reviewers of the novel tended to focus more on the evolution of Bea Pullman rather than on the complicated desires of Peola Johnson or her mother.

Imitation of Life was an extremely popular novel, one that revived the literary tradition of the tragic mulatto plot and shed new light on early 20th-century domesticity.

Bibliography

Caputi, Jane. "'Specifying' Fannie Hurst: Langston Hughes's 'Limitations of Life,' Zora Neale Hurston's *Their Eyes Were Watching God,* and Toni Morrison's *The Bluest Eye* as 'Answers' to Hurst's 'Imitation of Life,'" *Black American Literature Forum* 24, no. 4 (winter 1990): 697–716.

Kroeger, Brooke. *Fannie: The Talent for Success of Writer Fannie Hurst.* New York: Random House, 1999.

In Abraham's Bosom Paul Green (1926)

The PULITZER PRIZE–winning drama by white North Carolina playwright and professor PAUL GREEN. Critics hailed the play for its unrelenting examination of social violence and family tragedy. This was the first full-length work that Green, who had written several one-act plays, completed. It became part of the growing and increasingly influential canon of works on African-American themes by white writers. It also contributed to national awareness of LYNCHING as it showcased the simmering volatility and perpetual danger that African Americans faced in the American South.

The play's title recalls the biblical phrase that referred to one's ability to enjoy happiness and tranquillity. The plot, however, runs counter to the biblical meaning. The play is set in the South during Reconstruction and the early 20th century. It documents the life of Abraham McCranie, his white father, a former slave owner named Colonel McCranie, and the legitimate white heir, Lonnie. Abe, who works as a field hand on his father's plantation, is an ambitious young man determined to survive the brutal South. Other African-American men on the McCranie estate believe that the mixed-blood protagonist is not safe. They attribute his talkativeness, desire for education, and aspirations to being "bad mixed up all down inside." Green imagines Abe as a 25-year-old man whose "shaggy head, forehead, and jaw are marked with will and intelligence." He signals the impending racial conflict, however, by noting that the character's "wide nostril and a smoldering flash in his eye that now and then shows itself suggest a passionate and dangerous person when aroused." In sharp contrast to the potentially heroic Abe is his dissolute father, a "stout, run-down southerner, past middle age, with all the signs of moral and intellectual decadence upon him." The flawed and dysfunctional McCranie patriarch is soon threatened by a testy encounter between Abe and his white half brother Lonnie. The Colonel is forced to whip his son Abe when the struggle between the brothers comes to blows.

The domestic oppression of Abe McCranie and his family continues as the play progresses. Married to Goldie, a mulatto woman, the two have lost three children in infancy. Lonnie McCranie has desecrated the children's burial plots, and such malicious actions have thoroughly demoralized Abe and his wife. Just days after the couple have their fourth child, the colonel surprises the couple with a deed that makes them owners of their home

and 25 acres of land. Jubilant, Abe's faith in humanity and his own future is rekindled. He names his new son Douglass, after the formerly enslaved abolitionist leader. Abe regards his son as a "new Moses," one who will "bring the chillun out of bondage, ou'n sin and ignorance." Empowered by his domestic stability, Abe starts a school for the African-American children of the area. His rigidity and strong discipline anger the parents, however, and the school fails as the children withdraw in protest. He is alienated from his only son when he reacts violently to what he regards as idleness and dissolute behavior. Years later Abe is working as a miner. He still holds on to his dream of intellectual advancement even as the women of his household continually dream of burning his scholarly books. The tension in the play builds as Abe becomes determined to rally African Americans and to defy white power. He is engaged in a final and murderous altercation with Lonnie, and it is his own son who betrays him to the mob that wants to kill him. The play closes as Goldie discovers her husband dead in the front room of their home.

Green's play is a powerful story of a family ruined by years of oppression and hardship. It was a Broadway hit when it opened at the Provincetown Playhouse on BROADWAY on 30 December 1926. The troupe presented some 200 performances. Jasper Deeter directed the production presented by the PROVINCETOWN PLAYERS. This group, founded in Provincetown, Massachusetts, by Hutchins Hapgood, his wife EMILIE HAPGOOD, Neith Boyce, MABEL DODGE, and others, prided itself on staging works that engaged contemporary social questions and issues. *In Abraham's Bosom* won the 1927 Pulitzer Prize in drama.

Bibliography

Adams, Agatha B. *Paul Green of Chapel Hill.* Chapel Hill: University of North Carolina Library, 1951.

Avery, Lawrence G., ed. *A Southern Life: Letters of Paul Green, 1916–1918.* Chapel Hill: University of North Carolina Press, 1994.

Gassner, John. *Paul Green: Five Plays of the South.* New York: Hill and Wang, 1963.

Green, Paul. *The Field God and In Abraham's Bosom.* New York: R. M. McBride & Company, 1927.

Huggins, Nathan. *Harlem Renaissance.* New York: Oxford University Press, 1971.

Kenny, Vincent S. *Paul Green*. New York: Twayne, 1971.

Saunders, Frances. "'A New Playwright of Tragic Power & Poetic Impulse': Paul Eliot Green at UNC–Chapel Hill in the 1920s." *North Carolina Historical Review* 72, no. 3 (1995): 277–300.

Infants of the Spring Wallace Thurman
(1932)

The second novel by WALLACE THURMAN, an enterprising and popular writer of the Harlem Renaissance. The MACAULAY PUBLISHING COMPANY, which hired Thurman as a copy editor and reader, published the book. It appeared just two years before Thurman died of tuberculosis in 1934.

Infants of the Spring was a project that tested Thurman's patience and philosophies on writing. In a letter to friend HAROLD JACKMAN, he described his efforts to "make the novel elastic without having first learned the boundary lines so that I could steer a clear course." Like the writers ZORA NEALE HURSTON and LANGSTON HUGHES, Thurman's writing benefited from the timely financial assistance of a patron. Elisabeth Marbury, a well-traveled literary agent, responded to his request for $500, and it was these funds that enabled him to ensconce himself in the Jamaica, New York, home of THEOPHILUS LEWIS and to continue writing. Thurman dedicated the novel to his mother, Beulah. His inscription, which read "To Beulah the goose who laid a not so golden egg," reflected his troubled perception of his immediate family and by extension, perhaps, also of himself.

The novel takes its title from *Hamlet,* and Thurman invokes the Shakespearean play in one of the two epigraphs to the novel. The lines he chooses introduce the themes of mortality and premature ends that emerge so strongly in the novel: "The canker galls the infants of the spring / Too oft before their buttons be disclosed, / And in the morn and liquid dew of youth / contagious blastments are most imminent."

Infants of the Spring was an autobiographical narrative and one of the most vivid published exposés of contemporary life in HARLEM. Reminiscent of CLAUDE MCKAY's *HOME TO HARLEM* (1928), the novel traced the adventures of two male protagonists and the colorful, hectic worlds in which they moved. Thurman generated rather transparent parodies of friends, close associates, and figures whom he did not hold in high regard. When she read the work, Zora Neale Hurston wrote to CARL VAN VECHTEN to tell him that "You and I are in it in a small way" and characterized it as "[n]ot a bad book at all." Langston Hughes was extremely supportive of his friend. He characterized the work as "provoking" and "brave" and declared, "You have written a swell book . . . your potential soars like a kite breaking patterns for negro writers" (Rampersad, 213).

The primary setting is NIGGERATI Manor, a residence modeled after the actual rooming house at 267 West 136th Street in which Thurman lived. The protagonist is Raymond Taylor, a "small and slender Negro" with "smooth dark skin" and features that are "neither Nordic nor Negroid, but rather a happy combination of the two, retaining the slender outlines of the first, and the warm vigor of the second, thus escaping both Nordic rigidity, and African coarseness" (16). He is man of color who is given to assessing the motives and needs of those around him. The central characters with whom Taylor interacts are Samuel Carter, the singer Eustace Savoy, his friend Lucille, the artists Paul Arbian and Pelham Gaylord, and a visiting Canadian named Stephen Jorgenson. Over the course of the novel, the friendship between Taylor and Jorgenson deepens. Jorgenson is a relatively sheltered and naive COLUMBIA UNIVERSITY graduate student. He also is a man who is prone to making direct and troubling references about race. In the opening chapter, for instance, he confesses that he was "frightened" when he came to Harlem: "After all," he declares, "I had never seen a Negro before in my life, that is, not over two or three, and they were only dim, passing shadows with no immediate reality. New York itself was alarming enough, but when I emerged from the subway at 135th Street, I was actually panic stricken . . . I felt alien, creepy, conspicuous, ashamed. I wanted to camouflage my white skin, and assume some protective coloration" (15). Samuel Carter, another white friend, has other aspirations, though he finds himself thwarted and unable to become the "rebellious torchbearer, a persecuted spirit child of Eugene Debs and Emma Goldman, subject to frequent imprisonment, and gradually becoming inured to being put on the rack by the sadistic policemen who upheld the capitalistic regime" (28). There are a number of jarring events, revealing sexual encounters, and lively discussions, however, that serve to inject realism into Niggerati Manor, and ultimately the place is unable to fully accommodate its inhabitants or to contain their ideas.

Thurman satirized contemporary practices such as literary salons, interracial friendships, and discussions about appropriate demonstrations of African-American identity. He uses the character Stephen Jorgenson to trace the increasing immersion into Harlem of all the characters. It is Raymond, for instance, whose persuasive commentaries serve to educate Jorgenson. Ensconced in Niggerati Manor, he not only lives in Harlem but apparently becomes "a nigger." The group of friends with whom he now associates talk frankly about sexuality and race. The novel closes after Gaylord, a man described as "servile and deferential" is imprisoned for rape, Savoy is institutionalized in a mental hospital, Arbian commits suicide, and Jorgenson leaves America as a committed racist. The image of a renaissance in shambles is prevented only by the fact that Raymond Taylor has the prospect of a real relationship with Lucille and that the boardinghouse is to be redesigned as a settlement house for working women.

The novel clearly underscored Thurman's disappointment in certain aspects of the Harlem Renaissance. Despite his commitment to artistic excellence, he and several of his contemporaries had been frustrated by what they regarded as old-fashioned philosophies about race and sexuality. Thurman's efforts to establish FIRE!!, for instance, reflected his ambitions and investment in a more liberated and avant-garde cultural environment. Yet, the speedy failure of the magazine and the steady success of institutional publications such as THE CRISIS and OPPORTUNITY revealed the limitations placed upon him as an artist of color. Thurman scholar Eleonore van Otten suggests that Thurman's novel also critiqued white opportunism, caste prejudice, and gratuitous investments and parodies of blackness. Yet it was a novel criticized for being "clumsily written" with "incredibly bad" dialogue "which range[d] from elephantine witticisms to ponderous philosophizing" (NYT, 28 February 1932, BR7). THE NEW YORK TIMES review of the work did concede that at least "[s]ome of

the discussions are challenging" and that "[s]ome of the scenes . . . are shrewdly observed" but ultimately concluded that the book "lacks life and fails to awake in the reader the necessary emotional response" (NYT, 28 February 1932, BR7). Thurman himself authored a review of Infants of the Spring. In the unpublished assessment, he suggested that the "characters and their problems cried out for release" and "intruded themselves into . . . every alien thought" of the author. Ultimately, though, he concurred with his critics, suggesting that the novel was "unsatisfactory" and that the author had "certainly no excuse for having allowed it to be published." Thurman's words reflected his ambivalence about the work but also signaled his deep desire to quash the all-consuming frenzy that defined his experience of the Harlem Renaissance.

Bibliography

"Call Home The Heart and Other Works of Fiction," New York Times, 28 February 1932, BR7.

Kaplan, Carla. Zora Neale Hurston: A Life in Letters. New York: Doubleday, 2002.

Rampersad, Arthur. The Life of Langston Hughes: I, Too, Sing America. Vol. 1, 1902–1941. New York: Oxford University Press, 1986.

Thurman, Wallace. Infants of the Spring. Foreword by Amritjit Singh. Boston: Northeastern University Press, 1992.

van Notten, Eleonore. Wallace Thurman's Harlem Renaissance. Amsterdam: Rodopi, 1994.

Interne, The Wallace Thurman (1932)

The third novel of WALLACE THURMAN. The Interne appeared in the same year as the author's second book, INFANTS OF THE SPRING. Thurman collaborated with ABRAHAM FURMAN, a writer-attorney, on this tale of medical students, nurses, and the dramas that emerge in an urban hospital. The novel was based on a Thurman play of the same name. Like ZORA NEALE HURSTON, who published only one book featuring white characters, Thurman made his first and last attempt to depict white life in The Interne.

The novel chronicled the experiences of Carl Armstrong, a young white physician whose faith in medicine is shattered by the bureaucracy and heartlessness of the city hospital in which he comes to work. Eventually Armstrong himself is corrupted by the system that he initially despises. The novel closes as he makes an attempt to save himself by relocating to a rural environment and practicing medicine in a more humane and honest way.

Thurman's damning portrait of the politics and grim realities of a city hospital prompted him to tell LANGSTON HUGHES that he wanted to avoid being admitted to any such place. "If you ever hear of me being ill, don't let them send me to any city hospital," he advised his friend. "I am sure to be given the black bottle."

The novel received mixed reviews. It was praised by Clifford Mitchell of the *Washington Tribune* for its convincing profiles of "the motives and characteristics of the whites" depicted in the novel. *THE NEW YORK TIMES*, however, dismissed it as a "squalid" text that "flagrantly exaggerated" hospital conditions and the personalities of its staff. Two years after the novel's publication, however, Thurman's portrait of court-ordered sterilizations of poor people in *The Interne* became the basis for an independently produced film entitled *Tomorrow's Children*. That project and Thurman's subsequent work in films earned him the high weekly salary of $250.

Bibliography
van Notten, Eleonore. *Wallace Thurman's Harlem Renaissance.* Amsterdam: Rodopi, 1994.

Inter-State Tattler
The weekly newspaper that the NEW YORK CITY–based Inter-State Tattler Company began publishing in 1925. BENNIE BUTLER, GERALDYN DISMOND, and GEORGE B. JONES were among its editors. Writers for the newspaper included T. THOMAS FORTUNE, THEOPHILUS LEWIS, and MARY WHITE OVINGTON. It covered current events and was known for its juicy details about social events. The weekly also promoted entertainment and sporting events and generally covered news by and of interest to African Americans.

The paper, which ceased publication in 1932, was part of the city's dynamic African-American press, which included the *AMSTERDAM NEWS* and the *NEW YORK AGE*.

Isaacs, Edith Juliet (Rich) (1878–1956)
A Milwaukee, Wisconsin, native who became a highly respected figure in American drama circles and an advocate of American theater. Edith Juliet Rich, who married Lewis Isaacs, a New York City lawyer, began her professional life as a journalist. After stints at the *Milwaukee Sentinel*, she went on to write for the *Ladies' Home Journal* and *Ainslee's Magazine*. She became the editor of the journal *Theatre Arts* in 1918.

In the 1920s she collaborated with ALAIN LOCKE on an exhibition of African artifacts gathered during the Blondiau–*Theatre Arts* Expedition to the continent. Once the exhibit closed, Isaacs purchased the items and divided them between the Schomburg Center of the NEW YORK PUBLIC LIBRARY and HOWARD UNIVERSITY. The Schomburg collection includes several hundred sculptures and other artifacts.

J

Jackman, Harold (1901–1961)

A London-born teacher, model, and director who inspired both WALLACE THURMAN and CARL VAN VECHTEN to model characters based on their friend and associate. Jackman was one of the closest friends of poet COUNTEE CULLEN, a correspondent with ZORA NEALE HURSTON, and a well-known presence in the social world of the Harlem Renaissance. A student in the New York public school system, Jackman went on to graduate from NEW YORK UNIVERSITY in 1923. He earned a master's degree at COLUMBIA UNIVERSITY shortly thereafter.

An Alpha Phi Alpha brother, Jackman also was a member of the NATIONAL ASSOCIATION FOR THE ADVANCEMENT OF COLORED PEOPLE and the Urban League. He also was a high-ranking member of the Negro Actors Guild and an active member of the Ira Aldridge Society and the American Society of African Culture.

Some scholars speculate that his close friendship with Countee Cullen may have contributed to the breakdown of Cullen's short-lived marriage to YOLANDE DUBOIS, the only child of W. E. B. DUBOIS. Jackman, an openly gay man, was Cullen's best man, and the two men sailed for Europe, without Cullen's bride, two months after the wedding. The DuBois-Cullen marriage was officially over less than two years later. Cullen dedicated "Heritage," one of his most powerful poems, to Jackman.

Jackman and Zora Neale Hurston were good friends. In the winter of 1934 and spring of 1935, Hurston, a Columbia University graduate student at the time, lived in Jackman's Manhattan Avenue apartment. The two discussed her work, friends, and events of the period in their letters. In a 1944 note to Jackman, Zora Neale Hurston suggested that he and Cullen "come down for a few weeks this summer and rough it some." She continued, noting, "I could use two men to pull on ropes when coming into a dock." She was living on a houseboat in Daytona Beach at the time.

Jackman's participation in the Harlem Renaissance revolved around his involvement with theater and popular culture. He moved in some of the most visible and celebrated social circles. He was a frequent guest of Carl Van Vechten and also was a close friend of A'LELIA WALKER, the daughter of millionairess Madam C. J. Walker, both of whom were especially influential and high-profile society figures.

In 1924 the artist WINOLD REISS painted a portrait of Jackman just after his college graduation. Reiss, who titled the portrait *A College Lad*, captured the image of an impeccably dressed, serious, and handsome young man who embodied the TALENTED TENTH in whom DuBois, Locke, and other intellectuals believed. The image was included in the acclaimed issue of *SURVEY GRAPHIC* that was dedicated to African-American matters and edited by ALAIN LOCKE. Locke then reprinted the image in *HARLEM: MECCA OF THE NEW NEGRO*, the volume based on the journal issue.

Jackman was committed to preserving the legacy of Harlem Renaissance writers. It was he who worked with Carl Van Vechten to establish the Yale University James Weldon Johnson Memorial Collection of Negro Arts and Letters. In 1942 Jackman established the Countee Cullen Collection at Atlanta University, a substantial set of cultural, literary, and artistic materials and memorabilia relating to 20th-century African-American literature and the arts.

Bibliography

Ferguson, Blanche. *Countee Cullen and the Negro Renaissance.* New York: Dodd, Mead, 1966.
Kaplan, Carla. *Zora Neale Hurston: A Life in Letters.* New York: Doubleday, 2002.

Jackson, James A. (1878–unknown)

A former minstrel performer, waiter, and journalist whose widely circulated articles on entertainment made him the most popular African-American show business reporter. Jackson was born in Bellefonte, Pennsylvania, to Abraham Valentine and Nannie Lee Jackson. He and his wife, Cabrielle Bell Hill, who married in April 1909, had one child, a son named Albert. In the 1930s the Jacksons lived in WASHINGTON, D.C., and Jackson was working as a business specialist at the U.S. Department of Commerce.

He began writing for the local newspaper and later joined the staff of the *New York Globe* and the *New York Herald.* His expertise in entertainment later led to his appointment as theatrical editor at the *Washington Tribune.* The Clef Club in NEW YORK CITY made him an honorary member.

Jackson's career highlights also included the distinction of being the first African-American bank clerk in Illinois and one of only two African-American investigators for the U.S. Army's Military Intelligence Department. He was an army veteran who was commissioned to serve as adjutant of the First Provisional Regiment, an African-American unit that became the Fifteenth Regiment.

A member of the NATIONAL ASSOCIATION FOR THE ADVANCEMENT OF COLORED PEOPLE, Jackman was a high-ranking Mason and an active member of the National Negro Press Association and the Brotherhood of Sleeping Car Porters.

Jackson, Walter Clinton (1879–1959)

One of two North Carolina professors who coedited the 1924 ANTHOLOGY OF VERSE BY AMERICAN NEGROES. Jackson, a professor at the North Carolina

College for Women, was coeditor with NEWMAN IVEY WHITE, English professor and department chair of Trinity College, now Duke University. The volume, published by the newly established Trinity College Press in Durham, North Carolina, was one of the first anthologies of the Harlem Renaissance to showcase the work of African-American poets.

Jackson and White were part of the substantial group of white scholars and artists who publicized the substantial tradition of African-American letters and art.

Bibliography

White, Newman Ivey, and Walter Clinton Jackson, eds. *An Anthology of Verse by American Negroes.* Durham, N.C.: Trinity College Press, 1924.

J. B. Lippincott and Company

A long-standing publishing company in PHILADELPHIA. Joshua Ballinger Lippincott, a New Jersey native who was steeped in book culture and the publishing business from his early days, established the company in 1836. After several successful mergers, J. B. Lippincott and Company became one of the largest and most successful publishers in America.

The early history of the publishing company is linked to its production of works by Oscar Wilde, Sir Arthur Conan Doyle, Washington Irving, and Edgar Allan Poe.

Lippincott made overtures to ZORA NEALE HURSTON and in 1934 published the writer's first novel, *JONAH'S GOURD VINE.* Despite its interest in her work, Hurston was a bit dismayed by the company's seeming lack of familiarity with African-American authors and scholars. It was she, for instance, who had to insist that advance copies of *Jonah's Gourd Vine* be sent to prominent writers such as W. E. B. DuBois and JAMES WELDON JOHNSON. By 1942, however, company executives were working to broaden distribution of Hurston's work. As her biographer Melba Boyd notes, Hurston's colleague, the Rollins College professor Edwin Grover, was asked to help "to do everything possible to spread the good word" about the Hurston books that "do not get the distribution they deserve" (Boyd, 363).

The firm merged with Harper and Row in 1977.

Bibliography

Joshua B. Lippincott: A Memorial Sketch. Philadelphia: J. B. Lippincott Co., 1888.

Boyd, Valerie. *Wrapped in Rainbows: The Life of Zora Neale Hurston.* New York: Scribner, 2003.

Hinckley, Cornelius. *A Day at the Bookbindery of Lippincott, Grambo, & Co.* New Castle, Del.: Oak Knoll Books, 1988.

Jeffrey, Maurine L. (1900–unknown)

A southern writer from Texas who was part of the region's small but vibrant literary society during the Harlem Renaissance. Born in Longview, Texas, Jeffrey was raised in Dallas. She attended Prairie View State College. The school had important links to the North and to Boston's cultural circles through the writer and anthropologist MAUDE CUNEY HARE and Caroline Bond Day. Hare taught music at Prairie View in the late 1800s, and Day was English Department chair at the school. Maurine Jeffrey became a public school teacher but withdrew from her career when she married Jessie Jeffrey.

Jeffrey's poetry was featured in *Heralding Dawn,* a 1936 anthology of writers from Texas. The modest collection, edited by J. Mason Brewer, showcased two poems by Jeffrey and works by fellow Texans such as GWENDOLYN BENNETT and LAURETTA HOLMAN GOODEN. Jeffrey also published poems in several Texas newspapers. Her poems, which used dialect and standard prose, focused on family and religion.

Bibliography

Brewer, J. Mason. *Heralding Dawn: An Anthology of Verse.* Dallas: June Thomason, 1936.

Jelliffe, Rowena Woodham (1889–1994)

A sociologist who, with her husband, RUSSELL JELLIFFE, established a settlement house and legendary arts program in Cleveland, Ohio. Born in the utopian community of Albion, Ohio, she attended Oberlin College. She completed graduate work in sociology at the UNIVERSITY OF CHICAGO, earning a master's degree in 1915.

Woodham met Russell Jelliffe, a Mansfield, Ohio, native while at Oberlin. They both attended the University of Chicago as graduate students and married in 1915. They had one child, a son named Roger. The couple shared a passion for racial justice, and their marriage and partnership enabled them to realize their vision of an empowering and supportive interracial world.

The Jelliffes' link to the Harlem Renaissance is seen most clearly through their relationships with successful writers of the period. The poet LANGSTON HUGHES characterized Rowena Jelliffe and her husband as individuals who have "fought against both the intolerance of many whites and the bigotry of many Negroes composing the Cleveland community who wanted in one way or another to limit the scope of the players and their plays." Hughes, who moved at age 14 to Cleveland, was one of the talented young people who participated in the Neighborhood Association, or KARAMU HOUSE, programs. In addition to returning to teach at the center, Hughes later wrote six plays for the Gilpin Players, the talented theater company that was founded and in residence at the Karamu House. He maintained ties with the couple, and their correspondence reveals important collaborations and support during the Harlem Renaissance.

Jelliffe was caught up in the well-known 1930–31 controversy surrounding *MULE BONE,* the drama cowritten by Langston Hughes and ZORA NEALE HURSTON. She received the play and was enthusiastic about staging it with the Charles Gilpin Players, the African-American troupe that was founded and in residence at the Karamu House. Jelliffe contacted Hughes about the work, but he was alarmed to learn of its circulation because he had neither authorized its distribution nor been cited as coauthor. In the ensuing tense correspondence with Jelliffe, Hurston relayed the information that she had been told about Jelliffe. She accepted the idea that Jelliffe could be "trusted for integrity of script," but Hurston established strict terms for the play's production. Hurston instructed that "not one word must be altered except by me" and "script not to leave your hands." Despite delicate negotiations between the writers and the Jelliffes, the play was not performed. Hughes maintained a friendly relationship with the Jelliffes in the years following his time in Cleveland. In 1939 Langston Hughes forwarded a copy of *St. Louis Blues,* the ballet libretto that he composed and that was based on music by W. C. HANDY, to

Rowena Jelliffe. In 1940 he lobbied his influential friend CARL VAN VECHTEN for aid to support the Jelliffes as they tried to recover from a fire that devastated the theatrical venue. In the spring of 1941, Hughes encouraged ARNA BONTEMPS to see the couple's art exhibit at the Art Center in CHICAGO. Hughes also attended the phenomenal 1963 tribute to the Jelliffes. Held in Cleveland, the event drew more than 1,000 supporters, included entertainment by Noble Sissle and Eubie Blake, and, according to Hughes, "a moving program—a bit too long, of course, but not a soul left." Bontemps, who could not attend, contributed a poem that was read during the testimonial.

Rowena Jelliffe was a tireless advocate of the arts and racial justice. She was 105 years old when she died in 1994.

Bibliography

Berry, Faith, ed. *Langston Hughes: Before and Beyond Harlem.* Westport, Conn.: Lawrence Hill & Company, 1983.

Kaplan, Carla. *Zora Neale Hurston: A Life in Letters.* New York: Doubleday, 2002.

Nichols, Charles H. *Arna Bontemps–Langston Hughes: Letters 1925–1967.* New York: Paragon House, 1980.

Rampersad, Arnold. *The Life of Langston Hughes: I, Too, Sing America.* Vol. 1: *1902–1941.* New York: Oxford University Press, 1986.

———. *The Life of Langston Hughes: I Dream a World.* Vol. 2: *1941–1967.* New York: Oxford University Press, 1988.

Jelliffe, Russell (1891–1980)

A sociologist and the husband of ROWENA WOODHAM JELLIFFE who established the KARAMU HOUSE, a successful community, arts, and education center in Cleveland, Ohio. Born in Mansfield, Ohio, to Charles and Margaret Ward Jelliffe, he completed undergraduate work at Oberlin College in 1914 and a master's degree in sociology at the UNIVERSITY OF CHICAGO in 1915. He married Woodham, his college sweetheart, in May 1915, and the two moved to Cleveland.

The Jelliffes established the Neighborhood Association, an education and arts center. The organization was inspired by the settlement house, a type of institution that they had learned much about while in CHICAGO, home to pioneering settlement house leader Jane Hull. The center, which became known as the Karamu House, received much attention for its effective outreach to children. They developed art classes, recreational activities, and a respected children's theater. The organization later became home to the Gilpin Players, a highly respected dramatic troupe that performed the works of LANGSTON HUGHES, a former Karamu House attendee and art teacher.

The Jelliffes maintained an active role in national race politics and contributed much to the institutional life of central Harlem Renaissance-era organizations such as the NATIONAL ASSOCIATION FOR THE ADVANCEMENT OF COLORED PEOPLE. In addition to being a member of the NAACP and serving on the executive committee of the association's Cleveland branch, Jelliffe was instrumental in establishing the Cleveland chapter of the Urban League. The Jelliffes were honored by numerous organizations and feted in Cleveland for their untiring leadership and example.

Russell Jelliffe retired from Karamu House in 1963. He passed away in 1980.

Bibliography

Berry, Faith, ed. *Langston Hughes: Before and Beyond Harlem.* Westport, Conn.: Lawrence Hill & Company, 1983.

Kaplan, Carla. *Zora Neale Hurston: A Life in Letters.* New York: Doubleday, 2002.

Nichols, Charles H. *Arna Bontemps–Langston Hughes: Letters 1925–1967.* New York: Paragon House, 1980.

Rampersad, Arnold. *The Life of Langston Hughes: I, Too, Sing America.* Vol. 1: *1902–1941.* New York: Oxford University Press, 1986.

———. *The Life of Langston Hughes: I Dream a World.* Vol. 2: *1941–1967.* New York: Oxford University Press, 1988.

Jeremiah, the Magnificent Wallace Thurman and William Jourdan Rapp (1930)

An unpublished three-act play written by WALLACE THURMAN and WILLIAM JOURDAN RAPP. *Jeremiah* was the second play in *Color Play,* a series of three dramatic works. The first drama was

HARLEM: A MELODRAMA OF NEGRO LIFE, and the third was *Harlem Cinderella*. Of the three, only *Harlem and Jeremiah* were staged. *Harlem* opened at the APOLLO THEATRE in HARLEM, before traveling to BOSTON, CHICAGO, and Detroit. *Jeremiah, the Magnificent* was performed only once after Thurman's death in 1934.

The series focused on African-American families, migration, and the realities of urban life in modern America. *Jeremiah* was inspired by the West Indian nationalist MARCUS GARVEY and his campaigns to repatriate people of color to AFRICA.

Bibliography

Singh, Amritjit, and Daniel Scott III, eds. *The Collected Writings of Wallace Thurman: A Harlem Renaissance.* New Brunswick, N.J.: Rutgers University Press, 2003.

van Notten, Eleonore. *Wallace Thurman's Harlem Renaissance.* Amsterdam: Rodopi, 1994.

Jessye, Eva Alberta (1895–1992)

A teacher, poet, composer, and musical director whose lengthy career brought her into contact with prominent artists and influential people of and beyond the Harlem Renaissance. She worked with prominent American writers, performers, and composers. She was extremely active in the arts and drama communities of the Harlem Renaissance and enjoyed friendships with well-known figures such as AUGUSTA SAVAGE and LANGSTON HUGHES.

Her parents, Al and Julia Buckner Jessye, lived in Coffeyville, Kansas, at the time of their daughter's birth. A choir from the local Baptist church was on hand at the delivery, and scholars note the symbolic significance of such an event in the life of one of America's most accomplished choral directors. Her maternal grandmother, a woman of Cherokee and African-American descent, and her maternal aunts raised her when her parents separated.

Jessye, whose father worked as a chicken picker, had a deep love of books and music. She organized her first musical group when she was 12 years old. Jessye was denied access to high school in Kansas because of her race. She attended Western University in Quindaro, Kansas, the city known now as Kansas City, as a scholarship student. Admitted at the age of 13, she excelled and graduated in 1914. She also attended classes during three summer terms at Langston University in Oklahoma City, Oklahoma. Her coursework there resulted in a lifetime teaching certificate. With a degree in music theory and choral music, Jessye began working as a public school teacher in the Oklahoma towns of Taft, Haskell, and Muskogee.

Jessye relocated to Baltimore, Maryland, in 1920 and lived there for just over five years. She was an editorial staffer on the *Baltimore Afro-American* and also the choral director at Morgan State College. She relocated to NEW YORK CITY in 1926. She immersed herself in the arts community and developed an important professional relationship with WILL MARION COOK. She began to perform and enjoyed a successful career as a choral director for commercial ventures and professional theater. It was one of her former choral groups that performed the vocals for one of America's first radio advertisements. Jessye excelled as a choir director in entertainment and worked on films, radio, and in BROADWAY musicals. Her credits included the 1929 film *Hallelujah*, the first African-American musical, and working as the celebrated choral director for the 1935 GERSHWIN production of *PORGY AND BESS*. In 1934 she worked with Gertrude Stein and Virgil Thompson on their opera *Four Saints in Three Acts.* She and the Eva Jessye choir, a group known originally as the Dixie Jubilee Singers, appeared often at the Capitol Theatre in New York City. After World War II, the group traveled throughout Europe as part of a successful international concert tour. The group also performed at schools throughout the United States. In the 1960s Jessye directed the choir of *Tambourines for Glory: A Play with Songs,* a gospel play by Langston Hughes. In 1963 Jessye had the honor of directing the choir that performed at the historic Civil Rights March on Washington.

Jessye's lifelong love of music was reflected in her work on American Negro spirituals. She published *My Spirituals,* a collection of songs and stories based on the moving narratives that she had heard as a child, in 1929. Selections such as "Ain't Got Long to Stay Heah" and "Goin' to Pick Dis Cotton 'Till de Sun Go Down" both paid tribute to and illuminated the labor and lives of African-American laborers. Jessye published three additional books, including *The Life of Christ in Negro Spirituals* (1931) and *The Chronicle of Job* (1936) and saw at least one poem, "The Maestro," published in *Opportunity*.

Jessye donated her considerable collection of personal papers to Pittsburg State University in Pittsburg, Kansas, in 1977. Two years later, she was appointed artist-in-residence there. In 1976 the University of Michigan celebrated Jessye's accomplishments with a degree of determination. She received honorary degrees at Wilberforce University and Southern University and in 1988, an honorary doctor of art from Eastern Michigan University. A member of Sigma Gamma Rho, Jessye also belonged to the Songwriters Hall of Fame and to the American Society of Composers, Authors, and Producers (ASCAP).

After a stunning 75-year career in music and education, Jessye passed away in Ann Arbor, Michigan, on 21 February 1992.

Bibliography

The Eva Jessye papers are housed at the University of Michigan and at Pittsburg State University in Kansas.

Abdul, Raoul. *Blacks in Classical Music*. New York: Dodd, Mead, 1977.

Lanker, Brian. *I Dream a World*. New York: Stewart, Tabori and Chang, 1989.

Southern, Eileen. *Music of Black Americans*. New York: Norton, 1971.

Jim Crow

The term that was used to describe the laws that enforced racial segregation in America. The name "Jim Crow" was based on the contorted racist minstrel character and performances inaugurated by T. D. Rice in the 19th century. The laws upheld segregation in many public areas, schools, hospitals, restaurants, libraries, theaters, telephone booths, and cemeteries, and on buses, trains, and other modes of public transportation. The segregation legislated social relations as well, including restrictions on intermarriage, social interaction, athletics, and housing.

"John Redding Goes to Sea" Zora Neale Hurston (1926)

The first published story by ZORA NEALE HURSTON. It was published first in the May 1921 issue of *STYLUS*, the HOWARD UNIVERSITY literary magazine. The piece was republished five years later in the January 1926 issue of *OPPORTUNITY*. The tender and heartbreaking account of a young man's wanderlust is set in a northern Florida village near on the banks of the St. Johns River and near the city of Jacksonville. The story is enriched by details that link it to the author's family life and experiences.

The story revolves around John Redding, who as a boy would imagine himself "a prince riding away in a gorgeous carriage . . . a knight bestride a fiery charger prancing down the white shell road that led to distant lands. At other times he was a steamboat captain piloting his craft down the St. Johns River to where the sky seemed to touch the water." John's parents, Alfred and Matty, have conflicting opinions about their son's penchant to dream and to think beyond the narrow social expectations of his community. His father responds gently to John's vivid descriptions of the world around him and does not dismiss the young boy's unique visions. It is John's melancholy mother, a woman prone to self-pity and sobbing fits, who delays his journey out into the world. A spontaneous marriage to a beautiful village girl further distracts him from realizing his childhood goal of going out to sea and exploring distant lands. Ultimately, he decides to join the Navy. His wife and mother protest loudly and refuse to speak to him. On the eve of his departure, he volunteers to help a construction crew reinforce a bridge over the St. Johns River. The ensuing storm ends up destroying the bridge and injuring many of the workers. John Redding's family finally locates him, floating in the St. Johns River, killed by falling timber or steel. When crews prepare to retrieve his body, Alfred Redding commands them to stop. "Leave him g'wan. He wants tuh go. Ah'm happy 'cause dis maw'nin' mah boy is goin' tuh sea," he says earnestly, *"he's goin' tuh sea."* The story closes as John Redding, the young man who used to float twig ships in the river that flowed near his home, finally realizes his dream of exploration.

"John Redding" draws on the conventions of the picaresque, and it underscores the importance of imagination and the grim realities that can compromise dreamers. Hurston's own well-known wanderlust influences the story. Additional signs that the piece has shades of autobiography emerge in the names of the characters. Hurston assigns her stepmother's name to John's intractable mother, her father was named John, and her paternal grandfather was Alfred.

Hurston critics such as Robert Hemenway call attention to the use of folklore in the story, her exploration of signs and symbols that foretell John Redding's complicated yearnings and his fate. The story is one of several compelling Hurston pieces to feature aspiring, often misunderstood, travelers and their alluring quests. These include "DRENCHED IN LIGHT" (1924), which also appeared in *Opportunity*, and *THEIR EYES WERE WATCHING GOD* (1937).

Bibliography

Boyd, Valerie. *Wrapped in Rainbows: The Life of Zora Neale Hurston*. New York: Scribner, 2003.

Hemenway, Robert. *Zora Neale Hurston: A Literary Biography*. Urbana: University of Illinois, 1977.

Johnson, Charles Bertram (1880–1946)

A Missouri clergyman, teacher, and poet. He was born in Callao, Missouri, to James and Elizabeth Johnson. Johnson graduated from Western College in 1900 and pursued additional studies at Lincoln University in Missouri during 1901 and 1902, and at the UNIVERSITY OF CHICAGO during 1905. He earned his doctor of divinity degree from Western Seminary in 1932. He and his wife, Maud Maupin Johnson, had one child, a daughter named Ineth.

Johnson's literary career developed as he pursued a career in teaching and in the ministry. He taught at Western Seminary and in the Missouri public school system for some 11 years. His ministerial career spanned some 30 years and included a lengthy appointment at the Second Baptist Church in Jefferson, Missouri. He also was a member of the NATIONAL ASSOCIATION FOR THE ADVANCEMENT OF COLORED PEOPLE.

Johnson published three collections of poetry, the pamphlets entitled *Wind Whisperings* (1902) and *Songs of My People* (1918) and a book entitled *Mantle of Dunbar* (1918). Johnson made contributions to major Harlem Renaissance–era anthologies of the early 1920s. Two poems appeared in JAMES WELDON JOHNSON's anthology *THE BOOK OF AMERICAN NEGRO POETRY*, and his writing also appeared in the NEWMAN IVEY WHITE and WALTER JACKSON 1924 work entitled *ANTHOLOGY OF VERSE BY AMERICAN NEGROES*. In addition, Johnson published in *THE CRISIS* in 1923.

In his brief biographical sketch and editorial note that preceded Johnson's poems, editor James Weldon Johnson suggested that Johnson's work was "respectable, not varying in any great degree either up or down from that level." His poems ranged from lively dialect pieces to serious meditations. In "Negro Poets," the lengthy seven-stanza poem anthologized in the Johnson collection, the poet speculated on the moment when poetry would represent African-American matters. While "[f]ull many lift and sing / Their sweet imagining" he noted, "Whose pen with pregnant mirth / Will give our longings birth / And point our souls the way?" Johnson's poems reflected his interest in the production of African-American history and the preservation of black culture. His successful effort to produce a posthumous publication of his friend Roscoe Conkling Jamison underscored his belief in the power of literature and history. Jamison's volume, *Negro Soldiers: "These Truly Are the Brave" and Other Poems* appeared in 1918.

ALAIN LOCKE recognized Johnson as a part of the "pioneers and path-breakers in the cultural development and recognition of the Negro in the arts." In his powerful essay "Youth Speaks," written for the March 1925 special edition of *SURVEY GRAPHIC* that was devoted to Harlem and to African-American literature and issues, Locke hailed Johnson along with Paul Laurence Dunbar, GEORGIA DOUGLAS JOHNSON, and WALTER EVERETTE HAWKINS for their contributions to the African-American literary tradition.

Bibliography

Jamison, Roscoe C. *Negro Soldiers: "These Truly Are the Brave" and Other Poems*. 1918; reprint, New York: AMS Press, 1975.

Johnson, James Weldon. *The Book of American Negro Poetry*. New York: Harcourt, Brace and Company, 1922.

Johnson, Charles Spurgeon (1893–1956)

One of the most influential scholars and leaders of the Harlem Renaissance. Johnson, a sociologist, became a highly respected advocate for children, racial equality, and civil rights. He is perhaps best known for his longtime editorship of OPPORTU-NITY, the official publication of the NATIONAL URBAN LEAGUE, and for his years at FISK UNIVERSITY, where he served as a faculty member, department chair, and as president.

Born in Bristol, Virginia, he was the first of five children in the family of the Reverend Charles Henry and Winifred Branch Johnson. He and his siblings, Lillie, Sarah, Julia, and Maurice, grew up in a supportive family but a segregated southern town. Their father, whose own father had been enslaved in Virginia, was a dynamic Baptist minister who for 42 years presided over the historic Lee Street Baptist Church, which grew under his leadership from a modest shed to an expansive brick church with a distinctive spire. As scholar Kathleen Hauke notes, the Reverend Johnson, though not an overbearing personality, once used "force of personality and the Bible" to "so sham[e] a lynch mob that lynching ceased in Bristol" (Hauke, 147). Charles Johnson married Marie Antoinette Burgette of Milwaukee, Wisconsin, in November 1920. A graduate of the Wisconsin Conservatory of Speech and Fine Arts, she became an activist in her own right as she pursued a career in teaching following her landmark appointment as the first African-American employed in the Milwaukee library system. The couple had four children: Charles, Jr., a physician; Robert Burgette, a sociology professor and Cornell University Ph.D.; Patricia Marie, a Fisk University graduate; and Jeh Vincent, a COLUMBIA UNIVERSITY–educated architect and former student-body president of the School of Architecture. Marie Johnson, who was an active philanthropist and wife dedicated to maintaining her husband's legacy after his death in 1956, died nine years later.

Johnson was one of the many learned and accomplished figures of the Harlem Renaissance. He graduated in 1913 from Wayland Academy, a private school in Richmond, where his parents sent him in order to circumvent the intense racial prejudice of his hometown. He completed requirements for the bachelor's degree in three years and

Charles Spurgeon Johnson, editor of *Opportunity*, photographed by Carl Van Vechten. Permission granted by the Van Vechten Trust *(Yale Collection of American Literature, Beinecke Rare Book and Manuscript Library)*

graduated from the Virginia Union University, with which Wayland Academy was affiliated, in 1916. He then began graduate studies in sociology at the UNIVERSITY OF CHICAGO. There, he studied with the renowned sociologist Robert Park, a former reporter whose work on African and African-American issues included projects on the Belgian Congo and working as an aide, ghostwriter, and secretary to BOOKER T. WASHINGTON. He earned a Ph.B. degree in 1917 and by 1918 became a member of the armed forces. He joined the 803rd Pioneer Infantry of the American Expeditionary Forces and became part of the massive numbers of African Americans who fought in World War I. Johnson, a regimental sergeant major, was sent to the front lines in France, but as biographer Richard Robbins notes, he recorded very little about his military experience, which would have been marked for its intense racial segregation and limited options for qualified men of color. Johnson's return to the United States was marred by the violent racial targeting of veterans of color and by race riots such as the Chicago Riot of 1919. His first-hand experiences of war abroad and at home only prompted him to redouble his studies of race relations and methods by which African Americans could succeed in such a volatile nation. He was appointed to serve on the Chicago commission charged with investigating the riot and, after much research, published his substantial assessment of the race riot and his first major scholarly work, *The Negro in Chicago* (1922).

Johnson's role in the literary and cultural forums of the Harlem Renaissance grew out of his involvement with the National Urban League. The organization was founded in 1911. Johnson, who joined the organization in Chicago, served as director of research and investigations from 1917 to 1919. He and his family relocated to New York City in 1921 when Johnson was appointed research director of the organization. In 1923 he established and became the first editor of OPPORTUNITY, the organization's official journal. That venue soon emerged as one of the most important vehicles through which scholars, artists, and writers could share their work and contribute to the unprecedented advance in African-American art and letters.

Like JAMES WELDON JOHNSON, director of the NATIONAL ASSOCIATION FOR THE ADVANCEMENT OF COLORED PEOPLE, Johnson published collections that showcased the work of *Opportunity* writers and underwrote events that encouraged and rewarded creative productions. His 1927 anthology *EBONY AND TOPAZ: A COLLECTANEA*, which appeared two years after ALAIN LOCKE's *NEW NEGRO* and five years after Johnson's *BOOK OF AMERICAN NEGRO POETRY*, underscored further the breadth and diversity of African-American talent and intellectual interests. In his introduction to the volume, which the Urban League itself published, Johnson frankly declared that the collection "strangely enough, does not set forth to prove a thesis, nor to plead a cause, nor, stranger still, to offer a progress report on the state of Negro letters. It is a venture in expression," he stated, "shared, with the slightest editorial suggestion, by a number of persons who are here much less interested in their audience

than in what they are trying to say, and the life they are trying to portray." The volume was divided into four sections that dealt with African-American folklife, the diverse careers of African-American scholars, contemporary race issues, and essays on the future direction of African-American life. L. HOLLINGSWORTH WOOD, who provided the foreword for the volume, characterized it as a "challenging collection" that "focuses, as it were, the appraising eyes of white folks on the Negro's life and of Negroes on their own life and development in what seems . . . a new and stimulating way." The volume's 29 entries included an array of works, ranging from poems by STERLING BROWN, Elizabeth Barrett Browning, COUNTEE CULLEN, GEORGIA DOUGLAS JOHNSON, and Phillis Wheatley, to a one-act play by ZORA NEALE HURSTON, and stories by ARTHUR HUFF FAUSET and JOHN MATHEUS, and biographical and historical narratives by ARTHUR SCHOMBURG and JULIA PETERKIN.

Johnson, whom scholar Richard Robbins describes as "the entrepreneur of the Harlem Renaissance," (53) hosted two key social events that facilitated key alliances among artists, writers, editors, and patrons. At the urging of GWENDOLYN BENNETT and JESSIE FAUSET, Johnson organized the legendary Civic Club Dinner of March 1924. Originally planned as a celebration of Fauset's just-published novel *THERE IS CONFUSION*, the party included a rousing call from CARL VAN DOREN, *CENTURY MAGAZINE* editor and a prominent critic, for fresh, new work from the younger artists of the day. The special Harlem edition of *SURVEY GRAPHIC* that appeared shortly thereafter grew out of the Civic Club event as did *The New Negro*, Alain Locke's book version of the magazine edition.

Johnson's overtures to publishers and potential patrons of the arts benefited many writers and the Harlem Renaissance movement as a whole. He successfully courted Casper Holstein, a St. Croix native and the head of a profitable Harlem gambling organization, to sponsor prizes for what would become annual *Opportunity* literary competitions. In addition, he solicited African-American and white authors to serve as judges in the competitions, thus providing invaluable opportunities for beneficial exposure, potential collaborations, and contracts.

Johnson worked closely with numerous prominent figures of the Harlem Renaissance during and after his tenure as editor in chief of *Opportunity*. It was Johnson who encouraged Zora Neale Hurston, newly arrived in New York City, to submit her work for consideration in the *Opportunity* literary contests and to relocate to New York City. Hurston corresponded with him from time to time. She regarded Johnson as "an excellent man and full of zeal" (Kaplan, 109). Hurston's letters to him and the Johnson family, such as the December 1950 note written from New York City in which she announced, "I hate snow!", often were engaging and witty. In the mid-1930s, Hurston imagined herself "work[ing] out some of [her] visions at Fisk University" alongside Johnson, a man whom she believed had demonstrated "[h]is tremendous love of Negro creative instincts" and whose work "pulsates with the life of his people" (Kaplan, 318).

As the editor of *Opportunity*, Johnson was a contemporary of two other major editors, W. E. B. DuBois of *The Crisis* and A. Philip Randolph of *The Messenger*. Although scholars consider Johnson the least emphatic and strident of the three major figures, he remained a consistent race man and social critic. His unwavering belief in the power of literature and the arts also gave *Opportunity* a distinctive edge over the other two journals. Although *The Crisis* and *The Messenger* later included literature and creative work, *Opportunity* set aside significant space for such material from its beginnings. During its first year of publication, issues included articles such as "Our Young Negro Artists," book reviews by Alain Locke, and poems by Countee Cullen, Angelina Grimké, Leslie Pinckney Hill, Eunice Hunton, and Eric Walrond, and artwork by Meta Warwick Fuller. Johnson hired Countee Cullen as assistant editor and also to produce a popular monthly column on contemporary events and the vibrant literary and arts world of Harlem and beyond entitled "Dark Tower." Johnson also developed a close friendship with Arthur Schomburg and was instrumental in Schomburg's 1929 appointment to Fisk as curator of the university's library. Johnson also earned the respect of many writers with whom he corresponded during his tenure as editor. His careful notes and informed responses to authors such as Walter White and Angelina Grimké confirmed his deep commitment to maintaining productive relationships with the writers and artists whose work

was extremely important and propelled the race toward greater social and political advancement. His secretary Ethel Nance also was a key figure in the day-to-day operations at the journal. Her close relationship with Regina Andrews, who was a dynamic librarian and writer at the 135th Street Branch of the New York Public Library, also enriched the arts agendas of the journal.

Johnson's tenure at *Opportunity* ended in the spring of 1928. Later that year he joined the faculty at Fisk University, where he joined the sociology department and became chair of the social science department. In 1946, after 17 years on the faculty, he became the first African-American president of the historically black university where E. Franklin Frazier, James Weldon Johnson, and Elmer Imes, husband of Nella Larsen, also had taught and conducted research. He served through 1956 and was committed to establishing the school as a premier research institution and as the best of the historically black colleges and universities in the nation.

Johnson's own scholarship flourished during the Harlem Renaissance period and in the years following. He published several sociological studies, including *The Negro in American Civilization* (1930), *Shadow of the Plantation* (1934), *The Negro College Graduate* (1938), *Growing Up in the Black Belt: Negro Youth in the Rural South* (1941), and *Education and the Cultural Crisis* (1951). His prominence and continued professional and scholarly efforts also resulted in several honorary degrees and prizes. In addition to earning the Harmon Gold Medal in Science in 1930, he received honorary degrees from Virginia Union University, the University of Glasgow, Howard University, and Columbia University. In 1957 he was honored posthumously when he was admitted to the Ebony Hall of Fame.

Johnson was 63 years old when he died on 27 October 1956. The university president collapsed at the train station in Louisville, Kentucky, just before reboarding for his journey to a meeting of Fisk University trustees in New York City. *The New York Times* eulogized him as "one of the most profound observers of interracial matters." Johnson's legacy as a social scientist, civil rights activist, and race man made an undeniable impact on the Harlem Renaissance.

Bibliography

"Charles Johnson of Fisk U. Is Dead." *New York Times*, 28 October 1956, 88.

Johnson, Charles, ed. *Ebony and Topaz: A Collectanea.* 1927; reprint, North Stratford, N.H.: Ayer Company Publishers, Inc., 2000.

Kaplan, Carla. *Zora Neale Hurston: A Life in Letters.* New York: Doubleday, 2002.

Robbins, Richard. *Sidelines Activist: Charles S. Johnson and the Struggle for Civil Rights.* Jackson: University of Mississippi, 1996.

Hauke, Kathleen. "Charles S. Johnson." In *Dictionary of Literary Biography: Afro-American Writers from the Harlem Renaissance to 1940,* edited by Thadious Davis. Detroit: Gale Research Company, 1987, 146–152.

Johnson, Dorothy Vena (1898–1970)

A Los Angeles, California, poet and teacher. Johnson graduated from the University of Southern California and the Teachers College of the University of California at Los Angeles. The daughter of James and Namie Plumb Vena, Johnson became a teacher of journalism and creative writing in the Los Angeles public schools. She encouraged her students to publish as well, and the bimonthly children's magazine *Nuggets* featured their work.

Johnson was one of the 29 poets featured in the 1941 anthology *Golden Slippers: An Anthology of Negro Poetry for Young Readers.* ARNA BONTEMPS, editor of the volume, selected "Palace," a poem about sea shells, and "Twinkling Gown," a meditation on stars, for inclusion in the book section entitled "Sky Pictures." Also included in the section were poems by LANGSTON HUGHES, MARY EFFIE LEE NEWSOME, and GEORGIA DOUGLAS JOHNSON.

Despite her West Coast residence during the Harlem Renaissance, Johnson did establish friendships with active and visible members of the movement. She corresponded with Bontemps and Hughes in the years following the publication of *Golden Slippers.* In a fall 1941 letter to Hughes, Bontemps praised Johnson's scholarly thesis on "influencing race attitudes in children," noted that she cited their collaborative children's story POPO AND FIFINA, and concluded that the project was "very good." In May 1949 Hughes wrote to Bontemps asking whether or not Dorothy Johnson ever

shared with him her story of having "a youngster in her school whose first names are *Langston Arna.*" Johnson also received copies of Hughes's work from time to time.

Johnson was one of the many educators who contributed to the Harlem Renaissance through their own writing and their important outreach to children.

Bibliography

Bontemps, Arna. *Golden Slippers: An Anthology of Negro Poetry for Young Readers.* New York: Harper & Row, 1941.

Nichols, Charles H., ed. *Arna Bontemps–Langston Hughes Letters, 1925–1967.* New York: Paragon House, 1990.

Johnson, Fenton (ca. 1886/88–1958)

A poet, playwright, short story writer, and magazine publisher whose works appeared in THE CRISIS and in well-regarded anthologies, such as THE BOOK OF AMERICAN NEGRO POETRY (1922) edited by JAMES WELDON JOHNSON. Johnson was born in CHICAGO. He was an only child, whom his supporter ARNA BONTEMPS remembered as an extremely well-dressed young man who enjoyed motoring around Chicago in the early 1900s. Johnson attended both the UNIVERSITY OF CHICAGO and Northwestern University and also studied at the School of Journalism at COLUMBIA UNIVERSITY. He was a reporter for the *New York News* and the Eastern Press Association.

A talented playwright, Johnson was only 19 years old when the drama company at the Pekin Theatre located on South State Street in Chicago performed some of his works. He later became an independent publisher of magazines that he founded, *Correct English* and the *Champion Magazine.*

Johnson published three volumes of poetry in the decade leading up to the Harlem Renaissance. *A Little Dreaming* appeared in 1912 and was followed in quick succession by *Visions of Dusk* (1915) and *Songs of the Soil* (1916). A number of Johnson's poems appeared in *The Book of American Negro Poetry* (1922) and in the 1949 Bontemps-Hughes anthology, *The Poetry of the Negro, 1746–1949* (1949). In 1922 James Weldon Johnson lamented the fact that the man whom he regarded as "one of the first Negro revolutionary poets" had "[as] a poet . . . for ten years or more been almost silent." Johnson's immersion in journalism and the production of two magazines clearly took him away from his writing. In his discussion of Arna Bontemps's selfless mentoring of fellow writers, biographer Kirkland Jones characterizes Johnson as "a morose, aging poet" and suggests that his "career was boosted by Arna's encouragement and by the inclusion of several of his poems in the Bontemps-Hughes anthology" (Jones, 90). In the 1960s Bontemps was still promoting Johnson's work and noted enthusiastically to Langston Hughes that Johnson's Works Project Administration poems were to be published as part of a series, with an introduction that Bontemps would provide. Although Bontemps noted that the volume entitled *42 WPA Poems* was published posthumously, it appears that the work appeared as a pamphlet entitled *The Daily Grind* in 1994 and was edited and published by Paul Breman.

Johnson's poetry is powerful for what James Weldon Johnson referred to as its "fatalistic despair." Yet, poems such as "Children of the Sun" were soulful exhortations of a race that had borne up under great oppression. Johnson may have ceased to believe in true peace on earth, but he invested wholly in the notion of a restorative future. "We have come through cloud and mist, / Might men!" he exclaims. "Dusk has kissed our sleep born eyes, / Reared for us a mystic throne / In the splendor of the skies, That shall always be for us, Children of the Nazarene, Children who shall ever sing / Liberty! Fraternity!" Other poems such as "The New Day" maintained his critique of earthly violence and suffering. They also underscored Johnson's deep spiritual belief in a powerful redemption and victory ensured by an unwavering Christian faith.

Johnson published *Tales of Darkest America,* a collection of short stories, in 1920. His pre-Renaissance publications also included "The Servant," a story about a young southern domestic's maturation in the urban North that appeared in the August 1912 issue of *The Crisis.*

Bibliography

Johnson, Fenton. *The Daily Grind.* London: P. Breman, 1994.

———. *A Little Dreaming.* 1913, reprint, College Park, Md.: McGrath Publishing Company, 1969.

———. *Tales of Darkest America.* 1920, reprint, Freeport, N.Y.: Books for Libraries Press, 1971.

———. *Visions of the Dusk.* 1915, reprint, Freeport, N.Y.: Books for Libraries Press, 1971.

Johnson, James Weldon. *The Book of American Negro Poetry.* New York: Harcourt, Brace and Company, 1922.

Jones, Kirkland C. *Renaissance Man from Louisiana: A Biography of Arna Wendell Bontemps.* Westport, Conn.: Greenwood Press, 1992.

Johnson, Georgia Douglas (1877–1966)

The entry for Georgia Douglas Johnson in the 1930 *Who's Who of Colored America* identified her as "Housewife—Poet." Twenty years later, in 1950, the reference book listed her emphatically only as "Writer." Johnson was a dynamic, astute, and talented leader of the WASHINGTON, D.C., literary circle during and in the years following the Harlem Renaissance. Her works were anthologized more often than those of any other Harlem Renaissance writer. Her home was one of the most popular and engaging social and professional forums of the day. The "Round Table," as it was called, met weekly on Saturday evenings and often featured prominent writers, intellectuals, and influential figures of the day, ranging from W. E. B. DuBois and ANGELINA WELD GRIMKÉ to ALAIN LOCKE and MAY MILLER SULLIVAN.

Born Georgia Blanche Douglas Camp, she was the daughter of George and Laura Camp, who were both the children of interracial unions. Her paternal grandfather was a white Englishman who relocated to the United States and settled in Marietta, Georgia. Her maternal grandfather was an African-American builder and her grandmother was of Native American descent. Both died early and left their oldest daughter, Laura Camp, responsible for her six siblings. Johnson, who was born during the first of her mother's three marriages, had half brothers and a half sister as a result of her mother's subsequent unions. Johnson grew up in Rome, Georgia, and went on to study at the Normal School affiliated with ATLANTA UNIVERSITY. Following her graduation in 1893, she pursued studies in music at the OBERLIN CONSERVATORY and at Cleveland College of Music. She studied in a number of fields, including violin, piano, and voice, but as she increasingly immersed herself in poetry, she decided against a career as a composer or performer. Johnson taught school in Marietta, Georgia, and for one year before her marriage was appointed assistant principal at an Atlanta school.

In September 1903 she married Henry Lincoln Johnson, a native of Augusta, Georgia, and a public figure who enjoyed a 25-year career as "one of the outstanding leaders of the negro race, who served as Republican national committeeman from Georgia, and was a delegate at large to all Republican national conventions since 1896" (*NYT*, 11 September 1925, 23). Following his graduation from Atlanta University in 1888, he went on to attend law school at the University of Michigan and graduated in 1892. In 1912, Henry Johnson was appointed recorder of deeds, a historic post once held by Frederick Douglass. He resumed his law practice when his four-year appointment ended. He continued to be an active member of the Republican Party and national organization. He was active in numerous organizations, including the Colored Masons, the Colored Knights of Pythias, the National Order of Colored Elks for whom he served as grand legal adviser, and the Colored Odd Fellows of the World for whom he served as master. In September 1925, Henry Johnson suffered a fatal "stroke of apoplexy" at the family home on S Street. Following his death, Georgia Johnson accepted an appointment in the Labor Department from President Calvin Coolidge, who wanted to recognize her husband's years of service to the party. She eventually completed a biography of her husband entitled *The Black Cabinet, Being the Life of Henry Lincoln Johnson* but was unable to secure a publisher for the work. Following her husband's death, Johnson sought a number of jobs to sustain her family. As biographer Gloria Hull notes, she was employed in a variety of federal agencies and city departments, including the Public Schools Department of the District of Columbia and different offices within the Department of Labor.

Johnson's two sons inherited her love of education, and both parents ensured that both children had ample opportunities to advance their schooling. Their oldest son, Henry, attended Ashburnham Academy, Bowdoin College, and the law

school at HOWARD UNIVERSITY. The youngest son, Peter, who died in 1957, attended Williston Seminary, Dartmouth College, and the medical school at Howard University.

Johnson's emergence as a gifted poet preceded the Harlem Renaissance by a few years. Although she had published poetical works as early as 1905, she had to overcome her husband's insistence that she devote herself completely to domestic and family matters. Johnson counteracted the potential constraints that her husband placed on her by insisting on the importance of her writing and by developing supportive relationships outside of her marriage. Washington, D.C., did provide her with meaningful artistic support networks, however. KELLY MILLER, dean at Howard University and father of the writer May Miller Sullivan who later would befriend Johnson, encouraged her to share her works with the influential literary critic WILLIAM STANLEY BRAITHWAITE. Positive responses from Braithwaite raised her self-confidence, and she proceeded to publish works in *THE CRISIS*. She negotiated the social expectations and her own professional ambitions and published two important volumes of poems in 1918 and 1922. She dedicated both of these books to her husband. Following her husband's death in 1925, she was able to enjoy even more creative freedom and went on to produce additional works of poetry, plays, and a biography of her husband. Her first book, *THE HEART OF A WOMAN*, was marked for its works about deeply emotional matters and, as critics noted, did not include any poems dedicated strictly to racial matters. Four years later, she responded to the criticism and in *BRONZE: A BOOK OF VERSE* provided what she regarded as an "entirely racial" work (Shockley, 348). Six years later, she published her third collection of poems, *AN AUTUMN LOVE CYCLE*. W. E. B. DuBois, with whom she had a close relationship, provided the introduction for *Bronze*. ALAIN LOCKE provided the foreword for *An Autumn Love Cycle*, which was to be her final Harlem Renaissance volume. In 1951, she published *Share My World: A Book of Poems*, her last collection.

An earnest playwright, Johnson saw her status boosted by her successful showing in literary contests of the day. While she had been criticized for her apolitical poetry, few could ignore the powerful critiques of volatile race matters that Johnson tackled in her drama. In 1926 *BLUE BLOOD,* her play about interracial relationships, secured honorable mention in the *Opportunity* contest. In 1927 *PLUMES* focused on the emotional turmoil brought on by dire poverty and the ways in which ordinary, hardworking people grappled with tragedy and loss. Her moving portrait of tragic family life won first prize in the magazine's drama category. Between 1935 and 1939 she submitted five plays to the Federal Theatre Project for consideration. As critic Winona Fletcher notes, three of the works addressed issues of rape and LYNCHING, and the other two addressed issues of African-American enslavement in the South (Fletcher, 159). Included in the set were *Blue-Eyed Black Boy,* about the terrors of lynching, and her gripping family and antilynching drama entitled A *SUNDAY MORNING IN THE SOUTH.*

She published numerous short stories and, as she did while working as a journalist, wrote under pseudonyms. Of the many works she wrote, only three stories and one book review appear to be extant. The short stories "Free," "Gesture," and "Tramp Love" all appeared in *CHALLENGE* under Johnson's pseudonym of PAUL TREMAINE, and a review of a James Curley biography was published in the *New Republic* in 1957. Gloria Hull notes that Johnson sent the pieces to Harold Jackman for consideration and suggested that the stories were by a protégé who could benefit from direct criticism and advice. She later confessed the ruse, saying, "You see, Paul Tremaine is one of my pseudonyms. I used it on the stories. I rewrote them, you know, and feel a kind of pride in their reception" (Hull, *CSP,* 197). She also used the pseudonyms of JOHN TEMPLE and MARY STRONG. The latter was the name that she used for some 35 years while maintaining an extremely successful letter club that provided pen pals to those who joined the organization. Johnson also authored a syndicated weekly column that appeared in several leading African-American newspapers. Her feature, "Homely Philosophy," an encouraging commentary about home life and issues, was syndicated widely and published in papers such as the *New York News, CHICAGO DEFENDER, Boston Guardian,* and *Philadelphia Tribune.*

Johnson referred to her Washington, D.C., home on S Street as a "Halfway House." In the years after her husband's death, she freely accommodated, nurtured, and encouraged numerous writers including HAROLD JACKMAN, LANGSTON HUGHES, and ZORA NEALE HURSTON. Johnson's literary salons served as vital a purpose as those held in NEW YORK CITY, PHILADELPHIA, and BOSTON. They provided informal opportunities for writers and scholars to mingle, to debate, and to encourage each other's projects. Hurston, who studied at Howard University and made her literary debut while in Washington, D.C., was one of Johnson's most enthusiastic participants. "Please let me be a friend of yours always. I need you," she wrote earnestly in a July 1925 note to Johnson. In response to Johnson's own note to her, Hurston seized the opportunity to praise her colleague's talents. "This is my chance to say to you what a wonderful poet I think you are," she gushed before continuing in breathless fashion, "No, what a soulful poet I KNOW you are" (Kaplan, 61). ALICE DUNBAR-NELSON shared Hurston's enthusiasm. Dunbar-Nelson's journal entries include scintillating and lively details about the Johnsons and about her own interactions with Georgia Johnson. In 1921, during a visit when Henry Johnson was recovering from one of his first strokes, Dunbar-Nelson noted that "Georgia has done the big thing in letting [Alain] Locke, [W. E. B.] DuBois, and Braithwaite weed out her verses until only the perfect ones remain. What she has left are little gems, characterized by a finish of workmanship that is seldom seen in our people" (Hull, 88).

Unlike many of the writers with whom she associated, however, Johnson did not win prestigious fellowships that would have provided her with renewed professional credentials and, more importantly, time and funds to facilitate her writing. Scholars suggest that her tireless efforts to apply for awards such as the GUGGENHEIM FELLOWSHIP and JULIUS ROSENWALD FELLOWSHIP may have been thwarted by the tepid letters of support from her references. Referees such as JAMES WELDON JOHNSON and JEAN TOOMER, who socialized and corresponded often with her, tended to suggest that her work lacked poetical or political sophistication. Gloria Hull notes that Johnson was persistent even in the face of repeated rejection. In the years after the Harlem Renaissance, Johnson returned to music, her first love. She began composing songs and enjoyed a productive collaborative relationship with composer Lillian Evanti, a Washington, D.C.-born opera singer who became the first African American to perform with a formally organized European opera company. Evanti, who also founded the National Negro Opera Company in Pittsburgh, Pennsylvania, published at least three pieces with Douglas and worked on many more. Published songs such as "Beloved Mother" (1952) and "Hail to Fair Washington" (1953) included patriotic songs and loving tributes to mothers.

Johnson was active in civic, cultural, and political circles. A member of the League for the Abolition of Capital Punishment, she participated in the American Society of African Culture and the Writers' League Against Lynching. She also was a member of the Poet's Council of the National Women's Party, the Poet Laureate League, the Poets League of Washington, and the League of American Writers.

Her literary and political life continued to thrive after the Harlem Renaissance ended. She published her last book in 1962, just four years before her death. In 1965, Atlanta University bestowed an honorary degree upon her. Johnson suffered a stroke in May 1966 and was cared for in the Washington, D.C., Freedman's Hospital, the same facility in which her husband had been treated before he died. One of the most poignant images associated with Johnson emerged when her longtime friend May Miller, who used to visit her often, sat by her bedside, held her hand, and whispered repeatedly "Poet Georgia Douglas Johnson" (Fletcher, 163). Johnson was a vibrant and talented writer who felt constantly the pressure of daily responsibilities and her creative goals. Her close friends and colleagues were fully aware of the projects that she left unfinished. She clearly wanted to see more of her work published, confessing in a 1950 letter to Harold Jackman that she was "so eager to get to this writing before the taper is snuffed out. Am afraid of dying before I get the things done I hope to do" (Hull, *CSP,* 191).

Unfortunately, much of her massive collection of personal papers, including manuscripts in progress and completed works, was discarded haphazardly immediately after her death. Her friend OWEN DODSON was one of many close friends who lamented the sight of Johnson's papers heaped unceremoniously as garbage outside her home shortly after her funeral service. The Howard University Archives, however, did acquire a good amount of Johnson materials, and these include a rich variety of work and correspondence. Johnson's reputation and influence have been increasingly restored in the wake of absorbing scholarship and more frequently anthologized versions of her work.

Bibliography

Fletcher, Winona. "Georgia Douglas Johnson." In *Dictionary of Literary Biography.* Vol. 51: *Afro-American Writers from the Harlem Renaissance to 1940,* edited by Trudier Harris. Detroit: Gale Research Inc., 1987, 153–163.

Georgia Douglas Johnson Papers, Atlanta University, Oberlin College Archives, and Harmon Foundation Records, Library of Congress Manuscript Division. Other Johnson materials: Schomburg Center for Research in Black Culture, New York Public Library; Amistad Research Center, Tulane University; and Moorland-Spingarn Research Center, Howard University.

Hull, Gloria T. *Color, Sex, and Poetry: Three Women Writers of the Harlem Renaissance.* Bloomington: Indiana University Press, 1987.

Hull, Gloria, ed. *Give Us This Day: The Diary of Alice Dunbar-Nelson.* New York: W. W. Norton & Company, 1984.

Johnson, Georgia. *The Selected Works of Georgia Douglas Johnson.* Introduction by Claudia Tate. New York: G. K. Hall & Company, 1997.

Kaplan, Carla. *Zora Neale Hurston: A Life in Letters.* New York: Doubleday, 2002.

Shockley, Ann Allen. *Afro-American Women Writers, 1746–1933: An Anthology and Critical Guide.* Boston: G. K. Hall & Co., 1988.

Johnson, Guy Benton (1901–1991)

A Texan anthropologist, scientist, and sociologist who developed influential studies of race relations and contributed much to the American civil rights movement. In the 1930s Johnson worked alongside W. E. B. DuBois on the *Encyclopedia of the Negro* project.

Born in Caddo, Texas, and raised on a farm, Johnson completed undergraduate studies in sociology at Baylor University in 1921. He then earned his master's degree from the UNIVERSITY OF CHICAGO in 1922 and his Ph.D. in sociology from the University of North Carolina at Chapel Hill. He taught at Ohio Wesleyan University and at Baylor College for Women before joining the Institute for Research in Social Science established by HOWARD ODUM. He worked as a research assistant at the Institute and taught at Chapel Hill for 38 years. Johnson was highly respected for his work on the folk culture of African Americans in the south and taught the first anthropology courses offered at the university.

During the 1920s and 1930s, Johnson published studies on African Americans and Southern black folk culture including THE NEGRO AND HIS SONGS (1925) and Negro Workaday Songs (1926) with Howard Odum, Folk Culture on St. Helena Island (1929) and John Henry: Tracking Down a Negro Legend (1930). His writing on John Henry was selected for inclusion in EBONY AND TOPAZ: A COLLECTANEA (1927), edited by OPPORTUNITY editor and fellow sociologist CHARLES S. JOHNSON.

Guy Johnson continued to work on significant sociological projects and studies of race in the years after the Harlem Renaissance. His research analyses were instrumental to Gunnar Myrdal's An American Dilemma, a 1944 landmark study of American race relations.

Johnson, who was awarded the Anisfield Award for Research in Race Relations in 1937, continued to publish through the 1980s.

Bibliography

DuBois, W. E. B., and Guy B. Johnson. Encyclopedia of the Negro: Preparatory Volume with Reference Lists and Reports. New York: Phelps-Stokes Fund, 1945.

Johnson, Guy B., and Guion Griffis Johnson. Research in Service to Society: The First Fifty Years of the Institute for Research in Social Science at the University of North Carolina. Chapel Hill: University of North Carolina Press, 1980.

———, and Howard Odum. The Negro and His Songs; A Study of Typical Negro Songs in the South. 1925, reprint, New York: Negro Universities Press, 1968.

Johnson, Helene (1907–1995)

Born Helen Johnson in July 1907, this precocious BOSTON poet and short story writer was raised in Brookline, Massachusetts, and in the Martha's Vineyard island community of Oak Bluffs. She was the only child born to William and Ella Benson Johnson and was named after Helen Pease Benson, her maternal grandmother. Later in life, at the suggestion of her aunt Rachel Johnson West, she changed her name to Helene. She lived with her mother, who worked as a domestic for prominent Boston and Cambridge families, and with her extended maternal family including her aunts Rachel and Minnie. Johnson never met her father and knew little about him except that he might have been a Greek man from CHICAGO. Her maternal grandfather, Benjamin Benson, was a formerly enslaved man from Camden, South Carolina. He and Helen Pease Benson had three daughters, and when they migrated north, he and his wife relocated to Martha's Vineyard. Johnson's grandfather was a successful builder on the island but eventually returned to the South. Johnson's ties to the island off the coast of Massachusetts continued through the 20th century because her cousin DOROTHY WEST, also a successful Harlem Renaissance writer, lived there for many years in the decades of the Harlem Renaissance.

Johnson attended several Boston schools before going to college. She was a student at the Lafayette School and the Martin School and graduated from the prestigious Girls' Latin High School. Her high school years included piano lessons with Bessie Trotter, the daughter of WILLIAM MONROE TROTTER, the fiery, radical Boston Guardian newspaper editor. Her mother, Ella, took great pains to broaden Helene's horizons, and the two attended lectures and events featuring celebrated figures such as the Wright brothers. Johnson attended BOSTON UNIVERSITY before moving to NEW YORK CITY and enrolling at COLUMBIA UNIVERSITY. While in Boston, she also participated in the SATURDAY EVENING QUILL CLUB, an active literary group that saw many of its members go on to publish in mainstream journals and magazines.

In 1933, Johnson married William Warner Hubbell III, a motorman who encouraged his wife to continue writing. In September 1940 the couple had a daughter, Abigail Calachaly Hubbell, who would later graduate from Bard College, pursue a life in the theater, and become the owner of the Off-Center Theatre in New York City. A working mother, Johnson was employed at the Mount Vernon–based Consumers Union, where one of her coworkers was GWENDOLYN BENNETT. Johnson and Hubbell eventually separated, and Johnson relocated to Boston. She later returned to New York to live with her daughter and died in Manhattan in July 1995.

Johnson's writing career began while she was a college student. She placed first in a *Boston Chronicle* short story competition. While still in Boston, she began to submit work to the OPPORTUNITY literary contests when they first began in 1924. That year, she earned an eighth-place honorable mention for her poem "A Tree at Night." In 1926 her cousin Dorothy West tied for second place with ZORA NEALE HURSTON in the short story division. Johnson's work, a poem called "Fulfillment," won a first-place honorable mention. In 1927, the year in which she and West relocated to New York, Johnson won second prize in the Holstein literary and art competition sponsored by *Opportunity* for her poem "Summer Matures."

When she married, Johnson continued to write but withdrew from public life. Her daughter recalled that Johnson wrote "for herself because she enjoyed writing" and that Johnson "wrote a poem every single day, sometimes tossing out yesterday's piece, sometimes rewriting" (*NYT*, 11 July 1995, D19).

Despite her popularity and early visibility in the Harlem Renaissance circles, Johnson later slipped into obscurity. In addition to her decision to focus on her family, this may have been due in part to the fact that she did not publish a collected volume of her work. Scholars also propose that the universality of Johnson's work, rather than an overwhelming set of racially specific writing, may have led to her being overlooked. Critics have celebrated the diverse range of her writings and her compelling portraits of life, love, the natural world, and creativity. She engaged matters of race and developed poems that demonstrated her ability to craft insightful accounts of racial pride and social history.

New York City was Johnson's home for more than 50 years. During her time there, she developed a lively and caring friendship with Zora Neale Hurston, the Columbia anthropology student and dynamic prizewinning writer. Johnson, with her cousin Dorothy West, lived in the same West 66th Street apartment building as Hurston. In 1927, shortly after her first marriage, Hurston, who on various occasions addressed the writers as "Dear Little Sisters D & H" and "Dear Children," invited them to sublet her apartment. Hurston held the women in high regard and told them so. "I trust you and Helene more than anyone else in this world," she told West in a 1928 letter. "You are the fine gold in New York's show and shine," she declared. Johnson also enjoyed close friendships with Wallace Thurman and counted LANGSTON HUGHES and COUNTEE CULLEN among her friends. Zora Neale Hurston responded heartily to Johnson's work, even reading six of her poems at a 1929 lecture on poetry at the University of New Orleans.

Johnson published primarily in *Opportunity* and in other well-known magazines such as THE MESSENGER, CHALLENGE, and *Vanity Fair*. In 1926 she contributed "A Southern Road," a forthright, unflinching poem about lynching to the ambitious but short-lived journal *Fire!!* that her friend WALLACE THURMAN founded with Zora Neale Hurston, BRUCE NUGENT, Langston Hughes, and AARON DOUGLAS. Johnson's work was anthologized in major publications such as CAROLING DUSK (1927), THE BOOK OF AMERICAN NEGRO POETRY (1931), and *Golden Slippers: An Anthology of Negro Poetry for Young Readers* (1941). Her popularity continued after the Harlem Renaissance closed. Her works continue to be republished in collections of writings by African Americans and women. In 1967 her poem "Sonnet to a Harlem Negro" was part of "Poetry and Folk Music of American Negroes," a festive program sponsored by the New York Shakespeare Festival. Performers at the Delacorte Theatre in Central Park included Cicely Tyson and Roscoe Lee Brown on a night that was dedicated to an absorbing set of readings that, according to *New York Times* reporter Thomas Lask, reminded readers that "the patience of the oppressed is not endless" (Lask, 32).

Johnson was one of several Harlem Renaissance figures who inspired fictional characters. Novelist ARNA BONTEMPS celebrated Johnson's innocence and youth in his 1932 novel INFANTS OF THE SPRING. He modeled the character Hazel Jamison after Johnson.

Helene Johnson was eulogized as a "[p]oet of Harlem" when she died in July 1995.

Bibliography

Boyd, Valerie. *Wrapped in Rainbows: The Life of Zora Neale Hurston.* New York: Scribner, 2003.

Kaplan, Carla. *Zora Neale Hurston: A Life in Letters.* New York: Doubleday, 2002.

Lask, Thomas. "Poems and Songs by Negroes in Park." *New York Times,* 15 August 1967, 32.

Mitchell, Verner, ed. *This Waiting for Love: Helene Johnson, Poet of the Harlem Renaissance.* Amherst: University of Massachusetts Press, 2000.

Pace, Eric. "Helene Johnson, Poet of Harlem, 89, Dies." *New York Times,* 11 July 1995, D19.

Johnson, James Weldon (1871–1938)

A popular and effective race leader, scholar, lawyer, and writer whose professional and creative accomplishments underscore the impressive talent that shaped the Harlem Renaissance, James Weldon Johnson was the first of three children born to James and Helen Dillet Johnson. His parents, who were of Bahamian origin, met in NEW YORK CITY. His father was a studious, self-educated man who worked as a headwaiter at a posh hotel, and his mother was a schoolteacher and musician. Raised in Jacksonville, Florida, he responded to his parents' belief in the power of education and his mother's love for literature and art. When Johnson completed the program at the Stanton Central Grammar School, he had no opportunity to attend any high school because there was none for African Americans in the segregated city of Jacksonville. His intrepid parents were determined that his education continue and enrolled him in the rigorous preparatory program at ATLANTA UNIVERSITY. He completed his studies there and graduated in 1894. He returned to Jacksonville, established the *Daily American,* and became an enterprising principal at the Stanton School, the segregated grade school that he attended and at which his mother worked. He instituted new programs and established the state's first high school curriculum for African-American students. In 1897 he passed the Florida bar exam. He was the first African American in the state to be admitted to the bar and the first African-American attorney in Florida since Reconstruction.

Johnson relocated to New York City in 1901 and joined his brother J. Rosamond, a Boston Conservatory of Music graduate and emerging successful songwriter. The brothers collaborated on an impressive number of compositions, including the 1901 song "Lift Every Voice and Sing," the work that one day would be designated the Negro national anthem. The brothers also excelled as dramatists and saw several of their works open at New York City theaters such as the New Amsterdam Theatre and the Liberty Theatre. From 1903 through 1906 Johnson pursued graduate studies at COLUMBIA UNIVERSITY.

James Weldon Johnson, NAACP officer, activist, author, and diplomat *(Yale Collection of American Literature, Beinecke Rare Book and Manuscript Library)*

Johnson, a Republican, campaigned on behalf of Theodore Roosevelt. Thanks to endorsements by BOOKER T. WASHINGTON, Johnson was rewarded for his efforts with diplomatic appointments as consul to Venezuela and to Nicaragua. In 1904 he was one of several party members who established the Colored Republican Club in New York City.

He married Grace Nail in 1910. Nail was a native New Yorker and 15 years Johnson's junior. The couple, who had no children, enjoyed a happy and supportive relationship until the tragic car accident in Wicasset, Maine, that claimed Johnson's life in the summer of 1938.

Johnson began his noteworthy 14-year relationship with the NATIONAL ASSOCIATION FOR THE ADVANCEMENT OF COLORED PEOPLE (NAACP) in 1916. Appointed field secretary, he traveled throughout the country establishing branches and strengthening the organization's national and regional networks. One of his major accomplishments was in increasing the number of NAACP chapters in the South from a mere three outposts to 131 active branches. Johnson's international and political profile also resulted in opportunities to research U.S. military operations and tragic massacres in HAITI. Johnson also was active in the NAACP campaign to establish federal antilynching legislation. In 1920 he became the first African-American executive director of the organization. Johnson retired from the organization in 1930.

Before and during his tenure with the NAACP, Johnson published highly regarded anthologies and a novel. These included AUTOBIOGRAPHY OF AN EX-COLOURED MAN (1912, 1927), which he wrote while serving as consul in Venezuela, THE BOOK OF AMERICAN NEGRO POETRY (1922), and two volumes of African-American spirituals that appeared in 1925 and 1926. Johnson continued to hone his skills as a poet and to explore his deep love of black folk life and culture. In 1927 he published GOD'S TROMBONES: SEVEN NEGRO SERMONS IN VERSE, one of his most celebrated works. This book was inspired by the sermons that Johnson had heard during his Florida childhood and the preaching that he had encountered later in New York. His agnosticism did not prevent him from working to preserve a vital aspect of American religious life. Johnson, who believed that the "old-time Negro preacher is rapidly

passing," endeavored to "fix something of him" in his poetic tribute.

When he resigned from the NAACP in 1930, Johnson dedicated himself wholeheartedly to teaching and publishing. A JULIUS ROSENWALD FELLOWSHIP winner in 1930, he used his funds to complete *Black Manhattan*, the first African-American history of African Americans in New York. Johnson, who dedicated the work to John Nail, noted that his goal was "only to etch in the background of the Negro in latter-day New York, to give a cut-back in projecting a picture of Negro Harlem." He also published SAINT PETER RELATES AN INCIDENT OF THE RESURRECTION DAY (1930), a lengthy satiric poem that tackled race prejudice and illuminated its uselessness. He published ALONG THIS WAY, his autobiography, in 1933.

Johnson joined the faculty at FISK UNIVERSITY in 1932. He held an endowed professorship, the Adam K. Spence Chair of Creative Literature, and taught writing classes. Soon afterward, he had the opportunity to become a visiting professor at New York University and accepted.

His close friends included CARL VAN VECHTEN, the novelist and prominent society figure. Van Vechten, who wrote one of the early reviews of Johnson's BOOK OF AMERICAN NEGRO SPIRITUALS, cherished Johnson, whom he found to be "kind, gentle, helpful, generous, tolerant of unorthodox behaviour in others, patriarchal in offering good advice, understanding in not expecting it to be followed, moderate in his ways of living, and courageous in accepting the difficulties of life" (Kellner, 203). Johnson worked closely with W. E. B. DUBOIS, a fellow pioneering NAACP member and editor of *THE CRISIS*, the organization's official publication.

Johnson's many honors included honorary degrees from Atlanta University, Talladega College, and HOWARD UNIVERSITY. He was the 11th person to win a prestigious SPINGARN MEDAL, the highest award given by the NAACP. Johnson devoted his life to eradicating deadly misperceptions of African Americans and to sustaining resilient, inspiring, and multifaceted African-American literary, political, and cultural histories. He firmly believed that African-American life was affected more by the "national mental attitude toward the race than [by] actual conditions." He used his influence to generate opportunities that would allow African Americans to demonstrate their "intellectual parity . . . through the production of literature and art."

His untimely death in a car accident was marked by a moving funeral at the Harlem church of Rev. Frederick Cullen, the father of the poet COUNTEE CULLEN. More than 2,500 people attended. The pallbearers included W. C. HANDY, Carl Van Vechten, ARTHUR SPINGARN, WALTER WHITE, L. HOLLINGSWORTH WOOD, and HARRY BURLEIGH. In his eulogy, Gene Buck, the president of the American Society of Composers, Authors, and Publishers (ASCAP), remembered Johnson as a man of "nobility, culture, infinite taste and a burning desire for learning and tolerance that would not cease." Johnson was buried in the Greenwood Cemetery in Brooklyn.

Bibliography

James Weldon Johnson Papers, Beinecke Library, Yale University.

Johnson, James Weldon. *Along This Way: The Autobiography of James Weldon Johnson*, with an introduction by Sandra Kathryn Wilson. New York: Da Capo Press, 2000.

———. *The Autobiography of an Ex-Coloured Man*. Boston: Sherman, French, 1912; New York and London: Knopf, 1927.

———. *Black Manhattan*. New York: Knopf, 1930.

———. *God's Trombones; Seven Negro Sermons in Verse*. New York: Viking, 1927.

Kellner, Bruce. *Carl Van Vechten and the Irreverent Decades*. Norman: University of Oklahoma Press, 1968.

Levy, Eugene. *James Weldon Johnson: Black Leader, Black Voice*. Chicago: University of Chicago Press, 1973.

"Thousands Attend Johnson's Funeral." *New York Times*, 1 July 1938, 19.

Johnson, Mordecai Wyatt (1890–1976)

The first African-American president of HOWARD UNIVERSITY. He was born in Paris, Tennessee, to the Reverend Wyatt Johnson, a formerly enslaved mill engine operator, and Caroline Freeman Johnson, a domestic and housewife. Johnson began college studies at the Atlanta Baptist College, now MOREHOUSE COLLEGE. He studied with BEN-JAMIN BRAWLEY and so excelled as a student that the college hired him to teach immediately following his graduation. He earned a second bachelor's degree from the UNIVERSITY OF CHICAGO following two summers of study there in 1912 and 1913. He then earned a bachelor of divinity in 1916 from the Rochester Theological Seminary. In 1921 he began one year of studies at Harvard Divinity School and was awarded a master's degree in sacred theology in 1922.

The same year in which he completed his divinity studies at Rochester, Johnson married Anna Ethelyn Gardner. The couple, who went on to live in Charleston, West Virginia, had five children: Carolyn, Mordecai Jr., Archer, William, and Faith. In Charleston, Johnson established the first branch of the NATIONAL ASSOCIATION FOR THE ADVANCEMENT OF COLORED PEOPLE.

Johnson was only 33 years old when Howard University awarded him an honorary doctor of divinity degree. Three years later, in 1926, he was offered the prestigious post of president of the historic institution. He served for 34 years. Despite some faculty resistance to his administrative style and lack of advanced academic credentials, Johnson transformed the institution into an intellectual powerhouse. During his tenure, the faculty not only included Rhodes scholars such as ALAIN LOCKE but also Nobel Prize winners and internationally renowned scientists, historians, economists, and writers. The intellectual elite at Howard included professors Ralph Bunche, T. MONTGOMERY GREGORY, RAYFORD LOGAN, Charles Drew, and Charles Wesley. ZORA NEALE HURSTON, one of several successful graduates of Howard, described Johnson as a man with "great respect for established authority" and "tremendous prestige with both white and black in high places."

Johnson received a SPINGARN MEDAL in 1929 as a result of his successful efforts to revitalize Howard University and to secure its future as a premier institution of higher learning. He retired from Howard in 1960.

Bibliography

Logan, Rayford. *Howard University: The First Hundred Years, 1867–1967*. New York: New York University Press, 1969.

McKinney, Richard I. *Mordecai, The Man and His Message: The Story of Mordecai Wyatt Johnson.* Washington, D.C.: Howard University Press, 1998.

Mordecai Johnson Papers, Moorland-Spingarn Research Center, Howard University.

Johnson, S. Miller (1900–unknown)

A poet and short story writer whose works appeared in OPPORTUNITY and in THE MESSENGER. Born in Calhoun County, Arkansas, Johnson graduated from Hampton Institute in Hampton, Virginia.

Johnson published realistic, even racy poetry that celebrated African-American femininity and beauty. His "Variations on a Black Theme" was an extended meditation on the glorious nakedness of a woman named Nellie. The sweetheart of the woman with "comely hips," "swift black legs," "dimpled knees," and "bright red lips / Magnetic, honeydewed" transfixes her admirer. He is "wrapt in celestial bliss, wild-eyed" by the sight of her "dancing there naked on silver sand by / the Silver River for her lover, the Sun." Johnson's tantalizing account of voyeurism and unself-conscious pride appeared in the March 1927 issue of *Opportunity*.

Johnson's interest in tense, passionate, and unfulfilled relationships extended to his fiction. "THE GOLDEN PENKNIFE," a short story about two European immigrant families, revolved around dangerous and irrepressible female sexuality and frustrated male desire.

Jolson, Al (1886–1950)

The famous singer who became synonymous with blackface minstrelsy. Born Asa Yoelson in a Russian village that later became part of Lithuania, he arrived in America with his family in 1890.

In 1925 Jolson responded to GARLAND ANDERSON, a San Francisco hotel bellhop who became the first African-American playwright to see his work performed on BROADWAY. Anderson sent Jolson a copy of APPEARANCE, his play about a young bellboy who is falsely accused of rape. Jolson liked the story and financed Anderson's travel to the East Coast.

Jolson was a well-known performer who appeared in some of the first talking films. During the Harlem Renaissance, he appeared in *The Jazz Singer* (1927) and numerous stage shows.

Bibliography

Alexander, Michael. *Jazz Age Jews.* Princeton, N.J.: Princeton University Press, 2001.

Goldman, Herbert G. *Jolson: The Legend Comes to Life.* New York: Oxford University Press, 1988.

Jonah's Gourd Vine Zora Neale Hurston (1934)

The first novel by ZORA NEALE HURSTON. Inspired by her own family, it was a compelling account of life in EATONVILLE, Florida, the African-American town in which Hurston grew up. The novel was published by Lippincott, which gave the financially strapped Hurston, who endured eviction as she completed the novel, a $200 advance on the work. It included an introduction by FANNIE HURST, a celebrated writer and one of Hurston's supporters. Hurston completed this novel in less than four months. Her penchant for writing quickly emerged again in 1937 when she completed her groundbreaking novel THEIR EYES WERE WATCHING GOD in just seven weeks. The novel, which appeared in May 1934, was well-received and hailed by the NEW YORK TIMES as one of the most vibrant and authentic novels about African-American life to date.

The novel took its title and overall message from the Book of Jonah. Hurston focused on Chapter Four, verses 6–10. This section of the chapter refers to a great gourd that provides shade to the beleaguered prophet Jonah. Despite Jonah's pleasure, God then sends a worm to destroy the gourd and cause it to wither. Hurston used the biblical verses as a powerful allegory for the life-threatening actions of the protagonist John Buddy Pearson.

The novel follows the double life of John Pearson, an illegitimate Alabama laborer born to an enslaved woman named Amy, who works on the plantation of Alf Pearson, a white man. John, who loves women, is attracted to Lucy Potts, a schoolmate who marries him despite her family's objections to his poverty. The couple leave Alabama shortly after the birth of their third child and John's violent attack on Lucy's brother. The Pearsons relocate to Florida and begin life anew. John becomes a

Baptist pastor on Sundays and a troubled man who sins greatly during the week. The indiscretions of the minister who also writes poetry include adultery. He refuses to atone for his misdeeds even when confronted by his parishioners. His wife Lucy dies, and he promptly marries Hattie, his mistress. He uses powerful preaching to sustain himself in the face of negative campaigns against him but eventually steps down as minister. It is in his third marriage that he begins to gain some sense of accountability, but he is killed before he achieves true enlightenment. Hurston wrote to JAMES WELDON JOHNSON about what she had tried to accomplish in the novel. She regarded Johnson as a kindred spirit, writing "[we] seem to be the only ones even among Negroes who recognize the barbaric poetry in . . . sermons" by African-American preachers. Hurston offered the following explanation of her novel in an April 1934 letter to Johnson: "I have tried to present a Negro, preacher who is neither funny nor an imitation Puritan ram-rod in pants. Just the human being and poet that he must be to succeed in a Negro pulpit. I do not speak of those among us who have been tampered with and consequently have gone Presbyterian or Episcopal . . . I see a preacher as a man outside of the pulpit and so far as I am concerned he should be free to follow his bent as other men. He becomes the voice of the spirit when he ascends the rostrum" (Kaplan, 298). Her outspoken defense of *Jonah's Gourd Vine* continued in the weeks following its publication. She wrote forthright letters to the reviewers of her work, including Lewis Gannett of the *New York Herald-Tribune*. She assured Lewis, whom she thanked for his "understanding kindness," that "The preacher must satisfy [the] beauty-hunger" of the masses whom he served. "He *must* be a poet and an actor and possess a body and a voice. It is good if at the same time he is of high moral character" (Kaplan, 304).

Hurston was frustrated by the reviews, which, despite being highly complimentary, tended to overlook her overarching agenda. She protested the way in which reviewers cast doubt on the real poetry of African-American culture and the rich creative tradition in African-American religion. As Hurston biographer Robert Hemenway notes, Hurston's original dedication was telling. She offered the book to "the first and only Negro poets in America—the preachers, who bring barbaric splendor of word and song into the very camp of the mockers" (Hemenway, 195).

The novel is the first in a powerful series of Hurston's insightful and sophisticated tributes to African-American folk culture and creativity.

Bibliography
Hemenway, Robert. *Zora Neale Hurston: A Literary Biography.* Urbana: University of Illinois, 1977.

Kaplan, Carla. *Zora Neale Hurston: A Life in Letters.* New York: Doubleday, 2002.

Jones, Eugene Kinckle (1885–1954)
The cofounder of the NATIONAL URBAN LEAGUE and one of the African-American intellectual elite who comprised the "Black Cabinet," a group formed to advise President Roosevelt on race-related matters.

He was born to Joseph Endom and Rosa Daniel Kinckle Jones in Richmond, Virginia. His mother was a graduate of HOWARD UNIVERSITY and the New England Conservatory of Music. His father became one of the first African Americans in Virginia to earn a college degree when he graduated from Colgate (then Madison) University in Hamilton, New York, in 1876. Jones's parents were respected educators; his father was on the faculty at Richmond Theological Seminary, and his mother enjoyed a 40-year career at Hartshorn Memorial College.

Jones followed in the impressive intellectual example of his parents. He graduated from Virginia Union University with a B.A. in sociology and went on to study civil engineering at Cornell University. He transferred into the Department of Sociology when he realized the limited opportunities available to African-American engineers. At Cornell, he was the first man inducted into Alpha Phi Alpha and the fraternity's first president. He graduated in 1908 and married Blanche Ruby Watson one year later. He and his wife had two children, Eugene Jr., an attorney, and Adele, a social worker.

In 1911 he began his lifelong association with the National Urban League. He began working with George Haynes for the Committee on Urban Conditions among Negroes, the organization that was renamed the National Urban League in 1920. He became its first executive secretary and was actively supportive of his colleague and fellow sociologist CHARLES S. JOHNSON, who was the editor of OP-PORTUNITY, the organization's official publication.

Bibliography

Jones, Eugene Kinckle. *The First Forty Years of Service to the American People*. National Urban League 40th Anniversary Year Book, 1950. New York: National Urban League, 1951.

Parris, Guichard, and Lester Brooks. *Blacks in the City: A History of the National Urban League*. Boston: Little, Brown, 1971.

Weiss, Nancy J. *The National Urban League 1910–1940*. New York: Oxford University Press, 1974.

Jones, George B. (unknown)

An editor of the INTER-STATE TATTLER, the New York City newspaper known for its coverage of African-American social events. Jones became editor after BENNIE BUTLER and GERALDYN DIS-MOND, also editors, focused on theater and social events. The paper, which began publication in 1925, ceased in 1932.

Jones, Henry Joshua (1876–1953)

A South Carolina newspaper editor, poet, and writer who published primarily during the 1920s. Born in Orangeburg, South Carolina, Jones pursued a career in journalism after graduating from BROWN UNIVERSITY. He began at the *Providence News*. He relocated to BOSTON, where he worked at several newspapers, including the *Boston Advertiser*, where he became city editor. After working for four years as secretary to Boston mayor James Curley, Jones was appointed to the position of editor of the *City Record*.

Jones made his literary debut with HEART OF THE WORLD AND OTHER POEMS in 1919. Two years later, he published *Poems of the Four Seas* (1921). His poem "To a Skull," a vaguely morbid poem in which a "[g]hastly, ghoulish, grinning" skull is interrogated, was included in THE BOOK OF AMERICAN NEGRO POETRY, the 1922 anthology edited by JAMES WEL-DON JOHNSON. In 1924 Jones branched out into fiction and published BY SANCTION OF LAW, a novel in which he explored the cultural and social value of interracial marriage.

Journal of Negro History

The first American scholarly journal to focus explicitly on African-American history. The ASSOCI-ATION FOR THE STUDY OF NEGRO LIFE AND HISTORY established it in 1916. The HARVARD UNIVERSITY–educated scholar and SPINGARN MEDAL winner CARTER G. WOODSON was instrumental in the journal's production. The first editor of the publication, Woodson also invested $400 of his own money to finance the production of the first issue. The journal later was subsidized by funds from Harlem Renaissance–era philanthropists such as Julius Rosenwald.

In 2001, the journal was renamed the *Journal of African American History*.

Bibliography

Goggin, Jacqueline. *Carter G. Woodson: A Life in Black History*. Baton Rouge: Louisiana State University Press, 1993.

Greene, Lorenzo Johnston. *Working with Carter G. Woodson, the Father of Black History: A Diary, 1928–1930*. Baton Rouge: Louisiana State University Press, 1989.

Juliette Derricotte   Marion Vera Cuthbert (1933)

A biography of Juliette Derricotte, a graduate of Talladega College, and the dean of women at FISK UNIVERSITY. Written by MARION VERA CUTH-BERT, an activist and writer who, like Derricotte, was a member of the YOUNG WOMEN'S CHRIS-TIAN ASSOCIATION (YWCA), the book is a memorial biography to honor Derricotte, who died in 1931 when racist Atlanta hospitals refused to treat the life-threatening injuries that she sustained in a car crash.

Born in Athens, Georgia, in 1897, Derricotte was an exceptional scholar and highly respected figure in education. The first woman appointed to the Board of Trustees at Talladega College, she also served as national student secretary for the YWCA before joining the administration at Fisk University.

Bibliography

Cuthbert, Marion Vera. *Juliette Derricotte*. New York: Pilgrim Press, 1933.

Julius Rosenwald Fellowship

A fellowship established by Julius Rosenwald, the president of Sears, Roebuck and Company. The Rosenwald Fund, founded in CHICAGO in 1913, was a major philanthropic resource for African Americans. Rosenwald used the foundation to support African-American advances in science, education, politics, the arts, and literature. His generous investment in historically black colleges and universities also enabled the creation of the United Negro College Fund. The Fund awarded a grant to the NATIONAL ASSOCIATION FOR THE ADVANCEMENT OF COLORED PEOPLE during the GREAT DEPRESSION when the civil rights organization, like so many others, was staving off financial disaster. During the Harlem Renaissance, Edwin Embree served as the Rosenwald Fund's president.

The Rosenwald fellowship, offered first in 1929, recognized excellence and high potential of African-American scholars, artists, scientists, politicians, and writers. The award provided financial assistance that often allowed individuals to pursue academic studies, to immerse themselves in research and writing, and to make significant advances in their careers. Several winners, such as artist JACOB LAWRENCE, had major professional accomplishments immediately following their tenure as Rosenwald Fellows.

Julius Rosenwald Fellows included writers ARNA BONTEMPS, SHIRLEY GRAHAM DUBOIS, ZORA NEALE HURSTON, LANGSTON HUGHES, and JAMES WELDON JOHNSON. Winning artists included AUGUSTA SAVAGE, Jacob Lawrence, Eldzier Cortor, and RICHMOND BARTHÉ. The fellowship continued to be awarded after the Harlem Renaissance period ended. Later winners included James Baldwin, Jacob Lawrence, and Gordon Parks.

Winners of this fellowship often won or had earned other prestigious prizes such as the GUGGENHEIM FELLOWSHIP or HARMON AWARD.

K

Kansas State College

The poet CLAUDE McKAY transferred from TUSKEGEE INSTITUTE to Kansas State College in order to pursue his study of literature and poetry. He enrolled in the fall of 1912 and attended through the spring of 1914. Despite his efforts to immerse himself in literature, McKay wrote no poetry during his time in Manhattan, Kansas. It was in this Kansas college town that McKay's interest in radical American politics began to deepen. It also was during his time at Kansas State that McKay gained exposure to the powerful work of W. E. B. DuBois, specifically *SOULS OF BLACK FOLK* (1903).

Bibliography

Cooper, Wayne. *Claude McKay: Rebel Sojourner in the Harlem Renaissance.* New York: Schocken Books, 1987.

Karamu House

The CLEVELAND, OHIO, settlement house and neighborhood resource center established in 1915 by ROWENA JELLIFFE and her husband RUSSELL JELLIFFE. Originally called the Neighborhood Association Settlement, the institution was renamed the Karamu House in 1940. The new name of the organization was taken from the Swahili language. The word *Karamu*, which means "place of joyful gathering" and "center of the community," underscored the inspiring cultural activities and central role that the organization aspired to play in Cleveland.

The Jelliffes and the Karamu House had a connection to the Harlem Renaissance. LANGSTON HUGHES attended events at the house during his Cleveland childhood years and later returned to teach at the center. The Jelliffes, in collaboration with the Gilpin Players, the troupe established at the Karamu House, also produced several Hughes plays at the center during the Harlem Renaissance.

Bibliography

Berry, Faith, ed. *Langston Hughes: Before and Beyond Harlem.* Westport, Conn.: Lawrence Hill & Company, 1983.

France, Monroe. *The Karamu House and Its Impact on Social Change and the Community.* Available online. URL: http://www.coe.ohio-state.edu/EDPL/Gordon/courses/863/france/france.html

Karamu House Web site. Available online. URL: http://www.karamu.com.

Rampersad, Arnold. *The Life of Langston Hughes: I, Too, Sing America.* Vol. 1: *1902–1941.* New York: Oxford University Press, 1986.

———. *The Life of Langston Hughes: I Dream a World.* Vol. 2: *1941–1967.* New York: Oxford University Press, 1988.

Karamu Players

The troupe that was based in the KARAMU HOUSE, the oldest African-American theater company in the United States. The group was established in the Neighborhood Association Settlement, or as it came to be called in 1940, the Karamu House. During the tenure of founders ROWENA JELLIFFE and RUSSELL JELLIFFE, the group was founded first as the Dumas Drama Club. It was renamed the Gilpin

Players in 1923 in honor of the actor Charles Gilpin. Gilpin, whose visit to the troupe prompted the name change, received critical acclaim for his lead performance in the first production of EUGENE O'NEILL's *THE EMPEROR JONES* at the Province-town Playhouse in New York City. In 1940, after the Neighborhood Association organization was renamed, the troupe changed its name also.

The troupe became one of the most visible American theater organizations during the Harlem Renaissance. Since its inception, the troupe has performed works by the Harlem Renaissance literary giants LANGSTON HUGHES and ZORA NEALE HURSTON and, in later years, the acclaimed Lorraine Hansberry.

The Karamu Players are still in existence today and continue to advance the legacy of the organization's founders and earliest participants.

Bibliography

Berry, Faith, ed. *Langston Hughes: Before and Beyond Harlem.* Westport, Conn.: Lawrence Hill & Company, 1983.

Karamu House Web site. Available online. URL: http://www.karamu.com.

Krasner, David. *A Beautiful Pageant: African American Theatre, Drama, and Performance in the Harlem Renaissance, 1910–1927.* New York: Palgrave Macmillan, 2002.

Rampersad, Arnold. *The Life of Langston Hughes: I, Too, Sing America.* Vol. 1: *1902–1941.* New York: Oxford University Press, 1986.

———. *The Life of Langston Hughes: I Dream a World.* Vol. 2: *1941–1967.* New York: Oxford University Press, 1988.

Kelley, William Melvin, Sr. (1894–unknown)
A NATIONAL URBAN LEAGUE officer in CHICAGO, Illinois, who became an accomplished journalist and editor, Kelley was born in Chattanooga, Tennessee, in 1894 to Thomas and Sina Starks Kelley. In 1912 he completed high school at the Austin High School in Knoxville. He went on to WILBERFORCE UNIVERSITY but left after two semesters.

In 1913, the same year in which he left college, Kelley began his career in journalism and his longtime residency in NEW YORK CITY. In 1913 he began a two-year stint as circulation manager for the *New York News*. In 1915 he began working for the AMSTERDAM NEWS and married Gladys Caution. In 1916 the couple, who later divorced, had one child, a daughter named Sina Estelle. Kelley remarried in 1932; his wife was Narcissa Garcia.

After relocating to Chicago in 1917 Kelley worked as a member of the administrative staff of *Pearson's Magazine* and worked as the business manager for *Champion Magazine*. It was during this time that he was elected industrial secretary for the Chicago branch of the Urban League. In 1922 Kelley became editor of the New York–based *Amsterdam News* and held the post for many years.

Kellogg, Paul Underwood (1879–1958)
The longtime editor of *SURVEY GRAPHIC*, an important journal that was founded in 1923 and that focused on progressive politics, social work, and reform. Kellogg's major contribution to the Harlem Renaissance occurred when he published a special issue devoted to African-American matters. The "Harlem" issue showcased the innovative and scholarly work by and about African Americans.

Kellogg was born in Kalamazoo, Michigan, to Frank and Mary Foster Underwood Kellogg. He and his brother Arthur were raised primarily by their mother, Mary. Their father left the family when the family's lumber business failed. After working as a reporter and editor for the *Kalamazoo Daily Telegraph*, Kellogg moved to NEW YORK CITY in 1901. There he enrolled at COLUMBIA UNIVERSITY, where he would take classes for several years. He began working closely with the New York Charity Organization Society. In 1907 he was the leading researcher on the first comprehensive study of an urban community. His findings on Pittsburgh, Pennsylvania, secured his reputation as a rigorous sociological and cultural analyst.

Kellogg and his wife, Marion Pearce Sherwood, married in 1909. Before their divorce in 1934, they had two children. He married Helen Hall in 1935. When he died in 1958, Kellogg was living in New York City at the Henry Street Settlement, where his second wife served as director.

In 1909 Kellogg became editor of *Survey Magazine*, the journal produced by the New York

Charity Organization Society. He became editor in chief in 1912, and his brother Arthur joined the staff as managing editor. The magazine thrived for 40 years and was regarded as one of the nation's most influential social work and social reform publications.

Kellogg founded *Survey Graphic* in 1923. This monthly journal focused on pressing social, labor, and race issues. It was especially powerful for its attention to volatile events and issues such as police brutality. In the winter of 1924 Kellogg invited HOWARD UNIVERSITY professor ALAIN LOCKE to edit a special *Survey Graphic* issue that would focus on the Harlem Renaissance. The "Harlem" issue appeared in March 1925. Contributors included Locke, RUDOLPH FISHER, ANGELINA GRIMKÉ, JAMES WELDON JOHNSON, MELVILLE HERSKOVITS, KELLY MILLER, ARTHUR SCHOMBURG, and ANNE SPENCER. Locke later produced *THE NEW NEGRO,* an anthology that was an expanded version of the journal.

Bibliography

Chambers, Clarke A. *Paul U. Kellogg and the Survey.* Minneapolis: University of Minnesota Press, 1971.
Paul U. Kellogg Papers, University of Minnesota.

Kerlin, Robert T. (fl. 1923)

Editor of *NEGRO POETS AND THEIR POEMS,* an anthology published in 1923 by the Associated Publishers of WASHINGTON, D.C. One of the most comprehensive and inclusive anthologies of its day, the volume included works by CARRIE CLIFFORD, ALICE DUNBAR-NELSON, and ANNE SPENCER.

Kerlin also was one of several highly respected individuals invited to address the elite group of ministers who gathered weekly at the Baptist Education Center in NEW YORK CITY.

Knopf, Alfred Abraham (1892–1984)

The founder of one of America's most influential publishing houses, Alfred A. Knopf established an impressive and accomplished press that shaped literary trends and scholarship in and beyond the United States.

He was born in NEW YORK CITY to Samuel and Ida Japhe Knopf. His father remarried following Ida's death in 1896 and had two children with his second wife. Knopf was educated at the DE-WITT CLINTON HIGH SCHOOL in New York City and at the Mackenzie School in Dobbs Ferry. He attended COLUMBIA UNIVERSITY, where he studied with faculty who developed productive ties to the Harlem Renaissance. His professors included JOEL SPINGARN, after whom the NATIONAL ASSOCIATION FOR THE ADVANCEMENT OF COLORED PEOPLE named their most distinguished prize, and CARL VAN DOREN, also a Columbia alumnus, literary critic, and the literary editor of *THE NATION* from 1919 through 1922.

Knopf established ALFRED A. KNOPF, INC. in 1915. After two years as a clerk at Doubleday, Page and Company and a one-year appointment with the publisher Mitchell Kennerly, he embarked on an ambitious business venture with Blanche Wolf, whom he married in April 1916. As scholars have noted, the Knopfs became the first husband-and-wife team to succeed in book publishing. Their only child, Alfred A. Knopf, Jr., was born in 1918. He established Atheneum Publishers, his own firm, in 1959. Blanche Knopf passed away in 1966. One year later, Knopf married Helen Hedrick.

In 1923 Knopf collaborated with H. L. MENCKEN, a close friend, and George Jean Nathan and founded *AMERICAN MERCURY,* a well-received monthly journal of American social and political events. He served as publisher for 11 years, until the journal succumbed to financial difficulties in 1934 brought on by the GREAT DEPRESSION.

During Knopf's tenure, the publishing house produced more than 5,000 titles and saw an impressive number of its authors go on to win prestigious international and national prizes. By 1984, the year in which Knopf died, 16 Knopf authors had won Nobel Prizes, and 27 had been awarded PULITZER PRIZES. NELLA LARSEN, whose two novels were published with Knopf, was the first African-American woman to win a GUGGENHEIM FELLOWSHIP. Other Harlem Renaissance–era authors recruited by Knopf included RUDOLPH FISHER, LANGSTON HUGHES, and CARL VAN VECHTEN. Knopf Publishers became a subsidiary of Random House in 1960. Since then, the company has become part of the Bertelsmann media empire.

Alfred Knopf died in 1984 and was buried in Ferncliff Cemetery in Westchester County, New York.

Bibliography

Alfred A. Knopf, Sr., Papers, Harry Ransom Humanities Research Center, University of Texas at Austin.

Knopf, Alfred A. *Portrait of a Publisher, 1915–1965.* Vol. 1: *Reminiscences and Reflections.* New York: The Typophiles, 1965.

———. *Portrait of a Publisher, 1915–1965.* Vol. 2: *Alfred A. Knopf and the Borzoi Imprint: Recollections and Appreciations.* New York: Typophiles, 1965.

Madison, Charles Allan. *Jewish Publishing in America: The Impact of Jewish Writing on American Culture.* New York: Sanhedrin Press, 1976.

Krigwa Little Theatre Movement

W. E. B. DUBOIS, editor of THE CRISIS, established the Krigwa Little Theatre Movement in NEW YORK CITY in 1926. The group's name was an acronym for the "CRISIS GUILD OF WRITERS AND ARTISTS," a society established under the rubric of THE CRISIS, the official publication of the NATIONAL ASSOCIATION FOR THE ADVANCEMENT OF COLORED PEOPLE and the monthly magazine where DuBois served as editor. The Little Theatre Movement grew out of the successful pioneering productions of the Krigwa Players, a troupe established in 1924.

The Krigwa Little Theatre Movement, however, is most significant for its successful endorsement of African-American community theater and the preservation of folk theater traditions. It was one of nearly 500 little theater groups established between 1910 and 1930.

The movement was spurred on by DuBois's insistent call for theater by, about, and for African Americans. It was part of the significant dramatic tradition sustained during the Harlem Renaissance years. The counterparts of the Krigwa Little Theatre Movement included the HOWARD UNIVERSITY PLAYERS, established by T. MONTGOMERY GREGORY in 1919, the Cleveland, Ohio–based Charles Gilpin Players who were affiliated with the KARAMU HOUSE, and the HARLEM SUITCASE THEATRE established by Langston Hughes (1938).

The movement was realized through the creation of Krigwa theatres and troupes throughout the country. DuBois envisioned that these satellite troupes would provide much needed meaningful collective opportunities for communities of color. Companies performed in Cleveland, Ohio, in conjunction with KARAMU HOUSE and its founders RUSSELL JELLIFFE and ROWENA JELLIFFE, as well as at schools such as the celebrated DUNBAR HIGH SCHOOL in WASHINGTON, D.C.

The accomplished playwright WILLIS RICHARDSON, the first African American to see his work performed on BROADWAY, was one of those who contributed to DuBois's vision. The Richardson family hosted several meetings of the Krigwa Players in their home, and Mary Ellen Jones Richardson, the playwright's wife, served as secretary of the group for several years.

The history of the Krigwa Little Theatre Movement reflects the deliberate effort to secure forums that both enhanced and showcased African-American talent, history, and culture.

Bibliography

Gray, Christine Rauchfuss. *Willis Richardson, Forgotten Pioneer of African-American Drama.* Westport, Conn.: Greenwood Press, 1999.

Krasner, David. *A Beautiful Pageant: African American Theatre, Drama, and Performance in the Harlem Renaissance, 1910–1927.* New York: Palgrave Macmillan, 2002.

Krigwa Players

An innovative theater troupe established by W. E. B. DUBOIS and REGINA ANDREWS. The Krigwa Players were centrally located in Harlem. Based in the 135TH Street branch of the NEW YORK PUBLIC LIBRARY, their performances were accessible to residents and the aspiring writers and artists who frequented the library. The troupe performed groundbreaking pieces by contemporary African-American playwrights, and they enjoyed enthusiastic receptions in a number of American cities.

The repertoire of the Krigwa Players reflected the rich, politically conscious, and visionary tradition of African-American playwrights. The troupe's inaugural production featured EULALIE SPENCE's FOOL'S ERRAND and WILLIS RICHARDSON's COMPROMISE. Artist AARON DOUGLAS provided the set designs. The troupe also delivered a powerful 1926 production of GEORGIA DOUGLAS JOHNSON's antilynching play BLUE BLOOD (1927).

In 1931 they revisited the theme CLIMBING JACOB'S LADDER (1931), a riveting antilynching drama by Regina Andrews. The troupe later produced Andrews's historical drama *Underground* (1932), based on the Underground Railroad.

The Krigwa Players enjoyed an especially successful relationship with Willis Richardson, the talented dramatist and the first African American to see his work performed on Broadway. Author of the Broadway hit THE CHIP WOMAN'S FORTUNE, Richardson supported the efforts of the Krigwa Players and hosted rehearsals in his WASHINGTON, D.C., home. His wife, Mary Ellen Jones Richardson, was the secretary for the Washington, D.C.–based Krigwa Theatre troupe from 1926 through 1935. In addition to their debut performances of Richardson's play *Compromise,* they performed THE BROKEN BANJO in May 1926, THE HOUSE OF SHAM in February 1927, MORTGAGED and FLIGHT OF THE NATIVES in May 1927, and the *Nude Siren* and *The Chasm* in December 1928.

The Krigwa Players often staged their productions in accessible venues. In Washington, D.C., these included the renowned DUNBAR HIGH SCHOOL, the Phillis Wheatley YWCA, and the Dunbar Community Center.

The troupe ceased to be known as the Krigwa Players in 1928. It continued its vital contributions to American drama as the NEGRO EXPERIMENTAL THEATRE and as the HARLEM EXPERIMENTAL THEATRE.

Bibliography

Gray, Christine Rauchfuss. *Willis Richardson, Forgotten Pioneer of African-American Drama.* Westport, Conn.: Greenwood Press, 1999.

Krasner, David. *A Beautiful Pageant: African American Theatre, Drama, and Performance in the Harlem Renaissance, 1910–1927.* New York: Palgrave Macmillan, 2002.

Ku Klux Klan

An organization dedicated to white supremacy that was organized first in May 1866. Its founder was Nathan Bedford Forrest, a former Confederate army general. Members, known as Klansmen, covered their faces and bodies with white sheets, participated in ritual cross-burnings, promoted white supremacist ideology, and brutalized people of color throughout America. The organization, also known by its initials, KKK, supported racial violence such as LYNCHINGS and bombings and terrorized African Americans.

The Ku Klux Klan was extremely visible in the years after the Civil War. Their protest of African-American suffrage, as well as economic and intellectual advancement, prompted deadly attacks against and lynchings of African-American individuals, families, communities, and their supporters. The Ku Klux Klan also advocated the oppression of and violence toward Jews, Native Americans, Asians, and other peoples of color.

The organization was revitalized in 1915, on the eve of the Harlem Renaissance. Members were inspired by the controversial novel and film *Birth of a Nation* by D. W. Griffith. Following World War I, the group also targeted socialists and communists, as well as Roman Catholics. National membership reached nearly 4 million in 1925. Klansmen were elected to public office throughout the states and often used their power to uphold the racist and exclusionary principles of the organization.

The NATIONAL ASSOCIATION FOR THE ADVANCEMENT OF COLORED PEOPLE (NAACP) marshaled the most direct and effective institutional challenge to the Ku Klux Klan. In 1920 the organization held its annual meeting in Atlanta, Georgia, a hotbed of Klan activity. The NAACP was able to provide invaluable and damning firsthand coverage of Klan activities. One of its most intrepid reporters was WALTER WHITE, who worked as an undercover reporter for THE CRISIS, the official NAACP publication. Between 1918 and 1930 White investigated some 41 lynchings and eight race riots. His light skin and blue eyes suggested whiteness, and he used the misperception to gather evidence of horrific lynchings and racial violence for the NAACP.

The NAACP blasted MARCUS GARVEY for consorting with the Klan and used the details of the UNIVERSAL NEGRO IMPROVEMENT ASSOCIATION leader's appearance at a Klan rally to fuel Garvey's political demise. The NAACP also actively championed Robert Russa Moton's resistance to Klan aggression in Tuskegee, Alabama.

The organization still exists today. It has been linked to historic acts of violence such as the Civil

Rights–era church bombing in Atlanta that killed four young girls. Many Americans, including the Southern Poverty Law Center, protest the racism, divisive ideas, and violence that the group continues to sanction.

Bibliography

Chalmers, David Mark. *Hooded Americanism: The First Century of the Ku Klux Klan, 1865–1965.* Garden City, N.Y.: Doubleday, 1965.

Katz, William Loren. *The Invisible Empire: The Ku Klux Klan Impact on History.* Washington, D.C.: Open Hand Pub., 1986.

Turner, John. *The Ku Klux Klan: A History of Racism and Violence.* Montgomery, Ala.: Southern Poverty Law Center, 1981.

L

Lafayette Players Stock Company

A theater group founded in NEW YORK CITY in 1914 and the first stock theater company established in HARLEM. Anita Bush, owner of the LAFAYETTE THEATRE, hired the acclaimed actor Charles Gilpin to establish a viable theater company on-site. Soon after his arrival, Gilpin initiated efforts to organize the stock company. The group included a number of actors like Inez Clough, Charles Gilpin, and Evelyn Preer, who performed in historic and popular productions on and off BROADWAY.

During its 18-year existence, the troupe performed some 250 productions. These included a variety of works ranging from melodramas to classic plays such as *Faust, Othello,* and *The Count of Monte Cristo.* The Lafayette Players Stock Company disbanded in 1932.

Bibliography

Krasner, David. *A Beautiful Pageant: African American Theatre, Drama, and Performance in the Harlem 1910–1927.* New York: Palgrave Macmillan, 2002.

Lafayette Theatre

Located at 132nd Street and Seventh Avenue, a splendid and spacious venue that may have been the first theater in NEW YORK CITY to desegregate its seating. It was the theater in which Charles Gilpin established the first stock company in HARLEM. The Lafayette also was the venue in which WILLIS RICHARDSON's *THE CHIP WOMEN'S FORTUNE* was first produced, before it went on to become the first play by an African American to be staged on BROADWAY.

The Lafayette, which could seat 2,000, evolved during the Harlem Renaissance years. Before it closed in 1934, it had served as a theater, vaudeville house, movie theater, and church.

La Guardia, Fiorello (1882–1947)

The popular Republican mayor of NEW YORK CITY whose tenure began in 1933, during the last decade of the Harlem Renaissance. He was reelected to two more terms, in 1937 and again in 1941.

Born in Manhattan to Achille and Irene Coen La Guardia, he went on to attend New York University Law School. La Guardia's career in politics began when he was elected to Congress in 1917. During World War I he served in the army as a lieutenant with the aviation division, and while stationed in Italy he helped to train American pilots. La Guardia, who became New York City's 99th mayor, was known for his intolerance of corruption.

La Guardia was one of the prominent members appointed to the JAMES WELDON JOHNSON Memorial Committee. He served as honorary chairman of the group that was striving to erect a statue in honor of Johnson, who died tragically in 1938. Other members included chairman Theodore Roosevelt and secretary WALTER WHITE. The New York City mayor also worked closely with White on political issues, including representing federal interests during intense debates about discrimination in the workplace and in the military.

After battling pancreatic cancer, La Guardia died in 1947. Following a funeral at the Episcopal Cathedral of St. John the Divine, he was buried in New York City's Woodlawn Cemetery.

Bibliography

Elliott, Lawrence. *Little Flower: The Life and Times of Fiorello La Guardia.* New York: Morrow, 1983.

Fiorello La Guardia Papers, New York City Municipal Archives and Records Center.

Janken, Kenneth Robert. *White: The Biography of Walter White, Mr. NAACP.* New York: The New Press, 2003.

Kessner, Thomas. *Fiorello H. La Guardia and the Making of Modern New York.* New York: Penguin Books, 1991.

Moses, Robert. *La Guardia, a Salute and a Memoir.* New York, Simon and Schuster, 1957.

"Lai-Li" Mae Cowdery (1928)

The only published short story by MAE COWDERY, a PHILADELPHIA poet.

Cowdery's story of love, seduction, and death appeared in the June 1928 issue of BLACK OPALS, the journal of the literary society of which she was a part. Peppered with ellipses, the story chronicles the haunting and mysterious reunion between an island girl named Lai-Li and a sea captain who once romanced her. While it appears that the couple reunites, they meet only in death. The captain's body is discovered by two of his crewmen, who bury him on the island.

Cowdery's suggestive imagery plays on the stereotypes of island girls. The ultimate nature of the reunion, however, is part of a fleeting critique of conceptions of "the native" and the nature of romance.

Langston, John Mercer (1829–1897)

The maternal great-uncle of LANGSTON HUGHES, one of the most accomplished figures of the Harlem Renaissance.

Langston was born free in Louisa County, Virginia. His father, Ralph Quarles, was the owner of Lucy Langston, a woman of African and Native American heritage and a former slave on his Virginia plantation. Langston was orphaned at the age

of four. William Gooch, one of Quarles's executors, and his family in Chillicothe, Ohio, raised Langston. He later went to live with the abolitionist Richard Long when the Gooches relocated to Missouri, a slave state in which Langston's status and inheritance were threatened. He married Caroline Wall. She was an OBERLIN College student and, like Langston, also the daughter of an interracial union between a slave owner and a woman enslaved on his North Carolina plantation. Langston and Wall married in 1854 and went on to have five children.

Langston excelled at Oberlin College and passed the Ohio bar exam. In 1855, he became the first African-American elected to public office and served as clerk for two Ohio townships. Active in recruiting African Americans for the Massachusetts 54th and 55th Civil War Regiments, Langston went on to become a law professor and acting president of HOWARD UNIVERSITY in WASHINGTON, D.C. In 1877, he was appointed consul general to HAITI and served two terms. In 1890, he was elected to the U.S. House of Representatives and became the first African-American congressman from Virginia. Langston published his autobiography, *From the Virginia Plantation to the National Capitol,* in 1894.

Langston Hughes was very aware of his uncle's impressive political and scholarly achievements. His international travel, including trips to HAITI, and numerous readings at schools such as Virginia State College, allowed him to advance further his great-uncle's legacy of inspiring community outreach and racial uplift.

Bibliography

Berry, Faith, ed. *Langston Hughes: Before and Beyond Harlem.* Westport, Conn.: Lawrence Hill & Company, 1983.

Cheek, William F., and Aimee Lee Cheek. *John Mercer Langston and the Fight for Black Freedom, 1829–65.* Urbana: University of Illinois Press, 1989.

Langston, John Mercer. *From the Virginia Plantation to the National Capitol: or, The First and Only Negro Representative in Congress from the Old Dominion.* Hartford, Conn.: American Publishing Company, 1894. New York, Arno Press, 1969.

Rampersad, Arnold. *The Life of Langston Hughes: I, Too, Sing America.* Vol. 1: *1902–1941.* New York: Oxford University Press, 1986.

———. *The Life of Langston Hughes: I Dream a World.* Vol. 2: *1941–1967.* New York: Oxford University Press, 1988.

Larsen, Nella Marion (Nellie Walker, Nellye Larson, Nellie Larsen) (1893–1964)

One of the most talented writers of the Harlem Renaissance era and the first African-American woman to receive a prestigious GUGGENHEIM FELLOWSHIP. Larsen, who published two novels and three short stories, also pursued a career as a librarian and nurse. Larsen faded into obscurity after the Harlem Renaissance, but her career and accomplishments have once again attracted critical attention and continue to enrich contemporary scholarship on the Harlem Renaissance.

She was born in April 1893 in CHICAGO, Illinois, to Peter Walker, a West Indian cook, and Mary Hanson, a native of Denmark. Her parents separated shortly after their daughter's birth. Mary Hanson Walker then married Peter Larson, a white Iowan, and the couple had a daughter named Anna. Nella Larsen, as a result of her stepfather's encouragement, attended FISK UNIVERSITY, where she was enrolled in the high school division for one year, from 1909 through 1910. She then returned to Copenhagen, Denmark, where she had spent some time as a child with her mother in the late 1890s. During her stay there, she enrolled at the UNIVERSITY OF COPENHAGEN. After two years she returned to NEW YORK CITY and joined the prestigious nursing program at Lincoln Hospital. Following her nursing studies from 1912 through 1915, she returned to the South to work as an assistant superintendent of nurses at TUSKEGEE INSTITUTE in Alabama. After one year there, she joined the Lincoln Hospital staff as a registered nurse and worked for the New York City Department of Health. In 1922 she changed fields and joined the NEW YORK PUBLIC LIBRARY training program. She started as a volunteer but soon became an assistant librarian at the 135th Street Branch (HARLEM BRANCH). She eventually became the children's librarian. She worked with director Ernestine Rose, one of the most enterprising advocates of cultural and literary production during the Harlem Renaissance.

Portrait of Nella Larsen that the writer inscribed to her friends, Carl Van Vechten and his wife Fania Marinoff Van Vechten *(Yale Collection of American Literature, Beinecke Rare Book and Manuscript Library)*

Larsen married Dr. Elmer Imes in May 1919, one year after he had become the second African-American to earn a Ph.D. in physics. Imes, was born in Memphis, Tennessee, in 1883, to Elizabeth Rachel Wallace Imes, formerly enslaved in Natchez, Mississippi, and the Reverend Benjamin Albert Imes, an Oberlin College–educated minister (Davis, 118). Elmer Imes completed his undergraduate degree at Fisk University in 1903 and earned his M.A. at the University of Michigan in 1910. Eight years later, he completed his doctoral work in physics. In the years immediately following their marriage, Imes worked at a number of organizations until 1930, when he returned to Fisk as chair of the physics department. He remained at Fisk until he died 11 years later. An eminent man, he was a member of Sigma Pi Phi, a highly exclusive African-American professional men's organization whose members were selected on the basis of their "outstanding ability to compete success-fully with whites" and who were deemed to have "adhered to a code of unimpeachable personal conduct" (Davis, 127). The couple, who had no children, endured a painful, high-profile divorce, prompted by Imes's infidelity, in 1933.

Nella Larsen emerged as a new American literary talent during the 1920s. Her earliest published work appeared in THE BROWNIES' BOOK, the pioneering children's literature periodical founded by JESSIE FAUSET and W. E. B. DuBois. Larsen contributed two pieces, "Three Scandinavian Games" and "Danish Fun," to the June and July 1920 issues. Writing as Allen Semi, a pseudonym that was her married name written in reverse, she also contributed stories to *Young's Realistic Stories Magazine*. Her first published short story, "The Wrong Man," appeared in the January 1926 issue of *Young's Magazine*. Another work, "Freedom," appeared a few months later in the April 1926 issue.

During the course of her literary career, Larsen also had the opportunity to publish in OPPORTU-NITY, the official journal of the NATIONAL URBAN LEAGUE. She contributed book reviews to both *Opportunity* and THE MESSENGER. The enterprising writer WALLACE THURMAN invited Larsen to submit work to *Harlem*, a literary venture that ultimately did not succeed. Larsen's last and most controversial fictional work appeared in *Forum*.

Larsen made her debut as a novelist in 1928. She was part of an impressive cohort of writers celebrating publication that year. In addition to Larsen's QUICKSAND, four other works appeared: Jessie Fauset's PLUM BUN, RUDOLPH FISHER's THE WALLS OF JERICHO, CLAUDE MCKAY's HOME TO HARLEM, and W. E. B. DuBois's DARK PRINCESS. Her two novels, both of which were published by KNOPF, appeared in quick succession. The first, *Quicksand*, appeared in 1928 and earned her the first of several notable awards. The novel, which she completed in just over six months and dedicated to her husband, was awarded a HARMON FOUNDATION PRIZE. Her accomplishment was publicized in THE NEW YORK TIMES, and Larsen attended the prize ceremony with the other winners, the Reverend Channing Tobias and JAMES WELDON JOHNSON, who was representing winner Claude McKay because the latter was in Algiers at

the time. The ceremony, hosted by John Nail with prizes presented by Mayor Walker and speeches delivered by Rabbi Stephen Wise and by Helen Harmon, the vice president of the Harmon Foundation, was held at the Mother A.M.E. Zion Church on West 137th Street. Larsen received the second-prize bronze medal and $100; the poet and writer Claude McKay, who won first place, received a gold medal and $400 for his novel HOME TO HARLEM. Rabbi Wise, who delivered the main address that evening, noted that "The awards are to them whose inspirations and achievements alike are in the fields of life that matter to all of us." He also called attention to the fact that the presentation ceremony was held on "the birthday of the great American whose life, whose memory, whose name are become as a cherished symbol of both races. Was it not Lincoln," he asked, "who as much as any other human has led us to see that liberation from without means little unless it be supplemented by self-liberation?" (*NYT*, 13 February 1929, 13).

Larsen's own experiences as a biracial child and aspiring artist shaped the novel. It was roundly praised and prompted *Crisis* editor W. E. B. DuBois to state that it was the best work of African-American literature since the early 1900s. The work was reviewed widely and in a variety of forums including influential African-American publications such as *Opportunity*, *The Crisis*, the Baltimore *Afro-American*, and the CHICAGO DEFENDER. Reviews also appeared throughout the mainstream American press and in periodicals such as *The New York Times*, THE NEW REPUBLIC, and THE NATION. Writing in "The Ebony Flute," her monthly column published in *Opportunity*, GWENDOLYN BENNETT noted that "Nella Larsen's *Quicksand* has just arrived. And let me say that many folks will be interested to hear that this book does not set as its tempo that of the Harlem Cabaret—this is the story of the struggle of an interesting cultured Negro woman against her environment. Negroes who are squeamish about writers exposing our worst side will be relieved that Harlem night-life is more or less submerged by this author in the psychological struggle of the heroine" (Bennett, 153). Larsen's novel countered the graphic images of Harlem nightlife, intense sexuality, and domesticity in disarray that appeared in novels such as *Home to Harlem* (1928) by Claude McKay. Yet, as scholar Cheryl Wall suggests, Larsen did pursue issues that were of importance to her literary peers. It is the "bourgeois ethos of her novels," according to Wall, "that has unfortunately obscured the similarities" (Wall, 97).

One year later, in April 1929, Larsen published *PASSING*. This work, for which she had originally considered using the title "Nig," explored the plight of the modern woman and the complicated nature of racial and social politics. Larsen dedicated the novel to CARL VAN VECHTEN, author of the controversial and recently published *Nigger Heaven*, and his wife, Fania Marinoff Van Vechten. The book was part of an extended African-American literary tradition that explored race, social mobility, and identity. The novel's theme also echoed in other contemporary Harlem Renaissance works such as Jessie Fauset's *Plum Bun* (1928) and James Weldon Johnson's *Autobiography of an Ex-Coloured Man* (1912, 1927). Larsen's second novel revolves around the lengthy and complicated friendship between Clare Kendry and Irene Redfield and the ramifications of Kendry's decision to pass for white. The work, which historian Nathan Huggins describes as a study of "schizophrenia which results from racial dualism" (Huggins, 159), attracted critical attention and a number of reviews in respected literary journals such as the *Saturday Review of Literature*, *The Times Literary Supplement*, and the *New York Times Book Review*.

In 1930, Larsen became a member of an elite group when she became the first African-American woman to be awarded a Guggenheim Fellowship. She was the fourth person of color to win the award; previous winners included WALTER WHITE, COUNTEE CULLEN, and ERIC WALROND. Larsen made plans to travel extensively after she received the prize. Her sojourn abroad included visits to France, Portugal, and Spain. She established herself in Palma de Mallorca on the Balearic Islands and, according to biographer Thadious Davis, enjoyed flirtatious encounters and productive writing days. While in Spain, she corresponded with Henry Allen Moe of the Guggenheim Foundation who also was a regular correspondent of ZORA NEALE HURSTON during her tenure as a Guggenheim Fellow. In one of her most memorable notes to Moe, Larsen made a

very direct confession. "I do so want to be famous," she noted while updating him on the writings that she was producing (Davis, "NLHA" 245). While in Europe, Larsen began work on two new novels. Unfortunately, these works never were published and may have been lost after her death.

That same year, in 1930, her short story "SANCTUARY" elicited a heated public debate about plagiarism. Similarities were pointed out between her short story and an earlier published work, "Mrs. Adis" by white British writer Sheila Kaye-Smith, that appeared in a 1922 issue of *Century Magazine*. The controversy tarnished Larsen's reputation despite her assertions that she had been inspired to write the story after hearing it from one of her patients. Larsen's biographer Thadious Davis concludes that the similarities between the two works are indeed hard to overlook. Yet, Davis also mentions Larsen's previous publicly stated interest in stories about white protagonists that could be revised as works that are transformed by the introduction of race.

Larsen enjoyed friendships with well-known figures of the period including JEAN TOOMER, Carl Van Vechten, and Walter White. White played a significant role in Larsen's professional life. It was he who introduced her to Van Vechten, the well-known patron and writer who would enjoy a lengthy friendship with both Larsen and her husband, Elmer Imes. In his tireless efforts to support the creative efforts of emerging artists, White also provided Larsen with vital secretarial support as she completed her manuscript of *Passing*.

Larsen's departure from literary life coincided with the end of the Harlem Renaissance. She spent the last two decades of her life working as a highly respected nurse in New York City. She was on the staff at the Governeur Hospital, which later became affiliated with Beth Israel Medical Center and Hospital and the Metropolitan Hospital.

Despite her efforts to reconnect with her half sister, Larsen suffered a deep isolation from her family and was not acknowledged by her white sibling, Anna Larsen Gardner. Larsen died of heart failure on 30 March 1964. Unlike a number of her Harlem Renaissance peers, her published obituary had no full profile of her career of accomplishments. *The New York Times*, which listed her under her married name of Imes, noted only that she "died March 30, 1964, sister of Anna Larsen Gardener of Calif." (*NYT,* 7 April 1964, 35). It is sadly ironic that the obituary notice linked her both to her former husband and to her unresponsive sibling. Coworkers and her few close friends eulogized her as a dedicated and caring nurse.

Scholars such as Mary Helen Washington, Charles Larson, and Thadious Davis have spearheaded the reemergence of Larsen's work. Many scholars have considered Larsen's work in the context of racial passing and have used her writings to advance contemporary debates about figures such as the tragic mulatto and about issues such as African-American women's sexuality and the politics of middle-class life. Scholars continue to debate the circumstances of Larsen's life and to consider how the evolving conclusions about her origins, self-identification, and social mobility shaped her perspectives on the Harlem Renaissance in general, and on her own work in particular. The recovery of Larsen's work, and the painstaking reconstruction of her life have invigorated debate about the accomplishments of the period's most elusive and insightful writers.

Bibliography

"12 Negroes Honored for Achievements; Harmon Awards Presented Here to Claude McKay, Nella L. Imes and Dr. C. H. Tobias." *New York Times*, 13 February 1929, 13.

"Deaths." *New York Times*, 7 April 1964, 35.

Bennett, Gwendolyn. "The Ebony Flute." *Opportunity* (May 1928): 153.

Davis, Thadious M. *Nella Larsen, Novelist of the Harlem Renaissance: A Woman's Life Unveiled.* Baton Rouge: Louisiana State University Press, 1994.

———. "Nella Larsen's Harlem Aesthetic." In *The Harlem Renaissance: Reevaluations*, edited by Amritjit Singh, William S. Shiver, and Stanley Brodwin. New York: Garland Publishing, Inc., 1989. 245–256.

Huggins, Nathan. *Harlem Renaissance.* New York: Oxford University Press, 1971.

Hutchinson, George. "Nella Larsen and the Veil of Race." *American Literary History* 9, no. 2 (summer 1997): 329–349.

Larson, Charles, ed. *An Intimation of Things Distant: The Collected Fiction of Nella Larsen.* New York: Anchor Books, 1992.

———. *Invisible Darkness: Jean Toomer & Nella Larsen.* Iowa City: University of Iowa Press, 1993.

Wall, Cheryl. "Passing for What? Aspects of Identity in Nella Larsen's Novels." *Black American Literature Forum* 20, nos. 1–2 (summer 1986): 97–111.

Latimer, Catherine Allen (ca. 1895–unknown)

In 1920 Latimer became the first African-American woman appointed to the staff of the NEW YORK PUBLIC LIBRARY.

Born in Nashville, Tennessee, to H. W. Allen and Minta Bosley Allen, she was educated in Brooklyn, New York, and abroad in Germany and FRANCE. She completed undergraduate studies, including library-training courses, at HOWARD UNIVERSITY. She was a member of ALPHA KAPPA ALPHA sorority, one of four historic African-American Greek societies founded on the WASHINGTON, D.C., campus.

Before making her historic entry into the New York Public Library system, Latimer worked as an assistant librarian at TUSKEGEE INSTITUTE. Shortly after becoming a pioneering member of the New York Public Library staff, Latimer was appointed assistant branch reference librarian at the 135th Street Branch in HARLEM. In 1925 she was given charge of the newly established division of Negro Literature and History. There, she oversaw the extensive collection of Arthur Schomburg that, in addition to its artifacts, pamphlets, prints, and documents included more than 5,000 books relating to African-American and black life and culture. Latimer's career at the New York Public Library lasted 15 years.

Latimer preceded REGINA ANDREWS, who in 1936 became the first African-American supervising librarian in the New York Public Library system. Both women were influential professionals who used their positions at the 135th Street Branch to shape the Harlem Renaissance. They provided the community and artists with access to invaluable resources, showcased contemporary work, and supported the professional efforts of artists and writers.

Lawrence, Jacob (1917–2000)

One of America's most important artists and the most influential of African-American painters. Lawrence was an emerging talent when the Harlem Renaissance began, and he came of age professionally during that flowering of black arts, literature, and culture.

Lawrence was born in Atlantic City, New Jersey, in September 1917, the son of Jacob Lawrence, a coal miner and railroad employee, and Rosalie Armstead Lawrence, a domestic. Following his parents' separation in the mid-1920s, he and his two siblings relocated to HARLEM to live with his mother. Like his future friend and colleague LANGSTON HUGHES, who benefited from the community arts center in his Cleveland community, Lawrence began to develop his artistic talents in the Utopia Settlement House in Harlem. In 1941 he married Gwendolyn Knight, also a sculptor and artist, from Barbados, West Indies, whom he had met in the artists' community of New York City.

He worked closely with some of the most prominent and talented figures of the Renaissance period. In 1931 he began art studies at the Utopia House in New York City with Charles Alston. From 1934 through 1937, he continued his training at the Harlem Art Workshop, which met in the 135th Street Branch of the NEW YORK PUBLIC LIBRARY. In 1937 he earned a full scholarship to the American Artists School in New York City. His immersion in New York City culture soon brought him into contact with leading scholars and artists such as ROMARE BEARDEN, AARON DOUGLAS, RALPH ELLISON, Langston Hughes, ALAIN LOCKE, AUGUSTA SAVAGE, ARTHUR SCHOMBURG, and RICHARD WRIGHT. In 1938 he was hired by the Works Progress Administration on the recommendation of sculptor Augusta Savage.

His career began to blossom in the waning years of the Renaissance. He completed the first of his unique, multipart narratives in 1937. This series on Toussaint Louverture was followed in 1938 by a riveting series of 32 paintings devoted to the life and character of Frederick Douglass. In 1939 Lawrence completed another installation of more than 30 paintings on Harriet Tubman.

Lawrence won a JULIUS ROSENWALD FELLOWSHIP in 1940 and used the award's funds to secure a studio space. In that space, which he shared with CLAUDE MCKAY, WILLIAM ATTAWAY, and Romare Bearden, Lawrence created one of his most celebrated series, paintings that formed The Migration of the American Negro collection. The work debuted on December 7, 1941, in Manhattan's elite Downtown Gallery.

Lawrence continued to thrive in the decades following the Harlem Renaissance. He was awarded three JULIUS ROSENWALD FELLOWSHIPS, as well as the prestigious GUGGENHEIM FELLOWSHIP in 1946, the SPINGARN MEDAL given by the NATIONAL ASSOCIATION FOR THE ADVANCEMENT OF COLORED PEOPLE in 1970, and the National Medal of Arts in 1990. Lawrence taught at a number of colleges, including the New School for Social Research, the University of Washington at Seattle, and Brandeis University.

He died of lung cancer in Seattle, Washington, in June 2000.

Bibliography

Nesbett, Peter T., and Michelle DuBois, eds. *Over the Line: The Art and Life of Jacob Lawrence.* Seattle, Wash.: University of Washington Press in association with Jacob Lawrence Catalogue, 2000.

Wheat, Ellen Harkins. *Jacob Lawrence: American Painter.* Seattle: University of Washington Press, 1986.

Lee, George Washington (1894–1976)

An Indianola, Mississippi, native who began publishing fiction and poetry after establishing himself as a successful insurance executive. The son of George and Hattie Stingfeller Lee, the daughter of house servants, he went on to study at Alcorn Agricultural and Mechanical College. He financed his college studies by working during the summers as a bellhop in elite Memphis hotels.

Following his graduation in 1918, Lee was accepted into the Army's Officer Candidate School. He went on to serve with the 368th Negro Division in FRANCE and earned the French Croix de Guerre for bravery in battle. He was discharged at the rank of first lieutenant. Lee later received the honorary title of colonel.

Upon his return to America, Lee began working as an insurance salesman in Memphis. After jobs at the Mississippi Life Insurance and the Atlanta Life Insurance companies, he became director of the

Universal Life Insurance in 1927. An active community member and leader of the Republican Party of Tennessee, he also was a member of the American Legion, the Elks, and the Omega Psi Phi fraternity. He made his home in Memphis, Tennessee.

In 1934 Lee made his literary debut with the novel BEALE STREET: WHERE THE BLUES BEGAN. W. C. HANDY, the legendary blues musician and Lee's friend, provided the foreword. The novel, which was included in the BOOK-OF-THE-MONTH CLUB offerings for 1934, was inspired by Memphis and its rich music history. In 1937 Lee published his second novel, RIVER GEORGE. His third novel, *Beale Street Sundown,* appeared in 1942.

Bibliography

Tucker, David. *Lieutenant Lee of Beale Street.* Nashville: Vanderbilt University Press, 1971.

Lee, Ulysses (unknown)

Coeditor with STERLING BROWN and ARTHUR DAVIS of the 1941 anthology *The Negro Caravan.*

Lenox Avenue

A major thoroughfare in HARLEM. The well-known entertainment area known as Jungle Alley ran between Seventh Avenue and Lenox Avenue and included such legendary venues as the elegant COTTON CLUB, the opulent Savoy Ballroom, which came to be known as "The World's Most Beautiful Ballroom," and the Lenox Lounge, which opened in 1939 and was the venue in which Billie Holliday first performed "Strange Fruit," the most powerful song written about LYNCHING.

Lenox Avenue inspired writers, including LANGSTON HUGHES, whose poem "Lenox Avenue: Midnight" captures the complexity of life in Harlem. In "The Weary Blues" (1923), Hughes crafts a haunting image of an African-American musician playing "[d]own on Lenox Avenue the other night / By the pale dull pallor of an old gas light." The poem continues, calling attention to the artist's unself-conscious and expressive gestures: "He did a lazy sway . . . / He did a lazy sway . . . / To the tune o' those Weary Blues."

Lenox Avenue was one of the primary routes into and through Harlem. Major cultural and intellectual sites located on this busy road include the Schomburg Center for Research in Black Culture. The avenue is now known as Malcolm X Boulevard.

Let My People Go Lillian Wood (1922)

A novel by LILLIAN WOOD whose title evokes the powerful Old Testament challenge that the prophet Moses issued to Pharaoh. In the Book of Exodus, chapter 5, verse 1, Moses relays God's command to the Pharaoh, who holds Jews in bondage: "Let My people go that they may come and worship Me." Wood's book, published by the African Methodist Episcopal Church's publishing house, also considers the plight of oppressed people and the heroic efforts needed to secure their freedom and existence in a promised land of stability.

The protagonists are a young married couple, Helen Adams and Bob McComb. The novel chronicles their maturation as professionals and activists. Helen becomes a nurse, and Bob joins the army during World War I. The couple ultimately move to CHICAGO and intensifies their efforts to secure racial harmony. Bob becomes a member of Congress. There, he uses his influence and passion for civil rights to pass antilynching legislation.

The publication of Wood's novel coincided with historic public and federal debates about LYNCHING and antilynching legislation. In 1918, four years before her novel appeared, Congressman Dyer of Missouri introduced the most significant modern antilynching legislation ever brought to Capitol Hill. The NATIONAL ASSOCIATION FOR THE ADVANCEMENT OF COLORED PEOPLE (NAACP), which raised concerns about the potential unconstitutionality of the bill at first, ultimately supported the legislation. By 1919 the NAACP argued that the passage of the bill would demonstrate federal support for civil rights and constitute an emphatic condemnation of mob violence and brutal racial oppression. In January 1922 the Dyer Bill passed in the House. A Senate filibuster prevented it from becoming law.

Wood's novel explored the volatile issues of lynching. In the face of concerted opposition to antilynching amendments during the administrations of Woodrow Wilson and Warren Harding, Wood demonstrated the ways in which antilynching legislation could be realized.

Bibliography

Wood, Lillian. *Let My People Go*. Philadelphia: A.M.E. Book Concern, 1922.

Lewis, Frederick Allen (1890–1954)

A Bostonian and HARVARD UNIVERSITY graduate who became a well-known editor of *Harper's* and an important resource for Harlem Renaissance writers. Lewis was the son of the Reverend Frederick Baylies, an Episcopalian minister, and his wife, Alberta Lewis Allen. The younger Lewis's first wife was Dorothy Penrose Cobb. The couple had two children, Elizabeth and Oliver, before her death in 1930. Lewis married Agnes Rogers Hyde, a writer and editor with whom he collaborated, in September 1932. He passed away in February 1954 after suffering a cerebral hemorrhage.

Lewis's career in journalism began shortly after he graduated from Harvard in 1912 and completed a master's degree in 1913. He was a published writer whose works had appeared in THE ATLANTIC MONTHLY and *Punch* when he joined the staff of *The Atlantic Monthly* in 1914. He joined CARL VAN DOREN at THE CENTURY in 1916 and worked as managing editor there for one year. Lewis joined *Harper's Magazine* as an editorial assistant in 1923. By 1932 he was an associate editor, and in 1941 he began his 12-year appointment as the editor of the influential magazine.

Lewis was one of several notable white literary figures whom OPPORTUNITY editor CHARLES S. JOHNSON invited to the legendary CIVIC CLUB dinner in 1924. That historic event inaugurated a powerful tradition of high social and literary gatherings where emerging writers were feted among and by representatives from publishing.

Lewis is remembered for his enterprising work in journalism and his efforts to historicize and to preserve American culture. His Harlem Renaissance–era publications included a well-received book of photojournalism and one of his several works of social history. He and Agnes Rogers Allen coedited *The American Procession: American Life Since 1860 in Photographs* (1934). In 1931 he published *Only Yesterday: An Informal History of the Nineteen Twenties*. Lewis continued to publish in the years following the Harlem Renaissance.

Bibliography

Lewis, Frederick. *Frederick Baylies Allen; a Memoir*. Cambridge, Mass.: Riverside, 1929.
———. *Only Yesterday: An Informal History of the Nineteen-Twenties*. New York: Harper, 1935.
Payne, Darwin. *The Man of Only Yesterday: Frederick Lewis Allen, Former Editor of Harper's Magazine, Author, and Interpreter of His Times*. New York: Harper, 1975.

Lewis, Lillian Tucker (unknown)

Lewis was one of several Texas-born poets featured in *Heralding Dawn*, the 1936 anthology edited by J. Mason Brewer. Born in Corsicana, Texas, Lewis attended Prairie View College, the University of Denver, and Kansas University before pursuing a career in teaching.

A published poet, Lewis and her works have slipped into obscurity. *Heralding Dawn* includes only one poem by the writer, who apparently published in a number of Texas magazines and newspapers. "Longing" suggests Lewis's interest in religion, nature, and the finite nature of life.

Lewis, Sinclair (1885–1951)

A talented writer who, in 1930, became the first American to win the Nobel Prize in literature. Born in Sauk Centre, Minnesota, he was one of three sons born to Edwin and Emma Kermott Lewis. In 1892 his recently widowed father married Isabel Warner. Lewis enrolled at YALE UNIVERSITY in 1903. He graduated in 1908 after taking some time away from his studies to travel through England and Panama. He married Grace Livingston Hegger, a *Vogue* magazine staffer, in 1914. They had one son, Wells Lewis, a serviceman who died in World War II. Following his divorce from Hegger, Lewis married Dorothy Thompson, a journalist. The couple had one son, Michael, before their divorce in 1942. Sinclair Lewis died in Rome in January 1951 and was buried between his parents in Sauk Centre, Minnesota.

Lewis was catapulted to fame by *Main Street*, his seventh novel. Published by HARCOURT BRACE in 1920, the novel was a sensational hit that offered an absorbing and multifaceted critique of American culture.

Lewis published frequently throughout and after the Harlem Renaissance. He also supported the efforts to sustain the literary excellence of the period. With EUGENE O'NEILL and others, Lewis served as a judge in the highly regarded literary contests sponsored by THE CRISIS, the official journal of the NATIONAL ASSOCIATION FOR THE ADVANCEMENT OF COLORED PEOPLE (NAACP). He enjoyed a close and spirited friendship with WALTER WHITE, a fellow scholar and the intrepid undercover NAACP reporter who provided firsthand accounts of lynchings and mob violence. CARL VAN VECHTEN was one of the friends with whom White debated key aspects of his novels. The friendship between the two men began when Lewis read FIRE IN THE FLINT. Lewis provided a strong endorsement of the book, and the two began to correspond about the heated southern reception and protest of the novel about southern LYNCHING. It was White who facilitated the introduction between Lewis and CLAUDE MCKAY, the poet and novelist. The two met in Paris; Lewis wanted to meet the poet, journalist, and aspiring novelist. During their lengthy conversations over the course of two days, Lewis offered helpful and forthright evaluations of McKay's current writing project, *Color Scheme*. Impressed by McKay's writing and efforts, Lewis offered crucial support when he lobbied the Garland Fund to extend McKay's grant.

When Carl Van Vechten arrived in New York City in the early 1900s, the future well-connected critic and socialite lived in the same West 39th Street building as Lewis. The two men later became friends. From time to time, Lewis also reviewed the publications of his former neighbor. In response to Van Vechten's *Blind Bow Boy*, Lewis declared that the book was "impertinent, subversive, resolutely and completely wicked" and that Van Vechten had successfully "slap[ped] the tradition that highbrow American novels must be either lugubriously and literally 'realistic . . . or else acrobatically 'original' like . . . all the writers who are deriving from the solemn theology of Gertrude Stein" (Kellner, 147).

Lewis's novels were read widely by Harlem Renaissance authors including ZORA NEALE HURSTON. In 1927 she solicited help from friends DOROTHY WEST and HELENE JOHNSON, asking them to send along a copy of Lewis's *Elmer Gantry*

because her rural southern community was not one in which such books were available.

Bibliography
Bucco, Martin. *Critical Essays on Sinclair Lewis.* Boston: G. K. Hall, 1986.

Hutchisson, James. *The Rise of Sinclair Lewis, 1920–1930.* University Park: Pennsylvania State University Press, 1996.

Kellner, Bruce. *Carl Van Vechten and the Irreverent Decades.* Norman: University of Oklahoma Press, 1968.

Lingeman, Richard. *Sinclair Lewis: Rebel from Main Street.* New York: Random House, 2002.

Van Doren, Carol. *Sinclair Lewis: A Biographical Sketch.* Garden City, N.J.: Doubleday, Doran, 1933.

Lewis, Theophilus (1891–1974)

A self-educated theater writer who became one of the most visible and insightful drama critics during the Harlem Renaissance. He published widely during the era, and his reviews of books, drama, and short fiction appeared in such popular publications as OPPORTUNITY, INTER-STATE TATTLER, and the AMSTERDAM NEWS.

Born in Baltimore to Thomas and Anne Lewis, Theophilus Lewis had a spotty education before he joined the army and fought during World War I. He was a member of the American Expeditionary Forces. When he returned to the United States, he began working in NEW YORK CITY as a postal employee. He married in 1933 and had three children, Selma, Alfred, and Lowell. He became a Catholic in 1939 and began submitting work to numerous Catholic publications such as *Catholic World, Commonweal,* and *America.*

Lewis regarded the theater as an essential vehicle through which society could effect and consider social change and cultural development. His sentiments were akin to those of W. E. B. DuBois, T. MONTGOMERY GREGORY, LANGSTON HUGHES, and ZORA NEALE HURSTON, all of whom worked assiduously to establish a thriving African-American theater tradition for, by, and about the race. Lewis bemoaned the constraints placed on talented actors of color for whom there were not enough challenging and sophisticated roles. He praised the efforts of small community theaters, recognizing their important role in raising public interest in the arts and providing essential exposure to historical subjects and contemporary issues. Lewis, who assessed the careers of prominent performers such as Charles Gilpin, also wrote about the evolving relationship between the African-American theater and white theater. He noted the ways in which the two traditions borrowed from each other and noted what he regarded as a significant turning point, the increasing use of African-American material in white productions. Lewis also turned his attention to films and offered early, forthright critiques of works by black directors such as Oscar Micheaux.

The majority of Lewis's works appeared in THE MESSENGER, the journal that A. PHILIP RANDOLPH and CHANDLER OWEN established in New York City in 1917. He also published in African-American newspapers such as the *Pittsburgh Courier*. In addition to his extensive theater-related publications, Lewis wrote short fiction and coauthored with GEORGE SCHUYLER a regular *Messenger* column entitled "Shafts and Darts." In 1928 Lewis was poised to contribute several drama reviews to HARLEM: A FORUM OF NEGRO LIFE, an ambitious journal that WALLACE THURMAN hoped to establish. Lewis was one of several prominent writers who contributed to the first issue; unfortunately, the magazine failed.

Lewis combined his impressive writing record with a lengthy career with the U.S. Postal Service. In 1950 he was a founding member of the New York City Commission on Human Rights.

Bibliography

Bontemps, Arna, ed. *The Harlem Renaissance Remembered.* New York: Dodd, 1972.

Curtis, Susan. *The First Black Actors on the Great White Way.* Columbia: University of Missouri Press, 1998.

Krasner, David. *A Beautiful Pageant: African American Theatre, Drama, and Performance in the Harlem Renaissance, 1910–1927.* New York: Palgrave Macmillan, 2002.

Liberator

A literary magazine founded by MAX EASTMAN and colleagues with whom he had worked at *The Masses*, a political journal targeted under the ESPI-

ONAGE ACT. The *Liberator* was established when the *Masses* was banned due to its defiant criticism of the American World War I effort.

CRYSTAL EASTMAN, the sister of the founder, served as the editor of the *Liberator* for several years. Poet CLAUDE MCKAY, whose verse began appearing in the magazine in 1919, was a member of the editorial staff and enjoyed a close and enduring friendship with Max Eastman, a member of the American Left who went on trial twice for sedition. McKay's stirring and frequently republished poem "If We Must Die," prompted by the bloody race riots during the summer of 1919, appeared first in the *Liberator*.

The *Liberator* was transformed into *The Workers' Monthly* in 1922 when Robert Minor and the Communist Party took over the journal. The change in editorial policy and focus prompted many contributors to establish NEW MASSES in 1926.

Bibliography

Cantor, Milton. *Max Eastman.* New York: Twayne Publishers, 1970.

Cooper, Wayne. *Claude McKay: Rebel Sojourner in the Harlem Renaissance.* New York: Schocken Books, 1987.

Lewis, David Levering. *W. E. B. DuBois: The Fight for Equality and the American Century, 1919–1963.* New York: Henry Holt, 2000.

O'Neill, William. *The Last Romantic: A Life of Max Eastman.* New York: Oxford University Press, 1978.

Liberty Hall

The name for the main venues of the UNIVERSAL NEGRO IMPROVEMENT ASSOCIATION (UNIA), the organization that MARCUS GARVEY founded with black nationalist colleagues. Garvey, who had a longstanding interest in Irish political history, honored the efforts of James Connolly, a Socialist labor leader who established a Liberty Hall in Dublin, Ireland.

The first UNIA Liberty Hall was established in Kingston, Jamaica. When Garvey established his movement in HARLEM, he purchased an auditorium and named it Liberty Hall. This venue was used for NEW YORK CITY offices and UNIA events such as the 1922 UNIA convention. The organization also established businesses, such as restaurants, in these headquarters.

Bibliography

Burkett, Randall. *Black Redemption: Churchmen Speak for the Garvey Movement.* Philadelphia: Temple University Press, 1978.

Cronon, Edmund David. *Black Moses: The Story of Marcus Garvey and the Universal Negro Improvement Association.* Madison: University of Wisconsin Press, 1987.

Mackie, Liz. *The Great Marcus Garvey.* London: Hansib Publishers, 1987.

Liberty League

An ambitious political organization founded in 1917 by HUBERT HARRISON, a native of St. Croix, writer, and an early Socialist Party leader. The Liberty League was the first group to embody the ideals of the New Negro Movement. It stood as a powerful precursor of the Black Power Movement. The Liberty League philosophy insisted on importance of race matters over class issues. The organization was a strong political voice and advocated implementation of voting rights, civil rights, and antilynching legislation.

In July 1917 Harrison invited MARCUS GARVEY to make a public address, his first American speech, in New York City. Garvey became a member of the Liberty League in the years before he founded the UNIVERSAL NEGRO IMPROVEMENT ASSOCIATION (UNIA). His association with Harrison continued and included the appointment of Harrison as editor of *NEGRO WORLD*, the official UNIA publication.

Bibliography

Perry, Jeffrey, ed. *A Hubert Harrison Reader.* Middletown, Conn.: Wesleyan University Press, 2001.

Life's Sunshine and Shadows Mazie Earhart Clark (1940)

A collection of poems by MAZIE EARHART CLARK, an Ohio-born poet. Clark published the volume in 1929 with the Cincinnati-based Eaton Publishing Company. She used the pseudonym Fannie B. Steele for the book, which included a number of poems published in *GARDEN OF MEMORIES*, a collection published in 1932.

Clark's poems reflect her religious faith and her devotion to her husband, a sergeant in the U.S.

Army who died in 1919. She offered her poems to readers who might be in need of comfort. The central themes in her poems emerge from Clark's testimony about life after the death of a loved one, patriotism, romantic love, the soothing power of nature, and the rewards of Christian faith.

Bibliography

Boelcskevy, Mary Anne Stewart, ed. *Voices in the Poetic Tradition: Clara Ann Thompson, J. Pauline Smith, Mazie Earhart Clark.* New York: G. K. Hall, 1996.

Lincoln Memorial

A WASHINGTON, D.C., memorial built in honor of Abraham Lincoln, the 16th president of the United States. Construction began in 1914, and the memorial was dedicated in 1922 on Memorial Day. The architect Henry Bacon, sculptor Daniel Chester French, and artist Jules Guerin collaborated on the impressive structure. The memorial features a statue of Lincoln and 36 columns that represent the states over which Lincoln presided during his presidency. Copies of the Gettysburg Address and the speech that he delivered at his second inaugural ceremony also are housed at the site.

It was at this historic site that MARIAN ANDERSON, the acclaimed contralto, appeared on Easter Sunday, 1939. She performed at the Lincoln Memorial when the Daughters of the American Revolution, compelled by racism, denied her access to Constitution Hall. The concert drew some 75,000 people and did much to reveal the still-entrenched racism in American society.

Lincoln School for Nurses

Established in 1899, the Lincoln School for Nurses was one of the most prestigious African-American nursing programs. Its history dated back to the 1830s and efforts by Anne Mott and Mary Shotwell to establish a home for indigent people and the elderly. Known originally as the Home for the Colored Aged, the institution expanded its mission in the 1880s to include a hospital. The Lincoln School for Nurses graduated its first class, comprised of six students, in 1900. The organization received its official charter in 1902.

During the Harlem Renaissance era, the Lincoln School for Nurses was located at East 141st Street between Concord Avenue and Southern Boulevard in the Bronx. It was affiliated with the Lincoln Hospital and Home. In 1926 the school was sold to the city of New York, but the nursing school was preserved as a private venue.

The Lincoln School played an important role in the professionalization of African-American women. Its graduates and teachers included Ivy Nathan Tinkler, the first African American to be appointed director, and Ada Belle Samuel Thoms, an alumna who served for 18 years as assistant superintendent of nurses and a pioneer activist who worked to secure equal opportunities for African-American nurses within the American Red Cross and the U.S. Army Nurse Corps.

NELLA LARSEN, who worked as a nurse before and after she emerged as one of the most sophisticated writers of the Harlem Renaissance, began her nursing studies at the Lincoln School in 1912. One of her teachers was Adah Thoms. Larsen completed her training in 1915 and graduated with 10 other classmates. She then worked for two years at TUSKEGEE INSTITUTE as superintendent of nurses. She returned to New York and to the Lincoln Hospital in 1916 and worked for two years as a nurse.

Bibliography

Carnegie, Mary Elizabeth. *The Path We Tread: Blacks in Nursing, 1854–1990*. New York: National League for Nursing Press, 1991.

Davis, Thadious. *Nella Larsen, Novelist of the Harlem Renaissance: A Woman's Life Unveiled*. Baton Rouge: Louisiana State University Press, 1994.

Hine, Darlene Clark. *Black Women in the Nursing Profession: A Documentary History*. New York: Garland, 1985.

Thoms, Adah, and Belle Samuel. *Pathfinders: A History of the Progress of Colored Graduate Nurses*. New York: Kay Printing House, 1929.

Lincoln Theatre

One of the first two theaters established in HARLEM. Located at 56–58 West 125th Street, the Lincoln was an enormous venue that could accommodate some 1,000 patrons. The theater was the first home to the Anita Bush Players Company and featured African-American productions for its primarily African-American audiences.

Fats Waller was the longtime house organist who provided music for the silent films. The revival performances of THE EMPEROR JONES starring Jules Bledsoe were staged here. Ethel Waters made her New York debut at the Lincoln, and in 1919 and 1920 FLORENCE MILLS appeared at the Lincoln billed as "Harlem's dainty, sweet singer."

The Negro Playwrights Company leased the facility in 1940. Its first production, announced in the *New York Times*, was Theodore Powell's play *Big White Frog*, directed by Powell Lindsay.

Lincoln University

The Pennsylvania university that in 1854 became the first institution of higher learning for men of African descent. Its presidents included Horace Mann Bond. Within its first century, the school graduated approximately one-fifth of all African-American physicians and one-tenth of all African-American attorneys.

Located in Chester County, Pennsylvania, the school is some 45 miles southwest of Philadelphia and 55 miles north of Baltimore, Maryland. It became a coeducational institution in 1952 and in 1972 became one of Pennsylvania's state universities.

Some of its most accomplished graduates included ARCHIBALD GRIMKÉ, the nephew of white South Carolina abolitionists Angelina and Sarah Grimké, and Thurgood Marshall, the first African-American Supreme Court Justice. The school also maintained strong links to African nations, and its graduates include Nnamdi Asikiwe, a member of the class of 1930 and the first president of Nigeria, and Kwame Nkrumah, class of 1939 and the first president of GHANA.

A number of influential Harlem Renaissance writers and artists attended Lincoln. These included WARING CUNEY, William Allyn Hill, LANGSTON HUGHES, JAY SAUNDERS REDDING, and EDWARD SILVERA. In his application to Lincoln, poet Langston Hughes made an earnest appeal for admission. "I *must* go to college in order to be of more use to my race and America," wrote the recently published and feted poet. Hughes graduated in 1929. The university's Langston Hughes

Memorial Library honors one of the school's most distinguished alumni.

Bibliography

Bond, Horace Mann. *Education for Freedom: A History of Lincoln University, Pennsylvania.* Lincoln, Pa.: Lincoln University, 1976.

Lisping Leaves Ida Rowland (1939)

A collection of poems by IDA ROWLAND, who became the first Oklahoma woman of African descent to earn a Ph.D. *Lisping Leaves* comprised 47 poems that highlighted Rowland's love of nature, her race awareness, and her unwavering social optimism. The publication of the volume by Dorrance and Company of PHILADELPHIA coincided with Rowland's graduation from the University of Nebraska at Omaha, where she earned a master's degree.

The volume, which was the only collection that Rowland published, reflects her efforts to grapple with race, class, privilege, and disenfranchisement. Works such as "Heritage" and "Is It Not Enough" call attention to the overwhelming nature of racism and racial violence. The first-person complaint of "Is It Not Enough" is marked for its distress and frustration: "Is it not enough, / That I should suffer poverty and disease / Pay for crimes I do not commit, / Be burned at the stake for another's lust!" asks the speaker. The three-stanza poem ends on a sobering and bitter note. "No, it is not enough," concludes the speaker, "For I must have heaped upon / My already bowed head / The black prejudices of by-gone centuries." Other poems reveal Rowland's passionate protests of the constraints—physical and spiritual—that dictate the lives of African Americans. In "Negroid Things," Rowland rejects racial essentialism and the narrowness of stereotypes. "I cannot write of things negroid / I cannot feel the things that are black," asserts the speaker in the first lines before noting that she can "feel only life in its pulsing fullness: The joys, the grief and troubled cares / That come with every life." The poem ends with a powerful rejection of the blackness that is socially constructed and highly destructive. "And on that last day, When I must face a frowning Maker . . . / I shall say to him: / God, I could not feel the black," Rowland writes.

Lisping Leaves is a powerful meditation on transcendence, survival, and individuality.

Bibliography

Rowland, Ida. *Lisping Leaves.* Philadelphia: Dorrance & Co., 1939.

"Little Grey House, The" Anita Scott Coleman (1922)

One of the earliest published short stories by ANITA SCOTT COLEMAN. The piece appeared in two issues of *HALF-CENTURY* magazine, the July–August and September–October 1922 issues. The journal, based in CHICAGO, Illinois, was edited by Katherine Williams Irvin.

Little Heads: A One-Act Play of Negro Life Alvira Hazzard (1929)

A one-act play by ALVIRA HAZZARD that focuses on social racism and white expectations, and black performance.

The play features five characters: Mrs. Lee and her children, the 12-year-old twins Bee and Joe, and Frances, and a family friend named Edna. Mrs. Lee maintains a tranquil and enabling home environment for her children. In addition, she has a college-aged son named Bob who attends HOWARD UNIVERSITY. Mrs. Lee encourages her children to think of each other as smart and capable individuals who should not regard their race as an impediment to their professional goals.

Mrs. Lee, who may be a widow, is juggling family finances that include endowment policies based on interest derived from the family income. Frances, excited about the prospect of a social gathering, requests an advance on the fund so that she can dress well for the elite social gathering. Her twin siblings intercept the invitation to the gathering at Oak Manor, the school that Frances attends. They open the letter and to their dismay discover that Frances is invited but not as a guest. Her white schoolmate Dolores Page hopes that Frances will "help entertain" and "dress like—well, you know—sort of old fashioned, and sing some of those delightful spirituals." The children destroy the invitation and hope that they will be able to protect their sister from such a dreadful prospect.

Hazzard's play is an incisive critique of assimilation and its limits.

"Little Virgin, The" Langston Hughes (1927)

A vivid short story by LANGSTON HUGHES. Published in the December 1927 issue of THE MESSENGER, the story was inspired by Hughes's own adventures in the early 1920s as a shipmate aboard the SS *Malone,* a cargo ship that was bound for ports in Senegal, Guinea, Sierra Leone, and other African countries.

"The Little Virgin" is a young man aboard the *West Llana,* a ship with a multiracial crew that is bound for AFRICA. The protagonist, who is never identified by name, is nicknamed "The Little Virgin" because of his lack of sexual experience. He suffers mightily at the hands of the crew and becomes "the daily butt of sailors' jibes and vulgar jokes . . . everything the youngster did or said by day became a subject for ribald wit and ridicule on the after-hatch." The tormented sailor eventually finds a friend known as Mike from Newark. Unfortunately, however, shortly after the ship docks in Senegal, the two men are involved in a violent bar fight. In the melee that prompts the Little Virgin to lapse into heaving crying fits and melancholy, "a black woman spring[s] at Mike, her fingers like claws, and in her turn fall[s] backwards, struck in the face, among the tables and the feet of the sailors." The Little Virgin has attempted to come to the aid of the woman whom Mike from Newark has physically attacked. The story closes as the Little Virgin succumbs to delirium and is taken onshore in Calabar for medical treatment. He has been uttering the words, "Oughtn't to hit a woman . . . No, no, no . . ." and continues to do so even as he is removed from the ship.

Hughes's short story is rich for its caricatures of life aboard ship. It also is powerful for its suggestion that a young white man may be overcome by the specter of African womanhood and violent white male disregard for women of color.

Bibliography
Berry, Faith, ed. *Langston Hughes: Before and Beyond Harlem.* Westport, Conn.: Lawrence Hill & Company, 1983.

Liveright, Horace Brisbin (1886–1933)

A publisher, theater producer, and inventor who established himself in NEW YORK CITY during the Harlem Renaissance. He was born in Osceola Mills, Pennsylvania, to Henry and Henrietta Fleisher Liveright. An enterprising young man, he was 17 years old when he was on the verge of staging his first show, *John Smith,* a comic opera, in New York. He married Lucile Elas, the daughter of an International Paper Company executive, in 1911 and the couple had two children, Herman and Lucy, before they divorced in 1928. In 1931 Liveright remarried. His marriage to Elise Bartlett Porter, a divorced actress, ended quickly. The two were divorced in 1932.

Liveright's career in publishing began in 1917 when he became partners with ALBERT BONI. The two men, who met while working in the Alfred Wallerstein advertising agency, hoped to start their business by reprinting modern classics. Their company, BONI & LIVERIGHT, became known first for the Modern Library series. This collection included reprints of works by Oscar Wilde, August Strindberg, Guy de Maupassant, and Fyodor Dostoyevsky.

Boni's involvement ended shortly after the firm was established, but Liveright maintained the business and began to focus on American writers and the active literary community in New York City. Liveright also enjoyed publication successes with works by THEODORE DREISER, William Faulkner, Ernest Hemingway, and EUGENE O'NEILL. In 1923, shortly after Liveright attended the historic CIVIC CLUB dinner sponsored by CHARLES S. JOHNSON and *OPPORTUNITY,* the firm published *Cane,* the celebrated compilation of prose and poetry by JEAN TOOMER. Other prominent Harlem Renaissance publications were *PLUM BUN* (1929) by JESSIE FAUSET, the celebrated anthology *THE NEW NEGRO* (1925) edited by ALAIN LOCKE, and *TROPIC DEATH* (1926) by ERIC WALROND.

The demise of Boni & Liveright was quite dramatic. Liveright sold the popular and financially stable Modern Library division in 1925 but neglected to discuss his plans with company employees. Their efforts to halt the deal were thwarted when an outraged husband stormed the office. He wanted to kill Liveright, who was having an affair with his wife, and by the time the situation was defused, the paperwork for the sale had been processed. The new owner, Bennett Cerf, renamed the Modern Library division and called it Random House. During the early 1930s Liveright struggled to regain financial stability. Expenses and debts incurred by his divorces ruined him, and he filed for bankruptcy in 1931.

Liveright died from complications of pneumonia and emphysema in New York City in September 1933. He was 46 years old.

Bibliography

Dardis, Tom. *Firebrand: The Life of Horace Liveright.* New York: Random House, 1995.

Gilmer, Walker. *Horace Liveright, Publisher of the Twenties.* New York: D. Lewis, 1970.

Livingston, Myrtle Athleen Smith
(1902–1973)

A graduate of HOWARD UNIVERSITY and a professor at LINCOLN UNIVERSITY, Livingston emerged briefly as an aspiring playwright during the Harlem Renaissance.

The daughter of Samuel and Lula Hall Smith, Myrtle Livingston was born in Holly Grove, Arkansas. Following schooling in Denver, Colorado, Smith pursued pharmaceutical studies at Howard University and, while there, also joined the medical sorority Rho Psi Phi. After two years in WASHINGTON, D.C., she enrolled in the Colorado Teachers College in Greeley, Colorado. Although she did not graduate until 1926, she received a teacher's certificate and began teaching in Denver. Smith married William McKinley Livingston, a physician, in June 1924.

In 1925, Livingston won third place and a ten-dollar prize in the AMY SPINGARN literary competition for her play FOR UNBORN CHILDREN. The work, which was published in the July 1926 issue of THE CRISIS, revolves around a heart-wrenching interracial love affair and concludes as the protagonist faces a mob that is determined to lynch him. The play was not Livingston's work. She saw her works performed by sororities and fraternities. Details about these performances and texts, however, are limited.

Livingston retired to Hawaii, where she lived with her sister Ella, also a retired teacher. Livingston died in July 1973.

Locke, Alain (Arthur Le Roy Locke, Alain Leroy Locke) (1886–1954)

One of America's foremost scholars and an influential professor and writer whose passion for literary excellence and intellectual debate enriched the Harlem Renaissance. Proclaimed as the "dean" of the Harlem Renaissance, he exerted a considerable amount of influence over the movement, and his overtures, endorsements, support, and criticisms during the period affected both positively and negatively the careers of many individuals.

Born Arthur Locke, he was the son of schoolteachers. His father was Pliney Ishmael Locke, a mathematics instructor and Philadelphia court clerk. His mother, Mary Hawkins Locke, was a schoolteacher who was employed in the segregated

A 1926 portrait of Alain Locke with a dedication to James Weldon Johnson "in esteem and cordial regard" *(Yale Collection of American Literature, Beinecke Rare Book and Manuscript Library)*

Camden, New Jersey, schools. His paternal grandfather, Ishmael Locke, studied at Cambridge University and was a teacher and the headmaster of the Institute for Colored Youth in PHILADELPHIA. Alain Locke's father graduated from the Institute in 1867, before working as a teacher of freedmen in North Carolina and then obtaining a law degree from HOWARD UNIVERSITY Law School.

Locke was raised in Philadelphia and attended schools there and in New York City. Following his father's death in 1892, Locke began attending the newly established Ethical Culture School in New York City. Locke became ill from rheumatic fever and relocated to Philadelphia. He completed his high school education there at the Central High School.

Locke's college career began at the Philadelphia School of Pedagogy. He entered HARVARD UNIVERSITY as a transfer student and was elected to PHI BETA KAPPA during his second year. He graduated magna cum laude in 1907. He was one of the school's most accomplished students, won an impressive number of school awards, and even found time to be a coxswain for one of the school's crew teams. He immediately traveled to Oxford University in England as the first African American to win a RHODES SCHOLARSHIP. Despite his impressive intellectual record, Locke was rejected by several Oxford colleges on the basis of his race. He persevered and finally gained admission to Hertford College. There, he completed three years of study in Greek, Latin, literature, and philosophy and earned a B.Litt. degree. He then traveled to Europe, where he pursued graduate studies in philosophy and in English at the University of Berlin and in Vienna and Paris. In 1918 he became the first African American to earn a Ph.D. in philosophy at Harvard University.

Following his studies abroad, Locke returned to the United States. He joined the faculty of Howard University in WASHINGTON, D.C., in 1912 and began a 40-year career at the historic institution that was founded in 1866. His father had been a member of the university's first graduating law school class. Locke became chair of the Philosophy Department at the school in 1918, a position he held until his retirement. At Howard, he was instrumental in the founding of STYLUS, the school's literary magazine, and collaborated with T. MONT-GOMERY GREGORY in the acclaimed HOWARD UNIVERSITY PLAYERS, one of the nation's most highly respected college drama troupes. Locke also established the first Phi Beta Kappa chapter ever founded at a historically black institution of higher learning.

Locke was one of several prominent homosexual Harlem Renaissance figures. Scholar Thomas Wirth characterizes Locke as a "self-identified gay man" and notes that Locke made documented efforts to maintain a coterie that included other gay and bisexual artists, such as RICHMOND BARTHÉ, CLAUDE MCKAY, and RICHARD BRUCE NUGENT. Locke's attraction and deliberate overtures to Langston Hughes have been well documented. While Hughes, an emerging poet at the time, welcomed the opportunity to talk with Locke, he was not willing to indulge Locke's interest. Hughes, who was well known for maintaining his privacy, finally met Locke while abroad. It remains unclear whether or not the men had a romantic encounter before Locke left Hughes to fend for himself and negotiate his return to America when his passport was stolen. Locke was forthright in his overtures to Nugent, who recalled that "Locke offered me his body" and noted that he was "traumatized" and "disappointed" by the moment when "A professor of philosophy and a person old enough to be your father . . . lie[s] on a bed in their shorts and say[s], 'Do anything you want'" (Wirth, 24). The two men overcame the awkward encounter, and Locke became one of Nugent's professional mentors. Later, he even attempted to play the role of matchmaker when he tried to facilitate an introduction and potential relationship between Nugent and Richmond Barthé (Wirth, 25).

Locke's academic career also included short appointments to schools in Haiti, visiting appointments to the University of Wisconsin at Madison, City College of New York, and the New School for Social Research in New York City. He also forged important intellectual ties in the larger community of African-American scholars and was a member of the AMERICAN NEGRO ACADEMY and the Negro Society for Historical Research. The earliest of Locke's publications demonstrated his interest in history, philosophy, and literature. His scholarly works included literary studies such as *The Negro in American Literature* (1929), sociocultural studies such as *Americans All, Immigrants All* (1939), and historical works such as *Frederick Douglass: A Biography of Anti-Slavery* (1935).

Locke's major contributions to the Harlem Renaissance included the much-heralded collection of works by African Americans and about African-American life and culture. The 1925 publication of THE NEW NEGRO: AN INTERPRETATION signaled a new and deliberate stage in African-American studies and scholarship. This anthology grew out of his efforts to edit a special volume of SURVEY GRAPHIC on African-American issues. The opportunity to produce the volume came on the night of the famed 1924 celebration that *Opportunity* editor CHARLES S. JOHNSON hosted at the CIVIC CLUB in New York City in honor of JESSIE FAUSET and the publication of her first novel. On that evening, which also included Johnson's provocative pronouncement that Locke was the "virtual dean of the movement" (Rampersad, 96), Locke had the opportunity to talk at length with PAUL GREEN, founder of *Survey Graphic*. The Harlem issue of *Survey Graphic*, entitled HARLEM: MECCA OF THE NEW NEGRO, quickly led to the publication of Locke's anthology. The book included creative works by ANGELINA GRIMKÉ, LANGSTON HUGHES, ZORA NEALE HURSTON, Claude McKay, and ANNE SPENCER, artwork by WINOLD REISS and Richmond Barthé, and scholarly prose essays by Locke, MELVILLE HERSKOVITS, JAMES WELDON JOHNSON, ALBERT BARNES, WILFRED A. DOMINGO, KELLY MILLER, ARTHUR SCHOMBURG, and others. Published by ALBERT and CHARLES BONI, the volume was enthusiastically received. Promotion materials highlighted endorsements by individuals such as H. L. MENCKEN, who proclaimed that the book, priced at $5, was "a phenomenon of immense significance."

It was Locke who most notably advanced the notion of the New Negro, a figure whose intellectual, political, and social confidence heralded a new era in race consciousness, activism, and leadership. In his introduction to the 1925 anthology, he outlined the bold agendas of the collection. "This volume aims to document the New Negro culturally and socially," he wrote, "to register the transformations of the inner and outer life of the Negro in America that have so significantly taken place in the last few years." The work was meant to counteract the "voluminous literature on the Negro" that obscured the actual individual and resulted in familiarity with "the Negro problem rather than the Negro." Locke assured readers that movements such as the Harlem Renaissance signaled "a fresh spiritual and cultural focusing" and provided evidence of "a renewed race-spirit that consciously and proudly sets itself apart." His perspectives on African-American arts were in keeping with the TALENTED TENTH ideals that W. E. B. DUBOIS articulated and strove to realize during the period. As Ernest Mason notes, Locke was forthright about his desire to see African Americans advance purposefully in all areas of public life. "Both as an American and as a Negro," he wrote in the essay entitled "The High Cost of Prejudice" that appeared in the December 1927 issue of *Forum*, "I would much rather see the black masses going gradually forward under the leadership of a recognized and representative and responsible elite than see a group of malcontents later hurl these masses at society in doubtful but desperate strife" (Mason, 315).

Locke was more tolerant than his fellow Harvard graduate DuBois when it came to evaluating the moral responsibilities of Harlem Renaissance writers. He maintained a high level of reserve, though, and did not hesitate to comment on the explicit and often daring publications of writers like Wallace Thurman, Bruce Nugent, and others. According to Thomas Wirth, Locke "did not view art as a means of moral instruction, and he strongly opposed the conflation of art with propaganda. He valued, above all, authenticity of expression" and "was interested in establishing artistic traditions in which the sensibilities and life experiences that African Americans shared could be fully and freely expressed" (Wirth, 48). His evaluations reflected the inherent tensions of his perspectives, however, since he held writers of color to high and sometimes inflexible standards. He was particularly incensed by Claude McKay's critique of him as a self-important and unqualified evaluator of artistic enterprise and in response lambasted the West Indian writer's 1937 autobiography, *A Long Way from Home*. In "Spiritual Truant," his review published in the fall 1937 issue of *New Challenge*, Locke declared that McKay's "lack of common loyalty" to the race could not be disguised by "a fascinating style and the naivest egotism" and that McKay's re- jection of "all possible loyalties amounts to a self- imposed apostasy" (Cooper, 320). In sharp contrast to his assessments of Claude McKay were his opin- ions about COUNTEE CULLEN. According to Cullen biographer Blanche Ferguson, Locke regarded the young New Yorker as a writer who "blended the simple with the sophisticated so originally as almost to put the vineyards themselves into his crystal gob- lets" (Ferguson, 54).

When Cullen and his father, the Reverend Frederick Cullen of the SALEM METHODIST EPIS- COPAL CHURCH in Harlem, sailed to Europe in 1926 as they began an extensive voyage that would ultimately take them to the Middle East, they did so in the company of Locke, as well as with Dorothy Peterson and ARTHUR HUFF FAUSET. Zora Neale Hurston was outspoken in her evalua- tions of Locke and tended to take a dim view of the man whom she characterized in a 1938 letter to James Weldon Johnson as a "malicious litt[l]e snot that thinks he ought to be the leading Negro because of his degrees." Hurston, who was an- noyed by Locke's recent criticism in Opportunity of her novel THEIR EYES WERE WATCHING GOD (1937), suggested that Locke "lends out his pa- tronage and takes in ideas he soon passes off as his own. And God help you," she continued, "if you get on without letting him 'represent' you!" (Ka- plan, 413). Hurston's interactions with Locke were complicated by the fact that he had close ties to CHARLOTTE OSGOOD MASON, her white patron. After consultation with Mason, Locke would act as a go-between and deliver messages and advice to the dynamic and forthright anthropologist and writer. Hurston biographer Valerie Boyd notes that while Hurston would not "have deigned to explain herself so thoroughly to the meddling Locke" as she did following the dismal response to her musi- cal production entitled Great Day, "she felt com- pelled to give him the respect his position demanded" because "he claimed to be speaking with her on [Mason's] behalf" (Boyd, 234).

Hurston's complicated relationship with Locke was part of a larger tension that he had with women intellectuals and students. At Howard University, for instance, he was, according to Boyd, "notorious . . . for warning female students on the first day of class that they would likely receive C's,

regardless of their ability" (Boyd, 91). Jessie Fauset, who suffered an awful snub from Charles Johnson at the Civic Club party that was advertised as a celebration of her first novel but which became a fête of Locke and other men of the period instead, believed that his "failure as a writer" had affected him deeply and was responsible for the "utmost ar- rogance and obsequiousness to whites" that so in- formed his literary criticism (Boyd, 309).

Locke did not publish any primary creative works of his own, but he was instrumental in pub- lishing the works of promising artists. He edited FOUR NEGRO POETS in 1927, a collection of works by Countee Cullen, Langston Hughes, Claude McKay, and JEAN TOOMER. Also in 1927, he col- laborated with T. Montgomery Gregory, his dy- namic Howard University colleague, on PLAYS OF NEGRO LIFE: A SOURCEBOOK OF NATIVE AMERI- CAN DRAMA. Harper published the compilation that included illustrations by AARON DOUGLAS. Through his affiliation with the Associates in Negro Folk Education, an organization in which he served as secretary and editor, Locke also published The Negro and His Music (1936), Negro Art: Past and Present (1936), and The Negro in Art: A Picto- rial Record of the Negro Artist and of the Negro Theme in Art (1940). He also published widely in American periodicals including THE CRISIS, HARLEM: A FORUM OF NEGRO LIFE, OPPORTU- NITY, and Theatre Arts.

Like Zora Neale Hurston and Langston Hughes, Locke received support for his work from the philanthropist Charlotte Osgood Mason. Funds from Mason enabled him to travel and to begin collecting works by African Americans and peoples of African descent. He amassed an im- pressive collection of African art and organized many exhibitions to showcase the diversity of tal- ent and cultures. In 1925, at an impressive exhibit installed by the Harlem Art Committee at the YWCA on West 138th Street, Locke continued to protest racial essentialism. Locke addressed the audience gathered to see works by 64 African- American artists including the painter HENRY OS- SAWA TANNER and noted that "no art grows in a cultural vacuum" and insisted that "Negro art does not restrict the Negro artist to the use of the racial theme in art exclusively" (NYT, 18 March 1935, 24).

Locke was deeply committed to adult education and used his membership in the Associates in Negro Folk Education to strengthen educational offerings to adult learners. He contributed two detailed monographs to the *Bronze Book* series, a collection of works by highly regarded African-American intellectuals. In 1934 he was elected to the governing board of the American Association for Adult Education and in 1945 became the first African-American president of the organization.

Alain Locke, who was living at 12 Grove Street in New York City, died at age 67 in June 1954. He had no immediate surviving family members. His last book, *The Negro in American Culture* appeared in 1956, completed by his colleague and friend Margaret Just Butcher. In 1935, almost 20 years before his death, Locke described himself as a "philosophical mid-wife to a generation of younger Negro poets, writers, and artists." He was eulogized as "one of the leading interpreters of the cultural achievements of the Negro, and as one of the wisest analysts of his race and its relations with other races" (*NYT,* 10 June 1954, 31).

Shortly after his death, New York University arranged a series of lectures in honor of Locke's legacy and influence. Attendees at the seminars, which were offered under the general heading of "Alain Locke: Philosophy, Art and Human Relations," were able to "consider Dr. Locke's position in Negro literature in this country, his studies in African sculpture and his contributions in the field of philosophy" (*NYT,* 29 October 1955). He continues to be honored today, most recently by the Friends of African and African American Art who established the Alain Locke Awards in 1992. The annual prizes are given to individuals who emulate Locke's example and have "demonstrated dedication to the promotion and understanding of African American artistic culture" (*Michigan Citizen,* B1). Winners have included sculptor and artist Elizabeth Catlett, artists Dave Driskell and Sam Gilliam, and musician James Carter.

Bibliography

Alain Locke Letters, Moorland-Spingarn Collection, Howard University.
"Dr. Alain Locke, Teacher, Author: Howard University Professor 36 Years Dies—Noted for Race and Culture Writings." *New York Times,* 10 June 1954, 31.
"Locke Legacy." *Michigan Citizen,* 21 February 2004, B1.
"Locke Seminars at N.Y.U." *New York Times,* 29 October 1955, 8.
Boyd, Valerie. *Wrapped in Rainbows: The Life of Zora Neale Hurston.* New York: Scribner, 2003.
Cooper, Wayne. *Claude McKay: Rebel Sojourner in the Harlem Renaissance.* New York: Schocken Books, 1987.
Ferguson, Blanche. *Countee Cullen and the Negro Renaissance.* New York: Dodd, Mead, 1966.
Harris, Leonard, ed. *The Philosophy of Alain Locke: Harlem Renaissance and Beyond.* Philadelphia: Temple University Press, 1989.
Kaplan, Carla. *Zora Neale Hurston: A Life in Letters.* New York: Doubleday, 2002.
Linnemann, Russell, ed. *Alain Locke: Reflections on a Modern Renaissance Man.* Baton Rouge, Louisiana State University Press, 1982.
Locke, Alain LeRoy, ed. *The New Negro: An Interpretation.* New York, 1925.
Mason, Ernest D. "Alain Locke." *Dictionary of Literary Biography.* Vol. 51: *Afro-American Writers from the Harlem Renaissance to 1940,* edited by Trudier Harris. Detroit: Gale Research Inc., 1987. 313–321.
Rampersad, Arnold. *The Life of Langston Hughes: I, Too, Sing America.* Vol. 1, *1902–1941.* New York: Oxford University Press, 1986.
Washington, Johnny. *Alain Locke and Philosophy: A Quest for Cultural Pluralism.* Westport, Conn.: Greenwood Press, 1986.
Wirth, Thomas. *Gay Rebel of the Harlem Renaissance: Selections from the Work of Richard Bruce Nugent.* Durham, N.C.: Duke University Press, 2002.

Logan, Rayford (1897–1982)

A leading American historian who came of age professionally during the Harlem Renaissance. Logan worked alongside scholars whose pioneering studies of African-American life enriched the cultural and intellectual dimensions of the Harlem Renaissance.

Rayford Whittingham Logan was born in WASHINGTON, D.C., to Arthur Logan, a butler in the home of Connecticut senator Frederic Walcott, and Martha Whittingham Logan. He was the valedictorian of his class at the prestigious M STREET HIGH SCHOOL and graduated PHI BETA KAPPA from Williams College in 1917.

Logan enlisted in the U.S. Army during World War I. He served with the 372nd Infantry and achieved the rank of lieutenant before his discharge. His distaste for institutional racism in America prompted him to live in France for four years after the war ended. He collaborated with W. E. B. DuBois on plans for the successful Pan-African Congress meetings. Logan returned to the United States in 1924. After teaching at Virginia Union University and at ATLANTA UNIVERSITY, he became the assistant to renowned historian CARTER G. WOODSON. Logan worked with Woodson at the ASSOCIATION FOR THE STUDY OF NEGRO LIFE AND HISTORY. He later was instrumental in the push to train African-American pilots that culminated in the training programs that produced the Tuskegee Airmen.

Logan married Ruth Robinson, a Richmond, Virginia, native, talented soprano, and Howard University graduate, in 1927. The couple met at Virginia Union University, where she was working as a choir director. She passed away in 1966.

Logan published the majority of his works after the close of the Harlem Renaissance. This included his dissertation and landmark study, *The Diplomatic Relations of the United States with Haiti, 1776–1891* (1941), *The Negro and the Post-War World* (1945), and *The Negro in American Life and Thought: The Nadir 1877–1901* (1954). His greatest contribution to African-American history was completed just before his death. The *Dictionary of American Negro Biography* (1982), completed with coeditor Michael Winston, is an impressive compilation of biographies and rich social histories that illuminate the African-American history of enterprise and excellence.

Logan, a member of Alpha Phi Alpha, was honored in 1980 when the NATIONAL ASSOCIATION FOR THE ADVANCEMENT OF COLORED PEOPLE conferred upon him the SPINGARN MEDAL. An outspoken critic of segregation and black nationalism, Logan dedicated his life to achieving racial equality and civil rights for people of color.

Bibliography

Janken, Kenneth Robert. *Rayford W. Logan and the Dilemma of the African-American Intellectual.* Amherst: University of Massachusetts Press, 1993.

Logan, Rayford. *Howard University: The First Hundred Years, 1867–1967.* New York: New York University Press, 1969.

———. *The Attitude of the Southern White Press Toward Negro Suffrage, 1932–1940.* Washington, D.C.: The Foundation Publishers, 1940.

———. *The Betrayal of the Negro, from Rutherford B. Hayes to Woodrow Wilson.* New York: Collier Books, 1965.

Rayford Logan Papers, Moorland-Spingarn Research Center, Howard University; Manuscript Division, Library of Congress.

Sterling, Phillip, and Rayford Logan, eds. *Four Took Freedom: The Lives of Harriet Tubman, Frederick Douglass, Robert Smalls, and Blanche K. Bruce.* Garden City, N.Y.: Doubleday, 1967.

Loggins, Vernon (1893–1968)

A COLUMBIA UNIVERSITY professor who published one of the first serious analyses of early African-American literature.

Born in Hempstead, Texas, Loggins graduated from the University of Texas in 1914. He pursued graduate work at the UNIVERSITY OF CHICAGO and at Columbia University. He earned his master's degree in 1917 and then joined the U.S. Army. He was stationed in FRANCE during World War I. Loggins completed his Ph.D. at Columbia in 1931.

Loggins published *The Negro Author: His Development in America to 1900* in 1931. One of his best resources for the dissertation, which he then published, was the Schomburg Collection. This substantial set of African-American archival materials was housed in the 135th Street Branch of the NEW YORK PUBLIC LIBRARY.

Bibliography

Loggins, Vernon. *The Negro Author: His Development in America to 1900.* New York: Columbia University Press, 1931.

Lonesome Road: Six Plays for the Negro Theatre Paul Green (1926)

A collection of plays by PAUL GREEN, a white professor at the University of North Carolina at Chapel Hill and prolific playwright known for his works on African-American subjects.

Published in 1926, *Lonesome Road* included his well-known folk drama IN ABRAHAM'S BOSOM and the plays *White Dresses, The Hot Iron, The Prayer-Meeting, The End of the Row,* and *Your Fiery Furnace.* In the author's note that prefaced the work, Green explained his motivation to write and to collect the plays in the volume. He wrote specifically of African Americans in North Carolina, individuals whom he described as "the prey of his own superstition, suspicions and practices, beaten and forlorn before God Almighty himself." Green admitted that the plays represented "a first effort . . . to say something of what these people more recently have suffered and thought and done" especially now that "it seems apparent . . . that such things are worthy of record."

The anthology was published just one year before Green won the PULITZER PRIZE in drama, an award based on his accomplishments and the play *In Abraham's Bosom,* which the PROVINCE-TOWN PLAYERS had produced and notable NEW YORK TIMES drama critic J. Brooks Atkinson had praised.

Bibliography

Clark, Barrett. *Paul Green.* New York: Robert M. McBride & Company, 1928.

Green, Paul. *Lonesome Road: Six Plays for the Negro Theatre.* New York: R. M. McBride & Company, 1926.

Kenny, Vincent. *Paul Green.* New York: Twayne Publishers, 1971.

Roper, John. *Paul Green, Playwright of the Real South.* Athens: University of Georgia Press, 2003.

Long Way from Home, A Claude McKay (1937)

The autobiography of CLAUDE MCKAY. The volume was published in 1937 by Lee Furman, president of the MACAULAY PUBLISHING COMPANY.

Many of McKay's contemporaries read the work, and McKay was pleased to receive compliments on an absorbing and entertaining life story. According to McKay biographer Wayne Cooper, Edwin Embree praised the "cozy, companiable style" of the work, and JOEL SPINGARN thanked the poet-novelist for providing him with "real enjoyment" (Cooper, 319, 315).

There were others, however, who were disturbed by McKay's portraits of their personalities and careers. MAX EASTMAN, editor of the LIBERATOR, the journal for which McKay wrote, protested his former colleague's accounts of his interactions with the Communist Party. Others, such as SYLVIA PANKHURST and WALTER WHITE, protested McKay's accounts of their characters and certain professional encounters.

A Long Way from Home gave McKay the opportunity to represent his intellectual and political development. He divided his life story into six sections and offered an earnest, though at times misleading, chronicle of his professional life. The work prompted criticisms from figures such as ALAIN LOCKE, who criticized McKay for his political inconstancy. Overall, however, McKay's autobiography is powerful for its persuasive call for African-American unity and endorsement of collective resistance to racism and oppression.

Bibliography

Cooper, Wayne. *Claude McKay: Rebel Sojourner in the Harlem Renaissance.* New York: Schocken Books, 1987.

McKay, Claude. *A Long Way from Home.* 1937, reprint, New York: Harcourt, Brace & World, 1970.

Looking Glass, The

A HARLEM-based literary magazine. In 1925 writer WALLACE THURMAN, who recently had relocated to NEW YORK CITY, worked as a reporter and editor of the journal. His mentor THEOPHILUS LEWIS, the noted drama critic, was the publisher. Thurman's experience at *The Looking Glass* and his own enterprising efforts to establish OUTLET, a West Coast literary magazine, marked the beginning of his eventful life in magazine publishing. In later years, Thurman, who became managing editor of THE MESSENGER a year after he joined *The Looking Glass,* collaborated with figures such as ZORA NEALE HURSTON and LANGSTON HUGHES on innovative but short-lived literary journals. These publications included FIRE!! (1926) and HARLEM: A FORUM OF NEGRO LIFE (1928).

Bibliography

Johnson, Abby Arthur, and Ronald Maberry Johnson. *Propaganda & Aesthetics: The Literary Politics of*

African American Magazines in the Twentieth Century. Amherst: University of Massachusetts, 1979.

van Notten, Eleonore. *Wallace Thurman's Harlem Renaissance.* Amsterdam: Rodopi, 1994.

Lopez, Leon

One of the many pseudonyms that the writer CLAUDE MCKAY used during his career. He used this name and several others while working in London at the journal WORKER'S DREADNOUGHT.

Lost Zoo (A Rhyme for the Young, but Not Too Young), The Countee Cullen (1940)

A collection of poems by COUNTEE CULLEN, based on the animals that refused to take refuge on Noah's ark. The volume was one of two books of poetry that Cullen published for children. The verses were lively and reflected Cullen's ability to craft deft and colorful tales. He noted that the work was produced in partnership with Christopher Cat, his feline coauthor.

The work appeared in 1940, the same year in which Cullen married Ida Mae Roberson. It was one of the last works Cullen published before his death in 1946.

Louis, Joe (1914–1981)

The talented boxer who became the world heavyweight champion in 1937. Louis's victory, which coincided with the publication of ZORA NEALE HURSTON's *THEIR EYES WERE WATCHING GOD,* was cherished by many as a symbolic victory by African Americans over entrenched oppression and prejudice.

Louis, the son of an Alabama sharecropper, came of age as a boxer during the Harlem Renaissance. His major victories, against Jim Braddock, Max Schmelling, and Rocky Marciano, were legendary. Louis gained the title of world heavyweight champion in 1937 and defended it successfully for 11 years.

Bibliography

Hietala, Thomas. *The Fight of the Century: Jack Johnson, Joe Louis, and the Struggle for Racial Equality.* Armonk, N.Y.: M. E. Sharpe, 2002.

Louis, Joe, Edna Rust, and Art Rust, Jr. *Joe Louis: My Life.* New York: Harcourt Brace Jovanovich, 1978.

Louisiana J. Augustus Smith (1933)

A play by J. Augustus Smith that the Negro Theatre Guild performed in 1933. The play chronicled the efforts of a minister determined to see Christianity overcome voodoo beliefs.

The play opened at the 48th Street Theatre in late February 1933. It closed after eight performances. The 17-member cast included Smith as well as Laura Bowman, a popular actress who worked with Oscar Micheaux and WILLIS RICHARDSON, and the actresses Carrie Huff and Edna Barr.

The Negro Theatre Guild also produced *How Come, Lawd?,* a play written by Donald Heywood, in September 1937. Smith continued his collaborations with Harlem Renaissance writers and actors. In 1936 he was codirector of *CONJUR-MAN DIES,* a play by RUDOLPH FISHER. The project also involved the Negro Theatre Unit of the Federal Theater Project of the Works Progress Administration. The play opened at the Lafayette Theatre on Broadway and ran for some 24 performances.

Love, Rose Leary (1898–1969)

A first-grade teacher who published her first volume of children's literature in the late 1930s. She published numerous poems and short stories for children during her 39-year career as a teacher.

Love, a North Carolina native, shared a rich ancestry with the poet Langston Hughes. Love was the niece of abolitionist Lewis Sheridan Leary, whose widowed wife married Charles Langston and later became the grandmother of LANGSTON HUGHES. Leary, a skilled harness maker, was 24 when he joined the men who fought with abolitionist John Brown at Harper's Ferry. Leary was killed, and his wife, Rose, cherished the bloodstained shawl that one of his comrades returned to her. Rose eventually married Charles Langston, and their daughter Carrie was the mother of Langston Hughes.

Love attended Hampton Institute and COLUMBIA UNIVERSITY; she graduated from Barber Scotia Seminary and the Johnson C. Smith

University. With her husband George Love, she lived in Jakarta, Indonesia, for a year. While he worked as a technical adviser, she taught second grade at the International School in the capital.

Her first book, NEBRASKA AND HIS GRANNY, appeared in 1936. Published by the TUSKEGEE INSTITUTE Press, the work included illustrations by Preston Haygood. The volume, which followed the antics of a little boy named Nebraska and depicted his strong relationship with his grandmother, was part of a substantial canon of literature by and for children of color. Love's efforts contributed to the better-documented efforts of writers such as EFFIE LEE NEWSOME and JESSIE FAUSET, who edited THE BROWNIES' BOOK during her tenure with THE CRISIS, the official journal of the NATIONAL ASSOCIATION FOR THE ADVANCEMENT OF COLORED PEOPLE.

Love's memoir, Plum Thickets and Field Daisies, was published in 1997 by the Public Library of Charlotte and Mecklenburg County. The manuscript was donated by Love's friend Elizabeth S. Randolph and was praised for its detailed accounts of life in early 20th-century North Carolina.

Bibliography

Love, Rose Leary. A Collection of Folklore for Children in Elementary School and at Home. New York: Vantage Press, 1964.

———. Nebraska and His Granny. 1936, reprint, Tuskegee, Ala.: Tuskegee Institute Press, 1966.

Rose Leary Love Papers, Public Library of Charlotte and Mecklenburg County.

Lovinggood, Penman (1895–unknown)

A tenor, teacher, composer, and writer who, in 1921, published the first modern history of African-American music. A native of Austin, Texas, Lovinggood was the son of Reuben Lovinggood, first president of Samuel Houston College, an institution organized first as the Samuel Houston College and then the West Texas Conference School. The school, for African Americans, was the second college that the Freedman's Aid Society established in Texas. With donations from Samuel Houston and a gift of some 500 books from H. S. White, a Michigan Methodist, the school was eventually opened. Reuben Lovinggood was president from 1903 through 1917. His son Penman studied here before traveling north to New York. The institution merged with Tillotson College in 1952, and the historically black college is known now as Houston-Tillotson College.

Lovinggood established himself in NEW YORK CITY and worked as a teacher, soloist, and music reporter. Before his 1925 debut at Town Hall in New York City, Lovinggood also studied with J. Rosamond Johnson, brother of JAMES WELDON JOHNSON. His later collaborations included membership in one of Johnson's quartets and the W. C. HANDY orchestra.

In 1936 the American Negro Opera Association produced Menelek, Lovinggood's opera. He was one of several accomplished musicians to win a Wanamaker Prize, an award established by Rodman Wanamaker, a department store magnate and philanthropist.

Bibliography

Lovinggood, Penman. Famous Modern Negro Musicians. Brooklyn: Press Forum Company, 1921; reprint, New York: Da Capo Press, 1978.

Lulu Belle Charles MacArthur and Edward Sheldon (1926)

A play by Charles MacArthur and Edward Sheldon that revolved around the romantic machinations of Lulu Belle, a prostitute in HARLEM.

The play opened at the Belasco Theatre on BROADWAY in February 1926. The interracial cast that performed in nearly 500 performances included Evelyn Preer, veteran of WILLIS RICHARDSON plays; John Harrington; Edna Thomas, who in 1949 appeared in the Broadway debut of Tennessee Williams's A Streetcar Named Desire; and Elizabeth Williams, who appeared in HARLEM, the 1929 play by WALLACE THURMAN and WILLIAM JOURDAN RAPP.

lynching

The term used to describe lawless, violent, and often public murders of individuals. A form of vicious mob violence, lynching often targeted men and women of color, as well as whites and individuals whose ethnic or religious identities also provoked prejudice. Historian RAYFORD LOGAN characterized the brutal era of violence that flourished after Reconstruction as the American Dark Ages. Other scholars, such as Robert Gibson, regard this bloody era, which also included race riots and strengthened racist legislation and segregation, as the Black Holocaust.

Records of lynchings in America reveal the widespread nature of the violence. Between 1882 and 1968, murders occurred throughout the South, as far north as Maine, and as far west as California. According to the statistics collected by the TUSKEGEE INSTITUTE, between 1882 and 1968, there were nearly 4,800 lynchings in America. This tally included nearly 1,300 murders of whites and just under 3,500 murders of African Americans. The states in which the most lynchings occurred were primarily southern. Between 1882 and 1968, the Institute documented 581 in Mississippi, 531 in Georgia, 493 in Texas, 391 in Louisiana, 347 in Alabama, 284 in Arkansas, 282 in Florida, 251 in Tennessee, 205 in Kentucky, 160 in South Carolina, 122 in Missouri, and 100 in Virginia. Lynchings peaked in 1892, when some 230 individuals, 161 African Americans and 69 whites, were murdered. Between 1910 and 1919 there were 62 lynchings, and the racial violence continued through the Harlem Renaissance years of the 1920s, 1930s, and 1940s.

Lynching, often linked to the KU KLUX KLAN, was motivated by bloodthirsty mobs and used to maintain racial oppression. Victims of lynching included pregnant women such as Mary Turner of Georgia, who wanted to bring her husband's lynchers to justice, innocent men targeted by mobs bent on avenging social slights or deaths of white men, families of successful businessmen, and activists. Charges of rape and assault were among the most popular charges used to spur lynchings; another was robbery. Lynching also was used to punish individuals who registered to vote, were involved in interracial relationships, attempted to charge white men with crimes, used obscenities, or refused to relinquish their property to whites. According to historians such as Arthur Raper, many of the murdered victims were wrongly accused.

The African-American press was the first vehicle through which American lynching practices were systematically recorded and protested. The pioneering work of IDA B. WELLS-BARNETT, a Memphis journalist and activist, thrust lynching and its roots of racial hypocrisy and prejudice into the forefront of American social debate and racial protest. The Chicago Tribune, which Wells read and cited in her work, was the first organization to tabulate lynching records. In the early 1890s Tuskegee Institute began its records, and in 1912 the newly established NATIONAL ASSOCIATION FOR THE ADVANCEMENT OF COLORED PEOPLE (NAACP) began to maintain records and statistics. The NAACP established the Anti-Lynching Committee, and its members regularly publicized its findings in mainstream newspapers such as THE NEW YORK TIMES and The Atlanta Constitution. The organization also relied heavily on the courageous reportage of WALTER WHITE, who served as assistant executive secretary from 1918 through 1931. White, a light-skinned, blond, blue-eyed man of African descent, routinely infiltrated lynch mobs and Ku Klux Klan meetings and obtained firsthand information about lynchings and mob violence. He eventually used his research in his prizewinning study of lynching, ROPE AND FAGGOT: A BIOGRAPHY OF JUDGE LYNCH (1929).

The most effective early published works on lynching were pamphlets by the journalist Wells-Barnett, one of the cofounders of the NAACP. Her searing assessments of specific cases and evidence of local and federal collusion with lynch mobs catalyzed many to act and to protest the violence. Wells-Barnett's works included Lynch Law in Georgia (1890) and The Red Record (1895), the first publication to provide documented statistical assessments of lynching. In 1905 James Cutler's Lynch-Law chronicled the hideous methods of killing that included maiming, torture, dismemberment, castration, disembowelment, hanging, and burning at the stake. In 1919 the NAACP published Thirty Years of Lynching in the United States, 1889–1918. Its study was part of the organization's systematic effort to lobby for antilynching legislation. THE CRISIS, the organization's publication, also included regular commentary on the egregious practice.

The Dyer Anti-Lynching Bill was the first opportunity for the federal government to outlaw lynching. The bill passed in the House of Representatives, but southern senators effectively blocked the passage of the bill. They argued shamelessly that antilynching legislation was unconstitutional and that it interfered with states' rights. Undeterred by the failure of government to act, Americans rallied to establish organizations that would continue to protest lynchings. These included the Atlanta-based Association of Southern Women for the Prevention of Lynching and the Commission for Interracial Cooperation.

A number of Harlem Renaissance writers used their work to raise public awareness about lynching and its dreadful toll on American families. Scholars Kathy Perkins and Judith Stephens have identified some 10 plays written during the 1920s. The substantial set of antilynching dramas includes works such as *Frances* (1925) by G. D. Lipscomb, FOR UNBORN CHILDREN (1926) by MYRTLE SMITH LIVINGSTON, *RACHEL* (1916) by ANGELINA GRIMKÉ, *AFTERMATH* (1919) by MARY BURRILL, THE NOOSE (1919) by Tracy Mygatt, GRANNY MAUMEE (1914) by RIDGELEY TORRENCE, and *Mine Eyes Have Seen* (1918) by ALICE DUNBAR-NELSON.

Bibliography

Cutler, James E. *Lynch-Law: An Investigation into the History of Lynching in the United States.* Montclair, N.J.: Patterson Smith, 1969.

Gunning, Sandra, *Race, Rape, and Lynching: The Red Record of American Literature.* New York: Oxford University Press, 1996.

Hall, Jaquelyn Dowd. *Revolt Against Chivalry: Jessie Daniel Ames and the Women's Campaign Against Lynching.* New York: Columbia University Press, 1979.

Perkins, Kathy A., and Judith L. Stephens, eds. *Strange Fruit: Plays on Lynching by American Women.* Bloomington: Indiana University Press, 1998.

Stephens, Judith L. "'And Yet They Paused' and 'A Bill to Be Passed': Newly Recovered Lynching Dramas by Georgia Douglas Johnson." *African American Review* 33 (1999): 519–522.

Wells-Barnett, Ida B. *On Lynchings: Southern Horrors, a Red Record and Mob Rule in New Orleans.* New York: Arno Press, 1969.

Zangrando, Robert. *The NAACP Crusade against Lynching, 1909–1950.* Philadelphia: Temple University Press, 1960.

M

Macaulay Publishing Company

A NEW YORK CITY publishing company. Its editor in chief was Lee Furman, an aspiring writer who also established the Lee Furman publishing company. The enterprising writer WALLACE THURMAN joined the company as its first editor and reader of color. Macaulay later published two books, INFANTS OF THE SPRING and THE INTERNE (1932), which Thurman coauthored with ABRAHAM FURMAN, an attorney and a relative of the company founders. In addition, the Macaulay Company published the groundbreaking satirical novel BLACK NO MORE (1931) by George Schuyler and A LONG WAY FROM HOME (1937), the autobiography of poet CLAUDE MCKAY.

The company also published works of L. Ron Hubbard, Alfred Gordon Bennett, Frederick Faust, and Edward Newhouse.

Macmillan Company

A British publishing company that the Scottish brothers Daniel and Alexander Macmillan founded in 1843. Their early publications included works by Lewis Carroll, Thomas Hardy, Henry James, Rudyard Kipling, Alfred Lord Tennyson, and H. G. Wells.

The intrepid domestic and world-traveler JUANITA HARRISON saw her memoir, MY GREAT, WIDE, BEAUTIFUL WORLD, published by the company in 1936.

"Mademoiselle 'Tasie—A Story" Eloise Bibb Thompson (1925)

A short story by ELOISE ALBERTA VERONICA BIBB THOMPSON that appeared in the September 1925 issue of OPPORTUNITY. The plot revolved around the self-conscious Mademoiselle 'Tasie, a New Orleans Creole woman who is desperate to maintain an image of high class and racial superiority. She is undone, however, when hard economic times force her to seek employment with a family of dark-skinned people. Thompson's heroine ultimately learns her lesson about humanity and tolerance. This allows her to accept the marriage proposal of a man named Titus, a dark-skinned businessman.

Thompson's story was one of several insightful Harlem Renaissance–era works, including JESSIE FAUSET's PLUM BUN (1929) and NELLA LARSEN's PASSING (1929), that dealt with caste prejudice and social hypocrisy.

Magie Noire Paul Morand (1929)

A collection of short stories by PAUL MORAND, a Paris-born modernist writer and diplomat who was married to the Greek-born Romanian princess Hélène Soutzo. The volume, whose translated French title means "black magic," was inspired by Morand's extensive travels. Originally published in 1928, it was reprinted in the United States by Viking Press in 1929. The artist AARON DOUGLAS provided the illustrations for the volume.

The eight short stories in Magie Noire are marked for their sensational depictions of life and peoples of color in AFRICA, America, and the West Indies. In "The Black Tsar," Morand creates a troubled protagonist named Occide. A mulatto lawyer, Occide resides in 1920s HAITI during its U.S. occupation. He survives the occupation and is installed as tsar of the island nation.

Morand's work illustrated the deep fascination with African-American culture and the problematic tendency toward primitive, stereotypical representations in works about people of color.

Bibliography

Guitard-Auviste, Ginette. *Paul Morand.* Paris: Éditions Universitaires, 1956.

Lemaître, Georges. *Four French Novelists: Marcel Proust, André Gide, Jean Giraudoux, Paul Morand.* London: Oxford University Press, 1938.

Morand, Paul. *Black Magic,* translated by Hamish Miles. New York: Viking Press, 1929.

Ma Johnson's Harlem Rooming House
Mercedes Gilbert (1938)

A play by the writer and versatile film and stage actress MERCEDES GILBERT. The work was produced at the YOUNG MEN'S CHRISTIAN ASSOCIATION in HARLEM, New York.

It was the one of three dramas Gilbert wrote and the second published script by the actress-writer. Its production in NEW YORK CITY coincided with the publication of AUNT SARA'S WOODEN GOD, Gilbert's first and only novel.

"Makin' of Mamma Harris, The"
Ted Poston (1940)

A short story by the accomplished journalist TED POSTON. Published in the April 6, 1940, issue of *THE NEW REPUBLIC,* it was one of several short stories that Poston contributed to mainstream American journals.

The story chronicles the efforts of Mamma Harris, a woman determined to unionize her fellow workers in a tobacco company.

Bibliography

Hauke, Kathleen. *Ted Poston: Pioneer American Journalist.* Athens: University of Georgia Press, 1998.

———, ed. *The Dark Side of Hopkinsville: Stories by Ted Poston.* Athens: University of Georgia Press, 1991.

"Makin's, The" Marita Bonner (1939)

Published in the January 1939 issue of *OPPORTUNITY,* this short story by MARITA BONNER illus-

trated the awful toll that urban life could take on children.

The protagonist, a young boy named David, cannot persuade his overworked, underpaid, and frustrated parents to give him 10 cents. David wants the money in order to purchase seeds to plant in the nonexistent garden of his CHICAGO home. His grandmother, a religious woman, is also unable to provide him with the funds. By the story's end, David has purchased cigarettes for his father, played his mother's daily lottery number, and learned to curse. His mother's unlikely praise for her son's emerging aggression is a sobering suggestion about the evils and destructive effects of urban life.

Bibliography

Flynn, Joyce, and Joyce Occomy Stricklin. *Frye Street & Environs: The Collected Works of Marita Bonner.* Boston: Beacon Press, 1987.

Mamba's Daughters: A Novel of Charleston DuBose Heyward (1929)

A novel by DUBOSE HEYWARD, a Charleston, South Carolina, native and the author of PORGY, the work that inspired the Gershwin production of *PORGY AND BESS.*

Set in Charleston, the novel draws from Heyward's own life story and effort to embrace his heritage as a member of the white southern aristocracy. It chronicles the life of Mamba, a lower-class woman of color who takes a job as a servant in a white household. Aided by Maum Netta and the white children of the Wentworth family, Mamba is able to reinvent herself as a polished upper-class woman who is suitable to serve the white aristocracy. Mamba's savvy enables her to triumph over the paternalistic whites with whom she comes into contact. She is unable to prevent her daughter Hagar from getting into trouble and must enlist the help of the Atkinsons, a white family who grapple with the changing realities of the post–Civil War South. Her goal is to secure a bright future for Lissa, her granddaughter and a talented singer. Lissa ultimately succeeds as a result of her grandmother's determined efforts to build up savings. Lissa's triumph is secured when she travels to NEW YORK CITY and makes her successful debut as an opera singer at the new Metropolitan Opera House. Her grandmother and mother, in the audience, are able to share in the achievement that has been made possible by their own sacrifices and struggles. Lissa's life in New York is made more steady by the Reverend Thomas Grayson, a northern mulatto minister who failed to secure a southern church but leads a church in Harlem.

The novel was a financial success but received mixed reviews. White southerners tended to criticize the suggestions of racial equality in the novel. Others praised Heyward's efforts to portray the multifaceted nature of African-American experiences and characters. *Mamba's Daughters* was serialized in the *Woman's Home Companion* and in 1929 was chosen as a selection by the Literary Guild.

DuBose Heyward and his wife, Dorothy, collaborated to produce a dramatic script of *Mamba's Daughters*. The play debuted in 1939 and starred Ethel Waters. Her casting in the role of Hagar made her the first African-American actress ever to appear in a Broadway play in a dramatic role.

Bibliography

Durham, Frank. *DuBose Heyward's Use of Folklore in His Negro Fiction.* Charleston, S.C.: The Citadel, 1961.

Heyward, DuBose. *Mamba's Daughters: A Novel of Charleston.* 1929, reprint, Columbia: University of South Carolina Press, 1995.

Hutchisson, James. *DuBose Heyward: A Charleston Gentleman and the World of Porgy and Bess.* Jackson: University Press of Mississippi, 2000.

Slavick, William. *DuBose Heyward.* Boston: Twayne Publishers, 1981.

"Mammy" Dorothy West (1940)

A purposeful story by DOROTHY WEST about social welfare, PASSING, and unexpected family secrets. The story about a woman and her biracial daughter and granddaughter was inspired by West's own work as welfare investigator in NEW YORK CITY.

The protagonist is a young welfare investigator who bears the brunt of segregation even though she is a city worker. She hears the case of an older woman living in a Harlem boardinghouse and prepares to approve her petition for welfare relief. Before doing so, however, she travels to the Central Park West home of the woman's employer. There, she meets a white woman who relates Mammy's integral role in the home and her unmatched nursing of the ailing daughter. Satisfied that she can persuade the older lady to return, the welfare worker returns to Harlem. She breaks the news that she is denying the claim and, to the lady's dismay, begins to pack up the items in the room. As she does, the older lady, who has cursed her employer, reveals that the woman is not her employer but her daughter. The welfare investigator is stunned by the revelation and the intense deception that she has witnessed in the Central Park apartment. Yet, she adheres strictly to the policies of her agency and insists that the older woman return.

West's story is powerful for its subtle critique of passing and its exploration of the complicated realities of black migration from the South to the North.

Bibliography

Jones, Sharon. *Rereading the Harlem Renaissance: Race, Class, and Gender in the Fiction of Jessie Fauset, Zora Neale Hurston, and Dorothy West.* Westport, Conn.: Greenwood Press, 2002.

West, Dorothy. *The Richer, the Poorer: Stories, Sketches, and Reminiscences.* New York: Doubleday, 1995.

Mandrake, Ethel Belle

One of two pseudonyms that the writer, editor, and playwright WALLACE THURMAN used during his literary career.

Manhattan Civic Club

The site in which CHARLES S. JOHNSON, editor of OPPORTUNITY, hosted a groundbreaking celebration of African-American writers and artists on 21 March 1924. REGINA ANDREWS, a dynamic librarian at the 135th Street Branch of the NEW YORK PUBLIC LIBRARY, encouraged Johnson to organize the party at the venue located on Twelfth Street near FIFTH AVENUE. The event was intended originally as a celebration of JESSIE FAUSET, author of the newly published novel THERE IS CONFUSION.

The Civic Club gathering, which many scholars regard as the auspicious launch of the NEW

NEGRO movement, provided unprecedented opportunities for publishers, potential patrons, writers, and artists to meet and to network. The Civic Club dinner led to significant alliances and literary events, including the historic SURVEY GRAPHIC special issue on HARLEM that in turn prompted ALAIN LOCKE to edit the groundbreaking multidisciplinary anthology NEW NEGRO.

"Man Who Wanted to Be Red, The"
Frank Horne (1928)

FRANK HORNE's fantasy story of prejudice, superiority, and the value of humane and moral treatment of all peoples appeared in the July 1928 issue of THE CRISIS.

The story is set in Ur, a kingdom populated by the Greener tribe. The protagonist, Juda, is determined to transform the physical appearance of his disenfranchised tribe. By doing so, he hopes to lay claim to the good life enjoyed by the reds, a people "tall and straight with long hair, golden as the sky at the break of day" who have "skins a gorgeous red, like the heart of a flame, and a blazing ruby and the western sky when the sun goes down." Juda is a mixed-race man, born of Moda, a red tribe member and his former Greener servant, a woman who "slaved in Moda's house." Following his father's death, Juda develops scientific experiments that promise to transform his race. He is thrilled by the prospect of engineering, quite literally, the emancipation of his people. However, after a moving encounter with his mother and a reminder of the rich cultural history of the Greeners, Juda abandons his plans. As the story closes, he is on the verge of exploring ways to transform the oppressors instead.

Horne's story is a thinly veiled allegory of American society and the history of peoples of African descent in the United States. It taps into the theme of PASSING and also offers a sincere tribute to racial solidarity and cultural survival.

Maran, René (1887–1960)

The first author of African descent to publish a novel on African experiences under French colonial rule. Maran's powerful novel, BATOUALA (1921), earned him the Goncourt Prize, the prestigious French literary award, in 1922.

Maran, who was born in 1887 in Martinique, lived in Gabon and in the Bordeaux region of FRANCE. After graduating from the Lycée Talence and the Grand Lycée Michel Montaigne, he joined the French Colonial Service. Twenty years later, he settled in Paris and began working as an editorial staff member for political and literary journals.

Maran published his first novel, *Batouala*, in 1921. The English title of the work reads *Batouala: A True Black Novel*. The work, translated into 50 different languages, focused on the stories of Batouala, an elderly African chief. A member of the Banda tribe, Batouala and his people are confronted by the harsh realities of colonial rule. The enthusiastic American reception of *Batouala*, the only one of his seven novels to be translated into English, prompted Maran to begin to submit work to Harlem Renaissance journals such as OPPORTUNITY.

Maran had several close friends and colleagues in the Harlem Renaissance movement. He collaborated with WALTER WHITE on the French translation and publication of FIRE IN THE FLINT. He enjoyed a strong friendship with ALAIN LOCKE, whom he met in Paris in 1924.

Maran, who also published poetry, essays, and historical works, died in May 1960.

Bibliography
Cook, Mercer. *Five French Negro Authors*. Washington, D.C.: The Associated Publishers, 1943.

Irele, Abiola. *Literature and Ideology in Martinique: René Maran, Aimé Césaire, Frantz Fanon*. Buffalo, N.Y.: State University of New York at Buffalo, 1972.

Ojo-Ade, Femi. *René Maran, The Black Frenchman: A Bio-Critical Study*. Washington, D.C.: Three Continents Press, 1984.

Margetson, George Reginald
(1877–unknown)

A native of St. Kitts in the West Indies who became part of the active Harlem Renaissance–era literary circle there. Like a number of less well-known Harlem Renaissance writers, Margetson was unable to devote himself entirely to his writing because of family obligations and work responsibilities. Margetson began publishing poems in the early

1900s; three books of poems appeared between 1906 and 1910, and his first Harlem Renaissance–era volume was published in 1916. Margetson continued to write and to publish during the Harlem Renaissance, and his works were included in highly respected anthologies, newspapers, and in the SATURDAY EVENING QUILL, the first African-American literary journal produced in BOSTON during the Harlem Renaissance.

Margetson, who was born in St. Kitts in 1877, was educated at the Bethel Moravian School on the island. In 1897, two years after he graduated with honors from the school, he emigrated to the United States. Once here, he found work in a variety of fields. According to the biographical note published in one anthology that included his poems, he ultimately pursued a career as a stationary engineer (White and Jackson, 168). He married Elizabeth Matthews, of Cambridge, Massachusetts, in 1905, and the couple had several children. He may have been related to the celebrated Edward Margetson, a St. Kitt's native who settled in NEW YORK CITY, studied music at Columbia University, became a well-known composer, a HARMON FOUNDATION AWARD winner, and the founder of the Schubert Music Society.

Margetson's pre–Harlem Renaissance publications included *England in the West Indies: A Neglected and Degenerating Empire* (1906), *Ethiopia's Flight: The Negro Question; or, The White Man's Fear* (1907), and *Songs of Life* (1910). In 1916 he published *The Fledgling Bard and the Poetry Society*, a 100-page poem about a poet's quest to "find the new, the modern school, / Where Science trains the fledgling bard to fly, / Where critics teach the ignorant, the fool, / To write the stuff the editors would buy." It was this work that was anthologized most during the Harlem Renaissance. Margetson's writing also explored traditional religious themes and constituted classical poetic invocations of the muse. In "A Prayer," the work that NEWMAN WHITE and WALTER JACKSON included in their anthology of African-American poetry, Margetson's speaker prays earnestly for God to "[c]harge my soul with sacred fire, / To consume each low desire, / Let my raptured spirit rise, / In sweet cadence to the skies." Margetson was an enterprising writer who did not hesitate to invest in his own career. He self-published his first two books, and their success led to respectable contracts with Boston publishers. The

firm Sherman, French, which is perhaps best known as the publisher of the first edition of JAMES WELDON JOHNSON's *AUTOBIOGRAPHY OF AN EX-COLOURED MAN* (1912), published Margetson's *Songs of Life*. The Boston firm of R. G. Badger published his most successful work, *The Fledgling Bard*.

Margetson appears to have published one additional work during the early years of the Harlem Renaissance. His volume *The Immortal Twenty-Sixth Yankee Division* appeared in 1919. James Weldon Johnson, who included a selection of Margetson's writing in *THE BOOK OF AMERICAN NEGRO POETRY* (1922, 1931), noted that Margetson's poems "have been written in such moments as he could seize for that purpose." Johnson, commenting on Margetson's talent, also observed that "[a]mong Aframerican poets he has a good claim to originality, even though his originality may contain echoes from Byron."

Margetson became a member of the Boston-based SATURDAY EVENING QUILL CLUB and was one of the contributors whose work appeared in the first issue of the club's notable journal, the *Saturday Evening Quill*. Margetson, who lived in Cambridge, Massachusetts, during this time, was part of a prolific literary group that included WARING CUNEY, EUGENE GORDON, ALVIRA HAZZARD, HELENE JOHNSON, DOROTHY WEST, and others. Margetson also saw his work included in WILLIAM STANLEY BRAITHWAITE's 1916 anthology of poems. Margetson's poems also were included in James Weldon Johnson's celebrated *Book of American Negro Poetry* (1922), in ROBERT KERLIN's important collection entitled *NEGRO POETS AND THEIR POEMS* (1923), and in Newman White and Walter Jackson's *ANTHOLOGY OF VERSE BY AMERICAN NEGROES* (1924).

Bibliography
"Biographical Notes." *Saturday Evening Quill* (June 1928).

Marinoff, Fania   *See* VAN VECHTEN, FANIA MARINOFF.

"Marked Tree, The" Charles Chesnutt (1924, 1925)
An absorbing short story about southern folk and superstition by CHARLES CHESNUTT that appeared

in the December 1924 and January 1925 issues of *THE CRISIS*.

Written in the style of his famous dialect stories and earlier published collections, the "Marked Tree" is about a tree cursed by an indignant and wronged enslaved woman on the Spencer plantation. Phillis sees her son, who is born on the same day as the master's own son, sold years later to finance the wedding of the white heir. She curses the tree under which all Spencers have been baptized and married. When the narrator decides to purchase the property, he learns the awful history of the tree known as the Upas, or Tree of Death. In the final scene, a very distant cousin of the Spencers casually disregards the legends of death and destruction as figments of the imaginations of the foolish African Americans associated with the estate. Moments later, the disbelieving man, who sits on the stump of the tree, is killed by a rattlesnake. The narrator, who is dispatched to buy a home for his Ohio cousin, is undeterred and proceeds with his plans to purchase the property.

The story reflects Chesnutt's unwavering gift for crafting vivid tales of the encounters between whites and African Americans. Chesnutt also underscores the power of folk wisdom and illuminates the ways in which it is routinely underestimated as a reliable commentary on local life and history.

Bibliography

Andrews, William. *The Literary Career of Charles Chesnutt.* Baton Rouge: Louisiana State University Press, 1980.

Heermance, J. Noel. *Charles W. Chesnutt: America's First Great Black Novelist.* Hamden, Conn.: Archon Books, 1974.

Keller, Frances. *An American Crusade: The Life of Charles Waddell Chesnutt.* Provo, Utah: Brigham Young University Press, 1978.

McWilliams, Dean. *Charles Chesnutt and the Fictions of Race.* Athens: University of Georgia Press, 2002.

"Masks" Eloise Bibb Thompson (1927)

One of two short stories by ELOISE ALBERTA VERONICA BIBB THOMPSON THAT APPEARED IN *OPPORTUNITY*.

Set in New Orleans, the tale chronicles the tragic lives of Aristile Blanchard and his descendants. Blanchard, a Haitian quadroon, was foiled in his attempt to spy for the oppressed people of HAITI. Despite his exceedingly light skin, his African identity was discovered, and the French imprisoned him. Blanchard was rescued and was able to regain his freedom in New Orleans, but he spent the remainder of his years trying to create a mask that would confer white features upon its wearer. His granddaughter Julie has inherited her father's obsession with color and the explicit privileges available to lighter-skinned individuals. In an effort to ensure her status as an aristocratic Creole, she seizes the chance to marry Paupet, the whitest octoroon she has ever met. When their first child is born, however, Julie is quite literally shocked to death when she sees that her child bears a visible racial resemblance to her own dark-skinned mother. Her widowed husband honors his wife, a woman whom he knew best "only when she was expecting their offspring." He orders the inscription on her tombstone to read, "Because she saw with the eyes of her grandfather, she died at the sight of her babe's face."

Thompson's story is reminiscent of Kate Chopin's "Desiree's Baby," the haunting New Orleans story of maternal distress, betrayal, and race hysteria. Thompson's work also complements the novels of JESSIE FAUSET, NELLA LARSEN, DOROTHY WEST, and others who explored the often deadly implications of PASSING, racial obsessions, and caste prejudice.

Mason, Charlotte Louise Osgood
(1854–1946)

One of the most influential patrons of the Harlem Renaissance, Mason was the daughter of Peter Quick and Phoebe Vanderveer. She was born in Franklin Park, New Jersey. She became the second wife of Rufus Osgood Mason, a native of Sullivan, New Hampshire, and graduate of Dartmouth College. In 1859 he earned his M.D. degree from the College of Physicians and Surgeons and went on to become one of New York City's leading doctors. During the Civil War, Mason was an acting assistant surgeon. He later pursued his interests in metaphysical issues, hypnotism, and personality. He died in 1903 at the age of 73. His 51-year-old widow, Charlotte, began to use her wealth to promote anthropological research in Native American

Charlotte Osgood Mason, the legendary and exacting patron of Zora Neale Hurston and Langston Hughes *(Yale Collection of American Literature, Beinecke Rare Book and Manuscript Library)*

communities. She herself pursued fieldwork and lived with members of the Plains Indian tribes during the early 1900s.

During the Harlem Renaissance, Mason selected several promising writers to be her protégés. She was interested in primitivism, a perspective that suggested savagery and untamed natures were the best antidote to white notions of civilization. RICHMOND BARTHÉ, Miguel Covarrubias, LANGSTON HUGHES, ZORA NEALE HURSTON, Hall Johnson, ALAIN LOCKE, and LOUISE THOMPSON all benefited from financial support from the woman whom they were expected to address as

"Godmother." She, in turn, referred to the artists as her "children." Mason was an exacting patron who demanded absolute intellectual obedience and anonymity. Other artists, such as PAUL ROBESON, declined Mason's offers of patronage and support.

Alain Locke, who frequented Mason's Park Avenue residence and often brought emerging artists to call, introduced Mason to Zora Neale Hurston. Locke, who publicly endorsed the philosophy that African-American artists should not be constrained to examine only racial matters, suppressed such ideas in Mason's presence. He saw the opportunity to fund emerging artists and thus emphasized the value of articulating African themes in contemporary works.

Hurston and Mason met first in September 1927. Mason allocated generous amounts to fund Hurston's research. In exchange for the support, however, she forbade the COLUMBIA UNIVERSITY–trained anthropologist to publish any of her findings. Mason established a formal contract with Hurston, one that provided the writer with a $200 monthly stipend, a car, and a film camera and guaranteed Mason total control over all acquired materials that Hurston gathered in the course of her travels.

Hurston provided her patron with detailed sets of information about her anthropological research and wrote to her frequently about professional and personal matters. Hurston frequently wrote delightful notes in which she greeted Mason as "Darling my God-Flower" (Kaplan, 187) and signed off with phrases in which she pledged "All my love and gratitude and Devotion" (Kaplan, 263).

Mason maintained a tight control over Hurston's collaborations with scholars such as her former Columbia professor FRANZ BOAS and forced Hurston to develop research plans in secret. Ultimately, Hurston's intellectual independence hastened an end to the relationship.

Mason was the patron of Langston Hughes for some three and one-half years. According to Hughes biographer Faith Berry, the gifted but perennially financially strapped writer thought that Mason was "one of the most delightful women [he] had ever met, witty and charming, kind and sympathetic, very old and white-haired but amazingly modern in her ideas, in her knowledge of books and the theater, of Harlem, and of everything then taking place in the world" (Berry, 88). It was Mason who financed Langston Hughes so that he could publish his first novel, NOT WITHOUT LAUGHTER. She protested his inclinations to develop works of a political nature and advocated a much more narrow and insular focus on essentialist racial ideas and images. Mason dismissed potential collaborations between Hughes and Hurston, especially their plans to establish a formal theater program and their ill-fated work on MULE BONE. Hughes's relationship with Mason ended in December 1930. He proposed that they remain friends but asked for an end to her financial support and the restraints on his creative development. Mason predicted that he would fail without her. Hughes grappled with serious illness immediately after their tempestuous break. In 1931 the Harmon Literary Award winner sent the gold medals that he had received to Mason in an effort to smooth over the abrupt end to their relationship.

Hurston, like Hughes, chafing under the obsessive control and scripting of their creative genius, eventually broke ties with Mason. Mason hired Louise Thompson, former wife of WALLACE THURMAN, to work as secretary for Langston Hughes.

Mason believed in the power of the primitive and demanded that her protégés provide her with material that reinforced her views. According to Bruce Kellner, Mason dedicated more than $75,000 to the professional development of her artistic charges.

Mason died at Manhattan's New York Hospital in April 1946. She was actually a patient in residence, admitted in 1933 when she suffered a broken hip. Her rooms there were opulent, and she essentially maintained a private hospital residence for herself. Mason's death certificate listed her occupation simply as "housewife." Despite her prominence and influential role in New York society, THE NEW YORK TIMES refrained from publishing an obituary.

Bibliography

Bernard, Emily. *Remember Me to Harlem: The Letters of Langston Hughes and Carl Van Vechten.* New York: Knopf, 2001.

Berry, Faith, ed. *Langston Hughes: Before and Beyond Harlem.* Westport, Conn.: Lawrence Hill & Company, 1983.

Kaplan, Carla. *Zora Neale Hurston: A Life in Letters.* New York: Doubleday, 2002.

Rampersad, Arnold. *The Life of Langston Hughes: I, Too, Sing America.* Vol. 1: *1902–1941.* New York: Oxford University Press, 1986.

Massachusetts

The New England state that was home to several leading members of the Harlem Renaissance. In BOSTON, as in PHILADELPHIA, there were active literary circles that produced important Harlem Renaissance–era publications.

Massachusetts natives and residents who went on to enjoy successful careers in the arts included MARITA BONNER, WILLIAM STANLEY BRAITHWAITE, ANGELINA GRIMKÉ, Florence Marion Henderson, HELENE JOHNSON, and DOROTHY WEST. West later retired to Martha's Vineyard after a successful career in New York City during the heyday of the Harlem Renaissance.

The SATURDAY EVENING QUILL CLUB was the most active and well-known literary circle during the Harlem Renaissance. Its members included EDYTHE MAE GORDON, EUGENE GORDON, and FLORIDA RUFFIN RIDLEY. Writers such as Dorothy West, Helene Johnson, and Florence Harmon published in the SATURDAY EVENING QUILL, the organization's publication.

HARVARD UNIVERSITY, located in Cambridge, graduated some of the most accomplished men of the period. FREDERICK ALLEN LEWIS and ALAIN LOCKE were undergraduates who excelled and demonstrated the intellectual strength of the race that had been long thwarted by American segregation and exclusionary political and educational policies. Locke, a PHI BETA KAPPA and magna cum laude graduate in 1907 became the first African American selected for a RHODES SCHOLARSHIP. In 1896 W. E. B. DuBois became the first African American to earn a Ph.D. at Harvard, and Charles Hamilton Houston, a student at the law school, became the first African-American editor of the *Harvard Law Review.*

RADCLIFFE COLLEGE, the sister school of Harvard, was the alma mater of MARITA BONNER,

Caroline Bond Day, and EVA DYKES, one of the first women of color to earn a Ph.D. in an American institution. MARION CUTHBERT, Eugene Gordon, Helene Johnson, GERTRUDE MCBROWN, and Dorothy West attended BOSTON UNIVERSITY. MARY BURRILL and McBrown attended Emerson College. WARING CUNEY, poet, attended the Boston Conservatory of Music. Wellesley College graduates included ETHEL CAUTION-DAVIS, CLARISSA SCOTT DELANY, who graduated Phi Beta Kappa in 1923, and BRENDA RAY MORYCK. Charlotte Hawkins Brown, who attended the elite women's college for one year, was later granted honorary membership in the college's alumnae association.

The state also has an impressive literary and journalistic history. It was in Boston in 1857 that the *ATLANTIC MONTHLY* was founded. Writers such as Braithwaite wrote for local newspapers such as the *Boston Transcript*. Other well-known newspapers included the *Boston Globe*, the *Boston Guardian*, a paper edited by the fiery Harvard University Phi Beta Kappa graduate WILLIAM MONROE TROTTER, and the *Boston Post*, which included Eugene Gordon on its staff. Boston had an established publishing history. Companies included B. J. Brimmer, which worked with the poets Braithwaite and GEORGIA DOUGLAS JOHNSON. The Christopher Publishing House produced works by CLARA ANN THOMPSON and MERCEDES GILBERT. Also in the city were the Cornhill Press, which published SARAH LEE BROWN FLEMING, and the Stratford Company, which published early works by W. E. B. DuBois.

Bibliography

Brown, Richard. *Massachusetts: A Concise History.* Amherst: University of Massachusetts Press, 2000.

Cromwell, Adelaide. *The Other Brahmins: Boston's Black Upper Class, 1750–1950.* Fayetteville, University of Arkansas Press, 1994.

Hayden, Robert. *African-Americans in Boston: More Than 350 Years.* Boston: Trustees of the Public Library of the City of Boston, 1991.

Lewis, David Levering. *W. E. B. Du Bois: Biography of A Race.* New York: Henry Holt and Company, 1993.

Saunders, James Robert, and Renaie Nadine Shackelford, eds. *Dorothy West's Martha's Vineyard: Stories, Essays and Reminiscences by Dorothy West Writing in the Vineyard Gazette.* Jefferson, N.C.: McFarland, 2001.

Matheus, John Frederick (1887–1983)

A professor of modern languages, dramatist, and author who published some 50 works during his career. Born in Keyser, West Virginia, in September 1887, he was the son of John and Mary Brown Matheus. His father was a bank messenger and tanner. Matheus married Maude Roberts of Gallipolis, Ohio, in 1909. In 1973, eight years after his wife's death, the 86-year-old widower married Ellen Turner Gordon.

Matheus attended Western Reserve University, known now as Case Western Reserve. He graduated cum laude in 1910. He resumed his education a decade later, graduating with a master's degree from COLUMBIA UNIVERSITY in 1921. In the mid-1920s, he completed graduate courses at the SORBONNE in Paris and in 1927 attended courses at the UNIVERSITY OF CHICAGO. He joined the faculty at Florida Agricultural and Mechanical College as a professor of foreign languages and of Latin in 1911. In 1913, he relocated to West Virginia and began his lengthy tenure at West Virginia State College. He became chair of the modern languages department in 1922 and held the position until 1953. Matheus later held academic positions at Dillard University, Morris Brown College, Texas Southern University, Hampton Institute, and Kentucky State College.

Matheus emerged as a dynamic new voice when he won first prize for his short story "FOG" in the 1924–1925 *OPPORTUNITY* literary contest. The second- and third-place winners were ZORA NEALE HURSTON and ERIC WALROND, respectively. A year later, in 1926, Matheus was one of the most highly recognized writers in the *Opportunity* literary contest. He placed in four of the five literary categories. His short stories "CLAY" and "General Drums" and the poems "Lethe" and "The Frost" were awarded honorable mentions. A panel of three judges, which included EUGENE KINCKLE JONES, awarded first place to "Sand," Matheus's entry in the Personal Experience Sketches division. The play *C'RUITER* was selected over dramas by Zora Neale Hurston, MAY MILLER SULLIVAN, and GEORGIA DOUGLAS JOHNSON. Judges David Belasco, T. MONTGOMERY GREGORY, PAUL ROBESON, and Stark Young awarded Matheus second prize in the play division. In 1926 he won first place in the short story division of

THE CRISIS Literary Contest. CHARLES CHESNUTT, Otelia Cromwell, and Ernest Poole selected "Swamp Moccasin" as the first-place winner. Matheus adapted his one-act play TI YETTE (1929) for high school and college students.

Matheus wrote the libretto for *Ouanga!*, an opera dedicated to JULIUS ROSENWALD. Funds from Rosenwald, a well-known philanthropist, supported Matheus and celebrated violinist and composer Clarence Cameron White as they traveled to HAITI to complete their research on Jean-Jacques Dessalines, the first Haitian emperor and the figure whose life inspired their musical work. The opera, whose title means "voodoo charm," was billed as a work in four acts and was based on Matheus's "Haitian Drama." *Ouanga!* premiered in Chicago in 1932. Later productions of the prizewinning opera included the first stage performance in 1949 by the Burleigh Musical Association in South Bend, Indiana, and productions in Philadelphia and in NEW YORK CITY at Carnegie Hall and the Metropolitan Opera House.

Works by Matheus were selected for inclusion in prominent literary collections such as the anthology NEW NEGRO (1925), edited by ALAIN LOCKE; PLAYS OF NEGRO LIFE: A SOURCEBOOK OF NATIVE AMERICAN DRAMA (1927), edited by Locke and T. MONTGOMERY GREGORY with illustrations by AARON DOUGLAS; and *Negro Caravan: Writings by American Negroes* (1941), edited by STERLING BROWN, ARTHUR DAVIS, and ULYSSES LEE. He also published widely in academic periodicals such as the *Modern Language Journal* and the JOURNAL OF NEGRO HISTORY.

Matheus worked alongside *Opportunity* editor CHARLES S. JOHNSON in the late 1920s and early 1930s when the two men traveled to Liberia as part of a U.S. League of Nations Commission charged with investigating enslavement in Liberia. In the mid-1940s he was appointed director of the Inter-American Educational Foundation program that oversaw the teaching of English in Haiti.

Bibliography

Fleming, G. James, and Christian E. Burckel. *Who's Who in Colored America: An Illustrated Biographical Directory of Notable Living Persons of African Descent in the United States.* Yonkers-on-Hudson, N.Y.: Christian E. Burckel & Associates, 1950.

Matthews, Ralph, Sr. (1904–1978)

One of the best-known American journalists of color, Matthews became editor of the Baltimore *Afro-American*, one of the oldest African-American newspapers still in circulation. He joined the staff in 1924 and worked as a reporter until 1935, when he was appointed editor in chief. By the 1940s, the newspaper enjoyed a readership of more than 200,000.

Matthews was one of the cofounders of the Capital Press Club. The organization, founded in 1944, is the oldest African-American communications association. Its was established to combat racism and segregation in American journalism. At the time, African-American journalists were denied access to vital forums such as the National Press Club and the White House press groups. Matthews and other leading newspaper figures, such as Alfred Smith, founder of the *Chicago Daily Defender*, St. Claire Bourne of New York's AMSTERDAM NEWS, and Ric Roberts and J. Hugo Warren of the PITTSBURGH COURIER, worked to provide journalists of color with access to political figures and other newsmakers.

In 1977 Matthews was recognized by the National Newspaper Publishers Association for his commitment to civil rights and his lifelong efforts to use newspapers to draw public attention to the struggle for equal and civil rights.

Bibliography

Farrar, Hayward. *The Baltimore Afro-American: 1892–1950.* Westport Conn.: Greenwood Press, 1998.

Pride, Armistead. *A History of the Black Press.* Washington, D.C.: Howard University Press, 1997.

Vincent, Theodore. *Voices of a Black Nation: Political Journalism in the Harlem Renaissance.* Trenton, N.J.: Africa World Press, 1990.

Vogel, Todd. *The Black Press: New Literary and Historical Essays.* New Brunswick, N.J.: Rutgers University Press, 2001.

McBrown, Gertrude Parthenia (1902–unknown)

A teacher and writer who developed poetry and plays for children. A native of Charleston, South Carolina, McBrown attended schools in BOSTON before immersing herself in Harlem Renaissance literary circles. She attended the Emerson College of Drama and graduated in 1922. She earned a master's degree in education from BOSTON UNIVERSITY in 1926. While in Boston, McBrown joined the SATURDAY EVENING QUILL CLUB, a literary society whose membership included EUGENE GORDON, HELENE JOHNSON, and DOROTHY WEST. She published several poems in the journal in 1928.

McBrown relocated to WASHINGTON, D.C. There, she was part of the literary circles that revolved around poet GEORGIA DOUGLAS JOHNSON. McBrown established a drama studio in the capital and directed drama programs for children and adults. She later joined the *Negro History Bulletin* educational board. In the late 1960s, she and colleague Ruby Carter were instrumental in establishing the CARTER G. WOODSON Collection at the Queens Borough Central Library in New York.

McBrown's love of literature and history prompted her to produce several works that honored African-American figures. Her historical plays included *Birthday Surprise*, a work inspired by the life of Paul Laurence Dunbar, and *Bought with Cookies*, a drama about Frederick Douglass.

McBrown contributed several poems to the 1931 volume *Readings from Negro Authors for Schools and Colleges*. In 1935 she collaborated with Lois Maillou Jones, a renowned American artist, designer, and teacher, on *The Picture-Poetry Book*. The volume included gorgeous sketches of African-American children and family life. As a whole, the work challenged prevailing negative racial stereotypes and contributed to the larger effort by Harlem Renaissance writers to provide uplifting and authentic images of African-Americans.

Bibliography

McBrown, Gertrude. *The Picture-Poetry Book*. Washington, D.C.: Associated Publishers, 1935.

McCall, James Edward (1880–1963)

The journalist who coined the phrase *New Negro*. McCall was born in Montgomery, Alabama, on September 2, 1880. He attended Alabama State Normal School in Montgomery, HOWARD UNIVERSITY in WASHINGTON, D.C., and Albion College in Michigan. While at Howard, where he began medical studies, McCall contracted typhoid fever. The illness, which struck him when he was 20 years old, left him blind, and he never regained his sight. Unable to pursue his dream of becoming a physician, McCall turned to literature, another field in which he excelled. He enrolled at Albion College, a Methodist college that was one of the first coeducational institutions in the Midwest. With the aid of his sister, who joined him at Albion College, McCall graduated in 1905. Following his graduation, McCall returned to the South, and in Montgomery he began writing for several local newspapers. He founded *The Emancipator*, a weekly newspaper for and about African Americans. Some of McCall's peers nicknamed him "Blind Tom," a term inspired by Thomas Wiggins, a 19th-century blind, enslaved musical prodigy.

McCall married Margaret Thomas in 1914. Six years later, the couple moved to Detroit. There, he joined the *Detroit Independent* and worked as both city news editor and as an editorial writer. Margaret McCall worked closely with her husband and, according to one biographical profile of the writer, "ably assisted in his journalistic work" (Cullen, 34). McCall also began publishing poems, and his works appeared in a variety of newspapers, including the *New York World*.

McCall's poem "The New Negro" was included in COUNTEE CULLEN's CAROLING DUSK. The sonnet is powerful for its presentation of a figure who "scans the world with calm and fearless eyes" and is "[c]onscious within of powers long since forgot" (ll. 1–2). McCall envisioned a man impervious to the "man-made barriers" that would "bar his progress" (l. 3–4). His protagonist also was unfazed by the daunting power of the natural world that allows "thunder bursts and billows" that "surge and roll /. . . . while lightnings flash / Along the rocky pathway to his goal" (ll. 6–8). The New Negro, as McCall imagined him, was not only "wise and strong" but a man who possessed a "soul awakened" and who held "destiny within his hands" (ll. 13–14).

McCall maintained his love of poetry throughout his life. In his later years, he regularly shared his work with members of the Detroit and Eastern Michigan University communities. In 1960 he and his wife hosted a recording session of African-

American poetry in their Detroit home. On one occasion, he and Margaret Danner, a poet-in-residence at Wayne State University, held a reading together.

Bibliography

Cullen, Countee. *Caroling Dusk: An Anthology of Verse by Negro Poets.* New York: Harper & Brothers, 1927.

Papers relating to James McCall, Rosey Pool Papers, University of Sussex Library, England.

McCoo, Edward (unknown)

A Newport, Kentucky, playwright and minister in the African Methodist Episcopal (A.M.E.) Church. McCoo's play *Ethiopia at the Bar of Justice* (1924) was included in PLAYS AND PAGEANTS FROM THE LIFE OF THE NEGRO, a 1930 anthology edited by WILLIS RICHARDSON. The work met Richardson's standards, which called for materials that did not feature dialect and were accessible to young people. McCoo's play appeared alongside works by respected dramatists such as THELMA MYRTLE DUNCAN, JOHN MATHEUS, and MAY MILLER.

The biographical profile of McCoo included in *Plays and Pageants* notes that he had "given much attention to the strivings and achievements of the Negro." McCoo, like many authors, used his writing to "visualize" the inspiring history of African peoples. The work apparently became popular in Louisville, Kentucky. McCoo collaborated with Professor John Hawkins on a production of the work during the 1924 Quadrennial Conference of the A.M.E. Church. Its positive reception resulted in its repeated use during subsequent Negro History Week calendars.

McDougald, Gertrude Elise Johnson (1885–1971)

The first African-American principal in the NEW YORK CITY public school system, outspoken feminist, member of the YOUNG WOMEN'S CHRISTIAN ASSOCIATION, and essayist who published regularly in leading journals of the Harlem Renaissance era.

McDougald published in THE CRISIS and OPPORTUNITY as well as *Birth Control Review.* Her essay, "The New Day for the Colored Woman Worker" appeared in the special African-American issue of *Birth Control Review* that also included works by MARY BURRILL, W. E. B. DUBOIS, and ANGELINA WELD GRIMKÉ. In March 1925 she was one of only four women featured in the special Harlem issue of SURVEY GRAPHIC that included works by 23 influential scholars, artists, and writers. McDougald's essay "The Double Task: The Struggle of Negro Women for Sex and Race Emancipation" appeared in the section devoted to "Black and White—Studies in Race Contacts" that also included submissions by MELVILLE HERSKOVITS, WALTER WHITE, and KELLY MILLER. McDougald's essay offered a compelling social critique of African-American women's experiences. She concluded that the "Negro woman, figuratively, [is] struck in the face daily by contempt from the world about her." Harlem, she argued, provided a vital respite from the "cruder handicaps of primitive household hardships and the grosser forms of sex and race subjugation." This vibrant community provided the woman of color with "considerable opportunity to measure her powers in the intellectual and industrial fields of the great city." Despite the fact that "she knows little of peace and happiness," McDougald insisted that "the wind of the race's destiny stirs more briskly because of [her] striving." The journal also included a gorgeous WINOLD REISS portrait of McDougald.

McDougald's father, Peter Johnson, was involved in the founding of the NATIONAL URBAN LEAGUE. McDougald continued the family tradition of service and outreach through her affiliations with the New York City Board of Education and the U.S. Department of Labor.

Bibliography

"McDougald, Elise Johnson," *Survey Graphic* (March 1925): 689–691.

McKay, Claude (Claudius Festus McKay) (1889–1948)

The Jamaican poet whose evocative and incendiary 1919 poem "If We Must Die" is hailed often as a work that not only launched the Harlem Renaissance but also illustrated the keen political passion that informed the works of so many writers of the period. McKay was a prolific writer, publishing some four books of poetry, four novels, an autobiography, a social history of HARLEM, and several essays in diverse publications such as *The Nation, Ebony, Phylon,* and the *Interracial Review* during his lifetime.

Born in September 1889, McKay was the youngest of 11 children born to Thomas Francis McKay and his wife, Ann Elizabeth Edwards McKay, in Nairne Castle, Jamaica. The family, who made there living as farmers, were from Clarendon Parish in Jamaica. McKay's parents were ambitious and eventually owned some 100 acres of land in the area. Scholar Winston James notes that Thomas McKay, whose earliest employment was as a laborer, also became a successful sugar maker who had his own boiler and sugarhouse in which he manufactured sugar using his own highly prized Chattanooga mill exported from Tennessee (James, 98). McKay's parents provided him with his earli-

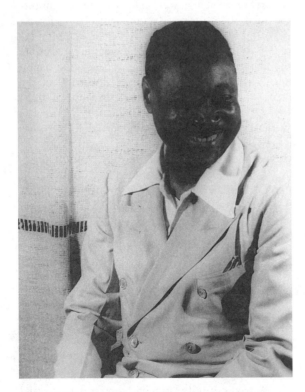

Claude McKay, author. Photograph by Carl Van Vechten. Permission granted by the Van Vechten Trust *(Yale Collection of American Literature, Beinecke Rare Book and Manuscript Library)*

est lessons in the power of literature and the inspiring history of peoples of African descent. His paternal grandfather, from the Ashanti tribe in West Africa, was enslaved, and Thomas McKay underscored the tragedy of such bondage for his son. McKay grew up in Jamaica while it was under colonial rule, and his formal education was based on traditional British materials and history. He learned much from his schoolteacher brother, Uriah, and took advantage of the opportunity to read widely from his brother's library. In 1911, after apprenticeships that included work with wheelwright Walter Jekyll, his first patron and an acquaintance of Robert Louis Stevenson, McKay joined the constabulary force in Spanish Town. He witnessed firsthand the racial politics that informed the justice system and developed an antipathy for the city that would not soon subside. He left before completing one year of service and returned to the more stable world of his family's home in Clarendon.

McKay's first published works, *Songs of Jamaica* and *Constab Ballads,* both of which were collections of dialect poetry, appeared in 1912. His mentor Walter Jekyll was of great assistance to McKay. He was instrumental in arranging the publication of McKay's two books and provided the introduction to *Songs of Jamaica.* McKay dedicated his first book to Sir Sydney Olivier, the governor of Jamaica and a friend of Jekyll's, whom he lauded as one who "by his sympathy with the black race has won the love and admiration of all Jamaicans" (Maxwell, 282). Jekyll, whose introduction attempted to clarify the patois, linguistic styles, and turns of phrase that McKay used in the poems, also noted that "[r]eaders of this volume will be interested to know that they here have the thoughts and feelings of a Jamaican peasant of pure black blood" who had "spent his early years in the depths of the country" (Maxwell, 285). Despite his discomfort and eventual rejection of life in the constabulary, McKay dedicated his volume *Constab Ballads* to his former supervisors, Inspector-General A. E. Kershaw and Inspector W. E. Clark. McKay was gracious in his tribute, noting that it was under these men that he had "had the honor of serving" and that he "respectfully and gratefully dedicated the volume." In his preface to the volume, McKay provided some insights into the challenges that he faced while on the police force. "Let me confess it at once," he wrote, "I had not in me the stuff that goes to the making of a good constable; for I am so constituted that imagination outruns discretion, and it is my misfortune to have a most improper sympathy with wrongdoers" (Maxwell, 295). He went on to make a quite liberal assessment that "We blacks are all somewhat impatient of discipline" and that "to the natural impatience of my race there was added, in my particular case, a peculiar sensitiveness which made certain forms of discipline irksome, and a fierce hatred of injustice" (Maxwell, 296). The response to his work was extremely positive and earned him the honor of becoming the first black Jamaican to win the medal of the island's Institute of Arts and Sciences.

McKay left Jamaica for the United States in 1912 and financed his travels with the prize money that he obtained from the Institute of Arts and Sciences. He headed first to TUSKEGEE INSTITUTE in Alabama. He transferred shortly thereafter to KANSAS STATE COLLEGE in Manhattan, Kansas. He relocated to NEW YORK CITY in 1914 and began what would become one of the most productive and inspiring literary careers of the Harlem Renaissance. McKay married EULALIE EDWARDS, his Jamaican childhood sweetheart. The marriage failed in less than six months, and a pregnant Edwards returned to Jamaica without McKay and there gave birth to their daughter, Rhue Hope Edwards. Known later as Hope McKay Virtue, McKay's daughter attended Columbia Teachers' College in New York City and corresponded with her father before his death. Tragically, their plans to meet for the first time were interrupted by his collapse and subsequent death due to congestive heart failure. Hope McKay passed away in 1992. McKay's extended family, many of whom still live in his former Jamaican village, include a set of twins, who are his great nephew and niece, named by Hartley McKay, their father, Claude and Claudette McKay in honor of their accomplished ancestor (James, "New Light," 98).

McKay traveled extensively throughout his life. He lived and worked in London, during the early 1920s and worked alongside SYLVIA PANKHURST and the staff at the socialist journal WORKER'S DREADNOUGHT. He also completed a substantial number of poems including the collection entitled SPRING IN NEW HAMPSHIRE. He financed his travels to Russia in 1923 by selling copies of his book HARLEM SHADOWS and then enjoyed a yearlong stay there. He was quite active in the COMMUNIST PARTY circles and took advantage of the opportunity to speak at the Kremlin and to participate in the Communist Party's Fourth Congress meeting. He then moved on to FRANCE, where he lived in Paris and was part of the large expatriate community that included a number of African Americans. He also traveled to North Africa and lived in Morocco for a time before returning to America in the mid-1930s.

McKay frequently published under pseudonyms in his early years. He used names inspired by his daughter, such as RHONDA HOPE and HUGH HOPE. He honored his former wife when he developed the pseudonyms E. Edwards, C. E. Edwards, Ness Edwards. He abandoned his use of these and other aliases, however, after 1920.

Claude McKay made his American literary debut in the LIBERATOR, a literary journal edited by socialist MAX EASTMAN. McKay's poem "If We Must Die" is one of the most frequently anthologized American poems. McKay exhorted people of African descent to defy the deadly oppression that threatened to undermine their communities, families, history, and ambitions. British prime minister Winston Churchill quoted McKay's lines during the Second World War. McKay's Liberator poems earned him a reputation as a poet who wrote searing protest poetry. He used graphic images of violence, vivid language, irony, and sarcasm to chronicle the effects of mob violence and to justify widespread resistance to oppression and subjugation. His early supporters included Eastman and his sister, CRYSTAL EASTMAN. The Eastmans influenced McKay's growing political consciousness and were responsible for introducing him to a number of people with links to the Communist Party. It was they who published the much-heralded poem "If We Must Die," which THE CRISIS, to which McKay first submitted the work, rejected. Another important literary ally was Pearson's Magazine editor FRANK HARRIS. Harris, an Irish immigrant and experienced journal editor, published a number of McKay's early American poems in 1918. The two men first met when Harris solicited poems from McKay for the magazine that he hoped "would reach and discover the obscure talents of America who were perhaps discouraged, engaged in uncongenial labor when they might be doing creative work" (Cooper, 89). After an extremely positive and lengthy first meeting, McKay contributed some five poems to the magazine.

McKay's poetry earned him praise, and he was included in major anthologies of the day. ALAIN LOCKE highlighted his work in the pioneering 1925 anthology NEW NEGRO. Two years later, Locke featured McKay in the highly selective 1927 volume entitled FOUR NEGRO POETS. McKay's works appeared alongside that of COUNTEE CULLEN, LANGSTON HUGHES, and JEAN TOOMER. McKay's first published American novel, HOME TO HARLEM (1928), propelled him further into the literary spotlight of the Harlem Renaissance. The work, which appeared some two years after the controversial and graphic novel NIGGER HEAVEN by Carl Van Vechten, often provoked comparisons between the two. Langston Hughes regarded McKay's work as "Nigger Hell" and noted that popular opinion was going against McKay's depictions of contemporary life in Harlem. "[T]he agreement seems to be," he wrote to his longtime friend and correspondent Van Vechten, "that Claude has gone much lower-down and betrayed the race to a much greater extent than you ever thought of doing" (Bernard, 62). Additional works followed in quick succession: BANJO: A STORY WITHOUT A PLOT (1929), a collection of short stories entitled GINGERTOWN (1932), and BANANA BOTTOM (1933). His autobiography, A LONG WAY FROM HOME, appeared in 1937 facilitated in part by McKay's work with the Federal Writers' Project in 1936. The publication fueled his long-standing frustration with Alain Locke, with whom he had a fractious professional relationship. McKay's frustration dated back to the mistakes that Locke made in the New Negro. McKay had chastised Locke for failing to consult him on his own biography and for publishing incorrect details about his life. McKay indulged in a biting critique of Locke in his A Long Way from Home, his autobiography, noting that the Harvard-educated professor and editor suffered from an "academic and pedestrian conception of art," which, "together with his editorial arrogance, made him totally unfit to serve as a spokesman for the black arts in America"

(Cooper, 320). In response, Locke published a scathing review of McKay's autobiography in which he targeted the friendship that he had with Harris, suggested that McKay was "the dark-skinned psychological twin of that same Frank Harris, whom he so cleverly portrays and caricatures," and characterized him as "the enfant terrible of the Negro Renaissance" (Cooper, 320). He was not the only one who regarded Locke as a problematic figure. Zora Neale Hurston, in a lively 1938 letter to James Weldon Johnson, declared, "Alain Locke is a malicious spiteful litt[l]e snot that thinks he ought to be the leading Negro because of his degrees" and that "[f]oiled in that, he spends his time trying to cut the ground from under everybody else" (Kaplan, 413).

McKay participated fully in the life of the Harlem Renaissance. Like many of his peers, however, his frequent and lengthy travels provided him with opportunities to write, forge new friendships, and gather rich material for his works. He had few close friendships with prominent writers, however. According to McKay scholar James Giles, the poet's closest friend was JAMES WELDON JOHNSON, a fellow writer and the executive director of the NATIONAL ASSOCIATION FOR THE ADVANCEMENT OF COLORED PEOPLE. It was Johnson who held a farewell party for McKay on the eve of his departure for Russia. The guest list, which included JESSIE FAUSET, WALTER WHITE, W. E. B. DuBois, and CARL VAN DOREN, certainly testified to McKay's standing. Biographer Wayne Cooper notes that McKay also enjoyed a steady and supportive friendship with ARTHUR SCHOMBURG, the bibliophile whose impressive collection of books and artifacts was transformed into the Schomburg Collection at the 135th Street Branch of the NEW YORK PUBLIC LIBRARY. As the Harlem Renaissance drew to a close, McKay continued to write. His history and sociological narrative, Harlem: Negro Metropolis, appeared in 1940, the same year in which he became a U.S. citizen.

During the last years of his life, McKay lived in CHICAGO, where he converted to Catholicism. He died there and was buried in New York City. His former colleagues continued to discuss his work after his death, and his accomplishments were celebrated on occasions such as the one organized at the Schomburg Library to celebrate the posthumous 1953 publication, *Selected Poems*. ARNA BON-TEMPS, who was involved in the arrangements for the evening, was struck by that fact that McKay's publishers "find out that some folks are STILL mad at Claude, even though he is daid and gone!" (Nichols, 305). In response to his friend's observation, Langston Hughes offered a sincere appraisal of the prolific and enterprising poet. "Either you or somebody else will have to write something objective about the controversial poet. It could be a book of widespread general interest if written quite frankly and with feeling," he told Bontemps. "Claude moved among interesting people at an exciting time. He wrote poignant and sometimes stirring lines. He reacted violently. He had secret loves and open battles. What better subject could a biographer want?" he asked. Claude McKay was one of the most earnest and hardworking writers of the Harlem Renaissance. A self-described "troubadour wandering," he dedicated himself to depicting life and humanity in all of its complexity and color.

Bibliography

Bernard, Emily. *Remember Me to Harlem: The Letters of Langston Hughes and Carl Van Vechten*. New York: Knopf, 2001.

Claude McKay Papers, Beinecke Library, Yale University; Lilly Library, Indiana University, Bloomington; Schomburg Library, New York City; Dillard University, New Orleans; Harvard University; and New York Public Library.

Cooper, Wayne. *Claude McKay: Rebel Sojourner in the Harlem Renaissance*. New York: Schocken Books, 1987.

Giles, James R. *Claude McKay*. Boston: Twayne Publishers, 1976.

Hathaway, Heather. *Caribbean Waves: Relocating Claude McKay and Paule Marshall*. Bloomington: Indiana University Press, 1999.

James, Winston. *A Fierce Hatred of Injustice: Claude McKay's Jamaica and His Poetry of Rebellion*. London: Verso Press, 2000.

———. "New Light on Claude McKay: A Controversy, a Document, and a Resolution." *Black Renaissance* 2, no. 2 (31 July 1999): 98.

Kaplan, Carla. *Zora Neale Hurston: A Life in Letters*. New York: Doubleday, 2002.

Maxwell, William J. *Complete Poems: Claude McKay*. Urbana: University of Illinois Press, 2004.

Nichols, Charles H., ed. *Arna Bontemps–Langston Hughes Letters, 1925–1967*. New York: Paragon House, 1990.

Tillery, Tyrone. *Claude McKay, Man and Symbol of the Harlem Renaissance, 1889–1948*. Amherst: University of Massachusetts Press, 1992.

Medea and Some Poems, The   Countee Cullen (1935)

The book by COUNTEE CULLEN that included his modern translation of *Medea*, the Greek drama by Euripides. Cullen was the first African-American writer to produce a substantial translation of the classic and the first modern writer of color to publish a major translation of a classical text. Cullen completed *Medea*, his last published collection of poems, during his tenure as a French and English teacher at the Frederick Douglass Junior High School in New York City.

Cullen's version of the often-translated Greek drama included accessible prose versions of the drama and poetical translations of the choruses. The PULITZER PRIZE–winning composer Virgil Garnett Thomson, who collaborated with Gertrude Stein in the 1920s, set Cullen's lyrical interpretations to music. The composer Daniel Pinkham updated the musical score in 1967. In his modern version, Cullen attributed Medea's awful power to render men blind to her beauty rather than to her extreme unattractiveness. Cullen underscored Medusa's all-encompassing grief at being abandoned by her husband, Jason. One of the most memorable scenes occurs when she murders her children. Medea urges herself into a state of denial and slips into a third-person address that signals her deeply fractured, traumatized state: "Lock up your heart against pity, Medea," she urges, "let mercy beat at the door, but do not hear. These are not my children. I never kissed them, nor held them to my heart. They were never dear to me. I never bore them! Believe these lies, today, my heart. Tomorrow you may break" (Cullen, 54). Cullen's interpretation tapped into the schizophrenia of the original Medea, who alternates between direct address to her friends and pained self-exhortation. In the original, for instance, Medea declares, "Away with cowardice! Give not one thought to thy babes, how dear they are or how thou art their mother. This one brief day forget thy children dear, and after that lament; for though thou wilt slay them yet they were thy darlings still, and I am a lady of sorrows" (Euripedes, ll. 1468–1471). Throughout the work as a whole, Cullen worked to transform the original script by Euripedes into more accessible modern prose.

In addition to the powerful translation of *Medea,* the volume included translations of poems by Baudelaire, compositions that Cullen wrote while in FRANCE, and an explosive meditation on the case of the Scottsboro Boys. Entitled "Scottsboro, Too, Is Worth Its Song: A Poem to American Poets," the three-stanza poem lamented the fact that writers failed to call attention to the explosive case. "I said, Now will the poets sing," (ll. 1–2) declares the speaker in the opening lines. "Remembering their sharp and pretty / Tunes for Sacco and Vanzetti, / I said: / Here too's a cause divinely spun / For those whose eyes are on the sun." The speaker is dismayed by the ways in which the "disgrace / And epic wrong" prompted major outcries within African-American communities but prompted little cultural examination in the wider American community. The poem ends with a pained observation: "Surely, I said, / Now will the poets sing. / But they have raised no cry. / I wonder why." The poem was reminiscent of earlier Cullen poems such as "Not Sacco and Vanzetti," which appeared in *The Black Christ and Other Poems* (1929) and continued Cullen's tradition of developing political critiques of provocative issues and historical events.

Unlike previous volumes, *The Medea and Some Poems* did not include a number of titled sections. The remaining poems in the volume were not arranged chronologically or according to theme. Included in the set of 27 poems were another poem about Medusa, meditations on Cullen's travels, and poems that addressed the power of emotional bonds and various relationships. In "Medusa," a poem written in first-person voice, the bold and foolhardy speaker recalls his first impressions of the legendary figure. "I was never one to be subdued / By any fear of aught not reason-bred," he recalls, "And so I mocked the ruddy word, and stood / To meet the gold-envenomed dart instead" (ll. 5–8). The poem

closes as the speaker reveals the limits of his immunity but rationalizes his loss of sight, the traditional penalty for those who would look upon Medusa, so that it reflects his unfailing romanticism: "Though blind, yet on these arid balls engraved / I know it was a lovely face I braved" (ll. 13–14).

Other more personal poems included "Three Nonsense Rhymes for My Three Goddaughters," which included three sections, one dedicated to "Diana," another to "Barbara who seldom smiles," and a final piece on "Mathematics for Carol not yet two." Cullen also included a number of formal, untitled sonnets on love that contemplated the glories of love and the limitations of human feeling. In "I have not loved you in the noblest way," the speaker assures his audience that "Loved have I much, but I have not been blind" (l. 8). Despite his apparent failings, however, he justifies himself and clarifies the high demands that noble feeling requires. "The noblest way is fraught with too much pain," he suggests, "Who travels it must drag a crucifix" (ll. 9–10). He concludes with a reference to the great mythological warrior Achilles, noting, "My mother never dipped me in the Styx, / And who would find me weak and vulnerable / Need never aim his arrow at my heel" (ll. 12–14). In "I would I could," the poet considers his desire for more inspiration, noting that "I would I might exchange this draggled plume / for one more exquisite, more brightly hued, / Snatched from a breast still singing in its doom" (ll. 9–11). Yet, despite his craving for a more rich and inspired pen, he realizes the power of authenticity. The poem closes as the speaker comes to the conclusion that "I can only sing of what I know, / And all I know, or ever knew, is woe" (ll. 13–14).

The last of Cullen's original volumes of poetry, *The Medea and Some Poems,* demonstrated the poet's classical training, investment in traditional forms, and efforts to use poetry to showcase universal themes that defy racial categorization.

Bibliography

Cullen, Countee. *Medea and Some Poems.* New York: Harper & Brothers, 1935.

Ferguson, Blanche. *Countee Cullen and the Negro Renaissance.* New York: Dodd, Mead, 1966.

Shucard, Alan. *Countee Cullen.* Boston: Twayne, 1984.

Meek Mose Frank Wilson (1928)

The BROADWAY play by FRANK WILSON, who would later see his play *Walk Together Chillun* (1936) staged on Broadway at the LAFAYETTE THEATRE. *Meek Mose* critiqued residential segregation, black disenfranchisement, and race pride.

The story revolves around a community that faces upheaval. Whites engineer the relocation of the community from "Blacktown" to "Badtown." Meek Mose, the title character, encourages his neighbors to accept the humiliating loss of their homes. The play's tragic plot ultimately evolves into a triumphant story of a dispossessed community that discovers oil and is able to profit from its natural resources.

The play opened on 6 February 1928 at the Princess Theatre and ran for some 24 performances. The premiere included speeches by New York City mayor Jimmy Walker and by Max Reinhardt, a theatrical producer from Europe. The director was George MacEntee, and the producer was Lester Walton.

The cast on opening night included LAURA BOWMAN, an actress who appeared in the celebrated 1923 productions of *THE CHIP WOMAN'S FORTUNE* and *Salome*, plays by the pioneering playwright WILLIS RICHARDSON. Also appearing was Alston Burleigh, who followed his Broadway debut in Wilson's play with an appearance in *HARLEM*, the play by WALLACE THURMAN and WILLIAM JOURDAN RAPP.

Mencken, Henry Louis (H. L. Mencken)
(1880–1956)

A well-known cultural critic, editor, and prolific journalist who was editor of *AMERICAN MERCURY* and who established friendships with well-known figures of the Harlem Renaissance such as JAMES WELDON JOHNSON, CARL VAN VECHTEN, and WALTER WHITE.

Born to August and Anna Abhau Mencken in Baltimore, he attended the Knapp's Institute, a school for children of the city's bourgeoisie, and Baltimore Polytechnic Institute. He began his career in journalism in 1899, just one day after his father passed away.

Mencken's views on racial matters included contempt for the KU KLUX KLAN and for ideas that African Americans were inferior to whites. He participated in events such as the legendary MANHATTAN CIVIC CLUB dinner hosted by CHARLES S. JOHNSON, editor of *OPPORTUNITY*, in March 1924.

Mencken regarded the Harlem Renaissance as an opportunity for African-American writers to retaliate against white culture for its abuse and caricatures of people of color. He believed in the necessity of the great African-American novel, a work in which a writer would expound upon specific areas in which African-Americans excelled above all others.

Mencken shared his ideas on the potential for the Harlem Renaissance in several forums, including an informative compendium of ideas on Negro art initiated by W. E. B. DUBOIS and published in *THE CRISIS*. CLAUDE MCKAY initiated a correspondence with Mencken in the hope that the latter would publish his work. While Mencken never promoted McKay, the two did share ideas about Russian history and other political matters. James Weldon Johnson was attracted to Mencken's use of satire and recommended that African Americans consider the narrative style as a weapon to use in the fight against oppression. In October 1922 Johnson, writing in the the *NEW YORK AGE*, proposed that "phases of the race question offer a great field for some colored writer who could employ the methods used by H. L. Mencken in attacking various foibles of civilization in general and of the American people in particular" (Scruggs, 58). ALAIN LOCKE challenged Mencken about his ideas and conceptions of the Harlem Renaissance but was one of the many intellectuals of color who read and discussed Mencken's work. Novelist and social critic GEORGE SCHUYLER published frequently in *American Mercury* during Mencken's tenure. He was appointed editor in 1924, when the journal was founded, and held the position until 1933.

Bibliography

H. L. Mencken Papers, New York Public Library.

Manchester, William. *Disturber of the Peace: The Life of H. L. Mencken.* Amherst: University of Massachusetts Press, 1986.

Scruggs, Charles W. *The Sage in Harlem: H. L. Mencken and the Black Writers of the 1920s.* Baltimore: Johns Hopkins University Press, 1984.

Stenerson, Douglas. *Critical Essays on H. L. Mencken.* Boston: G. K. Hall, 1987.

Yardley, Jonathan, ed. *My Life as Author and Editor by H. L. Mencken.* New York: Knopf, 1993.

Meschrabpom Film Corporation

The Russian film company that planned to produce BLACK AND WHITE, a film about race and racism in America. Known as the Meschrabpom Film of the Worker's International Relief, the company's interests were supported by an American organization, the Co-operating Committee on Production of a Soviet Film on Negro Life. The chair of the committee was W. A. DOMINGO. LOUISE THOMPSON volunteered her time to the committee and served as executive secretary. It was she who promoted *Black and White* and solicited her colleagues and friends to join. Domingo believed that the company would "trace the development of the Negro people in America, their work, their play, their progress, their difficulties" and do so in a film that was "devoid of sentimentality as well as of buffoonery" (Berry, 156).

Twenty-two individuals agreed to work with the company, and in 1932 they sailed for Russia to begin the project. Among those who went were LANGSTON HUGHES, Loren Miller, TED POSTON, Louise Thompson, and DOROTHY WEST. The company ultimately canceled the project under pressure from white investors who wanted to suppress the realistic and negative depictions of American society.

Langston Hughes, who had been called to testify in March 1953 before the Senate Permanent Subcommittee on Investigations of the Committee on Government Operations, endured questions about his travels in Russia.

Bibliography

Berry, Faith, ed. *Langston Hughes: Before and Beyond Harlem.* Westport, Conn.: Lawrence Hill & Company, 1983.

Rampersad, Arnold. *The Life of Langston Hughes: I, Too, Sing America.* Vol. 1: *1902–1941.* New York: Oxford University Press, 1986.

———. *The Life of Langston Hughes: I Dream a World.* Vol. 2: *1941–1967.* New York: Oxford University Press, 1988.

Messenger, The

The monthly journal that A. PHILIP RANDOLPH and CHANDLER OWEN established in NEW YORK CITY in 1917. It was the third most popular Harlem Renaissance African-American magazine and, unlike THE CRISIS and OPPORTUNITY, was not the official publication of an organization dedicated to achieving civil rights.

The magazine, which was published for 11 years, promoted socialist philosophies and advanced its theories for racial uplift and success. The editors sharply criticized the NATIONAL ASSOCIATION FOR THE ADVANCEMENT OF COLORED PEOPLE (NAACP) for what they deemed weak positions on critical issues such as segregation.

Its contributors included a number of writers whose works appeared also in *The Crisis* and *Opportunity.* These included COUNTEE CULLEN, ANGELINA WELD GRIMKÉ, WALTER EVERETTE HAWKINS, LANGSTON HUGHES, ZORA NEALE HURSTON, PAUL ROBESON, and DOROTHY WEST. Like its counterparts published by the NAACP and the NATIONAL URBAN LEAGUE, *The Messenger* was an interdisciplinary and multi-genre periodical. Issues featured fiction and poetry, book and drama reviews, and essays. Contributors of nonfiction included ALICE DUNBAR-NELSON, THOMAS MILLARD HENRY, CHANDLER OWEN, J. A. ROGERS, and GEORGE SCHUYLER. WALLACE THURMAN was one of the managing editors and the person responsible for building the literary dimensions of the journal.

According to Sondra Wilson, the journal advocated a strong position on race matters. Its editors believed in a New Negro, but one who would "no longer turn the other cheek" (Wilson, xxiii). Historian Manning Marable suggests that *The Messenger* was one of the most forthright critics of MARCUS GARVEY. The journal contributed to the dynamic world of African-American journalism and sparked many debates about contemporary issues such as PAN-AFRICANISM, black nationalism, segregation, and unionization. The outspoken views expressed in the periodical prompted the arrest of editors Randolph and Owen in August 1918 at an antiwar rally. Charges against them, filed under the ESPIONAGE ACT, were dropped because the judge expressed his doubts that the two men were experienced and old enough to have written and cultivated such antiwar and antigovernment opinions.

The Messenger offered readers an unapologetic forceful critique of social policy and current events. It provided another important forum in which writers could debate diverse social and political matters and present the dynamic ideas and absorbing work that so enriched the Harlem Renaissance period.

Bibliography

Anderson, Jervis. *A. Philip Randolph: A Biographical Portrait*. New York: Harcourt Brace Jovanovich, 1973.

Pfeffer, Paula. *A. Philip Randolph, Pioneer of the Civil Rights Movement*. Baton Rouge: Louisiana State University Press, 1990.

Wilson, Sondra, ed. *The Messenger Reader: Stories, Poetry, and Essays from The Messenger Magazine*. New York: Modern, 2000.

Millen, James Knox (unknown)

A southern playwright who incorporated African Americans in his casts and explored volatile issues such as LYNCHING. He worked with figures such as Howard Linsay, Chester Erskin, and Robin Sparks. His set designers included the celebrated Jo Mielziner.

Among the African-American actors who appeared in Millen's work were the veteran Rose McClendon, William L. Andrews, Viola Dean, and Leigh Whipper.

Millen's works, which often appeared on Broadway, included *Flame*, which was renamed and performed as *Never No More* (1932), *The Bough Breaks* (1937), and *Old Autumn*. The works appeared in such Broadway venues as the Hudson Theatre and Little Theatre. Millen's work was reviewed in major publications such as the *New York Times*. The highly respected drama critic J. Brooks Atkinson praised Millen for *Never No More*, a play that he described as "a harrowing, sincerely resolute play" (*NYT*, 8 January 1932, 27).

Bibliography

Atkinson, T. Brooks. "The Play: Lynching Bee." *New York Times*, 8 January 1932, 27.

"Theatrical Notes." *New York Times*, 12 December 1931, 23.

"The Openings." *New York Times*, 3 January 1932, X1.

"The Stage." *New York Times*, 17 September 1940, 33.

Miller, Kelly (1863–1969)

The first African American admitted to Johns Hopkins University, a dean at HOWARD UNIVERSITY, and the father of the accomplished playwright MAY MILLER SULLIVAN.

Miller, who is remembered as the first African-American graduate student in mathematics, was the sixth of 10 children born to Kelly Miller, a free African American and Confederate army soldier, and Elizabeth Roberts Miller, an enslaved woman.

Born in Winnsboro, South Carolina, he soon demonstrated his talent for mathematics. He won a scholarship to Howard University and earned his bachelor of science degree in 1886. Miller went on to study astronomy, physics, and mathematics at Johns Hopkins, one of the first universities to establish a graduate program in mathematics. Miller later earned a master's degree and an LL.D from Howard. He taught at the M STREET HIGH SCHOOL in WASHINGTON, D.C. He enjoyed a lengthy career at Howard, where he taught sociology and was one of the school's most highly regarded scholars and administrators.

Miller published much of his work in the years preceding the Harlem Renaissance.

He married Annie May Butler, a schoolteacher at the Baltimore Normal School, in July 1894. The couple had five children, including May, an accomplished playwright, active member of the literary circles in Washington, D.C., and close friend of playwright GEORGIA DOUGLAS JOHNSON.

Bibliography

Dyson, Walter. *Howard University, The Capstone of Negro Education, a History: 1867–1940*. Washington, D.C.: The Graduate School, Howard University, 1941.

Jackson, W. Sherman. *Kelly Miller and the Nadir of Race Relations in America*. New York: Garland, 1992.

Kelly Miller Papers, Moorland-Spingarn Research Center, Howard University.

Logan, Rayford. *Howard University: The First Hundred Years, 1867–1967*. New York: New York University Press, 1969.

Miller, Kelly. *Out of the House of Bondage: A Discussion of the Race Problem*. New York: T. Y. Crowell, 1914.

Miller, May *See* SULLIVAN, MAY MILLER.

Mims, Edwin (1872–1959)

A Vanderbilt University professor and the author of THE ADVANCING SOUTH. Mims, a professor in the English department, was a Vanderbilt alumnus and served as department chair from 1912 through 1942.

ALAIN LOCKE reviewed *The Advancing South* in the December 1926 issue of OPPORTUNITY. The book, published by Doubleday, Page & Company, focused on economic and social conditions in the American South. Locke praised Mims for his "cautiousness of tact rather than of timidity" and his efforts to provide "an adequate and convincing portrayal of the progressive and enlightened liberalism which is working out what has been aptly phrased as the 'second Reconstruction' in the South." Locke especially endorsed the book to African Americans. He proposed that Mims's work would "broade[n] . . . their inevitably narrowed vision of the South" and benefit from "the important realization that the race problem cannot be isolated from the other social problems of the Southland, and that a policy of isolation, either in thought or public interest of public action, is fatal under the circumstances of the present generation."

In 1986 Vanderbilt alumnus Lucius Burch, of the class of 1934, spearheaded the campaign to establish the Edwin Mims Professorship, an endowed chair in English.

Bibliography

Conkin, Paul. *Gone with the Ivy: A Biography of Vanderbilt University.* Knoxville: University of Tennessee Press, 1985.

Mims, Edwin. *The Advancing South: Stories of Progress and Reaction.* Garden City, N.Y.: Doubleday, Page & Company, 1926.

"Miss Kenny's Marriage" Eric Walrond (1923)

A short story by ERIC WALROND that was published in the September 1923 issue of *Smart Set,* a journal that promoted literary modernism and was edited by George Jean Nathan and H. L. MENCKEN.

Bibliography

Parascandola, Louis, ed. *Winds Can Wake Up the Dead: An Eric Walrond Reader.* Detroit: Wayne State University Press, 1998.

Mitchell, Joseph Solon (1891–unknown)

An Alabama-born attorney and playwright, Mitchell was born in Auburn, Alabama, in August 1891. He was the son of Solon and Elizabeth Switcher Mitchell. In 1923 he married Lucy Q. B. Miller, a native of Daytona Beach, Florida. The couple had a daughter, Laura Mitchell Holland, and a son, Joseph Mitchell, Jr.

Mitchell's education included undergraduate study at Talladega College and law studies at BOSTON UNIVERSITY. He earned his B.A. in 1913 and an LL.B. in 1917. He began working in the criminal justice and legal system in BOSTON. He held positions on the Massachusetts Parole Board and was assistant attorney general from 1945 through 1949. He was appointed assistant corporate counsel for the city of Boston in 1950.

An active member of the Republican Party, Mitchell belonged to several party organizations, including the Boston Republican club and the Suffolk County Republicans. He maintained a membership in the Boston Bar Association and was the director and treasurer of the Boston Center for Adult Education.

He was part of Boston's active literary circle during the Harlem Renaissance. He published in the SATURDAY EVENING QUILL, a monthly periodical produced by the literary society of the same name, whose members included EUGENE GORDON, FLORIDA RUFFIN RIDLEY, and DOROTHY WEST. Other prominent writers whose work appeared in the *Quill* included WARING CUNEY and ALVIRA HAZZARD. Mitchell's plays *Son-Boy* (1928) and *HELP WANTED* (1929) were published in the June 1928 and April 1929 issues of the *Quill,* respectively.

"Mob Madness" Marion Vera Cuthbert (1936)

One of several highly evocative works that focused on LYNCHING and its devastating effects on American families and society.

Written by MARION VERA CUTHBERT and published in the April 1936 issue of THE CRISIS, the story focuses on Lizzie, a white wife and mother who is driven to murder in the wake of a gruesome lynching in her town. Her husband, a "six-foot red-red-faced" man named Jim, is only too proud to relay the horrific graphic details of the lynching in which he has played an active role. When he produces an unidentifiable black object wrapped in a handkerchief to Little Jim, their son, Lizzie is thoroughly traumatized. She fails to respond to the neighbors who remind her of the recent violence or to the desperate, unidentified African-American woman who beseeches her for help in the wake of white violence against her family and home.

As the short story closes, Lizzie murders her daughter Bessie. She chooses to kill her daughter, rather than her son or husband, because she imagines Bessie as the object of potential violence. When her husband discovers the body, he assumes immediately that the killer is an African American and plans to launch another murderous spree to lynch the perpetrator. The sheriff ultimately convinces him that his own wife is the villain.

Cuthbert's story complemented the efforts to protest and outlaw lynching by THE CRISIS and its parent organization, the NATIONAL ASSOCIATION FOR THE ADVANCEMENT OF COLORED PEOPLE. The story also was part of the significant body of antilynching works by writers such as GEORGIA DOUGLAS JOHNSON, MARY BURRILL, and RIDGELY TORRENCE.

Bibliography
Gunning, Sandra. *Race, Rape, and Lynching: The Red Record of American Literature, 1890–1912.* New York: Oxford University Press, 1996.

Harris, Trudier. *Exorcizing Blackness: Historical and Literary Lynching and Burning Rituals.* Bloomington: Indiana University Press, 1984.

Mohammed Ali, Duse (1867–unknown)

A journalist and pan-Africanist and one of the persons who most influenced MARCUS GARVEY. The two men met in London in the early 1900s, and Garvey worked as a messenger for Mohammed when the latter founded *Africa and Orient Review,* a monthly anticolonization journal.

Mohammed, who was of Sudanese and Egyptian descent, later worked as a foreign affairs expert for *NEGRO WORLD,* the official newspaper of Garvey's UNIVERSAL NEGRO IMPROVEMENT ASSOCIATION.

Bibliography
Adi, Hakim. *Pan-African History: Political Figures from Africa and the Diaspora since 1787.* London: Routledge, 2003.

Cronon, Edmund. *Black Moses: The Story of Marcus Garvey and the Universal Negro Improvement Association.* Madison: University of Wisconsin Press, 1987.

Martin, Tony. *The Pan-African Connection: From Slavery to Garvey and Beyond.* Dover, Mass.: Majority Press, 1984.

Moods: A Book of Verse Idabelle Yeiser (1937)

A volume of poetry by IDABELLE YEISER, a COLUMBIA UNIVERSITY Ph.D., Dillard University professor, and member of the active literary circle in PHILADELPHIA during the Harlem Renaissance period.

Published in Philadelphia by the Colony Press, the collection was Yeiser's first published book of poetry. It included an array of works and was divided into five sections. Poems appeared in categories devoted to nature, children, love, and philosophy and included another with short works entitled Miniatures.

The collection revealed Yeiser's impatience with social and racial hypocrisy, her interest in considering the status of women, and her speculations about family life.

Moody Bible Institute

The CHICAGO religious school established in 1889 by Dwight Lyman Moody, a Northfield, MASSACHUSETTS native, an educator, and an evangelist.

Moody became a successful businessman in Chicago before traveling as an evangelist throughout America and England during the 1870s. The Chicago Bible school that he founded in 1889 was known first as the Bible Institute for Home and Foreign Missions. It was the third educational institute that Moody had established; in 1879 he established the Northfield Seminary for Young Ladies and in 1881, the Mt. Hermon School for Boys, both in western Massachusetts.

One of the school's best-known graduates was MARY MCLEOD BETHUNE. The enterprising educator, feminist, and civic leader received a scholarship to attend Moody. Bethune, who intended to become a missionary abroad, graduated in 1893. She became an educational pioneer, however, founding Bethune-Cookman Institute and developing national networks that brought her into contact with numerous Harlem Renaissance figures.

Bibliography

Findlay, James. *Dwight L. Moody, American Evangelist, 1837–1899.* Chicago: University of Chicago Press, 1969.

Hansen, Joyce. *Mary McLeod Bethune and Black Women's Political Activism.* Columbia: University of Missouri Press, 2003.

Moody, William. *D. L. Moody.* New York: Garland, 1988.

Robertson, Darrel. *The Chicago Revival, 1876: Society and Revivalism in a Nineteenth-Century City.* Metuchen, N.J.: Scarecrow Press, 1989.

Sterne, Emma. *Mary McLeod Bethune.* New York: Knopf, 1957.

Moore, Fred Randolph (1857–1943)

A journalist and founding member of the NATIONAL URBAN LEAGUE. Born in WASHINGTON, D.C., Moore worked first in the federal government as a messenger and served five secretaries of the Treasury. He became the owner of the NEW YORK AGE in 1907 and continued to write for the newspaper until he was in his 80s. He became editor of the *Colored American Magazine* when a hostile takeover, engineered by BOOKER T. WASHINGTON, ousted the accomplished writer and editor Pauline Hopkins from the Boston-based magazine. Moore also was a member of the National Negro Business League.

Bibliography

Johnson, Abby Arthur, and Ronald Maberry Johnson. *Propaganda & Aesthetics: The Literary Politics of African American Magazines in the Twentieth Century.* Amherst: University of Massachusetts, 1979.

Morand, Paul (1888–1976)

A French diplomat and writer who published numerous works, including two books about America and peoples of African descent, that generated critical interest during the Harlem Renaissance.

He was the son of Eugène and Marie-Louise Charrier Morand. His father was a curator at the Louvre and a dramatist, painter, and translator. As a result, Paul Morand met many influential artists and writers, including Auguste Rodin, Sarah Bernhardt, and Oscar Wilde. He was educated at the Lycée Carnot and the University of Paris, and he spent a year at Oxford. Morand married Hélène Soutzo, a Romanian princess, in 1927.

Morand was a prolific author and poet, and his earliest works were extremely well received. The poet Ezra Pound provided the English translation of Morand's second volume of poetry. Other esteemed writers such as Marcel Proust enjoyed his work.

During the late 1920s Morand's diplomatic career enabled him to travel widely throughout Europe, Africa, and the Caribbean. His travels influenced his 1928 volume MAGIE NOIRE, a book whose title means "black magic" and which included several short stories about people of color in African countries, the West Indies, and in America, often treated in a stereotypical and racist fashion. The artist AARON DOUGLAS provided the illustrations for the American publication of the work that was produced by Viking Press in 1929.

Morand supported the Vichy government during World War II and was subsequently exiled from France. He was able to return to his native country in 1953 and was elected to the Académie Française in 1968. He died in July 1976.

Bibliography

Guitard-Auviste, Ginette. *Paul Morand.* Paris: Éditions universitaires, 1956.

Lemaître, Georges. *Four French Novelists: Marcel Proust, André Gide, Jean Giraudoux, Paul Morand.* London: Oxford University Press, 1938.

Morand, Paul. *Black Magic,* translated by Hamish Miles. New York: Viking Press, 1929.

Morehouse College

A historically black college located in ATLANTA, Georgia, and the nation's only African-American college for men. It was founded in 1867 by William Jefferson White, a Baptist minister, and Richard

Coulter, a formerly enslaved man from Augusta. The men established the school in the basement of the Springfield Baptist Church in Augusta, Georgia, the oldest independent African-American church in the nation. Its first president was the Reverend Dr. Joseph Robert.

Known as the Augusta Institute, the school was dedicated to graduating men who would pursue careers as ministers and teachers. The school relocated to Atlanta in 1879 and was renamed the Atlanta Baptist Seminary. The school became Morehouse College in the early 1900s, named in honor of Henry Morehouse, a prominent Atlanta man and the corresponding secretary of the Atlanta Baptist Home Mission Society. The first president of the newly renamed Morehouse College was JOHN HOPE, a Phi Beta Kappa graduate of BROWN UNIVERSITY and the school's first African-American president.

Morehouse graduates went on to impressive careers and positions of influence in science, education, politics, journalism, and other fields. Among its most well known graduates are BENJAMIN BRAWLEY, a literary critic who later joined the faculty; MORDECAI JOHNSON, the first African-American president of HOWARD UNIVERSITY; Howard Thurman, an eminent theologian; Martin Luther King, Jr., the civil rights leader and Nobel Peace Prize winner; Hugh Gloster, president emeritus of Morehouse; journalist Lerone Bennett; Maynard Jackson, the first African-American mayor of Atlanta; David Satcher, a U.S. surgeon general; Samuel Jackson, an accomplished actor; and Spike Lee, a dynamic filmmaker and producer.

Bibliography

Butler, Addie. *The Distinctive Black College: Talladega, Tuskegee, and Morehouse.* Metuchen, N.J.: Scarecrow Press, 1977.

Jones, Edward. *A Candle in the Dark: A History of Morehouse College.* Valley Forge, Pa.: Judson Press, 1967.

Mortgaged Willis Richardson (1924)

A play by the pioneering playwright WILLIS RICHARDSON, a graduate of the M STREET HIGH SCHOOL. *Mortgaged* was the first play by a professional African-American playwright to be performed at HOWARD UNIVERSITY. The enterprising Howard University professors T. MONTGOMERY GREGORY and ALAIN LOCKE worked together to bring Richardson's work to the campus in the wake of his phenomenal success as the first African-American dramatist to see his works performed on BROADWAY.

The play revolves around two brothers whose obsessions with social appearance have awful consequences for their relationship. The protagonists are John and Tom Fields. John is a widowed chemist determined to finance his son's HARVARD UNIVERSITY education. Tom is a heartless landlord who uses the rent from his many dilapidated properties to finance the high-profile social life of his family. When John needs to borrow money from his brother to pay his son's college bills, his calculating brother demands that John give up his seemingly unprofitable chemical research and find another job. A dedicated father, John agrees to the terms but is saved from the Faustian bargain when a major chemical company invests in his research and purchases one of his chemical inventions. Freed from the potentially demeaning circumstances, John lectures his brother on the evils of oppression and poverty.

The play addresses African-American life, upward mobility, and racism in the workplace and in schools and underscores the value of education and scholarship.

Bibliography

Gray, Christine Rauchfuss. *Willis Richardson, Forgotten Pioneer of African-American Drama.* Westport, Conn.: Greenwood Press, 1999.

Moryck, Brenda Ray (1894–1949)

A WELLESLEY COLLEGE graduate, teacher, reporter, and author of prize-winning short stories.

Born in New Jersey, she was a descendant of the Reverend Charles Ray, a former blacksmith, active abolitionist, and Congregational minister who worked alongside other pastors such as Henry Highland Garnet and Samuel Ringgold in the effort to abolish American slavery and to achieve racial equality and advancement. Her grandmother was Henrietta Cordelia Ray, an accomplished poet and educator. In 1872, Moryck's great-aunt, Charlotte Ray, was the first African-

American woman to graduate from the HOWARD UNIVERSITY Law School.

Moryck, who graduated from Wellesley College in 1916, married Lucius Lee Jordan one year later. Following her marriage, she began working in the Newark Bureau of Associated Charities. By 1925 she was teaching in WASHINGTON, D.C., at the Armstrong Technical High School. While there, she collaborated with playwright and Howard University graduate MAY MILLER SULLIVAN.

She married again in 1930. Her second husband, Robert Francke, was an attorney and member of the Haitian legation in Paris. The couple had one child, Betty Osborne.

Moryck, an avid reader who had long cherished the idea of writing, made an impressive debut in OPPORTUNITY, the magazine edited by CHARLES S. JOHNSON and affiliated with the NATIONAL URBAN LEAGUE. In 1925 she won second prize for "A Man I Know," an essay evaluated by judges BENJAMIN BRAWLEY, VAN WYCK BROOKS, and Henry Goddard Leach. She earned a second-place honorable mention in the 1926–27 *Opportunity* contest for her essay "When A Negro Sings." In 1927 she placed second, behind MARITA BONNER, in the Literary Art and Expression Division of the contest sponsored by THE CRISIS, the journal of the NATIONAL ASSOCIATION FOR THE ADVANCEMENT OF COLORED PEOPLE (NAACP) that was edited by W. E. B. DUBOIS. Moryck was recognized for three short stories, "Old Days and New," "Days," and "Her Little Brother." Her essay "I, Too, Have Lived in Washington," published in the August 1927 issue of *Opportunity*, was a glowing testimonial of her experiences in Washington, D.C., and offered a direct contrast to the less favorable depictions of the city published by LANGSTON HUGHES in the same issue.

Moryck's work reflected her long-standing interest in social hierarchies, racial identity, and culture. Before her death from pneumonia in 1949, Moryck was rumored to have completed a novel. It was unpublished, however. She was an energetic presence in New York and in Washington, D.C. A member of the NAACP, she also participated in the NATIONAL COUNCIL OF NEGRO WOMEN.

Bibliography

Brown, Hallie Quinn, comp. *Homespun Heroines and Other Women of Distinction*. 1926, reprint, New York: Oxford University Press, 1988.

Moses, Man of the Mountain Zora Neale Hurston (1939)

The second of three novels that ZORA NEALE HURSTON published during the Harlem Renaissance. Her last novel, *Seraph on the Sewanee*, appeared in 1948. Published by the PHILADELPHIA company J. B. LIPPINCOTT, the novel was a racialized version of the Old Testament story of Moses and the Israelites. Hurston used dialect, colloquial phrases, folk humor, and elements of black religious thought in her novel about emancipation from bondage, caste, and racial prejudice, and faith. Her short story "THE FIRE AND THE CLOUD," published in 1934 in *CHALLENGE*, the ambitious but short-lived journal that DOROTHY WEST established, was a precursor to the novel. Five years later—after having worked on other projects, traveled in HAITI, and gained employment with the Florida Federal Writers' Project—Hurston finally returned to her hometown of EATONVILLE, Florida, and completed the novel.

Moses, Man of the Mountain offers stirring critiques of oppression, victimization, and assimilation. Hurston's portraits of a community besieged by Pharaoh and his soldiers are powerful and stark. Hurston offers a pointed commentary on the politics and potential revolutionary dimensions of reproduction and childbirth. In her foreword to the work, Hurston underscores the universal familiarity with Moses, a figure at the heart of legends in such diverse regions as Asia, the Near East, Europe, Africa, and the West Indies. She successfully contextualizes the Christian concept of Moses by narrating first in staccato fashion and including traditional, simplistic details such as "Moses was an old man with a beard" and "He died on Mount Nebo and the angels buried him there." Drawing on her own anthropological expertise, she reminds readers of his centrality in diverse cultures, including that of Haiti. There, states Hurston, "the highest god in the Haitian pantheon is Damballa Ouedo Ouedo Tocan Freda Dahomey and he is identified as Moses, the serpent god." She goes on, noting that "this deity did not originate in Haiti. His home is in Dahomey and is worshipped there extensively. Moses had his rod of power, which was a living serpent. So that in ever temple of Damballa there is a living snake, or the symbol." Hurston locates the life and power of Moses squarely within the African diaspora, noting earnestly that "[w]herever the children of Africa have been scattered by slavery, there is the acceptance of Moses as the fountain of mystic powers."

Hurston's Moses is a child of Ethiopian and Assyrian parentage and, as such, is central to her daring revisionist reading of the Bible and contemporary critique of American racism. As Hurston biographer Valerie Boyd notes, the writer's focus on this dimension of the biblical story calls attention to the protagonist's blackness. Hurston later uses Moses's decision to marry Zipporah, an Ethiopian woman, to challenge further notions of racial purity and to tease out the documented but underplayed evidence of racism in the Bible. According to Gloria Cronin, Hurston's story of enslavement, fugitive days, and emancipation was a vehicle through which she could "uncover the fundamental patriarchal error at the very foundations of historical Judeo-Christianity and provide a corrosive parallel commentary on both Nazi Germany and white America." Her retelling would equate America with Egypt, suggests Cronin, and Hurston's attention to unyielding hierarchies would "critique the gendered and racially ordered foundations of Judeo-Christianity, German and the U.S." (Cronin, 14). Biographer Robert Hemenway notes that the significance of *Moses, Man of the Mountain* is inextricably linked to the dominance of the Moses story in African-American culture. He suggests that "[t]o understand fully what Hurston attempted in this novel, one must remember the identification made by captive black slaves in America with the children of Israel in Egypt, and the resulting role that Moses played in Afro-American folklore" (Hemenway, 258). Hurston's depictions of Moses' evolution and increasing transcendence all function as persuasive allegories of African-American experiences in the passage from enslavement to emancipation. The novel also reflects Hurston's lifelong interest in folk culture. She incorporates elements of hoodoo, or what she describes as "sympathetic magic," into her repre-sentations of Moses, his family, and his emancipated but restless community of former slaves.

Hurston dedicated the novel to Edwin Osgood Grover, president of Rollins College and one of her supporters. In an October 1939 letter to him, she voiced her hopes that, unlike her, he would not be disappointed by the book. "I don't think that I achieved all that I set out to do," she wrote. "I thought that in this book I would achieve my ideal, but it seems that I have not reached it yet but I shall keep trying as I know you want me to" (Kaplan, 422). The reviews of the novel recognized its "racial vitality" and "dramatic intensity" but tended to critique its narrative style. Reactions from members of the Harlem Renaissance community varied greatly. ALAIN LOCKE dismissed it as "caricature" and RALPH ELLISON declared that it did nothing to advance the African-American literary tradition. Yet, CARL VAN VECHTEN praised the work and recommended heartily that his friend LANGSTON HUGHES seek it out. "I hope you will look into Zora's new book," he wrote in November 1939, less than three weeks after it appeared. "It is very good indeed," he insisted (Kaplan, 155).

Moses, Man of the Mountain is a compelling narrative, one informed by the belief about human agency that she considered in DUST TRACKS ON A ROAD, her 1942 autobiography. Hurston was convinced that human beings are responsible for their own destiny, that all have been "given a mind and will-power for that very purpose" (Hurston, 202). In *Moses, Man of the Mountain* she crafted a novel that emphasized the ways in which a range of individuals could effect their own transcendence and self-development in the public and private spheres.

Bibliography
Boyd, Valerie. *Wrapped in Rainbows: The Life of Zora Neale Hurston.* New York: Scribner, 2003.

Cronin, Gloria L. "Introduction: Going to the Far Horizon." In *Critical Essays on Zora Neale Hurston,* edited by Gloria Cronin. New York: G. K. Hall & Co., 1998.

Hemenway, Robert. *Zora Neale Hurston: A Literary Biography.* Urbana: University of Illinois Press, 1977.

Hurston, Zora Neale. *Dust Tracks on a Road.* 1942; reprint, New York: Harper Perennial, 1991.

Kaplan, Carla. *Zora Neale Hurston: A Life in Letters.* New York: Doubleday, 2002.

Mother Liked It Alvira Hazzard (1928)

A one-act play by ALVIRA HAZZARD that was published first in the SATURDAY EVENING QUILL, a BOSTON literary journal. Hazzard considered issues of deception and social conflict in the story about Jonas Smithly, a young man whose summer job is to appear in public as Ali Khan, an Indian Prince. The job enables him to pay his UNIVERSITY OF CHICAGO tuition.

Alta Fields, a character identified as one "[w]hose practical jokes misfire," and Tess, a woman who "takes life as she finds it," ridicule their friend Meena Thomas, a romantic who is completely enamored of the prince. Alta and Tess mastermind their own deception and hire Jay Windsor, another friend, to impersonate the false prince. Ultimately, the two men conspire to introduce Smithly to Meena, the "girl of the golden smile," whom he so admires. He reveals his true identity in a letter and notes that he will even change his real given name, even though "mother liked it." The play, set in a local theater and a trendy café, offers a concise examination of racial and social performance.

Mother Liked It, which does not appear to have been performed widely, was most likely staged by amateur theater groups that tended to perform other Hazzard plays.

M Street High School

One of the most prestigious high schools for African Americans in the country. Located in WASHINGTON, D.C., its roster of faculty and students was a daunting record of intellectual excellence. In 1916 the school, which was established originally as the Washington High School, was renamed DUNBAR HIGH SCHOOL.

Located at 128 M Street, the school's most celebrated principal was ANNA JULIA COOPER, the first African-American woman to earn a Ph.D. Cooper taught Latin and math there from 1887 until 1901, when she began a five-year tenure as principal. She was only the second woman to achieve the position of principal in the District of Columbia public schools. Cooper resumed teaching in 1910 and retired in 1929.

The accomplished faculty included MARY CHURCH TERRELL, the first president of the National Association of Negro Women; JESSIE FAUSET, who

taught Latin and French before becoming literary editor at THE CRISIS; and EVA BEATRICE DYKES, who, with fellow teacher Georgiana Simpson, became one of the first three African-American women to earn a Ph.D. from an American institution.

M Street students included James Butcher, a renowned artisan and creator of dollhouses; Sadie Mossell Tanner Alexander, daughter of African Methodist Episcopal Bishop Benjamin Tucker Tanner and the first woman to earn a Ph.D. in economics; Frank Coleman, head of the physics department at Howard University and cofounder of Omega Psi Phi Fraternity; Charles Hamilton Houston, the first African-American editor of the *Harvard Law Review* and counsel for the NATIONAL ASSOCIATION FOR THE ADVANCEMENT OF COLORED PEOPLE.

Mulatto Langston Hughes (1935)

A tragic melodrama by LANGSTON HUGHES that opened on BROADWAY at the Vanderbilt Theatre in October 1935. It was the longest-running African-American play on Broadway until Lorraine Hansberry's *A Raisin in the Sun* made its debut in March 1959.

Written by Hughes, the stage production of the three-act play was produced and directed by Martin Jones. The cast on opening night starred Rose McClendon and Morris McKenny who, between them, had appeared in Broadway productions of *Porgy* (1927, 1929), the Annie Nathan Meyer play *Black Souls* (1932), and the PAUL GREEN play *IN ABRAHAM'S BOSOM* (1926). McClendon, whom reviewers described as "an artist with a sensitive personality and a bell-like voice," delivered a performance that was hailed as one of the play's strengths.

The plot revolves around the tangled lives of a Colonel Norwood, a white widowed Georgia slave master, Cora, his enslaved housekeeper and the mother of three Norwood children, and Bert, his youngest and most irrepressible son, who ultimately kills his father and himself before a lynch mob descends upon his body. Hughes's focus on miscegenation and tragedy in the South complemented works on the southern racial tension and violence by writers such as MARION VERA CUTHBERT, Paul Green, and MYRTLE LIVINGSTON.

Hughes began to develop ideas for the play in earlier works, including his 1927 poem entitled "Mulatto" and the short story "Father and Son" (1933), which he included in THE WAYS OF WHITE FOLKS, a collection of short fiction published in 1933.

Reviews of the play, which ran for some 373 performances, suggested that it lacked a straightforward story line. The drama critic J. Brooks Atkinson penned a lengthy review in the 25 October 1935 issue of THE NEW YORK TIMES. In his article, entitled "Race Problems in the South the Theme of 'Mulatto,' a 'New Drama' by Langston Hughes," Atkinson welcomed the opportunity, "after a season dedicated chiefly to trash . . . to sit in the presence of a playwright who is trying his best to tell what he has in his mind." While he noted that the themes of racial tension, miscegenation, and family clearly were important to Hughes, Atkinson lamented the fact that Hughes's "ideas are seldom completely expressed" and that the "play is pretty thoroughly defeated by the grim mechanics of the stage." Despite Hughes's best efforts, Atkinson concluded that the "sympathies evoked . . . are muddled and diffuse." ALAIN LOCKE, discovered by Hughes when he visited Rose McClendon backstage shortly after the opening, pointedly criticized the work. He confronted Hughes with his negative impressions, insisting that "so grand and tragic a theme was prematurely exposed: the rarer the bitter it is unripe." Hughes scholars such as Joseph McLaren regard the play as an important, socially conscious work. According to McLaren, *Mulatto* is a strong protest play in which Hughes deliberately explores the links between tragedy and the multifaceted nature of injustice.

Bibliography

Atkinson, J. Brooks. "Race Problems in the South the Theme of 'Mulatto,' a 'New Drama' by Langston Hughes," *New York Times*. 25 October 1935. 25.

Berry, Faith, ed. *Langston Hughes: Before and Beyond Harlem*. Westport, Conn.: Lawrence Hill & Company, 1983.

Gates, Henry Louis, Jr., and Kwame Anthony Appiah, eds. *Langston Hughes: Critical Perspectives Past and Present*. New York: Amistad, 1993.

McLaren, Joseph. *Langston Hughes: Folk Dramatist in the Protest Tradition, 1921–1943*. Westport, Conn.: Greenwood Press, 1997.

Miller, R. Baxter. *The Art and Imagination of Langston Hughes*. Lexington: University of Kentucky Press, 1989.

Rampersad, Arnold. *The Life of Langston Hughes: I, Too, Sing America*. Vol. 1: *1902–1941*. New York: Oxford University Press, 1986.

———. *The Life of Langston Hughes: I Dream a World*. Vol. 2: *1941–1967*. New York: Oxford University Press, 1988.

Mule Bone Langston Hughes and Zora Neale Hurston (1930)

A play on which LANGSTON HUGHES and ZORA NEALE HURSTON collaborated. It is the work that tested and ultimately ruined their intense and otherwise supportive friendship.

It is ironic, given the debacle that ensued, that *Mule Bone* was based on Hurston's unpublished short story "The Bone of Contention." That work, set in EATONVILLE, Florida, revolved around an argument between two hunters, Dave Carter, who is known as the "local Nimrod" (212), and Jim Weston, "a constant disturber of the local peace" (214). Their dispute is based on the fact that they both shoot the same turkey. A trial is begun after one of the men uses a mule bone to attack his rival and to take possession of the disputed bird. The whole town, under the supervision of Joe Clarke, the omnipresent "mayor, postmaster, storekeeper and Pooh Bah general" (211), stages a trial in the town's Baptist church. At first, it seems as though Jim Weston is going to escape punishment because his accuser cannot persuade the court that a mule bone taken from the carcass of a long-dead "old, rawbony and mean" mule is in fact a legal murder weapon. In the court of folk justice, however, the Methodist Reverend Sims invokes the Bible and the story in Chapter 18 of the Book of Judges that describes how Samson uses the jawbone of an ass to kill some 3,000 people. The Reverend's winning point is that "if de jawbone is as dangerous as it says heah, in de Bible, by de time you gits clear back tuh his hocks hes rank pizen" (219). Within minutes, the case goes against Weston, who is then banned from the town.

Hurston transformed "The Bone of Contention" into a love story. Rather than have two men arguing about a prize wild turkey, in *Mule*

Bone she introduces a "plump, dark and sexy" domestic named Daisy, who sparks an intense rivalry between Dave Carter and Jim Weston, the same two protagonists of her short story. Carter is a "slightly arrogant, aggressive, somewhat self-important" Methodist who is "ready with his tongue" to engage in lively banter or argument. His primary challenger, Dave Carter, is a "soft, happy-go-lucky character, slightly dumb and unable to talk rapidly and wittily." The remaining cast members include Joe Clarke, church elders, and a host of minor characters. The first act contains much lively dialogue, delivered in rapid and vivid dialect to great effect. As in Hurston's novel THEIR EYES WERE WATCHING GOD (1937), the porch attached to the store of Joe Clarke is the primary stage upon which men indulge in verbal sparring and assess the world beyond them. Daisy flirts with both Jim and Dave, who at one point join forces to perform a lively song-and-dance act. When the two men come to blows in front of the store, Daisy is revealed as a self-absorbed woman. "Now, who's gonna take me home?" she wonders as Jim Clarke instructs that Jim be locked up in his barn, and others tend to the wounded Dave Carter.

Act Two revisits the courtroom scene, and the same logic that damns Jim Weston in the short story undoes his case here, too. He is found guilty of assault and instructed to leave Eatonville for a period of no less than two years. Hurston's final major revision of the short story comes in Act Three. Beyond the stares of the town and the men who gather regularly on Joe Clarke's porch, Daisy, Jim, and Dave encounter each other again. Daisy begs Jim, for whom she now has feelings, to live with her. Dave interrupts the encounter, and the two men begin to vie once more for Daisy's affections. They eventually realize that the words that an insightful old woman uttered long ago are true and that Daisy is more interested in having a provider than she is in having one of them. The men finally are disenchanted with Daisy, who is guilty of flirting with them equally and, in the aftermath of the fight, of tending to the hurt pride and injuries of both men. Jim and Dave unite against her. Their conflict becomes an opportunity for solidarity, and the play closes as the two men leave Daisy behind and return to Eatonville together.

LOUISE THOMPSON, whom the patron CHARLOTTE OSGOOD MASON hired to help Hughes, provided vital secretarial support to the writers and typed the manuscript. Thompson's involvement, and Hughes's proposal that she be paid one-third of the profits from the play, ultimately contributed to the messy conflict between the playwrights. Hurston's independent and seemingly covert efforts to negotiate with theater companies such as the Gilpin Players and ROWENA JELLIFFE at the KARAMU HOUSE in Cleveland further inflamed the row, and the play disappeared.

Each writer documented the upheaval in spirited letters to their patrons and friends, including Mason, JOEL SPINGARN, CARL VAN VECHTEN, and ARNA BONTEMPS. In 1931 Hurston wrote a candid letter to Hughes. She asserted that she was "very eager to do the play" and insisted to him that "anything you said would go over big with me. But scarcely had we gotten under way," she recalled, "before you made three propositions that shook me to the foundation of myself. First: That three-way split with Louise. Now, Langston, nobody has in the history of the world given a typist an interest in a work for typing it." Hurston went on to insist that the play was hers. "It was my story from beginning to end. It is my dialogue, my situations" (Kaplan, 202), she declared before earnestly noting that she was innocent of the conversations that had led to the play's unauthorized distribution.

Hughes grappled with the unexpected turn of events by enlisting the aid of close friends such as Carl Van Vechten. He asked Van Vechten to mediate between them, to "get in touch with Zora" and let her know that he, Hughes, was "not at all angry about her actions, because she always has been strange in lots of ways" (Bernard, 76). Van Vechten demurred, unwilling to suffer another "grand emotional scene" with Hurston and sure that "anything she might promise to do for me would have no effect whatever on her subsequent actions" (Bernard, 77). He also attempted to arrange a meeting in Cleveland with Hurston and the Jelliffes, who were interested in producing the play with the Gilpin Players, who had begun rehearsals on what Hughes discovered to be an unfinished draft of the work. Despite the fact that he was recovering from a tonsillectomy, Hughes hosted the three at his mother's Cleveland home. Hurston proved to be rather intractable. In his recollection of the event, which he included in his 1940 autobiography THE BIG SEA, Hughes remembered that Hurston "would not talk about the play! Not at all. She would speak only of things that did not concern the drama in question, one way or another. She spoke passionately, long, and loud, until the Jelliffes begged to be excused. They went home. Miss Hurston then got the last word and left without saying good-bye to my mother, whom she had known for years. That made my mother angry, so she pursued Miss Hurston into the hall to give her a piece of her mind. I had to get up out of bed and restrain my mother. It was an exciting afternoon for a tonsillectomy patient," he concluded dryly (Hughes, 248).

The play was not performed during the Harlem Renaissance era nor during the lifetimes of Hurston or Hughes. In 1991, some 60 years after its completion, the play debuted at Lincoln Center in NEW YORK CITY. The show ran from January through April, and its cast included Vanessa Williams, Kenny Neal, and Samuel E. Wright. Henry Louis Gates, Jr., who worked as a consultant with Hughes's literary executor, George Houston Bass, on the production, suggests that the controversy surrounding the play had much to do with the fact that it presented black vernacular as "the language of drama" (Gates, 225). He goes on to address the anxieties about representation of black life that frequently overshadow discussions of the work, asserting that "Hughes and Hurston develop their drama by imitating and repeating historical black folk rituals. Black folklore and southern rural black vernacular English served as the foundation for what they hoped would be a truly new art form" (225).

Bibliography

Bernard, Emily. *Remember Me to Harlem: The Letters of Langston Hughes and Carl Van Vechten.* New York: Knopf, 2001.

Berry, Faith, ed. *Langston Hughes: Before and Beyond Harlem.* Westport, Conn.: Lawrence Hill & Company, 1983.

Boyd, Valerie. *Wrapped in Rainbows: The Life of Zora Neale Hurston.* New York: Scribner, 2003.

Gates, Henry Louis Jr. "Why the *Mule Bone* Debate Goes On." In *Critical Essays on Zora Neale Hurston,* edited by Gloria Cronin, 225–228. New York: G. K. Hall & Co., 1998.

Hemenway, Robert. *Zora Neale Hurston: A Literary Biography.* Urbana: University of Illinois Press, 1977.

Hughes, Langston. *The Big Sea, an Autobiography.* New York: Knopf, 1940.

Kaplan, Carla. *Zora Neale Hurston: A Life in Letters.* New York: Doubleday, 2002.

Rampersad, Arnold. *The Life of Langston Hughes: I, Too, Sing America.* Vol. 1: *1902–1941.* New York: Oxford University Press, 1986.

Mules and Men   Zora Neale Hurston (1935)

The first published anthropological work by ZORA NEALE HURSTON. Published by the PHILADELPHIA company J. B. LIPPINCOTT, *Mules and Men* is a collection of 70 folktales. In her acknowledgements, Hurston paid special tribute to her patron, CHARLOTTE OSGOOD MASON. She thanked Mason, the "world's most gallant woman," for her providing a "hearty" and "spiritual" backing and for "financ[ing] the whole expedition in the manner of the Great Soul that she is." The artist Miguel Covarrubias provided 10 illustrations for the volume.

Hurston solicited FRANZ BOAS, her COLUMBIA UNIVERSITY anthropology professor and mentor, to write the introduction to the volume. Boas agreed to do so and praised Hurston for her "true work" and her "unusual contribution to our knowledge of the true inner life of the Negro." Boas also insisted on the high cultural and intellectual value of the primary materials that Hurston had assembled. The collection, he proposed, "throws into relief also the peculiar amalgamation of African and European tradition which is so important for understanding historically the character of American Negro life, with its strong African background in the West Indies, the importance of which diminishes with increasing distance from the south."

Hurston divided the book into two parts. The first, "Folklore," was made up of 10 chapters. The second, "Hoodoo," consisted of seven chapters. Also included in the book were classic folk stories, rituals on how to strengthen or revive love and to expel unwanted people from one's home, and methods for undoing curses. Hurston also included glossaries of folklore and hoodoo terms, folk song lyrics and music, and prescriptions from root doctors.

Hurston scholar Robert Hemenway suggests that *Mules and Men* "celebrates the art of the community" and that Hurston offered her readers the chance to "participate in collective rituals" of African-American life. Several of Hurston's compositions appeared in NEGRO, the anthology edited by NANCY CUNARD. The BOOK-OF-THE-MONTH CLUB awarded the collection an Honorable Mention in its Winter 1936 Club Award contest.

Bibliography

Boyd, Valerie. *Wrapped in Rainbows: The Life of Zora Neale Hurston.* New York: Scribner, 2003.

Cronin, Gloria. *Critical Essays on Zora Neale Hurston.* New York: G. K. Hall, 1998.

Glassman, Steve, and Kathryn Lee Seidel, eds. *Zora in Florida.* Orlando: University of Central Florida Press, 1991.

Hurston, Zora Neale. *Mules and Men.* 1935, reprint, New York: Perennial Library, 1990.

Kaplan, Carla. *Zora Neale Hurston: A Life in Letters.* New York: Doubleday, 2002.

Wall, Cheryl, ed. *Folklore, Memoirs and Other Writings: Zora Neale Hurston.* New York: Library of America, 1995.

Mumford, Lewis (1895–1990)

A distinguished architectural critic, urban planner, social philosopher, and essayist who published engaging and provocative essays on NEW YORK CITY architecture and culture in the *New Yorker* during the last decade of the Harlem Renaissance.

He was born in Flushing, Queens, in October 1895 to a housekeeper named Elvina Mumford and her employer, Lewis Charles Mack. Mumford, who bore the name of his mother's former husband, attended Stuyvesant High School and later attended classes at the City College of New York. He joined the U.S. Navy during World War I. When he returned to civilian life, Mumford's life as a journalist began. He worked as an associate editor at the *Dial* and contributed numerous essays to the AMERICAN MERCURY, *Harper's, Scribner's,* and to THE NEW REPUBLIC. The writer VAN WYCK BROOKS, who, with LANGSTON HUGHES, was committed to the success of the journal NEW MASSES, was one of his good friends. Mumford met Hughes during gatherings at the home of Noel Sullivan, one of his closest friends and a wealthy sup-

porter of the arts. His correspondence with Frank Lloyd Wright spanned some three decades.

The University at Albany, State University of New York, honored Mumford in 1998 when it established the Lewis Mumford Center for Comparative Urban and Regional Research.

Bibliography

Blake, Casey. *Beloved Community: The Cultural Criticism of Randolph Bourne, Van Wyck Brooks, Waldo Frank, and Lewis Mumford.* Chapel Hill: University of North Carolina Press, 1990.

Lewis Mumford Collection, Charles Patterson Van Pelt Library, University of Pennsylvania.

Miller, Donald. *Lewis Mumford, A Life.* New York: Weidenfeld & Nicholson, 1989.

Pfieffer, Bruce, and Robert Wojtowicz, eds. *Frank Lloyd Wright and Lewis Mumford: Thirty Years of Correspondence.* New York: Princeton Architectural Press, 2001.

Wojtowicz, Robert, ed. *Sidewalk Critic: Lewis Mumford's Writings on New York.* New York: Princeton Architectural Press, 1998.

Murphy, Beatrice Campbell (1908–1992)

A graduate of DUNBAR HIGH SCHOOL, editor, journalist, and poet, whose creative works were published in major Harlem Renaissance forums.

Born in Monessen, Pennsylvania, she was the daughter of Benjamin and Maude Campbell. She attended the highly regarded Dunbar High School in WASHINGTON, D.C., and began publishing shortly after her graduation in 1928. She worked at the Catholic University of America as secretary to the sociology department chair, established a circulating library, and became director of the Negro Bibliographic and Resource Center.

Murphy published poetry in THE CRISIS and several essays in the journals *Interracial Review* and *Our Colored Missions.* She carried on the important tradition of collecting and anthologizing the works of African-American poets. Like ALAIN LOCKE, LANGSTON HUGHES, and ARNA BONTEMPS, Murphy was committed to providing readers with ready access to African-American literature and to sustaining key networks among writers. She published three anthologies, including *Ebony Rhythm* (1948) and *Today's Negro Voices* (1978).

Bibliography

Murphy, Beatrice. *Ebony Rhythm: An Anthology of Contemporary Verse.* 1948; reprint, Salem, N.H.: Ayer Company, 1988.
———, ed. *Today's Negro Voices: An Anthology of Young Negro Poets.* New York: J. Messner, 1972.
———, and Nancy Arnez. *The Rocks Cry Out: Poems.* Detroit: Broadside Press, 1969.

Murray, Pauli (Anna Pauline Murray)
(1910–1985)

An accomplished poet, activist, feminist, and attorney who in 1977 became the first African-American woman to be ordained as a priest in the Episcopal Church.

Born in Baltimore, Maryland, Murray was the child of a school principal, William, and a nurse, Agnes Fitzgerald Murray. She was raised in Durham, North Carolina, following her mother's death in 1913 and her father's subsequent institutionalization in a mental hospital. She attended Hunter College in NEW YORK CITY and graduated in 1933 with a bachelor's degree in English. She earned an LL.B. from HOWARD UNIVERSITY Law School and graduated cum laude in 1944. A JULIUS ROSENWALD FELLOWSHIP enabled her to attend the University of California; she earned an LL.M. in 1945. She earned her master's degree in divinity from General Theological Seminary in 1976.

Murray demonstrated early her commitment to racial and social justice. She was a lifetime member of the NATIONAL ASSOCIATION FOR THE ADVANCEMENT OF COLORED PEOPLE, a NATIONAL URBAN LEAGUE field representative, a special field secretary for the Workers Defense League, and a member of the legal staff for the committee on Law and Social Action during the American Jewish Congress in New York. Her suit against the University of North Carolina at Chapel Hill to gain admission is credited as the move that initiated the federally mandated desegregation of the school. Murray's impressive legal career included her 1946 appointment as attorney general of California. She was the first woman of African descent to hold the post. She was an outspoken feminist and one of the founders of the National Organization of Women.

Murray published the bulk of her creative work after the Harlem Renaissance. During the era, however, she published poems in *OPPORTUNITY*. Her most celebrated works are *Proud Shoes: The Story of an American Family* (1956), a book that became a best-seller when it was republished in the 1970s, and *Dark Testament and Other Poems* (1970). The title work, "Dark Testament," was a poem completed in 1943. In 1988 she won the Robert F. Kennedy Book Award and the Christopher Award for her autobiography.

Murray received numerous awards and honors. Named the Woman of the Year in 1946 by the NATIONAL COUNCIL OF NEGRO WOMEN and by *Mademoiselle* magazine in 1947, she received honorary degrees from Dartmouth College, RADCLIFFE COLLEGE, and YALE UNIVERSITY.

Murray, a tireless, intrepid, and visionary figure, died of cancer on July 1, 1985. She was a resident of Pittsburgh, Pennsylvania, at the time. *The New York Times* recalled her impressive career achievements and unabating efforts to secure civil rights. Murray was survived by her sisters Mildred Fearing and Rosetta Stevens. A memorial service was held on July 5 in the National Cathedral in Washington, D.C.

Bibliography

"Obituary: Dr. Pauli Murray, Episcopal Priest." *New York Times,* 4 July 1985, A12.
Murray, Pauli. *Pauli Murray: The Autobiography of a Black Activist, Feminist, Lawyer, Priest, and Poet.* Knoxville: University of Tennessee Press, 1989.
O'Dell, Darlene. *Sites of Southern Memory: The Autobiographies of Katherine Du Pre Lumpkin, Lillian Smith, and Pauli Murray.* Charlottesville: University Press of Virginia, 2001.

"Muttsy" Zora Neale Hurston (1926)

A lively dialect story by ZORA NEALE HURSTON that won second place in the 1926 *OPPORTUNITY* literary contest. Published in the August 1926 issue, Hurston's story was one of several that showcased her hometown of EATONVILLE, Florida.

"Muttsy" is the story of Pinkie, an innocent country girl who moves north to HARLEM. She appears at the chaotic boardinghouse of Ma Turner. While she has little luggage, Pinkie has "everything she needed in her face—many, many trunks full." In Harlem she attracts the attention of Muttsy, a perennial gambler, who slips a diamond ring on her finger while she is sleeping. Pinkie, completely distraught by the wild ways of Ma Turner's clientele, leaves the house and Muttsy's ring and seeks her fortunes elsewhere. Her admirer eventually finds her and persuades her to marry him. One month later, a seemingly reformed Muttsy is the supervisor of 200 laborers on the New York waterfront. Unfortunately, he is unable to resist the lure of gambling. "What man can't keep one li'l wife an' two li'l bones?" he muses as he instructs a former rival from Ma Turner's to round up workers to play dice with him behind a crate on the dock.

Hurston's tale explores the irrepressible highlife of Harlem and urban northern communities. It also considers the stresses of modern American domesticity.

Bibliography

Jones, Sharon. *Rereading the Harlem Renaissance: Race, Class, and Gender in the Fiction of Jessie Fauset, Zora Neale Hurston, and Dorothy West.* Westport Conn.: Greenwood Press, 2002.

Wall, Cheryl. *Women of the Harlem Renaissance.* Bloomington: Indiana University Press, 1995.

My Great Wide Beautiful World Juanita Harrison (1936)

A colorful travel memoir by JUANITA HARRISON, a Mississippi-born domestic who financed her world tour by working throughout the United States. She left the United States in 1927, aged 36, for a series of voyages and expeditions that included stops in Egypt, France, India, Ireland, Italy, Japan, Spain, Turkey, and Hong Kong. After an immensely satisfying odyssey, during which she lived in 22 countries, Harrison settled in Hawaii in April 1935.

Harrison published portions of the text in the October and November 1935 issues of THE ATLANTIC MONTHLY. One year later, the book was published by the MACMILLAN COMPANY.

Harrison's title was inspired by a poem by W. B. Rands that contemplated the glory of the world and its far-flung and welcoming lands. She reprinted two stanzas of Rands's poem on the frontispiece of her book. The lines began, "Great, wide, beautiful, wonderful World, / With the wonderful water round you curled, /And the wonderful grass upon your breast, / World, you are beautifully dressed."

Mildred Morris provided an informative preface to Harrison's impressive travelogue and memoir. Morris was the daughter of Mrs. Felix Morris, for whom Harrison worked temporarily while in France. Morris provides the only known descriptions of Harrison, whom she describes as "an American colored woman, who undertook, at the age of thirty-six, to work her way around the world." She lost some $800 in savings when a Denver bank failed. Shortly thereafter, an employer and real estate broker named Mr. Dickinson invested her earnings and accumulated for her an annual income of $200. Harrison used that money to finance her travels. Morris notes that Harrison "[f]requently . . . adopted the garb of the country she visited and was accepted as a native. Her slight form, fresh olive complexion, long hair braided about her head, made her appear younger than her years."

The work was reprinted in 1996 with an introduction by Adele Logan Alexander.

Bibliography

Harrison, Juanita. *My Great Wide Beautiful World.* 1937, reprint, New York: G. K. Hall & Co., 1996.

N

Nance, Ethel Ray (1899–1992)

An effective secretary and administrator who facilitated dynamic networks among artists and scholars of the Harlem Renaissance period.

Born Ethel May Ray, she and her family resided in Duluth, Minnesota. Nance came of age in a town in which there were few African Americans. Her father, an advocate of African-American migration to northern cities, gave his daughter firsthand exposure to black activism and community outreach. Nance accompanied her father to the South in 1919 and was with him as he extolled the freedoms and possibilities for African Americans in the North. Her father later established the first Duluth chapter of the NATIONAL ASSOCIATION FOR THE ADVANCEMENT OF COLORED PEOPLE (NAACP). According to Nance, it was a horrific LYNCHING in Duluth in March 1920 that galvanized Minnesotans to work for civil and legal rights for African Americans. Thirteen African-American men, employees of the John Robinson Show Circus, were falsely accused of rape. Four of them were lynched before a bloodthirsty mob, whose size, historians debate, ranged between 5,000 and 10,000. The first activist Nance's father invited to address members of the newly established NAACP was W. E. B. DuBois, the scholar with whom Ethel Nance would later work closely.

Before she left Minnesota and relocated to NEW YORK CITY, Nance was an active member of several Minnesota organizations. She worked with the Red Cross and also became the first African-American policewoman in Duluth.

Nance's involvement with the Harlem Renaissance began in 1923. She began working as secretary for CHARLES S. JOHNSON, editor of *OPPORTUNITY*. Nance was one of the visionary women who encouraged the male leadership to generate forums that would promote African-American literary and artistic production. The fete at the Manhattan CIVIC CLUB was one of the most memorable events in which Nance played a major organizational role. Nance eventually relocated to Tennessee when Charles Johnson, who in 1946 would become the school's first African-American president, joined the faculty at FISK UNIVERSITY.

Nance developed close ties to the HARLEM BRANCH of the NEW YORK PUBLIC LIBRARY, located at 135th Street. Librarian REGINA ANDREWS was one of the women with whom Nance shared a flat in the SUGAR HILL neighborhood. With Louella Tucker, their third roommate, Nance and Andrews hosted regular gatherings of emerging artists and writers at the 580 St. Nicholas Avenue apartment that became well known, according to historian David Levering Lewis, as a "sort of Renaissance USO, offering a couch, a meal, sympathy, and proper introduction to wicked Harlem for newcomers on the Urban League approved list" (Lewis, 127). Lewis goes on to note that the apartment, which welcomed writers such as LANGSTON HUGHES, ZORA NEALE HURSTON, and ERIC WALROND, actually "functioned as a combination office and intelligence outpost for the Urban League" (Lewis, 128).

Nance also worked closely with W. E. B. DuBois. Years after her memorable first encounter with him in Duluth, Nance worked as a secretary and coordinator for DuBois. She was responsible for arranging the details relating to his activities and contacts on the West Coast. In 2000 her son Glenn Nance donated a set of 107 letters written by DuBois to his mother, to the Bancroft Library at the University of California at Berkeley.

Bibliography

Ethel Nance Papers, Bancroft Library, University of California at Berkeley; Special Collections, Fisk University.

Lewis, David Levering. *W. E. B. DuBois: The Fight for Equality and the American Century, 1919–1963.* New York: Henry Holt & Company, 2000.

Robbins, Richard. *Sidelines Activist: Charles S. Johnson and the Struggle for Civil Rights.* Jackson: University Press of Mississippi, 1996.

Nation, The

An important weekly political magazine. *The Nation,* founded in 1865, provided more comprehensive coverage of race-related issues during the Harlem Renaissance than any other periodical of its kind.

The periodical was established by abolitionists. Its first editor, Irish-born Edwin Godkin, declared his intent to use the magazine to support progressive issues such as women's suffrage and African-American civil rights. Writer and journalist William Dean Howells was one of the most frequent contributors to the magazine, and scholars suggest that it was his engaging writing that boosted circulation.

Editors of the magazine included descendants of William Lloyd Garrison, the tireless BOSTON abolitionist and editor of *The Liberator.* Henry Villard, a Garrison son-in-law and wealthy businessman, purchased the publication and the *New York Evening Post* in 1881. His son OSWALD GARRISON VILLARD became the editor and owner in 1918. Villard's tenure lasted until 1932. His membership in the NATIONAL ASSOCIATION FOR THE ADVANCEMENT OF COLORED PEOPLE influenced his editorial decisions at *The Nation.* The magazine reported on LYNCHINGs (including shocking eyewitness reports), race riots, civil rights activism, and African-American efforts to secure economic and political stability. It also published book reviews by leading activists such as WALTER WHITE. Villard also opposed the accommodationist philosophies of BOOKER T. WASHINGTON. Such ideas, accord to Villard, threatened the fight for African-American equality and were in direct contrast to the honest and forthright antislavery and abolitionist activism of the 19th century.

In later years, editors like Freda Kirchwey maintained the magazine's tradition of incisive, socially conscious journalism. During Kirchwey's tenure, *The Nation* was especially outspoken against fascism, Nazism, McCarthyism, and the intimidatory campaigns of the House Un-American Activities Committee.

Bibliography

Pages from The Nation: *Selections from the Contributions of the Editorial Staff for the Decade 1918–28.* New York: The Tenth Anniversary Committee of *Nation* Readers, 1928.

De Borchgrave, Alexandra Villard, and John Cullen. *Villard: The Life and Times of an American Titan.* New York: Doubleday, 2001.

Villard, Oswald Garrison. *Fighting Years: Memoirs of a Liberal Editor.* New York: Harcourt, Brace and Company, 1939.

National Association for the Advancement of Colored People (NAACP)

The oldest civil rights organization in the United States. Established in 1909, the National Association for the Advancement of Colored People (NAACP) became a leading champion of African-American social justice, civil and political rights, and social and economic equality. The multiracial group of founders included W. E. B. DuBois, MARY WHITE OVINGTON, IDA B. WELLS BARNETT, and OSWALD GARRISON VILLARD.

Morefield Storey was the first president of the organization. JOEL SPINGARN, the philanthropist after whom the NAACP named its most prestigious annual prize, succeeded him in 1929.

Other founding members and officers included influential public intellectuals, scholars, and activists. Oswald Garrison Villard, owner/editor of *THE NATION* and a descendant of William Lloyd Garrison, was appointed treasurer. In 1910 W. E. B. DuBois, a highly regarded scholar and an AT-

LANTA UNIVERSITY professor, began a lengthy appointment as publicity director and editor of THE CRISIS, the official NAACP publication. JAMES WELDON JOHNSON, a diplomat and novelist, became field secretary in 1916; four years later, he was promoted to the position of national secretary.

The NAACP experienced phenomenal growth in its membership rolls during the Harlem Renaissance years. Ten years after its founding, the organization had more than 300 national branches and some 90,000 members.

The NAACP had two distinct missions. The political wing of the organization focused on matters relating to African-American rights, disenfranchisement, and advancement. The NAACP was a vocal critic of political leaders such as Woodrow Wilson and Herbert Hoover. It was an active leader in antilynching campaigns and worked hard to document acts of murder and mob violence. NAACP agents such as WALTER WHITE infiltrated white supremacist organizations, and others filed numerous reports that confirmed KU KLUX KLAN activity and acts of violence and intimidation against African Americans. In the years after the Harlem Renaissance, the NAACP continued to represent African-American legal interests. It played a crucial role in the landmark 1954 Supreme Court decision in *Brown v. Board of Education*. Thurgood Marshall, NAACP legal consul on the *Brown* case, later became the first African American appointed to the U.S. Supreme Court.

The multifaceted monthly periodical *The Crisis* represented the cultural wing of the NAACP best. Under the watchful eye of DuBois and his literary editor, JESSIE FAUSET, *The Crisis* encouraged artistic and literary excellence, and it provided evidence of African-American cultural, professional, and educational advancement. *The Crisis* worked closely with patrons such as Joel Spingarn and his wife, AMY SPINGARN, who endowed literary contests and provided vital support to aspiring artists and writers.

During the 1930s the organization faced the economic pressures of the GREAT DEPRESSION and grappled with major turnover in its leadership. James Weldon Johnson and W. E. B. DuBois left the organization in 1928 and 1934, respectively. Yet, the organization rallied under the leadership of Walter White, who served from 1931 through 1955. Later presidents included Roy Wilkins (1955–77) and Benjamin Hooks (1977–93). Additional leaders have included Myrlie Evers-Williams, widow of the civil rights leader Medgar Evers, and former Congressman Kwesi Mfume of Maryland.

NAACP headquarters are located in Baltimore, Maryland. The organization has active chapters and affiliates throughout the United States and in Japan and Germany.

Bibliography
Janken, Kenneth Robert. *White: The Biography of Walter White, Mr. NAACP.* New York: New Press, 2003.
Wedin, Carolyn. *Inheritors of the Spirit: Mary White Ovington and the Founding of the NAACP.* New York: Wiley, 1998.

National Association of Colored Women (NACW)

Founded in 1896, the National Association of Colored Women (NACW) was an impressive organization dedicated to racial uplift and to the advancement of the race. Its motto, "Lifting As We Climb," signaled the dedication to collective advancement and strong community networks. NACW leaders included prominent activists, scholars, patrons, feminists, and writers from all walks of life and American communities. The founders included Ida B. WELLS-BARNETT, Frances Harper, MARY CHURCH TERRELL, Josephine St. Pierre Ruffin, and Harriet Tubman.

The NACW was a visionary national organization that often emerged as the first group to support vital political and social efforts such as women's suffrage. By 1915 the organization had more than 100,000 members and had numerous regional, state, and community chapters. NACW members established college scholarships for African-American women, provided job-training, organized child-care centers, founded settlement houses, advocated temperance, offered educational enrichment through classes and reading societies, and lobbied against such pervasive social ills as segregation and LYNCHING.

A number of Harlem Renaissance women writers had strong ties to the NACW. These included

HALLIE QUINN BROWN, MARY MCLEOD BETHUNE, FLORIDA RUFFIN RIDLEY, and CARRIE WILLIAMS CLIFFORD. Brown, a WILBERFORCE UNIVERSITY professor, TUSKEGEE INSTITUTE dean, and an active clubwoman, became NACW president in 1920. She published important feminist social histories during the Harlem Renaissance, including OUR WOMEN: PAST, PRESENT, AND FUTURE (1925) and HOMESPUN HEROINES AND OTHER WOMEN OF DISTINCTION (1926). The enterprising writer and activist Carrie Williams Clifford founded the Ohio Federation of Colored Women's Clubs in 1901. Like the NACW, Clifford's organization promoted suffrage and worked to improve women's lives. She later moved to Washington, D.C., where she developed professional friendships with Mary Church Terrell and other Harlem Renaissance figures such as W. E. B. DuBois, GEORGIA DOUGLAS JOHNSON, and ALAIN LOCKE. FLORIDA RUFFIN RIDLEY, daughter of well-known BOSTON clubwoman Josephine St. Pierre Ruffin, was part of the SATURDAY EVENING QUILL CLUB, Boston's most active Harlem Renaissance African-American literary society.

The organization continues to work on behalf of women of color.

Bibliography

Davis, Elizabeth. *Lifting As They Climb*. New York: G. K. Hall, 1996.

Jones, Beverly Washington. *Quest for Equality: The Life and Writings of Mary Eliza Church Terrell, 1863–1954*. Brooklyn, N.Y.: Carlson Publishers, 1990.

Terrell, Mary Church. *A Colored Woman in a White World*. New York: G. K. Hall, 1996.

National Colored Players

A short-lived theater group established in NEW YORK CITY in September 1929. The group's founder, Ida Anderson, was an experienced film actress who had worked with the pioneering filmmaker Oscar Micheaux and had starred in early African-American silent films such as Micheaux's *Son of Satan* (1924). Anderson hoped that the troupe would flourish and provide audiences with sobering and polished dramatic performances. Unfortunately, the company, which was housed in the West End Theatre at the intersection of St. Nicholas Avenue and 125th Street, dissolved after

only three fall 1929 productions. The plays that the National Colored Players produced were *Seventh Heaven*, *Crime*, and *The Gorilla*. The INTERSTATE TATTLER provided supportive reviews of the three weeklong productions.

Bibliography

Bowser, Pearl, and Louise Spence. *Writing Himself into History: Oscar Micheaux, His Silent Films, and His Audiences*. New Brunswick, N.J.: Rutgers University Press, 2000.

Green, J. Ronald. *Straight Lick: The Cinema of Oscar Micheaux*. Bloomington: Indiana University Press, 2000.

National Council of Negro Women

An organization founded in December 1935 by MARY MCLEOD BETHUNE, a pioneering educator and influential political figure. The key meetings in which influential women of color debated the focus and purpose of the organization were held in NEW YORK CITY at the 137th Street branch of the YOUNG WOMEN'S CHRISTIAN ASSOCIATION. Bethune's goal was to establish a cohesive parent organization for the diverse numbers of African-American women's professional, religious, and social societies.

The National Council of Negro Women (NCNW) existed for nearly six decades. There were four presidents during its 57 years: Mary McLeod Bethune, Dorothy Bolden Ferebee, Vivian Carter Mason, and Dorothy Height.

In addition to providing vital networks among numerous women's societies and organizations, the NCNW pursued public and political issues that affected all Americans. The organization worked with the leading race organizations such as the NATIONAL ASSOCIATION FOR THE ADVANCEMENT OF COLORED PEOPLE and the NATIONAL URBAN LEAGUE. It also collaborated with other national women's groups such as the YWCA, the League of Women Voters, the National Council of Jewish Women, and the National Council of Catholic Women. The NCNW also made alliances with labor unions and successfully documented employment statistics and workplace discrimination. The tireless efforts of the NCNW resulted in significant gains in civil rights such as the admission of African-American women to the Women's Army Corps and the establishment of the Fair Employment Practices Commission.

With the National Association of Colored Women, the parent organization of the 19th-century women's club movement, the NCNW maintained a cohesive campaign for women's advancement during and after the years of the Harlem Renaissance.

Bibliography
Fitzgerald, Tracey. *The National Council of Negro Women and the Feminist Movement, 1935–1975.* Washington, D.C.: Georgetown University Press, 1985.

Hanson, Joyce Ann. *Mary McLeod Bethune and Black Women's Political Activism.* Columbia: University of Missouri Press, 2003.

Height, Dorothy I. *Open Wide the Freedom Gates: A Memoir.* New York: Public Affairs, 2003.

McCluskey, Audrey Thomas, and Elaine M. Smith, eds. *Mary McLeod Bethune: Building a Better World: Essays and Selected Documents.* Bloomington: Indiana University Press, 1999.

National Council of Negro Women Papers, Bethune Museum and Archives National Historic Site, Washington, D.C.

National Ethiopian Art Theatre

One of numerous theater groups that were established in response to the call by W. E. B. DuBois, T. Montgomery Gregory, and others for a thriving national African-American theater culture.

The National Ethiopian Art Theatre was established in Chicago in the early 1920s. It appears to have made its New York City debut at the Frazee Theatre with a performance of Oscar Wilde's *Salome.* The cast in the eight shows of May 1924 included a number of well-known Harlem Renaissance figures including Laura Bowman, Evelyn Preer, and the actor and poet Lewis Alexander. Also involved were actors who would go on to perform in pioneering African-American shows. Marion Taylor, Solomon Bruce, and Sydney Kirkpatrick would appear just a week later in Willis Richardson's groundbreaking production *The Chip Woman's Fortune,* the first play by an African-American playwright to be staged on Broadway. Other actors such as Arthur Ray and Lionel Monagas would star in works such as Meek

Mose by Frank Wilson and *Conjur-Man Dies* by Rudolph Fisher, respectively. The production also included an actor named Walter White, but it is not clear that this man was the same Walter White who was associated with the National Association for the Advancement of Colored People and known best for his antilynching efforts during the 1920s and 1930s.

The company received critical attention from Theophilus Lewis and George Schuyler, drama critics for *The Messenger.* Shortly after the review of a 1924 summer recital, the troupe organized an impressive schedule of shows by and starring African Americans. These productions included *Being Forty* by Eulalie Spence and *Cooped Up* by Eloise Bibb Thompson. The calendar for 1925 included *Rider of Dreams,* the popular work by Ridgely Torrence.

The troupe appears to have disbanded in 1925.

Bibliography
Krasner, David. *A Beautiful Pageant: African American Theatre, Drama, and Performance in the Harlem Renaissance, 1910–1927.* New York: Palgrave Macmillan, 2002.

Lewis, Theophilus. "Theatre." *The Messenger* (August and November 1924).

Schuyler, George. "Theatre." *The Messenger* (November 1924).

National Medical Association

The medical association founded by Dr. Robert Fulton Boyd in 1895. African-American physicians were excluded from membership in the all-white American Medical Association. The National Medical Association (NMA) provided physicians with a professional society in which they could discuss medical advances and research, work to improve health care for all Americans, strategize about how best to combat racism in the medical field, and lobby against segregationist medical schools that would not admit qualified African-American applicants.

Rudolph Fisher, one of the most talented professionals of the Harlem Renaissance, was a Phi Beta Kappa graduate of Brown University, a highly regarded physician, and a pioneering roentgenologist. Fisher participated in the NMA and in 1929 delivered an address on X-ray technology, techniques, and interpretation at the 1929 NMA annual convention.

Like other race-based organizations, such as the NATIONAL URBAN LEAGUE and the NATIONAL ASSOCIATION FOR THE ADVANCEMENT OF COLORED PEOPLE, the NMA published its own journal. The *Journal of the National Medical Association* appeared first in 1909. Its editor was Dr. Charles V. Roman.

Nurses of color founded the National Association of Colored Graduate Nurses in 1908, in response to similar racist exclusionary practices of southern affiliates of the American Nurses Association. Novelist, librarian, and nurse NELLA LARSEN and her professional peers benefited immensely from the impressive examples of professionalism and scholarship of leaders such as Adah Thoms, Maria Clendenin, and Lula Warlick, who represented the excellence of nurses and health care professionals of color.

The NMA is still in existence. Its history of professional success, political activism, and dedication to social justice makes it one of the most important professional organizations in the country.

National Negro Bar Association

The professional association that was organized first in 1909 when lawyers who were members of the National Negro Business League established an African-American lawyers' auxiliary within the league. The group became an autonomous entity in 1925. The National Negro Bar Association (NNBA) was committed to establishing national links among attorneys of color, to supporting African-American business, and to protecting African-American civil rights.

In 1933 RAYMOND PACE ALEXANDER, an accomplished lawyer, judge, and politician and Ivy League graduate of the UNIVERSITY OF PENNSYLVANIA and HARVARD Law School, began a two-year term as president of the NNBA. Alexander, who published frequently about legal matters during the Harlem Renaissance, wrote persuasively about the role and responsibilities of African-American lawyers. In an address delivered before the NNBA and published later in the September 1931 issue of OPPORTUNITY, Alexander proposed

that "Negro members of the Bar of America face the unusual opportunity of making a lasting contribution to American Jurisprudence not yet attained by our white brothers." He went on to note that such groundbreaking accomplishments were directly related to the ways in which attorneys of color worked to "cultivat[e] . . . respect for the written law and by our actions, forcing our white contemporaries into a more tolerant and indulgent attitude with respect to the laws designed for the protection of our rights which are now ignored but which we can in this manner make them respect."

The NNBA, like the NATIONAL COUNCIL OF NEGRO WOMEN and the NATIONAL MEDICAL ASSOCIATION, was one of several professional organizations that contributed much to African-American advancement during and beyond the Harlem Renaissance period. The leaders and members of these groups published regularly in leading journals such as *Opportunity*, THE MESSENGER, and THE CRISIS and gained national recognition for their campaigns and outreach.

Bibliography

Alexander, Raymond Pace. "The Negro Lawyer." *Opportunity* (September 1931).

Boston, Thomas, ed. *A Different Vision: African American Economic Thought.* New York: Routledge, 1997.

Burrows, John H. *The Necessity of Myth: A History of the National Negro Business League, 1900–1945.* Auburn, Ala.: Hickory Hill Press, 1988.

Marable, Manning. *Black Leadership.* New York: Columbia University Press, 1998.

National Urban League

One of the most prominent American organizations and a group that greatly influenced and enriched the literary and political dimensions of the Harlem Renaissance. Founded in NEW YORK CITY in 1910, the group was known first as the National League on Urban Conditions Among Negroes. It became the National Urban League in 1920.

The organization was developed in response to massive migrations of African Americans from the South to the North. It was founded at a time when nearly 100,000 African Americans had relocated from southern states to New York City alone. Often referred to as the Urban League, the organization is committed to African-American economic and political advancement and to the abolition of racism and prejudice in America.

The founders of the Urban League included influential white and African-American men and women. Mrs. Ruth Standish Baldwin, a New York City philanthropist and widow of a railroad magnate, is recognized for her tireless commitment to purposeful social outreach. Baldwin is often recognized alongside Dr. George Edmund Haynes, a graduate of FISK UNIVERSITY and YALE UNIVERSITY and the first African American to earn a Ph.D. from COLUMBIA UNIVERSITY. Haynes served as director of the National Urban League until 1918. EUGENE KINCKLE JONES, whose term lasted through the Harlem Renaissance and ended in 1941, succeeded him. Whitney Young, Vernon Jordan, and John Jacob are among the directors who have served in recent years.

Like its fellow organization, the NATIONAL ASSOCIATION FOR THE ADVANCEMENT OF COLORED PEOPLE (NAACP), the Urban League has a significant number of chapters throughout the country. The local and regional divisions address issues relating to key areas such as housing, health care, and employment. It currently has some 115 branches in 34 states and in the District of Columbia.

The Urban League developed its own journal, OPPORTUNITY, in 1923. Although never as popular as THE CRISIS, the journal of the NAACP, Opportunity did much to promote African-American advancement, literary excellence, political debate, and cultural awareness. Its longtime editor, CHARLES S. JOHNSON, worked to cultivate a high profile for the journal and for its parent organization.

The emblem for the organization is a circle surrounding an equal sign. The symbol reiterates the Urban League's determination to achieve universal equality.

Bibliography

Dickerson, Dennis C. *Militant Mediator: Whitney M. Young, Jr.* Lexington: University Press of Kentucky, 1998.

Jordan, Vernon E. Jr., and Annette Gordon-Reed. *Vernon Can Read!: A Memoir.* New York: Basic Civitas Books, 2003.

Moore, Jesse Thomas Jr. *A Search for Equality: The National Urban League, 1910–1961.* University Park: Pennsylvania State University Press, 1981.

Weiss, Nancy J. *Whitney M. Young, Jr., and the Struggle for Civil Rights.* Princeton, N.J.: Princeton University Press, 1989.

———. *The National Urban League, 1910–1940.* New York, Oxford University Press, 1974.

Native Son Richard Wright (1940)

The groundbreaking novel by RICHARD WRIGHT that reflected the sharp turn into American literary modernism. The novel is associated with the emerging modernist period rather than with the Harlem Renaissance.

Wright did publish during the Harlem Renaissance, and he enjoyed close friendships with figures of the period such as RALPH ELLISON, LANGSTON HUGHES, and AUGUSTA SAVAGE.

The gripping story revolves around Bigger Thomas, a young man who accidentally kills the daughter of the white family for whom he works as a chauffeur. Wright's novel is powerful for its representation of Bigger's terrible angst, rage, decline, and ultimate victimization by an inhumane legal system.

The novel was an unqualified best-seller; it sold 250,000 copies in the first month. The novel appeared two years after Wright's UNCLE TOM'S CHILDREN: FOUR NOVELLAS (1938), a sobering collection of stories about devastated African-American families, deadly racism, and the ramifications of political choices.

Bibliography

Fabre, Michel. *The World of Richard Wright.* Jackson: University Press of Mississippi, 1985.

Gates, Henry Louis, Jr., and Kwame Anthony Appiah. *Richard Wright: Critical Perspectives Past and Present.* New York: Amistad, 1993.

Gayle, Addison. *Ordeal of a Native Son.* Garden City, N.Y.: Anchor Press/Doubleday, 1980.

Hakutani, Yoshinobu. *Critical Essays on Richard Wright.* Boston: G. K. Hall, 1982.

Webb, Constance. *Richard Wright: A Biography.* New York: Putnam, 1968.

Naumberg, Margaret (1890–1983)

The first wife of novelist WALDO FRANK. She was the founder of the Walden School, an educational facility that embraced the principles of the Montessori system. She was respected for her work with art and her use of art in therapeutic practice. Naumberg attended Vassar College and BARNARD COLLEGE before beginning graduate studies at COLUMBIA UNIVERSITY. She later pursued studies in psychology and other subjects at Oxford University and with scholars such as Maria Montessori in Italy.

It was Naumberg who introduced two of her most influential former professors to each other. Through her, Frederick Matthias Alexander, elocutionist and inventor of the Alexander Technique, came to know John Dewey, the well-known American philosopher and Naumberg's former professor at Columbia University. The two men enjoyed a fruitful professional relationship.

In 1914, Naumberg established the Children's School, an institution in NEW YORK CITY that later became known as the Walden School. She encouraged her teachers to have regular sessions with a psychoanalyst, believing that therapy would have a positive impact on their performance in the classroom. The Walden School faculty also included Florence Cane, her sister and an art educator.

Naumberg divorced Waldo Frank in 1923, shortly after the couple had a son together. She later became the lover of JEAN TOOMER, one of Frank's colleagues and a writer with whom he shared his work. Naumberg's affair with Toomer ended in 1926.

Naumberg was a dynamic and versatile figure who had ties to Harlem Renaissance literary circles in and beyond New York City. She also participated in the movement advanced by GEORGES IVANOVITCH GURDJIEFF and strengthened her ties to Jean Toomer as they explored the psychological and spiritual benefits of Gurdjieff's philosophies together. Naumberg also was a recognized writer who published poems and plays, as well as many academic and professional papers on education and art. She returned to Columbia University as a professor and taught there until she was well into her 80s.

Bibliography

Carter, Paul. *Waldo Frank.* New York: Twayne Publishers, 1967.

Kerman, Cynthia Earl, and Richard Eldridge. *The Lives of Jean Toomer: A Hunger for Wholeness.* Baton Rouge: Louisiana State University Press, 1987.

Trachtenberg, Alan, ed. *Memoirs of Waldo Frank.* Amherst: University of Massachusetts Press, 1973.

Naxos

The fictional campus in *QUICKSAND* (1927), the first novel of NELLA LARSEN. The school, whose name can be rearranged to read "Saxon," represented a searing critique of the highly regimented and stifling environment of an overly racially conscious environment.

Larsen modeled her fictional school on TUSKEGEE INSTITUTE, the industrial education facility that BOOKER T. WASHINGTON founded in Alabama. She had worked there as a head nurse from 1915 through 1916.

Bibliography

Davis, Thadious M. *Nella Larsen, Novelist of the Harlem Renaissance: A Woman's Life Unveiled.* Baton Rouge: Louisiana State University Press, 1994.

Larsen, Nella. *Quicksand,* edited with an introduction and notes by Thadious M. Davis. New York: Penguin Books, 2002.

Near Calvary Willis Richardson (ca. 1930-34)

A play by WILLIS RICHARDSON, the first African-American playwright whose work was produced on BROADWAY and the first to edit a collection of African-American plays for children.

Near Calvary was one of five Richardson plays that were included in *NEGRO HISTORY IN THIRTEEN PLAYS,* the 1935 anthology that Richardson coedited with playwright MAY MILLER SULLIVAN. The work appeared alongside three works by May Miller and dramas by RANDOLPH EDMONDS, GEORGIA DOUGLAS JOHNSON, and Helen Webb Harris.

Bibliography

Gray, Christine Rauchfuss. *Willis Richardson, Forgotten Pioneer of African-American Drama.* Westport, Conn.: Greenwood Press, 1999.

Richardson, Willis, and May Miller. *Negro History in Thirteen Plays.* New York: Associated Publishers, 1935.

Nearing, Scott (1883–1983)

A teacher, conservationist, and eloquent and committed pacifist who believed in the power of living in accord with nature. Born in Morris Run, Pennsylvania, he went on to attend the UNIVERSITY OF PENNSYLVANIA. He returned to his alma mater to teach economics. In 1915 the university fired him for writing and speaking out about the commercial interests that motivated American military ventures and wars. He joined the faculty at Toledo University but again was ousted because of his political views. He later joined the faculty at the Rand School of Social Science, a school in Manhattan established by members of the American Socialist Society.

During the Harlem Renaissance, Nearing published works on racism and society. His study, *Black America,* published in 1924, was followed eight years later by *Free Born.*

In the early 1930s the Nearings moved to Vermont and then to Maine. They established Forest Farm, a homestead on Penobscot Bay that was visited by thousands interested in the back-to-the-land movement. The site still stands today and is open to the public.

Nearing worked with individuals who had a significant impact on the Harlem Renaissance and on American society during the period. For example, Nearing served with JAMES WELDON JOHNSON on the American Fund for Public Service. The writer JEAN TOOMER, newly arrived in New York City in 1917, intent on immersing himself in intellectual and literary circles, sought out lectures by Nearing and several other noteworthy scholars and public intellectuals. Poet LANGSTON HUGHES also benefited from Nearing's ideas. Like Toomer, Hughes sought out numerous lectures at the Rand School when his classes and schoolmates at COLUMBIA UNIVERSITY failed to provide him with stimulating intellectual opportunities.

Nearing is best known for *Living the Good Life: How to Live Sanely and Simply in a Troubled World,* a book that he cowrote with his wife Helen Knothe Nearing and published in 1954. Nearing died in Harborside, Maine, in 1983 at the age of 100.

Bibliography

Nearing, Helen. *Loving and Leaving the Good Life.* Post Mills, Vt.: Chelsea Green Pub., 1992.

Nearing, Scott. *Black America.* New York: Vanguard Press, 1929.

———. *The Making of A Radical: A Political Autobiography.* New York: Harper & Row, 1972.

Saltmarsh, John. *Scott Nearing: An Intellectual Biography.* Philadelphia: Temple University Press, 1991.

Nebraska and His Granny Rose Leary Love (1936)

A popular story for children by ROSE LEARY LOVE, a North Carolina writer and teacher. The book, illustrated by Preston Haygood, was part of a vital movement to produce satisfying and positive literature for and about children of color. It complemented efforts by JESSIE FAUSET and W. E. B. DuBOIS that resulted in the publication of THE BROWNIES' BOOK, an invaluable and vivid resource for children of color.

Nebraska and His Granny was published by the press affiliated with TUSKEGEE INSTITUTE, the industrial education school established in Alabama by BOOKER T. WASHINGTON. Love's story revolved around a little brown-skinned boy named Nebraska and his loving and industrious grandmother. The story was divided into days of the week and was especially moving because of the loving relationship between the two. The book also included seven poems, each of which alluded to the topic of the coming chapter.

Bibliography

Love, Rose Leary. *Nebraska and His Granny.* 1936; reprint, Tuskegee, Ala.: Tuskegee Institute Press, 1966.

Negritude

A term coined by the French Martinican writer Aimé Césaire and used to describe literary works and cultural movements that address the collective and diverse experience of peoples of African descent who are part of the African diaspora and survivors of Western colonialism and oppression. Negritude often is linked to the works of francophone writers and intellectuals of color such as Frantz Fanon, RENÉ MARAN, and Léopold Sédar Senghor. The movement values and privileges blackness and African origin and critiques the threatening principles and devastating history of colonial invasion and African cultural suppression. Césaire's use of the term also insisted upon the alienating effects of colonial experience and charted the efforts of black subjects to reclaim their identity.

Writers of the Harlem Renaissance embraced the principles of Negritude in their work and philosophies. CLAUDE MCKAY, a Jamaican whose experience of British colonialism informed his views on black society, has been regarded by some as a powerful representative of the rich scope of Negritude. His works, which include vivid accounts of peoples of African descent in postcolonial worlds and critiques of colonial ideology, underscore the ways in which blackness and racial identity evolve in and beyond the original contexts of African origin. Like McKay, LANGSTON HUGHES, JAMES WELDON JOHNSON and COUNTEE CULLEN also explored the notions of cultural dispersion, racial assimilation, and racial identity. Other figures such as MARCUS GARVEY embodied, and even enacted, principles of Negritude before Césaire's articulation began to circulate. Garvey's unwavering and insistent race pride informed his international movement to reclaim a powerful and profitable African identity and homeland.

White European artists and scholars such as Jean Cocteau, André Gide, Pablo Picasso, and Jean-Paul Sartre also invested and explored concepts of Negritude.

Bibliography

Davis, Gregson. *Aimé Césaire.* Cambridge; New York, N.Y.: Cambridge University Press, 1997.

Jack, Belinda Elizabeth. *Negritude and Literary Criticism: The History and Theory of "Negro-African" Literature in French.* Westport, Conn.: Greenwood Press, 1996.

Popeau, Jean Baptiste. *Dialogues of Negritude: An Analysis of the Cultural Context of Black Writing.* Durham, N.C.: Carolina Academic Press, 2003.

Negro, The W. E. B. DuBois (1915)

The first English-language history of peoples of African descent. Written by W. E. B. DuBOIS, the volume offered a comprehensive overview of contemporary scholarship and emerging theories of African history and culture.

In his preface to the volume, DuBois noted that new and emerging scholarship in African history, archaeology, and anthropology indicated that "the time has not yet come for a complete history of the Negro peoples." DuBois noted the need for "intensive monographic work in history and science . . . to clear mooted points and quiet the controversialist who mistakes personal desire for scientific proof." Yet, in the absence of such substantial literature, he ventured to provide an initial history of Negro peoples. "I have not been able to withstand the temptation to essay such short general statements of the main known facts and their fair interpretation," he confessed.

The volume included 12 chapters that included subjects such as "The Coming of Black Ben," "The War of Races at Land's End," and "The Negro Problems." In addition to the chapters, *The Negro* included relevant maps and suggestions for further reading. British and American editions appeared in May 1915.

Reviewers generally praised this DuBois volume, an essential contribution to Afrocentric scholarship. *The Negro* represented an ambitious and masterful reinterpretation of African history and culture.

Bibliography

Lewis, David Levering. *W. E. B. DuBois: Biography of a Race, 1868–1919.* New York: Henry Holt and Company, 1993.

Negro Americans: What Now? James Weldon Johnson (1934)

A pamphlet by JAMES WELDON JOHNSON that attempted to assess the state of African Americans. Its forceful theses influenced the work of Gunnar Myrdal as he completed his epic sociological study, *An American Dilemma.*

Johnson published the work in the wake of suggestions by W. E. B. DuBOIS that segregation could be an empowering and protective state for African Americans. In the essay, published by Viking Press, Johnson considered five main options before African Americans: exodus, physical force, revolution, isolation, or integration. He endorsed efforts that would produce racial equality and called for unity, an intensification of race pride, black political autonomy, and strategic, ambitious African-American economic advancement that was not constrained by efforts to reach only consumers of color.

Negro Americans concluded with a powerful assertion. "My inner life is mine," wrote Johnson, "and I shall defend and maintain its integrity against all the powers of hell." The pamphlet endorsed racial uplift, self-preservation, and forceful activism to achieve racial advancement in diverse areas of American life and society.

Bibliography

Johnson, James Weldon. *Along This Way: The Autobiography of James Weldon Johnson.* 1933, reprint, New York, Da Capo Press, 1973.

Levy, Eugene. *James Weldon Johnson, Black Leader, Black Voice.* Chicago, University of Chicago Press, 1973.

Negro and His Songs, The: A Study of Typical Negro Songs in the South
Howard Odum and Guy Johnson (1925)

An anthology of songs compiled by HOWARD ODUM and GUY JOHNSON, two white University of North Carolina professors. The volume included the texts, but not music, of a variety of songs from African-American life. Odum and Johnson included work, religious, and everyday social songs as well as a commentary on the ways in which the works influenced, and were themselves shaped by, white music.

ARTHUR HUFF FAUSET, reviewing the volume in the November 1925 issue of *OPPORTUNITY*, lamented the presentation of the rich material. "The pity of it is that all who read this splendid volume," he wrote, "must content themselves with the mere seeing. Negro song is not something to be looked at; to appreciate it and understand it you must hear it." Fauset recognized the enthusiasm of the editors, suggesting that they had "devoured what came across their paths, and apparently made a good meal of it." He also noted that some of the commentary in the book would provoke "lively debates." Comments about the "vulgar and indecent content" of "a great mass of material," for instance, attempted to explain that much primary material

was not suitable for inclusion. Ultimately, Fauset concluded that "[m]any will be inclined to laugh as they read the words which Odum and Johnson have recorded so faithfully and interpreted with such evident carefulness." Despite the distinct possibility of such reception, however, he firmly believed that such a volume would reveal "the soul which underlies and permeates these songs of black folk" and recognize it as "the same one which in latter years has burst forth into the luxuriant, mellifluous outpourings from the hearts of such children as Dunbar, DuBois, and COUNTEE CULLEN."

Bibliography

Fauset, Arthur Huff. "The Negro's Cycle of Song," *Opportunity* (November 1925).

Odum, Howard W., and Guy B. Johnson. *The Negro and His Songs: A Study of Typical Negro Songs in the South.* 1925; reprint, New York: Negro Universities Press, 1968.

"Negro Art Hokum" George Schuyler
(1926)

One of the most provocative and controversial essays published during the Harlem Renaissance. Written by journalist and novelist GEORGE SCHUYLER, "Negro Art Hokum" took direct aim at the principles underlying the Harlem Renaissance and contributed to the ongoing debates of the day about the authenticity of African-American art, the responsibilities of artists of color, and the expectations of the American public in general, and the African-American audience in particular.

Schuyler published the scathing essay in the June 1926 issue of *THE NATION*, but it appeared nearly one year after he submitted it for consideration and after editor Freda Kirchwey had circulated it among numerous African-American leaders in order to gauge potential national reaction. A tone of impatience marked the essay, which opened with the bold assertion that "Negro art there has been, is, and will be among the numerous black nations of Africa; but to suggest the possibility of any such development among the ten million colored people in this republic is self-evident foolishness." Schuyler was advancing his theories in the wake of the acclaimed 1925 *SURVEY*

GRAPHIC Harlem issue and the subsequent anthology THE NEW NEGRO: AN INTERPRETATION (1925) that ALAIN LOCKE had edited.

Schuyler's theses seemed to challenge the very notion on which Locke and others presented their work and championed the powerful idea of a Harlem Renaissance. According to Schuyler, there was nothing distinctive about creative work produced by people of color in America. "As for the literature, painting, and sculpture of Aframericans—such as there is," he stated, "it is identical in kind with the literature, painting, and sculpture of white Americans." He then proposed that "the Aframerican is merely a lampblacked Anglo-Saxon" who "[a]side from his color, which ranges from very dark brown to pink, your American Negro is just plain American." Schuyler concluded by asking, "Why should the Negro artists of America vary from the national artistic norm when Negro artists in other countries have not done so? . . . One contemplates the popularity of the Negro-art hokum and murmurs 'How come?'"

Critic Michael Peplow suggests that Schuyler's "real purpose" was to "discredit long-standing and entrenched stereotypes." He also wanted to endorse a retroactive assimilationism, one that recognized the ways in which people of African descent in America were completely interwoven into the fabric of the nation. Schuyler's essay appeared alongside a rebuttal piece authored by Langston Hughes. *Nation* editor Freda Kirchwey asked Hughes to comment on the Schuyler essay and to provide "an independent positive statement of the case for a true Negro racial art" (Rampersad, 130). As Hughes biographer Arnold Rampersad notes, it took the poet-activist less than one week to generate "THE NEGRO ARTIST AND THE RACIAL MOUNTAIN," "the finest essay of Hughes's life" (Rampersad, 130). In his piece, which appeared in the same June 1926 issue of *The Nation* in which Schuyler's writing was published, Hughes suggested that Negro art could be a reality and that its creation was in fact frustrated by a "racial mountain," the "urge within the race toward whiteness, the desire to pour racial individuality into the mold of American standardization, and to be as little Negro and as much American as possible" (Rampersad, 130). The essay and the additional debate that it prompted called attention to the intense racial politics of the day and the degree to which the movement was inherently political during a time when many people of color contended with segregation, mob rule, and stereotypes even as they saw the history and creative genius of African Americans highlighted like never before.

Bibliography

Leak, Jeffrey. *Rac(e)ing to the Right: Selected Essays of George S. Schuyler.* Knoxville: University of Tennessee Press, 2001.

Peplow, Michael. *George S. Schuyler.* Boston: Twayne Publishers, 1980.

Rampersad, Arnold. *The Life of Langston Hughes: I, Too, Sing America.* Vol. 1, 1902–1941. New York: Oxford University Press, 1986.

"Negro Artist and the Racial Mountain, The" Langston Hughes (1926)

An influential essay by LANGSTON HUGHES published in the June 1926 issue of THE NATION, the influential American political magazine. Freda Kirchwey, editor in chief, on the recommendation of JAMES WELDON JOHNSON, solicited Hughes and asked him to generate an essay on African-American art. Her request was motivated in part by a just-published essay in *The Nation*, "NEGRO ART HOKUM" by GEORGE SCHUYLER.

Hughes offered a powerful set of observations about the prejudice of audiences and patrons who declared their interest in ethnic art and then disregarded works by gifted African-American artists and performers. He also directed sharp criticism at African-American artists who believed that they must transcend race in order to achieve greatness. After recounting an anecdote in which a young African-American poet confessed his desire to "be a poet—not a Negro poet," Hughes made an emphatic evaluation of the obstacles to black creative excellence. The racial mountain to which the essay's title refers is, according to Hughes, a "mountain standing in the way of any true Negro art in America" and defined as an "urge within the race toward whiteness, the desire to pour racial individuality into the mold of American standardization, and to be as little Negro and as much American as possible."

Hughes, who was enrolled at LINCOLN UNIVERSITY in Pennsylvania when he wrote the essay, concluded with an exhortation to young writers of color whom, he declared, "now intend to express our individual dark-skinned selves without fear or shame. If white people are pleased, we are glad. If they are not, it doesn't matter. We know we are beautiful. And ugly too. The tom-tom cries and the tom-tom laughs. If colored people are pleased, we are glad. If they are not, their displeasure doesn't matter either. We build our temples for tomorrow, strong as we know how, and we stand on top of the mountain, free within ourselves." The essay, which echoed the angst of writers like COUNTEE CULLEN and JEAN TOOMER, also reinforced the ambitions of Hughes's visionary friends and colleagues like ZORA NEALE HURSTON and WALLACE THURMAN with whom he would collaborate on innovative creative ventures to produce creative works or new literary journals such as *FIRE!!*.

Bibliography

Berry, Faith, ed. *Langston Hughes: Before and Beyond Harlem*. Westport, Conn.: Lawrence Hill & Company, 1983.

Rampersad, Arnold. *The Life of Langston Hughes: I, Too, Sing America*. Vol. 1: *1902–1941*. New York: Oxford University Press, 1986.

Negro Art Theatre of Harlem

One of the many theater groups established in response to the call for a vibrant black theater for and about African Americans. The Negro Art Theatre was established in the historic ABYSSINIAN BAPTIST CHURCH in NEW YORK CITY in 1925. It may have staged prize-winning works such as ZORA NEALE HURSTON's COLOR STRUCK as early as 1925, but its formal debut appears to have occurred some four years later in 1929. The troupe's first complete production was the show *Wade in the Water* starring Adam Clayton Powell, Jr., and LAURA BOWMAN.

In a November 1925 letter to Annie Nathan Meyer, president of BARNARD COLLEGE and one of her supporters, Zora Neale Hurston noted that "The Negro Art Theatre of Harlem is fairly launched now and the first program will include my 'Color Struck.'" Three years later, the Baltimore *Afro-American*, which kept its readers apprised of diverse events in African-American arts

and culture circles, published an update on the troupe. According to a brief August 1928 article, the "merciless heat proved too much for the summer activities of the Negro Art Theatre here in GREENWICH VILLAGE." The troupe shortened its advertised 10-week performance schedule to four weeks.

Bibliography

"Heat Defeats Art Theatre." *Baltimore Afro-American*, 18 August 1928, 8.

Kaplan, Carla. *Zora Neale Hurston: A Life in Letters*. New York: Doubleday, 2002.

Negro Authors and Composers of the United States W. C. Handy (1935)

One of five books published by WILLIAM CHRISTOPHER HANDY, the gifted musician regarded as the father of the blues. It was a useful history of writers and composers that complemented early encyclopedic texts such as *Music and Some Highly Musical People* (1881) by James Monroe Trotter and *The Negro and His Music* (1936) by ALAIN LOCKE.

Bibliography

Handy, W. C., and Arna Bontemps, ed. *Father of the Blues: An Autobiography*. 1941, reprint, New York: Da Capo Press, 1985.

Negro Champion

The official publication of the American Negro Labor Congress, a short-lived Communist organization that was founded in CHICAGO in 1925. Its editor was Lovett Fort-Whiteman, a militant antiwar activist and Marxist organizer who was instrumental in arranging the first conference. The offices of the newspaper were located in the Bronzeville section of Chicago.

Negro Experimental Theatre

A theater group founded by Dorothy Peterson and REGINA ANDREWS in February 1929 and based in the 135TH Street Branch (HARLEM BRANCH) of the NEW YORK PUBLIC LIBRARY. The company was known first as the KRIGWA PLAYERS and evolved into the troupe known as the Negro Experimental Theatre. It attracted the attention of other influential figures such as W. E. B. DuBois, Jessie Fauset, and Theophilus Lewis, all of whom actively supported the efforts of the troupe that was committed to developing African-American theater for and about African Americans.

The company put on a celebrated production of *Plumes*, a play by Georgia Douglas Johnson, under the direction of Harold Jackman. By 1931 the group had moved from the library to quarters at the Saint Philip's Protestant Episcopal Church. There, it continued to produce acclaimed dramas including works by and about African Americans such as *The Rider of Dreams* (1917) by Ridgely Torrence and "Climbing Jacob's Ladder" (1931) and *Underground* (1932) by Regina Andrews.

The troupe is credited with inspiring myriad theater troupes and with helping to develop the little-theater movement advocated by DuBois and others.

Bibliography

Krasner, David. *A Beautiful Pageant: African American Theatre, Drama, and Performance in the Harlem Renaissance, 1910–1927.* New York: Palgrave Macmillan, 2002.

Negro History in Thirteen Plays May Miller and Willis Richardson (1935)

An important drama anthology compiled by May Miller Sullivan and Willis Richardson. The volume showcased the works of five playwrights: Miller, Richardson, Georgia Douglas Johnson, Randolph Edmonds, and Helen Webb Harris.

The works showcased historical, literary, and biblical figures whose lives and accomplishments made significant contributions to the history of America and to the world. Works included American history plays on Crispus Attucks, Frederick Douglass, William and Ellen Craft, Nat Turner, Sojourner Truth, and Harriet Tubman. Additional works profiled Alexandre Dumas, the Elder, Antonio Maceo, and King Menelek.

Bibliography

Gray, Christine Rauchfuss. *Willis Richardson, Forgotten Pioneer of African-American Drama.* Westport, Conn.: Greenwood Press, 1999.

Richardson, Willis, and May Miller. *Negro History in Thirteen Plays.* New York: Associated Publishers, 1935.

Negro in American Fiction, The Sterling Brown (1937)

Published by Sterling Brown, a Phi Beta Kappa graduate of Williams College, poet, and Howard University professor of English. The volume appeared in the same year that Brown was awarded a Guggenheim Fellowship. It was the sixth monograph in the Bronze Booklet series edited by Alain Locke and produced by the Washington, D.C.–based group Associates in Negro Folk Education.

The volume comprises 12 chapters that cover diverse literary topics. Chapters range from "The Plantation Tradition: Pro-Slavery Fiction," "Antislavery Fiction," "Counter-Propaganda—Beginning Realism," "The Urban Scene," and "Historical Fiction." Each chapter concludes with a set of probing discussion questions.

Brown did not mince words in his forthright introduction. The volume begins with his assertion that "[t]he treatment of the Negro in American fiction, since it parallels his treatment in American life, has naturally been noted for injustice. Like other oppressed and exploited minorities, the Negro has been interpreted in a way to justify his exploiters." Brown recognized writers such as Herman Melville and George Washington Cable for their sympathetic treatments of African Americans but concluded with an insistent call for African-American writing that echoed the sentiments of early 20th century writers such as Pauline Hopkins. According to Brown, since "[m]any authors who are not hostile to the Negro and some who profess friendship still stress a 'peculiar endowment' at the expense of the Negro's basic humanity," it was vital that writers of color develop their own substantial literary tradition. "Negro novelists," he declared, "must accept the responsibility of being the ultimate portrayers of their own."

The book offers a rich overview of American canonical literature and women's writing. It includes brief plot summaries, close readings, and literary critiques. These lively discussions underscore Brown's larger argument about the ways in which racial stereotypes, national mythologies, and cultural ideals both shape and are advanced by literature.

Bibliography

Brown, Sterling. *The Negro in American Fiction*. Albany, N.Y.: The J. B. Lyon Press, 1937.

Gabbin, Joanne. *Sterling A. Brown: Building the Black Aesthetic Tradition*. Westport, Conn.: Greenwood Press, 1985.

Negro in Art, The: A Pictorial Record of the Negro Artist and of the Negro Theme in Art Alain Locke, ed. (1940)

A highly regarded history of art that ALAIN LOCKE edited and published in 1940. It was one of three works that Locke published with the Associates in Negro Folk Education, the WASHINGTON, D.C.–based organization with which he was affiliated and served as secretary. He had, since 1936, edited the Bronze Booklet series for the Associates group and had overseen works on African-American literature, art, and culture.

This volume appeared four years after Locke published *Negro Art: Past and Present* (1936), the third installment in the Bronze Booklet series. It is regarded as one of the most popular of his works, after the influential anthology, *THE NEW NEGRO* (1925).

Locke, who earned a doctorate in philosophy, had a deep interest in African-American art. He was intrigued by the ways in which this body of work was influenced and shaped by African art. He challenged those who regarded African art as primitive and simplistic; instead, he argued, such works had a sophisticated artistry and demonstrated intricate techniques. Locke also used this work to encourage African-American artists to seek out native African art traditions and to incorporate these styles and themes in their own works.

Bibliography

Linneman. Russell. *Alain Locke: Reflections on a Modern Renaissance Man*. Baton Rouge: Louisiana State University, 1982.

Locke, Alain. *Negro Art: Past and Present*. Washington, D.C.: Associates in Negro Folk Education, 1936.

———, ed. *The Negro in Art: A Pictorial Record of the Negro Artist and of the Negro Theme in Art*. 1940; reprint, New York: Hacker Art Books, 1971.

Negro in Art, The: How Shall He Be Portrayed? A Symposium (1926)

In 1926 W. E. B. DuBois initiated a seven-month-long discussion in *THE CRISIS* about the artistic and literary representations of African Americans. Convinced that all art was propaganda, DuBois endeavored to engage his contemporaries in serious debate about the responsibilities, tendencies, and philosophies of writers who pursued racial themes and subjects in their works. DuBois and his literary editor JESSIE FAUSET distributed some seven questions, developed apparently by CARL VAN VECHTEN, to prominent African-American and white writers, literary figures, and scholars. Their answers were published in seven issues of *The Crisis* during 1926.

The respondents included SHERWOOD ANDERSON, COUNTEE CULLEN, JOHN FARRAR, Jessie Fauset, DuBOSE HEYWARD, LANGSTON HUGHES, ALFRED KNOPF, SINCLAIR LEWIS, GEORGIA DOUGLAS JOHNSON, Vachel Lindsay, H. L. MENCKEN, JULIA PETERKIN, Carl Van Vechten, and WALTER WHITE.

Van Vechten, whose novel *NIGGER HEAVEN* was forthcoming, suggested that the "squalor of Negro life, the vice of Negro life, offer a wealth of novel, exotic, picturesque material to the artist." He also suggested that the real issue at hand was whether or not "Negro writers are going to write about this exotic material while it is still fresh or will they continue to make free gift of it to white authors who will exploit it until not a drop of vitality remains?" Countee Cullen argued for artistic freedom and encouraged others to generate literature that was "representative" of the race. John Farrar, a prominent book critic and cofounder of the publishing house Farrar, Strauss and Giroux, proposed that African Americans be forthright and confident, showing "as little self-consciousness as possible." H. L. Mencken, the writer and satirist, suggested that African Americans fight pernicious stereotypes by crafting equally devastating images of their oppressors. Walter White called for genuine, polished, and diverse representations of African-American life and, like Vachel Lindsay, the poet who catapulted Langston Hughes into the spotlight, proposed that publishers refrain from projects that contained sloppy and divisive works.

The debate about the politics of artistic representation, the nature of African-American images, and the relationship among art, history, and realism continued throughout the Harlem Renaissance. The tensions between more conservative thinkers like DuBois and the emerging younger artists like Hughes, WALLACE THURMAN, and ZORA NEALE HURSTON produced some of the most dynamic and volatile works and discussions of the period.

Bibliography

Lewis, David Levering. *W. E. B. DuBois: The Fight for Equality and the American Century, 1919–1963*. New York: Henry Holt and Company, 2000.

Negro Life in New York's Harlem: A Lively Picture of a Popular and Interesting Section Wallace Thurman (1928)

An engaging narrative by WALLACE THURMAN on HARLEM and the diverse populations and cultural activities of the NEW YORK CITY neighborhood. Thurman provided information on the religious life, artistic ventures, energetic social scenes, and range of parties that included rent parties to raise funds to cover housing costs, cabaret locations, and gambling.

The lengthy essay appeared first in triple fall/winter issue of the Kansas-based *Haldeman-Julius Quarterly* in 1928. It was then republished as an installment in the Little Blue Book Series that the press produced. The monograph appeared in the same year that Thurman attempted to publish the promising but short-lived periodical, HARLEM: A FORUM OF NEGRO LIFE.

Bibliography

McIver, Dorothy Jean. *Stepchild in Harlem: The Literary Career of Wallace Thurman*. Ann Arbor, Mich.: University Microfilms International, 1995.

van Notten, Eleonore. *Wallace Thurman's Harlem Renaissance*. Amsterdam: Rodopi, 1994.

Negro Mother and Other Dramatic Recitations, The Langston Hughes (1931)

A popular pamphlet published by the Golden Stair Press that contained six dramatic monologues composed by LANGSTON HUGHES. The white artist Prentiss Taylor, who founded the Golden Stair Press in Greenwich Village with help from Hughes and CARL VAN VECHTEN, provided illustrations that were described as "decorations." The press produced 1,700 copies, including 17 rare hand-colored copies with Hughes's and Taylor's autographs.

Priced at 25 cents, the pamphlet sold briskly, especially when Hughes completed a rousing reading and audiences flocked to local bookstores to purchase copies of his works. According to Hughes biographer Arnold Rampersad, the poet sold some 100 copies at a New York YOUNG MEN'S CHRISTIAN ASSOCIATION branch, including some 18 copies sold in an elevator by the attendant. In the fall of 1931 Hughes himself packed copies of the work and took them with him to distribute during what was planned as a lengthy eight-month lecture and reading tour throughout the South.

The volume included the powerful title work, "The Negro Mother," and five other pieces: "The Colored Soldier," "Broke," "The Black Clown," "The Big-Timer," and "Dark Youth." The title poem, written in the first person, was a moving exhortation from a woman to her descendants. "Children, I come back today / To tell you a story of the long dark way / That I had to climb, that I had to know / In order that the race may live and grow," declares the resurrected narrator in the poem's opening lines. The female speaker goes on to recount the physical labor that she endured, the evils of segregation, the range of mistreatment, and the faith that sustained her through life. The poem ends with an emphatic reminder of the rights that long-suffering elders have already won for contemporary people of color. She encourages others to "march every forward, breaking down bars. / Look ever upward at the sun and the stars." The highly evocative last lines of the poem are directed at children of the race: "Oh, my dark children, may my dreams and my prayers / Impel you forever up the great stairs—/ For I will be with you till no white brother / Dares keep down the children of the Negro mother."

Selections from the work also were included in the 1938 production *Don't You Want to Be Free?*, a multi-genre piece that included a range of Hughes's dramatic works set to music.

Bibliography

Berry, Faith, ed. *Langston Hughes: Before and Beyond Harlem*. Westport, Conn.: Lawrence Hill & Company, 1983.

Hughes, Langston. *The Negro Mother, and Other Dramatic Recitations, with decorations by Prentiss Taylor.* 1931; reprint, Salem, N.H.: Ayer, 1990.

Rampersad, Arnold. *The Life of Langston Hughes: I, Too, Sing America.* Vol. 1, *1902–1941.* New York: Oxford University Press, 1986.

Negro Musicians and Their Music
Maude Cuney Hare (1936)

A comprehensive collection of works by musicians of African descent published by MAUDE CUNEY HARE. Hare, a folklorist, music historian, teacher, playwright, and founder of the Allied Arts Center in BOSTON, gathered materials for the book during her travels throughout the Caribbean, Mexico, and the United States. The volume included works from Puerto Rico, the Virgin Islands, Cuba, Mexico, and the United States.

The volume was Hare's last work and was published in 1936, the year of her death.

Bibliography

Hales, Douglas. *A Southern Family in White and Black: The Cuneys of Texas.* College Station: Texas A&M University Press, 2003.

Maude Cuney Hare Papers, Atlanta University Center Archives.

Negro Poetry and Drama Sterling Brown
(1937)

An influential work of literary criticism by STERLING BROWN, a PHI BETA KAPPA graduate of WILLIAMS COLLEGE, published poet, and HOWARD UNIVERSITY English professor.

Brown published the work with the Associates in Negro Folk Education, the WASHINGTON, D.C., organization with which fellow Howard University colleague ALAIN LOCKE was affiliated.

The volume appeared in the same year as Brown's shorter monograph THE NEGRO IN AMERICAN FICTION. This work was part of the Bronze Booklet series for which Locke was editor. As he did in the Bronze Booklet volume, Brown generated discussion questions and a secondary-source reading list at the end of each chapter in *Negro Poetry and Drama.*

Brown used *Negro Poetry and Drama* to discuss issues pertinent to the Harlem Renaissance. He in-

cluded such chapters as "Contemporary Negro Poetry," in which he considered the works and styles of "The New Negro" poets, individuals whom he believed "shared in the [Harlem Renaissance] movements reaction against sentimentality, didacticism, optimism, and romantic escape." Writers such as FENTON JOHNSON, GEORGIA DOUGLAS JOHNSON, ALICE DUNBAR-NELSON, CARRIE CLIFFORD, and JAMES WELDON JOHNSON shaped what Brown touted as the invaluable literary aspects of "New Negro Renaissance": "(1) a discovery of Africa as a source for race pride (2) a use of Negro heroes and heroic episodes from American history (3) propaganda of protest (4) a treatment of the Negro masses (frequently of the folk, less often of the workers) with more understanding and less apology and (5) franker and deeper self revelation."

Brown's pioneering articulation and review of the African-American literary tradition engaged with scholars such as W. E. B. DuBois and Alain Locke who, with other writers such as LANGSTON HUGHES, COUNTEE CULLEN, JESSIE FAUSET, and ZORA NEALE HURSTON, debated about the uses of African-American writing and art and the politics explicit in contemporary representation of African-American experiences.

Bibliography

Brown, Sterling. *Negro Poetry and Drama.* 1937, reprint, New York: Arno Press, 1969.

Gabbin, Joanne. *Sterling A. Brown: Building the Black Aesthetic Tradition.* Westport, Conn.: Greenwood Press, 1985.

Negro Poets and Their Poems Robert T. Kerlin
(1923)

An invaluable literary and historical resource written by ROBERT T. KERLIN and published in 1923. It includes works by at least 60 poets, many of whom achieved prominence during and after the Harlem Renaissance and also excelled in additional professions.

The volume opens with a heartfelt dedication "To the Black and Unknown Bards who gave to the world the priceless treasure of those 'canticles of love and woe,' the camp-meeting Spirituals; more particularly, to those untaught singers of the old plantations of the South, whose melodious lullabies to the babes of both races entered with genius-quickening power into the souls of Poe and Lanier, Dunbar and Cotter." It is "to them, for whom any monument in stone or bronze were but mockery," that Kerlin "dedicate[s] this monument of verse, builded by the children of their vision."

There are eight lengthy chapters, each containing several subsections devoted to a profile of an author and his or her works. Chapters include "The Present-Day Negro Heritage of Song," "The Present Renaissance of the Negro," "The Heart of Negro Womanhood," "Ad Astra Pera Aspera," "The New Forms of Poetry," "Dialect Verse," "The Poetry of Protest," and a final chapter entitled "Conquest by Poetry: A Miscellany." The volume also includes a section devoted to biographical and bibliographical notes pertaining to each of the writers.

Kerlin's assessment of the African-American poetry tradition is enriched by detailed contextual information and his efforts to consider the works of lesser-known poets from all walks of life. He provides information on traditional and well-known early poets such as Phillis Wheatley, George Moses Horton, and Frances Harper but extends his conversations to include notes on J. Mord Allen, Charles Reason, and Albery Whitman. In subsequent chapters, he incorporates the works of journalists, invalids, and felons and explores the pathos of their verse in relation to more established works by writers such as Paul Laurence Dunbar, WILLIAM STANLEY BRAITHWAITE, JAMES WELDON JOHNSON, and WALTER EVERETTE HAWKINS. Chapter 3, devoted specifically to women writers, addresses the works of seven individuals: EVA JESSYE, Mrs. J. W. Hammond, ALICE DUNBAR-NELSON, GEORGIA DOUGLAS JOHNSON, ANGELINA GRIMKÉ, ANNE SPENCER, and JESSIE FAUSET. This chapter does not represent the sum of Kerlin's discussions of women's writing. Kerlin includes works by other women writers such as CARRIE CLIFFORD, CLARISSA SCOTT DELANY, GWENDOLYN BENNETT, and MARGARET WALKER in other chapters.

Negro Poets and Their Poems also includes an impressive number of illustrations and portraits. The book's frontispiece is adorned by a reproduction of a Meta Warrick Fuller sculpture entitled *Emancipation*. Other images of writers are included, offered by bibliophile ARTHUR SCHOMBURG for inclusion in the book.

Bibliography
Kerlin, Robert T. *Negro Poets and Their Poems.* Washington, D.C.: Associated Publishers, Inc., 1923.

Negro's Contribution to American Culture, The: The Sudden Flowering of a Genius-Laden Artistic Movement
Walter White (1927)

A work of social and cultural history published by WALTER WHITE, just one year after he was awarded a GUGGENHEIM FELLOWSHIP. White would become executive director of the NATIONAL ASSOCIATION FOR THE ADVANCEMENT OF COLORED PEOPLE in 1930.

White's pamphlet was published as part of the Little Blue Books series produced by E. Haldeman-Julius and Henry Haldeman. Other works in that series by notable Harlem Renaissance figures included *THE NEGRO MOTHER AND OTHER DRAMATIC RECITATIONS* (1931) by LANGSTON HUGHES.

Bibliography
Janken, Kenneth Robert. *White: The Biography of Walter White, Mr. NAACP.* New York: The New Press, 2003.

Negrotarians

A popular Harlem Renaissance term coined by ZORA NEALE HURSTON. The word refers to wealthy whites who had a strong interest in the New Negro movement and whose philanthropic efforts included an explicit commitment to sustaining African-American artists and writers.

Bibliography
Boyd, Valerie. *Wrapped in Rainbows: The Life of Zora Neale Hurston.* New York: Scribner, 2003.

Hemenway, Robert. *Zora Neale Hurston: A Literary Biography.* Urbana: University of Illinois Press, 1977.

Negro Voices: An Anthology of Contemporary Verse
Beatrice Campbell Murphy (1938)

A collection of poems edited by BEATRICE CAMPBELL MURPHY, a poet, journalist, and longtime resident of WASHINGTON, D.C. The volume includes works by Murphy and other prominent writers such as LANGSTON HUGHES. With this work, Murphy established herself as one of the few American women who published compilations of primary works by African Americans. The volume was a companion piece to other compilations such as the celebrated ALAIN LOCKE anthology *NEW NEGRO* (1925), Robert Kerlin's study *NEGRO POETS AND THEIR POEMS* (1923), and the WALTER CLINTON JACKSON and NEWMAN IVEY WHITE volume *AN ANTHOLOGY OF VERSE BY AMERICAN NEGROES* (1924).

Negro Voices was the first of three anthologies that Murphy published during her career. She once described anthologies as "something like a bowl of mixed chocolates," a treat that individuals could "dig into . . . and find almost any kind which suits your fancy."

Murphy's second anthology, *Ebony Rhythm*, appeared in 1948. Her third poetry collection, entitled *Today's Negro Voices: An Anthology by Young Negro Poets*, was published in 1970.

Bibliography

Murphy, Beatrice. *Negro Voices: An Anthology of Contemporary Verse*. New York: Henry Harrison, 1938.

——. *Ebony Rhythm: An Anthology of Contemporary Negro Verse*. 1948, reprint, Salem, N.H.: Ayer Company, 1988.

——. *Today's Negro Voices: An Anthology by Young Negro Poets*. New York: Messner, 1970.

Negro World

The official publication of the UNIVERSAL NEGRO IMPROVEMENT ASSOCIATION (UNIA), the organization that MARCUS GARVEY established in 1914. It became a popular publication and could boast of a readership of some 200,000 in its best years.

The first issue of the weekly newspaper appeared in NEW YORK CITY on August 17, 1918, a date that also was Garvey's birthday. The editors and reporters were prominent activists and included Garvey, who was actively involved through the early 1930s. HUBERT HARRISON, the founder of the Liberty League and the man who invited Garvey to make his first address in New York, also served as editor of the paper, as did WILFRED ADOLPHUS DOMINGO, a West Indian nationalist.

Amy Jacques Garvey, the second wife of Marcus Garvey, served as associate editor from 1924 to 1927. Duse Mohammed Ali, Garvey's mentor, served as a foreign affairs expert for a period. The intellectual John E. Bruce also was a regular contributor to *Negro World.*

In 1923 Garvey and his editors developed a Spanish-language section; one year later, *Negro World* also included a French-language section as well. The paper sold for five cents in New York City, seven cents elsewhere in the United States, and ten cents abroad.

The paper was extremely popular and enjoyed an international readership. Its black nationalist message, however, was thoroughly critical of colonial rule and philosophies. As a result, the publication was banned in several colonies in the Caribbean and in Africa. Travelers, students, and seamen of color often smuggled copies of the paper into circulation and thus disseminated Garvey's fervent messages about black emancipation and political triumph despite government prohibitions.

The regular features of the newspaper included an editorial by Garvey, coverage of current events, and news about UNIA events and campaigns. The editors published articles by prominent Harlem Renaissance–era figures such as W. A. Domingo, T. THOMAS FORTUNE, ZORA NEALE HURSTON, ERIC WALROND, and ARTHUR SCHOMBURG. *Negro World* also publicized works by emerging writers. In 1922, for instance, it celebrated the publication of *BATOUALA*, the award-winning novel by RENÉ MARAN, the first person to publish a novel on the experiences of Africans living under French rule.

The paper ceased publication in 1932. It resumed publication again for a brief period in October 1933, but Garvey officially disbanded the newspaper later that year.

Bibliography

Cronon, E. David. *Black Moses: The Story of Marcus Garvey and the Universal Negro Improvement Association*. Madison: University of Wisconsin Press, 1987.

Garvey, Amy J., ed. *Philosophy and Opinions of Marcus Garvey*. New York: The Universal Publishing House, 1923–1925.

Hill, Robert, ed. *The Marcus Garvey and Universal Negro Improvement Association Papers*. Berkeley: University of California Press, 1983.

Lewis, Rupert. *Marcus Garvey: Anti-Colonial Champion*. Trenton, N.J.: Africa World Press, 1988.

Stein, Judith. *The World of Marcus Garvey: Race and Class in Modern Society*. Baton Rouge: Louisiana State University Press, 1986.

Stephens, Michelle. "Black Transnationalism and the Politics of National Identity: West Indian Intellectuals in Harlem in the Age of War and Revolution," *American Quarterly* 50, no. 3 (1988): 592–608.

Negro Year Book

An annual publication compiled by Monroe N. Work, the director of the Department of Records and Research at TUSKEGEE INSTITUTE in Alabama.

Work began publishing the volumes, which detailed the life, history, accomplishments, and statistics relating to peoples of African descent, in 1918. The annual yearbooks were recommended highly to a wide array of American audiences, including "Mission Study classes, Y.M.C.A. and Y.W.C.A. classes and literary clubs" and was "especially adapted for use in schools where sociological and historical courses on the Negro are given."

During the 1920s the volume was priced at $1 for paperback editions and $1.50 for hardcover versions.

Negry v Amerike   Claude McKay (1923)

Published in the former Soviet Union in 1923, this collection of essays by CLAUDE MCKAY was based on writings he completed during his early-1920s sojourns abroad in Russia and North Africa. It was published less than a year after McKay, who had recently been working with SYLVIA PANKHURST and others in the offices of the *WORKER'S DREADNOUGHT* in England, addressed the Comintern in 1922.

The translated title of the volume reads, "Negroes in America." The book, which McKay completed in six months, shed light on his understanding of Marxism and Communism and revealed his opinions about African-American labor issues and politics. The volume included

chapters on "Labor Leaders and Negroes," "Negroes in Sports," and "Sex and Economics."

Bibliography
Cooper, Wayne. *Claude McKay: Rebel Sojourner in the Harlem Renaissance*. New York: Schocken Books, 1987.

Giles, James R. *Claude McKay*. Boston: Twayne Publishers, 1976.

Neighborhood Playhouse

A NEW YORK CITY theater built in 1915 by the philanthropist sisters Alice and Irene Lewisohn. Both women were actively involved in the settlement house movement, and they oversaw artistic productions at the Henry Street Settlement House on the Lower East Side. It was one of the first venues designated as an "off-Broadway" theater.

The first production at the venue was JEPHTHAH'S DAUGHTER, a tragedy by CARRIE MORGAN FIGGS, based on the Old Testament story of Jephtha, a man forced to sacrifice his own child, in the Book of Judges. Additional productions at the venue included *Carlos Among the Candles*, a 1917 play by Wallace Stevens. The November 1920 debut of THE EMPEROR JONES by EUGENE O'NEILL starred Charles Gilpin in the title role, and the show ran for some 204 performances. The theater also accommodated lectures and nondramatic performances. It was there that JEAN TOOMER, MARGARET NAUMBERG, and others attended presentations by members of the Gurdjieff movement.

The Neighborhood Playhouse closed in 1927. Its legacy continued to shape American theater, however. In 1928 the Lewisohn sisters collaborated with Rita Wallach Morgenthau and established the Neighborhood Playhouse School of the Theatre. Its celebrated faculty included Martha Graham and Agnes De Mille.

Bibliography
Blood, Melanie Nelda. *The Neighborhood Playhouse, 1915–1927: A History and Analysis*. Evanston, Ill.: Northwestern University, 1994.

Krasner, David. *A Beautiful Pageant: African American Theatre, Drama, and Performance in the Harlem Re-*

naissance, 1910–1927. New York: Palgrave Macmillan, 2002.

"Nettleby's New Year, The" Anita Scott Coleman (1920)

A short story by ANITA SCOTT COLEMAN. The story, published in the January 1920 issue of THE HALF CENTURY magazine, was one of several short stories that Coleman published in the Chicago-based African-American periodical.

Never No More James Knox Millen (1932)

A play by JAMES KNOX MILLEN that opened at the Hudson Theatre on BROADWAY in January 1932. The show, which starred Rose McClendon, Leigh Whipper, and Lew Payton, closed after only 12 performances.

The play revolved around a besieged family who is targeted by a mob intent on lynching one of its sons who has accidentally strangled a young white girl. In defense of her child, the mother threatens to detonate a bomb that will annihilate the mob.

New Challenge

A journal that DOROTHY WEST established in 1937. The title recalled West's first publishing venture with CHALLENGE, a popular literary periodical that featured works by her contemporaries and friends such as ZORA NEALE HURSTON, COUNTEE CULLEN, CLAUDE MCKAY, CARL VAN VECHTEN, and others.

West collaborated with RICHARD WRIGHT on the *New Challenge* venture. She appointed him associate editor of the quarterly magazine and promptly published his pioneering essay "Blueprint for Negro Writing," in the fall 1937 issue. West solicited contributions to the journal from well- and lesser-known figures of the Harlem Renaissance. *New Challenge* included poetry by FRANK MARSHALL DAVIS, Margaret Walker, STERLING BROWN, and Owen Dodson, as well as short fiction by Norman Macleod, Clarence Haill, and Benjamin Appel. In addition to Wright's essay, *New Challenge* also included essays by Verna Arvey and Eugene Holmes and book reviews by figures such as Henry Lee Moon, RALPH ELLISON, and ALAIN LOCKE.

Wright and West had a number of editorial arguments about the scope and focus of the revived magazine that led to its untimely demise after one issue.

Bibliography

West, Dorothy. *The Richer, the Poorer: Stories, Sketches, and Reminiscences.* New York: Doubleday, 1995.

New Masses

A journal founded by left-wing writers and thinkers in 1926. Michael Gold and John Sloan founded *New Masses* when the journal THE LIBERATOR became a vehicle of the American Communist Party. Its name recalled an earlier socialist journal, *Masses,* for which the writer MAX EASTMAN had worked as editor.

New Masses published works by prominent and outspoken American writers. RALPH ELLISON was one of the magazine's volunteer literary reviewers, and other contributors included Ezra Pound, RICHARD WRIGHT, LANGSTON HUGHES, Carl Sandburg, WALDO FRANK, and EUGENE O'NEILL. Hughes published his powerful verse drama, SCOTTSBORO LIMITED, in *New Masses* before including it in the moving 1932 collection of the same name. The journal also commented on Harlem Renaissance writers and literature. CLAUDE MCKAY was one of the writers whose work was critiqued in the journal and criticized for what was deemed an inadequate class consciousness in his works.

The journal was a monthly periodical during most of its publication years. It became a weekly publication from 1933 through early 1948. After 22 years of publication, the journal ceased in mid-January 1948.

Bibliography

Jackson, Lawrence. *Ralph Ellison: Emergence of Genius.* New York: John Wiley & Sons, Inc., 2002.

O'Neill, William. *The Last Romantic: A Life of Max Eastman.* New York: Oxford University Press, 1978.

New Negro, The: An Interpretation
Alain Locke, ed. (1925)

The celebrated and influential anthology that articulated the cultural, artistic, and scholarly momentum in African-American letters and research. ALAIN LOCKE edited and published the volume shortly after the acclaimed Harlem issue of SURVEY GRAPHIC appeared. *The New Negro,* published by the New York firm A. Boni, included "book decoration and portraits" by WINOLD REISS.

In his introduction to the volume, Locke described the goals of the powerful anthology. The book aimed "to document the New Negro culturally and socially—to register the transformations of the inner and outer life of the Negro in America that have so significantly taken place in the last few years." The book allowed "the Negro [to] speak for himself," an important move that had been called for by authors such as Pauline Hopkins, W. E. B. DU BOIS, ARTHUR HUFF FAUSET, and others. Locke characterized the diverse contents of the anthology as evidence of "an unusual outburst of creative expression" and the inspiring "renewed race spirit that consciously and proudly sets itself apart." Critics praised the collection and emphasized the intriguing appeal that it would have to a vast number of readers. Reviewer Dorothy Scarborough insisted that the volume was "a book of surprises" and "an extraordinarily interesting page of history, an impressive record of achievement." "Here," she wrote, "Harlem, home of the new negro speaks" and "[n]o matter how well-informed the reader, he will find here facts that he has not known about the progress of the negro in America" (Scarborough, BR 19).

Locke used the anthology to advance further his beliefs that powerful sociocultural forces continued to impact African-American life and were responsible for the creation of the New Negro. Migration was one of the key factors in the evolution of this figure for it was responsible for creating new diverse communities of color, ones that were quick to learn from each other and to develop new and intriguing histories. "Here in Manhattan is not merely the largest Negro community in the world," he wrote, "but the first concentration in history of so many diverse elements of Negro life. . . . Each group has come with its own separate motives and for its own special ends, but their greatest experience has been the finding of one another . . . Within this area, race sympathy and unit have determined a further fusing of sentiment and experience. So what began in terms of segregation

becomes more and more, as its elements mix and react, the laboratory of a great race-welding." Locke's essay on the "New Negro," a figure who came to embody the diverse and progressive goals of the Renaissance, has been of lasting significance in American literary history. His overview of the cultural and social evolutions, the impact of migration, and the literary trends make the essay a rich guide to the major transformations that defined the Harlem Renaissance. Locke delighted in the "New Negro," a figure whom he described as one that often defied easy characterization.

The volume included authors published in the *Survey Graphic* issue, and it presented the work in a format similar to that found in the periodical. In "The Negro Renaissance," the first of the book's two sections, Locke included creative works by writers such as COUNTEE CULLEN, JESSIE FAUSET, LANGSTON HUGHES, GEORGIA DOUGLAS JOHNSON, JAMES WELDON JOHNSON, WILLIS RICHARDSON, ANNE SPENCER, JEAN TOOMER, and ZORA NEALE HURSTON. The section also included writers' essays on literary politics such as Hughes's thoughtful meditation "THE NEGRO ARTIST AND THE RACIAL MOUNTAIN." The second section, "The New Negro in a New World," contained nonfiction and scholarly prose articles by sociologists CHARLES JOHNSON and anthropologists such as MELVILLE HERSKOVITS alongside articles by W. A. DOMINGO, ELISE JOHNSON MCDOUGALD, KELLY MILLER, Robert Moton, and WALTER WHITE.

The preparations leading up to the publication of *The New Negro* were not without controversy. The writer Jean Toomer, who came to resist invitations to submit his work for inclusion in African-American anthologies, also rejected Locke's call for an entry. Yet, as Toomer recalled with some horror, "when Locke's book came out . . . there was a story from *CANE,* and there in the introduction, were words about me which have caused me . . . misunderstanding." As far as Toomer was concerned, "Locke tricked and misused" him, and he was quite forthright about the fact that "[f]or a short time after the appearance of Locke's book I was furious." Toomer's primary objection to Locke was rooted in his preference to keep *Cane* intact and not "dismembered" (Byrd, 216). CARL VAN VECHTEN was alarmed when Locke showed him the draft of the volume because of the contribution that he saw attributed to his friend Langston Hughes. He wrote immediately to Hughes, cautioning him about the legal aspects of republication and the problems that could arise from the reprinting of two Hughes poems. "Of course, you know that you cannot publish in book form anything included in your own book without permission from Mr. Knopf," he wrote earnestly. While he admitted "there could be no objection to using the poems in the *Survey Graphic*," he noted that "Locke had a further section labeled 'Jazzonia,' and I think it would be a decided mistake to publish any of the jazz poems in book form before your book appeared." Van Vechten could not stop there; he was quite concerned about how any sense of impropriety might jeopardize his young colleague's pending publication and future reputation. "You see," he wrote, "this anthology will appear a good three months before your book appears; everybody will buy it and if it contains a sufficient number of your best poems it will take the edge off the sale and reviews of your own book. If it were coming out after your book there could be no such objection. Even so, it is the part of wisdom to be sparing in contributions to anthologies" (Bernard, 23).

The New Negro was one of the most well-known anthologies of the Harlem Renaissance period. Locke's efforts to present a persuasive and absorbing collection of writings ultimately resulted in one of the most earnest assessments of African-American culture, literature, and history.

Bibliography

Bernard, Emily. *Remember Me to Harlem: The Letters of Langston Hughes and Carl Van Vechten.* New York: Knopf, 2001.

Byrd, Rudolph. "Jean Toomer and the Writers of the Harlem Renaissance: Was He There with Them?" In *The Harlem Renaissance: Reevaluations,* edited by Amritjit Singh, William S. Shiver, and Stanley Brodwin. New York: Garland Publishing, Inc., 1989, 209–218.

Linneman, Russell, ed. *Alain Locke: Reflections on a Modern Renaissance Man.* Baton Rouge: Louisiana State University, 1982.

Locke, Alain. *The New Negro: An Interpretation.* 1925; reprint, New York: Arno Press, 1968.

Scarborough, Dorothy. "From Cotton Field and Levee to the Streets of Harlem." *New York Times,* 20 December 1925, DR 19.

New Negro Arts Movement

The name that was used first to describe the literary and cultural awakening known as the HARLEM RENAISSANCE.

New Negro Art Theatre

A theater company based in NEW YORK CITY and founded by Hemsley Winfield, a dynamic figure in the world of dance and theater who was committed to creating a respected and sophisticated African-American dance tradition. The theater company included a number of extremely talented individuals, including Ollie Burgoyne, Edna Guy, and Randolph Sawyer.

Winfield was a recognized presence in the New York performance world. He made his debut in 1927 in *Wade in the Water,* a play by his mother that was produced at the Cherry Lane Theatre in Greenwich Village. In 1933 he would choreograph and perform dances in the Metropolitan Theatre ballet productions of EUGENE O'NEILL's *THE EMPEROR JONES.*

The year 1931 was a stellar one for Winfield. In addition to founding the New Negro Art Theatre, he and Guy had starred in a groundbreaking dance performance in April that was billed as the "First Negro Dance Recital in America."

Bibliography

Perpener, John O., III. *African American Concert Dance: The Harlem Renaissance and Beyond.* Urbana: University of Illinois Press, 2001.

New Republic, The

One of the nation's most prominent political weekly journals, founded in 1914 by Dorothy and Willard Straight and journalist Herbert Croly. Croly served as the magazine's first editor. The magazine was a left-wing and liberal publication dedicated to providing its readers with scrupulous reports and analyses of current issues, society and culture, and government policies. In its early years, the magazine endorsed President Theodore Roosevelt and was an advocate of the Progressive movement. Croly later supported Woodrow Wilson and the efforts to wage war against Germany. The decision prompted criticism from fellow political editors such as MAX EAST-MAN of *The Masses.*

The magazine had a modest readership of fewer than 1,000 readers during its first year. In 1915, however, circulation numbers exploded and reached 15,000.

The magazine had lost its founder, Willard Straight, during the devastating influenza epidemic of 1918. Straight's widow, Dorothy, however, remained committed to the journal and worked tirelessly to cultivate contributors and to maintain the financial stability of the journal. During the 1930s, Bruce Bliven served as editor. He was succeeded by Henry Wallace, a dynamic figure who increased the readership to 100,000 before leaving the post to run for the presidency of the United States. In 1947, Michael Whitney Straight, son of the journal's founders, was appointed editor.

During the Harlem Renaissance, the journal published dynamic writers such as ERIC WAL-ROND, WALLACE THURMAN, the writer and enterprising founder of several literary magazines, and HUBERT HARRISON, the outspoken labor organizer and *NEGRO WORLD* editor. Other contributors of note included Willa Cather, John Dos Passos, and H. L. MENCKEN.

Bibliography

Peterson, Merrill D. *Coming of Age with the New Republic, 1938–1950.* Columbia: University of Missouri Press, 1999.

Seideman, David. *The New Republic: A Voice of Modern Liberalism.* New York: Praeger, 1986.

Newsome, Mary Effie Lee (1885–1979)

A native of PHILADELPHIA, Newsome became a writer of children's stories and literature. Born Mary Effie Lee on 19 January 1885, she was the daughter of Mary Elizabeth Ashe Lee and Benjamin Franklin Lee. Her father was a journalist and bishop, who also served as president of WILBER-FORCE UNIVERSITY. Her father's work in the church resulted in the family's frequent relocation to cities such as Wilberforce, Ohio, and Waco, Texas. Her older brother, Benjamin, born while the family was living in Wilberforce, Ohio, went on to become a member of the NATIONAL URBAN LEAGUE, an active member of the YOUNG MEN'S CHRISTIAN ASSOCIATION, and the executive secretary of the Civic League in Cincinnati, Ohio.

Effie Lee attended several universities between the years 1901 and 1914. These included Wilberforce University between 1901 and 1903, OBERLIN College for one year from 1904 through 1905, and the Philadelphia Academy of Fine Arts for an additional year in 1907. She appears to have completed her college education at the UNIVERSITY OF PENNSYLVANIA in 1914, but as biographers Lorraine Roses and Ruth Randolph note, there is no evidence that she graduated from any of these institutions.

In August 1920 Lee married Henry Nesby Newsome, a widowed African Methodist Episcopal minister, president of the Safety Banking and Realty Company in Mobile, Alabama, and father of six children. The couple soon settled in Birmingham, Alabama. There, Mary Lee Newsome organized the Boys of Birmingham Club in 1925. The couple eventually moved back to Wilberforce, Ohio. Newsome, who had a passion for writing literature for children, worked as an elementary school librarian.

Newsome began publishing before her marriage. Her poems began appearing in *THE CRISIS* as early as 1917. She continued to publish with the official journal of the NATIONAL ASSOCIATION FOR THE ADVANCEMENT OF COLORED PEOPLE for almost two decades. On occasion she used the pseudonym "Johnson Ward"; it was under this name that she won an honorable mention in 1926 for the poem "The Bird in the Cage" that she submitted to a *Crisis* literary contest.

Her poems, which tended to focus exclusively on children, their experiences, and family relationships, were diverse in form and setting. She developed caring narratives about young people who managed to overcome the racism of their worlds and who were capable of loving sincerely despite hardships. In addition, Newsome helped to advance *THE CRISIS* to young children of color. She authored "The Little Page," a regular feature that included informative columns about diverse subjects, her own poetry, letters from children, and even the submissions that she received from some of her young readers.

Newsome published two books, *Our Young People's Book of Verse* in 1923 and *GLADIOLA GAR-*

DENS: POEMS OF OUTDOORS AND INDOORS FOR SECOND GRADE READERS (1940). The renowned artist Lois Maillou Jones provided the illustrations for this volume.

Newsome's work merited recognition and was selected for inclusion in two highly regarded anthologies of the Harlem Renaissance. COUNTEE CULLEN published eight Newsome poems in his 1927 collection entitled CAROLING DUSK. In 1941 ARNA BONTEMPS selected seven of her works for inclusion in *Golden Slippers: An Anthology of Negro Poetry for Young Readers*. The biographical note included in the Bontemps collection reflected Newsome's engaging character. "Mary Effie Lee Newsome would rather not talk about how long it has been since she was a child," it reads before noting that with her sister, Consuelo, she developed a love of reading, writing, and illustrating. As children, reports the profile, the Newsome sisters "sent their work to children's pages of magazines, and before long they were winning prizes."

Newsome's writings are part of the substantial canon of African-American children's literature that emerged during the Harlem Renaissance era. Her contemporaries in this field included JESSIE FAUSET, the literary editor of *The Crisis*, Arna Bontemps, NELLA LARSEN, and ROSE LEARY LOVE.

Bibliography

Bontemps, Arna. *Golden Slippers: An Anthology of Negro Poetry for Young Readers.* New York: Harper & Row, 1941.

Newsome, Effie Lee. *Gladiola Gardens: Poems of Outdoors and Indoors for Second Grade Readers.* Washington, D.C.: Associated Publishers, 1940.

New Song, A Langston Hughes (1938)

A collection of poems by LANGSTON HUGHES. Its publication was sponsored by the International Workers Order (IWO). The organization was a fraternal order based in NEW YORK CITY, and its membership was made up primarily of immigrants and individuals from numerous ethnic groups. *A New Song* was the first literary pamphlet in the series that the IWO hoped to publish in the coming years.

The foreword to *A New Song* noted that the organization "publishes these poems in the desire to make available literature which would otherwise be out of the reach of wage earners." Gold also noted that the selection of Hughes was prompted by the IWO's desire to "create a better understanding and closer solidarity between nationalities." The preface, penned by Michael Gold, noted that the initial publication run was 10,000 copies, "a rare and startling figure in the American poetry world." Gold encouraged the 140,000 members of the IWO to embrace the work, noting that if they as "members can create a great people's audience for poetry here, [the IWO] will have contributed mightily to the rise of that democratic culture of which Walt Whitman prayed and dreamed." Gold praised Hughes for articulating "the hopes, the dreams, and the awakening of the Negro people" and for doing so "naturally, like a bird in the woods."

A New Song, published as a modest booklet, contained 17 poems, among them "Let America Be America Again," "Chant for May Day," "Ballad of Lenin," "Lynching Song," and "Open Letter to the South." Some of the works, like "A New Song," had been published previously in well-read journals of the Harlem Renaissance such as OPPORTUNITY.

Hughes's poems reiterated themes established in his earlier works. The lament about exile within America pervaded works like "Let America Be America Again." In this earnest piece, the speaker takes on the identity of oppressed peoples in America, including "the poor white, fooled and pushed apart," "the Negro bearing slavery's scars," "the red man driven from the land," and the "immigrant clutching . . . hope." The poem also included the moving parenthesized aside and confession that "America never was America to me." Other works like "Park Bench" underscored the class divide that separated individuals in the same city and environment. "I live on a park bench. / You, Park Avenue" declared the speaker before making the acerbic observation "Hell of a distance / Between us two." The volume included militant poems like "Pride" and "The Ballad of Ozie Powell," a moving piece that chronicled the hate-filled LYNCHING of a young man in Alabama. This piece and "Lynching Song" were compelling laments for justice denied to young men of color and the unchecked mob violence that was allowed to reign in America. The volume also included forthright political poems, such as the "Ballad of Lenin" and "Song of Spain," that exhorted workers to seize their rightful due. A *New Song* concluded with the poem entitled "Union," a piece that recognized racial differences and the need for all to work together to "shake the pillars of those temples / Wherein the false gods dwell / And worn-out altars stand / Too well defended."

Hughes had several links to the IWO. His friend LOUISE THOMPSON, the wife of WALLACE THURMAN, worked for the organization. In April 1938 the Harlem branch of the IWO, at Thompson's suggestion, sponsored the debut performance of Hughes's newly established HARLEM SUITCASE THEATRE and its multi-genre show entitled *Don't You Want to Be Free?* Following the publication of *A New Song*, the IWO invited Hughes to present several lectures to their membership in different American cities.

Bibliography

Berry, Faith, ed. *Langston Hughes: Before and Beyond Harlem.* Westport, Conn.: Lawrence Hill & Company, 1983.

Hughes, Langston. *A New Song.* New York: International Workers Order, 1938.

Rampersad, Arnold. *The Life of Langston Hughes: I, Too, Sing America.* Vol. 1, *1902–1941.* New York: Oxford University Press, 1986.

New York Paul Morand (1930)

A travel book by PAUL MORAND, author of *MAGIE NOIRE.* First published in 1929, the English translation of 1930 was completed by Hamish Miles and published by the Henry Holt Company. The volume included illustrations by Joaquin Vaquero.

The volume included narratives about HARLEM, the New York Stock Exchange, Prohibition, BROADWAY, and other notable features and institutions of NEW YORK CITY.

Bibliography

Lemaître, Georges. *Four French Novelists: Marcel Proust, André Gide, Jean Giraudoux, Paul Morand.* London: Oxford University Press, 1938.

Morand, Paul. *New York.* New York: H. Holt and Company, 1930.

New York Age

NEW YORK CITY newspaper that was founded, in part, by T. THOMAS FORTUNE, who served as its editor until 1907. The newspaper eventually became a blatant pro–BOOKER T. WASHINGTON vehicle when it was taken over by FRED R. MOORE, a faithful Washington ally who served as editor until 1930. Despite contributions from writers like CLEVELAND ALLEN, the paper never achieved the stature of other African-American newspapers such as New York–based publications like the *AMSTERDAM NEWS* or the *CHICAGO DEFENDER.*

Bibliography

Johnson, Abby Arthur, and Ronald Maberry Johnson. *Propaganda & Aesthetics: The Literary Politics of African American Magazines in the Twentieth Century.* Amherst: University of Massachusetts, 1979.

Osofsky, Gilbert. *Harlem: The Making of a Ghetto: Negro New York, 1890–1930.* New York: Harper & Row, 1966.

New York Amsterdam News   See AMSTERDAM *NEWS.*

New York City

The thriving urban city in New York State and the location that was synonymous with the NEW NEGRO ARTS MOVEMENT, or Harlem Renaissance.

Numerous members of the Harlem Renaissance period lived, worked, or studied in New York City. Among those who relocated to the bustling city were W. E. B. DUBOIS, RALPH ELLISON, JESSIE FAUSET, LANGSTON HUGHES, HELENE JOHNSON, NELLA LARSEN, WALLACE THURMAN, and DOROTHY WEST. It was home to influential patrons such as CHARLOTTE OSGOOD MASON, JOEL and AMY SPINGARN, Madame C. J. Walker and her daughter A'LELIA WALKER, JULIUS ROSENWALD.

The city's rich educational resources also attracted talented teachers and students. Individuals attended COLUMBIA UNIVERSITY, NEW YORK UNIVERSITY, the Rand School, and BARNARD COLLEGE, and taught at high schools such as the HARLEM ACADEMY and the DEWITT CLINTON HIGH SCHOOL. Writers like RUDOLPH FISHER and NELLA LARSEN also pursued demanding careers in the prestigious medical facilities of the city. The intellectual circles attracted figures like JEAN TOOMER, LANGSTON HUGHES, and others.

Known for its unmatched theatrical community and performance venues, New York City was a vital forum in which African-American playwrights established themselves and advanced the black dramatic tradition. Legendary entertainment venues such as the COTTON CLUB, the APOLLO THEATRE, and the Savoy were located in the heart of HARLEM, a predominantly African-American community in the northern area of Manhattan. The active arts community inspired pioneers like ROMARE BEARDEN, who enrolled at Columbia.

Harlem, one of New York City's most vibrant historic communities, was the cultural, political, and social mecca during the Harlem Renaissance period. The area now boasts the largest number of landmark districts in Manhattan. Notable neighborhoods within Harlem include STRIVER'S ROW in the St. Nicholas historic district and the SUGAR HILL community that was home to W. E. B. DuBOIS, ADAM CLAYTON POWELL, SR., PAUL ROBESON, EULALIE SPENCE, and others.

Religious life in the city revolved around historic churches such as the ABYSSINIAN BAPTIST CHURCH, the Episcopal Church of St. John the Divine, St. George's Episcopal Church, and the Salem Street Episcopal Church, which was pastored by the REVEREND FREDERICK CULLEN, father of the poet COUNTEE CULLEN.

The city is home to the NEW YORK PUBLIC LIBRARY and its numerous branches. Of these, the 135th Street branch (HARLEM BRANCH) was one of the most active and enterprising. The Schomburg Center for Research in Black Culture is one of the area's most prestigious academic libraries and regarded as an unmatched contemporary resource for scholars and students of African and African-American history and culture.

The city supported an impressive and diverse number of Harlem Renaissance–era publishing ventures. These included OPPORTUNITY and THE CRISIS, the official publications of the NATIONAL URBAN LEAGUE and the NATIONAL ASSOCIATION FOR THE ADVANCEMENT OF COLORED PEOPLE, respectively, and the independent monthly, THE MESSENGER. In addition, the city was home to influential newspapers such as the AMSTERDAM NEWS, the NEW YORK AGE, the INTER-STATE TATTLER, and the NEGRO WORLD.

The city of New York inspired several Harlem Renaissance–era publications. These included NEW YORK (1930) by PAUL MORAND and HARLEM: NEGRO METROPOLIS (1940) by CLAUDE McKAY.

Bibliography

Lankevich, George. *American Metropolis: A History of New York City.* New York: New York University Press, 1998.

Schoener, Allon, ed. *Harlem on My Mind: Cultural Capital of Black America.* New York: Random House, 1969.

Wetzsteon, Ross. *Republic of Dreams: Greenwich Village, The American Bohemia, 1910–1960.* New York: Simon & Schuster, 2002.

New York Public Library

Established formally in February 1901, the New York Public Library's history dates back to the 19th-century institutions of the Astor Library, the Lenox Library, and donations from the wealthy family of Governor Samuel Tilden, who before his death in 1886 bequeathed nearly $2.5 million to the city so that it could construct a free lending library and reading room for New Yorkers. The New York Public Library was founded when the two early reference libraries merged with the New York Free Circulating Library. The industrialist Andrew Carnegie provided more than $5 million to create library branches throughout the city.

The main branch of the New York Public Library is located on FIFTH AVENUE in New York City. It opened in May 1911 with a collection of more than one million books. Present at the historic opening ceremony were President William Taft, Governor John Allen Dix, and Mayor William Gaynor. Between 30,000 and 50,000 people visited the institution on its first day. The library's hallmark statues, two lions referred to as "Patience" and "Fortitude," created by sculptor Edward Clark Potter and made from pink Tennessee marble, are among the most well-known symbols of the city.

One of the most important local branches during the Harlem Renaissance was located in Harlem at 135th Street (see HARLEM BRANCH OF

THE NEW YORK PUBLIC LIBRARY). It was there that librarians ERNESTINE ROSE, NELLA LARSEN, and REGINA ANDREWS worked to create an empowering, intellectually rich environment and community center. The 135th Street branch accommodated lectures and was home to dramatic troupes and companies as well.

Bibliography

Dain, Phyllis. *The New York Public Library: A History of Its Founding and Early Years*. New York: New York Public Library, 1972.

Lydenberg, Harry. *History of the New York Public Library: Astor, Lenox and Tilden Foundations*. New York, 1923.

New York Times, The

One of the most highly respected newspapers in the world, *The New York Times* was published first on 18 September 1851. Its founders were Henry Jarvis Raymond and George Jones. Raymond, a fervent antislavery advocate, became the director of the newly organized Associated Press in 1856. He later served a two-year term as a U.S. Congressman for New York. The newspaper began publishing Sunday editions in 1861, in response to readers' desire for information about the Civil War. That also was the year in which the newspaper began incorporating illustrations in its issues.

During the Harlem Renaissance, the newspaper often featured stories of interest to its African-American readers. It also included reviews of and advertisements for upcoming theatrical and entertainment productions.

Bibliography

Davis, Elmer. *History of the New York Times, 1851–1921*. 1921; reprint, New York: Greenwood Press, 1969.

Diamond, Edwin. *Behind the Times: Inside the* New York Times. New York: Villard Books, 1994.

Tifft, Susan, and Alex Jones. *The Trust: The Private and Powerful Family Behind the* New York Times. Boston: Little, Brown, 1999.

New York University

Founded in April 1831 by Albert Gallatin, secretary of the treasury during Thomas Jefferson's administration, New York University was designed to accommodate all students, not only those of the upper classes. Its initial enrollment was 158 students, and it had 14 faculty members. The university has grown significantly since its early days and now counts some 48,000 students in its 14 schools and colleges and six Manhattan branches.

Harlem Renaissance figures who studied and taught at New York University include CLEVELAND ALLEN, a music journalist; HUBERT HENRY HARRISON, editor of the *NEGRO WORLD* who was appointed lecturer at the school; and CLEMENT WOOD, a white Alabama writer who was a poetry lecturer.

Bibliography

Dim, Joan, and Nancy Cricco. *The Miracle on Washington Square: New York University*. Lanham, Md.: Lexington Books, 2001.

Frusciano, Thomas, and Marilyn Pettit. *New York University and the City: An Illustrated History*. New Brunswick, N.J.: Rutgers University Press, 1997.

Jones, Theodore. *New York University: 1832–1932*. New York: The New York University Press, 1933.

New York World

One of several NEW YORK CITY newspapers. It was established in 1860. In 1883 Hungarian immigrant and American Civil War veteran Joseph Pulitzer bought the newspaper from Jay Gould for just under $350,000. At the *New York World*, Pulitzer encouraged his reporters to develop human-interest reports, sensational stories about everyday people, and to pursue news relating to immigrants. The paper, which had been floundering before his takeover, became an extremely popular daily. One of his most celebrated reporters was Elizabeth Jane Cochran, the journalist known best as Nellie Bly, who in 1889 succeeded in traveling around the globe in fewer than 80 days and sustaining an enormous publicity campaign designed to draw attention to the newspaper. Bly was an extremely successful and intrepid investigative reporter whose exposés of poverty, problematic health care, and deadly working conditions prompted many vital social and political reforms.

A fierce competition with rival William Randolph Hearst and the *New York Journal* resulted in yellow journalism, a term that is used to describe the unseemly and wild promotional schemes that a newspaper uses to generate sales.

After Pulitzer died in 1911, the paper began a steady decline and ultimately merged with the *New York Evening Telegram* to become the *New York World-Telegram.*

Before his death, Pulitzer made plans to establish a school of journalism at COLUMBIA UNIVERSITY. He also endowed the PULITZER PRIZES, awards that recognized individuals who made significant achievements in a variety of fields and professions.

Bibliography
Juergens, George. *Joseph Pulitzer and the New York World.* Princeton, N.J.: Princeton University Press, 1966.

Seitz, Don Carlos. *Joseph Pulitzer: His Life and Letters.* 1924; reprint, Garden City, N.Y.: Garden City Publishing Company, 1927.

Niagara movement

The movement that began in 1905 with a clandestine and productive meeting near Niagara Falls, New York. The group met in the Buffalo, New York, home of MARY B. TALBERT, an outspoken member of the community. The conference, inspired by the nearby Niagara Falls, chose to call itself the Niagara movement.

A number of the 27 activist intellectuals and professionals who attended the first of several annual meetings were instrumental in the formation of the NATIONAL ASSOCIATION FOR THE ADVANCEMENT OF COLORED PEOPLE in 1910. In later years, meetings were held in Harpers Ferry, West Virginia, and at Faneuil Hall in BOSTON, Massachusetts.

W. E. B. DuBOIS, the first African-American Ph.D. at HARVARD UNIVERSITY, and WILLIAM MONROE TROTTER, a PHI BETA KAPPA graduate of Harvard and the editor of the *Boston Guardian*, were the primary organizers of the movement. Also involved were ATLANTA UNIVERSITY president JOHN HOPE, journalist J. Max Barber, Alonzo Herndon, and Clement Morgan. The conference and resulting movement were dedicated to challenging the violent political, economic, and social disenfranchisement of African Americans. The participants also were unified in their rejection of BOOKER T. WASHINGTON's accommodationist philosophies. The manifesto of the conference underscored the impatience and intent of its members: "We want full manhood suffrage and we want it now . . . We are men! We want to be treated as men. And we shall win."

The Niagara movement ended in 1910 when the NAACP was established.

Bibliography
Broderick, Francis. *W. E. B. Du Bois, Negro Leader in a Time of Crisis.* Stanford, Calif.: Stanford University Press, 1959.

Dennis, Rutledge. *W. E. B. Du Bois: The Scholar as Activist.* Greenwich, Conn.: JAI Press, 1996.

Fox, Stephen. *The Guardian of Boston: William Monroe Trotter.* New York: Atheneum, 1970.

Jack, Robert. *History of the National Association for the Advancement of Colored People.* Boston: Meador Publishing Company, 1943.

Jackson, Florence. *The Black Man in America, 1905–1932.* New York: Watts, 1974.

Lewis, David Levering. *W. E. B. Du Bois: Biography of a Race, 1868–1919.* New York: Henry Holt and Company, 1993.

Nickel and a Prayer, A   Jane Edna Harris Hunter (1940)

The autobiography of JANE EDNA HARRIS HUNTER, an enterprising social activist, nurse, and attorney. The volume chronicles Hunter's experiences as she worked to establish the Phillis Wheatley Association, a residence and training school for African-American women in Cleveland.

The history that Hunter recalls in her autobiography provides vital details about the uplift activities, educational accomplishments, and economic ventures of African Americans before and during the Harlem Renaissance era.

A Nickel and a Prayer was one of several autobiographies published by Harlem Renaissance figures. Others included *A LONG WAY FROM HOME* (1937) by CLAUDE MCKAY, *THE BIG SEA* (1940) by LANGSTON HUGHES, and *DUST TRACKS ON A ROAD* (1942) by ZORA NEALE HURSTON.

Bibliography
Hunter, Jane Edna. *A Nickel and a Prayer.* Nashville, Tenn.: Parthenon Press.

Jones, Adrienne Lash. *Jane Edna Hunter: A Case Study of Black Leadership, 1910–1950.* Brooklyn, N.Y.: Carlson Publishers, 1990.

Sowash, Rick. *Heroes of Ohio: Twenty-three True Tales of Courage and Character.* Bowling Green, Ohio: Gabriel's Horn Publishing Company, 1998.

Nigger: A Novel Clement Wood (1922)

One of several novels about African Americans written by white American authors. Published in 1923, it was written by CLEMENT WOOD, a Tuscaloosa, Alabama, native and YALE UNIVERSITY–educated lawyer. Wood, who relocated to GREENWICH VILLAGE before the Harlem Renaissance began, held various jobs, including dean of the Barnard School for Boys and poetry instructor at NEW YORK UNIVERSITY.

The tragic and melodramatic tale traces the life and descendants of Jake, an enslaved orphan, and Phoebe, his mulatto wife. The couple survive the deaths of four of their five children. Their only living child, Isaac, goes on to marry and have seven children. While this might seem to be a turning point for the besieged family, Isaac and his wife die shortly after the birth of the seventh child, and Jake and Phoebe become responsible for their grandchildren. Unfortunately, the family is devastated by violence and poverty despite Jake's desire to acquire education and opportunities for his kin.

The especially bleak account of African-American life that included dialect was, according to reviewers, complemented by "delicate touches" that illustrated Wood's "apt understanding of certain of the simpler forms of behavior." CHARLES S. JOHNSON, editor of OPPORTUNITY, reviewed the work in the January 1923 issue of his magazine. He characterized the work as "serious, honest, and tremendously impressive—a real tragedy." He praised Wood for representing the "Negro . . . as a human being capable of some aspirations and standards enough to feel his disappointment over failure to attain them." Finally, Johnson noted that a "race drama involving highly controversial issues between the white and Negro populations of the South is not easy to write," and he praised Wood for his literary triumph in this regard.

Bibliography

Johnson, Charles S. "Nigger: A Novel by Clement Wood." *Opportunity* (January 1923).

Wood, Clement. *Nigger: A Novel.* New York: E. P. Dutton & Company, 1922.

Niggerati

A slang term coined by ZORA NEALE HURSTON, WALLACE THURMAN, and others to describe members of the African-American literary circles of the Harlem Renaissance. Hurston and Thurman, who collaborated on projects such as the short-lived periodical *FIRE!!*, referred to the boardinghouse that was popular with Harlem Renaissance writers and artists at 267 West 136th Street as "Niggerati Manor." Thurman later incorporated this same building into his last novel, *INFANTS OF THE SPRING: A NOVEL* (1932).

Nigger Heaven Carl Van Vechten (1926)

The controversial novel by CARL VAN VECHTEN, a white native of Cedar Rapids, Iowa, that refueled the intense Harlem Renaissance debates about the representation by whites of African-American lives and experiences. It was one of several satirical novels about the delights and evils of decadence that Van Vechten published during the 1920s. With this novel, Van Vechten became the first white writer to publish a novel based on African-American life in HARLEM.

The title, which certainly incorporates a racial epithet, refers as a whole to the segregated balcony areas in which African Americans were forced to sit during the era of JIM CROW racial segregation. Van Vechten did worry that the title would alienate potential friends and readers. Yet, while friends LANGSTON HUGHES and JAMES WELDON JOHNSON urged him to consider alternative titles, others like WALTER WHITE delighted in the catchy phrase and thought it eminently marketable.

Van Vechten, who dedicated the work to his wife FANIA MARINOFF VAN VECHTEN, used four lines from the moving COUNTEE CULLEN poem entitled "Heritage" as an epigraph to the novel. The quoted lines, which read, "All day long and all night through / One thing only must I do: Quench my pride and cool my blood, / Lest I perish in the flood," introduced a cautionary note about the value of self-restraint and the politics of survival in an aggressive world.

The story revolves around the unfortunate figure of Byron Kasson, who, like so many people of color, finds his aspirations derailed by racism and limited, even nonexistent opportunities for advancement. Kasson, an aspiring writer, is employed as an elevator attendant. His sweetheart is Mary Love, a young woman who works as a librarian. The plot twists include Kasson's unfortunate seduction and encounters with Lasca Sartoris, a flamboyant Harlem heiress whose character suggests the real-life figure of A'LELIA WALKER. After a series of seedy encounters with gamblers, prostitutes, and other less-than-uplifting characters, Byron finds himself enmeshed in the unsavory world that he has worked so hard to avoid. The novel closes as he shoots another man, Randolph Pettijohn, a lover of Lasca Sartoris, and realizes that his imminent arrest will separate him forever from the virtuous Mary Love.

Nigger Heaven sold briskly when it appeared. The first run of 16,000 copies sold out within days, and the press had to produce nine more printings of the work within the first four months of the novel's release. In order to avoid a lawsuit for copyright infringement, Van Vechten was forced to delete the lyrics of a popular song that he had incorporated in the novel without permission. In a frantic move, he appealed to Langston Hughes for help, and the poet produced a new set of lyrics for incorporation into the novel. Van Vechten paid Hughes $100 for his taxing and life-saving night of work.

The novel satirizes the energetic, chaotic, vibrant, and colorful world of Harlem in the 1920s. It revolves around a librarian and a writer whose love affair is doomed by the hardships and racial realities of the world around them, and it includes thinly transparent parodies of numerous well-known figures and locations of the Harlem Renaissance.

The book has enjoyed numerous reprintings, including a later edition for which Langston Hughes, Van Vechten's close friend, provided poems. The book prompted many to respond to its content and politics. W. E. B. DuBois, the eminent scholar and editor of *THE CRISIS*, despised the work. After admitting that he read the book "and read it through because [he] had to," DuBois concluded emphatically that it was "a blow in the face, an affront to the hospitality of black folk and to the intelligence of white" (Lewis, 180). In a memorable December 1926 *Crisis* article, DuBois blasted Van Vechten for "express[ing] all of Harlem life in its cabarets . . . Such a theory of Harlem is nonsense. The overwhelming majority of black folk there never go to cabarets. The average colored man in Harlem is an everyday laborer, attending church, lodge and movie and as conservative and conventional as ordinary working folk everywhere." Others agreed with DuBois. HUBERT HARRISON, writing for the *PITTSBURGH COURIER*, decried it as an awful dialect book that also revealed Van Vechten's fascination with unsavory elements of life. CLEVELAND ALLEN nearly prompted a riot when he denounced the work before a large meeting at the 135th Street Branch Library and prompted other outraged Harlemites to speak out vehemently at the gathering.

JAMES WELDON JOHNSON, who, like DuBois, was affiliated with the NATIONAL ASSOCIATION FOR THE ADVANCEMENT OF COLORED PEOPLE, liked the work. He suggested that the real debate was not about the title but the content of the book itself. In his review of the novel, published in *OPPORTUNITY*, Johnson suggested that Van Vechten had "achieved the most revealing, significant, and powerful novel based exclusively on Negro life yet written." He went on to praise Van Vechten for paying "colored people the rare tribute of writing about them as people rather than as puppets." In the Harlem community, prominent and wealthy socialites like A'LELIA WALKER, whose identity Van Vechten parodied in the novel, refused to associate with Van Vechten and refused him entry to social gatherings and parties.

Published three years after CLEMENT WOOD's *NIGGER: A NOVEL*, Van Vechten's story was marketed by the Knopf publishing company as a serious meditation on African-American life. The publicity was in keeping with Van Vechten's regard for the material. He had insisted frequently that the novel was focused specifically on Negroes and their daily lives rather than on the more controversial, explosive elements of their lives in America.

Bibliography

Bernard, Emily. *Remember Me to Harlem: The Letters of Langston Hughes and Carl Van Vechten.* New York: Knopf, 2001.

Berry, Faith, ed. *Langston Hughes: Before and Beyond Harlem.* Westport, Conn.: Lawrence Hill & Company, 1983.

Coleman, Leon. *Carl Van Vechten and the Harlem Renaissance: A Critical Assessment.* New York: Garland Publishers, 1998.

Kellner, Bruce. *Carl Van Vechten and the Irreverent Decades.* Norman; University of Oklahoma Press, 1968.

———. *Letters of Carl Van Vechten.* New Haven: Yale University Press, 1987.

Lewis, David Levering. *W. E. B. Du Bois: The Fight for Equality and the American Century, 1919–1963.* New York: Henry Holt and Company, 2000.

Lueders, Edward. *Carl Van Vechten.* New York: Twayne Publishers, 1965.

Van Vechten, Carl. *Nigger Heaven.* Introduction by Kathleen Pfeiffer. Urbana: University of Illinois Press, 2000.

No Alabaster Box Evelyn Crawford Reynolds (1936)

The first of three books of verse that EVELYN CRAWFORD REYNOLDS published and the only volume that she produced during the Harlem Renaissance. The PHILADELPHIA-based publishers, Alpress, produced some 350 copies in the first run of the work. The book appeared as the work of Eve Lynn, the name that Reynolds used as a pseudonym.

Reynolds's title alludes to the New Testament story of Mary, sister of Martha and Lazarus, who broke an expensive alabaster jar so that she could use the expensive perfume within it to minister to Jesus.

A Philadelphia poet, Reynolds tended to write about religious themes, racial issues, citizenship, and patriotism. The volume received positive reviews, including an endorsement by literary critic BENJAMIN BRAWLEY.

Reynolds's subsequent works reflected her social prominence and connections as the wife of Hobson Richmond Reynolds, a highly respected Pennsylvania assemblyman and magistrate. The educator and activist MARY MCLEOD BETHUNE provided the introduction for her second work, *To No Special Land: A Book of Poems* (1953), and the celebrated contralto MARIAN ANDERSON penned the introduction for her third collection, *Put a Daisy in Your Hair* (1963).

Bibliography

Reynolds, Evelyn Crawford. *No Alabaster Box.* Philadelphia: Alpress, 1936.

No Hiding Place Sterling Brown (unpublished)

A collection of poems that author and HOWARD UNIVERSITY professor STERLING BROWN could not get published. Works that he had intended for the volume, such as "Sharecropper," a rousing tribute to agricultural workers in the South, were published later in other collections.

Brown was a talented poet whose intense poetical renderings of African-American folklife, dialect, spirituals, blues, and jazz earned him praise from many in and beyond the Harlem Renaissance literary world. Unfortunately, however, his colleagues at Howard held his writing in lower regard, and that criticism made it extremely difficult for the poet to acquire a publisher for his GREAT DEPRESSION–era second volume.

After failing to publish *No Hiding Place,* Brown turned to literary criticism, and it was 40 years before he published another volume of verse, *The Last Ride of Wild Bill,* in 1975.

Bibliography

Gabbin, Joanne. *Sterling Brown: Building the Black Aesthetic Tradition.* Westport, Conn.: Greenwood Press, 1985.

Harper, Michael. *The Collected Poems of Sterling A. Brown.* Chicago: TriQuarterly Books, 1989.

Sanders, Mark. *Afro-Modernist Aesthetics and the Poetry of Sterling A. Brown.* Athens, Ga.: University of Georgia, 1999.

"Nomah—a Story" John Matheus (1931)

A short story by JOHN MATHEUS, a COLUMBIA UNIVERSITY graduate and college professor, that appeared in the July 1931 issue of *OPPORTUNITY.* Set in Monrovia, Liberia, the tale focuses on the drowning death of Kadah Watu and the deep mourning of his devoted daughter Nomah.

Nomah, now orphaned, is a Catholic, as her deceased mother was. Distressed by the fact that her father's body was not recovered from the ocean, she seeks out the local priest in an effort to organize a burial ceremony nonetheless. When she realizes that she does not have money enough to pay for her father's coffin, she decides to marry the persistent old suitor Kufu. A man of means who works for a colonial English business interest, Kufu becomes miserly and mean after the marriage ceremony. Nomah, desperate to sustain herself now that she truly has no financial stability even in marriage, makes the momentous decision to use her father's old canoe and go fishing. As she overcomes her grief, prompted again by the sight of the vessel that bore her father out to his death, she realizes that the boat has been sabotaged. Sure that the systematic set of bored holes in its floor are the work of her scheming husband, she kills him.

Matheus's absorbing story of family devotion, revenge, African beliefs, and rituals was one of many works that underscored the richness of African heritage and its relevance to contemporary American life.

"Noose, The" Octavia Wynbush (1927)

A haunting short story by OCTAVIA WYNBUSH, author of several short stories that were published in *THE CRISIS*, "The Noose," which appeared in the December 1931 issue of *Crisis*, centered on a cuckolded man named King who seeks revenge on the man who seduced his wife, Nomia. The story begins as Nomia's sister, Leora, seeks out King for news of Jed, the fast-talking, charming man who returned to the plantation community after Nomia's death in an unnamed wintry Northern city.

King, who has waited to avenge his loss, reports to Leora that a jury has not only tried Jed but found him guilty and executed him. Her belief in Jed's innocence begins to prey on King. As he goes to sleep that evening, he is frightened by what he thinks is a noose hanging from the rafters. After realizing that it is an errant piece of rope, he douses the light and goes to sleep. When he wakes the next morning, however, he is convinced that a rope is around his neck. Panicked, he does his best to shed the "thing" whose "cords were growing thicker and tighter." Leora and neighbors discover

King's dead body, upon which there are remnants of a spider's web around his neck, a few days later.

"The Noose" is a tragic story of savage realism and gothic horror. Wynbush crafted a memorable portrait of southern life and a stirring exploration of the powers of human guilt and the unconscious.

North Carolina College for Negroes at Durham

The North Carolina College for Negroes at Durham was known first as the National Religious Training School and Chautauqua. It received its charter in 1909 and accepted its first students in 1910. Its founder and first president was Dr. James Shepard. It was the first state-supported African-American liberal arts college.

The institution relied on student tuition fees and private donations. One of its chief benefactors was Mrs. Russell Sage. The school became a public institution in 1923 when the General Assembly of North Carolina passed legislation that allocated funds for the purchase of the institution and its upkeep. The legislature also approved the change in name to Durham State Normal School but in 1925 voted approved the school's new name, The North Carolina College for Negroes. In 1947 the school's name was changed again, to North Carolina College at Durham. It is known now as North Carolina Central University,

In 1939, the university received legislative approval of its law school. This was the same year in which ZORA NEALE HURSTON joined the faculty as a drama instructor. During her time in Durham, she had the opportunity to meet PAUL GREEN, the white playwright and University of North Carolina at Chapel Hill drama professor. Other prominent intellectuals who were part of the college faculty and staff included Dr. John Hope Franklin, the eminent historian, and his wife, Aurelia Whittington Franklin, who was a law librarian at the school. The school conferred an honorary master's degree on Charlotte Hawkins Brown, a tireless North Carolina educator, feminist, and historian.

Bibliography

Roebuck, Julian. *Historically Black Colleges and Universities: Their Place in American Higher Education.* Westport, Conn.: Praeger, 1993.

Whiting, Albert. *Guardians of the Flame: Historically Black Colleges Yesterday, Today, and Tomorrow.* Washington, D.C.: American Association of State Colleges and Universities, 1991.

Willie, Charles, and Ronald Edmonds, eds. *Black Colleges in America: Challenge, Development, Survival.* New York: Teachers College Press, 1978.

Northwestern University

Located in Evanston, Illinois, and the institution at which pioneering anthropologist MELVILLE HERSKOVITS founded the first African-American studies program in the nation.

The school was established in 1850 as a Christian university that would prepare individuals to minister and educate the populations in the Northwestern Territories. It was based in Ridgeville, a village some 12 miles away from CHICAGO. The town of Evanston was named after John Evans, one of the school's founders. The school had 10 students when it opened for classes in 1855 and a faculty of two, mathematics professor Henry Noyes and Greek language and literature professor William Godman. Its first president was the Reverend Randolph Sinks Foster, a minister from New York State.

Melville Herskovits, who was a member of the sociology department at Northwestern, established the African-American studies program in 1948.

Bibliography

Simpson, George. *Melville Herskovits.* New York: Columbia University Press, 1973.

Ward, Estelle. *The Story of Northwestern University.* New York: Dodd, Mead and Company, 1924.

Williamson, Harold, and Payson Wild. *Northwestern University: A History, 1850–1975.* Evanston, Ill.: Northwestern University, 1976.

"Nothing New" Marita Bonner (1926)

A savage short story by MARITA BONNER about the evils of race prejudice and the tragedies that can befall its visionary and talented victims of color, "Nothing New" appeared in the November 1926 issue of *THE CRISIS.* In a narrative that foreshadowed the turf wars rendered so painstakingly in RICHARD WRIGHT's "Ethics of Living Jim Crow," the story described the life of Denny Jackson. Jackson is a young boy living in Frye Street, Bonner's fictional ethnic and racist CHICAGO community. There are two epic battles in the story. The first occurs when Denny wants to pick a beautiful flower but is prevented from doing so by an obnoxious white child who insists that Denny stay out of the "white kids' side." A thrashing from his mother prompts him to wonder about the justice in the world, but he preserves his love of beauty nonetheless. Denny's penchant for noticing beautiful things prompts his teachers to recommend that he be admitted to a selective art school. After some time, however, he and a white female student are seen in each other's company at an art exhibit. Denny is falsely accused of preying on the girl, and a vicious fight breaks out when an incensed white male student attacks him in the classroom. Denny inadvertently kills the boy and is sentenced to death. The violence prompts the school to renege on its policy of integrated classrooms, and the community is divided in its opinions about what "ruined Denny" and made it impossible for him to live in modern society. Bonner's story is a stark critique of northern racism, racial hysteria, and the earnest but fragile nature of African-American life.

Bibliography

Flynn, Joyce, and Joyce Occomy Striklin. *Frye Street & Environs: The Collected Works of Marita Bonner.* Boston: Beacon Press, 1987.

Not Without Laughter Langston Hughes (1930)

A prizewinning book and the first novel by LANGSTON HUGHES. *Not Without Laughter* was awarded first prize, a gold medal and $400, in the HARMON FOUNDATION Literary Contest of 1930. Published by the New York–based ALFRED A. KNOPF INC., the autobiographical novel that Hughes dedicated to philanthropists JOEL and AMY SPINGARN was hailed by critics for its sincerity of presentation and its insightful portraits of African-American lives.

Hughes began work on the manuscript while he was a student at LINCOLN UNIVERSITY. While his own family was the primary inspiration for the book, he realized that his was "not a typical Negro family." As a result, he "created around [himself] what seemed to [him] a family more typical of Negro life in Kansas." *Not Without Laughter* was an autobiographical venture, one in which Hughes indulged himself fully. "I gave myself aunts that I didn't have," he revealed in his autobiography *The BIG SEA* (1940), "modeled after other children's aunts whom I had known but I put in a real cyclone that had blown my grandmother's front porch away. And I added dances and songs I remembered" (Hughes, 228–229). The philanthropist CHARLOTTE OSGOOD MASON, Hughes's exacting patron, provided him with funds that enabled him to sequester himself and to write. He spent his entire senior year of college revising the book and, following graduation, "stayed on the campus in a big, empty theological dormitory all alone" and "cut and polished, revised and re-wrote" while "the people in the book seemed to walk around the room and talk, to me, helping me write" (Hughes, 229). He was grateful for the help of LOUISE THOMPSON, "a sympathetic and excellent typist" with whom he would later work on the ill-fated *MULE BONE* and who "must have done certain pages over . . . so often she could have recited by heart their varying versions" (Hughes, 229). Mason critiqued the early drafts of his manuscript and also critiqued the early versions of the titles, *So Moves This Swift World* and *Roots of Dawn*. Her first response to the finished draft came in the form of a 24-page letter with detailed notes about the writing and suggestions for revisions. The book enjoyed a wide national and international distribution to such places as Tokyo, Bombay, Paris, and Melbourne. Unfortunately, however, the publication of *Not Without Laughter* coincided with the onset of the GREAT DEPRESSION, and sales were affected.

The plot focuses on Sandy, a young boy who lives in Kansas with his Christian grandmother, Hager Williams. Aunt Hager, a hardworking laundress, is a pillar of her community and "[a]ll the neighborhood, white or colored, called [her] when something happened. She was a good nurse, they said, and sick folks liked her around . . . sometimes they paid her and sometimes they didn't" (10). Hager has three daughters: Tempy, a respectable middle-class wife, Anjee, a free-spirited woman and wife, and Harriet, a blues singer and prostitute. The youngest of the three girls, Harriet suffers it seems, because she essentially "had no raising, even though she was smart" (34).

Sandy is the son of Anjee and her husband Jimboy Rogers. Rogers is a laborer, and when the novel opens he has left his family for yet another lengthy absence. His departures are due in part to the limited employment opportunities available to people of color. "[W]hat was there in Stanton anyhow," muses Anjee shortly after she receives a letter from her husband, "for a young colored fellow to do except dig sewer ditches for a few cents an hour or maybe porter around a store for seven dollars a week. Colored men couldn't get many jobs in Stanton, and foreigners were coming in, taking away what little work they did have" (33). Like his father, to some degree, Sandy too is a perennial wanderer. He also is a gifted musician, and he eventually becomes a powerful blues singer. He steadily becomes the child of his father, a man who, on his return from his latest expedition to secure work, quickly begins to play for his family, letting his fingers run "[s]oftly . . . light as a breeze, over his guitar strings, imitating the wind rustling through the long leaves of the corn" (55).

The novel chronicles the migrations of Hager's children, journeys that are prompted by a range of desires. Ultimately, Anjee leaves, and the young protagonist Sandy is the only one left living with his grandmother. The relative quiet in the house allows Sandy to hear even more stories from his cherished, hardworking grandmother, and he absorbs them all. They sit, "the black wash-woman with the grey hair and the little brown boy" and he listens to her "Slavery-time stories, myths, folktales like the Rabbit and the Tar Baby; the war, Abe Lincoln, freedom." Hager's stories are enriched by "years of faith and labor, love and struggle," and her grandson, who "was getting to be too big a boy to sit in his grandmother's lap and be rocked to sleep as in summers gone by . . . sat on a little stool beside her, leaning his head on her legs when he was tired. Or else he lay flat on the floor of the porch listening, and looking up at the stars" (188–189).

These tender and unforgettable moments enable Hager to have a strong and loving impact on her grandson. As a result, Sandy is less inclined to indulge his musical calling so that it jeopardizes the relationships that he cherishes. Despite his love of music and his desire to pursue it, Sandy honors his grandmother's lessons about the most important elements of life. He does not descend into the tantalizing world about which his father would sing or into the amoral environment of vaudeville that seduced his aunt Harriet and played havoc with all their lives as a result. Hager encourages her grandson to pursue dreams that will enable him to be a "great man." "'I wants you to be a great man, son,' she often told him, sitting on the porch in the darkness, singing, dreaming, calling up the past, creating dreams within the child. I wants you to be a great man'" (314). Her gentle insistence and her unwavering belief in his potential enable Sandy to straddle two worlds, the public world of entertainment and the private world in which he continues his schooling and advances himself.

Having weathered much upheaval in his family life and benefited from his grandmother's steadiness, Sandy eventually comes to understand the strategies that African Americans can use to survive the tolls of everyday life, the evils of segregation, and the devastating nature of racial violence. The novel closes as he and his mother, Anjee, agree implicitly to honor the wishes of Hager and as they revel in uplifting, rather than seductive song, in lyrics that are "vibrant and steady like a stream of living faith" (324).

Bibliography

Bernard, Emily. *Remember Me to Harlem: The Letters of Langston Hughes and Carl Van Vechten.* New York: Knopf, 2001.

Berry, Faith, ed. *Langston Hughes: Before and Beyond Harlem.* Westport, Conn.: Lawrence Hill & Company, 1983.

Gates, Henry Louis, Jr., and Kwame Anthony Appiah. *Langston Hughes: Critical Perspectives Past and Present.* New York: Amistad, 1993.

Hughes, Langston. *The Big Sea: An Autobiography.* 1940; reprint, edited by Joseph McLaren. Columbia: University of Missouri Press, 2002.

Rampersad, Arnold. *The Life of Langston Hughes: I, Too, Sing America.* Vol. 1, *1902–1941.* New York: Oxford University Press, 1986.

Shields, John P. "Never Cross the Divide": Reconstructing Langston Hughes's *Not Without Laughter. African American Review* 28, no. 4 (1994): 601–613.

Trotman, C. James. *Langston Hughes: The Man, His Art, and His Continuing Influence.* New York: Garland Publishers, 1995.

Nugent, Richard Bruce (1906–1987)

Nugent was born in WASHINGTON, D.C., to Richard Henry and Paulina Minerva Bruce. His parents were members of the African-American upper class in Washington, D.C. His father, who worked as a Pullman porter, doorman at the Supreme Court, and Capitol Hill elevator operator, also was a member of the Clef Club quartet that performed in the city. His mother, a talented pianist and schoolteacher, was descended from Scottish and Native American ancestors. Nugent attended DUNBAR HIGH SCHOOL, where his teachers included writer ANGELINA WELD GRIMKÉ. The Nugents fostered their children's love of the arts and exposed them to contemporary and pioneering groups, such as the LAFAYETTE PLAYERS STOCK COMPANY. The family moved to NEW YORK CITY after Nugent's father died from tuberculosis and asthma. Nugent worked as a delivery boy, errand boy, and bellhop in an effort to support the family and to supplement the wages that his mother, who was light-skinned enough to pass for white and gain higher paying jobs, earned as a domestic worker and waitress. While in New York, Nugent began taking classes in art at the New York Evening School of Industrial Arts and at the Traphagen School of Fashion. His brother, Gary Lambert Nugent, known as Pete Nugent, was a dancer who appeared on Broadway and in Irving Berlin wartime productions, and later worked as road manager for the Temptations during the 1960s.

In 1952 Richard Bruce Nugent married Grace Elizabeth Marr. The couple had a platonic relationship that lasted for 17 years until her suicide in 1969. Marr was a successful graduate of the Harlem Hospital School of Nursing, a microbiology instructor in the COLUMBIA UNIVERSITY nursing education program, and, ultimately, the first African-American supervisor of nursing in the New York State Department of Education. Nugent, who was living in Hoboken, New Jersey, at the end of his life, suffered congestive heart failure and passed away on 27 May 1987.

Nugent was one of the most eclectic and unconventional figures in the Harlem Renaissance community. He had an unabashed interest in men and was not at all secretive about his homosexual preferences. He was known for his playful and inventive nature. A light-skinned man, he did experiment with passing as white but did not pursue this for any extended period of time. One especially memorable anecdote features him, his good friend LANGSTON HUGHES, and WARING CUNEY strolling through the streets of Washington, D.C., pretending to be mysterious foreigners and speaking gibberish to each other.

Nugent enjoyed a close and supportive friendship with Langston Hughes, whom he met at one of the literary salons hosted by GEORGIA DOUGLAS JOHNSON, the Washington, D.C., poet and mentor. It was Hughes who retrieved a discarded poem of Nugent's that eventually became the writer's first published poem when it appeared in OPPORTUNITY. He wrote his first short story, "Sadhji" (1925) in response to a request from ALAIN LOCKE who wanted a narrative to accompany a Nugent sketch of an African woman. Locke included the work in his pioneering 1925 anthology, THE NEW NEGRO. Two years later, Locke and his HOWARD UNIVERSITY colleague T. MONTGOMERY GREGORY included a revised and dramatic version of the work in PLAYS OF NEGRO LIFE: A SOURCE-BOOK OF NATIVE AMERICAN DRAMA (1927), their acclaimed anthology. "Sadhji" was subsequently performed as a one-act ballet in 1932 at the Eastman School of Music in Rochester, New York.

Nugent was part of the enterprising set of young emerging and insurgent writers and artists of the Harlem Renaissance. He collaborated with Hughes, WALLACE THURMAN, with whom he shared an apartment at 267 West 136th Street, the boarding house populated with artists and writers and nicknamed NIGGERATI Manor, for two years, and ZORA NEALE HURSTON on FIRE!!, the short-lived journal produced in 1926. His short story in the first and only issue of Fire!! was entitled "SMOKE, LILIES, AND JADE." It was the first narrative of the period to feature openly homosexual themes. Nugent continued to work with Thurman, one of the most visionary and energetic figures of the Harlem Renaissance. He collaborated with Thurman and worked as associate editor of HARLEM: A FORUM OF NEGRO LIFE. Unfortunately, that journal, to which Nugent contributed theater reviews, also suffered from financial woes and ceased publication after its first issue appeared

in November 1928. Nugent inspired Thurman's character Paul Arbian, the artist and writer in his second and last novel, INFANTS OF THE SPRING (1932).

He also collaborated with AARON DOUGLAS at a time when the acclaimed artist was designing murals for Harlem nightclubs. Other colleagues and collaborators included GWENDOLYN BENNETT and DOROTHY WEST.

Nugent inherited his parents' flair for performance. He auditioned and was chosen to be in the cast of the 1929 and 1930 productions of DUBOSE HEYWARD's PORGY. In 1933 he appeared as a dancer in Run, Little Chillun, a drama by Hall Johnson that ran on BROADWAY for four months before going on tour. In the years after the Harlem Renaissance ended, he also joined the Negro Ballet Company, a troupe founded in 1939 by Wilson Williams.

Like RICHARD WRIGHT, Zora Neale Hurston, and others, Nugent contributed to the Federal Writers' Project during the 1930s. He worked with Roi Ottley and compiled numerous biographical profiles of African Americans in New York City. Nugent published frequently in diverse publications of the Harlem Renaissance. His fiction, poems, and drawings appeared in The Crisis, the Dorothy West journals CHALLENGE and NEW CHALLENGE, PALMS, Topaz, and Trend. With HAROLD JACKMAN, he served as executor for the estate of L. S. Alexander Gumby, the avid book collector who had ambitious plans to produce the GUMBY BOOK STUDIO QUARTERLY, a literary journal.

Bibliography

Garber, Eric. "Richard Bruce Nugent." In Dictionary of Literary Biography. Vol. 51, edited by Trudier Harris and Thaddeus Davis. Detroit: Gate, 1987.

Lewis, David Levering, When Harlem Was in Vogue. New York: Knopf, 1981.

McBreen, Ellen. "Biblical Gender Bending in Harlem: The Queer Performance of Nugent's Salome," Art Journal 57, no. 3 (fall 1998): 22–28.

Nugent, Richard Bruce. "Sadhji." In The New Negro, edited by Alain LeRoy Locke. New York: Boni, 1925. 113–114.

———. "Smoke, Lilies, and Jade." Fire!! (November 1926), 405–408.

Wirth, Thomas. *Gay Rebel of the Harlem Renaissance: Selections from the Work of Richard Bruce Nugent.* Durham: Duke University Press, 2002.

———. "Richard Bruce Nugent." *Black American Literature Forum* 9 (spring 1985): 16–17.

Nuggets of Gold Carrie Law Morgan Figgs
(1921)

A collection of poems by CARRIE LAW MORGAN FIGGS, *Nuggets of Gold* included 19 works that reflected Morgan's deep love of family and interest in African-American folk and religion. The volume included poems that praised African-American women and promoted uplifting images of family life. In "The Black Queen," Figgs applauded the strength of women of color, individuals upon whom men of the race could depend for unqualified and reliable support. She also wrote forthright poems, such as "The Negro's Upward Flight," that exhorted African-American men in their daily life. Figgs encouraged her readers to claim their rightful and due equality, realizing that they were "the equal of any man / Found anywhere."

Morgan's title poem, "Nuggets of Gold," was dedicated to her children and expressed Figgs's pleasure in motherhood. Cast in simple rhymes, she noted that she, the woman who "own[ed] three golden nuggets," was the "happiest woman in the world."

Figgs financed the publication of *Nuggets of Gold*. The CHICAGO firm, Jaxon Printing Company, produced the modest collection.

Oberlin Conservatory of Music

Located in Oberlin, Ohio, the highly regarded conservatory founded in 1865 is the oldest continuously operating American music school. The conservatory became part of Oberlin College, the liberal arts school founded in 1833 and the first American college to admit women, in 1867.

A number of prominent Harlem Renaissance–era figures attended Oberlin Conservatory. Composer WILL MARION COOK received his training there before going on to work with writers Paul Laurence Dunbar, WALLACE THURMAN, and COUNTEE CULLEN. A pioneering composer and the first African American to conduct a professional symphony orchestra, WILLIAM GRANT STILL studied at Oberlin.

Sue Bailey Thurman, the feminist activist editor and wife of the influential theologian and activist Howard Thurman, graduated from Oberlin in 1926. She was the first African-American student to earn the bachelor of science degree in music from the Conservatory. Other figures with ties to the school include musician and poet LUCY ARIEL WILLIAMS HOLLOWAY, who earned a bachelor's degree in music from the conservatory. Playwright and poet GEORGIA DOUGLAS JOHNSON, who also attended the Cleveland College of Music, studied music at Oberlin and completed her studies there in 1906.

Bibliography

Barnard, John. *From Evangelicalism to Progressivism At Oberlin College, 1866–1917*. Columbus: Ohio State University Press, 1969.

Fletcher, Robert Samuel. *A History of Oberlin College from Its Foundation Through the Civil War*. Oberlin: Oberlin College, 1943.

Rockicky, Catherine. *James Monroe: Oberlin's Christian Statesman and Reformer, 1821–1898*. Kent, Ohio: Kent State University Press, 2002.

O Canaan! Waters Turpin (1939)

Published in 1939, this novel by Waters Turpin chronicled the lives and experiences of Mississippians who journeyed north as part of the Great Migration. Turpin's novel appeared at a time when many African Americans were enduring severe hardships brought on by the economic and social upheaval of the GREAT DEPRESSION.

The novel is divided into four parts: "Into Canaan," "Wilderness," "The Tides of Spring," and "Rock in a Weary Land." The story, which begins in Mississippi, offers detailed accounts of life in CHICAGO, and HARLEM. The novel's protagonist, Joe Benson, is an earnest and visionary field worker, the son of the plantation's overseer and the husband of Christine Lawson, a light-skinned octoroon teacher who returns to Mississippi after completing her education in New Orleans. Benson, in the wake of LYNCHINGs and yet another boll weevil attack on his cotton crops, rallies his family and several members of his community to abandon the violent and unrewarding world of Mississippi.

Benson, a powerfully built man whose "bigness . . . whenever he was indoors, reminded one of a caged animal," organizes a migration to

Chicago, the urban city known to many as Canaan, celebrated as a "[l]usty, virile, and boisterous city . . . city of the high, the low, the merchant prince and the consuming pauper . . . of the polyglot racial spawns spewed from all the quarters of the globe." The Bensons take a formidable work ethic with them and succeed in establishing themselves as a respectable family in Chicago. Their son Sol joins the Eighth Illinois, an army division that earns the nickname "The Black Devils" after their heroic battles in FRANCE during World War I. Sol departs, confident in his abilities to fight but concerned that violence against African-American families at home will not cease. He and his regiment return to a hero's welcome, but the city erupts into a vicious race riot that targets Sol and his community just days later. Over the course of the novel, Turpin explores the community and social dynamics that sustain and exhaust families. The Bensons weather their children's emotional distress and impromptu marriages because of pregnancy. They also see the next generation honor the Benson family traditions of fortitude and will.

Hailed as a "novel of prime human significance on a theme never before approached in American literature," *O Canaan!* also was celebrated as an "unforgettable story, told with sweep and power."

Bibliography

Turpin, Waters. *O Canaan!* 1939, reprint, New York: AMS Press Inc., 1975.

Odum, Howard Washington (1884–1954)

A sociologist whose published studies of African-American folk music and folklore contributed much to the ongoing scholarship on race relations and African-American culture.

Born in Bethlehem, Georgia, to William Pleasants Odum and Mary Ann Thomas Odum, he spent his childhood on the family's modest farm. Following the family's relocation to Oxford, Georgia, he attended Emory College and graduated with a degree in classics and in English. Odum began teaching immediately after graduation and also proceeded to work toward a master's degree in classics from the University of Missis-

sippi. In 1909 he completed his first Ph.D., at Clark University, in psychology and in 1910 he completed his second in sociology at COLUMBIA UNIVERSITY. Odum was on the faculty at the University of Georgia and at Emory University before he began a 34-year career in 1920 as the Kenan Professor of Sociology at the University of North Carolina at Chapel Hill. He married Anna Louise Kranz, a Clark University graduate student whom he met while pursuing his doctoral studies at the Worcester, Massachusetts, school. The couple wed on Christmas Eve 1910 and went on to have three children.

During the Harlem Renaissance, Odum published several works on African-American culture. These included *THE NEGRO AND HIS SONGS* (1925), coauthored with GUY BENTON JOHNSON, and a trilogy of works about a quasi-fictional hero referred to as Black Ulysses. The collection consisted of *Rainbow Round My Shoulder: The Blue Trail of Black Ulysses* (1928), *Wings on My Feet: Black Ulysses at the Wars* (1929), and *Cold Blue Moon: Black Ulysses Afar Off* (1931).

Bibliography

Brazil, Wayne. *Howard W. Odum: The Building Years, 1884–1930.* New York: Garland Press, 1988.

Howard Odum Papers, University of North Carolina at Chapel Hill.

Odum, Howard. *American Sociology: The Story of Sociology in the United States through 1950.* New York: Longmans, Green, 1951.

———, and Guy Benton Johnson. *The Negro and His Songs: A Study of Typical Negro Songs in the South.* 1925; reprint, New York: Negro Universities Press, 1968.

———, and Guy Benton Johnson. *Negro Workaday Songs.* 1926; reprint, New York: Negro Universities Press, 1969.

Sosna, Morton. *In Search of the Silent South: Southern Liberals and the Race Issue.* New York: Columbia University Press, 1977.

O'Keeffe, Georgia Totto (1887–1986)

An accomplished artist celebrated for her pioneering modernist work, O'Keeffe also was the first woman painter to have her works featured in a solo exhibit at the Museum of Modern Art.

Born in Sun Prairie, Wisconsin, to Francis O'Keeffe, a farmer, and his wife, Ida Ten Eyck Totto, O'Keeffe attended the Art Institute in CHICAGO and the Art Student League in NEW YORK CITY. She held art-related jobs in Amarillo Texas, the University of Virginia, and Columbia College in South Carolina before she began exhibiting her work. It was ALFRED STIEGLITZ, her future husband, who engineered the first exhibit without O'Keeffe's knowledge or consent, in 1917. O'Keeffe lived in NEW YORK CITY with Stieglitz between 1918 and 1928. It was during this period that she became part of the circle of artists and intellectuals that included WALDO FRANK, SHERWOOD ANDERSON, LEWIS MUMFORD, HART CRANE, and JEAN TOOMER.

O'Keeffe's connection to the Harlem Renaissance was established through her relationship with Jean Toomer, a writer and poet with whom she had a love affair and a shared interest in spiritual and mystical matters, particularly the teachings and practices of mystic GEORGES GURDJIEFF. O'Keeffe and Toomer, who had been friends for at least a decade, became intimate in late 1933. In letters to Toomer, O'Keeffe confessed her "wish so hotly to feel you hold me very very tight" and admitted that she "like[d] knowing the feel of your maleness and your laugh (Kerman and Eldridge, 216). In 1934, Toomer married Marjorie Content, one of O'Keeffe's close friends. O'Keeffe, despite some sense of loss about her relationship with Toomer, did maintain contact with Toomer and Content after their wedding. O'Keeffe died in Santa Fe, New Mexico, in March 1986.

Bibliography

Castro, Jan Garden. *The Art and Life of Georgia O'Keeffe.* New York: Crown, 1985.

Eisler, Benita. *O'Keeffe and Stieglitz: An American Romance.* New York: Penguin Books, 1992.

Kerman, Cynthia Earl, and Richard Eldridge. *The Lives of Jean Toomer: A Hunger for Wholeness.* Baton Rouge: Louisiana State University Press, 1987.

Lisle, Laurie. *Portrait of an Artist: A Biography of Georgia O'Keeffe.* Albuquerque: University of New Mexico, 1986.

Messinger, Lisa Mintz. *Georgia O'Keeffe,* New York: Thames & Hudson, 2001.

Ollie Miss George Wylie Henderson (1935)

The first novel of GEORGE WYLIE HENDERSON, an Alabama native and former TUSKEGEE INSTITUTE student. The story centers on the figure of Ollie Miss, an itinerant young woman who joins an Alabama farm community in Macon County. A hard worker, she receives support from Uncle Alex, the man who provides her with an abode and the opportunity to reap some profits from her labors in the field. Ollie's true love is a handsome but emotionally elusive man named Jule. He and Ollie now live apart from one another, but she travels back to find him once she has settled into a routine with Uncle Alex.

Ollie is reminiscent of the winsome, desired women in *CANE*, JEAN TOOMER's acclaimed sketches of the South. She maintains control over her sexuality in spite of the intense physical desire that the men in the community have for her. She is unafraid about living alone in a small cabin, and much to the chagrin of some of the older religious ladies of the community, she defends her right to use tobacco and keep company with whomever she chooses. Like Janie, the protagonist of ZORA NEALE HURSTON's *THEIR EYES WERE WATCHING GOD* (1937), Ollie Miss suffers the intense scrutiny of her community. Her voracious appetite makes her both plaintive and threatening to some of the women; her unself-conscious allure and apparent lack of interest in local men drives her fellow male workers to complete distraction.

Critic Blyden Jackson remarks that the "the tone of *Ollie Miss* . . . is neither polemical nor tractarian. "A lyricism," he suggests, "genuinely sweet, tempers *Ollie Miss* from its opening pages to its last, making of [the novel] truly a poem in prose." The novel's sparse prose, evocative images, and absorbing narrative contribute to Henderson's haunting images of life in the black belt region of the South.

Bibliography

George Wylie Henderson. *Ollie Miss with an Introduction by Blyden Jackson.* 1935, reprint, Tuscaloosa: The University of Alabama Press, 1988.

"On Being a Domestic" Eric Walrond (1923)

A fictional documentary sketch by ERIC WALROND that illuminated the types of unrelenting and demanding conditions that domestic servants, butlers, and maids faced in the workplace. Published in the May 1923 issue of OPPORTUNITY, the piece chronicled a day in the life of a harassed and hardworking houseman in an unidentified lodging that may be an upscale boardinghouse or hotel.

The piece is narrated in the first person and includes sobering comments on what it means to be a domestic laborer. According to the protagonist, this work is "low, mean, degrading," "thrives on chicanery," and "dams up the [Negro's] fountains of feeling and expression." The unnamed houseman concludes that "It is hell, I say, to be a domestic."

Bibliography

Parascandola, Louis, ed. *Winds Can Wake Up the Dead: An Eric Walrond Reader.* Detroit: Wayne State University Press, 1998.

"On Being Black"   Eric Walrond   (1922)

A pointed narrative by ERIC WALROND that documents the nature of enduring racism in the public sphere. Published in the 1 November issue of THE NEW REPUBLIC, the piece is divided into three sections and represents three different alienating experiences. All three protagonists are anonymous and recall their interactions in understated first-person narratives.

The first narrator recounts an insulting encounter with a Jewish optician who assumes that the African-American man before him is a colored chauffeur. When the nameless protagonist corrects him, the optician responds with an "atrociously cynical smile" that forces his would-be patron to leave the store. The second narrator is a stenographer in search of work. The narrator is extremely diligent and makes a systematic effort to seek out each and every office on lower Broadway. Despite these efforts and a record of prior achievements, however, the self-confessed "ignorantly optimistic" job seeker is unable to secure work. The third narrator is a husband who wants to send his wife to the tropics in order to improve her health. When he calls a steamship company, he receives one set of fares. When he appears in person, the rates have increased, and suddenly there is a limited availability. Although he is shocked by the blatant racism

of the desk clerk, the husband does his best to challenge the exorbitant fees. Forced to leave the office because it is closing, he vows to return, and because he is determined to improve his wife's health, he also intends to pay the higher fee. "It pays to be black," he notes, in the searing last line of the narrative.

"On Being Black" is one of Walrond's most memorable and scathing sketches of urban life and its challenges for middle-class African Americans.

Bibliography

Parascandola, Louis, ed. *Winds Can Wake Up the Dead: An Eric Walrond Reader.* Detroit: Wayne State University Press, 1998.

"On Being Young—a Woman—and Colored"   Marita Bonner   (1925)

A prize-winning essay by MARITA BONNER that was published in THE CRISIS. Judges Edward Bok, JOEL SPINGARN, and BENJAMIN BRAWLEY awarded Bonner's essay first prize in its literature and art contest and chose essays by LANGSTON HUGHES and G. A. Steward for second and third place, respectively.

Bonner wrote the essay while she was living in WASHINGTON, D.C., and part of the dynamic literary circle that her friend the poet GEORGIA DOUGLAS JOHNSON hosted regularly in her Washington, D.C., home. The essay, with its unabashed second-person narration, is immediately engaging. "You start out after you have gone from kindergarten to sheepskin covered with sundry Latin phrases," remarks the narrator in the essay's opening lines. Over the course of the essay, the narrator seems to talk directly to her female audience, one she imagines as insightful and ambitious. "At least you know what you want life to give you," she notes before probing away at the psychological turmoil that begins to emerge in the face of social limitations and racism.

Bonner charts the effects of racism over the course of the essay. She calls attention to the ways in which both the body and psyche are affected and threatened by the "Jim-Crow train" and the "petty putrid insult dragged . . . like pebbled sand on your body where the skin is tenderest." Yet, Bonner suggests that enlightenment is within reach for the patient woman of color. "You must sit quietly without a chip," she writes, "quiet; quiet. Like Buddha—who brown like I am—sat entirely at ease, entirely sure of himself; motionless and knowing." The essay ends with a celebration of transcendence, the ability to absorb life energy that enables the watchful woman to "gather, as it passes, the essences, the overtones, the tints, the shadows" and to "draw understanding to yourself." The essay reflects Bonner's awareness of the vital need for self-preservation in the face of daily hardships and obstacles. She exhorts her readers to resist bitterness and resentment, encouraging them instead to cultivate their potential for liberating self-assertion and race pride.

Bibliography

Flynn, Joyce, and Joyce Occomy Striklin. *Frye Street & Environs: The Collected Works of Marita Bonner.* Boston: Beacon Press, 1987.

"One Boy's Story" Marita Bonner (1927)

A gripping story by MARITA BONNER about a mixed-race boy who inadvertently kills his white father. Bonner, who published the work under a pseudonym in the November 1927 issue of THE CRISIS, explored the fraught family and social relations brought on by illegitimacy and infertility.

Louise Gage, an industrious African-American seamstress, has an observant 10-year-old son named Donald, who realizes that his mother is involved in some sort of tense relationship with Dr. Swyburne, the husband of one of her regular, and noticeably sad, clients. Donald overhears snatches of heated conversations between Louise and Dr. Swyburne but never has the opportunity to confirm his identity as Swyburne's son. When Mr. Frazier, Louise Gage's former suitor and a soldier, reappears, the story becomes especially frantic as Louise struggles to end her relationship with Swyburne. When Donald sees his mother threatened physically, he uses his slingshot to defend her. Unfortunately, his shot is deadly, and his father dies immediately. In a tragic turn evocative of the Greek tragedies that Donald loves to read, the young boy receives a dreadful wound to his tongue, one that forces doctors to cut it out and leave him mute. His mother, who understands that her son

has killed his father, is relieved that her son will never be able to confess to the act. Dr. Somerset, a man who also has suffered at the hands of Dr. Swyburne, aids her.

Bonner's story of a complicated childhood, interracial alliances, and fate reflects her interest in social realism and American domesticity. "One Boy's Story" is a measured narrative that explores how women of color negotiate their sexuality and domestic autonomy. Bonner's use of the young boy as narrator contributes to the compelling story and underscores the awful loss of innocence and voice that can befall individuals.

Bibliography

Flynn, Joyce, and Joyce Occomy Striklin. *Frye Street & Environs: The Collected Works of Marita Bonner.* Boston: Beacon Press, 1987.

135th Street Library *See* HARLEM BRANCH OF THE NEW YORK PUBLIC LIBRARY.

O'Neill, Eugene Gladstone (1888–1953)

A winner of the Nobel Prize in literature and a four-time PULITZER PRIZE–winning playwright whose substantial canon invigorated the American dramatic world during the Harlem Renaissance and included provocative dramas on race matters.

Born in NEW YORK CITY, he was the third son of popular actor James O'Neill and his wife Ella Quinlan O'Neill. He began college studies at PRINCETON UNIVERSITY in 1906 and pursued drama classes at HARVARD UNIVERSITY from 1914 through 1915. At Harvard, he was part of the "47 Workshop," the well-known drama workshop of George Pierce Baker. O'Neill married three times and had three children, two sons and a daughter. His son Eugene, Jr., born to O'Neill and his first wife, Kathleen Jenkins, committed suicide when he was 40 years old. With Agnes Bolton, O'Neill had two children, but following the birth of his third child and first daughter Oona, he divorced Bolton. He later disinherited both of his children with Bolton because he disapproved of their lifestyle and marriage choices. In 1928 he abandoned his family and married Carlotta Monterey, an actress who lived with him and supported his career in later life. The couple settled in Danville, California, where O'Neill became a reclusive figure.

His career as a playwright began formally in 1914, following a suicide attempt and bout with tuberculosis. The PROVINCETOWN PLAYERS, a troupe founded in 1915 by Susan Glaspell and George Cram, produced his earliest works. Based first in Massachusetts, the troupe later developed a site in GREENWICH VILLAGE. O'Neill joined the group and became one of its most prolific and frequently produced writer members. During the Harlem Renaissance era, O'Neill won the Pulitzer Prize three times, in 1920, 1922, 1928. He was awarded the Pulitzer again in 1958. In 1936 the accomplished writer won the Nobel Prize for Literature. He died in BOSTON in November 1953.

O'Neill is recognized by scholars as a writer whose attention to racial matters in his work and the opportunities and talents of African-American performers made important advances in the field. Works such as *The Dreamy Kid* (1919), *THE EMPEROR JONES* (1920), and *ALL GOD'S CHILLUN GOT WINGS* (1923) included integrated casts, featured African Americans in lead roles, and presented audiences with new, and sometimes controversial, scenarios such as interracial marriage and unapologetic black nationalism. Like PAUL GREEN, O'Neill was one of several well-known white playwrights who explored African-American life and experiences in their works. O'Neill's play *The Emperor Jones* featured PAUL ROBESON in the 1925 production and represented one of the earliest leading roles for an actor of African descent in an American play. The performer Charles Gilpin, after whom the respected Gilpin Players of the well-known Cleveland, Ohio-based KARAMU HOUSE were named, also starred in *The Emperor Jones* and helped to advance opportunities for other actors of color.

The author of such compelling modern tragedies as *The Iceman Cometh* and *Long Day's Journey into Night* died of pneumonia in November 1953. He was buried in the Forest Hills Cemetery in Boston, Massachusetts.

Bibliography

Gelb, Arthur, and Barbara Gelb. *O'Neill.* New York: Harper & Row, 1974.

Manheim, Michael, ed. *The Cambridge Companion to Eugene O'Neill.* Cambridge: Cambridge University Press, 1998.

Maufort, Marc. *Eugene O'Neill and the Emergence of American Drama.* Amsterdam: Rodopi, 1989.

Moorton, Richard Jr., ed. *Eugene O'Neill's Century: Centennial Views on America's Foremost Tragic Dramatist.* New York: Greenwood Press, 1991.

One Way to Heaven Countee Cullen (1932)

The first and only novel by COUNTEE CULLEN. Published in February 1932 by HARPER & BROTHERS, the book was referred to as "a Harlem story." The novel revolves around church, faith, religious hypocrisy, and social pressures. The hero, Sam Lucas, is a manipulative itinerant who habitually seeks out revivals, pretends to abandon his sinful habits of gambling and fighting, and then takes advantage of the welcoming congregation. On New Year's Eve he tries his luck again. On this occasion, the presiding minister sees through Lucas's pretense but, in the interest of honoring the genuine conversions of the moment, decides not to expose the faithless impostor. Sam wins the heart of Mattie, a woman of great and earnest faith. Their wedding, organized by Constancia Brandon, a polished social leader and RADCLIFFE COLLEGE graduate, is a high point of the season. Yet, neither Sam nor the minister is willing to reveal what they know about Sam's true state because they do not want to threaten her faith. Sam is unable to maintain himself as an upright believer and is ultimately mortally wounded. When he hears that Mattie will be comforted only if she knows that he is saved, he makes one final false testament of faith in order to please his wife.

Reviewed in *THE NEW YORK TIMES*, *One Way to Heaven* was praised for its "convincing picture of life in Harlem" and for its "amusing and brilliant" sketches of HARLEM's diverse community. *New York Times* reviewer Elizabeth Brown mused that "it must always be a difficult task to interpret one's own race to another; and though a novelist's work is written as a novel and not as an interpretation, yet it is almost unavoidable that a white reader, knowing Mr. Cullen's reputation, should look at it from that point of view" (NYT, 28 February 1932, BR7).

Four years after the publication of *One Way to Heaven*, Cullen prepared a dramatic version of the novel. His play of 10 scenes, described as "a mixture of satire and comedy," was to be the first play presented in a series of "Negro plays" organized at the Hedgerow Theatre at Rose Valley in Philadelphia (NYT, 29 September 1936, 35). The cast of 14 featured 12 actors of color, a detail to which the *New York Times*, in its brief mention of the upcoming play, called the attention of its readers.

Bibliography

Cullen, Countee. *One Way to Heaven*. New York: Harper & Brothers, 1932.

Ferguson, Blanche. *Countee Cullen and the Negro Renaissance*. New York: Dodd, Mead, 1966.

On the Fields of France Joseph Seamon Cotter, Jr. (1920)

A posthumously published one-act play written by JOSEPH SEAMON COTTER, JR. Published in June 1920 in *THE CRISIS*, the play appeared 16 months after Cotter's death from tuberculosis in February 1919.

Set on a battlefield in northern FRANCE during the FIRST WORLD WAR, the play features two speakers, a "White American Officer" and a "Colored American Officer." Both men, according to the stage directions, are "mortally wounded," and they spend their last moments sharing water, reminiscing about their homes in America, lamenting the divisive nature of caste and race prejudice. Cotter insisted on an elusive equality, signaled by the white officer's opening overtures to the other dying soldier. The white American addresses the African-American as "my good fellow" and introduces himself as "a fellow officer, my friend." The two take each others hands as they feel death approaching and they share a vision of heavenly figures that herald their arrival in heaven. The white officer sees George Washington, "a white haired figure clad in the Old Continentals, standing there within the gates of heaven . . . beckoning for me." While the officer of color also sees the first president and former slave owner, he then sees Crispus Attucks next to Washington, the runaway slave who was the first to die in the Boston Massacre. Attucks appears with "his swarthy chest bare and

torn" and beckons to the African-American veteran just moments before the figure of William Carney, the heroic Civil War–era soldier who served with the Massachusetts 54th Regiment and who, in the deadly assault on Fort Wagner, made sure that the flag never touched the ground. Carney, accompanied by Shaw and "his black—heroes" has come for their symbolic descendant.

The play closes as the soldiers muse about the fact that they, like their angelic soldiers, "stand hand in hand over there and we died hand in hand over here on the fields of France." In a climactic moment of national pride and racial unity, the two shout, "America!" in unison and then "fall back hand in hand as their life blood ebbs away."

The play reflected Cotter's deep interest in the First World War and in the contributions and experiences of the soldiers who fought in the segregated ranks. This play, like his "Sonnet to Negro Soldiers," recognized the sacrifices that men of color made for their country, despite the systematic efforts to disenfranchise them and the race as a whole.

Bibliography

Cotter, Joseph Seamon, Jr. *The Band of Gideon, and Other Lyrics*. 1918; reprint, College Park, Md.: McGrath Publishing Company, 1969.

Payne, James Robert, ed. *Complete Poems: Joseph Seamon Cotter, Jr.* Athens: University of Georgia Press, 1990.

Oppenheim, James (1882–1932)

An editor and outspoken radical who immersed himself in the literary and activist worlds of NEW YORK CITY during the Harlem Renaissance, James Oppenheim was born in St. Paul, Minnesota, to Joseph Oppenheim, a former Minnesota legislator, and Matilda Schloss Oppenheim. The family, which relocated to New York City shortly after Oppenheim's birth, suffered the death of Joseph Oppenheim in 1890. In 1901, James began studies at COLUMBIA UNIVERSITY. He was enrolled through 1903 and left before the start of his senior year. He chose instead to pursue work as a teacher and as a social worker with the Lower East Side communities of the city. Shortly after his 1905 marriage to Lucy Seckel, with whom he would have two sons,

Oppenheim became the superintendent of the Hebrew Technical School for Girls. His radical ideas about education, however, prompted the school to call for his resignation. He worked there for two years before deciding to dedicate himself full-time to writing. Following his 1914 divorce from Seckel, Oppenheim enjoyed a longtime companionship with Gertrude Smith. Following Smith's death, he married Linda Gray, who tended him until his untimely death at age 50.

Oppenheim, the author of several novels, collections of poetry, and many pieces of short fiction, became the editor of the avant-garde monthly literary magazine THE SEVEN ARTS in 1916. The associate editors were WALDO FRANK and VAN WYCK BROOKS. Founded in 1916, the magazine was one of several short-lived journals that appeared during the Harlem Renaissance. Although it was published only for one year, *The Seven Arts* was a promising literary venue. It published the works of major writers such as SHERWOOD ANDERSON, John Dos Passos, THEODORE DREISER, H. L. MENCKEN, CLAUDE MCKAY, and EUGENE O'NEILL. Oppenheim was one of the outspoken literary critics who encouraged African-American writers like Claude McKay to write only on racial matters. The magazine suffered when its editors criticized the war effort; Oppenheim was labeled a traitor, and funding for the magazine was halted.

Oppenheim, who contracted tuberculosis, died in St. Paul, Minnesota, in August 1932.

Opportunity

The official journal of the NATIONAL URBAN LEAGUE, *Opportunity* was first published in 1923, 13 years after the founding of its parent organization. Like influential race journals such as the *Colored American Magazine* and THE CRISIS, *Opportunity* was a multidisciplinary journal that focused on literature, the arts, politics, and social issues of the day. The title of the journal was inspired by the motto of the Urban League: "Not Alms, but Opportunity."

CHARLES SPURGEON JOHNSON, a respected sociologist and UNIVERSITY OF CHICAGO graduate, was the first editor of *Opportunity*. He used his position to generate vital support for African-American artists and writers and to advance the

campaigns spearheaded by the Urban League. In the first issue of the monthly periodical, Urban League director Eugene Kinckle Jones noted that the magazine was designed to "depict Negro life as it is with no exaggerations" and that issues would include "careful scientific surveys and . . . facts gathered from research." According to historians Abby and Ronald Johnson, there were some 4,000 readers of *Opportunity*'s first issue in 1923. Four years later, circulation totaled approximately 11,000 readers. The magazine received vital annual operating funds from the Carnegie Foundation that, according to the Johnsons, in 1921 began to provide some $8,000 to the National Urban League.

Opportunity evolved deliberately and expanded gradually to include literature and art. The first works of poetry were published in the April 1923 issue, but it was not until October 1925 that the magazine published short fiction. It also included regular features such as the social columns "EBONY FLUTE," written by GWENDOLYN BENNETT, and "DARK TOWER," written by COUNTEE CULLEN. Both columns ran for almost two years. Bennett's feature column appeared from August 1926 through May 1928, and Cullen's contributions were published from December 1926 through September 1928.

Under Johnson's editorship, the magazine inaugurated the dynamic tradition of Harlem Renaissance literary and arts contests. The magazine was known for its celebratory awards dinners. Johnson recruited notable white and African-American scholars, activists, artists, and writers as judges. The panels included well-known Harlem Renaissance figures such as COUNTEE CULLEN, RUDOLPH FISHER, and PAUL ROBESON and other notable figures such as WITTER BYNNER, THEODORE DREISER, FANNIE HURST, JAMES WELDON JOHNSON, Vachel Lindsay, MARY WHITE OVINGTON, and Carl Sandburg.

Johnson encouraged African Americans to submit their work for consideration. The celebratory awards presentations provided winners and their peers with opportunities to meet each other as well as to make contact with prospective publishers and patrons. Contest winners received a modest cash prize, publication of their work, and critical acclaim that often led to book contracts and additional publications. In 1924, the year of the first contest, first-place winners included JOHN MATHEUS, LANGSTON HUGHES, and E. FRANKLIN FRAZIER.

The journal's future began to change dramatically in the spring of 1928. Charles Johnson resigned as editor and moved to Nashville, where he joined the faculty of FISK UNIVERSITY and would, in 1946, become the first African-American president of the institution. The journal's editorial staff now included Ira De Reid as research director and ELMER CARTER as editor. During the World War II era, the monthly journal became a quarterly publication. The last issue was published in the winter of 1947.

Opportunity was one of the most influential publications of the Harlem Renaissance era. Each issue shed light on the key political agendas of the day, the range of cultural awareness and trends, and the nature of the art and literary aesthetics of the period.

Bibliography

Gilpin, Patrick, and Marybeth Gasman. *Charles S. Johnson: Leadership Beyond The Veil in the Age of Jim Crow.* Albany: State University of New York Press, 2003.

Johnson, Abby Arthur, and Ronald Maberry Johnson. *Propaganda & Aesthetics: The Literary Politics of African-American Magazines in the Twentieth Century.* Amherst: University of Massachusetts, 1979.

Robbins, Richard. *Sidelines Activist: Charles S. Johnson and the Struggle for Civil Rights.* Jackson: University Press of Mississippi, 1996.

Our Women: Past, Present, and Future
Hallie Quinn Brown (1925)

One of two books that HALLIE QUINN BROWN, an accomplished educator, elocutionist, and women's activist, published in 1925. *Our Women* appeared one year before HOMESPUN HEROINES: WOMEN OF DISTINCTION (1926), perhaps her most well-known compilation. The Eckerle Printing Company of Xenia, Ohio, republished the book in 1940.

Brown published the work just one year after she completed an active four-year term as president of the NATIONAL ASSOCIATION OF COLORED WOMEN. The volume represented her continued commitment to documenting the heroic accomplishments of African-American women and to exhorting her contemporaries to work together to improve the social conditions and professional opportunities for women of color.

Bibliography

Daniel, Sadie Iola, Charles Wesley, and Thelma Perry. *Women Builders.* Washington, D.C.: Associated Publishers, 1970.

Kates, Susan. *Activist Rhetorics and American Higher Education, 1885–1937.* Carbondale: Southern Illinois University Press, 2001.

McFarlin, Annjennette Sophie. *Hallie Quinn Brown: Black Woman Elocutionist.* Ann Arbor, Mich.: University Microfilms, 1975.

Outlet

The first of several literary magazines that the enterprising writer WALLACE THURMAN founded during the Harlem Renaissance. Thurman developed plans for *Outlet* in 1924 while he was living in Los Angeles and working as associate editor at the African-American newspaper *The Pacific Defender.*

It was Thurman's hope that the magazine would become a West Coast complement to East Coast literary magazines such as THE CRISIS and OPPORTUNITY that celebrated African-American creativity and published emerging writers of the day. The journal lasted for six months before Thurman ceased publication and relocated to NEW YORK CITY, where he became an integral part of the Harlem Renaissance movement.

Bibliography

van Notten, Eleonore. *Wallace Thurman's Harlem Renaissance.* Amsterdam: Rodopi, 1994.

Ovington, Mary White (1865–1951)

One of the most influential reformers of the 20th century and a cofounder of the NATIONAL ASSOCIATION FOR THE ADVANCEMENT OF COLORED PEOPLE (NAACP).

Born in Brooklyn, New York, to Unitarians and abolitionists Theodore and Ann Ketcham Ovington, she was part of the activist world of late 19th-century America. She was a student at

Packer Collegiate Institute and went on to pursue studies in economics at RADCLIFFE COLLEGE. She attended the school from 1891 through 1893, but a downturn in the family finances prevented her from continuing her studies and graduating. In 1893 she became a social worker and by the early 1900s based herself at the Greenwich House Settlement in Manhattan, an organization whose clientele was predominantly people of color.

Ovington's political awareness and commitment to racial equality and African-American civil rights intensified as she came into contact with such influential thinkers and activists as W. E. B. DuBois. In 1909, Ovington, who joined the Socialist movement, worked alongside DuBois and other visionary activists to develop plans for the formation of the NAACP. She enjoyed a 40-year affiliation with the organization during which she served as vice president, chair of the board, and treasurer. It was Ovington who lobbied for the organization to dedicate itself to achieving equal funding for white and African-American schools. Her intervention in this regard is viewed as an important contribution to the protests and legal challenges to segregated education, including the 1954 *Brown v. Board of Education* case in which the NAACP played a vital leadership role. The NAACP celebrated Ovington's tireless contributions to the advancement of people of color and recognized her as "the Mother of the New Emancipation."

During the Harlem Renaissance, Ovington was actively involved in the publishing and literary world of the time. In addition to working on the editorial staff at THE CRISIS, she published a variety of works, including articles, book reviews, children's books, and historical biographical sketches. Her history, *Portraits of Color*, which included profiles of leading African Americans of the past and present, was published in 1927. During 1932 and 1933 she contributed articles to the *Baltimore Afro-American* about the NAACP. Those pieces were republished as *Black and White Sat Down Together: The Reminiscences of an NAACP Founder* in 1995. Ovington also contributed articles to several newspapers and scholarly journals, including *The New York Evening Post*, JOURNAL OF NEGRO HISTORY, and *Survey*. Her history of the NAACP, *The Walls Come Tumbling Down*, was published in 1947, the year that she retired from the organization.

Ovington, who moved to Massachusetts after her retirement, died in her sister's Newton Highland's home in July 1951.

Bibliography

Ovington, Mary White. *Black and White Sat Down Together: The Reminiscences of an NAACP Founder.* Ralph Luker, ed. New York: Feminist Press at the City University of New York, 1995.

Wedin, Carolyn. *Inheritors of the Spirit: Mary White Ovington and the Founding of the NAACP.* New York: Wiley, 1998.

Owen, Chandler (1889–1967)

An activist, journalist, and cofounder of THE MESSENGER magazine, Owen Chandler was born in Warrenton, North Carolina. He went on to attend Virginia Union University, from which he graduated in 1913. He then pursued studies in political science and sociology as a student at the New York School of Philanthropy, a branch of COLUMBIA UNIVERSITY. His studies were financed by one of the first social work fellowships that the NATIONAL URBAN LEAGUE awarded. While a student in NEW YORK CITY, Owen met A. PHILIP RANDOLPH, the activist with whom he would share a rich, lifelong friendship.

Owen and Randolph founded *The Messenger* in New York City in 1917. The two men, who both were members of the Socialist Party, were known throughout Harlem as "Lenin" and "Trotsky." Unlike the two other leading monthly periodicals, THE CRISIS and OPPORTUNITY, *The Messenger* was not affiliated with a civil rights organization. The magazine had a specifically political focus and regularly called attention to the overwhelming injustices visited upon African Americans. During World War I, Owen and Randolph were charged with treason after they encouraged Americans to become politically active and lobby their elected officials to work toward peace. The case against them was dismissed, however. Owen published a number of political pamphlets and books during and after the Harlem Renaissance. He collaborated with Randolph in 1917 to publish *Terms of Peace and The Darker Races* and the antilynching study entitled *The Truth About Lynching: Its Causes and Effects*. In the years immediately following the Harlem Renaissance, Owen also published works directly related to World War II, including the pamphlet *What Will Happen to the Negro If Hitler Wins* (1941) and *Negroes and the War* (1942).

When *The Messenger* ceased publication in 1928, Owen relocated to CHICAGO. There, he joined the staff of the *Chicago Bee* as managing editor. He eventually founded a public-relations company and was a speechwriter for well-known politicians including Dwight Eisenhower and Lyndon Baines Johnson. Chandler Owen died in November 1967.

Bibliography

Owen, Chandler. *Negroes and the War*. Washington, D.C.: Government Printing Office, 1942.

Randolph, A. Philip, and Chandler Owen. *Terms of Peace and The Darker Races*. New York: Poole Press Association, 1917.

———— and Chandler Owen. *The Truth About Lynching: Its Causes and Effects*. New York: Cosmo-Advocate Publishing Company, 1917.

Oxford University

One of the most prestigious universities in the world and the oldest university in the English-speaking world. Located in Oxford, England, the university was teaching students in the early 11th century.

The university itself comprises 39 colleges, the first of which, University College, was established in the 13th century. In 1884 women were admitted to classes, but, were prevented from earning degrees until 1920.

Winners of the RHODES SCHOLARSHIPS, awards established by Cecil Rhodes for students from the British colonies, America, and Germany, pursue post-baccalaureate study at colleges of Oxford University. In 1907 ALAIN LOCKE, a PHI BETA KAPPA and magna cum laude graduate of HARVARD UNIVERSITY, became the first man of African descent to win a Rhodes scholarship. Unfortunately, his race prompted several Oxford colleges to deny him entry. Refusing to accept the racist rejections, Locke, who would later become the first African-American to earn a Ph.D. in philosophy from Harvard, pursued his right to study and eventually gained admission to Hertford College, the Oxford institution founded in 1874. Locke studied Greek, Latin, literature, and philosophy and graduated in 1910 with a B. Litt.

Bibliography

Linneman, Russell, ed. *Alain Locke: Reflections on a Modern Renaissance Man*. Baton Rouge: Louisiana State University Press, 1982.

Morris, Jan, ed. *The Oxford Book of Oxford*. New York: Oxford University Press, 2002.

Tames, Richard. *A Traveller's History of Oxford*. New York: Interlink Publishing Group, 2002.

P

Pace Phonograph Company

Established in 1921, the Pace Phonograph Company was the first African-American recording company in the United States. The organization was based first in Pace's New York City home on West 138th Street. Harry H. Pace, a professor turned music industry executive, founded the company. He had already made a name for himself in the business through his collaboration with musician W. C. HANDY. The two men formed the Pace and Handy Music Company, the first African-American publisher of music, in 1908. Their partnership lasted through 1913.

Pace was an enthusiastic sponsor of Harlem Renaissance cultural and artistic events. He was one of several successful entrepreneurs who financed the Krigwa Awards, a competition organized by W. E. B. DuBois. Shortly after Pace organized the company, he renamed it the Black Swan Phonograph Corporation in honor of Elizabeth Taylor Greenfield, a celebrated 19th-century diva of color.

Pace, who regarded DuBois as one of his mentors, gained public recognition for his pioneering work to produce the works of African-American artists and to cater to African-American audiences. DuBois was well aware of the company's cultural and professional significance. During his chief address at the third Pan-African Conference in London in 1923, the eminent scholar and CRISIS editor included remarks about the Pace company's efforts to defend itself from predatory competitors who wanted to engineer the company's bankruptcy.

The impressive Black Swan client list included Ethel Waters, Revella Hughes, Alberta Hunter, and musicians such as William Grant Still and members of Frank Henderson's Novelty Orchestra. The Black Swan had the opportunity to sign Bessie Smith but, based on Pace's criticism of her style, chose not to do so. In 1924 Pace sold the company and it became part of the Paramount Record Company.

Bibliography

Handy, W. C., and Bontemps, Arna, eds. *Father of the Blues: An Autobiography.* 1941, reprint, New York: Da Capo Press, 1985.

Kenney, William. *Recorded Music in American Life: The Phonograph and Popular Memory, 1890–1945.* New York: Oxford University Press, 1999.

Padmore, George (Malcolm Ivan Meredith Nurse) (1902–1959)

A Trinidad-born activist and influential communist who is regarded as the "Father of African Emancipation." During the Harlem Renaissance, Padmore's accomplishments included editorship of the HARLEM LIBERATOR, the publication formerly known as NEGRO WORLD.

Padmore was born Malcolm Nurse in Arouca, Trinidad. His father, James Hubert Alfonso Nurse, was a respected and talented teacher. After beginning a career as a reporter in Trinidad, Padmore, who counted the scholar C. L. R. James as one of his close childhood friends, emigrated to the United States. Once in America, he changed his name to George Padmore and joined the COMMUNIST PARTY. He pursued studies in social work and in premedicine at COLUMBIA UNIVERSITY, FISK UNIVERSITY, and HOWARD UNIVERSITY before beginning law school at NEW YORK UNIVERSITY. Padmore also published articles in *The Daily Worker,* the Communist Party newspaper.

Padmore's professional successes included two prominent posts that gave him the opportunity to impact international debates about labor, unions, and worker's rights. In 1929, serving as the director of the Negro Bureau of the Red International of Labour Unions, he traveled to the Soviet Union. Two years later, in 1931, he was appointed head of the International Trade Union Committee of Negro Workers (ITUCNW) in Germany. After being expelled from the Soviet Union's Comintern in 1933 because he protested the nation's dissolution of the ITUCNW, Padmore relocated to England. There, he continued to work as a journalist and to publish on colonial and African issues. He corresponded with W. E. B. DuBois, who would later claim citizenship in Ghana, and worked with him on the international Pan-African conferences of the 1930s.

Padmore's books *How Britain Rules Africa* and *Africa and World Peace* were published in 1936 and 1937, respectively. The 1971 edition of *Pan Africanism or Communism? The Coming Struggle for Africa* (1956) included a foreword by RICHARD WRIGHT. Padmore's last appointment, which began in 1957, was as an adviser to Ghanaian president Kwame Nkrumah, whom he had met in London through a letter of introduction from C. L. R. James in the early 1940s. Nkrumah held Padmore in high regard and mourned the death of the man whom he regarded as a close friend and as a brother.

Padmore, who contracted dysentery in Liberia in 1959, died in London, England, where he had sought medical care. He is buried in Accra, Ghana, at Christianborg Castle.

Bibliography

Hooker, James. *Black Revolutionary: George Padmore's Path from Communism to Pan-Africanism.* New York: Praeger, 1967.

LaGuerre, John. *The Social and Political Thought of the Colonial Intelligentsia.* Mona, Jamaica: Institute of Social and Economic Research, University of the West Indies, 1982.

Padmore, George. *History of the Pan-African Congress: Colonial and Coloured Unity, A Programme of Action.* 1945, reprint, London: Hammersmith Bookshop, 1963.

———. *The Gold Coast Revolution: The Struggle of an African People from Slavery to Freedom.* London: D. Dobson, 1953.

Palms

The magazine founded in 1923 by Idella Purnell, a longtime resident of Guadalajara, Mexico. Purnell, who attended the University of California at Berkeley and had classes with WITTER BYNNER, recruited her former teacher and friends to assist with the publication. Bynner and Agustin Basave were the contributing editors while Barbara Burks and Vernon King, former Berkeley classmates, were appointed associate editors.

Palms was a journal that involved much innovation. Limited funds prevented Purnell from paying contributors, many of whom were new and emerging writers. The magazine, which required Purnell to perform a number of the tasks required to ensure publication, publicity, and circulation, had a readership of at least 2,000.

The first issue of *Palms* featured works by the editors Basave and Bynner and later included contributions by such well-known writers as D. H. Lawrence and Mabel Dodge Luhan. The fall 1926 issue was devoted to African-American writers. Purnell invited COUNTEE CULLEN to serve as guest editor. The volume included prose and poetry contributions from 17 well-known Harlem Renaissance figures, six women and 11 men. There were multiple works by LEWIS ALEXANDER, W. E. B. DuBois, JESSIE FAUSET, GWENDOLYN BENNETT, and LANGSTON HUGHES. Other contributors of single works included ARNA BONTEMPS, WILLIAM STANLEY BRAITHWAITE, Countee Cullen, WARING CUNEY, CLARISSA SCOTT DELANY, GEORGIA DOUGLAS JOHNSON, HELENE JOHNSON, ALAIN LOCKE, RICHARD BRUCE NUGENT, ALBERT RICE, ANNE SPENCER, and WALTER WHITE.

John Weatherwax, Purnell's husband, assumed the role of *Palms* publisher in 1927. His responsibilities ceased when the marriage dissolved in 1929. Purnell's future second husband, Remi Stone, became business manager for the magazine in the fall of 1929. Purnell ceased publication of the journal in May 1930. Later, however, in 1932, she was approached by the Reverend Elmer Nicholas, a poetry enthusiast. The Indiana minister negotiated with Purnell, who agreed to sell the name, rights, and list of subscribers for the price of the outstanding magazine debts. Nicholas then began republishing *Palms*.

Bibliography
Idella Purnell Stone and *Palms Magazine* Papers, Harry Ransom Humanities Research Center, University of Texas at Austin.

Pan-African Congresses

The international conferences established by W. E. B. DuBois in 1919 and designed to provide a forum in which leaders of African descent and their supporters could meet to discuss pressing political and social issues of the day. The first congress was held in 1919 in Paris, the second two years later, in 1921 in London, Brussels, and Paris. The third congress was held in 1923 in London, Paris, and Lisbon, the fourth in 1927 in New York City, and the fifth in 1947, originally slated for Tunis, was relocated to Manchester, England.

Bibliography
Lewis, David Levering. *W. E. B. DuBois: The Fight for Equality and the American Century, 1919–1963.* New York: Henry Holt and Company, 2000.

pan-Africanism

A long-standing philosophy and political ideology geared toward establishing strong links among African nations and among peoples of African descent throughout the world. Efforts to combat enslavement, colonialism, and disenfranchisement prompted activists to organize conferences in order to develop cohesive strategies of resistance and black empowerment. In addition, pan-Africanists used the press and their own writings to call attention to widespread and global injustice and violence and to publicize the progress and accomplishments of peoples of African descent.

During the Harlem Renaissance, pan-Africanist thought and consciousness were highlighted through works by writers such as LANGSTON HUGHES, ZORA NEALE HURSTON, CLAUDE MCKAY,

IDABELLE YEISER, and others that celebrated the shared history of Africa. In addition, pan-Africanism was strengthened through political movements and organizations such as MARCUS GARVEY's UNIVERSAL NEGRO IMPROVEMENT ASSOCIATION and the PAN-AFRICAN CONGRESSES organized by W. E. B. DuBois.

Bibliography
Adi, Hakim, and Monica Sherwood. *Pan-African History: Political Figures from Africa and the Diaspora Since 1787.* New York: Routledge, 2003.
Lewis, David Levering. *W. E. B. DuBois: The Fight for Equality and the American Century, 1919–1963.* New York: Henry Holt and Company, 2000.
Martin, Guy. *Africa in World Politic: A Pan-African Perspective.* Trenton, N.J.: Africa World Press, 2002.

Pankhurst, Sylvia (Estelle Sylvia Pankhurst) (1882–1960)

The white British activist, writer, and artist known for her tireless work and unflinching self-sacrifice to secure voting rights for women.

She was born in Manchester, England, to Richard and Emmeline Pankhurst. Her father, a lawyer with whom she was very close, died when she was 16 years old. Pankhurst was a talented artist and won scholarships to fund her advanced schooling. She pursued art studies in Venice and at London's Royal College of Art. Pankhurst delivered pro-suffrage speeches throughout the United States during her travels of 1911 and 1912. She worked alongside her sister, Christabel, and with her mother, Emmeline, who founded the Women's Social and Political Union in 1903, an organization that ultimately approved violence as an acceptable means by which to secure the vote. Her political work led to numerous imprisonments, and Pankhurst also staged hunger strikes to draw attention to her causes.

Differences in opinion about World War I led to an estrangement from her mother. Pankhurst, who opposed England's role in the war, later became involved in the movement to secure Ethiopian independence from Italy. Pankhurst, who never married, advocated reproductive freedom for all women, not just those who were married. Her son, Richard, born when Pankhurst was

45 years old, went on to become a professor at University College in Addis Ababa, Ethiopia. His mother never publicly revealed the identity of her son's father.

The Harlem Renaissance poet CLAUDE MCKAY worked with Pankhurst during his sojourn in England. In 1919 McKay relocated from the United States to England, where he took up residence in London. In 1920 he joined the staff of Pankhurst's WORKER'S DREADNOUGHT, the influential newspaper that was founded originally as the *Women's Dreadnought*. McKay did not earn wages but rather gained room and board when he agreed to work at the paper. He was able to publish a number of poems and articles, and he frequently used pseudonyms, including the name RHONDA HOPE, in order to protect himself from political persecution. Pankhurst was familiar with McKay before he joined her staff; she had published in the *Worker's Dreadnought* a set of his poems and a copy of a letter to the editor that he had submitted to the British *Daily Herald*. McKay biographer Wayne Cooper notes that the poet held Pankhurst in high regard and that "McKay recalled that she was a plain little Queen-Victoria sized woman with plenty of long, unruly, bronze-like hair . . . her eyes were fiery, even a little fanatic, with a glint of shrewdness. . . . And in the labor movement she was always jabbing her hat pin into the hides of the smug and slack labor leaders" (Cooper, 115). McKay's tenure at the *Worker's Dreadnought* ended when Scotland Yard raided the offices and arrested Pankhurst and some of her supporters. McKay, who took care to remove incriminating articles from the office, eluded arrest.

Pankhurst died in Addis Ababa in September 1960. She was 78 years old.

Bibliography

Bullock, Ian, and Richard Pankhurst. *Sylvia Pankhurst: From Artist to Anti-Fascist.* New York: St. Martin's Press, 1992.

Cooper, Wayne. *Claude McKay: Rebel Sojourner in the Harlem Renaissance.* New York: Schocken Books, 1987.

Curtin, Patricia. *E. Sylvia Pankhurst: Portrait of a Radical.* New Haven, Conn.: Yale University Press, 1987.

Winslow, Barbara. *Sylvia Pankhurst: Sexual Politics and Political Activism.* New York: St. Martin's Press, 1996.

"Parasites, The" Hazel Campbell (1936)

A short story by HAZEL CAMPBELL that appeared in the September 1936 issue of *OPPORTUNITY*. The second of two works that Campbell published during the Harlem Renaissance, the story focuses on an impoverished family who have an unhealthy dependence on welfare assistance. The family, a married couple and their son, face a threat to their otherwise steady existence when the husband is appointed to a ditch-digging crew. Campbell, like writer DOROTHY WEST and others, used the story to expose the dangers of enforced poverty and the complicated evils of federal support.

"Part of the Pack: Another View of Night Life in Harlem" Hazel Campbell (1935)

The first of two stories that HAZEL CAMPBELL published in *OPPORTUNITY*. "Part of the Pack," published in the August 1935 issue, is a grim tale about one couple's desperate efforts to survive during the GREAT DEPRESSION. Set in HARLEM, the story chronicles the tension that grows between Lu and her husband, Steve. Like "THE PARASITES" (1936), Campbell's second *OPPORTUNITY* story, "Part of the Pack" focuses on the limits of federal assistance and the challenges that upstanding people face in moments of dire need.

passing

The term that is used to denote the act of self-transformation and reinvention. It is often used to refer to racial passing, when an individual of African descent, and usually of light skin tone, passes for white. The act of passing, however, is not limited to African Americans passing for white; it includes all variations of self-re-presentation. The term can also refer to social passing, in which individuals pose as members of another class and claim otherwise elusive and restricted privileges for themselves.

Passing was a popular subject during the Harlem Renaissance. Authors such as MARITA BONNER, JESSIE FAUSET, JAMES WELDON JOHNSON, RUDOLPH FISHER, NELLA LARSEN, WALTER WHITE, and others tackled the theme in their fictional works. Fisher's prizewinning short story "HIGH YALLER" chronicles the trials of a young

African-American couple who endure social os- tracism because their difference in skin tone prompts others to regard them as an interracial couple. Larsen's novel, *Passing,* is a gripping tale of two women and former friends whose decisions about race and the different ways in which they grapple with social bias and their own desires.

In addition to emerging as a significant theme in Harlem Renaissance literature, passing also func- tioned as a political tool during the period. Writers and activists such as Walter White used their abil- ity to pass to secure evidence against white supremacists and the KU KLUX KLAN. As a member of the NATIONAL ASSOCIATION FOR THE AD- VANCEMENT OF COLORED PEOPLE, the blond- haired and blue-eyed African-American White infiltrated Klan rallies, lynchings, and mobs to gather information and facts to support antilynch- ing protests and activism. Activists such as LOUISE THOMPSON, frustrated by prejudice against people of African descent and the inability to obtain em- ployment, passed for Mexican and obtained work as a secretary in San Francisco. Others, such as WARING CUNEY, impersonated foreigners on occa- sion to secure lodging. With his friend LANGSTON HUGHES, Cuney also was known for his playful public impersonations of foreigners and audible use of other languages meant to corroborate his impersonations.

Bibliography

Ginsberg, Elaine, ed. *Passing and the Fictions of Identity.* Durham, N.C.: Duke University Press, 1996.

Pfeiffer, Kathleen. *Race Passing and American Individual- ism.* Amherst: University of Massachusetts Press, 2003.

Sollors, Werner. *Neither Black Nor White Yet Both: The- matic Explorations of Interracial Literature.* New York: Oxford University Press, 1997.

Wald, Gayle. *Crossing The Line: Racial Passing in Twenti- eth Century U.S. Literature.* Durham, N.C.: Duke University Press, 2000.

Passing Nella Larsen (1929)

The second of two novels by NELLA LARSEN, the first African-American woman to win a GUGGEN- HEIM FELLOWSHIP. Published by the NEW YORK CITY company Alfred Knopf and originally entitled *Nig,* the novel emerged in April 1929 under the less explosive but still provocative title, *Passing.* Larsen dedicated the novel to CARL VAN VECHTEN and his wife FANIA MARINOFF, both of whom supported her literary efforts and with whom Larsen and her husband, Elmer Imes, socialized often.

Passing begins with a tantalizing epigraph from COUNTEE CULLEN's poem "Heritage" and the lines "One three centuries removed / From the scenes his father loved, / Spicy grove, cinnamon tree, / What is Africa to me?" The lines set the stage for a story about a quest for self-definition, reunion, and an affirming racial identity. The story, which is or- ganized into three sections entitled "Encounter," "Re-Encounter," and "Finale," centers on two women, Irene Redfield and Clare Kendry. Both women are light-skinned African Americans and able to pass for white should they choose to do so. When the two meet each other after a separation of many years, they are both passing. Redfield, who has established herself in a stable, middle-class African-American world, passes only occasionally and only when it is socially convenient for her. Her childhood friend Clare, however, has committed wholly to the white world and even married a man with racist views. Clare has survived a much more tumultuous background than her former friend. The orphaned daughter of Bob Kendry, an alco- holic prone to violent outbursts, she becomes the ward of two great-aunts who essentially treat her not as kin but as a live-in domestic. The novel opens with Irene's recollections of Clare, a young girl whom she imagines as "[c]atlike" and period- ically "hard and apparently without feeling at all; sometimes . . . affectionate and rashly impulsive . . . capable of scratching, and very effectively too" who also possessed "an amazing soft malice, hidden well away until provoked" (7).

Prompted by a profound loneliness and desire to see her friend, Clare initiates the reunion be- tween herself and Irene. In a passionate and un- self-conscious letter to Irene, she confesses, "For I am lonely, so lonely . . . cannot help longing to be with you again, as I have never longed for any- thing before; and I have wanted many things in my life" (8).

The tension of the novel increases when the two women and their respective spouses recon- nect. Clare, who has been living life as the white

Mrs. John Bellew, is determined to maintain her newly resurrected friendship with Irene despite the risks to her social status, marriage, and personal safety. Her insistence gives Irene ample opportunity to study her old friend and to assess the benefits and drawbacks of passing, and the nature of life in the white world. While Clare reveals that passing has given her "everything I want, except, perhaps a little more money" (44), Irene notes that her friend's physical loveliness is something innate, and independent of her feigned racial status. Clare, she notes, "always had that pale gold hair . . . lips . . . sweet and sensitive and a little obstinate" and eyes that were "magnificent! dark, sometimes absolutely black, always luminous, and set in long, black lashes. Arresting eyes, slow and mesmeric, and with, for all their warmth, something withdrawn and secret about them" (45). Clare's identity is perpetually under scrutiny, a point reaffirmed by the nickname that her white financier husband John applies to her. During Irene's first visit to the couple's apartment, John Bellew arrives and greets his wife as "Nig," a name that he uses now because "When we were first married," he explains, "she was as white as—as—well as white as a lily. But I declare she's gettin' darker and darker" (67). When Irene presses him to consider the possibility that she might be "one or two per cent coloured," he is emphatic in his racist rejection. "'Oh no, Nig,' he declared, 'nothing like that with me. I know you're no nigger, so it's all right. You can get as black as you please as far as I'm concerned, since I know you're no nigger. I draw the line at that. No niggers in my family. Never had been and never will be'" (68). At this defining moment, Irene becomes complicit in Clare Kendry Bellew's racial masquerade. She refrains from revealing her own identity and does nothing to refute John Bellew's racism.

The tension continues to build as Irene Redfield grapples with the overtures from Clare and the prospect of becoming a sort of racial mediator for her former friend. "I've no intention of being the link between her and her poorer darker brethren," she insists to her husband, physician Brian. Yet, Irene's efforts to avoid Clare and her husband are ultimately undone. John Bellew meets Irene out in public and in an instant sees her as an African-American woman, rather than as the white woman he believed her to be. At a dinner party, his rage about his wife's association with Irene explodes. In an effort to protect her friend, Irene steps in to protect her friend, determined not to have "Clare Kendry cast aside by Bellew" (209). In the intense and fleeting scene that follows, Clare plummets to her death from the apartment balcony: "One moment Clare had been there, a vital glowing thin, like a flame of red and gold. The next she was gone" (209). Larsen artfully constructs the scene so that it is impossible to determine whether Irene, who is last seen with her "hand on Clare's bare arm," has made an effort to "save" her friend by pushing her to her death, or whether Clare committed suicide.

According to Larsen biographer Thadious Davis, the novel is a deliberately organized work that reflects Larsen's interest in probing the psyche of African-American women with middle-class aspirations. Larsen, notes Davis in a comprehensive study, based the character of Irene Redfield on her own childhood friend Pearl Mayo and on a well-known YWCA officer and Fisk graduate, Irene McCoy. The novel prompted a series of positive reviews that praised Larsen for the "sharpness and definition of [her] mind" (Davis, 329). The novel seems to have confirmed Larsen's formidable talent as a writer, although recent critical assessments tend to regard the work as less powerful than her debut work, QUICKSAND (1928). It is worth noting that Larsen completed the novel during an especially trying time in her personal life. She discovered that her husband, FISK UNIVERSITY professor Elmer Imes, was involved in an extramarital affair with Ethel Gilbert, the woman he would marry when his divorce from Nella Larsen Imes was finalized. Yet, despite the personal frustration with which she was dealing, Larsen crafted a novel that would catapult her into the literary elite and result in her selection as a Guggenheim Fellow in 1930. Her award also ranked as the first Guggenheim prize given to an African-American woman.

Contemporary assessments of the Harlem Renaissance and Larsen's contributions to the movement note that her novel tackled prevailing major questions relating to race, mixed-race identity, and the complex double-consciousness that scholar and CRISIS editor W. E. B. DuBois articulated in his pioneering volume, SOULS OF BLACK FOLK

(1903). Nathan Huggins, who draws parallels between the works of Larsen and JESSIE FAUSET, notes that Larsen "moved away from the conventional genteel formula" that was a hallmark of Fauset's writing (Huggins, 160). According to Huggins, Larsen went further and "exposed the psychological narrowness of Negro life, its avoidance of experiment, chance-taking and daring." He also suggested that "[w]hile she toyed with the notion of the Negro's basic sensuality, she could not let it overwhelm her credo" (Huggins, 161).

Recent scholarship has explored the degree to which the novel also represents a critique and exploration of lesbian desire. Critics Deborah McDowell and Beverly Haviland suggest that Larsen may have used race as a foil in order to accommodate the intense psychosexual drama embedded in the novel and in the relationship between the two female protagonists. Yet, as critic Nell Sullivan cautions, while race may be a pretext that allows a writer to consider additional issues, *Passing* is a novel that is "profoundly concerned with racial identity" (Sullivan, 373). *Passing* illustrates the impressive ways in which women writers were grappling with contemporary social issues, political debates about race, and enduring discussions of domesticity, female desire, and self-preservation.

Bibliography

Davis, Thadious M. *Nella Larsen, Novelist of the Harlem Renaissance: A Woman's Life Unveiled.* Baton Rouge: Louisiana State University Press, 1994.

Haviland, Beverly. "Passing from Paranoia to Plagiarism: The Abject Authorship of Nella Larsen." *Modern Fiction Studies* 43, no. 2 (1997): 295–318.

Huggins, Nathan. *Harlem Renaissance.* New York: Oxford University Press, 1971.

Larsen, Nella. *Passing.* New York: Alfred A. Knopf, 1929.

Larson, Charles. *Invisible Darkness: Jean Toomer and Nella Larsen.* Iowa City: University of Iowa Press, 1993.

McLendon, Jacquelyn. *The Politics of Color in the Fiction of Jessie Fauset and Nella Larsen.* Charlottesville: University Press of Virginia, 1995.

Sullivan, Nell. "Nella Larsen's *Passing* and the Fading Subject." *African American Review* 32, no. 3 (autumn 1998): 373–386.

Wall, Cheryl. *Women of the Harlem Renaissance.* Bloomington: Indiana University Press, 1995.

"Patch Quilt" Marita Bonner (1940)

A tragic tale of betrayal and domestic distress by MARITA BONNER, "Patch Quilt" is one of several sobering short stories about family life and social upheaval that Bonner published during the Harlem Renaissance. Appearing in the March 1940 issue of THE CRISIS, the tale focuses on Sara, a devoted and hardworking wife who hopes to celebrate her husband's new job and long-awaited paycheck. Unable to wait for Jim, her spouse, to return from his construction job, Sara raids her precious savings and sets out for the market to purchase delicacies for a celebratory dinner. On the way, she encounters a number of individuals who make what she regards as bizarre comments about her mission and one of her neighbors, Miss Drake. On her way home, however, Sara uncovers the truths behind her community's nervous asides and discovers Jim with his light-skinned lover, Marie Drake. In a fit of blind rage, Sara attacks the couple with her newly purchased ice pick. As a result of the injuries sustained in the attack, the scarred and half-blinded Marie Drake never leaves her home, and Jim, wounded in the arm, is unable to do manual labor and resume his job on the construction crew. Sara, the wronged wife, now is forced to work doubly hard to support herself and her erstwhile husband.

Bibliography

Flynn, Joyce, and Joyce Occomy Striklin. *Frye Street & Environs: The Collected Works of Marita Bonner.* Boston: Beacon Press, 1987.

Patterson, Louise Thompson *See* THOMPSON, LOUISE.

Pa Williams' Gal Frank Wilson (1923)

A melodrama about African-American family life by FRANK WILSON, the actor and playwright whose other works included such BROADWAY productions as *Meek Mose* (1928) and *Walk Together Chillun* (1936). Wilson also had a role in the popular play *PORGY* alongside PAUL ROBESON.

The play opened in HARLEM at the LAFAYETTE THEATRE at 132nd Street and Seventh Avenue.

The leading role was played by Richard Barry Harrison. Harrison was a formerly enslaved man who in 1895 became the first African-American graduate of the Chicago Conservatory of Music. He later became a celebrated actor during the Harlem Renaissance. THE NEW YORK TIMES described Harrison's performance as "a brief engagement in an otherwise unimportant play" (NYT, 15 March 1935). Historian Bruce Kellner suggests that Wilson's work was a substantial contribution because it presented African-American issues in a serious rather than comedic and stereotypical fashion.

Pen Pictures of Pioneers at Wilberforce
Hallie Quinn Brown (1937)

The last of several important histories published by HALLIE QUINN BROWN, influential educator and reformer. The volume was a substantial tribute to the pioneers of WILBERFORCE UNIVERSITY, Brown's alma mater. Completed when she was 82 years old, Pen Pictures was an earnest tribute to the founders of Wilberforce, its beloved and influential professors and their wives, and the school itself. As scholar Robin Kilson notes, the volume shed light on the tight-knit community that encouraged its scholars and students in their efforts to achieve academic and professional excellence.

Brown dedicated the work to "the pioneers and to perpetuate the beginnings of Wilberforce— Who wrought more wisely than they knew." Brown provided engaging profiles of Bishop Daniel Payne and Bishop James Shorter, rich descriptions of the extended families who taught and were involved with the school, and memorable narratives about homes on the campus and in the nearby community. The volume closed with an earnest tribute to Shorter Hall, one of the historic campus buildings that had been destroyed recently by fire. Brown ended the work with a call to rebuild and to "make of this a blessing instead of a calamity."

Brown's work and legacy reveal an important aspect of the race pride that was nurtured during the Harlem Renaissance. Social histories such as Pen Pictures grounded contemporary writers and scholars and provided Americans with access to an all-too-frequently overlooked history of African-American achievement.

Bibliography
Kilson, Robin, ed. Hallie Quinn Brown—Pen Pictures of Pioneers at Wilberforce. New York: G. K. Hall & Company, 1997.

Perlman, William J. (ca. 1889–1954)

A playwright and the owner of the Mayfair Theatre, the BROADWAY venue in which a revival of the EUGENE O'NEILL play THE EMPEROR JONES was held in 1926. The Mayfair Theatre was located on West 44th Street. In addition to staging the O'Neill production, the theater also was used for performances of Sarah Hyman's The Seventh Heart (1927), Sean O'Casey's Juno and the Paycock (1926), and Perlman and John Tucker Battle's The Bottom of the Cup (1927).

The Mayfair production of The Emperor Jones, which ran for some 61 performances, was directed by Charles Gilpin, who also starred in the leading role as Brutus Jones. Other cast members included Moss Hart, Arthur Ames, Hazel Mason, and Mae Ford.

Peterkin, Julia Mood (1880–1961)

A white South Carolina writer who published sketches of African-American life, plantation culture, and southern society. Peterkin was one of several white writers known during the Harlem Renaissance period for their writings on race and African-American life.

The daughter of Julius and Alma Archer Mood, she was raised in Laurens County, South Carolina. The death of her mother prompted her physician father to turn her care over to an African-American nanny. Peterkin's exposure to her nurse's Gullah community and traditions sparked a lifelong interest in African-American life. Peterkin became a teacher after a chaotic stint at Columbia College, from which she was expelled, and from Converse College, where she earned both bachelor's and master's degrees in 1896 and 1897, respectively. She married William Peterkin, member of a wealthy plantation family, in 1903. The couple, had a son named William George. Julia Peterkin weathered her husband's debilitating illness, agricultural disaster, and the deaths of workers. Ultimately, she prevailed as mistress of Lang Syne estate when her husband was unable to oversee affairs, and she succeeded in maintaining the large farming operations and its enormous workforce of some 500 Gullah people.

Peterkin began writing in 1921, and Carl Sandburg encouraged her to publish her work. Her submission to *Smart Set,* the magazine of H. L. MENCKEN, soon led to book contracts. She published her first collection, *Green Thursday,* in 1924 and her first novel, *Black April,* in 1927. Her 1928 novel *Scarlet Sister Mary,* which sold more than 1 million copies, was awarded a PULITZER PRIZE. Additional works included the novel *Bright Skin* (1932), *Roll, Jordan, Roll* (1933), a collection of essays about Gullah life that included photographs by Doris Ullman, and *A Plantation Christmas* (1934), a volume about southern plantation life.

Peterkin was both lauded and criticized for her portraits of African Americans. Her prizewinning novel *Scarlet Sister Mary* prompted outrage in certain quarters of the South because it featured a powerful heroine of African descent. Peterkin later was criticized by African-American scholars and activists who regarded her work as excessive and fantastical local-color writing without substantive attention to pertinent social and political realities.

Peterkin, published additional works in the 1930s, died in Orangeburg, South Carolina, in 1961. She was buried in the Peterkin Cemetery in Fort Motte, South Carolina.

Bibliography

Durham, Frank, ed. *Collected Short Stories of Julia Peterkin.* Columbia: University of South Carolina Press, 1970.

Landess, Thomas. *Julia Peterkin.* Boston: Twayne Publishers, 1976.

Williams, Susan Millar. *A Devil and a Good Woman, Too: The Lives of Julia Peterkin.* Athens: University of Georgia Press, 1997.

Peterson, Jerome Bowers (1859–1943)

A journalist whose lively Brooklyn home and the legendary meetings there between white and African-American artists and scholars prompted novelist CARL VAN VECHTEN to immortalize the site in his novel *NIGGER HEAVEN.*

A self-made journalist, Peterson was a staff writer for the New York *Globe* before he established the NEW YORK AGE, a paper that came to be allied closely with BOOKER T. WASHINGTON and his accommodationist policies. He worked closely with T. THOMAS FORTUNE, a contributing editor for the *Age* and Peterson's partner in founding the New York *Freeman.* In 1904 he was appointed consul to Venezuela. His daughter Dorothy Peterson participated in the Harlem Renaissance through her work at the 135th Street branch (HARLEM BRANCH) of the NEW YORK PUBLIC LIBRARY. His son Sidney Peterson was a physician who worked with the New York City Board of Health.

The Jerome Bowers Peterson Memorial Collection held at the University of New Mexico includes some 200 photographs of African Americans, including 82 portraits that Carl Van Vechten took during the 1920s and 1930s.

Bibliography

Harlan, Louis, ed. *The Booker T. Washington Papers.* Vol. 4: *1895–1898.* Urbana, University of Illinois Press, 1975.

Johnson, Abby Arthur, and Ronald Maberry Johnson. *Propaganda & Aesthetics: The Literary Politics of African American Magazines in the Twentieth Century.* Amherst: University of Massachusetts, 1979.

Petry, Ann Lane (1908–1997)

A New England–born novelist and the first African-American writer to publish a book that sold more than 1 million copies. Petry, who achieved success in the years after the Harlem Renaissance, moved to New York City, and her time there as a reporter had a great impact on her literary sensibilities and writing.

Petry was born in 1908 in Old Saybrook, Connecticut, to Peter and Bertha Clarke. Her parents were respected, middle-class professionals. Her father was a pharmacist, and her mother was a shop owner, chiropodist, and hairdresser. Petry attended the University of Connecticut and graduated with a doctorate in pharmacy in 1931. She joined the family business, following in the footsteps of her father, grandfather, aunt, and uncle. She married George Petry in February 1938, and the couple, who moved to New York City following their wedding, had one child, Elisabeth Ann. In New York, Petry joined the staff of the AMSTERDAM NEWS and began to realize her dream of becoming a published writer. While in New York, Petry returned to school. She attended COLUMBIA UNIVERSITY for one year in 1943.

Petry published her first fictional work in THE CRISIS. "On Saturday the Siren Sounds at Noon," which was included in the November 1943 *Crisis*, garnered her almost immediate attention. Houghton Mifflin solicited her, hoping that she was at work on a novel. One year later, when they received preliminary chapters for a novel entitled *The Street*, the press awarded Petry, who was working full-time to help support her family, a Houghton Mifflin Literary Fellowship of $2,400 to facilitate her writing. Two years later, the novel was published. *The Street* was an immediate sensation, selling more than 1.5 million copies.

The Petrys returned to Old Saybrook, and Petry continued to write. Her second novel, *A Country Place*, was published in 1947. Her third novel, *The Narrows*, was published in 1953. Petry also published children's books, including *Harriet Tubman: Conductor on the Underground Railroad* (1955) and the acclaimed *Tituba of Salem Village* (1964).

She was awarded honorary degrees from Suffolk University in 1983, the University of Connecticut in 1988, and Mount Holyoke College in 1989.

Bibliography

Barrett, Lindon. *Blackness and Value: Seeing Double.* Cambridge: Cambridge University Press, 1999.

Ervin, Hazel. *Ann Petry: A Bio-Bibliography.* New York: G. K. Hall, 1993.

Holladay, Hilary. *Ann Petry.* New York: Twayne Publishers, 1996.

Phi Beta Kappa

An academic honor society that is the oldest and largest organization of its kind in the United States. Founded in 1776 at the College of William and Mary, the society was, in its early years, a secret organization that accepted only men. Early charters were distributed to select universities such as HARVARD UNIVERSITY and YALE UNIVERSITY,

thus ensuring that the organization would be able to sustain itself despite the upheaval of war.

Women were admitted to Phi Beta Kappa in 1875, nearly 100 years after its founding. The pioneering female members gained admission through the University of Vermont.

A number of Harlem Renaissance writers and leaders were elected to Phi Beta Kappa during their undergraduate years. JESSIE FAUSET, a student at Cornell University, was the first African-American woman elected to the honor society. Other Phi Beta Kappa members with ties to the Harlem Renaissance included COUNTEE CULLEN at NEW YORK UNIVERSITY, STERLING BROWN and RAYFORD LOGAN at WILLIAMS COLLEGE, CLARISSA SCOTT DELANY at WELLESLEY COLLEGE, RUDOLPH FISHER and JOHN HOPE at BROWN UNIVERSITY, ESTHER POPEL at Dickinson College, and JAY SAUNDERS REDDING and WILLIAM MONROE TROTTER at HARVARD UNIVERSITY. ALAIN LOCKE, who also was a member of Phi Beta Kappa at Harvard, went on to establish the first Phi Beta Kappa society at HOWARD UNIVERSITY.

Bibliography

Current, Richard Nelson. *Phi Beta Kappa in American Life: The First Two Hundred Years.* New York: Oxford University Press, 1990.

Philadelphia

A city in Pennsylvania and home to one of the most active Harlem Renaissance–era literary communities beyond NEW YORK CITY. The city was home to well-known Harlem Renaissance figures. It was the birthplace of singer MARIAN ANDERSON, art collector ALBERT BARNES, attorney RAYMOND ALEXANDER, scholar ALAIN LOCKE, and writer EFFIE LEE NEWSOME. Philadelphia also was home to sculptor Meta Warrick Fuller, who went on to attend the Philadelphia College of Art and later establish a studio in the city. The writers NELLIE BRIGHT, BESSIE CALHOUN BIRD, MAE COWDERY, ARTHUR HUFF FAUSET, JESSIE FAUSET, OTTIE BEATRICE GRAHAM, and IDABELLE YEISER also lived in Philadelphia, as did the painter JACOB LAWRENCE, who relocated with his mother to Philadelphia during the Great Migration in the 1920s.

The city's history of excellent educational opportunities also enriched the lives of Harlem Renaissance figures who lived there. The major universities and colleges there include Saint Joseph's University, Temple University, and the UNIVERSITY OF PENNSYLVANIA. Jessie Fauset, highly regarded for her influential role at *The Crisis* and her visionary outreach to emerging writers, attended the highly regarded Philadelphia High School for Girls. Following her graduation from Cornell University, she enrolled at the University of Pennsylvania and earned a master's degree in French. LEWIS ALEXANDER, Raymond Alexander, Nellie Rathborne Bright, ALICE DUNBAR-NELSON, Arthur Fauset, and others also attended the University of Pennsylvania, and Albert Barnes was a graduate of the University of Pennsylvania Medical School.

The city, which had a significant African-American population, also proved to be an ideal site in which to conduct research on African-American experiences. W. E. B. DuBois interviewed more than 2,000 Philadelphians for *The Philadelphia Negro*, his groundbreaking study of African-American urban life.

Literary life in the city was fueled by active clubs and societies that, like their counterparts in NEW YORK CITY and BOSTON, provided intellectuals and artists with the opportunity to meet their peers, to share their work, and to engage in lively debates. In Philadelphia, these African-American social and literary organizations included the PIRANEAN CLUB, the Beaux Arts Club, and the Black Opals Society.

Philadelphia also featured in Harlem Renaissance–era literature such as the short story "EMMY" (1912–13) by Jessie Fauset and the one-act play entitled THE HUNCH (1927) by EULALIE SPENCE. Important publishing companies such as J. B. Lippincott, the press with which Zora Neale Hurston was affiliated, were based for many years in Philadelphia. Other presses that worked with writers of the period included the Alpress Company and the African Methodist Episcopal Book Concern.

Bibliography

Jubilee, Vincent. *Philadelphia's Afro-American Literary Circle and the Harlem Renaissance.* Ann Arbor, Mich.: University Microfilms, 1982.

Pickens, William (1881–1954)

A South Carolina educator who dedicated more than two decades to the NATIONAL ASSOCIATION FOR THE ADVANCEMENT OF COLORED PEOPLE (NAACP).

The son of Jacob and Fannie Porter Pickens, he was born in Anderson County, South Carolina. Three years after his graduation from Talladega College in Alabama, he married Minnie Cooper McAlpine in 1905, and the couple had three children. After earning his bachelor's degree from Talladega College, Pickens went on to earn a second bachelor's degree from YALE UNIVERSITY, where he distinguished himself as an orator and was elected to membership in PHI BETA KAPPA. He earned a Master's degree from FISK UNIVERSITY in 1908.

Pickens returned to his Alabama alma mater to teach Latin and German. He relocated to Wiley College in Marshall, Texas, the school from which he would earn a law degree in 1920, and taught Greek and sociology. In 1915 he accepted the post of dean at Morgan College and held it until 1920. In that year, Pickens began his lengthy administrative career with the NAACP as field secretary. With W. E. B. DuBois, Pickens represented NAACP interests, serving at one time with DuBois on the All-America Anti-Imperialist League, a group founded in 1925 in order to prevent further aggressions against oppressed peoples in the name of American imperialism.

During the Harlem Renaissance, the period in which he was teaching and working with the NAACP, Pickens published BURSTING BONDS (1923), his autobiography. He also published poetry and prose works in contemporary journals of the era, including THE MESSENGER.

A member of the AMERICAN NEGRO ACADEMY and the fraternity Omega Psi Phi, Pickens published numerous works before and during the Harlem Renaissance. In the years preceding the Renaissance, Pickens produced a biography of Abraham Lincoln, a historical study entitled *Frederick Douglass and the Spirit of Freedom*, and *The Heir of Slaves*, the first of two autobiographies. His later works included *The Ultimate Effects of Segregation and Discrimination* (1915), *The New Negro* (1916), and *Bursting Bonds* (1923).

Bibliography

Andrews, William, ed. *Bursting Bonds: Enlarged Edition of The Heir of Slaves: The Autobiography of a 'New Negro.'* Bloomington: Indiana University Press, 1991.

Avery, Sheldon. *Up from Washington: William Pickens and the Negro Struggle for Equality, 1900–1954.* Newark: University of Delaware Press, 1989.

Picture-Poetry Book, The Gertrude Parthenia McBrown (1935)

The only collection of poetry by the South Carolina poet and playwright GERTRUDE PARTHENIA MCBROWN. Associated Publishers, the WASHINGTON, D.C., group with which CARTER G. WOODSON and ALAIN LOCKE were associated, published the volume. *The Picture-Poetry Book,* which was republished in 1946, also included illustrations by the accomplished artist Lois Maillou Jones.

Pierce, Billy (1890–1934)

A HOWARD UNIVERSITY graduate and journalist who enjoyed professional success during the Harlem Renaissance as a dance teacher, Pierce managed the Broadway Dancing School, a popular venue in which many white patrons sought out lessons in the dance styles of the day such as the Charleston. His students included CARL and FANIA MARINOFF VAN VECHTEN and many other celebrities. In the years before he immersed himself in the entertainment business, Pierce worked as a reporter for well-known newspapers such as the *CHICAGO DEFENDER* and the *INTER-STATE TATTLER.*

Bibliography

Cunard, Nancy, ed. *Negro: An Anthology.* 1925, reprint, New York: Ungar Publishing Company, 1970.

"Pink Hat, The" Caroline Bond Day (1926)

A short story by Caroline Bond Day that addressed the issue of PASSING and self-acceptance in an intriguing manner. Published in the December 1926 issue of *OPPORTUNITY,* the story traced the adventures, misfortune, and newfound life of an anonymous narrator whose pink hat obscures her African-American identity.

In an engaging first-person account, the story chronicles the moment when the female narrator finds that she "had been mistaken for other than a Negro" despite the fact that she "look[ed] like hundreds of other colored women—yellow-skinned and slightly heavy featured with frizzy brown hair." The hat, which she refers to as an "Aladdin's lamp," grants her access to previously prohibited places. Shopkeepers cater to her, and life seems much easier to manage. When she realizes what she can gain, she makes the conscious decision to pass. "I deliberately set out to deceive," she declares. "Now, I decided, I would enjoy all that had previously been impossible." The farce ends abruptly when the narrator's body betrays her. Anxious about being found out and the kind of violence brought on by "hooded figures and burning crosses" that might ensue, she attempts to hurry her way through a crowd. Unfortunately, she breaks an ankle, is taken home, and thus is reinstated as a woman of color with her family, "a colored family—in a colored section of the town." As she manages her painful recuperation and deals with substandard medical care, the narrator rediscovers the joys of her community. "Who'd want a hat?" she asks at the story's end.

Day's analysis of passing was part of a substantial canon of Harlem Renaissance literature that grappled with the implications of segregation, social mobility, and personal ambition. Like JESSIE FAUSET, NELLA LARSEN, and RUDOLPH FISHER, Day considered the private and public dimensions of passing and provided readers with a provocative meditation on the subject.

Piranean Club

A Harlem Renaissance–era literary club based in PHILADELPHIA. Its members included BESSIE CALHOUN BIRD, a writer who hosted gatherings at her Philadelphia home.

The Piranean Club, like the Beaux Arts Club, contributed to local publications such as the *BLACK OPALS* literary magazine as well as to national magazines such as *THE CRISIS, OPPORTUNITY,* and *THE MESSENGER.* Like its counterparts in NEW YORK CITY, BOSTON, and WASHINGTON, D.C., the Piranean Club provided writers, intellectuals, and professionals an opportunity to meet regularly, to share their work, and to participate in forums that sustained their creativity.

Bibliography

Jubilee, Vincent. *Philadelphia's Afro-American Literary Circle and the Harlem Renaissance.* Ann Arbor, Mich.: University Microfilms, 1980.

Pittsburgh Courier

The most widely read African-American newspaper of the Harlem Renaissance era. Established in 1910, the newspaper achieved an impressive readership of some 250,000 during the 1920s. The press generated some 14 editions of the newspaper for circulation in Pittsburgh.

The *Pittsburgh Courier* flourished under the leadership of Robert L. Vann, an attorney who served first as legal counsel for the newspaper before becoming its editor and publisher. It reflected Vann's political commitment to African-American uplift and advancement. When Vann, disillusioned with the Republican Party, became a Democrat in the early 1930s, he prompted many *Courier* readers to reevaluate their own political affiliations. Scholars note the paper's unwavering support of A. Philip Randolph and his labor reform efforts, particularly in his work to establish the Brotherhood of Sleeping Car Porters.

The newspaper attracted well-known and outspoken writers. Its reporters included GEORGE SCHUYLER and JOEL A. ROGERS. Vann enjoyed a lengthy career as editor and publisher, serving until he died in October 1940.

Bibliography

Buni, Andrew. *Robert L. Vann of the Pittsburgh Courier: Politics and Black Journalism.* Pittsburgh: University of Pittsburgh Press, 1974.

Simmons, Charles. *The African American Press: A History of News Coverage During National Crises, with Special Reference to Four Black Newspapers, 1827–1965.* Jefferson, N.C.: McFarland & Co., 1998.

Plays and Pageants from the Life of the Negro Willis Richardson, ed. (1930)

A collection of plays edited and collected by WILLIS RICHARDSON, one of the leading figures in American drama during the Harlem Renaissance era. As editor, Richardson was asked to select plays that adhered to a specific set of criteria: "plays must be written by Negro authors, must be for the most part not in dialect, and must have subject matter suitable for young people of school age." Historian CARTER G. WOODSON assisted Richardson in the process and "made all the corrections as to names, dates, and historical inaccuracies." As Richardson notes in his introduction, however, Woodson "was too modest to allow his name to be printed along with the author on the title page of the book."

Published by the Associated Publishers, the WASHINGTON, D.C., press with which ALAIN LOCKE was affiliated, the volume included eight plays and four pageants. The works were deemed suitable for "every reasonable need of School, Church, or Little Theatre group." In addition, the pageant selections also contained material that could involve children as young as two years of age.

Nine writers were featured in the volume. The six women were THELMA DUNCAN, MAUD CUNEY HARE, MAY MILLER SULLIVAN, Inez Burke, Dorothy Guinn, and Frances Gunner. The three men featured were JOHN MATHEUS, WILLIS RICHARDSON, and EDWARD MCCOO. Gregory's brief biographical remarks about the writers underscored their potential, called attention to their previous literary accomplishments, and insisted on the relevance of the works to contemporary African-American communities.

The scripts ranged from materials prepared in HOWARD UNIVERSITY drama workshops to plays developed for church groups. Included in the list of eight plays, three of which were by Richardson and two by Miller, were Cuney Hare's ANTAR OF ARABY, Miller's RIDING THE GOAT and GRAVEN IMAGES, Matheus's TI YETTE, and Duncan's SACRIFICE. The four pageants included Burke's *Two Races* and McCoo's *Ethiopia at the Bar of Justice*, a popular work that had been "used extensively in connection with Negro History Week" following its debut at an African Methodist Episcopal Convention.

Plays and Pageants was an important collection designed to provide African Americans with sophisticated scripts and to confirm the breadth of talent and subject matter produced by American writers of color.

Bibliography

Rauchfuss, Christine Gray. *Willis Richardson: Forgotten Pioneer of African American Drama*. Westport, Conn.: Greenwood Press, 1999.

Richardson, Willis, ed. *Plays and Pageants from the Life of the Negro*. Washington, D.C.: The Associated Publishers, 1930.

Plays of Negro Life: A Sourcebook of Native American Drama Alain Locke and T. Montgomery Gregory, eds. (1927)

A dynamic collection of plays by and about African Americans. Edited by HOWARD UNIVERSITY professors ALAIN LOCKE and THOMAS MONTGOMERY GREGORY, the volume included illustrations by AARON DOUGLAS.

Published by HARPER AND BROTHERS, *Plays of Negro Life* republished plays that had appeared in popular Harlem Renaissance periodicals such as THE CRISIS and OPPORTUNITY. The editors also provided a comprehensive set of materials that shed light on the plays and playwrights, including cast lists, performance chronologies, and production photographs.

The writers represented in the *Plays of Negro Life* were among the most talented and promising figures of the day. The collection featured African-American and white writers who had explored race and related issues in their works. Included were PAUL GREEN, THELMA MYRTLE DUNCAN, GEORGIA DOUGLAS JOHNSON, RICHARD BRUCE NUGENT, EUGENE O'NEILL, J. W. Rogers, EULALIE SPENCE, JEAN TOOMER, and RIDGELEY TORRENCE.

Bibliography

Linneman, Russell, ed. *Alain Locke: Reflections on a Modern Renaissance Man*. Baton Rouge: Louisiana State University, 1982.

Locke, Alain, and Montgomery Gregory. *Plays of Negro Life: A Source-Book of Native American Drama*. 1927; reprint, Westport, Conn.: Negro University Press, 1970.

Plum Bun: A Novel Without a Moral Jessie Fauset (1929)

The third of four novels by JESSIE FAUSET, one of the most enterprising and visionary figures of the Harlem Renaissance. *Plum Bun*, published by Frederick Stokes publishing company of New York City and priced at $2.50, tackled the complicated issue of PASSING. Fauset dedicated the novel to her father and mother, Redmon and Anna Fauset.

The title of *Plum Bun* is derived from the children's rhyme that reads "To Market, To Market, / to Buy Plum Bun; / Home again, Home again, / Market is done" (McDowell, xii). Fauset divided the novel into five sections that evoke the refrain from the popular children's song: "Home," "Market," "Plum Bun," "Home Again," and "Market Is Done." The Murrays live in a neighborhood whose very aura foreshadows the insidious upheaval that soon will face the family. Their apartment is part of a neighborhood that "has no mystery, no allure, either of exclusiveness or of downright depravity," and they reside in one of the several three-story apartment buildings on Opal Street. The Murrays live in one of these apartments that "contain[s] six boxes called by courtesy, rooms." The protagonist is Angela Murray, the daughter of Junius Murray, a carpenter and former coachman, and his wife Matty, a former domestic who was employed in the household of a "famous actress," and sister of Virginia, a young woman with "rosy bronzeness and . . . deeply waving black hair." Angela, a talented art student who "had no high purpose in life," has light skin that prompts many with whom she comes into contact to assume that she is white. When her true identity is discovered, however, Angela is repeatedly hurt by the unpleasant reactions that she has to endure. She experiences this trauma as a young schoolgirl when one of her friends abandons her. "Coloured! Angela, you never told me that you were coloured!" is the refrain that plagues the young girl whose response is marked by its "tragic but proud bewilderment" (38). She also sees firsthand how her father, a dark-skinned man, is forced to deny his marriage to Matty, who, because of her light skin, is one day admitted to a white hospital after a fainting spell.

When Mrs. Murray dies shortly thereafter, Angela loses not only her mother but the companion with whom she would shop and easily transgress the public rules of racial segregation. Eventually, Angela decides to accept the consistent public misreadings of her identity and to pursue her professional goals as an artist. At the local academy, she neglects to identify herself, thinking that "[a]rtists were noted for their broad-mindedness" and "were the first persons in the world to judge a person for his worth rather than by any hall-mark" (63). Unfortunately, she experiences a racial unveiling that is eerily reminiscent of her unfortunate encounter as a young schoolgirl. She changes her name to Angéle Mory and relocates to New York City, where she is determined to pass. Angela's decision requires that she divorce herself from her family, however, and when her parents both pass away, she is able to proceed even more deliberately toward her goal of social and professional advancement. She tries to rationalize her decision, telling her sister Jinny that "it isn't being coloured that makes the difference, it's letting it be known" (78). Ultimately, however, her philosophy forces her to abandon her darker-skinned sister Virginia in an extremely painful public way in order to preserve her fabricated whiteness.

Angela's decision to pass is quickly complicated by her romantic possibilities. She has two strikingly different suitors. The first is Anthony Cross, a light-skinned, reticent artist whose impoverished background is in stark contrast to the steady life that Angela hopes to acquire for herself. The second suitor, Roger Fielding, is a wealthy white man who can offer Angela much in the way of material luxuries and social privileges. While she benefits enormously from life as a white woman, Angela ultimately cannot ignore the racism and injustice perpetuated on people of African descent. Her relationship with Fielding, a man whom she regards as "so gay, so beautiful, like a blond glorious god, so overwhelming, so persistent" (129), demands compromise; she becomes his mistress, and he ultimately abandons her because he does not consider her to be wealthy enough. He shares with her his interracial family history and the horrific details of his father's murder and mother's grief. Faced with his overwhelming pain, Angela sees an opportunity to redeem herself and how she might "completely . . . surprisingly . . . change" his own tragic circumstances. Unfortunately, when she plans to reveal her own background, she finds out that Cross has given her up and, completely unaware of the family relationship, become engaged to her sister Virginia. As the novel comes to a close, Angela is one of two stu-

dents awarded an art scholarship. When the committee deprives the African-American student of the prize because it fears public protest, Angela reveals her true identity and refuses to accept her own scholarship. Her courageous act prompts Cross to reveal that he, too, has been passing. The two are able to renew their commitment to each other in a meaningful and promising manner. Virginia finds personal and professional satisfaction as a teacher of music in a Harlem school, and with a little encouragement from Angela, Matthew Henson resumes his pursuit of Virginia. Overwhelmed by her adventures and trials, Angela relocates to Paris, and it is there, some time later, that Anthony Cross finds her once again.

The novel was reviewed in the NEW YORK TIMES alongside a lengthy evaluation of a modern reprint of CHARLES CHESNUTT's *The Conjure Woman*. The article on Fauset's work entitled " 'White' Negroes" praised her for sustaining a "simple fidelity to character which has nothing to do with race or creed or color." Despite the promise of the work, however, the review predicted that the timing of the book's publication would diminish its impact and popularity. "Coming as this novel does on the heels of more sensational studies of negro life," wrote the reviewer, "it seems likely that it will not receive all the attention it deserves. For *Plum Bun* is not in the least sensational. It deals with that impulse of the less favored races, now more generally recognized than formerly, to cross the color line—to obtain by some means the privileges and freedom of movement which the Northern European races ordinarily reserve for themselves." The *New York Times* reviewer was somewhat disappointed by the "highly coincidental character of the story's solution" and concluded that on the basis of this, *Plum Bun* "is very justly subtitled 'A Novel Without a Moral.'"

HAROLD JACKMAN, a close friend of COUNTEE CULLEN's and one of the many writers who availed themselves of Fauset's hospitality and participated in the literary salons that she hosted in her New York City apartment, railed against the text in a letter to Cullen. The novel is "lousy, absolutely terrible," he insisted. "Really, I don't see how the publishers could take it. Jessie doesn't know men, she doesn't write prose well; it is bad, bad, bad . . . [I]t is one of the worst books I have read in a long time" (Davis, 303). Other critics, however, note that the coincidental ending, which evokes the traditional American sentimental novel, does have a moral and that it successfully insists on the need for self-assertion and demonstrates the inherent value of race pride. As Deborah McDowell observes, "On its face, *Plum Bun* is just another novel of racial passing" but "to read it simply as such is to miss the irony and subtlety of its artistic technique. The novel is a richly-textured and ingeniously-designed narrative. . . . In this rich tapestry, the passing plot is just one thread, albeit an important one, woven into the novel's over-arching frame, the *bildungsroman*, or novel of development" (McDowell, xi). Scholar Kathleen Pfeiffer concludes that "*Plum Bun* extends and complicates the analysis of identity, citizenship, and community life taking place in the public discourse of the 1920s and therefore represents a 'linking up' of the Harlem Renaissance's concerns with those of American intellectual culture generally" (Pfeiffer, 80).

It is useful to consider Fauset's *Plum Bun* in relation to other seminal Harlem Renaissance–era works that explored passing, such as JAMES WELDON JOHNSON's *AUTOBIOGRAPHY OF AN EX-COLOURED MAN* (1912, 1927) and NELLA LARSEN's *PASSING* (1929), which appeared in the same year as Fauset's novel. In *Plum Bun*, Fauset develops a meditative bildungsroman that sheds new light on African-American consciousness, mobility, and self-presentation.

Bibliography

Fauset, Jessie. *Plum Bun.* 1929, reprint, Boston: Beacon Press, 1987.

Davis, Thadious M. *Nella Larsen, Novelist of the Harlem Renaissance: A Woman's Life Unveiled.* Baton Rouge: Louisiana State University Press, 1994.

Jones, Sharon. *Rereading the Harlem Renaissance: Race, Class, and Gender in the Fiction of Jessie Fauset, Zora Neale Hurston, and Dorothy West.* Westport, Conn.: Greenwood Press, 2002.

McDowell, Deborah, ed. *Plum Bun: A Novel Without a Moral.* Boston: Pandora Press, 1985.

Pfeiffer, Kathleen. "The Limits of Identity in Jessie Fauset's *Plum Bun.*" *Legacy* 18, no. 1 (2001): 79–93.

Sylvander, Cheryl. *Jessie Redmon Fauset, Black American Writer.* Troy, N.Y.: Whitson Pub. Co., 1981.

Wall, Cheryl. *Women of the Harlem Renaissance.* Bloomington: Indiana University Press, 1995.

Plumes: Folk Tragedy Georgia Douglas Johnson (1927)

A one-act play by GEORGIA DOUGLAS JOHNSON that focuses on an impoverished mother's battle to save her child and prepare a respectable funeral. *Plumes*, which won first place in the 1927 OPPORTUNITY literary contest, is centered on the plight of Charity Brown, a widow who has suffered the loss of not only her husband but also one of her two children. Her daughter Emmerline, who never appears on stage, is suffering greatly from a condition that may warrant a costly but not lifesaving operation.

The play is set in Brown's modest two-room cottage. Brown sits there with her friend Tildy, who offers to help Charity, a hardworking laundress, complete the white dress that Emmerline has always wanted. The two women debate delicately about the length of the hem because it may be used for a funeral shroud rather than an outfit fit for a celebratory social occasion. Charity laments the high price of the doctor's fees and her determination to provide a respectable service for the last of her family. She is clearly hurt by the unceremonious arrangements that she had to make for her husband and infant child. The sight of an ornate funeral procession, complete with plumed horses, ornate floral arrangements, and several carriages for the grieving family and mourners, strengthens her own resolve to have plumed horses in her child's funeral procession.

The conflicting nature of maternal love intensifies throughout the play. Johnson's protagonist is a devoted mother, and it is clear that she is devastated by the specter of losing her child. Yet, Johnson complicates the domestic scenario by allowing her maternal figure to consider her own desires and the ways in which she will finally achieve power over her otherwise oppressive circumstances. When Tildy reads the coffee grounds in her friend's cup, she predicts a large gathering that suggests a funeral. The doctor's efforts to charge Charity $50 for an operation, the very amount needed to purchase plumes for the mortuary's horses, illuminate her daunting resolve to do the best that she can for her child. The play ends with Emmerline's sudden death, an event that prevents Charity from enduring challenges and harsh criticism for the choice that she makes.

Critic Claudia Tate notes that the play suggests Johnson's efforts to examine "the inevitability of death and Johnson's steadfast conviction that only love can preserve human dignity" [Tate, lx]. Indeed, the play is one of several Johnson dramas that underscore the complexity of family life and the ways in which African Americans grapple with conflicting social expectations, grief, and loss.

Bibliography

Hull, Gloria. *Love, Sex, and Poetry: Three Women Writers of the Harlem Renaissance.* Bloomington: Indiana University Press, 1987.

Johnson, Georgia Douglas. *The Selected Works of Georgia Douglas Johnson* with an introduction by Claudia Tate. Boston: G. K. Hall, 1997.

Tate, Claudia. Introduction to *The Selected Works of Georgia Douglas Johnson.* Boston: G. K. Hall, 1997.

Poems Sarah Collins Fernandis (1925)

One of the books that the poet, teacher, and activist SARAH COLLINS FERNANDIS published in 1925. *Poems* included a number of celebratory race poems and writings on nature and on urban life.

Works such as "The Torch Bearer," written in honor of BOOKER T. WASHINGTON, founder of TUSKEGEE INSTITUTE and a proponent of accommodationism, reveal Fernandis's penchant for flowery and romantic imagery. Written after Washington's death, the poem imagines him as a "dusky, untried youth," who went on to enjoy a "rich life spent to uplift a race / With self-effacement, and achievement rare!"

Other poems, such as "A Blossom in an Alley," combine classical prose with contemporary observations about urban life. The somewhat jarring juxtaposition of narrative styles reveals the clash between the natural world and the uncaring world of the city.

Fernandis, whose poetry appeared in the journal SOUTHERN WORKMAN, included a number of those published poems in her 1925 collection.

Poet and Other Poems, The Raymond Dandridge (1920)

The second of three volumes of poetry that RAYMOND DANDRIDGE published in his lifetime. Dedicated to Oscar William Dandridge, his deceased brother, the volume included works in dialect and in standard prose. Dandridge, a paralyzed writer living in Cincinnati, saw his work published by a local publisher, Powell and White. The volume included more than 60 poems, ranging from deliberate tributes to historic figures to playful dialect poems.

In his foreword to the volume. Winston Morrow assured readers that the "fame of the author has exceeded the limits of his boyhood suburb and his new book will no doubt add many new friends and admirers." Morrow provided a moving description of the poet, noting that he was "[s]hut in within four walls by a strange decree of nature for many long years, racked at times by the most excruciating pains, denied free intercourse among his fellow-men and handicapped in a thousand other ways." He also insisted that Dandridge was "a true product of Cincinnati" and that his writing more than earned him "a prominent place among the poets of the Ohio valley and a commanding position among the literary minded of his race."

The collection included patriotic and nationalistic poems such as "Roosevelt" and "Toussaint L'Ouverture" and religious musings such as "Old Glory" and "Eternity." Dandridge revealed his uncompromising vision in religious poems such as "To an Unhanged Judas," a harsh castigation of a "blasphemer of sacred trust," a "Cannibalistic vulture, / Grown fat upon [his] brother's blood." In stirring race poems such as "Time to Die" he encouraged all "Black Brother[s]" to "If necessary, your life give / For something, ere in vain you die." The dialect poems, scattered throughout the volume, tend to focus on situational crises and folk character. In "Sprin' Fevah," Dandridge's narrator confesses to "a lazy, sortah hazy / Feelin' " that "grips me, thoo an' thoo" and wonders about the "thief dat steals embition in de win'."

The Poet and Other Poems was an eclectic mix of narrative styles and subjects. Overall, however, the collection clearly established Dandridge in the role of outspoken social critic and uncompromising race man.

Poetic Pearls Carrie Law Morgan Figgs (1920)

The first of two collections of poetry by CARRIE LAW MORGAN FIGGS, a writer who also enjoyed success as a children's playwright. According to

Figgs's own notes in NUGGETS OF GOLD (1921), a subsequent volume of poetry, *Poetic Pearls* sold well and enjoyed "enormous sales." In her foreword to the work, Figgs noted that "[i]t has been the great desire of my heart to scatter sunshine and contribute something to the world." She declared that she was "sending this little book out into the world" and that while she could "not tell into whose hands this book may fall," it was her "sincere hope that every one who reads it will find something interesting and inspiring."

The volume, which Figgs "lovingly dedicated" to her mother, consisted of some 23 pieces, including a tribute to her deceased father and a copy of a speech delivered to the Woman's Mite Missionary Society in 1919. The first poem in the collection, "To My Mother," was an earnest tribute to the "queenliest woman on earth," the "woman who gave me birth," "who made of me all that I am," and "fashioned my life by your own plan." Additional poems revealed Figgs's keen observations of everyday life, conversations between couples, and the natural world. In works such as "It's Hard to Keep a Good Man Down," she encouraged her readers to recognize and to praise the indomitable will of the man who "may be white . . . black / . . . red or brown" who will "dodge your blow and grow and go / Because you can't keep a good man down." Melodramatic and tortured poems such as "The Meanest Man on Earth" and "Lamentations of a Deceived Woman" infused the volume with notes of genuine grief, outrage, and sorrow. Figgs also used *Poetic Pearls* to honor her local community and the inspiring efforts of its African-American residents. Works such as "Tribute to the Business Men of Jacksonville" and "The Negro Has Played His Part" revealed her confidence in the African-American spirit and history of achievement. "Today finds [the Negro] progressive, / No more content with that ox cart," she writes in "The Negro Has Played His Part," before assuring "America, dear America / Mother of all Americans thou art" that she "need not grieve" since "your black boy won't leave / He's going to stay and continue to do his part."

Although Figgs does not appear to have been part of a cohesive Harlem Renaissance literary community, her efforts to publish reveal the widespread allure of literature during this time and testify to the breadth of African-American literary tradition.

Bibliography
Clifford, Carrie Williams, and Carrie Law Morgan Figgs. *Writings of Carrie Williams Clifford and Carrie Law Morgan Figgs with an introduction by P. Jane Splawn.* New York: G. K. Hall & Co., 1997.

Popel, Esther A. B. (1896–1958)
A poet whose work appeared in major Harlem Renaissance publications such as THE CRISIS, and OPPORTUNITY. She was educated in Harrisburg, Pennsylvania, and became the first woman of color to attend Dickinson College in Pennsylvania. She graduated PHI BETA KAPPA in 1919, having immersed herself in foreign-language studies. After college, Popel began a short stint as a civil servant before moving to WASHINGTON, D.C. There, she capitalized on her undergraduate studies and began teaching French and Spanish at the junior high school level.

Popel was part of the lively literary salon community hosted by GEORGIA DOUGLAS JOHNSON in Washington, D.C., and she emerged as a Harlem Renaissance writer during the mid-1920s. In the 1924–25 *Opportunity* literary contest, she earned a second-place honorable mention for her poem "Symphonies" and a first-place honorable mention for her personal sketch "Cat and the Saxophone." Her impressive showings in the competition motivated her to submit additional work for consideration. She published the majority of her poems in *Opportunity* but also saw her work appear in *The Crisis* and in the *Journal of Negro Life*. In 1934 she published *A Forest Pool* with the Washington, D.C.–based company Modernistic Press.

According to scholars Lorraine Roses and Ruth Randolph, Popel enjoyed an active public life in the capital, one informed by her membership in the Lincoln Memorial Congregational Temple and participation in women's uplift organizations.

Bibliography
Roses, Lorraine Elena, and Ruth Elizabeth Randolph. *Harlem's Glory: Black Women Writing, 1900–1950.* Cambridge, Mass.: Harvard University Press, 1996.

Popo and Fifina: Children of Haiti
Arna Bontemps and Langston Hughes (1932)
A novel for children on which ARNA BONTEMPS and LANGSTON HUGHES, lifelong friends, collaborated.

The emerging artist E. Simms Campbell provided the illustrations. *Popo and Fifina* was the first of many books for children that Bontemps would publish during his lifetime.

The inspiration for the book came from Hughes, who had spent time traveling through the Caribbean. The duo submitted their proposal for the book, which, according to Hughes biographer Faith Berry, they envisioned as a "travel story," to Macmillan Publishers in 1932, the same year in which it was published (Berry, 139).

The story revolved around two Haitian children, Popo and Fifina, and their family life. The story recounts the children's adventures at play and the family's move from a farm to a coastal village. The volume is marked for its picturesque images of life in HAITI and the winsome adventures of the children. ALAIN LOCKE described the work as "a flimsy sketch, a local-color story of Haitian child life" (Berry, 184). Yet, according to Arnold Rampersad, more than a decade after its publication, some 500 copies of the book still were being sold annually. The lasting popularity of *Popo and Fifina* prompted at least one translation into Japanese, decades after its initial publication.

Bibliography

Berry, Faith, ed. *Langston Hughes: Before and Beyond Harlem.* Westport, Conn.: Lawrence Hill & Company, 1983.

Bontemps, Arna, and Langston Hughes. *Popo and Fifina.* 1932; reprint, New York: Oxford University Press, 1993.

Rampersad, Arnold. *The Life of Langston Hughes: I, Too, Sing America.* Vol. 1, *1902–1941.* New York: Oxford University Press, 1986.

Porgy DuBose Heyward (1925)

The novel by DUBOSE HEYWARD that became the basis of a celebrated BROADWAY musical. Set in Charleston, South Carolina, the novel revolves around the Gullah community of Catfish Row, a gritty Charleston neighborhood. The protagonist is Porgy, a crippled man who regularly gambles away the alms that he receives during the day. Porgy begins to change for the better when Bess, a lively and energetic woman, comes into his life. Unfortunately, his happiness is short-lived because Bess succumbs to the evils of drugs and decides to abandon Porgy for Crown, a violent gambler with whom she was involved in the past.

Heyward, who initially drafted his protagonist as Porgo, used his own observations of the Charleston docks and African-American neighborhoods to inform his novel. The novel opens with the bold and revisionist assertion that "Porgy lived in the Golden Age. Not the Golden Age of a remote and legendary past, nor yet the chimerical era treasured by every man past middle life, that never existed except in the heart of youth; but an age when men, not yet old, were boys in an ancient, beautiful city that time had forgotten before it destroyed." The relationship between Porgy and Bess is restorative for them both. In the wake of her time with Porgy, "Bess had undergone a subtle change that became more evident from day to day. Her gaunt figure had rounded out, bringing back a look of youthful comeliness, and her face was losing its hunted expression. The air of pride that had always shown in her bearing, which had amounted almost to disdain, that had so infuriated the virtuous in her evil days, was heightened, and in her bettered condition forced a resentful respect from her feminine traducers."

JOHN FARRAR, editor of the *Bookman* and a representative of the George Doran publishing company, was instrumental in the publication of *Porgy.* Due to Farrar's support, the novel appeared in three installments in the *Bookman* and went on to receive critical acclaim when the book version appeared. Many of Heyward's white southern peers in Charleston praised the author for having "gotten so close to the life of the Negro." Brisk book sales prompted a second edition in 1928, and the new volume included sketches and illustrations by Heyward's Charleston neighbor, Elizabeth O'Neill Verner.

Bibliography

Durham, Frank. *DuBose Heyward: The Man Who Wrote Porgy.* Port Washington, N.Y.: Kennikat Press, 1965.

Hutchisson, James. *DuBose Heyward: A Charleston Gentleman and the World of Porgy and Bess.* Jackson: University Press of Mississippi, 2000.

Slavick, William. *DuBose Heyward.* Boston: Twayne Publishers, 1981.

Porgy **DuBose Heyward and Dorothy Heyward** (1927)

A drama cowritten by DUBOSE HEYWARD and DOROTHY HEYWARD that was based on DuBose Heyward's popular novel *PORGY*. The play, directed by Rouben Mamoulian, debuted on BROADWAY in October 1927 at the Guild Theatre on West 52nd Street. It ran for more than 200 performances before beginning a successful national tour and returned to Broadway for an additional 150-plus performances.

The Heywards were committed to using an African-American cast, rather than actors in blackface, for the production. Heyward biographer Frank Durham notes that in the absence of an organized national Negro theater, the Heywards found themselves "taken aback" by the "group of people from whom they were to select those entrusted with the interpretation of the comedy and drama and pathos of their story." After lengthy rehearsals, however, the play took shape as an absorbing piece, one enriched by the talents of the cast that included the celebrated veteran Rose McClendon.

Despite its popularity, the Heyward version of *Porgy* was eclipsed by the 1935 GEORGE GERSHWIN musical adaptation of the novel.

Bibliography

Durham, Frank. *DuBose Heyward: The Man Who Wrote Porgy*. Port Washington, N.Y.: Kennikat Press, 1965.

Hutchisson, James. *DuBose Heyward: A Charleston Gentleman and the World of Porgy and Bess*. Jackson: University Press of Mississippi, 2000.

Slavick, William. *DuBose Heyward*. Boston: Twayne Publishers, 1981.

Porgy and Bess (1935)

The GEORGE GERSHWIN adaptation of DUBOSE and DOROTHY HEYWARD's play *PORGY* (1927). Heyward's play was in turn based on his 1925 novel of the same name.

Porgy and Bess opened on BROADWAY at the Alvin Theatre in October 1935. Gershwin collaborated with the Heywards and with Rouben Mamoulian, the director of the Heyward production. In 1935 Mamoulian was responsible for staging the musical; Heyward wrote the libretto and collaborated with Ira Gershwin on the lyrics.

On opening night, 10 October 1935, the cast featured Anne Wiggins Brown in the starring role of Bess and Todd Duncan in the leading role of Porgy. Also appearing in the Gershwin debut was J. Rosamond Johnson, brother of JAMES WELDON JOHNSON. The Eva Jessye Choir, under EVA JESSYE's direction, performed as the musical ensemble.

Unlike the first adaptation of the novel, Heyward's own 1927 production that opened on Broadway, the Gershwin musical failed to garner critical acclaim or generate substantial audience interest. It closed after only five months and 124 shows. The play continues to be staged.

Bibliography

Durham, Frank. *DuBose Heyward: The Man Who Wrote Porgy*. Port Washington, N.Y.: Kennikat Press, 1965.

Hutchisson, James. *DuBose Heyward: A Charleston Gentleman and the World of Porgy and Bess*. Jackson: University Press of Mississippi, 2000.

Hyland, William. *George Gershwin: A New Biography*. Westport, Conn.: Praeger, 2003.

Jablonski, Edward. *Gershwin*. Boston: Northeastern University Press, 1990.

Slavick, William. *DuBose Heyward*. Boston: Twayne Publishers, 1981.

"Possible Triad on Black Notes, A"
Marita Bonner (1933)

A set of three jarring short stories by MARITA BONNER that earned her first honorable mention in the 1932–33 *OPPORTUNITY* literary contest. The collection included a foreword and three vignettes, "There Were Three," "Of Jimmy Harris," and "Corner Store." All three were set in the Frye Street community of CHICAGO that Bonner created and invoked repeatedly in her fiction. The multiracial and multiethnic community was a place in which "All the World" exists, in which identity is both fluid and inflexible. On Frye Street, an observer may "wonder whether Russians are Jews, or Jews, Russians—and finally . . . wonder how the Negroes there manage to look like all men of every other race and then have something left over for their own distinctive black-browns." It is in this bustling cultural milieu that Bonner sets her tragic tales of families on the verge of ruination.

"There Were Three" is a disturbing account of a single mother named Lucille and her two children, Little Lou and Robert. Lucille's creamy skin and blondness are coupled with her voluptuous body and air of sensuality that, according to the narrator, "made you know that underneath . . . there lay a black man—a black woman." Although she is a loving mother who dotes on her children, Lucille is despised by the women in her Frye Street neighborhood. They regard her as a "flamboyant symbol of uncleanness that always sets the psalm-singers of all earth into rhapsodies." Despite his mother's prohibition, Robert gets work as a bellboy in a downtown Chicago hotel. One fateful evening, he delivers champagne to a room and discovers that the prostitute in the room is his mother. The client, angry about the bellboy's seeming inappropriate reaction and clearly unaware of the relationship between the mother and son, hurls Robert out of the hotel window and to his death. The vignette closes with shocking glimpses of an institutionalized Lucille ranting and suffering from visions of the fateful night.

"Of Jimmy Harris," the shortest of the three stories, recounts the sudden death of Harris, a 38-year-old man with "seal-smooth skin coupled with the straight cast features and hair of a natural smooth waviness that constitutes 'a good-looking brown.'" Jimmy, who prefers to stitch his clothes rather than gamble with the men of Frye Street, falls unconscious. The hysterical reactions of his mother are not enough to rouse him from his stupor. At one point, Jimmy seems to rally, is aware of his condition, and struggles to gain control of his body. Unable to do so, however, he becomes "reconciled to die," and within moments, he is gone.

"Corner Store," the final piece of the story triad, features a Jewish shopkeeper and his family who, despite their best efforts to maintain their culture, become involved with individuals outside their religion. Anton Steinberg, a besieged man who cannot bear to look at his wife Esther and her "flabby body, slouched in faded grey house dress and muffled in ragged black sweater," falls into a caring relationship with one of his customers. His wife encounters a woman in the shop, one who appears to be Semitic but who, upon closer inspection, is African American. When Anton appears and shoos away his wife, she goes to deal with her daughter Meta, who wants to date an African American. When she returns to find her husband engaged in a clearly caring conversation with the unidentified woman, Esther runs back into her house and, symbolically, in the hallway between the public shop and her private home, begins to scream.

Bonner's grim portraits of real life, betrayal, and encroachment are especially powerful for their depiction of human nature and desire. Like her other works of short fiction, *A Possible Triad on Black Notes* addresses the overwhelming and often disorienting aspects of daily life.

Bibliography

Flynn, Joyce, and Joyce Occomy Striklin. *Frye Street & Environs: The Collected Works of Marita Bonner.* Boston: Beacon Press, 1987.

Poston, Robert Lincoln (1890–1924)

A journalist who became an ally of MARCUS GARVEY and a leading figure in the UNIVERSAL NEGRO IMPROVEMENT ASSOCIATION (UNIA). Poston, a native of Kentucky, was the son of Ephraim and Mary Cox Poston. Two of his siblings, Ulysses and Ted, pursued careers in journalism. Poston first forged his connection with the Garvey movement by joining the staff of *NEGRO WORLD*, the official newspaper of the UNIA.

In 1923, the year in which he married AUGUSTA SAVAGE, the renowned sculptor, he represented the UNIA in a mission to Liberia. The December voyage with Henrietta Vinton Davis and J. Milton Van Lowe was a serious effort to make arrangements for Garvey followers and UNIA members to settle in Liberia. Despite the seemingly positive interactions with Liberian officials, the plans failed to gain Liberian government approval.

Poston died in March 1924 when he contracted pneumonia. At the time of his death, he was sailing from Liberia following the close of his unsuccessful 1923 meetings.

Bibliography

Cronon, Edmund. *Black Moses: The Story of Marcus Garvey and the Universal Negro Improvement Association.* Madison: University of Wisconsin Press, 1987.

Vincent, Theodore, ed. *Voices of a Black Nation: Political Journalism in the Harlem Renaissance.* Trenton, N.J.: Africa World Press, 1990.

Poston, Theodore (Ted) Roosevelt
(1906–1974)

Born in Hopkinsville, Kentucky, Poston, a journalist who distinguished himself as a reporter while working in NEW YORK CITY during and after the Harlem Renaissance, was the youngest son born to Ephraim and Mary Cox Poston. His older brothers, Ulysses and Robert, also were journalists of note. Poston's brother Frederick was a veteran. After graduating from Tennessee State Agricultural and Industrial College in 1928, Poston relocated to New York and joined the staff of the *New York Contender.* In 1929 he began working at the PITTSBURGH COURIER, and in 1930 he returned to New York City as a reporter for the AMSTERDAM NEWS. He held that post for six years before becoming a feature writer, investigative reporter, and "rewrite man" for the *New York Post.* After a five-year stint at the National Defense Advisory Commission during World War II, Poston returned to the *Post* and resumed his extremely successful career. In 1949 Long Island University recognized his work with the George Polk Memorial plaque for best national reporting. One year later, in 1950, he was awarded the American Newspaper Guild's Heywood Broun award for outstanding reporting.

Highlights of Poston's career included his coverage of Father Divine (GEORGE BAKER) and violence directed toward the spiritual leader and mission founder. Poston, a member of the NATIONAL ASSOCIATION FOR THE ADVANCEMENT OF COLORED PEOPLE and the fraternity Omega Psi Phi, also provided invaluable coverage of the Scottsboro case and, decades after the Harlem Renaissance, the historic March on WASHINGTON, D.C.

Bibliography

Detweiler, Frederick. *The Negro Press in the United States.* College Park, Md.: McGrath Publishing Company, 1968.

Vincent, Theodore, ed. *Voices of a Black Nation: Political Journalism in the Harlem Renaissance.* Trenton, N.J.: Africa World Press, 1990.

Wolseley, Roland. *The Black Press, U.S.A.* Ames, Iowa: State University Press, 1972.

Pot Maker, The (A Play to Be Read)
Marita Bonner (1927)

A one-act play by MARITA BONNER that is reminiscent of the biblical parable of the talents. The Jackson family comprises Elias, a minister, his erstwhile wife Lucinda, and his parents, Nettie and Luke.

The play, like much of Bonner's work, explores themes of betrayal and treachery. Lucinda, described vividly as "a woman who must have sat down in the mud" has eyes that "are dirty. [The mud] has filtered through . . . her speech is smudged. Every inch of her body, from the twitch of an eyebrow to the twitch of muscles lower down in her body, is soiled." Lucinda has no patience for her husband or his earnest sermons. She also is filled with contempt for her in-laws and thinks nothing of delving into Nettie's wardrobe without asking permission. Bored with her marriage, she takes a lover, Lew Fox, a man who occupies the set but says nothing. Fox, according to the pointed stage directions, "must be an over-fat, over-facetious, over-friar, over-bearing, over-pleasant, over-confident creature." Over the course of the play, Elias rehearses his sermon for the upcoming Sunday meeting. The subject of his address is a pot maker who lived during the time of Jesus. As Elias tells it, the pot maker indulges his pots, which when cracked, refuse to be filled until the pot maker gently repairs them without wondering how they become damaged. After a night in which some of the pots obey his orders and others do not, the pot maker decides which of his creations will be gold, silver, brass, or tin. Elias draws a persuasive parallel between the pot maker and God, the ultimate Creator who "won't ask you how you got cracked" but will "heal you."

The play reaches a climax when Lucinda attempts to reunite with her lover, Lew, even while her husband Elias is with her at home. When Lew stumbles into a well by accident, the overwrought Elias bids his wife to try and save her lover. Unable to resist helping her, he finally runs out into the dark night. Bonner closes the play in melodramatic style, staging only noises that suggest that all three have fallen victim to the well.

The play is a straightforward glimpse into family frustrations and a meditation on the life-threatening consequences of infidelity.

Bibliography

Flynn, Joyce, and Joyce Occomy Striklin. *Frye Street & Environs: The Collected Works of Marita Bonner.* Boston: Beacon Press, 1987.

Powell, Adam Clayton, Sr. (1865–1953)

The influential minister known for his leadership of the ABYSSINIAN BAPTIST CHURCH and legacy of social reform in and beyond HARLEM.

Powell was born in Franklin County, Virginia, to Anthony Powell, a German man, and Sally Dunning Powell, a formerly enslaved woman of African and Native American descent. After Powell's father died during the Civil War, his mother joined the family of Anthony Dunn, a former slave. Powell, who lived with his family in West Virginia before striking out on his own, moved to Washington, D.C., in the late 1880s. A newly converted Christian, he enrolled at Wayland Seminary in Washington, D.C.

Powell, who married his childhood sweetheart Mattie Fletcher Schaefer in 1890, graduated from the seminary in 1892. In 1908, he was appointed minister at the Abyssinian Baptist Church, a historic congregation founded in the early 19th century by Boston minister Thomas Paul and several disenfranchised New York City African Americans who were not satisfied with the church options open to them in the segregated city. Mattie Powell, with whom Adam Powell had two children, a son, Adam Jr., and a daughter, Blanche, died in 1945. Adam Sr. remarried one year later. His second wife was Inez Means, a native of Clifton, South Carolina.

During the Harlem Renaissance, Powell Sr. was an active advocate of social justice who used his powerful position to lobby on behalf of African-Americans rights. He worked alongside Ruth Standish Baldwin and George Edmund Haynes to establish the National League on Urban Conditions among Negroes, the group that in 1920 was renamed the NATIONAL URBAN LEAGUE. Powell Sr. also played a visible role in the NATIONAL ASSOCIATION FOR THE ADVANCEMENT OF COLORED PEOPLE, serving on the organization's first board of directors.

Powell retired from the Abyssinian Baptist Church in 1937. His dynamic son, Adam Clayton Powell, Jr., assumed his position and maintained the family's impressive history of evangelism, social outreach, and political activism.

Bibliography

Clingan, Ralph. *Against Cheap Grace in a World Come of Age: An Intellectual Biography of Clayton Powell, 1865–1953.* New York: P. Lang, 2002.

Prancing Nigger Ronald Firbank (1924)

A novel by RONALD FIRBANK, a prolific white British writer, that focuses on the Mouths, a West Indian family of color with high social aspirations and whose patriarch often is referred to by his wife as "Prancing Nigger." The work, originally entitled *Sorrow in Sunlight,* was solicited by the publishing firm of ALBERT AND CHARLES BONI and was published in America by the NEW YORK CITY firm of Brentano's.

The novel opens as Miami Mouth considers her mother's plans to move from the family home in Mediaville to "the Celestial city of Cuna-Cuna" (Firbank, 593). Miami's ruminations about how one enters society set the tone for the rather convoluted and melodramatic tone of the novel. "In what way, she reflected, would the family gain by *entering Society,* and how did one enter it at all? There would be a gathering, doubtless, of the elect (probably armed), since the best Society is exclusive and difficult to enter. And then? Did one burrow? Or charge?" (Firbank, 593). Mrs. Ahmadou Mouth, the matriarch of the family, is perennially distressed by the lack of good suitors for her daughters and the potential options for her son. She is motivated to relocate in order to secure a better education and social prospects for them all. Her husband, Mr. Mouth, however, does not share her sense of urgency. On one occasion, the frustrated Ahmadou accosts him: "Prancing Nigger, from dis indifference to your fambly be careful let you do arouse de vials ob de Lord's wrath" (Firbank, 595). The novel taps into popular Harlem

Renaissance-era uses of dialect in stories about the social aspirations of African Americans. Its use of dialect introduce a comedic aspect to a tragic tale. By novel's end, the Mouth daughters are in no way positioned to realize their mother's dream. Miami takes the veil and commits to life with a community of penitent women, and her sister Edna makes an unfortunate choice to love a feckless man who is bound to abandon her.

CARL VAN VECHTEN, who worked to promote Firbank's work, provided an introduction for the novel and it was he who retitled the work *Prancing Nigger*. According to Firbank biographer Miriam Benkovitz, Van Vechten assured his friend that the new title would "'beyond a doubt' sell 'at least a thousand more copies'" (Benkovitz, 251). Firbank was thrilled by the prospect of additional sales. He had no qualms about using the controversial racial epithet for his work, "declared himself speechless with pleasure," and insisted that the new title was "delicious" (Benkovitz, 251).

Reviews of the book tended to applaud Firbank's "jewel-like insouciance" and his "elusive, subtle, elliptical" nature. In a *NEW YORK TIMES* review of new books, the unidentified commentator relished the "glorious black-face minstrel show" that the book presented. "The reader's curiosity is immediately aroused," he asserted, "but he is also thrown on guard against a heavy-footed, wooden attempt to write down to a presumptive aboriginal inferiority. Firbank, it proves, has written up to a very high level of naiveté" (*NYT*, 23 March 1924, BR8). The reviewer concluded in glowing terms, insisting that Firbank had concocted a story that was "at once aged and ageless . . . obliquely visual, as though it were witnessed in entirety from aloof yet discerningly selective eyes" (*NYT*, 23 March 1924, BR8). It appeared that Firbank was poised to reap even greater rewards for his work when he entered into discussions of a GEORGE GERSHWIN musical version of the novel. Those plans did not materialize, however.

Bibliography

Benkovitz, Miriam. *Ronald Firbank: A Biography*. London: Weidenfeld & Nicholson, 1970.

Brophy, Brigid. *Prancing Novelist: A Defence of Fiction in the Form of a Critical Biography in Praise of Ronald Firbank*. New York: Barnes & Noble Books, 1973.

Firbank, Ronald. *Prancing Nigger* in *The Complete Ronald Firbank*. London: Gerald Duckworth & Co. Ltd., 1967.

Pratt Institute

A college in Brooklyn, New York, that is known for its rigorous art and design programs. During the Harlem Renaissance era, the writers and artists GWENDOLYN BENNETT and MAE COWDERY attended Pratt Institute. The school was founded in 1887 by Charles Pratt, a successful industrialist and philanthropist. The school, which began as a non-degree-granting institution, awarded its first degrees in 1938. Students had the opportunity to enroll in graduate programs in 1950. The library at Pratt Institute, established in 1896, was the first free public library to open in Brooklyn. The institution currently offers degrees in four schools that focus on art and design, architecture, information and library science, and professional studies.

Price, Doris D. (unknown)

A still-obscure playwright whose contributions to the Harlem Renaissance included four plays, only three of which appear to have been published during the period.

Price's works THE BRIGHT MEDALLION and THE EYES OF THE OLD were included in the third volume of *University of Michigan Plays*, a collection edited by George Wahr. A third play, TWO GODS: A MINARET, was published in the December 1932 issue of *OPPORTUNITY*.

Princeton University

An Ivy League institution located in Princeton, New Jersey, and the alma mater of several prominent Harlem Renaissance figures.

Founded in 1746, the school originally was known as the College of New Jersey and was located in Elizabeth, New Jersey. The school relocated to Princeton one decade later, in 1756. The school became Princeton University in 1896, in the year of its sesquicentennial. In 1947 the university issued a diploma to an African-American student for the first time. Women were admitted as formal students in 1969. In 2001 Shirley Tilghman became the first woman president of the institution.

The playwright EUGENE O'NEILL, author of the popular Harlem Renaissance play *The EMPEROR JONES*, began his college studies at Princeton in 1906.

"Prison Bound, The" Marita Bonner (1926)

A melancholy vignette by MARITA BONNER that features little dialogue and much angst in the home of an unhappily married couple. Published in the September 1926 issue of *THE CRISIS*, the story opens as Maggie, a dissatisfied and depressed housewife, wonders how her cup of tea has salt in it. Over the course of her silent wonderings, she gazes around the awful apartment that she shares with a husband for whom she has little desire. When Charlie looks up at his wife and sees her crying, he is overcome by distaste and beats a hasty retreat. The story closes as Maggie begins to clean up the dishes and hopes that heaven will help her to overcome. The story closes, as it opens, with lines from a prayer: "God help the prison-bound / Them within the four iron / walls this evening!"

"The Prison Bound" is one of several portraits that Bonner created of unrealized happiness and distressed couples. Her relentless critique of dysfunctional domesticity and frustrated women contributed to the literary realism that was so much a part of the Harlem Renaissance.

Bibliography

Flynn, Joyce, and Joyce Occomy Striklin. *Frye Street & Environs: The Collected Works of Marita Bonner.* Boston: Beacon Press, 1987.

"Prologue to a Life" Dorothy West (1929)

A heartfelt story and tragic romance by DOROTHY WEST that appeared in the April 1929 issue of the *SATURDAY EVENING QUILL* magazine.

The protagonists, Lily Bemis and Luke Kane, embark on a new life when they get married. Lily came north when the white southern family for whom she worked moved to Springfield, Massachusetts. Luke is a longtime resident of the state but has had no desire to move away from his close-knit and watchful family in Springfield. Luke falls in love with Lily; her affection for him is based on her strong desire to have a child. According to the narrator, Lucy regards a man as a means to the ends of her grand reproductive plans: "In her supreme egoism she believed the male seed would only generate it," notes the narrator. "She would not conceive of [the seed] becoming blood of her child's blood, and flesh of her child's flesh. Men were chiefly important as providers. She would have married any healthy man with prospects." Lucy gives birth to twin boys, James and John, who have her "soft yellow skin and fine brown eyes." Her devotion to them is absolute and "[t]o her, they were gods."

The twins drown together when they fall through the ice on a pond during the winter. Lily is devastated and withdraws completely from her husband and her mother-in-law. "She had given no thought to death before the death of her twins," the narrator reveals. Yet, in the wake of her loss, "she had thought of her going as only a dreamless sleeping and a waking with her sons." Luke does his best to comfort his wife, and in time she finds that she is pregnant again. Her attitude toward childbearing has changed completely, however. She berates him inhumanely, telling him that this child is his. "I've borne my babies," she exclaims, "And I've buried them. This is your little black brat, d'you hear? You can keep it or kill it." Lily does not live long after she delivers the child. The unnamed infant also struggles for life. In a fit of desperation, Luke pumps her chest and blows air into her lungs. The baby girl responds, and as she does, he names her after her mother. "Lily was dead, and Lily was not dead," observes the narrator quietly before delivering the final philosophical perspectives on the exhausting events that have unfolded. "A mother is the creator of Life. And God cannot die."

West's story anticipates some of her later short fiction in which she continues to grapple with unloving parent-child relationships and the desperation to which some women succumb in their marriages.

Provincetown Players

An enterprising and dynamic theater group established in 1914 in Provincetown, Massachusetts, by wealthy and progressive New York intellectuals.

The founders included Hutchins Hapgood, EMILY BIGELOW HAPGOOD, and MABEL DODGE, and later members included EUGENE O'NEILL. George Cram Cook had a major influence on the group in its formative years.

The troupe, which began staging productions in 1915, included works by O'Neill and is credited with launching the career of the Nobel Prize– and PULITZER PRIZE–winning writer. The Provincetown Players relocated to GREENWICH VILLAGE at the end of 1916 and there became a vital part of the avant-garde theater community. It worked with writers such as Edna St. Vincent Millay and PAUL GREEN, the white Pulitzer Prize–winning playwright whose works included *IN ABRAHAM'S BOSOM*, a drama that the Players produced in 1926 to much acclaim. The Provincetown Players lasted for some 15 years and presented their final productions in 1929.

Bibliography

Sarlos, Robert. *Jig Cook and the Provincetown Players: Theatre in Ferment*. Amherst: University of Massachusetts Press, 1982.

Pulitzer Prize

A prestigious award given to individuals who demonstrate excellence in such fields as literature, journalism, and music. Joseph Pulitzer, an intrepid and entrepreneurial Hungarian-American publisher, endowed the prizes in his will. Pulitzer, who also allocated funds to establish the Columbia School of Journalism, indicated that the prizes should be awarded in the fields of journalism, letters, drama, and education, and also include four prizes to fund travel.

The first prizes were given in 1917. During the Harlem Renaissance, winners included PAUL GREEN for his play *IN ABRAHAM'S BOSOM* (1926); writer ZONA GALE, who in 1924 helped to judge the annual *Opportunity* literary contest; MARC CONNELLY for his play *THE GREEN PASTURES: A FABLE* (1930); novelist JULIA MOOD PETERKIN; and composer Virgil Thomson, who collaborated with COUNTEE CULLEN in the 1930s on musical adaptations of the poet's work.

Bibliography

Hohenberg, John. *The Pulitzer Diaries: Inside America's Greatest Prize*. Syracuse, N.Y.: Syracuse University Press, 1997.

Juergens, George. *Joseph Pulitzer and the New York World*. Princeton, N.J.: Princeton University Press, 1966.

Seitz, Don Carlos. *Joseph Pulitzer: His Life and Letters*. 1924; reprint, Garden City, N.Y.: Garden City Publishing Company, 1927.

Purple Flower, The   Marita Bonner (1928)

An abstract one-act play by MARITA BONNER. Published in the January 1928 issue of *THE CRISIS*, the play centers on "Sundry White Devils" and their competition, "The Us's." Set on an "open plain" that is "bounded distantly on one side by Nowhere and faced by a high hill—Somewhere," the play contemplates issues of oppression, encroachment, and survival.

The Us's are made up of figures who could "be as white as the White Devils, as brown as the earth, as black as the center of a poppy" and who "may look as if they were something or nothing." The group, whose description suggests that they symbolize African Americans, bemoan their plight at the hands of the elitist "Sundry White Devils" and plot how best to overcome their tormentors. The group, intent on scaling the high hill on the horizon, realizes the need for capable leaders and the importance of group solidarity.

Bonner used the play to advance her critique of contemporary American society.

Bibliography

Flynn, Joyce, and Joyce Occomy Striklin. *Frye Street & Environs: The Collected Works of Marita Bonner*. Boston: Beacon Press, 1987.

Q

Quicksand Nella Larsen (1928)

The first of two novels by NELLA LARSEN. *Quicksand* is a compelling story about a young woman who strives to claim a place for herself. There are autobiographical undertones in the novel, whose protagonist teaches at, lives in, and travels to locations to which Larsen herself had ties.

The story of Helga Crane, a 22-year-old lonely mixed-race woman, begins in NAXOS, a college in the Black Belt. Crane, born of a white mother and a father of African descent, is a teacher at the school whose location, with rearranged letters, reveals the degree to which Anglo-Saxon, ideas hold sway. Helga, who does not forge friendships with her fellow teachers and sequesters herself in her richly textured and decorated private rooms, ultimately leaves the school in a rage, unable to overcome what she regards as limitations on her own self-development. She travels to CHICAGO and obtains employment that takes her to HARLEM. There, under the watchful eye of Mrs. Jeanette Hayes-Rore, she attempts to meld into upper-middle-class African-American society. Her patron, however, advises her to suppress the facts of her mixed ancestry, specifically the details about her white lineage. She becomes close to Anne Grey, a widow who provides Helga with further opportunities to move in African-American circles. The alliance with Mrs. Grey begins to unravel, however, when Helga tires of the woman's vocal antipathy toward whites despite her efforts to emulate white social practices and fashions.

The arrival of a $5,000 check from her maternal white relatives saves Helga from the increasingly suffocating Harlem network in which she finds herself. She uses the money to finance a visit, and potential permanent relocation, to Denmark. Once there, however, instead of having to suppress her white identity, she finds her African origins highlighted dramatically. She attracts a great deal of attention because of her African origins and is regarded as a fascinating exotic. Her family prompts her to dress in vivid colors that accentuate her difference from the majority of Danish people, and Helga struggles now to take control of her body and projected self-image. An accomplished artist, Axel Olsen, is in love with her, but Helga refuses to marry him. She is concerned, in part, that despite his promises of love he eventually will turn on her and despise her because of her race. Helga leaves Denmark with a sharper sense of how race and identity are both manipulated and malleable; she has an epiphany about her own father's hunger for restorative racial environments and ties.

Shortly after her return to Harlem, Helga Crane marries the Reverend Green, a minister whom she meets in a storefront church. The couple relocates to Alabama, but Helga's speedy repatriation into the African-American world does not bode well. She begins to suffocate under the burdens of childbearing, motherhood, and domestic responsibilities. The final scenes of the book reveal that she is pregnant with her fifth child soon after the birth of her fourth; Helga is a woman with no control over her body. The novel closes with the specter of Helga's demise rather than her restoration, a woman suffering in a racial and personal quagmire from which there may be no escape.

Larsen, who published the novel with the ALFRED A. KNOPF, dedicated the work to her husband. She also included a telling epigraph from "Cross," a moving LANGSTON HUGHES poem about a mixed-race child whose "old man died in a fine big house" and "ma died in a shack. / I wonder where I'm going to die / Being neither white nor black." Larsen's strategic use of the epigraph signaled the novel's focus on mixed-race identity, class and race divisions, racial assimilation, and deadly social alienation.

According to Larsen biographer Thadious Davis, *Quicksand* was well-received, and Larsen was pleased by the response to her debut novel. Davis notes that white reviews praised the book for its orderly presentation, style, and aesthetics. African-American reviews, however, tended to focus on Larsen's investigations of racial matters and praised the new approach and contexts that Larsen used to explore race and identity in the contemporary world. Davis notes that ARTHUR HUFF FAUSET celebrated Larsen's intervention and regarded the work as "a step forward" (Davis, 279). GWENDOLYN BENNETT, whose first comments on the work appeared in "THE EBONY FLUTE," her regular OPPORTUNITY column, celebrated the fact that "this book does not set as its tempo that of the Harlem cabaret . . . and that Harlem night-life is more or less submerged by this author in the psychological struggle of the hero-

ine" (Davis, 278–279). The eminent *CRISIS* editor W. E. B. DUBOIS celebrated the work as a sharp relief from the chaos of works like CLAUDE MCKAY's *HOME TO HARLEM*. DuBois characterized Larsen's work as "fine, thoughtful and courageous" and confidently asserted that it was "on the whole, the best piece of fiction that Negro America has produced since the heyday of Chesnutt" (Davis, 280). ALAIN LOCKE agreed, praising the novel as a "social document of importance, and as well, a living, moving picture of a type not often in the foreground of Negro fiction, and here treated for the first time with adequacy" (Davis, 281). The high praise buoyed Larsen immensely and fueled her as she worked to complete her second novel, *PASSING* (1929). *Quicksand* still stands as one of the most sophisticated and compelling works of the Harlem Renaissance.

Bibliography

Davis, Thadious M. *Nella Larsen, Novelist of the Harlem Renaissance: A Woman's Life Unveiled.* Baton Rouge: Louisiana State University Press, 1994.

Larson, Charles. *Invisible Darkness: Jean Toomer and Nella Larsen.* Iowa City: University of Iowa Press, 1993.

McLendon, Jacquelyn. *The Politics of Color in the Fiction of Jessie Fauset and Nella Larsen.* Charlottesville: University Press of Virginia, 1995.

Wall, Cheryl. *Women of the Harlem Renaissance.* Bloomington: Indiana University Press, 1995.

R

Rachel Angelina Weld Grimké (1916)

A sobering feminist play about LYNCHING, racism, and African-American domesticity by ANGELINA WELD GRIMKÉ. The play's production history, though limited, is important to note. The play is the earliest known 20th-century play to be performed publicly with an all-African-American cast. Grimké, who wrote the play in response to a call from the NATIONAL ASSOCIATION FOR THE ADVANCEMENT OF COLORED PEOPLE (NAACP) for race plays, saw it performed under the auspices of that organization. It debuted in Washington, D.C., at the Myrtilla Miner School. Two subsequent productions were staged in New York City at the Neighborhood Theatre on April 26, 1917, and in Cambridge, Massachusetts, in May 1917. The play was published for the first time four years later, in 1920.

Rachel is a three-act play that explores African-American middle-class life and family values in the North. Grimké takes great pains to document the material signs of the Lovings' respectability. The meticulous stage directions that precede Act One reveal the playwright's determination to dispel stereotypes about African-American domesticity. As the play opens, Mrs. Loving, a seamstress hard at work before her sewing machine, is ensconced in a "room scrupulously neat and clean and plainly furnished." Included in the numerous items that suggest the family's stability, religiosity, and worth are "white sash curtains," a "bookcase full of books," "a simply framed, inexpensive copy of Millet's 'The Reapers,'" a copy of Burne-Jones's "Golden Stairs," matched vases on the mantelpiece, and a piano above which hangs a copy of the "Sistine Madonna" by Raphael. Tragically, however, none of these items offers any protection from the prejudice and racial intolerance. The Lovings, while clearly nurtured in their own home, are unable to avoid the uncivilized masses that taunt the African-American children of the apartment building in school or those who reject Tom Loving's job applications because of his race.

The family's experience of mob violence is withheld from the second generation of Lovings. Eventually, the widowed Mrs. Loving reveals that her husband and the children's father and brother were lynched. The two men were murdered because they dared to protest the lynching of an innocent man. The Loving children endure a painful, private coming of age when they learn that they were asleep while their father and stepbrother were lynched. Their father was an outspoken journalist whose "daring" articles were reminiscent of those written by pioneering antilynching journalist IDA B. WELLS-BARNETT. Eventually, he receives an intimidating message from outraged whites that calls for him to retract an especially insistent piece written to protest the lynching of an innocent man. He refuses and a short time later is taken forcefully from his home and family. His wife's son George attempts to defend his father but is murdered by the mob as well. Once Rachel hears this awful story, she makes an almost immediate connection between racial violence and maternal anguish. She recognizes her mother's double loss and, as Act One closes, Rachel suggests that "this nation—this

438

white Christian nation—has deliberately set its curse upon the most beautiful—the most holy thing in life—motherhood!" Overcome by the family tragedy and the larger implications of such violence, she collapses in the arms of her mother.

Act Two is set seven years later, a symbolic passage of time that suggests Rachel's maturation and growth. She has become the adoptive mother of Jimmy, a young neighbor who reminds Mrs. Loving of her murdered son George. Rachel seems to be thriving in her new role and prides herself on providing Jimmy with much love and attention. Her confidence is shaken, however, when Mrs. Lane, a new neighbor, shares her harrowing stories about her daughter's abuse in the neighborhood school. At the end of the women's conversation, Mrs. Lane shocks Rachel with her philosophies about bearing children of color into the modern American world. When Rachel inquires as to whether the woman has any other children, Mrs. Lane makes the following startling reply: "(dryly) Hardly! If I had another—I'd kill it. It's kinder." As she leaves, Mrs. Lane instructs Rachel to avoid motherhood altogether. "Don't marry," she says. Act Two ends as Rachel's "honey boy," the light-skinned Jimmy, shares his tales of children targeting him with stones and harsh racial epithets. "The stone hurts me there, Ma Rachel," the child says, "but what they called me hurts and hurts here."

As the act ends, Rachel sinks prostrate to the floor and vows to God that "no child of mine shall ever lie upon my breast, for I will not have it rise up, in the terrible days that are to be—and call me cursed." The biblical Old Testament rhetoric that Grimké employs underscores the intensity of the feminine distress and reproductive crisis prompted by racist social aggression.

Grimké's meditation on African-American women's responses to lynching and racial violence intensifies as the play continues. Rachel accepts and then rejects her suitor's proposal of marriage. The distraught young woman descends into a melodramatic depression. Ultimately she decides that she can never bring children into a cruel and fallen world. Her politicized abstinence and self-imposed sterility are nonnegotiable. Ultimately they are literally maddening. Rachel descends into an inaccessible melancholy and is lost to her family and community.

The play *Rachel* was published in 1920. Critics like Gloria Hull note that the play is perhaps more powerful as a written than a performed piece.

Bibliography
Hull, Gloria. *Color, Sex, and Poetry: Three Women Writers of the Harlem Renaissance.* Bloomington: Indiana University Press, 1987.

Miller, Ericka. *The Other Reconstruction: Where Violence and Womanhood Meet in the Writings of Wells-Barnett, Grimké, and Larsen.* New York: Garland, 2000.

Radcliffe College

In 1999 Radcliffe College ended its 120-year role as an undergraduate institution for women. It merged with HARVARD UNIVERSITY and became the Radcliffe Institute for Advanced Study at Harvard.

The school was named after Lady Ann Radcliffe Mowlson, who in 1643 became the first individual to establish a scholarship fund at Harvard College. Elizabeth Cary Agassiz, widow of Harvard professor Louis Agassiz, served as the first president. Radcliffe was part of an influential consortium of women's colleges known as the Seven Sisters. Its six sister colleges were Barnard, Bryn Mawr, Mount Holyoke, Smith, Vassar, and Wellesley.

Radcliffe students did not have full privileges at Harvard University. It was not until 1943 that the two schools agreed to joint instruction. The schools enjoyed their first combined commencement in 1970.

Accomplished Radcliffe graduates who shaped the Harlem Renaissance include MARITA BONNER, Caroline Stewart Bond Day, and EVA DYKES. Bonner, who majored in English and comparative literature, also composed her class song and founded the Radcliffe chapter of DELTA SIGMA THETA. Dykes, a graduate of DUNBAR HIGH SCHOOL and HOWARD UNIVERSITY, completed graduate studies at Radcliffe and was one of the first women of color to receive a Ph.D. in the United States.

Bibliography
Howells, Dorothy. *A Century to Celebrate: Radcliffe College, 1879–1979.* Cambridge, Mass.: Radcliffe College, 1978.

Kendall, Elaine. *"Peculiar Institutions": An Informal History of the Seven Sister Colleges*. New York: Putnam, 1976.

McCord, David. *An Acre for Education, Being Notes on the History of Radcliffe College*. Cambridge, Mass.: Crimson Printing Company, 1954.

Sollors, Werner, Caldwell Titcomb, and Thomas Underwood, eds. *Blacks at Harvard: A Documentary History of African American Experience at Harvard and Radcliffe*. New York: New York University Press, 1993.

Randolph, A(sa) Philip (1889–1979)

One of America's greatest activists and labor leaders and the man whose unflinching challenge of racism led to the desegregation of the U.S. military.

Born in Crescent City, Florida, Asa was the youngest of two sons born to James and Elizabeth Robinson Randolph. His father was a tailor and African Methodist Episcopal minister, and the family was immersed in the world of the church. In 1903 Randolph and his older brother James began school at the Cookman Institute, the first high school for African Americans in Florida. After graduating at the head of his class, Randolph migrated to New York City in 1911 with hopes of pursuing a career in the theater. Shortly after he arrived in Harlem, Randolph enrolled at City College, where he attended night classes. His studies in economics, history, and philosophy primed him for the vibrant political milieu of New York City and the perspectives of such visible public figures as Hubert Harrison, a provocative soapbox orator on the streets of New York. In 1915 he married Lucille Campbell Green, a beautician who had received her training from the self-made millionairess Madam C. J. Walker and enjoyed a close friendship with Walker and with her daughter A'Lelia. The Randolphs had no children. Lucille Randolph died in 1963, just before the historic March on Washington, in which her husband walked in the lead procession.

Randolph and his lifelong friend CHANDLER OWEN, whom he met through his wife Lucille, founded THE MESSENGER. It was one of the three most widely circulated African-American periodicals of the Harlem Renaissance. Randolph served as editor, manager, and publisher of the monthly journal that produced its first issue in November 1917. Writer GEORGE SCHUYLER joined the staff in 1924 and became a managing editor who incorporated more literary and cultural materials into the periodical. Lucille Randolph was the primary financial supporter of the journal that featured work by ROBERT BAGNALL, COUNTEE CULLEN, CLAUDE MCKAY, LANGSTON HUGHES, THEOPHILUS LEWIS, WILLIAM PICKENS, and WALLACE THURMAN.

The *Messenger* was an outspoken advocate of socialism, racial justice, and civil rights. It did not hesitate to make pointed criticisms of the government or of matters of global import such as World War I. Randolph and Owen were jailed because of their antiwar views, and the periodical was even banned from the U.S. mail. During its heyday, *The Messenger* enjoyed a circulation of more than 25,000 copies in 1919, but in the 1920s readership dropped dramatically to 5,000 copies. The journal ceased publication in 1925.

Randolph emerged as a major political figure during the Harlem Renaissance. He was known for his fiery public lectures, many of which he delivered like HUBERT HARRISON, on the corner of 135th Street and LENOX AVENUE in HARLEM. In the years before the founding of the Brotherhood of Sleeping Car Porters, Randolph and Owen organized the United Brotherhood of Elevator and Switchboard Operators.

In 1925 Randolph became one of the cofounders of the Brotherhood of Sleeping Car Porters. It was the first African-American union, and its potential power prompted the Pullman company, the primary employers of the sleeping car porters and maids, to offer Randolph a $10,000 bribe to cease his organizing efforts. Despite opposition from many quarters, including the American Federation of Labor, the labor union was finally recognized. Randolph went on to become the first African-American vice president of the AFL-CIO, the American Federation of Labor and Congress of Industrial Organizations, a formidable consortium of American unions.

Randolph continued to shape American policy and race relations in the decades after the Harlem Renaissance. His plans in 1941 to mobilize 50,000 African Americans for a march on Washington to protest discriminatory practices in the military and in the federal government forced

President Roosevelt to issue executive orders that prohibited discrimination in the defense industry.

In 1948 Randolph's eloquent and tireless campaign against the segregated military culminated in his pledge to become a martyr for the cause. His willingness to suffer imprisonment prompted a recalcitrant President Truman to desegregate the military. In 1963 Randolph was with Martin Luther King, Jr., for the historic March on Washington and witnessed firsthand the stirring "I Have a Dream Speech" that the civil rights leader delivered on the Mall in Washington, D.C., on August 28. In his address to the marchers, Randolph made a stirring declaration: "We are the advance guard of a massive moral revolution for jobs and freedom," he exclaimed before insisting that "[t]his revolution reverberates throughout the land, touching every village where black men are segregated, oppressed, and exploited" (*NYT,* 17 May 1979, A1).

A. Philip Randolph, the winner of the 1942 SPINGARN MEDAL, the most prestigious award given by the NAACP, and the 1964 Presidential Medal of Freedom, passed away in his Manhattan home on May 16, 1979. He was 90 years old. His longtime protégé Bayard Rustin, who at the time was director of the A. Philip Randolph Institute, described his mentor as a man tireless in his dedication to achieving equality and social justice. "No individual did more to help the poor, the dispossessed and the working class in the United States and around the world than A. Philip Randolph," said Rustin. "With the exception of W. E. B. DuBois, he was probably the greatest civil rights leader of this century until Martin Luther King" (*NYT,* 17 May 1979, A1). The National Urban League mourned his passing. President Vernon Jordan honored Randolph as a "noble and dedicated humanitarian" whose "brilliance of . . . mind, magnificence of . . . voice, and his refusal to succumb to pressure, made him a living legend." Shortly after his death, more than 1,500 people gathered to honor Randolph's life and inspiring legacy at a public memorial service at Avery Fisher Hall at Lincoln Center.

Bibliography

Anderson, Jervis. *A. Philip Randolph: A Biographical Portrait.* New York: Harcourt Brace Jovanovich, 1973.

A. Philip Randolph, cofounder and coeditor of *The Messenger (Yale Collection of American Literature, Beinecke Rare Book and Manuscript Library)*

Harris, William. *Keeping the Faith: A. Philip Randolph, Milton P. Webster, and the Brotherhood of Sleeping Car Porters, 1925–1937.* Urbana: University of Illinois Press, 1977.

Pfeffer, Paula. *A. Philip Randolph, Pioneer of the Civil Rights Movement.* Baton Rouge: Louisiana State University Press, 1990.

Wintz, Cary, ed. *African American Political Thought, 1890–1930: Washington, DuBois, Garvey, and Randolph.* Armonk, N.Y.: M. E. Sharpe, 1996.

Rand School of Social Science

The school founded by Carrie Rand and her husband, George Davis Herron. The institution, which in 1917 was established in the Union

Square neighborhood of New York City, received major support from the American Socialist Society.

The school's mission to educate workers reflected the Herron-Rand's political commitment to socialism. Courses focused primarily on economics and history but also included a number of other subject areas. Its faculty included A. PHILIP RANDOLPH and CHANDLER OWEN, the founders of THE MESSENGER, one of the three most widely circulated Harlem Renaissance–era African-American periodicals. Additional faculty included Charles Beard, Mary Beard, George Willis Cooke, and SCOTT NEARING. The writer-poet LANGSTON HUGHES frequently attended lectures at the school during his year at COLUMBIA UNIVERSITY.

The school closed in 1956 due to financial hardships brought on by a sharp decline in enrollment.

Bibliography
Rand School of Social Science. *The Case of the Rand School.* New York: The School, 1919.

Ransom, Birdelle Wycoff (1914–   )

A Texas poet whose work appeared in the southern anthology *Heralding Dawn: An Anthology of Verse* (1936).

Born in Beaumont, Texas, Ransom began publishing her work in the *Houston Informer* following her graduation from the Houston Junior College in 1933. In 1956 Ransom, who completed a thesis on Charles Dickens and social reform, earned a master's degree from Texas Southern University. She was one of six women whom folklorist J. Mason Brewer selected for inclusion in *Heralding Dawn*, his 1936 anthology of African-American Texan poets. Brewer praised her for the "accuracy and skill" with which "her verse portrays in a very vivid manner, race consciousness." Ransom's poem "Night" celebrated the kinship between the poet and the night, a time in which "infinite shade was manifest." Despite the fact that Ransom was part of an important southern Harlem Renaissance literary tradition, she appears to have slipped into obscurity.

Bibliography
Brewer, J. Mason. *Heralding Dawn: An Anthology of Verse.* Dallas, Tex.: Superior Typesetting, 1936.

Rapp, William Jourdan (1895–1942)

Rapp, a white NEW YORK TIMES reporter and editor of *True Story Magazine,* collaborated with WALLACE THURMAN to write and produce an ambitious play about life in Harlem. Rapp and Thurman saw their first collaboration, HARLEM: A MELODRAMA OF NEGRO LIFE, open on BROADWAY's Apollo Theatre on February 20, 1929. A few months later, the play enjoyed a 16-show revival at the Eltinge 42nd Street Theatre. Edward Blatt was the producer for both productions. The two joined forces again to write the three-act play JEREMIAH, THE MAGNIFICENT, a play inspired by the life and ambitions of black nationalist MARCUS GARVEY. *Jeremiah* was not produced until after Thurman's death in 1934.

Rapp, who enjoyed a lifelong friendship with Thurman, went on to write at least three additional plays after *Harlem* was produced. His play *Whirlpool,* directed by Edwin Morse, was produced by the group American Playwrights. The play had only three performances at the Biltmore Theatre on Broadway in early December 1929. In the fall of 1935 *Substitute for Murder* opened and, in December 1936, *The Holmeses of Baker Street* ran for some 53 performances at the Theatre Masque.

Bibliography
van Notten, Eleonore. *Wallace Thurman's Harlem Renaissance.* Amsterdam: Rodopi, 1994.

Rawlings, Marjorie Kinnan (1896–1953)

An accomplished writer who may be best known as the author of *The Yearling* (1938), the PULITZER PRIZE–winning novel about a boy and the deer that he befriends. Rawlings was born in Washington, D.C., and moved to Florida with her husband, Charles Rawlings, in 1928 in an unsuccessful attempt to save their marriage. Rawlings remained in Cross Creek, Florida, and began publishing regularly while supervising the orange grove on the property.

Rawlings met ZORA NEALE HURSTON in Florida shortly after the end of the Harlem Renaissance. The two enjoyed a lively tea at Rawlings's apartment in the segregated hotel that Norton Sanford Baskin, her second husband, owned.

Rawlings struggled with her desire to develop a friendship with the talented writer and the unyielding racism that frowned on such social interaction and equality. The two writers corresponded in the years that followed, and Rawlings facilitated Hurston's introduction to editors at the publishing house of Charles Scribner's Sons, a meeting that ultimately resulted in a book contract and advance for *Seraph on the Suwanee*.

Bibliography

Bellman, Samuel. *Marjorie Kinnan Rawlings*. New York: Twayne Publishers, 1974.

Boyd, Valerie. *Wrapped in Rainbows: The Life of Zora Neale Hurston*. New York: Scribner, 2003.

Kaplan, Carla. *Zora Neale Hurston: A Life in Letters*. New York: Doubleday, 2002.

Silverthorne, Elizabeth. *Marjorie Kinnan Rawlings: Sojourner at Cross Creek*. Woodstock, N.Y.: Overlook, 1988.

"Red Cape, The" Gertrude Schalk (1929)

A compelling short story by GERTRUDE SCHALK about the frailty of love and the awful effects of mistrust and impatience. Published in the 1929 annual issue of the SATURDAY EVENING QUILL, "The Red Cape" features Peter, a newlywed sailor who has been away from his bride for six months. He and his wife had only three months together before he joined a crew and mission that took him to sea. Peter is anxious to see his wife and his honorable, romantic feelings about her are in sharp contrast to the more callous sentiments of his shipmates who plan to get drunk and head to the brothel closest to the pier. When he alights, Peter sees a woman swathed in a red cape running into town. Unfortunately, he does not realize that she is running past the cemetery near the ocean and thinks instead that she is hurrying away from the brothel. Assuming the worst, he hurries home and in a dreadfully unfortunate conversation filled with inferences rather than direct statements, accuses her of being unfaithful. She thinks that someone has told him about the tragedy that has befallen him and, in her distress, fails to realize that he is talking about her alleged infidelity.

Peter storms out of the house and secures a two-year tour on a ship called the *Beacon*. Mean-

while, his wife, whom a motherly neighbor is unable to console, goes back to the Baptist cemetery on Sea Street. There, she "stared with agonized eyes at the head-stone. Peter Jr. Born April 15, 1928. Died April 30, 1928." The story ends as the young devastated wife falls "violently . . . on the damp grave and her red cape fluttered defiantly to the breeze." The story's setting, intense emotional plot, and vivid imagery made it one of the most riveting works in the *Saturday Evening Quill*.

Redding, Jay Saunders (1906–1988)

The first African American to join the faculty at an Ivy League College, Redding was a gifted teacher, editor, and writer. Born in Wilmington, Delaware, he was the third of seven children of Lewis and Mary Ann Holmes Redding, a HOWARD UNIVERSITY graduate and former schoolteacher. His father, also a Howard University graduate, was a postal employee and secretary of the local chapter of the NATIONAL ASSOCIATION FOR THE ADVANCEMENT OF COLORED PEOPLE. Lewis Redding was an industrious man committed to racial uplift, and it was he who established the first YOUNG MEN'S CHRISTIAN ASSOCIATION for African Americans in Wilmington. In 1929 he married Esther James, a teacher from Newark, Delaware, and the couple had two sons, Conway and Lewis.

Redding began his college studies at LINCOLN UNIVERSITY, the alma mater of WARING CUNEY, LANGSTON HUGHES, KWAME NKRUMAH, the first president of Ghana, and Thurgood Marshall, the first African-American Supreme Court justice. He went on to complete his undergraduate degree at BROWN UNIVERSITY, the alma mater of his brother Louis, who went on to become the first African-American lawyer in the state of Delaware. After earning a bachelor of philosophy, Redding completed a master's degree from Brown in 1926 that also earned him membership in PHI BETA KAPPA. He started teaching at MOREHOUSE COLLEGE in Atlanta, Georgia, in 1926 following his graduation from Brown. Subsequent teaching posts included as department head at Southern University in Baton Rouge, Louisiana, and at State Teachers College in Elizabeth City, North Carolina, and an endowed chair as the James

Weldon Johnson Professor of Literature and Creative Writing at Hampton Institute. In 1949 the two-time GUGGENHEIM FELLOWSHIP winner returned to Brown and became the first professor of color to teach at an Ivy League institution. In 1970 he joined the faculty at Cornell University in Ithaca, New York. He was the first African-American professor in the university's College of Arts and Sciences.

Redding published "Delaware Coon," his first short story, in the *Brown University Quarterly* in December 1928. His first book appeared just as the Harlem Renaissance was coming to a close. TO MAKE A POET BLACK (1939) was a work of literary criticism that examined the evolution of the African-American literary tradition. In the years that followed, Redding secured a reputation for excellent scholarship. Later works included *No Day of Triumph* (1942), a study of African-American life in the South, his only novel, *Stranger and Alone* (1950), and *They Came in Chains: Americans from Africa* (1950), a comprehensive history of people of African descent in America. He published 10 books, book reviews for the Baltimore *Afro-American,* and numerous articles that appeared in prestigious periodicals such as the *Atlantic Monthly* and *Phylon.*

Redding received an impressive number of academic and professional honors during his lengthy career. He was a Rockefeller and Ford Foundation fellow, the winner of two Guggenheim fellowships, and the winner of the 1950 NATIONAL URBAN LEAGUE Citation for Outstanding Achievement. Several colleges and universities bestowed honorary degrees upon him, including Brown University, Dickinson College, Wittenberg University, Hobart College, and Virginia State College.

Redding died in Ithaca, New York, in March 1988.

Bibliography

Berry, Faith, ed. *A Scholar's Conscience: Selected Writings of J. Saunders Redding, 1942–1977.* Lexington: University Press of Kentucky, 1992.

Fraser, C. Gerald. "J. Saunders Redding, 81, Is Dead; Pioneer Black Ivy League Teacher." New York Times. 5 March 1988: 33.

Redding, J. Saunders. *To Make a Poet Black.* Chapel Hill: University of North Carolina Press, 1939.

Red Scare

The phrase that describes the period in which the U.S. government targeted communists in America, challenged labor unions, and intimidated liberal constituencies. Woodrow Wilson appointed A. Mitchell Palmer to the post of attorney general in 1919, and it was he who established the Federal Bureau of Investigation (FBI). Palmer also appointed J. Edgar Hoover as FBI director. Hoover used the organization to gather information about Americans whose actions and politics were deemed to be radical. Among the many targeted were Jane Addams and Charles Beard.

During the Harlem Renaissance period, there were deportations to Russia, unsanctioned home invasions, and arrests made without warrants or charges filed. In 1920, some 6,000 individuals were arrested and jailed and denied access to counsel.

The Red Scare was prompted in part by fears of communism and the possibility that communists emboldened by the revolution in Russia were plotting to overthrow the U.S. government. It also was shaped by the massive labor movement that in 1919 saw more than 3,000 strikes nationwide.

In 1950 Wisconsin senator Joseph McCarthy revived the Red Scare when he began a ruthless campaign against communism and communists and their supporters in America.

Bibliography

Kornweibel, Theodore. *Seeing Red: Federal Campaigns Against Black Militancy, 1919–1925.* Bloomington: Indiana University Press, 1998.

Landis, Mark. *Joseph McCarthy: The Politics of Chaos.* Selinsgrove, Pa.: Susquehanna University Press, 1987.

Schmidt, Regin. *Red Scare: FBI and the Origins of Anti-Communism in the United States, 1919–1943.* Copenhagen: Museum Tusculanum Press, University of Copenhagen, 2000.

Woods, Jeff. *Black Struggle, Red Scare: Segregation and Anti-Communism in the South, 1948–1968.* Baton Rouge: Louisiana State University, 2004.

Red Summer of 1919

The phrase that refers to the violent summer of 1919 in which some 26 race riots occurred in major cities throughout the United States. The violence was prompted in large part by the return of African-American veterans from World War I. Evidence of African-American patriotism and entrepreneurship, coupled with increasingly outspoken calls for racial justice, prompted many whites to resent African-American success and potential. In addition, the violence was prompted by white workers who resented what they regarded as black encroachment on their jobs. The Great Migration period, which resulted in thousands of African Americans relocating from the South to the North, intensified competition for jobs and housing. Violent race riots ensued.

Cities such as Baltimore, CHICAGO, Houston, Little Rock, New Orleans, NEW YORK, and WASHINGTON, D.C., all saw major rioting and civil disobedience during the summer of 1919. Riots began with individual acts of violence such as the stoning of Eugene Williams in Chicago as he tried to swim ashore at the 29th Street Beach. When police refused to arrest the murderer, five days of rioting ensued. Some 38 people died, and nearly 300 were wounded. In Elaine, Arkansas, African-American sharecroppers were attacked by some 1,000 white men and army soldiers after they protested unfair compensation by plantation owners for their crops. According to Grif Stockley, the African-American death toll during the brutal massacre that historian David Levering Lewis has characterized as an incident of "collective barbarism" may have been as high as 856.

The Red Summer of 1919 was not the only period of sustained and widespread violence during the Harlem Renaissance period. Two years later, the Tulsa Race Riot left between 300 and 3,000 African Americans dead and 7,800 homeless, and more than 600 African-American businesses in ruins. The cohesive and prosperous Tulsa community known as Black Wall Street was ransacked, bombed by air, and dynamited by whites.

Bibliography

Stockley, Grif. *Blood in Their Eyes: The Elaine Race Massacres of 1919.* Fayetteville: University of Arkansas, 2001.

Tuttle, William Jr. *Race Riot: Chicago in the Red Summer of 1919.* Urbana: University of Illinois Press, 1996.

Williams, Lee, and Lee Williams, II. *Anatomy of Four Race Riots: Racial Conflict in Knoxville, Elaine (Arkansas),* *Tulsa, and Chicago, 1919–1921.* Hattiesburg: University and College Press of Mississippi, 1972.

Reid, Ira De Augustine (1901–1968)

An eminent sociologist, educator, veteran, Quaker, activist, and OPPORTUNITY editor known for his invaluable research on African-American life and experience. Born in Clifton Forge, Virginia, Reid was the son of Daniel Augustine, a Baptist minister, and his wife, Willie Roberta James Reid. He married Gladys Russell Scott in the fall of 1925. They adopted a daughter, Enid Harriet. In 1958, two years after his wife Gladys passed away, Reid married Anne Cooke. He died in Bryn Mawr, Pennsylvania, of emphysema in the fall of 1968.

He spent most of his childhood in Harrisburg and PHILADELPHIA, Pennsylvania. When his father was transferred to Savannah, Georgia, during Reid's high school years, Reid attended Morehouse Academy in ATLANTA, the only Georgia high school available to African Americans. He returned to Atlanta after his World War I military service. He attended MOREHOUSE COLLEGE at the urging of its president, JOHN HOPE, and graduated in 1922. He hoped to pursue additional studies at the UNIVERSITY OF CHICAGO but attended only briefly before returning home to his family, who by then were living in West Virginia. He eventually resumed master's degree studies at the University of Pittsburgh and in 1925 received his degree in sociology. In 1939 he earned his Ph.D. in sociology from COLUMBIA UNIVERSITY. That year, as a JULIUS ROSENWALD FELLOWSHIP winner, he traveled to England and studied at the London School of Economics.

Reid's affiliation with the NATIONAL URBAN LEAGUE began in 1924 when he won a fellowship from the Pittsburgh Urban League. He then joined the staff of the New York Urban League as an industrial secretary. In 1928 Reid, whose research had been published in *Opportunity,* the official Urban League publication, succeeded CHARLES S. JOHNSON, with whom he had worked closely as a research assistant, as research director and *Opportunity* editor. Reid held the position until 1934, when he joined the faculty at ATLANTA UNIVERSITY, where he later became head of the sociology department and editor of the Atlanta University–based scholarly journal *Phylon: The Atlanta University Review of Race and Culture.*

Reid's publications during the Harlem Renaissance included a number of works on African Americans, labor, education, and family life. He published studies such as *Negro Membership in American Labor Unions* (1930), *The Problem of Child Dependency Among Negroes* (1936), *Adult Education Among Negroes* (1936), and *The Urban Negro Worker in the United States, 1925–1936* (1938).

Bibliography

Moore, Jesse Thomas, Jr. *A Search for Equality: The National Urban League, 1910–1961.* University Park: Pennsylvania State University Press, 1981.

Parris, Guichard, and Lester Brooks. *Blacks in the City: A History of the National Urban League.* Boston: Little, Brown, 1971.

Weiss, Nancy. *The National Urban League, 1910–1940.* New York: Oxford University Press, 1974.

Reinhardt, Max (1873–1943)

An Austrian writer and director who founded the Salzburg Theatre Festival and directed and produced more than 500 plays during his lifetime. Billed as a "prophet in the theater" who had a "pronounced 'sixth sense' with respect to drama," he spoke to ALAIN LOCKE about the future of African-American theater. Locke was committed to facilitating a viable and sustainable African-American theater tradition. While at HOWARD UNIVERSITY, he had collaborated with the inspired drama professor T. Montgomery Gregory and inaugurated the HOWARD UNIVERSITY PLAYERS, the university's first theater troupe and a nationally respected amateur company.

Locke's interview with Reinhardt appeared in the May 1924 issue of OPPORTUNITY. The piece, entitled "Max Reinhardt Reads the Negro's Dramatic Horoscope," included what Locke believed readers would regard as "penetrating and quite prophetic observations." In response to Locke's questions about the damage that exploitation wreaked upon African-American actors and theatrical projects, Reinhardt insisted that African Americans "must not even try to link up to the dramas of the past, to the European drama. That is why there is no American drama as yet," he pronounced before making the bold assertion that "if there is to be [an American drama], it will be yours." Reinhardt's assertion echoed the sentiments of leading Harlem Renaissance figures such as Locke,

Gregory, W. E. B. DuBois, and the visionary playwrights of the period such as GEORGIA DOUGLAS JOHNSON, ANGELINA WELD GRIMKÉ, and WILLIS RICHARDSON. The KRIGWA LITTLE THEATRE movement and the founding of small theater companies such as LANGSTON HUGHES's Little Suitcase Theatre provided playwrights with opportunities to explore African-American folk material and to generate scripts that grappled with other absorbing aspects of American society and human experience.

Bibliography

Brown-Guillory, Elizabeth. *Their Place on the Stage: Black Women Playwrights in America.* New York: Greenwood Press, 1988.

Hay, Samuel. *African American Theatre: A Historical and Critical Analysis.* Cambridge: Cambridge University Press, 1994.

Hill, Errol. *A History of African American Theatre.* Cambridge: Cambridge University Press, 2003.

Manuel, Carme. "Mule Bone: Langston Hughes and Zora Neale Hurston's Dream Deferred of an African American Theatre of the Black Word," *African American Review* (2001).

Reinhardt, Gottfried. *The Genius: A Memoir of Max Reinhardt.* New York: Knopf, 1979.

Styan, J. L. *Max Reinhardt.* Cambridge: Cambridge University Press, 1982.

Reiss, Winold (1886–1953)

A Bavarian painter who immigrated to the United States with the intention that he would paint Native Americans. Reiss's love of portraiture prompted him to engage many potential subjects in NEW YORK CITY, and he soon became an artist well known for his sketches of ethnic peoples.

The son of Fritz Reiss, a landscape painter, he went on to study with the German artist Franz von Stuck. He groomed himself as a portrait painter in Sweden, Holland, and Germany where he painted different groups of folk peoples. He emigrated to the United States in 1913 and supported himself by working as an interior designer and commercial artist. He was celebrated for his art designs in hotels, restaurants, shops, and other public venues. He later immersed himself in Native American art, forging a professional relationship with the Blackfeet Indians in Montana. Reiss established his own school at

Glacier Park in Montana and between 1934 and 1937 offered art classes there during the summer.

The historic March 1925 SURVEY GRAPHIC issue that was devoted to Harlem and African-American issues featured artwork by Reiss. In his editorial comments, guest editor ALAIN LOCKE noted that the images offered "a graphic interpretation of Negro life, freshly conceived after its own patterns" (Locke, 651). Locke also praised Reiss as a "folk-lorist of the brush and palette, seeking always the folk character back of the individual, the psychology behind the physiognomy" (Locke, 653). Reiss also produced a series of drawings of Harlem Renaissance personalities including Locke, COUNTEE CULLEN, and W. E. B. DuBOIS.

Bibliography

Locke, Alain. "Harlem Types: Portraits by Winold Reiss," *Survey Graphic* (March 1925): 651–654.

Stewart, Jeffrey. *To Color America: Portraits by Winold Reiss.* Washington, D.C.: Smithsonian Institution Press, 1989.

———. *Winold Reiss: An Illustrated Checklist of His Portraits.* Washington, D.C.: National Portrait Gallery, 1990.

Renaissance Ballroom

The ballroom located in the Renaissance Casino located at 133rd Street and Seventh Avenue. The African-American-owned business also included a casino and film auditorium. In 1923 the Sares Realty Company agreed to transform the ballroom into a basketball arena for the Spartan Braves, an African-American team. Renamed the Renaissance Big Five, the team became the first professional basketball team with an African-American owner and players.

Bibliography

Thurman, Wallace. *Negro Life in New York's Harlem: A Lively Picture of a Popular and Interesting Section.* Haldeman-Julius Quarterly, 2, no. 1 (October–November–December 1927).

"Replica"   Eunice Hunton Carter   (1924)

An intriguing vignette by EUNICE HUNTON CARTER and one of the four stories that she published in OPPORTUNITY during the Harlem Renaissance. "Replica" appeared in the September 1924 issue under the name Eunice Roberta Hunton, which she continued to use after her 1924 marriage. The issue also included poems by COUNTEE CULLEN and articles on French colonial policy by ALAIN LOCKE and RENÉ MARAN.

The vignette focuses on a summer gathering in Georgia on a blisteringly hot day. Despite the "hot and languid" breezes and the "angry red dust" that conspires to "settle back heavily on all who dared the road," the members of the large unidentified party gather to celebrate a holiday. The scene is enlivened by Carter's vivid descriptions. In addition to enticing details about the "food of the great Negro South," she provides evocative profiles of the range of people gathered under "the cool shadow of the mammoth trees." Included are "romping children" and "slim brown girls whose comely bodies stood silhouetted as streaks of light pierced thin and clinging garments." The events suddenly take a turn, however, when a compelling drumbeat begins to emanate from the nearby grove. Within moments, a striking female elder emerges. This unnamed woman, described as "a weird figure," is "burnt black with the suns of many summers and worn thin with the burdens of years." Despite her unusual appearance and advanced age, however, the woman is able to captivate the audience before her. Soon after she begins to dance with "astounding agility and abandon," a young, barefooted girl joins her. The two women dance un-self-consciously, and the gestures of the younger woman transform the moment into a scene of seduction. The narrator notes that "the dusky mane of her hair tumbled down, her full red lips drooped slightly apart, the swell of her ripe young breasts rose and fell with drumbeat after drumbeat, and the youths in the circle watched spellbound." The story ends as the women in the crowd rush to dance, "throwing away restraint" and prompting the mass dance to "increas[e] in abandon and barbarity as the minutes slipped away." The story credits memories of a long-lost African past for the enthusiastic response. The women, it appears, are overcome by a collective "memory of jungle nights, of stagnant heat, of prowling beasts, of glowing fires, of the tom tom's pulsing beat, of naked bodies gleaming in the firelight, dancing, dancing, dancing, and the strong black arms of a belted chief."

Hunton's story anticipates the powerful imagery of the poem "Heritage" by Countee Cullen, a poem in which a contemplative narrator wonders "What is Africa to me?" and considers the African myths and American realities that define his identity. The piece also builds on memorable Harlem Renaissance–era profiles of African-American life and examples of local-color writing. This piece appeared just one year after celebrated works such as CANE (1923) by JEAN TOOMER, for instance. "Replica" is powerful for Hunton's focused efforts to grapple with the liberatory implications of African-American links to a powerful, demonstrative African past.

"Return of a Modern Prodigal, The"
Octavia Wynbush (1937)

One of several short stories that OCTAVIA WYNBUSH published in THE CRISIS during the Harlem Renaissance. Wynbush adapted, but dramatically revised, the biblical parable of the prodigal son.

The story opens as the protagonist, Slim Sawyer, makes his way home to the South. Some 25 years earlier, he succumbed to the call of the road and simply abandoned his mother and father and their simple way of life. His experiences in the urban North recall the dissolution in Paul Laurence Dunbar's seminal novel *Sport of the Gods* (1901). Slim falls prey to the common vices of the street and in a drunken stupor allegedly kills a man. Imprisoned for almost a decade, he is finally freed, and after a year of "trying to lose the prison traces," he begins his journey home.

His reunion with his parents does not proceed as he had hoped. He assumes a false identity, and although he recognizes his mother, she does not recognize him. Mrs. Sawyer offers him her son's room and prepares to host the gentleman who is stopping with them for a night. Mr. Sawyer may realize that the visitor is his son but does not make this assertion. When the three talk generally about why the Sawyer son disappeared and what may explain his silence after 25 years, Slim comes to believe that he will only bring shame upon his parents if he reveals his identity and sordid past. He leaves again without saying good-bye but encloses $1,000 in a short note to the mother whom he will not acknowledge plainly.

Wynbush's story considers the implications of migration, the dangers of urban life, and the nature of southern family dynamics.

Reynolds, Evelyn Crawford (1900–unknown)

A reporter, teacher, poet, and member of the PHILADELPHIA literary circle during the Harlem Renaissance who published the first of her three collections of poetry during the Harlem Renaissance period.

Reynolds, who married Hobson Richmond Reynolds in December 1927, was active in the Philadelphia community. She contributed regular columns to the PITTSBURGH COURIER that detailed current social and cultural events of interest to the African-American community. Under the pseudonym Eve Lynn, she documented social events and visits by prominent people to the city, and she commented on fashion trends of the day.

Reynolds published NO ALABASTER BOX, a volume of poems, in 1936. The Alpress Company of Philadelphia produced 350 copies of the work that contained poems on traditional themes such as nature and love. Her next volume, *To No Special Land: A Book of Poems* (1953) was published 17 years later and included an introduction by MARY MCLEOD BETHUNE. Her third and final work, *Put a Daisy in Your Hair,* appeared in 1953 and featured an introduction by the celebrated diva MARIAN ANDERSON.

Reynolds, a member of the Beaux Arts Club, was part of the Harlem Renaissance literary and arts circle that included BESSIE CALHOUN BIRD, MAE COWDERY, and OTTIE BEATRICE GRAHAM. Her marriage to Hobson Reynolds catapulted her into prominent social circles and into the local spotlight. A mortician by profession, Hobson became an influential state legislator and magistrate.

Bibliography
Jubilee, Vincent. *Philadelphia's Afro-American Literary Circle and the Harlem Renaissance.* Ann Arbor, Mich.: University Microfilms, 1982.

Reynolds, Evelyn Crawford. *No Alabaster Box.* Philadelphia: Alpress, 1936.

Rhodes Scholarship

The prestigious academic scholarship established and named after Cecil Rhodes, the white British businessman, founder of the De Beers Consolidate Mines, imperialist, and Oxford University graduate for whom the African nation Rhodesia (present-day Zimbabwe) was renamed.

The awards, established in 1902, provide winners with two or three years of study at Oxford University. Applicants are selected from the United States, Commonwealth Caribbean nations, and select African and European nations. The fellows are chosen on the basis of several criteria, including academic achievement, character, and leadership qualities.

In 1907, HARVARD UNIVERSITY graduate ALAIN LOCKE became the first African-American to be awarded a Rhodes Scholarship. His intellectual achievements, however, did not prevent a number of the Oxford Colleges from refusing to admit him because of his race. He finally gained admission to Hertford College and during his fellowship years studied Greek, Latin, literature, and philosophy. Locke was the only African-American to win the award until 1960.

Bibliography

Elton, Godfrey. *The First Fifty Years of the Rhodes Trust and the Rhodes Scholarships, 1903–1953*. Oxford: Blackwell, 1955.

Schaeper, Thomas, and Kathleen Schaeper. *Cowboys Into Gentlemen: Rhodes Scholars, Oxford, and the Creation of an American Elite*. New York: Berghahn Books, 1998.

Thomas, Antony. *Rhodes*. New York: St. Martin's Press, 1997.

Rice, Albert (1903–unknown)

A WASHINGTON, D.C., poet who thoroughly enjoyed his access to the literary salons hosted by fellow Washingtonian GEORGIA DOUGLAS JOHNSON. Rice lived in the nation's capital until he graduated from the renowned DUNBAR HIGH SCHOOL. After a brief and unsatisfying stint as a civil servant in Washington, D.C., he relocated to NEW YORK CITY in 1926. That same year, his work appeared in the African-American issue of *PALMS*, a literary journal that had published established writers such as D. H. Lawrence and Mabel Dodge Luhan. Rice's poem "Black Madonna" appeared alongside works by LEWIS ALEXANDER, W. E. B. DUBOIS, JESSIE FAUSET, HELENE JOHNSON, ALAIN LOCKE, ANNE SPENCER, and others.

The primary source of information about Rice's evolution as a poet and his participation in the Harlem Renaissance is his forthright autobiographical statement in COUNTEE CULLEN's 1927 anthology, *CAROLING DUSK: AN ANTHOLOGY OF VERSE BY NEGRO POETS*.

According to Rice, once in New York, he "served an apprenticeship in literary vagabondage with the bizarre and eccentric young vagabond poet of High Harlem, Richard Bruce." Rice was a self-confessed fan of CLAUDE MCKAY and his "favorite poet." He "abhor[red] all things Anglo-Saxon" and "love[ed] New York because it is crowded and noisy and an outpost of Europe."

Caroling Dusk, which included illustrations by AARON DOUGLAS, featured two poems by Rice, the previously published poem "The Black Madonna" and "To a Certain Woman." The first was inspired by a church visit in which Rice, "lost in contemplation before Our Lady" at St. Mary's the Virgin, "thought of a Madonna of swart skin, a Madonna of dark mien." The 24-line poem with three-line verses suggested a particular kinship between the Holy Mother and the worshipper at her feet. "Not as the white nations / know thee / O Mother!" initiated Rice's reclamation of the Madonna as the embodiment of white womanhood. The second poem, "To a Certain Woman" was a celebration of multiethnic womanhood. The narrator's enthusiastic compliments to the woman before him prompted thoughts of "Black diamonds / Of Hindustan / Figure silks / Of Lahore / Scarlet flames / Of Fuji-Yama." The poem turned into a set of unfortunate realizations, however, about the woman's poisonous vows, kisses, and deceits.

Bibliography

Cullen, Countee. *Caroling Dusk: An Anthology of Verse by Negro Poets*. 1927, reprint, New York: Harper & Row, 1968.

Wirth, Thomas. *Gay Rebel of the Harlem Renaissance: Selections from the Work of Richard Bruce Nugent*. Durham: Duke University Press, 2002.

Richardson, Willis (1889–1977)

A talented and pioneering playwright who became the first African-American dramatist to see his work performed on BROADWAY. A native of Wilmington, North Carolina, he was the son of Willis and Agnes Harper Richardson. The family left North Carolina following the violent Wilmington Riots in 1898. In 1906 Richardson began attending the M STREET HIGH SCHOOL in WASHINGTON, D.C. There, he excelled in academics and in sports. In addition to being a champion marksman among students at segregated African-American schools and the captain of the football team, he also demonstrated his gifts as a writer. Playwright MARY BURRILL, his English teacher, and ANGELINA GRIMKÉ, also on the faculty, thought that his work was promising and worthy of publication, and they encouraged him to continue developing his talents.

Richardson earned a scholarship to HOWARD UNIVERSITY but was unable to accept it because of his family's financial needs. He began working immediately following high school in order to supplement his family's income, securing jobs in the Library of Congress and at the Bureau of Engraving and Printing. In 1916, while working full time, he began two years of correspondence courses in poetry and drama with the Springfield, Massachusetts–based Home Correspondence School. In 1914 Richardson married Mary Jones of Washington, D.C., whom he met when they both were working at the Bureau of Engraving and Printing. The couple had two daughters, Jean and Shirley, and one son, Noel.

Richardson, whose teachers wholeheartedly exhorted him to write, was inspired to immerse himself in the world of drama when he witnessed the 1916 Washington, D.C., debut of RACHEL, Angelina Grimké's powerful antilynching play. He was an active member of the literary salon that poet and playwright GEORGIA DOUGLAS JOHNSON hosted in her Washington, D.C., home. During his successful career, Richardson would become a nationally known playwright and respected essayist. In 1920 and 1921 he published his first plays in THE BROWNIE'S BOOK, the groundbreaking monthly magazine for children of color that JESSIE FAUSET and W. E. B. DUBOIS produced under the auspices of THE CRISIS and the NATIONAL ASSOCIATION FOR THE ADVANCEMENT OF COLORED PEOPLE. The works were both accessible to young readers and were historically grounded and politically forthright about the hardships brought on by poverty and enslavement. *The King's Dilemma* (1920), his first *Brownie's Book* play, was staged some six years later in Washington, D.C. Additional plays for children included *The Children's Treasure*, a work in which children band together to raise money enough to save an elderly lady from eviction. Richardson's plays appeared in THE CRISIS, THE MESSENGER, and OPPORTUNITY, and they were performed by such talented troupes as the ETHIOPIAN ART PLAYERS, the Gilpin Players, and the HOWARD UNIVERSITY PLAYERS. For example, his first play for adult audiences, THE DEACON'S AWAKENING, was published in the November 1920 issue of *The Crisis* and was promptly prepared for the stage by the St. Paul Players based in Minnesota.

In 1923, Richardson made history when his play THE CHIP WOMAN'S FORTUNE opened on Broadway. One week after opening first at the LAFAYETTE THEATRE in HARLEM, the play opened at the Frazee Theatre on Broadway in May 1923. It was the first nonmusical drama by an African-American to be featured on Broadway. Richardson's works contributed much to the growing African-American theater movement and provided good material to up-and-coming troupes such as the KRIGWA PLAYERS and the Howard University Players. In 1924 Richardson became the first African-American playwright to see his work performed at Howard University by the Howard University Players. The respected school troupe that drama professor THOMAS MONTGOMERY GREGORY founded in 1919 staged Richardson's play MORTGAGED, a compelling play about two brothers and their different perspectives on material and professional success. Six years later, Richardson's play won fourth place in a drama competition when it was performed by the Dunbar Dramatic Club of Plainfield, New Jersey (Perry, 239). In 1925 ALAIN LOCKE selected *Mortgaged* for inclusion in THE NEW NEGRO, his landmark anthology of writings by and about African Americans.

Richardson developed a reputation for his insightful domestic dramas, plays that examined recognizable everyday families of color. His characters ranged from middle-class northerners, who worked to preserve their domestic stability and grappled with their desires to advance, to southern families persecuted by 19th-century enslavement and by

20th-century mob rule and the threat of lynching. Richardson also developed an absorbing set of mythical, historical, and biblical plays that celebrated the accomplishments and explored the examples of powerful and privileged figures. These included *The King's Dilemma,* set in "The Future," *The Last Kingdom of the World, Antonio Maceo,* and *Attucks the Martyr,* inspired by the life of Crispus Attucks, the first man to fall in the Boston skirmish that provoked the American Revolution. Richardson also contributed to the efforts to generate a substantial and visible African-American theater tradition. Like fellow Washingtonians T. Montgomery Gregory and Alain Locke, he published collections of plays, including PLAYS AND PAGEANTS FROM THE LIFE OF THE NEGRO (1930). He was initially prompted to compile the volume by CARTER G. WOODSON, the established historian with whom he unofficially coedited the work. Five years later, he coedited NEGRO HISTORY IN THIRTEEN PLAYS (1935) with MAY MILLER SULLIVAN.

Richardson, who remained based in Washington, D.C., participated fully in the Harlem Renaissance movement and sought out opportunities to showcase his work. He participated in the literary contests sponsored by *Opportunity* and by *The Crisis.* He submitted a play for consideration in the first *Opportunity* literary contest, held in 1924. Judges T. Montgomery Gregory, Alexander Woollcott, Robert C. Benchley, and Edith Isaacs awarded his play *Fall of the Conjurer* the second honorable mention in the competition that saw the first four prizes go to G. D. Lipscomb, Warren McDonald, ZORA NEALE HURSTON, and May Miller. Undeterred, Richardson entered the upcoming *Crisis* competition for 1925, which would give awards to some 15 writers. On this occasion, judges EUGENE O'NEILL, Charles Burroughs, and Lester Walton awarded Richardson first prize for THE BROKEN BANJO. The second and third prizes went to RUTH GAINES-SHELTON and to MYRTLE SMITH LIVINGSTON, respectively. The following year, Richardson's play *Boot-Black Lover* edged out works by EULALIE SPENCE and RANDOLPH EDMONDS and won first place in the 1926 *Crisis* literary contest. Richardson received his prize, also referred to as the Amy Spingarn Prize for Negro Literature and Art in honor of the philanthropist who funded the awards, from W. E. B. DuBois, editor of *The Crisis,* at the International House in New York City in October.

Richardson, although an exemplary playwright, combined his playwriting career with his full-time job at the Bureau of Engraving, where he was employed until he retired in 1955. He maintained his membership in the NATIONAL ASSOCIATION FOR THE ADVANCEMENT OF COLORED PEOPLE (NAACP) and in the NATIONAL URBAN LEAGUE. The NAACP awarded Richardson a Spingarn prize in 1925 and 1926 for two of his dramatic works, *The Broken Banjo* and *Boot-Black Lover,* respectively. He was wholeheartedly devoted to the advancement of African-American theater, which he saw as a powerful vehicle by which writers could educate, challenge, and invigorate audiences in general and African-American communities in particular. Richardson's passion for theater, which was unwavering during his lifetime, was evident when he was just beginning his career. As he confessed in a letter to his longtime colleague T. Montgomery Gregory in 1922, "Negro drama has been, next to my wife and children, the very hope of my life" (Martin, 1). His works have benefited from recent republication and have enjoyed a modest set of contemporary productions such as the Black Theater Alliance Festival show of *The Chip Woman's Fortune* at the Brooklyn Academy of Music in the fall of 1973. Richardson's work was part of the popular three-week festival hosted by a group of African-American theaters in New York City that functioned as "vital grass-roots community centers" and, in addition to producing plays, offered a variety of drama instruction and workshops (*NYT,* 17 November 1973). Such events underscore the lasting power of Richardson's lifelong mission to make theater an integral part of American community life.

Bibliography
Gray, Christine Rauchfuss. *Willis Richardson, Forgotten Pioneer of African-American Drama.* Westport, Conn.: Greenwood Press, 1999.
Martin, George-McKinley. "Willis Richardson." Available online. URL:http://www.dclibrary.org/blkren/bios/richardsonw.html. Accessed June 28, 2005.

"Rich Man, Poor Man" Anita Scott Coleman (1920)
One of three short stories that ANITA SCOTT COLEMAN published in the CHICAGO-based THE

HALF-CENTURY magazine edited by Katherine Williams Irvin. "Rich Man, Poor Man," which appeared in the May 1920 issue of *The Half Century*, addressed African-American domesticity and the consequences that racism had on African-American employment and families.

The protagonist, Drusilla, is determined to marry a man who can provide for her. She falls in love with John Condon. A baker by trade, Condon is a good prospect, but he is unable to secure employment because of his race. When he falls ill, Drusilla is forced to revisit her pledge not to work for any man. To meet their debts and to generate some income during John's illness, Drusilla begins to sell her fine clothes. In spite of the contemporary belief that a woman of color can always find work while a man of color cannot, Drusilla is determined that she will not become the primary or sole provider for her family. Invested in the reality and promise of black masculinity, Drusilla prevails and maintains her pledge to share, but not assume, domestic responsibilities.

The story's focus on African-American womanhood, marriage, and family complemented other works that Coleman published in *The Half-Century*, THE CRISIS, and OPPORTUNITY.

Rideout, Ransom (unknown)

The playwright and screenwriter known best for his 1928 play GOIN' HOME, a play about World War I soldiers in FRANCE. *Goin' Home*, which opened on BROADWAY in 1928 at the Hudson Theatre, gave him the opportunity to work with producer Brock Pemberton. One year later, in 1929, Rideout was involved in the making of *Hallelujah*, the major African-American Hollywood musical production directed by King Vidor. Other Rideout works include the play *Boots* (1924) which opened at the Pasadena Playhouse in May 1924.

Rider of Dreams, The Ridgely Torrence (1917)

One of three plays by the white poet, writer, and NEW REPUBLIC editor RIDGELY TORRENCE that were created expressly for "a Negro Theatre." The plays in the collection, published by Macmillan in 1917, included *The Rider of Dreams*, GRANNY MAUMEE, and SIMON THE CYRENIAN. The accom-

plished performer PAUL ROBESON made his stage debut in the last. The three plays, which focused on African-American life and were tailored to African-American casts, positively influenced the national effort to constitute an African-American theater movement.

The Rider of Dreams opened in early April at the Garden Theatre. In mid-April, the production was relocated to the Garrick Theatre. As producer of the three plays, the philanthropist and theater enthusiast EMILIE HAPGOOD invested thousands of dollars in the shows. The troupe that performed Torrence's work included Inez Clough and Opal Cooper and was referred to as the EMILIE HAPGOOD PLAYERS.

The one-act play, written in dialect, revolves around the Sparrow family of Lucy, Madison, and Booker. Lucy, a God-fearing woman and hardworking washerwoman, does her best to inculcate spiritual awareness in her son, Booker, and to rein in the reckless schemes of her husband, Madison. Madison returns home one evening with a guitar and with plans to go into business with a wily friend. Lucy soon finds out not only that the guitar is stolen but also that her husband and his friend have forged her signature and withdrawn the hard-earned savings that she has amassed over 12 years. In the mayhem that ensues when Madison discovers that he has lost the money, their neighbor Uncle Wilson stops by on the pretense of buying one of their appliances. As the play ensues, the neighbor finally reveals that he is the rightful owner of the guitar and that he retrieved the money from Madison when he accidentally dropped it. Uncle Wilson, the owner of the Sparrows' cottage, intervenes, restores Lucy's dream of purchasing the house, and challenges Madison to use the guitar to advance his dreams and to provide for his wife and child. The play closes as Madison bemoans the fact that he is always subject to other people's directions and unable to indulge himself in his own dreams.

The play's focus on domesticity provided a traditional, even stereotypical view of African-American men. Torrence's play was deemed of value, however, because it offered a substantial, rather than comedic and caricatured, presentation of African-American life.

Bibliography

Clum, John. *Ridgely Torrence*. New York: Twayne, 1972.

Ridgely Torrence Papers, Rare Books and Special Collections, Princeton University Library.

Torrence, Ridgely. *Granny Maumee, The Rider of Dreams, Simon the Cyrenian: Plays for a Negro Theatre*. New York: The Macmillan Company, 1917.

Riding the Goat May Miller (1929)

A one-act play by MAY MILLER SULLIVAN that was selected for inclusion in the WILLIS RICHARDSON anthology PLAYS AND PAGEANTS FROM THE LIFE OF THE NEGRO (1930). Sullivan, who published the play as May Miller, adapted the work so that it was appropriate for use by high school and college students.

The play, set in contemporary times, revolved around the South Baltimore community that was on the verge of a summer parade. William Carter, a physician and the grand master of the United Order of Moabites, has no desire to lead the parade. His unwillingness is fueled by his exhaustion from conducting house calls and his frustration with the closed society that the Order represents. The primary action of the play occurs in the home of Aunt Hetty, grandmother to Ruth Chapman, the young woman whom Carter loves. Ruth soon learns that Christopher Columbus Jones, a childhood friend and privileged jealous man, plans to upstage and confront Carter. When Carter refuses to agree to lead the march, Ruth dons his costume and mask and does so in his stead. Jones chases the impostor, determined to reveal the scam and to justify Carter's ouster from the lodge. Carter emerges heroically, just in time to save his sweetheart from Jones's threats. The play ends as both Dr. Carter and Ruth celebrate their triumph and newfound sense of collaboration.

Miller's play explored the social roles of ritual, accommodation, and heroism. As a love story, the play also introduced a fearless heroine whose example inspires others to noble action.

Ridley, Florida Ruffin (1861–1943)

A BOSTON writer, editor, social worker, and activist who was part of the SATURDAY EVENING QUILL CLUB, the city's Harlem Renaissance–era literary society. Born Amelia Yates Ruffin, she was the daughter of George and Josephine St. Pierre Ruffin. The Ruffins were leading members of Boston's African-American social and professional elite. Her father, a musician and a journalist for the *New York Anglo-African*, in 1869 became the first African-American to graduate from the Harvard Law School. He went on to become the first African-American municipal court judge in the United States. Ruffin's mother was an influential member of the racial uplift and women's club movements. In 1894 both Josephine St. Pierre Ruffin and her daughter Florida made history when they established *The Woman's Era*, the first newspaper that was owned, managed, and published by African-American women.

Florida Ruffin graduated from the Boston Teacher's College and began teaching at the Grant School in Boston. In 1888 she married Ulysses Ridley, a native of Georgia who was a successful Boston tailor. The couple had two children, Constance and Ulysses, Jr. In the years before the Harlem Renaissance, Florida Ruffin Ridley was active in the women's club movement and in efforts to improve the lives of children. She was the corresponding secretary of the Women's Era Club and the National Federation of Afro-American Women. She also was one of the few members of color in the Twentieth Century Club and the Women's City Club of Boston, two predominantly white New England organizations. She founded and was president of the Association for Promotion of Child Training in the South and spent three years in ATLANTA as the organizer of a kindergarten. Ridley also served as editor of the *Social Service News*, a publication of the Cooperative Social Agencies.

During World War I, Ridley completed secretarial courses that familiarized her with the administrative needs of various war-related organizations. She worked with the Soldier's Comfort Unit and the War Camp Community Service following her graduation from the Boston University Secretarial War Course.

Ridley's Harlem Renaissance literary debut came in 1925 when she won second place in the Personal Experience category of the OPPORTUNITY literary contest. She also published stories in the SATURDAY EVENING QUILL, the periodical that was founded in 1925 and edited by fellow Bostonian

EUGENE GORDON. Her works included the gripping June 1928 short story "HE MUST THINK IT OUT," in which a white man grapples with his newly revealed African-American heritage. As a member of the Saturday Evening Quill Club, Ridley discussed literature and the arts with WARING CUNEY, EDYTHE MAE GORDON, ALVIRA HAZZARD, HELENE JOHNSON, DOROTHY WEST, and others. Ridley's writings, including those that appeared in the *Quill*, frequently addressed issues of PASSING, race pride, African-American history, and personal integrity.

Ridley's long-standing New England family history prompted her involvement with the Society of the Descendants of Early New England Negroes. She was appointed president of the organization in 1931 and served in that capacity for several years.

Bibliography

Davis, Elizabeth. *Lifting As They Climb*. New York: G. K. Hall, 1996.

Dorman, Franklin. *Twenty Families of Color in Massachusetts*. Boston: New England Historic Genealogical Society, 1998.

Wesley, Charles. *The History of the National Association of Colored Women's Clubs: A Legacy of Service*, Washington, D.C.: The Association, 1984.

"Ringtail" Rudolph Fisher (1925)

A gripping short story, by RUDOLPH FISHER, of racial tension, West Indian immigrant life, and revenge. Published in the May 1925 issue of *THE ATLANTIC MONTHLY*, the story revolves around Cyril Sebastian Best, a man proud of his British West Indian heritage. Best, a native of Trinidad, is a resourceful young man who thinks nothing of being dishonorable in his efforts to reach America. Once in the United States, Best prides himself on what he regards as a superior identity, one that elevates him above African Americans, who have no claim on British history and civilization.

One Sunday afternoon, an extremely well-dressed Best is targeted by an unruly group of young men. Ready to make fun of his attire and attitude, they trip him up, assault him physically, and finally hurl insults at him, calling him a "ringtail monkey chaser." Best, who fights back with curses picked up during his time at sea, is ultimately unable to defend himself. Aggrieved and physically wounded in the incident, he manages to extricate himself from the scene. Despite his efforts and compelling case, he fails to find a lawyer who will protest the street brawl and prosecute the ruffians on his behalf.

Best is distracted from the unpleasantness of the melee by his job as an elevator operator and switchboard operator. He soon comes to think that Hilda Vogel, one of the building's residents and a Bermudan woman whom he has admired greatly, may be in love with him. One afternoon, he intercepts a call to Hilda from Punch, the man who attacked him on Seventh Avenue. When Punch comes to call, he suffers an awful accident in the elevator that Best operates. The story ends as the villain is taken away in an ambulance whose wails sound like "receding derisive laughter." Best has achieved revenge and has done so without resorting to public violence.

Fisher's story, set in NEW YORK CITY, is a biting commentary on the tensions between West Indian immigrants and American-born people of color. The insults to Best and the negative comments about MARCUS GARVEY hint at the uneasy relations that existed to some degree during the Harlem Renaissance. "Ringtail" is compelling for its detailed and eloquent presentation of the experiences and aspirations of immigrants of color.

Bibliography

McCluskey, John Jr. *The City of Refuge: The Collected Stories of Rudolph Fisher*. Columbia: University of Missouri Press, 1987.

Perry, Margaret, ed. *The Short Fiction of Rudolph Fisher*. New York: Greenwood Press, 1987.

River George George Washington Lee (1937)

The second in a series of three novels about Beale Street in Memphis by GEORGE WASHINGTON LEE. *River George* appeared three years after Lee's first novel, *BEALE STREET: WHERE THE BLUES BEGAN*. That novel, with its detailed portraits of respectable, colorful, and sometimes unsavory life in Memphis, was the first book by an African-American that the BOOK-OF-THE-MONTH CLUB chose to advertise.

In *River George*, Lee, a southerner from Mississippi, continues to explore the richness of the

South. His critique of northern life, especially the world of Harlem, was part of his effort to suggest that African Americans did not have to migrate north in order to find true fulfillment and stability.

Bibliography

Tucker, David. *Lt. Lee of Beale Street.* Nashville, Tenn.: Vanderbilt University Press, 1971.

Robeson, Eslanda Cardozo Goode
(1896–1965)

A scholar, writer and activist who, with her husband, PAUL ROBESON, advocated tirelessly for the rights and freedoms of African Americans and people of color around the world. The granddaughter of Francis Cardozo, a South Carolina congressman with a distinguished mixed-race heritage, she was born in WASHINGTON, D.C., in December 1896. Her parents, Eslanda Cardozo and John Goode, faced some opposition from the Cardozo family, who disapproved of the match between the light-skinned Eslanda and John, a dark-skinned West Indian from CHICAGO. John Goode died when his daughter was six years old. A Northwestern University graduate and lawyer, he became a postal clerk in Washington, D.C., because racism severely limited his ability to practice law. The family moved to NEW YORK CITY in 1905. There, Eslanda Robeson, a talented student, attended the Wadleigh High School for three years and earned a scholarship to the University of Illinois. When the university denied her admission because it preferred that its students complete four years of high school work, she transferred to COLUMBIA UNIVERSITY. She graduated with a B.S. in chemistry from the

The acclaimed performer Paul Robeson and his wife, Eslanda Goode Robeson *(Yale Collection of American Literature, Beinecke Rare Book and Manuscript Library)*

Teacher's College in 1920. She promptly became the first African American hired by the city's Presbyterian Hospital when she was employed to oversee the Surgical Pathological Laboratory. Robeson earned a B.S. from the UNIVERSITY OF CHICAGO in 1923. From 1937 to 1938 she studied at the University of London and at the London School of Economics. She earned her Ph.D. in anthropology from the Hartford Seminary in Connecticut in 1945.

Robeson met her future husband, Paul Robeson, in New York City. The couple, who married in August 1921, had one child, Paul Jr. In 1925 she left her job at the Presbyterian Hospital to become her husband's business manager. It was she who urged Paul Robeson to accept the leading role in SIMON THE CYRENIAN, one of three plays in a series by RIDGELY TORRENCE. That debut represented the successful beginning of Robeson's lengthy and impressive career as a performer. The couple lived abroad in England for 11 years, and while there, Eslanda Robeson published *Paul Robeson, Negro,* a biography of her husband. When the couple returned to the United States, they settled in Enfield, Connecticut, at a rural home that they named "The Beeches."

In the latter years of the Harlem Renaissance, Robeson intensified her profile as an international activist. She published *African Diary* in 1936, an account of her time in Africa.

In the years following the Harlem Renaissance, she continued to play an instrumental role in international, especially African, affairs. In 1941 she was a cofounder of the Council on African Affairs. A decade later, in 1951, she and two other activists protested the United Nations post-World Genocide Conference. In 1958 she attended the All-African Peoples Conference in GHANA. Targeted by Joseph McCarthy and the House Un-American Activities Committee in the early 1950s, she refused to cooperate when called to testify.

Robeson, suffering from breast cancer, passed away in December 1965.

Bibliography

Boyle, Sheila Tully, and Andrew Buni. *Paul Robeson: The Years of Promise and Achievement.* Amherst: University of Massachusetts Press, 2001.

Duberman, Martin. *Paul Robeson.* New York: Knopf, 1989.

Robeson, Paul Jr. *The Undiscovered Paul Robeson: An Artist's Journey, 1898–1939.* New York: J. Wiley, 2001.

Robeson, Paul (1898–1976)

The versatile and talented actor, singer, linguist, and activist whose public career made unprecedented advances for African Americans in the arts and whose political persecution brought much attention to the plight of oppressed peoples in the United States and around the world.

Paul Robeson was born in Princeton, New Jersey, in April 1898. He was the son of William, a self-emancipated, formerly enslaved man and Lincoln University graduate, and Maria Bustill Robeson, a noted schoolteacher and descendant of abolitionists. He married ESLANDA CARDOZO GOODE ROBESON, a gifted scholar, in 1921. The couple had one son, Paul Robeson, Jr.

Robeson completed high school with honors and after beginning college at his father's alma mater, he became the third African American to attend the school now known as Rutgers University. There, he excelled in academics and in athletics. He earned a stunning 17 varsity letters, won the class prize for oratory every year, and gained admission to PHI BETA KAPPA. Robeson, who became the first African American recognized as an all-American in football, was the valedictorian of his class and was admitted into the honorary Senior Society of Cap and Skull. After graduating from Rutgers, he began law school at COLUMBIA UNIVERSITY.

Robeson made his theatrical debut with the encouragement of his wife. In 1921 he appeared in the production of SIMON THE CYRENIAN by RIDGELY TORRENCE at the 135th Street YOUNG MEN'S CHRISTIAN ASSOCIATION. Still in law school at the time, he began to develop his skills as a performer and soon left the law to immerse himself fully in the world of theater. He joined the PROVINCETOWN PLAYERS and became familiar with EUGENE O'NEILL, one of the group's most prolific members. Robeson's professional debut came in 1922 in *Taboo,* a play by Mary Hoyt Wiborg. Subsequent appearances included leading roles in ALL GOD'S CHILLUN GOT WINGS and THE EMPEROR JONES by Eugene O'Neill, PORGY by DUBOSE and DOROTHY HEYWARD, *The Hairy Ape, Basilisk, Toussaint L'Ouverture, Black Boy,* and *John Henry*. In London he appeared in the title role in productions of William Shakespeare's *Othello*.

Robeson's talents made it inevitable that he would soon appear in films. He made his debut in Oscar Micheaux's *Body and Soul* (1924). He then appeared in nationally circulated films such as *The Emperor Jones*, *Showboat*, *King Solomon's Mines*, *The Proud Valley*, *Jericho*, and *Tales of Manhattan*.

In addition to his stellar career as a stage and film actor, Robeson also excelled as a singer. He was a member of the Harmony Kings, an acclaimed quartet that joined the successful *Shuffle Along* musical company organized by Eubie Blake and Noble Sissle, during the summer of 1921. In April 1925 he appeared with pianist Lawrence Brown, whom he met while performing in *Othello* in London, to perform in the first American concert of African-American music by solo artists. The concert at the Greenwich Village Theatre earned substantial accolades, and audience enthusiasm prompted the two to appear in a repeat performance.

In the years after the Harlem Renaissance, Robeson became increasingly outspoken about civil rights and labor issues. He supported the World War II effort by giving concerts as part of the United Service Organization and also sang patriotic songs on the radio. In 1945 the NATIONAL ASSOCIATION FOR THE ADVANCEMENT OF COLORED PEOPLE awarded Robeson the SPINGARN MEDAL, the organization's most prestigious prize. Robeson, who spoke some 20 languages and was motivated to study them in order to strengthen bonds with peoples across cultures, came under siege after World War II, however. His activities were scrutinized by the Federal Bureau of Investigation, and he was summoned to appear before Senator Joseph McCarthy and the House Un-American Activities Committee in 1946. He was branded a communist and blacklisted as a performer. Four years later, in 1950, the State Department revoked his passport in response to his support for the Soviet Union, where he had enjoyed a rousing welcome in 1934. After a successful suit against the federal government, he won his passport back in 1958. That year, he reappeared on stage at Carnegie Hall before going to perform in Europe and in the Soviet Union.

Paul Robeson relocated to PHILADELPHIA after the death of his wife, Eslanda. He died there in January 1976 at age 77.

Paul Robeson, actor and activist *(Yale Collection of American Literature, Beinecke Rare Book and Manuscript Library)*

Bibliography

Boyle, Sheila Tully, and Andrew Buni. *Paul Robeson: The Years of Promise and Achievement.* Amherst: University of Massachusetts Press, 2001.

Duberman, Martin. *Paul Robeson.* New York: Knopf, 1989.

Paul Robeson Papers, Robeson Family Archives, Moorland Spingarn Research Center, Howard University.

Robeson, Paul. *Here I Stand.* Boston: Beacon Press, 1958.

Robeson, Paul, Jr. *The Undiscovered Paul Robeson: An Artist's Journey, 1898–1939.* New York: J. Wiley, 2001.

Robeson, Susan. *The Whole World in His Hands: A Pictorial Biography of Paul Robeson.* Seacaucus, N.J.: Citadel Press, 1981.

Rogers, Joel Augustus (ca. 1880–1966)

A Jamaican-born journalist, novelist, and historian whose studies of African-American history were pioneering contributions to the field of American history. Born in Negril, Jamaica, Rogers was one of four children born to Samuel, a teacher and plantation supervisor, and Emily Rogers. Following his wife's death, Samuel Rogers remarried and had seven additional children. Joel Rogers completed high school and, without the benefit of further formal education, proceeded to become a self-educated historian and journalist. After high school, he joined the British army and served for four years as an artillery man. He arrived in the United States in 1906 and became a citizen 11 years later in 1917. He married Helga Bresenthal. Rogers passed away in Harlem, in September 1966.

Rogers's first work, *From 'Superman' to Man* (1917), appeared in the same year that he became an American. The volume was prompted by Rogers's experiences of American racism and his growing interest in documenting the evolution and dissemination of prejudices and racist ideologies. In his research for the work, Rogers taught himself French, German, Portuguese, and Spanish and conducted extensive research in Africa and Europe.

Rogers began writing for the PITTSBURGH COURIER, the most widely circulated African-American newspaper during the Harlem Renaissance, during the 1930s. Following successful reports on the 1930 coronation of Ethiopian Emperor Haile Selassie, he became the first American war correspondent of African descent when he covered the war between Ethiopia and Italy in 1935. He also published in well-known periodicals such as JOURNAL OF NEGRO HISTORY, AMERICAN MERCURY, SURVEY GRAPHIC, and *Freedomways*.

Rogers enjoyed memberships in the American Academy of Political Science and the American Geographical Society as well as the French organization, Société d'Anthropologie.

Rogers published throughout and after the Harlem Renaissance period. His works included *As Nature Leads: An Informal Discussion of the Reason Why Negro and Caucasian Are Mixing in Spite of Opposition* (1919), *The Maroons of the West Indies and South America* (1921), *The Ku Klux Klan Spirit: A Brief Outline of the History of the Ku Klux Klan Past and Present* (1923), *World's Greatest Men of African Descent* (1931), and *100 Amazing Facts About the Negro, with Complete Proof: A Short Cut World History of the Negro* (1934). He published two novels, *Blood Money* (1923) and *The Golden Door* (1927), during the Harlem Renaissance.

Bibliography

Kinya Kiongozi, ed. *Selected Writings of Joel Augustus Rogers.* New York: Pyramid, 1988.

Pinckney, Darryl. *Out There: Mavericks of Black Literature,* New York: BasicCivitas Books, 2002.

Roll Sweet Chariot: A Symphonic Play of the Negro People Paul Green (1934)

A tragic play about suffering, betrayal, and murder in the deep South by PAUL GREEN, the white PULITZER PRIZE–winning playwright known for his works on African-American experiences and culture.

The play is set primarily in Potter's Field, a depressed community named after a former plantation owner but one that increasingly takes on the characteristics of a burial ground. The boardinghouse of Quiviene Lockley stands at the center of this depressed community of undertakers, laborers, would-be sweethearts, abandoned children, and convicts. Milly Wilson, wife of the imprisoned Bantam Wilson, hopes to secure a divorce from her husband in order to marry Tom Sterling, a fellow boarder at the Lockleys'. Before the two can wed and escape the awful community, Bantam returns to claim his wife. A dreadful and violent confrontation ensues, and before long, Bantam is dead, shot to death by Sterling. Milly is shocked by the double loss, and her pain only increases when Sterling is sentenced to 10 years of hard labor on the chain gang. Aware that Sterling is ill, Milly finds the prison crew and tries unsuccessfully to get medicine to Sterling. When he finally succumbs to illness and drops to the ground, one of the prison guards shoots Sterling in the back and kills him. The play closes as a bright light rises above Potter's Field and as the convicts, unable to stop and to mourn, continue to work.

Roll Sweet Chariot debuted some seven years after Green's nationally acclaimed play IN ABRAHAM'S BOSOM won the Pulitzer Prize in drama. The show, which opened in October 1934 at the Cort

Theatre on BROADWAY, had a brief run of only seven performances. It was directed by Margaret Hewes, EM JO BASSHE, and Stanley Pratt. The cast included Rose McClendon, Frank Wilson, a veteran actor whose credits included appearances in the original and revival shows of DUBOSE and DOROTHY HEYWARD's PORGY, and Lionel Monagas, a member of the ETHIOPIAN ART THEATRE troupe, who staged Oscar Wilde's *Salome* in 1923 and would later star in RUDOLPH FISHER's 1936 CONJURE-MAN DIES. The play appeared in published form in 1935 and included a comprehensive list of the cast who appeared in the October 1934 debut.

Bibliography

Clark, Barrett. *Paul Green*. New York: Robert M. McBride & Company, 1928.

Krasner, David. *A Beautiful Pageant: African American Theatre, Drama, and Performance in the Harlem Renaissance, 1910–1927*. New York: Palgrave Macmillan, 2002.

Roper, John. *Paul Green, Playwright of the Real South*. Athens: University of Georgia Press, 2003.

Rope and Faggot: A Biography of Judge Lynch Walter White (1929)

A documentary history of LYNCHING by antilynching activist and investigator WALTER WHITE. The title referred to the rope and firewood often used by lynch mobs to murder their victims. White, who published the book in 1929 with ALFRED A. KNOPF, dedicated the work to JAMES WELDON JOHNSON, his longtime colleague at the NATIONAL ASSOCIATION FOR THE ADVANCEMENT OF COLORED PEOPLE (NAACP).

White, who because of his light skin, blond hair, and blue eyes was able to pass for white and infiltrate mobs that targeted African Americans, noted that he "tried to discuss the problem [of lynching] in as temperate and unbiased a manner as possible, but to write about lynching without discussing religion and sex among its causes is to leave the root of the matter unexplained." The book's nine chapters tackled such issues as "The Economic Foundations of Lynch-Law," "The Mind of the Lyncher," and "Sex and Lynching." White also included an appendix with statistics about the frequency of lynchings nationwide, details about the race of those lynched, and the ratio between foreign-born residents and lynchings in each state.

The book, which was White's first work of nonfiction, is powerful for its efforts to link ruthless mob violence to racism, stereotypes, class conditions, and religious ideologies.

Bibliography

Janken, Kenneth Robert. *White: The Biography of Walter White, Mr. NAACP*. New York: The New Press, 2003.

White, Walter. *A Man Called White: The Autobiography of Walter White*. 1948; reprint, Athens: University of Georgia Press, 1995.

Wilson, Sondra, ed. *In Search of Democracy: The NAACP Writings of James Weldon Johnson, Walter White, and Roy Wilkins (1920–1977)*. New York: Oxford University Press, 1999.

Rose, Ernestine (fl. 1920)

An intrepid librarian whose leadership at the 135th Street branch (HARLEM BRANCH) of the NEW YORK PUBLIC LIBRARY helped to make it a beacon in the Harlem community and one of the most successful branches in the city.

Rose, a white woman, joined the staff at the 135th Street Library in 1920 and stayed on for 22 years. She was determined to make the library accessible to the community, to stock it with absorbing materials that would appeal to the predominantly African-American patrons, and to insist that events were of a high caliber and always free of charge. According to scholar Nancy Tolson, Rose was selected for the post because of her previous successes in organizing libraries for ethnic groups. Rose's staff included NELLA LARSEN, Augusta Baker, and REGINA ANDREWS, a resourceful librarian and talented playwright who was actively involved in the theater productions and cultural events held at the library. With her staff, Rose made the library available for lectures, readings, book discussions, receptions, and plays.

As a member of the Citizen's Committee, Rose worked to establish an impressive and unprecedented collection of African-American materials. The committee's officers included HUBERT HARRISON, JAMES WELDON JOHNSON, John Nail, and ARTHUR SCHOMBURG. During her tenure, the

Division of Negro Literature, History, and Prints was founded. The collection received a major donation of materials from bibliophile Arthur Schomburg that included more than 3,000 manuscripts, 5,000 works, 2,000 pieces of artwork, and thousands of additional items. Rose predicted correctly that the collection would be unmatched in scope and value. The library was renamed in honor of Arthur Schomburg following his death in 1938.

Ernestine Rose's leadership, vision, and unwavering commitment to the community and its children made the 135th Street Branch an invaluable asset to Harlem and to the greater New York City community.

Bibliography

Tolson, Nancy. "Making Books Available: The Role of Early Libraries, Librarians, and Booksellers in the Promotion of African American Children's Literature," *African American Review* no. 32 (spring 1998): 9–16.

Roseanne Nan Bagby Stephens (1923)

A play by Nan Bagby Stephens that failed when it opened with a white cast on BROADWAY and reopened three months later when it starred the accomplished actors Rose McClendon and Charles Gilpin. Stephens's play, originally described as "a play . . . dealing with negro life in Georgia," was performed first by a white cast. The revival of the show featured an African-American cast and enabled its director and producer to transform the work drastically by using completely different actors and contexts.

The play deals with seduction, moral judgments, and LYNCHING in a community whose minister seduces one of its young women to whom he is supposed to provide religious training. When the unsavory actions of the Reverend Cicero Brown are discovered, Roseanne, the young woman's foster mother, addresses the church and calls for a lynching. Ultimately, however, she realizes that God can provide the best judgment, and she withdraws her call for violence.

The play opened at the Greenwich Village Theatre in late December, 1923. It was produced by Mary Kirkpatrick. Early reports named Rachel Crothers as director, but when it opened, the di-

rector was John Kirkpatrick. The first show ran for 41 performances. The notion that it had "suffered an untimely fate on the occasion of its recent Broadway presentation" prompted the directors to organize a revival of the work (*NYT*, 11 March 1924, 16). Stephens featured Negro spirituals in the work and in a January 1924 article for *THE NEW YORK TIMES* discussed the value of such material. She described the songs as works "long hidden from any but the Southern people, who, having always accepted them as part of the very fibre of their existence, did not recognize their full value." Stephens suggested that "the words of . . . spirituals seldom mean what the music makes of them, but we accept them as fitting without exactly knowing why. The songs must not be analyzed if one would keep their value." Stephens's own potential to appreciate the complexity and richness of the songs may have been limited even though she thoroughly enjoyed concerts at FISK UNIVERSITY and applauded the TUSKEGEE INSTITUTE chorus that traveled nationwide.

In March 1924 the show opened for a one-week run at the Shubert-Riviera Theatre. According to *The New York Times*, audiences were most interested in seeing Charles Gilpin and "what [he] would do with the role of the rascally preacher." Reviewers were disappointed with Gilpin's performance, especially in light of his recent powerful presentations in the title role of EUGENE O'NEILL's *THE EMPEROR JONES*. While Gilpin, in the role of Cicero Brown apparently was only able to "str[ike] a genuine note for a few minutes," Rose McClendon provided a "frequently moving" performance.

Bibliography

"Negroes Play 'Roseanne." *New York Times*, 11 March 1924, 16.

"Mary Kirkpatrick's Plays." *New York Times*, 6 August 1923, 14.

Stephens, Nan Bagby. "Negro Spirituals." *New York Times*, 27 January 1924, X4.

Rowland, Ida (1904–unknown)

A published poet and teacher, and the first African American from Oklahoma to earn a Ph.D., Ida

Rowland was born in Texas but spent her high school years in Oklahoma. She attended college as an older student and pursued concentrations in English and philosophy while working toward a bachelor's degree in sociology. Following the completion of her college studies in 1936, Rowland entered a master's program at the University of Nebraska and graduated in 1939 having completed a thesis entitled "An Analysis of Negro Ritualistic Ceremonies as Exemplified by Negro Organizations in Omaha." In 1939 she completed doctoral studies in the social sciences at Laval University in Quebec and became the first Oklahoman woman of African descent to earn a Ph.D.

Rowland wrote one volume of poetry during the Harlem Renaissance. *LISPING LEAVES*, published by the Philadelphia firm Dorrance & Company, included nearly 50 poems on nature, self-determination, racial awareness, and humanity.

Rowland published poetry and numerous works relating to African-American history. Through her own press, Bell Enterprises, located in Pine Bluff, Arkansas, she published the series entitled *Black Heroes and Heroines* that featured profiles of figures such as MARY McLEOD BETHUNE, PAUL LAURENCE DUNBAR, JAMES WELDON JOHNSON, and Phillis Wheatley. A collection of poetry, *Idylls of the Seasons, Poems* was published in 1978.

S

Sacrifice Thelma Myrtle Duncan (1930)

An earnest play about sacrifices and honor by THELMA DUNCAN that was included in *PLAYS AND PAGEANTS FROM THE LIFE OF THE NEGRO* (1930), the selective anthology edited by WILLIS RICHARDSON.

Set in a "large eastern city," the play features the Payton family of three and Roy, a friend. Mrs. Payton, a widowed laundress, is suffering from the hard labor that she routinely does to support herself and two children. Her daughter Ina, a light-hearted and caring woman, has an office job that represents a significant advance in the family's prospects. Ina's younger brother Billy, however, is the one on whom Mrs. Payton has pinned all of her hopes. She longs for his graduation from high school and looks forward to seeing him succeed.

The crisis in the play revolves around Billy's faulty decision to steal the notes for an upcoming chemistry exam. Faced with the prospect of expulsion, he is unable to return the notes or to confess his deed to his teacher. His friend Roy, who hopes to win the heart of Ina Payton, ultimately comes to his aid. Roy's efforts, which may jeopardize his own law school studies, not only protect his friend but give him an opportunity to prove himself to Ina.

Duncan modified the play when it was selected for inclusion in *Plays and Pageants*. Her editorial note indicates that the one-act drama was "[a]dapted to the capacity of children of the eighth grade." The work is an important contribution to the African-American theater tradition that evolved substantially during the Harlem Renaissance period. The value of Duncan's work lies in its steady examination of moral values, ambition, domestic life, and heroism within the African-American community.

Sad-Faced Boy Arna Bontemps (1937)

A novel for children by ARNA BONTEMPS that explores the allure of HARLEM. Republished in 1937 by Houghton Mifflin, the story focuses on an enterprising young boy named J. P. Morgan. Much like his entrepreneurial, self-confident namesake, Bontemps's protagonist has the opportunity to make a name for himself in the world beyond his rural Alabama home. He sets off for Harlem with his friends named Slumber, Rags, and Willie. Unfortunately, gangsters beset the hopeful adventurers. They lose their shoes and, with their battered pride, are forced to make their way home again. The group's misfortune, however, allows them to value their home anew and to cherish their connections there.

Sad-Faced Boy was read aloud on national radio in 1940, some three years after its publication. The publicity prompted Bontemps to note in a letter to longtime friend and correspondent LANGSTON HUGHES that the airing was reviving interest in the book "from the trade angle" and that the show might be of use to librarians and teachers who wanted to promote children's literature.

Bibliography

Jones, Kirkland C. *Renaissance Man from Louisiana: A Biography of Arna Wendell Bontemps.* Westport, Conn.: Greenwood Press, 1992.

Nichols, Charles H., ed. *Arna Bontemps–Langston Hughes Letters, 1925–1967*. New York: Paragon House, 1990.

Saint Mark's Methodist Episcopal Church

One of the most prominent churches of HARLEM during the Renaissance era. Located at 138th Street and St. Nicholas Avenue, the church was known for its formal services, high sacred music performances, and grandly attired choir and ministers.

It was there in 1908 that more than 50 nurses, denied membership and professional privileges in the racially exclusionary American Nurses Association, established the National Association of Colored Graduate Nurses.

Saint Peter Relates an Incident: Selected Poems   James Weldon Johnson (1935)

The last published collection of poems by JAMES WELDON JOHNSON, the influential civil rights activist and author of the intriguing novel *AUTOBIOGRAPHY OF AN EX-COLOURED MAN*. The volume included a small group of new works and a majority of the poems published 18 years earlier in *Fifty Years and Other Poems*. Johnson began work on the title poem once he heard a startling report about the segregated transportation provided to African-American and white mothers who had lost sons in World War I and were traveling to Europe to see the graves of their children. Determined to counter the narrow-mindedness of racism, he penned a long, satirical poem that transformed the biblical rapture into an innovative, modern-day critique of racism. That work was published separately in 1930 and then was included in the 1935 collection.

The title poem, "Saint Peter Relates an Incident of the Resurrection Day," is divided into six sections and totals some 161 lines. In the poem's organized set of four-line stanzas, Johnson provides an intriguing glimpse of heaven and humanizes the angels there through his suggestion that they, like mortals, relish a good story. "Tell us a tale, Saint Peter, they entreated; / And gathered close around where he was seated." The bearded saint, who "fumbled with his keys" for inspiration before be-

ginning the tale, then launches into a vivid tale of the Resurrection morning. The archangel Gabriel sounds his horn, and the world below begins to give up the dead: "A shudder shook the world, and gaping graves / Gave up their dead. / Out from the parted waves / Came the prisoners of old ocean. The dead belonging / To every land and clime came thronging." The process seems to be in keeping with the script outlined in the Bible until a "special order" is issued "within the American border." That instruction requires that veterans of all American wars, including the Civil War, "Mexican, Spanish, Haitian," the "Trustees of the patriotism of the nation," and the "Confederate Veterans and the Ku-Klux Klan" assemble themselves on the edge of the Potomac River to "escort the unknown soldier up to heaven."

The patriots and veterans are responsible for emancipating the unknown soldier from his grave, and they work "with a will / . . . toiled with a pick, with crowbar, and with drill / To cleave a breach" wide enough to accommodate the "towering form" that eventually "loomed big and bigger." They are stunned however, to see that the man they have released is African American and they "all fell back aghast." The soldier represents legions of veterans of color, many of whom have long remained unacknowledged despite their sacrifices in wars dating back to the French and Indian Wars of the 18th century to World War I. While his audience grapples with its racist reaction and disbelief, he celebrates his new destination and the long-awaited experience of glory. The "unknown soldier, dust-stained and begrimed" begins his upward journey and soon becomes a "tall, black soldier-angel" whose "clear and strong" song resonates throughout heaven "until heaven took up the song." The satisfying conclusion, which is rooted in the promise of eventual redemption and triumph over one's persecutors and enemies, is made more rich by the response of the angelic host. "The tale was done," reports the narrator, "The angelic hosts dispersed, / but not till after / There ran through heaven / Something that quivered / twixt tears and laughter."

The conclusion of "Saint Peter Relates" has been used to characterize the poem as a humorous indictment of racism. Certainly, the reaction seems directed away from the stalwart and long-suffering soldier and toward the shocked white hordes who have been deluded in their tributes to the unknown soldier. Johnson renders them both central and peripheral to the Rapture. He also succeeds in crafting a provocative narrative about the actual Tomb of the Unknown Soldier that was established at the center of Arlington National Cemetery in 1921.

Other poems in the volume reiterated the themes of African-American patriotism, endurance, and optimism that pervaded the title poem of the collection. One of the most powerful additional works was "Lift Every Voice and Sing," the poem that Johnson created with his brother J. Rosamond Johnson, and that African Americans enthusiastically adopted as the Negro National Anthem.

Bibliography

Fleming, Robert. *James Weldon Johnson*. Boston: Twayne Publishers, 1987.

Saint Philip's Protestant Episcopal Church

One of the most well-known churches in NEW YORK CITY and a vital community resource for citizens in the years before and during the Harlem Renaissance. Founded in 1818, the church was established in Brooklyn in 1899 and then relocated to HARLEM in 1911. It encouraged African Americans to purchase real estate and was in large part responsible for the rapid growth in and popularity of Harlem among people of color.

The church, whose congregation was one of the wealthiest in the city, was known for its impressive financial resources. A'LELIA WALKER, daughter of the successful entrepreneur Madame C. J. Walker, hosted the extravagant wedding of her daughter Mae, at St. Philip's in 1923. In November 1954 the funeral service of composer and entertainer J. Rosamond Johnson, brother of JAMES WELDON JOHNSON, was held at St. Philip's Church.

The church also was respected for its long-standing history of community outreach and support of the arts. One of its earliest and best-known programs was the St. Christopher Club, a Bible study group that evolved into an acclaimed basketball team associated with the African-American

Olympian Athletic League. In 1931 the church hosted the HARLEM EXPERIMENTAL THEATRE Group, a troupe based in the HARLEM BRANCH of the NEW YORK PUBLIC LIBRARY. The drama group made its professional debut in the parish house of St. Philip's.

Bibliography

Dodson, Howard, Christopher Moore, and Roberta Yancy. *The Black New Yorkers: The Schomburg Illustrated Chronology*. New York: John Wiley & Sons, Inc., 2000.

Watson, Steven. *The Harlem Renaissance: Hub of African-American Culture, 1920–1930*. New York: Pantheon Books, 1995.

Salem Methodist Episcopal Church

Located at 129th Street and Seventh Avenue, this was the church of the Reverend FREDERICK CULLEN, father of poet COUNTEE CULLEN.

The Salem Methodist Episcopal Church was located first in a humble storefront. Reverend Cullen established the congregation in 1902 when he arrived in NEW YORK CITY. Twenty-two years later, in 1924, the congregation moved to HARLEM. The membership was substantial, numbering some 2,500 by the mid-1920s.

Bibliography

Ferguson, Blanche. *Countee Cullen and the Negro Renaissance*. New York: Dodd, Mead, 1966.

Shucard, Alan. *Countee Cullen*. Boston: Twayne, 1984.

"Sanctuary"   Nella Larsen (1930)

A provocative and controversial short story by NELLA LARSEN that appeared in the January 1930 issue of *FORUM*. Accompanying the story were four illustrations by WINOLD REISS, an accomplished artist known for his ethnic and folk sketches.

The story, which is divided into four sections, traces a tumultuous set of events that involve Annie Poole, the protagonist, who lives in the South near the sea. Poole lives in a deserted area that is near the "old fields of ruined plantations" and whose "partly grown-over road . . . still shows traces of furrows made by the wheels of wagons that have long since rotted away or been cut into firewood" (250). One evening, she takes in Jim Hammer, a fugitive from the law "with pale brown eyes in which there was an odd mixture of fear and amazement" (250–251). Hammer also happens to be a friend of Poole's son Obadiah. He announces to Annie that he is in trouble because he has shot another man and persuades her to hide him there because that is what her son would urge her to do. Poole is hiding under the covers in her bed when the sheriff arrives with the body of Obadiah and reveals that Poole is the man who killed him. Despite the awful tragedy and Hammer's heinous betrayal, Annie does not divulge his whereabouts to the police. When they leave, she gives in to a "raging fury" and then orders him to "Get outen mah feather baid, Jim Hammer, an outen mah house, an' don' nevah stop thankin' you' Jesus he done gib you dat black face" (255). In a moment of supreme charity, Annie spares Jim Hammer's life. The story's powerful conclusion demonstrates the degree to which racial solidarity can trump personal desire or tragedy. It also honors the staggering example of maternal charity that Annie Poole is able to muster in the face of an overwhelming loss. She is clearly unwilling to become complicit with the white southern system in which African Americans are so rarely granted equal or just treatment.

Shortly after the publication of "Sanctuary," Larsen was accused of plagiarizing the story. The rumors began to circulate widely throughout the Harlem Renaissance community. HAROLD JACKMAN, a longtime friend of COUNTEE CULLEN, told his friend that he had "literary dirt" to share and noted that the work was "an exact blue print" of another story. One of Larsen's most vocal critics, he urged Cullen to "get ahold of the *Forum*" and the original story by Sheila Kaye-Smith, in order to "compare them. But isn't this a terrible thing," he wrote, "It remains to be seen whether the *Forum* people will find this out" (Davis, 348). Additional Larsen supporters included Countee Cullen, who urged caution in assessing Larsen's literary guilt, and CARL VAN VECHTEN, with whom Larsen socialized often.

The original version of the tale, which featured white characters rather than the African-American figures whom Larsen used, was entitled "Mrs. Adis" and was written by Sheila Kaye-Smith. The work appeared in *Joanna Godden Married, and Other Stories*, a collection of stories published in 1926. According to Larsen biographer Thadious Davis, Jackman's assertions were correct even though class, rather than race, explained the decision of Mrs. Adis. Although both pieces shared striking similarities in structure, imagery, and plot, Larsen defended her work as an example of a standard story in African-American culture. Her editors at *Forum* supported her statements, noting that she had submitted several drafts to them before the piece was published.

The controversy surrounding the publication of "Sanctuary" was enough to bring her promising career to a halt. Although she began and completed two additional novels, she published neither one. As the 1930s proceeded, she began to withdraw from the literary and social circles in which she had been active. The death of her husband and the subsequent loss of alimony, combined with her apparent literary caution, prompted her to return to nursing. In this new career, in which she worked for some two decades, Larsen thoroughly suppressed the literary career that she had enjoyed and that had given her splendid opportunities for travel and personal advancement.

Bibliography

Davis, Thadious M. *Nella Larsen, Novelist of the Harlem Renaissance: A Woman's Life Unveiled.* Baton Rouge: Louisiana State University Press, 1994.

Kaye-Smith, Sheila. *Joanna Godden Married, and Other Stories.* London: Cassell and Company Ltd., 1926.

Larson, Charles, ed. *The Complete Fiction of Nella Larsen.* New York: Anchor Books, 2001.

San Juan Hill District

A neighborhood in Midtown Manhattan that became home to many African Americans during the Great Migration and Harlem Renaissance periods. The community was home to such well-known figures as bibliophile ARTHUR SCHOMBURG and his family, and to Lionel Canegata, better known as Canada Lee, a prizefighter and actor who starred in and earned much acclaim for his performance in the 1941 production of *NATIVE SON*.

Saturday Evening Quill

The literary magazine that the BOSTON-based SATURDAY EVENING QUILL CLUB published during the Harlem Renaissance. The organization hoped to produce annual issues and was quite firm in its resolve only to circulate, rather than sell, copies to members and a small number of interested supporters. Members also hoped to use the publication as part of their own efforts to improve their writing rather than to acquire fame or simply to draw attention to themselves.

The first issue, which appeared in June 1928, three years after the founding of the club, provided readers with a detailed note about the missions of the Quill Club members. Editor EUGENE GORDON, a *Boston Post* journalist and Quill Club president, insisted that the magazine's purpose was "chiefly to present original work of Saturday Evening Quill Club members *to themselves*" and that "this publication is *not* for sale." Gordon explained that "Members are not particularly desirous of hearing praise of what is found herein, but will listen to it, as, also, they will listen to adverse criticism." "Nor have the members an exalted opinion of their work," he revealed. "They had not published it because they think any of it 'wonderful' or 'remarkable,' or 'extraordinary,' or 'unusual,' or even promising. They have published it because being human, they are possessed of the very human traits of vanity and egotism." He also noted matter-of-factly that the publication would be produced only if "it annually has something to publish and sufficient money with which to pay the printer."

There were three annual issues of the magazine published from 1928 through 1930 and approximately 250 copies of each issue produced. The group refrained from printing additional copies even when besieged by "numerous requestors." Unlike some of the more daring magazines and editorial groups, the *Quill* maintained an air of literary propriety and prided itself on the respectable material that appeared in each issue. The issues featured poems, plays, essays, short stories, and book reviews, many of which were sophisticated creative works.

A number of prominent figures published their work in the *Saturday Evening Quill*. Among those featured in the magazine were LEWIS ALEXANDER, EDYTHE GORDON, FLORENCE HARMON, ALVIRA HAZZARD, HELENE JOHNSON, and DOROTHY WEST. *Saturday Evening Quill* members devoted the April 1929 issue to member and poet A. Aloysius

Greene, one of the youngest members, who had just passed away tragically at age 23 and for whom "the inevitability of [his] brilliant future only death could hinder."

The *Saturday Evening Quill* earned high critical praises from leading figures of the Harlem Renaissance. W. E. B. DuBois, longtime editor of the New York City–based CRISIS, suggested that "[o]f the booklets issues by young Negro writers in New York, Philadelphia, and elsewhere, this collection from Boston is the most interesting and best." He went on to insist that not only was it "well printed and readable" but that it "maintains a high mark of literary excellence." The widely read *New York* AMSTERDAM NEWS predicted that the existence of the Quill Club and its magazine was encouraging. "Of such things good literature will come," it predicted. "Harlem writers should follow their example" (*Saturday Evening Quill*, April 1929).

Although it was a short-lived literary enterprise, the *Saturday Evening Quill* magazine was a significant Harlem Renaissance endeavor.

Saturday Evening Quill Club

The BOSTON-based literary club established during the Harlem Renaissance. Like similar literary societies in Philadelphia and Washington, D.C., the group, also known as the Boston Quill Club, met regularly to discuss literary matters and new works. The club's publication, the SATURDAY EVENING QUILL, referred to the club as "an organization of Boston writers," most of whom "are unprofessionals, and all, incidentally, are Negroes, although anybody who is eligible may become a member."

Members of the Quill Club included prominent Bostonians and others who went on to achieve fame during the Harlem Renaissance. The membership roll included Alice Furlong, EDYTHE GORDON, EUGENE GORDON, GERTRUDE PARTHENIA McBROWN, Grace Vera Postles, FLORIDA RUFFIN RIDLEY, GERTRUDE SCHALK, and Roscoe Wright.

In 1928 the group began to publish the *Saturday Evening Quill*, a short-lived but significant publication of the period. Eugene Gordon edited the annual publication that was circulated, rather than sold, to members and supporters. During its three years of publication, the magazine featured works by members who attained national visibility such as LEWIS ALEXANDER, WARING CUNEY, ALVIRA HAZZARD, FLORENCE HARMON, HELENE JOHNSON, and DOROTHY WEST.

Bibliography
Saturday Evening Quill 1, no. 1 (June 1928).

Savage, Augusta Christine Fells
(1892–1962)

One of the most talented, decorated, and prominent American artists of the Harlem Renaissance period. The only woman of color invited to participate in the 1939 World's Fair, Savage was an intrepid and gifted artist who worked to ensure that other aspiring artists of color had opportunities to study and to showcase their works.

Savage was the seventh child of 14 born to Edward and Cornelia Murphy Fells. Savage was born in Green Cove, Florida, and her father, a minister, supported the family by working as a house painter. She was married three times. She was widowed after several years of marriage to John T. Moore, her first husband and the only husband with whom she had a child. Their daughter, Irene, would later care for Savage when she was afflicted with cancer in the last years of her life. Her marriage to James Savage, her second husband, ended in divorce. Her third husband was ROBERT LINCOLN POSTON, a journalist, ally of MARCUS GARVEY, and influential member of the UNIVERSAL NEGRO IMPROVEMENT ASSOCIATION. Poston contracted pneumonia and died just six months after he and Savage wed.

Savage, who began modeling clay figures during her childhood, was educated in the public schools of Florida. She studied at the State Normal School in Tallahassee before heading north to attend prestigious Cooper Union in NEW YORK CITY. She spent three years studying at the Woman's Art School. In addition, Savage studied abroad at institutes such as the Académie de la Chaumière and in Belgium and Germany.

Savage's career was marked for its publicity and her impressive talent and the controversies that threatened to impede her meteoric rise in the American and international art worlds. In 1923 she was denied a prestigious summer fellowship to study in France because of her race. Savage did not hesitate to reveal the despicable nature of the rejection and succeeded in generating much public sympathy for her cause. She enjoyed national and international acclaim for her work and received impressive citations. These included a 1931 Colonial Exposition medallion from the French government and citations for exhibits at various French salons including the Salon Automne and Salon Printemps at Grande Palace.

Savage worked closely with a number of well-known Harlem Renaissance figures. She was well acquainted with artist JACOB LAWRENCE. It was Savage whose recommendation led to Lawrence's employment in the Works Progress Administration (WPA) projects of the late 1930s. He was one of the approximately 200 artists of color whom she promoted to WPA officials. Her protégés went on to produce much public art as part of the organization's nationwide outreach and community programs. Savage was friendly with many in the Harlem community including EVA JESSYE. Savage was one of the first people whom RALPH ELLISON met when he arrived in New York City. She provided Ellison with numerous and profitable introductions into the vibrant cultural circles of Harlem.

Savage earned numerous honors during her career, and she established impressive records in African-American art history. She was a three-time winner of the prestigious JULIUS ROSENWALD FELLOWSHIP, and her work was featured on the covers of widely circulated periodicals such as *OPPORTUNITY*. She designed sculptures and portraits of leading Harlem Renaissance figures such as W. E. B. DUBOIS, MARCUS GARVEY, W. C. HANDY, and JAMES WELDON JOHNSON. Her most celebrated and mythic work, an enormous sculpture entitled "Lift Every Voice and Sing," was created for the 1939 World's Fair. She was the first African-American woman admitted to membership in the National Association of Women Painters and Sculptors.

Savage reestablished herself in the New York City area and dedicated herself to providing educational and professional opportunities for aspiring artists of color. In addition to establishing the Savage Studio of Arts and Crafts that was funded initially by a generous $1,500 grant from the Carnegie Foundation, she also was the first director

"Lift Every Voice and Sing," the impressive sculpture that Augusta Savage crafted for the 1939 World's Fair. Photographed by Carl Van Vechten. Permission granted by the Van Vechten Trust *(Yale Collection of American Literature, Beinecke Rare Book and Manuscript Library)*

at the Harlem Art Center, one of the largest WPA-sponsored organizations of the day. Her interests also included politics, and in 1933 she organized the Vanguard Club, a regular gathering of intellectuals and artists. Savage ceased to sponsor the group when it eventually became a haven for Communists and their supporters.

At the end of the Harlem Renaissance, Savage left New York City for the Catskill Mountains. She established a studio in Saugerties, New York. Poor health prompted her to move back to New York City, where she could live with her daughter. Augusta Savage died of cancer in March 1962.

Bibliography

"Augusta Savage, 62 [sic], Sculptor, Is Dead." *New York Times*, 27 March 1962, 31.

Bibby, Deirdre. *Augusta Savage and the Art Schools of Harlem*. New York: Schomburg Center for Research in Black Culture, 1988.

Leininger-Miller, Theresa. *New Negro Artists in Paris: African American Painters and Sculptors in the City of Light, 1922–1934*. New Brunswick, N.J.: Rutgers University Press, 2001.

Savage Rhythm Harry Hamilton and Norman Foster (1931)

A play by Harry Hamilton and Norman Foster that featured an African-American cast in the story of a Harlem star who, upon her return to her southern home, gains important powers through the conjure magic of her female kin.

Savage Rhythm opened at the John Golden Theatre on New Year's Eve, 1931. This was the same theater in which ZORA NEALE HURSTON staged the single performance of her multi-genre production entitled *The Great Day*. Produced by John Golden, it was directed by Robert Burton. The 16-member cast on opening night included Mamie Carter, Georgette Harvey, Inez Clough, Alvin Childress, and Ernest Whitman.

The play revolves around the Mississippi community of Tuckaloo, a town that, according to the program guide's author's note, did in fact exist under a different name. During a community barbeque, a deadly conflict breaks out, and the female lover of a married man is stabbed to death. The community decides to depend on itself in order to identify and to punish the murderer. The matriarchs of the community, two conjure women, who have now tragically lost one of their granddaughters, endow Orchid, their surviving granddaughter, with magical powers. She helps the people to Tuckaloo to reveal the "sweetback" whose adulterous actions prompted the deadly fight. Despite the fact that he is not the actual murderer, the community gangs up on him and forces him into a deadly swamp on the edge of town.

THE NEW YORK TIMES theater critic Brooks Atkinson complimented the play, noting that it was "an intelligent drama of Negro sorcery" that was "respectably thought out and . . . respectably produced." Ultimately, though, Atkinson lamented that "the authors have not given much significance to their pictures of domestic life" and that the play was "virtually themeless until the final scene." In closing, Atkinson referred to a popular DUBOSE HEYWARD hit when he suggested that the play "needs some of the *Porgy* rhythm." Atkinson's review concluded with the damning note that "[a]t the present moment most of the savage rhythm in New York is scrambling and jostling outside this office window" (*NYT*, 1 January 1932, 30).

The play closed after 12 performances.

Bibliography

Atkinson, J. Brooks. "The Play: 'Way Down South," *New York Times*, 1 January 1932, 30.

"Theatrical Notes," *New York Times*, 31 December 1931, 21.

Scarborough, Dorothy (1875–1935)

A white Texas-born writer, teacher, and folklorist who supported the Harlem Renaissance in general and the efforts of OPPORTUNITY editor CHARLES S. JOHNSON to direct attention to emerging African-American artists in particular. Born in Mt. Carmel, Texas, she was one of four children born to John and Mary Ellison Scarborough. After graduating from high school, she attended Baylor University. She earned her B.A. in 1896 and her M.A. in 1898. The university offered her a job, and she became the first professor to teach journalism and creative writing, with an emphasis on the short story, in the Southwest. Scarborough was an energetic scholar and pursued opportunities to attend summer sessions at the UNIVERSITY OF CHICAGO and to study at OXFORD UNIVERSITY in England during a sabbatical. She earned her Ph.D. in English from COLUMBIA UNIVERSITY in 1917 and, as she had at Baylor, promptly joined the faculty. She moved up the faculty ranks at Columbia, becoming an associate professor of English in 1931.

Scarborough was a recognized folklorist and a writer with a demonstrated interest in ghost stories. A member of the Texas Folklore Society, she eventually served a one-year term as president of the organization. She made her literary debut in 1912 with *Fugitive Verses*. Scarborough's publications during the Harlem Renaissance period included *Famous Modern Ghost Stories* (1921), *Humorous Ghost Stories* (1921), and novels that included *In the Land of Cotton* (1923), *The Wind* (1925), *Griselda* (1927), and *The Stretch-Berry Smile* (1932). African-American culture was part of her folklore studies, and in 1925 she published *On the Trail of Negro Folk-Songs* (1925).

In 1924, Scarborough was one of several prominent individuals whom Charles Johnson invited to serve as judges in the first *Opportunity* literary contest. Scarborough accepted enthusiastically, noting that she was "very much interested in the development of the talents, artistic and otherwise, of the Negroes" and that she thought Johnson's "plan excellent for arousing interest" in African-American accomplishments and potential.

In 1927 Johnson included Scarborough in *EBONY AND TOPAZ: A COLLECTANEA*, the anthology that appeared in 1927. Scarborough's piece, "New Light on an Old Song," appeared alongside works by LANGSTON HUGHES, GEORGIA DOUGLAS JOHNSON, ARTHUR SCHOMBURG, DONALD HAYES, BLANCHE TAYLOR DICKINSON, and many others.

Dorothy Scarborough died prematurely, struck down by influenza while living in New York City.

Bibliography
Scarborough, Dorothy. *On the Trail of Negro Folk-Songs.* 1925, reprint, Hatboro, Pa.: Folklore Associates, 1963.

Schalk, Gertrude (Lillian Schalk)
(1906–unknown)

A writer, editor, and member of the SATURDAY EVENING QUILL CLUB of BOSTON, Lillian Schalk was born in Boston in 1906 to Theodore and Mary Wilkerson Schalk. She attended BOSTON UNIVERSITY in the early 1920s in order to study journalism. In 1946 she married John Johnson.

As a member of the Saturday Evening Quill Club, Schalk had the opportunity to discuss her work and her professional goals with well-established journalist EUGENE GORDON, an editor at the *Boston Post*. According to scholars Lorraine Roses and Ruth Randolph, Schalk began to use the name Gertrude once she began to write and to publish.

Schalk published in the SATURDAY EVENING QUILL, an annual literary magazine that was produced by members of the literary group that included WARING CUNEY, HELENE JOHNSON, JOSEPH MITCHELL, FLORIDA RUFFIN RIDLEY, and DOROTHY WEST. Her works included the tragic love story entitled "THE RED CAPE" (1929) and "FLOWER OF THE SOUTH" (1930), a stark story about LYNCHING. The brief biographical note that appeared in the magazine reveals that in 1929 Schalk was the editor of a literary magazine named *Sunburst* that was "recently established in Boston." She was also identified as a "frequent contributor to the *Illustrated Feature Section* of the Negro Press and her brief short stories have been widely distributed by the Wheeler Syndicate, Inc., among scores of daily and weekly newspapers of the country." Schalk, who went on to join the staff of the *PITTSBURGH COURIER* as the editor of the women's page, seems to have slipped into obscurity following her marriage.

Bibliography
Saturday Evening Quill (April 1929): 81.

Roses, Lorraine Elena, and Ruth Elizabeth Randolph. *Harlem's Glory: Black Women Writing, 1900–1950.* Cambridge, Mass.: Harvard University Press, 1996.

Schomburg, Arthur (Arturo Alfonso Schomburg) (1874–1938)

A lawyer, cofounder of the Negro Society for Historical Research, and the celebrated bibliophile whose unmatched collection of materials on peoples of African descent formed the basis of the impressive Division of Negro Literature, History, and Prints at the HARLEM BRANCH OF THE NEW YORK PUBLIC LIBRARY.

Born in San Juan, Puerto Rico, Arthur Schomburg was the child of an unmarried couple, Mary Joseph, a laundress and midwife from St. Thomas, and Carlos Schomburg, a German businessman. Details about Schomburg's early life are elusive, but biographer Elinor Des Verney Sinnette notes that he spent much of his childhood with his maternal family in St. Croix. He attended St. Thomas College in the Danish West Indies and the Instituto de Instrucción in San Juan before arriving in the United States in 1917. In New York City, Schomburg became an active member of the Puerto Rican community and a leading voice in its political movements. He was a member of the liberation group Las Dos Antillas, an organization dedicated to achieving Puerto Rican and Cuban independence. In the late 1890s the death of José Martí and subsequent reorganizations in the American-based Caribbean political movements prompted Schomburg to immerse himself in African-American issues. He became a Mason when he joined a lodge whose members were primarily of Cuban and Puerto Rican descent. By 1926 he was an officer in the Prince Hall Lodge and served as grand secretary and master.

Schomburg married Elizabeth Hatcher of Virginia in 1895, and the couple had three sons, Maximo; Arthur, Jr.; and Kingsley. Following his wife's death in 1900, Schomburg remarried. In 1902 he wed Elizabeth Morrow Taylor, with whom he had two sons, Reginald and Nathaniel. Widowed for a second time, Schomburg married Elizabeth Green, with whom he had three more children, Fernando, Dolores, and Placido.

Schomburg was an astute and visionary man who believed in the emancipatory and political power of knowledge. With his lifelong friend, JOHN EDWARD BRUCE, he founded the Negro Society for Historical Research in 1911. Schomburg also was a member of the AMERICAN NEGRO ACADEMY, the organization that Alexander Crummell founded in 1897 and the nation's first learned African-American society.

Schomburg is perhaps best known and celebrated for his impressive collection of books, artifacts, and materials by and about peoples of African descent. In 1925 his collection, which included thousands of books, manuscripts, pamphlets, art, and other collectible items, formed the foundation of the Division of Negro Literature, History, and Prints housed at the Harlem Branch of the NEW YORK PUBLIC LIBRARY on 135th Street. The collection, bought for the library by the Carnegie Corporation for $10,000, was unprecedented in scope and wholly invaluable to scholars, artists, and students. The writer James Baldwin often crept up into the library, which catered primarily to adults, and could be found immersed in the extensive literature collection that, according to the 1937 *Who's Who in Colored America*, was the "rarest private collection of Africana and of Negro Americana in this country" [460].

Schomburg, who in 1922 became president of the American Negro Academy, was an active writer and editor. In 1916 he published *A Bibliographical Check List of American Negro Poetry*, the first comprehensive reference on African-American poets. Additional works included an edition of *The Collected Works of Phillis Wheatley* (1915), *A Plea for Negro History* (1918), and a persuasive essay entitled "The Negro Digs Up His Past," which appeared first in the March 1925 Harlem issue of SURVEY GRAPHIC that led to ALAIN LOCKE's pioneering anthology, THE NEW NEGRO (1925). Schomburg's essays appeared in leading periodicals of the time, including *Negro Digest*, THE MESSENGER, and NEGRO WORLD.

Schomburg received prestigious honors during his lifetime. He was one of the first winners of the HARMON FOUNDATION Awards, prizes established by magnate Elmer Harmon to recognize outstanding African-American achievements.

A longtime employee at Bankers Trust Company, Schomburg retired from his post as head of the mail department in 1930 to join the faculty and staff at FISK UNIVERSITY. There, as curator of the Negro Collection, he created a substantial special collections archive and succeeded in generating much excitement at and beyond the university with conferences and academic gatherings focused on African-American history and literature. He left Nashville for New York City in 1932 when he received an offer to become the curator of the Schomburg Collection at the 135th Street branch of the New York Public Library.

Arthur Schomburg died of complications from an infection on June 10, 1938. He was buried in Brooklyn at the Cypress Hills Cemetery.

Bibliography

Arthur Schomburg Papers, Schomburg Center for Research in Black Culture; Moorland-Spingarn Research Center, Howard University; James Weldon Johnson Collection, Yale University; Charles Johnson Collection, Fisk University.

Moss, Alfred. *The American Negro Academy*. Baton Rouge: Louisiana State University Press, 1981.

Piñeiro de Rivera, Flor. *Arthur A. Schomburg: A Puerto Rican's Quest for His Black Heritage*. San Juan: Centro de Estudios Avanzados de Puerto Rico y el Caribe, 1989.

Sinnette, Elinor Des Verney. *Arthur Alfonso Schomburg, Black Bibliophile and Collector: A Biography*. New York: New York Public Library, 1989.

Schuyler, George (1895–1977)

A prolific and outspoken writer and journalist, George Samuel Schuyler is credited with publishing the first African-American satirical novel. Born in Providence, Rhode Island, he was the son of chef George Schuyler and his wife Eliza Jane Fisher [Fischer] Schuyler. Following the death of his father, Schuyler and his mother relocated to Syracuse, New York. His mother remarried, and his stepfather was a porter for the New York Central Railroad. He married Josephine Codgill Lewis, a white Texan with liberal views on race, in January 1928. The couple had one child, daughter Philippa, a gifted pianist, composer, and missionary who, like her father, also pursued a career in journalism. Philippa Schuyler, whose IQ was measured at 185 when she was five years old, died tragically in 1967 while working as a war correspondent in Vietnam. Her mother was devastated by the loss and committed suicide in 1969. Schuyler passed away eight years later, in August 1977.

Schuyler left high school before graduation and joined the army in 1912. His six years of service included deployment with the 25th Infantry, a segregated infantry unit during World War I. Following his discharge at the rank of first lieutenant, Schuyler relocated to New York City. He

soon gained exposure to the UNIVERSAL NEGRO IMPROVEMENT ASSOCIATION and the philosophies of MARCUS GARVEY and became a colleague of A. PHILIP RANDOLPH and CHANDLER OWEN. Schuyler joined Randolph and Owen at THE MESSENGER, the journal that they founded in 1917. He worked as associate editor from 1923 through 1928. In 1937 Schuyler joined the staff of THE CRISIS, where he worked as business manager through 1944. His articles appeared in the major African-American periodicals of the Harlem Renaissance and in other mainstream publications such as THE NATION and AMERICAN MERCURY. His association with the *Mercury* during the tenure of editor H. L. MENCKEN earned Schuyler a reputation as "the colored Mencken" (Kellner, 196). In June 1926 one of his most controversial essays, "THE NEGRO ART HOKUM," appeared in *The Nation* and prompted a lively public debate about the priorities, integrity, and direction of African-American artistic production.

Schuyler enjoyed a lengthy and accomplished career in journalism. In addition to working as a special undercover correspondent from Liberia for the *New York Evening Post* in 1931, Schuyler published for many years in the PITTSBURGH COURIER, the newspaper where he also worked as chief editorialist and associate editor. In addition, he served as editor of the *National News*, literary editor at the *Manchester Union Leader*, and analysis editor for the *Review of the News*.

Schuyler's literary debut came in 1931 when he published BLACK NO MORE: *Being an Account of the Strange and Wonderful Workings of Science in the Land of the Free, A.D. 1933–1940* with MACAULAY, the same company that published works by WALLACE THURMAN and CLAUDE MCKAY. In 1932 he published his second novel, *Slaves Today*, a work based on his investigative reporting on the African slave trade.

In the years following the Harlem Renaissance, Schuyler continued to be an outspoken social and political critic. He championed African-American support for World War II, viewing it as a means to challenge racism at home and to generate new domestic opportunities for people of color. He published *Black and Conservative*, his autobiography, in 1966.

Bibliography

Leak, Jeffrey, ed. *Rac(e)ing To the Right: Selected Essays of George S. Schuyler*. Knoxville: University of Tennessee Press, 2001.

Kellner, Bruce. *The Letters of Carl Van Vechten*. New Haven, Conn.: Yale University Press, 1987.

Peplow, Michael. *George S. Schuyler*. Boston: Twayne Publishers, 1980.

Schuyler, Philippa. *Adventures in Black and White*. New York: Robert Speller and Sons, 1960.

Talalay, Kathryn. *Composition in Black and White: The Life of Philippa Schuyler*. New York: Oxford University Press, 1995.

Williams, Harry Jr. *When Black Is Right: The Life and Writings of George Schuyler*. Ann Arbor, Mich.: University Microfilms International, 1990.

Scotia Seminary

The North Carolina school from which the influential educator MARY MCLEOD BETHUNE graduated in 1893. The Presbyterian Church, which founded the school in 1867, established the campus in West Concord, North Carolina. Scotia Seminary was dedicated to educating African-American women for careers in education and in social work. Scotia Seminary was renamed Scotia Women's College in 1916. In 1930 the school merged with the Alabama institution Barber Memorial College and was renamed Barber-Scotia College.

Bethune, one of the school's most accomplished alumni, established BETHUNE-COOKMAN COLLEGE in Daytona Beach, Florida. Barber-Scotia later honored her by naming one of the buildings on its modest campus after the visionary educator and political adviser. The school continues to thrive today as a historically black coeducational institution.

Bibliography

Roebuck, Julian, and Komanduri Murty. *Historically Black Colleges and Universities: Their Place in American Higher Education*. Westport, Conn.: Praeger, 1993.

Whiting, Albert. *Guardians of the Flame: Historically Black Colleges Yesterday, Today, and Tomorrow*. Washington, D.C.: American Association of State Colleges and Universities, 1991.

Scott, Clarissa M. *See* DELANY, CLARISSA M. SCOTT.

Scottsboro Limited: Four Poems and a Play in Verse Langston Hughes (1932)

A politically motivated collection by writer LANGSTON HUGHES that focused on the explosive, false rape charges by two white prostitutes against nine young African-American men aged 13 to 19 (eight of the nine were sentenced to death; see SCOTTSBORO TRIAL). Hughes donated profits from the work to the Scottsboro Defense Fund. Published by the NEW YORK CITY–based Golden Stair Press, the volume was priced at 50 cents and included moving illustrations by Prentiss Taylor, a white WASHINGTON, D.C., artist who collaborated with Hughes on his 1931 collection, *THE NEGRO MOTHER AND OTHER RECITATIONS*.

Scottsboro Limited included a verse drama that had been published earlier in *NEW MASSES* and four other previously published works, poems that had appeared in journals such as the University of North Carolina at Chapel Hill student newspaper *CONTEMPO* and *OPPORTUNITY*. The four poems were "Justice," "The Town of Scottsboro," "Christ in Alabama," and "Scottsboro." Each was an evocative manifesto marked for its graphic images of violence, oppressed African-American figures, and worlds devoid of justice.

The first poem in the collection is a stark, four-line poem entitled "Justice." The narrator notes wryly and without hesitation "That Justice is a blind goddess / Is a thing to which we black are wise." The sobered narrator, notes, however, that the goddess, like the justice she represents, is in crisis and unwhole. The classic blindfold that covers Justice's eyes is transformed into a "bandage," one that "hides two festering sores / That once perhaps were eyes." In "Scottsboro," Hughes is unabashed in his indictment of white southern hypocrisy, prejudice, and inclination toward violence. "8 BLACK BOYS IN A SOUTHERN JAIL / WORLD, TURN PALE!" the narrator declares before posing jarring observations and a haunting question: "8 black boys and one white lie. Is it much to die?" The pointed evaluation in "The Town of Scottsboro," declares that "Scottsboro's just a little place: No shame is writ across its face— / Its court, too weak to stand against a mob, / Its people's heart, too small to hold a sob." The portraits of victims and aggressors in the volume are poignant and direct.

The play *Scottsboro Limited* staged confrontations and interactions among "Eight Black Boys, A White Man, Two White Women, Eight Workers, [and] Voices in the Audience." The set directions are minimal, calling only for a single chair that represents the electric chair used in capital punishment cases, to be placed on the stage. The play opens as the eight characters representing the Scottsboro boys, "chained by the right foot, one to the other, walk slowly down the center aisle from the back of the auditorium." Their entrance is disrupted when the single white man of the cast who has been seated in the audience, rises up to challenge their arrival. The boys and man engage in a spirited set of arguments. "We come in chains / To show our pain," says one boy; another insists that "death can't kill" a "sense of injustice," and another declares that they have come "So the people can see / What it means to be / A poor black workman / In this land of the free." The play progresses with the boys and the man involved in a set of clarifications, rebuttals, and challenges. Racial epithets become part of the heated exchange as tempers begin to flare. The girls who claim to have been raped appear, and each boy responds to the charges that the young women and the judge make. As the courtroom scene comes to a close, voices of a mob are heard. The level of intimidation, both within and beyond the courtroom, is rising considerably. The judge's final words confirm this. "Don't worry folks, the law will take its course. They'll burn, and soon at that," he says to the audience as he exits, "talking and smiling" with the alleged victims. Once the representatives of southern mob law and racist white society leave, a "murmur" of "red voices" begins. The "red voices" counter the threats of the mob and help to rally the young boys. The Scottsboro boys then team up with the workers in an effort to achieve justice and racial unity. "The voice of the red world / Is our voice too," says one boy as another declares, "With all of the workers, / Black or white, / We'll go forward / Out of the night." The play ends as the audience begins to chant, "Fight! Fight! Fight! Fight!" The stage directions call for the singing of the "Internationale" and the raising of the red flag.

Some scholars suggest that the play never was performed, but by May 1932 Hughes was able to report to his longtime friend and correspondent CARL VAN VECHTEN that the play had been "produced quite effectively by the Rebel Players in Los Angeles . . . before a big audience." Hughes also contributed to the performance, noting that he "read a mass-chant and every one yelled beautifully at the proper moments" (Bernard, 97).

The collection represents Hughes's capacity for searing political critique and powerful artistic renderings of crises and challenges.

Bibliography

Bernard, Emily. *Remember Me to Harlem: The Letters of Langston Hughes and Carl Van Vechten.* New York: Knopf, 2001.

Berry, Faith, ed. *Langston Hughes: Before and Beyond Harlem.* Westport, Conn.: Lawrence Hill & Company, 1983.

Rampersad, Arnold. *The Life of Langston Hughes: I, Too, Sing America.* Vol. 1, *1902–1941.* New York: Oxford University Press, 1986.

Scottsboro trial

The explosive case against nine young men ranging in age from 13 to 19 years who were accused of raping two white prostitutes in Alabama. The events, which began in March 1931, evolved into several years of legal struggles, national outpouring of support, petitions to presidents, physical violence against the accused, and intervention by the U.S. Supreme Court. The case was one of the most gripping American legal proceedings and captured the attention of many Harlem Renaissance figures and writers.

The Scottsboro Boys, as the nine came to be called, were Olen Montgomery, Clarence Norris, Haywood Patterson, Ozie Powell, Willie Roberson, Charlie Weems, Eugene Williams, Andy Wright, and Roy Wright. All but one were sentenced to death for a crime that they did not commit. One of the alleged victims, Ruby Bates, later admitted that she had lied and that the charges against the nine were false.

The legal defense for the young men was both highly publicized and extremely politicized. The International Labor Defense Fund hired Clarence

Darrow, the legendary criminal defense attorney, to defend the nine accused. WALTER WHITE of the NATIONAL ASSOCIATION FOR THE ADVANCEMENT OF COLORED PEOPLE (NAACP), however, advised Darrow to withdraw from the case. The NAACP found itself in conflict with the COMMUNIST PARTY, which wanted to lead the defense. The latter prevailed and hired Samuel Leibowitz to chair the defense team.

The Alabama Supreme Court upheld the conviction of seven of the nine, but in 1932, the U.S. Supreme Court reversed the convictions on the grounds that the state of Alabama had failed to provide adequate counsel to the accused. Additional upheaval in the case, however, led to Alabama courts imposing death sentences for Patterson and Norris. In 1935 the U.S. Supreme Court again intervened, this time noting that the two had been denied a trial by their peers because African Americans had been prohibited from serving as jurors. Four of the nine Scottsboro Boys saw the charges against them dropped. The others began serving lengthy sentences that ranged from 75 years to 99 years. Weems, Norris, Wright, and Powell were paroled in the 1940s. Haywood Patterson, who escaped from prison in 1946, was later captured and eventually died in jail. The last survivor of the group, Clarence Norris, died in 1989 at the age of 76.

Leading publications of the Harlem Renaissance era covered the trial and the plight of the nine young men, one of whom was almost blind and all of whom were subjected to violence and abuse from their jailers. The AMSTERDAM NEWS and the *Daily Worker* were two of the newspapers that offered consistent coverage of the case. Noted international academics, writers, and professionals protested the unjust treatment of the Scottsboro Nine. Among those who called for justice were Albert Einstein, Edna St. Vincent Millay, George Bernard Shaw, and Virginia Woolf.

Poet LANGSTON HUGHES crafted one of the most notable creative responses to the Scottsboro Case. SCOTTSBORO LIMITED (1932), a collection of four poems and a verse drama, rallied supporters and further outraged protestors. In addition, COUNTEE CULLEN composed "Scottsboro, Too, Is Worth Its Song," and playwright John Wexley wrote *They Shall Not Die* (1934), a one-act verse play that ran on BROADWAY. Additional works included NANCY CUNARD's "Scottsboro—and Other Scottsboro," a documentary-style work with quotes derived from the events that appeared in her 1933 anthology *Negro Anthology Made by Nancy Cunard, 1931–1933*. Cunard's work prompted poet Kay Boyle to publish "A Communication to Nancy Cunard" in the June 1937 THE NEW REPUBLIC, shortly after the Scottsboro Boys were scheduled for yet another trial.

The Scottsboro case and the literary responses to it illuminated the tragic nature of southern racial injustice and the volatile nature of social and sexual dynamics in the South and throughout the nation.

Bibliography

Carter, Dan. *Scottsboro: A Tragedy of the American South.* Baton Rouge: Louisiana State University Press, 1979.

Goodman, James. *Stories of Scottsboro: The Rape Case That Shocked 1930s America and Revived the Struggle for Equality.* New York: Vintage Books, 1994.

Norris, Clarence, and Sybil Washington. *The Last of the Scottsboro Boys: An Autobiography.* New York: Putnam, 1979.

Wexley, John. *They Shall Not Die: A Play.* 1934; reprint, New York: French, 1950.

"Sealed Pod, A" Marita Bonner (1936)

A short story about betrayal by MARITA BONNER. One of several stories that Bonner published in OPPORTUNITY, "A Sealed Pod" appeared in the March 1936 issue of the NATIONAL URBAN LEAGUE periodical.

The story is set, as many of Bonner's works are, in the CHICAGO neighborhood of Frye Street. The multiethnic neighborhood is home to Ma Davis, a very dark-skinned woman, and her daughter Violette, a young woman who was "kitten-soft with the golden flesh and golden hair that marks the mixed-blood female." Violette entertains many men while her mother works at a night job cleaning offices in downtown Chicago. One night, her fugitive lover, Joe Tamona, an Italian man sought in a bar murder, returns to claim his sweetheart. Unfortunately, he finds her with Dave Jones, a married man with two children. Tamona hides inside the apartment in a closet all night long until Jones finally leaves. Tamona emerges and kills Violette in her bed. No one sees him race out of the apartment building and down toward the river and a freighter that is just moving out from the shore. Dave Jones is falsely accused of the murder on the basis of his proud assertions that he was going to spend the night with Violette. Jones is hanged, and Tamona escapes. The story closes with the detached observation that "everything and everybody in the case was side by side—like peas in the pod. But the pod was sealed. And the peas did not touch each other."

"A Sealed Pod" is one of Bonner's stark fictional accounts of gritty urban life, marital unhappiness, and the deadly consequences of betrayal.

Bibliography

Flynn, Joyce, and Joyce Occomy Striklin. *Frye Street & Environs: The Collected Works of Marita Bonner.* Boston: Beacon Press, 1987.

Second Comin', The George Bryant (1931)

A shocking three-act play by white playwright George Bryant that revolved around African-American religious life and the interracial treachery that could pervade supposedly sanctified communities. The Reverend Wilbur, a white minister, attempts to save an African-American church by performing a major miracle. One of the members, aptly named Nicodemus, dares the minister to create a black Jesus. Wilbur does so but through devious and sinful means. He hypnotizes and then has intercourse with Glory, the woman Nicodemus loves. Wilbur then predicts that Glory is a modern Virgin Mary and will bear a child. She does, but the child is white-skinned. The church erupts in chaos: The misguided, predatory reverend drops dead, the church bell atop the steeple falls to the ground, and Nicodemus is beside himself with rage.

The play opened at the Provincetown Playhouse on 8 December 1931. There were eight performances. The cast was "largely composed of Negroes" (*NYT*, 8 December 1931, 36) and as such represented the emerging works about African-American culture by white writers that increasingly featured actors of color. A. B. Comathiere starred as Nicodemus, Irving Hopkins as Wilbur, and Enid Raphael as Glory. The programs distributed for the shows included a comment from Bryant in which he noted that he had intended to "present an authentic study of the emotional phases of the Negro as they are expressed in their search for religion" (*NYT*, 9 December 1931, 32).

Respected *NEW YORK TIMES* drama critic J. Brooks Atkinson characterized *The Second Comin'* as a "weird brew of truthful observation and reasoning, of worried drama writing and of a solemn accouchement mercifully conducted off-stage." Atkinson suggested that the realism that Bryant had sought emerged only when "the Negroes were alone on the stage, singing, swaying and arguing." Bryant apparently failed to achieve the persuasive authenticity of writers like MARC CONNELLY, the Pulitzer Prize–winning author of the acclaimed play *THE GREEN PASTURES: A FABLE* (1930).

Bibliography

Atkinson, J. Brooks. "The Play: The Parson's Dilemma." *New York Times*, 9 December 1931, 32.
"Theatrical Notes." *New York Times*, 8 December 1931, 36.

Selected Gems of Poetry, Comedy, and Drama Mercedes Gilbert (1931)

A self-edited collection of works that the multitalented actress and writer MERCEDES GILBERT published in 1931. The volume, produced by the Boston-based Christopher Publishing House, included a variety of Gilbert's previously published works.

Bibliography

Gilbert, Mercedes. *Selected Gems of Poetry, Comedy, and Drama; Aunt Sara's Wooden God.* Introduction by Susanne Dietzel. New York: G. K. Hall, 1997.

Select Plays: Santa Claus Land, Jepthah's Daughter, The Prince of Peace, Bachelor's Convention Carrie Law Morgan Figgs (1923)

A self-published collection of plays by poet and playwright CARRIE LAW MORGAN FIGGS. The title page made a pointed note that "Production of these Plays is FREE to Amateurs, but the sole *Professional Rights* are reserved by the *Author. Moving Picture Rights reserved.*" Two of the four works were based on biblical stories, one was a children's play, and another was a contemporary "comedy drama."

Santa Claus Land was a short two-act play for children and featured a governess named Alice and her three charges, a young girl named Fluffy and her two brothers, Stuffy and Toughy. The group is in search of Santa Claus and gets help from a kindly Queen of the Fairies. When Fluffy is on the verge of being kidnapped by a King of the Goblins, her outspoken brother Toughy saves her. His gruff manner and disregard for magic embarrass his sister, but as he points out in the closing scene, "you weren't ashamed of me when them Goblins was after you, and you're ashamed now?" The play has no overwhelming moral message but does build on children's interest in Santa Claus and suggests the benefits of patience and curiosity.

Bachelor's Convention is a satire of the relationships between men and women. A group of shipwrecked nurses seek shelter in a disorganized male sanctuary known as Bachelor's Headquarters. Over the course of the three acts, the men, whose names range from James Disgusted to Richard Sleepyhead, set aside their protests of female influence and accept the improved domestic arrangements that the women make. By play's end, the bachelors ask the ladies to marry them and agree to the strict terms that the women institute. These house rules enable the ladies to attend their own club meetings and to leave any children in the care of their fathers, and give control of household finances to the women.

The two biblical plays were based on sobering stories of self-sacrifice and female bravery. The first, *Jepthah's Daughter,* was a three-act play that condensed the story of Jepthah found in the Old Testament book of Numbers. Figgs created a fast-paced version of the tragic story that culminates in a father's necessary sacrifice of his only child. The outcast, but eventually victorious, soldier Jepthah makes a promise to God in order to secure military triumphs. When he returns home, he is forced to sacrifice Adah, his daughter and only child, in order to honor his pledge to God. The play closes as characters sing "Swing Low, Sweet Chariot," one of the several spirituals that Figgs has interspersed throughout the play. The second biblical play, *The Prince of Peace,* reenacts the days preceding the birth of Jesus in the course of three brief acts. The play includes well-known scenes of Mary's visitation, Herod's pronouncement, and the birth of the child. It concludes with the hymn "Silent Night" as characters gather around Mary and the child in the manger.

Bibliography

Clifford, Carrie Williams, and Carrie Law Morgan Figgs, *Writings of Carrie Williams Clifford and Carrie Law Morgan Figgs with an introduction by P. Jane Splawn.* New York: G. K. Hall & Co., 1997.

Seven Arts

A progressive socialist literary arts magazine that, despite its short-lived publication period, contributed significantly to the advance of the Harlem Renaissance.

The *Seven Arts* editors VAN WYCK BROOKS, WALDO FRANK, and JAMES OPPENHEIM hoped to introduce fresh and dynamic works by emerging and established writers. The journal featured writers such as Sherwood Anderson, John Dos Passos, THEODORE DREISER, Robert Frost, Amy Lowell, and EUGENE O'NEILL. *Seven Arts* also became the first white literary magazine of the Harlem Renaissance period to publish the work of a writer of color. In 1917 the journal published the sonnets "The Harlem Dancer" and "Invocation" by CLAUDE MCKAY, who on this momentous occasion used the pseudonym ELI EDWARDS.

Despite its promising and substantial start, the *Seven Arts* lasted only one year before it merged with *The Dial,* a magazine that published JEAN TOOMER and Waldo Frank. The outspoken political views of Oppenheim, who voiced his opposition to World War I, resulted in a severe loss of funding, and the magazine merged with *The Dial.*

Bibliography

Carter, Paul. *Waldo Frank.* New York: Twayne Publishers, 1967.

Cooper, Wayne. *Claude McKay: Rebel Sojourner in the Harlem Renaissance.* New York: Schocken Books, 1987.

Giles, James R. *Claude McKay.* Boston: Twayne Publishers, 1976.

Seventh-Day Adventist Harlem Academy
See HARLEM ACADEMY.

"Seven Years for Rachel" Theophilus Lewis
(1924)

A lengthy story by THEOPHILUS LEWIS that appeared in three installments of the *THE CRISIS*—the November 1923 and January and February 1924 issues. The story title recalls the Old Testament narrative of Jacob and his efforts to secure Rachel, daughter of Laban and sister of Leah, as his wife. Laban who substitutes Leah, his oldest daughter, as the bride, thwarts Jacob. Jacob, who has worked the negotiated seven years for Rachel, then commits to working another seven years to obtain the hand of the wife he truly desires.

The male protagonist in Lewis's story is Sam Jones, a married man who has developed feelings for Rachel Pettus, a much younger woman. The two eventually confess their feelings for each other, but Rachel demurs from developing a relationship. Her Christian values and unwillingness to break the seventh commandment prompt her to refrain from seeing Jones as much as she would like. Sam's frustration prompts him to seek out Zeb Hicks, a witchdoctor known for conjuring spells to punish wicked people. Hicks suggests that Sam sell his soul to the devil for seven years in exchange for the desires of his heart. In short order, Sam's wife dies and Sam is able to marry Rachel. After six months of wedded bliss, however, Rachel becomes ill and dies as well. Her deathbed musings about God's blessings on them and their honorable efforts to avoid adulterous behavior torment Sam. He is convinced that he has betrayed not only God but also the innocent woman that he loves. When Rachel dies, Sam realizes that his request of the devil was incomplete; he asked only to have Rachel but failed to specify that he wanted to enjoy a lifetime of happiness. The story closes somewhat abruptly as Sam seeks absolution and counsel from a minister who pronounces him damned and sinful.

Shades and Shadows Randolph Edmonds
(1930)

The first of two anthologies that university professor RANDOLPH EDMONDS published during the Harlem Renaissance. A third collection, *The Land of Cotton and Other Plays,* appeared in 1943. The collected plays included *The Devil's Price, Hewers of Wood, Shades and Shadows, Everyman's Land, The Tribal Chief,* and *The Phantom Treasure.*

Shaw University

Founded by Baptist missionaries in 1865, it is the oldest historically black college in the South. Reverend Henry Martin Tupper offered the first classes, and it was his sessions with Southern freedmen just after the end of the Civil War that eventually led to the foundation of the school in Raleigh, North Carolina. Established first as Raleigh Institute, the coeducational school became Shaw Collegiate Institute in 1870. It was named in honor of Elijah Shaw, the donor who financed the construction of Shaw Hall, the first building on campus. In 1875 the school was renamed Shaw University.

Shaw's impressive academic history is rooted in its commitment to excellence and preparation of its students for successful professional lives. The first undergraduate class graduated in 1878. The medical school, established in 1885 and the first southern four-year medical school open to African-American students, graduated its first students in 1886. The school has since intensified its focus on liberal arts and functions as a college, rather than as a university.

IDA B. WELLS-BARNETT studied at Shaw, which was known as Rust College until 1890. Activist Ella Baker attended Shaw, graduated in 1927, and headed north to New York City where she became immersed in the Harlem Renaissance and began working with the NATIONAL ASSOCIATION FOR THE ADVANCEMENT OF COLORED PEOPLE.

Bibliography

Morehouse, Henry. *H. M. Tupper, D.D. A Narrative of Twenty-Five Years' Work in the South, 1865–1890.* New York: American Baptist Home Mission Society, 1890.

Roebuck, Julian. *Historically Black Colleges and Universities: Their Place in American Higher Education.* Westport, Conn.: Praeger, 1993.

Whiting, Albert. *Guardians of the Flame: Historically Black Colleges Yesterday, Today, and Tomorrow.* Washington, D.C.: American Association of State Colleges and Universities, 1991.

Willie, Charles, and Ronald Edmonds, eds. *Black Colleges in America: Challenge, Development, Survival.* New York: Teachers College Press, 1978.

Sheen, Edwin Drummond (unknown)

A native of Decatur, Illinois, Sheen was a journalist who also wrote fiction during the Harlem Renaissance. He enrolled at James Milliken University, an institution founded in 1901 that was affiliated with the Presbyterian Church. Sheen graduated with honors in 1925. Two years later, he completed his second bachelor's degree at the University of Illinois.

Sheen won the second prize in the 1926 CRISIS literary contest. His short story "THE DEATH GAME" was one of four notable works identified by the judges CHARLES CHESNUTT, Otelia Cromwell, and Ernest Poole. This story appears to be the only work of fiction that Sheen published during the Harlem Renaissance.

Sherman, French, and Company

One of several small Boston publishing houses and the firm that in 1912 published the first edition of *THE AUTOBIOGRAPHY OF AN EX-COLOURED MAN* by JAMES WELDON JOHNSON. The firm also published works by GEORGE REGINALD MARGETSON, a Boston-based West Indian poet who participated in the city's SATURDAY EVENING QUILL CLUB and contributed works to the *SATURDAY EVENING QUILL.*

"Silk Stockings" Anita Scott Coleman (1926)

A frenetic short story about unfulfilled desires and domesticity by ANITA SCOTT COLEMAN. Published in the August 1926 issue of *THE MESSENGER*, the story was part of the journal's efforts to diversify its contents and to include more literary materials.

The story begins as a type of intervention, one meant to tell the "plain tale of plain people," the "plain everyday folks" in whose lives one can find "tragedies from which drama is woven." Protagonist Nancy Meade marries John Silas Light after an unsuccessful but educational dalliance with Gerald Lincoln McKay. An industrious woman and talented seamstress, she creates a wardrobe that is the envy of many of her coworkers. The items that Nancy cannot make, however, are silk stockings. Following the birth of her baby, she skillfully transforms a portion of her wardrobe into baby clothes. After enduring his wife's direct hints, her husband buys her stockings. Unfortunately, they are neither attractive nor made of silk. Disillusioned, she allows herself to question her marriage and to reconsider McKay as a sweetheart. She and McKay enjoy a number of outings and kisses but one night, the sight of a laundry line with men's socks, women's cream stockings, and a pair of baby's stockings jars Nancy back into reality. She flees McKay and hurries home to her husband and child.

Coleman's story, like a number of works by fellow Harlem Renaissance writers, examines the material realities and desires that sometimes threaten marriages. The themes of self-indulgence, betrayal, and recommitment, however, transform this potentially tragic tale into a meditation on recuperation and reunion.

Silvera, Edward S., Jr. (1906–1937)

A Florida native who, before his untimely death, was an emerging and promising poet of the Harlem Renaissance. Silvera moved north with his family to New Jersey. He pursued undergraduate studies at LINCOLN UNIVERSITY, the first American institution of higher learning for African-American men. Silvera thrived at Lincoln, the alma mater of ARCHIBALD GRIMKÉ, Thurgood Marshall, and Kwame Nkrumah. Lincoln also was the alma mater of LANGSTON HUGHES, WARING CUNEY, and William Hill. In 1930 the works of Silvera, Hughes, Cuney, and Hill were featured in "FOUR LINCOLN UNIVERSITY POETS," a celebratory university sponsored pamphlet.

Silvera was one of several writers featured in *FIRE!!*, the dynamic, controversial, and short-lived journal edited by WALLACE THURMAN. In November 1926 his poem "Jungle Taste" appeared in *Flame From the Dark Tower*, a collection of poems that also featured the writings of LEWIS ALEXANDER, ARNA BONTEMPS, Waring Cuney, COUNTEE CULLEN, Langston Hughes, and HELENE JOHNSON. The poem celebrates the private racialized knowledge that is available only to people of specific and shared ancestries. In his tribute to "the songs of black men" and to the "faces of black women," Silvera reveled in the idea that what was a "weird strangeness" to others "sounds not strange to me." The poem closed with the assertion that the "Jungle beauty / And mystery" and "Dark hidden beauty" in African-American women was not wholly accessible, a beauty "Which only black men / see." The poem is marked for its heightened race pride and self-assured possessive sensibility.

Silvera received recognition from established Harlem Renaissance figures for his writing. In 1927 he placed second behind poet MAE COWDERY in *THE CRISIS* literary competition. His "Song to a Dark Girl" was one of three prizewinning works selected that year.

Bibliography

Bond, Horace Mann. *Education for Freedom: A History of Lincoln University, Pennsylvania.* Lincoln University, Pa.: Lincoln University, 1976.

Simon the Cyrenian Ridgely Torrence (1917)

A pioneering verse play by RIDGELY TORRENCE that was part of his groundbreaking trilogy of plays created specifically for African-American actors. The three-play collection published in 1917 also included *GRANNY MAUMEE* and *THE RIDER OF DREAMS*.

The play, which is the only religious drama in the trilogy, focuses on Simon the Cyrenian, a brave man and leader of Roman slave revolts who shares the burden of the cross with Jesus in the moments leading up to the Crucifixion. Initially determined to rescue the criminal Barabas from imprisonment, Simon of Cyrene is transfixed by the gaze of Jesus when he encounters him briefly. Jesus, betrayed by Judas, is captured by guards while praying on the Mount of Olives. It is there that Simon "saw men come with torches and seize a man. / I hurried near," he notes, "and through the olive leaves / His eyes looked into mine, / His eyes burned into mine. I have seen them since, / Waking or sleeping." Simon later endeavors to help Jesus and does not hesitate to take up the heavy cross upon which Jesus is to be crucified. He later bears a crown of thorns and vows to "wear this / I will bear this till [Jesus Christ] comes into his own." The play fea-

tures a hero of Northern Africa who is determined to honor his faith despite the threat of violent retribution and ostracism.

As Torrence biographer John Clum notes, the playwright was quite explicit about his claims that the work honored an African hero. Torrence provided a detailed explanation of his racial rationale, stating that "It has been the author's design that all the characters in this play should be represented by persons entirely or partly of Negro blood. . . . Simon is a full-blooded Negro . . . The Roman characters are played by persons of a slighter Negroid strain." Torrence also addressed the historical and anthropological facts that supported his claims. He explained that "Although Cyrene was in Northern Africa, the wall-paintings in the vast Cyrenian tombs depict black people instead of brown" and that "Jesus' cross bearer was a black man, as the early painters represented him." Torrence's recuperation of the biblical and historical facts endowed the play with a pointed historical agenda that reinforced his contemporary goal of crafting serious dramas that featured people of color in central roles.

Philanthropist and theater enthusiast EMILIE HAPGOOD was the producer of *Simon the Cyrenian*. The play opened first on BROADWAY at the Garden Theatre on April 4, 1917. Nearly two weeks later, on April 16, 1917, it opened at the Garrick Theatre and ran for just over one additional week. The cast on opening night at the Garden Theatre included Inez Clough, who would later appear in WALLACE THURMAN and WILLIAM RAPP's *HARLEM* (1929); the multitalented performer, director, writer, and lyricist Alex Rogers; and Jesse Shipp, a veteran of early African-American musicals and a founding member with J. Rosamond Johnson, Bert Williams, George Walker, and others of the African-American theater professionals group known as The Frogs.

In 1920 the Harlem YWCA staged an amateur production of *Simon the Cyrenian*. PAUL ROBESON, then a law student at COLUMBIA UNIVERSITY, followed the suggestion of his wife, ESLANDA GOODE ROBESON, who coached sports at the facility, and auditioned for the play. Robeson was cast in the play and made his theatrical debut when it opened in the June 1920. His performance at the Harlem YWCA, witnessed by members of the

PROVINCETOWN PLAYERS, led to their immediate recruitment of Robeson and his subsequent appearance in EUGENE O'NEILL's ALL GOD'S CHILLUN GOT WINGS and to Robeson's historic leading role in O'Neill's THE EMPEROR JONES.

Bibliography
Clum, John. *Ridgely Torrence.* New York: Twayne, 1972.

Torrence, Ridgely. *Granny Maumee, The Rider of Dreams, Simon the Cyrenian: Plays for a Negro Theater.* New York: The Macmillan Company, 1917.

Six Plays for the Negro Theatre
Randolph Edmonds (1934)
The second of two drama collections that RANDOLPH EDMONDS published during the Harlem Renaissance. The volume appeared in the same year as JONAH'S GOURD VINE by ZORA NEALE HURSTON and THE WAYS OF WHITE FOLKS by LANGSTON HUGHES.

Six Plays, published by the BOSTON firm of W. H. Baker, included a foreword by Frederick Koch. The volume featured six works by Edmonds: *Bad Man, Old Man Pete, Nat Turner, Breeders, Bleeding Hearts,* and *The New Window.* Of this group, only *Nat Turner* had been previously published. That play was included in NEGRO HISTORY IN THIRTEEN PLAYS (1935), the collection that WILLIS RICHARDSON and MAY MILLER edited and published with Associated Publishers, the WASHINGTON, D.C., company with which CARTER G. WOODSON and ALAIN LOCKE were affiliated.

Bibliography
Edmonds, Randolph. *Six Plays for the Negro Theatre.* 1934, reprint, Ann Arbor, Mich.: University Microfilms, 1986.

"Slackened Caprice" Ottie Graham (1924)
The only short story that OTTIE GRAHAM published in OPPORTUNITY during the Harlem Renaissance.

"Slackened Caprice" was published in the November 1924 issue of the NATIONAL URBAN LEAGUE's monthly magazine. The unnamed narrator is traveling with a friend named Carlotta. The two women stop at the Jamieson home and there encounter the son of Carlotta's friend. A mysterious man, he plays the piano for them several times. His major composition, a caprice, was inspired initially by the sight of children playing in a nearby park. Unfortunately, the soldier also witnessed the children's ejection by a racist park watchman. From that moment on, he is unable to complete his composition or to perform it without lapsing into a dramatic panic. Some time passes before the narrator returns to the Jamiesons' hometown. She finds that the family has dispersed and that their home has been demolished and replaced by a theater. She is able to attend the theater and there hears another musician perform the unfinished composition by Jamieson. In an unexpected moment, the lost veteran-artist appears on the stage and performs his music. In the mayhem that follows his unscheduled appearance, Jamieson collapses. The narrator attempts to take responsibility for him, but he dies there on the site of his former home just moments after leaving the stage. She sells her rings in order to cover the costs of his funeral.

Graham's tale of a talented but disturbed veteran underscores the kind of major damage that prejudice, not world war, could impose upon individuals.

Slaves Today: A Story of Liberia George Schuyler (1931)
The second and last novel that GEORGE SCHUYLER published during his career and a work influenced by his investigative work in Liberia during a three-month period in early 1931. Schuyler, recruited by George Palmer Putnam, was in the African nation working as an undercover reporter in Liberia for the *New York Post.* Schuyler's investigative findings would be considered in a case against the African nation brought by the League of Nations. Upon his return, Putnam's publishing house, Brewer, Warren, and Mason, collected the serialized installments of the work that had appeared in an array of American newspapers and published the volume in the fall of 1931.

Schuyler hoped that the novel, a fictionalized documentary based on actual individuals and events, would draw attention to the global practice of enslavement. The author's foreword reveals the intensity of Schuyler's hopes for the novel and for its impact on many nations. He writes plainly that "[i]f this novel can help arouse enlightened world opinion against this brutalizing of the native population in a Negro republic, perhaps the conscience of civilized people will stop similar atrocities in native lands ruled by proud white nations that boast of their superior culture."

Slaves Today focuses on the oppressive labor practices in Liberia and the exploitation of native peoples. In his foreword, Schuyler notes that "[r]egardless of the polite name that masks it while bloody profits are ground out for white and black masters," modern slavery "differs only in slight degree from slavery in the classic sense, except that the chattel slaves's lives were not held so cheaply." Schuyler's literary exposé contributes to the larger pan-African interest in African social, economic, and political matters. His story, however, focuses on the ways in which Africans exploited their kinsmen, rather than on the evils of white colonialism.

Schuyler critic Michael Peplow, who proposes that Slaves Today is the first novel about AFRICA by an African American, notes that the novel was markedly controversial. The most tragic aspect of Schuyler's fictional narrative revolves around Zo and Pameta, a newlywed and native African couple. Before the wedding festivities are completed, the couple is brutally separated by slave raiders. Zo is sold into bondage and transported out of the country. His wife, Pameta, becomes a slave in a harem. After grueling experiences that include sickness, efforts to escape, and betrayal, the couple is reunited. Pameta dies in her husband's arms. Enraged by her death, Zo plots to murder the commissioner who instigated the initial raid on the wedding ceremony. He succeeds in killing Commissioner Jackson but loses his life immediately when a guard shoots him in the commissioner's compound.

Slaves Today also illuminates the political machinations that both facilitate and maintain slavery. Schuyler develops thinly veiled portraits of contemporary officials and political leaders. The persistent corruption and the failure of reform and resistance efforts mean ultimately that slavery is not abolished.

Bibliography

Peplow, Michael. *George Schuyler*. Boston: Twayne Publishers, 1980.

Schuyler, George. *Slaves Today: A Story of Liberia*. 1931; reprint, New York: AMS Press, 1969.

"Sleeper Wakes, The" Jessie Fauset (1920)

A moving short story about emerging racial consciousness by JESSIE FAUSET that appeared in three installments in THE CRISIS. One of several stories that appeared in the monthly magazine of the NATIONAL ASSOCIATION FOR THE ADVANCEMENT OF COLORED PEOPLE, "The Sleeper Wakes" appeared in the August, September, and October 1920 issues.

The protagonist is Amy, a light-skinned, mixed-race woman who, after living with a white family, becomes the charge of an African-American family named the Boldins. Amy has no information about her background, only the memory of a "tall, proud white woman" who drives her to the Boldins' home in Trenton, New Jersey. When she is 17, Amy resolves to run away in order to express herself fully and to enjoy the world. She makes her way to NEW YORK CITY and there takes up with a lively artist named Zora Harrison. Living as a white woman in New York, Amy has the opportunity to marry an older, rich white man. She does so, even though she does not love him. Her life is good, but Stuart James Wynne is a southerner with no inclination to be civil to his African-American domestic staff. After witnessing a series of confrontations with the help, Amy intervenes when a young male servant whom she likes threatens revenge on Wynne. As she tries to justify her intervention, she reveals to her husband that she is a colored woman. Predictably, Wynne divorces her, and she begins life anew. When, after some time, he finds her and offers to take her back, she is stunned to realize that he does not want her as a wife but as a mistress. She refuses and, at that point, realizes that she wants desperately to reconnect with the Boldins, the family who loved her unconditionally. The story closes as she prepares to reunite with the family who has missed her and looks forward to her return.

Fauset's story foreshadows the themes of racial consciousness, female desire, and social responsibility that emerge in her novels. "The Sleeper Wakes" is a substantial meditation on the power of self-assertion and reclamation in the face of supposed ostracism and domestic upheaval. Fauset's resilient heroine takes responsibility for her life, and her maturation depends on her willingness to evaluate the limits of white privilege and the emancipatory, uplifting possibilities available in the African-American world.

Bibliography

Jones, Sharon. *Rereading the Harlem Renaissance: Race, Class, and Gender in the Fiction of Jessie Fauset, Zora Neale Hurston, and Dorothy West.* Westport, Conn.: Greenwood Press, 2002.

Sylvander, Carolyn. *Jessie Redmon Fauset, Black American Writer.* Troy, N.Y.: Whitson Pub. Co., 1981.

Wall, Cheryl. *Women of the Harlem Renaissance.* Bloomington: Indiana University Press, 1995.

Small Wisdom Anita Scott Coleman (1937)

ANITA SCOTT COLEMAN published this volume of poems under the pseudonym of Elizabeth Stapleton Stokes. It was the first of three collections that Coleman published during the career and the only one that she produced during the Harlem Renaissance.

Published by the New York publisher H. Harrison, *Small Wisdom* includes 53 poems that address subjects such as mortality, romance, the act of writing, and childhood. The title poem, "Small Wisdom," sets the stage for the volume's overall theme of reminiscence. "This small wisdom, then, / From all the year's design! / Filtered / drop by tedious drop, / In quintessential wine," declares the speaker in the first stanza. The three-stanza poem closes on a note of distress. The speaker clearly is alarmed that the labor that produced the poem and, by extension, the volume, could arrive too late for readers: "But oh! if hands that grope for stars / Stiffen with the chill, / And eager eyes be one with dust / Before the cup distill!" Other works such as "Plea for Immortality," "Fragment," "Irony," and "Words" further explore the tension between the passage of time and a poet's intensive, though often deliberate, efforts to produce works. Other poems consider the beauty of the writing process. In "Little Words,"

Coleman delights in the romance of creativity even as she ponders the limitations of the physical act of creation. "This radiant, hushed expectant page! / Potential with divine / And infinite dreams—" the speaker observes, before admitting that the page is "bound / By little words of mine!" Other poems explore family bonds, childhood, and maturation. In "Night," Coleman considers how "each span of darkness lessens them, / These boys, grown suddenly so tall; / Fetters their confident interval / Of light; and by some timeless stratagem, / Annuls the years." Other works, such as "A Small Boy Practising" and "For a Small Boy Just Arrived at Camp," are poignant notes about the unknown, the prospect of adventure, and the rituals of life. In the latter, the speaker focuses on a young boy, "Straight and gallant, khaki-clad" whose "eager freckled face" reveals his "brave belief his world would bring / High adventure." Additional poems, such as "Prayer" and "Souvenir of a Journey" reflect the speaker's disillusionment with adult responsibilities and desire to triumph over the passage of time.

Smith, J. Pauline (unknown)

A poet of the Midwest whose works primarily appeared in religious and civic publications during the Harlem Renaissance. Little is known about Smith, who published a volume of collected poems in 1922. That volume, EXCEEDING RICHES AND OTHER VERSE, was published by the PHILADELPHIA-based A.M.E. Book Concern. That organization, part of the African Methodist Episcopal Church, established in 1818, was the oldest department of the church that may be best known for publishing the *Christian Recorder,* the world's oldest continuously published periodical published by people of African descent.

Smith, who may have lived in Detroit, Michigan, published poems in local periodicals such as the *Detroit Club Woman* and the *Detroit Free Press.* She also published poems in the *AME Christian Recorder.*

Bibliography

Smith, J. Pauline. *Exceeding Riches and Other Verse.* Philadelphia: A.M.E. Book Concern, 1922.

"Smoke, Lilies, and Jade" Richard Bruce Nugent (1926)

A daring, homoerotic story by RICHARD BRUCE NUGENT published in the first and only issue of *FIRE!!* Nugent's story, which appeared in November 1926, is set in contemporary times and features a number of Harlem Renaissance figures, including PAUL ROBESON, LANGSTON HUGHES, and ZORA NEALE HURSTON. Nugent also makes reference to GEORGES GURDJIEFF, JEAN TOOMER, H. L. MENCKEN, and COUNTEE CULLEN, among others.

The story, which is infused throughout with ellipses and staccato-like phrases, follows the musings of Alex, a fatherless male protagonist whose itinerant life and immersion in the world of artists and writers distresses his mother and family. Alex enjoys his contacts with the colorful figures of the Harlem Renaissance and distracts himself from his distressing past, which includes the death of his father, by imagining artistic projects. These include crafting a portrait of Fania, a character clearly based on FANIA MARINOFF VAN VECHTEN, wife of CARL VAN VECHTEN, the man who photographed so many Harlem Renaissance figures. Alex is attracted to two different individuals, a woman named Melva and an intriguing, seductive male persona named Beauty. After physical encounters with both, Alex concludes that "one *could* love two at the same time." The story ends without any definitive choice on Alex's part. Nugent signals that the story itself is not over, noting that it is "To Be Continued." The cessation of *Fire!!*, however, meant that Nugent was unable to publish additional installments of his story.

Bibliography

Wirth, Thomas. *Gay Rebel of the Harlem Renaissance: Selections from the Work of Richard Bruce Nugent*. Durham: Duke University Press, 2002.

"Snakes" Eric Walrond (1924)

A short story by ERIC WALROND that provides a glimpse of West Indian interactions in NEW YORK CITY. Published in the February 1924 issue of *THE MESSENGER*, the story is narrated by a figure who is prompted to assert that Lloyd, the main character, is a West Indian man because "[to] say this is vital if I am to get over the idea of this sketch." The narrator then provides insights about Lloyd, a Jamaican man who fought for the British in France and Mesopotamia before arriving in HARLEM. During the course of the two men's evening stroll through Harlem, they come across all sorts of gatherings including impromptu dances of the Charleston on the street corner. Before long, the two men come across a Haitian man who is writhing on the street. The man, who complains loudly of the snakes in his belly, offers Lloyd $200 for his help. Lloyd listens to the man's story about the loss of 300 gold coins, and the suspected treachery of his wife and best friend. Believing himself cursed by snakes, 300 of them, the man has left Haiti for Harlem and is desperate to be rid of the snakes that now plague his belly. Lloyd finally takes the $200 and writes him a prescription for "aloe and scrutcheoneel" that he may fill at a West Indian apothecary nearby.

Walrond's sketch, written in the form of a local-color anecdote, is part of the substantial body of literature on West Indian life in New York City.

Bibliography

Parascandola, Louis, ed. *Winds Can Wake Up the Dead: An Eric Walrond Reader*. Detroit: Wayne State University Press, 1998.

Sorbonne

One of the oldest educational institutions in Europe, the Sorbonne is one of the 13 educational facilities that make up the University of Paris. Founded in 1253, the University of Paris became known first for its teachings of theology. In 1257, French theologian Robert de Sorbon established the Sorbonne, which was known originally as La Communauté des Pauvres Maîtres Etudiants en Théologie, (the community of poor scholars).

During the Harlem Renaissance, a number of gifted scholars, artists, and writers studied in FRANCE and at the Sorbonne. Dr. ANNA JULIA COOPER, principal of the highly respected M STREET HIGH SCHOOL in WASHINGTON, D.C., became the first African-American woman to earn a Ph.D. from the Sorbonne and the fourth woman of color in America to earn the degree. Cooper, aged 65, wrote a dissertation entitled "The Attitude of France on the Question of Slavery Between 1789 and 1848" and graduated from the Sorbonne in 1925.

The demonstrated excellence of several Harlem Renaissance figures resulted in scholarships to study at the Sorbonne. Writer and artist GWENDOLYN BENNETT was one of several emerging artists who studied at the prestigious institution. Following her graduation from PRATT INSTITUTE in NEW YORK CITY and appointment to the faculty at HOWARD UNIVERSITY, Bennett accepted a $1,000 scholarship to pursue studies in art at the Sorbonne. In 1928 COUNTEE CULLEN won a GUGGENHEIM FELLOWSHIP that facilitated his studies at the Sorbonne.

Artist ROMARE BEARDEN enrolled at the Sorbonne following his schooling at COLUMBIA UNIVERSITY and his stint in the army. He used the GI Bill to fund his six months of study in Paris. In addition, artist James Porter, a highly respected Howard University professor who is heralded as the father of African-American art history, studied baroque art at the Sorbonne.

JESSIE FAUSET, the era's most acclaimed mentor and the most published woman writer of the Harlem Renaissance, enrolled at the Sorbonne following her graduation from the UNIVERSITY OF PENNSYLVANIA, where she had earned a master's degree in French. Fauset traveled to France and furthered her studies in French literature and language before returning to New York City, where she became a leading literary figure.

JOEL AUGUSTUS ROGERS, the self-educated anthropologist, historian, and journalist, represented a set of Harlem Renaissance–era intellectuals who had ties to French institutions and academic communities. Rogers, who was an elected member of the Paris Society of Anthropology, lectured at the Sorbonne.

Souls of Black Folk W. E. B. DuBois (1903)

W. E. B. DuBois's best-known publication, *Souls of Black Folk*, cemented his reputation as an intellectual and as the main challenger to the accommodationist philosophies of BOOKER T. WASHINGTON.

The volume consists of a series of 14 probing autobiographical, historical, sociological, and fictional narratives. These essays, which include titles such as "Of the Training of Black Men," "Of

Mr. Booker T. Washington and Others," "Of Our Spiritual Strivings" and a biographical tribute to Alexander Crummell, constitute, according to Peter Coviello, "an impassioned, often surpassingly lyrical account of the trauma of race in America" and a staggeringly intricate account of the intimate life of race" (Coviello, 2). DuBois's prefatory words to readers, published in the "Forethought" to the volume, offer a memorable and confident characterization of the work. "Herein lie buried many things which if read with patience may show the strange meaning of being black here at the dawning of the Twentieth Century," he wrote. In keeping with the traditionally deferential tone and studied humility of many late 19th-century writers, he asked his "Gentle Reader" to "receive my little book in all charity, studying my words with me, forgiving mistake and foible for sake of the faith and passion that is in me, and seeking the grain of truth hidden there" (DuBois, xxxi). He also authorized himself as one able to provide a reliable and convincing assessment of African-American life, noting that he was "bone of the bone and flesh of them that live within the Veil" (DuBois, xxxii).

DuBois outlined the deliberate structure of the work and called attention to the systematic ways in which he had attempted to address the lives and histories of African Americans, the "ten thousand thousand Americans" who had to contend with and survive bondage and ruthless oppression. "I have tried to show what Emancipation meant to them," he wrote, before noting that additional chapters tackled subjects such as "the slow rise of personal leadership," "the two worlds within and without the Veil," "the struggles of the massed millions of the black peasantry," and "the present relations of the sons of master and man." Finally, he noted that he had, on behalf of his readers, "stepped within the Veil, raising it that you may view faintly its deeper recesses,—the meaning of its religion, the passion of its human sorrow, and the struggle of its greater souls." The first essay included one of the most powerful conceits ever applied to the African-American condition. In "Spiritual Strivings," DuBois articulated his conception of double consciousness, a "peculiar sensation, this double-consciousness, this sense of always looking at one's self through the eyes of others, of measuring one's soul by the tape of a world that looks on in amused contempt and pity." He continued, noting that "One ever feels his twoness,—an American, a Negro; two souls, two thoughts, two unreconciled strivings; two warring ideals in one dark body, whose dogged strength alone keeps it from being torn asunder" (DuBois, 3).

In *Souls of Black Folk*, DuBois emphasized an investment in the intellectual and political advancement of people of color and, according to historian Nathan Huggins, constituted an explicit rejection of what DuBois and his colleagues regarded as Booker T. Washington's "sell-out of the Negro's political and social rights" and his "anti-intellectual position against higher education for the Negro man of ability" (Huggins, 20).

Bibliography

Coviello, Peter. "Intimacy and Affliction: DuBois, Race, and Psychoanalysis," *Modern Language Quarterly* 64 (1) 2003. 1–32.

DuBois, W. E. Burghardt. *Souls of Black Folk*. 1903; reprint, New York: Bantam Books, 1989.

———. *The Autobiography of W. E. B. DuBois: A Soliloquy on Viewing My Life from the Last Decade of Its First Century*. New York: International Publishers, 1968.

Huggins, Nathan. *Harlem Renaissance*. New York: Oxford University Press, 1971.

Sundquist, Eric. *The Oxford W. E. B. DuBois Reader*. New York: Oxford University Press, 1996.

Southern Road Sterling Brown (1932)

A collection of diverse and moving poems by STERLING BROWN. The volume, which Brown dedicated to fellow poet ANNE SPENCER, elicited high praise from leading literary figures and race leaders such as ALAIN LOCKE and JAMES WELDON JOHNSON. Locke knighted Brown as the "New Negro Folk Poet" and praised him earnestly for his presentation of racial themes and avoidance of stereotype. Johnson, affiliated at the time with FISK UNIVERSITY, praised Brown for crafting a number of poems that "admit of no classification or brand" and others that reflect the poet's capacity for transforming folk poems "without diluting [their] primitive frankness and raciness" and for present-

ing these foundational African-American poetic ideas "with artistry and magnified power" (Johnson, xxxvii).

The volume, which appeared just one year after Brown published his influential anthology entitled THE BOOK OF AMERICAN NEGRO POETRY (1931), included previously published poems and a number of new works. The book was divided into four sections. The two longest sections were Part One, entitled "Road So Rocky," with 21 poems, and Part Two, entitled "On Restless River," with 18 poems. The last two and the shortest sections were Part Three, "Tin Roof Blues," and Part Four, "Vestiges," which contained nine and 10 poems, respectively. Brown combined traditional poetical forms such as sonnets with work songs, ballads, and sermons.

The volume opens with a series of poems that reflect the intense history of African-American labor and migration. In the first, "Odyssey of Big Boy," the narrator, Big Boy, provides a sobering autobiographical record that includes mining, tobacco harvesting, corn shucking, rice planting, and dock work. "Done worked and loafed on such like jobs / Seen what dey is to see," muses the narrator, before he shifts his attention to the myriad social experiences that have accompanied, if not softened, his grueling work life. "Done had my time wid a pint on my hip / An' a sweet gal on my knee, / Sweet mommer on my knee," he notes. Big Boy is proud to assert that he "Done took my livin' as it came, / Done grabbed my joy, done risked my life" and as he contemplates his own mortality, asks only "Lemme be wid John Henry, steel drivin' man, / Lemme be wid old Jazzbo" when "time comes fo' to go." The reflective hardworking hero who emerges in Big Boy continues to examine his own philosophies about masculinity, domesticity, and emotional ties. In "Long Gone," the speaker confesses his inability to settle in one place. In the poem, which functions as a one-sided conversation between two lovers, Big Boy confesses that although he "laks yo' kin' of lovin' " and "Ain't never caught you wrong," "it jes' ain' nachal / Fo' to stay here long." He confesses that "I don't know which way I'm travelin'—/ Far or near, / All I knows fo' certain is / I cain't stay here." In the face of his lover's understandable distress, he tries to reassert his powerlessness to resist the deep and uncontestable desire to move on: "Ain't no call at all, sweet woman / Fo' to carry on—/ Jes' my name and jes' my habit / To be Long Gone."

Southern Road is powerful for its moving and illuminating profiles of everyday people doing their best to maintain their families, to become spiritually enriched, and to support each other in times of crisis. It also offers striking portraits of lives in disrepair and fraught with emotional tension. In "Seeking Religion," a man named Jim saves Lulu, a woman desperate to become religious. Jim finds Lulu in a "dusky graveyard" where she "[f]ought her fears and sat among ghostlike stones. / Waiting for her visions," ultimately offers her love that redeems her, and allows her to "[find] religion in a chubby baby boy." Other poems, like "Bessie," chronicle the decline that can wreak havoc on innocence and beauty. "Who will know Bessie now of those who loved her," asks the narrator as he introduces "Bess . . . this woman, gaunt of flesh and painted / Despair deep bitten in her soft brown eyes." She is one of many who "left behind the stupid, stifling shanties, / And took her to the cities to get her share of fun." Bessie no longer is "Bessie with her plaited hair, / Bessie in her gingham, / Bessie with her bird voice, and laughter like the sun," and the narrator gives thanks that her parents died without seeing the state of their "darling," the girl whom they "talked of . . . at night, and dreamt dreams so." Other works, like "Pardners," profile the kinds of difficulties that arise as men and women attempt to forge relationships. The realities of urban decay, corrupted innocence, and the toll that both take on the victim and her family are reminiscent of works by MARITA BONNER, JESSIE FAUSET, RUDOLPH FISHER, CLAUDE MCKAY, and others who assessed the toll that migration and distance from family could have upon individuals, communities, and the nation.

The collection also cultivates the image of the African-American observer, a marginalized but invaluable figure with clear appreciation of racial hierarchies, white power, and African-American legacy. Works like "Strong Men," which begins with a quote from Carl Sandburg, provide a graphic account of enslavement, racial oppression, and modern-day segregation and racial violence. Brown recounts this history in italics and thus underscores its unspeakable, haunting, and nightmar-

ish nature. This daunting narrative is punctuated by a refrain printed in plain text. Over the course of the poem, the refrain "The strong men keep a'comin on / The strong men git stronger," evolves and intensifies, and the poem ends with the words "The strong men . . . comin' on / The strong men gittin' stronger. / Strong men. . . . / Stronger." The last lines suggest African-American resilience even as they also signal, through Brown's use of ellipses, utter weariness in the face of relentless predation. Brown also honors the optimism and earnest hopes of the many who work the land in an effort to secure domestic stability for their families. In one of the volume's most moving poems, "After Winter," he profiles a nameless farmer who "snuggles his fingers / In the blacker loam" and "[t]hough he stands ragged / An old scarecrow" thinks about how the land will enable him to plant favorite crops for his womenfolk and provide "[r]unnin' space" for "de little feller" in their family. The poem contains a catalog of vegetables and other plants, all of which are part of the farmer's plan to host his neighbors and to sustain his family during the seasons to come. It is on the "[t]en acres unplanted" that this farmer attempts "[t]o raise dreams" as he comforts himself with the refrain, "Butterbeans fo' Clara / Sugar corn fo' Grace / An' fo' de little feller / Runnin' space."

James Weldon Johnson, who penned the introduction for the first edition of the work, suggested that Brown was among the elite group of five poets of color who had cultivated a national reputation for themselves. Johnson proposed that Brown and Claude McKay, JEAN TOOMER, COUNTEE CULLEN, and LANGSTON HUGHES were part of what he deemed a group of "younger poets" who were "on the whole newer in their response to what still remains the principal motive of poetry written by Negroes—race." He went on to note that this pioneering group of talented poets were, "[i]n their approach to 'race' . . . less direct and obvious, less didactic or imploratory; and, too, they are less regardful of the approval or disapprobation of their white environment" (Johnson, xxxvi).

Contemporary literary critics continue to examine Brown's deft presentations of African-American life and his articulations of the blues and folk traditions. As Stephen Henderson notes, "The hallmark of Sterling Brown's poetry is its exploration of the bitter dimension of the blues, which he links with a view of humankind that he shares with writers like Sandburg, Frost, and Edwin Arlington Robinson . . . and he extends the literary blues without losing their authenticity" (Henderson, 32). The volume presents what scholar Charles Rowell has aptly described as "a kaleidoscopic picture of black folk character and life in America—a picture that is constant with the folk themselves." The volume's testament to African-American ambition, fortitude, romance, and endurance made it one of the seminal publications of the Harlem Renaissance era. Unfortunately, it would be some 40 years before Brown published another volume. Intolerance for his investment in the folklife by his professional colleagues at Howard, coupled with the financial upheaval of the GREAT DEPRESSION, made it difficult for him to secure a publisher for the next volume that he completed shortly after *Southern Road* appeared.

Bibliography

Brown, Sterling. *Southern Road: Poems by Sterling A. Brown.* 1932; reprint, Boston: Beacon Press, 1972.

Gabbin, Joanne V. *Sterling A. Brown: Building the Black Aesthetic Tradition.* Westport, Conn.: Greenwood Press, 1985.

Henderson, Stephen. "The Heavy Blues of Sterling Brown: A Study of Craft and Tradition," *Black American Literature Forum* 14, no. 1 (spring 1980): 32–44.

Johnson, James Weldon. Introduction to *Southern Road: Poems by Sterling A. Brown.* 1932, reprint, Boston: Beacon Press, 1972.

Rowell, Charles. "Sterling A. Brown and the Afro-American Folk Tradition." In *Harlem Renaissance Re-Examined: A Revised and Expanded Edition,* edited by Victor Kramer and Robert Russ. Troy, N.Y.: The Whitson Publishing Company, 1997.

Sanders, Mark. *Afro-Modernist Aesthetics & the Poetry of Sterling A. Brown.* Athens: University of Georgia Press, 1999.

Southern Workman

The official publication of the Hampton Folk-Lore Society, one of the earliest professional groups dedicated to the collection of American folk materials. The society and the journal were both based at Hampton Institute, a historically black institution founded in 1872 and located in Hampton, Virginia.

The journal, which was published monthly from 1872 through 1939, included regular profiles of educational practices at Hampton Institute. In addition, it included detailed articles about and informative images relating to African-American and Native American folklife, practices, and history.

Bibliography

Armstrong, Samuel Chapman. *The Founding of the Hampton Institute.* Boston: Directors of the Old South Work, 1904.

Engs, Robert. *Educating the Disenfranchised and Disinherited: Samuel Chapman Armstrong and Hampton Institute, 1839–1893.* Knoxville: University of Tennessee Press, 1999.

Schall, Keith. *Stony the Road: Chapters in the History of Hampton Institute.* Charlottesville: University Press of Virginia, 1977.

"South Lingers On, The" Rudolph Fisher (1925)

Published in the historic March 1925 Harlem issue of SURVEY GRAPHIC, this short story by RUDOLPH FISHER offered a series of moving portraits of southerners grappling with the realities and temptations of life in the urban North.

Divided into five sections, the stories focus on generational differences, the hopes of the older generations, and the frustrated goals and realized aspirations of youth. "The South Lingers On" begins with the evocative story of Reverend Ezekiel Taylor, a humble southern minister who, on the invitation of his former community, has traveled north to HARLEM. Taylor's efforts to establish a church have failed as the young people have succumbed to the evils of the city. Taylor, almost convinced that Harlem is a godless place with numberless souls in need of salvation, stumbles upon a brownstone church that is peopled in part by some of his former southern neighbors. Much to the distress of the current pastor, a "reformed" gambler who profits from his congregation, Taylor is welcomed and immediately embraced by congregants who desire to establish a new church with him as their pastor.

Other portions of Fisher's profile of city life include the unsuccessful efforts of Jake, a young farmer from Virginia, who is unqualified for much but eager to work. Despite his desire, however, he is unable to secure a job. He is determined, though, to refrain from the potentially lucrative but unsavory world of gambling and its associated vices.

The sections that focus on female protagonists offer starkly contrasting images of assimilation. The sketch about Majutah reveals the efforts of one young woman to elude her watchful and religious grandmother. Despite her best efforts, Majutah is unable to hide her plans to go to late night dance clubs. The sketch closes as her grandmother kneels by her bed and prays for the child's salvation. The second sketch to feature young women is much more uplifting. Anna, the child of parents who received little formal education, is not only accepted to COLUMBIA UNIVERSITY but is awarded a scholarship to fund her studies. Her parents rejoice with her, proud of their daughter's major accomplishment and the sure sign of the advancement of their family and the race.

Bibliography

McCluskey, John, Jr. *The City of Refuge: The Collected Stories of Rudolph Fisher*. Columbia: University of Missouri Press, 1987.

Spence, Eulalie (1894–1981)

One of the most prolific playwrights of the Harlem Renaissance and the first African-American woman to have her work performed on BROADWAY.

Born in Nevis, West Indies, she and her family emigrated to the United States. Her father was a sugar planter and her mother, a seamstress. Spence was a teacher in the years before she turned to writing plays. She attended Wadleigh High School, and her interest in a teaching career prompted her to enroll at the New York Training School for Teachers. In 1918 she began teaching high school. In 1927 she began her lengthy career at Eastern District High School in Brooklyn. Her students there included Joseph Papp, the accomplished Brooklyn-born director and producer. In 1937, following her successful Harlem Renaissance years, Spence returned to school. She earned a B.S. from NEW YORK UNIVERSITY in 1937 and completed an M.A. in speech at COLUMBIA UNIVERSITY in 1939. Spence retired from Eastern District High in 1958

after some 31 years of teaching English, drama, and elocution and coaching the drama club.

Spence is known to have written 14 plays during her career. Of these, 13 were one-act plays, and seven were staged. Paramount Productions optioned, but never produced, her only full-length play, the three-act comedy THE WHIPPING that was based on a novel by Ray Flanagan.

Spence enjoyed the prestige that winners in THE CRISIS and OPPORTUNITY annual literary contests enjoyed. In the 1926 *Crisis* literary contest, Spence, the only woman to place in the category, won second prize for her play FOREIGN MAIL. The winner was WILLIS RICHARDSON, and the panel of judges, which included T. MONTGOMERY GREGORY, awarded RANDOLPH EDMONDS two honorable mention awards. One year later, Spence's plays *Hot Stuff* and UNDERTOW won third prize in the Literary Art and Expression category.

In the 1926–27 *Opportunity* contest, judges PAUL GREEN, PAUL ROBESON, Edith Isaacs, and Lula Vollmer awarded her second prize for THE HUNCH and a split third prize for THE STARTER that she shared with Randolph Edmonds, author of *Bleeding Hearts*. That year, it was GEORGIA DOUGLAS JOHNSON who won first place for her wrenching drama entitled PLUMES.

The year 1927 was especially rewarding for Spence. She was one of the playwrights whom T. Montgomery Gregory and ALAIN LOCKE featured in PLAYS OF NEGRO LIFE, their pioneering 1927 collection of plays by and about African Americans. Her work appeared alongside plays by Paul Green, EUGENE O'NEILL, Willis Richardson, JEAN TOOMER, Georgia Douglas Johnson, Richard Bruce, and others. In addition, she was one of 16 writers featured in the May 1927 HARLEM issue of *Carolina Magazine*. Guest editor Lewis Alexander, who included writers such as COUNTEE CULLEN and ANGELINA WELD GRIMKÉ, selected Spence's recent prize-winning play *The Hunch* for inclusion in the issue. Two years later, in April 1929, Spence's *Undertow* appeared in another issue of *Carolina Magazine* alongside works by JOHN MATHEUS, Willis Richardson, and LEWIS ALEXANDER.

An especially prolific writer during the 1920s, Spence wrote a number of one-act plays and saw them performed in a variety of contexts. The KRIGWA PLAYERS, an enterprising troupe organized by REGINA ANDREWS and W. E. B. DuBois, performed FOOL'S ERRAND in the Little Theatre Tournament, a well-known annual national competition. The play won second prize in the rigorous competition. Published by the New York company of Samuel French, *Fool's Errand* subsequently was staged at the Frolic Playhouse on Broadway in May 1927 and became the first work by an African-American woman to open on Broadway.

Spence collaborated with several small but notable drama troupes of the period. These included the Dunbar Garden Players. She worked closely with her sister Dora Spence, an aspiring actress who was cast as an understudy in Paul Green's PULITZER PRIZE–winning play IN ABRAHAM'S BOSOM.

Spence, who never married, died in March 1981.

Spencer, Anne Bethel Scales Bannister
(1882–1976)

A poet, librarian, civil rights activist, and avid gardener known for her gentility, high morality, and intellectual engagement with leading figures of the Harlem Renaissance period. Born on the R. J. Reynolds plantation in Henry County, West Virginia, Spencer was the only child of Joel Cephus and Sarah Louise Scales Bannister. Her parents were both of mixed-race ancestry. Her father was of African-American and Seminole Indian ancestry, and her mother was the daughter of a formerly enslaved woman and a white Virginian. Spencer, who did not begin formal schooling until she was 11 years old, spent much time at the Martinsville, Virginia, saloon that her father owned. In 1887 the Bannister marriage ended, and Sarah relocated to Bramwell, West Virginia, with her daughter. Anne became the foster child of Mr. and Mrs. William Dixie while her mother worked full-time as a cook to support the family. Sarah Bannister's insistence that her daughter receive the best education led to her enrollment in an African-American boarding school in Lynchburg, Virginia. She began studying at the Virginia Seminary, known formerly as the Lynchburg Baptist Seminary, in 1893. Spencer's hard work, demonstrated commitment to academics, and dynamic personality resulted in selection as class valedictorian when she graduated in 1899.

In May 1901, two years after her graduation from Virginia Seminary and College, she married Edward Spencer, who was a fellow student at Virginia Seminary, her former science tutor, and a fellow member of the class of 1899. Spencer worked on the railroad when they married but soon became the first parcel postman in Lynchburg, Virginia. The couple had three children, Bethel, Alroy, and Chauncey, an accomplished aviator. After 65 years of marriage, Edward Spencer passed away. He died at age 88 in 1964. Spencer survived her husband for some 11 years. In July 1975 the 92-year-old poet died of cancer.

Spencer's civil rights work and interests had significant implications for her literary career. In 1918 she led the effort to establish the first Lynchburg, Virginia, chapter of the NATIONAL ASSOCIATION FOR THE ADVANCEMENT OF COLORED PEOPLE. She worked directly with JAMES WELDON JOHNSON to establish the local organization, and it was he who introduced her work to editor and critic H. L. MENCKEN. Johnson also encouraged the emerging writer to publish under the name "Anne Spencer." Spencer's first published poem, "Before the Feast of Shushan," appeared in THE CRISIS in February 1920. Additional works appeared in SURVEY GRAPHIC, PALMS, and OPPORTUNITY. In addition, Spencer's poems appeared in major literary anthologies. Her early mentor James Weldon Johnson included her work in his 1922 edition entitled THE BOOK OF AMERICAN NEGRO POETRY. She also was featured in Robert Kerlin's NEGRO POETS AND THEIR POEMS (1923) and was the only woman of color featured in Louis Untermeyer's *American Poetry Since 1900* (1923). In 1925 Spencer's poems were included in ALAIN LOCKE's THE NEW NEGRO, the celebrated and influential 1925 collection of works by and about African Americans. Her work also appeared in two major anthologies published in 1927, COUNTEE CULLEN's CAROLING DUSK and Charles Johnson's EBONY AND TOPAZ. Cullen featured 10 of Spencer's poems. In 1941, just after the close of the Harlem Renaissance, her work appeared in STERLING BROWN's THE NEGRO CARAVAN. In 1963 ARNA BONTEMPS included three of her works in *American Negro Poetry*.

During the Harlem Renaissance, Spencer was based primarily in Lynchburg, Virginia. In 1923 she

Anne Spencer *(Yale Collection of American Literature, Beinecke Rare Book and Manuscript Library)*

began a lengthy career as a librarian. She worked at the Jones Memorial Library and also at the DUNBAR HIGH SCHOOL library until her retirement in 1945. The Spencer home was an active literary salon, one that catered regularly to lively gatherings of contemporary scholars, artists, and writers. Spencer developed friendships with leading poets of the period including Langston Hughes, Georgia Douglas Johnson, and Claude McKay. In addition, her home at 1313 Pierce Street was where influential public figures such as GEORGE WASHINGTON CARVER, W. E. B DUBOIS, ADAM CLAYTON POWELL, SR., and PAUL ROBESON gathered.

Spencer combined her literary career with social activism. Her efforts to secure educational opportunities for African-American students led to the establishment of a library at Dunbar High School. In addition, her protests on behalf of African-

American teachers who were denied employment opportunities because of their race eventually led to their hiring in Lynchburg's segregated schools. Virginia Seminary and College celebrated Spencer's career by awarding her an honorary degree in 1975.

Bibliography

Anne Spencer Papers, Anne Spencer House Historic Landmark, Lynchburg, Virginia; Beinecke Rare Book and Manuscript Library, Yale University.

Greene, J. Lee. *Time's Unfading Garden: Anne Spencer's Life and Poetry.* Baton Rouge: Louisiana State University, 1977.

Stetson, Erlene. "Anne Spencer." *CLA Journal* 21 (March 1978): 400–409.

Spingarn, Amy (1883–1980)

One of the best-known white patrons of the Harlem Renaissance. In December 1895 she married JOEL SPINGARN, the first Jewish professor at COLUMBIA UNIVERSITY and a dedicated member and officer of the NATIONAL ASSOCIATION FOR THE ADVANCEMENT OF COLORED PEOPLE (NAACP). The Spingarns dedicated themselves to civil rights reforms and were generous supporters of the Harlem Renaissance literary and arts movements.

The daughter of David Einstein and the sister of the American scholar and diplomat Lewis Einstein, Amy Spingarn inherited considerable wealth from her father, a New Jersey mill owner and landowner. After schooling abroad, she enrolled at BARNARD COLLEGE but did not graduate. While there, she fell in love with Columbia professor Joel Spingarn and proposed marriage to him. The couple had four children, Hope, Honor, Stephen, and Edward. In addition to their home in New York City, the Spingarns owned Troutbeck, a spacious country estate in Amenia, New York. Guests as the 18th-century home included SINCLAIR LEWIS, Ernest Hemingway, LANGSTON HUGHES, and President Theodore Roosevelt.

Spingarn, who had interests in art and literature, also published during the Harlem Renaissance. In the summer of 1924, writing under her maiden name, Einstein, she published a poem in *THE CRISIS*.

In 1925 Spingarn established a literary contest that was run in conjunction with *The Crisis*, the official publication of the NAACP. The prizes in literature and art attracted numerous submissions from established and emerging artists. Like *The Crisis* and OPPORTUNITY literary contests, the Spingarn awards competition involved judges who were notable literary and public figures. In the first year, judges included H. G. Wells, CHARLES CHESNUTT, MARY WHITE OVINGTON, LESLIE PINCKNEY HILL, and EUGENE O'NEILL. First-place winners in the first Spingarn literary contest were RUDOLPH FISHER for his short story "HIGH YALLER," COUNTEE CULLEN for his poem "Two Moods of Love," WILLIS RICHARDSON for his play "THE BROKEN BANJO," and MARITA BONNER for her essay "ON BEING YOUNG—A WOMAN—AND COLORED." In subsequent years, winners included ARNA BONTEMPS, MAE COWDERY, and JOHN MATHEUS.

Spingarn also made specific contributions to individual artists. After meeting with Langston Hughes, she offered to help with his education. It was she who financed his studies at LINCOLN UNIVERSITY. Spingarn also worked to raise public awareness about vital issues such as LYNCHING. She sponsored an antilynching art exhibit that traveled to East Coast cities throughout the 1930s.

Bibliography

Van Deusen, Marshall. *J. E. Spingarn.* New York: Twayne Publishers, 1971.

Spingarn, Arthur Barnett (1878–1971)

An attorney, civil rights activist, and member of the influential Spingarn family who worked closely with the NATIONAL ASSOCIATION FOR THE ADVANCEMENT OF COLORED PEOPLE (NAACP). Born in NEW YORK CITY, Arthur Spingarn was the son of Elias and Sarah Barnett Spingarn. His father was an Austrian Jewish immigrant and successful businessman who hoped to see his son become an attorney. He enrolled at COLUMBIA UNIVERSITY, and by 1900 he had received his B.A., M.A., and J.D. In 1918, in the midst of two years military service in the U.S. Army, he married Marion Mayer. He and his wife, who was a social worker, had no children.

Shortly after the founding of the NAACP in 1909, Spingarn became counsel for the organization. His brother Joel, a civil rights activist, editor,

and highly regarded horticulturalist, established the SPINGARN MEDAL, the highest award given by the NAACP, and later served as president of the organization. Arthur Spingarn, spurred on by pervasive racial discrimination in America, became one of the most active members of the NAACP. In 1911 he became vice president and also served as chairman of the organization's national legal committee. In 1940, following the death of his brother Joel Spingarn, who was president at the time, Arthur Spingarn became president. His tenure lasted some 26 years, until 1966. He was an earnest admirer of W. E. B. DUBOIS, who served as editor of *THE CRISIS*, and the two worked closely during their association with the NAACP.

Arthur Spingarn developed a substantial collection of materials by African Americans and individuals of African descent. In 1946 HOWARD UNIVERSITY purchased his collection of some 5,000 items. His collection became part of the university's impressive Moorland-Spingarn Research Center, a research library and archive that also is named after donor Reverend Jesse Moorland.

Bibliography

Arthur Spingarn Papers, Moorland-Spingarn Research Center, Howard University, Washington, D.C.

Spingarn, Joel Elias (1875–1939)

A civil rights activist, university professor, poet, literary critic, and respected horticulturist known best for his leadership within the NATIONAL ASSOCIATION FOR THE ADVANCEMENT OF COLORED PEOPLE (NAACP) and his philanthropic support of African-American excellence and leadership.

The oldest of four children born to Elias and Sarah Barnett Spingarn, Joel attended Collegiate Institute before enrolling at New York's City College. After one year there, he transferred to Columbia College and graduated in 1895. He married AMY SPINGARN, daughter of a wealthy New Jersey landowner, David Einstein, in 1896. The couple, who met while Amy was a Barnard student and Spingarn was a member of the COLUMBIA UNIVERSITY faculty, had four children, Hope, Honor, Stephen, and Edward.

In the years preceding his work with the NAACP, Spingarn pursued careers in politics and academia. He ran for Congress and was an enthusiastic Progressive Party member. He taught comparative literature at Columbia, where he honed his reputation as an expert on the Italian philosopher Benedetto Croce, but his decision to support a dismissed colleague resulted in his own firing in 1911.

Spingarn was one of the leading white supporters of the NAACP. He worked closely with the organization and held a number of influential positions. In 1913 he began a six-year term as chairman of the board of trustees. He became treasurer of the organization in 1919 and held the post until 1930, when he was appointed president. He held that post until his death in 1939. His brother ARTHUR SPINGARN, an accomplished lawyer, succeeded Spingarn as president. During his decades of service with the NAACP, Spingarn dedicated substantial funds to efforts that would recognize African-American leadership. In 1913 he established a trust fund for the SPINGARN MEDAL, the highest prize that the NAACP awarded in recognition of high achievement and leadership by an African American. Spingarn also offered direct support to aspiring and established artists of the Harlem Renaissance. It was he who introduced CLAUDE MCKAY's work to SEVEN ARTS editors JAMES OPPENHEIM and WALDO FRANK. McKay's work, which was published in the December 1917 issue, represented a landmark in American publishing history when Seven Arts became the first white literary magazine of the period to publish the work of a writer of color.

Spingarn had a rich and multifaceted career before and during the years of the Harlem Renaissance. He was a highly regarded expert on the clematis and was one of the founding members of the American Legion. In addition, Spingarn's career also included World War II military service and work as the owner and publisher of the Amenia Times and as an overseer of two active mills. He was a cofounder of the publishing company HARCOURT, BRACE & COMPANY, which was established in 1919, and served as a literary adviser for the firm until his retirement in 1932.

Joel Spingarn died in July 1939. THE NEW YORK TIMES obituary for Spingarn hailed him as an "uncompromising critic in diverse fields" and a man who "fought for Negro rights."

Bibliography

"J. E. Spingarn Dies; Author and Critic." *New York Times*, 27 July 1939, 25.

Ross, B. Joyce. *J. E. Spingarn and the Rise of the NAACP, 1911–1939*. New York: Atheneum, 1972.

Van Deusen, Marshall. *J. E. Spingarn*. New York: Twayne Publishers, 1971.

Philanthropist, professor, and longtime chairman of the NAACP Board of Directors, Joel Spingarn. The portrait, inscribed to James Weldon Johnson, is offered "with warm friendship and admiration of J. E. Spingarn." *(Yale Collection of American Literature, Beinecke Rare Book and Manuscript Library)*

Spingarn Medal

A prestigious award and the highest honor bestowed by the NATIONAL ASSOCIATION FOR THE ADVANCEMENT OF COLORED PEOPLE (NAACP). JOEL SPINGARN, literary critic, activist, and COLUMBIA UNIVERSITY professor, established the award in 1914 while he was chairman of the NAACP's board of directors. Spingarn ensured the long-term existence of the prize by dedicating a $20,000 trust fund for the prize. The Spingarn Medal, which also carried initially a prize of $100, recognized outstanding achievements by African Americans. The first prize was awarded in 1915, and the organization continues to honor accomplished American men and women of color.

Spingarn medalists during the Harlem Renaissance era represented major achievements in the arts, the sciences, politics, education, and numerous other areas. The first recipient was Ernest Just in 1915. The first woman to win the award was Mary B. Talbert. Winners during the 1920s and 1930s included singer MARIAN ANDERSON, MARY MCLEOD BETHUNE, GEORGE WASHINGTON CARVER, CHARLES CHESNUTT, W. E. B. DUBOIS, Charles Gilpin, ARCHIBALD GRIMKÉ, Roland Hayes, JOHN HOPE, Robert Russa Moton, WALTER WHITE, and CARTER G. WOODSON.

Since the Harlem Renaissance, Spingarn Medal winners have included Myrlie Evers-Williams, John Hope Franklin, Leon Higginbotham, Lena Horne, LANGSTON HUGHES, Jesse Jackson, Dr. Martin Luther King, Jr., and L. Douglas Wilder.

Bibliography
Ross, Barbara Joyce. *J. E. Spingarn and the Rise of the NAACP, 1911–1939.* New York: Atheneum, 1972.
Van Deusen, Marshall. *J. E. Spingarn.* New York: Twayne Publishers, 1971.

Spivak, John Louis (1897–1981)

A white investigative journalist whose publications during the Harlem Renaissance included explosive exposés about the KU KLUX KLAN, American prison camps, and African-American chain gangs. Spivak was a native of New Haven, Connecticut, born in June 1897. He went on to enjoy a successful career in journalism. In addition to working with newspapers in NEW YORK CITY, he also was appointed to posts abroad as news bureau director for papers in Moscow and Berlin.

Spivak's turn to fiction was informed by his years of investigative reporting. During the Harlem Renaissance, he became part of a recognized group of white writers that included figures such as PAUL GREEN, DUBOSE HEYWARD, and JULIA PETERKIN, who considered African-American issues and characters in their works. Spivak published GEORGIA NIGGER in 1932. The novel was a blend of documentary reporting and fiction. Set in Georgia, it focused on the plight of African-American members of a chain gang. The book, which was published by the New York press of Brewer, Warren and Putnam, also included riveting photographs of convicts whose excessive chains clearly evoked the age of American enslavement. Additional images included men working on various construction projects and pictures of the barbaric conditions under which the imprisoned were forced to live.

Spivak was a social critic who also addressed the issues facing the working class. Additional works included *America at the Barricades* (1935), a study of the working class, poverty, and socioeconomic conditions, and *Europe Under the Terror* (1936), a study of Europe and fascism in the post–World War I era.

Bibliography
Lichtenstein, Alex. "Chain Gangs, Communism & the 'Negro Question': John Spivak's Georgia Nigger." *Georgia Historical Quarterly* 79 (fall 1995): 633–658.
Spivak, John. *Georgia Nigger.* Montclair, N.J.: Patterson Smith, 1969.

Spokesman, The

A short-lived and eclectic NEW YORK CITY periodical. Published from 1925 through 1926, the magazine featured a range of articles on issues relating to health, current events, and political matters. ZORA NEALE HURSTON was a contributing editor, and WILLIAM FERRIS, literary editor of *Negro World,* was a literary editor for the journal.

Spring in New Hampshire and Other Poems Claude McKay (1920)

The third volume of poetry by CLAUDE MCKAY and the first of two that he published in the United States during his career. McKay wrote and compiled the modest collection of 31 poems for *Spring in New Hampshire* while he was living in England. He had relocated from New York City to London in 1919 and spent almost one year abroad. C. K. Ogden, a Cambridge University professor to whom McKay was introduced during his sojourn in the United Kingdom, facilitated the volume's first publication in London. Ogden also published several of McKay's newest poems in the *Cambridge Magazine.*

McKay republished the volume in the United States in 1922 under the new title of HARLEM SHADOWS. There were plans to produce a simultaneous American version of the British manuscript, but that did not occur. McKay had hoped that the playwright George Bernard Shaw would contribute a preface to the volume. Shaw demurred, however. The influential British scholar I. A. Richards ultimately provided the introduction to the volume that was republished in expanded form as *Harlem Shadows* in the United States in 1922. In his introduction, Richards provided brief autobiographical details about McKay and developed an emphatic assessment of the ways in which he deserved respect as a powerful race writer. "Claude McKay is a pure blooded Negro," he wrote, "and though we have recently been made aware of some of the more remarkable achievements of African Art typified by the sculpture from Benin, and in music by the 'Spirituals,' this is the first instance of success in poetry with which we in Europe at any rate have been brought into contact" (Maxwell, 307). The revised version of the book that appeared in America received strong support from influential figures of the day. JOEL SPINGARN supported McKay's efforts to publish the work, and the new volume contained an enthusiastic preface by MAX EASTMAN, editor of the *LIBERATOR* and one of McKay's longtime friends.

Spring in New Hampshire included a number of poems inspired by McKay's sojourn in the United States. Among these were "Spring in New Hampshire," "Harlem Shadows," "The Harlem Dancer," "The Lynching," and "On Broadway." The book also included works such as "Reminiscences," "Love Song," and "Sukee River," which he had recently published in the Summer 1920 issue of *Cambridge Magazine*. "Reminiscences" was a tender poem, one in which the speaker's memories warm him during winter "[w]hen the day is at its dimmest / And the air is wild with snow, / And the city's at its grimmest." The elements are unable to prevent the speaker from remaking the landscape before him. The winter scene is replaced by "an old world sugarmill / Where the southern sun is inking—/ Gold and crimson—o'er the hill" and by a "white stream dashing / Gay and reckless through the brake, / O'er the root-entwined rocks washing / Swiftly, madly to the lake." The poem "Love Song" extended McKay's

reveries about the power of the natural world. In the two-stanza poem, he celebrated the richness of flowers and the glories of the skies. Ultimately, however, not even the "[h]eart of the saffron rose / Lines of the lily red, / Gold of the buttercup, / Dew of the daisies' bed" or the "[r]ime of the silver morn / Fair on the green of trees" and the "[s]cent of the coffee blooms" could exceed the glories of his love affair. The speaker confesses that such sights are "[r]are . . . to see / But more than all and more / Is your fond heart to me." In "Sukee River," McKay considered themes that would recur in his later volumes. "When from my early wandering I returned / did I not promise to remain for aye," muses the speaker who is clearly dismayed by the powerful wanderlust that prompts him to immediately contemplate leaving once again. "Yet instantly for other regions yearned / And wearied of thee in a single day," he confesses, "No wonder that my feet are faltering ever," he concludes, "I have been faithless to thee, Sukee River."

As biographer Wayne Cooper notes, the poems in *Spring in New Hampshire* represent a "heightened poetic creativity" (Cooper, 132). McKay would preserve the creative momentum that he began to realize in the volume and would use it to full advantage when he returned to the United States and began to establish himself as a major literary figure in the Harlem Renaissance community.

Bibliography

Cooper, Wayne. *Claude McKay: Rebel Sojourner in the Harlem Renaissance*. New York: Schocken Books, 1987.

Giles, James R. *Claude McKay*. Boston: Twayne Publishers, 1976.

Maxwell, William J., ed. *Complete Poems: Claude McKay*. Urbana: University of Illinois Press, 2004.

"Spring of '65, The"   William Moore (1925)

A Civil War–era short story by William Moore about the plot to assassinate President Abraham Lincoln. Published in the February 1925 issue of *The Messenger*, "The Spring of '65" revolves around a clandestine meeting in NEW YORK CITY of co-conspirators. A man named Dick Jackson travels to New York from WASHINGTON, D.C., to meet with partners who are determined to accomplish the killing of the president whom they regard as a Negro-lover.

Much to the dismay and outrage of his fellows, however, he brings his mixed-race sweetheart with him. Josephine, a woman of "supernal loveliness," is anxious, and in a moment of desperation, she breaks in on the meeting and threatens to reveal all unless Dick withdraws from the plan. Jackson's comrades quickly see him in the same light as they do President Lincoln, one whose interest in African-American people is both undesirable and threatening.

News of General Lee's surrender finally reaches the men, and they disband just before police descend on their meeting place. The story closes with the cryptic reference to the death of Josephine. Murdered and discarded, her body is found in the East River. The story is an elusive tale that builds on the conspiracy theories that emerged in the wake of Lincoln's assassination.

"Spunk" Zora Neale Hurston (1920)

A prizewinning short story about courage and retribution by ZORA NEALE HURSTON that appeared in OPPORTUNITY a few months before its author was honored in the journal's prestigious annual literary contest. In the 1925 *Opportunity* literary contest, a panel of nine judges that included FANNIE HURST, CARL VAN DOREN, ALAIN LOCKE, Dorothy Canfield Fisher, and ZONA GALE awarded second prize to Hurston for "Spunk." First prize went to JOHN MATHEUS for his story entitled "FOG," and third prize was awarded to ERIC WALROND for "THE VOODOO'S REVENGE." ALAIN LOCKE later selected the prizewinning tale for inclusion in THE NEW NEGRO (1925), his pioneering anthology of works by and about African Americans.

"Spunk" tells the tale of Spunk Banks, a burly mill worker who believes that his physical might makes him invincible. Banks, who "ain't skeered of nothin' on God's green footstool," begins a public affair with Lena Kanty, a married woman. Joe Kanty, the cuckolded husband, is no match for Banks, but after a humiliating conversation in the local store he decides to "fetch" his wife and end the torturous gossip. Kanty, a man in whom "one could actually *see* the pain he was suffering," in-

tends to use a razor to kill Banks and to reclaim his honor and his wife. Unfortunately, Banks kills Kanty with little effort. Then he plans to marry Lena, and during the first night that the couple spend together, a black bobcat circles the house repeatedly. The bully believes that the cat is a manifestation of Kanty. When Banks is pushed by an invisible force into the saw at the mill, he uses his last breath to tell onlookers that he intends to pursue Kanty in the afterworld and seek vengeance for his own death. The story ends as the town files into Lena's home for the wake. Joe Kanty's father stands over the dead man, "leering triumphantly" now that he, too, has been felled, and the women of the community begin to wonder about the next man whom Lena will compromise.

Hurston's story was part of the rich oeuvre of folk narratives that she crafted during her career. "Spunk," like several of her novels and other works of short fiction, delivered an evocative portrait of long-suffering individuals prompted to heroic, though not necessarily victorious, action.

Bibliography

Gates, Henry Louis Jr., and K. A. Appiah, eds. *Zora Neale Hurston: Critical Perspectives Past and Present.* New York: Amistad, 1993.

Harris, Trudier. *The Power of the Porch: The Storyteller's Craft in Zora Neale Hurston, Gloria Naylor, and Randall Kenan.* Athens: University of Georgia Press, 1996.

Starter, The: A Comedy of Negro Life
Eulalie Spence (1927)

A fast-paced prize-winning one-act play about HARLEM by EULALIE SPENCE. Written in the fall of 1926, the play garnered much praise the following year when Spence was honored by the NATIONAL URBAN LEAGUE and was selected for inclusion in a prominent collection of plays by and about African Americans.

The Starter features two primary and two peripheral characters. Set in a park in "Present day Harlem" on a sweltering summer day, the play focuses first on the thoughts and antics of T. J. Kelly. Kelly is an ambitious but professionally thwarted young man. Current racial prejudice keeps him working as a hotel bellman. Despite his frustrations, Kelly imagines himself as a "starter" but only "one step better'n the man who runs the [elevator]." After he flirts with and harasses two women who want to share his park bench, Kelly is joined by his sweetheart, an earnest woman named Georgia. The two embrace passionately, much to the dismay of the irked women who have gone off in search of somewhere else to sit. Kelly and Georgia commiserate about their employment situations. Georgia, who works as a seamstress in a factory, notes wryly that they make quite a pair. Kelly is a starter, and she is a finisher by trade, one who makes the final adjustments to dresses. Eventually the two begin a fretful conversation about marriage. Despite Georgia's pointed questions about the state of Kelly's limited savings, the two decide to wed. The play closes as they marvel at the sight of Harlem's lights and the gorgeous moon above.

The Starter explores African-American aspirations and romance. Spence considers the realities that conspire against African Americans. She also develops a realistic and resilient couple, one whose capacity for romance and for dreaming thrives despite the difficulties that they face.

Spence saw two of her plays honored in the 1927 annual literary contest sponsored by OPPORTUNITY. A panel of judges that included Paul Green, Edith Isaacs, and PAUL ROBESON awarded her play *The Hunch* second prize behind GEORGIA DOUGLAS JOHNSON's moving play PLUMES. *The Starter* tied for third place with *Four Eleven*, a play by William Jackson. In addition, ALAIN LOCKE selected *The Starter* for inclusion in his 1927 anthology entitled PLAYS OF NEGRO LIFE. Spence was one of only four women playwrights included in the volume of plays by 18 contemporary African-American and white dramatists.

Bibliography
Burton, Jennifer. *Zora Neale Hurston, Eulalie Spence, Marita Bonner, and Others: The Prize Plays and Other One-Acts Published in Periodicals.* New York: G. K. Hall, 1996.

Stieglitz, Alfred (1864–1946)

A pioneering American photographer, writer, and editor, Stieglitz was one of six children born to Hedwig Werner Stieglitz and her husband Edward Stieglitz, a German Jewish immigrant and merchant. Born in Hoboken, New Jersey, he grew up in Manhattan where his love of art and photography intensified. He studied at City College before relocating to Germany with his family. There, he continued his schooling, including a course in mechanical engineering at the University of Berlin.

Stieglitz, who had endured an unhappy marriage, eventually divorced. In 1922 he married GEORGIA O'KEEFFE, a talented painter who shared his passion for art and innovation. Stieglitz's connection to the Harlem Renaissance came through his wife's contacts with JEAN TOOMER. Toomer visited the couple at their upstate New York home in Lake George.

During the Harlem Renaissance period, Stieglitz opened An American Place, a Manhattan gallery that showcased works by American artists. WALDO FRANK, a colleague and friend of Toomer's, was instrumental in publishing a volume honoring Stieglitz's work during the period. The volume *America and Alfred Stieglitz,* which Frank coedited with Lewis Mumford and Dorothy Norman, was published in 1934.

Bibliography
Eisler, Benita. *O'Keeffe and Stieglitz: An American Romance.* New York: Penguin Books, 1992.
Frank, Waldo, Lewis Mumford, and Dorothy Norman. *America and Alfred Stieglitz: A Collective Portrait.* New York: Literary Guild, 1934.
Kerman, Cynthia Earl, and Richard Eldridge. *The Lives of Jean Toomer: A Hunger for Wholeness.* Baton Rouge: Louisiana State University Press, 1987.
Richter, Peter-Cornell. *Georgia O'Keeffe and Alfred Stieglitz.* Munich: Prestel, 2001.
Whelan, Richard. *Alfred Stieglitz: A Biography.* Boston: Little, Brown, 1995.

Still, William Grant (1895–1978)

One of America's most gifted and accomplished musicians and composers, Still was the first African-American composer to conduct a major American orchestra, the first composer of color to see his works performed by an American orchestra, and the first African American whose opera was performed by a major company. He compiled a diverse collection of works that ranged from choral pieces, symphonic works, and operas to spirituals. Still worked with leading artists, writers, and entertainers of the Harlem Renaissance period, including ZORA NEALE HURSTON, LANGSTON HUGHES, and W. C. HANDY.

He was born in Woodville, Mississippi, in May 1895 to William Grant Still, a math professor, and to Carrie Lena Fambro Still, a teacher. Still, whose mother fostered his passion for classical music, went on to study at WILBERFORCE UNIVERSITY. Controversial charges about his relationship with Grace Bundy, a fellow student, ended his college career. Nonetheless, he married Bundy in 1915, and the couple had four children. After years of separation, they divorced in 1939, and Still remarried that same year. His second wife, Verna Arvey, was a concert pianist.

During his college years and premedical studies, Still emerged as a formidable talent. He organized popular quartets, staged concerts, and served as the school's band conductor. In the years after Wilberforce, Still joined the Navy during World War I and later established a professional relationship with W. C. Handy. He joined the staff of Pace and Handy, the first African-American-owned music publishing firm. Handy co-owned the business with Harry Pace, who went on to establish the PACE PHONOGRAPH COMPANY.

Still's musical successes included performing in the first orchestra of the all-popular musical *Shuffle Along* and working as musical director for the Black Swan Phonograph Company, the organization originally known as the Pace Phonograph Company.

Still's greatest professional triumphs came during the Harlem Renaissance. In 1931 his "Afro-American Symphony" became the first work by an African-American composer to be performed by a major American orchestra. The Rochester Symphony Orchestra performed the multifaceted piece that included an eclectic mix of musical forms including spirituals, blues, and jazz rhythms. In 1929 he provided music for the ballet *Sahdji*, a performance that included a story written by ALAIN LOCKE. In 1935, he completed the score for *Pennies From Heaven*, the Hollywood film starring Bing Crosby.

In the years following the Renaissance, Still collaborated with Langston Hughes on *Troubled Island*, an opera for which Hughes composed the libretto.

Still worked with Zora Neale Hurston on *Caribbean Melodies*, a work centered around her folklore research and findings. The impressive orchestras that performed his works included the New York Philharmonic, the London Symphony, the Tokyo Philharmonic, and the Berlin Philharmonic.

Still's talents and potential earned him national recognition as the dean of African-American composers. In addition to receiving numerous honorary degrees, Still was the recipient of several prestigious prizes, including a HARMON FOUNDATION AWARD in 1927, GUGGENHEIM FELLOWSHIPS in 1934 and 1935, and JULIUS ROSENWALD FELLOWSHIPS in 1939 and 1940.

Bibliography

Arvey, Verna. *In One Lifetime.* Fayetteville: University of Arkansas Press, 1984.

Parson, Catherine. *William Grant Still: A Study in Contradictions.* Berkeley: University of California Press, 2000.

Still, Judith, ed. *William Grant Still and the Fusion of Cultures in American Music.* Flagstaff, Ariz.: MasterPlayer Library, 1995.

Stokes, Elizabeth Stapleton

The pseudonym that ANITA SCOTT COLEMAN used when she published *Small Wisdom*, a book of poems, in 1937.

"Stone Rebounds, The" Eric Walrond (1925)

A fictionalized confessional narrative by ERIC WALROND that appeared in the September 1925 issue of *OPPORTUNITY*. The piece revolves around a Jewish anthropologist named Kraus, who regards himself as an "intellectual anarchist." Kraus, who is "interested in the Negro problem," accompanies his friend Earl into "dark Harlem."

After a dismal reception at Barrett House, an artistic colony favored by his white friends, Kraus accepts Earl's offer to meet elsewhere. His arrival in Harlem and his visit to a basement club subject him to the same scrutiny usually visited upon African Americans by whites. His conversations with various individuals in the club are not entirely productive, and soon he is "conscious of an enveloping silence" and the awareness that his whiteness is prompting his companions to stare at him. The piece closes with a terse, but apparently enlightening observation. "I am white," concludes Kraus.

Walrond explores racial awareness and objectification in "The Stone Rebounds." The piece, like "ON BEING A DOMESTIC," which appeared in *Opportunity* in May 1923, uses the power of a first-person narrative to create a story of persuasive social realism.

Bibliography
Parascandola, Louis, ed. *Winds Can Wake Up the Dead: An Eric Walrond Reader.* Detroit: Wayne State University Press, 1998.

Stribling, Thomas Sigismund (1881–1965)
An editor, teacher, and PULITZER PRIZE–winning novelist known for his popular novels about the South. According to Bruce Kellner, Stribling was the first white author since Harriet Beecher Stowe to publish a novel featuring an African-American protagonist.

He was born in March 1881 in Clifton, Tennessee, to Amelia Waits and Christopher Columbus Stribling. After completing high school, Stribling enrolled at Southern Normal College in Huntingdon, Tennessee, for two years before going on to pursue a teacher-training course at the Florence Normal College in Alabama. He graduated with a B.A. in 1903 and then started studying law. He earned an LL.B. from the University of Alabama at Tuscaloosa in 1905. He published *The Cruise of the Dry Dock*, his first novel, in 1917. It was his second work, *BIRTHRIGHT* (1922), however, that secured him national recognition. The novel revolves around a mixed-race HARVARD UNIVERSITY graduate named Peter Siner who is forced to confront the pernicious JIM CROW segregation laws of the South when he returns home.

Stribling published several works during the Harlem Renaissance. They included *Fombombo* (1923), *Teeftallow* (1926), *Red Sand* (1924), and his Pulitzer Prize–winning novel *The Store* (1933).

Bibliography
Eckley, Wilton. *T. S. Stribling.* Boston: Twayne Publishers, 1975.
Piacentino, Edward J. *T. S. Stribling: Pioneer Realist in Modern Southern Literature.* Lanham, Md.: University Press of America, 1988.

Striver's Row
An upscale residential HARLEM neighborhood located between 138th and 139th Streets and Seventh and Eighth Avenues. Striver's Row was known for its elegant European-style town houses, which were designed by the architect Stanford White. The area was home to such notable figures as Eubie Blake, AARON DOUGLAS, W. C. HANDY, and Ethel Waters. Successful professionals such as Dr. Ernest Alexander, a dermatologist, and his wife, Lillian, often hosted sophisticated gatherings that celebrated Harlem Renaissance artists and facilitated continued conversation between them and interested parties.

The neighborhood was featured in "On Striver's Row," a 1940 satire by Abram Barrington Hill, future cofounder of the American Negro Theatre, and staged by the Rose McClendon Players. The play was revived in 2003 by the Black Theatre Troupe at Phoenix College.

Bibliography
Bailey, S. Peter, A. Peter Bailey, Edith J. Slade, and David N. Dinkins. *Harlem Today: A Cultural and Visitors Guide.* New York: Gumbs & Thomas Publishers, 1986.
Watson, Steven. *The Harlem Renaissance: Hub of African-American Culture, 1920–1930.* New York: Pantheon Books, 1995.

Strong, Mary
One of several pseudonyms that the poet, playwright, and songwriter GEORGIA DOUGLAS JOHNSON used during her career. Johnson used the name "Mary Strong" when she developed a letter-writing club in which she would provide members with a "generous list" of people with whom they shared interests. According to biographer Gloria Hull, Johnson began using the pseudonym in 1930 when she opened a mailbox for the club and continued to use it through 1965, the year before she passed away.

Bibliography

Hull, Gloria. *Love, Sex, and Poetry: Three Women Writers of the Harlem Renaissance.* Bloomington: Indiana University Press, 1987.

Stylus

The literary magazine of HOWARD UNIVERSITY. Established in 1916 by professors ALAIN LOCKE and THOMAS MONTGOMERY GREGORY, *Stylus* also was the first literary magazine published at a historically black American college or university. The journal was named after a college literary society of the same name, one with which Locke and Gregory also played key founding roles.

The debut issue included works by Howard University students as well as prominent figures of the period such as JAMES WELDON JOHNSON and WILLIAM STANLEY BRAITHWAITE. Later issues featured contributions by CHARLES CHESNUTT, W. E. B. DuBois, and ARTHUR SCHOMBURG. The magazine resumed publication in 1921 in the wake of World War I. It was there that "JOHN REDDING GOES TO SEA," the first published work of ZORA NEALE HURSTON, then a Howard University student, appeared in May 1921.

Bibliography

Johnson, Abby Arthur, and Ronald Maberry Johnson. *Propaganda & Aesthetics: The Literary Politics of African American Magazines in the Twentieth Century.* Amherst: University of Massachusetts, 1979.

Linneman, Russell, ed. *Alain Locke: Reflections on a Modern Renaissance Man.* Baton Rouge: Louisiana State University, 1982.

"Subversion" Edythe May Gordon (1928)

A haunting short story by EDYTHE MAE GORDON that appeared in the June 1928 issue of the SATURDAY EVENING QUILL. Gordon's story, one of only two that she published during the Harlem Renaissance, revolves around betrayal and death. John Marley is dying and grappling with the awful news he has received from his physician. On the way home, the financially strapped music teacher slips and falls on the wet and icy sidewalk. He soaks his coat and is quite disheveled as he makes his way to the home of longtime friend Charlie Delany. Delany is a good-natured fellow, an unmarried man, and a successful realtor from whom Marley hopes to borrow some money. Delany gives him cash and also insists that Marley take his plush coat. Being ensconced in the rich, "beaver-lined coat, with the beaver collar and cuffs . . . made him feel different," and Marley is imbued with a sense of purpose once again. Buoyed up by a renewed sense of pride, he uses some of his borrowed cash to buy small gifts for his wife and son.

The story takes a tragic turn when Marley appears at his home. Since his keys are in the coat that he left at Delany's, he rings the doorbell, and Lena answers. In the dark of the hallway, however, she feels only the coat and fails to recognize the man wearing it. Believing that Delany is before her, she whispers words that immediately reveal her affair with the family friend. Marley is devastated by his wife's betrayal and by the fact that his son is not his but Delany's. Marley maintains his composure, and when his deceptive friend appears for Thanksgiving dinner the next day, he asks him to "be kind to Lena and the boy" because he "can think of not more appropriate person to ask such a favor of." The two guilty parties are silenced by their shame and Marley's suffering.

Gordon's story complements the number of writings about domesticity, family life, and betrayal. "Subversion," like Gordon's "If Wishes Were Horses" (1929), "Patch Quilt" (1940) by Marita Bonner, and other works, explores the awful pain of infidelity and domesticity gone awry.

Bibliography

Gordon, Edythe Mae. *Selected Works of Edythe Mae Gordon with introduction by Lorraine Elena Roses.* New York: G. K. Hall & Co., 1996.

Sudom Lincha Claude McKay (1923)

CLAUDE MCKAY published *Sudom Lincha* in Russian. The English-language version, whose title translates to "Trial by Lynching," was one of two works that the writer published in Russian. The second work, *Negry v. Amerike*, translated as *The Negroes in America*, appeared in 1925.

According to scholar Kate Baldwin, *Sudom Lincha* is especially valuable for the insights it provides into McKay's perspectives on race, class, and gender. The volume, whose subtitle is "Stories about Negro Life in America," contains stories that shed light on the "black-belt thesis," a Russian communist belief that the American South could not only function as a black nation but also could be groomed to become a part of what Baldwin referred to as the "global Soviet."

Bibliography

Baldwin, Kate. *Beyond the Color Line and the Iron Curtain: Reading Encounters Between Black and Red, 1922–1923.* Durham, N.C.: Duke University Press, 2002.

Sugar Cain Frank Wilson (1926)

A one-act play by actor and playwright FRANK WILSON that won first prize in the 1926 OPPORTUNITY literary contest. Set in Waynesboro, Georgia, the play revolves around sexual violence, the threat of LYNCHING, and one family's efforts to preserve their honor and integrity in the face of a daughter's alleged sexual impropriety. The Cain family lives in an extremely modest home, one that the stage directions characterize as the abode of "honest, but poor people." The daughter Celia, known by the nickname Sugar, is overwhelmed by the gossip and secrets surrounding the birth of her child, Ora. Her parents are convinced that the father is a young and enterprising man named Howard who has gone north for his education. Paul Cain has threatened to kill Howard, and Sugar is paralyzed with fear when she learns that Howard has returned to the neighborhood.

Paul Cain and his son Fred are engaged in fretful conversations about their white neighbors, the Draytons, and about white people in general. Fred believes that his father places too much stock in whites; Paul, in turn, suggests that Lee Drayton, the son of the widowed Mary Drayton, is "alright" and that subterfuge and feigned submission, not violence, are the most effective way to best white people and to provide for his family. When Howard appears, Paul Cain attempts to shoot him, and the explosive scene forces Sugar to reveal the secret about the child's paternity. The ne'er-do-well boy Lee Drayton attacked her when she took laundry down to the Drayton home. In addition to assaulting her, he then threatened to call down the

KU KLUX KLAN upon her family if she ever revealed what had happened. In a desperate attempt to save Howard's life, she reveals once again that Lee Drayton is the father of her child. In the flurry of fevered activity that follows, Howard attacks Drayton, the Cains believe that a lynch mob is descending upon their house, and Fred Cain saves Mary Drayton from a fire in her home. The play ends as the Cains find out that Lee Drayton, wounded in the encounter with Howard, crawled into his mother's home and died there in the fire.

The play is a powerful narrative that focuses on the ramifications of sexual oppression, the tyranny of racial intimidation, and the power of heroic and divine intervention.

Sugar Hill

A HARLEM neighborhood that was home to the African-American aristocracy. Located between 145th and 155th Streets and between Edgecombe and Amsterdam Avenues, the area included the famous apartment building at 409 Edgecombe Avenue that was known simply as 409.

Among the intellectual and social elite who lived in Sugar Hill were WILLIAM STANLEY BRAITHWAITE, W. E. B. DuBois, AARON DOUGLAS, Thurgood Marshall, WALTER WHITE, and Roy Wilkins. DUKE ELLINGTON's "Take the A Train (Up to Sugar Hill)" (1940) is a tribute to the prestigious neighborhood that still is thriving today.

Bibliography

Bailey, S. Peter, A. Peter Bailey, Edith J. Slade, and David N. Dinkins. *Harlem Today: A Cultural and Visitors Guide.* New York: Gumbs & Thomas Publishers, 1986.

Watson, Steven. *The Harlem Renaissance: Hub of African-American Culture, 1920–1930.* New York: Pantheon Books, 1995.

Sullivan, May Miller (1899–1995)

A playwright, poet, and active member of the WASHINGTON, D.C., literary and cultural circles during the Harlem Renaissance. She was one of five children born to KELLY MILLER and his wife Anna May Butler Miller. Her father was a talented intellectual. He became the first African American to enroll at Johns Hopkins University, a pioneer in the field of sociology, and one of the cofounders of the impressive Moorland-Spingarn collection at Howard University. May Miller grew up in WASHINGTON, D.C., and was fortunate to be ensconced in the encouraging and motivated intellectual African-American communities of the city. She attended DUNBAR HIGH SCHOOL and, like Willis Richardson and others, gained much from teachers MARY BURRILL and ANGELINA WELD GRIMKÉ. She went on to study at Howard and graduated in 1920. She became a teacher at the Frederick Douglass High School in Baltimore. She taught dance, drama, and speech at the school where she remained on staff for some 20 years. Miller married John "Bud" Sullivan, a Washington, D.C., high school principal and later an accountant with the U.S. Postal Service, in 1940. She retired from teaching three years later and devoted much of her time to writing poetry and promoting African-American literature.

An especially enthusiastic writer, Miller began writing at an early age. Her schooling allowed her to refine further her skills. It was MARY BURRILL whose encouragement prompted her to complete her first play, *Pandora's Box,* a work that was published in 1914 in the school magazine. At Howard University she joined the HOWARD UNIVERSITY PLAYERS, a talented undergraduate troupe that university professor WILLIS RICHARDSON established in 1919 with support from his colleague ALAIN LOCKE. She received enormous encouragement from her professor T. MONTGOMERY GREGORY and was the first student to receive a prestigious award for drama. At the time of her graduation from Howard, she was awarded a prize for *Within the Shadows,* a one-act play. In 1925 her prizewinning play *The Bog Guide* signaled her potential as a leader in the burgeoning theater movement of the Harlem Renaissance. She was awarded third prize by judges Montgomery Gregory, Robert Benchley, and others for the work that she submitted to the 1924–25 *Opportunity* literary contest that also saw ZORA NEALE HURSTON win second prize for her play COLOR STRUCK. The following year, Miller won one of the four honorable mention certificates for her play *The Cuss'd Thing* in the competition that saw first and second prizes go

to FRANK WILSON and JOHN MATHEUS, respectively. Miller also saw her work featured in notable issues of periodicals such as the April 1929 issue of *Carolina Magazine* that was devoted to African-American plays. Her work, *Scratches,* appeared alongside plays by LEWIS ALEXANDER, EULALIE SPENCE, Willis Richardson, and John Matheus.

Miller's works reflected her awareness of contemporary social and political issues, her appreciation of racial tensions, and her commitment to promoting African-American history. Her collection of historical plays included works that honored intrepid antebellum women and that revisited moving biblical themes. Miller collaborated with Willis Richardson, a pioneering Washington, D.C., playwright, on an important anthology entitled NEGRO HISTORY IN THIRTEEN PLAYS. That volume included four of her own compositions, *Christophe's Daughters, Harriet Tubman, Samory,* and *Sojourner Truth.* In 1930 she contributed two plays to Richardson's innovative anthology PLAYS AND PAGEANTS FROM THE LIFE OF THE NEGRO. The collection of plays for children and young people also featured contributions by MAUD CUNEY HARE, John Matheus, and EDWARD McCOO. Richardson called attention to Miller, in particular, in his introduction, noting that she was "[o]ne of the most promising of the Negro playwrights" of the day. The collection included GRAVEN IMAGES, a work about Moses, his sister Miriam, and racial prejudice, and RIDING THE GOAT, a comedic critique about African-American lodge life and expectations. Miller also contributed to numerous periodicals including the THE NATION, THE NEW YORK TIMES, *Poetry, Phylon, Arts Quarterly,* and *Writer.*

Sullivan was an integral part of the Washington, D.C., literary community, and she enjoyed especially close ties to GEORGIA DOUGLAS JOHNSON, an earnest poet, insightful playwright, and beloved mentor of many. It was Sullivan who sat with Johnson as she lay on her deathbed. Her tender attention to Johnson is perhaps best illustrated by the fact that she held her friend's hand and repeated over and over, "Poet Georgia Douglas Johnson," an act of love that continued to reinforce Johnson's tireless and ambitious efforts to sustain a writing career.

Sullivan continued to publish long after the Harlem Renaissance ended. Her last play, *Free-*

dom's Children on the March (1943), was performed at that year's graduation ceremony at Douglass High School. Additional later works included volumes of poetry entitled *Into the Clearing* (1959), *Not That Far* (1973), *Dust of an Uncertain Journey* (1975), *The Ransomed Wait* (1983), and *Collected Poems* (1989). She also maintained close ties to academia and accepted invitations to become poet-in-residence at schools such as the University of Wisconsin-Milwaukee, Phillips-Exeter Academy, and Monmouth College.

Sullivan enjoyed a most productive literary career during the Harlem Renaissance. Her influence on the movement testifies to the mentoring that she received and bestowed, and to the power of collaborative enterprise with fellow writers.

Bibliography

Brown-Guillory, Elizabeth, ed. *Wines in the Wilderness: Plays by African-American Women from the Harlem Renaissance to the Present.* Westport, Conn.: Greenwood Press, 1990.

Gray, Christine Rauchfuss. *Willis Richardson: Forgotten Pioneer of African-American Drama.* Westport, Conn.: Greenwood Press, 1999.

Richardson, Willis, ed. *Plays and Pageants from the Life of the Negro.* Washington, D.C.: Associated Publishers, 1930.

Roses, Lorraine Elena, and Ruth Elizabeth Randolph. *Harlem Renaissance and Beyond: Literary Biographies of 100 Black Women Writers.* Boston: G. K. Hall & Co., 1990.

"Summer Tragedy, A" Arna Bontemps
(1932)

A moving tale of love and desperation by ARNA BONTEMPS. Judges FANNIE HURST, STERLING BROWN, and Richard Walsh named Bontemps the winner in the 1932 *OPPORTUNITY* literary contest. His story was chosen over four other works awarded honorable mention, among them fiction by EUGENE GORDON and MARITA BONNER. "A Summer Tragedy" became one of Bontemps's most frequently anthologized works.

The story is set in the South on Greenbriar Plantation, an estate that now profits from the labors of African-American sharecroppers. Jeff and Jennie Patton, an elderly couple, have been on the land for four and half decades. Facing sickness and death brought on by their years of hard labor and minimal profits at the hands of Major Stevenson, their employer, the couple consider how best to preserve their dignity and domestic stability. After much consideration, the two decide to kill themselves and proceed with the plan that allows them to die together, much as they have lived in a loving and supportive fashion together.

Bontemps's stirring tale was inspired by his own ties to the South, a region from which his father moved the family in light of its violence and several specific intolerable racist incidents.

Bibliography

Bontemps, Arna. *The Old South: "A Summer Tragedy" and Other Stories of the Thirties.* New York: Dodd, Mead, 1973.

Jones, Kirkland C. *Renaissance Man from Louisiana: A Biography of Arna Wendell Bontemps.* Westport, Conn.: Greenwood Press, 1992.

Sunday Morning in the South, A
Georgia Douglas Johnson (1925)

A chilling antilynching drama by GEORGIA DOUGLAS JOHNSON that illuminated the devastating effects of racial hysteria and violence upon African-American families. Set in a generic "town in the South" in 1924, the drama opens on the home of Sue Jones, a grandmother who is caring for her two grandsons, aged 19 and seven. Tom, the oldest, is a hardworking and respectful young man who slept soundly on Saturday evening having exhausted himself working. The Jones's preparations for Sunday morning services are upset, however, when a contingent of police officers arrive with a victim of an alleged attack. After impatient and pointed directions from the police, the victim suggests that Tom resembles the man who assaulted her. Despite the protestations of his family, Tom is hauled away. Sue Jones, counseled by her neighbor Liza, hopes to alert the white woman whom she nursed and took care of for years. She hopes in vain, however, that "Miss Vilet" and her father, who is a judge, will be able to intervene. It is only a matter of moments, however, before the shaken grandmother receives the news that her innocent grandson has been lynched. The play closes as Sue Jones collapses, and strains from the nearby church repeat the phrase "Lord have mercy."

Johnson completed the play in the same year that she began hosting literary salons in her WASHINGTON, D.C., home. The play is one of several piercing antilynching plays that Johnson wrote during her career. *A Sunday Morning in the South*, like her other works, underscores the random nature of racial violence and the particular upheaval that it wrought in respectable African-American homes. Johnson's work contributed much to the systematic protest of LYNCHING, mob violence, and the KU KLUX KLAN that continued throughout the Harlem Renaissance. She wrote the play some six years after the NATIONAL ASSOCIATION FOR THE ADVANCEMENT OF COLORED PEOPLE (NAACP) published *Thirty Years of Lynching in the United States, 1889–1918* (1919), its comprehensive study of lynching practices. Johnson, along with playwrights such as MARY BURRILL, ALICE DUNBAR-NELSON, and ANGELINA GRIMKÉ, succeeded in raising public awareness about the violence. Their works contributed to political efforts by the NAACP and other organizations to protest the insufficient governmental efforts to combat the practice.

Bibliography

Gunning, Sandra. *Race, Rape, and Lynching: The Red Record of American Literature.* New York: Oxford University Press, 1996.

Johnson, Georgia Douglas. *The Selected Works of Georgia Douglas Johnson* with an introduction by Claudia Tate. Boston: G. K. Hall, 1997.

Perkins, Kathy A., and Judith L. Stephens, eds. *Strange Fruit: Plays on Lynching by American Women.* Bloomington: Indiana University Press, 1998.

Zangrando, Robert. *The NAACP Crusade Against Lynching, 1909–1950.* Philadelphia: Temple University Press, 1960.

Survey Graphic

A periodical that was linked to *Survey Magazine*, the leading American social work journal of the 1920s. *Survey Graphic*, published from 1921 through 1948, was the monthly illustrated companion publication of *Survey*. Founded by PAUL KELLOGG, the journal represented a shift away from its primary audience of professional social workers toward a larger socially and politically conscious reading public.

In March 1925, *Survey Graphic* published its most well-known and historic issue when it focused on African-American writers, issues, culture, and scholarship. ALAIN LOCKE, who was a HOWARD UNIVERSITY professor, HARVARD UNIVERSITY graduate, and the first African American awarded a RHODES SCHOLARSHIP, was the guest editor of the issue entitled *HARLEM: MECCA OF THE NEW NEGRO*. The volume included works by and about African Americans. The Harlem issue featured artwork by WINOLD REISS and creative writing by a number of notable figures including COUNTEE CULLEN, ANGELINA GRIMKÉ, LANGSTON HUGHES, CLAUDE MCKAY, ANNE SPENCER, and JEAN TOOMER. ALBERT BARNES, George Haynes, MELVILLE HERSKOVITS, ELISE MCDOUGALD, J. A. ROGERS, and ARTHUR SCHOMBURG were among those who contributed essays and scholarly articles. Locke promptly capitalized on the tremendous set of materials and later that year published *THE NEW NEGRO* (1925), an anthology that included many of the works published in *Survey Graphic*.

Bibliography

Chambers, Clarke. *Paul U. Kellogg and the Survey: Voices for Social Welfare and Social Justice.* Minneapolis: University of Minnesota Press, 1971.

Finnegan, Cara. *Picturing Poverty: Print Culture and FSA Photographs.* Washington, D.C.: Smithsonian Books, 2003.

"Sweat" Zora Neale Hurston (1926)

Published in the first and only issue of the avant-garde periodical *FIRE!!*, the story was one of two works that ZORA NEALE HURSTON contributed to the controversial and short-lived publication that hoped to mark the emergence of a new generation of Harlem Renaissance writers. Critics regard "Sweat" as one of Hurston's most powerful and sophisticated works.

The protagonist, Delia, is an earnest, hardworking, and long-suffering laundress. Her marriage to Sykes, a domineering and insensitive man, is draining and demoralizing. Sykes's efforts to humiliate Delia, the woman whose labors maintain their home, intensify when he takes a mistress. He intends to dislodge Delia from the home that she has made, the place where she has begun a pathetic but meaningful little garden. Determined to oust Delia, Sykes preys on her fear of snakes. He hides an enormous rattlesnake in the laundry basket that his wife uses, and it frightens her so badly that she seeks refuge in the barn. Unfortunately for Sykes, the snake targets him when he returns home. Delia, crouched in the flowerbed that lies beneath the bedroom window, listens to the awful commotion that ensues as Sykes battles for his life. She refrains from helping the man who has tormented her and so regains her freedom from domestic tyranny.

The story offers a poignant example of woman's efforts to preserve her dignity. The fallen nature of the world in which Delia finds herself and the fate that ultimately befalls the evil man in her life rewrite the Creation story and biblical narratives about Eden and Eve's temptation by the serpent. This short story and other powerful works such as "DRENCHED IN LIGHT" (1924), and THEIR EYES WERE WATCHING GOD (1937) reinforced Hurston's reputation as a skilled writer of works that considered the complicated ways in which individuals in general, and women in particular, secured their freedom and established their domestic autonomy.

Bibliography

Boyd, Valerie. Wrapped in Rainbows: The Life of Zora Neale Hurston. New York: Scribner, 2003.

Hemenway, Robert. Zora Neale Hurston: A Literary Biography. Urbana: University of Illinois Press, 1977.

"Symphonesque" Arthur Huff Fauset (1926)

A stirring short story by ARTHUR HUFF FAUSET. Judges ZONA GALE, JEAN TOOMER, CARL VAN DOREN, and others awarded "Symphonesque" first prize in the 1925 OPPORTUNITY literary contest. Fauset's work edged out submissions by ZORA NEALE HURSTON, DOROTHY WEST, and EUGENE GORDON.

Divided into three sections, the story is fashioned in the modes of a musical composition. Sections such as "Allegro Non Troppo," "Crescendo," and "Agitato" follow the increasingly frenzied actions and thoughts of Cudjo, a 17-year-old boy in Gum Ridge, Texas. He sets out from the dilapidated cabin that he shares with a man identified only as Old Ben, intent on watching the Sunday afternoon baptismal exercises in the Tougaloo River. His shouts, antics, and seemingly uncontrollable dancing eventually prompt members of the annoyed congregation to physically remove him from the scene. Cudjo then focuses his attention on Amber Lee, a young girl who, like him, is prone to dancing outdoors. Overtaken by his desire for her, Cudjo snatches her but refrains from assaulting her when he sees the fear in her eyes. He struggles to assure Amber Lee that he cherishes her; she responds by telling him that she saw a demon in his eyes, one that was replaced by a savior. Utterly confused by the feverish events of the day, Cudjo eventually makes his way to the summit of a nearby hill, and the story closes as the sun sets on this lonely, frustrated character.

T

Taboo Mary Hoyt Wiborg (1922)

A short-lived play about voodoo, curses, and slavery by Mary Hoyt Wiborg. The show opened in April 1922 on BROADWAY at the Sam H. Harris Theatre. The play is set on a Louisiana plantation during a devastating drought. Eventually some of the enslaved plantation workers decide that the drought and the ruined crops are the results of a curse directed toward the Gaylords, their owners. They decide that the mute white grandchild of the plantation mistress must be sacrificed in order to alleviate the suffering. Plans are interrupted by the arrival of Jim, an itinerant musician. Jim's arrival prompts a drastic change in time and scenery as the play turns its attention to long-ago African scenes and history. Jim is reintroduced as a voodoo king whose wife is Mrs. Gaylord. Jim, now an authority on the African roots of voodoo, clarifies the origin of the Louisiana curse. The play ends as the child speaks, but the surprise of the event prompts Mrs. Gaylord to die from shock at the sudden turn of events.

Taboo appears to be the only Broadway play that Wiborg, a NEW YORK CITY socialite and the daughter of a rich banker, staged during her career. It lasted only four performances. Produced by Augustin Duncan, its predominantly African-American cast on opening night included PAUL ROBESON. Robeson, who would make his name in EUGENE O'NEILL's THE EMPEROR JONES some three years later, left the Harmony Kings to take the lead role in Wiborg's play. The play also included African dances and musical accompaniments provided by the Clef Club Orchestra.

Bibliography

Boyle, Sheila Tully, and Andrew Buni. *Paul Robeson: The Years of Promise and Achievement.* Amherst: University of Massachusetts Press, 2001.

Duberman, Martin. *Paul Robeson.* New York: Knopf, 1989.

Talbert, Mary Burnett (1866–1923)

A visionary activist, educator, and clubwoman who, in 1923, became the first African-American woman to win the prestigious SPINGARN MEDAL. Born in 1866 in Oberlin, Ohio, Talbert was one of eight children born to Cornelius and Caroline Nicholls Burnett. Burnett's parents were visible citizens of Oberlin and, as owners of a barbershop, boardinghouse, and restaurant, also among the city's most enterprising entrepreneurs. Burnett attended Oberlin College, the alma mater of HALLIE QUINN BROWN, ANNA JULIA COOPER, and MARY CHURCH TERRELL. Following her graduation from Oberlin, Burnett began teaching in Arkansas. In 1887 she became the state's first African-American principal.

Burnett married William Talbert, a Buffalo native, in 1891. The couple's only child, Sarah May, was born one year later. Sarah May Talbert, a gifted musician, went on to attend the New England Conservatory of Music and enjoyed a career as a composer and pianist.

In the years before the Harlem Renaissance, Talbert played a leadership role in two major national organizations, the NATIONAL ASSOCIATION FOR THE ADVANCEMENT OF COLORED PEOPLE

(NAACP) and the NATIONAL ASSOCIATION OF COLORED WOMEN (NACW). When W. E. B. DuBois, WILLIAM MONROE TROTTER, and others met in Buffalo to establish the NIAGARA MOVEMENT, a forerunner of the NAACP, the group met secretly in the Talberts' Buffalo home.

Talbert was instrumental in forging links between the NACW and the newly established NAACP. She was president of the national women's organization for four years, from 1916 through 1920. Talbert, who is recognized as one of the cofounders of the NAACP, served as vice president of the organization from 1918 through 1923, the year of her death. During her tenure, she called attention to the horrors of LYNCHING and lobbied intensely for antilynching legislation such as the Dyer Bill, brought before Congress in the early 1920s. One of her last efforts was to preserve the historic Anacostia, Maryland, home of Frederick Douglass.

Bibliography

Davis, Elizabeth Lindsay. *Lifting As They Climb.* New York: G. K. Hall, 1996.

Talented Tenth

The phrase coined by W. E. B. DuBois that refers to the African-American intellectual elite. The phrase was a direct challenge to the accommodationist philosophies of BOOKER T. WASHINGTON, who advocated industrial training, rather than intellectual advancement, as a means of securing better conditions for blacks. DuBois was distressed that the emphasis on African-American labor would relegate the race to perpetual second-class citizenship and prevent diverse, powerful, and multifaceted African-American development and achievement.

DuBois first used the phrase in 1903 in *The Negro Problem.* Biographer David Levering Lewis suggests that DuBois's perspectives on intellectual potential informed his work several years before the HARVARD UNIVERSITY Ph.D. and future editor of THE CRISIS used the term in print.

Bibliography

Lewis, David Levering. *W. E. B. DuBois: Biography of a Race, 1868–1919.* New York: Henry Holt and Company, 1993.

"Tale of the North Carolina Woods, A"
Arthur Huff Fauset (1922)

A southern local-color story by ARTHUR HUFF FAUSET that appeared in the January 1922 issue of *THE CRISIS.* The evocation of folk history, local mysteries, and the vital role of an African-American sage are reminiscent of the acclaimed regionalist writings and sketches of CHARLES CHESNUTT.

The story involves a set of racially unidentified young men who live in a North Carolina community but know very little about the folk history of the place. One afternoon, while sitting on the branches of an ancient tree, they seize the opportunity to learn about the tree's history and the reasons that might explain its unique form. They decide to question Aunt Sedalia, a sprightly, elderly woman whose "face was dark brown in color, her eyes somewhat slanty, black, and sparkling, with the fire of a maniac." She eventually tells them about the tree, which is rooted on one side of a river but spans the entire breadth of that same body of water. According to the self-identified Queen of Sedalia, the tree began to grow in the days following the death of a young white boy. After a snake fatally poisons the son of Colonel Marks, Queen Sedalia, as she also refers to herself, begins to pray regularly on the very spot where the child died. Eventually, a tree begins to grow, and she is convinced that it has sprouted from the blood spilled on that site. The story closes without a dramatic resolution or evidence of the effect that the story has had on the demanding but untutored audience.

Fauset's story suffers somewhat from its uncomplicated stock characters and unpersuasive story line. It appeared some two years before "The Marked Tree," a much more riveting local-color story by Charles Chesnutt that appeared in the December 1924 and January 1925 issues of *The Crisis.*

Tales My Father Told Me Hallie Quinn Brown (1925)

One of several works that HALLIE QUINN BROWN published during the HARLEM RENAISSANCE. The volume honored her father, Thomas Brown, and included numerous examples of his selfless and charitable efforts to improve the lives of others. The volume reflected Brown's determination to provide American readers with evidence of African-American heroism, high morality, and civic pride.

Tanner, Henry Ossawa (1859–1937)

One of America's finest painters and an artist whose evocative art and professional example inspired many American painters and leading artists of the Harlem Renaissance. Tanner was the first of seven children born to Rev. Benjamin Tanner and his wife, Sarah Elizabeth Miller Tanner. Born in Pittsburgh and raised in PHILADELPHIA, Henry Tanner studied art at the Pennsylvania Academy of the Fine Arts located in Philadelphia. He studied with the renowned artist Thomas Eakins before going on to pursue his studies in FRANCE at the Académie Laurens. His successes in prestigious European art competitions led to honors and enabled Tanner to establish an art studio of his own. He continued to work in France, at the Trépied, an artists' colony.

Tanner's best-known paintings include a series of moving portraits of African-American families. His portrait entitled *The Banjo Lesson* (1893) was one of several in which he represented children learning from their elders, and the scenes were especially moving for the highly attentive and loving interaction between the subjects. Tanner later developed a series of powerful biblical paintings that included such works as *The Annunciation* (1898), *Christ Learning to Read* (1910–1914), and *Christ and His Mother Studying the Scriptures* (1910).

Tanner married Jessie Macauley Olssen, a musician of Swedish descent, in 1899. She was a model for several of Tanner's paintings including *The Annunciation*. The couple's only child, Jessie Ossawa Tanner, was born in 1903. Their son went on to study at Cambridge University and the Royal School of Mines before suffering a nervous breakdown. Thanks to his father's care, Jessie recovered and went on to live a full and productive life. Jessie Tanner died in 1925, a victim of pleurisy. Tanner passed away in May 1937.

During the Harlem Renaissance, the emphasis on African-American themes did generate criticism of Tanner's work that, by that point, did not include an overwhelming amount of African-American material. However, his steady career, in-sightful visions, and lifelong dedication to art could not diminish his status as one of the most highly regarded American painters.

Bibliography

Mathews, Marcia. *Henry Ossawa Tanner, American Artist.* Chicago: University of Chicago Press, 1969.

Mosby, Dewey. *Across Continents and Cultures: The Art and Life of Henry Ossawa Tanner.* Kansas City, Mo.: Nelson-Atkins Museum of Art, 1995.

Tarry, Ellen (1906–unknown)

An Alabama-born author, teacher, and journalist who began her successful literary career just as the Harlem Renaissance came to a close. The daughter of John and Eula Meadows Tarry, she was born in Birmingham, Alabama. Raised as a Protestant, she converted to Catholicism in 1922. Tarry completed her education in Alabama at the State Normal School and began teaching in public schools in Birmingham. She began her journalism career at the *Birmingham Truth,* the official publication of the Knights of Pythias. The majority of her publications related to African-American history and culture, published under a regular column entitled "Negroes of Note."

Tarry relocated to New York City in 1929 and became part of the city's active African-American literary and intellectual circles. She became a member of the Negro Writer's Guild, an organization with which ARTHUR SCHOMBURG, CLAUDE MCKAY, STERLING BROWN, and other prominent writers were associated.

In 1940 Tarry published "Native Daughter," a feminist response to RICHARD WRIGHT's recently published NATIVE SON. Later that year, she published *Janie Bell,* the first of several children's books that she would write during her career.

Tarry enjoyed a successful and diverse career in the years following the Harlem Renaissance. In addition to writing children's stories, she published a variety of essays on race and religion. Her work appeared in publications such as *Catholic World* and *Inter-Racial Review.* She contributed articles to the AMSTERDAM NEWS and continued to publish African-American historical works. These included *Katherine Drexel: Friend of the Neglected* (1958), *Young Jim: The Early Years of James Weldon*

Johnson (1967), and *The Other Toussaint: A Post-Revolutionary Black* (1981).

Bibliography

Tarry, Ellen. *The Third Door: The Autobiography of an American Negro Woman.* 1955; reprint, Westport, Conn.: Negro Universities Press, 1971.

Temple, John

One of the pseudonyms that writer GEORGIA DOUGLAS JOHNSON used during her career. She used the name when she submitted her prizewinning play *PLUMES* to the 1927 *OPPORTUNITY* literary contest.

Tenderloin District

The NEW YORK CITY district located in mid-Manhattan near Pennsylvania Station. Also known as Herald Square, the area was home to a significant African-American community that developed in the early 1900s. Many of the residents were part of the large-scale African-American migration to the North that occurred during the Harlem Renaissance era, between World Wars I and II.

Terrell, Mary Eliza Church (1863–1954)

An influential activist and outspoken civic leader who was especially well known for her leadership in the NATIONAL ASSOCIATION OF COLORED WOMEN (NACW) and the NATIONAL ASSOCIATION FOR THE ADVANCEMENT OF COLORED PEOPLE (NAACP).

Born into a southern family of interracial heritage, Terrell was raised in Memphis, Tennessee. She was the first child born to Robert and Louisa Church, both of whom had been enslaved in the South. Robert Church was the son of his slave owner, Charles Church. Terrell's parents' industrious and successful entrepreneurial efforts provided the family with many material comforts and social advantages. By the 1880s, Robert Church, whose estate was valued at close to $1 million, reportedly was the richest African-American in the South.

Terrell went on to attend Oberlin College and graduated in 1884. Despite her father's wishes that she not pursue a professional life, Terrell began teaching. After a stint at WILBERFORCE UNIVERSITY in Ohio, she relocated to WASHINGTON, D.C., and began teaching at the Colored High School. She met Robert Terrell, a HOWARD UNIVERSITY–educated teacher and principal of the M Street High School, who later became an influential municipal judge. The couple married in 1891. Their only child, Phyllis, was born in 1898. In 1905 the adoption of Terrell's niece, named Terrell Church, expanded the family.

Terrell's accomplishments as a highly respected public figure, women's advocate, and race woman grew out of her work with the NACW in the early 1900s. She was one of the cofounders of the NAACP and enthusiastically accepted the invitation of W. E. B. DuBois to become one of the organization's charter members. During the Harlem Renaissance, Terrell continued to lobby for equal rights, was a forceful antilynching activist, and challenged many of the segregation practices in Washington, D.C., businesses and organizations.

Terrell's only book, *A COLORED WOMAN IN A WHITE WORLD* (1940), appeared as the Harlem Renaissance drew to a close. Her autobiography, which included a preface by writer H. G. Wells, was an invaluable record of achievement and perseverance.

She died in July 1954, shortly after the U.S. Supreme Court decision in the *Brown v. Board of Education* case. She was buried in Lincoln Memorial Cemetery.

Bibliography

Jones, Beverly Washington. *Quest for Equality: The Life and Writings of Mary Church Terrell.* Brooklyn, N.Y.: Carlson Publishers, 1990.

Sterling, Dorothy. *Black Foremothers: Three Lives.* New York: Feminist Press, 1988.

Terrell, Mary Church. *A Colored Woman in a White World.* 1940; reprint, New York: Arno Press, 1980.

Their Eyes Were Watching God Zora Neale Hurston (1937)

The most celebrated and well known of ZORA NEALE HURSTON's novels. The novel, which was underestimated and disregarded when it was first published, is hailed now as a seminal work of American literature, a definitive text of the

Harlem Renaissance, and a powerful African-American feminist *bildungsroman.*

Hurston completed the manuscript in less than two months. At the time, she was living in HAITI on a GUGGENHEIM FELLOWSHIP and, as her biographers suggest, also recovering from what she regarded as "the real love affair of my life" with a West Indian man whom she had met first in New York in 1931 and with whom she reconnected briefly some time later. Their respective career goals, his idealized vision of her as wife who would devote herself to him wholly, and her increasingly ambitious professional desires tested the relationship. It was with much sadness that Hurston ended the affair with the man whom she identifies in *DUST TRACKS* only as A. W. P. In her autobiography, *Dust Tracks on a Road* (1942), Hurston recalled that the novel was "dammed up in me, and I wrote it under internal pressure in seven weeks." She later regretted that she could not "write it again. In fact, I regret all of my books," she continued dramatically. "It is one of the tragedies of life that one cannot have all the wisdom one is ever to possess in the beginning" (Hurston, 155).

The novel's protagonist is Janie, a young woman who returns to her hometown of EATONVILLE after living intensely and surviving tragic and traumatic events that have given her a powerful foundation on which to construct and to reconstruct the story of her life. The narrator establishes immediately that Janie is a survivor and witness; her story will be as much autobiography as it will be testimony: "[T]his was a woman and she had come back from burying the dead. Not the dead of sick and ailing with friends at the pillow and the feet. She had come back from the sodden and the bloated; the sudden dead, their eyes flung wide open in judgment." Over the course of 20 chapters, Janie relates her gripping and evocative tales to Phoeby Watson, her dear friend.

The major stories in *Their Eyes* revolve around domesticity, desire, and marriage. Janie Crawford is being raised by her God-fearing grandmother, who aspires to situate Janie in a marriage that will save her from the oppressive circumstances that all too often overwhelm women of color. That plan eventually collides with Janie's romanticism, a sensibility that comes alive during a powerful epiphany beneath the pear tree on her grandmother's prop-

erty. In this most memorable scene of the novel, Janie spends as much time as she can over a three-day period watching a blossoming pear tree come alive. She is unable to resist the call "to come and gaze on a mystery" that emanates from the tree. As she watches, it changes from "barren brown stems to glistening leaf-buds; from the leaf-buds to snowy virginity of bloom." Janie watches the bees pollinate the buds and is overwhelmed by the sensual nature of the natural process. "So this was a marriage!" she concludes after watching "the dust-bearing bee sing into the sanctum of the bloom" and the "thousand sister-calyxes arch to meet the love embrace and the ecstatic shiver of the tree from root to tiniest branch creaming in every blossom and frothing with delight." Her grandmother quickly interrupts Janie's dewy-eyed vision of the world and overtures to a young man whom she regards as a less than satisfactory match for her granddaughter. Nanny marries Janie off to Logan Killicks, owner of some 60 acres, a man whom she thinks will provide the best "protection" of her charge after she passes away.

Marriage, which can function as an alternating symbol of high domesticity and the institutionalized oppression of women, is central in the novel. Janie has three marriages to very different men. She leaves Logan Killicks when he ceases to treat her adoringly and takes up with the entrepreneurial, bossy, and loquacious Joe Starks. The two travel to Eatonville, where Starks purchases some 200 acres and proceeds to install himself as the most powerful man in town. That marriage disintegrates as their mutual desire subsides, and Hurston suggests that Starks dies when Janie challenges him in public about his perceived, and perhaps actually nonexistent, all-powerful manhood. With the death of Starks, Janie is free to revel in the attentions of Vergible "Tea Cake" Woods, a man younger than herself and the most enlightened of the men she has met. Janie does not hesitate to accompany Tea Cake as he lives his itinerant laboring life. Their bliss is savagely undone when they are endangered by a hurricane in the Everglades, and in the dreadful days following the natural disaster, Tea Cake is attacked by a rabid dog. He contracts rabies, and in his delusion he attempts to shoot Janie. She fires back in self-defense and, tragically, kills him. She journeys back to Eatonville, and it is there, on the back steps of her house, that she retraces the phases of her epic journey aloud with Phoeby. The novel ends with a moment of anointing and expansive acceptance as Janie ascends to her bedroom. The lamp in her hand becomes "a spark of sun-stuff washing her face in fire" and the open windows of her room "had broomed out all the fetid feeling of absence and nothingness." Tea Cake's spirit returns, "prancing around her," and the "kiss of his memory" makes "pictures of love and light against the wall." In this instance, she finds peace, which is seamlessly "pulled in her horizon like a great fishnet. Pulled it in from around the waist of the world and draped it over her shoulder. So much of life in its meshes! She called in her soul to come and see." This final synthesis of stories told and images beheld brings the novel to a inspired close.

The response to Hurston's incisive and passionate literary endeavor was mixed. Ralph Thomson, writing for THE NEW YORK TIMES, was impressed by Hurston's talent and the distinctive ways in which she was writing race fiction. Unlike a host of white authors who write "*about* the Negro," he observed, "Miss Hurston writes *out* of the Negro and this distinction makes comparison dangerous if not downright futile" (Thomson, 23). While Thomson did find fault with this "unusual piece of work" and was unimpressed, for instance, by the strength of the dialect, he did admit that "Miss Hurston does not forget her sober interest when writing fiction." "[T]his novel has passages, even pages," he intoned, "that are as faithful expressions of Negro character as one could find in an anthropologist's notebook," and the novel as a whole left "no question that it is further evidence of a marked and honest talent." "Those who have overlooked Miss Hurston thus far," he insisted, "will make no mistake in beginning to read her now." (Thomson, 23).

Hurston suffered the criticism of her literary colleagues and some prominent Harlem Renaissance leaders, however. RICHARD WRIGHT lamented the fact that the book reinforced the notion that the "Negro folk-mind" was uncomplicated and apolitical. STERLING BROWN agreed, proposing that "Her characters eat and laugh and cry and work and kill; they swing like a pendulum eternally in that safe and narrow orbit in which America likes to see the Negro live; between laughter and tears"

(Hemenway, 241). In January 1938 ALAIN LOCKE savaged the book in a 1937 review of books by and about African Americans. His most generous comment referred to the work as "folklore fiction at its best," but he insisted that the book had no intellectual heft, political sensibility, or social critique. He suggested that Hurston's literary endeavors elicited serious questions about her vocation and philosophical engagement. "When will the Negro novelist of maturity, who knows how to tell a story convincingly—which is Miss Hurston's cradle gift, come to grips with motive fiction and social document fiction?" he asked (Boyd, 310). The attack left Hurston steaming, and she penned a rebuttal to OPPORTUNITY, but editor CHARLES S. JOHNSON refused to publish it. In a February 1938 letter to JAMES WELDON JOHNSON, Hurston revealed that she thought the shoddy evaluation to be part of a pattern of "envious picking on me" and she was tired of it. "[I]f you will admit the truth," she wrote to Johnson, "you know that Alain Locke is a malicious, spiteful, litt[l]e snot that thinks he ought to be the leading Negro because of his degrees. Foiled in that, he spends his time trying to cut the ground from under everybody else. He lends out his patronage and takes in ideas which he soon passes off as his own" (Kaplan, 413). As biographer Valerie Boyd notes, Hurston was dedicated to creating work that exceeded the narrow constraints of "social document fiction" that Locke and others glorified. Hurston rallied to her own defense, insisting that writers of color had the right to creative freedom and that they should not be scripted by the white majority or the African-American elite to focus solely on race.

Contemporary evaluations of *Their Eyes Were Watching God* side with Hurston's insistent claim. The book has enjoyed a revival that has secured its author's reputation as an impassioned, insightful, and innovative writer, one who transforms anthropological details into absorbing narrative and whose creative work is steadied by her penchant for keen and farsighted cultural analysis. It inspired a movie made for television, coproduced by Oprah Winfrey.

Bibliography
Boyd, Valerie. *Wrapped in Rainbows: The Life of Zora Neale Hurston.* New York: Scribner, 2003.

Cronin, Gloria, ed. *Critical Essays on Zora Neale Hurston.* New York: G. K. Hall & Co., 1998.

Hemenway, Robert. *Zora Neale Hurston: A Literary Biography.* Urbana: University of Illinois Press, 1977.

Kaplan, Carla. *Zora Neale Hurston: A Life in Letters.* New York: Doubleday, 2002.

Thomson, Ralph. "Books of the Times." *New York Times,* 6 October 1937, 23.

There Is Confusion Jessie Fauset (1924)

The first novel by JESSIE FAUSET, influential CRISIS editor and mentor to numerous Harlem Renaissance writers. It established Fauset's interest in representing the African-American middle class and issues of racial PASSING and the complicated politics of acculturation and assimilation. Fauset contracted with the New York publishing firm of BONI & LIVERIGHT, the same firm that had published CANE by JEAN TOOMER to much acclaim. The book, however, was printed in England because Boni & Liveright had sold the rights to her novel to the London-based firm of Chapman & Hall (*NYT,* 7 September 1924, BR18). The press publicized Fauset's forthcoming novel as part of its own efforts "to give a fair hearing to young writers." The firm's spring 1924 publicity for the novel introduced Fauset to readers as the author who "discloses the life of the cultured negroes in New York and Philadelphia" (*NYT,* 27 April 1924, BR32).

The plot revolves around Joanna Marshall, a talented singer and aspiring dancer who struggles with the contemporary prejudices and stereotypes that would undermine her professional successes. The daughter of a man from whom she loved to hear stories as a child, she longs for venues in which she can practice and perfect her art. Even church becomes a forum in which she can advance her secular goals. As the soloist in the choir, she is able to attract "throngs to the church every Sunday" because of her "mezzo voice full and pulsing and gold" (73). She is quite different from her siblings, both of whom pursue different kinds of lives. Her sister Sylvia is "like a firefly in comparison with Joanna's steady beaconlike flood of light," a woman who "dashed about, worked as quickly as she thought and produced immediate and usually rather striking results" (17). Her brother Phillip, an activist and World War I veteran who dies at

home, was gassed during the war and eventually is nursed by his wife, Maggie Ellersley. Maggie, whose early experiences of domestic upheaval and of poverty prompt her to link emotional security with financial stability, eventually finds real love and fulfillment.

Set in PHILADELPHIA and in NEW YORK CITY, the novel is a tempestuous love story. Joanna is involved with Peter Bye, a multitalented but indolent man whose "dark arresting beauty" catches Joanna's eye. The narrator attributes Bye's penchant for laziness to his heredity, a background that "had become a tradition, of a tradition that had become warped, that had gone astray, and had carried Peter and Peter Bye's father along in its general wreckage" (21–22). That background dates back to the early years of American enslavement, includes an ancestor who fought nobly in the American Revolution, and a pioneering educator who resented the ways in which his white owners and their descendants enjoyed success that was essentially financed by the labors of their slaves. Peter becomes convinced that "the world owes me a living." It is this perspective, in addition to his deep-rooted hatred of white people, that he must overcome in order to participate fully in the modern world. Ultimately, the two are able to recognize the potential value and protective powers of the love that they share. Joanna chooses to abandon her career, and she does so in order to devote herself wholly to her marriage. As she tells Peter, "I learned that nothing in the world is worth as much as love. For people like us, people who can and must suffer—*Love* is our refuge and strength" (283–284). The novel closes once Fauset has crafted this idyllic image of stable domesticity and self-aware commitment to racial solidarity and emotional uplift.

Contemporary analyses of *There Is Confusion* explore the ways in which Fauset highlighted the intense scrutiny with which African Americans dealt in the public sphere. Critics also note Fauset's discussion of domesticity and femininity and the degree to which modern women had to negotiate their professional and public desires with the expectations and responsibilities of the private sphere. Thadious Davis suggests, however, that Fauset contrives the final message about high domesticity. She proposes that "Joanna's reversal comes too completely and too abruptly" and that "she embraces an ideal external to the novel proper, but she underscores its conclusion: that the African-American woman must subordinate gender issues and personal ambitions to the advancement of the race through the male's attainment of parity—notwithstanding the fact that she is his equal" (Davis, xxi).

The publication of *There Is Confusion* inspired CHARLES S. JOHNSON, editor of *OPPORTUNITY*, to organize a celebratory publication dinner at the CIVIC CLUB. Much to Fauset's dismay, however, the March 1924 event evolved into an occasion on which many notable figures such as W. E. B. DUBOIS and JAMES WELDON JOHNSON directed attention away from Fauset and toward the emerging and predominantly male writers of the Harlem Renaissance instead. Fauset's publishers used the occasion to advance their publicity of the work. They characterized the event as a birthday celebration for "a new sort of book about colored people—the birthday of a fine novel about Negroes of the upper classes of New York and Philadelphia—as impressive and vital in their special environment as the upper class whites whom Edith Wharton or Archibald Marshall love to write about . . . Yes, there's something new under the sun," the press exclaimed, "and it is *There Is Confusion*" (Sylvander, 71). The poet and writer GWENDOLYN BENNETT celebrated Fauset's novel by dedicating a poem, "To Usward," to *The Crisis* literary editor and Cornell University graduate.

The novel garnered significant praise from leading members of the Harlem Renaissance intellectual elite. ALAIN LOCKE declared that the novel articulated the issues at the core of the Harlem Renaissance and that it was "the novel that the Negro intelligentsia [had] been clamoring for" [Miller, 208]. Locke's HOWARD UNIVERSITY colleague T. MONTGOMERY GREGORY, who reviewed it in the June 1924 issue of *Opportunity*, praised it for its decisive portrayals of African Americans, images that defied the pervasive racial stereotypes that usually relegated people of color to subservient social roles. According to Gregory, "the great value of this novel [lies] in interpreting the better elements of our life to those who know us only as domestic servants, 'uncles,' or criminals" (181). GEORGE SCHUYLER, who admitted that the

book had kept him completely absorbed, endorsed the novel for readers of *THE MESSENGER*. Literary critic Ernest Boyd saw the novel as more powerful than "the ordinary story of negro life." In his June 1924 *NEW YORK TIMES* article, "Charting the Sea of Fiction," he insisted that the novel "assumes the proportions of an important book; it is well executed, so well, in fact, that no Ku Kluxer could stand it" (*NYT,* 22 June 1924, BR1).

There Is Confusion is a provocative meditation on the politics of domesticity, female empowerment, and the potentially alienating nature of the public sphere. Fauset's critique of self-indulgence and of self-sacrifice enriches the novel and provides Harlem Renaissance readers with a meaningful study of racial advancement and gender politics.

Bibliography
"Books and Authors." *New York Times,* September 1924, BR18.

Boyd, Ernest. "Charting the Sea of Fiction," *New York Times,* 22 June 1924, BR1.

Davis, Thadious. Foreword in *There Is Confusion,* by Jessie Fauset. Boston: Northeastern University Press, 1989.

Fauset, Jessie. *There Is Confusion.* 1924, reprint, Boston: Northeastern University Press, 1989.

Gregory, Montgomery. "The Spirit of Phillis Wheatley." *Opportunity* (June 1924): 181.

Jones, Sharon. *Rereading the Harlem Renaissance: Race, Class, and Gender in the Fiction of Jessie Fauset, Zora Neale Hurston, and Dorothy West.* Westport, Conn.: Greenwood Press, 2002.

Miller, Nina. "Femininity, Publicity, and the Class Division of Cultural Labor: Jessie Redmon Fauset's *There Is Confusion.*" *African American Review* 2 (summer 1996): 205–220.

Sylvander, Cheryl. *Jessie Redmon Fauset, Black American Writer.* Troy, N.Y.: Whitson Pub. Co., 1981.

They That Sit in Darkness Mary Burrill (1919)

A compelling one-act drama by MARY BURRILL that considers the life-threatening nature of excessive work and unrelenting domestic labor. Set in the South, the drama focuses on the impoverished Jasper family. Malinda Jasper, the mother of seven children, has survived repeated pregnancies and the deaths of two infants. Despite her husband's toil and Malinda's tireless efforts to take in laundry, the couple are unable to gain any financial stability. The most recent pregnancy that Lindy, as Malinda is called, has endured has jeopardized her weak heart. The visiting nurse, a Massachusetts woman named Elizabeth Shaw, insists that Lindy rest in order to protect her health. Unfortunately, the advice is difficult to take, given the need to feed the six children at home. The nurse encourages Lindy to take control of her reproductive life, but restrictive state laws prevent her from elaborating on the birth control methods that would be effective. Nurse Shaw is able only to recommend that Lindy "be careful"; the besieged 38-year-old mother notes emphatically that "Dat's all you nu'ses say!" and challenges the health care provider when she insists that she "got'a be tellin' me sumpin' better'n dat, Mis' Liz'-beth!" Despite the desperate need for information, the nurse honors the nurse's oath and "the law [that] forbids [her] telling . . . what you have a right to know!" The play ends tragically as Malinda, exhausted by a rigorous day of laundry and incessant child care, dies.

Burrill's play appeared in *Birth Control Review*, the periodical that the intrepid birth control advocate Margaret Sanger established in 1917. *They That Sit in Darkness* was one of several works by African-American writers that appeared in the September 1919 issue, devoted to the works of African-American writers and a discussion of issues related to people of color. The play appeared alongside writings by ANGELINA WELD GRIMKÉ, GERTRUDE MCDOUGALD, AUGUSTUS GRANVILLE DILL, W. E. B. DUBOIS, and CHANDLER OWEN. The play is notable for its stark realism and its forthright critique of oppressive legal statutes that perpetuate poverty and domestic instability.

Bibliography

Perkins, Kathy A. *Black Female Playwrights: An Anthology of Plays before 1950.* Bloomington: Indiana University Press, 1989.

Thompson, Clara Ann (1869–1949)

An Ohio poet who fashioned a career for herself as a writer for the people in her communities. Born in Rossmoyne, Ohio, she was the daughter of John Henry and Carla Jane Gray Thompson. Her parents, both of whom were formerly enslaved Virginians, had five children, three of whom pursued their love of poetry and became writers. Her sister Priscilla lovingly dedicated *Gleanings of Quiet Hours,* a collection of poems "mostly of which are closely associated with a proscribed race" to "my sister and brothers." Clara Thompson, who never married, became a teacher in Ohio public schools.

Thompson published *Songs by the Wayside,* the first of four collections, in 1908. She dedicated the volume to her brother and sister, Garland and Priscilla. The Rossmoyne press of Aaron Thompson, her brother, produced the book. His press also supported the efforts of sibling Priscilla Jane Thompson, who published *Gleanings of Quiet Hours* in 1907, just one year before her sister Clara made her literary debut. In 1921 she collaborated with her brother's press again and produced *What Means This Bleating of the Sheep.* A second edition of this work appeared just two years later in 1923. That year, Thompson saw the publication of *There Came Wise Men* by the BOSTON-based Christopher Publishing House, the same press that had published works by MERCEDES GILBERT. In 1926, Thompson collaborated again with the Christopher Publishing House to produce *A GARLAND OF POEMS,* her most frequently cited collection. The volume included poems about an impressive range of topics. Thompson, who published frequently in local newspapers, addressed subjects such as World War I and the role of African-American soldiers, religious themes and celebrations, and history. That year, Thompson received special recognition for her work when HALLIE QUINN BROWN, author of *HOMESPUN HEROINES* (1926), included a moving excerpt from a Thompson poem in her dedication of the volume. Brown, who dedicated her substantial women's history to members of the American and Canadian branches of the NATIONAL ASSOCIATION OF COLORED WOMEN, included the following lines by Thompson: "Through all the blight of slavery / They kept their womanhood, / And now they march with heads erect, / To fight for all things good, / Nor care for scorn nor seek for praise, / Just so they please their God."

Thompson lived for many years with her two siblings, Priscilla, a poet, public reader, and elocutionist, and Garland. She was a member of the NA-TIONAL ASSOCIATION FOR THE ADVANCEMENT OF COLORED PEOPLE and an active participant in the YOUNG WOMEN'S CHRISTIAN ASSOCIATION.

Bibliography

Thompson, Clara Ann, J. Pauline Smith, and Mazie Earhart Clark. *Voices in the Poetic Tradition: Clara Ann Thompson, J. Pauline Smith, Mazie Earhart Clark.* With an introduction by Mary Anne Stewart Boelcskevy. New York: G. K. Hall, 1996.

Thompson, Eloise Alberta Veronica Bibb (1878–1928)

A writer and journalist who prided herself on crafting meaningful responses to vital and controversial issues of her day. Born in New Orleans, Louisiana, she was the daughter of Charles and Catherine Adele Bibb. Her father was a U.S. customs inspector. She was part of the upper-class circle that included ALICE DUNBAR-NELSON, one of her literary contemporaries and a close friend. She attended the Oberlin Academy school from 1899 through 1901. In 1903, after a short stint as a teacher, she traveled north to attend the Teachers' College at HOWARD UNIVERSITY. Following her graduation in 1908, Bibb began working in WASHINGTON, D.C., at the Colored Social Settlement, a university-run organization. She married journalist Noah Thompson, and the couple relocated to California. In Los Angeles, Eloise Thompson became a regular contributor to local newspapers such as the *Los Angeles Sunday Tribune.* An active member of the Catholic community, she also wrote frequently for religious periodicals.

Thompson made her literary debut in 1895, when she was 17 years old. *Poems,* published by the BOSTON-based Monthly Review Press, reflected her ties to the New Orleans community and honored her friendship with Alice Dunbar-Nelson. Indeed, the two talented, young writers shared their literary debut; Dunbar also published *Violets and Other Tales,* her first book, with the Monthly Review Press in the same year.

Thompson's debut as a playwright drew intense public scrutiny and prompted much debate. *A Reply to the Clansman* (1915) was a pointed response to the racist novel *The Clansman* by

Thomas Dixon that in 1915 became the film *Birth of A Nation,* produced by D. W. Griffith. Thompson's play was considered for theatrical and film production but ultimately was set aside because of its direct engagement and challenge to the white-authored texts by Dixon and Griffith. Subsequent plays included *A Friend of Democracy* (1920) CAUGHT (1920), *Africans* (1922), and COOPED UP (1924), and Thompson saw her works performed widely. COOPED UP earned an honorable mention from judges T. MONTGOMERY GREGORY, Edith Isaacs, Alexander Woolcott, and Robert Benchley in the 1924–25 OPPORTUNITY literary contest. The ETHIOPIAN ART PLAYERS later produced the work.

Thompson published two short stories in *Opportunity* during her literary career. "MADEMOISELLE 'TASIE" and "MASKS" appeared in September 1925 and October 1927, respectively.

There are few details about Thompson's last years and her death in 1928. *Opportunity* noted her passing in its February 1928 issue.

Bibliography

Beasley, Delilah L. *Negro Trailblazers of California.* 1919; reprint, New York: G. K. Hall, 1997.

Thompson, Louise (1901–1999)

The last surviving member of the Harlem Renaissance era, Thompson was an energetic participant in the literary, social, and political circles of the period.

Born in CHICAGO in September 1901, she was the daughter of William and Lula Brown Toles. She lived with her mother following her parents' separation in 1903. Lula Toles and her daughter relocated to Berkeley, California, and Lula's marriage to Hadwick Thompson soon followed. Louise attended Oakland High School and then went on to study economics at the University of California-Berkeley. When she graduated cum laude in 1923, she became one of the first African-American women to earn a degree from the institution. Widespread racism prompted her to pass in order to acquire employment. She adopted a Mexican persona and was able to gain work in San Francisco as a secretary. She and her mother returned to Chicago in 1925.

Thompson's connection to the Harlem Renaissance began in the mid-1920s, when, after relocating to Chicago, she came into contact with W. E. B. DuBois. She previously had met the eminent scholar and *CRISIS* editor at a lecture in Berkeley. After this second meeting, she benefited directly from his help. DuBois's assistance netted Thompson teaching positions at Southern College and at Hampton Institute. She and Susan Bailey, the future wife of educator Howard Thurman, left Hampton after chafing against the double standards of etiquette and the restrictive environment. Bailey and Thompson moved to NEW YORK CITY. Thompson, the recipient of a scholarship from the NATIONAL URBAN LEAGUE, began studies at the New School for Social Research.

In New York, Thompson pursued sociology studies and immersed herself in the vibrant world of Harlem. She became friends with LANGSTON HUGHES, AARON DOUGLAS, and WALLACE THURMAN. In August 1928 she married Thurman, an ingenious literary talent and writer. Although many of Thurman's acquaintances knew of his homosexual preferences, Thompson apparently did not. The marriage soon dissolved, but Louise Thurman's efforts to secure a divorce were frustrated by family illnesses and limited financial resources.

Six years after Thurman's tragic death in 1934, Thompson remarried. Her second husband, William Patterson, was a well-known political activist. Their daughter, Mary Louise, was born in 1943. The couple, who met at a meeting sponsored by the NATIONAL ASSOCIATION FOR THE ADVANCEMENT OF COLORED PEOPLE, became tireless proponents of civil rights and workers' rights. William defied Senator Joseph McCarthy and his efforts to suppress free speech and to target suspected Communist Party supporters. He also was instrumental in the SCOTTSBORO TRIAL, the legal fight to defend nine youths in Alabama falsely accused of rape.

Louise Thompson, like GEORGIA DOUGLAS JOHNSON, ETHEL RAY NANCE, and REGINA ANDREWS, used her home to foster connections among emerging writers and thinkers of the period. Intellectuals gathered often at her Convent Avenue apartment to participate in the Vanguard Salon, a gathering that reflected Thompson's leftist political views and interest in addressing issues re-

lating to African-American life. She also developed close friendships with several prominent Harlem Renaissance figures, including Langston Hughes and CHARLOTTE OSGOOD MASON. It was Mason who funded Thompson so that she could work as administrative and secretarial support for Hughes, and it was Thompson who typed the manuscript of his novel *GOD SENDS SUNDAY* (1931).

She also worked with Hughes when he collaborated with ZORA NEALE HURSTON on their ill-fated comedy *MULE BONE* (1930). Thompson had met Hurston and hosted her and Hughes many times at her New York City apartment. The duo employed her to type the *Mule Bone* manuscript. Eventually, however, Hurston was outraged when Hughes lobbied on Thompson's behalf and proposed that she receive one-third of the profits. The partnership between the two writers was unduly strained by events relating to *Mule Bone* and by what Hurston regarded as a full-fledged conspiracy between Thompson and Hughes. Hughes's efforts to reward Thompson for her work frustrated Hurston and contributed to the explosive demise of the project and the friendship between the two authors. Hughes later dedicated *Shakespeare in Harlem* (1942), a volume of poems, to Thompson. "Would you like to have a book of poems dedicated to you?" he asked her in a letter. "Such is *Shakespeare in Harlem*, the present collection I'm assembling for Knopf. Folk, blues, and lyric verse in the lighter manner—but not too light" (Berry, 299).

In the early 1930s, Thompson volunteered her time to the Co-Operating Committee on Production of a Soviet Film on Negro Life. Working alongside W. A. DOMINGO, she publicized *BLACK AND WHITE*, the film project that the MESCHRABPOM FILM CORPORATION was preparing to begin. She, Hughes, DOROTHY WEST, and TED POSTON were among the 22 writers, artists, and scholars who sailed for Russia. Challenged by conservative white American businessmen who were working in Russia, the film company was forced to halt the project. Thompson's early optimism about the project prompted some of her colleagues to nickname her "Madame Moscow."

Thompson's turn toward activism intensified during the 1930s and in the years following the

Harlem Renaissance. She joined the International Worker's Order, an organization dedicated to protecting workers' rights. In 1937, at Thompson's suggestion, Hughes established the HARLEM SUITCASE THEATRE in the New York City space that the IWO branch was leasing at the time.

Thompson was one of the signatories of the 1951 "We Charge Genocide" petition that challenged the United Nations to address American violence against African Americans. She also worked closely with PAUL ROBESON, who attended her wedding to Patterson, when he was targeted for his political views. She helped to organize Robeson's legendary Peekskill, New York, concerts and his appearances before African-American audiences during the years when he was blacklisted. In 1970 Thompson was again at the forefront of public agitation for civil rights and social justice. She was chair of the New York committee working to achieve the freedom of Angela Davis.

Thompson died in New York City on August 27, 1999 at the age of 97. Upon her death, Thompson was recognized as a champion of political, civil, and social rights. The *People's Weekly* reminded its readers that colleagues such as Frank Chapman of the National Alliance Against Racist and Political Repression had regarded her as one who had "seen the trials and tribulations of our century not as an observer but as a participant." *The New York Times* hailed her as "an advocate of civil rights and leftist causes, a participant in the Harlem Renaissance and a longtime associate of one of its leading figures, the poet Langston Hughes" (*NYT,* 2 September 1999).

Bibliography

"Louise Patterson Dies at 97." *People's Weekly World* (7 September 1999). Available online. URL: http://www.hartford-hwp.com/archives/45a/140.html. Accessed June 1, 2005.

Berry, Faith, ed. *Langston Hughes: Before and Beyond Harlem.* Westport, Conn.: Lawrence Hill & Company, 1983.

Boyd, Valerie. *Wrapped in Rainbows: The Life of Zora Neale Hurston.* New York: Scribner, 2003.

Boynton, Robert. "The Lives They Lived: Louise Patterson, b. 1901; The Red and the Black." *New York Times,* 2 January 2000, 22.

Goldstein, Richard. "Louise Patterson, 97, Is Dead; Figure in Harlem Renaissance." *New York Times,* 2 September 1999, C20.

Rampersad, Arnold. *The Life of Langston Hughes: I, Too, Sing America.* Vol. 1, *1902–1941.* New York: Oxford University Press, 1986.

———. *The Life of Langston Hughes: I Dream a World.* Vol. 2, *1941–1967.* New York: Oxford University Press, 1988.

Woo, Elaine. "Louise Patterson, Harlem Social Activist." *Chicago Sun-Times,* 20 September 1999, 54.

"Three Dogs and a Rabbit" Anita Scott Coleman (1926)

This short story by ANITA SCOTT COLEMAN placed third in the 1925 *CRISIS* literary contest. The narrative evolves as an absorbing story about true womanhood and empathy. The loquacious narrator, Timothy Phipps, is a self-conscious storyteller who recognizes characters, setting, and mood as the vital elements of any story. He "unreel[s] his yarn" during the course of a meal, his words satisfying himself and his audience almost as much as the "copious helping[s]" that he piles upon his own plate.

Phipps relates the story of the widow Ritton, a white woman whose "natural curliness" of hair suggests to the perceptive observer that she may in fact have African ancestry. The widow has been charged with harboring a fugitive. Three stout white gentlemen have brought the case against her. In her own defense, the widow takes the stand and begins to testify. She quickly notes that doing so will force her to reveal a lifelong secret. In the course of her narration, she reveals that she was an enslaved child who, when traveling with her master's family, was able to save a rabbit from three hunting dogs. Despite the family's desperate hunger, the young girl refused to hand over the rabbit that she had ensconced in her skirt pocket. She withstood the violent beating that she got from her master for not noting the rabbit's path and refused to surrender the defenseless animal. Her courage stirred up a newfound respect in Howard Ritton, the master's son, and he later freed and married the brave slave girl. Mrs. Ritton's testimony finishes as she justifies her decision to offer sanctuary to the man who entered her home, desperate to escape the three hunters on his trail. "The black man who was running so wildly was only a little terror-mad rabbit," she declares from the stand before noting that the "three stout gentlemen there . . . and the crowd which followed after . . . had the visage of my master." The story closes as the narrator Phipps reveals that it was he who was "the running black gentleman" of the widow's story.

Through Sepia Eyes Frank Marshall Davis (1938)

The third of six volumes of poetry that FRANK MARSHALL DAVIS published during his career. Davis enjoyed a productive literary period in the last decade of the Harlem Renaissance. His first volume, *BLACK MAN'S VERSE*, appeared in 1935, and the second, *I AM THE AMERICAN NEGRO*, was published in 1937. *Through Sepia Eyes* appeared just one year later. Davis wrote the volume during his tenure as executive editor for the Associated Negro Press.

Bibliography

Tidwell, John Edgar, ed. *Livin' The Blues: Memoirs of a Black Journalist and Poet—Frank Marshall Davis.* Madison: University of Wisconsin Press, 1992.

Thurman, Wallace Henry (1902–1934)

An enterprising, multitalented writer, editor, and playwright whose visionary projects repeatedly challenged the Harlem Renaissance community to determine its literary and political priorities, artistic goals, and racial agendas. Born in Salt Lake City, Utah, Wallace Henry Thurman was the son of Oscar and Beulah Thurman. His father moved to California when Wallace was a young boy, and the two were not particularly close. His mother remarried several times, and it may have been the series of domestic changes that encouraged the young boy to become especially close to his maternal grandmother, Emma Jackson.

Following his graduation from the public schools in Salt Lake City, Thurman enrolled at the University of Utah. Biographers differ in their accounts of Thurman's academic ventures. Some suggest that he completed the premedical program

at the University of Utah, excelled in chemistry and pharmacy, and completed the program in record time. Others suggest that he suffered a nervous breakdown, withdrew from the program abruptly, and later relocated to California to resume his medical studies. Thurman did relocate to Los Angeles in 1923, and it was in that year that he enrolled at the University of Southern California. After a year of postgraduate study, Thurman abandoned his preprofessional studies and decided to pursue a career in journalism. He also supported himself by taking a job in the Post Office. It was there that he met ARNA BONTEMPS, a fellow aspiring writer with whom he would one day live in NEW YORK CITY.

In August 1928 he married LOUISE THOMPSON, a graduate of the University of California at Berkeley, teacher, and political activist whom he had met in New York City. The marriage, which came as a surprise to many who knew of Thurman's homosexual interests, dissolved some six months later. Thompson, who had deep feelings for Thurman, was, "hurt and baffled" by the marriage's decline. As Arnold Rampersad notes, she disclosed later that she "*never* understood Wallace. He took nothing seriously. He laughed about everything. He would often threaten to commit suicide but you knew he would never try it. And he would never admit that he was a homosexual. *Never, never,* not to me at any rate" (Rampersad, 172). Thurman continued to deny that his homosexual interests, which on one occasion in the fall of 1925 had resulted in an embarrassing arrest, were responsible for the marriage's dissolution. He insisted instead that Thompson was to blame and that the sexual difficulties that they experienced were as a result of her inadequacies. The couple attempted to divorce, but heated negotiations about alimony, a family illness to which Thompson had to attend, and limited funds ultimately prevented Thompson from completing the legal proceedings. The couple separated, but the marriage did not officially end until Thurman's death in 1934. Thompson went on to marry William Patterson, a prominent attorney and activist.

Thurman's impressive career revolved around writing, a passion that he had nurtured since his childhood and that enabled him to finish his first novel when he was only 10 years old. His insatiable appetite for books also made him a formidable writer, and later in his life his friends marveled at the speed at which he read. In his autobiography entitled *THE BIG SEA*, LANGSTON HUGHES described Thurman as a voracious reader and "strangely brilliant black boy," one "who could read eleven lines at a time" and "who had read everything and whose critical mind could find something wrong with everything he read." Thurman produced an impressive amount of writing, including short fiction for periodicals such as *True Story* that he submitted under the pseudonyms of PATRICK CASEY and ETHEL BELLE MANDRAKE. He founded three literary journals, worked at several newspapers, published three novels, saw one of his several plays produced on BROADWAY, completed two screenplays, and published numerous other writings in contemporary periodicals and newspapers such as the *Los Angeles Sentinel*, *NEGRO WORLD*, *THE NEW REPUBLIC*, *THE NEW YORK TIMES*, and the *Independent*. His nonfiction writing often featured Harlem. Essays such as "Harlem: A Vivid Picture of the World's Greatest Negro City," which appeared in *THE ATLANTIC MONTHLY*, "Harlem Facets" in the *World Tomorrow*, and "Harlem's Place in the Sun" in *Dance Magazine* expanded the perspectives of American readers about the thriving place where Thurman had immersed himself.

Thurman began his journalism career at the *Los Angeles Sentinel*, an African-American newspaper, where he worked as a staff reporter and also produced a regular column entitled "Inklings." In 1924, inspired by the thriving Harlem Renaissance movement, Thurman attempted to launch a West Coast literary magazine. He hoped that the publication would mirror the artistic efforts of his contemporaries on the East Coast. His first journal, *OUTLET*, lasted only six months, but it illustrated Thurman's commitment to providing a forum for writers of color and to drawing attention to the rich tradition of African-American writing.

When he relocated to New York City in 1925, Thurman shared rooms with Arna Bontemps, his former Post Office colleague. Thurman found work soon after his arrival. He began working as an elevator operator and then made contact with THEOPHILUS LEWIS, publisher of *THE LOOKING GLASS*. Thurman then began work as a reporter and editor for the publication. As scholar Phyllis

Wallace Thurman *(Yale Collection of American Literature, Beinecke Rare Book and Manuscript Library)*

Klotman notes, Thurman, who received no pay but did get regular meals for his work, was an "everything man" at *The Looking Glass*, where he was an "editorial writer, reporter, assistant make-up man, and errand boy." In 1926, with the help of an enthusiastic recommendation from Lewis, Thurman joined the staff of *THE MESSENGER*, the journal that A. PHILIP RANDOLPH and CHANDLER OWEN established in 1917. Thurman was appointed managing editor of the journal and filled the post recently held by GEORGE SCHUYLER. Like JESSIE FAUSET at *THE CRISIS* and later DOROTHY WEST at *CHALLENGE*, Thurman used his contacts with writers to solicit manuscripts that would enrich the publication. It was he who published the first short stories by Langston Hughes, a friend whom he would later describe as "the most close-mouthed and cagey individual I had ever known when it came to personal matters" and one who "fended off every attempt to probe into his inner self and did this with such an unconscious and naive air" (Rampersad, 119). During the early 1930s his unfortunate involvement with the increasingly controversial work by ZORA NEALE HURSTON and LANGSTON HUGHES entitled MULE BONE led to a cooling in the friendship that he had with Hughes. Yet, Hughes rallied again to support Thurman's publication efforts. Thurman, who published a number of his own pieces in the monthly periodical, eventually left the position to become circulation manager at THE WORLD TOMORROW, another New York City newspaper. In 1929 Thurman became the first African-American editor to work at the MACAULAY PUBLISHING COMPANY.

Thurman published THE BLACKER THE BERRY, the first of his three novels, in 1929. He dedicated the work, which was well received by many of his peers and by reviewers, to his grandmother, Emma Jackson. That same year, he also explored his interest in drama. He completed HARLEM: A MELODRAMA OF NEGRO LIFE, his first play and a work coauthored with WILLIAM JOURDAN RAPP, a white journalist and the future editor of True Story, with whom he would have a lasting friendship. In the wake of a successful theater run and a national tour, Thurman anticipated a trilogy of plays that would be known as Color Parade. He proceeded to complete the next installment, JEREMIAH, THE MAGNIFICENT (1930), a work inspired by the political agenda and back-to-Africa movement spearheaded by MARCUS GARVEY. The third play, Harlem Cinderella, was never completed. Thurman wrote Savage Rhythm (1931) and Singing the Blues (1932), two additional plays. The works remained unpublished and were never produced, however. The year 1932 was especially productive for Thurman. In addition to completing Singing the Blues, he published two novels, INFANTS OF THE SPRING and THE INTERNE. The Interne, published by Macaulay, was a coauthored novel about the sobering aspects of New York City hospital life. Thurman collaborated with ABRAHAM FURMAN, legal counsel for and a relative of the Macaulay Publishing Company founders.

Thurman was one of the most energetic, optimistic, and unrelenting figures of the Harlem Renaissance period. He lived at the DARK TOWER, the legendary Harlem residence owned by A'LELIA WALKER. He was well known as the host of regular and lively parties, and he was part of the most dynamic circles of writers and intellectuals. His closest friends and colleagues included AARON DOUGLAS, Langston Hughes, Zora Neale Hurston, and RICHARD BRUCE NUGENT. With them, he decided to establish FIRE!!, an avant-garde literary publication that would reflect more accurately the unconventional and daring imagination of emerging African-American writers. Thurman, who was the editor and publisher, provided most of the $1,000 required to produce the magazine. Despite its high goals and the determination of its founders, Fire!! failed after only one issue. The toll of organizing the venture prompted Thurman to sacrifice regular meals, fall behind in his rent, and grow quite desperate for any means of sustaining the venture. He overcame the staggering odds and limitations brought on by inadequate funding, however. The memorable table of contents for the first and only issue included the first installment of a two-part story entitled SMOKE, LILLIES, AND JADE by Nugent, the first openly gay story of the period; striking images by Aaron Douglas, who also provided the cover art; Hurston's short story "Sweat"; and additional contributions by writers such as GWENDOLYN BENNETT, Arna Bontemps, HELENE JOHNSON, COUNTEE CULLEN, and EDWARD SILVERA. The deans of the movement, W. E. B. DuBois and others, were not impressed by what they regarded as reckless and salacious material that threatened to undermine African-American cultural and literary progress. In 1928 Thurman, who had spent the past four years covering the debts incurred by Fire!!, attempted to establish another literary magazine. HARLEM: A FORUM OF NEGRO LIFE appeared in 1928. Unfortunately, it lasted for only two issues. That year, Thurman joined McFadden Publications as a member of the editorial staff.

Thurman's last professional venture was into the world of film and screenwriting. He returned to the West Coast in 1934. That same year he signed a contract to write for Foy Productions and relocated to Hollywood to "be sold down the river," as he described it to Langston Hughes (van Notten, 297). Thurman, who was making about $1,000 a month, took advantage of his time in the lively West Coast world. He completed *Tomorrow's Children*, a provocative and controversial screenplay about poverty and enforced sterilization that actually included a scene of a vasectomy in progress. He also completed *High School Girl*, another work with intense sexual content that focused on pregnancy and abortion. Thurman left Hollywood and returned to New York in May 1934, his health failing.

Thurman defied the reality of his physical decline, insisting that he live life to the fullest for as long as possible. An alcoholic known for his preference for gin, Thurman eventually contracted tuberculosis. In July 1934 he collapsed at the party that he threw to celebrate his return to New York. He was admitted to City Hospital, the very institution that he had featured in *The Interne*. His estranged wife, Louise Thompson, cared for him despite the tension that marked their relationship, but scholars suggest that his former friends essentially abandoned Thurman. Although Thurman wrote to Hughes from his sickbed, Hughes did not reply with any regularity. After six months of hospitalization, Thurman succumbed to the disease. Funeral services were held in the St. James Presbyterian Church on Christmas Eve. The popular mystery writer and playwright Hughes Allison composed the eulogy. "There was one word," he recalled, "which Wallace Thurman used to describe a situation or a book or a play or a joke or anything which he thought superior and outstanding—'Priceless.'" Allison then insisted that Thurman's "life, his work, his success characterize that word—the word and his name are synonymous. Wallace Thurman was Priceless" (Klotman, 273). Thurman was laid to rest in Silver Mount Cemetery on Staten Island.

Bibliography

Fire!! 1926, reprint, Metuchen, N.J.: Fire!! Press, 1982.

Henderson, Mae. "Portrait of Wallace Thurman." In *The Harlem Renaissance Remembered*, edited by Arna Bontemps. New York: Dodd, Mead, 1972.

Klotman, Phyllis. "Wallace Thurman." In *Dictionary of Literary Biography*. Vol. 51: *Afro-American Writers from the Harlem Renaissance to 1940*, edited by Trudier Harris. Detroit: Gale Research Inc., 1987. 260–273.

Lewis, David Levering. *When Harlem Was in Vogue*. New York: Knopf, 1981.

McIver, Dorothy. *Stepchild in Harlem: The Literary Career of Wallace Thurman*. Ann Arbor, Mich.: University Microfilms International, 1985.

"Obituary: Wallace Thurman." *New York Times*, 23 December 1934, 17.

Rampersad, Arnold. *The Life of Langston Hughes: I, Too, Sing America*. Vol. 1, *1902–1941*. New York: Oxford University Press, 1986.

Singh, Amritjit, and Daniel Scott, eds. *The Collected Writings of Wallace Thurman: A Harlem Renaissance Reader*. New Brunswick, N.J.: Rutgers University Press, 2003.

Thurman, Wallace. *Infants of the Spring*. 1932, reprint, New York: Modern Library, 1999.

———. *The Blacker the Berry*. 1929, reprint, New York: Scribner Paperback Fiction, 1996.

van Notten, Eleonore. *Wallace Thurman's Harlem Renaissance*. Amsterdam: Rodopi, 1994.

Wallace Thurman Papers, Beinecke Library, Yale University; Moorland-Spingarn Research Center, Howard University; William Jourdan Rapp Collection, University of Oregon.

Wright, Shirley Haynes. *A Study of the Fiction of Wallace Thurman*. Ann Arbor, Mich.: University Microfilms International, 1985.

"Ticket Home" Octavia Wynbush (1939)

One of several short stories that OCTAVIA WYNBUSH published in THE CRISIS during the 1930s. "Ticket Home" explored the challenges of reclaiming a difficult past and reconnecting with family abandoned. The protagonist, Margaret, finally decides to return to her country home in order to face the daughter whom she left some 14 years earlier. In the course of her journey, she meets a young woman who is in fact her daughter. The girl has no idea that she is in the company of her mother. Margaret uses their time together to assure the girl of her mother's love, and the story ends without any revelation of Margaret's true identity.

The escapism that is implicit in "Ticket Home" is moderated somewhat by Wynbush's exploration of the great psychic and emotional pain of her selfish and desperate protagonists.

"Tin Can" Marita Bonner (1934)

A bleak short story about delinquency and the limits of salvation by MARITA BONNER. Published in the July and August 1934 issues of OPPORTUNITY, the story focused on the impoverished CHICAGO community that Bonner invented and used in most of her fiction. The protagonist, an energetic but scheming young adolescent named Jimmie Joe, does all that he can to impress his gang and the schoolgirl he likes. Idolized by his younger brother, Jimmie Joe stops at nothing, including stealing from his mother, in order to indulge his desires and macho adventures. His mother, an earnest and hardworking domestic, attempts to correct her son's behavior by taking him to church. The sermon on the pitfalls of thievery fails to change her son, however. Ultimately, he is involved in a fight and framed by members of an opposing gang. He is sentenced to death and electrocuted. One day, overwhelmed by her grief, his mother collapses in the street. In an especially heartless closing scene, policemen who see her prone on the sidewalk assume that she is drunk, put her into the paddy wagon, and transport her to jail.

Like much of her published short fiction, "Tin Can" reveals the sincere efforts that families of color make to save their children. Bonner offers a pointed commentary on the high, even life-threatening, cost of domestic labor for others and the suffering perpetuated by unrelenting racism.

Bibliography

Flynn, Joyce, and Joyce Occomy Striklin. *Frye Street & Environs: The Collected Works of Marita Bonner.* Boston: Beacon Press, 1987.

Ti Yette John Matheus (1929)

A one-act play by the popular writer JOHN MATHEUS. Set in New Orleans, Louisiana, during the spring of 1855, the play opens as Ti Yette, a light-skinned Creole woman, and Racine, her dark-skinned brother, debate about their plight as people of African descent. Racine is obsessed with HAITI and the island's powerful history. He is determined to abandon the restrictive and demoralizing American society and to establish himself and his sister in this empowering, albeit idealized, Caribbean nation. Ti Yette, who increasingly prefers her given name Henriette, is in love with Joseph Rhubotham, a scheming white man who is determined to forge documents that will allow him to marry Ti Yette and claim her extensive property holdings that she has inherited from her white father. The plans of both men ultimately converge as Mardi Gras celebrations reach their highest peak. A heated argument ensues between the men, and Racine, blinded by his sister's seeming betrayal, stabs her to death. Rhubotham abandons his sweetheart once the police draw near; Racine, devastated by his actions and the awful end to his dream, holds his sister in his arms and sobs.

Ti Yette appeared in the 1930 anthology PLAYS AND PAGEANTS FROM THE LIFE OF THE NEGRO, the pioneering anthology edited by WILLIS RICHARDSON and published by the Associated Publishers, Inc., the WASHINGTON, D.C., press with which CARTER G. WOODSON and ALAIN LOCKE were associated. Matheus and the other playwrights featured in the collection modified their contributions so that they were suitable for school-age children and youths to perform.

"To a Wild Rose" Ottie Beatrice Graham (1923)

A short story by OTTIE BEATRICE GRAHAM that focuses on the legacy of slavery and the efforts to preserve an ennobling Afrocentric identity. Published in the June 1923 issue of THE CRISIS, the story is inspired by the 18th-century Aphra Behn tale entitled *Oroonoko*. The narrator is a spunky, formerly enslaved man who shares his insightful observations about antebellum life and intraracial prejudice. The female protagonist in "To a Wild Rose" is Flo, a slave girl who believes herself to be a direct descendant of Oroonoko, the enslaved African prince who strove to protect Imoinda, his true love, who was abducted and forced to endure life in a harem. Flo chooses to escape north to freedom with the narrator, a fellow slave whom she names "Red Boy" in light of his skin color. The two settle in different places, but Red Boy maintains his ties to Flo. Eventually, he reveals his feelings for her and proposes marriage. In response, Flo "threw back her curly head, but she didn't smile her bright smile. She closed her black eyes lak as though she was in pain, an' lak as though the pain come from pity." Dejected by Flo's refusal, Red Boy leaves for some two years.

When Red Boy eventually returns to the North, he finds Flo to be a changed woman. No longer the "Wild Blood" and outspoken person that he knew, she instead seems like a "wild, helpless thing like a thistle blowed to pieces—a wild, helpless thing lak a spirit chained to earth." She is devastated by the tattered, but nevertheless illuminating, scrap of paper on which her mother has recorded the circumstances of her child's birth. The now-pregnant Flo, who has married a Moroccan in an effort to preserve her supposedly unbroken link to Africa, is devastated to learn that she is the product of a rape that occurred when her enslaved mother was attacked by her owner. Flo stays on with Red Boy until the birth of her child. Before she dies, Flo instructs her lifelong friend to tell her daughter that she has royal blood. He resists at first, and when, 20 years later, he finds Flo's child, it is clear that she is proud of her identity and not at all in need of a vexed and elusive African genealogy.

To Make a Poet Black   J. Saunders Redding (1939)

Published by poet, teacher, and writer J. SAUNDERS REDDING, *To Make a Poet Black* is a significant contribution to American literary history. Redding proposed that his book was a "study of the literature of . . . dark Americans" and that such a critical enterprise was "a practical, as opposed to a purely speculative exercise." He asserted the impressive link between race and literature, noting that "no one who studies even superficially the history of the Negro in America can fail to see the uncommon relationship of his letters to that history" and that "from the very beginning the literature of the Negro has been literature either of purpose or necessity." Redding examined the works of writers such as Jupiter Hammon, Phillis Wheatley, Charles Remond, Frances Harper, Paul Laurence Dunbar, and W. E. B. DuBois. In his final chapter, entitled "Emergence of the New Negro," Redding examined the works of Harlem Renaissance era writers such as JESSIE FAUSET, RUDOLPH FISHER, JAMES WELDON JOHNSON, and others.

Redding's volume is invaluable for its steady and insightful appraisal of African-American literature and its efforts to advance the formal African-American tradition of literary criticism.

Bibliography

Redding, J. Saunders. *To Make a Poet Black.* 1939; reprint, Ithaca, N.Y.: Cornell University Press, 1988.

Berry, Faith, ed. *A Scholar's Conscience: Selected Writings of K. Saunders Redding, 1942–1977.* Lexington: University Press of Kentucky, 1992.

Tom-Tom   Shirley Graham DuBois (1929)

A music-drama by SHIRLEY GRAHAM DuBOIS, considered by many scholars to be the first opera written by an African-American woman. Graham completed the work while she was a sophomore at Oberlin College. In 1932, three years after its first production, the work was debuted in Cleveland, Ohio. Organized by the Cleveland Opera Company and staged at the Cleveland Stadium in Ohio, it starred Jules Bledsoe in the title role.

Bibliography

Horne, Gerald. *The Lives of Shirley Graham DuBois.* New York: New York University Press, 2000.

Toomer, Nathan Eugene (Jean) (1894–1967)

One of the most enigmatic writers of the Harlem Renaissance, Toomer produced lyrical documentary fiction, plays, and poetry and was known for his philosophical considerations, spiritual pursuits, and complicated perspectives on race and its impact on the Harlem Renaissance.

Born in WASHINGTON, D.C., he was the son of Nathan and Nina Pinchback Toomer. Toomer's immediate and extended family were of mixed race, and this ancestry impacted his own self-definition and politics. Nathan Toomer, who may have been born free, was the child of a mixed race woman and a white Georgia planter. Jean Toomer's maternal grandfather, Pinckney Benton Stewart Pinchback, was of mixed-race ancestry, too, the son of Eliza Stewart, an enslaved mulatto woman, and her white master. Pinchback became a member of the

Corps d'Afrique (a legendary Civil War regiment from Louisiana) and a popular elected official whose posts included the lieutenant governorship of Louisiana and culminated in his election to the U.S. Senate. Jean Toomer's early life was complicated by his father's desertion in 1895, less than one year after Jean was born. Toomer, who lived with his mother and her parents for several years, was not free to discuss his father and was encouraged to identify himself as a Pinchback. It was not until he began writing seriously that Toomer reclaimed his father's surname. Toomer and his mother moved to New Rochelle, New York, in 1906. Three years later, in 1909, Nina Pinchback Toomer passed away unexpectedly due to complications from appendicitis and surgery. Toomer, now effectively orphaned, returned to live with his maternal grandparents until his graduation from high school.

After graduating from the acclaimed DUNBAR HIGH SCHOOL in 1914, Toomer gained entry to the University of Wisconsin at Madison. Biogra-

phers note that his college applications signal Toomer's efforts to protect and to advance himself. In response to college forms that requested racial information, Toomer, a light-skinned man, identified himself as white or provided no information at all. He was motivated to do this in part because of his genealogy that he believed included several ethnicities, including Scotch, Welsh, German, Dutch, and Spanish. He also refrained from self-identifying as an African-American man in order to ward off racial discrimination, isolation, or harassment. Toomer left Wisconsin after only one semester and began a fretful period as an itinerant student. During the next few years, he attended and withdrew from several universities. These included the UNIVERSITY OF CHICAGO, the College of Physical Training in Chicago; the Massachusetts College of Agriculture in Amherst, Massachusetts; NEW YORK UNIVERSITY; and the City College of New York.

Toomer had a series of intense love relationships during his life that included tragic and steadying marriages as well as soulful affairs with close friends and well-known artists. One of Toomer's most memorable alliances involved MARGARET NAUMBERG, the wife of his close friend and fellow writer WALDO FRANK. The couple met in 1923 when the Franks' marriage was deteriorating. Naumberg was an enthusiastic believer in the philosophies of the Russian mystic GEORGES GURDJIEFF and shared a spiritual compatibility with Toomer that fueled their affair.

Margery Latimer, a wealthy white writer whom Toomer met in Wisconsin, became his first wife in 1931. The couple had one child, named Margery after her mother. Tragically, however, Margery Latimer Toomer died shortly after the birth of their daughter. A few years later, Toomer began one of his most intense and legendary relationships when he became involved with the gifted painter GEORGIA O'KEEFFE. The two met in NEW YORK CITY, where they both were part of the same vibrant intellectual circle that included Waldo Frank, SHERWOOD ANDERSON, LEWIS MUMFORD, and HART CRANE. Toomer and O'Keeffe shared deep spiritual interests and became lovers in late 1933, following the death of Toomer's first wife. Toomer married Marjorie Content, one of O'Keeffe's close friends, in the fall of 1934. O'Keeffe weathered the loss of

Jean Toomer, author. White Studio, New York *(Yale Collection of American Literature, Beinecke Rare Book and Manuscript Library)*

her relationship with Toomer and maintained contact with Toomer and Content once they were married.

Toomer and Content settled in Doylestown, Pennsylvania, with Toomer's daughter, Margery. The couple, who named their rural farm home Mill House, lived there together until Toomer's death in 1967. Mill House, while a respite from the world, also was the site of a small, private press that produced Toomer's later publication efforts.

Toomer's introduction to the Harlem Renaissance and his subsequent immersion in the literary life began when he moved to New York City in 1919. It was there that he became part of an avant-garde literary and arts circle that included VAN WYCK BROOKS, WITTER BYNNER, Georgia O'Keeffe, and Waldo Frank. Toomer's major literary accomplishments, however, did not come easily. In 1921 he began a formative journey through the South that ultimately involved a short-term position as head teacher in a small Sparta, Georgia, school. Within months of returning to New York, Toomer began writing CANE (1923), the volume that would catapult him into the literary limelight.

Toomer's first significant publication appeared in the spring of 1922, when "Song of the Son," a piece that he would include in Cane, appeared in THE CRISIS. Subsequently, excerpts from the collection appeared in the LIBERATOR. Additional works included two plays. The first, BALO, was a one-act folk play that was later staged by the impressive college drama troupe the Howard University Players. Balo also was included in the valuable anthology PLAYS OF NEGRO LIFE edited by ALAIN LOCKE and MONTGOMERY GREGORY. Toomer's second play, the unpublished Natalie Mann, focused on African-American life in Washington, D.C. The play, which was not staged during Toomer's lifetime, was published for the first time in 1980. During the mid-1920s, Toomer also published several short stories in a variety of venues including The Dial and anthologies such as The New American Caravan, edited by Alfred Kreymborg. Toomer's few published poems appeared in The Crisis in 1922 and 1932, in Pagany, and again in the New American Caravan anthology. Toomer also produced several unpublished manuscripts during his career. These include the novels The

Gallonwerps, written in 1927; Transatlantic, completed in 1929; and Caromb, written in 1932.

Toomer eventually withdrew from the New York literary world in which he enjoyed critical acclaim and prestige. Enamored by the teachings of Gurdjieff, he became a committed disciple and leader in the spiritualist movement. For some 10 years, he traveled extensively, advocating Gurdjieff's principles and teachings. In 1934, however, troubled by problematic financial arrangements within the movement, he withdrew.

Toomer, who suffered from several ailments, including arthritis and arteriosclerosis, died in March 1967.

Bibliography

Byrd, Rudolph P. Jean Toomer's Years with Gurdjieff: Portrait of an Artist, 1923–1936. Athens: University of Georgia Press, 1990.

Jones, Robert B., and Margery Toomer Latimer, eds. The Collected Poems of Jean Toomer. Chapel Hill: University of North Carolina Press, 1988.

Kerman, Cynthia Earl, and Richard Eldridge. The Lives of Jean Toomer: A Hunger for Wholeness. Baton Rouge: Louisiana State University Press, 1987.

McKay, Nellie Y. Jean Toomer, Artist: A Study of His Literary Life and Work, 1894-1936. Chapel Hill: University of North Carolina Press, 1984.

O'Daniel, Therman B., ed. Jean Toomer: A Critical Evaluation. Washington, D.C.: Howard University Press, 1988.

Turner, Darwin T., ed. The Wayward and the Seeking: A Collection of Writings by Jean Toomer. Washington, D.C.: Howard University Press, 1982.

Torrence, Ridgely (1874–1950)

A white American playwright who invigorated the nation's dramatic tradition during the early years of the Harlem Renaissance and is credited with developing the earliest BROADWAY plays by a white American writer to feature African-American characters in absorbing, non-stereotypical roles. Torrence was active in publishing and literary circles, worked as an editor at several well-known periodicals, and produced a variety of literary works ranging from poems to plays during his lengthy career.

Born in Xenia, Ohio, he was the oldest child of Findley David Torrence, a former Civil War officer and a lumber merchant, and his wife, Mary Ridgeley, a descent of the fifth president of the College of New Jersey, the school that later became PRINCETON UNIVERSITY. Torrence entered Miami College of Ohio in 1893. Two years later, he enrolled at Princeton University but withdrew due to medical issues. He relocated to NEW YORK CITY and began his work in publishing. Torrence eventually returned to academia in his later years. He became a visiting professor at Miami University in 1920 and again in 1942. In 1938 he joined the faculty at Antioch College as a visiting professor. In 1936 he was considered seriously for the high honor of Ohio Poet Laureate but was not selected. Torrence, suffering from lung cancer, passed away on Christmas Day, 1950.

In the years before the Harlem Renaissance, Torrence held editorial posts at such well-known periodicals as *The Critic, Cosmopolitan,* and *THE NEW REPUBLIC,* where he served as poetry editor for more than a decade. His work appeared in respected journals such as CENTURY MAGAZINE and in THE ATLANTIC MONTHLY. In 1934 he became a cofounder of the Academy of American Poets, the organization of which he became chairman in 1937.

On April 5, 1917, Torrence gained critical attention as a playwright when *Plays for a Negro Theatre,* a collection of three works, THE RIDER OF DREAMS, GRANNY MAUMEE, and SIMON THE CYRENIAN, opened at the Garden Theatre. The plays then moved to the Garrick Theatre for an additional week of performances. Torrence's producer was Mrs. EMILIE BIGELOW HAPGOOD, a wealthy philanthropist, dedicated theater patron, and respected stage designer. Hapgood's financial and intellectual support of the Torrence plays ultimately transformed the casts of the plays into the EMILIE HAPGOOD PLAYERS.

Torrence maintained his interest in African-American theater and subjects following his documented success with the Negro plays. Biographer John Clum notes the ways in which Torrence's interest in African-American material was influenced by his limited childhood interactions with African Americans in Xenia, Ohio, and by his later interests in Irish history and literature. In a 1917 CRISIS article entitled "The New Negro Theatre," Torrence asserted plainly that he had "sometimes imagined that the Negro, all other things being equal, might produce the greatest, most direct, the most powerful drama in the world." In 1939 he used a Rockefeller Foundation grant to generate a study of African-American theater. Torrence affiliated himself with a major Ohio and African-American dramatic center, the Karamu Theatre in Cleveland, which was established by ROWENA JELLIFFE and her husband, RUSSELL JELLIFFE, during his fellowship period. He produced an invaluable bibliography of plays written by African-American playwrights and explored the kinds of initiatives that dramatists and companies might consider employing to increase their audiences and to generate additional attention to their dramatic ventures.

Bibliography

"The New Negro Theatre," *Crisis* (June 1917).

Clum, John. *Ridgeley Torrence.* New York: Twayne Publishers, 1972.

Torrence, Ridgeley. *Granny Maumee, The Rider of Dreams, Simon the Cyrenian: Plays for a Negro Theater.* New York: The Macmillan Company, 1917.

Toussaint L'Ouverture   Leslie Pinckney Hill (1928)

A play by playwright and poet LESLIE PINCKNEY HILL that was included in the 1928 collection entitled *Toussaint L'Ouverture: A Dramatic History.* In his prefatory remarks, Hill noted that his study of Toussaint Louverture was reflected in his own efforts to contribute to the necessary and growing tradition of African-American perspectives on history. "The Negro youth of the world has been taught that the black race has no great traditions, no characters of World importance, no record of substantial contributions to civilization," asserted Hill. His play was an intervention in the pernicious miseducation of African-American children and of Americans in general.

According to Edward Ako, Hill's play reflects a desire to adhere closely to the known historical facts about Louverture, the enslaved man known as the "Black Napoleon," who led the successful and bloody fight in HAITI for the nation's independence. According to Ako, Hill's Haitian hero is "an individual who hardly breaks his word . . . someone who knows how to repay past acts of kindness" (Ako, 194). Hill humanizes and deifies his defiant general. He presents him as a man anointed by God to emancipate his people. Hill underscores Louverture's democratic principles as a warrior. In an early scene, Louverture asserts the true motivation for his battle against the French. He declares that "It is not, then, to make one race supreme / that we must fight, but to make all men free." Hill's protagonist is a powerful humanist, one whose war on French colonizers is in fact a metaphor for his fight to achieve universal, rather than local, West Indian, freedom.

Bibliography

Ako, Edward O. "Leslie Pinckney Hill's *Toussaint Louverture*." *Phylon* 48, no. 3 (1987): 190–195.

James, C. L. R. *The Black Jacobins: Toussaint Louverture and the San Domingo Revolution.* New York: Vintage Books, 1963.

Ros, Martin. *Night of Fire: The Black Napoleon and the Battle for Haiti.* New York: Sarpedon, 1994.

Trelling, Ursula (Ursala Trelling)

The pseudonym that REGINA ANDREWS, playwright, COLUMBIA UNIVERSITY graduate, and NEW YORK PUBLIC LIBRARY librarian, used during the Harlem Renaissance. Andrews's plays, such as CLIMBING JACOB'S LADDER (1931) and *Underground* (1932), appeared under the pseudonym.

Tremaine, Paul

The pseudonym that poet and playwright GEORGIA DOUGLAS JOHNSON used on occasion. Much of the work that she attributed to Paul Tremaine was and remains unpublished.

Tri-Arts Club

Based at the Harlem branch of the YOUNG WOMEN'S CHRISTIAN ASSOCIATION, the Tri-Arts Club was one of several small drama troupes established during the Harlem Renaissance era. According to historian Bruce Kellner, members included John Wilson, Lillian Mattison, Marie Santos, and Ruppert Marks. The Tri-Arts Club was established in 1923 and seems to have disbanded within a year.

The club received critical attention when THEOPHILUS LEWIS, drama critic for THE MESSENGER, evaluated its efforts. The group, which was short-lived, appears to have produced only three plays. None of the works was devoted to African-American issues. Each catered instead to generic popular themes of the day.

Tropic Death Eric Walrond (1926)

A riveting collection of short stories by ERIC WALROND. Published in 1926, the volume is regarded as Walrond's most significant and influential work. The volume, published by BONI & LIVERIGHT, includes 10 works that grapple with issues specific to the West Indies and Caribbean. As scholar Louis Parascandola suggests, however, Walrond's title raises the specter of deadly forces at work in the paradise that the writer explores.

The collection begins with "Drought," a gritty story about an impoverished Barbadian family, previously published in the NEW YORK AGE. The protagonist, Coggins Rum, is fighting to preserve himself, a battle underscored by the narrator's description of him as a "black, animate dot" upon the "broad road" that leads to work. Coggins has an exacting life as a laborer, one that constantly threatens to reduce him to nothingness. The story begins with a series of disembodied references about the men as they pause for an 11 o'clock break: "Throats parched, grim, sun-crazed blacks cutting stone on the white burning hillside . . . Hunger—pricks at stomachs inured to brackish coffee and cassava pone . . . Helter-skelter dark, brilliant black faces of West Indian peasants moved along, in pain . . . dissipating into the sun-stuffed void the radiant forces of the incline" (19). These stark images reveal the overwhelming nature of the work and also dispel immediately any illusion that the islands are idyllic places. Walrond uses this story to begin his forceful treatise on the nature of death in the tropics.

"The Palm Porch" is a multifaceted meditation on the invasive effects of the Panama Canal construction, sexuality and controversial morality, and the degree to which family life can be corrupted in the modern day. Like "Drought," it, too, focuses on the stonecutting industry and opens with gripping scenes of overworked laborers. "Black men behind wheelbarrows slowly ascended a rising made of spliced boards and emptied the sand rock into the maw of a mixing machine," observes the narrator. "More black men," he notes, "a peg down, behind wheelbarrows, formed a line which caught the mortar pouring into the rear organ of the omnivorous monster" (85). The protagonist of the story is Miss Buckner, a mysterious mulatto woman who presides, with her five daughters, over a salon that hosts men. There is intense curiosity about the madam who prevails over the Palm Porch: "[W]hether she was the result of a union of white and black, French and Spanish, English and Maroon—no one knew. Of an equally mystical heritage were her daughters, creatures of a rich and shining beauty. Of their father the less said the better" (91). The pathos of this story emerges through Miss Buckner's impressive ability to prevail even as her "home" is overtaken by drunken sailors and their captains. It is clear that she has not got complete control over her daughters; some of them embark on relationships of which she does approve, while others have children out of wedlock. Yet, in the chaos of the overwhelmingly male environment in which she lives and plies her trade, Miss Buckner seems to be untouched.

The title story, and the last in the collection, "Tropic Death" is a moving account of life that draws heavily from Walrond's own experiences. The semiautobiographical tale chronicles the migrations of Gerald Bright, whose sea voyage to Panama constitutes an awful, contemporary version of the Middle Passage. The opening scene of the story focuses on a "dainty little boy, about eight years of age" who wears "a white stiff jumper jacket, the starch on it so hard and shiny it was ready to squeak; shiny blue-velvet pants, very tight and very short—a little above his carefully oiled knees, a brownish green bow tie, bright as a cluster of dewy crotons; an Eton collar, an English sailor hat, with an elastic band so tight it threatened to dig a gutter in the lad's bright brown cheeks." The child is "overwhelmed" by the "fluid activity" that is underway as he watches "a police launch carry a load of Negro country folk out to a British packet smoking

blackly in the bay." The narrator is deliberately opaque about the circumstances involved here, and it is unclear whether the transport is for legal reasons. Eventually it is revealed that the young boy Gerald and his mother are part of the exodus, and that they, too, must take the police launch in order to begin their journey to Panama and a reunion with Gerald's father. In Panama, Bright is reunited with his unsavory father, a man whom he struggles to love in the face of degradation and sickness. The collection ends with this alienating scene of domesticity denied and yet another example of the relentless type of social death that can and does occur in the tropics.

Additional stories such as "The Wharf Rats," "Panama Gold," "Subjection," and "The Yellow One" explore the chaos and unpredictability of islanders striving to preserve themselves and to prevail against challenges of poverty, migration, and taxing environmental realities. Written during Walrond's tenure at OPPORTUNITY, the volume received critical acclaim. W. E. B. DuBois praised it as a "human document of deep significance," and the noted critic Benjamin Brawley mused that the book was "the most important contribution made by a Negro to American letters since the appearance of Dunbar's *Lyrics of Lowly Life.*"

Bibliography

Parascandola, Louis, ed. *Winds Can Wake Up the Dead: An Eric Walrond Reader.* Detroit: Wayne State University Press, 1998.

Walrond, Eric. *Tropic Death.* New York: Boni & Liveright, 1926; reprint, New York: Collier Books, 1972.

Trotter, William Monroe (1872–1934)

The first African-American student to be elected to PHI BETA KAPPA at HARVARD UNIVERSITY, Trotter was a purposeful social critic, an intrepid race activist, and the visionary editor of *The Guardian,* one of BOSTON's most outspoken newspapers.

Born in Chillicothe, Ohio, Trotter was the son of James and Virginia Isaacs Trotter. His father, who became the recorder of deeds in WASHINGTON, D.C., a post formerly held by Frederick Douglass, was a well-known advocate of African-American Civil War soldiers. He lobbied successfully for equal pay for and fair treatment of black veterans.

Following his graduation from the Hyde Park High School, where he was elected senior class president, Trotter enrolled at Harvard College in 1891. He graduated magna cum laude and Phi Beta Kappa in 1895. He married Geraldine Pindell, a member of a prominent and politically active Boston family, in 1899.

In 1901, Trotter established *The Guardian*, a weekly newspaper dedicated to anti-accommodationism and the political philosophies and strategies advanced by BOOKER T. WASHINGTON and his supporters. In 1905 Trotter collaborated with W. E. B. DuBois, a fellow Harvard University graduate, on the movement that ultimately led to the formation of the NATIONAL ASSOCIATION FOR THE ADVANCEMENT OF COLORED PEOPLE. Trotter's daring, coupled with his piercing intellectual powers, made him a formidable social critic. In 1914 he made front-page news when he challenged President Woodrow Wilson to address racial segregation in federal agencies. Trotter, representing the National Independence Equal Rights League, traveled to Washington to meet with Wilson. THE NEW YORK TIMES reported Trotter's scathing evaluation of Wilson's tolerance of segregation, including his memorable reminder to Wilson that "Two years ago you were thought to be a second Lincoln" (*NYT*, 13 November 1914, 1). Trotter was instrumental in the 1915 Boston protest of BIRTH OF A NATION, the racist film that promoted the KU KLUX KLAN and pernicious racial stereotypes. In 1919 Trotter advocated in France for the Versailles Treaty to address issues of racial equality.

Trotter, one of the most forceful and dynamic leaders of the early 20th century, passed away in Boston in 1934.

Bibliography

Fox, Stephen. *The Guardian of Boston: William Monroe Trotter.* New York: Athenaeum, 1970.

Johnson, Abby Arthur, and Ronald Maberry Johnson. *Propaganda & Aesthetics: The Literary Politics of African American Magazines in the Twentieth Century.* Amherst: University of Massachusetts, 1979.

Puttkammer, Charles W., and William Worthy. "William Monroe Trotter." *Journal of Negro History* 43 (October 1958): 298–316.

Tucker, Louella (unknown)

The apartment mate of ETHEL RAY NANCE, the secretary to OPPORTUNITY editor and NATIONAL URBAN LEAGUE officer CHARLES S. JOHNSON, and REGINA ANDREWS, a NEW YORK PUBLIC LIBRARY branch librarian and playwright. The three women shared a residence in the SUGAR HILL district of HARLEM.

One of the most famous photographs of Harlem Renaissance writers was taken during a celebration hosted by these celebrated hostesses and ardent supporters of the Harlem Renaissance. The photo, taken on the roof of the apartment building, features LANGSTON HUGHES, Charles Johnson, E. FRANKLIN FRAZIER, RUDOLPH FISHER, and Hubert Delaney.

Tuneful Tales Bernice Love Wiggins (1925)

The only volume that the prolific Texas poet BERNICE LOVE WIGGINS published during her career. Wiggins's work appeared in diverse newspapers such as the *El Paso Herald* and the CHICAGO DEFENDER. In 1925 she self-published *Tuneful Tales*, an impressive collection of some 100 poems.

The volume included vivid race poems that conveyed the horrors of LYNCHING and poems that addressed contemporary issues such as women's work, religious life, and poverty. The poems reflect Wiggins's versatility and social awareness. Sobering works such as "Ethiopia Speaks" complement the fierce call for racial solidarity and race protest articulated by COUNTEE CULLEN, LANGSTON HUGHES, and others. Wiggins links her comment on lynching and the loss of a son "Somewhere in the South, the 'Land of the Free'" to the historic sacrifice that African-American families have already made. "When the flag was in danger they answered the call / I gave them black sons, ah! yes, gave them all" exclaims the speaker. Wiggins's deft intervention here suggests that lynching not only savages the African-American family but also dishonors the significant and willing sacrifice that many made to acquire freedom and justice in America.

In the poem "And Now Goodnight," Wiggins's speaker makes a direct address to readers. "I have told you tuneful tales / Gathered from the hills and dales / Wheresoever mine own people chanced to dwell," notes the speaker. The following lines suggest the poet's own hopes for the volume: "If the tales have brought you mirth, / Brought more laughter to the earth, / It is well." *Tuneful Tales* is a polished collection that represents the wide variety of contributions and African-American literary communities of the Harlem Renaissance era.

Bibliography

Dailey, Maceo, Jr., and Ruthe Winegarten. *Tuneful Tales by Bernice Love Wiggins.* Lubbock: Texas Tech University Press, 2002.

Turner, Lucy Mae (1884–unknown)

A published poet, educator, and granddaughter of Nat Turner, the leader of the nation's most effective and bloody slave revolt. Born in Zanesville, Ohio, she was the daughter of a formerly enslaved man named Gilbert Turner who survived the traumatic and enforced separation from his family during a sale of slaves. Once Gilbert Turner achieved his freedom and then purchased his wife and children, the family settled in Zanesville. Lucy Mae, a gifted student, earned a scholarship to Ohio State University. Unfortunately, she was unable to attend because the family could not afford the room-and-board costs. Turner enrolled instead at WILBERFORCE UNIVERSITY and graduated in 1908. In 1934, having begun a career in teaching, Turner resumed her studies. She returned to Ohio State and in 1934 earned her B.S. In 1942 she completed graduate studies at the University of Illinois and earned a master's degree. Turner's passion for learning prompted her to enroll at the St. Louis University Law School when it finally decided to accept African-American students. She was awarded an LL.B. in 1950. Despite her record of achievement and demonstrated commitment to professional advancement, Turner was denied admission to the Ohio bar.

Four years after she graduated from Ohio State, Turner published her only volume of poems. *'BOUT CULLED FOLKSES* (1938) included 38 poems that addressed contemporary life, survival strategies in a world hostile to African Americans, and the power of women.

Bibliography

Turner, Lucy Mae. "The Family of Nat Turner, 1831–1854." *Negro History Bulletin* (March 1955): 127–132, 145; (April 1955): 155–158.

Tuskegee Institute

Located in Tuskegee, Alabama, the school opened on July 4, 1881. BOOKER T. WASHINGTON, a former slave, was appointed president of the Tuskegee Normal School for Colored Teachers that came to be called Tuskegee Institute.

Washington served as president from 1881 until his death in 1915. During his tenure, the school became synonymous with industrial education. Robert Russa Moton succeeded Washington as president of the institution. Moton's legacy included the establishment of the Tuskegee Veteran's Administration Hospital. The facility, which opened its doors in 1923, was the first and only American hospital with an entirely African-American staff. When Frederick Patterson became president in 1935, he extended the school's professional mission to include the School of Veterinary Medicine. It was Patterson who oversaw the programs that trained the legendary Tuskegee Airmen, the squadrons of African-American pilots whose excellence, stunning record, and professionalism defied the racism that continued to rationalize segregation in the armed forces.

Tuskegee Institute's faculty included George Washington Carver, E. FRANKLIN FRAZIER, and LESLIE PINCKNEY HILL. HALLIE QUINN BROWN served as dean of women, and NELLA LARSEN was appointed assistant superintendent of nurses at the school before she relocated to NEW YORK CITY and immersed herself in the literary world of the Harlem Renaissance. CATHERINE LATIMER, the first African-American woman appointed to the staff of the NEW YORK PUBLIC LIBRARY, began her library career at Tuskegee. Monroe Work, a respected historian and editor of the *NEGRO YEAR BOOK*, was director of the Department of Records and Research at the school.

Tuskegee graduates included CLAUDE ALBERT BARNETT as well as a number of students who began their studies at the Alabama institute. Students who attended included GEORGE WYLIE HENDERSON, CLAUDE MCKAY, and RALPH ELLISON, who left in 1936, after his junior year, to pursue opportunities in New York City.

The school was invoked in several Harlem Renaissance works including QUICKSAND (1928) by NELLA LARSEN and THEY THAT SIT IN DARKNESS (1919) by MARY BURRILL.

Bibliography

Thrasher, Max Bennett. *Tuskegee: Its Story and Its Work.* Boston: Small, Maynard & Co., 1900.

Verney, Kevern. *The Art of the Possible: Booker T. Washington and Black Leadership in the United States, 1881–1925.* New York: Routledge, 2001.

Walker, Anne Kendrick. *Tuskegee and the Black Belt: A Portrait of a Race.* Richmond, Va.: The Dietz Press, Inc., 1944.

Washington, Booker T., ed. *Tuskegee & Its People: Their Ideals and Achievements.* 1905; reprint, New York: Negro Universities Press, 1969.

Twelve Negro Spirituals Ruby Berkley Goodwin (1937)

A multi-genre work by Ruby Berkley Goodwin that included Goodwin's stories about African-American life and songs and spirituals by acclaimed composer and musician William Grant Still. The New York–based Handy Brothers Music Company published the work.

Two Gods: A Minaret Doris Price (1932)

A provocative play by DORIS PRICE that suggests the inflexibility of the church and the survival strategies that might empower traumatized believers. Published in the December 1932 issue of OPPORTUNITY, the one-act play focuses on the tension between a bereft woman and her watchful, but unsupportive, local and church communities. Corinne Barber is a widow and the lone living member of her immediate family. The play opens as she prepares an apple pie with fruit harvested from the tree cultivated by her recently deceased husband. When Amy Grey, a well-meaning but somewhat insensitive friend, stops by, the two talk about Corinne's lasting anguish about her losses.

The arrival of the local minister intensifies the conversation about Corinne's unwillingness to resume regular church attendance and participation in the choir. The minister's chiding and his emphasis on God's unwillingness to accommodate backsliders ultimately drives Corinne to deny God's existence. "Dare ain no God! Yer heah me—Dere ain no God!" she declares with a "wild distraught expression" upon her face. Moments after the emotional outburst, a friend named Virginia Kelton arrives. Her headdress, a green scarf bound around her head, is similar to the one that Corinne now wears. When Kelton leaves, the minister accosts Corinne one last time and, in a violent gesture, snatches at the scarf on her head. It unfurls and reveals the widow's shaved and reddened scalp. The sight of it forces the minister into an "awed and trembling silence," but that gives way to a final violent set of condemnations and curses. The play closes as the minister curses his former parishioner and renders her, for all intents and purposes, to a vexed exile from what should be a nurturing, loving community.

Price's presentation of unrewarding domesticity and unfulfilled female longing for kindness is evocative of the pain that female protagonists experience in works by NELLA LARSEN, ZORA NEALE HURSTON, and MARITA BONNER. Price challenges her audiences to cultivate greater compassion and tolerance in the face of overwhelming loss and despair.

Bibliography

Burton, Jennifer, ed. *Zora Neale Hurston, Eulalie Spence, Marita Bonner and Others: The Prize Plays and Other One-Acts Published in Periodicals.* New York: G. K. Hall & Co., 1996.

"Typewriter, The" Dorothy West (1926)

A prizewinning short story and the second work that DOROTHY WEST published in a major Harlem Renaissance periodical. The nameless protagonist is a southerner living in Boston. An "abject little man of fifty-odd years" who works as a janitor in the heart of Boston's business district, he is quietly frustrated by the limited opportunities for people of color in the North. His home life is not entirely rewarding; his wife Net shows little domestic ingenuity, and his second job as the caretaker of the apartment building requires that he deal with obstreperous and demanding tenants. One evening, he begins a fateful collaboration with his daughter Millie, a young woman who hopes to practice her stenographic and secretarial skills. Each night, for a few weeks, Millie types the letters that her father dictates to powerful businessmen and tycoons of the day. The evenings with Millie allow for a "chameleon change of a Court Street janitor to J. Lucius Jones, dealer in stocks and bonds." The father relishes the chance to engage, even in fantasy, in serious business dealings that test his mettle and indulge his own thwarted professional aspirations. He begins to "stride up and down, earnestly and seriously debating the advisability of buying copper with the market in such a fluctuating state" (14). He begins to mail the letters that he writes to himself and takes secret pleasure in his correspondence. When Millie sells the typewriter without any warning, her father suffers a great and perhaps life-threatening shock. "Silence . . . crowded in on him, engulfed him. That blurred his vision, dulled his brain. Vast, white, impenetrable . . . His ears strained for the old, familiar sound. And silence beat upon them" (17). The story ends in dramatic fashion as "J. Lucius Jones crashed and died" (17).

The story is a jarring and insightful commentary on the effect that thwarted ambitions can have on earnest and imaginative individuals. The pathos of the story is reinforced by the seemingly impenetrable alienation that the nameless everyman who comes to life as J. Lucius Jones experiences. The story is one of several piercing commentaries on the tragic and sometimes unrelenting nature of modern domestic life that West published during the Harlem Renaissance.

"The Typewriter," published in the July 1926 issue of OPPORTUNITY, tied for second place with "Muttsy" by ZORA NEALE HURSTON in the magazine's annual literary competition. Judges of the short story entries, who awarded first prize to ARTHUR HUFF FAUSET for "SYMPHONESQUE," included JEAN TOOMER, CARL VAN DOREN, ZONA GALE, and BLANCHE WILLIAMS.

Bibliography

Saunders, James Robert, and Renae Shackelford. *The Dorothy West Martha's Vineyard: Stories, Essays, and Reminiscences by Dorothy West Writing in the Vineyard Gazette.* Jefferson, N.C.: McFarland, 2001.

West, Dorothy. "The Typewriter." In *The Richer, the Poorer: Stories, Sketches, and Reminiscences,* by Dorothy West. New York: Doubleday, 1995.

U

Uncle Tom's Children: Four Novellas
Richard Wright (1938)

A collection of powerful and tragic novellas by RICHARD WRIGHT that marked the turn toward stark realism and naturalism as the Harlem Renaissance came to a close. Published in 1938, two years before his bestseller NATIVE SON, Uncle Tom's Children included "Big Boy Leaves Home," "Down by the Riverside," "Long Black Song," and the prize-winning piece entitled "Fire and Cloud." Wright's literary success with Uncle Tom's Children was enriched by the fact that this also was the year in which he met RALPH ELLISON, the writer who became one of his closest friends and intellectual allies. A second edition, published later in 1938, appeared under the title Uncle Tom's Children: Five Long Stories. The fifth piece added to the collection was "BRIGHT AND MORNING STAR," a short story that Wright published in NEW MASSES in 1938 and saw included in Best American Short Stories. A third edition of the collection appeared in 1940 with HARPER AND BROTHERS, the company that published Native Son, and this edition included Wright's stark autobiographical narrative entitled "The Ethics of Living Jim Crow."

The stories illuminate the ways in which African-American self-determination and domestic stability are under perpetual threat. He explores the inhumane nature of violence, contests notions of southern honor, and produces a thoroughly overwhelming set of stories about modern communities in crisis. The stories are rooted in an explosive American South that is prone to LYNCHING and to acts of devastating white violence against people of color. The first story, "Big Boy Leaves Home," for instance, is an earnest tale about Big Boy, a daring young man whose recklessness endangers him and his friends. After a fateful decision to go skinny-dipping in Harvey's Pond located on white-owned land, the boys are unable to recover their clothes easily when a white woman arrives on the scene. The predictable conflict that emerges escalates rapidly, and within minutes Big Boy, in an effort to stem the hysteria that incites white lynch mobs, becomes a murderer who is forced to flee his home and family. "Down by the Riverside" showcases the nature of awful, deadly indecision that can make life for people of color in the South an unrelenting source of moral and emotional distress. "Long Black Song" represents a narrative departure for Wright in that it features a female protagonist. Yet again, however, Wright hones in on the permeability and fragility of African-American homes. Sarah, a young wife, is tragically seduced by a traveling salesman who calls when her husband is away. She is found out when Silas, her cuckolded husband, discovers the white man's hat by the bedside. Enraged, he attacks and kills two white men and then is set upon by a lynch mob that descends upon the house. The story is informed by Wright's own life and the vicious murder of his own uncle Silas Hopkins in Elaine, Arkansas. Wright, his mother, and his siblings had relocated to Elaine to live with Hopkins and Wright's maternal aunt. In 1916 a mob of white men, determined to acquire the property of Hopkins, murdered him, and their brutality forced the family to flee for their own lives.

ZORA NEALE HURSTON, writing in the *Saturday Review of Literature*, characterized the work as one "about hatreds" in which Wright "serve[d] notice by his title that he [spoke] of people in revolt, and his stories [were] so grim that the Dismal Swamp of race hatred must be where they live." The collection identified Wright as a powerful emerging literary figure, and it contributed significantly to his selection as a GUGGENHEIM FELLOWSHIP winner in 1939.

Bibliography

Butler, Robert. *The Critical Response to Richard Wright.* Westport, Conn.: Greenwood Press, 1995.

Fabre, Michel. *The World of Richard Wright.* Jackson: University Press of Mississippi, 1985.

Gates, Henry Louis, Jr., and Kwame Anthony Appiah, eds. *Richard Wright: Critical Perspectives Past and Present.* New York: Amistad, 1993.

Rowley, Hazel. *Richard Wright: The Life and Times.* New York: Henry Holt and Company, 2001.

Uncommon Sense: The Law of Life in Action Garland Anderson (1933)

A work of nonfiction by GARLAND ANDERSON, a California bellhop turned BROADWAY playwright. Anderson, the first African American to have a full-length play staged on Broadway, published the work while serving as the Minister of Constructive Thinking at an institute known as the Truth Center. Published two years before Anderson's death, the volume advanced his optimistic ideas about how best to live in the world.

Undertow Eulalie Spence (1927)

A tragic prize-winning one-act play by EULALIE SPENCE that revolves around a troubled marital relationship, illegitimacy, and faithfulness. The play features four central characters. Dan, Hattie, and their son Charley are an unhappy family of three who fail to relate to each other in healthy and empowering ways. Clem, a former friend and lover of Dan's, reappears unexpectedly and soon makes a claim on Dan's affections when she finds out how unhappy he is in his marriage. Dan, who receives no kindness from his wife, has begun to contemplate leaving her for Clem and the daughter

named Lucy who was borne of their relationship. Clem decides to face her competition and, after six evenings of keeping company with Dan, arrives at his home to confront his wife and the friend whom she betrayed. Clem, who is a more sympathetic character only because she responds to the pain she sees in her beloved, requests that Hattie grant her husband a divorce. Although Dan has been ready to quit his marriage, it is Clem who hopes that he can acquire a legally binding separation and thus be free to marry her. Clem hopes desperately to provide her daughter, now on the verge of marriage, with a respectable family history. When Hattie threatens to reveal Clem to her daughter as a prostitute, Dan intervenes. In an unfortunate accident, Hattie strikes her head and dies. Desperate to save Clem from the law and implication in Hattie's death, Dan instructs his longtime sweetheart and only hope of domestic bliss to leave him. The story closes as Dan apologizes to the unresponsive figure of his wife and suffers the painful irony that he now is finally freed from his oppressive marriage but still unable to act independently and for his own benefit.

Undertow won recognition from CRISIS in its annual literary competition. In 1927 Spence was awarded third prize for two of her plays, *Undertow* and *Hot Stuff,* in the journal's competition in literature and art. First and second prize went to MARITA BONNER and to BRENDA RAY MORYCK, respectively. Two years later, *Undertow* was published in *Carolina Magazine,* and the play was one of four by African-American playwrights that appeared in the April 1929 issue. In addition to Spence's work, the periodical included BLACK DAMP by JOHN MATHEUS, *Scratches* by MAY MILLER SULLLIVAN, and THE IDLE HEAD by WILLIS RICHARDSON.

Scholar James Hatch notes that *Undertow* is powerful for Spence's invocation of universal, rather than racial, themes in the work. Indeed, Spence succeeds in exploring difficult issues such as emotional abuse, infidelity, and problematic parenting skills without indicting the African-American characters or suggesting that their struggles are specific to the race.

Bibliography

Burton, Jennifer, ed. *Zora Neale Hurston, Eulalie Spence, Marita Bonner and Others: The Prize Plays and Other*

One-Acts Published in Periodicals. New York: G. K. Hall & Co., 1996.

Underwood, Edna Worthley (1873–1961)

A gifted linguist, novelist, translator, and mentor who became best known for her English translations of foreign works. Born in Phillips, Maine, Underwood was raised in Arkansas City, Kansas. Her parents, Albert and Alice Howard Worthley, were committed to her intellectual advancement and provided private tutors for her. By 1888, the year in which she graduated from high school, Worthley had already prepared the bulk of an anthology on Slav literature that she planned to publish. Following her graduating from the University of Michigan in Ann Arbor in 1892, she returned to Kansas. In 1897 she married Robert Earl Underwood. In 1904 the couple decided to relocate to NEW YORK CITY.

Underwood's career is impressive for the sheer scope of her literary endeavors. From 1921 through 1938, she published fiction, poetry, and numerous English translations that included detailed biographical and contextual information about the work and the author. Her impressive translations included a 1903 edition of Evenings in Little Russia by Nikolai Gogol; Moons of Nippon, a 1917 edition of Japanese poetry; the Anthology of Mexican Poets (1932), which was the first English translation ever published of Mexican poetry; Flemish Short Stories (1934); and The Poets of Haiti, 1782–1934 (1934), which included a glossary of terms and a set of woodcut images. In addition, Underwood produced a variety of her own creative writings in the early years of the Harlem Renaissance. These included The Garden of Desire: Love Sonnets to a Spanish Monk (1913), Book of the White Peacocks (1915), and The Whirlwind: A Novel of the Russian 18th Century (1919). She also published a trilogy of novels set in 19th-century Russia: The Penitent (1923), The Passion Flower (1924), and The Pageant Maker (1926).

Underwood represented the dynamic range in intellectual interests and creative production that African Americans could produce and were producing during the Harlem Renaissance. She was one of the nine judges who served in the first OPPORTUNITY literary contest, and her own work was included in the rich 1927 anthology EBONY AND TOPAZ: A COLLECTANEA, edited by CHARLES JOHNSON and published by the NATIONAL URBAN LEAGUE.

Underwood, who had been widowed since 1944, died in June 1961 in her hometown of Arkansas City, Kansas.

Bibliography
Underwood, Edna. Anthology of Mexican Poets from the Earliest Times to the Present Day. Portland, Maine: The Mosher Press, 1932.

———. Short Stories From the Balkans, Translated into English by Edna Worthley Underwood. Boston: Marshall Jones Company, 1919.

———. The Slav Anthology: Russian, Polish, Bohemian, Serbian, Croatian, Translated by Edna Worthley Underwood. Portland, Maine: The Mosher Press, 1931.

———. The Taste of Honey: The Notebook of a Linguist. Portland, Maine: The Mosher Press, 1930.

"Unfinished Masterpieces" Anita Scott Coleman (1927)

A meditative short story about life experiences and the passage of time by prize-winning writer ANITA SCOTT COLEMAN. Published in the March 1927 issue of THE CRISIS, the story proceeds in the fashion of Charles Dickens's A Christmas Carol (1868) as an omniscient narrator considers the past encounters and the value of reminiscence. "Backward ho, through the mazes of the past," declares the narrator, who then proceeds to focus on two individuals whom the invisible and unnamed protagonist has known. Coleman presents first Dora Johns, a child who, despite the lack in her life "seem[ed] not to heed the seething bubbles upon the other side" and could often be found "shaping, shaping marvelous things out of mud." The narrator concludes that Dora, a true innocent, is one of the "Master's unfinished shapes which He will some day gather to mould anew into the unfinished masterpiece." The second individual featured in the story is Mr. William Williams, a 51-year-old man who "wear[s] a child's simplicity, the sort that is so sad to see upon a man." More concerned with gambling money than investing it, Williams is a "lump of mud," one who has not been shaped and for whom death, or the "gathering up," will provide the only opportunity to "be moulded anew into the finished masterpiece." The piece ends with a rather generous exhortation to all about the value of heaven and its welcome of "white and black, rich and poor, of whatever caste or creed many enter and find comfort and ease and food and drink." Coleman uses a nontraditional narrative style in "Unfinished Masterpieces," and the story suffers slightly from its lack of momentum, true crisis, or satisfying resolution.

"Unimportant Man, An" Dorothy West
(1928)
A short story by DOROTHY WEST published in the Boston-based SATURDAY EVENING QUILL. It is a heart-wrenching story of one man's unsuccessful efforts to create a career and family.

Bibliography
Jones, Sharon. Rereading the Harlem Renaissance: Race, Class, and Gender in the Fiction of Jessie Fauset, Zora Neale Hurston, and Dorothy West. Westport, Conn.: Greenwood Press, 2002.

Universal Negro Improvement Association (UNIA)
An impressive, global organization dedicated to the uplift, political independence, and economic success of peoples of African descent. Founded in 1914 in Kingston, Jamaica, by MARCUS GARVEY, the UNIA, as it was called, became one of the best-known race organizations of the Harlem Renaissance era.

Garvey established the first American UNIA branch in HARLEM shortly after he arrived in 1916. By the 1920s, the organization had chapters throughout the Caribbean, Latin America, sub-Saharan AFRICA, and the United States. The UNIA was dedicated to political independence, articulating race pride, and challenging colonial rule throughout the world. Garvey garnered much attention because of the pomp and circumstance that he incorporated into UNIA events, his activism, and his searing critiques of the NATIONAL ASSOCIATION FOR THE ADVANCEMENT OF COLORED PEOPLE. In addition, his bold financial ventures, which included the establishment of factories, restaurants, and the ill-fated Black

Star shipping line, explained his success and the degree to which he was deemed a threat by federal agencies that ultimately succeeded in jailing him on mail fraud charges and then deporting him.

The official publication of the UNIA was NEGRO WORLD, a popular weekly newspaper. Its editorial leadership and staff included WILFRED ADOLPHUS DOMINGO, a nationalist and fellow West Indian, Amy Jacques Garvey, the second wife of the UNIA leader, and HUBERT HARRISON, the individual who first invited Garvey to address African Americans in New York City.

Bibliography
Cronon, Edmund. Black Moses: The Story of Marcus Garvey and the Universal Negro Improvement Association. Madison: University of Wisconsin Press, 1987.
Hill, Robert, ed. The Marcus Garvey and Universal Negro Improvement Association Papers. Berkeley: University of California Press, 1983–95.
Lewis, Rupert. Marcus Garvey: Anti-Colonial Champion. Trenton, N.J.: Africa World Press, 1988.
Smith-Irvin, Jeannette. Footsoldiers of the Universal Negro Improvement Association: Their Own Words. Trenton, N.J.: Africa World Press, 1989.
Stein, Judith. The World of Marcus Garvey: Race and Class in Modern Society. Baton Rouge: Louisiana State University Press, 1986.

University of Chicago
The university founded by John D. Rockefeller after the demise during the 1880s of the first institution of the same name that was established in 1856. The institution opened in 1892, and its first president was William Rainey Harper, a gifted scholar who earned a Ph.D. from YALE UNIVERSITY when he was 18 years old. The university recruited leading scholars of the day to join its faculty. It also achieved academic history by founding some of the first major departments in American colleges. The university was home to the nation's first sociology department.

Many Harlem Renaissance figures had strong ties to the university. REGINA ANDREWS, BENJAMIN BRAWLEY, ALLISON DAVIS, Katherine Dunham, JOHN HOPE, CHARLES BERTRAM JOHNSON, and

CHARLES S. JOHNSON, editor of *OPPORTUNITY* and one of the most influential figures of the Harlem Renaissance movement, were among those who attended the institution. ARNA BONTEMPS earned a master's degree in library science, E. FRANKLIN FRAZIER earned a Ph.D. in 1931, and MELVILLE HERSKOVITS, the founder of African-American studies, completed his undergraduate studies there in 1920. RUSSELL JELLIFFE and ROWENA WOODHAM JELLIFFE, pioneers in the Karamu Theatre organization of Cleveland, both completed graduate studies in sociology at the university.

Bibliography

Goodspeed, Thomas. *The Story of the University of Chicago, 1890–1925*. Chicago: The University of Chicago Press, 1925.

University of Copenhagen

Founded in 1479 in the Danish capital city of Copenhagen, the university is the nation's largest academic institution in what now is the largest Scandinavian city. NELLA LARSEN attended the University of Copenhagen during her two-year stay in Denmark in the early 1900s. In 1921, EDWARD FRANKLIN FRAZIER, the first American to receive the prestigious American Scandinavian Foundation Fellowship, used his award to finance a year of studies at the university.

University of Pennsylvania

Located in PHILADELPHIA, Pennsylvania, it was established by Benjamin Franklin and a small group of monied philanthropists. The university was home to the first American medical school and to the first graduate school in the country.

The University of Pennsylvania was the alma mater of ARTHUR HUFF FAUSET, who earned a B.A., M.A., and Ph.D. from the institution during his tenure as a principal in the Philadelphia public school system. Writer LEWIS ALEXANDER also attended the university. Other famous alumni include Kwame Nkrumah, the first president of GHANA and a LINCOLN UNIVERSITY graduate; William Brennan, a U.S. Supreme Court justice; linguist Noam Chomsky; and the former U.S. surgeon general C. Everett Koop.

Bibliography

Thomas, George, and David Brownlee. *Building America's First University: An Historical and Architectural Guide to the University of Pennsylvania*. Philadelphia: University of Pennsylvania Press, 2000.

Thorpe, Francis, ed. *Benjamin Franklin and the University of Pennsylvania*. Washington, D.C.: Government Printing Office, 1893.

"Unquenchable Fire, The" Robert Bagnall (1924)

An eerie story by ROBERT BAGNALL that explores the impact of LYNCHING upon the instigators of the murder and those who survive the murderous violence against their kin and households. Published in the November 1924 issue of *THE MESSENGER*, the story proceeds in a gothic, dark style evocative of the works of Edgar Allan Poe. A nameless traveler seeks shelter in a farmhouse guarded by two enormous dogs. The owner is John Tower, a white man and a "once powerful figure over six feet four, now emaciated and worn." The other occupants of the house include a sullen mulatto housekeeper and a disheveled white woman, who appears to be mad. The traveler is sure that he has heard of his host, whose white hair stands upright upon his head as if in response to a great shock. However, it is not until the wee hours of the morning, when he is awakened by plaintive cries of the madwoman, that the traveler remembers what he has heard about the house and its inhabitants. He then reconstructs the tale of Tower, a widower raising his beautiful daughter alone. After he hires a mulatto housekeeper with a six-year-old child, rumors begin to circulate that the child is his. Years pass, and the children become especially close. Eventually, Tower's daughter becomes ill, and Tower finds out that she is expecting a child. When she finally reveals that she and Jimmy have been having a secret relationship during the past year, Tower is incensed. He goads a mob of white men into action by claiming that Jimmy has raped his daughter. When they find the young man, it is Tower who gives the order to murder him. The story ends as the traveler makes an effort to leave the home that many believe is haunted by the ghost of Jimmy. On his way out, he spies a Bible open to a passage that refers to an unquenchable fire.

Bagnall's short story is part of the substantial Harlem Renaissance–era literature about lynching. His work reveals the horrific and personal nature of mob violence. It also considers the living hell experienced by those who lodge deadly charges against others, claims that not only devastate the immediate families of the accused but also clearly victimize the supposedly avenged white families.

Urban League Bulletin

The first official publication of the NATIONAL URBAN LEAGUE and the precursor to OPPORTUNITY, the popular and influential monthly magazine that emerged in 1923. CHARLES S. JOHNSON, editor of *Opportunity,* served as editor for the bimonthly *Bulletin.*

According to historians Abby Arthur Johnson and Ronald Johnson, the *Bulletin* focused primarily on events and issues that pertained directly to the organization. Charles S. Johnson, however, made an effort to include illuminating editorials about contemporary issues and trends related to African-American life, communities, and progress. His example fueled the efforts of EUGENE KINCKLE JONES and other Urban League members who wanted to develop a more widely circulated and influential publication.

Bibliography

Johnson, Abby Arthur, and Ronald Maberry Johnson. *Propaganda & Aesthetics: The Literary Politics of African American Magazines in the Twentieth Century.* Amherst: University of Massachusetts, 1979.

Moore, Jesse. *A Search for Equality: The National Urban League, 1910–1961.* University Park: Pennsylvania State University Press, 1981.

Parris, Guichard, and Lester Brooks. *Blacks in the City: A History of the National Urban League.* Boston: Little, Brown, 1971.

Weiss, Nancy. *The National Urban League, 1910–1940.* New York: Oxford University Press, 1974.

Valentine, C.

The pseudonym that the editor, journalist, and activist CYRIL VALENTINE BRIGGS used during his career. While he published the majority of his major political works under his own name, Briggs regularly used his pseudonym to publish articles on African history, African-American figures, and other issues in journals such as *The Crusader*, the monthly periodical of which he was editor.

Van Doren, Carl Clinton (1884–1950)

A highly respected white literary critic and historian who supported the Harlem Renaissance–era efforts to sustain a vibrant African-American literary tradition. Born in Hope, Illinois, to Charles Lucius and Dora Anne Butz Van Doren, Carl Van Doren was the oldest of five sons and brother to poet Mark Van Doren. After graduating from the University of Illinois-Urbana in 1907, Van Doren relocated to New York City to begin graduate work at COLUMBIA UNIVERSITY. He earned his Ph.D. in 1911 and by 1919 was a persuasive critic working as literary editor at THE NATION.

Van Doren's career during the Harlem Renaissance era included stints as headmaster of the Brearley School and as instructor in the English department at Columbia. Throughout the 1920s Van Doren oversaw important comprehensive literary projects and publication efforts. He was literary editor of CENTURY MAGAZINE, managing editor of the *Cambridge History of American Literature*, and author of critical studies on the writers SINCLAIR LEWIS and Branch Cabell. In 1936

Harper and Brothers published *Three Worlds*, Van Doren's autobiography.

In 1924 Van Doren participated in the historic celebratory CIVIC CLUB dinner organized, ostensibly, to celebrate the publication of THERE IS CONFUSION, the first novel by JESSIE FAUSET. The event, however, became a festive meditation on the potential impact of a literary movement and the accomplishments of many emerging male writers and thinkers of the time. On this occasion, Van Doren suggested that African Americans had the potential to infuse new and much-needed vitality in to the American literary tradition.

In 1924, with FANNIE HURST, EDNA WORTHLEY UNDERWOOD, ALAIN LOCKE and others, Van Doren participated as a judge in the first *Opportunity* literary contest. He lent his expertise to the short story division of the 1925–26 contest that saw works by ARTHUR HUFF FAUSET, ZORA NEALE HURSTON, DOROTHY WEST, Lee Wallace, and EUGENE GORDON take top honors. Van Doren served for a third and final term in 1926–27 and, with fellow judges THEODORE DREISER, ERIC WALROND, and his daughter Irita Van Doren, awarded first-place honors to writers EUGENE GORDON and Cecil Blue.

Bibliography

Van Doren, Carl. *Three Worlds.* New York: Harper and Brothers, 1936.

Vanity Fair

A popular magazine that was one of the first mainstream publications to feature the works of

African-American writers and artists. Founded in 1913 by Condé Nast, the magazine was dedicated to celebrating contemporary high society, fashion, and issues of interest. Its editor, FRANK CROWNINSHIELD, revealed the aesthetic and material splendors that upper-class individuals enjoyed and also provided regular commentary on entertainment and cultural events. During the Harlem Renaissance, the works of well-known figures of the era appeared in the monthly issues. The magazine published works by LANGSTON HUGHES, COUNTEE CULLEN, Miguel Covarrubias, and CARL VAN VECHTEN. The magazine ceased publication in 1936.

Vann, Robert L. (1879–1940)

A lawyer and the longtime influential editor of the *PITTSBURGH COURIER*, Robert L. Vann was born in rural North Carolina to a cook named Lucy Peoples, who gave her son the surname of her aristocratic employers. Following abbreviated schooling in the severely limited segregated schools of the area, Vann went on to study at the Waters Training School. Despite some necessary breaks in order to earn money to support himself, he graduated as class valedictorian. He attended Virginia Union University and eventually went on to earn a law degree from Western University of Pennsylvania in 1909.

Vann became involved with the *Courier* in 1910 after providing some clients with the legal papers necessary to establish the newspaper. Founded by Edwin Harleston, the paper struggled to survive early on. Under Vann's leadership, however, the weekly newspaper achieved a stunning national circulation of 400,000 at its peak and was well known as an eloquent and passionate advocate of African-American affairs.

Vann combined his journalism and law careers. He also served as Pittsburgh's city solicitor for nearly two decades. As an active Republican, he worked to elect Calvin Coolidge. When he changed party allegiances, however, he supported the election of Franklin Roosevelt. In 1932 Vann was appointed special assistant to the U.S. Attorney General in honor of his enthusiastic support of Roosevelt during the 1932 election.

Vann died in October 1940.

Bibliography

Buni, Andrew. *Robert L. Vann of the Pittsburgh Courier: Politics and Black Journalism*. Pittsburgh: University of Pittsburgh Press, 1974.

Van Vechten, Carl (1880–1964)

A novelist, journalist, photographer, social critic, and legendary patron of the Harlem Renaissance era. Van Vechten was a dedicated historian of the Harlem Renaissance and preserved stunning images of many figures of the era. He also created substantial collections of primary materials by and about the artists and writers of the period. Van Vechten achieved a deep intimacy with many of the creative individuals associated with the Harlem Renaissance. His connection was in large part fueled by his belief that one had a responsibility to come to know individuals as completely as possible. "[I]f my profession kept me from knowing anybody I really wanted to know," he noted on one occasion, "I should relinquish that profession without hesitation" (*NYT*, 22 December 1964, 29). He enjoyed lasting friendships with many celebrities and literary personalities including GEORGE GERSHWIN, EUGENE O'NEILL, LANGSTON HUGHES, and Gertrude Stein.

A native of Cedar Rapids, Iowa, he was the youngest son of banker Charles Van Vechten and his wife, Ada. While he had a stable home life and benefited much from his parents' love of the arts and middle-class status, he later recalled that he "eventually escaped" from Cedar Rapids, a town "which [he] loathed from the first" (*NYT*, 22 December 1964, 29). He attended the UNIVERSITY OF CHICAGO and graduated in 1903. Immediately after college, Van Vechten worked as a reporter for the *Chicago American*. He relocated to NEW YORK CITY in 1906 after being released from the Chicago paper for "lowering the tone of the Hearst publications" (*NYT*, 22 December 1964, 29) and made his first contacts in the literary and theater communities there. In the city that he regarded as "enchanting," he provided reviews of plays for the *New York Press*. He also wrote for *Broadway Magazine* and its novelist-editor Sinclair Lewis and published music reviews in *THE NEW YORK TIMES*, where he worked as an assistant music critic. Between 1908 and 1909, he lived in Europe, working for the *New York Times* as its Paris correspondent. In 1925, with generous amounts of information and text that he solicited from Langston Hughes, he published a series of articles in *VANITY FAIR* about a variety of African-American entertainment figures and subjects.

Van Vechten's first marriage, to a Cedar Rapids high school friend named Ann Snyder, took place in London in 1907. After five years, the marriage ended badly, and Van Vechten had to contend with his ex-wife's demands for money. Ultimately, the couple settled on a $1,000 payment, for which Van Vechten went into debt. Ann Snyder's life ended tragically after years of self-imposed exile in Europe. In 1933, sick with cancer, she committed suicide by leaping to her death from a Paris sanatorium (Kellner, 91). In 1914 Van Vechten married Fania Marinoff, an actress from Odessa who had immigrated to the United States in the 1890s. According to Van Vechten biographer Bruce Kellner, Fania, whose mother died when Fania was an infant, was secreted under her stepmother's skirts during much of the journey so that the family could avoid paying additional fares. The Marinoffs settled in Boston, Massachusetts, and Fania, who in school was known as Fanny Epstein, eventually followed her brother to Denver, Colorado. Her career on the stage began in Colorado, and by the age of 12 she had joined a traveling theater troupe. She eventually arrived in New York City, and it was there that Van Vechten met the woman whom the newspapers described as "a darksome and delightful slip of a girl" (Kellner, 63). Although the couple was extremely close and appeared together quite frequently at the numerous celebratory events in Harlem, scholars like Arnold Rampersad note that FANIA MARINOFF VAN VECHTEN "didn't care much for Van Vechten's hard drinking and Harlem club-crawling" (Rampersad, 108).

Van Vechten stopped writing criticism in 1920, when he was 40 years old, noting that at that age, "a man experienced intellectual hardening of the arteries which made him unfit for criticism" (*NYT*, 22 December 1964). While he did publish an occasional review after his dramatic pronouncement, he turned his attention away from the writing that many viewed as an indispensable facet of the arts scene. The work that he had produced to date gen-

Carl Van Vechten, author, photographer, and patron. Photographed by Mark Lutz. Permission granted by the Van Vechten Trust *(Yale Collection of American Literature, Beinecke Rare Book and Manuscript Library)*

erated high praise. His assessments of dance, even when read years later, were deemed by many to be "as sound as they ever were and the prescience they exhibit in an art in which America (in common with most of the rest of the world) was abysmally illiterate bespeaks a remarkably sensitive and forward-looking mind. That they played a major part in the creation of public taste cannot be gainsaid" (*NYT*, 18 June 1961, X15). Van Vechten's "passionate collecting of items pertaining to the Negro contribution to American life" included "photos, manuscripts, 100 early phonograph records by Negro musicians, letters and the like" (*NYT*, 22 December 1964, 29).

Throughout the 1920s Van Vechten turned his creative energies toward writing fiction. Journalist Leo Lerman described the works, which varied in theme and settings, as "novels that abound in dance minutiae" (*NYT*, 18 June 1961, X15). Van Vechten published several novels during his career. The first, a somewhat autobiographical work entitled *Peter Whiffle: His Life and Works* (1922), was followed quickly by other works such as *The Blind Bow-Boy* (1923), *The Tattooed Countess* (1924), and *Fire-crackers* (1925). It was Van Vechten's sixth novel, however, that drew the most fire and praise. *NIGGER HEAVEN* (1926) was inspired by Van Vechten's immersion in dynamic African-American social and literary circles in New York City. The novel, controversial because of its use of the vicious racial epithet, was a satire of Harlem Renaissance life. Responses to it were varied and included book burnings at public rallies such as the one convened in late December 1926 to protest the lynchings of a young South Carolina woman and her two brothers. At the rally organized by the National Negro Development Union and the National Negro Centre Political Party, WILBERFORCE UNIVERSITY professor S. R. Williams tore two pages from a copy of the novel. "After reading several passages he asked what should be done with them to show proper resentment of their contents." In response, the crowd of approximately 400 people "shouted 'Burn 'em up'" and "he ignited the two pieces of paper" and then noted that "there might be a later ceremony for the burning of the entire book" (*NYT*, 12 December 1926, 15). Leading figures such as W. E. B. DuBois and ALAIN LOCKE vigorously protested the novel, but Van Vechten received support for his work from equally visible figures such as JAMES WELDON JOHNSON and Langston Hughes. Van Vechten, whose friendship with Hughes began in 1924, frequently discussed the novel in its early stages, confessing in December 1925 that he was "very unsettled" about the work and that he was "too emotional when writing it and what one needs in writing is a calm, cold eye" (Bernard, 34). Hughes also provided a set of lyrics for the novel in order to help Van Vechten avoid a costly suit for using unauthorized verses from a popular song of the day.

Scholar Emily Bernard, who published a comprehensive collection of letters between Hughes and Van Vechten, notes that Van Vechten was well aware of the potential damage that his novel might do. His choice of title, for instance, had "turned [COUNTEE CULLEN] white with hurt," and he en-

couraged his editor at Knopf to begin the publicity campaign well in advance of the book's appearance so that "the kind of life I am writing about will not come as an actual shock" (Bernard, 41). Van Vechten's nervousness was not easily diminished despite the fact that he had been urged by such keen activists as James Weldon Johnson and WALTER WHITE to proceed. Historian David Levering Lewis notes that Johnson "urged Carl Van Vechten to write it in the first place because 'no acknowledged American novelist has yet made use of this material'" (Lewis, 180). Still, Van Vechten had to contend with the obvious rejection of his work and companionship, which a number of people now regarded suspiciously. Since its publication, however, scholars such as Lewis have suggested that "[n]ot only is it not a memorable literary work, it is not even up to Van Vechten's usual polish" (Lewis, 181). The novel reflects much about the racial stakes that shaped the Harlem Renaissance and contributes to ongoing studies of how white writers like Van Vechten, PAUL GREEN, and others grappled with and presented African-American subjects. The novel also provides rich insights into the African-American response to such literature and the ways in which writers articulated their specific racial agendas in the face of potential literary and artistic poaching or appropriation.

Van Vechten enjoyed photography, and in the early 1930s he began taking portraits of many friends, colleagues, and newly emerging figures. His images of well-known figures and writers included those of ZORA NEALE HURSTON, NELLA LARSEN, EUGENE O'NEILL, and Anna May Wong. The images often are evocative and powerful and constitute one of the most impressive modern collections of Harlem Renaissance–era portraits. Van Vechten developed his prints in his own darkroom and was known to be especially proud of the fact that throughout his photography career, he had never had to crop an image. One of his colleagues, Edward Steichen, characterized Van Vechten's portraits as "darned good," noting that Van Vechten "had a good opportunity to do the kind of work he was interested in, and he did it very well." Van Vechten, who proudly noted that he had "photographed everybody from Matisse to Isamu Noguchi," also recalled that his "first subject was

Anna May Wong, and my second was Eugene O'Neill" (*NYT,* 22 December 1964, 29). Other subjects included Tallulah Bankhead, Marc Chagall, F. Scott Fitzgerald, Billie Holliday, Joe Louis, RICHARD BRUCE NUGENT, Bessie Smith, and Thomas Wolfe. Van Vechten's love of photography often propelled him into the darkroom in the early morning hours, and he was working on images up until the morning before he passed away.

Van Vechten was a close friend of Langston Hughes, with whom he corresponded frequently for decades. During the course of their friendship, which began in the mid-1920s and lasted through 1964, the two men exchanged nearly 1,500 letters (Bernard, xxix). Hughes introduced Van Vechten to Richard Bruce Nugent, who reflected that the contact was arranged because Hughes knew that Van Vechten "could be helpful to me. I knew that when he introduced me. I knew it wasn't just that [Hughes] was interested and intrigued and amused that I thought Carl was a white monkey" (Wirth, 226). Hughes worked closely with Van Vechten, the patron who succeeded in obtaining a publishing contract for Hughes's first volume of poems in less than three weeks. Another of Van Vechten's close friends was writer Gertrude Stein. Their relationship evolved, from the early days when Van Vechten would publish reviews of her work, to Stein's appointment of him as literary executor of her estate.

Van Vechten was a steady supporter of African-American ventures during the Harlem Renaissance. In addition to donating funds to support *OPPORTUNITY,* he facilitated numerous introductions, negotiated publishing contracts for writers, and participated in formal debates about the nature of African-American art and creativity. In 1926 he collaborated with JESSIE FAUSET to generate a questionnaire about the "The Negro in Art." Van Vechten also took advantage of his intense familiarity with Harlem nightspots and social circles to become what David Levering Lewis has described as "white America's guide through Harlem." FISK UNIVERSITY honored Van Vechten with an honorary degree in 1955. He received the Yale University Gold Medal that same year.

On December 21, 1964, Van Vechten died in his Central Park West apartment. The New York City icon, whose 75th birthday party had been held in the 135th Street branch (HARLEM BRANCH) of the NEW YORK PUBLIC LIBRARY, was remembered as an "enthusiastic discoverer of young or overlooked talent and lover of cats." He was celebrated for using fiction to create a "documentary study of the nineteen-twenties" and a series of "thinly veiled portraits of the era's leading bohemians." The man who "adored celebrities" had a lasting impact on American letters and made deliberate efforts to preserve the legacies of the Harlem Renaissance. As historian Bruce Kellner notes, Van Vechten established several major archival collections of Harlem Renaissance materials including the well-known James Weldon Johnson Memorial Collection of Negro Art and Letters at YALE UNIVERSITY and collections of manuscripts and photographs at FISK UNIVERSITY, the University of New Mexico, and HOWARD UNIVERSITY.

Bibliography

Bernard, Emily, ed. *Remember Me to Harlem: The Letters of Langston Hughes and Carl Van Vechten.* New York: Knopf, 2001.

Byrd, Rudolph, ed. *Generations in Black and White: Photographs by Carl Van Vechten.* Athens: University of Georgia Press, 1993.

Kellner, Bruce. *Carl Van Vechten and the Irreverent Decades.* Norman: University of Oklahoma Press, 1968.

Lerman, Leo. "Dance: June Walk." *New York Times,* 18 June 1961, X15.

———. *Letters of Carl Van Vechten.* New Haven: Yale University Press, 1987.

Lewis, David Levering. *When Harlem Was in Vogue.* New York: Knopf, 1981.

Lueders, Edward. *Carl Van Vechten.* New York: Twayne Publishers, 1964.

———. *Carl Van Vechten and the Twenties.* Albuquerque: University of New Mexico Press, 1955.

Mauriber, Saul, comp. *Portraits: The Photography of Carl Van Vechten.* Indianapolis: Bobbs-Merrill, 1978.

Wirth, Thomas, ed. *Gay Rebel of the Harlem Renaissance: Selections from the work of Richard Bruce Nugent.* Durham: Duke University Press, 2002.

Van Vechten, Fania Marinoff (1890–1971)

The second wife of CARL VAN VECHTEN, one of the most energetic, enterprising figures of the Harlem Renaissance. Marinoff, a native of Odessa, emigrated from Russia to the United States with her Jewish family. The Marinoffs settled in Boston, but Fania soon joined her older siblings, who had relocated to Denver, Colorado. Marinoff enjoyed an early and successful start in theater and joined troupes such as the Camilla Martins St. George Company that enabled her to travel throughout the West and the Midwest. She met her future husband when she began performing in New York City. According to biographer Bruce Kellner, Van Vechten was smitten by the "darksome and delightful slip of a girl" (Kellner, 63). The couple married in 1914 and were together until Van Vechten's death in 1964.

Bibliography
Kellner, Bruce. *Carl Van Vechten and the Irreverent Decades.* Norman: University of Oklahoma Press, 1968.

Vengeance of the Gods and Three Other Stories of Real American Color Line Life
William Pickens (1922)

A collection of short stories by WILLIAM PICKENS, a PHI BETA KAPPA graduate of YALE UNIVERSITY and field secretary of the NATIONAL ASSOCIATION FOR THE ADVANCEMENT OF COLORED PEOPLE. The volume, published by the PHILADELPHIA-based A.M.E. Book Concern, included "The Vengeance of the Gods," "The Superior Race," "Passing the Buck," and "Tit for Tat."

"Vignettes of the Dusk" Eric Walrond
(1924)

Five vignettes by ERIC WALROND that provide perspectives on negotiations of the color line in 1920s America. Walrond's story is part of his rich collection of fiction that examines the social realities and survival strategies of people of color in the modern world.

Published in the January 1924 issue of *OPPORTUNITY*, the piece ranges from first-person anecdotes to omniscient narratives marked for their observations of the practical and whimsical strategies that individuals use to preserve their sense of self and racial pride. The narrator of the first sketch circumvents segregation in an upscale restaurant that does not cater to African Americans. The narrator achieves the goal—even though the order is given in a take-out bag. Other sketches honor the irreverent sensibilities of migrants of color who, despite 20 years of life in the United States, are not prepared to become citizens. As a Mr. Williams of New Jersey, husband to a "pretty wife, a jewel of one of the best colored families of Baltimore," notes, "America is all right . . . but I ain't taking no chances!" The collection ends with intraracial exchanges about skin color and caste.

Bibliography
Parascandola, Louis, ed. *Winds Can Wake Up the Dead: An Eric Walrond Reader.* Detroit: Wayne State University Press, 1998.

Villa Lewaro

An opulent mansion and the home of A'LELIA WALKER, daughter of the successful hair-care entrepreneur Madam C. J. Walker, the first self-made African-American woman millionaire. The villa, located in Irvington, N.Y., and the place in which Madam Walker died, was designed by Vertner Woodson Tandy, the first African-American architect who was licensed to practice in New York State. The legendary tenor Enrico Caruso suggested the name for the 20-room mansion that cost $250,000 to build.

Harlem Renaissance figures often enjoyed splendid weekend parties at the Villa Lewaro. In keeping with the wishes of Madam Walker, her daughter bequeathed the estate to the NATIONAL ASSOCIATION FOR THE ADVANCEMENT OF COLORED PEOPLE. The high maintenance costs and the toll of the Great Depression, however, forced the organization to sell the property. The buyers used the estate as a home for the elderly. The mansion has been designated a National Historic Landmark.

Bibliography
Bundles, A'Lelia Perry. *Madam C. J. Walker.* New York: Chelsea House Publishers, 1991.
———. *On Her Own Ground: The Life and Times of Madam C. J. Walker.* New York: Scribner, 2001.

Lowry, Beverly. *Her Dream of Dreams: The Rise and Triumph of Madam C. J. Walker.* New York: Alfred A. Knopf, 2003.

Villard, Oswald Garrison (1872–1949)

A journalist, activist, and grandson of William Lloyd Garrison, the pioneering abolitionist and *Liberator* editor. Born in Wiesbaden, Germany, he was the son of German-born businessman Henry Villard and his wife, Helen Frances Garrison Villard. The family returned to the United States in 1876, after a lengthy stay abroad that was intended to restore Henry Villard's health. Oswald, the third of four children, attended HARVARD UNIVERSITY and graduated in 1893. Several years after the boating enthusiast established *Yachting Magazine,* Villard became editor of THE NATION, a progressive weekly magazine that reported on civil and social injustices and the efforts to achieve various equalities in the United States. Villard held the post from 1918 until 1932.

Villard followed in the footsteps of his famous grandfather and committed himself to working for racial equality. With W. E. B. DuBois and others, he was a cofounder of the NATIONAL ASSOCIATION FOR THE ADVANCEMENT OF COLORED PEOPLE. While serving as chairman of the organization, he met with President Woodrow Wilson but was dismayed by Wilson's lack of interest in matters pertaining to racial injustice.

Villard suffered a stroke and died in New York City in 1949. He was buried in Tarrytown, New York, at the Sleepy Hollow Cemetery.

Bibliography

Humes, Dollena. *Oswald Garrison Villard, Liberal of the 1920s.* Syracuse, N.Y.: Syracuse University Press, 1960.

Villard, Oswald Garrison. *Fighting Years: Memoirs of a Liberal Editor.* New York: Harcourt, Brace and Company, 1939.

"Virginia Idyll" John Aubrey (1931)

A mournful short story by JOHN AUBREY, set in the home of an impoverished southern family with a sick child. Published in the April 1931 issue of OPPORTUNITY, the terse narrative chronicles the efforts of a nameless mother who is determined to secure medicine for her child. Her husband, however, does not share her sense of urgency and resists his wife's request that he seek out medicine for the dying child. She makes desperate efforts, sending her husband out with the last of the wheat she has set aside for bread in order to buy medicine at the store. He returns, but only to tell her that the owner took the wheat to cover the tobacco bill that he had run up at the store. In an act of extreme need, the wife turns a rifle on her husband, who is determined to go to bed. She urges him to take their only calf to a white landowner, get money, and buy medicine. Hours later, the man returns, drunk from the alcohol purchased from the small sum made from the sale of the calf. The story ends as the husband delivers a slurred speech in the presence of his wife who, despite her best efforts, has been unable to prevent the death of her infant child.

Aubrey's story is an uncompromising portrait of domesticity gone awry and the muted but piercing ways in which the larger society contributes to the demise of its less powerful citizens.

Vision Sarah Collins Fernandis (1925)

The second of two volumes of poetry by SARAH COLLINS FERNANDIS. Unfortunately, *Vision,* published by a small BOSTON company, has escaped critical attention and seems to have disappeared from circulation altogether.

"Voodoo's Revenge, The" Eric Walrond (1925)

A prize-winning short story by ERIC WALROND about a misanthropic activist in a West Indian island community. Published in July 1925, the two-part story introduces Nestor Villaine, a stowaway from Anguilla who has sequestered himself in the forests of another French Caribbean island to which he originally came to work. Eventually Nestor becomes the editor of a political paper that supports the Liberal Party. Unfortunately, a brawl with a political critic lands them both in court, and without any regard for Nestor's political fidelity, the judge sentences both men to 60 days in jail. The bewildered Nestor, unable to comprehend how his sacrifice on behalf of the judge and the party he represents, feels "Revolution surg[e] through him," and he resorts to "plotting, plotting" during his term of hard labor.

"The Voodoo's Revenge" won third prize in the first literary contest sponsored by OPPORTUNITY, the official publication of the NATIONAL URBAN LEAGUE. First and second prizes went to JOHN MATHEUS for "FOG" and ZORA NEALE HURSTON for "SPUNK," respectively. Walrond's fiction often examines the psychological torment of characters, and his focus on West Indian communities also explores the brusque and blind nature of colonial rule.

Bibliography
Parascandola, Louis, ed. *Winds Can Wake Up The Dead: An Eric Walrond Reader.* Detroit: Wayne State University Press, 1998.

Walker, A'Lelia (1885–1931)

A businesswoman, an enthusiastic patron of the arts, and the only daughter of Madam C. J. Walker, the self-made business phenomenon known for her innovations in African-American hair care.

Walker, who inherited millions from her mother, was one of the most flamboyant and energetic hostesses of the Harlem Renaissance period. She had three primary residences, an Edgecombe Avenue apartment, a mansion on 136th Street, and VILLA LEWARO, a splendid mansion located at Irvington-on-Hudson, New York.

Walker was an enthusiastic supporter of the arts and engaged frequently with literary figures of the period. It was she who established a regular salon that came to be known as the DARK TOWER. The meetings, held on one floor of her home on 136th Street, were part of a traditional salon culture that enriched the literary and cultural endeavors and relationships in such cities as BOSTON, PHILADELPHIA, New York, and WASHINGTON, D.C.

She died in 1931. The luminaries of the movement attended her funeral. Speakers included the Rev. ADAM CLAYTON POWELL, SR., who read the eulogy, LANGSTON HUGHES, who shared his poem "To A'Lelia," and educator MARY MCLEOD BETHUNE.

Bibliography

Bundles, A'Lelia Perry. *Madam C.J. Walker.* New York: Chelsea House Publishers, 1991.

———. *On Her Own Ground: The Life and Times of Madam C. J. Walker.* New York: Scribner, 2001.

Lowry, Beverly. *Her Dream of Dreams: The Rise and Triumph of Madam C. J. Walker.* New York: Knopf, 2003.

Socialite, patron, and heiress, A'Lelia Walker *(Yale Collection of American Literature, Beinecke Rare Book and Manuscript Library)*

Neihart, Ben. *Rough Amusements: The True Story of A'Lelia Walker, Patroness of the Harlem Renaissance's Down-Low Culture.* New York: Bloomsbury, 2003.

Walker, Margaret Abigail (1915–1998)

A celebrated poet, educator, and novelist whose impressive career was shaped by the Harlem Renaissance. She was born in Birmingham, Alabama, in July 1915 to the Reverend Sigismund Walker and his wife, Marion Dozier Walker, a music teacher. The family relocated to New Orleans in 1925, and Walker went on to attend New Orleans University, known now as Dillard University. After two years there, she transferred to NORTHWESTERN UNIVERSITY and earned her B.A. in English in 1935. She later earned an M.A. in creative writing from the University of Iowa and a Ph.D. in 1965.

Walker's immersion in the Harlem Renaissance culture began in the mid-1930s. She joined the Federal Writers' Project efforts in Chicago in 1936 and until 1939 worked alongside writers such as Gwendolyn Brooks and Frank Yerby. In Chicago she also was an active participant in the South Side Writers Group and through it became a close friend and colleague of RICHARD WRIGHT.

Margaret Walker's literary career began in the final years of the Harlem Renaissance. She published her powerful and frequently cited poem "For My People" in *Poetry* magazine in 1937. The poem, included in the influential collection *The Negro Caravan* (1941), became the title piece of *For My People* (1942), Walker's first collection of poems. *For My People* was awarded the Yale Younger Poets Award. In 1944 Walker won a JULIUS ROSENWALD FELLOWSHIP. In later years she also was the recipient of other prestigious awards and fellowships including Ford, Fulbright, and National Endowment for the Humanities fellowships.

Walker's later works and accomplishments include the publication of *Jubilee* (1966) and the formation of the Institute for the Study of History, Life and Culture of Black People at Jackson State College. The center has been renamed in honor of Walker and is known now as the Margaret Walker Alexander National Research Center.

Bibliography

Graham, Maryemma, ed. *Conversations with Margaret Walker.* Jackson: University Press of Mississippi, 2002.

———. *Fields Watered with Blood: Critical Essays on Margaret Walker.* Athens: University of Georgia Press, 2001.

———. *How I Wrote Jubilee and Other Essays on Life and Literature.* New York: Feminist Press at the City University of New York, 1990.

Walker, Margaret. *For My People.* 1942, reprint, Salem, N.H.: Ayer, 1987.

Walls of Jericho, The Rudolph Fisher (1928)

The first novel by RUDOLPH FISHER, a pioneering medical researcher and prolific writer credited with publishing one of the earliest non-serialized African-American detective novels. Critics differ in their opinions about whether the novel presents a sophisticated satire of HARLEM life and the archetypes of 1920s society or whether it mocks the stock figures who explore the African-American community and aspire to support the creative aspirations of its artists.

The firm of ALFRED A. KNOPF published the work and, on the frontispiece of Fisher's volume, noted that it was part of a series entitled "The Negro in Unusual Fiction." That list included *THE AUTOBIOGRAPHY OF AN EX-COLOURED MAN* by JAMES WELDON JOHNSON, *NIGGER HEAVEN* by CARL VAN VECHTEN, *THE FIRE IN THE FLINT* and *FLIGHT* by WALTER WHITE, and *Latterday Symphony* by Romer Wilson.

Fisher's title, *The Walls of Jericho,* evokes the Old Testament reference to the supposedly impenetrable walls around the city of Jericho that come tumbling down when Joshua and his men circle the walls seven times while sounding their musical horns insistently. Fisher included two lines from a spiritual on Joshua on the title page of the book. The novel itself evokes the besieged city of Jericho. It is set in modern-day Harlem, whose days of glory have long passed. The protagonist of the novel is a 20th-century Joshua, a hardworking piano and furniture mover named Joshua Jones who is also known as "Shine." Jones loves Linda Young, a maid employed by Agatha Cramp, a conservative, racist white philanthropist. The two sweethearts experience wholly different aspects and realities of New York City because of their jobs. Linda's employer is a spinster and inadvertently becomes attracted to Fred Merritt, a successful, light-skinned attorney. Not aware that Merritt could be anything other than a white man, Cramp invites him to call upon her after the two meet at the annual ball hosted by the General Improvement Association, an African-American society. The matter becomes even more complicated by the fact that Merritt has just purchased a home in the elite neighborhood in which Agatha Cramp resides.

The plot intensifies as residential and domestic politics embroil the characters increasingly volatile circumstances. Merritt hires Linda as a maid in his home. Much to her sweetheart's dismay, she is almost raped. Merritt's home is set ablaze, and Merritt suspects his white neighbors but finds out that he has been victimized by Henry Patmore, a villainous saloon keeper who has a vendetta against Merritt because the lawyer successfully tried a case against him and forced Patmore to pay restitution to him in the amount of $10,000. Eventually, however, Shine, who has firsthand knowledge of Patmore's boasts about the fire and has had contact with Merritt because he helped to move his household belongings, comes to the aid of the besieged lawyer. Shine also is motivated to act on Merritt's behalf because he learns that it is Patmore, rather than the attorney, who attempted to rape Linda. Fisher's novel ends with a hopeful and strategic message about African-American solidarity and honorable masculinity. Merritt, on the verge of buying out the moving company for which Shine works, offers his defender a major promotion from laborer to manager of the company.

The novel provides one of the most comprehensive portraits of African-American social life in Harlem during the 1920s. Scholar David Levering Lewis suggests that *The Walls of Jericho* sidesteps the "decadence" of Carl Van Vechten's *Nigger Heaven* and the "graceless realism" of Claude McKay's *Home to Harlem* (Lewis, 229). Contemporary reviews, however, veered toward heavy-handed descriptions of the worlds and people whom Fisher represented in the novel. Featured as the leading item in an August 1928 *NEW YORK TIMES* book review, *The Walls of Jericho* prompted one reviewer to dwell at length on images of Harlem as a "negro colony," as an "urban jungle of . . . standardized tenements," and ultimately as "Darkest Harlem." The unidentified reviewer went on to note the value of Fisher's glossary, a tool that in combination with the narrative "provides a considerably informing picture of negro life as it has developed in [Harlem] . . . jungle which hides under the deadly monotony of its outside, lurking places among us for colonies, larger or smaller, of most of the races under the sun" (*NYT*, 5 August 1928, 54).

Fisher's novel also functions as an astute and daring contemporary social and political critique. It included thinly veiled portraits of well-known figures associated with the Harlem Renaissance such as CHARLOTTE OSGOOD MASON, the demanding philanthropist and patron of ZORA NEALE HURSTON, LANGSTON HUGHES, ALAIN LOCKE, and others. David Levering Lewis suggests that the

novel "expose[s] the cleavages within the Afro-American world," a perspective that differs sharply from one contemporary 1928 review that acknowledges that "Dr. Fisher's view of the relations of the races" is "touched with irony which reveals at once a strong prejudice and a certain fairness" but goes on to suggest that he "makes fun of the 'uplifters' of his people and does not conceal his contempt for the whites who profess to be lovers of the race for the pose's sake or for profit" (*NYT*, 5 August 1928, 54). The novel's value lies in its richly textured portrait of Harlem, its considerations of African-American domesticity and solidarity, and its realistic exploration of the racial tensions that can both endanger and empower people of color.

Bibliography

Fisher, Rudolph. *The Walls of Jericho*. 1928; reprint, Ann Arbor: University of Michigan Press, 1994.

Gable, Craig, ed. *Rudolf Fisher Newsletter*. Available online. URL: http://www.fishernews.org. Accessed June, 1, 2005.

Lewis, David Levering. *When Harlem Was in Vogue*. New York: Knopf, 1981.

"*The Walls of Jericho* and Other Works of Fiction." *New York Times*, 5 August 1928, 54.

Walrond, Eric Derwent (1898–1966)

A journalist, writer, and one of several prominent West Indian writers who made significant contributions to the Harlem Renaissance. Born in Georgetown, British Guyana, Walrond moved in 1906 with his mother, Ruth, to her home near Black Rock in Barbados after his parents' marriage foundered. In 1910 he and his mother made an earnest effort to relocate Walrond's father. In the course of their search, the two traveled to the Panama Canal Zone because the majority of laborers recruited to work on the massive construction project were from Guyana and other West Indian countries such as Jamaica. Mother and son eventually settled in Colón, Panama, where Walrond was educated in the public school system and by tutors. He became a civil servant in the health department of the Canal commission. In 1916 he began his career in journalism with the *Panama Star-Herald* and later that year, intrigued by stories he had heard of the United States, immigrated to NEW YORK CITY.

Walrond immigrated to America in 1918 when he was 21 years old. He settled in New York City and began attending classes at the City College of New York. Historian David Levering Lewis notes that Walrond made quite an impression in Harlem, especially on ETHEL NANCE and her two roommates, who shared an apartment in the SUGAR HILL district that was well known as a welcoming place for African-American artists and writers. His "flashing eyes," combined with his "alert and very alive face" and "accented, rippling wit, his urbanity and fearless independence," made him one of the more memorable figures to join the Harlem circle. In 1924 he began a two-year affiliation with COLUMBIA UNIVERSITY, where he enrolled in creative writing courses. Walrond's background in journalism enabled him to become deeply involved in the Brooklyn and Long Island *Informer*. He be-

came co-owner, editor, and reporter for the African-American newspaper that was a contemporary of the established AMSTERDAM NEWS and the BALTIMORE AFRO-AMERICAN. He also joined the editorial staff of NEGRO WORLD, the official newspaper of the UNIVERSAL NEGRO IMPROVEMENT ASSOCIATION that Jamaican activist, writer, and entrepreneur MARCUS GARVEY established. When he left the staff of *Negro World*, Walrond joined the prestigious literary offices of OPPORTUNITY and for two years worked as business manager.

Walrond was married twice. He eventually was divorced from Edith, his first wife and a native of Jamaica. He remarried while in Europe. Walrond was the father of three daughters, Dorothy, Jean, and Lucille.

Walrond published in an array of well-known American literary journals and popular magazines such as OPPORTUNITY, VANITY FAIR, THE NEW REPUBLIC, THE MESSENGER, *Smart Set*, and the *Saturday Review of Literature* in the early 1920s. The first stories that he published in the United States reflect what critic Jay Berry regards as Walrond's "profound disillusionment and disgust with race relations in America" (Berry, 297). Indeed, the first two publications, "ON BEING BLACK" (1922) and "ON BEING A DOMESTIC" (1923), published in THE NEW REPUBLIC and *Opportunity*, respectively, testify to the dehumanization and invisibility of African Americans, many of whom are at the center of American daily life. His essay "The Color of the Caribbean," published in the May 1927 issue of THE WORLD TO-MORROW, confirms the alienating experiences imposed upon people of color and on West Indian immigrants in America. Walrond asserted that "On coming to the United States, the West Indian often finds himself out of patience with the attitude he meets here respecting the position of whites and Negroes. He is bewildered . . . at being shoved down certain blocks and alleys 'among his own people.' He is angry and amazed at the futility of seeking out certain types of employment for which he may be specially adapted. And about the cruelest injury that could be inflicted upon him is to ask him to submit to the notion that because he is black it is useless for him to aspire to be more than . . . a Red Cap in Pennsylvania Station, or a clerk in the Bowling Green Post Office" (Parascandola, 146).

Walrond published eight short stories in the years leading up to the publication of his first and

Eric Walrond *(Yale Collection of American Literature, Beinecke Rare Book and Manuscript Library)*

only collection of short fiction in 1926. Six appeared in *Opportunity,* and in addition to his literary debut in *The New Republic* he published one short story, "MISS KENNY'S MARRIAGE," in the September 1923 issue of *Smart Set.* Walrond also published four works of nonfiction from 1923 through 1925 in the journals *Current History, The Messenger,* and the *Independent.* These demonstrated his study of the African-American political scene, controversial figures such as BOOKER T. WASHINGTON and Marcus Garvey, and major socioeconomic realities such as African-American migration from the South.

TROPIC DEATH, Walrond's first collection of short fiction, appeared in 1926 to much acclaim. The 10 short stories ranged in subjects and included portraits of young immigrant families, Panamanian life, and tragic conflicts that resulted in murder. His work was anthologized in pioneering collections of African-American work. His story "The Palm Porch" was included in ALAIN LOCKE's THE NEW NEGRO (1925) alongside works by COUNTEE CULLEN, W. E. B. DuBois, WALTER WHITE, and ZORA NEALE HURSTON. Additional works appeared in *The American Caravan* (1927), edited by VAN WYCK BROOKS. Walrond's literary output began to wane after the publication of *Tropic Death,* but he had a number of promising projects in the works. In 1927 and 1928 he was awarded three significant fellowships. He won a Harmon Award in Literature, a ZONA GALE scholarship that enabled him to study at the University of Wisconsin, and a GUGGENHEIM FELLOWSHIP. Walrond left the United States in the fall of 1928, ostensibly to begin his Guggenheim research, but he was never to return to America.

When he was awarded a Guggenheim Fellowship in 1928, Walrond was planning to complete a study of the Panama Canal and publish it with the firm of BONI & LIVERIGHT, the company that had published *Tropic Death.* The *New York Times,* which published a brief notice about his $2,500 award, called attention to his "plans to travel in the West Indies gathering material for books" and described him as one who "had considerable success as a free lance writer in New York City" (*NYT,* 29 April 1928). The book for which Walrond hoped to begin research during his Guggenheim year was tentatively entitled *The Big Ditch.* It was the final

project that Walrond was working on when he died in 1966. Walrond spent time in Panama and traveled widely throughout the West Indies as a Guggenheim fellow.

In the summer of 1929 he relocated to Paris and was there until 1932. During his time there, he met up with Countee Cullen, who, like many African Americans, was enjoying the rich culture and less racially charged environment of FRANCE, and the two eventually shared an apartment. Later that year, Zora Neale Hurston entertained the notion of accompanying her friend DOROTHY WEST to Paris. In a letter to LANGSTON HUGHES, Hurston noted that West's rationale was based on the growing list of intriguing writers who had settled in Paris. "She wants me to come to Paris with her," wrote Hurston, "Says Eric and Countee and A[u]gusta Savage are there and so she and I ought to be there" (Kaplan, 158). The year before, however, Hurston had been quick to express to Hughes her disdain for what appeared to be a growing trend among her peers to leave America for Europe. "What, I ask with my feet turned out, are Countee and Eric going aboard to study?" she asked Hughes. "In the words of H—Hannibal, 'O Carthage, I see thy fate! . . . A negro goes to Whiteland to learn his trade! Ha!" (Kaplan, 116).

Walrond eventually moved on from France to England. In London he reconnected with Marcus Garvey, the enigmatic figure with whom he had worked briefly while in the United States. He also resumed his writing, publishing in both American and British journals. Essays and short stories appeared from the 1930s through the 1950s in journals such as *Roundway Review, The Spectator,* the *London Evening Standard, The Crisis, Arena,* and the *People's Voice,* a magazine that Harlem-based minister and politician Adam Clayton Powell, Jr., edited during the 1940s. In 1958 he coedited with Rosey Pool an anthology entitled *Black and Unknown Bards: A Collection of Negro Poetry.* According to Louis Parascandola, editor of the first comprehensive collection of Walrond's writings, Walrond was "driven to excel as a writer." Yet, speculates Parascandola, Walrond's creativity may have been dampened by the oppressive racism that was an entrenched part of the British and American worlds in which he moved. Walrond took seriously the plight and challenges of West Indian and

Latin American immigrants, and his writings reflect his earnest efforts to investigate alternative political philosophies that might prove emancipatory and empowering for peoples of color.

Though he was quite removed from the New York circles in which he used to participate, news of his passing in 1966 circulated among American writers. In a letter to Walrond's dear friend Langston Hughes, ARNA BONTEMPS asked whether or not he had "heard that Eric Walrond died in England a couple of weeks ago." Bontemps went on to note that Walrond, who had suffered some four heart attacks previously, was struck down by a fifth while walking "on a street in London" (Nichols, 474).

Eric Walrond, like the Jamaican-born CLAUDE MCKAY, generated incisive critiques of American society and African-American identity during the Harlem Renaissance. As a West Indian with experiences in England and the United States, Walrond was poised to become a multifaceted commentator on the experiences of people of color, nationalism, and the legacies of colonialism. Walrond's important contributions to the Harlem Renaissance period lie in the diversity of literature that he produced and in the richness of the social realism and political commentary that he generated during his career.

Bibliography

Berry, Jay. "Eric Walrond." *Dictionary of Literary Biography*, Volume 51: 296–300.

Kaplan, Carla. *Zora Neale Hurston: A Life in Letters*. New York: Doubleday, 2002.

"Negro Author's $2,500 Fellowship." *New York Times*, 29 April, 1928, 16.

Nichols, Charles H., ed. *Arna Bontemps-Langston Hughes Letters, 1925–1967*. New York: Paragon House, 1990.

Parascandola, Louis, ed. *Winds Can Wake Up the Dead: An Eric Walrond Reader*. Detroit: Wayne State University Press, 1998.

Walton, Lester A. (1882–1965)

A journalist, drama critic, and leader in the African-American theater community of the Harlem Renaissance, Walton arrived in New York several years before the Harlem Renaissance began. In 1908 he joined the staff of the NEW YORK AGE as drama critic. He became managing editor of the newspaper before he resigned in 1914.

Walton's involvement in theater demonstrated his love of the craft, support for the emerging community, and vision for the future. He was a member of The Frogs, a small group of African-American men dedicated to excellence in theater. Founded in 1908 by George Walker, the group included legendary performers and entertainment veterans such as Bert Williams, Jesse Shipp, James Reese Europe, and J. Rosamond Johnson, brother of JAMES WELDON JOHNSON, the writer, diplomat, and staff member of the NATIONAL ASSOCIATION FOR THE ADVANCEMENT OF COLORED PEOPLE. The group, which became a highly respected club for African-American professionals in diverse fields, worked to develop archival holdings relating to African-American history and to establish a library devoted to the African-American theater tradition.

Walton succeeded in securing the LAFAYETTE THEATRE, the first NEW YORK CITY theater to desegregate its seating. Under his management, the Anita Bush Company affiliated with the Lafayette and became the Lafayette Players Stock Company.

Walton continued to be involved in African-American uplift and was dedicated to the economic advancement of the race. He was a member of the National Negro Business League and continued to participate in efforts to secure civil and equal rights for people of color.

Bibliography

"The Frogs." Schomburg Center for Research in Black Culture. Available online. URL: http://www.si. umich.edu/CHICO/Harlem/text/frogs.html. Downloaded December 2004.

Krasner, David. *A Beautiful Pageant: African American Theatre, Drama, and Performance in the Harlem Renaissance, 1910–1927*. New York: Palgrave Macmillan, 2002.

Washington, Booker Taliaferro (1856–1915)

Washington, who died just as the Harlem Renaissance was beginning, established an institution that impacted the lives of many writers associated with the literary period. The school, which represented

Washington's endorsement of industrial training, was established first to train African-American teachers. Robert Russa Moton succeeded Washington as president and in 1920 Moton published his autobiography, *FINDING A WAY OUT*. Tuskegee Institute students and graduates included CLAUDE BARNETT, RALPH ELLISON, GEORGE HENDERSON, and CLAUDE McKAY. The Institute faculty and administration included HALLIE QUINN BROWN, GEORGE WASHINGTON CARVER, E. FRANKLIN FRAZIER, LESLIE PINCKNEY HILL, and Monroe Work.

SARA DELANEY, a librarian, was on staff at the Tuskegee Veteran's Administration Hospital; novelist NELLA LARSEN served as assistant superintendent of nurses at the school; and Catherine Latimer worked as an assistant librarian before becoming the first African-American woman librarian hired by the NEW YORK PUBLIC LIBRARY. Journalist T. THOMAS FORTUNE was the legendary ghostwriter for many of Washington's own works.

Bibliography

Harlan, Louis. *Booker T. Washington: The Wizard of Tuskegee, 1901–1915*. New York: Oxford University Press, 1983.

Smock, Raymond, ed. *Booker T. Washington in Perspective: Essays of Louis R. Harlan*. Jackson: University Press of Mississippi, 1988.

Washington, D.C.

The capital of the United States and the city in which a vibrant literary and arts community flourished during the Harlem Renaissance period. The city was home to impressive African-American educational institutions such as the prestigious M STREET HIGH SCHOOL, later renamed DUNBAR HIGH SCHOOL, and HOWARD UNIVERSITY. Graduates of the M Street-Dunbar High School, included WILLIS RICHARDSON and LEWIS ALEXANDER. The faculty included playwright MARY BURRILL, philosopher and feminist ANNA JULIA COOPER, and JESSIE FAUSET. Howard University students and graduates included ZORA NEALE HURSTON, MAY MILLER, LEWIS ALEXANDER, and WARING CUNEY. Writer MARITA BONNER taught at the Armstrong Colored High School, a pioneering facility that was the first African-American manual training school established in the capital.

Washington, D.C., enjoyed its own literary and arts renaissance during the 1920s and 1930s. It supported innovation in theater and saw the development of a vibrant drama tradition. The HOWARD UNIVERSITY PLAYERS, founded in 1919 and also known as the HOWARD PLAYERS, was one of the nation's premier college drama troupes and presented the work of emerging and established white and African-American writers. Its chief director, T. MONTGOMERY GREGORY, was on the faculty at Howard and collaborated frequently with ALAIN LOCKE, a faculty colleague. ANGELINA WELD GRIMKÉ saw her antilynching play *RACHEL* staged in Washington, D.C., in 1916.

The city's most celebrated residents included GEORGIA DOUGLAS JOHNSON, who hosted regular literary salons in her home and was responsible for mentoring and supporting numerous writers and artists of color. EDWARD CHRISTOPHER WILLIAMS, a playwright, translator, and poet, and husband to CHARLES CHESNUTT's daughter Ethel, was a dynamic Washington, D.C., resident. The former headmaster of the Dunbar High School, he became the head librarian at Howard while teaching as a professor of German and Romance languages. CARRIE CLIFFORD, an editor, poet, and active member of the NATIONAL ASSOCIATION FOR THE ADVANCEMENT OF COLORED PEOPLE, also was known for the dynamic salons that she hosted in her Washington, D.C., home.

Eminent historian CARTER G. WOODSON, founder of the ASSOCIATION FOR THE STUDY OF NEGRO LIFE AND HISTORY and editor of the Associated Press, was one of the city's most respected citizens. The offices of the *JOURNAL OF NEGRO HISTORY*, which Woodson edited and where poet LANGSTON HUGHES worked for a time as Woodson's assistant, were located in Washington, D.C.

Bibliography

Dyson, Walter. *Howard University: The Capstone of Negro Education, a History: 1867–1940*. Washington, D.C.: Howard University Press, 1940.

Logan, Rayford, W. *Howard University: The First Hundred Years, 1867–1967*. New York: New York University Press, 1969.

Moore, Jacqueline. *Leading the Race: The Transformation of the Black Elite in the Nation's Capital, 1880–1920*. Charlottesville: University Press of Virginia, 1999.

Shannon, Alexander. *The Negro in Washington: A Study in Race Amalgamation.* New York: W. Neale, 1930.

Ways of White Folks, The Langston Hughes (1934)

A collection of 12 startling short stories by poet and political activist LANGSTON HUGHES. The title is reminiscent of THE SOULS OF BLACK FOLK, the seminal work by W. E. B. DuBois, and Hughes scholars suggest that the author was inspired by that work when he devised the title. It was translated into several foreign languages. Hughes donated a copy of the French version, entitled *Histories de Blancs,* to the FISK UNIVERSITY Library when his close friend ARNA BONTEMPS was head librarian there.

Hughes completed the manuscript while living in the Carmel, California, beach home of Noel Sullivan, a wealthy, outgoing gay man who had transformed a former family property that had belonged to Robert Louis Stevenson and then become a home for Carmelite nuns into a writers' sanctuary and gathering place. Hughes dedicated the volume to Sullivan, who became a close friend and generous supporter. In the letter to Sullivan that accompanied a draft copy of the manuscript, Hughes told his friend that he had "helped . . . with them . . . listened to many of them before they were ever written . . . read them all, given me the music, and the shelter of your roof, and the truth of your friendship, and the time to work" (Berry, 201). CARL VAN VECHTEN, who received the manuscript from Blanche Knopf, "tackle[d] it with a great deal of hope" in December 1933. In one of his many letters to Hughes, he told "Dear old Langston" with much gusto that "all my hopes were realized." He advised Hughes to include two works that Hughes was completing and then celebrated his friend's accomplishments with the triumphant last line, "Laurel wreaths to you, brown Genius!" (Bernard, 115).

Published by the New York–based company Knopf in 1934, the volume included "Cora Unashamed," "A Good Job Gone," "Berry," "Passing," "Father and Son," and "Red-Headed Baby," stories that explore the shocking racial and social dynamics of the times. Hughes grapples with the pain of rejection, hypocrisy, and intolerance. He also considers, to great effect, the underlying threat of violence that seems to plague interracial relationships. In "Red-Headed Baby," a white sailor named Clarence returns to find that Betsy, his African-American lover, has borne their child. Clarence, a man already beset by his world, can barely grapple with the fact that his son not only possesses red hair but also is deaf and dumb. The gripping tale in "Father and Son" spirals out of control as the mixed-race and illegitimate son of a white plantation owner and his African-American housekeeper returns home and refuses to be compromised by the oppressive racial codes of the South. The family is completely devastated through madness, suicide, and LYNCHING and ends with a stunning message about the kind of self-denial required in order to survive in America.

Hughes continued his explication of unyielding and unsatisfying American domesticity in "Cora Unashamed." The story revolves around Cora Jenkins, a 40-year-old woman who works as a domestic in the emotionally repressive household of the white Studevants family. Cora is a "maid of all work—washing, ironing, cooking, scrubbing, taking care of kids, nursing old folks, making fire, carrying water." Despite the fact that the family holds her in bondage, Cora also becomes an indispensable source of love for Jessie, the Studevantses' only child. The outraged, omniscient narrator of the piece suggests that Cora's lack of autonomy is due to "the teeth in the trap of economic circumstance that kept her in [the Studevantses'] power practically all her life." Cora's own home life is desperate; her mother has eight children, and her father is a "closet-cleaning, ash-hauling and junk-dealing" man, one whose wages tend to go toward "the stuff that makes you forget you have eight kids." Cora weathers the painful loss of Josephine, the child borne of her only love affair, an encounter with a young white man named Joe, who came to Melton, "was some kind of foreigner . . . [h]ad an accent, and yellow hair, big hands, and grey eyes." Eventually she becomes an ally for Jessie, who falls in love with a young immigrant boy of whom her parents do not entirely approve. When Jessie becomes pregnant, is forced by her mother to have an abortion, and then dies as a result of the procedure, Cora finally speaks out against the oppressive hypocrisy that she has both witnessed and endured in the household. The story was adapted for television and premiered on PBS in

2000. It starred Regina Taylor in the role of Cora Jenkins and Cherry Jones as Mrs. Studevants.

Hughes scholar Faith Berry proposes that "every story in the book was biting, trenchant, and critical of the prevailing attitudes of whites toward African Americans at the time" [Berry, 201]. Contemporary reviews of the work also noticed Hughes's dramatic departure from "the singing, vibrant rhythm" that so defined his poetry and commented on the "suppressed, almost weary, quality of bitterness" found in the story "One Christmas Eve" and that permeated the rest of the volume. Reviewer John Chambers suggested that Hughes was well equipped to write "stories of life at the edge of the colored line." "[H]e knows the conditions of Negro existence in a callous white world," Chambers asserted, and is "able to discount disappointment before it hits him. The tragedies of his stories are undeniably real. But they sound, in the telling, like an old man recalling the troubles and defeats of his youth. An old man recalling tragedy does so with an air of 'Well, it was fated so to happen.' Mr. Hughes's stories have this air of finality about them" (Chambers, 21).

The Ways of White Folks is a definitive and haunting meditation on American society, and it confirmed Hughes's status as one of America's most insightful writers and eloquent social critics.

Bibliography

Bernard, Emily. *Remember Me to Harlem: The Letters of Langston Hughes and Carl Van Vechten.* New York: Knopf, 2001.

Berry, Faith, ed. *Langston Hughes: Before and Beyond Harlem.* Westport, Conn.: Lawrence Hill & Company, 1983.

Chambers, John. "Books of the Times." *New York Times,* 28 June 1934, 21.

Nichols, Charles H., ed. *Arna Bontemps–Langston Hughes Letters, 1925–1967.* New York: Paragon House, 1990.

Rampersad, Arnold. *The Life of Langston Hughes: I, Too, Sing America.* Vol. 1, *1902–1941.* New York: Oxford University Press, 1986.

Weary Blues, The Langston Hughes (1926)

The first published work of poet LANGSTON HUGHES. Hughes dedicated to his mother the volume that he completed with much encouragement and advice from CARL VAN VECHTEN. The prestigious New York company ALFRED A. KNOPF published the book in 1926. The magazine VANITY FAIR, impressed by the work, bought prepublication rights to several of the poems and published them in the magazine. Miguel Covarrubias, a Mexican artist who became a major contributor to the Harlem Renaissance art tradition, designed the dust jacket of the book. Van Vechten, who had submitted the manuscript to Knopf on Hughes's behalf, wrote the introduction to the volume.

The poems are divided into seven sections, and most include a poem that incorporates the section title. These sections include "The Weary Blues," "Dream Variations," "The Negro Speaks of Rivers," "A Black Pierrot," "Water Front Streets," "Shadows in the Sun," and "Our Land." "Proem," an independent piece that underscored the pan-Africanist perspectives that endowed many Hughes poems with such power, was the first poem in the volume and preceded the rest of the works that were organized into specific groups. In "Proem" the speaker notes all of the different roles that he plays in the world. These include being a Negro, slave, worker, singer, and victim. "I am a Negro," the speaker declares in the opening stanza, "Black as the night is black, / Black like the depths of my Africa." He goes on to bridge time and space, linking the great accomplishments of unacknowledged Africans to those of disregarded but indispensable African Americans: "I've been a worker: / Under my hand the pyramids arose. / I made mortar for the Woolworth Building." Hughes also incorporates an explicit political commentary that is capable of galvanizing readers to protest the global persecution of peoples of color. In one of the poem's most moving stanzas, he writes "I've been a victim: / The Belgians cut off my hands in the Congo. / They lynch me now in Texas."

The refrain in the title poem, "The Weary Blues," originates from "a black man's soul" and reveals a lasting hunger for a life that apparently is out of reach. "I got the Weary Blues / And I can't be satisfied. / Got the Weary Blues / And can't be satisfied—/ I ain't happy no mo' / And I wish that I had died." Additional poems in the opening section such as "Negro Dancers," "The Cat and the Saxophone," "To Midnight Nan at Leroy's," and "Harlem Night Club" maintain the focus on music, performance, longing, and desire. Other poems present a more studied and quietly intimate vision of Harlem and the women who survive there. In "Nude Young Dancer," Hughes wonders, "What jungle tree have you slept under, / Night-dark girl of the swaying hips? What star-white moon has been your mother? / To what clean boy have you offered your lips?" In "Young Prostitute," the speaker shares a more matter-of-fact and depressing conclusion about the woman he sees. "Her dark brown face / Is like a withered flower / On a broken stem," he notes. Yet, the last two lines of the short poem offer a challenge or potential acceptance of that image of depressed womanhood: "Those kind come cheap in Harlem / So they say."

Additional sections reflect Hughes's penchant for observation. The poems in "Shadows in the Sun" include "Beggar Boy," a work in which a speaker wonders "[w]hat is there within this beggar lad / That I can neither hear nor feel nor see, / That I can neither know nor understand / And still it calls to me?" The lone figure in "Troubled Woman" seems untouched by the speaker's gaze. She "stands / In the quiet darkness . . . / Bowed by / Weariness and pain, / Like an / Autumn flower / In the frozen rain. / Like a / Wind-blown autumn flower / That never lifts it head / Again."

"Our Land," the very last section of the volume, includes some of Hughes's most often anthologized works, including the poignant "Mother to Son." The penultimate work is "Epilogue," the inspired manifesto that challenges American racism and disregard for its citizens of color. "I, too, sing America," declares the resolute speaker, the "darker brother" who is banished "to eat in the kitchen / When company comes." The poem ends with the speaker's rejection of the flawed "logic" of segregation. "They'll see how beautiful I am / And be ashamed,—" he predicts, "I too, am America."

In 1926, Hughes met his friend WARING CUNEY for the first time, and their contact was facilitated by the publication of *The Weary Blues*. As Hughes would recall later in his autobiography *THE BIG SEA* (1940), he met Cuney on a "street car in Washington. . . . He had a *CHICAGO DEFENDER*, oldest American Negro paper, in his hand, and my picture was in the *Defender* with the announcement of the forthcoming publication of *The Weary*

Blues. Cuney looked from the picture to me, then asked if I were one and the same. I said yes. Then he said he wrote poetry, too. I said I'd like to see it, so later he brought some of his poems to show me" (173–174).

Blanche Knopf, a central figure at the publishing house with which Hughes would have a long and productive relationship, assured him that the book contained "delightful verse" and that "we want to publish it" (Rampersad, 1109). The volume is especially powerful for its colorful and studied portraits of HARLEM and its delicately phrased perspectives on the multifaceted and contemplative residents of that diverse community.

Bibliography

Hughes, Langston. *The Big Sea: An Autobiography.* 1940; reprint, edited by Joseph McLaren. Columbia: University of Missouri Press, 2002.

———. *The Weary Blues.* New York: Knopf, 1926.

Berry, Faith, ed. *Langston Hughes: Before and Beyond Harlem.* Westport, Conn.: Lawrence Hill & Company, 1983.

Rampersad, Arnold. *The Life of Langston Hughes: I, Too, Sing America.* Vol. 1, *1902–1941.* New York: Oxford University Press, 1986.

"Wedding Day" Gwendolyn Bennett (1926)

The short story that GWENDOLYN BENNETT contributed to *FIRE!!,* the short-lived avant-garde literary magazine. The protagonist, Paul Watson, is a talented musician, former prizefighter, and American expatriate living in Paris. Watson, known well to musicians and residents in the Montmartre district of Paris, despises white Americans. He does not hesitate to lash out violently at individuals who use racial epithets in their conversations with or about him. Eventually, Watson is imprisoned for shooting two white American sailors who disrespect him. He is released in time to join the French army during World War I. Eventually, Watson succumbs to the tears and plaintive request for attention from a white woman named Mary. Despite his hatred of white Americans, he falls in love with her, and the two decide to marry. On the morning of his wedding day, Paul gets a terse note from Mary in which she confesses that her race and low class status prevent her from marrying him. The story closes as Watson, disoriented by his betrayal and his own willingness to marry into the race he despises, boards a French train without a clear sense of his own destination.

"Wedding Day," Bennett's only published work of fiction, reflected her efforts to assess the damage of racism, the various manifestations of race pride, and the survival strategies that Americans of color used to preserve their sense of purpose and possibility.

Weeden, Lula Lowe (1918–   )

A teacher, poet, and literary phenomenon who was only nine years old when six of her poems were selected for inclusion in CAROLING DUSK: AN ANTHOLOGY OF NEGRO VERSE, the prestigious volume edited by COUNTEE CULLEN. A native of Lynchburg, Virginia, she was the daughter of Lula and Henry Weeden, a dentist. The family lived adjacent to ANNE SPENCER, a gifted poet, active member of the WASHINGTON, D.C., literary community, and avid horticulturist. Spencer mentored the young girl and was one of her most attentive teachers.

In his introduction to *Caroling Dusk,* Cullen savored the valuable perspectives that Weeden brought to the collection. As the "youngest poet in the volume . . . [she] is too young to realize that she is colored in an environment calculated to impress her daily with the knowledge of this pigmentary anomaly." Despite her gift for writing and demonstrated promise, Weeden ceased writing during her teenage years.

We Lift Our Voices and Other Poems
Mae Cowdery (1936)

The only volume of poetry that MAE COWDERY published during the Harlem Renaissance. The volume included an introduction by critic WILLIAM STANLEY BRAITHWAITE.

Cowdery, who showed great promise as a poet, published in leading journals of the day including THE CRISIS and OPPORTUNITY. Her work also was included in special magazine issues and anthologies devoted to African-American writing. *We Lift Our Voices* included a range of Cowdery's work and demonstrated her straightforward writing style, in-

terest in nature, and efforts to praise and celebrate individuals with whom she was familiar.

Wells-Barnett, Ida B. (1862–1931)

An intrepid journalist, eloquent social critic, feminist, and tireless antilynching activist. Wells overcame great family tragedy to become the most influential advocate in the United States against LYNCHING.

A native of Holly Springs, Mississippi, she was born into slavery in July 1862. Wells-Barnett was the first of eight children of James and Elizabeth Wells, whose mixed-race ancestries included white, Native American, and African heritage. In 1878 a devastating yellow fever epidemic claimed the lives of both parents and one of the Wells children. Although she was only 16 years old at the time, Wells-Barnett insisted on keeping the family together and worked to provide for them all.

Before becoming a journalist, Wells-Barnett was a teacher. She obtained her own schooling at Rust College, the institution formerly known as SHAW UNIVERSITY. It was adversity and racism that propelled Wells-Barnett to begin her lifelong crusade against injustice. One of the most well-known incidents involved her refusal to surrender her first-class ticket and ride in the smoker car of a Chesapeake and Ohio train. She won a settlement of $500 but was denied her rightful claim when the Tennessee Supreme Court overruled the decision.

The savage lynching of three close friends in 1892 galvanized Wells-Barnett into action. She was determined to protest vigorously the deaths of Thomas Moss, Calvin McDowell, and William Stewart by a mob in Memphis. In the pages of the *Free Speech,* the outspoken newspaper where she worked as editor and partner, Wells made pointed critiques of white mob violence and the myths in which lynchers invested in order to justify their lawlessness. Her articles prompted some whites to destroy the *Free Speech* offices and to threaten Wells-Barnett with bodily harm if she ever returned to the city.

Wells-Barnett was an impressive lecturer, and her presentations to American and to European audiences did much to raise awareness about American racial violence and injustice. In 1913, she established the Alpha Suffrage Club in

Chicago, the first African-American suffrage organization. She was an impassioned clubwoman and with colleagues such as MARY CHURCH TERRELL helped to advance the practical and ambitious goals of the African-American women's club movement. In 1924 she ran for president of the National Association of Colored Women but lost to MARY MCLEOD BETHUNE.

Wells-Barnett played a significant role in the formation of the NATIONAL ASSOCIATION FOR THE ADVANCEMENT OF COLORED PEOPLE (NAACP). She was a member of the organization's executive committee and advocated that there be an official publication to reflect and communicate the organization's agenda. She also was involved in the founding of the NATIONAL URBAN LEAGUE and was one of the only two women who signed the documents calling for the formation of the NAACP. In 1930 she became one of the first African-American women to run for public office when she campaigned for an Illinois state senate seat.

Wells-Barnett died in 1931 as a result of uremic poisoning. The leadership, commitment to African-American suffrage, advancement, and success that embodied her life were at the heart of what many in the Harlem Renaissance movement hoped to realize.

Bibliography

The Ida B. Wells-Barnett Papers are held at the University of Chicago Library, Special Collections Research Center, Chicago, Illinois.

Duster, Alfreda. *Crusade for Justice: The Autobiography of Ida B. Bells.* Chicago: University of Chicago Press, 1972.

Schecter, Patricia. *Ida B. Wells-Barnett and American Reform, 1880–1930.* Chapel Hill: University of North Carolina Press, 2001.

McMurry, Linda. *To Keep the Waters Troubled: The Life of Ida B. Wells.* New York: Oxford University Press, 1998.

West, Dorothy (1907–1998)

A writer, editor, actress, and journalist who, at the time of her death, was the last surviving member of the Harlem Renaissance. West, who enjoyed her status as the youngest of the Harlem Renaissance artists and writers among whom she circulated, was one of the most enthusiastic and enterprising writers of the period. Her reminiscences of the literary figures, many of whom she counted as friends, have provided invaluable insights on the period.

Born in BOSTON, she was the only child of Isaac and Rachel Pease Benson West. Her father was an enterprising businessman who had enjoyed financial success in Springfield, Massachusetts, before establishing himself in a wholesale fruit business located directly across from the historic Faneuil Hall. West was a gifted student and benefited from her early tutoring. Her teachers included Bessie Trotter, sister of the brilliant *Boston Guardian* editor WILLIAM MONROE TROTTER. West graduated from the Girls' Latin High School in 1923 and went on to attend BOSTON UNIVERSITY. She later pursued courses at the Columbia School of Journalism.

West was part of a close extended family that included her cousin and fellow aspiring writer HELENE JOHNSON. The two relocated to NEW YORK CITY together in 1926 and took rooms at the YOUNG WOMEN'S CHRISTIAN ASSOCIATION branch in HARLEM. They later became house sitters for ZORA NEALE HURSTON and shared an apartment in the heart of Harlem. West participated fully in the dynamic social networks that fueled the literary movement. She had the opportunity to work and to socialize with PAUL ROBESON, and of her memorable 1929 visit to his luxurious London home, she recalled, "They had five white servants . . . The Robesons were 'gentility' as much as the whites these servants had worked for in the past and we [the African-American guests] were not. It was almost funny" (Boyle and Buni, 208). She enjoyed a close relationship with Zora Neale Hurston and was clearly inspired by her friend's ebullience, autonomy, and determination. Hurston's letters to West reveal her confidence in West's potential. Writing to West in the fall of 1928, Hurston assured her friend that she was "near my heart and always will be. I trust you and Helene more than anyone else in this world," she wrote before declaring, "You are the fine gold in New York's show and shine" (Kaplan, 130).

Like a number of Harlem Renaissance figures, West had a variety of creative interests. She developed her love of drama and pursued it with great success. In 1927 she was cast in the original performance of DuBose Heyward's *Porgy* and was part of the cast that traveled to England for a three-month tour. West later joined some 20 African Americans for an eventful but not entirely successful venture to Russia to participate in *Black and White,* a film based on African-American experiences in the United States. The participants included Henry Lee Moon, Louise Thompson, Theodore Poston, Langston Hughes, and a number of students, social workers, and individuals drawn from a variety of other professions. Though the film production was jeopardized and ultimately halted by protests from white Americans with business interests in Russia, West seized the opportunity to stay on in the country when the majority of the other participants returned to the United States. News of her father's death, however, prompted her to abandon her new ventures, which included working with Russian filmmakers, and to return home.

West's literary career began with the selection of "The Typewriter" as a prizewinning short story in the 1926 literary contest sponsored by *Opportunity.* She had published her first short fiction in Boston newspapers and continued to write regularly for *Opportunity.* She also was part of the serious literary society known as the Saturday Evening Quill Club. She had published in the society's short-lived but important publication, the *Saturday Evening Quill.* In New York, West contributed work to *Opportunity* and sought out additional venues for her literary interests such as the *New York Daily News.* She was one of several writers whom Walter White mentored.

She founded the literary magazine Challenge in 1934. The quarterly magazine represented West's efforts to provide a professional forum for African-American writers. It was printed in Boston by the *Boston Chronicle.* Annual subscriptions were $15, and single copies were priced at 15 cents each. Founded with $40 and a lot of will, the magazine debuted in March 1934. Its four sections, "Stories," "Special Articles," "Heard Songs," and "Departments," featured contributions by a number of recognizable Harlem Renaissance artists such as Arna Bontemps, Countee Cullen, Langston Hughes, Helene Johnson, Pauli Murray, Lucia Mae

Novelist, editor, and essayist, Dorothy West. Photographed by Carl Van Vechten, 1948 *(Yale Collection of American Literature, Beinecke Rare Book and Manuscript Library)*

Pitts, and Zora Neale Hurston. Hurston heartily supported West's venture and responded positively to West's request for submissions. "Yes, to all questions," Hurston declared in a March 1934 letter to her friend. "I'm too delighted at your nerve in running a magazine not to help all I can," she announced. "I *love* your audacity," she continued. "You have learned at last the glorious lesson of living dangerously" (Kaplan, 296). Later issues included book reviews, editorials, and letters, as well as profiles of the contributors to each issue.

West reorganized the magazine three years later as New Challenge. The masthead revealed that she and Marian Minus were the editors and that Richard Wright, her main collaborator, was the associate editor. Another noticeable shift that signaled the new directions of the journal was the extensive list of contributing editors. Included in the list of nine names were STERLING BROWN, Robert Hayden, Langston Hughes, and MARGARET WALKER. Advertised as a "Literary Quarterly," the magazine was now based in New York City. Subscriptions dropped to $1 for the year, and individual copies were available for 25 cents. Wright published his well-known "Blueprint for Negro Writing" in the first issue. Ultimately, she abandoned the project because she resisted its increasing politicization by colleague and associate editor Richard Wright. While the loss of the magazine may have been devastating, West may have been buoyed by the spirited words of her friend Hurston who, when West revealed her plans, told her, "Let the sun go down on you like King Harold at the battle of Hastings—fighting gloriously. Maybe a loser, but what a loser! Greater in defeat than the Conqueror. Certainly not a coward that rusted out lurking in his tent" (Kaplan, 296).

Like many other Harlem Renaissance writers, she sought employment unrelated to her writing that would sustain her. Before becoming part of the extensive Works Progress Administration's Federal Writers' Project, she worked for a year and a half as a welfare investigator in New York City. Her experiences influenced her writing, and her sobering story "MAMMY" was based on her encounters during that time. She also continued to write during this period, publishing a number of stories in the *New York Daily News*. Her association with the Federal Writers' Project ended in the mid-1940s, and West relocated to Martha's Vineyard in 1947. It was while living there that she published *The Living Is Easy*, her first novel. The thinly veiled autobiographical novel appeared in 1948, almost 10 years after the close of the Harlem Renaissance.

West cherished her time on Martha's Vineyard. "The island is my yearning," she confessed in a *Vineyard Gazette* article. "All my life, wherever I have been, abroad, New York, Boston, anywhere, whenever I yearned for home, I yearned for the island" (Beech, 16). Her family had been one of the few African-American families to vacation and then own property on the island. Despite the small numbers of people of color, however, West revealed that her family regarded it as "an agreeable number. There was enough of us to put down roots, to stake our claim to a summer place, so that the chil-

dren who came after us would take for granted a style of living that we were learning in stages" (Allen, 23).

On the island off the coast of Massachusetts, she became a regular contributor to the *Vineyard Gazette*, the local paper. She also initiated a regular column entitled the "Cottagers Corner," which was named in honor of the philanthropic group organized by the few African-American women who owned cottages on the island. The group of about 12 women included West and Helen Brooke, mother of Senator Edward Brooke, the first African American elected to the U.S. Senate since Reconstruction. The column, which is somewhat evocative of GWENDOLYN BENNETT's "EBONY FLUTE" and Countee Cullen's "Dark Tower," was devoted exclusively to issues relating to the African Americans with links to Martha's Vineyard.

West's later publications included a memoir of WALLACE THURMAN. She published her much anticipated second novel, *The Wedding*, in 1995 with support from editor and fellow islander Jackie Kennedy Onassis. The book inspired a television production financed by Oprah Winfrey and starring Halle Berry and Carl Lumbly.

West was unmarried all her life. She proposed marriage in 1933 to her close friend Langston Hughes, whose nickname for her was "The Kid," but he declined. Countee Cullen proposed marriage to her, but she turned him down. In a 1995 interview, West declared that "[a]s a child, I decided I never wanted to be the last leaf on the tree . . . and now here I am, the last leaf" (Cardwell, SM47). Two years later, First Lady Hillary Clinton, in attendance at the memorable 90th birthday celebration for West, declared the intrepid writer a "national treasure" (Yarrow, A29). West did not hesitate to talk with the many people who sought her out on the island. She regarded conversation with visitors as a serious responsibility. "I know that I will not live forever so therefore I have to pass on my knowledge. It is a duty that I owe," she mused in a 1995 interview (Beech, 16). She was feted during the last years of her life. On the occasion of her 90th birthday, luminaries and distinguished guests gathered at the Union Chapel on the island to honor West. Among those in attendance were Hillary Clinton, Jessye Norman, Anita Hill, and Charles Ogletree. Hundreds more gathered outside the chapel to celebrate the dynamic and outgoing authoress.

West died in August 1998. Scholar Henry Louis Gates remembered her as one who "[t]o her death . . . maintained that the only truthful way to write about black Americans was as a diversity of colors, of classes, and of sensibilities—united only by a common history and, at times, a common enemy. As a twentieth-century writer, she knew that depicting the lives of colored people with unsparing intimacy, and without ideology or argument, might just be the most revolutionary thing she could do" (*The Journal of Blacks in Higher Education*, 31 October 1998, 109). West's passing signaled for some the end of the Harlem Renaissance, but the ways in which the period remained so vibrant in her mind also reminded many that the period remains an incredibly rich and evocative period in American literary history.

Bibliography

Allen, Joan H. "Harlem Renaissance writer Dorothy West celebrates her 90th birthday." *New York Amsterdam News*, 11 September 1997, 23.

Beech, Wendy. "Dorothy West: A Lone Voice Survives." *Philadelphia Tribune*, 24 November 1995, 16.

Boyle, Sheila Tully, and Andrew Buni. *Paul Robeson: The Years of Promise and Achievement*. Amherst: University of Massachusetts Press, 2001.

Cardwell, Diane. "Last Leaf on the Tree." *New York Times*, 3 January 1999, SM 47.

Dorothy West Papers, Mugar Memorial Library, Boston University; James Weldon Johnson Memorial Collection, Yale University.

Jones, Sharon. *Rereading the Harlem Renaissance: Race, Class, and Gender in the Fiction of Jessie Fauset, Zora Neale Hurston, and Dorothy West*. Westport, Conn.: Greenwood Press, 2002.

Kaplan, Carla. *Zora Neale Hurston: A Life in Letters*. New York: Doubleday, 2002.

Saunders, James Robert, and Renae Shackelford. *The Dorothy West Martha's Vineyard: Stories, Essays, and Reminiscences by Dorothy West Writing in the Vineyard Gazette*. Jefferson, N.C.: McFarland, 2001.

West, Dorothy. *The Living Is Easy*. 1948, reprint, London: Virago, 1987.

———. *The Richer, the Poorer: Stories, Sketches, and Reminiscences*. New York: Doubleday, 1995.

———. *The Wedding*. New York: Doubleday, 1995.

Yarrow, Andrew. "Dorothy West, a Harlem Renaissance Writer, Dies at 91." *New York Times*, 19 August 1998, A29.

Wetmore, Judson Douglass (unknown)

A close friend of writer JAMES WELDON JOHNSON whose experiences as a light-skinned African American who could pass informed the *AUTOBIOGRAPHY OF AN EX-COLOURED MAN*, Johnson's pioneering 1912 novel. Wetmore, who met Johnson in ATLANTA, attended the University of Michigan Law School as a white man.

Wexley, John (1907–1985)

A white playwright and screenwriter who was inspired to create a political play based on the plight and trial of the Scottsboro Boys, nine young men falsely accused and imprisoned on charges of rape. Wexley's play, *They Shall Not Die*, opened on BROADWAY in February 1934. It was his third Broadway play and was preceded by *The Last Mile* (1930) and *Steel* (1931).

Whipping, The Eulalie Spence (1933)

A three-act play by EULALIE SPENCE that she adapted from the novel of the same name by Ray Flanagan. The play, which was never published, was scheduled to open in Connecticut, but that did not occur. The play, the only work that Spence claimed to have made money from, was later optioned by Paramount Pictures. Unfortunately, the company never produced the film version of the work.

Bibliography

Roses, Lorraine Elena, and Ruth Elizabeth Randolph. *Harlem Renaissance and Beyond: Literary Biographies of 100 Black Women Writers, 1900–1945*. Boston: G. K. Hall & Co., 1990.

White, Newman Ivey (1892–1948)

One of the two editors who produced the 1924 collection entitled *AN ANTHOLOGY OF VERSE BY AMERICAN NEGROES*. At the time, White was an English professor and chairman of the department at Trinity College, now Duke University. He collaborated with Walter Clinton Jackson, a professor at the North Carolina College for Women.

Bibliography

White, Newman Ivey, and Walter Clinton Jackson. *An Anthology of Verse by American Negroes, edited with a critical introduction, biographical sketches of the authors, and bibliographical notes by Newman Ivey White and Walter Clinton Jackson, with an introduction by James Hardy Dillard.* 1924, reprint, Durham, N.C.: Moore Pub Co., 1968.

White, Walter Francis (1893–1955)

A central figure in the fight for civil rights, an antilynching crusader, writer, and officer in the NA-TIONAL ASSOCIATION FOR THE ADVANCEMENT OF COLORED PEOPLE (NAACP). Born on July 1, 1893, in Atlanta, he was the fourth child of seven born to Madeline Harrison White and George White. White's parents were of mixed-race and were extremely light-skinned. White, a blue-eyed, blond Negro, would later use his appearance to infiltrate white society and to expose the violence and truths of LYNCHING. White attended high school at ATLANTA UNIVERSITY, which offered a curriculum to students for whom the state provided no high school classes, and then entered the college. He graduated in 1916. Following graduation, he became an insurance salesman with the Standard Life Insurance Company of Harry Pace, founder of PACE PHONOGRAPH COMPANY and Black Swan Records.

In 1922 he married Leah Powell, a fellow NAACP staff member. The couple, who had two children, Jane and Walter Carl Darrow, lived at 409 Edgecombe Avenue, one of HARLEM's most desirable locations. White married Poppy Cannon, a white woman, in 1949, following his divorce from Powell.

White's foray into public political life came through his involvement with the NAACP. He was one of the most outspoken members of the organization, which he joined as a member of the administration in 1918. White, who worked closely with JAMES WELDON JOHNSON, became one of the NAACP's primary investigators of lynching. His reports enabled the organization to publish damn-ing statistics about the prevalence and rationales of lynch mobs and to craft antilynching legislation proposals. In 1929 he published ROPE AND FAG-GOT, an extended study of lynching and race violence. He succeeded James Weldon Johnson, his mentor and friend, as executive secretary of the NAACP in 1930.

White combined his extensive political work with his literary interests. In 1924 he published FIRE IN THE FLINT, for which he completed the draft in less than two weeks. Publisher JOHN FAR-RAR read the manuscript with great interest, but his publishing firm, George Doran and Company, rejected the book, in part because the author would not soften his unflattering portraits of whites. The novel, is a gripping and ruthless account of lynching and false accusations. His second novel, FLIGHT, considers the pain and politics of racial passing. White completed work on this

Walter White. Photographed by Carl Van Vechten, 1938. Permission granted by the Van Vechten Trust *(Yale Collection of American Literature, Beinecke Rare Book and Manuscript Library)*

book while abroad in France on a GUGGENHEIM FELLOWSHIP. White was solicited to contribute works to major Harlem Renaissance–era collections, including ALAIN LOCKE's 1925 *NEW NEGRO* anthology. He was a well-known figure in literary circles and was especially supportive of COUNTEE CULLEN and CLAUDE MCKAY. He also opened his home to "hungry literati," notes scholar Cary Wintz, and helped to facilitate CARL VAN VECHTEN's interactions with African-American writers of the day. White continued to write in the years following the Harlem Renaissance. His autobiography, *A Man Called White*, appeared in 1948.

Funeral services for Walter White, who died in March 1955, were held at Saint Martin's Episcopal Church in Harlem.

Bibliography

Cannon, Poppy. *A Gentle Knight: My Husband, Walter White*. New York: Rinehart, 1956.

Janken, Kenneth. *White: The Biography of Walter White, Mr. NAACP*. New York: New Press, 2003.

Waldron, Edward. *Walter White and the Harlem Renaissance*. Port Washington, N.Y.: Kennikat Press, 1978.

White, Walter. *A Man Called White*. New York: Viking, 1948.

Wilson, Sondra, ed. *In Search of Democracy: The NAACP Writings of James Weldon Johnson, Walter White, and Roy Wilkins (1920–1977)*. New York: Oxford University Press, 1999.

"Who Gives Himself" Eunice Hunton Carter (1924)

One of two short stories that EUNICE HUNTON CARTER published in *OPPORTUNITY* during 1924. "Who Gives Himself" appeared alongside "DRENCHED IN LIGHT" (1924) by ZORA NEALE HURSTON, and articles by EUGENE GORDON, ANGELINA GRIMKÉ, PAUL ROBESON, and RENÉ MARAN.

The account of Christmas Eve and Christmas Day begins with a dismayed narrator who is "marooned in a boarding school in the far South in Louisiana." The pithy first-person account of Christmas tracks the narrator's growing appreciation of the season, despite the fact that she finds herself in a land where the weather defies her traditional notions of the holiday. The narrator is responsible for overseeing the distribution of holiday baskets that also are accompanied by modest gifts of 50 cents. She eventually rouses herself from sleep and dreams of "sugar cane stalks, muddy roads, draughty cabins and Christmas baskets chasing each other." She is humbled by the earnest and beautiful carols that prompt her to rise and to greet the day. The story ends as the narrator and the other students involved in the distribution mission make their first call and experience a stirring encounter with an impoverished, grateful new mother. The woman, described as "gaunt" and dressed in a "drab and faded gingham dress" accepts the "gifts regally but her thanks [are] broken and breathless." Just before the group leaves, one of the young students asks to hold the woman's newborn baby. The mother "surrender[s]" her child and then plucks a white rose from the bush that is blooming near her front door. After peeling off its thorns, she offers it to the narrator, who accepts it humbly as part of her holiday corsage. The gesture prompts the narrator to note that "[i]t was Christmas morning and the mother of a new born babe had given me a rose." The story ends as the narrator contemplates the significance of the encounter and realizes that seemingly contrary environments cannot diminish the rich symbolism of meaningful religious holidays and interactions with earnest folk.

"Who Gives Himself" reflects Carter's interest in dispelling myths about the South as a place alienated from tradition or the past. Like "Replica" (1924), this short story encourages readers to consider the powerful nature of human interaction and the uplifting bonds that African Americans can share in an often oppressive and seemingly disempowering environment.

Wiggins, Bernice Love (1897–unknown)

A Texas native who was part of the small, ambitious circle of African-American women writing in the Southwest during the Harlem Renaissance.

Wiggins graduated from public schools in El Paso and appears to have begun writing without any formal training. According to biographers Lorraine Roses and Ruth Randolph, Wiggins published regularly in Texas newspapers such as the *El Paso Herald* and in northern publications such as the *CHICAGO DEFENDER*.

Wiggins saw her work included in the important 1925 Texas collection, *Heralding Dawn*, edited by J. Mason Brewer. That same year, she published TUNE-FUL TALES, a collection of more than 100 poems that ranged widely in subject matter and style.

Bibliography

Roses, Lorraine Elena, and Ruth Elizabeth Randolph. *Harlem's Glory: Black Women Writing, 1900–1950.* Cambridge: Harvard University Press, 1996.

Wilberforce University

The oldest private African-American institution of higher learning and the first American college to have an African-American president. Founded in 1856 and located in Wilberforce, Ohio, the school was named in honor of William Wilberforce, the British abolitionist. The school is affiliated with the African Methodist Episcopal Church and still thrives today as a liberal arts institution. Its alumni include educator, historian, and women's rights leader HALLIE QUINN BROWN, playwright and librarian REGINA ANDREWS, and civil rights activist Bayard Rustin.

Bibliography

Brown, Hallie Quinn. *Pen Pictures of Wilberforce.* Xenia, Ohio: Aldine Publishing Company, 1937.

Ransom, Reverdy. *School Days at Wilberforce.* Springfield, Ohio: The New Era Company, 1892.

Williams, Blanche Colton (1879–1944)

A popular white novelist, editor, and biographer who supported the efforts to advance and to celebrate literary achievements by African-American writers of the Harlem Renaissance era. Williams was a judge in the first OPPORTUNITY literary contest. In a note of acceptance to CHARLES S. JOHN-SON, the editor who extended the invitation to join the judges' panel, Williams noted that she would "gladly serve" and that the awards "cannot but be helpful to more than one young man and woman" (Wilson, xxvi). During the Harlem Renaissance, Williams, who would publish biographies of John Keats, George Eliot, and Clara Barton, published several works. These included an edited volume of the *Best American Short Stories: O. Henry Memorial*

Prize Winning Stories, 1919–1932 and an instructive guide to Old English.

Bibliography

Wilson, Sondra Kathryn, ed. *The Opportunity Reader.* New York: The Modern Library, 1999.

Williams, Edward Christopher
(1871–1929)

A teacher, writer, translator, librarian, and playwright who was part of the dynamic Harlem Renaissance literary community in WASHINGTON, D.C. Born in Cleveland, Ohio, he was a mixed-raced son of the African-American Daniel Williams and the Irish Mary Kilary Williams. He married Ethel Chesnutt, a daughter of writer CHARLES CHESNUTT, in 1902. The couple had one son.

After graduating from the Cleveland public schools, Williams attended Case Western Reserve's Adelbert College, where he was elected to PHI BETA KAPPA and graduated as valedictorian of his class. Williams began working immediately after graduation in the college library. He later completed an M.A. in library science at the New York State Library School in Albany.

Williams relocated to Washington, D.C., for professional reasons and was principal of the M STREET HIGH SCHOOL for several years. He then became head librarian at HOWARD UNIVERSITY and joined the faculty as a professor of German and Romance languages.

Williams emerged as an insightful social critic. His articles on African-American society in the capital appeared in *The MESSENGER*. According to biographer Paul Mills, Williams also became a member of the Mu-So-Lit Club, an African-American men's literary society in the capital. He later cofounded the Literary Lovers, a social group of men and women that encouraged members to consider issues of race. He contemplated joining a group such as the fictionalized Blue Vein Society in Charles Chesnutt's short story "The Wife of His Youth," but despite interactions with JEAN TOOMER and participation in early meetings he declined to pursue any formal involvement in the group of mixed-race people.

Williams's writings often reflected his own academic interests in the Romance languages and in African-American literature. He published poems and fiction under the Italian pseudonym of Bertuccio Dantino. He also completed *Exile,* an Italian drama, and *Sheriff's Children,* a play inspired by the Charles Chesnutt short story.

In 1929 Williams began doctoral studies in library science at COLUMBIA UNIVERSITY but died suddenly. Funeral services for Williams were held on the campus of Howard University, and the school's president, Dr. MORDECAI JOHNSON, conducted the event. Williams was buried at Lincoln Cemetery in Suitland, Maryland.

Bibliography

Dyson, Walter. *Howard University: The Capstone of Negro Education, a History: 1867–1940.* Washington, D.C.: Howard University Press, 1940.

Josey, E. J. "Edward Christopher Williams: Librarian's Librarian." *Negro History Bulletin* 33 (March 1970): 70–77.

Logan, Rayford, W. *Howard University: The First Hundred Years, 1867–1967.* New York: New York University Press, 1969.

Wilson, Frank (1886–1956)

A playwright and an accomplished stage and film actor who performed with some of the most promising dramatic troupes and in some of the best-known plays of the Harlem Renaissance period. Wilson's professional experience was informed by his education at the American Academy of Dramatic Art and his early performances with the LAFAYETTE PLAYERS STOCK COMPANY. In 1926 he appeared with PAUL ROBESON in EUGENE O'NEILL's *ALL GOD'S CHILLUN GOT WINGS* and two years later, in 1926, in the PULITZER PRIZE–winning play by Paul Green, *IN ABRAHAM'S BOSOM.* Wilson was eventually catapulted into the leading role in that play and received high praise from theater critics for his polished performances. In 1927 he played the title role of Porgy in DU-BOSE HEYWARD's early dramatic adaptation of his novel *PORGY.*

Wilson wrote several plays, but their reception and impact were uneven. In 1922 he completed *PA WILLIAMS' GAL,* a play that was performed in Harlem before modest audiences. Williams won first prize in the 1925–26 *OPPORTUNITY* literary contest. His work, judged by David Belasco, T.

MONTGOMERY GREGORY, PAUL ROBESON, and Stark Young, edged out submissions by JOHN MATHEUS, ZORA NEALE HURSTON, GEORGIA DOUGLAS JOHNSON, and MAY MILLER SULLIVAN. In 1928, *MEEK MOSE* opened on BROADWAY but did not meet with overwhelming success.

Wings of Oppression Leslie Pinckney Hill (1921)

A collection of poems by LESLIE PINCKNEY HILL, the HARVARD UNIVERSITY–educated president of the Cheyney Training School for Teachers. Dedicated to his wife Jane Clark Hill, the volume was published by Stratford Company of BOSTON, Massachusetts.

In his preface, Hill declared that "Nothing in the life of the nation has seemed to me more significant than the dark civilization which the colored man has built up in the midst of a white society organized against it." He went on to note that in *Wings of Oppression* he "desired to exhibit something of [the] indestructible spiritual qualities of my race." Hill's political sensibilities and race pride shaped the collection and reflected his effort to contribute to the engaged race literature of the period.

The volume contained poems that had been published previously in leading journals of the day, such as *THE CRISIS, The Outlook,* and *The Independent.* It began with the title poem, "The Wings of Oppression," and then included poems divided into five sections. Hill developed categories such as "Poems of My People," "Poems of the Times," "Poems of Appreciation," "Songs," and "Poems of the Spirit." He provided contextual remarks for some works, such as "Armageddon," a poem published in *The Crisis* as "Die Zeitgeist" and prompted by the start of World War I, "Matto Grosso," "Brixton Prison," which honored Lord Mayor McWiney of Cork, who martyred himself for Irish freedom, and "So Quietly," a haunting poem on LYNCHING that was inspired by a murder reported in *THE NEW YORK TIMES.* Poems such as "My Race" reflected Hill's patriotism and desire to seek out places "[w]herever the light of dreams is shed / And faith and love to toil are bound" so that he may "stay to break the bread / For there my kinsmen will be found." Hill's poems conveyed his optimism about African-American success, and

Hill used works such as "Ode to Patriotism," "A Call to Poets," and "To All Leaders of Men" to exhort readers and poets to debate the power and destiny of the race. The volume is a powerful example of the uncompromising race literature of the Harlem Renaissance.

Bibliography
Hill, Leslie Pinckney. *Wings of Oppression.* Boston: Stratford Company, 1921.

Wood, Clement (1880–1950)
A white, American author who in 1925 celebrated the publication of the Harlem issue of SURVEY GRAPHIC and noted that "There is no more significant transition in America today than that of the Negro from the position of an awakening chattel to that of full manhood, economically, politically, socially, and artistically." Wood also was one of several white judges who participated in the annual OPPORTUNITY literary contests. He judged poetry submissions in the 1924 and 1925 contests and in 1928 judged entries in the August round of the CHARLES WADDELL CHESNUTT Honoraria.

Wood was the author of NIGGER (1922), a work that preceded the controversial NIGGER HEAVEN (1926) by CARL VAN VECHTEN. He published several works on poetry as well as biographies of Amy Lowell and Julius Caesar.

Bibliography
Survey Graphic. May 1925.
Wood, Clement. *Nigger: A Novel.* New York: E. P. Dutton & Company, 1922.

Wood, L. Hollingsworth (1873–1956)
Vice chairman of the Board of Trustees of FISK UNIVERSITY. He provided the foreword to the volume EBONY AND TOPAZ: A COLLECTANEA that CHARLES S. JOHNSON, future president of the university, edited and published in 1927.

Wood, Lillian (fl. 1922)
A teacher and still obscure writer who published a single novel during the Harlem Renaissance. In 1922 Wood published LET MY PEOPLE GO, a moving novel about LYNCHING and the power of organized and visionary political protest. The book, published by the respected PHILADELPHIA A.M.E. Book Concern, included a preface by the Methodist Episcopal Bishop Robert Jones, a former editor and the former president of Wiley University, Samuel Houston College, and New Orleans University.

Bibliography
Wood, Lillian. *Let My People Go.* Philadelphia: A.M.E. Book Concern, 1922.

Woodson, Carter Godwin (1875–1960)
Regarded as the "Father of Black History," Woodson was a pioneering scholar, author, and editor who shaped the scholarship and intellectual tenor of African-American history. It was he who inaugurated "Negro History Week," the forerunner of Black History Month, in an effort to honor Frederick Douglass and Abraham Lincoln, both of whom had February birthdays.

The son of Ann and James Henry Woodson, formerly enslaved people, was born in New Canton, Virginia. One of nine children, he worked alongside his sharecropper parents when he was not attending the impoverished school for African-American children that was open for only four months of the year. The family, who valued education and cultivated Woodson's love of learning and appreciation of the political power of education, relocated to Huntington, West Virginia. There, 20-year-old Woodson received a more steady education at the Frederick Douglass High School. Following his graduation, he enrolled at Berea College for two years, from 1896 through 1898. In 1903, after having begun a teaching career and attending the UNIVERSITY OF CHICAGO for one year, he returned to Berea and completed his B.A. in 1903. He later reenrolled at the University of Chicago, where he worked toward both a B.A. and an M.A. He enrolled at HARVARD UNIVERSITY and began doctoral studies in history. He taught at the selective M Street High School, also known as DUNBAR HIGH SCHOOL, while completing the requirements for his Ph.D., which he received in 1912.

Woodson was one of the most eminent and attentive members of the vibrant WASHINGTON, D.C., intellectual and literary community during the Harlem Renaissance. He collaborated with ALAIN LOCKE at the Associated Publishers, a company that published several works relating to African-American life and culture. Woodson, a member of the AMERICAN NEGRO ACADEMY, founded the ASSOCIATION FOR THE STUDY OF NEGRO LIFE AND HISTORY in 1915. He was a prolific author whose impressive works included *A Century of Negro Migration* (1918), *The Education of the Negro* (1919), *The History of the Negro Church* (1921), and *The Negro in Our History* (1922). A winner of the prestigious SPINGARN MEDAL in 1926, he was celebrated for his tireless commitment to documenting and making African-American history accessible to all.

Bibliography

Conyers, James Jr. *Carter G. Woodson: A Historical Reader.* New York: Garland Publishing, 2000.

Goggin, Jacqueline. *Carter G. Woodson: A Life in Black History.* Baton Rouge: Louisiana State University Press, 1993.

Greene, Lorenzo, and Arvarh Strickland, ed. *Working with Carter G. Woodson, The Father of Black History: A Diary, 1928–1930.* Baton Rouge: Louisiana State University Press, 1989.

Work, John Wesley, III (1901–1967)

A composer, writer, and teacher, Work was part of an impressive family of African-American musicians and cultural activists. Born in Tullahoma, Tennessee, he was the son of John and Agnes Haynes Wesley. He married Edith McFall, a Charleston, South Carolina, native, in 1928, and the couple had two sons, John IV and Frederick.

A graduate of FISK UNIVERSITY, Work earned his M.A. from COLUMBIA UNIVERSITY in 1923 and his Mus.B. from YALE UNIVERSITY in 1933. He also won a JULIUS ROSENWALD FELLOWSHIP that enabled him to study music at the Juilliard Institute. Work joined the faculty of Fisk University, his father's alma mater, and was a longtime member of the music department. During his tenure as music director at Fisk, Work composed numerous choral arrangements, won first prize from the Fellowship of American Composers in 1946, and had the opportunity to collaborate with well-known figures of the

Harlem Renaissance such as ARNA BONTEMPS, for whom he created a musical version of Bontemps's *Golgotha Is a Mountain.* Work also published in leading journals of the period, and his essays on Negro folk songs appeared in publications such as *OPPORTUNITY.*

Bibliography

Work, John Wesley. *Folk Song of the American Negro.* 1915; reprint, New York: Negro Universities Press, 1969.

Worker's Dreadnought

A British trade workers' journal founded by SYLVIA PANKHURST. The journal was known first as the *Women's Dreadnought,* but in the wake of World War I and the Russian Revolution, Pankhurst transformed the journal into the *Worker's Dreadnought* and affiliated the publication with the Worker's Socialist Federation.

Poet CLAUDE MCKAY joined the staff of the magazine during his sojourn in England in the early 1920s. McKay published more than a dozen works in the magazine during 1920, including "To 'Holy' Russia," "The Beast," "Joy in the Woods," "Samson," "Song of the New Soldier and Worker," and "Summer Morn in New Hampshire."

Bibliography

Bullock, Ian, and Richard Pankhurst, eds. *Sylvia Pankhurst: From Artist to Anti-Fascist.* New York: St. Martin's Press, 1992.

Cooper, Wayne. *Claude McKay: Rebel Sojourner in the Harlem Renaissance.* New York: Schocken Books, 1987.

Giles, James R. *Claude McKay.* Boston: Twayne Publishers, 1976.

Romero, Patricia. *E. Sylvia Pankhurst: Portrait of a Radical.* New Haven, Conn.: Yale University Press, 1987.

Pugh, Martin. *The Pankhursts.* London: Penguin Books, 2002.

World Tomorrow, The

A Protestant journal that was dedicated to peace and Socialist principles. Founded in NEW YORK CITY in 1918, the periodical was marketed first as

New World but became *The World Tomorrow* some six months after it began. Its editors and major contributors included Socialist Party leader Norman Thomas and Quaker mystic and Haverford College professor Rufus Jones. The paper ceased publication in 1934 but was incorporated into the magazine *Christian Century*.

Writer and editor WALLACE THURMAN was on staff at the white-owned journal during the fall of 1926 during the period when he was working to produce *FIRE!!* The journal published ERIC WALROND's "The Color of the Caribbean" in its May 1927 issue. His piercing essay on the demoralizing nature of emigration to the United States was an extremely forthright and searing articulation of the racial stereotypes that white society upheld and the ways in which people of color were so carelessly and violently abused of their self-confidence, qualifications, and goals. In May 1928 the journal published ZORA NEALE HURSTON's memorable essay "HOW IT FEELS TO BE COLORED ME." She had submitted the work in an effort to generate monies to cover the production costs associated with *Fire!!*

Bibliography

Boyd, Valerie. *Wrapped in Rainbows: The Life of Zora Neale Hurston.* New York: Scribner, 2003.

Hemenway, Robert. *Zora Neale Hurston: A Literary Biography.* Urbana: University of Illinois Press, 1977.

Kaplan, Carla. *Zora Neale Hurston: A Life in Letters.* New York: Doubleday, 2002.

Thurman, Howard. *With Head and Heart: The Autobiography of Howard Thurman.* New York: Harcourt Brace Jovanovich, 1979.

Wright, Richard (1908–1960)

One of America's foremost literary figures and an accomplished scholar whose emergence represented the end of the Harlem Renaissance and the inauguration of American modernism. Born in September 1908 in Mississippi, Wright was the son of sharecropper Nathan Wright and teacher Ella Wilson Wright. The family moved frequently during Wright's early years and later settled in Arkansas with his maternal kin. The brutal murder of his uncle Silas Hopkins by a white lynch mob forced the family to flee from their home in Elaine,

Richard Wright. Photographed by Carl Van Vechten. Permission granted by the Van Vechten Trust *(Yale Collection of American Literature, Beinecke Rare Book and Manuscript Library)*

Arkansas. Wright's itinerant childhood was marked by poverty and violence. He was able to focus on schooling by 1921 and immediately demonstrated his deep love of literature and writing. He moved with his family to CHICAGO, and it was there that his writing career began.

Wright's early publications included "Superstition," a short story that appeared in the African-American-owned *ABBOTT'S MONTHLY* magazine. As he became immersed in communism and political groups, he also began to publish in journals such as *NEW MASSES* and *The Left Front*. In 1935 he joined the Federal Writers' Project, a movement affiliated with the Works Progress Administration and the organization with which ARNA BONTEMPS, Gwendolyn Brooks, CLAUDE MCKAY, RICHARD

Bruce Nugent, Margaret Walker, Dorothy West, Frank Yerby, and other prominent writers were involved.

Wright relocated to New York City in the late 1930s. He collaborated with Dorothy West on New Challenge, a revised version of the journal Challenge that West had founded in 1934. His essay "Blueprint for Negro Writing" was published in the journal's first and only issue. Wright began to receive critical praise for his writing with the publication of "Fire and Cloud," a prizewinning short story that appeared in Story Magazine. In 1938 he published Uncle Tom's Children: Four Novellas and secured a reputation as a gifted and incisive writer. In 1940, as the Harlem Renaissance came to a close and the new era of American modernism began, Wright published Native Son, a phenomenal best seller. The book was hailed by critics for its stark realism and studied examination of African-American subjectivity. It also had its critics, among them George Schuyler and Carl Van Vechten. Both men, who were well known for their inventive representations of racial "reality," thought that Native Son was "an over-rated book if there ever was one," and Van Vechten went so far as to suggest to Harold Jackman that the book "has done the Negro an unconscionable amount of harm in the minds of many an ofay who has read it" (Kellner, 176).

In the years following the Harlem Renaissance, Wright continued to publish widely. Later works included Black Boy (1945), Black Power: A Record of Reactions in a Land of Pathos (1954), and the novels Pagan Spain (1958) and The Long Dream (1958). In 1941 the National Association for the Advancement of Colored People awarded him its most prestigious award, the Spingarn Medal. In 1947 he became an American expatriate when he took up permanent residence in France. Wright, who succumbed to a heart attack, was buried in the Père Lachaise Cemetery with a copy of Black Boy.

Bibliography

Fabre, Michel. The Unfinished Quest of Richard Wright. Urbana: University of Illinois Press, 1993.

Gayle, Addison. Richard Wright: Ordeal of a Native Son. Garden City, N.Y.: Anchor Press, 1980.

Hakutani, Yoshinobu. Critical Essays on Richard Wright. Boston: G. K. Hall, 1982.

Kellner, Bruce, ed. Letters of Carl Van Vechten. New Haven, Conn.: Yale University Press, 1987.

Kinnamon, Kenneth, and Michel Fabre. Conversations with Richard Wright. Jackson: University Press of Mississippi, 1993.

Richard Wright Papers, Richard Wright Archive, Beinecke Rare Book and Manuscript Library, Yale University.

Walker, Margaret. Richard Wright: Daemonic Genius. New York: Warner Books, 1988.

Wright, Zara (fl. 1920)

A still obscure author who published two novels during the Harlem Renaissance. Black and White Tangled Threads and its sequel, Kenneth, were published in 1920. Wright dedicated both books, which received positive reviews in the Chicago Defender, to her husband, J. Edward Wright.

Wynbush, Octavia Beatrice (1894–1972)

A teacher, poet, and writer whose publications included works for children. The biographical details about Wynbush are gleaned from notes that prefaced some of her published works. She was born in Pennsylvania and went on to graduate from Oberlin College. She later pursued an M.A. in English at Columbia University and graduated in 1934. She became a college teacher and taught at several institutions, such as Straight College, Arkansas State College, and Philander Smith College. In later life she resided in Missouri and taught high school. Biographers Lorraine Roses and Ruth Randolph, who have combed through the Oberlin College archives, note that Wynbush married Lewis Strong in 1963 when she was in her sixties.

Wynbush published several evocative short stories in The Crisis and in Opportunity during the late 1930s and early 1940s. She made her Harlem Renaissance debut with "The Noose," an eerie short story published in the December 1931 issue of Opportunity. Her fiction, which often is set in Louisiana and focuses on small communities and issues of betrayal, seduction, and self-preservation, includes "Bride of God," "Conjure Man," "The Return of a Modern Prodigal," and "The

CONVERSION OF HARVEY." Wynbush was featured on the cover of the March 1936 *Crisis*, and her productivity suggested that she would continue to develop as one of the period's accomplished writers. Her only published children's book is *The Wheel That Made Wishes Come True* (1941).

Bibliography

Roses, Lorraine Elena, and Ruth Elizabeth Randolph. *Harlem's Glory: Black Women Writing, 1900–1950.* Cambridge: Harvard University Press, 1996.

Wynbush, Octavia. *The Wheel That Made Wishes Come True.* Philadelphia: Dorrance & Company, 1941.

Yale University

Founded in 1701 and part of the Ivy League, a group of eight prestigious northeastern universities, Yale was renamed in 1718 after Elihu Yale, a British merchant and the school's benefactor. Distinguished alumni of the school that is located now in New Haven, Connecticut, include Samuel Morse, William Howard Taft, Noah Webster, and Eli Whitney.

A number of individuals who shaped the literary and political traditions of the Harlem Renaissance attended Yale University and its law school. OWEN DODSON earned an M.F.A. from the renowned School of Drama, and SHIRLEY GRAHAM DUBOIS enjoyed a two-year residency there on a JULIUS ROSENWALD FELLOWSHIP. Among those who completed undergraduate and graduate work there were JOSEPH DANDRIDGE BIBB, SHEPPARD RANDOLPH EDMONDS, JOHN FARRAR, WILLIAM FERRIS, WALDO FRANK, George Edmund Haynes, WILLIAM PICKENS, and CLEMENT WOOD. ARNA BONTEMPS became the chief archivist of the impressive JAMES WELDON JOHNSON collection, held in the university's Beinecke Library.

Bibliography

Kelley, Brooks. *Yale: A History*. New Haven: Yale University Press, 1974.

Yeiser, Idabelle (1897–unknown)

An active member of the literary circles in PHILADELPHIA during the Harlem Renaissance, a poet, and a prize-winning essayist. There are limited biographical details about Yeiser's early and late life. The details that she herself provided in autobiographical prefaces to her works reveal that she spent part of her life in New Jersey and graduated from the State Normal School in Montclair. Yeiser, who attended the UNIVERSITY OF PENNSYLVANIA for a time, earned her Ph.D. in French from COLUMBIA UNIVERSITY. After time abroad, she returned to Philadelphia and began a teaching career.

During the Harlem Renaissance, Yeiser published in the major journals THE CRISIS and OPPORTUNITY. Her travels in Europe and the Middle East inspired her essay "AN ECHO FROM TOULOUSE," published in the July 1926 *Crisis*. One year later she published "Letters," an autobiographical travel narrative. In 1937 Yeiser published MOODS, her first collection of poems and her only Harlem Renaissance–era book. Her second collection, *Lyric and Legend*, appeared in 1947.

Yeiser appears to have settled in Louisiana after the Harlem Renaissance. In 1945 she was identified as a professor of education at Dillard University and celebrated as one of several faculty members who had "distinguished themselves not only as teachers but as writers and scholars" (*Dillard Bulletin*, 1945).

Bibliography

Dillard Bulletin, December 1945. Available online. URL: http://books.dillard.edu/ Archives/Bulletin. Accessed June 1, 2005.

Yellow Peril: A One-Act Play George Schuyler (1925)

A comical but pointed play by GEORGE SCHUYLER about intraracial sexual mores and mischief. The play is set in the Seventh Avenue apartment of Corinne, a light-skinned woman who has cultivated numerous male sweethearts and providers. One evening, however, her usually choreographed dalliances begin to go haywire, and she is forced to deal with a seemingly unpredictable and unrelenting flow of male callers. Each man brings her expensive items, and the treats range from expensive shoes to rent money. Finally, her policeman beau is alerted to the possibility that she has criminals lurking on the balcony outside her window. In the mayhem that ensues, all six of the men whom she has staged in various places in her apartment are revealed to each other. Dismayed by Corinne's treachery, they retrieve their gifts and abandon her.

Yellow Peril, whose title invokes the colloquial and mildly pejorative phrase "high yaller" that denotes light-skinned people, appeared in the January 1925 issue of THE MESSENGER.

Bibliography
Leak, Jeffrey. *Rac(e)ing to the Right: Selected Essays of George S. Schuyler.* Knoxville: University of Tennessee Press, 2001.

Peplow, Michael. *George S. Schuyler.* Boston: Twayne Publishers, 1980.

Williams, Harry. *When Black Is Right: The Life and Writings of George S. Schuyler.* Ann Arbor, Mich.: University Microfilms International, 1990.

York Beach Jean Toomer (1929)

A truncated version of a novel that JEAN TOOMER intended to complete. First entitled *Istil*, the novel was influenced significantly by Toomer's own experiences as an aspiring writer. The protagonist Nathan Antrum, whose name itself recalls Toomer's own Christian name, comes to terms with life and his own desires as a writer. In 1929, with the help of Paul Rosenfeld, who also featured in the novel, Toomer published a 70-page version of the work.

Bibliography
Kerman, Cynthia Earl, and Richard Eldridge. *The Lives of Jean Toomer: A Hunger for Wholeness.* Baton Rouge: Louisiana State University Press, 1987.

You Can't Pet a Possum Arna Bontemps and Langston Hughes (1934)

A story for children that ARNA BONTEMPS cowrote with LANGSTON HUGHES. The story, which featured a child named Shine Boy and his hound named Butch, was published by William Morrow in 1934, two years after the successful children's book *POPO AND FIFINA: CHILDREN OF HAITI* (1932), also cowritten by Bontemps and Hughes. The work also appeared some two years before Bontemps completed his powerful historical novel, *BLACK THUNDER* (1936), based on the slave revolt led by Gabriel Prosser in 1800. *You Can't Pet a Possum* was one of several works for children that Bontemps published during his lengthy and successful career. His commitment to providing absorbing literature for young readers was inspired by his desire both to write and to provide delightful and unfettered imaginative stories for his six children and many others.

Bibliography
Jones, Kirkland C. *Renaissance Man from Louisiana: A Biography of Arna Wendell Bontemps.* Westport, Conn.: Greenwood Press, 1992.

Young, Nathan Benjamin (1894–1993)

Young published sporadically during the Harlem Renaissance, but his work garnered critical attention and praise. In the first literary contest sponsored by OPPORTUNITY, Young saw two of his works honored. "THE BOLL WEEVIL STARTS NORTH" won first honorable mention, and "All God's Chillun Got Shoes" earned a sixth-place honorable mention. In 1927 Young competed in THE CRISIS literary contest and was one of several writers, among them JOHN MATHEUS and RANDOLPH EDMONDS, who earned honorable mention for their entries.

Limited autobiographical information in the periodicals that published his work makes it difficult to confirm Young's background. It is possible that he was in fact, Nathan Benjamin Young, Jr., a Tuskegee, Alabama, native who graduated from Yale Law School in 1918, became a forceful organizer in Birmingham, Alabama, for the NATIONAL ASSOCIATION FOR THE ADVANCEMENT OF COLORED PEOPLE (NAACP), and then relocated with his wife to St. Louis, Missouri. In St. Louis, that figure became the first African-American municipal judge, and he founded the *St. Louis American*, a weekly African-American newspaper, and served as publisher and frequent contributor for more than four decades. He also continued to immerse himself in art and music and to produce numerous portraits and paintings. Judge Nathan Young died at the age of 98 in 1993.

Bibliography

Waide, John. "Two Narratives: Edna Patterson-Petty and Nathan B. Young, Jr." St. Louis University Museum of Art. January 2002. Available online. URL: http://sluma.slu.edu/past_ex_two_narr.html. Accessed June 2, 2005.

Young, Benjamin. "The Boll Weevil Starts North: A Story." *Opportunity* (February 1926).

"Young Blood Hungers, The" Marita Bonner (1922)

Published in the May 1928 issue of THE CRISIS, MARITA BONNER's unconventional philosophical meditation on the plight of the younger generations referred only to Young Blood, a figure or force hungering for guidance and success. The brief story, classified by scholars as fiction or as an essay, is informed by religious themes, social realities, and anxieties about survival. It conveys Bonner's interests in progress but does not compete with her more grim and searing narratives based on the fictional CHICAGO neighborhood of Frye Street.

Bibliography

Flynn, Joyce, and Joyce Occomy Striklin. *Frye Street & Environs: The Collected Works of Marita Bonner.* Boston: Beacon Press, 1987.

"Young Glory of Him, The" Langston Hughes (1927)

A moving and tragic short story about unrequited love by LANGSTON HUGHES. Published in the April 1927 issue of THE MESSENGER, the story focused on the inevitable corruption of an innocent girl named Daisy Jones. A sheltered daughter of white New England missionaries to Africa, she falls in love with one of the sailors aboard the freight ship carrying them to their foreign post. The narrator, who is the cabin boy aboard the ship the *West Ilana*, has the opportunity to read Daisy's diary and finds out that her feelings for Eric Gynt, the blond sailor, are quite sincere and passionate. Over the course of the voyage,

however, it is clear that the virtuous affection that she offers is not what she can expect in return. Following a disastrous trip into Dakar, one evening when the ship docks there, Daisy Jones becomes withdrawn and intensely upset. She eventually jumps overboard and drowns. Her suicide note reveals that Gynt had betrayed her affection and did not love her truly.

Hughes's portrait of the callous and sincere nature of attraction is powerful for its evocative portrait of innocence betrayed. Like "BODIES IN THE MOONLIGHT" and "THE LITTLE VIRGIN," "The Young Glory of Him" was inspired by Hughes's own travels aboard the SS *Malone* in the years before he achieved literary fame.

Bibliography

Berry, Faith, ed. *Langston Hughes: Before and Beyond Harlem.* Westport, Conn.: Lawrence Hill & Company, 1983.

Rampersad, Arnold. *The Life of Langston Hughes: I, Too, Sing America.* Vol. 1, *1902–1941.* New York: Oxford University Press, 1986.

Young Men's Christian Association

The first Young Men's Christian Association (YMCA) was established in 1844 in London, England. Founder George Williams, a draper, founded the group with a number of fellow workers. The men hoped to use the organization to minister to the itinerant and migrant workers who were flooding London. In less than 10 years, the more than two dozen YMCA branches in England had nearly 3,000 members. The YMCA movement spread rapidly throughout Europe and in 1855 resulted in a World Conference in Paris that succeeded in establishing the World Alliance of YMCAs. The first YMCA in the United States was founded in Boston in December 1851, just over one month after the first YMCA in North America was established in Montreal, Canada. A formerly enslaved man named Anthony Bowen established the first YMCA for African Americans, in WASHINGTON, D.C, in 1853.

The national YMCA, from its founding until 1946, was an organization that adhered to a strict policy of racial segregation. African Americans were prohibited from joining, residing, or participating in the events of white YMCA branches.

African Americans did, however, establish their own branches, which became vital and thriving cultural and community spaces.

The HARLEM branches of the YMCA and its sister organization, the YOUNG WOMEN'S CHRISTIAN ASSOCIATION (YWCA), were located in the heart of Harlem and in close proximity to the popular 135th Street branch (HARLEM BRANCH) of the NEW YORK PUBLIC LIBRARY, a community gathering place and center for cultural and intellectual events. Harlem had had YMCA branches as early as 1900, but in 1932 construction on the neighborhood's official center was completed. Four years later, in 1936, the site was officially named the Harlem Branch of the YMCA.

The Harlem YMCA also provided rooms to African-American men who had been denied accommodations in segregated city hotels. During the era of the Harlem Renaissance, a number of aspiring literary figures lived at the 135th Street branch. Langston Hughes boarded at the YMCA when COLUMBIA UNIVERSITY failed to provide him with dormitory housing when he enrolled. RALPH ELLISON took rooms in the Harlem YMCA when he relocated from Alabama to New York City. It was in the lobby of the building that he first met both ALAIN LOCKE and LANGSTON HUGHES, both of whom proved instrumental in his acclimation to the city. Artist AARON DOUGLAS was commissioned to create murals for several major buildings in the city, and, in addition to providing art for the New York Public Library, he generated art work to adorn the walls of the Harlem YMCA.

Bibliography

Hopkins, Charles. *History of the YMCA in North America.* New York: Association Press, 1951.

Mjagki, Nina, and Margaret Spratt, eds. *Men and Women Adrift: The YMCA and the YWCA in the City.* New York: New York University Press, 1997.

Young Women's Christian Association

The organization founded in England in 1887 by Emma Robarts and Lady Kinnaird that became the oldest international women's organization in the world. The Young Women's Christian Association (YWCA) was formed in 1858 by Mrs. Marshall Roberts in NEW YORK CITY under the name "Ladies' Christian Association." One year later, the city of Boston, in which the first American Young Men's Christian Association had been established in 1851, became the first to refer to the organization as the YWCA. In 1889 in Dayton, Ohio, the first African-American YWCA opened. One year later, in 1890, the first YWCA branch for Native American women opened in Chilocco, Oklahoma.

The YWCA was dedicated to providing safe accommodations for working women. Like its brother organization, the YMCA, the YWCA did at first adhere to a racial segregation policy. In 1915 the organization reflected its willingness to engage across racial lines and staged the first interracial conference of any kind in the South. In 1936 SHAW UNIVERSITY, a historically black institution, hosted the first interracial coed student conference in the South. The YWCA worked to improve the home life of and professional options for women. It opened nurseries for children, offered classes in typing, provided the first English as a Second Language courses offered, and organized training schools for practical nursing.

A number of Harlem Renaissance figures were active members of and leaders in the YWCA. MARION CUTHBERT, dean of Talladega College, was a board member who authored the biography of Juliette Derricote, the national student secretary of the YWCA, a member whose untimely death was hastened by racist segregation practices and the refusal of treatment to African Americans by Atlanta hospitals. ADDIE HUNTON and Kathryn Johnson were two especially enterprising members. They are perhaps best remembered for their pioneering work during World War I with the American Expeditionary Forces, experiences that they documented in their collaborative memoir. NELLA LARSEN was inspired by Irene McCoy, a prominent YWCA officer, and a character in her celebrated novel PASSING is based on Larsen's longtime friend and active YWCA member. The writers DOROTHY WEST and HELENE JOHNSON were among the many who, upon their arrival in New York City, sought accommodations at the HARLEM YWCA.

The YWCA also worked with influential African-American organizations such as the NATIONAL COUNCIL OF NEGRO WOMEN (NCNW). In 1935, for instance, the NCNW held its organizational meetings in the 137th Street Harlem branch of the YWCA.

Bibliography

Mjagki, Nina, and Margaret Spratt, eds. *Men and Women Adrift: The YMCA and the YWCA in the City.* New York: New York University Press, 1997.

Weisenfeld, Judith. *African American Women and Christian Activism: New York's Black YWCA, 1905–1945.* Cambridge: Harvard University Press, 1997.

Young Women's Christian Association of the U.S.A. National Board. *Handbook of the Young Women's Christian Associations of the United States of America.* New York, 1910.

Z

Zalka Peetruza and Other Poems
Raymond Garfield Dandridge (1928)

A collection of poems by RAYMOND GARFIELD DANDRIDGE. The volume includes new works as well as poems that had been published previously in his 1928 collection, *THE POET AND OTHER POEMS*. Produced by the McDonald Press of Cincinnati, the volume references the poem "Zalka Peetruza" that was one of five Dandridge poems had been included six years earlier in JAMES WELDON JOHNSON's anthology, *THE BOOK OF AMERICAN NEGRO POETRY* (1922). This poem, whose title was followed by the parenthetical note that Zalka Peetruza was a woman "Christened Lucy Jane," chronicled the transformation of an ordinary woman into an exotic other. "She danced, near nude, to tom-tom beat, / With swaying arms and flying feet," reports the absorbed and observant speaker. Yet, despite the "swirling spangles, gauze, and lace," it is the face of Lucy Jane, aka Zalka Peetruza, that does not participate in the performance.

Dandridge's poem suggests the alienation of the woman performer whose "eyes [are] obsessed with vacant stare" and whose "heart stood still" throughout the dance. The distance that Lucy Jane maintains suggests that her appearance is staged on a number of levels and that it has discernible traumatic implications. The dance by Zalka Peetruza is cultivated for the sake of audience gratification rather than personal satisfaction, and in this way it speaks to the unfeeling and dehumanizing commodification of particular bodies and experiences for "art's" sake.

SELECTED BIBLIOGRAPHY OF HARLEM RENAISSANCE–ERA WORKS BY LEADING FIGURES

ARNA BONTEMPS

Books

God Sends Sunday. New York: Harcourt, Brace, 1931.

Popo and Fifina: Children of Haiti. With Langston Hughes. New York: Macmillan, 1932.

You Can't Pet a Possum. New York: Morrow, 1934.

Black Thunder. New York: Macmillan, 1936.

Sad-Faced Boy. Boston: Houghton Mifflin, 1937.

Drums at Dusk. New York: Macmillan, 1939.

Periodical Publications

The Crisis

"Hope." August 1924: 176.

"Spring Music." June 1925: 93.

"Dirge." May 1926: 25.

"Holiday." July 1926: 121.

"Nocturne at Bethesda." December 1926: 66.

"Tree." April 1927: 48.

"A Summer Tragedy." June 1933: 174–177, 190.

New Challenge

"Barrel Staves." March 1934: 16–24.

COUNTEE CULLEN

Books

Color. New York & London: Harper, 1925.

The Ballad of the Brown Girl: An Old Ballad Retold. New York & London: Harper, 1927.

Caroling Dusk: An Anthology of Verse by Negro Poets. New York: Harper & Brothers Publishers, 1927.

Copper Sun. New York & London: Harper, 1927.

The Black Christ and Other Poems. New York & London: Harper, 1929.

One Way to Heaven. New York & London: Harper, 1932.

The Medea and Some Poems. New York & London: Harper, 1935.

The Lost Zoo (A Rhyme for the Young, but Not Too Young). New York & London: Harper, 1940.

Periodical Publications

The Crisis

"Hope Deferred." September 1914.

Opportunity

"Poet on Poet—*The Weary Blues.*" 4 February 1926: 73.

"The Dark Tower," 4 December 1926: 388; 5 February 1927: 53–54; 5 March 1927: 86–87; 5 April 1927: 118–119; 5 May 1927: 149–150; 5 June 1927: 180–181; 5 July 1927: 210–211; 5 August 1927: 240–241; 5 November 1927: 336–337; 5 December 1927: 373–374; 6 January 1928: 20–21; 6 February 1928: 52–53; 6 March 1928: 90; 6 April 1928: 120; 6 July 1928: 210; 6 September 1928: 271–273.

W. E. B. DuBois

Books

Black Folk Then and Now: An Essay in the History and Sociology of the Negro Race. New York: Henry Holt, 1939.

Dark Water: Voices from Within the Veil. New York: Harcourt, Brace, 1921.

Dusk of Dawn: An Essay Toward an Auto-biography of a Race Concept. New York: Harcourt, Brace, 1940.

JESSIE FAUSET

Books

There Is Confusion. New York: Boni & Liveright, 1924.
Plum Bun. London: Mathews & Marrot, 1928.
The Chinaberry Tree. New York: Frederick A. Stokes, 1931.
Comedy, American Style. New York: Frederick A. Stokes, 1933.

Periodical Publications

The Crisis
"'There Was One Time,' A Story of Spring." April 1917: 272–277; May 1917: 11–15.
"Again It Is September." September 1917.
"The Return." January 1919: 118.
"Mary Elizabeth." December 1919: 51–56.
"Oriflamme." January 1920: 128.
"New Literature on the Negro," June 1920: 78–83.
"The Sleeper Wakes." August 1920: 168–173; September 1920: 226–229; October 1920: 267–274.
"La Vie C'est La Vie." July 1922: 124.
"Dilworth Road Revisited." August 1922: 167.
"Song for a Lost Comrade." November 1922: 22.
"When Christmas Comes." December 1922: 61–63.
"Double Trouble." August 1923: 155–159; September 1923: 205–209.
"Rencontre." January 1924: 122.
"Here's April." April 1924: 277.
"Rain Fugue." August 1924: 155.
"Stars in Alabama." January 1928: 14.
"Courage! He Said." November 1929: 378.

RUDOLPH FISHER

Books

The Walls of Jericho. New York: Knopf, 1928.
The Conjure-Man Dies: A Mystery Tale of Dark Harlem. New York: Covici, Friede, 1932.

Periodical Publications

American Mercury
"The Caucasian Storms Harlem." August 1927: 393–398.

The Atlantic Monthly
"The City of Refuge." February 1925: 178–187.
"Ringtail." May 1925: 652–660.
"The Promised Land." January 1927: 37–45.
"Blades of Steel." August 1927: 183–192.

Baltimore Afro-American
"Common Meter." 8 and 15 February 1930.

The Crisis
"High Yaller." October 1925: 281–286; November 1925: 33–38.

Junior Red Cross News
"Ezekiel." March 1932: 151–153.
"Ezekiel Learns." February 1933: 123–125.

McClure's
"The Backslider." August 1927: 16–17, 101–104.
"Fire by Night." December 1927: 64–67, 98–102.

Metropolitan, a Monthly Review
"John Archer's Nose." January 1935.

Opportunity
"Dust." February 1931: 46–47.
"Guardian of the Law." March 1933: 82–85, 90.

Story
"Miss Cynthie." June 1933: 3–15.

Survey Graphic
"The South Lingers On." March 1925: 644–647.

Play

Conjure-Man Dies. 1936.

Unpublished Fiction

"Across the Airshaft."
"The Love Lost Blues."
"The Man Who Passed."
"The Lindy Hop."

LANGSTON HUGHES

Books

The Weary Blues. New York: Knopf, 1926.
Fine Clothes to the Jew. New York: Knopf, 1927.
Not Without Laughter. New York & London: Knopf, 1930.
The Negro Mother and Other Dramatic Recitations. New York: Golden Stair Press, 1931.
Dear Lovely Death. Amenia, N.Y.: Troutbeck Press, 1931.
Popo and Fifina. With Arna Bontemps. New York: Macmillan, 1932.
The Dream Keeper and Other Poems. New York: Knopf, 1932.

Scottsboro Limited: Four Poems and a Play. New York: Golden Stair Press, 1932.

A Negro Looks at Soviet Central Asia. Moscow & Leningrad: Co-operative Publishing Society of Foreign Workers in the U.S.S.R., 1934.

The Ways of White Folks. New York: Knopf, 1934.

A New Song. International Workers Order, 1938.

The Big Sea: An Autobiography. New York: Knopf, 1940.

ZORA NEALE HURSTON

Books

Jonah's Gourd Vine. Philadelphia and London: Lippincott, 1934.

Mules and Men. Philadelphia and London: Lippincott, 1935.

Their Eyes Were Watching God. Philadelphia and London: Lippincott, 1937.

Tell My Horse. Philadelphia and London: Lippincott, 1938.

Moses, Man of the Mountain. Philadelphia and London: Lippincott, 1939.

Periodical Publications

Howard University Record
"Poem." February 1922: 236.

Stylus
"O Night." 1 May 1921: 42.

Fire!!
Color Struck: A Play in Four Scenes. 1 November 1926: 7–15.

Opportunity
"Drenched in Light." December 1924: 371–374.
"Spunk." June 1925: 171–173.
"John Redding Goes to Sea." January 1926: 16–21.

New York Herald Tribune
"Full of Mud, Sweat and Blood": Review of *God Shakes Creation* by David M. Cohn. 3 November 1935: 8.

Saturday Review
"Stories of Conflict": Review of *Uncle Tom's Children* by Richard Wright. 2 April 1938: 32.

Washington Tribune
"Race Cannot Become Great Until It Recognizes Its Talent." 29 December 1934.

World Tomorrow
"How It Feels to Be Colored Me." May 1928: 215–216.

Plays and Musicals

The First One: A Play. In *Ebony and Topaz: A Collectanea*, edited by Charles S. Johnson. New York: National Urban League, 1927.

Mule Bone: A Comedy of Negro Life in Three Acts. Coauthored with Langston Hughes. New York: Harper-Perennial, 1931.

Fast and Furious. Coauthored with Clinton Fletcher and Tim Moore. In *Best Plays of 1931–1932*, edited by Burns Mantle and Garrison Sherwood. New York: Dodd, Mead & Co., 1932.

CHARLES S. JOHNSON

Books

The Negro in American Civilization: A Study of Negro Life and Race Relations in the Light of Social Research. New York: Holt, 1930.

Shadow of the Plantation. Chicago: University of Chicago Press, 1934.

Race Relations: Adjustment of Whites and Negroes in the United States. Coauthored with Willis Duke Weatherford. Boston: Heath, 1934.

The Collapse of Cotton Tenancy: Summary of Field Studies and Statistical Surveys, 1933–1935. Coauthored with Edwin R. Embree and W. W. Alexander. Chapel Hill: University of North Carolina Press, 1935.

A Preface to Racial Understanding. New York: Friendship, 1936.

The Negro College Graduate. Chapel Hill: University of North Carolina Press, 1938.

Edited Collection

Ebony and Topaz: A Collectanea. New York: Urban League, 1927.

GEORGIA DOUGLAS JOHNSON

Books

The Heart of Woman, and Other Poems. Boston: Cornhill, 1918.

Bronze: A Book of Verse. Boston: B. J. Brimmer, 1922.

An Autumn Love Cycle. New York: H. Vinal, 1928.

Plays

A Sunday Morning in the South: A One Act Play. Washington, D.C.: 1924.

Blue Blood. New York: Appleton Publishing, 1927.

Plumes: Folk Tragedy. New York: French, 1927.

Attucks. (never produced) 1930s.
Frederick Douglass. (never produced) 1930s.
The Starting Point. (never produced) 1930s.
William and Ellen Craft. (never produced) 1930s.

Periodical Publication
Liberator
"A Song of Courage." September 1924: 23.

JAMES WELDON JOHNSON

Books
Autobiography of an Ex-Coloured Man. 1912, reprint, New York: Knopf, 1927.
Fifty Years and Other Poems. Boston: Cornhill, 1917.
God's Trombones: Seven Negro Sermons in Verse. New York: Viking, 1927.
Black Manhattan. New York: Knopf, 1930.
Along This Way: The Autobiography of James Weldon Johnson. New York: Viking, 1933.
Negro Americans: What Now? New York: Viking, 1934.
Saint Peter Relates an Incident. New York: Viking, 1935.

Edited Collections
The Book of American Negro Poetry. New York: Harcourt, Brace and Company, 1922.
The Book of American Negro Spirituals. New York: Viking, 1925.
The Second Book of Negro Spirituals. New York: Viking, 1926.

Translation
Fernando Periquet. *Goyescas; or, The Rival Lovers* (opera libretto). New York: G. Schirmer, 1915.

NELLA LARSEN

Books
Quicksand. New York: Knopf, 1928.
Passing. New York: Knopf, 1929.

Periodical Publications
The Brownie's Book
"Three Scandinavian Games." June 1920: 191–192.
"Danish Fun." July 1920: 219.

Forum
"Sanctuary." January 1930: 15–18.

Opportunity
"Review of *Black Sadie.*" January 1929: 24.

Young's Realistic Stories Magazine
Semi, Allen. "The Wrong Man." January 1926: 243–246.
———. "Freedom." April 1926: 241–243.

ALAIN LOCKE

Books
A Decade of Negro Self-Expression. Charlottesville, Va.: Michie Co., 1927.
The Negro in America. Chicago: American Library Association, 1933.
The Negro and His Music. Washington, D.C.: Associates in Negro Folk Education, 1936.
Negro Art: Past and Present. Washington, D.C.: Associates in Negro Folk Education, 1936.
The Negro in Art: A Pictorial Record of the Negro Artist and of the Negro Theme in Art. Washington, D.C.: Associates in Negro Folk Education, 1940.

Edited Collections
The New Negro: An Interpretation. New York: Boni, 1925.
Four Negro Poets. New York: Simon & Schuster, 1927.
Plays of Negro Life: A Source-Book of Native American Drama. With Montgomery Gregory. New York: Harper, 1927.

CLAUDE MCKAY

Books
Spring in New Hampshire, and Other Poems. London: Richards, 1920.
Harlem Shadows: The Poems of Claude McKay. New York: Harcourt, Brace, 1922.
Negry v Amerike. Edited by Alan L. McLeod. Translated from the Russian by Robert J. Winter. 1923, reprint, Port Washington, N.Y.: Kennikat Press, 1979.
Sudom Lincha. Edited by Alan L. McLeod. Translated from the Russian by Robert Winter. 1925, reprint, Mysore, India: Institute of Commonwealth and American Studies and English Language, 1989.
Home to Harlem. New York: Harper, 1928.
Banjo: A Story Without a Plot. New York: Harper, 1929.
Gingertown. New York: Harper, 1932.
Banana Bottom. New York: Harper, 1933.
A Long Way from Home. New York: Furman, 1937.
Harlem: Negro Metropolis. New York: Dutton, 1940.

WILLIS RICHARDSON

Edited Collections

Plays and Pageants From the Life of the Negro. Washington, D.C.: Associated Publishers, 1930.

Negro History in Thirteen Plays. Coauthored with May Miller. Washington, D.C.: Associated Publishers, 1935.

Plays

The Chip Woman's Fortune. 1923.

Mortgaged. 1924.

Compromise 1925.

The Black Horseman. 1931.

Periodical Publications

The Brownies' Book

The King's Dilemma. December 1920.

The Gypsy's Finger Ring. March 1921.

The Children's Treasure. June 1921.

The Dragon's Tooth. October 1921.

Carolina

The Idle Head. April 1927.

The Flight of the Natives. April 1927.

The Crisis

"The Hope of a Negro Drama." November 1919: 338–339.

The Broken Banjo. February and March 1926.

The Deacon's Awakening: A Play in One Act. November 1920.

Opportunity

"The Negro and the Stage." October 1924: 310.

"The Negro Audience." April 1925: 123.

"Characters." June 1925: 183.

"The Unpleasant Play." September 1925: 282.

WALLACE THURMAN

Books

The Negro Life in New York's Harlem. Girard, Kans.: Haldeman-Julius, 1928.

The Blacker the Berry. New York: Macaulay, 1929.

Infants of the Spring. New York: Macaulay, 1929.

The Interne. Coauthored with Abraham Furman. New York: Macaulay, 1932.

Periodical Publications

American Monthly

"Harlem: A Vivid Picture of the World's Greatest Negro City." May 1927: 19–20.

Bookman

"Negro Poets and Their Poetry." July 1928: 555–561.

Dance Magazine

"Harlem's Place in the Sun." May 1928: 23, 54.

Fire!!

"Cordelia the Crude." November 1926: 17.

Independent

"Nephews of Uncle Remus." 24 September 1927: 296–298.

The Messenger

"Confession." June 1926: 167.

"Grist in the Mill." June 1926: 165–167.

Negro World

"Harlem—As Others See It." Coauthored with William Jourdan Rapp. 13 April 1929: 3.

The New Republic

"Negro Artists and the Negro." 31 August 1927: 37–39.

Opportunity

"The Last Citadel." April 1926: 128.

"God's Edict." July 1926: 216.

Outlet

"Eugene O'Neill's 'All God's Chillun Got Wings.'" October 1924: 19–20.

"You Never Can Tell." September and October 1924: 6–8, 14–15.

The World Tomorrow

"Harlem Facets." November 1927: 465–467.

Screenplays

Tomorrow's Children. 1934.

High School Girl. 1935.

Unpublished Work

Jeremiah the Magnificent.

CARL VAN VECHTEN

Books

Music after the Great War. New York: Schirmer, 1915.

Music and Bad Manners. New York: Knopf, 1916.

Interpreters and Interpretations. New York: Knopf, 1917.

The Merry-Go-Round. New York: Knopf, 1918.

The Music of Spain. New York: Knopf, 1918.

In the Garret. New York: Knopf, 1920.

The Tiger in the House. New York: Knopf, 1920.

Peter Whiffle: His Life and Works. New York: Knopf, 1922.

The Blind Bow-Boy. New York: Knopf, 1923.

Red. New York: Knopf, 1925.

Firecrackers. New York: Knopf, 1925.

The Tattooed Countess. New York: Knopf, 1926.

Nigger Heaven. New York: Knopf, 1926.

Excavations. New York: Knopf, 1926.

Spider Boy. New York: Knopf, 1928.

Parties. New York: Knopf, 1930.

Feathers. New York: Random House, 1930.

Sacred and Profane Memories. New York: Knopf, 1932.

Edited Collection

Lords of the Housetops, Thirteen Cat Tales. New York: Knopf, 1921.

ERIC WALROND

Book

Tropic Death. New York: Boni & Liveright, 1926.

Periodical Publication

Current History

"The New Negro Faces America." 17 February 1923: 786–788.

DOROTHY WEST

Periodical Publications

Black World

"Elephant's Dance: A Memoir of Wallace Thurman." 20 November 1970: 77–85.

The Messenger

"Hannah Byde." July 1926: 197–199.

Opportunity

"The Typewriter." July 1926: 220–222.

"The Black Dress." May 1934: 140, 158.

"Mammy." October 1940: 298–302.

Saturday Evening Quill

"An Unimportant Man." June 1928: 21–32.

"Prologue to a Life." April 1929: 5–10.

1909

The National Association for the Advancement of Colored People is founded.

1910

The National Urban League is founded.

W. E. B. DuBois is appointed editor of *The Crisis*, the official journal of The National Association for the Advancement of Colored People. He serves as editor of the influential journal until 1934.

1912

James Weldon Johnson publishes *The Autobiography of an Ex-Coloured Man*, the first version of the novel that he later republishes under his own name in 1927.

1914

Joel Spingarn, one of the founders of the National Association for the Advancement of Colored People, endows the Spingarn Medal. The annual award, which is still bestowed today, recognizes outstanding achievement by an African American.

Marcus Garvey organizes the Universal Negro Improvement Association, an organization dedicated to achieving African and West Indian independence from colonial rule.

World War I begins in Europe.

1915

Booker T. Washington passes away.

1916

Carter G. Woodson establishes the *Journal of Negro History*

1917

A. Philip Randolph and Chandler Owen begin publishing *The Messenger*, a journal that ceases publication in 1928.

The Silent Protest March occurs in Manhattan on July 28. Civil rights leaders such as the Reverend Frederick Cullen, W. E. B. DuBois, and James Weldon Johnson organize the march, which includes between 10,000 and 15,000, in order to protest lynchings and the inadequate federal response to mob law, racial violence, and segregation.

The United States enters World War I.

1918

Georgia Douglas Johnson makes her literary debut with *The Heart of a Woman.*

Marcus Garvey and the Universal Negro Improvement Association begin publishing *Negro World*, the official newspaper of the organization. It ceases publication in 1933.

World War I ends. The United States has benefited from the military service of some 370,000 African Americans during the conflict.

1919

Race riots erupt throughout the nation, prompting James Weldon Johnson to coin the term *Red Summer*, to denote the bloodshed in the 25 cities affected by the upheaval.

T. Montgomery Gregory organizes the Howard Players, one of the nation's first African-American undergraduate theater troupes.

W. E. B. DuBois organizes the first Pan-African Conference, and the meeting is held in Paris, France.

The Nineteenth Amendment, which grants women the right to vote, is passed.

1920

The Universal Negro Improvement Association, headed by Marcus Garvey, organizes its First International Convention of the Negro Peoples of the World in New York City.

The Emperor Jones by Eugene O'Neill, and the play that will feature Charles Gilpin and Paul Robeson in the legendary title role, opens in New York City.

James Weldon Johnson becomes the first African-American officer of the National Association for the Advancement of Colored People. He will serve in this post for 10 years.

1921

Jessie Fauset and W. E. B. DuBois begin publication of *The Brownies' Book*, a magazine for children of color.

1922

James Weldon Johnson publishes *The Book of American Negro Poetry*, the first comprehensive anthology of 20th-century African-American poetry.

Claude McKay publishes *Harlem Shadows*, a celebrated work that many regard as the first major work of the Harlem Renaissance.

William Elmer Harmon establishes the Harmon Foundation, an organization that dispenses prestigious awards to promising and established artists of color.

1923

The National Urban League begins publication of *Opportunity: A Journal of Negro Life* and appoints Charles S. Johnson as its first editor. The journal continues publication until 1949.

Willis Richardson, author of *The Chip Woman's Fortune*, becomes the first African American to have a nonmusical drama performed on Broadway.

Jean Toomer publishes *Cane*.

1924

Jessie Fauset publishes *There Is Confusion*, the first novel by an African-American woman of the Harlem Renaissance.

The notable Civic Club dinner, organized by Charles Johnson in honor of Jessie Fauset and often regarded as one of the most celebrated gatherings of the Harlem Renaissance, is held in New York City.

1925

Opportunity begins sponsoring annual literary contests that become one of the most celebrated aspects of the period.

Survey Graphic, the leading American social work journal, devotes its March issue to African-American writers and subjects. Alain Locke is the guest editor of the periodical volume, entitled "Harlem: Mecca of the New Negro," that leads to his edited anthology entitled *The New Negro: An Interpretation*.

Countee Cullen makes his literary debut with the publication of *Color*.

Garland Anderson, the author of *Appearances*, becomes the first African-American playwright to see a full-length production of his work staged on Broadway.

The *Inter-State Tattler*, a New York City–based newspaper, is established and is published through 1932.

A. Philip Randolph is instrumental in the founding of the Brotherhood of Sleeping Car Porters, the first African-American union to be affiliated with the American Federation of Labor.

1926

The innovative but short-lived journal *Fire!!*, edited by Wallace Thurman, makes its debut.

W. E. B. DuBois, editor of the *The Crisis*, Regina Andrews, and Gwendolyn Bennett establish The Crisis Guild of Writers and Artists, known by the acronym Crigwa, at the 135th Street Branch of the New York Public Library.

Arthur Schomburg's unmatched collection of artifacts relating to African and African-American history and culture becomes part of the holdings of the 135th Street Branch of the New York Public Library.

Langston Hughes publishes *The Weary Blues*, his first volume of poetry.

Carl Van Vechten publishes *Nigger Heaven*.

Eric Walrond publishes *Tropic Death*.

1927

A number of impressive edited collections of poems, prose, and drama are published. Works include Charles Johnson's *Ebony and Topaz: A Collectanea*, Countee Cullen's *Caroling Dusk*, Alain

Locke's *Four Poets*, and T. Montgomery Gregory and Locke's *Plays of Negro Life*.

James Weldon Johnson republishes his 1912 *Autobiography of an Ex-Coloured Man*.

1928
Claude McKay's *Home to Harlem*, the author's first novel, becomes the first African-American novel to be included on the *New York Times* best seller list.

Nella Larsen publishes *Quicksand*, her first novel.

W. E. B. DuBois publishes *Dark Princess*, his second novel and the only work of fiction that he published during the Harlem Renaissance.

Harlem: A Forum of Negro Life, a journal edited by Wallace Thuman, is published but ceases publication after the first issue.

1929
Two notable novels about passing are published in this year: Jessie Fauset's *Plum Bun* and Nella Larsen's *Passing*.

Wallace Thurman publishes his first novel, *The Blacker the Berry*.

V. F. Calverton publishes the *Anthology of American Negro Literature*, one of the early collections of African-American writing.

Walter White publishes a history of lynching in the United States entitled *Rope and Faggot: A Biography of Judge Lynch*.

The historic stock market crash that signals the beginning of the Great Depression occurs in late October.

1930
Nella Larsen becomes the first African-American woman to receive a Guggenheim Fellowship.

James Weldon Johnson publishes *Black Manhattan*, a cultural history of African Americans in New York.

Langston Hughes publishes *Not Without Laughter*, his first novel.

1931
George Schuyler publishes *Black No More: Being an Account of the Strange and Wonderful Workings of Science in the Land*, one of the earliest African-American satirical novels.

Arna Bontemps publishes *God Sends Sunday*, his first novel.

A'Lelia Walker, the well-known socialite and daughter of the successful Madam C. J. Walker, passes away.

The trial of nine young men known as the Scottsboro Boys who are falsely accused of rape in Alabama begins.

1932
Rudolph Fisher publishes *The Conjure-Man Dies: A Mystery Tale of Dark Harlem*. It is one of the earliest non-serialized African-American mystery novels.

Sterling Brown publishes *Southern Road*, his first volume of poems.

Claude McKay publishes *Gingertown*, his only collection of short stories.

Charles Chesnutt, novelist and 1928 Spingarn Medalist, passes away.

1934
Nancy Cunard edits *Negro Anthology*.

Zora Neale Hurston makes her debut as a novelist and publishes *Jonah's Gourd Vine*.

W. E. B. DuBois resigns as editor of the *The Crisis* and from the National Association for the Advancement of Colored People.

Rudolph Fisher passes away.

Wallace Thurman passes away.

1935
A major riot occurs in Harlem, prompted by discriminatory practices by shop owners.

The federal Works Progress Administration is founded. Known later as the Works Projects Administration, the organization employs a number of artists and writers for social, literary, and arts projects. It remains in existence until 1943.

George Henderson publishes *Ollie Miss*, the first of his two novels.

Langston Hughes's play *Mulatto*, which will become the longest-running African-American play on Broadway until Lorraine Hansberry's 1959 *Raisin in the Sun*, opens.

1936
Arna Bontemps publishes *Black Thunder*, one of the earliest African-American novels about an American slave revolt.

John Mason Brewer publishes *Heralding Dawn: An Anthology of Verse*, an edited anthology of works by Texan poets of color.

Mae Cowdery publishes *We Lift Our Voices and Other Poems,* her only Harlem Renaissance–era volume of poetry.

1937

Zora Neale Hurston publishes *Their Eyes Were Watching God.*

Claude McKay publishes *A Long Way from Home,* his autobiography.

Idabelle Yeiser publishes *Moods: A Book of Verse,* her first collection of poems.

Dorothy West begins editing *New Challenge,* her second journal.

1938

Mercedes Gilbert publishes *Aunt Sara's Wooden God,* her first and only novel.

Langston Hughes establishes the Harlem Suitcase Theater.

Beatrice Campbell Murphy publishes *Negro Voices: An Anthology of Contemporary Verse,* one of the few collections of poetry edited by a woman during the Harlem Renaissance.

Richard Wright publishes *Uncle Tom's Children: Four Novellas.*

National Association for the Advancement of Colored People officer, writer, and diplomat James Weldon Johnson passes away.

Renowned bibliophile and collector Arthur Schomburg passes away.

1939

Arna Bontemps publishes *Drums at Dusk,* a novel about Toussaint Louverture and the Haitian Revolution.

Zora Neale Hurston publishes *Moses, Man of the Mountain.*

Ida Rowland, the first African-American woman from Oklahoma to earn a Ph.D., publishes *Lisping Leaves,* her first volume of poems.

William Attaway publishes *Let Me Breathe Thunder* (1939), his first novel.

J. Saunders Redding publishes *To Make a Poet Black,* his only Harlem Renaissance–era volume

and a highly respected work of American literary history and criticism.

Marian Anderson, the legendary contralto, is denied access by the Daughters of the American Revolution to Constitution Hall. She delivers a historic concert on the steps of the Lincoln Memorial as a result of intervention by Eleanor Roosevelt and others.

Joel Spingarn, longtime National Association for the Advancement of Colored People member, passes away.

Garland Anderson, pioneering playwright, passes away.

1940

Claude McKay publishes *Harlem: Negro Metropolis,* a cultural overview of Harlem and its dynamic arts and culture community.

Langston Hughes publishes *The Big Sea: An Autobiography,* the first of his two published memoirs.

Jane Harris Hunter, a civil rights leader and an officer in the National Association of Colored Women, publishes *A Nickel and a Prayer,* her autobiography.

Mary Effie Lee Newsome publishes *Gladiola Gardens: Poems of Outdoors and Indoors for Second Graders.* The volume includes illustrations by the celebrated painter Lois Mailou Jones.

Countee Cullen publishes *The Lost Zoo (A Rhyme for the Young, but Not Too Young),* one of his two volumes of poetry for children.

Mary Church Terrell publishes her autobiography, *A Colored Woman in a White World.*

Richard Wright publishes *Native Son,* a novel that reinforces the end of the Harlem Renaissance and the turn toward American literary modernism.

Marcus Garvey passes away in England.

DuBose Heyward, author of *Porgy,* passes away.

Robert Abbott, founder and editor of the influential *Chicago Defender,* passes away.

Robert Vann, longtime editor of the respected *Pittsburgh Courier,* passes away.

BIBLIOGRAPHY OF
SECONDARY SOURCES

Abrahamson, Doris E. *Negro Playwrights in the American Theatre, 1925–1959.* New York: Columbia University Press, 1969.

Alexander, Eleanor. *Lyrics of Sunshine and Shadow: The Tragic Courtship and Marriage of Paul Lawrence Dunbar and Alice Ruth Moore: A History of Love and Violence Among the African-American Elite.* New York: New York University Press, 2002.

Anderson, Jervis. *This Was Harlem: A Cultural Portrait, 1900–1950.* New York: Farrar, Straus and Giroux, 1982.

Arata, Esther, and Nicholas Rotoli, eds. *Black American Playwrights, 1800 to the Present: A Bibliography.* Metuchen, N.J.: Scarecrow Press, 1976.

Avery, Laurence G., ed. *A Southern Life: Letters of Paul Green, 1916–1981.* Chapel Hill: The University of North Carolina Press, 1994.

Awkward, Michael, ed. *New Essays on Their Eyes Were Watching God.* New York: Cambridge University Press, 1990.

Baker, Houston A., Jr. *A Many-Colored Coat of Dreams: The Poetry of Countee Cullen.* Detroit: Broadside Press, 1974.

———. *Afro-American Poetics: Revisions of Harlem and the Black Aesthetic.* Madison: University of Wisconsin Press, 1988.

———. *Modernism and the Harlem Renaissance.* Chicago: University of Chicago Press, 1987.

Bascom, Lionel C. *A Renaissance in Harlem: Lost Essays of the WPA, by Ralph Ellison, Dorothy West, and Other Voices of a Generation.* New York: Amistad, 2001.

Bassett, John Earl. *Harlem in Review: Critical Reactions to Black American Writers, 1917–1939.* Selinsgrove, Pa.: Susquehanna University Press, 1992.

Bell, Bernard W. *The Afro-American Novel and Its Tradition.* Amherst: University of Massachusetts Press, 1987.

Bell, Roseann, Bettye Parker, and Beverly Guy-Sheftall, eds. *Sturdy Black Bridges: Visions of Black Women in Literature.* Garden City, N.Y.: Anchor-Doubleday, 1979.

Bernard, Emily. *Remember Me to Harlem: The Letters of Langston Hughes and Carl Van Vechten.* New York: Knopf, 2001.

Berry, Faith, ed. *Langston Hughes: Before and Beyond Harlem.* Westport, Conn.: Lawrence Hill & Company, 1983.

———, ed. *Good Morning Revolution: The Uncollected Social Protest Writing of Langston Hughes.* New York: Lawrence Hill, 1973.

Bloom, Harold, ed. *Black American Poets and Dramatists of the Harlem Renaissance.* New York: Chelsea House, 1995.

Bloom, Harold, ed. *Black American Prose Writers of the Harlem Renaissance.* New York: Chelsea House Publishers, 1994.

———, ed. *Zora Neale Hurston.* New York: Chelsea House, 1986.

———, ed. *Zora Neale Hurston's Their Eyes Were Watching God.* New York: Chelsea House, 1987.

Boelcskevy, Mary Anne Stewart, ed. *Voices in the Poetic Tradition: Clara Ann Thompson, J. Pauline Smith, Mazie Earhart Clark.* New York: G. K. Hall, 1996.

Bone, Robert A. *Down Home: A History of Afro-American Short Fiction from Its Beginnings to the End of the Harlem Renaissance.* New York: Putnam, 1975.

———. *The Negro Novel in America.* New Haven, Conn.: Yale University Press, 1965.

Bonner, Pat E. *Sassy Jazz and Slo' Draggin' Blues: Music in the Poetry of Langston Hughes.* New York: P. Lang, 1996.

Bontemps, Arna Wendell, ed. *Golden Slippers: An Anthology of Negro Poetry for Young Readers.* New York: Harper & Row, 1941.

———. *The Harlem Renaissance Remembered: Essays with a Memoir.* New York: Dodd, Mead, 1972.

Bordelon, Pamela. *Go Gator Muddy the Water: Writings By Zora Neale Hurston from the Federal Writers' Project with Biographical Essays.* New York: W. W. Norton & Company, 1999.

Boyd, Valerie. *Wrapped in Rainbows: The Life of Zora Neale Hurston.* New York: Scribner, 2003.

Boyle, Sheila Tully, and Andrew Buni. *Paul Robeson: The Years of Promise and Achievement.* Amherst: University of Massachusetts Press, 2001.

Bronz, Stephen H. *Roots of Negro Racial Consciousness: The 1920's: Three Harlem Renaissance Authors.* New York: Libra, 1964.

Brown, Sterling. *The Negro in American Fiction: Negro Poetry and Drama.* 1937, reprint, New York: Atheneum, 1972.

Brown-Guillory, Elizabeth, ed. *Wines in the Wilderness: Plays by African American Women from the Harlem Renaissance to the Present.* New York: Praeger, 1990.

Burton, Jennifer, ed. *Zora Neale Hurston, Eulalie Spence, Marita Bonner, and Others: The Prize Plays and other One-Acts Published in Periodicals.* New York: G. K. Hall, 1996.

Butcher, Margaret J. *The Negro in American Culture: Based on Materials Left by Alain Locke.* New York: Knopf, 1956.

Byrd, Rudolph P., ed. *Generations in Black and White: Photographs by Carl Van Vechten from the James Weldon Johnson Memorial Collection.* Athens: University of Georgia Press, 1993.

Campbell, Josie. *Student Companion to Zora Neale Hurston.* Westport, Conn.: Greenwood Press, 2001.

Chambers, Clarke A. *Paul U. Kellogg and the Survey.* Minneapolis: University of Minnesota Press, 1971.

Chauncey, George. *Gay New York: Gender, Urban Culture, and the Making of the Gay Male World, 1890–1940.* New York: Basic Books, 1994.

Clarke, John Henrik, et al., eds. *Black Titan: W. E. B. Du Bois: An Anthology by the Editors of Freedomways.* Boston: Beacon Press: 1970.

Cooper, Floyd, *Coming Home: From the Life of Langston Hughes.* New York: Philomel Books, 1994.

Cooper, Wayne. *Claude McKay: Rebel Sojourner In the Harlem Renaissance.* New York: Schocken Books, 1987.

———, ed. *The Passion of Claude McKay: Selected Poetry and Prose, 1912–1948.* New York: Schocken, 1973.

Cronin, Gloria L., ed. *Critical Essays on Zora Neale Hurston.* New York: G. K. Hall, 1998.

Cronon, Edmund. *Black Moses: The Story of Marcus Garvey and the Universal Negro Improvement Association.* Madison: University of Wisconsin Press, 1987.

Cullen, Countee. *Caroling Dusk: An Anthology of Verse by Negro Poets.* New York: Harper & Brothers Publishers, 1927.

Curtis, Susan. *The First Black Actors on the Great White Way.* Columbia: University of Missouri Press, 1998.

Dace, Tish, ed. *Langston Hughes: The Contemporary Reviews.* New York: Cambridge University Press, 1997.

Davis, Arthur P. *From the Dark Tower: Afro-American Writers, 1900–1960.* Washington, D.C.: Howard University Press, 1974.

Davis, Thadious M. *Nella Larsen, Novelist of the Harlem Renaissance: A Woman's Life Unveiled.* Baton Rouge: Louisiana State University Press, 1994.

De Jongh, James. *Vicious Modernism: Black Harlem and the Literary Imagination.* Cambridge: Cambridge University Press, 1990.

Dickinson, Donald C. *A Bio-Bibliography of Langston Hughes, 1902–1967.* Hamden, Conn.: Archon Books, 1967.

Dietzel, Susanne B., ed. *Mercedes Gilbert: Selected Gems of Poetry, Comedy, and Drama.* New York: G. K. Hall, 1997.

Dodson, Howard, Christopher Moore, and Roberta Yancy. *The Black New Yorkers: The Schomburg Illustrated Chronology.* New York: John Wiley & Sons, Inc., 2000.

Du Bois, Shirley Graham. *His Day Is Marching On: A Memoir of W. E. B. Du Bois.* Philadelphia: Lippincott, 1971.

Dutty, Susan, ed. *The Political Plays of Langston Hughes.* Carbondale: Southern Illinois University Press, 2000.

duCille, Ann. *The Coupling Convention: Sex, Text, and Tradition in Black Women's Fiction.* New York: Oxford University Press, 1993.

Egar, Emmanuel E. *Black Women Poets of the Harlem Renaissance.* Lanham, Md.: University Press of America, 2003.

Emanuel, James. *Langston Hughes*. New York: Twayne, 1967.

Fabre, Genevieve, and Michel Feith, eds. *Jean Toomer and the Harlem Renaissance*. New Brunswick, N.J.: Rutgers University Press, 2001.

Fabre, Michel. *From Harlem to Paris: Black American Writers in France, 1840–1980*. Urbana: University of Illinois Press, 1991.

———. *The World of Richard Wright*. Jackson: University Press of Mississippi, 1985.

Favor, J. Martin. *Authentic Blackness: The Folk in the New Negro Renaissance*. Durham, N.C.: Duke University Press, 1999.

Felgar, Robert. *Student Companion to Richard Wright*. Westport, Conn.: Greenwood Press, 2000.

Ferguson, Blanche. *Countee Cullen and the Negro Renaissance*. New York: Dodd, Mead, 1966.

Fishbein, Leslie. *Rebels in Bohemia: The Radicals of the Masses, 1911–1917*. Chapel Hill: University of North Carolina Press, 1982.

Fleming, G. James, and Christian E. Burckel. *Who's Who in Colored America: An Illustrated Biographical Directory of Notable Living Persons of African Descent in the United States*. Yonkers-on-Hudson, N.Y.: Christian E. Burckel & Associates, 1950.

Fleming, Robert. *James Weldon Johnson*. Boston: Twayne Publishers, 1987.

Flynn, Joyce, and Joyce Occomy Striklin. *Frye Street & Environs: The Collected Works of Marita Bonner*. Boston: Beacon Press, 1987.

Franklin, John Hope, and August Meier, eds. *Black Leaders of the Twentieth Century*. Urbana: University of Illinois Press, 1982.

Fullilove, Maggie Shaw. *Who Was Responsible?: Stories from Half Century*. Introduction by P. Gabrielle Foreman. New York: G. K. Hall, 1996.

Gable, Craig, ed. *Ebony Rising: Short Fiction of the Greater Harlem Renaissance Era*. Bloomington: Indiana University Press, 2004.

———. Rudolph Fisher Newsletter: Online News and Resources for Rudolph Fisher and the Harlem Renaissance. Available online. URL: http://www.fishernews.org.

Gates, Henry Louis, Jr., and Kwame Anthony Appiah, eds. *Langston Hughes: Critical Perspectives Past and Present*. New York: Amistad, 1993.

———. *Zora Neale Hurston: Critical Perspectives Past and Present*. New York: Amistad, 1993.

Gayle, Addison, Jr. *Claude McKay: The Black Poet at War*. Detroit: Broadside, 1972.

———. *The Way of the New World: The Black Novel in America*. Garden City, N.Y.: Anchor Press, 1976.

Gibson, Donald B., ed. *Five Black Writers*. New York: New York University Press, 1970.

Gilpin, Patrick, and Marybeth Gasman. *Charles S. Johnson: Leadership Beyond the Veil in the Age of Jim Crow*. Albany: State University of New York Press, 2003.

Glassman, Steve, and Kathryn Lee Seidel, eds. *Zora in Florida*. Orlando: University of Central Florida Press, 1991.

Gray, Christine Rauchfuss. *Willis Richardson, Forgotten Pioneer of African-American Drama*. Westport, Conn.: Greenwood Press, 1999.

Greenberg, Cheryl Lynn. *Or Does It Explode? Black Harlem in the Great Depression*. New York: Oxford University Press, 1997.

Greene, J. Lee. *Time's Unfading Garden: Anne Spencer's Life and Poetry*. Baton Rouge: Louisiana State University Press, 1977.

Grider, Sylvia Ann and Lou Halsell Rodenberger, eds. *Texas Women Writers: A Tradition of Their Own*. College Station, Tex.: A & M University Press, 1997.

Gunning, Sandra. *Race, Rape, and Lynching: The Red Record of American Literature, 1890–1912*. New York: Oxford University Press, 1996.

Hamilton, Virginia. *W. E. B. Du Bois: A Biography*. New York: T. Y. Crowell, 1972.

Hardy, Gayle. *American Women Civil Rights Activists: Bio-bibliographies of 68 Leaders, 1825–1992*. London: McFarland & Company, Inc., 1993.

Harris, Leonard, ed. *The Philosophy of Alain Locke: Harlem Renaissance and Beyond*. Philadelphia: Temple University Press, 1989.

Harris, Trudier. *The Power of the Porch: The Storyteller's Craft in Zora Neale Hurston, Gloria Naylor, and Randall Kenan*. Athens: University of Georgia Press, 1996.

———, and Thadious Davis, eds. *Afro-American Writers from the Harlem Renaissance to 1940*. Dictionary of Literary Biography, Vol. 51. Detroit: Gale Research Co., 1987.

Hatch, James V., and Leo Hamalian. *Lost Plays of the Harlem Renaissance 1920–1940*. Detroit: Wayne State University Press, 1996.

Hatch, James V., and Ted Shine, eds. *Black Theatre, U.S.A.: Forty-Five Plays by Black Americans, 1847–1974*. New York: Free Press, 1974

Hatch, Shari, and Michael Strickland, eds. *African-American Writers: A Dictionary*. Santa Barbaran, Calif.: ABC-CLIO, 2000.

Helbling, Mark. *The Harlem Renaissance: The One and the Many*. Westport, Conn.: Greenwood Press, 1999.

Hemenway, Robert. *Zora Neale Hurston: A Literary Biography*. Urbana: University of Illinois Press, 1977.

Hill, Anthony. *Pages from the Harlem Renaissance: A Chronicle of Performance*. New York: Peter Lang, 1996.

Hill, Christine. *Langston Hughes: Poet of the Harlem Renaissance*. Springfield, N.J.: Hanslow Pub., 1997.

Hill, Lynda Marion. *Social Rituals and the Verbal Art of Zora Neale Hurston*. Washington, D.C.: Howard University Press, 1996.

Holloway, Karla. *The Character of the Word: The Texts of Zora Neale Hurston*. New York: Greenwood Press, 1987.

Honey, Maureen. *Shadowed Dreams: Women's Poetry of the Harlem Renaissance*. New Brunswick, N.J.: Rutgers University Press, 1989.

Howard, Lillie P. *Zora Neale Hurston*. Boston: Twayne, 1980.

———, ed. *Alice Walker and Zora Neale Hurston: The Common Bond*. Westport, Conn.: Greenwood Press, 1993.

Huggins, Nathan. *Harlem Renaissance*. New York: Oxford University Press, 1971.

Hull, Gloria. *Color, Sex, and Poetry: Three Women Writers of the Harlem Renaissance*. Bloomington: Indiana University Press, 1987.

Hull, Gloria, ed. *Give Us Each Day: The Diary of Alice Dunbar-Nelson*. New York: W. W. Norton & Company, 1984.

Hutchinson, George. *The Harlem Renaissance in Black and White*. Cambridge, Mass.: Belknap Press of Harvard University Press, 1995.

Jackson, Lawrence. *Ralph Ellison: Emergence of Genius*. New York: John Wiley & Sons, Inc., 2002.

Janker, Kenneth Robert. *Rayford W. Logan and the Dilemma of the African-American Intellectual*. Amherst: University of Massachusetts Press, 1993.

———. *White: The Biography of Walter White, Mr. NAACP*. New York: The New Press, 2003.

Johnson, Abby Arthur, and Ronald Maberry Johnson. *Propaganda & Aesthetics: The Literary Politics of African American Magazines in the Twentieth Century*. Amherst: University of Massachusetts Press, 1979.

Johnson, Eloise E. *Rediscovering the Harlem Renaissance: The Politics of Exclusion*. New York: Garland Publishing, 1997.

Johnson, James Weldon. *Along This Way: The Autobiography of James Weldon Johnson*. 1933; reprint, New York: Da Capo Press, 2000.

———, ed. *The Book of American Negro Poetry*. New York: Harcourt, Brace and Company, 1922.

Jones, Kirkland C. *Renaissance Man From Louisiana: A Biography of Arna Wendell Bontemps*. Westport, Conn.: Greenwood Press, 1992.

Jones, Robert B. *Jean Toomer and the Prison-House of Thought: A Phenomenology of the Spirit*. Amherst: University of Massachusetts Press, 1993.

Jones, Sharon L. *Rereading the Harlem Renaissance: Race, Class, and Gender in the Fiction of Jessie Fauset, Zora Neale Hurston, and Dorothy West*. Westport, Conn.: Greenwood Press, 2002.

Jordan, William E. *Black Newspapers and America's War for Democracy*. Chapel Hill: The University of North Carolina Press, 2001.

Jubilee, Vincent. *Philadelphia's Afro-American Literary Circle and the Harlem Renaissance*. Ann Arbor, Mich.: University Microfilms, 1982.

Kaplan, Carla. *Zora Neale Hurston: A Life in Letters*. New York: Doubleday, 2002.

Kellner, Bruce. *Carl Van Vechten and the Irreverent Decades*. Norman: University of Oklahoma Press, 1968.

———, ed. *Keep a-Inchin' Along: Selected Writings of Carl Van Vechten about Black Art and Letters*. Westport, Conn.: Greenwood Press, 1979.

———, ed. *Letters of Carl Van Vechten*. New Haven, Conn.: Yale University Press, 1987.

Kerlin, Robert Thomas, ed. *Negro Poets and Their Poems*. Washington, D.C.: Associated Publishers, Inc., 1923.

Kerman, Cynthia Earl, and Richard Eldridge. *The Lives of Jean Toomer: A Hunger for Wholeness*. Baton Rouge: Louisiana State University Press, 1987.

Knox, Marcy, ed. *The Sleeper Wakes: Harlem Renaissance Stories by Women*. New Brunswick, N.J.: Rutgers University Press, 1993.

Kornweibel, Theodore, Jr. *No Crystal Stair: Black Life and the Messenger, 1917–1928*. Westport, Conn.: Greenwood Press, 1975.

Kramer, Victor, and Robert Russ, eds. *The Harlem Renaissance Re-Examined*. Troy, N.Y.: Whitson Pub., 1997.

Krasner, David. *A Beautiful Pageant: African American Theatre, Drama, and Performance in the Harlem Renaissance, 1910–1927*. New York: Palgrave Macmillan, 2002.

Kyvig, David E. *Daily Life in the United States, 1920–1939: Decades of Promise and Pain.* Westport, Conn.: 2002.

Larson, Charles R., ed. *An Intimation of Things Distant: The Collected Fiction of Nella Larsen.* New York: Anchor, 1992.

———. *Invisible Darkness: Jean Toomer and Nella Larsen.* Iowa City: University of Iowa Press, 1993.

Leak, Jeffrey. *Rac(e)ing to the Right: Selected Essays of George S. Schuyler.* Knoxville: University of Tennessee Press, 2001.

Lemert, Charles and Esme Bhan, eds. *The Voice of Anna Julia Cooper: Including A Voice from the South and Other Important Essays, Papers, and Letters.* Lanham, Md.: Rowman & Littlefield, 1998.

Lester, Neal A. *Understanding Zora Neale Hurston's Their Eyes Were Watching God: A Student Casebook to Issues, Sources, and Historical Documents.* Westport, Conn.: Greenwood Press, 1999.

Levy, Eugene. *James Weldon Johnson: Black Leader, Black Voice.* Chicago: University of Chicago, 1973.

Lewis, David Levering. *W. E. B. Du Bois: Biography of A Race, 1868–1919.* New York: Henry Holt and Company, 1993.

———. *W. E. B. Du Bois: The Fight for Equality and the American Century, 1919–1963.* New York: Henry Holt & Company, 2000.

———. *When Harlem Was in Vogue.* New York: Knopf, 1981.

Linneman, Russell, ed. *Alain Locke: Reflections on a Modern Renaissance Man.* Baton Rouge: Louisiana State University, 1982.

Locke, Alain, ed. *The New Negro.* Introduction by Arnold Rampersad. New York: Atheneum, 1992.

———, and Montgomery Gregory, eds. *Plays of Negro Life: A Source-book of Native American Drama.* New York: Harper & Brothers, 1927.

Logan, Rayford, ed. *W. E. B. Du Bois: A Profile.* New York: Hill and Wang, 1971.

Lowe, John. *Jump at the Sun: Zora Neale Hurston's Cosmic Comedy.* Urbana: University of Illinois Press, 1994.

Lueders, Edward. *Carl Van Vechten.* New York: Twayne, 1965.

———. *Carl Van Vechten and the Twenties.* Albuquerque: University of New Mexico Press, 1955.

Lyons, Mary E. *Sorrow's Kitchen: The Life and Folklore of Zora Neale Hurston.* New York: Scribners, 1990.

Marable, Manning. *W. E. B. DuBois: Black Radical Democrat.* Boston, G. K. Hall, 1986.

Martin, Tony. *Literary Garveyism: Garvey, Black Arts, and the Harlem Renaissance.* Dover, Mass.: Majority Press, 1983.

Maxwell, William J., ed. *Complete Poems: Claude McKay.* Urbana: University of Illinois Press, 2004.

McClaren, Joseph. *Langston Hughes: Folk Dramatist in the Protest Tradition, 1921–1943.* Westport, Conn.: Greenwood Press, 1997.

McCluskey, John, Jr. *The City of Refuge: The Collected Stories of Rudolph Fisher.* Columbia: University of Missouri Press, 1987.

McLendon, Jacquelyn Y., ed. *Sarah Lee Brown Fleming: Hope's Highway and Clouds and Sunshine.* New York: G. K. Hall, 1995.

Meltzer, Milton, *Langston Hughes: A Biography.* New York: Crowell, 1968.

Miller, R. Baxter. *The Art and Imagination of Langston Hughes.* Lexington: University Press of Kentucky, 1989.

Mishkin, Tracy. *The Harlem and Irish Renaissances: Language, Identity, and Representation.* Gainesville: University Press of Florida, 1998.

Mitchell, Angelyn, ed. *Within the Circle: An Anthology of African American Literary Criticism from the Harlem Renaissance to the Present.* Durham, N.C.: Duke University Press, 1994.

Mitchell, Verner, ed. *This Waiting for Love: Helene Johnson, Poet of the Harlem Renaissance.* Amherst: University of Massachusetts Press, 2000.

Moon, Henry Lee, ed. *The Emerging Thought of W. E. B. Du Bois.* New York: Simon & Schuster, 1972.

Moses, Norton H., comp. *Lynching and Vigilantism in the United States: An Annotated Bibliography.* Westport, Conn.: Greenwood Press, 1997.

Nichols, Charles H., ed. *Arna Bontemps–Langston Hughes Letters, 1925–1967.* New York: Paragon House, 1990.

O'Daniel, Therman B., ed. *Langston Hughes: Black Genius, a Critical Evaluation.* New York: Morrow, 1971.

———, ed. *Jean Toomer: A Critical Evaluation.* Washington, D.C.: 1988.

Parascandola, Louis, ed. *Winds Can Wake Up the Dead: An Eric Walrond Reader.* Detroit: Wayne State University Press, 1998.

Patterson, Lindsay. *Anthology of the American Negro in the Theatre: A Critical Approach.* New York: Publishers Company, 1967.

Peplow, Michael. *George S. Schuyler.* Boston: Twayne Publishers, 1980.

Perkins, Kathy A., ed. *Black Female Playwrights: An Anthology of Plays before 1950*. Bloomington: Indiana University Press, 1989.

Perry, Jeffrey, ed. *A Hubert Harrison Reader*. Middletown, Conn.: Wesleyan University Press, 2001.

Perry, Margaret. *Silence to the Drums: A Survey of the Literature of the Harlem Renaissance*. Westport, Conn.: Greenwood Press, 1976.

———, ed. *The Short Fiction of Rudolph Fisher*. New York: Greenwood Press, 1987.

Peters, Pearlie Mae Fisher. *The Assertive Woman in Zora Neale Hurston's Fiction, Folklore, and Drama*. New York: Garland, 1997.

Peterson, Bernard L. *Contemporary Black American Playwrights and Their Plays: A Biographical Directory and Dramatic Index*. Westport, Conn.: Greenwood Press, 1988.

———. *The African-American Theatre Directory, 1816–1960: A Comprehensive Guide to Early Black Theatre Organizations, Companies, Theatres, and Performing Groups*. Westport, Conn.: Greenwood Press, 1997.

Plant, Deborah. *Every Tub Must Sit on Its Own Bottom: The Philosophy and Politics of Zora Neale Hurston*. Urbana: University of Illinois Press, 1995.

Porter, Dorothy. *North American Negro Poets: a Bibliographical Checklist of Their Writings, 1760–1944*. Hattiesburg, Miss.: Book Farm, 1945.

Price, Kenneth, and Lawrence J. Oliver, ed. *Critical Essays on James Weldon Johnson*. New York: G. K. Hall, 1997.

Pride, Armistead Scott, and Clint C. Wilson. *A History of the Black Press*. Washington, D.C.: Howard University Press, 1997.

Pryse, Marjorie, and Hortense J. Spillers, eds. *Conjuring: Black Women, Fiction, and Literary Tradition*. Bloomington: Indiana University Press, 1985.

Rampersad, Arnold. *The Life of Langston Hughes: I, Too, Sing America*. Vol. 1, *1902–1941*. New York: Oxford University Press, 1986.

———. *The Life of Langston Hughes: I Dream a World*. Vol. 2, *1941–1967*. New York: Oxford University Press, 1988.

Rauchfuss, Christine Gray. *Willis Richardson: Forgotten Pioneer of African American Drama*. Westport, Conn.: Greenwood Press, 1999.

Reardon, Joanne, and Kristine Thorsen. *Poetry by American Women, 1900–1975: A Bibliography*. Metuchen, N.J.: Scarecrow Press, 1979.

Reed, Adolph L. Jr. *W. E. B. Du Bois and American Political Thought: Fabianism and the Color Line*. New York: Oxford University Press, 1999.

Robbins, Richard. *Sidelines Activist: Charles S. Johnson and the Struggle for Civil Rights*. Jackson: University Press of Mississippi, 1996.

Roses, Lorraine Elena, ed. *Selected Works of Edythe Mae Gordon*. New York: G. K. Hall, 1996.

———, and Ruth Elizabeth Randolph. *Harlem Renaissance and Beyond: Literary Biographies of 100 Black Women Writers, 1900–1945*. Boston: G. K. Hall & Co., 1990.

Roses, Lorraine Elena, and Ruth Elizabeth Randolph, eds. *Harlem's Glory: Black Women Writing, 1900–1950*. Cambridge: Harvard University Press, 1996.

Rudwick, Elliot. *W. E. B. Du Bois, Propagandist of Negro Protest*. New York: Atheneum, 1968.

Rush, Theressa, Carol Myers, and Esther Arata. *Black American Writers Past and Present: A Biographical and Bibliographical Dictionary*. Metuchen, N.J.: Scarecrow Press, 1975.

Schafer, Yvonne. *American Women Playwrights, 1900–1950*. New York: Peter Lang, 1997.

Schwarz, A. B. Christa. *Gay Voices of the Harlem Renaissance*. Bloomington: Indiana University Press, 2003.

Scruggs, Charles. *The Sage in Harlem: H.L. Mencken and the Black Writers of the 1920s*. Baltimore: Johns Hopkins University Press, 1984.

Shockley, Ann Allen. *Afro-American Women Writers 1746–1933*. Boston: G. K. Hall, 1988.

Shucard, Alan. *Countee Cullen*. Boston: Twayne, 1984.

Singh, Amritjit. *The Novels of the Harlem Renaissance: Twelve Black Writers, 1923–1933*. University Park: Pennsylvania State University Press, 1976.

———, and Daniel Scott, eds. *The Collected Writings of Wallace Thurman: A Harlem Renaissance Reader*. New Brunswick, N.J.: Rutgers University Press, 2003.

———, William S. Shiver, and Stanley Brodwin, eds. *The Harlem Renaissance: Reevaluations*. New York: Garland Publishing, Inc., 1989.

Sinnette, Elinor Des Verney. *Arthur Alfonso Schomburg: Black Bibliophile and Collector*. Detroit: New York Public Library and Wayne State University Press, 1989.

Slavic, William H. *Dubose Heyward*. Boston: Twayne Publishers, 1981.

Smethurst, James Edward. *The New Red Negro: The Literary Left and African-American Poetry, 1930–1946*. New York: Oxford University Press, 1999.

Smith, Katharine Capshaw. *Children's Literature of the Harlem Renaissance.* Bloomington: Indiana University Press, 2004.

Sochen, June. *The New Woman: Feminism in Greenwich Village, 1910–1920.* New York: Quadrangle/The New York Times Book Co., 1972.

Solomon, Mark. *The Cry Was Unity: Communists and African Americans, 1917–36.* Jackson: University Press of Mississippi, 1998.

Southern, Eileen, ed. *Famous Modern Negro Musicians.* New York: Da Capo Press, 1978.

Splawn, P. Jane, ed. *Writings of Carrie Williams Clifford and Carrie Law Morgan Figgs.* New York: G. K. Hall, 1997.

Stafford, Mark. *W. E. B. Du Bois.* New York: Chelsea House, 1989.

Stewart, Jeffrey. *The Critical Temper of Alain Locke: A Selection of His Essays on Art and Culture.* New York: Garland Publishing, 1983.

Sundquist, Eric. *The Hammers of Creation: Folk Culture in Modern African-American Fiction.* Athens: University of Georgia Press, 1992.

———, ed. *The Oxford W.E.B. DuBois Reader.* New York: Oxford University Press, 1996.

Sylvander, Cheryl. *Jessie Redmon Fauset, Black American Writer.* Troy, N.Y.: Whitson Publishing Company, 1981.

Tate, Claudia, ed. *The Selected Works of Georgia Douglas Johnson.* Boston: G. K. Hall, 1997.

Tillery, Tyrone. *Claude McKay: A Black Poet's Struggle for Identity.* Amherst: University of Massachusetts Press, 1992.

Tracy, Steven. *Langston Hughes & The Blues.* Urbana: University of Illinois Press, 1988.

Trotman, C. James. *Langston Hughes: The Man, His Art, and His Continuing Influence.* New York: Garland, 1995.

Turner, Darwin T. *In a Minor Chord: Three Afro-American Writers and Their Search for Identity.* Carbondale: Southern Illinois University Press, 1971.

Tyler, Bruce. *From Harlem to Hollywood: The Struggle for Racial and Cultural Democracy, 1920–1943.* New York: Garland, 1992.

van Notten, Eleonore. *Wallace Thurman's Harlem Renaissance.* Amsterdam: Rodopi, 1994.

Vincent, Theodore G., ed. *Voices of a Black Nation: Political Journalism in the Harlem Renaissance.* Trenton, N.J.: Africa World Press, 1990.

Vogel, Todd, ed. *The Black Press: New Literary and Historical Essays.* New Brunswick, N.J.: Rutgers University Press, 2001.

Wagner, Jean. *Black Poets of the United States.* Urbana: University of Illinois Press, 1973.

Walden, Daniel, ed. *W. E. B. Du Bois: The Crisis Writings.* Greenwich, Conn.: Faucett Publications, 1972.

Walker, Alice, ed. *I Love Myself When I Am Laughing . . . and Then Again When I Am Looking Mean and Impressive: A Zora Neale Hurston Reader.* New York: Feminist Press, 1979.

———. *Langston Hughes, American Poet.* New York: HarperCollins, 1988.

Wall, Cheryl. *Women of the Harlem Renaissance.* Bloomington: Indiana University Press, 1995.

Washington, Johnny. *A Journey into the Philosophy of Alain Locke.* Westport, Conn.: Greenwood Press, 1994.

———. *Alain Locke and Philosophy: A Quest for Cultural Pluralism.* Westport, Conn.: Greenwood Press, 1986.

Watson, Steven. *The Harlem Renaissance: Hub of African-American Culture, 1920–1930.* New York: Pantheon Books, 1995.

Weiss, Nancy J. *The National Urban League.* New York: Oxford University Press, 1974.

White, Newman Ivey, and Walter Clinton Jackson, eds. *An Anthology of Verse by American Negroes.* Durham, N.C.: The Seaman Printery Incorporated, 1924.

Wilson, Sondra, ed. *The Crisis Reader: Stories, Poetry, and Essays from the N.A.A.C.P.'s Crisis Magazine.* New York: The Modern Library, 1999.

———. *The Messenger Reader: Stories, Poetry, and Essays from The Messenger Magazine.* New York: Modern, 2000.

———. *The Opportunity Reader: Stories, Poetry, and Essays from the Urban League's Opportunity Magazine.* New York: The Modern Library, 1999.

Wintz, Cary D. *Black Culture and the Harlem Renaissance.* College Station, Tex.: A&M University Press, 1997.

———, ed. *The Politics and Aesthetics of "New Negro" Literature.* New York: Garland Pub., 1996.

———, ed. *The Emergence of the Harlem Renaissance.* New York: Garland Pub., 1996.

Wirth, Thomas. *Gay Rebel of the Harlem Renaissance: Selections from the Work of Richard Bruce Nugent.* Durham: Duke University Press, 2002.

Witcover, Paul. *Zora Neale Hurston.* New York: Chelsea House, 1991.

Woodson, Jon. *To Make a New Race: Gurdjieff, Toomer, and the Harlem Renaissance.* Jackson: University Press of Mississippi, 1999.

Woll, Allen. *Dictionary of the Black Theatre: Broadway, Off-Broadway, and Selected Harlem Theatre.* Westport, Conn.: Greenwood Press, 1983.

Wright, Shirley Haynes. *A Study of the Fiction of Wallace Thurman.* Ann Arbor, Mich.: University Microfilms International, 1983.

Yenser, Thomas. *Who's Who in Colored America: A Biographical Dictionary of Notable Living Persons of African Descent in America. 1933–1937.* Brooklyn: Thomas Yenser, 1937.

Young, James O. *Black Writers of the Thirties.* Baton Rouge: Louisiana State University Press, 1973.

INDEX

Boldface page numbers indicate major treatment of a topic. Page numbers in *italic* indicate photographs.

OVER NIGHT BOOK

This book must be returned before the first class on the following school day.

DATE DUE
